CRIMINAL LAW

Text, Cases, and Materials

SEVENTH EDITION

Jonathan Herring

OXFORD

UNIVERSITY PRESS

OXFORD

UNIVERSITY PRESS

Great Clarendon Street, Oxford, OX2 6DP,
United Kingdom

Oxford University Press is a department of the University of Oxford.
It furthers the University's objective of excellence in research, scholarship,
and education by publishing worldwide. Oxford is a registered trade mark of
Oxford University Press in the UK and in certain other countries

Fourth edition 2010
Fifth edition 2012
Sixth edition 2014

Impression: 1

Public sector information reproduced under Open Government Licence v2.0
(http://www.nationalarchives.gov.uk/doc/open-government-licence/open-government-licence.htm)

Published in the United States of America by Oxford University Press
198 Madison Avenue, New York, NY 10016, United States of America

British Library Cataloguing in Publication Data
Data available

Library of Congress Control Number: 2015958006

ISBN 978-0-19-875304-9

Printed in Italy by
L.E.G.O. S.p.A.

For Kirsten, Laurel, Joanna, and Darcy

NEW TO THIS EDITION

This new edition has been completely updated to take into account the latest statistics and case law. The following are particularly notable developments:

- A new offence of domestic violence.
- Developments in the law on joint enterprise, including coverage of *R v Jogee*.
- A recent case on the defence of diminished responsibility and loss of control.
- Judicial considerations of the meaning of consent in sexual offences.
- Major developments on the law on attempts.

PREFACE

Usually, students greatly enjoy criminal law. The facts of the cases are readily understandable and provide a revealing insight into the bizarre and grotesque. But many students miss out on the intellectual fascination that the subject has to offer. This is in part because much of the theoretical material on criminal law has been presented with such sophistication that it is inaccessible to students. It is one of the primary aims of this book to make the theoretical material on criminal law more readily comprehensible to undergraduates. Therefore, each chapter (apart from the first) has two parts. The first part sets out the law, with extracts from the leading cases. The second part describes some of the theoretical material, extracting some of the writing from leading commentators. The hope is that the reader will have a secure grasp of the law itself, but also an introduction to the complex philosophical and ethical debates concerning criminal law.

The selection of materials in books of this kind is far harder than might be thought. The articles and books which might be the leading authorities on the topics are sometimes not readily susceptible to having short passages extracted. I have therefore included throughout the book suggestions for further reading. These will enable a reader who wishes to pursue a particular issue in further detail to do so.

The book seeks to set out the law at 1 September 2015.

Jonathan Herring
Exeter College, Oxford

AUTHOR'S APPROACH

Two-part chapter structure

This book takes a unique approach to the study of criminal law. Each chapter is split into two parts. The first part looks at what the law actually is at the moment—the 'black letter' law—and provides many extracts from key cases. The second part looks at the theory behind the law, analyses the law, and provides critical and analytical extracts from secondary sources, including articles and books.

Cross-references

In order to relate the black letter part of each chapter to the theoretical part, the author has provided clear cross-references throughout the text. These are indicated in the text by the use of arrows with numbers to help you find the corresponding reference, for example, →1 and ←1. Therefore, when studying the black letter law, readers can refer forwards in the chapter to the theoretical discussion of this aspect of the law, and vice versa by finding the corresponding number.

Central issues

At the start of each chapter, the author has provided a list of the central issues that will be covered, outlining the major areas of discussion and issues within each topic.

Further reading

The author has provided lists of further reading interspersed throughout the text so that readers can quickly and easily locate relevant additional sources on particular aspects of law.

Definitions

Definitions of key legal terms and concepts are provided and highlighted throughout the text.

Questions and examination tips

Questions both to test the reader's understanding of the actual law, as well as more theoretical questions, are included throughout each chapter. Examination tips are also provided, including resources such as flowcharts to help determine what sort of crime has been committed, and guidelines on approaching specific questions or scenarios.

Online resources

This book is accompanied by an Online Resource Centre at www.oxfordtextbooks.co.uk/orc/herringcriminal7e/. This provides regular updates to the law following publication—a particularly important resource in this fast-moving area. A selection of key annotated web links is also offered, guiding readers towards useful websites, along with online guidance on answering a selection of the questions posed in the text. Questions with online guidance are highlighted in the text by the following: 'For guidance on answering this question, please visit the Online Resource Centre that accompanies this book: www.oxfordtextbooks .co.uk/orc/herringcriminal7e/'. A test bank of interactive multiple-choice questions is also provided as a lecturer resource. In addition to this, a full bibliography for the text is available on the site.

Finally, there is a video of the author talking about the study of criminal law and his approach to the subject.

OUTLINE TABLE OF CONTENTS

CONTENTS

2   *ACTUS REUS*: THE CONDUCT ELEMENT   71

3   *MENS REA*: THE MENTAL ELEMENT   132

4 STRICT LIABILITY 211

5   HOMICIDE   231

6 NON-FATAL NON-SEXUAL OFFENCES AGAINST THE PERSON — 314

7 SEXUAL OFFENCES

407

8   THEFT, HANDLING, AND ROBBERY   495

15 COMPLICITY   830

ABBREVIATIONS

AC	Appeal Cases
ALJR	Australian Law Journal Reports
All ER	All England Reports
ASBO	Anti-social behaviour order
BMLR	Butterworths Medico-Legal Reports
BWS	Battered Women's Syndrome
C & P	Craig & Phillips
CA	Court of Appeal
Cald	Caldecott's Magistrates' and Settlement Cases
CAR	Commonwealth Arbitration Reports (Aust.)
Car & M	Carrington & Marshman's Nisi Prius Reports
CCR	Crown Cases Reserved
Cl & F	Clark & Finnelly's House of Lords Cases
CLR	Commonwealth Law Reports (Aust.)
CMAC	Courts-Martial Appeal Court
Cox CC	Cox's Criminal Cases
CPS	Crown Prosecution Service
Cr App R	Criminal Appeal Reports
Crim LR	Criminal Law Review
CSEW	Crime Survey for England and Wales
D & B	Dearsley & Bell
DC	Divisional Court
DLR	Dominion Law Reports (Can.)
DPP	Director of Public Prosecutions
East	East's Term Reports, King's Bench
ECHR	European Convention on Human Rights
ECtHR	European Court of Human Rights
EHRR	European Human Rights Reports
ER	English Reports
EWCA	England and Wales Court of Appeal
EWHC	England and Wales High Court
F & F	Foster & Finlayson's Nisi Prius Reports
FCR	Family Court Reporter
GM	Genetically Modified
HL	House of Lords
HRA	Human Rights Act 1998
JP	Justice of the Peace Reports
KB	King's Bench
Le & Ca	Leigh & Cave's Crown Cases Reserved
Lew CC	Lewin's Crown Cases Reserved

LT	Law Times Reports
Med LR	Medical Law Reports
Mod Rep	Modern Reports
Mood & R	Moody & Robinson's Nisi Prius Reports
Mood CC	Moody's Crown Cases Reserved
NI	Northern Ireland Law Reports
NZLR	New Zealand Law Reports
P & CR	Property, Planning & Compensation Reports
PC	Privy Council
Plowd	Plowden's Commentaries
QB	Queen's Bench
QBD	Queen's Bench Division
RTR	Road Traffic Reports
Russ & Ry	Russell & Ryan's Crown Cases Reserved
SC	Supreme Court
SCR	Supreme Court Reports (Can.)
TLR	Times Law Reports
UKHL	United Kingdom House of Lords
UKPC	United Kingdom Privy Council
UKSC	United Kingdom Supreme Court
WLR	Weekly Law Reports

ACKNOWLEDGEMENTS

I am very grateful to many colleagues who have offered intellectual and practical support in the writing of this book. I am particularly grateful to several anonymous reviewers who, with great care, provided comments on the first edition. I have also greatly benefited from conversations with the following people who have (sometimes unknowingly) assisted in the writing of the book: Alan Bogg, Michelle Madden Dempsey, Charles Foster, Stephen Gilmore, George P. Smith, Rachel Taylor, and Rebecca Williams. The many students to whom I have taught criminal law have greatly influenced this book by their constant questioning of the accepted view on a topic and their insistence on no-nonsense answers. I also owe a great debt, as do countless other students, to Roy Stuart, who as my tutor introduced me to the study of criminal law. The team at Oxford University Press has been excellent in their advice, assistance, and attention to detail. Above all, I am grateful to my wife, Kirsten Johnson, and children, Laurel, Joanna, and Darcy, for their encouragement, love, and laughter.

Jonathan Herring
Exeter College

SOURCE ACKNOWLEDGEMENTS

Grateful acknowledgement is made to all the authors and publishers of copyright material which appears in this book, and in particular to the following for permission to reprint material from the sources indicated:

Extracts from unreported case reports, Law Commission Reports, Consultation papers, and Home Office reports and statistics are Crown copyright material and are reproduced under Class Licence Number C2006010631 with the permission of the Controller of OPSI and the Queen's Printer for Scotland. Extracts from House of Lords Reports (UKHL) are Parliamentary copyright and are reproduced by permission of the Controller of HMSO on behalf of Parliament.

F. J. Abbate: extract from 'The Conspiracy Doctrine: A Critique' in M. Gorr and S. Harwood (eds) *Controversies in Criminal Law* (Boulder, CO: Westview, 1992).

Ashgate Publishing: extract from V. Tadros, 'The Limits of Manslaughter' in C. Clarkson and S. Cunningham (eds) *Criminal Liability for Non-Aggressive Death* (2008).

Cambridge Law Journal and the authors: extracts from J. Gardner, 'Rationality and the Rule of Law in Offences against the Person' (1994) *CLJ* 502; and G. Williams, 'Oblique Intention' (1987) *CLJ* 417.

Cambridge University Press and the author: extract from A. Norrie, *Crime Reason and History: A Critical Introduction to Criminal Law* (3rd edn, 2014).

N. Cobb: extract from 'Compulsory Care-Giving: Some Thoughts on Relational Feminism, the Ethics of Care and Omissions Liability' (2008) 39 *Cambrian Law Review* 11.

Hart Publishing Ltd, an imprint of Bloomsbury Publishing plc: extracts are © A.P. Simester, J.R. Spencer, G.R. Sullivan, and G. Virgo, *Simester and Sullivan's Criminal Law: Theory and Doctrine* (4th edn, 2010); © W. Wilson, *Central Issues in Criminal Theory* (2002); and © M. Moore, 'The Moral Worth of Retribution' in A. von Hirsch and A. Ashworth (eds), *Principled Sentencing* (1998).

Incorporated Council of Law Reporting: extracts from the Law Reports: Appeal Cases (AC), Queen's Bench Division (QB), Family Court Reports (Fam), United Kingdom House of Lords (UKHL), and United Kingdom Supreme Court (UKSC).

National Law School of India Review: extract from J. Herring, 'Rape and the Defence of Consent' (2014) 16 *National Law School of India Review* 62.

Oxford University Press: extracts from A. Ashworth and J. Horder, *Principles of Criminal Law* (7th edn, 2013); A. Duff, *Criminal Attempts* (1996); G. Fletcher, *Basic Concepts of Criminal Law* (1998); J. Horder, *Excusing Crime* (2004); F. Leverick, *Killing in Self-Defence* (2006); M. Moore, *Act and Crime* (1993); M. Moore, *Placing Blame* (1997); V, Tadros, *Criminal Responsibility* (2005); C. Wells, *Corporations and Criminal Responsibility* (2nd edn, 2001); L. Zedner, *Criminal Justice* (2005); A. Simester and G. Sullivan, 'The Nature and Rational of Property Offences' in R.A. Duff and S.P. Green (eds) *Defining Crimes: Essays on the Special Part of Criminal Law* (2005); A. Ashworth, 'Belief, Intent and Criminal

Liability' in J. Eekelaar and J. Bell (eds) *Oxford Essays in Jurisprudence* (1987); J. Gardner and S. Shute, 'The Wrongness of Rape', and N. Lacey, 'Philosophical Foundations of the Common Law: Social Not Metaphysical' in J. Horder (ed.) *Oxford Essays in Jurisprudence* (4th Series, 2000); N. Lacey, 'Legal Constructions of Crime' in M. Maguire, R. Morgan, and R. Reiner (eds) *The Oxford Handbook of Criminology* (2007); V. Tadros, 'Recklessness and the Duty to Take Care' in S. Shute and A. Simester (eds) *Criminal Law Theory* (2002); A. Simester, 'Is Strict Liability Always Wrong?' in A. Simester (ed.) *Strict Liability* (2005); R.A. Duff, 'Subjectivism, Objectivism, and Criminal Attempts', J. Gardner, 'Justifications and Reasons', G. Lamond, 'Coercion, Threats, and Blackmail', and G.R. Sullivan, 'Making Excuses' in A. Simester and A. Smith (eds) *Harm and Culpability* (1996); L. Alexander and K. Kessler Ferzan, 'Beyond the Special Part' in S. Green and R.A. Duff (eds) *Philosophical Foundations of Criminal Law* (2011); L. Farmer, 'Definitions of Crime' in P. Cane and J. Conaghan (eds) *The New Oxford Companion to Law* (2008); T. Hörnle, 'Theories of Criminalization', V. Bergelson, 'The Defense of Consent', V. Munro, 'Sexual Autonomy', S. Green, 'Propery Offences', S. Buell, '"White Collar" Crimes', and M. Cahill, 'Inchoate Crimes' in M. Dubber and T. Hörnle (eds) *The Oxford Handbook of Criminal Law* (2014); W. Sinnott-Armstrong and K. Levy, 'Insanity Defenses' and K. Kessler Ferzan, 'Justification and Excuse' in J Deigh and D Dolinko (eds) *The Oxford Handbook of Philosophy of Criminal Law* (2011); M. Madden Dempsey, 'Public Wrongs and the "Criminal Law's Business": When Victims Won't Share' in R. Cruft, M. Kramer, and M. Reiff (eds) *Crime Punishment and Responsibility* (2011); H.L.A. Hart, 'Negligence, *Mens Rea*, and Criminal Responsibility' in H.L.A. Hart, *Punishment and Responsibility* (1968).

Oxford University Press Journals: extracts from *Oxford Journal of Legal Studies*: C. Clarkson, 'Attempt: The Conduct Requirement' (2009) 29 *OJLS* 25; M. Madden-Dempsey and J. Herring, 'Why Sexual Penetration Requires Justification' (2009) 27 *OJLS* 467; G.R. Sullivan, 'Is Criminal Law Possible?' (2002) 22 *OJLS* 747; and V. Tadros, 'Rape without Consent' (2007) 26 *OJLS* 515. Extract from the *Medical Law Review*: J. Herring, 'Escaping the Shackles of Law at the End of Life' (2013) 21 *Med L Rev* 487. Extract from *International Journal of Law Policy and the Family*: S. Choudhry and J. Herring, 'Righting Domestic Violence' (2006) 20: 95.

RELX (UK) Limited, trading as LexisNexis: extracts from the All England Law Reports (ALL ER).

S.H. Pillsbury: extract from 'Crimes against the Heart: Recognizing the Wrongs of Forced Sex' (2002) 35 *Loyola of Los Angeles Law Review* 845.

Santa Clara Law Review: extract from J. Dressler, 'Some Brief Thoughts (Mostly Negative) about "Bad Samaritan" Laws' (2000) 40 *Santa Clara Law Review* 971.

Springer Science & Business Media: extracts from A. Ashworth and L. Zedner, 'Defending Criminal Law: Reflections on the Changing Character of Crime, Procedure, and Sanctions' (2008) 2 *Criminal Law and Philosophy* 21; J. Gardner, 'Complicity and Causality' (2007) 1 *Criminal Law and Philosophy* 127; and N. Lacey, 'Space, Time and Function: Intersecting Principles of Responsibility across the Terrain of Criminal Justice' (2007) 1 *Criminal Law and Philosophy* 233.

Sweet & Maxwell Ltd reproduced by permission of THOMSON REUTERS (PROFESSIONAL) UK LTD: extracts from *Criminal Appeal Reports*; extracts from *Law Quarterly Review*: A. Ashworth, 'Is Criminal Law a Lost Cause?' (2000) 116 *LQR* 225; S. Gardner, 'Appropriation in Theft: The Last Word?' (1993) 109 *LQR* 194; A.P. Simester, 'The

Mental Element in Complicity' (2006) 123 *LQR* 578; and R. Williams, 'Deception, Mistake and Vitiation of the Victim's Consent' (2008) 124 *LQR* 132; and extracts from *Criminal Law Review*: A. Ashworth, 'Robbery Re-assessed' (2002) *Crim LR* 851 and 'Principles, Pragmatism and the Law Commission's Recommendations on Homicide Law Reform' (2007) *Crim LR* 333; I. Dennis, 'Reverse Onuses and the Presumption of Innocence: In Search of Principle' (2005) *Crim LR* 901; S. Gardner, 'Direct Action and the Defence of Necessity' (2005) *Crim LR* 371; E. Griew, 'Dishonesty: The Objections to *Feely* and *Ghosh*' (1985) *Crim LR* 341; J. Herring, 'Mistaken Sex' (2005) *Crim LR* 511; J. Horder, 'Reconsidering Psychic Assault' (1998) *Crim LR* 392 and 'Transferred Malice and the Remoteness of Unexpected Outcomes from Intentions' (2006) *Crim LR* 383; R. Mackay, 'The Coroners and Justice Act 2009—Partial Defences to Murder (2) The New Diminished Responsibility Plea' (2010) *Crim LR* 290; A. Norrie, 'The Coroners and Justice Act 2009—Partial Defences to Murder (1) Loss of Control' (2010) *Crim LR* 275; D. Ormerod, 'The Fraud Act 2006—Criminalising Lying?' (2007) *Crim LR* 193; D. Ormerod and R. Fortson, 'Serious Crime Act 2007: The Part 2 Offences' (2009) *Crim LR* 389; W. Wilson and D. Ormerod, 'Simply Harsh to Fairly Simple: Joint Enterprise Reform' (2015) *Crim LR* 3; S. Shute, 'Appropriation and the Law of Theft' (2002) *Crim LR* 445; G. Virgo, 'Joint Enterprise Liability is Dead: Long Live Accessorial Liability' (2012) *Crim LR* 850; M .Weait, 'Knowledge, Autonomy and Consent: *R v Konzani*' (2005) *Crim LR* 763; and G. Williams, 'Temporary Appropriation Should be Theft' (1981) *Crim LR* 129; *Hashman and Harrup v United Kingdom* (Application No. 25594/94) (2000) 30 EHRR 241 (ECtHR); B. Crewe, A. Liebling, N. Padfield, and G. Virgo, 'Joint Enterprise: The Implications of an Unfair and Unclear Law' (2015) *Crim LR* 4; *R v Geddes* (1996) *Crim LR* 894 (CA).

Taylor & Francis Books UK: extracts from N. Lacey, 'General Principles of Criminal Law? A Feminist View' and A. McColgan, 'General Defences' in D. Nicolson and L. Bibbings (eds) *Feminist Perspectives on Criminal Law* (Cavendish Press, 1996).

University of Arizona and the author: extracts from D.N. Husak, 'The Nature and Justifiability of Nonconsummate Offenses' (1995) 37 *Arizona Law Review* 151, copyright © 1995 by the Arizona Board of Regents and Douglas N. Husak.

University of California, Hastings College of the Law: extract from S.P. Green, 'Lying, Misleading, and Falsely Denying: How Moral Concepts Inform the Law of Perjury, Fraud and False Statements' (2001) 53 *Hastings Law Journal* 157.

University of California Press Journals: extracts from *New Criminal Law Review*: A. Duff, 'Harms and Wrongs' (2001) 5 *New CLR* 13; V. Nourse, 'Heart and Minds: Understanding the New Culpability' (2002) 6 *New CLR* 361; and A.P. Simester, 'On the So-called Requirement for Voluntary Action' (1998) 1 *New CLR* 403; D. Baker, 'The Moral Limits of Consent as a Defense in the Criminal Law' (2009) 12 *New CLR* 93.

University of Chicago Press: extract from C.A. MacKinnon, 'Feminism, Marxism, Method and the State: Toward Feminist Jurisprudence' (1983) 8 *Signs* 635.

University of Michigan Law School: extract from M.A. Gomez, 'The Writing on Our Walls: Finding Solutions through Distinguishing Graffiti Art from Graffiti Vandalism' (1993) 26 *University of Michigan Journal of Law Reform* 633.

University of Southern California Law School: extract from G.E. Mueller, 'The Mens Rea of Accomplice Liability' (1988) 61 *Southern California Law Review* 2169.

University of Western Ontario: extracts from *The Canadian Journal of Law and Jurisprudence:* D. Klimchuck, 'Causation, Thin Skulls and Equality' (1998) 11 *CJLJ* 115; and N. Lacey, 'Unspeakable Subjects, Impossible Rights: Sexuality, Integrity and Criminal Law' (1998) 11 *CJLJ* 47.

Vathek Publishing: extracts from J. Stannard, 'Sticks, Stones and Words: Emotional Harm and the English Criminal Law' (2010) 74 *Journal of Criminal Law* 533; N. Wake, 'Battered Women, Startled Householders and Psychological Self-Defence: Anglo-Australian Perspectives' (2013) 77 *Journal of Criminal Law* 433; and C. Withey, 'The Fraud Act 2006—Some Early Observations and Comparisons with the Former Law' (2007) 30 *Journal of Criminal Law* 220.

Wiley-Blackwell Publishing: extracts from *Modern Law Review:* J. Gobert, 'The Corporate Manslaughter and Corporate Homicide Act 2007—Thirteen Years in the Making but Was It Worth the Wait?' (2008) 71 *MLR* 413; and N. Lacey, 'A Clear Concept of Intention: Elusive or Illusory?' (1993) 56 *MLR* 621.

Yale Law Journal Company: extract from V. Nourse, 'Passion's Progress: Modern Law Reform and the Provocation Defense' (1997) 106 *Yale Law Journal* 1331.

Every effort has been made to trace and contact copyright holders prior to publication but this has not been possible in every case. If notified, the publisher will undertake to rectify any errors or omissions at the earliest opportunity.

TABLE OF CASES

Where extracts from cases are reproduced, the relevant page numbers are shown in **bold**.

TABLE OF LEGISLATION

Where sections are reproduced in full the page number is shown in **bold**.

1

AN INTRODUCTION TO CRIMINAL LAW

CENTRAL ISSUES

1. It is extremely difficult to answer the question: 'What is a crime?' An important distinction is drawn between the criminal law, where the aim of the court is to punish the wrongdoing of the defendant, and the civil law, where the aim of the court is to compensate the victim for injuries wrongfully caused by the defendant.

2. There are certain principles which are generally thought to underpin the criminal law. These include the principle of legality (that crimes should be clearly defined), the principle of responsibility (that a person should only be guilty if they are to be blamed for their actions), the principle of minimum criminalization (that the criminal law should be used only where absolutely necessary), the principle of proportionality (that the sentence given for an offence should reflect its seriousness), and the principle of fair labelling (that the description of the offence should accurately describe the wrong involved).

3. The criminal law is made up of a mixture of statutes and common law principles. Some people believe that the law would be in a better state if the criminal law was put into a single Criminal Code. However, others think that this would make the law too inflexible.

4. There has been much debate about how the government should decide which acts are criminal. A popular approach is to say that the criminal law should only be concerned with acts which cause other people harm.

5. There is extensive dispute between criminal lawyers on how to determine the extent to which a defendant can be blamed for his or her actions.

6. Criminal lawyers tend to focus on the definitions of criminal offences. In practice, the procedures that lead to a person facing a criminal court are also extremely important.

7. The Human Rights Act 1998 now plays a central role in several parts of the criminal law.

8. Feminist and critical scholars have done much to challenge some of the unspoken assumptions that underlie the criminal law.

1 WHAT IS A CRIME?

You probably think you know what crimes are: murder, rape, theft, and so forth. But is it possible to define a crime? A wide range of conduct can be the basis for criminal offences. Everything from murder to shoplifting; from pollution offences to speeding. Can a definition of 'a crime' be found which includes all these offences?

As the following extract demonstrates, the answer to the question 'What is a crime?' depends on your perspective:[1]

L. Farmer, 'Definitions of Crime' in P. Cane and J. Conaghan (eds) *The New Oxford Companion to Law* (Oxford: OUP, 2008), 263–4

There is no simple and universally accepted definition of crime in the modern criminal law, a feature that probably reflects the large and diverse range of behaviours that have been criminalized by the modern state. It is now widely accepted that crime is a category created by law—that is, a law that most actions are only criminal because there is a law that declares them to be so—so this must be the starting point for any definition.

Most modern definitions of crime fall into two main categories, the moral and the procedural. Moral definitions of crime are based on the claim that there is (or should be) some intrinsic quality that is shared by all acts criminalized by the state. This quality was originally sought in the acts themselves—that all crimes were in an important sense moral wrongs, or *mala in se*—and that the law merely recognized this wrongful quality. The weakness of this approach was that it could extend to certain actions which seemed morally neutral (often refered to as *mala prohibita*), such as speeding or failing to register the birth of a child, which have been made crimes by statute. Accordingly, it is argued crimes are such because criminal law recognizes public wrongs as violations of rights or duties owed to the whole community, that is, that the wrong is seen as the breach of the duty owed to the community to respect the law. This definition covers a broader range of offences, as well as recognizing the sociological fact that many acts are criminal only by virtue of being declared so by the law. The strength of this type of definition is less a description of the object of the crimination law, than as an account of the principles which should limit the proper scope of the criminal law.

Procedural definitions, by contrast, define crimes as those acts which might be prosecuted or punished under criminal procedure. The most influential definition of this type was produced by legal theorist, Glanville Williams, in 1955. He sought a purely formal definition of crime. For him, a crime is

> an act capable of being followed by criminal proceedings having a criminal outcome, and a proceeding or its outcome is criminal if it has certain characteristics which mark it as criminal.

This is undeniably circular (something is criminal if it is criminal), and seems to avoid definition of the term 'criminal' and so might appear to be of little use. However, it arguably reflects more accurately the reality of the modern criminal law, where the scope of the law has extended to include large numbers of regulatory offences tried under criminal proceedings,

---

[1] Lacey (1998a). For the benefits of considering the law from different perspectives, see Lavi and Schneebaum (2014) on sociology, Lacey (2001c) on history, Nelken (1987) on economics, Ainsworth (2000) on psychology, Gurnham (2014) on literature, and Fletcher (2001) on philosophy.

the content of which go far beyond conduct which can easily be regarded as moral or even public wrongs. However, given the diverse range of sanctions and procedures which can be adopted, from forms of treatment or reparation to mediation or restorative justice, it is not obvious that this definition alone can help to determine what is or is not a criminal proceeding.

As this extract suggests, whether a particular kind of conduct should be regarded as criminal can change over time as a response to political and social factors and depends on where in the world you live. For example, the legal response to homosexual sexual activity[2] has changed over the decades in response to a variety of social, political, and legal influences.

The definition of a crime comes into focus when it is necessary to distinguish crimes from civil wrongs. If you hit someone you may be prosecuted for the criminal offence of assault and receive a fine. You may also be sued by the victim for damages in the civil law of tort. Both proceedings in a sense result in the same outcome for the defendant: a loss of money; but these legal proceedings have crucial differences. It is the censure and punishment that are attached to a criminal conviction which can explain the difference between civil and criminal proceedings.[3] A fine carries with it moral blame, while an award of damages may signify that a person is responsible for the loss, but not carry the sense of condemnation that a criminal sanction does. This has led Andrew von Hirsch and others to suggest that it is the censure that attaches to a criminal penalty which most clearly distinguishes criminal wrongs from other legal wrongs.[4] Not everyone is convinced by this argument. It is, for example, possible to award punitive damages in civil proceedings if the court regards the tort or breach of contract as a particularly blameworthy one. A different explanation of the difference between civil and criminal proceedings is provided by Andrew Simester, John Spencer, Bob Sullivan, and Graham Virgo:

Assault involves an interference with fundamental rights of the victim, rights which the State is perceived to have a duty to protect. By contrast, individuals are normally able to protect themselves against breach of contract, and can satisfactorily undo any damage suffered with the aid of the civil law.[5]

They, therefore, argue that the state intervenes with the criminal law to protect citizens when people are unable to protect themselves or receive adequate compensation through the civil courts.

In the following passage, Lucia Zedner warns against defining crimes simply in terms of the official legal response.[6] She starts by setting out the official legal classifications of what crimes are, before challenging them:

L. Zedner, *Criminal Justice* (Oxford: OUP, 2005), 58–63

Thinking about crime as a legal category poses problems for students of criminal justice. It tends to downplay the contingency of crime and, by imposing fixed definitions, to deny

---

[2] Lesbian sexual behaviour has not been the subject of specific prohibition under the criminal law.
[3] G. Williams (1955).　　[4] von Hirsch (1993: 9–12).
[5] Simester, Spencer, Sullivan, and Virgo (2013: 2).
[6] See J. Edwards (2011), who is concerned that too often the government does not make it clear why something has been made criminal.

its open and contested nature. Understanding the central components of the legal classification of crime is indispensable but it is also fraught with difficulties.

First, central to the legal classification of crime is its public quality. A wrong that arises primarily in respect of the rights and duties owed only to individuals is the subject of civil law, whether as a tort, a breach of contract or trust and property rights. A crime is differentiable by the fact that the wrong is deemed to offend against duties owed to society. Just to complicate matters, the same conduct (or inaction) may be both a civil and a criminal wrong; in which case proceedings may generally be taken in both civil and criminal court simultaneously. For example, an assault is potentially both a tort and a crime, and a deception may entail a tort, a breach of contract or trust or be treated as a crime. Given this overlap it is important to identify the differences that determine whether civil or criminal liability, or both, arise. The liability of the civil wrongdoer is based principally upon the loss he or she has occasioned, whereas the criminal wrong resides, in principle at least, in the voluntary action of the perpetrator, their culpability, and the harm caused. And whereas in civil law proceedings are generally brought by the injured party in order to secure compensation or restitution, it is generally the state that prosecutes and punishes crime. A serious problem with the legal classification of crime as public wrong is that it is uninformative: a crime is that which is legally designated as criminal. But the classification does not tell us how, why, or to what end that legal designation has arisen. It cannot explain why some forms of deviance attract the response of the law and not others. It does not explain what determines whether that response is criminal, or civil, or both.

A second facet of the legal classification of crime is that every crime must be so designated by statute or case law and its component parts clearly specified. Every crime consists of a conduct element and, unless it is a crime of strict liability, an accompanying mental element. The conduct element specifies the act or conduct, omission, consequence, or state of affairs that is the substance of the offence. The mental element specifies the state of mind that the prosecution must prove the defendant had at the time of committing the offence. Both must be set down in law to define an offence and both must be proven in order to secure a conviction. For lawyers, this definition has some important attractions. It honours the principle that there be no crime without law and that liability arises only in respect of actions or omissions already proscribed by law as criminal. This principle allows people to go about their daily business free from fear of arbitrary punishment. It gives fair warning to those who choose to offend against the law that they may expect punishment to ensue. It respects the presumption of innocence by making it improper to speak of someone as a criminal until all aspects of liability for a crime have been proven in a court of law. If it is right to refer to suspects, not offenders, in the pre-trial process, then it must be right also to talk only of alleged crimes and alleged victims until the case has been proven in court.

As a substantive definition of crime, however, legal classification is problematic. Although it specifies the structural conditions (principally the mental and conduct elements) that must be met before a court of law will convict, it provides little purchase on the social phenomenon that is crime. To say both that criminal law responds to crime and that crime is defined by the criminal law creates an unfortunate circularity. Taken at face value, it suggests that without criminal law there can be no crime or even that the criminal law, in some bizarre sense, is the formal cause of crime.

A third aspect is that legal ideology makes certain claims as to the objectivity and political neutrality of legal doctrine and the autonomy of legal reasoning by which judgment is reached. Critical scrutiny of the criminal law allows the student of criminal justice to understand that doctrinal framework and the larger values and political factors that underlie it. For example, attention to the centrality of the mental element in the general part of the criminal law attests to its importance as a mechanism for assigning responsibility. But legal ideology can be problematic too. The proclaimed authority of the judgment and bringing in of the guilty verdict are brutal techniques for imposing order on social strife or messy disputes in which attribution of blame is often far less clear-cut than the law pretends.

A fourth aspect of legal classification is the requirement that crime be subject to a distinctive set of procedures. The rules of evidence, the standard of proof, the requirement that crime be adjudicated in a designated forum, subject to its own procedural rules, and staffed by its own personnel, are all intrinsic to the legal definition of crime. The requirement of proof beyond all reasonable doubt, the principle of morality, and the rules and conventions of the adversarial system combine with the legal institutions of the magistracy, judiciary, and lay jury as distinctive features of the criminal process. Understood this way, crime can be defined as that which is the subject of the criminal process: without prosecution and conviction, no liability for crime can be said to have occurred. The chief problem with this approach is that it is doubtful whether defining crime by reference to laws of evidence and procedure takes one much further.

For the student of criminal justice, the larger problem lies less in the elements so far discussed than the fact that most criminal law scholarship does not address the ways in which law is in practice applied by police, prosecutors, defence lawyers, magistrates, and judges. A simple application of legal definitions misses important variations in social attitudes and moral judgments that determine how those definitions are in practice imposed. And it cannot account for disparities in the application of the law according to the age, sex, class, and race of the supposed perpetrator.

To think about crime, as some criminal law textbooks still do, as comprising discrete, autonomous legal categories remote from the social world, is to engage in an absorbing but esoteric intellectual activity. The exercise of the law is not an arcane clerical task of filing different behaviours in discrete and precisely labelled boxes to achieve nothing more than a semblance of order. Of course, conceptual clarification and normative critique are essential elements of criminal law. Criminal law must define crimes clearly and crimes so defined should be worthy of their label. But the emphasis given by some textbooks to the legal requirements of mental and conduct elements is at odds with the practice of the criminal law, where these concepts play a more marginal role. To illustrate, students of criminal law typically begin their studies by minute examination of the intricacies of the mental elements of crime. They are less often asked to begin by reflecting upon the fact that the great bulk of the 8,000 offences in English criminal law are crimes of strict liability and, as such, require no intention. The sheer number of offences of strict liability raises doubts about the centrality of intention to criminal liability and about the centrality of individual responsibility. It might even be said to place in question what the criminal law is for. With respect to offences of strict liability at least, it is difficult to sustain the notion that crime is principally defined by culpable wrongdoing.

The misapprehension that practising lawyers devote their energies to tortured discussion about the degree of certainty needed to infer or find intention from evidence of foresight would similarly be dispelled by observation of the caseload and working patterns of magistrates' courts where intention is rarely at issue. Likewise, although university courses generally focus on serious offences such as murder, manslaughter, assault, and rape, in practice petty property, public order, and driving offences are the staple work of the lower courts. It is not surprising that generations of students of criminal law are misled into thinking that serious offences and jury trials are the norm, and that sentences of imprisonment are common punishment. Attention to the statistics of recorded crime; to the proportion of cases going to magistrates' and Crown courts; and to patterns of punishment quickly reveals another truth.

Most importantly, for a criminologist to accept that crime is that which is defined by law would lead to some perverse results. To proceed from the idea that crime exists only in law and only insofar as it has been proven in a court of law would excise from criminology a good part of its present subject matter, scope, and interest. By this definition there could be no dark figure of unrecorded crime since, legally, it is not crime at all. It would also require that the *British Crime Survey* be renamed the British Survey of Alleged Crime and its respondents called not victims but claimants. Official criminal statistics, on the other hand, would enjoy a perfect fit with crime. For by definition only those acts and omissions proven to satisfy the legal requirements of crime before a court of law and recorded as such would count as crime. Studies of attrition rates would also need to be re-conceptualized. There could be no gap between the commission and reporting of crime, nor between reporting of crime and recording by police, and no failure of clear-up rates either. Likewise there could be no offenders other than those convicted, nor any victim whose offender has not been so convicted. In sum, the possibility of hidden crime, of unreported crime, of unsolved crime, or of unknown or undisclosed victims would evaporate and much criminological endeavour with it.

This emphatically doctrinal account of criminal law is diminishing as legal and criminological scholarship converge. Criminal lawyers have fruitfully extended their scrutiny to the social world in which the laws they study are constructed, applied, and enforced. And criminologists reflect more and more upon the legal categorization of activities as criminal: to ask not only why people offend, but also why this behaviour, but not that, is legally designated criminal. If, as is currently the case in England, the study of criminal justice increasingly takes place within law schools, then a conception of crime that speaks little to its legally trained students must be undesirable. But convergence is not union and criminal justice scholars sitting at the margins of the two disciplines have to hold two different definitions of crime, the criminological and the legal, simultaneously in play. Those reading their work had better be quite clear which meaning they employ on each occasion. The crime that is the verdict of a jury persuaded beyond all reasonable doubt of the guilt of the offender is, of necessity, a different phenomenon from the crime concealed in the dark field that has yet to face the bright light of the legal process.

FURTHER READING

Finkelstein, C. (2000) 'Positivism and the Notion of an Offense' *California Law Review* 88: 335.

Husak, D. (2002) 'Limitations on Criminalization and the General Part of the Criminal Law' in S. Shute and A. Simester (eds) *Criminal Law Theory* (Oxford: OUP).

Lamond, G. (2007) 'What is a Crime?' *Oxford Journal of Legal Studies* 27: 609.

Williams, G. (1955) 'The Definition of Crime' *Current Legal Problems* 107.

---

2 THE ROLE OF CRIMINAL LAW

What should the aim of the criminal law be?

The American Model Penal Code, section 1.02

(1) The general purposes of the provisions governing the definition of offenses are:

    (a) to forbid and prevent conduct that unjustifiably and inexcusably inflicts or threatens substantial harm to individual or public interests;

(b) to subject to public control persons whose conduct indicates that they are disposed to commit crimes;

(c) to safeguard conduct that is without fault from condemnation as criminal;

(d) to give fair warning of the nature of the conduct declared to constitute an offense;

(e) to differentiate on reasonable grounds between serious and minor offenses.

Of course, not everyone will agree with all of these. Even if they are accepted, these principles will often conflict, and where they do there will be disagreement over how they should be balanced.[7] Take the example of bullying. This is behaviour which clearly falls within (a) as conduct which harms another. But there is great difficulty in defining precisely what bullying is as is required by (d). The law must then decide either to enact legislation which is rather vague but will mean that bullying can be prosecuted, or enact legislation which is precise, but might allow some bullies to 'get away' with their wrongdoing.[8]

While many commentators see the role of criminal law in political terms—such as ensuring that there is order on the streets—Antony Duff argues that the central role of the criminal law is part of a moral conversation: 'The criminal law provides the institutional framework within which, and procedures through which, perpetrators of public wrongs can be called to account (held responsible) for those wrongs.'[9] He develops this in the following summary of his thinking of the role of the criminal law:

R.A. Duff, 'Responsibility Citizenship and Criminal Law' in S. Green and R.A. Duff (eds) *Philosophical Foundations of Criminal Law* (Oxford: OUP, 2011), 127

The criminal law, in its substantive dimension, defines certain types of conduct as criminal (and defines certain defences for those who commit such criminal conduct). In so doing, it defines and condemns such conduct as wrong: not merely, and trivially, as legally wrong, as a breach of the rules of this particular game, but as morally wrong in a way that should concern those to whom it speaks, and that warrants the further consequences (trial, conviction, and punishment) that it attaches to such conduct. To say that it defines such conduct as wrong is not, however, to say that it creates that wrongfulness: although it is trivially true that criminal conduct is criminally wrongful only because the criminal law so defines it, it is substantively false to say that such conduct is morally wrongful only because the criminal law defines it as wrong. The criminal law does not (cannot) turn conduct that was not already wrongful into a moral wrong: it does not determine, but presupposes, the moral wrongfulness of the conduct that it defines as criminal; it determines which pre-criminal wrongs should count as 'public' wrongs whose perpetrators are to be called to public account. Its adjectival dimension then specifies the procedures through which those accused of perpetrating such wrongs are called to account: the criminal trial, as the formal culmination of the criminal process, summons a defendant to answer to a charge of public wrongdoing, and to answer for that wrongdoing if it is proved; if he cannot offer an exculpatory answer, he is convicted and thus condemned as a wrongdoer. Finally, in its penal dimension, the criminal law provides for the determination and administration of punishments for those convicted of such public wrongdoing.

---

[7] P. Robinson (2002: 79).

[8] See also the problems that arise in seeking to make extremely violent pornography unlawful (Rowbottom 2006).

[9] Duff (2011: 126).

3 THE STATISTICS OF CRIMINAL BEHAVIOUR

We will consider the statistics for particular offences when we deal with them separately. But here are some general statistics which give a picture of criminal behaviour in England and Wales. It should be noted that there is a significant difference between reported offences (those reported to the police and officially recorded) and surveys which interview people and try and find out whether they have been the victims of crimes, even if not reported to the police (e.g. the Crime Survey for England and Wales (CSEW)). Studies suggest the following:

(1) Around 9.2 million people, a fifth of the adult population, have a criminal record.[10] In one survey,[11] 61 per cent of people admitted some kind of offence against the government, their employers, or businesses. One survey found that 47 per cent of cars travelling on a motorway were travelling over the speed limit.[12] Over half of Britain's motorists break the speed limit every day, according to a survey by the RAC.[13] So most readers of this book are likely to have committed, or will commit, a crime at some point in their lives. If you don't want to fall into this majority read the following chapters carefully!

(2) The CSEW estimates that for the years 2014/15 there were 6.8 million crimes committed against adults[14] in England. Of these, 3.8 million were reported to the police.[15] The CSEW estimate is the lowest figure since records began in 1981, belying the common perception that crime is becoming ever more prevalent.

(3) Two out of every 100 adults aged 16 and over experienced a crime against the person in the previous 12 months before March 2015.[16] In 1995 the figure had been five in every 100 adults, showing a steep drop; although the victimization rate depends significantly on a range of socio-economic factors and age.

(4) The detection rate of reported offences was 28.9 per cent for 2012/13.[17]

(5) The general public grossly overestimates the incidence of violent crime and grossly underestimates the length of sentences that are typically awarded.[18]

QUESTIONS

1. Do any of these statistics surprise you? Why?

2. Why is it that the general public appears to have such an inaccurate view of criminal behaviour?

FURTHER READING

Office for National Statistics (2015) *Crime in England and Wales, Year Ending March 2015* (London: ONS).

---

[10] Howard (2013).   [11] BBC News Online (2007b).   [12] Chorley (2014).
[13] BBC News Online (2005a).
[14] In addition there were 709,000 offences committed against children.
[15] Office for National Statistics (2015a).   [16] *Ibid*.
[17] Office for National Statistics (2013c).   [18] Mattinson and Mirrlees Black (2000: vii).

4 'PRINCIPLES' OF CRIMINAL LAW

We will now turn to some of the so-called principles of criminal law. These are principles which some academic commentators and some judges have suggested underpin the English and Welsh criminal law. It must be emphasized that these are not in any sense strict rules which are followed throughout the criminal law. Rather they are proposed by some academics as principles to which the law should aspire. It should be stressed that some commentators are wary of stating principles that apply across the whole of criminal law and think it is more appropriate to consider the issues as they relate to particular offences.

4.1 THE PRINCIPLE OF LEGALITY

This is the principle that criminal offences should be clearly enough defined to enable people who wish to be law abiding to live their lives confident that they will not be breaking the law.[19] Consider living in a state which had a criminal law: 'It is a criminal offence to behave badly.' You would not know what 'behaving badly' meant. You may try as hard as you could to live a lawful life but still find that the authorities have regarded a particular piece of conduct as 'bad'. This principle is often viewed as a key aspect of the 'Rule of Law', a notion many constitutional lawyers promote as a central plank of a sound legal system. The principle is now enshrined in our criminal law through the Human Rights Act 1998, as we shall see.

This principle has a number of specific aspects, including the following:

(1) The law must be clear.
(2) The law must be capable of being obeyed. A law which prohibited breathing in public would clearly infringe the principle.
(3) The law must be readily available to the public. If all the laws were kept secret, then even if they were written in the clearest language you would not be able to keep them.

An example of an offence which arguably infringes this principle is section 5 of the Public Order Act 1986, which states that it is an offence to engage in disorderly behaviour or threatening, abusive, or insulting behaviour likely to cause 'harassment, alarm or distress'. This is a potentially very wide offence, and indeed it provides a discretion for police officers to arrest people for conduct of which they do not approve.[20]

4.2 THE PRINCIPLE OF RESPONSIBILITY

This is the principle that people should only be guilty in respect of conduct for which they are responsible. So, people should not be guilty for conduct over which they had no control. This principle might be infringed if the criminal law punished a person for behaviour he carried out while suffering from an epileptic fit, for example.

---

[19] See Westen (2007) for further discussion.
[20] See e.g. *Masterson v Holden* [1986] 1 WLR 1017, where the Divisional Court held that the magistrates were entitled to say that two men kissing were 'insulting' passers-by. The defendants were charged under the Metropolitan Police Act 1839, s. 54(13).

4.3   THE PRINCIPLE OF MINIMAL CRIMINALIZATION

This principle suggests that the criminal law should prohibit something only if absolutely necessary.[21] There are practical reasons for such a principle: our courts and prisons are overcrowded enough as it is without creating an ever increasing number of offences. But there is also a principled reason for it. A criminal sanction conveys the message that the conduct was not just bad, but bad enough to involve criminal proceedings. This censure function will be lost if less serious conduct is criminalized.[22] The criminal law, it should be remembered, is only one way of influencing behaviour that is seen as undesirable. Education, rewarding good behaviour, shaming, and civil proceedings are alternatives that the law has at its disposal for dealing with bad behaviour.[23] So, it must be asked whether it is necessary to have around 8,000 statutes which create criminal offences. Chalmers and Leverick[24] claim that recent governments have been especially productive with 1,395 offences created solely in the year 1997/98 and 634 in 2010/11. Although in later research the authors find that there are no more newly created offences now than there were in previous decades.[25] Many academic commentators have expressed concern that we have far too much criminal law.[26] Many law students would agree! In particular there is a concern that creating a new criminal offence is an easy response for politicians to the 'issue of the day'. Dennis Baker has suggested we need to recognize a right not to be criminalized.[27]

In the following extract, Andrew Ashworth argues that the state has become too keen to use the criminal law to deal with 'troublesome' behaviour:[28]

A. Ashworth, 'Is Criminal Law a Lost Cause?' (2000) 116 *Law Quarterly Review* 225

The number of offences in English criminal law continues to grow year by year. Politicians, pressure groups, journalists and others often express themselves as if the creation of a new criminal offence is the natural, or the only appropriate, response to a particular event or series of events giving rise to social concern. At the same time, criminal offences are tacked on to diverse statutes by various government departments, and then enacted (or, often, re-enacted) by Parliament without demur. There is little sense that the decision to introduce a new offence should only be made after certain conditions have been satisfied, little sense that making conduct criminal is a step of considerable social significance. It is this unprincipled and chaotic construction of the criminal law that prompts the question whether it is a lost cause. From the point of view of governments it is clearly not a lost cause: it is a multi-purpose tool, often creating the favourable impression that certain misconduct has been taken seriously and dealt with appropriately. But from any principled viewpoint there are important issues—of how the criminal law ought to be shaped, of what its social significance should be, of when it should be used and when not—which are simply not being addressed in the majority of instances.

. . .

Despite the disorderly state of English criminal law, it appears that the Government does profess some principles for criminalisation. In response to a parliamentary question, Lord

---

[21] Husak (2008).   [22] Feinberg (1986: ch. 5).   [23] Card and Ashworth (2000).
[24] Chalmers and Leverick (2013).   [25] Chalmers, Leverick, and Shaw (2015).
[26] See e.g. Baker (2011b).   [27] Baker (2011b).
[28] See also the use of ASBOs (anti-social behaviour orders) (see Squires (2008), Burney (2005), and von Hirsch and Simester (2006)). See Baker (2007) for a discussion of broader issues surrounding remote harms.

Williams of Mostyn has stated that offences 'should be created only when absolutely necessary', and that

'In considering whether new offences should be created, factors taken into account include whether:

- the behaviour in question is sufficiently serious to warrant intervention by the criminal law;
- the mischief could be dealt with under existing legislation or by using other remedies;
- the proposed offence is enforceable in practice;
- the proposed offence is tightly-drawn and legally sound; and
- the proposed penalty is commensurate with the seriousness of the offence.

The Government also takes into account the need to ensure, as far as practicable, that there is consistency across the sentencing framework.'

. . .

Although I have tried in this essay to give some flavour of the proliferation of legal forms and structures for the guidance of conduct, and thereby to demonstrate a blurring of the boundaries between criminal and regulatory and between criminal and civil, the main purpose has been to develop two lines of argument.

The first is that the criminal law is indeed a lost cause, from the point of view of principle. The Government's purported criteria for creating new crimes are not followed in practice, nor have they been in the recent past. *Pace* Lord Williams, new offences have been created to penalise non-serious misbehaviour, sometimes with maximum sentences out of proportion to other maxima. The empirical basis for this claim was illustrated by examples from the 1997 statute book, and particularly the offence in section 1 of the Crime and Disorder Act 1998 of breaching an anti-social behaviour order. The plain fact is that governments often take the view that the creation of a new crime sends out a symbolic message that, in blunt terms, may 'get them off a political hook'—even though the new crime fails to satisfy Lord Williams' criteria on one or more grounds.

The second line of argument is more constructive, in seeking to identify a principled core of criminal law. The core consists, it is submitted, of four interlinking principles:

The principle that the criminal law should be used, and only used, to censure persons for substantial wrongdoings. The principle recognises that the prevention of such misconduct is a reason for criminalising it: if serious wrongdoing can be identified, it is of social importance that its incidence be reduced. However, this should be distinguished from the less acceptable propositions *(a)* that the prevention of misconduct is a sufficient reason for criminalisation, and *(b)* that the criminal law is, either on its own or in combination with other social policies, necessarily an effective means of prevention. The tendency to overestimate the deterrent efficacy of criminal sentencing has already been mentioned. As for crime prevention strategies, these are usually designed to minimise the risk that certain situations or opportunities will come about, or that certain individuals will find it attractive to behave in particular ways. Appropriately targeted social, educational and housing policies may well have a greater preventive effect than the enactment of a criminal offence and the conviction of (what is likely to be) a relatively small proportion of offenders, a point rarely acknowledged in the political and media discussions that lead to the creation of new crimes. However, methods of crime prevention also raise questions of moral and social principle that should be kept in view.

The principle that criminal laws should be enforced with respect for equal treatment and proportionality. The implication is that enforcement authorities and their policies ought to be reorganised so as to reflect the relative seriousness of the wrongdoing with which they are dealing, and should not remain hidebound by traditional divisions of responsibility that fail to reflect proper assessments of the culpable wrongs involved.

The principle that persons accused of substantial wrongdoing ought to be afforded the protections appropriate to those charged with criminal offences, i.e. *at least the minimum protections declared by Articles 6.2 and 6.3 of the European Convention on Human Rights.* These minimum protections ought to be regarded as an inherent element of criminal procedure, and this principle as interlinked with the others. Thus, if wrongdoing is regarded as serious enough to warrant the creation of an offence, and if it is thought so serious as to require a substantial maximum sentence, it would be a violation of this principle for a government to avoid or whittle down the protections that a person facing such a charge ought to be accorded. This, it will be recalled, is one objection to the offence of failing to comply with an anti-social behaviour order contrary to section 1 of the Crime and Disorder Act 1998. A maximum penalty of five years' imprisonment has been provided for what is a strict liability offence, all the substantive issues having been determined in earlier civil proceedings without the Article 6 safeguards. Civil-criminal hybrids designed to circumvent Convention rights are wrong in principle.

The principle that maximum sentences and effective sentence levels should be proportionate to the seriousness of the wrongdoing. The implication here, as with the second principle, is that there needs to be a root-and-branch change—a thorough revision of maximum penalties and a re-assessment of sentence levels and of differentials between them.

These are put forward as core principles. It is not claimed that they should be regarded as absolute rules, and indeed at various points above some possible qualifications to them have been discussed. Derogations from them should be argued as derogations, and should be principled in themselves.

The principles also lead in other directions that cannot be examined fully in this context. At the core is the idea that, if a particular wrong is thought serious enough to justify the possibility of a custodial sentence, that wrong should be treated as a crime, with fault required and proper procedural protection for defendants. This has implications for those minor wrongs that are presently made the subject of criminal offences simply because the criminal courts offer themselves as a quick and cheap means of dealing with them: many of the 1997 offences fall into this category, as do hundreds of other strict liability offences. A fine solution would be to create a new category of 'civil violation' or 'administrative offence' which would certainly be non-imprisonable and would normally attract a financial penalty; procedures would be simplified but would preserve minimum rights for defendants, such as access to a criminal court. Another implication of the principles should be that any new criminal code for this country ought to declare the most serious offences in English law, rather than simply those traditional offences that have been the focus of textbooks over the years.

What are the prospects for thus re-structuring and restoring integrity to the criminal law? Political reality suggests that they are unpromising: in this sense, the criminal law may be a lost cause. Even governments with large parliamentary majorities, and which profess certain criteria for the creation of new offences, may either give way to the allure of media popularity or simply not care sufficiently to adhere to their own principles. In such political circumstances it is all the more necessary to re-kindle debate about the functions and characteristics that the criminal law ought to have, and to ensure that the close interconnections between criminal law, criminal procedure and sentencing are kept at the forefront of that debate.

4.4 THE PRINCIPLE OF PROPORTIONALITY

The sentence accorded to a crime should reflect the seriousness of the offence. This is, in a way, obvious.[29] It would clearly be wrong if murder carried a less serious sentence than assault. But there are more complex arguments over whether one offence is more or less serious than another: is rape more or less serious than having a hand cut off?

To deal with such harder cases, we need a way of grading the seriousness of the harm suffered by the victim. Joel Feinberg suggests focusing on the victim's loss of opportunity or range of choices. Clearly, therefore, murder is the most serious offence as it completely destroys the victim's range of opportunities or choices. Andrew von Hirsch and Nils Jareborg have suggested another, which focuses on the following[30] four kinds of interests:

(1) physical integrity: health, safety, and the avoidance of physical pain;

(2) material support and amenity: includes nutrition, shelter, and other basic amenities;

(3) freedom from humiliation or degrading treatment;

(4) privacy and autonomy.

In assessing the degree of harm suffered you should first determine which interests of the victim have been interfered with and then consider the extent of the interference. This involves considering how far it affects the victim's 'living standard': the basic things a person needs to achieve a good life. An assessment of harm will also involve considering the blameworthiness of the defendant.

Such an approach has the benefit of providing a focus for determining the extent of harm: how far it impedes victims in living a good life. However, that leaves open the question of what is a good life. It also focuses on the impact of the crime on the victim, and does not capture the sense that a crime involves a public wrong. This concept is explored in the following extract:

A. Ashworth and J. Horder, *Principles of Criminal Law* (7th edn, Oxford: OUP, 2013), 29–30

[Another] aspect, in addition to harmfulness and wrongfulness, is the public element in wrongs. One manifestation of this consists of those general obligations of citizens that are so important that the criminal sanction may be justified to reinforce them. A core of offences against state security may be justified on these grounds, as may some offences against the taxation and benefits system, so long as the limiting effect of the minimalising principle . . . is kept in view. These are public wrongs, inasmuch as the victim is not an individual but the community as a whole, and it is right that the more serious among them are considered suitable for criminalization—not least where the gain or advantage obtained is as great as, or greater than, that obtained in the typical offence with an individual victim. But it is to the latter kind of offence that we must now turn, and this is where the public element becomes problematic. How can we tell which wrongs done to the individual are sufficiently 'public' to warrant the condemnation of the criminal law? As Antony Duff [(2007)]

---

[29] Although see von Hirsch and Ashworth (2005) and Koffman (2006) for a discussion of the difficulties in putting this principle into practice.

[30] von Hirsch and Jareborg (1991).

argues, the answer lies not in an aspect of the wrong itself, but in the public valuation of the wrong:

> We should interpret a 'public' wrong, not as a wrong that injures the public, but as one that properly concerns the public, i.e. the polity as a whole . . . A public wrong is thus a wrong against the polity as a whole, not just the individual victim: given our identi-fication with the victim as a fellow citizen, and our shared commitment to the values that the rapist violates, we must see the victim's wrong as also being our wrong.

The public element does not have anything to do with location: unkind remarks made to a friend in public would not 'concern the public' unless they tended to provoke a breach of the peace, and a very public breaking of a promise to attend a certain event may not be regarded as sufficiently important for the polity as a whole to be required to take action. Contrast those instances with domestic violence (e.g. a substantial beating) which, even if it occurs entirely in the private realm of a home, is a moral and social wrong that the community should regard as a wrong that ought to be pursued through the public channels of prosecution and trial. Thus, as Grant Lamond [(2007)] has argued, the question is whether the community is appropriately responsible for punishing these wrongs. The supporting argument here is pre-sumably that the state should protect and promote the basic value of security and freedom from physical attack by prosecuting assaults wherever they occur (leaving aside questions of consent and its proper limits), and that the fact that an assault occurs in a domestic context should make no difference to this. It does not follow from this that adultery is a good can-didate for criminalization, harmful and wrongful though it may be in many instances, since the question is whether the value of marriage as an institution is so central and fundamental to the political community that the state is expected to prosecute through the criminal law those whose conduct threatens it.

4.5 THE PRINCIPLE OF FAIR LABELLING

This principle requires that the description of the offence should match the wrong done.[31] If the definition of a crime in law departs too markedly from the definition as understood by the general public then the law may fall into disrepute. When defining a crime it is helpful to distin-guish the loss a victim suffers and the wrong done to a victim. This point can be made by way of an example: Alf steals Ben's book; Catherine destroys Davina's book. Both Ben and Davina suffer the same loss: their books are gone. But the wrongs done to them are different: the way their property was lost matters in moral terms. Hence the criminal law distinguishes between criminal damage and theft.[32] There is more to this point than that. Imagine that both Edward and Fred are pushed over, but Fred was deliberately pushed over and Edward accidentally. They may have suffered the same harm, but the wrong done to them was different. Edward might laugh the event off as an accident, expecting an apology at most. However, Fred would regard the incident as a serious invasion of his right to bodily integrity.[33] So the state of mind of the defendant is an important aspect of the wrong done to the victim.

One uncertainty surrounding the issue of labels, is the question of to whom the labels in criminal law are addressed. Are we seeking descriptions which will carry meaning for mem-bers of the general public, or meanings which have significance for professionals working in the criminal justice system?[34]

---

[31] Chalmers and Leverick (2008); Mitchell (2001).   [32] Duff (2002: 6).
[33] J. Gardner (1998a: 211).   [34] Chalmers and Leverick (2008).

FURTHER READING

Ashworth, A. (2000c) 'Is the Criminal Law a Lost Cause?' *Law Quarterly Review* 116: 225.

Ashworth, A. (2004) 'Social Control and Anti-Social Behaviour' *Law Quarterly Review* 120: 263.

Baker, D. (2007) 'The Moral Limits of Criminalizing Remote Harms' *New Criminal Law Review* 10: 370.

Baker, D. (2011b) *The Right Not to be Criminalized* (Aldershot: Ashgate).

Chalmers, J. and Leverick, F. (2008) 'Fair Labelling in Criminal Law' *Modern Law Review* 71: 217.

Husak, D. (2008) *Overcriminalization: The Limits of the Criminal Law* (Oxford: OUP).

Jareborg, N. (1995) 'What Kind of Criminal Law Do We Want?' in A. Snare (ed.) *Beware of Punishment* (Oslo: Pax Forlag).

Mitchell, B. (2001) 'Multiple Wrongdoing and Offence Structure: A Plea for Consistency and Fair Labelling' *Modern Law Review* 64: 393.

Tadros, V. (2012) 'Fair Labelling and Social Solidarity' in L. Zedner and J. Roberts (eds) *Principles and Values in Criminal Law and Criminal Justice: Essays in Honour of Andrew Ashworth* (Oxford: OUP).

5 PROPOSALS FOR A CRIMINAL CODE

The failure of English and Welsh criminal law to live up to the principles we have just been discussing has led some to suggest that the government should produce a Criminal Code. This would be a single statute which would seek to describe the criminal law (or the important parts of criminal law) in one document in clear language. In producing such a Code, it would be possible to seek to adhere to the principles mentioned in Section 4 as much as possible. Indeed the Law Commission undertook the job of drafting such a Code.[35] However, in 2008 the Law Commission indicated that it had abandoned its work on the Code.[36] Instead, it decided to focus its work on producing proposals to reform particular areas of the law. In an editorial entitled 'RIP: The Criminal Code (1968–2008)' the editors of the *Criminal Law Review* expressed their grave disappointment at this news, saying it was a 'sad end for a noble ideal'.[37] Although, at first, the idea of a Code might be thought an unmitigated blessing (especially for law students!), in fact it has not proved universally popular.[38]

5.1 ARGUMENTS IN FAVOUR OF A CODE

(1) **Certainty** The argument in favour of codification is that it will create a clearly stated rule which will govern whether a person is guilty. This avoids the common law

---

[35] For another version of a Code, see P. Robinson (1997) (criticized in Mitchell (2001) and Duff (2002)).
[36] Law Commission (2008).   [37] Editor of the *Criminal Law Review* (2009).
[38] Although for a recent attempt to revive the argument in favour of the Code, see Lavery (2010).

approach of having rather vaguely defined offences whose interpretation can be expanded or contracted by the judge to fit the justice of the particular case. Of course, codification will not produce a criminal law which is absolutely clear in every regard and it would be wrong to think that all common law offences are utterly vague, but the argument is that a Criminal Code should reduce the circumstances in which the principle of legality is breached. The point can also be made in constitutional terms—that a Code would help uphold the separation of powers: that the creation of the law should be for Parliament not the judiciary.

(2) **Accessibility** If a member of the public wanted to find out what the criminal law was at present, she or he could not find one document that sets out the criminal law. To get hold of all the statutes and all the case law to provide an effective guide to the present law would be a marathon task.[39] Toulson LJ has made a forceful attack on the lack of access to statutes. Indeed he has said it is 'profoundly unsatisfactory' if statutory law is not accessible, and he says that statutes are not even readily accessible to courts.[40] In theory, if the entire criminal law could be found in a Code it could become readily available to the general public at all good booksellers.

Such arguments have led Paul Robinson[41] to propose a Code which distinguishes between rules of conduct and rules of attribution.[42] He sees the rules of conduct as primarily aimed at sending clear messages[43] to citizens telling them what they can and cannot do in simple terms.[44] Controversially, this means that the conduct rules do not include references to the results that arise from the acts or to states of mind.[45] By contrast, rules of attribution are directed towards judges or juries telling them when a particular person should be convicted for infringing a rule of attribution. This distinction has the benefit, he claims, of keeping the rules of conduct (which are directed to the general public) as brief and clear as possible.

Critics of Robinson's approach have argued that rules of conduct can be of little use if they do not include an indication of a state of mind. Take rape: a citizen who was seeking to obey the law would conduct his or her sex life quite differently if the law on rape was a strict liability offence than if it was an intention-based offence.[46] Antony Duff has suggested that it is unlikely that members of the public will read a Code and that it is more important that the Code makes moral sense in that it reflects community values rather than that it is linguistically clear.[47]

(3) **Efficiency** The benefits mentioned so far—certainty and accessibility—would also work, it is argued, to make courts more efficient. The judge will be able to give a clear direction on the law to the jury, making the jury's job easier and lessening the need for appeals to the Court of Appeal following a misdirection by judges.

(4) **Consistency** Proponents of a Code argue that in drafting it the contradictions and ambiguities in the law can be removed.

(5) **Updating** The Code would provide the opportunity to rid the law of 'old fashioned offences', which might have made sense when they were passed, but seem bizarre in the

---

[39] Purchasing a textbook on the criminal law would be much easier!
[40] *Chambers* [2008] EWCA Crim 2467.   [41] P. Robinson (1997); P. Robinson (1990).
[42] P. Robinson (1997). See also Dan-Cohen (2002: ch. 2).
[43] He describes rules of conduct as having a 'communicative function'.
[44] P. Robinson (1997: 128).   [45] For criticism of this, see Husak (1999a).
[46] Duff (2002: 69).   [47] Duff (2002). For arguments against Duff's view, see Alldridge (2002).

twenty-first century. Is it really necessary to have the offence of 'assaulting a clergyman in the discharge of his duties in a place of worship or burial place'?[48]

5.2 DISADVANTAGES OF THE CODE

The following are some of the alleged disadvantages of a Criminal Code:

(1) **Obsession with 'consistency'** There is a concern that if the Code were to become obsessed with guiding principles and internal consistency this might overlook the fact that apparent contradictions within the criminal law in fact reflect the complexity of the many political, ethical, and practical issues involved in developing the law for a particular offence.[49] Apparently, contradictory aspects of the criminal law may in fact prove to be a workable compromise for those areas of the law. Further, the views of the public on what may be an acceptable criminal law are not always consistent or rational. This may justify a criminal law which, although 'irrational', perhaps reflects the public morality.

(2) **The benefits of a Code are overemphasized**[50] It is not realistic that *The Code* will hit the bestseller list. Further, hard cases are hard cases because they involve a clash of important principles. For example, the infamous conjoined twins case[51] (see Chapter 12) raised extremely difficult questions for law and morality. That case would have been no easier were there a Code in place.

FURTHER READING

de Búrca, G. and Gardner, S. (1990) 'The Codification of the Criminal Law' *Oxford Journal of Legal Studies* 10: 559.

Farmer, L. (2014) 'Codification' in M. Dubber and T. Hörnle (eds) *The Oxford Handbook of Criminal Law* (Oxford: OUP).

Robinson, P. (1998) *Structure and Function of Criminal Law* (Oxford: OUP).

---

6 WHAT CONDUCT SHOULD BE CRIMINAL?

How should the state decide which conduct should, or should not, be criminal? Why should Parliament not make swearing in a public place an offence?[52] We shall shortly consider the extensive academic analysis of this question. But before doing so it is worth emphasizing that in practice a government's decision on whether to criminalize something is normally a matter of political expediency, rather than fine-sounding principles.[53] For example, in 1990 there was a media campaign against the horrors of 'killer dogs', featuring horrific photographs of children attacked by vicious dogs. The campaign called upon Parliament to 'do

---

[48] Offences Against the Person Act 1861, s. 36. [49] de Búrca and Gardner (1990).
[50] Clarkson (1994). [51] *Re A (Conjoined Twins: Medical Treatment)* [2000] 4 All ER 961 (CA).
[52] Although it might be necessary first to repeal the Human Rights Act 1998 (which protects the freedom of speech).
[53] See Ashworth (2000c).

something'. In the light of such a campaign, it is hard for politicians not to react, not least for fear that in due course there might be other children harmed by dogs and the press would then say 'if only you had passed legislation this child would have been saved'. Indeed in due course the Dangerous Dogs Act 1991 was passed.[54] The political pressure to increase the number of criminal offences has led some academics to argue that we need to articulate principles to restrict the tendency to create new offences.

These are some of the principles academics have suggested should govern Parliament's decisions on criminalization.

6.1 AUTONOMY

To many commentators the right of autonomy, the right to live one's life as one likes, is of fundamental importance.[55] Making decisions for ourselves means that we can be proud of the good things that we do, but also that we can be ashamed of, and deserve blame for, the bad things we do. Autonomy plays three crucial roles in defining the criminal law:

(1) It justifies the existence of the criminal law. Without the criminal law, other people could, without punishment, interfere with my right to live my life as I choose. In other words, the criminal law is necessary to prevent one person's exercise of autonomy interfering with another's.

(2) It restricts the extent of the criminal law. The criminal law impinges on people's autonomy. If the criminal law made it illegal for same-sex couples to engage in consenting sexual relationships, this would interfere with how many people would like to live their lives. The autonomy principle therefore explains why it is only where the activity causes a significant amount of harm to others or to society that the law is justified in prohibiting it.

(3) It justifies censure. If we are autonomous citizens, able to live our lives as we choose, then we should be responsible for the bad choices we make as well as the good ones. In other words, the autonomy principle explains why people should be liable for making the wrong choice, and also explains that where people do not have a free choice to act as they should the criminal law provides a defence (e.g. where they are acting under duress).

It should not be thought that the autonomy principle is uncontroversial. First, there are some who point out that the right to choose how to live our lives may be available for the rich, the able, and advantaged, but it may be regarded as a chimera for the poor, the disabled, and the disadvantaged.[56] Indeed one of the leading proponents of the importance of autonomy, Joseph Raz, has argued that if the state wants to take the right of autonomy seriously it must ensure that the social conditions necessary for the exercise of full autonomy are provided.[57]

For others there are concerns that the autonomy principle overemphasizes individualism.[58] It talks about the right for me to pursue my vision of the 'good life', but for many people

---

[54] Arguably another example is the substantial amount of terrorist legislation which was passed as a swift response to the events of 11 September 2001 (for discussion, see Fenwick (2002)).

[55] Raz (1985).   [56] Hudson (1994).   [57] Raz (1986).

[58] Herring (2009a) and Fineman (2004).

their vision of the good life is tied up with families, friends, and communities.[59] For them the promotion of the good life might mean the promotion of the good of groups of people. Criminal law may be required to ensure proper regulation of common life. So seen, far from criminal law undermining autonomy it may be essential to enable people to exercise their autonomy.

There are many offences which appear to protect people from themselves and cannot readily be justified by the autonomy principle.[60] One well-known example is the requirement that people travelling in cars wear seat belts. We feel that although we respect people's choices, there comes a point where the law states 'we will not allow you to do such a dangerous thing'.

The autonomy principle is behind one of the most popular theories explaining when a state may criminalize: the harm principle.[61]

6.2 THE HARM PRINCIPLE

The leading exposition of the harm principle is provided by John Stuart Mill with his famous essay, *On Liberty*. At the heart of his argument is the following:

> The only purpose for which power can be rightfully exercised over any member of a civilized community against his will is to prevent harm to others. His own good, either physical or moral, is not sufficient warrant. He cannot rightfully be compelled to do or forbear . . . because in the opinion of others to do so would be wise or even right.[62]

Essentially, then, the harm principle is that each person should be allowed to do and say what he or she likes provided that this does not harm the interests of others. Simply because an activity is seen as immoral or harmful to the actor is not a good enough reason to justify criminalizing it.[63] The harm principle tells us what sorts of behaviour should *not* be criminalized. Just because conduct harms others does not mean that supporters of the harm principle would necessarily support criminalizing it.[64] Indeed Hamish Stewart has argued that in respect of some kinds of conduct people have a right to engage in it, however harmful it might be.[65] Further, there is a wide range of ways that the state could use to respond to undesirable activity, criminalization being only one of them.[66]

In recent times, the harm principle has received powerful support from the work of Joel Feinberg, who in three highly influential books has sought to interpret and justify a modern

---

[59] Herring (2013d).

[60] This leads Dan-Cohen (2000) to argue that the concept of dignity, rather than autonomy or welfare, should be the basis of the law.

[61] For further discussion, see Baker (2011a and 2011b); Herring (2012b: ch. 1).   [62] Mill (1991).

[63] See further Gross (2007: 225–7) who sees human rights as an important tool in ensuring criminal law is not used to promote moral values, rather than protecting against harm.

[64] Gardner (1998: 229) suggests that an activity needs to be both harmful and base or worthless to justify criminalization.

[65] Stewart (2009). He does not provide specific examples, but consensual sexual acts in private might be seen by some as one example.

[66] Tadros (2010).

understanding of the principle. In the following extract, Douglas Husak summarizes and discusses Feinberg's theory:

D. Husak, 'The Nature and Justifiability of Nonconsummate Offences' (1995) 37 *Arizona Law Review* 151 at 155–9

Most theorists agree that the criminal sanction should be imposed only for blameworthy and wrongful conduct. This necessary condition of justified criminal legislation might be called the *wrongfulness* requirement. The most persuasive of many possible arguments in support of this requirement focuses on the institution of criminal punishment. Violations of the criminal law, by definition, are subject to the penal sanction. This sanction involves the deliberate infliction of a hardship. The deliberate infliction of a hardship requires a justification. It is hard to see how punishment could be justified unless a person deserves to be punished, and it is unclear how a person could deserve to be punished unless his conduct is blameworthy and wrongful.

There are principled reasons not to criminalize all wrongful and blameworthy conduct, even if the practical difficulties of enforcement could be overcome. Immorality is a necessary, but not a sufficient condition for criminalization. Commentators have struggled to identify that subclass of wrongful conduct that is eligible for punishment. The *harm* requirement provides the most plausible solution to this problem. Joel Feinberg's work represents the most ambitious and impressive defence of what he calls a *liberal* theory of law, characterized as the thesis that the only good reason to subject persons to criminal punishment is to prevent them from wrongfully causing harm to others.

According to Feinberg, 'the sense of "harm" as that term is used in the harm principle must represent the overlap of [normative and non-normative senses]: only setbacks of interests that are wrongs, and wrongs that are setbacks to interest, are to count as harms in the appropriate sense.' In the 'normative' sense of harm, A harms B 'by wronging B, or by treating him unjustly.' In the 'non-normative' sense of harm, A harms B 'by invading, and thereby setting back, his interest.' The need for an overlap of these two senses should be apparent. Harmful but permissible conduct is not eligible for criminal penalties because it fails to satisfy the wrongfulness requirement. Person A might set back the interests of person B—thereby placing B in a 'harmed condition'—through a legitimate competition, for example. But A's conduct should not be criminalized because B has not been wronged or treated unjustly. The interests of B may have been set back and *infringed*, but they have not been *violated*. Conversely, harmless but impermissible conduct is not eligible for criminal penalties because it does not set back anyone's interests. Person A might behave immorally without victimizing anyone. But A's conduct should not be criminalized because no one has been harmed.

The 'overlap' of these two senses of harm can be expressed succinctly by invoking the concept of rights: All wrongful conduct that sets back the interests of others violates their rights. Thus Feinberg's liberal framework establishes the moral limits of the criminal law by reference to the rights of persons. As expressed succinctly, 'criminal prohibitions are legitimate only when they protect individual rights.'

Feinberg claims no originality on behalf of his general thesis, which he locates squarely in the tradition of John Stuart Mill. The novelty of his approach lies in the details of his explication of the harm principle. In particular, Feinberg's interpretation provides a response to two reservations that have long been expressed about the harm requirement, even by theorists who tend to sympathize with it. First, many commentators have feared that the harm requirement is empty, trivial, tautological, or vacuous. If *any* undesirable consequence can be countenanced as a harm, all serious candidates for criminal legislation will satisfy the harm requirement. Second, many commentators have endorsed the harm principle because they believe that the criminal law should not be used to enforce morality. According to these theorists it is harm, rather than immorality, that should be prevented by the criminal law. Thus harm is sometimes thought to represent an alternative to the proposal that the criminal law should enforce morality.

Among Feinberg's central achievements are his responses to each of these two reservations. He interprets the harm requirement as nontrivial and full of substantive content, much of which is clearly moral in nature. Applications of his liberal theory entail that criminal intervention is unjustified in principle unless (a) the rights of someone are set back by (b) wrongful conduct. According to this view, the harm requirement cannot function as a genuine alternative to the claim that the criminal law should enforce morality, but rather identifies that subclass of immoral conduct that the criminal law should proscribe.

A detailed account of the specific instances of legislation that should be rejected as incompatible with a liberal theory of law requires at least two supplementary theories: first, a theory of moral rights, and second, a theory of wrongful conduct. Feinberg is well aware of the need for these two supplementary theories. He is equally aware that neither of these theories is easy to produce, and he does not pretend to have completed the task. Still, a virtue of Feinberg's account is that it clearly identifies the kinds of work that remain to be completed in order to provide a comprehensive theory of the moral limits of the criminal law.

Even without these two supplementary theories, one would anticipate few difficulties in applying Feinberg's views to justify enactment of the most familiar criminal offenses in Anglo-American law. Consider theft. Rights in personal property that are set back by acts of theft are a familiar part of virtually all theories of rights. In addition, the wrongfulness of theft is widely acknowledged. Thus the application of a liberal theory to justify the creation and enforcement of the offense of theft seems unproblematic.

Moreover, Feinberg's views are equally plausible when applied to reveal the deficiencies in proposals to create new criminal legislation that most everyone would denounce as an unjustifiable exercise of state authority. Consider a hypothetical proposal to enact criminal legislation to prohibit persons from dropping out of school prior to graduation. No one doubts the utility of an educated citizenry. But does someone who fails to complete his education act wrongfully (as opposed to foolishly or imprudently)? Does he set back anyone's rights (apart from his own long-term interests)? Unless both of these questions can be answered affirmatively, a liberal theory of law, as explicated by Feinberg, would preclude enacting criminal legislation for this purpose.

Of course, a sponsor of such legislation could always insist that rights *are* set back, and that conduct *is* wrongful, whenever persons drop out of school. It may be impossible to persuade such a sponsor without actually providing supplementary theories of rights and wrongful conduct. In the absence of these two supplementary theories, one can only hope that the intuitive implausibility of these claims would be recognized. In this context, this hope seems reasonable. The judgment that persons should be punished for failing to graduate is not easily brought into 'reflective equilibrium' with other judgments about rights and wrongful conduct, both specific and general, that persons tend to endorse. Thus Feinberg's liberal theory of law, when accompanied by widely shared judgments about the supplementary theories required by its application, seems to escape the charge that the harm principle is trivial and vacuous. His theory supports criminal legislation of which most everyone approves, and condemns criminal legislation of which most everyone disapproves. A liberal theory—according to which the criminal law should not be used except to prevent persons from violating the moral rights of others—is enormously valuable to help identify the moral limits of the criminal law.

As this passage indicates, the harm principle itself is fairly straightforward. But at its heart is the concept of harm, and it is far from clear what that means. There is little disagreement that cuts, bruises, and death count as harms, but other issues are less straightforward. Indeed some commentators have argued that the principle is so vague that it can justify pretty much whatever conclusion you want to reach.[67] Nevertheless, debates over harm play a central role in the debates over when it should be illegal to smoke in public.[68] A key point that swayed that debate was that passive smoking caused harm to other people.

Is offence harm?

Is this offence 'harm' for the purposes of the harm principle?[69] In *DPP v Gough*[70] the conviction of Stephen Gough for an offence under section 5 of the Public Order Act 1986 was upheld. For the past ten years he has been walking around Britain 'wearing only walking boots, socks, a hat, a rucksack and a compass on a lanyard around his neck'. He is a committed naturist and believes people should be free to walk around naked if they wish. Two women gave evidence they were disgusted when seeing him walk through a town. Sir Brian Leveson P explained:

> the district judge was clearly entitled to conclude that, by walking through a town centre entirely naked, he was violating public order or, in the language of the case contributing "to a breakdown of peaceful and law-abiding behaviour as evidenced by the reactions of the public": he was thus disorderly. There was nothing passive about his conduct in that he knew full well (not least from his past experience) that many members of the public would both be alarmed and distressed by sight of his naked body whether or not others would take a more benign view and whatever the origins or psychological reasons for that alarm and distress. Furthermore, he was being deliberately provocative in order to support his own stance.

But is the disgust or discomfort of others sufficient to justify a criminal conviction? Joel Feinberg supports the prohibition of conduct that causes offence. But he uses a strict definition of 'offence'. Offence involves more than concern or disapproval. An example might be the feelings relatives would have if they found that the body of their loved one had been horribly desecrated. It is unlikely the women's disgust in the *Gough* case would be sufficient. For other academics no degree of offence is sufficient to constitute a 'harm'. To permit offence to be harm enables one set of people to impose their moral values on others. Indeed the more hard line they are, the more likely they are to be profoundly disturbed, and so the more likely to fall within Feinberg's definition of 'offence'.

Is harm to future generations harm?

This issue is relevant in particular to environmental legislation. If it is demonstrated that an activity will not harm anyone presently living but will have long-term environmental damage which might harm future generations, would this be harm for the purposes of the harm principle?

---

[67] Harcourt (1999).   [68] Ferguson (2011).
[69] See Simester and von Hirsch (2002) and Feinberg (1986b).   [70] [2013] EWHC 3267 (Admin).

Are potential harms harm?

What about conduct which in itself is not harmful but which carries the risk of causing harm?[71] For example, the criminal law prohibits possession of a firearm. The prohibition is not based on the fact that possession itself harms society; rather the possession of firearms generally is likely to increase their use, which can be regarded as a harm.[72] To some there are grave dangers in accepting potential harms as harms.[73] All kinds of activity are potentially harmful.

Is damage to the public good a harm?

What about offences which are designed not to prevent the harm to individuals, but harm to society generally?[74] Some traffic laws, building regulations, and state security regulations cannot be said to protect identifiable people, but rather are justified for the good running of society as a whole.[75] Are these reconcilable with the harm principle? Robin West, writing from a feminist perspective, has argued that the law should recognize harms to groups and to society. She complains that too often the law sees harm in terms of the harm to individuals rather than harm to people as connected individuals in relationships.[76] Susan Marshall and Antony Duff have discussed the way in which a criminal offence harms not just the victim but the wider community.[77] Others are concerned that once 'harms' to groups are taken into account the floodgates may be opened. These concerns are elaborated in the following passage by Michael Madden Dempsey.

**M. Madden Dempsey, 'Public Wrongs and the "Criminal Law's Business":
When Victims Won't Share' in R. Cruft, M. Kramer, and M. Reiff (eds) *Crime,
Punishment, and Responsibility* (Oxford: OUP, 2012), 270–1**

To review, my argument regarding victims who refuse to share runs as follows. Some communities (indeed, most communities of which I am aware) suffer (more or less) from what we can think of as character flaws grounded in structural inequalities such as racism and patriarchy. These communities, we might say, are racist or patriarchal in character. Moreover, the character of some kinds of wrongs committed within these communities can be constituted, at least in part, by the tendency these wrongs have to sustain or perpetuate these vicious character traits. As I have argued elsewhere, for example, we can understand the wrong of domestic violence as being partly constituted by its tendency to sustain or perpetuate the structural inequality of patriarchy, thereby reinforcing the community's patriarchal character.

Criminal justice officials often stand in a particularly good position to act on behalf of their communities so as to condemn the structural inequalities that partially constitute wrongs such as domestic violence, racist violence, rape, gay-bashing, etc. Moreover, if their condemnatory response to such structural inequalities is habituated, it has the potential to reconstitute the character of the community as less patriarchal, less racist, less homophobic, and so forth. It is (in part) because the criminal justice officials act as representatives of their

---

[71] See Oberdiek (2009) for discussion.   [72] von Hirsch (1996).
[73] von Hirsch (1985). See also the excellent discussion in Baker (2009).
[74] Howe (1991).   [75] Husak (2005); Duff and Green (2005: 8); and Brudner (1993).
[76] West (1988).   [77] See Madden Dempsey (2009b) for a rejection of this view.

communities—rather than merely as representatives of the individual victims—that they are particularly well-positioned to realize the value of reconstituting the character of their communities in these valuable ways. They are, in other words, often particularly well-suited to fulfilling the criminal law's constitutive function.[3]

Insofar as criminal justice officials do fulfil the criminal law's constitutive function, we can begin to explain the justification of criminal law's intervention in cases when Gardner's displacement function does not apply. In other words, criminal law's intervention can be justified even in cases where people are not inclined to retaliate against wrongdoers, indeed even in cases in which the victim refuses to share the wrong done to her. For if the criminal law's response to wrongs can realize the value of (re)constituting the character of the State and/or community in valuable ways, then criminal intervention can be (partly) justified even when no one desires retaliation and even when the victim refuses to share the wrong with her community. Moreover, *pace* Duff, the victim's refusal to share need not be unreasonable in order for pursuit of these wrongs to remain within the ambit of the criminal law's business. Rather, these wrongs become and remain the criminal law's business simply insofar as criminal justice officials are well-positioned to fulfil the criminal law's constitutive function.

Moral principles

One of the key elements of the harm principle is that an activity cannot be criminalized simply because it is regarded as immoral.[78] However, some people argue that there are some moral principles which are central to the well-being of society. Consider the debate over fox hunting. Leaving aside all the other issues, one argument that can be made is that our society is a less civilized and more cruel society if we allow fox hunting. It diminishes society and what it stands for. Many people will disagree. But these kinds of arguments suggest that when thinking about society's welfare there will be a wide range of views on what is good for society. Lord Devlin[79] has argued that there is a 'moral cement' that helps to keep society together, and that the state is entitled to use the criminal law to protect that cement from being damaged by behaviour which infringes those principles. He suggests that the extent of disgust felt by society at a particular kind of activity would indicate whether it challenged a fundamental value that underpinned society.[80]

There is much about this argument which can be challenged. For example, in a multicultural, multi-faith society, is it true there are moral principles which can be regarded as so fundamental to the way people live their lives that they are society's 'cement'? Even if you think there are, is it true that the fact that a few people break those moral taboos harms that cement? Was Devlin correct to suggest that disgust indicates how precious a moral value is to society?[81] Many people experience great disgust at the picking of a nose, but that does not indicate that it reflects a fundamental moral principle!

There has been somewhat of a revival in support for moralism as a basis for criminal law.[82] One benefit is that it makes the law more predictable. If the law seeks to match general moral standards in society this may make it easier for citizens to predict what the law is and may make it more 'in tune' with general attitudes within society.[83] We have already mentioned Antony Duff's argument that criminal law should involve a 'moral conversation' with a criminal.[84] If a conviction for criminal law is to convey censure, as

---

78 See the discussions in J. Gardner (2007); Alldridge (2002). 79 Devlin (1965).
80 See further Wall (2013). 81 Hart (1963). 82 Peterson (2010); Zaibert (2011).
83 Goodin (2011). 84 Duff (2010).

it is commonly argued, does that not imply that the law is involved in recognizing that morality is playing a role in the definition of a crime? Steven Wall, promoting moralism, explains moralism this way:

> It is a proper function of the criminal law to promote good character, and to restrain or discourage people from engaging in activities that cause moral harm to themselves or to others. Having and sustaining a good character is part of living well. And the law, including the criminal law, may have a role to play in enabling or assisting those who are subject to it in achieving this good.[85]

What this observation may overlook is that compelling people to act in a good way may deprive them of the opportunity to be virtuous, by choosing to do good. It is a better society if everyone chooses to be good, than if everyone is compelled to be good.[86]

Michael Moore[87] is a prominent supporter of modern legal moralism. His support for it flows from the fact he sees punishment as about retribution: it is valuable to punish those who commit moral wrongs. Punishment should be restricted to moral wrongdoing. However, he accepts that the reasons in favour of criminalizing moral wrongdoing may be outweighed by other concerns. He does not, for example, support criminalizing queue jumping. The expense would outweigh the benefits of doing that.

6.3 PRACTICALITY

Although much of the academic debate over criminalization has focused on the controversy surrounding the enforcement of morality, a very important issue is whether or not a law is practically enforceable.[88] There is no point rendering conduct criminal, if it is unlikely the police will ever be able to prove it has happened, or only if extensive police resources are employed. As this indicates there may be some conduct which should be criminal but there is no point in making it criminal because there would be no way of proving it. A more interesting argument is that if people are largely complying with the law anyway there may be a good case for not using the criminal law as that will deny people the good of behaving well through their own choice, rather than compulsion by the state.[89]

6.4 WHEN IS CRIMINALIZATION REQUIRED?

Generally the debates about criminalization discuss the 'limits' of criminalization. In this passage Tatjana Hörnle discusses when the state is required to punish criminal behaviour.

T. Hörnle, 'Theories of Criminalization' in M. Dubber and T. Hörnle (eds) *The Oxford Handbook of Criminal Law* (Oxford: OUP, 2014), 700–1

> Criminalization theories usually take the question of whether the state may punish certain conduct as their starting point (either implicitly or explicitly). The point of developing

---

[85] S. Wall, 'Enforcing Morality' (2013) 7 *Criminal Law and Philosophy* 455.   [86] Hörnle (2015).
[87] Moore (1997).   [88] Walker (1987: 148–52).   [89] Herring and Madden Dempsey (2010).

arguments in this field is usually to contend that certain reasons for criminalizing behavior are wrong reasons. From the viewpoint of critical policy review, the question whether the state *may* punish has priority over the question whether the state *must* punish. Modern legislatures tend toward overcriminalization rather than undercriminalization. However, from a theorist's point of view, one should not exclude a priori the question of whether conduct *must* be prohibited with criminal laws, that is, whether the state has a duty of protection toward citizens whose rights would be infringed by the conduct in question. The premises of this perspective are disputed and must therefore be elaborated on. Should the role of constitutional rights be extended from their defensive functions (rights *against the state*) to protective rights, which is a categorically different right? And what does "protection" mean in this context: prevention only or is it also a right to have wrong-doing correctly labeled? Consider the following thought-experiment: a state abolishes its criminal laws on rape and introduces elaborate preventative and effective (e.g. educative) programs instead. Would there still be reason to demand criminal law norms? Defendants of protective rights take the following position: it is not only prevention that matters, but also categorizing the significance of certain behavior and the adequacy of reactions to the rare events of "lapses."

Moving away from thought-experiments to the realities of contemporary legal systems, it is hard to find examples where, all things considered, one could plausibly claim a strict duty to criminalize. If we examine existing criminal codes, we find that they tend to penalize conduct that violates others' rights in a comprehensive way. Wrongdoing that violates important rights of others usually will be labeled a criminal offense in positive criminal law. If the argument of a gap within criminal law is nevertheless raised in policy disputes (e.g. with the argument that the state is under a duty to introduce criminal laws against abortion), the crucial point in such debates will be the issue of countervailing rights. When there are some doubts about which rights ought to prevail, a *in dubio pro liberate* [in cases of doubt favour liberty] principle should be applied . . . A strict duty to criminalize would presuppose that countervailing rights are of much lesser significance. This constellation will hardly ever be present in those relatively rare cases where protective rights might be a prima facie case for protection—if one takes both side-constraints and *in dubio pro liberate* seriously.

QUESTIONS

1. In the light of the issues discussed so far, what arguments can be made for or against fox hunting? What about incest? (See Temkin (1991).)

2. William Wilson asks (Wilson 2002: 44): 'How can the state justify censuring and punishing the possession of a few grams of cannabis for one's own use, while possessing a cellar full of wine for the consumption of the diners of Herefordshire risks only the award of the Michelin rosette?' Do you have a good reply for him?

3. Is the argument 'it is wrong to enforce morality' itself a moral principle which its proponents are seeking to enforce?

4. I suspect that if many people were asked at the end of their lives what had caused them the most harm it would not be those things that concern the criminal law, but issues such as broken relationships, which are not covered by the criminal law. Does this mean that the law needs to rethink its understanding of harm?

For guidance on answering this question, please visit the Online Resource Centre that accompanies this book: www.oxfordtextbooks.co.uk/orc/herringcriminal7e/.

5. Harcourt (1999) discusses attempts in the city of Chicago to prohibit liquor stores. This is not on the basis of the evils of alcohol, but on the harm such stores are said to cause to the atmosphere and ambience of parts of the city. Is this a good reason for criminalization?

FURTHER READING

Baker, D. (2008) 'Constitutionalizing the Harm Principle' *Criminal Justice Ethics* 27: 3.

Baker, D. (2011b) *The Right Not to be Criminalized* (Aldershot: Ashgate).

Devlin, P. (1965) *The Enforcement of Morals* (Oxford: OUP).

Duff, R.A. (2013) 'Relational Reasons and the Criminal Law' in L. Green and B. Leiter (eds) *Oxford Studies in Philosophy of Law* (Oxford: OUP).

Duff, R.A., Farmer, L., Marshall, S., Renzo, M., and Tadros, V. (2013) *The Constitution of the Criminal Law* (Oxford: OUP).

Dworkin, G. (1999) 'Devlin was Right: Law and the Enforcement of Morality' *William and Mary Law Review* 40: 927.

Feinberg, J. (1984) *Harm to Others* (New York: OUP).

Feinberg, J. (1986a) *Harm to Self* (New York: OUP).

Feinberg, J. (1986b) *Offense to Others* (New York: OUP).

Feinberg, J. (1988) *Harmless Wrongdoing* (New York: OUP).

Goodin, R. (2010) 'An Epistemic Case for Legal Moralism' *Oxford Journal of Legal Studies* 30: 615.

Hart, H. (1963) *Law, Liberty, and Morality* (Oxford: OUP).

Hörnle, T. (2014) 'Theories of Criminalization' in M. Dubber and T. Hörnle (eds) *The Oxford Handbook of Criminal Law* (Oxford: OUP).

Husak, D. (2002) 'Limitations on Criminalization and the General Part of Criminal Law' in S. Shute and A. Simester (eds) *Criminal Law Theory* (Oxford: OUP).

Lacey, N. (1995a) 'Contingency and Criminalisation' in I. Loveland (ed.) *The Frontiers of Criminality* (London: Sweet & Maxwell).

Raz, J. (1988) *The Morality of Freedom* (Oxford: OUP).

Schonsheck, J. (1994) *On Criminalization* (Dordrecht: Kluwer).

Simester, A. and von Hirsch, A. (2011) *Crimes, Harms, and Wrongs: On the Principles of Criminalisation* (Oxford: Hart).

Stewart, H. (2001b) 'Harms, Wrongs, and Set-Backs in Feinberg's Moral Limits of the Criminal Law' *Buffalo Criminal Law Review* 5: 47.

Thorburn, M. (2011) 'Constitutionalism and the Limits of the Criminal Law' in R.A. Duff, L. Farmer, S. Marshall, M. Renzo, and V. Tadros (eds) *The Structures of the Criminal Law* (Oxford: OUP).

Wilson, W. (2002) *Central Issues in Criminal Theory* (Oxford: Hart), ch. 1.

7 CULPABILITY

For a crime, it is normally not enough to show that the offender caused harm to another; it must also be shown that the defendant was blameworthy in harming the other person. In other words it must be shown that the defendant was responsible for the harm.[90] At a minimum this requires that the defendant was capable of acting differently from the way he or she did.[91]

The traditional way of analysing offences is to divide them up into the harmful act of the accused (the *actus reus*) and the blameworthy state of mind of the accused (the *mens rea*). Even where both the *actus reus* and *mens rea* are present the law provides defences, such as self-defence or duress (e.g. where the defendant commits a crime because he or she has been threatened with death if he or she does not).

In the following extract, Nicola Lacey sets out the standard conceptual framework for analysing offences. She explains that through a range of devices the law seeks to ensure that only blameworthy individuals are punished:

N. Lacey, 'Legal Constructions of Crime' in M. Maguire, R. Morgan, and R. Reiner (eds) *The Oxford Handbook of Criminology* (4th edn, Oxford: OUP, 2007), 185–7

The Conceptual Framework of Criminal Law

Contemporary codes and commentaries on criminal law in both the common and the civilian traditions tend to be organized around a core framework which sets out the general conditions under which liability may be established. This core framework is often known as the 'general part', or 'general principles', of criminal law—in other words, the set of rules and doctrines which apply across the whole terrain of criminal law rather than to specific offences. In the UK, this framework consists of four main elements: capacity, conduct, responsibility, and (absence of) defence.

1. Capacity

Only those who share certain basic cognitive and volitional capacities are regarded as the genuine subjects of criminal law. One might regard defences such as insanity as defining certain kinds of people as simply outwith the system of communication embodied by criminal law. Since law operates in terms of general standards, the line between criminal capacity and criminal incapacity is a relatively crude one from the point of view of other disciplines. For instance, almost every criminal law system exempts from criminal liability people under a certain age, whatever their actual capacities.

2. Conduct

Criminal conviction is founded, secondly, in a certain kind of conduct specified in the offence definition: appropriating another person's property in the case of theft; causing a person's death in the case of homicide; having sexual intercourse with a person without their consent in the case of rape; driving with a certain level of alcohol in one's blood in the case of driving while intoxicated. Though there are exceptions in the UK's criminal law doctrine, it

---

[90] Honoré (1999).   [91] Hart (1968).

is generally asserted that mere thoughts, being of a certain status rather than doing an act, and, in the absence of a specific duty to act, omitting to do something rather than acting positively, are insufficient to found criminal liability.

3. Responsibility/fault

Criminal liability is generally said to depend, thirdly, on the capable subject being in some sense responsible for or at fault in committing the conduct specified in the offence definition: we do not hold people liable, to put it crudely, for accidents. Responsibility or fault conditions generally consist of mental states or attitudes such as intention, recklessness, knowledge, belief, dishonesty, or negligence. To revert to the examples above, the relevant conditions consist in a dishonest intention permanently to deprive in the case of theft; an intention to kill or cause some less serious kind of harm, or gross negligence in relation to these results, in the case of homicide; recklessness as to the victim's lack of consent in the case of rape. The fourth example—driving while intoxicated—provides an exception to what is generally represented as the general principle that a discrete responsibility element must be proven by the prosecution: only the driving and the blood alcohol level need be established by the prosecution. Notwithstanding their 'exceptional' status, however, these offences of so-called 'strict' liability are in fact empirically dominant in English criminal law today. This division between offences of 'strict' liability and offences requiring proof of fault is the way in which the division between the 'quasi-moral' and 'instrumental/regulatory' terrains of criminal law is purportedly mapped on to legal doctrine. However, as the example of driving while intoxicated—an offence which thirty years ago was regarded as a quintessentially regulatory offence, yet which today carries a marked moral stigma—illustrates, this line is in fact far from clear.

4. Defences

Even where a capable subject has committed the relevant conduct with the requisite degree of fault, a range of defences may operate to preclude or mitigate his or her liability. For example, if the defendant has committed a theft while under a threat of violence, she may plead the defence of duress; if a person kills, intentionally, in order to defend himself against an immediate attack, he may plead self-defence; and if she kills under provocation, she may be convicted of a lesser degree of homicide. 'General defences' apply not only to crimes which require proof of responsibility, but also to those of strict liability. Hence, for example, a person who drives while intoxicated because of duress, whether in the form of a threat or in the form of highly compelling circumstances, may be able to escape liability. Defences are often thought to fall into three main groups—*exemptions, justifications*, and *excuses*—each relating to the other three components of liability already mentioned. The defence of insanity, for example, arguably operates to recognize that the defendant's *incapacity exempts* him or her from the communications of criminal law; the defence of self-defence may be seen as amounting to a claim that the *conduct* in question was, in the circumstances, *justified* and hence not the sort of *conduct* which criminal law sets out to proscribe; the defence of duress may be viewed as *excusing* the defendant on the basis that the conditions under which she formed the relevant *fault* condition—in cases of duress, this would generally be intention—are such that the usual inference of *responsibility* is blocked. The defences may be seen as fine-tuning, along contextualized and morally sensitive lines, the presumptive inferences of liability produced by the first three elements.

At one level, this conceptual framework is analytic: it simply provides a set of building blocks out of which legislators and lawyers construct criminal liability. On the other hand—as the description of the framework as a set of 'general principles' suggests—it contains an implicit set of assumptions about what makes the imposition of criminal liability legitimate. The ideas, for example, that there should be no punishment for mere thoughts, or that defendants should not be convicted unless they were in some sense responsible for their conduct, or in circumstances in which some internal incapacity or external circumstance deprived them of a fair opportunity to conform to the law, express a normative view of criminal law not merely as an institutionalized system of coercion but rather as a system which is structured around certain principles of justice or morality. This normative aspect of the 'general part' of criminal law becomes yet clearer in the light of two broad procedural standards which characterize most modern systems. The first of these is *the principle of legality*: criminal law must be announced clearly to citizens in advance of its imposition. Only those who know the law in advance can be seen as having a fair opportunity to conform to it. Principles such as clarity and non-retroactivity are therefore central tenets of the liberal ideal of the rule of law. The second procedural doctrine is the *presumption of innocence*: a crime must be proven by the prosecution (generally the state, and hence far more powerful than the individual defendant) to a very high standard. Criminal law is therefore implicitly justified not only in terms of its role in proscribing, condemning, and, perhaps, reducing conduct which causes or risks a variety of harms, but also in treating its subjects with respect, as moral agents whose conduct must be assessed in terms of attitudes and intentions, and not merely in terms of effects. And underlying this normative framework is a further set of assumptions about the nature of human conduct: about voluntariness, will, agency, capacity as the basis for genuine human personhood and hence responsibility.

The various assumptions underlying the conceptual framework within which criminal liability is constructed should be of great interest to criminological and criminal justice scholars. For they give us insight into the processes of interpretation in the courtroom—one key site in the process of criminalization. They also provide some interesting points of both contrast and similarity when compared with the assumptions on the basis of which other practices within the criminal process are founded. Are the assumptions of responsible subjecthood that constitute the core of criminal law thinking the same as, or even consistent with, those that underpin the development of policing strategy, sentencing decision-making, probation practice, or prison regimes? If not, does it matter? And what does it signify?

Having presented the orthodox position, Nicola Lacey goes on to critically assess the description of the law she has just provided. As her discussion shows, the position is not as straightforward as might at first appear:

N. Lacey, 'Legal Constructions of Crime' in M. Maguire, R. Morgan, and R. Reiner (eds) *The Oxford Handbook of Criminology* (4th edn, Oxford: OUP, 2007), 188–90

'General Principles' of Criminal Law: A Critical Assessment

The need to bring criminal justice and criminal law analyses into relation with one another is therefore clear. However, it is equally clear that criminal justice scholars ought to be wary of taking the 'general principles' of criminal law on lawyers' terms. For the fact is that the 'general principles of criminal law' are honoured in many systems, and certainly in the UK, as much in the breach as in the observance. The preponderance of criminal offences in fact derogates from these principles in some way: by imposing 'strict' liability without fault; by requiring proof of responsibility in relation only to certain components of the offence; or by modifying the prosecution's burden of proof by imposing evidential, or occasionally, legal burdens on the defence. The fact that a substantial number of these derogations occur in serious offences such as sexual, financial, and drug-related crime suggests that the 'general principles' are as much an ideological as an actual feature of criminal law's operations. In this respect, the criminal justice scholar will gain some enlightenment from the more critical genre of criminal law scholarship which has subjected the 'general principles' of criminal law to a searching examination.

Conventional criminal law scholars, as we have seen, generally provide a brief résumé of the moral/retributive, regulatory/deterrent aspects of criminal justice. They go on to give a terse statement of the competing concerns of fairness and social protection, due process, and crime control which are taken to inform the development and implementation of criminal law in liberal societies. From this point on, they take the idea of 'crimes' as given by acts of law-creation. In this way both political and criminological issues are quietly removed from the legal agenda. In contrast, critical criminal lawyers assume that the power and meaning of criminal laws depend on a more complex set of processes and underlying factors than the mere positing of prohibitory norms to be enforced according to a particular procedure. Most obviously, they assume that the influences of political and economic power permeate not only the statutory construction of crime but also the practice of doctrinal interpretation. Yet their view is not the reductive, instrumental one of Realism or the Chicago School. Rather, critical criminal lawyers argue that judicial practice is shaped by tensions between competing values whose power infuses all social practices, and which cannot be reconciled by either legislative reform or feats of rationalizing interpretation. From this perspective, further links between the legal and social construction of crime appear. For it seems, a priori, likely that the evaluative and pragmatic tensions which shape the development of criminal law will also manifest themselves, albeit to different degrees and in different ways, in other criminal justice practices.

The primary aim of early critical criminal law scholarship was to develop an internal or 'immanent' critique of the doctrinal framework within which different areas of law have been taken to be organized. Taking a close interest in the way in which criminal liability is constructed within legal discourse, critical scholars took as their focus the structure of 'general principles' which are usually taken to underpin criminal law in liberal societies. These included not only the liberal ideals about the fair terms under which criminal punishment may be imposed upon an individual agent, which we considered above, but also the aspirations of neutrality, objectivity, and determinacy of legal method which are associated with the rule of law (Norrie 2001). For example, Kelman's work scrutinized the basis of the responsibility/fault doctrine which purports to structure and justify the attribution of criminal responsibility to the free individual via the employment of standards of fault such as intent and recklessness. He showed that fault requirements veer in an unprincipled way between 'subjective' standards, in which attributions of responsibility depend on what the defendant actually intended or contemplated, and 'objective' standards such as negligence, which impute to the defendant the state of mind of the 'reasonable man'. Following from this, Kelman emphasized the fact that criminal law doctrine evinces no consistent commitment to either a free-will or a determinist model of human behaviour.

Furthermore, Kelman and others demonstrated the manipulability and indeterminacy of the generally accepted doctrinal framework according to which criminal liability is constructed in terms of the four elements discussed above: capacity, conduct, responsibility or fault, and absence of defence. For example, the issue of mistake could be conceptualized with equal doctrinal propriety as a matter pertaining to the existence of the conduct or fault elements of a crime, or to the existence of a defence. A person who assaults another person in the mistaken belief that that other person is in the process of committing an assault on a third party could, in other words, be regarded as having a defence (of mistaken self-defence), or as lacking the conduct (no 'unlawful' act) or (in certain circumstances) fault/responsibility (no relevant intention) elements of a crime. Since these conceptualizations sometimes affect the outcome of the legal analysis, this entails that doctrinal rules are not as determinate as the conventional theory of legal reasoning assumes. Moreover, the outcome of legal reasoning is contingent upon factors such as the time frame within which the alleged offence was set. For example, whether or not a person is regarded as negligent, in the sense of having failed to reach a reasonable standard of care or awareness, may depend on what range of conduct the court is able to examine. What appears an unreasonable lapse judged in itself may look more reasonable if evidence about its history can be admitted. This broadening of the time frame or context is precisely what the defences often effect. Yet the influence of the framing process is not acknowledged within the doctrinal structure, which accordingly fails to regulate judicial interpretation in the way which is generally supposed.

The critical enterprise here is to hold criminal law up to scrutiny in terms of the standards which it professes to instantiate; and in doing so, to reveal that, far from consisting of a clear, determinate set of norms, based on a coherent set of 'general principles', it rather exemplifies a contradictory and conflicting set of approaches which are obscured by the superficial coherence and determinacy of legal reasoning. By scrutinizing carefully the form which criminal legal reasoning takes, it becomes possible to reveal that practice as having important ideological dimensions, rationalizing and legitimating a system which serves a variety of powerful interests by representing criminal law as a technical and apolitical sphere of judgement. An important part of this process is the (re)reading of cases not merely as exercises in formal legal analysis, but also as texts whose rhetorical structure is at least as important as their superficial legal content. In this kind of reading, critical scholars emphasize the significant symbolic aspect of the power of criminal law, along with the implicit yet powerful images of wrongdoing and rightful conduct, normal and abnormal subjects, guilt and innocence which legal discourse draws upon and produces.

7.1 THE SUBJECTIVISM/OBJECTIVISM DEBATE

There has been much debate over whether, when assessing the blameworthiness of a defendant, the law should adopt a subjectivist or objectivist perspective. In short, a subjectivist account argues that criminal liability should be determined by looking inside the mind of the defendant and considering his or her intentions or foresight.[92] An objectivist account focuses on the behaviour of the defendant and asks whether the defendant acted as a reasonable person would.

In the following extract, Antony Duff describes the key elements of subjectivism and objectivism:

R.A. Duff, 'Subjectivism, Objectivism and Criminal Attempts' in A. Simester and A. Smith (eds) *Harm and Culpability* (Oxford: OUP, 1996), 19–22

It is no doubt sometimes unhelpful to portray controversies about the proper principles of criminal liability as controversies between 'subjectivism' and 'objectivism'. Certainly neither term picks out a single, unitary, position. Furthermore, some disagreements rather concern the scope of the 'subjective' itself: for example, should we analyse recklessness in terms of conscious risk-taking or of 'practical indifference', both of which could be portrayed as

---

[92] For a powerful recent statement of subjectivism, see Alexander and Kessler Ferzan (2010).

'subjective' aspects of the agent's conduct? Nor can we always draw a clear distinction between the 'subjective' and the 'objective'. If we justify an ascription of recklessness by saying that an agent failed to notice some obvious risk because he did not care about it, we are not simply explaining his failure to notice that risk in morally neutral terms: we are, rather, interpreting his conduct in the light of some normative, non-subjective, standard of appropriate care.

In some contexts, however, there does seem to be a clear distinction between 'subjectivist' and 'objectivist' principles of criminal liability, and controversies which embody that distinction. One such context is the law of attempts. . . .

'Subjectivists' and 'objectivists' disagree about the appropriate criteria for action ascriptions. An agent is criminally liable only if an action matching the law's definition of an offence can justly be ascribed to her. But how should we decide what actions can justly be ascribed to an agent; what criteria should determine our ascriptions? Subjectivists insist that the criteria should be 'subjective'; the actions that are to be ascribed to an agent, for which she is to be held liable, must be described in 'subjective' terms. By contrast objectivists argue that what is 'mine' as an agent cannot be defined or delimited in purely 'subjective' terms, but must be described in partly 'objective' terms.

But what are 'subjective', or 'objective', terms or descriptions? We can say that the 'subjective' is a matter of the agent's psychological states: but that is too vague to be helpful. Any more precise account of the 'subjective', however, would have to be an account of the different conceptions of the 'subjective' expressed in *different* forms of subjectivism. The two most familiar contemporary subjectivist theories, the 'choice' and the 'character' accounts of criminal liability, embody different accounts of the 'subjective'. 'Choice' theorists insist that we can properly ascribe to an agent only those actions that he *chose* to perform; any action for which he is to be held liable must be described in terms of his choices. Choice, as constituting the 'subjective', can then be (minimally) defined in terms of intention and belief; I choose to do what I intend to do, or believe myself to be doing. 'Character' theorists, by contrast, hold that we should ground criminal liability in the character traits manifested in the agent's conduct; for them, the 'subjective' consists in those dispositions, attitudes, or motives which constitute legally relevant character traits.

I will focus in this paper on the 'choice' conception of criminal liability, which is the dominant version of subjectivism. Though the objectivist grounding for the law of attempts which I will sketch is opposed to both types of subjectivism, the implications of each type for the law of attempts differ; and the arguments that I will offer against the 'choice' conception are not the same as those that might be offered against the 'character' conception.

The 'choice' version of subjectivism can be defined by Ashworth's 'intent' and 'belief' principles: agents should be held 'criminally liable for what they intended to do, and not according to what actually did or did not occur', and must be 'judged on the basis of what they believed they were doing, not on the basis of actual facts and circumstances which were not known to them at the time'. This does not mean that agents are to be held liable for their intentions and beliefs *rather than* for their actions. The claim is that the *actions* for which agents are to be held liable should be identified in terms of what they intended to do or believed they were doing: agents are liable for their actions qua chosen.

A subjectivist might argue, or might avow principles which imply, that the action ascriptions which generate criminal liability should be determined by *purely* subjective criteria: the actions we ascribe to an agent must be described purely in terms of her intentions and beliefs. By contrast, 'objectivists' (as I shall use the notion) do not hold that criminal liability should be based on *purely* objective criteria: that agents' actual intentions or beliefs should be wholly irrelevant to their criminal liability. They deny, rather, that the subjective dimensions of the agent's conduct are all that matter for criminal liability: its 'objective' aspects may also be crucial. But what are these 'objective' aspects?

They are of two kinds. One consists in what actually occurs or is actually the case: for example, in the fact of whether the shot that I intend should hit, or believe will hit, V actually hits or misses; in the fact of whether the woman on whom I press sexual intercourse, believing her to consent to it, actually consents or not. The other consists in what a 'reasonable' person would believe, or realize: in the fact that what I take to be a person is obviously (i.e. would be immediately seen by any reasonable person to be) a tree; or that the means by which I hope to achieve a criminal goal are obviously (i.e. would be seen by any reasonable person to be) utterly inadequate; or that my action creates an obvious risk of harm which would be recognized by any reasonable persons.

Now in many contexts subjectivist principles play an *exculpatory* role, exempting from criminal liability those who might otherwise be held liable. Thus someone who does not realize that her action might damage another's property should not be convicted of criminal damage—even if her act 'in fact creates an obvious risk' (one that would be obvious to the 'ordinary prudent' person) of such damage: for she has not chosen to risk damaging another's property. A man who honestly believed that the woman with whom he had intercourse consented to it should not be convicted of rape—even if his belief was both mistaken and unreasonable: for he did not choose to have, or to take a risk of having, 'intercourse with a woman who [did] not consent to it'.

In the following passage from a Law Commission report on manslaughter, the benefits and disadvantages of an objectivist and subjectivist approach are explored:

Law Commission Report No. 237, *Legislating the Criminal Code: Involuntary Manslaughter* (London: HMSO, 1996), paras 4.4–4.23

Orthodox Subjectivist Theory

4.4 The legal philosophy traditionally applied in mainstream English criminal law and by this Commission is known as 'subjectivist theory'. It rests on the principle that moral guilt, and hence criminal liability, should be imposed only on people who can be said to have *chosen* to behave in a certain way or to cause or risk causing certain consequences. The roots of subjectivism lie in a liberal philosophy that regards individuals as autonomous beings, capable of choice, and each deserving of individual respect. It is called 'subjectivism' because of the significance that it accords to the individual's state of mind at the time of the prohibited conduct.

4.5 Three principles have been identified as inherent in this basis of liability. The first of these is the '*mens rea* principle', which imposes liability only for outcomes which were *intended* or *knowingly risked* by the alleged wrongdoer. The second principle, the 'belief principle', judges a defendant according only to what *she* believed she was doing or risking. Thirdly, according to the 'principle of correspondence', subjectivists insist that the fault element of a crime *correspond* to the conduct element; for example, if the conduct element is 'causing serious injury', the fault element ought to be 'intention or recklessness as to causing serious injury'. This ensures that the defendant is punished only for causing a harm which she *chose* to risk or to bring about.

4.6 Subjectivist philosophy applies widely in the criminal law today. A man cannot be convicted of rape, for example, if he genuinely believed, albeit unreasonably, that his victim consented to sexual intercourse, because this belief would be incompatible with the intention to have intercourse with a woman *without her consent*, or recklessness as to that possibility, which are the mental states required for rape.

. . .

Criticisms of the Subjectivist *Mens Rea* Principle: Can Liability Based on Inadvertence ever be Justified?

4.12 Orthodox subjectivist theory, then, requires the defendant to have been, at least, *aware* of the risk of causing the prohibited harm. However, there is a body of criticism, from very distinguished commentators, of the orthodox subjectivist *mens rea* principle. One ground of criticism is that it is based on a simplistic view of what constitutes knowledge or awareness of risk:

> . . . while we do indeed sometimes make our knowledge of what we are doing explicit to ourselves in . . . silent mental reports, it is absurd to suggest that such knowledge can be actual only if it is made thus explicit. When I drive my car, my driving is guided by my (actual) knowledge of my car and of the context in which I am driving: but my driving is not accompanied by a constant silent monologue in which I tell myself what to do next, what the road conditions are, whether I am driving safely or not, and all the other facts of which I am certainly aware while I am driving. . . . The occurrence or the non-occurrence of certain explicit thoughts is irrelevant to whether I am actually aware of what I am doing: my actions can manifest my awareness even if no explicit thoughts about the relevant facts pass through my mind at the time.[93]

4.13 On this view of what constitutes a mental state, the contrast between awareness and lack of awareness of risk is not as stark as in conventional subjectivist accounts, and it is less clear why inadvertence ought not to be classified, as *mens rea* in certain circumstances.

4.14 The main argument in favour of criminalizing some forms of inadvertent risk-taking, however, is that in some circumstances a person is *at fault in failing to consider* the consequences that might be caused by her conduct. The example given by R A Duff is that of a bridegroom who misses his wedding because it slipped his mind when he was in the pub. An orthodox subjectivist would point to his lack of intention or awareness, and deem him consequently less culpable. The bride, however, would rightly condemn him, because it is plain from his conduct that he did not care, and this attitude is sufficient to make him blameworthy. Duff argues that this account retains a subjective element, because attitudes are subjective.

4.15 A similar argument was used by Lord Diplock in the famous case on criminal damage, *Caldwell*:

> If it had crossed his mind that there was a risk that someone's property might be damaged but because his mind was affected by rage or excitement or confused by drink, he did not appreciate the seriousness of the risk or trusted that good luck would prevent it happening, this state of mind would amount to malice in the restricted meaning placed upon that term by the Court of Appeal; whereas if, for any of these reasons, he did not even trouble to give his mind to the question whether there was any risk of damaging the property, this state of mind would not suffice to make him guilty of an offence under the Malicious Damage Act 1861. *Neither state of mind seems to me to be less blameworthy than the other.* . . .[94]

4.16 Professor Hart some years ago attacked the assumption that to allow criminal liability for negligence would be to set aside the requirement of *mens rea* as a precondition of punishment. His argument was that since 'negligence' implies a failure to do what ought to have been done, it is therefore more than inadvertence, it is *culpable* inadvertence:

> Only a theory that mental operations like attending to, or thinking about, or examining a situation are somehow 'either there or not there', and so utterly outside our control,

---

[93] Duff (1990: 160).   [94] [1982] AC 341, 352 (emphasis added).

can lead to the theory that we are *never* responsible if, like the signalman who forgets to pull the signal, we fail to think or remember. . . .

What is crucial is that those whom we punish should have had, when they acted, the normal capacities, physical and mental, for doing what the law requires and abstaining from what it forbids, and a fair opportunity to exercise these capacities. Where these capacities and opportunities are absent, as they are in different ways in the varied cases of accident, mistake, paralysis, reflex action, coercion, insanity etc, the moral protest is that it is morally wrong to punish because 'he could not have helped it' or 'he could not have done otherwise' or 'he had no real choice'. But, as we have seen, there is no reason (unless we are to reject the whole business of responsibility and punishment) *always* to make this protest when someone who 'just didn't think' is punished for carelessness. For in some cases at least we may say 'he could have thought about what he was doing' with just as much rational confidence as one can say of any intentional wrongdoing 'he could have done otherwise'.[95]

Professor Ashworth also concedes that negligence may be an appropriate standard for criminal liability where the harm risked was great, the risk obvious and the defendant had the capacity to take the required precautions.

What Makes Inadvertence *Culpable*?

4.17 In all the sources cited in paragraphs 4.12–4.16, the view is taken that it may be justifiable to impose criminal liability for the *unforeseen* consequences of a person's acts, at any rate where the harm risked is great and the actor's failure to advert to this risk is *culpable*, we are persuaded by this reasoning, in the following paragraphs, therefore, we consider the criteria by which *culpable inadvertence* should be judged if it is to attract the sanctions of the criminal law when death results.

4.18 The first criterion of culpability upon which we must insist is that the harm to which the accused failed to advert was at *least foreseeable*, if not strikingly foreseeable or obvious. If the accused is an ordinary person, she cannot be blamed for failing to take notice *of* a risk if it would not have been apparent to an *average person* in *her position*, because the criminal law cannot require an *exceptional* standard of perception or awareness from her. If the accused held herself out as an expert of some kind, however, a higher standard can be expected from her; if she is a doctor, for example, she will be at fault if she fails to advert to a risk that would have been obvious to the average doctor in her position.

4.19 As a matter of strict principle, the accused ought only to be held liable for causing death if the risk to which she culpably failed to avert was a risk of *death*. In practice, however, there is a very thin line between behaviour that risks serious injury and behaviour that risks death, because it is frequently a matter of chance, depending on such factors as the availability of medical treatment, whether serious injury leads to death. Admittedly it is possible for conduct to involve a risk of serious injury (such as a broken limb) though not a risk of death; but intention to cause serious injury constitutes the *mens rea* of murder although the *actus reus* is the causing of death, and we see no compelling reason to distinguish between murder and manslaughter in this respect. We consider, therefore, that it would not be wrong in principle if a person were to be held responsible for causing death through failing to advert to a clear risk of causing death *or* serious injury—subject of course to a second criterion, to which we now turn.

[95] Hart (1968: 151–2).

4.20 The second criterion of culpability which we consider to be essential is that the accused herself would have been *capable* of perceiving the risk in question, had she directed her mind to it. Since the fault of the accused lies in her failure to consider a risk, she cannot be punished for this failure if the risk in question would never have been apparent to her, no matter how hard she thought about the potential consequences of her conduct. If this criterion is not insisted upon, the accused will, in essence, be punished for being less intelligent, mature or capable than the average person.

. . .

4.22 . . . A person cannot be said to be morally at fault in failing to advert to a risk if she lacked the capacity to do so.

4.23 If the criteria in paragraphs 4.17–4.22 are satisfied, we consider that it is appropriate to impose liability for inadvertently causing harm in cases where the harm risked is *very serious*. Where a person embarks on a course of conduct which inherently involves a risk of causing death or serious injury to another, society is justified in requiring a higher standard of care from her than from someone whose conduct involves a lesser risk or no risk at all. J L Austin made this point graphically when he wrote 'We may plead that we trod on the snail inadvertently: but not on the baby—you ought to look where you're putting your great feet'.[96]

FURTHER READING

Bandes, S. (2010) 'Is It Immoral to Punish the Heedless and Clueless? A Comment on Alexander, Ferzan and Morse: Crime and Culpability' *Law and Philosophy* 433.

Duff, R.A. (2005a) 'Theorizing Criminal Law: A 25th Anniversary Essay' *Oxford Journal of Legal Studies* 25: 353.

Smith, A. (1978) 'On *Actus Reus* and *Mens Rea*' in P. Glazebrook (ed.) *Reshaping the Criminal Law* (London: Sweet & Maxwell).

Sullivan, G.R. (1996a) 'Making Excuses' in A. Simester and A. Smith (eds) *Harm and Culpability* (Oxford: OUP).

Tadros, V. (2005a) Criminal Responsibility (Oxford: OUP).

Tur, R. (1993) 'Subjectivism and Objectivism: Towards Synthesis' in S. Shute, J. Gardner, and J. Horder (eds) *Action and Value in Criminal Law* (Oxford: OUP).

Wells, C. (1982) 'Swatting the Subjectivist Bug' *Criminal Law Review* 209.

---

8 THE VICTIM IN CRIMINAL LAW

Until fairly recently criminal lawyers and criminologists have focused on the defendant and assessments of her or his liability.[97] The victim, in much writing on criminal law, is a shadowy figure who appears to be an irrelevance. Consider a case of alleged rape where a defendant wrongly but reasonably believed that the victim was consenting. This 'easy' case would be dealt with by the law saying that such a defendant lacks the *mens rea* for rape and so no offence is committed. But that is to look at the question entirely from the defendant's point of view. As for the victim, she was raped in that she was penetrated without her

---

[96] Austin (1956: 1).   [97] S. Edwards (2004); Doak (2003).

consent. Another aspect of this issue is that the defendant has no defence based on the fact that the crime was partly the 'victim's fault'. It is no defence for a burglar to say that the victim had left their front door unlocked. However, some academics have suggested that there is a case for providing a defence where the victim contributed to the harm done to them by the defendant.[98] Such suggestions are highly controversial, although they do highlight the fact that it is easy to paint a picture of the 'bad criminal' and the 'good victim', whereas the truth may be somewhat more complex.

There have been suggestions that victims owe responsibilities. For example, that individuals should be expected to protect themselves from crime. Another is that victims have a responsibility to report crime. In a recent controversial case, a woman who had been raped by her husband but withdrew her complaint out of terror, was convicted of perverting the course of justice.[99] That seems to have been particularly harsh in the context of that case where the woman was the victim of domestic violence and marital rape.[100] She needed the protection of the law, not prosecution by it.

FURTHER READING

Cancio Meliá, M. (2004) 'Victim Behavior and Offender Liability' *Buffalo Criminal Law Review* 7: 513.

Edwards, S. (2012) 'The Duplicity of Protection—Prosecuting Frightened Victims: An Act of Gender-Based Violence' *Journal of Criminal Law* 76: 29.

Hall, M. (2009) *Victims of Crime: Policy and Practice in Criminal Justice* (Cullompton: Willan).

Herring, J. (2013c) 'Victims as Defendants: When Victims Participate in Crimes against Themselves' in A. Reed and M. Bohlander (eds) *Participation in Crime* (Aldershot: Ashgate).

Johnstone, G. (2002) *Restorative Justice* (Cullompton: Willan).

von Hirsch, A. *et al* (2003) *Restorative Justice and Criminal Justice* (Oxford: Hart).

---

9 THE CRIMINAL PROCESS

Statistics on the number of convictions for particular offences are a poor guide to which crimes are actually committed. It is estimated that only 6 per cent of crimes committed result in a conviction.[101] This is because victims often do not report the crimes to the police, and if they do the offender is rarely caught. Even if the offender is found, the police may still decide not to charge him. If the police decide to charge, then the Crown Prosecution Service (CPS) may decide not to pursue a prosecution.[102] There have been concerns over how these decisions not to prosecute are reached. In particular there are concerns that race, sex, and economic background can improperly play a role in the decision.[103] The CPS, even if it does decide to prosecute, may charge a lesser offence than the one committed. This might be done for various reasons: the CPS might believe that it would be easier, in order to obtain a

---

[98] See Gruber (2004) and Bergelson (2007a). For a rejection of such arguments, see Herring (2013c).
[99] *R v A* [2012] EWCA Crim 434.   [100] S. Edwards (2012).   [101] Bamber (2002).
[102] See Rogers (2006b) for a discussion of this decision-making process.
[103] Ashworth and Horder (2013: ch. 1).

conviction, to do so; or the defendant might have offered to plead guilty to the lesser charge, but would plead not guilty to the more serious charge;[104] or charging the lesser offence may mean that the case will be heard before magistrates, rather than the Crown Court, and so be cheaper.[105]

A particularly topical issue is assisted suicide. Following the decisions of the House of Lords in *R (Purdy) v DPP*[106] and *R (Nicklinson) v Ministry of Justice*[107] the CPS was required to produce and then redraft guidance which set out when they would or would not prosecute cases of assisted suicide.[108] The current position of assisted suicide is somewhat ambiguous. While still technically a crime it is clear that in some cases it will not be prosecuted. John Spencer has queried whether this is consistent with basic democratic principles:

> Is it really compatible with the rule of law that, when an Act of Parliament makes a certain form of behaviour a criminal offence, the DPP should in effect decriminalise it, in whole or in part, by saying when it will and will not be prosecuted? The orthodox answer, forcibly expressed by the Court of Appeal in the judgment which the House of Lords reversed, is 'no': once Parliament has created an offence, only Parliament has the authority to redraw its boundaries so that it catches fewer people in its net. For any other organ of the State to attempt to do so is to infringe the first rule of the constitution, which is the supremacy of Parliament.[109]

He goes on to note that in recent times Parliament has been drafting such over-broad laws that some discretion over prosecution must be exercised.

In the following passage, Andrew Ashworth and Lucia Zedner describe ways from which the orthodox approach towards criminal procedure is being departed. Traditionally, for a person to be guilty of a crime they are charged with an offence, there is then a trial at which they are found either guilty or not guilty. If the former, they are then sentenced. The authors start by setting out the reasons used by politicians to explain why this traditional approach is not appropriate for some offences in recent years. They then explain why they think such departures should be opposed:

A. Ashworth and L. Zedner, 'Defending the Criminal Law: Reflections on the Changing Character of Crime, Procedure, and Sanctions' (2008) 2 *Criminal Law and Philosophy* 21

> We will outline five avenues of challenge to the paradigmatic sequence of prosecution-trial-conviction-sentence:
>
> (a) Not cost-effective: it is argued that, as the cost of trials rises, they are not a cost-effective means of fulfilling their purpose. Jury trials should therefore be reserved for the most serious charges where the defendant pleads not guilty, and even summary trials should be reserved for cases in which a court hearing really is necessary.

---

104 This is sometimes called 'plea bargaining'.
105 For an interesting discussion on how the cutbacks in legal aid may affect the advice given by lawyers to their clients on how to plead, see Tata and Stephen (2006).
106 [2009] UKHL 45. 107 [2014] UKSC 38.
108 CPS (2010). See Daw and Solomon (2010).
109 Spencer (2009: 495). See also Rogers (2011) and Greasley (2010).

(b) Not preventive: it is argued that bringing a defendant to court, with a view to conviction and sentence, may not have preventive effects and may even be counterproductive. This has been a prominent argument in youth justice, where the experience of being accused in court may reinforce a youth's self-identification with lawbreakers and impose the stigma of conviction. It also appears that for some adult offenders conviction and sentence have no greater preventive effect than a form of diversion. This challenge assumes that the purpose of the criminal law and its processes is preventive, at least to some degree.

(c) Not necessary: it is argued that court proceedings are unnecessary where the defendant is willing to plead guilty, and that for some lesser forms of offending a court hearing may not need to examine the defendant's fault or may not be necessary at all for minor offences, since almost all defendants are willing to accept some lesser, swifter resolution of the case.

(d) Not appropriate: it is argued that the criminal trial is not well suited to dealing with ongoing conduct and continual offending, because it focuses on specific charges without examining broader issues and continuing patterns of misconduct.

(e) Not effective: it is argued that in some cases it may not be possible to have a trial, if the canons of procedural fairness are observed, because witnesses are likely to be in fear or otherwise reluctant, and the charge will therefore have to be dropped. For some kinds of crime, high attrition rates (i.e., a low proportion of detected cases going to trial) suggest that aspects of criminal procedure may have the effect of preventing some defendants from being brought to trial.

[They describe in detail some of the recent innovations in criminal law which impact on the traditional procedures used where a crime is alleged. These include (1) diversion, (2) fixed penalties, (3) summary trials, (4) hybrid civil–criminal processes, (5) strict criminal liability, (6) incentives to plead guilty, (7) preventive orders.]

Conviction of an individual for an offence is the strongest form of condemnation of conduct that the state can muster. Conviction for an offence also opens the possibility of a coercive sentence, ordered by a court within the limits of what legislation permits. To justify the creation of a certain crime is therefore to justify the imposition of the censure of conviction and the imposition of a punishment. It is the special significance and gravity of these consequences, with all their legal and social implications, that supports the argument for safeguards in the shape of the procedural requirements of human rights law—the presumption of innocence, the need for proper notice of the charge, adequate time and facilities for preparing a defence, state-funded legal assistance, the right to confront witnesses, the free assistance of an interpreter, the privilege against self-incrimination and various other rights.

Yet we have shown how the existence of these human rights protections has stimulated the development of alternative channels of control that enable the state to avoid the more onerous procedural requirements that now apply to the criminal process. The panoply of preventive, civil, administrative, and hybrid orders introduced in England and Wales in recent years is to a large extent the consequence of just such an imaginative skirting of the burdens of the Convention.

FURTHER READING

Ashworth, A. (2014) 'A Decade of Human Rights in Criminal Justice' *Criminal Law Review* 325.

Ashworth, A. and Redmayne, M. (2010) *The Criminal Process* (4th edn, Oxford: OUP).

Rogers, J. (2010) 'Prosecutorial Policies, Prosecutorial Systems, and the *Purdy* Litigation' *Criminal Law Review* 543.

Saunders, A. and Young, R. (2007) 'From Suspect to Trial' in M. Maguire, R. Morgan, and R. Reiner (eds) *The Oxford Handbook of Criminology* (Oxford: OUP).

10 CRIMINAL LAW AND THE HUMAN RIGHTS ACT 1998

10.1 THE SIGNIFICANCE OF THE HUMAN RIGHTS ACT 1998

At many points throughout this book we will consider the potential impact of the Human Rights Act 1998 (HRA) on the interpretation of the offence. This section will not therefore seek to summarize the impact of the Act on English and Welsh criminal law,[110] but will outline how the Act works.[111] The Human Rights Act 1998 is designed to ensure the protection of individuals' rights under the European Convention on Human Rights (ECHR). The HRA protects the rights in the ECHR in two main ways:

(1) Section 3 requires judges to interpret legislation in a way which complies with the ECHR so far as is possible. It states:

> So far as it is possible to do so, primary legislation and subordinate legislation must be read and given effect in a way which is compatible with the Convention rights.

As section 3 makes clear, if the wording of a statute is ambiguous and can be interpreted either in a way which is compliant with the Convention rights or in a way which is not, then the statute should be read so as to be compliant. The key phrase is 'so far as it is possible'. Only time will tell how far the courts will be willing to stretch the meaning of words to comply with the statute. The House of Lords has given some guidance on this by saying that section 3 is to be used to interpret, but not amend, legislation.[112] If the court is unable to interpret a statute in line with the Convention rights, then it must apply the statute as it stands and issue a declaration of incompatibility, as a result of which Parliament should consider whether the legislation needs to be amended.[113]

(2) Section 6 requires public authorities to act in a way which is compatible with the Convention rights. Section 6 states:

> (1) It is unlawful for a public authority to act in a way which is incompatible with a Convention right.
>
> (2) Subsection (1) does not apply to an act if—
>
>   (a) as the result of one or more provisions of primary legislation, the authority could not have acted differently; or

---

[110] See Ashworth and Strange (2003); Ashworth (2000b).

[111] For more detail, see Choudhry and Herring (2010: chs 1 and 2).

[112] *Re S; Re W* [2002] 1 FCR 577 (HL), para. 38.

[113] See *Bellinger v Bellinger* [2003] UKHL 21 for an example of a case where a declaration of incompatibility was issued.

> (b) in the case of one or more provisions of, or made under, primary legislation which cannot be read or given effect in a way which is compatible with the Convention rights, the authority was acting so as to give effect to or enforce those provisions.

Importantly for criminal lawyers, the definition of a public authority includes the police, the CPS, and a court.[114] The significance of section 6 for criminal lawyers is as follows:

(1) Under sections 3 and 6 of the HRA the court must interpret that offence (if possible) in line with the Convention.[115]

(2) When the CPS is considering whether or not to bring a prosecution, it is bound by section 6 because it is a public body. However, in *R v G*[116] a majority of the House of Lords rejected an argument that to charge a defendant with a particular crime amounted to an interference with his human rights.[117]

(3) If a defendant has been convicted of an offence which infringes the Convention rights (e.g. a statutory offence which could not be interpreted in line with the Convention) then it can be argued that the court should impose only a nominal sentence (e.g. an absolute discharge). To impose a substantial sentence would infringe an individual's Convention rights, which section 6 prohibits.

DEFINITION

It is important to appreciate that the HRA can affect the definition of a criminal offence in two ways:

(1) a defendant may argue that to convict him or her of a particular offence would infringe his or her Convention rights;

(2) a victim (or potential victim) may argue that the state has infringed his or her rights by not protecting him or her under the criminal law.[118] In *A v UK*[119] the fact that the stepfather could hit his stepson without being liable to punishment under the criminal law infringed the stepson's rights under Article 3. This subsequently led the Court of Appeal in *H*[120] to reinterpret the circumstances in which a parent can rely on the defence of reasonable chastisement when facing a charge of assault.

10.2 THE IMPORTANT ARTICLES IN THE EUROPEAN CONVENTION

The following are the most important rights under the ECHR for criminal lawyers:

---

[114] Human Rights Act 1998, s. 6(3)(a).

[115] Note that s. 3 applies only when the court is interpreting a statutory offence; s. 6 would be relevant if the offence is a common law one.

[116] [2008] UKHL 37.

[117] Followed in *R (E) v DPP* [2011] EWHC 1465 (Admin), but see Malkani (2011).

[118] Ashworth (2013: ch. 8); Herring (2013b).   [119] (1998) 27 EHRR 611.

[120] [2002] 1 Cr App R 59.

The European Convention on Human Rights

Article 2—Right to life

1. Everyone's right to life shall be protected by law. No one shall be deprived of his life intentionally save in the execution of a sentence of a court following his conviction of a crime for which this penalty is provided by law.

2. Deprivation of life shall not be regarded as inflicted in contravention of this Article when it results from the use of force which is no more than absolutely necessary:

   (a) in defence of any person from unlawful violence;

   (b) in order to effect a lawful arrest or to prevent the escape of a person lawfully detained;

   (c) in action lawfully taken for the purpose of quelling a riot or insurrection.

Article 3—Prohibition of torture

No one shall be subjected to torture or to inhuman or degrading treatment or punishment.

Article 5—Right to liberty and security

1. Everyone has the right to liberty and security of person. No one shall be deprived of his liberty save in the following cases and in accordance with a procedure prescribed by law:

   (a) the lawful detention of a person after conviction by a competent court;

   (b) the lawful arrest or detention of a person for non-compliance with the lawful order of a court or in order to secure the fulfilment of any obligation prescribed by law;

   (c) the lawful arrest or detention of a person effected for the purpose of bringing him before the competent legal authority on reasonable suspicion of having committed an offence or when it is reasonably considered necessary to prevent his committing an offence or fleeing after having done so;

   (d) the detention of a minor by lawful order for the purpose of educational supervision or his lawful detention for the purpose of bringing him before the competent legal authority;

   (e) the lawful detention of persons for the prevention of the spreading of infectious diseases, of persons of unsound mind, alcoholics or drug addicts or vagrants;

   (f) the lawful arrest or detention of a person to prevent his effecting an unauthorised entry into the country or of a person against whom action is being taken with a view to deportation or extradition.

2. Everyone who is arrested shall be informed promptly, in a language which he understands, of the reasons for his arrest and of any charge against him.

3. Everyone arrested or detained in accordance with the provisions of paragraph 1(c) of this Article shall be brought promptly before a judge or other officer authorised by law to exercise judicial power and shall be entitled to trial within a reasonable time or to release pending trial. Release may be conditioned by guarantees to appear for trial.

4. Everyone who is deprived of his liberty by arrest or detention shall be entitled to take proceedings by which the lawfulness of his detention shall be decided speedily by a court and his release ordered if the detention is not lawful.

5. Everyone who has been the victim of arrest or detention in contravention of the provisions of this Article shall have an enforceable right to compensation.

Article 6—Right to a fair trial

1. In the determination of his civil rights and obligations or of any criminal charge against him, everyone is entitled to a fair and public hearing within a reasonable time by an independent and impartial tribunal established by law. Judgment shall be pronounced publicly but the press and public may be excluded from all or part of the trial in the interest of morals, public order or national security in a democratic society, where the interests of juveniles or the protection of the private life of the parties so require, or to the extent strictly necessary in the opinion of the court in special circumstances where publicity would prejudice the interests of justice.

2. Everyone charged with a criminal offence shall be presumed innocent until proved guilty according to law.

3. Everyone charged with a criminal offence has the following minimum rights:
   (a) to be informed promptly, in a language which he understands and in detail, of the nature and cause of the accusation against him;
   (b) to have adequate time and facilities for the preparation of his defence;
   (c) to defend himself in person or through legal assistance of his own choosing or, if he has not sufficient means to pay for legal assistance, to be given it free when the interests of justice so require;
   (d) to examine or have examined witnesses against him and to obtain the attendance and examination of witnesses on his behalf under the same conditions as witnesses against him;
   (e) to have the free assistance of an interpreter if he cannot understand or speak the language used in court.

Article 7—No punishment without law

1. No one shall be held guilty of any criminal offence on account of any act or omission which did not constitute a criminal offence under national or international law at the time when it was committed. Nor shall a heavier penalty be imposed than the one that was applicable at the time the criminal offence was committed.

2. This Article shall not prejudice the trial and punishment of any person for any act or omission which, at the time when it was committed, was criminal according to the general principles of law recognised by civilised nations.

Article 8—Right to respect for private and family life

1. Everyone has the right to respect for his private and family life, his home and his correspondence.

2. There shall be no interference by a public authority with the exercise of this right except such as is in accordance with the law and is necessary in a democratic society in the interests of national security, public safety or the economic well-being of the country, for the

prevention of disorder or crime, for the protection of health or morals, or for the protection of the rights and freedoms of others.

Article 9—Freedom of thought, conscience and religion

1. Everyone has the right to freedom of thought, conscience and religion; this right includes freedom to change his religion or belief and freedom, either alone or in community with others and in public or private, to manifest his religion or belief, in worship, teaching, practice and observance.

2. Freedom to manifest one's religion or beliefs shall be subject only to such limitations as are prescribed by law and are necessary in a democratic society in the interests of public safety, for the protection of public order, health or morals, or for the protection of the rights and freedoms of others.

Article 10—Freedom of expression

1. Everyone has the right to freedom of expression. This right shall include freedom to hold opinions and to receive and impart information and ideas without interference by public authority and regardless of frontiers. This Article shall not prevent States from requiring the licensing of broadcasting, television or cinema enterprises.

2. The exercise of these freedoms, since it carries with it duties and responsibilities, may be subject to such formalities, conditions, restrictions or penalties as are prescribed by law and are necessary in a democratic society, in the interests of national security, territorial integrity or public safety, for the prevention of disorder or crime, for the protection of health or morals, for the protection of the reputation or rights of others, for preventing the disclosure of information received in confidence, or for maintaining the authority and impartiality of the judiciary.

Article 11—Freedom of assembly and association

1. Everyone has the right to freedom of peaceful assembly and to freedom of association with others, including the right to form and to join trade unions for the protection of his interests.

2. No restrictions shall be placed on the exercise of these rights other than such as are prescribed by law and are necessary in a democratic society in the interests of national security or public safety, for the prevention of disorder or crime, for the protection of health or morals or for the protection of the rights and freedoms of others.

This Article shall not prevent the imposition of lawful restrictions on the exercise of these rights by members of the armed forces, of the police or of the administration of the State.

Article 14—Prohibition of discrimination

The enjoyment of the rights and freedoms set forth in this Convention shall be secured without discrimination on any ground such as sex, race, colour, language, religion, political or other opinion, national or social origin, association with a national minority, property, birth or other status.

10.3 POTENTIAL CONSEQUENCES OF THE HRA ON THE CRIMINAL LAW

Throughout this book we will mention the potential impact of the HRA on specific offences. But here we will consider some of the general principles of the ECHR which will affect the whole of the criminal law.

Certainty

The state is permitted under the ECHR to create criminal offences which interfere with citizens' Convention rights, such as rights to private and family life (Article 8) and freedom of expression (Article 10), but only if the interferences are in accordance with a 'law'. The European Court of Human Rights (ECtHR) has interpreted 'law' in an interesting way.[121] A rule can be a law only if it is defined with sufficient precision to enable the citizen to know how to behave in accordance with the law.[122] In the following case the ECtHR held that the power under English law to bind the defendant to keep the peace on the basis that his conduct was *contra bonos mores* ('contrary to the public good') was so imprecise that it did not amount to a law, and therefore was an impermissible infringement of the individual's rights.

Hashman and Harrup v United Kingdom
(Application No. 25594/94) (2000) 30 EHRR 241 (ECtHR)

The applicants were bound over to keep the peace and to be of good behaviour by a UK court after they had disrupted the Portman hunt. They claimed that the finding that they had behaved in a manner *contra bonos mores* and the binding over order interfered with the exercise of their rights under Article 10 in a way which was not 'prescribed by law'.

31. The Court recalls that one of the requirements flowing from the expression 'prescribed by law' is foreseeability. A norm cannot be regarded as a 'law' unless it is formulated with sufficient precision to enable the citizen to regulate his conduct. At the same time, whilst certainty in the law is highly desirable, it may bring in its train excessive rigidity and the law must be able to keep pace with changing circumstances. The level of precision required of domestic legislation—which cannot in any case provide for every eventuality—depends to a considerable degree on the content of the instrument in question, the field it is designed to cover and the number and status of those to whom it is addressed. (See generally in this connection, *Rekvenyi v. Hungary*: 20 May 1999, para. 34.)

32. The Court further recalls that prior restraint on freedom of expression must call for the most careful scrutiny on its part. (See, in the context of the necessity for a prior restraint, *The Sunday Times v. United Kingdom (No. 2)*, loc. cit., para. 51.)

33. The Court has already considered the issue of 'lawfulness' for the purposes of Article 5 of the Convention of orders to be bound over to keep the peace and be of good behaviour. (In *Steel v. United Kingdom*, loc. cit., paras. 71–77.) In that case, the Court found that the elements of breach of the peace were adequately defined by English law. (ibid., para. 75.)

. . .

---

[121] *Silver v UK* (1983) 5 EHRR 347.
[122] *Norris v Government of the United States of America* [2008] UKHL 16.

35. It is a feature of the present case that it concerns an interference with freedom of expression which was not expressed to be a 'sanction', or punishment, for behaviour of a certain type, but rather an order, imposed on the applicants, not to breach the peace or behave contra bonos mores in the future. The binding-over order in the present case thus had purely prospective effect. It did not require a finding that here had been a breach of the peace. The case is thus different from the case of *Steel*, in which the proceedings brought against the first and second applicants were in respect of breaches of the peace which were later found to have been committed.

36. The Court must consider the question of whether behaviour contra bonos mores is adequately defined for the purposes of Article 10(2) of the Convention.

37. The Court first recalls that in its *Steel* judgment, it noted that the expression 'to be of good behaviour' was particularly imprecise and offered little guidance to the person bound over as to the type of conduct which would amount to a breach of the order (para. 76). Those considerations apply equally in the present case, where the applicants were not charged with any criminal offence, and were found not to have breached the peace.

38. The Court next notes that conduct contra bonos mores is defined as behaviour which is 'wrong rather than right in the judgment of the majority of contemporary fellow citizens' (para. 13). It cannot agree with the Government that this definition has the same objective element as conduct 'likely to cause annoyance', which was at issue in the case of *Chorherr* (para. 29). The Court considers that the question of whether conduct is 'likely to cause annoyance' is a question which goes to the very heart of the nature of the conduct proscribed: it is conduct whose likely consequence is the annoyance of others. Similarly, the definition of breach of the peace given in the case of *Percy v. Director of Public Prosecutions* (para. 11)—that it includes conduct the natural consequences of which would be to provoke others to violence—also describes behaviour by reference to its effects. Conduct which is 'wrong rather than right in the judgment of the majority of contemporary citizens', by contrast, is conduct which is not described at all, but merely expressed to be 'wrong' in the opinion of a majority of citizens.

39. Nor can the Court agree that the Government's other examples of behaviour which is defined by reference to the standards expected by the majority of contemporary opinion are similar to conduct contra bonos mores as in each case cited by the Government, the example given is but one element of a more comprehensive definition of the proscribed behaviour.

40. With specific reference to the facts of the present case, the Court does not accept that it must have been evident to the applicants what they were being ordered not to do for the period of their binding over. Whilst in the case of *Steel* the applicants had been found to have breached the peace, and the Court found that it was apparent that the bind over related to similar behaviour, the present applicants did not breach the peace, and given the lack of precision referred to above, it cannot be said that what they were being bound over not to do must have been apparent to them.

41. The Court thus finds that the order by which the applicants were bound over to keep the peace and not to behave contra bonos mores did not comply with the requirement of Article 10(2) of the Convention that it be 'prescribed by law'.

. . .

43. It follows that there has been a violation of Article 10 of the Convention.

Violation of Article 10 found.

It should not be thought that a court will readily find that an offence is too vaguely defined to constitute law and hence potentially infringe the European Convention. In *Steel v UK*[123]

[123] (1999) 28 EHRR 603.

it was held that the English offence of breach of the peace (defined as 'when an individual causes harm to persons or property or acts in a manner the natural consequences of which would be to provoke others to violence') was sufficiently precise to amount to 'law'. In *Tagg*[124] the Court of Appeal rejected an argument that the offence of being drunk on an aircraft[125] was insufficiently precise to amount to a law.

One of the reasons why law must not be too vague is that otherwise it will, in effect, be judges or juries, rather than Parliament, which decide what is criminal. In *Jones*[126] Lord Bingham emphasized that

> an important democratic principle in this country [is] that it is for those representing the people of the country in Parliament, not the executive and not judges, to decide what conduct should be treated as lying so far outside the bounds of what is acceptable in our society as to attract criminal penalties.

Burden of proof

Most members of the public know that under English and Welsh criminal law a person should be presumed innocent unless proved guilty.[127] Lord Sankey LC in *Woolmington v DPP*[128] declared that 'throughout the web of the English criminal law one golden thread is always to be seen—that it is the duty of the prosecution to prove the prisoner's guilt'. The principle is justified on the basis that the consequences of a conviction and punishment are so severe that the state prefers to run the risk of acquitting people who may in fact have committed the offence than convicting people who are in fact innocent. The principle also reflects the fact that the prosecution will have all the resources and power of the state on its side, while the defendant will usually have comparatively limited resources.

The reality is that the presumption of innocence is honoured more in the breach than the observance. Even of the more serious offences which are triable in the Crown Court, 40 per cent include some form of departure from the presumption of innocence, according to Andrew Ashworth and Meredith Blake.[129] Lord Steyn in *Lambert*[130] found that 219 of the 540 offences then triable in the Crown Court had provisions which required the defendant to prove their innocence. A common way of departing from the presumption is to create strict liability offences (where it is necessary to prove only that the defendant caused a particular result or state of affairs, and it is not necessary to show that the defendant had a particular state of mind or even behaved unreasonably). Many such offences then have a defence of 'due diligence' or 'no intent' for which the defendant is obliged to produce evidence.

Any departure from the presumption of innocence must now be considered in the light of the HRA. The presumption of innocence is reinforced by Article 6(2) of the ECHR, which declares: 'Everyone shall be presumed innocent until proved guilty according to the law.' However, perhaps surprisingly, the ECtHR has not interpreted that article as strictly as it might. The Court's approach in *Salabiaku v France*[131] and *Phillips v UK*[132] is that presumption

---

[124] [2001] EWCA Crim 1230. See also *Cotter* [2002] Crim LR 824, where it was held that the offence of perverting the course of justice was sufficiently clear to be compatible with the European Convention.

[125] Air Navigation (No. 2) Order 1995, SI 1995/1970, art. 57 and the Civil Aviation Act 1982, s. 61.

[126] [2006] UKHL 16, para. 29.

[127] A leading work on the presumption of innocence is Stumer (2010).

[128] [1935] AC 462, 481 (HL).   [129] Ashworth and Blake (1996).   [130] [2002] 2 AC 545, 569.

[131] (1988) 13 EHRR 379.   [132] [2001] Crim LR 217.

of guilt or the placing of the burden of proof on the defendant does not contravene Article 6 if it is confined within 'reasonable limits'. The House of Lords examined the issue in *Kebelene*[133] and held that the key issue was the difference between persuasive and evidential burdens of proof:

(1) A persuasive burden of proof means that the party must prove the matter at issue.

(2) An evidential burden of proof means that the party must introduce sufficient evidence to establish the reasonable possibility that a particular issue is true.

For example if D faces a charge of assault and wishes to raise the defence of duress, D has an evidential burden of establishing some evidence to show that he might have been acting under duress. If he or she introduces some evidence to show that that might be true, the prosecution has the persuasive burden of proof of showing beyond reasonable doubt that the defendant was not acting under duress.

The House of Lords in *Kebelene*[134] explained that reverse burdens of proof were more likely to be compatible with Article 6 if they were evidential rather than persuasive burdens. The court will need to consider the relative difficulty of proving the relevant matter for the defendant and the prosecution, and the seriousness of the threat at which the criminal offence is directed. In other words, a persuasive burden will be justifiable only if it involves an issue which is very easy for the defendant to establish (e.g. to prove that he or she has a licence to perform the activity)[135] or the burden is necessary for the protection of the public. Therefore, in the light of the HRA, section 3, any statutory burden of proof on the defendant would be interpreted to be evidential if at all possible.[136] It will be interpreted as a persuasive burden only if there is a 'pressing necessity'[137] for there to be a persuasive burden.

The House of Lords has considered the issue in three cases: *Lambert*,[138] *Johnstone*,[139] and *Sheldrake*:

Sheldrake v Director of Public Prosecutions; Attorney-General's Reference (No. 4 of 2002) [2005] 1 AC 264

Two cases concerning burdens of proof were heard by the House of Lords together. In the first Peter Sheldrake was charged with the offence under section 5(1)(b) of the Road Traffic Act 1988 of being in charge of a motor vehicle after having consumed so much alcohol that the proportion of it in his breath exceeded the prescribed limit. He sought to rely on the defence under section 5(2), which cast upon the defendant the legal burden of proving that there was no likelihood of his driving the vehicle while over the limit. He was convicted by the magistrates. He argued before the House of Lords that this burden of proof was not compliant with the presumption of innocence guaranteed by Article 6(2) of the ECHR.

In the *Attorney-General's Reference* case, the defendant was charged with belonging to a proscribed organization contrary to section 11(1) of the Terrorism Act 2000. He sought to rely on the defence in section 11(2) that the organization had not been

---

133 *R v DPP, ex p Kebelene* [1999] 4 All ER 801 (HL).　　134 *Ibid.*
135 cf. *DPP v Barker* [2006] Crim LR 140 and *R v Makuwa* [2006] Crim LR 911.
136 See *Webster* [2010] EWCA Crim 2819.　　137 *Lambert* [2001] 3 WLR 206 (HL).
138 [2001] 3 WLR 206 (HL). For criticism, see Beyleveld, Kirkham, and Townend (2002).
139 [2003] 1 WLR 1736.

proscribed at the time when he became a member or professed to be a member of it and that he had not taken part in any of the organization's activities since it had been proscribed. At the trial the Crown conceded that the defence in section 11(2) imposed an evidential, but not legal, burden on the defendant. The Attorney General referred to the Court of Appeal the question of whether the defence in section 11(2) imposed a legal or evidential burden on the defendant and if a legal one, then whether it was compatible with Article 6(2).

Lord Bingham of Cornhill

[Having reviewed the relevant case law from the ECtHR, **Lord Bingham** stated:]

21. From this body of authority certain principles may be derived. The overriding concern is that a trial should be fair, and the presumption of innocence is a fundamental right directed to that end. The Convention does not outlaw presumptions of fact or law but requires that these should be kept within reasonable limits and should not be arbitrary. It is open to states to define the constituent elements of a criminal offence, excluding the requirement of *mens rea*. But the substance and effect of any presumption adverse to a defendant must be examined, and must be reasonable. Relevant to any judgment on reasonableness or proportionality will be the opportunity given to the defendant to rebut the presumption, maintenance of the rights of the defence, flexibility in application of the presumption, retention by the court of a power to assess the evidence, the importance of what is at stake and the difficulty which a prosecutor may face in the absence of a presumption. Security concerns do not absolve member states from their duty to observe basic standards of fairness. The justifiability of any infringement of the presumption of innocence cannot be resolved by any rule of thumb, but on examination of all the facts and circumstances of the particular provision as applied in the particular case.

. . .

30. Both *R v Lambert* [2002] 2 AC 545 and *R v Johnstone* [2003] 1 WLR 1736 are recent decisions of the House, binding on all lower courts for what they decide. Nothing said in *R v Johnstone* suggests an intention to depart from or modify the earlier decision, which should not be treated as superseded or implicitly overruled. Differences of emphasis (and Lord Steyn was not a lone voice in *R v Lambert*) are explicable by the difference in the subject matter of the two cases. Section 5 of the Misuse of Drugs Act 1971 and section 92 of the Trade Marks Act 1994 were directed to serious social and economic problems. But the justifiability and fairness of the respective exoneration provisions had to be judged in the particular context of each case. I have already identified the potential consequence to a section 5 defendant who failed, perhaps narrowly, to make good his section 28 defence. He might be, but fail to prove that he was, entirely ignorant of what he was carrying. By contrast, the offences under section 92 are committed only if the act in question is done by a person 'with a view to gain for himself or another, or with intent to cause loss to another.' Thus these are offences committed (if committed) by dealers, traders, market operators, who could reasonably be expected (as Lord Nicholls pointed out) to exercise some care about the provenance of goods in which they deal. The penalty imposed for breaches of section 92 may be severe (see, for example, *R v Gleeson* [2002] 1 Cr App R (S) 485), but that is because the potential profits of fraudulent trading are often great.

31. The task of the court is never to decide whether a reverse burden should be imposed on a defendant, but always to assess whether a burden enacted by Parliament unjustifiably infringes the presumption of innocence. It may none the less be questioned whether (as the Court of Appeal ruled in para 52d) 'the assumption should be that Parliament would not have

made an exception without good reason'. Such an approach may lead the court to give too much weight to the enactment under review and too little to the presumption of innocence and the obligation imposed on it by section 3.

Sheldrake v Director of Public Prosecutions

. . .

41. It may not be very profitable to debate whether section 5(2) infringes the presumption of innocence. It may be assumed that it does. Plainly the provision is directed to a legitimate object: the prevention of death, injury and damage caused by unfit drivers. Does the provision meet the tests of acceptability identified in the Strasbourg jurisprudence? In my view, it plainly does. I do not regard the burden placed on the defendant as beyond reasonable limits or in any way arbitrary. It is not objectionable to criminalise a defendant's conduct in these circumstances without requiring a prosecutor to prove criminal intent. The defendant has a full opportunity to show that there was no likelihood of his driving, a matter so closely conditioned by his own knowledge and state of mind at the material time as to make it much more appropriate for him to prove on the balance of probabilities that he would not have been likely to drive than for the prosecutor to prove, beyond reasonable doubt, that he would. I do not think that imposition of a legal burden went beyond what was necessary. If a driver tries and fails to establish a defence under section 5(2), I would not regard the resulting conviction as unfair, as the House held that it might or would be in *R v Lambert* [2002] 2 AC 545. I find no reason to conclude that the conviction of Mr Sheldrake was tainted by any hint of unfairness.

. . .

44. I would allow the Director's appeal, reinstate the justices' decision and answer the certified question by saying that the burden of proof provision in section 5(2) of the Road Traffic Act 1988 imposes a legal burden on an accused who is charged with an offence contrary to section 5(1)(b) of that Act.

Attorney-General's Reference (No. 4 of 2002)

. . .

54. In penalising the profession of membership of a proscribed organisation, section 11(1) does, I think, interfere with exercise of the right of free expression guaranteed by article 10 of the Convention. But such interference may be justified if it satisfies various conditions. First, it must be directed to a legitimate end. Such ends include the interests of national security, public safety and the prevention of disorder or crime. Section 11(1) is directed to those ends. Secondly, the interference must be prescribed by law. That requirement is met, despite my present doubt as to the meaning of 'profess'. Thirdly, it must be necessary in a democratic society and proportionate. The necessity of attacking terrorist organisations is in my view clear. I would incline to hold subsection (1) to be proportionate, for article 10 purposes, whether subsection (2) imposes a legal or an evidential burden. But I agree with Mr Owen that the question does not fall to be considered in the present context, and I would (as he asks) decline to answer this part of the Attorney General's second question.

. . .

Lord Carswell

79. My Lords, I have had the advantage of reading in draft the opinion of my noble and learned friend, Lord Rodger of Earlsferry. I agree with his reasons and conclusions and wish to add only a few observations of my own.

80. The issue common to these appeals is whether it is unfair to the accused to have to undertake the burden of proving the defence provided for in the governing legislation and, if so, whether the relevant provisions should be 'read down' as an evidential rather than a legal or persuasive burden. My noble and learned friend, Lord Bingham of Cornhill, has reviewed in detail in his opinion the applicable provisions of the European Convention on Human Rights and the decisions of the European Court of Human Rights, together with the domestic decisions which affect the issues before us, and I do not wish to add anything to the discussion of the law set out in his opinion and that of Lord Rodger of Earlsferry. I shall consider in this opinion the application of the law to the two appeals before us, observing only that the objective of article 6 of the Convention is to require a fair trial and that the presumption of innocence contained in article 6(2) is one aspect of that requirement, rather than constituting a free-standing obligation. For that reason, as accepted by the European Court of Human Rights in *Salabiaku v France* 13 EHRR 379, inroads into the obligation of the prosecution to prove beyond reasonable doubt all the matters in issue in a criminal trial may be permissible in certain circumstances. The reversal of the ordinary burden of proof resting upon the prosecution may accordingly be justified in some cases and will not offend against the principle requiring a fair trial. Where the question arises, it has to be determined, first, whether it is fair and reasonable in the achievement of a proper statutory objective for the state to deprive the defendant of the protection normally guaranteed by the presumption of innocence whereby the burden of proof is placed upon the prosecution to prove beyond reasonable doubt all the matters in issue. Secondly, one must determine whether the exception is proportionate, that is to say, whether it goes no further than is reasonably necessary to achieve that objective.

. . .

[**Lord Carswell** in considering the *Sheldrake* case stated:]

84. The ultimate risk may be that the defendant may elect to drive the vehicle, but it is not in my view the gravamen of the offence. Being in charge of a vehicle while over the limit is in itself such an anti-social act that Parliament has long since made it an offence. A person who has drunk more than the limit should take steps to put it out of his power to drive. Section 5(2) gives him an escape route, which it is quite easy for him to take in a genuine case, as he is the person best placed to know and establish whether he was likely to drive the vehicle. Conversely, the prosecution might be able readily enough to establish that the defendant was in a position to drive the vehicle if he elected to do so, but it could well be difficult to prove beyond reasonable doubt that there was a likelihood of his driving it.

85. An example may be posed to test these propositions. The owner of a car, who has drunk enough alcohol to take him over the limit, decides to wash the car. He takes his keys with him, which he uses to open the doors to get access to all the surfaces to be washed and to clean the inside. It is indisputable that during this process he is in charge of the vehicle. He may have started off with the sole intention of confining himself to cleaning the car, but the possibility exists that he may change his intention and drive it on some errand, perhaps to fill the tank with petrol. The person who knows best whether there was a real risk of that occurring is the defendant himself. I see nothing unreasonable or disproportionate in requiring him to prove on the balance of probabilities that there was no likelihood of his doing so. He should in my opinion have to do so, by adducing evidence which may be duly tested in court.

Appeal allowed. Order of Divisional Court set aside. Order of Court of Appeal (Criminal Division) affirmed in regard to the first question referred and set aside in regard to the second question referred. Defendant's costs on reference in Court of Appeal and House of Lords out of Central Funds.

In the following extract, Ian Dennis usefully summarizes the current state of the law:

I. Dennis, 'Reverse Onuses and the Presumption of Innocence: In Search of Principle' [2005] *Criminal Law Review* 901 at 912–17

The first stage of the decision-making process deals with the question whether a statute imposes a burden of any kind on the defendant, and, if so, whether it is a legal or an evidential burden. This question is settled by ordinary principles of statutory construction. These include the effect of s.101 of the Magistrates Courts Act 1980, as explained and expanded by Edwards and Hunt. If the burden is an evidential one no problem of compatibility with Art.6 arises. If the burden is a legal one, the issue of compatibility must be considered.

The second stage of decision-making requires a court to decide the issue of compatibility according to whether the reverse onus (legal burden) is justified as a proportionate measure in pursuance of a legitimate aim. It is at this stage that the main problems and uncertainties arise. The debate is almost entirely about proportionality, but analysis of the case law shows considerable disagreement and inconsistency about the use of one or more of six relevant factors in determining this question. If no broader principles for applying the relevant factors can be identified, the decisions as to the justifiability of particular reverse onuses will continue to resemble a forensic lottery. A search for principle suggests that issues of moral blameworthiness should be proved by the prosecution. These issues will include, in addition to the relevant prohibited acts, any requisite culpable mental states, any objective fault such as negligence, and the unavailability of any common law defences raised by the defendant. Exceptionally, legal burdens can be placed on defendants to prove formal qualifications to do certain regulated acts, and in cases where the defendant accepts the burden of proof of exculpation by virtue of voluntarily participating in a regulated activity from which he intends to derive benefit. Lord Bingham in *Sheldrake* adopted a further principle that where the scope of an offence is so wide as to include defendants who are not blameworthy a reverse onus on the defendant to prove lack of culpability is disproportionate. Conversely, an onus to prove facts taking the defendant outside the rationale of the offence, meaning the danger with which the prohibited, morally blameworthy, conduct is intended to deal, may be upheld. There are advantages to Lord Bingham's principle, but also significant problems.

If the reverse onus is justified as proportionate to a legitimate aim no further decision is necessary. If it is not justified according to these criteria the third stage of decision-making requires the court to read down the legal burden to an evidential burden if it is possible to do this using s.3 of the HRA. On the basis of *Sheldrake* it seems that it will almost always be possible to do this; it is hard to envisage a case that would not come within the scope of Lord Bingham's reasoning. Accordingly a declaration of incompatibility of a reverse onus will almost never be necessary.

Prosecution policy

In *R v G*[140] a 15-year-old boy had sexual intercourse with a girl who was aged under 13. The case proceeded on the basis that the act was consensual. As such he could have been prosecuted either for the offence of rape of a 13-year-old (section 5 of the Sexual Offences Act 2003) or the less serious offence of committing a sexual act with a child (section 13). He was

---

[140] [2008] UKHL 37.

charged and convicted of rape. He appealed to the House of Lords claiming that the charge infringed his rights under Articles 6 and 8.

All of their Lordships agreed that there was no breach of Article 6. That was because Article 6 was concerned with the fairness of the procedure and could not be used to challenge the substantive law.[141]

Lords Hoffmann and Mance and Baroness Hale held that Article 8 did not cover the decision by a prosecution authority to charge a defendant with one offence rather than the other. Therefore, it did not, in this case, infringe G's rights to prosecute him under section 5 (rape of an under-13-year-old) rather than the lesser offence under section 13. Lords Hope and Carswell disagreed holding that to prosecute G for the section 5 offence was a breach of his Article 8 rights.

The impact of the HRA on particular offences

As already mentioned, at many points throughout this book we will consider the impact of the HRA on particular offences. Here just a couple of examples will be given. As the following examples indicate, although defendants may often seek to raise a defence on the basis of the HRA, rarely have they been successful:

(1) *Smethurst*:[142] a defendant charged with the creation of an indecent photograph sought to argue that to convict him of the offence interfered with his right to freedom of expression or right to respect for private life. His argument was rejected.

(2) *Taylor*:[143] a Rastafarian defendant unsuccessfully claimed that to convict him of a drugs offence interfered with his right to religious freedom.

(3) *H*:[144] the Court of Appeal interpreted the defence of reasonable chastisement in a way which was compatible with the victim's rights under the ECHR.

(4) *Concannon*:[145] the defendant argued that the law on accessories operated unfairly in the context of murder, and that therefore his right to a fair trial under Article 6 was breached. His argument failed, with the Court of Appeal emphasizing that Article 6 concerned the fairness of criminal trials, not the fairness of the law itself.

(5) *Rimmington*:[146] the House of Lords rejected an argument that the offence of causing a public nuisance was too vague to satisfy the requirements of Article 6.

(6) *Howitt*:[147] the Divisional Court rejected a claim that the bar on smoking in pubs in the Health Act 2006 breached articles of the ECHR.

FURTHER READING

Ashworth, A. (2002a) *Human Rights, Serious Crime and Criminal Procedure* (London: Sweet & Maxwell).

Buxton, R. (2000) 'The Human Rights Act and the Substantive Criminal Law' *Criminal Law Review* 311.

---

[141] Followed in *R (E) v DPP* [2011] EWHC 1465 (Admin), but see Malkani (2011).
[142] [2001] Crim LR 657.   [143] [2001] EWCA Crim 2263.   [144] [2002] 1 Cr App R 59.
[145] [2002] Crim LR 213 (CA).   [146] [2005] 3 WLR 982 (HL).
[147] *R (Howitt) v Preston Magistrates' Court* [2009] EWHC 1284 (Admin).

Dennis, I. (2005) 'Reverse Onuses and the Presumption of Innocence: In Search of Principle' *Criminal Law Review* 901.

Dingwall, G. (2002) 'Statutory Exceptions, Burdens of Proof and the Human Rights Act 1998' *Modern Law Review* 65: 40.

Duff, R.A. (2005c) 'Strict Liability, Legal Presumptions, and the Presumption of Innocence' in A. Simester (ed.) *Appraising Strict Liability* (Oxford: OUP).

Emmerson, B. and Ashworth, A. (2001) *Human Rights and Criminal Justice* (London: Sweet & Maxwell).

Hamer, D. (2007) 'The Presumption of Innocence and Reverse Burdens: A Balancing Act' *Cambridge Law Journal* 66: 142.

Roberts, P. (2005) 'Strict Liability and the Presumption of Innocence' in A. Simester (ed.) *Appraising Strict Liability* (Oxford: OUP).

Stumer, A. (2010) *The Presumption of Innocence: Evidential and Human Rights Perspectives* (Oxford: Hart).

11 CRITICAL CRIMINAL LAW

In recent times much attention has been paid to critical analysis of criminal law. Critical analysts claim that the attempts of the judiciary and commentators to paint a picture of a law which is rational and logical have failed and that in fact criminal law is replete with irrationality. This reflects political and social tensions within society.[148] We have already seen a fine example of critical analysis in Nicola Lacey's analysis of the general principles of criminal law excerpted in Section 7. Might it not be more useful to look at what makes police officers decide to arrest someone or what really influences juries in order to convict or acquit,[149] rather than what the law 'in the books' is?

One of England's leading critical criminal lawyers is Alan Norrie, whose work will be excerpted at various points in this book. Here we will extract an analysis of his work by G.R. Sullivan. He focuses on Norrie's claim that criminal law cannot be just because of its failure to consider the potential impact of social and economic inequalities in society.[150] He challenges Norrie—a challenge he often faces—to suggest an alternative criminal law which would be more just. This is a common criticism of critical scholars; they are brilliant deconstructors, but what is to replace the rubble they have created?

G.R. Sullivan, 'Is Criminal Law Possible?' (2002) 22 *Oxford Journal of Legal Studies* 747 at 750–4

Norrie is right to accord a central place to a concern with the nature of the justice or injustice that the criminal law engenders. For Norrie, the maintenance of order in a 40/30/30 society

---

148 Norrie (2002).
149 Thomas (2010) for a fascinating (and rather reassuring) survey of the fairness of juries.
150 Of particular concern are the racial aspects of crime: see Phillips and Bowling (2002). On the wider issue of the link between crime and social exclusion, see Green (2011); J. Young (2002); and Tadros (2009). Garland (2001) discusses the use of crime as a form of social control.

entails that the criminal law operates in a fundamentally unjust manner, albeit an injustice tempered by a concern with the requirements of (too limited) a model of justice.

Many will agree with Norrie that large inequalities of resources and power are a bad thing and that many civic advantages would flow from establishing a more egalitarian, less materialistic society. The link between social deprivation and the incidence of criminal offending is undeniable. Anyone with the most cursory knowledge of the day to day realities of the criminal justice system will know the questionable nature of many of its decisions and their consequences when assessed in terms of justice and fairness. Norrie argues that if the criminal justice system is to advance the cause of justice for defendants, the grip of the Kantian model must be eased. Norrie does not dismiss as chimeras the Kantian values of autonomy and freedom. He acknowledges that there is a place in moral judgments for responsibility based on personal agency. His argument is that an exclusive stress on personal agency excludes far too much of the whole picture. He emphasizes time and again that conduct is a compound of the social and the personal. Accordingly, the pressures and exigencies of social circumstances and forces should feature in determining criminal liability—a relational account grounded in social reality.

There is considerable force in Norrie's arguments. Yet it is unclear what consequences for the form and content of the criminal law would be entailed by a relational account. He returns frequently to his contention that the principal role of the criminal law is to maintain the status quo for a society profoundly unequal. This perspective would allow claims that at least certain criminal acts are justified forms of defiance and/or appropriate exercises in distributive justice. A functioning legal order could not accept such claims as the basis of exemption from the norms of the criminal law. Thus his argument moves in the direction of displacing the current legal order. Yet Norrie insists he is not bent on a dismissal of legal ordering and legal values. His project is one of reconstruction, albeit radical reconstruction. In keeping with that, he nowhere claims directly that social disadvantage justifies criminal acts. Indeed, he seems to allow that findings of guilt must be made even within the current dispensation. His position seems to be that social factors should constitute grounds of *excuse* and that these excuses currently go unheard because of the Kantian model. Thus we are not dealing with a macro rejection of the right of the institutions of an unjust society to condemn and punish. We are within the realm of the micro examination of the circumstances of individuals, the realm of excuses.

Thus Norrie requires a theory of excuse which accommodates the exculpatory force of certain kinds of social circumstances and pressures. Yet the possibility of such a theory is unexamined by Norrie. The link between the macro unfairness of society and the micro circumstances of individuals is not made. There is merely a pervasive assumption that exculpation would frequently follow *ipso facto* from an holistic appraisal of all the salient circumstances of disadvantaged defendants. Norrie is aware that an holistic appraisal would be very difficult to fit in with any kind of criminal law which aspired to be a rule based system. He seemingly envisages forms of adjudication which reflect systems of popular justice which have emerged from time to time in certain countries, usually in revolutionary or immediate post-revolution times. Norrie's reconstruction is effectively a dismissal of the possibility of a just and principled criminal law for our current form of liberal capitalist society.

Norrie, with his preoccupation with societal forces, gives little if any attention to the psychological determinants of human agency. It is fair to say that he adopts the Standard Social Science Model of human conduct, allowing pre-dominant effect to the formative influence of social structures and cultural norms. As stated, the individual and individual agency are part of Norrie's ontology and yet the mechanics of individual agency are unexplored. He accepts the premise of free will required by the Kantian paradigm, albeit a free will heavily conditioned by social circumstances. Yet the acceptance of free will, in however socially conditioned a form, makes the accommodation of excuses based on non-exceptional social circumstances very difficult to accommodate.

Undeniably, social deprivation has a vast impact on the range and nature of options available to an agent. But, of course, there is more in the mix than the constriction of resources and legitimate opportunities. Family circumstances, maleness and age clearly correlate with the incidence of offending. And yet the majority of socially disadvantaged males under the age of 25 from single parent households are not consistent offenders. Clearly, the particulars of an individual's psychology and the vagaries of chance and luck are important too. We may be confident that D would not Φ, if he had been placed in different social circumstances, and yet the majority of his contemporaries in similar social and familial circumstances to him do not Φ. Indeed, a focus on the psychological make-up of the individual defendant may open the way for a more destabilizing critique of the foundations of judgments of culpability than the socially orientated account offered by Norrie.

In the past decade, due to developing imaging techniques, remarkable progress has been made into the understanding of the nature of the brain and its processes. It would be foolish to claim that the increase in the scientific understanding of brain processes eliminates the possibility of an empirically grounded account of free-will. Indeed, so complex is the brain and its processes, a full scientific account of human agency and consciousness may never be had. Yet enough information is already to hand to persuade any open minded person that deterministic accounts of human activities, including complex cerebral activities, cannot be refuted by metaphysics alone.

A striking feature arising from what is known of the workings of the brain is the automaticity of the neuro-chemical processes that are triggered by responses to threats and opportunities arising from the agent's environment. These processes may initiate complex behaviours which are non-volitional if volition implies unconditioned, voluntary choice. It becomes entirely plausible to suppose that different agents, otherwise in like cases, might respond to the same threat or opportunity according to their brain-conditioned psychology. This does not deny for one moment the salience of social circumstances in the construction of conduct. Agent E may be in a position either to offer immediate resistance to a threat or to seek legal redress thereafter. Agent D may lack the option of legal redress. Clearly such socially conditioned data will affect the brain's responses. Yet whether D resists the threat (and thereby commits an offence) or succumbs to it will be a product of her brain-conditioned psychology in addition to her social situation. Whether her conduct is to be conceived as a natural product or as arising from a capacity for choice which she can exercise within some haven of reasons sequestered from the natural order is moot. Yet even if we still cling to the latter view, we must at least concede that it is a contingent hypothesis. Unfortunately, for many criminal lawyers and theorists, free-will will continue to be a confidently held article of faith, supplying vitality to the malign Kantian heritage of punishment as a good in itself rather than a regrettable and problematic necessity. By contrast, receptiveness to the possibility that determinism, even in its hardest versions, may be true should encourage rethinking about the whole process of punishment and stimulate the pursuit of more rational, humane forms of social control.

Accordingly, for persons coming from a very different direction than Norrie, a great deal of scepticism may arise about the criminal law as a system of justice. But just or otherwise, the criminal law will remain as a system of control for the indefinite future. Popular sentiment, quite understandably, would still be moved to condemn wrongdoing and wrongdoers whatever the level of acceptance among scientists and theorists that a deterministic account was the most plausible account of human conduct. Indeed popular sentiment may be fortified by moral theories which do not make voluntarism a necessary condition of blame. In any event, whatever the ultimate legitimacy of these forms of popular sentiment and varieties of moral theory, an atomistic and conflictual society such as our own could not, for Hobbesian reasons, dispense with State coercion and control in respect of anti-social conduct. As a system of control, Norrie conceives the criminal law as predominantly a resource for the powerful to deploy against the excluded. This, it is suggested, is too monolithic a picture.

It is true, that notwithstanding the advent of the Serious Fraud Office and the Financial Services Authority, the criminal law is of very limited effectiveness in punishing property and fraud offences perpetrated by persons in commercial and professional settings. But then the clear-up rates for domestic burglaries are low, in some police authorities appallingly so. The criminal law and its agencies are not necessarily perceived as an alien occupying force even in the most impoverished of neighbourhoods. Not infrequently, the inhabitants of such neighbourhoods seek more effective protection from the criminal law and explore alternatives to police protection where it is ineffectual. Vulnerable classes of victim such as victims of domestic violence, child abuse, racial attack, corporate disregard for safety look to the criminal law to correct imbalances of power. On occasion, protection may not be forthcoming because the provision of protection may be too disruptive of vested interests. Nonetheless some of the greatest upheavals in doctrine arise when protection is extended to a vulnerable victim in circumstances not obviously within the letter of the law.

The criminal law, its agencies, its punitive infrastructure are problematic, overly politicized facets of modern society. If society is too unfair to command the support of the majority of agents subjected to its criminal law, it follows that the norms of the criminal law will be rejected along with other civic obligations. Yet if the calculus is that the civic order of current society is, all things considered, worth preserving, notwithstanding the unfair distribution of goods in that society, the question arises of whether a criminal law can be achieved which combines effectiveness with legitimacy. The fact that any system of criminal law currently conceivable must, perforce, cause significant injustice to least advantaged citizens must be compatible with an all things considered judgment favouring the criminal law's legitimacy. We must face too the real possibility that the criminal law employs a model of human conduct at variance with the facts of the natural order. These are large caveats, perhaps too large to be set aside. If they are conceded however, central to its legitimacy is whether criminal law is a legal domain or merely a particular form of political decision making.

A particularly influential form of critical theory is critical race theory, which seeks to show how the law can reflect and perpetuate racial hierarchies. This is summarized in the following extract by Bennett Capers.

B. Capers, 'Critical Race Theory' in M. Dubber and T. Hörnle (eds) *The Oxford Handbook of Criminal Law* (Oxford: OUP, 2014), 26

[Critical Race Theory (CRT) is]...committed to challenging racial hierarchy, and indeed hierarchy and subordination in all of its various forms. To that end, CRT insists on progressive race consciousness, on systemic analysis of the structures of subordination, on the inclusion of counter-accounts of social reality, and on a critique of power relationships that is attentive to the multiple dimensions on which subordination exists. Beyond this, a review of the key writings that formed the movement reveals some recurring themes and tenets. First, that "formal," color-blind laws often serve to marginalize and obscure social, political, and economic inequality. Secondly, that legal reforms that ostensibly benefit minorities occur only when such reforms also advance the interests of the white majority, a requirement most often referred to as "interest convergence." Thirdly, that race is biologically insignificant; rather, the concept of race is, to a large extent, socially and legally constructed. Fourthly, CRT rejects crude essentialism and recognizes that oppression and subordination operate on multiple axes. For example, a black working-class lesbian in one part of the United States likely experiences oppression differently than a black male investment banker in another part of the United States. Fifthly, that race is often elided in the law; much CRT thus involves making race visible, or as I have described it elsewhere, "reading black." While there is no one methodology in CRT, much of the literature incorporates personal narrative, or what is often referred to as "legal storytelling." In addition, in the past decade, CRT scholars have increasingly turned to research on implicit biases to support their claims.

FURTHER READING

Baker, D. (2011a) 'The Impossibility of a Critically Objective Criminal Law' *McGill Law Journal* 56: 349.

Duff, R.A. (1998b) 'Principle and Contradiction in the Criminal Law: Motives and Criminal Liability' in R.A. Duff (ed.) *Philosophy and the Criminal Law* (Cambridge: Cambridge University Press).

Lacey, N. (1998a) 'Contingency, Coherence and Conceptualism' in R.A. Duff (ed.) *Philosophy and the Criminal Law* (Cambridge: Cambridge University Press).

Lacey, N. (2014) 'Community, Culture and Criminalization' in W. Kymlicka, C. Lernestedt, and M. Matravers (eds) *Criminal Law and Cultural Diversity* (Oxford: OUP).

Lacey, N., Wells, C., and Quick, O. (2010) *Reconstructing Criminal Law* (4th edn, Cambridge: Cambridge University Press).

Norrie, A. (2001) *Crime, Reason and History* (2nd edn, London: Butterworths).

Norrie, A. (2002) *Punishment, Responsibility, and Justice* (Oxford: OUP).

Tadros, V. (2009) 'Poverty and Criminal Responsibility' *Journal of Value Inquiry* 43: 391.

12 FEMINIST LEGAL THOUGHT

Feminist analysis has proved a powerful influence on the study of criminal law.[151] Much work has been done on highlighting injustices to women within the criminal justice system. Consider, for example, the following indictment of the criminal justice system:

Domestic violence accounts for a quarter of all crime, and yet only 5% of recorded cases of domestic violence end in conviction, less than 20% of rapes and sexual assaults are reported to the police, and less than 6% of rapes result in conviction. There are now over 4,500 women in prison, an increase of 194% in the last ten years. Most women are convicted of non-violent offences, such as shoplifting. One woman out of 12 judges in the House of Lords, five women out of 43 police Chief Constables, 18 women out of 42 Chief Officers of Probation, seven women out of 42 Chief Crown Prosecutors, 31 women out of 138 Prison Governors. There was evidence of sexual harassment and discrimination experienced by women working in the system.[152]

---

[151] See Naffine (1997 and 2002) and Wells (2004) for a discussion generally on feminist approaches to law.
[152] Dustin (2004).

It should be noted that of the just over 4,000 women in prison over half are themselves the victims of domestic violence and over a third have suffered sexual abuse.[153] Feminists have expressed concern that too often women who are in an abusive relationship end up being convicted of crimes they are coerced to do by their abusers.[154]

It must not be thought that feminism's sole contribution is to point out examples of gender stereotyping amongst the judiciary or lawyers (rape cases are replete with these) or examples of where the law unjustifiably treats men and women differently (coercion may be an example of this in that it is available as a defence for wives but not husbands). As the following extracts by Nicola Lacey and Prabha Kotiswaran suggest, there is much more to a feminist perspective than this:

N. Lacey, 'General Principles of Criminal Law? A Feminist View' in D. Nicolson and L. Bibbings (eds) *Feminist Perspectives in Criminal Law* (London: Cavendish, 1996), 92–9

Probably the most *distinctively* feminist objection to the idea of criminal law as based on general principles lies, however, in the claim that generalisations—appeals to universally valid categories or concepts—tend to obscure important differences between persons, actions or situations. From a liberal point of view, for example, the move from the standard of a 'reasonable man' to that of a 'reasonable person' is an advance. But feminists may question whether the abstract person is implicitly understood in terms of characteristics, contexts and capacities more typical of men's than of women's lives and, moreover, is so understood in generalised terms which render exposure of sex/gender issues yet more difficult than in the days of sex-specific language.

This argument comes in more and less radical forms. The more radical version is summed up by Catharine MacKinnon's witty comment that 'I refer: to women and men because you don't see many persons around'. MacKinnon implies that sex/gender is such a fundamental feature of human identity that the idea of a gender-neutral subjectivity simply makes no sense. This might be taken to mean that the very idea of a standard of 'reasonableness' engages in a totalising discourse, flattening out relevant differences between persons and contexts and brutally assimilating the vast array of human difference to a specific norm. Of course, this is not an *exclusively* feminist argument: it can be (and has been) reproduced around other indices of differentiation, such as ethnicity or class. But it is an argument which has been of sufficient salience in feminist thought to count as one of the distinctive questions posed by feminist scholarship for the general principles.

There are two reasons, however, why this argument fails to generate an entirely convincing critique of the substance of criminal law's general principles. In the first place, the argument proves too much; if it were genuinely persuasive, it would undermine all forms of generalisation, feminist analysis and other forms of critical social theory included. Secondly, a strong form of the argument entails a decisive objection not only to the idea of criminal law as based on general principles, but also to the very idea of criminal law, which is, inevitably, in the business of applying general standards across a range of persons and in a variety of situations. This, of course, does not mean that key political questions about proper respect for relevant differences of history or circumstance do not arise for criminal law. But it does suggest that the implementation of substantive offences and rules of evidence, rather than

---

[153] Loveless (2010). See further Seal (2010) for a detailed discussion of prejudice shown to female offenders.
[154] Loveless (2010); Herring (2007c).

the general principles, should be the primary object of critical attention. This is because the contextual factors which may be normatively relevant to the application of a general standard to a particular case need to be understood in relation to the types of situation in which they arise.

A less sweeping version of the argument about the capacity of generalisations to obscure important questions of sexual difference has been articulated by Hilary Allen. In a subtle analysis of interpretations of the reasonable person in a series of provocation cases, Allen has revealed the way in which the gender-neutral person is nonetheless fleshed out in judicial discourse in highly (and often stereotypically) sex-specific terms. The construct of the reasonable person cannot entirely conceal the fact that the judges themselves find it difficult to conceive of a legal standard of reasonable behaviour applicable across the sexes. From Allen's point of view, this is highly problematic, because it is inconsistent with the tenet that women are properly accounted full and equal citizens and legal subjects. This does not imply, however, that the different situations of men and women in certain contexts should not be taken into account by criminal law. In relation to provocation, this cashes out in terms of an argument that the level of self-control to be expected should indeed be that attributable to a reasonable legal subject, irrespective of sex, while sexually-specific aspects affecting the gravity of the provocation to a particular woman or man should, like other salient, social differences, indeed be taken into account. Allen's argument implies the more general, prescriptive proposition that criminal law should show sensitivity to inequalities of impact along sexually patterned lines, but that its basic conceptualisation of its subjects should not be sexually differentiated. This argument has something in common with Donald Nicolson's suggestion that the appropriate approach is to ask what it is reasonable to expect of particular defendants in the light of their history, circumstances and so on.

As Allen's argument suggests, another promising ground for feminist analysis lies in the normative aspect of the appeal to general principles. The post-enlightenment vision of responsible human agency which underpins the normative appeal of the general principles is one which was thought valid for women considerably later than for men. Arguably, the gradual recognition of women's agency represents the crowning triumph of feminism's immanent critique of liberalism. Nonetheless, there remains a significant and disturbing difference of degree in the willingness to interpret women's behaviour as the product of psychological or medical pathology, rather than responsible choice. This point is underscored by Allen's excellent *Justice Unbalanced*, a study which demonstrates sentencing courts' willingness to interpret female offending as the product of mental disorder and a corresponding unwillingness so to interpret male offending.

It is often argued, however, that liberal legal orders conjure up an inappropriately atomistic vision of the social world—a world peopled by competitive individuals whose relations with one another are structured primarily or even exclusively by the pursuit of self-interest. And some feminists have argued that this vision of the social world has particularly baleful implications in marginalizing the relations of care, nurturing and reciprocity which have, as a matter of history, been more central to women's lives than to men's. Interestingly, this is a less salient feature of criminal law than of, say, contract law; criminal law is, after all, in the business of articulating reciprocal responsibilities. One might argue, on the other hand, that the inexorable shift towards subjectivism as the dominant interpretation of the general principles reinforces an individualistic and decontextualised interpretation of human behaviour. By contrast, the reasonableness test, whose allegedly 'objective' nature has been controversial among some feminists, is anything but atomistic. It is, at root, all about a vision of the obligations which human beings owe to one another. Yet again, important feminist questions are likely to arise not merely about the content of these obligations, but also about the kinds of evidence which should be relevant to determining whether they have been breached and about the law's proper response where those obligations have a radically unequal impact on women and men.

. . .

Sexing the Subject of Criminal Law?

In recent years, feminist criminal law theory has shifted away from questions about how a pre-existing category, 'women', are treated (or ignored) by legal doctrine in favour of questions about legal doctrine's dynamic role in *constituting* women and men as legal and social subjects. This shift was presaged in Cousins' argument that: '[A feminist approach] must analyse how particular legal forms of agency are more or less implicated in the organization of sexual difference and what effect they have on that differentiation.' A good example of this sort of approach is Ngaire Naffine's analysis of the law of rape, which traces a particular and highly sexually differentiated conception of heterosexual relations, even into the 'post-feminist', gender-neutral reconstructed Australian sexual assault provisions. Similarly, one could interpret the critical analysis of the immediacy requirements structuring self-defence and of the loss of self-control model of provocation as contributions to this more recent project.

This sort of argument engages directly with aspects of the general principles of criminal law; it exposes the assumptions which underlie allegedly general concepts, such as consent, belief, foresight or reasonableness and reveals the ways in which they are implicated in the constitution of sexually differentiated social relations. But, crucially, it does so not merely in terms of engagement with the general principles themselves, but rather in terms of the combined effects of a number of much more concrete factors. These include not only widely applied concepts, but also the substance of particular offences; the nature of the time frame and the breadth of the social context defined as relevant by rules of evidence; and the context in which offences are interpreted. Only in relation to this broader set of factors can a specifically feminist analysis of aspects of the general principles be realised. A good example is the well known argument about criminal law's reflection of a dualistic view of human beings as divided between the mental and the material, between mind and body, which is vividly reflected in the distinction between *actus reus* and *mens rea*. This, along with the understanding of *mens rea* in terms of capacities of reason, understanding and self-control has been argued to have distinctively feminist implications. The strong cultural association of men and the masculine with the mind and with reason, and of women and the feminine with the body and with emotion, inevitably, so the argument goes, constructs women as nonstandard subjects of the rationalist discourse of criminal law.

This is a potentially important insight, but it takes on different complexions according to the context in which it is deployed. It might be argued that the contemporary theoretical emphasis on mental conditions of responsibility—on culpability, rather than harmful conduct—indeed reflects a highly gendered world view, in which the standard model of responsible behaviour is implicitly marked as masculine. Ironically, this might be taken to imply a greater willingness to regard men as potentially criminally responsible and hence to prosecute and punish them. In the context of rape law, the emphasis on the mental linchpin of consent implies something rather different: the doctrinal marginalisation of the embodied aspect of the wrong. At the level of defences based on mental incapacities, it might be expected to lead to a marginalisation of women's full responsibility. These are, of course, questions which are susceptible of empirical research.

In order to interpret the feminist significance of the conceptual building blocks out of which criminal liability is constructed, we therefore have to contextualise those building blocks within the actual offences which they help to create. And, as analysis of the law of rape illustrates, one of the most important issues in tracing criminal law's 'implication in the organisation of sexual difference' will be the relevant rules of evidence, which shape the relevant context and time frame within which the subject is conceptualised. The sexing of criminal law's subjects—indeed, their subjectification—happens in the enactment and interpretation of substantive offences and of the rules of evidence. Though certain aspects of criminal law's normative ideals or conceptual framework may be more often implicated in the construction of sexual difference than are others, their significance varies dramatically across the offences and defences. A dynamic analysis of criminal law's role in maintaining sexual difference is likely to be obstructed, therefore, by the contemporary scholarly practice of placing primary emphasis on the general part.

Finally, it is important to notice that the contours of the general principles, focused as they are on the construction of criminal liability, form an unduly narrow basis for an evaluation of criminal law's sexing of its subjects. For, as feminist analyses of the operation of the law of rape demonstrate, criminal law's constitution of sexed subjects relates not only to defendants, but also to victims and witnesses in the criminal process. To take a doctrinal example, the sexually differentiated position of the incest victim tells us something just as important as the sexually-specific definition of the incest offender's conduct. An adequate feminist analysis of criminal law could never, therefore, confine itself to the conceptual framework or normative underpinnings of liability.

P. Kotiswaran, 'Feminist Approaches to Criminal Law' in M. Dubber and T. Hörnle (eds) *The Oxford Handbook of Criminal Law* (Oxford: OUP, 2014), 60–2

[T]he reach of the feminist project in criminal law is extensive. One only has to consider the compulsory first-year criminal law curriculum to get a sense of likely arenas for feminist intervention. Teaching English criminal law, one can hardly fail to note early on in the law of causation, that the cases of *Steel and Malcherek* are about women who were murdered because they refused the sexual advances of male defendants. Feminists have contributed to theorizing the duty of care in the context of omissions liability. Du-bois Pedain has drawn on care feminism to criticize decisions like *R. v. Bland* and argue that viewed through the lens of "care morality," the doctor–patient duty of care might well exceed the demands of the criminal law and its "stranger morality." Other feminists have interrogated the extent to which specific offenses, like homicide, rape, and grievous bodily harm reflect women's experiences. Seizing upon the contingency of the common law and the inability of outdated statutes to deal with domestic violence, for instance, English feminists have argued that a husband be held guilty of constructive manslaughter when his severely mentally abused wife commits suicide after being physically assaulted by him. They have energetically sought to reconfigure defenses such as provocation, diminished responsibility, and self-defense in the interests of female offenders....

Feminist energy so far has not, however, been expended only on these turgid matters of first-year criminal law doctrine but has significantly contributed to a steady expansion of the remit of the criminal law, as it relates to the spheres of the family and the market. The feminist critique of the public–private divide within criminal law has led to the conceptualization of private harms such as child abuse, marital rape, date rape, homosexual rape, and domestic violence in terms of crime, leading to the creation of new offenses....

In the United States and the United Kingdom, feminists have been successful in pushing forth legislation on a range of public harms against women such as sexual harassment, pornography, prostitution, voyeurism, rape, and stalking. Feminists have also been instrumental in re-envisioning how the criminal law relates to the market by delineating the conditions under which exploitative labor conditions can be prosecuted as trafficking. Implicit in this are judgments about the types of labor that may qualify as legitimate work.

Many feminists have pointed to the obvious, but too easily forgotten, fact that men are responsible for the vast majority of crimes.[155] Men's violence against women and children is often denied or legitimated within society.[156] The study of male violence has led to an increase in interest in masculinity and what it is that creates such a strong link between the male identity and the commission of crime.[157] There will, no doubt, be an increasing amount of academic interest in that subject.

FURTHER READING

Forell, C. and Matthews, D. (2000) *The Reasonable Woman as a Measure of Man* (New York: New York University Press).

Kotiswaran, P. (2014) 'Feminist Approaches to Criminal Law' in M. Dubber and T. Hörnle (eds) *The Oxford Handbook of Criminal Law* (Oxford: OUP).

Lacey, N. (1996) 'General Principles of Criminal Law? A Feminist View' in D. Nicolson and L. Bibbings (eds) *Feminist Perspectives in Criminal Law* (London: Cavendish).

Moran, M. (2003) *Rethinking the Reasonable Person* (Oxford: OUP).

Naffine, N. (1998) *Law and the Sexes* (Sydney: Allen and Unwin).

Nicolson, D. and Bibbings, L. (eds) (2001) *Feminist Perspectives on Criminal Law* (London: Cavendish).

Romito, P. (2008) *A Deafening Silence: Hidden Violence Against Women and Children* (Bristol: Polity Press).

Smart, C. (1992) 'The Woman of Legal Discourse' *Social and Legal Studies* 1: 29.

Wells, C. (2004) 'The Impact of Feminist Thinking on Criminal Law and Justice' *Criminal Law Review* 503.

Young, A. (1996) *Imagining Crime* (London: Sage).

---

13 PUNISHMENT

Theories of why we punish offenders are crucial to the understanding of criminal law.[158] Knowing why we punish people can assist us in knowing what offences should be criminal. After all there is little point in finding guilty of offences people who we do not think deserve any kind of punishment.

In fact it is not easy to define punishment.[159] Why do we regard the payment of taxes as not a punishment: is it really different from a fine? Is detention under the Mental Health

---

[155] Heidensohn (2002).   [156] Romito (2008).   [157] Walklate (2001).
[158] A very useful collection of readings can be found in von Hirsch and Ashworth (1998).
[159] See Lacey (1988: 7–8) and Hart (1968: 4–5).

Act different from imprisonment? There is, not surprisingly, no agreement over what exactly punishment is. It is generally thought to contain some of the following elements:[160]

(1) It must be unpleasant.

(2) It is inflicted by the state.

(3) It is imposed on those who have broken the law.

(4) Its purpose is not to compensate the victim.

(5) It carries censure of what the defendant did.

The starting point is that punishment is something that requires strong justification.[161] For the state to deprive a citizen of his or her liberty by detaining him or her in prison is a huge invasion of a citizen's basic rights and requires the best of reasons.[162]

Theories of punishment can be broken down into those which are consequentialist (that claim that there are good consequences that result from punishment and therefore justify it) and those which are non-consequentialist (that claim that there are other reasons apart from its consequences which justify punishment). As can be imagined, a whole book could easily be written on the theories of punishment and here the topic can only be covered in outline.[163]

13.1 CONSEQUENTIALIST THEORIES OF PUNISHMENT

Consequentialist justifications include the following:

(1) **Personal deterrence** By punishing the offender he or she will be deterred from committing a crime again.[164]

(2) **General deterrence** By punishing the offender the general public (and particularly those of a criminal bent), on learning of the punishment, will be deterred from committing offences.[165] This may be directly (a person deciding not to commit a crime for fear of the punishment) or indirectly (the law and punishment may affect the moral attitudes of society, which thereby leads to people not taking up crime).[166]

(3) **Rehabilitation** The punishment may reform and educate the offender so that he or she does not commit an offence again.[167]

(4) **Incapacitation** The offender is removed from society (by imprisonment) and so prevented from causing (for a period of time) more harm to society.[168]

(5) **Restorative justice** There are two main versions of this theory. One focuses on the notion that the response of the criminal law should be analogous to conflict resolution. The criminal law should seek to mediate and mend the broken relationship

---

[160] See Lacey (1988: 7–8).   [161] J.G. Murphy (1994).

[162] For some discussion on why we punish, see Duff and Garland (1994).

[163] Often one's views on punishment reflect wider social, political, and even religious views.

[164] Walker (1994).

[165] For a startling example, see *Attorney-General's Reference (No. 4 of 2002)* [2002] Crim LR 333, which suggested sentences of five years for robbery of mobile phones in order to deter others.

[166] Edmundson (2002).   [167] Richards (1998).

[168] N. Morris (1994). One particularly controversial proposal is that those deemed particularly dangerous should be incapacitated for longer than those deemed non-dangerous who commit similar offences (see von Hirsch (1998a and 1998b) and Prins (2003)). For a broader discussion of the issues, see Ashworth, Zedner, and Tomlin (2013).

between the victim and the offender. The other aims to compensate the victim for the wrong done. The link between these themes is that they seek to undo or rectify the harm or some of the harm done by the defendant to the victim.[169]

Critics of consequentialist theories claim that they can lead to injustice. They could lead to one offender receiving a far longer sentence than he or she deserved in order to deter others from committing a crime, or to reform the offender him or herself. Imagine that researchers told the Home Secretary that if she announced that every year ten people who had been convicted of theft would be selected at random and have their hands cut off, this would reduce the number of thefts by half. This research would still not justify the cutting off of the hands of the unlucky few involved.

There are also objections that in fact punishment does not achieve the desired aims. For example:

(1) There is little evidence that imprisonment deters offenders from reoffending.[170]

(2) The evidence that people can be reformed is inconclusive.[171]

(3) There is even evidence that prison may make people more likely to commit offences on their release.[172]

These points, however, should not mean that the consequentialist theories must be abandoned. It may be, for example, that better systems of treating prisoners may improve the reformation rates.[173] Or, if conviction rates were higher, it might be that the deterrent effect of punishment would be more effective.

13.2 NON-CONSEQUENTIALIST THEORIES

The most popular non-consequentialist theory is retributive theory.[174] This is that, quite simply,[175] punishment is justified because the offender deserves it.[176] It is good in and of itself to punish, regardless of any consequences of the punishment. Through punishment, the law treats people as human beings who are able to make choices and take the consequences of those choices.[177] To some retributivists punishment is linked to a concept of the offender paying his or her dues to society. Having suffered the penalty, the offender can return to society as a fully acceptable member. To others an offender has gained an unfair advantage over law-abiding citizens by breaking the law, and this needs to be removed by imposing the burden of a punishment.[178] This last theory has difficulties in the context of serious crime. It is uncomfortable saying that a rapist has gained an advantage by raping.

Retributive theories would also indicate that the level of punishment should reflect the amount of punishment the offender deserves. This seems obvious, but it is significant in that it means that a person should not be given a longer sentence than he or she might otherwise receive on the basis that to do so would be for his or her own good, or for society's

---

[169] Christie (1998).   [170] The evidence is discussed in Beyleveld (1998).

[171] von Hirsch and Maher (1998).   [172] Martinson (1974).

[173] Brody (1998) discusses the effectiveness of various rehabilitative techniques.

[174] Walker (1998).

[175] M. Moore (1987) claims that retributive theories reflect a natural intuition.

[176] Kant (1965: 100).

[177] Duff (1998a) emphasizes the importance of seeing punishment as a form of communication between the state and offenders.

[178] N. Morris (1969).

good. We should therefore not, for example, impose an especially high sentence on people who have stolen a mobile phone in order to discourage others from stealing, or imprison shoplifters just in order to ensure they receive treatment for their drug addiction. In both these cases, we would be imposing a higher sentence than their crimes deserve. Rather, what should be done is to impose a sentence which is proportional to the wrong they have done.[179]

Another non-consequentialist theory of punishment is that punishment is an expression of censure (see the extract at What is a Crime?, p.2). Punishment expresses the denunciation by society of the kind of conduct done by the offender.[180] This helps to promote social cohesion and channels public outrage, thereby avoiding vigilantism. This theory provides a clear explanation of why taxation is not equivalent to a fine: a fine, but not a tax demand, carries with it condemnation of the actions of the recipient. The difficulty with the censure theory is that it does not explain why it is necessary to impose a punishment in order to do the censuring task.[181] The censure theory is seen by one of its chief proponents as complementary to retributivism:[182]

M. Moore, 'The Moral Worth of Retribution' in A. von Hirsch and A. Ashworth (eds) *Principled Sentencing* (Oxford: Hart, 1998), 153–4

Retributivism is a very straightforward theory of punishment: we are justified in punishing because and only because offenders deserve it. Moral culpability (desert) is in such a view both a sufficient as well as a necessary condition of liability to punitive sanctions. Such justification gives society more than merely a right to punish culpable offenders. It does this, making it not unfair to punish them, but retributivism justifies more than this. For a retributivist, the moral culpability of an offender also gives society the *duty* to punish. Retributivism, in other words, is truly a theory of justice such that, if it is true, we have an obligation to set up institutions so that retributivism is achieved.

[Moore then turns to defend retributivism from two common criticisms:]

1. First and foremost there is the popularly accepted belief that punishment for its own sake does no good. 'By punishing the offender you cannot undo the crime', might be the slogan for this point of view. I mention this view only to put it aside, for it is but a reiteration of the consequentialist idea that only further good consequences achieved by punishment could possibly justify the practice. Unnoticed by those who hold this position is that they abandon such consequentialism when it comes to other areas of morals. It is a sufficient justification not to scapegoat innocent individuals, that they do not deserve to be punished; the injustice of punishing those who did not deserve it seems to stand perfectly well by itself as a justification of our practices, without need for further good consequences we might achieve. Why do we not similarly say that the injustice of the guilty going unpunished can equally stand by itself as a justification for punishment, without need of a showing of further good consequences? It simply is not the case that justification always requires the showing of further good consequences.

Those who oppose retributivism often protest at this point that punishment is a clear harm to the one punished, and the intentional causing of this harm requires some good thereby achieved to justify it; whereas *not* punishing the innocent is not a harm and thus does not stand in need of justification by good consequences. Yet this response simply begs the question against retributivism. Retributivism purports to be a theory of justice, and as such claims

---

[179] von Hirsch (1985).   [180] N. Morris (1994).   [181] Feinberg (1994).   [182] *Ibid.*

that punishing the guilty achieves something good—namely, justice—and that therefore reference to any other good consequences is simply beside the point. One cannot defeat the central retributivist claim—that justice is achieved by punishing the guilty—simply by assuming that it is false.

The question-begging character of this response can be seen by imagining a like response in areas of tort, property, or contract law. Forcing another to pay tort or contract damages, or to forgo use and possession of something, is a clear harm that corrective justice theories of tort, promissory theories of contract, or natural right theories of property are willing to impose on defendants. Suppose no one gains anything of economic significance by certain classes of such impositions—as, for example, in cases where the plaintiff has died without heirs after his cause of action accrued. 'It does no good to force the defendant to pay', interposed as an objection to corrective justice theories of tort, promissory theories of contract, or natural right theories of property simply denies what these theories assert: that something good *is* achieved by imposing liability in such cases—namely, that justice is done.

This 'harm requires justification' objection thus leaves untouched the question of whether the rendering of justice cannot in all such cases be the good that justifies the harm all such theories impose on defendants. I accordingly put aside this initial objection to retributivism, relying as it does either on an unjustifiable discrimination between retributivism and other deontological theories, or upon a blunderbuss assault on deontological theories as such.

2. A second and very popular suspicion about retributive judgments is that they presuppose an indefensible objectivism about morals. Sometimes this objection is put metaphysically: There is no such thing as desert or culpability (Mackie, 1982). More often the point is put as a more cautious epistemological modesty: 'Even if there is such a thing as desert, we can never know who is deserving'. For religious people, this last variation usually contrasts us to God, who alone can know what people truly deserve. We might call this the 'don't play God' objection.

A striking feature of the 'don't play God' objection is how inconsistently it is applied. Let us revert to our use of desert as a limiting condition on punishment: We certainly seem confident both that it is true and that we can know that it is true, that we should not punish the morally innocent because they do not deserve it. Neither metaphysical scepticism nor epistemological modesty gets in our way when we use lack of moral desert as a reason not to punish. Why should it be different when we use the presence of desert as a reason to punish? If we can know when someone does *not* deserve punishment, mustn't we know when someone *does* deserve punishment? Consider the illogic in the following passages from Karl Menninger (1968):

> It does not advance a solution to use the word justice. It is a subjective emotional word . . . The concept is so vague, so distorted in its applications, so hypocritical, and usually so irrelevant that it offers no help in the solution of the crime problem which it exists to combat but results in its exact opposite—injustice, injustice to everybody. (10–11)

Apparently Dr. Karl knows injustice when he sees it, even if justice is a useless concept. Analogously, consider our reliance on moral desert when we allocate initial property entitlements. We think that the person who works hard to produce a novel deserves the right to determine when and under what conditions the novel will be copied for others to read. The novelist's labour gives him or her the moral right. How can we know this—how can it be true—if desert can be judged only by those with godlike omniscience, or worse, does not even exist? Such scepticism about just deserts would throw out a great deal that we will not throw out. To me, this shows that no one really believes that moral desert does not exist or that we could not know it if it did. Something else makes us suspect our retributive judgments than supposed moral scepticism or epistemological modesty.

13.3 MIXED THEORIES

One very influential theory, propounded by Herbert Hart, has sought to mix both consequentialist and non-consequentialist theories together. He relies on a retributivist theory in order to explain who should be punished and a consequentialist theory to explain how people should be punished. In other words only those who deserve punishment should be punished, but the form of punishment can be decided on the basis of the consequentialist aims of deterrence, incapacitation, or reform.

FURTHER READING

Brooks, T. (2012) *Punishment* (Abingdon: Routledge).

Duff, R.A. (1986) *Trials and Punishments* (Cambridge: Cambridge University Press).

Duff, R.A. and Garland, D. (eds) (1994) *A Reader on Punishment* (Oxford: OUP).

Hart, H. (1968) *Punishment and Responsibility* (Oxford: OUP).

Norrie, A. (2000) *Punishment, Responsibility, and Justice* (Oxford: OUP).

Tadros, V. (2013) *The Ends of Harm* (Oxford: OUP).

von Hirsch, A. (1993) *Censure and Sanctions* (Oxford: OUP).

---

14 SENTENCING

Of course a conviction is not the end of the trial. If there is a conviction, the judge still needs to go on to consider the appropriate sentence to be imposed. In the following extract, Alan Norrie[183] has noted that the flexibility in matters of sentencing is in marked contrast to the 'strictness' of the criminal law. Although the jury get to decide whether the defendant is guilty or not, it is the judge who determines sentencing and has considerable flexibility in doing so. It is, therefore, understandable that several commentators[184] have argued that criminal law can only be properly understood by having a secure grasp of not only the definition of criminal offences, but also criminal procedure and the law on sentencing. That would certainly be an ideal, but for students it would mean that criminal law courses would have to last three times as long as they do at present. Also, criminal law textbooks would be even bigger.

FURTHER READING

Ashworth, A. (2005) *Sentencing and Criminal Justice* (Cambridge: Cambridge University Press).

Easton, S. (2008) *Sentencing and Punishment* (Oxford: OUP).

von Hirsch, A. and Ashworth, A. (eds) (1998) *Principled Sentencing* (Oxford: Hart).

Wasik, M. (2001) *Emmins on Sentencing* (London: Blackstone).

---

[183] Norrie (2001).   [184] e.g. Lacey (2002).

15 CONCLUDING THOUGHTS

This chapter should have demonstrated that the concepts of 'crime' and 'criminal law' are far less straightforward than might be thought. Indeed it has proved very difficult to even define what a crime is. Academics have been keen to produce fine-sounding theories seeking to restrict the use of criminal law to those circumstances in which it is absolutely necessary and, where it is needed, to ensure the response of the criminal law is proportionate and predictable. It should not be surprising that these theories are honoured far more in the breach than the observance. The criminal law is an easy tool for politicians to use to 'deal with' politically troublesome issues and provide an easy way to pander to the tabloid press. The criminal law, therefore, although capable of being presented as reflecting certain key philosophical and political principles, more often reflects the rough and tumble of everyday political life.

2

ACTUS REUS:
THE CONDUCT ELEMENT

CENTRAL ISSUES

1. The traditional method of analysing the definition of an offence is to separate out the *actus reus* (which describes the acts of the defendant and their consequences) and the *mens rea* (which describes the required mental state of the defendant).

2. A defendant is only guilty if she or he has performed a voluntary act.

3. Normally people will not be guilty of a crime because they omitted to act.

However, they can be guilty for an omission if they were under a duty to act.

4. Many crimes require proof that the defendant caused a particular result. A defendant will be held to have caused a result if but for his or her actions the result would not have occurred and there has been no intervening act of a third party.

PART I: THE LAW

1 DISTINGUISHING THE COMPONENT ELEMENTS OF A CRIME

DEFINITION

Actus reus: the conduct element of the offence. The *actus reus* describes what the defendant must be proved to have done (or sometimes failed to do), in what circumstances, and with what consequences in order to be guilty of a crime.

Mens rea: the mental element of the offence. This may be, for example, intention, recklessness, or negligence.

The traditional way of analysing criminal offences is to divide a crime up into the conduct of the accused (known as the *actus reus* or conduct element) and the state of mind of the accused (the *mens rea* or mental element).[1] For example, in a murder case the prosecution must show that the defendant caused the death of the victim and that he or she intended to kill or cause grievous bodily harm to the victim. The *actus reus* of murder is causing the death of the victim; the *mens rea* is an intention to kill or cause grievous bodily harm. Only if both the *actus reus* and *mens rea* are proved will the defendant be guilty.[2] In this chapter we will consider the *actus reus*, and in Chapter 3 the *mens rea* will be discussed. In Part II of this chapter we will examine the benefits and disadvantages of dividing crimes into the *mens rea* and *actus reus* elements. →1 (p.104)

So what is the *actus reus* of a crime? One popular way of explaining it is to define its role, namely that it identifies the conduct which the criminal law considers harmful. The *actus reus* of an offence tells us what we can and cannot do: killing, damaging another's property, and injuring another person are examples of forbidden kinds of conduct. By contrast the *mens rea* and defences enable us to decide whether the defendant was to blame for his or her wrongful acts. Another popular way of defining an *actus reus* is by describing what it is not: the *actus reus* is that part of the crime which is not concerned with the accused's state of mind.

The exact nature of the *actus reus* depends on the particular crime: in murder it involves killing; in theft it involves taking another's property. The *actus reus* of a crime may involve three different aspects:

(1) proof that the defendant did a particular act,

(2) proof that the act caused a particular result, and

(3) proof that the act or result occurred in certain circumstances.

Not all *actus rei*[3] involve all three of these. For example, the offence of bigamy requires the act of marriage in certain circumstances (the defendant is already married), but there is no need to prove any result. It is useful to distinguish between conduct crimes and result crimes:

(1) Conduct crimes require proof only that the defendant did an act. There is no need to demonstrate that the act produced a particular result. Possession of prohibited drugs would be an example.

(2) Result crimes require proof not only that the defendant performed a particular act but that that act produced certain results. For example, murder requires proof that the defendant's act caused the death of the victim.

Are there any common threads that link the *actus reus* of every crime? There is much debate over this issue and this chapter will now consider three particular questions:

(1) Do all *actus rei* require an act?

(2) Do all *actus rei* require a *voluntary* act?

---

[1] In *Miller* [1983] 2 AC 161, 174 Lord Diplock suggested that it would be preferable not to use the Latin terminology and refer instead to 'the conduct of the accused and his state of mind'. Despite these objections the Latin terminology is still very widely used by the judiciary and commentators.

[2] The Latin maxim is *actus non facit reum nisi mens sit rea*—'an act is not criminal in the absence of a guilty mind'.

[3] *Actus rei* is the plural of *actus reus*.

(3) If the *actus reus* of a crime requires proof that the defendant caused a particular result, what does 'cause' mean?

2 THE VOLUNTARY ACT 'REQUIREMENT'

DEFINITION

The 'voluntary act requirement': many criminal offences require proof that the defendant performed a voluntary act. But not all do: sometimes offences can be committed by an omission, some only require proof of a state of affairs, and sometimes a defendant can be convicted in respect of the actions of another.

Usually you cannot commit a crime without doing an act. Sitting in a room thinking the most evil of thoughts and conjuring up the most heinous of plans is not an offence.[4] Indeed if evil thoughts were to constitute criminal offences, the prisons would be very full indeed! Not only must there be an act; there must be a voluntary act. Lord Denning[5] explained: '[T]he requirement that it should be a voluntary act is essential . . . in every criminal case'.[6] Where the defendant is not acting voluntarily he or she is said to be acting as an automaton and will not be guilty of an offence because the *mens rea* and *actus reus* will not be proved. If Barbara was holding a valuable vase when Andre came up behind her and said 'boo' in a loud voice, causing Barbara to drop the vase, then this (the dropping of the vase) would not be seen as Barbara's act, and so she could not be convicted of unlawfully damaging the vase.[7] The detail of the law on automatism, or involuntary acts, is discussed in Chapter 12. →2 (p.106)

The general principle that a crime must involve an act of the defendant is subject to two important caveats. First, it is far from clear what is meant by the word 'act' here. The question how to define an act will be considered in detail in Part II of this chapter. Second, there are a number of crimes which appear to be exceptions to the rule. In fact there are so many exceptions that some commentators argue that the rule does not really exist.[8] In brief, the exceptions include the following:

(1) Sometimes a failure to act, an omission, can give rise to criminal liability. In such cases the failure to act can constitute the *actus reus* of the crime.

(2) Sometimes the *actus reus* of an offence is defined as a state of affairs or set of circumstances, which may or may not involve an actual act. For example, possession of a firearm can, in some circumstances, amount to an offence.

(3) Under some circumstances a defendant can be responsible for the acts of another person.

It should be noted that whether these are or are not true exceptions in part depends on how one defines an act. Let us now consider these exceptions to the 'rule' that a criminal offence must require an act in more detail.

---

[4] Dan-Cohen (2002: ch. 6).
[5] *Bratty v Attorney-General of Northern Ireland* [1963] AC 386 (HL).
[6] See also *Kay v Butterworth* (1945) 173 LT 191.   [7] Indeed it may be seen as Andre's act.
[8] G. Williams (1992: 31).

2.1 OMISSIONS

Generally a person will not be liable for simply failing to act. Criminal lawyers often point out that if a person comes across a child drowning in a pond and simply walks by leaving the child to die, there is no criminal liability. Some countries have statutes that make it a criminal offence not to offer aid to those you come across who are in peril, when it is reasonably practical for you to do so. But there is no such general duty in English and Welsh law. This is not to say that a defendant is never criminally liable for an omission: a defendant can be criminally liable for an omission where there is a duty to act in a particular way.

> **DEFINITION**
> A summary of the criminal law on omissions: a defendant is only guilty of a crime when failing to act, where he or she is under a duty to act.

The discussion of liability for omissions will be divided into four sections. First, we will note that there are some crimes which can never be committed by omission. Second, we will consider when a defendant will be under a duty to act. Third, we will ask what is required of a defendant who is under such a duty. Fourth, the difficult question of how acts and omissions can be distinguished will be tackled. →3 (p.110)

Crimes that cannot be committed by omission

There are certain crimes that cannot be committed by an omission. These are statutory crimes which in their definition require an act to be committed. For example, in *Ahmad*[9] the defendant was charged with an offence under the Protection from Eviction Act 1977 which required proof of the defendant 'doing acts calculated to interfere with [the victim's] peace and comfort'. The defendant, a landlord, failed to carry out alterations on the victim's house and this left the premises uninhabitable, thereby interfering with the tenant's peace and comfort. The failure to carry out the alterations was not an 'act' and so the landlord was not guilty of the offence.

When the defendant is under a duty to act

The duty to act can arise in the following eight ways:

Statutory duty

There are a large number of statutory duties requiring people to act in a particular way. For example, under section 6 of the Road Traffic Act 1988 a driver who fails to provide a sample of breath when required to do so by a constable under certain circumstances commits a criminal offence. There are too many examples of statutory duties to act for them all to be listed here.[10]

---

[9] (1986) 52 P & CR 346 (CA).

[10] There are a few common law offences which can be said to involve liability for omission, e.g. cheating the Revenue and misconduct in a public office (*Mavji* [1987] 1 WLR 1388 (CA)).

Duties of law enforcement

Police officers are under a duty to assist members of the public in danger. So, a police officer who failed to protect a citizen who was being kicked to death was held to have committed an offence.[11] Further, if a police officer calls upon a citizen to assist him or her to restore the peace, the citizen is under a duty to offer the assistance.

Contractual duty

Where a person is under a contractual duty to help another he or she may be under a duty under criminal law to do so. For example, in *Pittwood*[12] the defendant was employed as a gatekeeper on a railway line. One day he failed to perform his duties and did not close the gate when required. This led to an accident in which a train hit a cart and a man was killed. It was held that he could be liable for manslaughter because he was required under his contract of employment to ensure that the gate was shut. His omission, in failing to shut the gate, was in breach of his contractual duty and so could constitute a criminal offence.[13]

Assumed duties

People who voluntarily assume responsibility for another's welfare will be under a duty to care for him or her. The assumption of responsibility may be expressed (e.g. where a person explicitly agrees to look after a vulnerable person) or implied (a person has regularly offered assistance to another and so a mutual understanding of responsibility can be assumed[14]).

Some duties arise automatically: a parent is automatically responsible for caring for a child. So, if a parent fails to feed a child and the child dies of starvation then the parent might be liable even though the failure to feed was an omission.[15] Similarly, a parent who stands by and lets another person harm his or her child might be guilty of an offence.[16] In *Sheppard*[17] it was held that there was no duty owed by a parent to an 18-year-old daughter. This suggests that once a child reaches majority the legal duty towards the child may come to an end.[18]

Whether a duty will be assumed in the context of other relationships is less clear. It is generally assumed that spouses (and presumably long-term partners[19]) owe a duty to assist each other if they are in peril.[20] It may be that older children owe duties towards their elderly

---

[11] *Dytham* (1979) 69 Cr App R 387 (CA).   [12] (1902) 19 TLR 37.

[13] It should be noted that the contractual duty to shut the gate was owed not to the victim but to the employer.

[14] In *Charlotte Smith* (1865) 10 Cox CC 82 a master was found guilty of the homicide of his servant after he failed to give her sufficient food and general care.

[15] *Gibbons and Proctor* (1919) 13 Cr App R 134 (CA); *Lowe* [1973] 1 QB 702 (CA). The Domestic Violence, Crime and Victims Act 2004, s. 5 creates a specific offence of causing or allowing the death of a child.

[16] *Emery* (1993) 14 Cr App R (S) 394 (CA).

[17] (1862) Le & Ca 147. The age of majority was, at that time, 21.

[18] It should be noted that under the Children and Young Persons Act 1933, s. 1 there is a duty not to neglect the child, which ends when the child reaches the age of 18. It is also an offence under the Mental Capacity Act 2005, s. 44 wilfully to neglect a person lacking mental capacity. See further *R v Patel* [2013] EWCA Crim 965.

[19] Although in an American case, *People v Beardsley* 113 NW 1128 (1907), it was held that a man did not owe a duty to his lover who took morphine in his presence.

[20] *Hood* [2003] EWCA Crim 2772; *Bonnyman* (1942) 28 Cr App R 131 (CA).

parents, but the existence or extent of such a duty is yet to be tested in the courts.[21] It may be that outside the parent–child relationship the duty that will be imposed will depend on the nature of the relationship between the two parties. In *R v Nicholls*[22] a grandmother was said not necessarily to owe a duty to care for a grandchild, although on the facts of the case she did because she had taken on care of the child. Similarly in *Barrass*[23] an adult who had taken on caring for his elderly mother owed her a duty of care.

In *Evans (Gemma)*[24] a mother who failed to summon help for her 16-year-old daughter who collapsed after taking heroin was convicted of manslaughter. Her older half-sister was held not to be under a duty of care simply by virtue of their blood relationship. However, the fact she had supplied the drugs could create the duty. The court will be reluctant to impose a duty between two spouses who have separated, but may be very willing to impose a duty if one person is disabled and depends on a friend for their well-being. In *Lewin v CPS*[25] a young man left his friend asleep and intoxicated in a car on a very hot day. The friend died, but no prosecution was brought. The decision not to prosecute was upheld in the High Court. This suggests friendship alone is insufficient. Andrew Ashworth's detailed analysis concludes with the suggestion that outside the core cases of parent–child relationships,

> The strongest criterion is D's assumption of responsibility for V's welfare, combined with the requirement that D be aware, or ought reasonably to be aware, that V is in a life-threatening condition. The assumption of responsibility can derive from an explicit statement or agreement, or it can be inferred from a settled relationship of mutual interdependence.[26]

Controversially, a duty of care was held to exist in the following case:

R v Stone; R v Dobinson
[1977] QB 354 (CA)

The appellants were John Edward Stone (a man aged 67, of below average intelligence, partially deaf, and almost blind) and Gwendoline Dobinson (aged 43 and described by the court as 'ineffectual and inadequate'). Stone's sister, Fanny, aged 50, came to live with them and their son Cyril. She suffered from anorexia nervosa and so often denied herself food and stayed in her room for days at a time. Once she was found by the police wandering the street and the appellants then tried to find her doctor but were unable to do so. Fanny grew weaker and became confined to bed. The appellants did nothing to get help for her, despite requests from neighbours. Subsequently she was found dead: naked, very dirty, and in appalling conditions. The appellants were convicted of manslaughter and appealed.

Lord Justice Geoffrey Lane

There is no dispute, broadly speaking, as to the matters on which the jury must be satisfied before they can convict of manslaughter in circumstances such as the present. They are: (1) that the defendant undertook the care of a person who by reason of age or infirmity was

---

[21] Simester, Spencer, Sullivan, and Virgo (2013: 70) argue that children do not owe their parents a duty.
[22] (1874) 13 Cox CC 75.   [23] [2011] EWCA Crim 2629.   [24] [2009] EWCA Crim 650.
[25] [2002] EWHC 1049 (Admin).   [26] Ashworth (2015).

unable to care for himself; (2) that the defendant was grossly negligent in regard to his duty of care; (3) that by reason of such negligence the person died. It is submitted on behalf of the appellants that the judge's direction to the jury with regard to the first two items was incorrect.

At the close of the Crown's case submissions were made to the judge that there was no, or no sufficient, evidence that the appellants, or either of them, had chosen to undertake the care of Fanny.

. . .

This court rejects that proposition. Whether Fanny was a lodger or not she was a blood relation of the appellant Stone; she was occupying a room in his house; Mrs Dobinson had undertaken the duty of trying to wash her, of taking such food to her as she required. There was ample evidence that each appellant was aware of the poor condition she was in by mid-July. It was not disputed that no effort was made to summon an ambulance or the social services or the police despite the entreaties of Mrs Wilson and Mrs West. A social worker used to visit Cyril [Stone's disabled son]. No word was spoken to him. All these were matters which the jury were entitled to take into account when considering whether the necessary assumption of a duty to care for Fanny had been proved.

This was not a situation analogous to the drowning stranger. They did make efforts to care. They tried to get a doctor; they tried to discover the previous doctor. Mrs Dobinson helped with the washing and the provision of food. All these matters were put before the jury in terms which we find it impossible to fault. The jury were entitled to find that the duty had been assumed. They were entitled to conclude that once Fanny became helplessly infirm, as she had by 19th July, the appellants were, in the circumstances, obliged either to summon help or else to care for Fanny themselves.

Appeals against conviction dismissed. Appeal by the appellant Stone against sentence allowed; sentence varied (from three years to twelve months).

At the heart of this decision is the finding that Stone and Dobinson had voluntarily assumed responsibility to care for Fanny. The decision is highly controversial because of the low capabilities of the two accused. It appears they had enough difficulty looking after themselves effectively, let alone being expected to offer a reasonable level of care to Fanny. It is not clear from *Stone and Dobinson* what was crucial to the finding of a duty. Was it the biological relationship, the undertaking of especial responsibility for the victim's welfare, or a combination of these two factors? →4 (p.114)

Ownership or control of property

It may be that if someone owns a piece of property and another person in his or her presence commits a crime using that property the owner is under a duty to seek to prevent the crime in so far as is reasonable.[27] There certainly have been some cases where the courts have found an owner criminally liable under such circumstances, although this is normally based on liability for aiding and abetting the other person. For example, in *Tuck v Robson*[28] a publican failed to intervene to prevent customers on his premises drinking after hours. He was found to have aided and abetted their crime.[29] The precise scope of this duty is unclear until we have further guidance from the courts.[30]

---

[27] Ashworth (1989: 446).   [28] [1970] 1 WLR 741.

[29] Another example can be found in *DuCros v Lambourne* [1907] 1 KB 40.

[30] It may be argued that one neighbour owes a limited duty to another neighbour, e.g. to ensure that a fire does not spread from his or her house, relying on the tort case of *Smith v Littlewoods* [1987] 1 All ER 710 (HL).

Continuing act

The courts have held that some cases which appear to be cases involving omissions have, in fact, involved a 'continuing act'. This can be best explained by referring to an example. In *Fagan v Metropolitan Police Commissioner*[31] Fagan drove his car accidentally onto a policeman's foot. When the policeman asked him to remove it he refused to do so. Fagan was convicted but appealed on the basis that the only act he did was driving onto the foot and that was performed without *mens rea*. By the time he realized his car was on the foot (and he had *mens rea*) he was not doing an act. The Divisional Court, however, upheld Fagan's conviction on the basis that he was committing the *actus reus* of battery (exercising force on the policeman's foot) for the whole of the time he had his car on the constable's foot. Fagan was guilty once he was aware of the harm he was causing to the policeman because then he had both the *actus reus* and *mens rea* of the offence at the same time.

Creation of the danger

Where someone has created a dangerous situation they may be under a duty to act to prevent harm resulting. The leading case on this is the following:

R v Miller
[1983] 2 AC 161 (HL)

James Miller, who was drunk, fell asleep with a lighted cigarette in his hand in the house in which he was staying. He subsequently woke to discover that his cigarette had set his mattress on fire. He simply moved out of the room into a neighbouring room. He was convicted of arson. The Court of Appeal dismissed his appeal but gave leave to appeal to the House of Lords, certifying the following question of law: '[W]hether the *actus reus* of the offence of arson is present when a defendant accidentally starts a fire and thereafter, intending to destroy or damage property belonging to another or being reckless as to whether any such property would be destroyed or damaged, fails to take any steps to extinguish the fire or prevent damage to such property by that fire?'

Lord Diplock

. . .

The first question to be answered where a completed crime of arson is charged is: did a physical act of the accused start the fire which spread and damaged property belonging to another . . .?

The first question is a pure question of causation. It is one of fact to be decided by the jury in a trial on indictment. It should be answered 'No' if, in relation to the fire during the period starting immediately before its ignition and ending with its extinction, the role of the accused was at no time more than that of a passive bystander. In such a case the subsequent questions to which I shall be turning would not arise. The conduct of the parabolical priest and Levite on the road to Jericho may have been indeed deplorable, but English law has not so far developed to the stage of treating it as criminal and if it ever were to do so there would be difficulties in defining what should be the limits of the offence.

---

[31] [1969] 1 QB 439.

If, on the other hand, the question, which I now confine to: 'Did a physical act of the accused start the fire which spread and damaged property belonging to another?', is answered 'Yes', as it was by the jury in the instant case, then for the purpose of the further questions the answers to which are determinative of his guilt of the offence of arson, the conduct of the accused, throughout the period from immediately before the moment of ignition to the completion of the damage to the property by the fire, is relevant so is his state of mind throughout that period.

Since arson is a result-crime the period may be considerable, and during it the conduct of the accused that is causative of the result may consist not only of his doing physical acts which cause the fire to start or spread but also of his failing to take measures that lie within his power to counteract the danger that he has himself created. And if his conduct, active or passive, varies in the course of the period, so may his state of mind at the time of each piece of conduct. If, at the time of any particular piece of conduct by the accused that is causative of the result, the state of mind that actuates his conduct falls within the description of one or other of the states of mind that are made a necessary ingredient of the offence of arson by s 1(1) of the Criminal Damage Act 1971 (i.e. intending to damage property belonging to another or being reckless whether such property would be damaged), I know of no principle of English criminal law that would prevent his being guilty of the offence created by that subsection. Likewise I see no rational ground for excluding from conduct capable of giving rise to criminal liability conduct which consists of failing to take measures that lie within one's power to counteract a danger that one has oneself created, if at the time of such conduct one's state of mind is such as constitutes a necessary ingredient of the offence. I venture to think that the habit of lawyers to talk of '*actus reus*', suggestive as it is of action rather than inaction, is responsible for any erroneous notion that failure to act cannot give rise to criminal liability in English law.

No one has been bold enough to suggest that if, in the instant case, the accused had been aware at the time that he dropped the cigarette that it would probably set fire to his mattress and yet had taken no steps to extinguish it he would not have been guilty of the offence of arson, since he would have damaged property of another being reckless whether any such property would be damaged.

I cannot see any good reason why, so far as liability under criminal law is concerned, it should matter at what point of time before the resultant damage is complete a person becomes aware that he has done a physical act which, whether or not he appreciated that it would at the time when he did it, does in fact create a risk that property of another will be damaged, provided that, at the moment of awareness, it lies within his power to take steps, either himself or by calling for the assistance of the fire brigade if this be necessary, to prevent or minimise the damage to the property at risk.

. . .

The recorder, in his lucid summing up to the jury (they took 22 minutes only to reach their verdict), told them that the accused, having by his own act started a fire in the mattress which, when he became aware of its existence, presented an obvious risk of damaging the house, became under a duty to take some action to put it out. The Court of Appeal upheld the conviction, but its ratio decidendi appears to be somewhat different from that of the recorder. As I understand the judgment, in effect it treats the whole course of conduct of the accused, from the moment at which he fell asleep and dropped the cigarette onto the mattress until the time the damage to the house by fire was complete, as a continuous act of the accused, and holds that it is sufficient to constitute the statutory offence of arson if at any stage in that course of conduct the state of mind of the accused, when he fails to try to prevent or minimise the damage which will result from his initial act, although it lies within his power to do so, is that of being reckless whether property belonging to another would be damaged.

My Lords, these alternative ways of analysing the legal theory that justifies a decision which has received nothing but commendation for its accord with common sense and justice have, since the publication of the judgment of the Court of Appeal in the instant case, provoked academic controversy. Each theory has distinguished support. Professor J C Smith espouses the 'duty theory' (see [1982] Crim LR 526 at 528). Professor Glanville Williams who, after the decision of the Divisional Court in *Fagan v Metropolitan Police Comr* [1968] 3 All ER 442, [1969] 1 QB 439 appears to have been attracted by the duty theory, now prefers that of the continuous act (see [1982] Crim LR 773). When applied to cases where a person has unknowingly done an act which sets in train events that, when he becomes aware of them, present an obvious risk that property belonging to another will be damaged, both theories lead to an identical result and, since what your Lordships are concerned with is to give guidance to trial judges in their task of summing up to juries, I would for this purpose adopt the duty theory as being the easier to explain to a jury though I would commend the use of the word 'responsibility' rather than 'duty' which is more appropriate to civil than to criminal law since it suggests an obligation owed to another person, i.e. the person to whom the endangered property belongs, whereas a criminal statute defines combinations of conduct and state of mind which render a person liable to punishment by the state itself.

Appeal dismissed.

This case was a difficult one for the House of Lords. The problem was the requirement that the *actus reus* and *mens rea* of the offence must exist at the same moment in time. At first sight in *Miller* the *actus reus* was the dropping of the cigarette, setting off the fire, but at that point there was no *mens rea*. However, at the time when the defendant had the *mens rea* (when he realized there was a fire) he was not doing anything. The House of Lords upheld the conviction by finding that Miller was under a duty to stop the fire because he had started it and that on leaving the room in breach of his duty to act he was therefore committing the *actus reus* of the offence.

The House of Lords' reasoning was applied in *Evans*,[32] where the Court of Appeal held that a young woman who supplied her sister with drugs, owed her a duty of care. When the sister collapsed and the woman failed to seek help, she could be liable for manslaughter on the basis that she owed her sister a duty to summon help because she had created the dangerous situation by supplying the drugs, and had breached that duty.

Novel situations

It seems that the list of exceptions is not necessarily a closed list. The courts may be willing to create new circumstances under which there is a duty to act.[33]

QUESTIONS

1. Lord Diplock in Miller acknowledged that there were two ways of explaining why Miller was liable: (a) the duty theory (Miller was under a duty to stop the fire because he had started it (albeit unintentionally)), (b) the continuing act theory (Miller's

---

[32] [2009] EWCA Crim 650.

[33] Although it might be argued that to do so would constitute retrospective legislation and so be in breach of Art. 6 of the European Convention on Human Rights (ECHR). In *CR v UK* [1996] 1 FLR 434 the European Court of Human Rights held that case-by-case development of the common law by analogy with established cases would not necessarily constitute retrospective legislation.

initial act was regarded as a continuing act until the result was produced). Which of the two theories do you think a jury would more readily understand?

2. In *Khan and Khan* [1998] Crim LR 830 (CA) the defendants supplied a 15-year-old girl with some heroin. It seems that she had not tried the drug before. She took twice the normal amount and collapsed in a coma. The defendants left without summoning medical help and she died. Do you think the defendants had a duty to summon help? (Without deciding the question the Court of Appeal suggested that it 'may be correct that such a duty does arise'.)

For guidance on answering this question, please visit the Online Resource Centre that accompanies this book: www.oxfordtextbooks.co.uk/orc/herringcriminal7e/.

What is required if there is a duty to act?

The simple answer to this question is that the defendant must do what is reasonable. What is reasonable will be decided by the jury. If a mother finds her child drowning in a shallow pond and she can easily save her child she should do so and if she does not she will have committed the offence of murder or manslaughter. If, however, the child is drowning in a tempestuous sea and she can attempt to rescue the child only by placing her own life in grave danger there is no legal obligation to do so. It may be that the reasonable thing to do is not to rescue the victim but to summon help. In *Singh (Gurphal)*[34] a landlord and his agent were responsible for failing to bring in experts when tenants complained that their gas fires were not working properly and subsequently a tenant died from escaping carbon monoxide.

One issue that is not yet resolved is whether the defendant is required to do what is reasonable *for him or her* or what would be reasonable for an ordinary person in his or her shoes. The Court of Appeal in *Stone and Dobinson*,[35] quoted previously, did not directly address the issue, but seemed to ignore the defendant's disabilities and require the defendants to act as ordinary people.

In *R (Jenkins) v HM Coroner for Portsmouth and South East Hampshire and Cameron and Finn*[36] a man became seriously ill. His partner and friends advised him to see a doctor. However, due to his beliefs he refused to see one. The court rejected an argument that his partner or friends breached their duty to him to summon help because it was his choice to refuse help and his friends correctly respected his decision.[37] It would have been different if he was a child or lacked mental capacity.

It must be shown that the omission caused the harm. In other words, had the defendant acted reasonably in accordance with his or her duty the harm would not have occurred. For example, in *Dalloway*[38] the defendant was driving a cart without keeping a proper grip on the reins. A young child ran out in front of the cart and was killed. It was held that if the defendant was to be convicted it had to be shown that had he been driving properly and holding onto the reins he would have been able to avoid injuring the child.[39] Similarly, if a father sees his child drowning in a pond and does nothing to help he is not criminally

---

[34] [1999] Crim LR 582 (CA).   [35] [1977] QB 354 (CA).   [36] [2009] EWHC 3229 (Admin).
[37] See Herring (2010b).   [38] (1847) 2 Cox CC 273.
[39] There is some debate over whether it needs to be shown that if the defendant had acted as he ought the victim would not have suffered the harm, or whether it is enough that there is evidence that the victim might not have suffered the harm. In *Marby* (1882) 8 QBD 571 the defendant was convicted of manslaughter after failing to summon medical help which *might* have saved the life of the victim.

responsible for causing the child's death if it is shown that even if he had tried to save the child it would have been too late to do so.[40]

Distinguishing between omissions and acts

Although the law draws a sharp line between acts and omissions there can be great difficulties in distinguishing between the two.[41] This has led some commentators to question whether it is proper to place so much weight on the distinction. Andrew Ashworth and Jeremy Horder argue that 'although there are some clear cases of omission and some cases of act, there are many ambiguous cases in which the act–omission distinction should not be used as a cloak for avoiding the moral issues.'[42] An example of the difficulty in drawing the distinction between acts and omissions is *Speck*.[43] In that case a child innocently placed her hand on a man's genital area and he did nothing to move her hand. Was this an act or an omission by the man? It was held in effect to be an act by the man, although it might more naturally be regarded as an omission.

A leading case demonstrating the difficulty in drawing the distinction between acts and omissions is *Bland*. In order to understand the House of Lords' judgment it is necessary to appreciate two important points of medical law. The first is that a doctor must not force the treatment on a patient who is competent and refuses to consent, even if without the care the patient will die.[44] The second is that if a patient is unable to express a view a doctor must act in the best interests of the patient.[45] As the reasoning in *Bland* demonstrates, this does not mean that everything must be done to prolong the life of the patient.[46] Sometimes it will be in the patient's interests not to receive treatment which could prolong a painful life, but this does not permit a doctor to do an act to end a patient's life.

Airedale NHS Trust v Bland
[1993] AC 789 (HL)

Tony Bland, then aged 17, was horrifically injured at a disaster at the Hillsborough football ground. He was diagnosed as suffering from a condition known as persistent vegetative state. The medical opinion was that there was no hope of any improvement in his condition or recovery. The consultant in charge of his case, with the support of his parents, sought from the court a declaration permitting the discontinuation of all life-sustaining treatment.

Lord Keith of Kinkel

[I]t is, of course, true that in general it would not be lawful for a medical practitioner who assumed responsibility for the care of an unconscious patient simply to give up treatment in circumstances where continuance of it would confer some benefit on the patient. On the other hand a medical practitioner is under no duty to continue to treat such a patient where

---

[40] He may, nevertheless, be guilty of the offence of child neglect (Children and Young Persons Act 1933, s. 1) for failing to ensure that the child did not get into a dangerous situation.
[41] See the discussion in Elliott and Ormerod (2008).   [42] Ashworth and Horder (2013: 100).
[43] [1977] 2 All ER 859.   [44] *St George's v S* [1999] Fam 26.
[45] *Re F (Mental Patient: Sterilisation)* [1990] 2 AC 1. The law is now found in the Mental Capacity Act 2005.
[46] du Bois-Pedain (2014).

a large body of informed and responsible medical opinion is to the effect that no benefit at all would be conferred by continuance. Existence in a vegetative state with no prospect of recovery is by that opinion regarded as not being a benefit, and that, if not unarguably correct, at least forms a proper basis for the decision to discontinue treatment and care: *Bolam v. Friern Hospital Management Committee* [1957] 1 W.L.R. 582.

Given that existence in the persistent vegetative state is not a benefit to the patient, it remains to consider whether the principle of the sanctity of life, which it is the concern of the state, and the judiciary as one of the arms of the state, to maintain, requires this House to hold that the judgment of the Court of Appeal was incorrect. In my opinion it does not. The principle is not an absolute one. It does not compel a medical practitioner on pain of criminal sanctions to treat a patient, who will die if he does not, contrary to the express wishes of the patient. It does not authorise forcible feeding of prisoners on hunger strike. It does not compel the temporary keeping alive of patients who are terminally ill where to do so would merely prolong their suffering. On the other hand it forbids the taking of active measures to cut short the life of a terminally ill patient. In my judgment it does no violence to the principle to hold that it is lawful to cease to give medical treatment and care to a P.V.S. patient who has been in that state for over three years, considering that to do so involves invasive manipulation of the patient's body to which he has not consented and which confers no benefit upon him.

Lord Goff of Chieveley

. . . I start with the simple fact that, in law, Anthony is still alive. It is true that his condition is such that it can be described as a living death; but he is nevertheless still alive. . . .

It is on this basis that I turn to the applicable principles of law. Here, the fundamental principle is the principle of the sanctity of human life—a principle long recognised not only in our own society but also in most, if not all, civilised societies throughout the modern world, as is indeed evidenced by its recognition both in article 2 of the European Convention for the Protection of Human Rights and Fundamental Freedoms (1953) (Cmd. 8969), and in article 6 of the International Covenant o[n] Civil and Political Rights 1966.

But this principle, fundamental though it is, is not absolute. Indeed there are circumstances in which it is lawful to take another man's life, for example by a lawful act of self-defence, or (in the days when capital punishment was acceptable in our society) by lawful execution. We are not however concerned with cases such as these. We are concerned with circumstances in which it may be lawful to withhold from a patient medical treatment or care by means of which his life may be prolonged. But here too there is no absolute rule that the patient's life must be prolonged by such treatment or care, if available, regardless of the circumstances.

First, it is established that the principle of self-determination requires that respect must be given to the wishes of the patient, so that if an adult patient of sound mind refuses, however unreasonably, to consent to treatment or care by which his life would or might be prolonged, the doctors responsible for his care must give effect to his wishes, even though they do not consider it to be in his best interests to do so: see *Schloendorff v Society of New York Hospital* (1914) 105 N.E. 92, 93, per Cardozo J.; *S. v. McC. (orse S.) and M. (D.S. Intervener); W. v. W.* [1972] A.C. 24, 43, per Lord Reid; and *Sidaway v. Board of Governors of the Bethlem Royal Hospital and the Maudsley Hospital* [1985] A.C. 871, 882, per Lord Scarman. To this extent, the principle of the sanctity of human life must yield to the principle of self-determination (see ante, pp. 826H–827A, per Hoffmann L.J.), and, for present purposes perhaps more important, the doctor's duty to act in the best interests of his patient must likewise be qualified. . . .

I must however stress… that the law draws a crucial distinction between cases in which a doctor decides not to provide, or to continue to provide, for his patient treatment or care which could or might prolong his life, and those in which he decides, for example by administering a lethal drug, actively to bring his patient's life to an end. As I have already indicated, the former may be lawful, either because the doctor is giving effect to his patient's wishes by withholding the treatment or care, or even in certain circumstances in which (on principles which I shall describe) the patient is incapacitated from stating whether or not he gives his consent. But it is not lawful for a doctor to administer a drug to his patient to bring about his death, even though that course is prompted by a humanitarian desire to end his suffering, however great that suffering may be: see *Reg. v. Cox* (unreported), 18 September 1992. So to act is to cross the Rubicon which runs between on the one hand the care of the living patient and on the other hand euthanasia—actively causing his death to avoid or to end his suffering. Euthanasia is not lawful at common law. It is of course well known that there are many responsible members of our society who believe that euthanasia should be made lawful; but that result could, I believe, only be achieved by legislation which expresses the democratic will that so fundamental a change should be made in our law, and can, if enacted, ensure that such legalised killing can only be carried out subject to appropriate supervision and control. It is true that the drawing of this distinction may lead to a charge of hypocrisy; because it can be asked why, if the doctor, by discontinuing treatment, is entitled in consequence to let his patient die, it should not be lawful to put him out of his misery straight away, in a more humane manner, by a lethal injection, rather than let him linger on in pain until he dies. But the law does not feel able to authorise euthanasia, even in circumstances such as these; for once euthanasia is recognised as lawful in these circumstances, it is difficult to see any logical basis for excluding it in others.

At the heart of this distinction lies a theoretical question. Why is it that the doctor who gives his patient a lethal injection which kills him commits an unlawful act and indeed is guilty of murder, whereas a doctor who, by discontinuing life support, allows his patient to die, may not act unlawfully—and will not do so, if he commits no breach of duty to his patient?…

I agree that the doctor's conduct in discontinuing life support can properly be categorised as an omission. It is true that it may be difficult to describe what the doctor actually does as an omission, for example where he takes some positive step to bring the life support to an end. But discontinuation of life support is, for present purposes, no different from not initiating life support in the first place. In each case, the doctor is simply allowing his patient to die in the sense that he is desisting from taking a step which might, in certain circumstances, prevent his patient from dying as a result of his pre-existing condition; and as a matter of general principle an omission such as this will not be unlawful unless it constitutes a breach of duty to the patient. I also agree that the doctor's conduct is to be differentiated from that of, for example, an interloper who maliciously switches off a life support machine because, although the interloper may perform exactly the same act as the doctor who discontinues life support, his doing so constitutes interference with the life-prolonging treatment then being administered by the doctor. Accordingly, whereas the doctor, in discontinuing life support, is simply allowing his patient to die of his pre-existing condition, the interloper is actively intervening to stop the doctor from prolonging the patient's life, and such conduct cannot possibly be categorised as an omission. The distinction appears, therefore, to be useful in the present context in that it can be invoked to explain how discontinuance of life support can be differentiated from ending a patient's life by a lethal injection. But in the end the reason for that difference is that, whereas the law considers that discontinuance of life support may be consistent with the doctor's duty to care for his patient, it does not, for reasons of policy, consider that it forms any part of his duty to give his patient a lethal injection to put him out of his agony.

Lord Mustill

After much expression of negative opinions I turn to an argument which in my judgment is logically defensible and consistent with the existing law. In essence it turns the previous argument on its head by directing the inquiry to the interests of the patient, not in the termination of life but in the continuation of his treatment. It runs as follows. (i) The cessation of nourishment and hydration is an omission not an act. (ii) Accordingly, the cessation will not be a criminal act unless the doctors are under a present duty to continue the regime. (iii) At the time when Anthony Bland came into the care of the doctors decisions had to be made about his care which he was unable to make for himself. In accordance with *In re F.* [1990] 2 A.C. 1 these decisions were to be made in his best interests. Since the possibility that he might recover still existed his best interests required that he should be supported in the hope that this would happen. These best interests justified the application of the necessary regime without his consent. (iv) All hope of recovery has now been abandoned. Thus, although the termination of his life is not in the best interests of Anthony Bland, his best interests in being kept alive have also disappeared, taking with them the justification for the non-consensual regime and the co-relative duty to keep it in being. (v) Since there is no longer a duty to provide nourishment and hydration a failure to do so cannot be a criminal offence.

My Lords, I must recognise at once that this chain of reasoning makes an unpromising start by transferring the morally and intellectually dubious distinction between acts and omissions into a context where the ethical foundations of the law are already open to question. The opportunity for anomaly and excessively fine distinctions, often depending more on the way in which the problem happens to be stated than on any real distinguishing features, has been exposed by many commentators, including in England the authors above-mentioned, together with *Smith & Hogan on Criminal Law*, 6th ed. (1988), p. 51, H. Beynon at [1982] Crim.L.R. 17 and M.J. Gunn and J.C. Smith at [1985] Crim.L.R. 705. All this being granted we are still forced to take the law as we find it and try to make it work....

I therefore consider the argument to be soundly-based. Now that the time has come when Anthony Bland has no further interest in being kept alive, the necessity to do so, created by his inability to make a choice, has gone; and the justification for the invasive care and treatment, together with the duty to provide it have also gone. Absent a duty, the omission to perform what had previously been a duty will no longer be a breach of the criminal law.

[Speeches were also given by **Lord Lowry** and **Lord Browne-Wilkinson** agreeing that the appeal should be dismissed.]

Appeal dismissed.

QUESTIONS

1. Professor Smith asks: 'If a doctor is keeping a patient alive by cranking the handle of a machine and he stops, this looks like a clear case of omission. So too if the machine is electrically operated but switches it off every 24 hours and the doctor deliberately does not restart it. Switching off a functioning machine looks like an act; but is it any different in substance from the first two cases?' (J.C. Smith 2002: 64).

2. Lord Goff in *Bland* stated: 'I also agree that the doctor's conduct is to be differentiated from that of, for example, an interloper who maliciously switches off a life support

> machine because, although the interloper may perform exactly the same act as the
> doctor who discontinues life support, his doing so constitutes interference with
> the life-prolonging treatment then being administered by the doctor. Accordingly,
> whereas the doctor, in discontinuing life support, is simply allowing his patient to
> die of his pre-existing condition, the interloper is actively intervening to stop the
> doctor from prolonging the patient's life, and such conduct cannot possibly be cat-
> egorized as an omission.' Does it make sense that a happening which is regarded as
> an action when done by one person (an interloper) is regarded as an omission when
> done by another (a doctor)?
>
> For guidance on answering this question, please visit the Online Resource Centre that
> accompanies this book: www.oxfordtextbooks.co.uk/orc/herringcriminal7e/.

2.2 SITUATIONAL OFFENCES

Analogous to offences involving omissions are cases where the defendant is guilty for
being in a particular situation or state of affairs.[47] Examples are being drunk while in
charge of a vehicle,[48] or possessing a drug[49] or offensive weapon.[50] (Possession offences
will be discussed further in Chapter 4.) Such offences can be seen as being compatible
with the voluntary act requirement as they will at least involve an earlier act. Take being
drunk in charge of a vehicle. It can be said that getting drunk and getting into a vehicle
are acts.

A particularly controversial case concerning a situational offence was *Larsonneur*,[51]
in which the defendant was convicted of the offence of being found in the UK while
being 'an alien to whom leave to land in the United Kingdom had been refused', contrary to articles 1(3) and 18(1)(b) of the Aliens Order 1920, as amended. The case was
controversial because the defendant was in the UK only because she had been forcibly
returned to the UK by the Irish police.[52] Whether it was correct to punish her when
she had performed no voluntary act to put herself in the criminal situation is hotly
debated.[53]

2.3 LIABILITY FOR THE ACTS OF OTHER PEOPLE

There are certain circumstances under which a party is criminally responsible for the
acts of a third party. In such a case a defendant is not punished for his or her own acts,
but the acts of someone else. Two examples are particularly relevant: vicarious liability
and the doctrine of innocent agency. Under vicarious liability an employer, under certain circumstances, may be criminally responsible for the acts of an employee. This is
explored further in Chapter 13. Under the doctrine of innocent agency if A causes B (who
is insane or a child) to cause harm to another then A can be made criminally responsible for the consequences of B's act. The doctrine of innocent agency is discussed in
Chapter 15.

---

[47] See generally Glazebrook (1978: 108).   [48] Road Traffic Act 1988, s. 4(2).
[49] Misuse of Drugs Act 1971.   [50] Prevention of Crime Act 1953.   [51] (1933) 149 LT 542.
[52] The background to the case is explained in Lanham (1976).
[53] See also *Winzar v Chief Constable of Kent* The Times, 28 March 1983.

3 CAUSATION

We mentioned earlier that for some crimes it is necessary to show not only that the defendant performed an act, but that that act caused a particular consequence. For example, in murder it must be proved that the accused has caused the death of the victim. In many cases causation will be straightforward. If the defendant chops off the victim's head and the victim dies, it will be hard to deny that the defendant has caused the victim's death. It is only where there is a rather unusual set of facts that there is any dispute over the question. The most difficult cases are ones where it is not clear which of two or more people caused the result.

Imagine the following scenario: David, who was abused by his father as a child, has recently been made redundant by his employer and turned to drink. After a heavy drinking session Victor hurls a racial insult at him. David flies into a rage and stabs Victor. A passer-by phones for an ambulance, which takes a long time to arrive because of traffic jams and bad weather. When Victor arrives at the hospital there is a long delay before he is seen by a doctor because of the staff shortages in the NHS. By then Victor has died.

Who or what caused Victor's death? It would be possible to blame David, David's father, David's employer, the brewery who produced the alcohol he drank or the pub which sold it to him, Victor for the racial insult, the government for failing to prevent traffic congestion or fund the NHS adequately, the NHS trust at the relevant hospital, or even God for the weather! Indeed it would not be surprising if a doctor, a sociologist, a lawyer, a politician, a theologian, or a member of the public all answered the question: 'Who caused Victor's death?' in different ways. The important point to make is that there is no magic formula to answer the question correctly; rather the law must decide which of the many possible approaches to take.

The courts have consistently stated that causation is simply a matter of common sense[54] and it is not a question of philosophical analysis. Stephen Shute has explained: '[T]he law tends to regard causation in terms of broad generalisations based on common sense principles, rather than attempting to mimic the more obscure approach to causation often taken by the philosopher or the scientist.'[55] Therefore the courts tend to see causation as a question of fact for the jury. However, it is not always that straightforward and the House of Lords has acknowledged that sometimes it is necessary for a judge to direct the jury to apply special legal rules and not just leave the causal question to the common sense of the jury.[56] Indeed if it is clear to the judge that in law the defendant could not be said to have caused the result, the judge should withdraw the case from the jury.[57]

At the heart of the law's understanding of causation is an assumption that each person is responsible for his or her actions. Arguments such as 'my background made me act this way' or 'society caused me to do this' carry no weight in the law's understanding of causation. The effect of this is that if there is a voluntary act of an individual immediately connected to the result the law's analysis stops. The individual caused the result and there is no need to ask if anything made him or her act in that way or enquire into the reasons for his or her action. →5 (p.128)

Although the issue of causation is a legal one the judiciary appears to apply the rules flexibly. Some commentators feel that in fact policy issues and moral judgments affect the law's attitude to causation. In other words the questions 'Should the defendant be held responsible

---

[54] See e.g. *Kennedy* [2007] UKHL 38, para. 15. [55] Shute (1992: 584).

[56] *Empress Car Co (Abertillery) Ltd v National Rivers Authority* [1998] 1 All ER 481 (HL).

[57] *Malcherek* [1981] 2 All ER 422 (CA).

for this result?' and 'Did the defendant legally cause the result?' merge together. We will consider this further in Part II of this chapter.

It is now necessary to look at the law's understanding of causation and start by considering factual or 'but for' causation.

3.1 FACTUAL OR 'BUT FOR' CAUSATION

> **DEFINITION**
>
> 'But for' causation: the defendant's act is a 'but for' cause of a result, if, but for the defendant's act, the result would not have occurred.

'But for' or factual causation is an important aspect of the criminal law on causation.[58] Something cannot be a legal cause unless it is a factual cause, but it does not follow that just because an act is a factual cause that it is also a legal cause. The test for factual causation requires the jury to consider whether, but for the defendant's unlawful actions, the harm would have occurred at the same time and in the same way that it did. Contrast these two cases:

(1) In *Dyson*[59] the victim was dying from meningitis when Dyson injured him. The victim died as a result of the injuries. The evidence was that because of the injuries the victim died sooner than he would have done from the meningitis. Dyson could be held to have caused the victim's death. But for Dyson's actions the victim would not have died at the time and place that he did.[60]

(2) In *White*[61] the defendant put poison into the victim's drink. The victim suffered a heart attack, having taken a few sips. Medical evidence suggested that the poison was unrelated to the heart attack. The victim would have died in exactly the same way and at the same time had the defendant not put the poison in the drink, and therefore it could not be said that the poison was a factual cause of the death.

The Supreme Court in *Hughes*[62] helpfully summarized the importance of but for causation in this way (using the terminology *sine qua non* to mean but for causation):

> The law has frequently to confront the distinction between "cause" in the sense of a sine qua non without which the consequence would not have occurred, and "cause" in the sense of something which was a legally effective cause of that consequence. The former, which is often conveniently referred to as a "but for" event, is not necessarily enough to be a legally effective cause. If it were, the woman who asked her neighbour to go to the station in his car to collect her husband would be held to have caused her husband's death if he perished in a fatal road accident on the way home. In the case law there is a well recognised distinction between conduct which sets the stage for an occurrence and conduct which on a common sense view is regarded as instrumental in bringing about the occurrence.

---

[58] This is sometimes known as *sine qua non* causation.   [59] [1908] 2 KB 454 (CA).
[60] There was, however, no conviction for manslaughter because the victim did not die within a year and a day of the defendant's actions. That year and a day rule is no longer part of the law (Law Reform (Year and a Day Rule) Act 1996).
[61] [1910] 2 KB 124 (CA).   [62] [2013] UKSC 56.

As the Supreme Court recognized, factual causation cannot be used as the general rule for causation because it is far too wide. For example, in a murder case a defendant's parents could be said to have caused a victim's death: but for the defendant's parents bringing him into the world, the victim would not have died. However, 'but for causation' is useful in that it tells us who *cannot* be regarded as a cause of death. If the victim would have died in the same way and at the same time had the defendant not been there, then the defendant cannot be said to have caused the death in the eyes of the law.

3.2 THE KEY TEST FOR LEGAL CAUSATION

From the factual causes the law selects the one or ones which are the legal cause. A legal cause is 'an operating and substantial cause'. The Court of Appeal in *Mellor* stressed that there may be several operating and substantial causes of the result.[63] So, the mere fact that both the defendant and another person contributed to the harm does not mean that the defendant cannot be responsible. What do the two terms 'substantial' and 'operating' mean? →6 (p.122)

Substantial

The defendant's act must be a substantial cause of the result. It must contribute to the end result to a significant extent;[64] not be a 'slight or trifling link'.[65] It must make more than an 'insubstantial or insignificant contribution'.[66] In *R v L*[67] it was suggested that it was sufficient if the defendant's act had been a more than negligible contribution. The Supreme Court in *Hughes*[68] said it had to be substantial: it had to be more than a 'de minimis or minimal' cause. The courts have avoided speaking in mathematical terms. In *Hennigan*[69] a judge who directed the jury that a defendant was not guilty if he was less than one-fifth to blame was held to have given a misdirection. Imagine Edwin stabbed Thelma in the leg and then Fred shot her and medical evidence established that she had died from the shot, but as she had been slightly weakened by the stabbing she died a second earlier than she would have done without the stab wound. In such a case, the stabbing would be regarded as a minimal contribution to the death and so not a cause.

Operating

The defendant's act must be an operating cause of the result. The most common way for a defendant to deny that his or her act was an operating cause is to argue that there has been a 'break in the chain of causation' or a *novus actus interveniens*. This means that the act of someone else has taken over responsibility for the chain of events and the defendant is no longer responsible. For example, in *Rafferty*[70] the defendant and his friends, Taylor and Thomas, hit the victim. The defendant then ran away. Taylor and Thomas then drowned the victim in the sea. The actions of Taylor and Thomas were held to be a *novus actus interveniens* and Rafferty was not held to have caused the victim's death. He was, however, still guilty of the assault.

---

[63] *Mellor* [1996] 2 Cr App R 245.   [64] *Cheshire* [1991] 3 All ER 670 (CA).
[65] *Kimsey* [1996] Crim LR 35 (CA).   [66] *Cato* [1976] 1 All ER 260 (CA).
[67] [2010] EWCA Crim 1249.   [68] [2013] UKSC 56.   [69] [1971] 3 All ER 133.
[70] [2007] EWCA Crim 1846.

It is necessary to take a further look at the notion of a *novus actus interveniens*. It is useful to distinguish three different situations: where it is the acts of a third party which break the chain, where it is the victim's acts which are said to break the chain, and where it is a 'natural event' or 'act of God' which is said to break the chain.

3.3 ACTS OF THIRD PARTIES BREAKING THE CHAIN OF CAUSATION

EXAMINATION TIP

If you are dealing with a question in which A injured the victim and then B inflicted a further injury on the victim after which the victim died, the following would be four possible results a court could reach:

(1) If the evidence was that the victim died as a combination of both injuries it could be found that both A and B caused the death. This is known as 'concurrent causes'.

(2) It could be found that B's act was a *novus actus interveniens* so A no longer could be said to have caused the death, but B could.

(3) It could be that B's act was of negligible effect (e.g. if B had only scratched the victim), then it may be found that A caused the death, but B did not.

(4) It could be found that neither of the acts caused the death, for example if the victim died from a heart attack unconnected with either injury.

You should consider which of these possibilities covers the set of facts with which you are dealing.

As these points indicate, if two people both harm the victim there are a number of different legal interpretations of what has happened. Here we will concentrate on where one person's act is a *novus actus interveniens* and breaks the chain of causation.

DEFINITION

A *novus actus interveniens*: a free, voluntary and informed act of a third party which renders the original act no longer a substantial and operating cause of the result.

The importance of the doctrine of *novus actus interveniens* has been affirmed by the House of Lords in the following decision:[71]

R v Kennedy
[2008] AC 269

Simon Kennedy had prepared a syringe of heroin for Marco Bosque. Bosque injected himself and died shortly after. Kennedy was charged with supplying a class A drug

[71] See W. Wilson (2008b) for an excellent discussion of the issues raised.

and manslaughter, and convicted on both charges. On appeal the Court of Appeal held that the crucial question was whether the appellant could be held to be jointly responsible for carrying out the injection. This issue, it was felt, was adequately covered by the trial judge's direction and therefore the appeal was dismissed. Subsequently the Criminal Cases Review Commission referred the case back to the Court of Appeal on the basis that later cases had cast doubt on the reasoning of the original Court of Appeal case and that the judge had failed adequately to explain to the jury that the free, voluntary, and informed act of the victim in injecting himself with heroin would break the chain of causation between the appellant's act of supplying the drugs and the victim's death.

[The report was delivered on behalf of all their Lordships:]

14. The criminal law generally assumes the existence of free will. The law recognises certain exceptions, in the case of the young, those who for any reason are not fully responsible for their actions, and the vulnerable, and it acknowledges situations of duress and necessity, as also of deception and mistake. But, generally speaking, informed adults of sound mind are treated as autonomous beings able to make their own decisions how they will act, and none of the exceptions is relied on as possibly applicable in this case. Thus D is not to be treated as causing V to act in a certain way if V makes a voluntary and informed decision to act in that way rather than another. There are many classic statements to this effect. In his article "*Finis for Novus Actus?*" (1989) 48(3) CLJ 391, 392, Professor Glanville Williams wrote:

> "I may suggest reasons to you for doing something; I may urge you to do it, tell you it will pay you to do it, tell you it is your duty to do it. My efforts may perhaps make it very much more likely that you will do it. But they do not cause you to do it, in the sense in which one causes a kettle of water to boil by putting it on the stove. Your volitional act is regarded (within the doctrine of responsibility) as setting a new 'chain of causation' going, irrespective of what has happened before."

In chapter XII of *Causation in the Law*, 2nd ed (1985), p 326, Hart and Honoré wrote:

> "The free, deliberate, and informed intervention of a second person, who intends to exploit the situation created by the first, but is not acting in concert with him, is normally held to relieve the first actor of criminal responsibility."

This statement was cited by the House with approval in *R v Latif* [1996] 1 WLR 104. The principle is fundamental and not controversial.

15. Questions of causation frequently arise in many areas of the law, but causation is not a single, unvarying concept to be mechanically applied without regard to the context in which the question arises. That was the point which Lord Hoffmann, with the express concurrence of three other members of the House, was at pains to make in *Environment Agency (formerly National Rivers Authority) v Empress Car Co (Abertillery) Ltd* [1999] 2 AC 22....

17. In his article already cited Professor Glanville Williams pointed out (at p 398) that the doctrine of secondary liability was developed precisely because an informed voluntary choice was ordinarily regarded as a *novus actus interveniens* breaking the chain of causation:

> "Principals cause, accomplices encourage (or otherwise influence) or help. If the instigator were regarded as causing the result he would be a principal, and the conceptual division between principals (or, as I prefer to call them, perpetrators) and accessories would vanish. Indeed, it was because the instigator was not regarded as causing the crime that the notion of accessories had to be developed. This is the

irrefragable argument for recognising the *novus actus* principle as one of the bases of our criminal law. The final act is done by the perpetrator, and his guilt pushes the accessories, conceptually speaking, into the background. Accessorial liability is, in the traditional theory, 'derivative' from that of the perpetrator."

18. This is a matter of some significance since, contrary to the view of the Court of Appeal when dismissing the appellant's first appeal, the deceased committed no offence when injecting himself with the fatal dose of heroin. It was so held by the Court of Appeal in *R v Dias* [2002] 2 Cr App R 96, paras 21–24, and in *R v Rogers* [2003] EWCA Crim 945, [2003] 1 WLR 1374 and is now accepted. If the conduct of the deceased was not criminal he was not a principal offender, and it of course follows that the appellant cannot be liable as a secondary party. It also follows that there is no meaningful legal sense in which the appellant can be said to have been a principal jointly with the deceased, or to have been acting in concert. The finding that the deceased freely and voluntarily administered the injection to himself, knowing what it was, is fatal to any contention that the appellant caused the heroin to be administered to the deceased or taken by him.

24. It is possible to imagine factual scenarios in which two people could properly be regarded as acting together to administer an injection. But nothing of the kind was the case here. As in *R v Dalby* and *R v Dias* the appellant supplied the drug to the deceased, who then had a choice, knowing the facts, whether to inject himself or not. The heroin was, as the certified question correctly recognises, self-administered, not jointly administered. The appellant did not administer the drug. Nor, for reasons already given, did the appellant cause the drug to be administered to or taken by the deceased.

25. The answer to the certified question is: "In the case of a fully-informed and responsible adult, never". The appeal must be allowed and the appellant's conviction for manslaughter quashed.

The principle confirmed by their Lordships from these cases appears straightforward.[72] If A does an act after which B does an act, then if B's act is

(1) a free, voluntary, and informed act; and

(2) it renders A's act no longer a substantial and operating cause,

A will not have caused the result. B's act will be a *novus actus interveniens*. More needs to be said about these requirements.

A free, voluntary, and informed act

Only the free, voluntary, and informed acts of a third party will break the chain of causation. What then will constitute a free, voluntary, and informed act? The following points will be of some assistance:

(1) Where a person, D, is not acting voluntarily his or her 'action' will not be a *novus actus interveniens*. So if Guy pushes Mary into Ivy who suffers injuries then Guy is said to have caused the injuries, as Mary was not acting in a voluntary way and so her 'act' could not be regarded as a *novus actus interveniens*. It is not quite clear how far this may be taken. In *Wise*

---

[72] While the decision has been widely welcomed, Cherkassky (2008) argues that it fails to follow the earlier line of cases which established that only unforeseeable 'free, voluntary and informed acts' break the chain of causation.

v Dunning[73] a religious preacher gave an anti-Catholic speech. He realized that there were Catholics in the audience and that they would react violently to his speech, which they did. The court was willing to accept that the preacher caused the spontaneous violence. It seems the court took the view that the violence was an instinctive reaction of the listeners, and so was not truly voluntary. Some commentators regard this case as stretching the meaning of 'voluntary' too far.

(2) Where a person is acting in a way which is justified his or her action is not free, voluntary, or informed.[74] To give three examples:

(a) If someone is acting in order to preserve his or her own life or limb the act will not be free, voluntary, or informed. So if Tim throws an object at Penelope who, in order to protect herself, deflects the object but it then hits Fred, Tim will be said to have caused Fred's injuries. Penelope's act will not break the chain of causation because she was justified in acting as she did.[75] In *Gnango*[76] the defendant and another man had engaged in a shooting match and the other man had accidentally shot a passer-by. A minority of their Lordships held that the defendant could be said to have caused the death of the passer-by. The majority did not take this approach because the other man was not acting in self-defence but had been, from the start, trying to kill Gnango and so was not justified in acting as he did. He was, therefore, responsible for his own actions.

(b) If someone is acting in order to assist law enforcement this will not be a break in the chain of causation. So in *Pagett*[77] a defendant was said to have caused his girlfriend's death after he kidnapped her and she was killed by police marksmen trying to secure her release. It was found that he had caused the police to act in this way and the police were acting lawfully and therefore their actions did not break the chain of causation.

(c) It may be that acts in accordance with a moral obligation will not break the chain of causation. For example, if a passer-by came across an injured person and tried to administer first aid, but did so in such a way that in fact the victim died, the passer-by's act may not break the chain of causation.[78] Certainly sound medical practice will not break the chain of causation. In *Malcherek and Steel*[79] a doctor who switched off a life support machine in accordance with approved medical procedures was held not to have caused the patient's death.

(3) If a person does not know the circumstances of his action it may not break the chain of causation. If Charles posts a parcel bomb which is delivered by Tina (a postal worker) and injures someone, Charles will be said to have caused the injury. Although the delivery of the bomb by Tina was free and voluntary it was not 'informed'.[80]

Rendering the defendant's action no longer an operating and substantial cause

To amount to a *novus actus interveniens* the act of the third party must have rendered the defendant's original act no longer an operating and substantial cause. Many of the

---

[73] [1902] 1 KB 167.   [74] *Latif* [1996] 1 All ER 353 (HL).
[75] *Scott v Shepherd* (1773) 96 ER 525.   [76] See Chapter 15 for a lengthy discussion of this case.
[77] *Pagett* (1983) 76 Cr App R 279 (CA). cf *Latif* [1996] 1 All ER 353 (HL).
[78] Hart and Honoré (1985: 335).   [79] [1981] 1 WLR 690 (CA).
[80] Similarly if D is a child or suffers from a lack of mental capacity his actions will not be free, voluntary, and informed.

cases have involved a defendant who has injured a victim; the victim has then received bad medical treatment and died. The defendant then claims that the bad medical treatment the victim subsequently received broke the chain of causation. The courts have been very reluctant to accept such arguments. They have clearly been persuaded by the response that the victim would not have required medical treatment had the defendant not injured him or her. It therefore hardly lies in the mouth of the defendant to complain about the standard of the medical treatment he or she necessitated. Indeed it has been suggested that bad medical treatment cannot be regarded as 'abnormal'. Inevitably in busy hospitals treatment of emergencies cannot always be of the highest possible standard.

One of the very few cases where medical treatment did break the chain of causation was *R v Jordan*.[81] Here the defendant stabbed the victim. The victim was taken to hospital, where the wound had almost healed when a doctor administered a drug to which the victim was allergic. The drug killed the victim. The court heard evidence that the doctor should have known that the victim was intolerant to the drug. The Court of Appeal held that the medical treatment and not the defendant caused the death of the victim. There were two crucial facts in the case which led to this conclusion:

(1) The original wound had virtually healed at the time of death. In medical terms the wound inflicted by the defendant had not contributed to the death of the deceased.

(2) The treatment provided by the hospital was 'abnormal', 'palpably wrong', or 'grossly negligent'. It should have been known by the doctor that the victim was intolerant to the antibiotic.

Of course, although Jordan was held not to be responsible for the death he was still responsible for the original assault.

Jordan has been regarded as exceptional: only in the most unusual of circumstances will medical treatment, however negligent, break the chain of causation. A more representative example of the case law is *Cheshire*,[82] in the following extract, where, even though the treatment was not as it should have been, it did not break the chain of causation. In *Malcherek*[83] D inflicted wounds upon P, who had to be put on a life support machine. Several days later the machine was switched off by doctors. The Court of Appeal accepted that there was no doubt that the injury was an operating and substantial cause of the death. After all, what did the victim die from when the machine was switched off, if not the injuries inflicted by the defendant?

William Wilson[84] has suggested that in a case where a victim suffers death in hospital it is necessary to distinguish two kinds of cases:

(1) The death of the victim was a result of bad medical treatment which was attempting to treat the victim's injuries. In such a case the treatment must be palpably wrong if it is to break the chain of causation.

(2) The death of the victim was caused by things done in a hospital not connected to treatment of the injuries inflicted by the defendant (e.g. food poisoning from the hospital food, catching a disease from a fellow patient, a doctor deliberately harming

---

81 (1956) 40 Cr App R 152 (CA).   82 *Cheshire* [1991] 3 All ER 670 (CA).
83 [1981] 2 All ER 422 (CA).   84 W. Wilson (2003: 112–13).

a victim out of maliciousness), which do not have to be palpably wrong to break the chain of causation.

The argument behind this distinction is that although the defendant can reasonably be said to have necessitated the provision of medical treatment there is a looser connection between the defendant and other things that may happen to the victim in hospital. Although the courts have not been explicit in drawing such a distinction, they may well be attracted to such an approach in an appropriate case.

The following case is a good example of how the courts treat cases where it is alleged that medical treatment has broken the chain of causation:

R v Cheshire
[1991] 3 All ER 670 (CA)[85]

David Cheshire (the appellant) shot the victim (Trevor Jeffrey) in the leg and stomach during an argument in the Ozone fish and chip shop. The victim was taken to hospital and placed in intensive care. A tracheotomy tube was inserted in his windpipe because he was having breathing difficulties. Two months after the shooting the victim died because the windpipe had narrowed where the tracheotomy had been performed. This was a rare but not unknown complication of such a procedure. The defendant was convicted of murder. He appealed on the basis that the trial judge had wrongly directed the jury that only if the medical treatment could be described as reckless could the appellant be said not to have caused the victim's death.

Lord Justice Beldam

In the criminal law, and in particular in the law of homicide, whether the death of a deceased was the result of the accused's criminal act is a question of fact for the jury, but it is a question of fact to be decided in accordance with legal principles explained to the jury by the judge.

[Having quoted from Hart and Honoré's *Causation in the Law*, **Beldam LJ** continued:]

As Professors Hart and Honoré comment, treatment which falls short of the standard expected of the competent medical practitioner is unfortunately only too frequent in human experience for it to be considered abnormal in the sense of extraordinary. Acts or omissions of a doctor treating the victim for injuries he has received at the hands of an accused may conceivably be so extraordinary as to be capable of being regarded as acts independent of the conduct of the accused but it is most unlikely that they will be.

We have not been referred to any English authority in which the terms of the direction which should be given to a jury in such a case have been considered. We were referred to *R v Jordan* (1956) 40 Cr App R 152, in which the appellant, who had been convicted of murder, sought leave to call further evidence about the cause of the victim's death. The application was granted and evidence was received by the court that the stab wound from which the victim died eight days later was not the cause of the victim's death. The deceased had died from the effects of sensitivity to Terramycin which had been given to him after his intolerance to it was established and in abnormal quantity. The court considered that the introduction into the system of the victim of a substance shown to be poisonous to him and in quantities which were so great as to result in pulmonary oedema leading to pneumonia were factors which ought to have been before the jury and which in all probability would have affected their decision.

R v Jordan was described in the later case of *R v Smith* [1959] 2 QB 35 as a very particular case dependent upon its exact facts. The appellant in *R v Smith* had been convicted at court-martial of the murder of another soldier by stabbing him. The victim had been dropped twice while being taken to the medical reception station and was subsequently given treatment which was said to be incorrect and harmful. Lord Parker CJ, giving the judgment of the Court Martial Appeal Court, rejected a contention that his death did not result from the stab wound. He said ([1959] 2 QB 35 at 42–43):

'It seems to the court that, if at the time of death the original wound is still an operating cause and a substantial cause, then the death can properly be said to be the result of the wound, albeit that some other cause of death is also operating. Only if it can be said that the original wounding is merely the setting in which another cause operates can it be said that the death does not result from the wound. Putting it in another way, only if the second cause is so overwhelming as to make the original wound merely part of the history can it be said that the death does not flow from the wound.'

Both these cases were considered by this court in *R v Malcherek, R v Steel* [1981] 2 All ER 422, in which it had been argued that the act of a doctor in disconnecting a life support machine had intervened to cause the death of the victim to the exclusion of injuries inflicted by the appellants. In rejecting this submission Lord Lane CJ, after considering *R v Jordan* and *R v Smith*, said ([1981] 2 All ER 422 at 428):

'In the view of this court, if a choice has to be made between the decision in *R v Jordan* and that in *R v Smith*, which we do not believe it does (*R v Jordan* being a very exceptional case), then the decision in *R v Smith* is to be preferred.'

Later in the same judgment Lord Lane CJ said ([1981] 2 All ER 422 at 428–429):

'There may be occasions, although they will be rare, when the original injury has ceased to operate as a cause at all, but in the ordinary case if the treatment is given bona fide by competent and careful medical practitioners, then evidence will not be admissible to show that the treatment would not have been administered in the same way by other medical practitioners. In other words, the fact that the victim has died, despite or because of medical treatment for the initial injury given by careful and skilled medical practitioners, will not exonerate the original assailant from responsibility for the death.'

In those two cases it was not suggested that the actions of the doctors in disconnecting the life support machines were other than competent and careful. The court did not have to consider the effect of medical treatment which fell short of the standard of care to be expected of competent medical practitioners.

[Having considered passages from the judgments in the Supreme Court of Victoria in *R v Evans and Gardiner (No 2)* [1976] VR 523, **Beldam LJ** continued:]

It seems to us that these two passages demonstrate the difficulties in formulating and explaining a general concept of causation but what we think does emerge from this and the other cases is that when the victim of a criminal attack is treated for wounds or injuries by doctors or other medical staff attempting to repair the harm done, it will only be in the most extraordinary and unusual case that such treatment can be said to be so independent of the acts of the accused that it could be regarded in law as the cause of the victim's death to the exclusion of the accused's acts.

Where the law requires proof of the relationship between an act and its consequences as an element of responsibility, a simple and sufficient explanation of the basis of such relationship has proved notoriously elusive.

In a case in which the jury have to consider whether negligence in the treatment of injuries inflicted by the accused was the cause of death we think it is sufficient for the judge to tell the jury that they must be satisfied that the Crown have proved that the acts of the accused caused the death of the deceased, adding that the accused's acts need not be the sole cause or even the main cause of death, it being sufficient that his acts contributed significantly to that result. Even though negligence in the treatment of the victim was the immediate cause of his death, the jury should not regard it as excluding the responsibility of the accused unless the negligent treatment was so independent of his acts, and in itself so potent in causing death, that they regard the contribution made by his acts as insignificant.

It is not the function of the jury to evaluate competing causes or to choose which is dominant provided they are satisfied that the accused's acts can fairly be said to have made a significant contribution to the victim's death. We think the word 'significant' conveys the necessary substance of a contribution made to the death which is more than negligible.

. . . Although for reasons we have stated we think that the judge erred when he invited the jury to consider the degree of fault in the medical treatment rather than its consequences, we consider that no miscarriage of justice has actually occurred. Even if more experienced doctors than those who attended the deceased would have recognised the rare complication in time to have prevented the deceased's death, that complication was a direct consequence of the appellant's acts, which remained a significant cause of his death. We cannot conceive that, on the evidence given, any jury would have found otherwise.

Accordingly, we dismiss the appeal.

Appeal dismissed.

QUESTIONS

1. In *Bush v Commonwealth* 78 Ky 268 (1880) (Kentucky Court of Appeals) the defendant injured the victim. A medical officer then attended the victim and inadvertently infected him with scarlet fever and he died of that. Did the defendant cause the victim's death?

2. In *Martin* (1827) 172 ER 390 a father offered his son a sip from his alcoholic drink, but the child took the whole drink and died. This was held not to be foreseeable (perhaps surprisingly!) and so the father had not caused the death. Do you think the same result would be reached today?

3.4 OMISSIONS OF THIRD PARTIES BREAKING THE CHAIN OF CAUSATION

Although the courts have not said so explicitly, it is submitted that omissions of a third party cannot break the chain of causation. This is because an omission cannot render the defendant's act no longer an operating and substantial cause. If the defendant stabbed the victim, who was taken to hospital but died because no medical treatment was offered, then the defendant would be said to have caused the death.[86]

3.5 ACTS OF THE VICTIM BREAKING THE CHAIN

What about cases where the defendant alleges that the acts of the victim have broken the chain of causation? There are two leading cases on this which need to be contrasted, *Roberts* and *Blaue*:

R v Roberts
(1971) 56 Cr App R 95 (CA)

Kenneth Roberts was giving the victim a lift in his car after a party when he made indecent suggestions to her. He threatened her and started to touch her coat. She jumped out of the car injuring herself. Roberts was convicted of causing her actual bodily harm, contrary to section 47 of the Offences Against the Person Act 1861. The judge directed the jury that if they felt sure that the victim was induced to jump out of the car they should convict the defendant. Roberts appealed on the basis that the judge had misdirected the jury.

Lord Justice Stephenson

We have been helpfully referred to a number of reported cases, some well over a century old, of women jumping out of windows, or jumping or throwing themselves into a river, as a consequence of threats of violence or actual violence. The most recent case is the case of *Lewis* [1970] Crim. L. R. 647. An earlier case is that of *Beech* (1912) 7 Cr. App. R. 197, which was a case of a woman jumping out of a window and injuring herself, and of a man who had friendly relations with her, whom she knew and might have had reason to be afraid of, being prosecuted for inflicting grievous bodily harm upon her, contrary to section 20 of the Offences against the Person Act. In that case the Court of Criminal Appeal (at p. 200) approved the direction given by the trial judge in these terms: 'Will you say whether the conduct of the prisoner amounted to a threat of causing injury to this young woman, was the act of jumping the natural consequence of the conduct of the prisoner, and was the grievous bodily harm the result of the conduct of the prisoner?' That, said the Court, was a proper direction as far as the law went, and they were satisfied that there was evidence before the jury of the prisoner causing actual bodily harm to the woman. 'No-one could say', said Darling J. when giving the judgment of the Court, 'that if she jumped from the window it was not a natural consequence of the prisoner's conduct. It was a very likely thing for a woman to do as the result of the threats of a man who was conducting himself as this man indisputably was.'

  This Court thinks that that correctly states the law, and that Mr. Carus was wrong in submitting to this Court that the jury must be sure that a defendant, who is charged either with inflicting grievous bodily harm or assault occasioning actual bodily harm, must foresee the actions of the victim which result in the grievous bodily harm, or the actual bodily harm.

---

[86] In such a case it is arguable that the hospital trust also caused the death.

That, in the view of this Court, is not the test. The test is: Was it the natural result of what the alleged assailant said and did, in the sense that it was something that could reasonably have been foreseen as the consequence of what he was saying or doing? As it was put in one of the old cases, it had got to be shown to be his act, and if of course the victim does something so 'daft,' in the words of the appellant in this case, or so unexpected, not that this particular assailant did not actually foresee it but that no reasonable man could be expected to foresee it, then it is only in a very remote and unreal sense a consequence of his assault, it is really occasioned by a voluntary act on the part of the victim which could not reasonably be foreseen and which breaks the chain of causation between the assault and the harm or injury.

Appeal dismissed.

It should be noted that the test in *Roberts* is not whether the victim acted reasonably, but whether the reaction was reasonably foreseeable. The significance of this distinction is that it is foreseeable that, put into an emergency situation, a victim may react irrationally. *Roberts* was approved by the Court of Appeal in *Williams and Davis*,[87] but with a slight modification of the test. It suggested the question for the jury in these kinds of cases was

whether the deceased's reaction in jumping from the moving car was within the range of responses which might be expected from a victim placed in the situation in which he was. The jury should bear in mind any particular characteristic of the victim and the fact that in the agony of the moment he may act without thought and deliberation.

In *Lewis*[88] the Court of Appeal suggested the jury could consider whether the victim's response 'might have been expected' as a result of the defendant's acts and if it was then it was caused by the defendant. *Roberts* was also followed in the Court of Appeal's decision in *Marjoram*,[89] which emphasized that when deciding whether the victim's reaction was reasonably foreseeable the question was whether the reaction was foreseeable to an ordinary person and not whether it was reasonably foreseeable to a person of the defendant's age and characteristics. →7 (p.124)

R v Blaue
[1975] 3 All ER 446 (CA)[90]

Robert Blaue stabbed Jacolyn Woodhead, piercing her lung. She was taken to hospital and was told that a blood transfusion was necessary. She refused to consent to the operation which was contrary to her beliefs as a Jehovah's Witness. She was told that without the transfusion she would die, but she stuck by her refusal and died the next day. The appellant was subsequently convicted of manslaughter, but appealed, arguing that the victim's refusal to have a blood transfusion broke the chain of causation between the stabbing and death.

---

[87] [1992] 2 All ER 183 (CA).   [88] [2010] EWCA Crim 151.
[89] *Marjoram* [2000] Crim LR 372 (CA).   [90] [1975] 1 WLR 1411, (1975) 61 Cr App R 271.

Lord Justice Lawton

The physical cause of death in this case was the bleeding into the pleural cavity arising from the penetration of the lung. This had not been brought about by any decision made by the deceased girl but by the stab wound.

Counsel for the appellant tried to overcome this line of reasoning by submitting that the jury should have been directed that if they thought the girl's decision not to have a blood transfusion was an unreasonable one, then the chain of causation would have been broken. At once the question arises—reasonable by whose standards? Those of Jehovah's Witnesses? Humanists? Roman Catholics? Protestants of Anglo-Saxon descent? The man on the Clapham omnibus? But he might well be an admirer of Eleazar who suffered death rather than eat the flesh of swine (See 2 Maccabees, ch 6, vv 18–31) or of Sir Thomas Moore who, unlike nearly all his contemporaries, was unwilling to accept Henry VIII as Head of the Church in England. Those brought up in the Hebraic and Christian traditions would probably be reluctant to accept that these martyrs caused their own deaths.

As was pointed out to counsel for the appellant in the course of argument, two cases, each raising the same issue of reasonableness because of religious beliefs, could produce different verdicts depending on where the cases were tried. A jury drawn from Preston, sometimes said to be the most Catholic town in England, might have different views about martyrdom to one drawn from the inner suburbs of London. Counsel for the appellant accepted that this might be so; it was, he said, inherent in trial by jury. It is not inherent in the common law as expounded by Sir Matthew Hale and Maule J. It has long been the policy of the law that those who use violence on other people must take their victims as they find them. This in our judgment means the whole man, not just the physical man. It does not lie in the mouth of the assailant to say that his victim's religious beliefs which inhibited him from accepting certain kinds of treatment were unreasonable. The question for decision is what caused her death. The answer is the stab wound. The fact that the victim refused to stop this end coming about did not break the causal connection between the act and death.

Appeal dismissed.

At first sight these two cases seem to be offering different tests. The *Blaue* decision focuses on the rule that defendants must take their victims as they find them, whatever their peculiarities. This is an application of the 'thin skull' rule, which will be discussed in Section 3.6.[91] The *Roberts* decision focuses on whether the victim's response was reasonably foreseeable. The two tests are quite different. Had the *Roberts* test been applied in the *Blaue* decision it might have been decided that it was not reasonably foreseeable that the victim would be a Jehovah's Witness and refuse a blood transfusion. Although the cases appear to conflict, commentators have suggested a number of ways to reconcile them:

(1) The crucial fact in the *Blaue* decision was that the victim's act was in effect an omission. She failed to consent to the blood transfusion. By contrast, in *Roberts* the victim acted by jumping out of the car. This interpretation suggests that the *Blaue* rule is that an omission of the victim will not break the chain of causation, whereas the *Roberts* rule explains that the act of a victim might, if the act was unforeseeable or 'daft'. Such a position could be readily justified because it would fit in well with the criminal law's general approach of not attaching causal significance to omissions. Indeed the courts have consistently held that a victim who is injured

---

[91] *Martin* (1832) 5 C & P 128. For a case where the victim actually had a thin skull, see *Simpson* [2002] EWCA Crim 25.

by a defendant, but decides not to seek medical treatment and dies, will be found to have been killed by the defendant.[92] After all, if the victim neglects the injury and dies, what else does the victim die from, but the injury inflicted by the defendant? Although there is much to be said in favour of this argument, based on whether the victim performs an act or an omission, it must be admitted that it is not one that is made explicit by the courts themselves.

(2) It might be argued that there is no conflict between the two approaches given the modification of the *Roberts* test in *Williams and Davis* which required the jury to consider whether the response was reasonably foreseeable, *given the victim's characteristics*. In *Blaue* it was reasonably foreseeable that a victim with the characteristic of being a Jehovah's Witness would refuse a blood transfusion. The difficulty with such a test is that it could be argued that it will always be satisfied. In *Corbett*[93] it was held that the victim's conduct in running away and falling in front of a car was foreseeable, given that the victim was 'immensely drunk'. Further, if that was the correct interpretation then the Court of Appeal in *Blaue* should have considered whether the victim acted as a reasonable Jehovah's Witness. But, they never asked that question.

(3) It may be argued *Blaue* was a special case which was in fact about freedom of religion. The argument could be that normally the jury should consider whether the victim's response was reasonably foreseeable, but that the court was unwilling to ask that question in *Blaue* because that might require the jury to consider whether the exercise of a religious belief was unreasonable.

A more recent rather problematic decision which is not readily reconcilable with either *Roberts* or *Blaue* is *Dear*,[94] where the victim was stabbed by the defendant. The victim died from the wounds, although it was unclear whether the victim had reopened the wounds himself. With a minimum of discussion of the legal issues, the Court of Appeal held that the jury was entitled to find that, even if the victim had deliberately reopened the wounds, the defendant's actions could be found to have been an operating and substantial cause of the victim's death. The point is that the victim had died from the blood seeping from the very wounds inflicted by the defendant.

In *Dhaliwal*[95] the Court of Appeal appeared willing to accept that a husband who had been continually abusive to his wife had caused her to commit suicide. The outcome of the case turned on other issues (see Chapter 5), and there was little discussion of the causation issue. It might be argued that subjecting someone to a lengthy campaign of abuse in an intimate relationship could foreseeably cause the victim to commit suicide. Another argument is that 'the destructive effect domestic abuse has on the victim's autonomy can be regarded as rendering the defendant criminally responsible for the victim's suicide'.[96] In other words, the defendant, through the abuse, has made suicide something the victim was not truly free to avoid.

QUESTIONS

1. Marion slashes Steve's face with a knife. Steve is a vain model and is so distressed with the resulting scar that he commits suicide. Has Marion caused Steve's death? Consider how the cases of *Roberts*, *Blaue*, and *Dear* could be relevant to this case.

For guidance on answering this question, please visit the Online Resource Centre that accompanies this book: www.oxfordtextbooks.co.uk/orc/herringcriminal7e/.

---

[92] *Holland* (1841) 2 Mood & R 351.   [93] [1996] Crim LR 594.   [94] [1996] Crim LR 595.
[95] [2006] EWCA Crim 1139.   [96] Horder and McGowan (2006: 1042).

2. Timothy stabs Yvonne. When Yvonne gets to hospital she is converted to the faith of the Jehovah's Witnesses by a nurse and therefore refuses to consent to a blood transfusion which is needed to save her life. Yvonne dies. Has Timothy caused Yvonne's death?

3.6 THE 'THIN SKULL' RULE

The 'thin skull' rule states that defendants must take their victims as they find them. In other words, it is no defence for a defendant to say that the injuries or death were caused by the physical condition of the victim.[97] In *Hayward*[98] there was a violent argument between the defendant and his wife. Hayward chased his wife out of the house and she collapsed and died. The medical evidence suggested that the wife had an abnormal medical condition which meant that if she suffered fright or physical exertion she might die. Ridley J confirmed that the husband could be said to have caused the wife's death. The fact that the wife's death had resulted in part from her medical condition was irrelevant: the husband's act had caused her death. A less obvious application of the rule was *McKechnie*,[99] where, owing to the injuries inflicted by the defendant, the victim was not able to receive the medical treatment that he needed for an ulcer (which had nothing to do with the injuries caused by the defendant) and died as a result. It was held that the defendant had caused the victim's death. As we have seen in *Blaue*[100] the Court of Appeal said that under the thin skull rule the defendant must take the victim as the 'whole person'. This includes not only their physical characteristics, but also, in that case, their religious beliefs. The defendant will also have to take the victim with her own emotional and psychological condition. What is not clear is whether the thin skull rule can be extended to apply to cases where as a result of the injury inflicted by the defendant the victim acts in a way which causes a further harm. It is submitted that such an extension would be taking the thin skull rule too far and it is better to restrict it to cases where the victim does not do anything to make their condition worse.

3.7 A NATURAL EVENT ('ACTS OF GOD')

A natural event will not normally break the chain of causation. If the defendant injures the victim and leaves his or her body on the sea shore and the sea comes in and drowns the victim then the sea coming in does not break the chain of causation.[101] However, where there is a freak of nature this may break the chain of causation. Imagine that the defendant had injured the victim and left his body in a field, and a bolt of lightning struck and killed the victim. In such a case the bolt of lightning could constitute a break in the chain of causation because it would be an 'extraordinary' event. In *Gowans*[102] the defendant attacked the victim, putting him in a coma. The victim then caught a serious infection and died. As being in a coma had put the victim in an especially vulnerable state to any infections, it was held the defendant's act was an operating and substantial cause of the death. The infection could not be seen as an 'act of God' which broke the chain of causation.

---

[97] *Watson* [1989] 2 All ER 865 (CA).   [98] (1908) 21 Cox CC 692.
[99] (1992) 94 Cr App R 51 (CA).   [100] [1975] 3 All ER 446 (CA).
[101] In *Hart* [1986] 2 NZLR 408 the New Zealand Court of Appeal found the defendant guilty on similar facts.
[102] [2003] EWCA Crim 3935.

3.8 INTENDED RESULTS

Some commentators have suggested that if a defendant acts intending to produce a particular result and that result occurs then the defendant will automatically be found to have
caused that result.[103] It should be stressed that this would be true only if the 'but for test' was
satisfied. Mary could not be convicted of John's murder if he died shortly after she had stuck
pins into a voodoo doll of him, intending that this should lead to his death (assuming it cannot be proved that the voodoo caused the death!).

Despite some academic support for the proposition there is little case law on the point.
In *Michael*[104] the defendant wished her baby dead and so gave a bottle of poison to a nurse,
saying that it was medicine for the baby. The nurse placed the medicine on the mantel-
piece, unaware that it was poison. A 5-year-old child removed the poison and gave it to the
baby. Even though the turn of events was unexpected, the end result was what the defendant
wanted, and so she could be said to have caused it. However, the case can also be explained
on the basis that the actions of the nurse and child were not free, voluntary, and informed
actions and so could not be *novus actus interveniens*.

FURTHER READING

Cherkassky, L. (2008) '*Kennedy* and Unlawful Act Manslaughter: An Unorthodox
Application of the Doctrine of Causation' *Journal of Criminal Law* 387.

Elliot, C. and De Than, C. (2006) 'Prosecuting the Drug Dealer When a Drug User Dies:
R v Kennedy (No 2)' *Modern Law Review* 69: 986.

Hart, H. and Honoré, A. (1985) *Causation in the Law* (2nd edn, Oxford: OUP).

Shute, S. (1992) 'Causation: Foreseeability v Natural Consequences' *Modern Law
Review* 55: 584.

Williams, R. (2005a) 'Policy and Principle in Drugs Manslaughter Cases' *Cambridge
Law Journal* 64: 66.

Williams, R. (2005b) 'Drugs Manslaughter and Unorthodox Doctrine on Causation'
Cambridge Law Journal 64: 537.

PART II: *ACTUS REUS*: THEORY

4 CLASSIFICATION OF OFFENCES

As suggested at the start of this chapter, the most common way of analysing a criminal
offence is to divide it into three elements:[105]

(1) the *actus reus*,

(2) the *mens rea*,

(3) defences which the defendant may rely on.

---

[103] See the discussion in J.C. Smith (2002: 55).   [104] (1840) 9 C & P 356.
[105] e.g. Lanham (1976).

However, this is by no means the only way of separating out the elements of the offence. Andrew Ashworth, for example, uses four requirements:

(1) act and causation requirements,

(2) absence of justification,

(3) capacity and fault requirements, and

(4) excusatory defences.[106]

By contrast Glanville Williams argues that there are only two elements of an offence, the *actus reus* and *mens rea*.[107]

You may well be wondering whether it really matters very much how we divide up the elements of an offence and how we decide into which category a particular requirement falls.[108] Is this not just academics desperately trying to create a tidy picture of the criminal law? Well, there are both practical and theoretical benefits which some claim for such analysis.[109] Here are some: ←1 (p.72)

(1) **Evidential rules** Such divisions may assist when considering burdens of proof. As a very basic rule the prosecution must prove beyond reasonable doubt the *actus reus* and *mens rea*. However, the defendant has an evidential burden in relation to a defence.[110] Unfortunately there are exceptions to this. For example, a justification (e.g. self-defence) has been regarded by the courts as an element of the *actus reus*,[111] but the defendant carries the evidential burden in relation to the justification.

(2) **Substantive law** There are some occasions on which the substantive law requires attention to whether or not the *actus reus* of the crime has occurred. For example, strict liability offences require proof of the *actus reus*, but not the *mens rea*.

(3) **Theory** It can be claimed that the distinction between *actus reus* and *mens rea* assists in theoretical analysis of offences in that it separates the issues: what is the wrong with which this offence is concerned (the *actus reus* question) and when will the defendant be held sufficiently blameworthy for the offence (the *mens rea* question). Several commentators have objected to this kind of reasoning and claimed that the wrong done to the victim sometimes depends on the state of mind with which an act is done. Antony Duff[112] gives an example: 'Robbery is not just a physical attack or threat, *plus* theft: the character of the attack or the threat as a particular kind of wrong is determined in crucial part by the fact that it is made in order to steal.' In his view, then, the definition of the wrong done to the victim can include elements of both the *actus reus* and *mens rea*.

---

[106] Ashworth (2009: 85).

[107] G. Williams (1961: 20) argues that defences are included in the meaning of the *actus reus*. By contrast Kadish (1968) claims that the *mens rea* involves blameworthiness and therefore includes both the required mental element and the absence of a defence.

[108] See the discussion in P. Robinson (1993).   [109] See Chiao (2014) for further discussion.

[110] i.e. the defendant must introduce some evidence in support of the defence. If he or she does so then the prosecution must prove beyond reasonable doubt that the defendant does not have the defence.

[111] *Williams (Gladstone)* [1987] 3 All ER 411 (CA).   [112] Duff (2002: 59).

FURTHER READING

Robinson, P. (1993) 'Should the Criminal Law Abandon the *Actus Reus/Mens Rea* Distinction?' in S. Shute, J. Gardner, and J. Horder (eds) *Action and Value in Criminal Law* (Oxford: OUP).

Robinson, P. (1997) *Structure and Function in Criminal Law* (Oxford: OUP).

Smith, A. (1978) 'On *Actus Reus* and *Mens Rea*' in P. Glazebrook (ed.) *Reshaping the Criminal Law* (London: Sweet & Maxwell).

5   THE NEED FOR A VOLUNTARY ACT

Contrast these two examples:

(1)   Alfred was a mathematician and was so taken up with considering a novel algebraic problem that he did not look where he was going when he bumped into Beth, who then fell over.

(2)   Chau was walking along when he was pushed from behind by Danielle, causing him to bump into Edith, who also fell over.

In both cases Alfred and Chau did not intend to bump into anyone. But there is an important difference between the cases. Although we can say that Alfred's acts caused Beth to fall over in case 1, it is not clear that Chau acted at all. Indeed Danielle was the one who acted and Chau was more like an object than a person.[113] Something was done *to him*, rather than something being done *by him*.[114] This distinction is reflected in legal terms by the fact that Alfred would be found not guilty because he lacked *mens rea* (he was not acting intentionally or recklessly), while Chau would be found not guilty on the basis that he did not commit the *actus reus* (he did not do anything).

As mentioned in Part I, it is often stated that a defendant can be convicted of a crime only if he or she has performed a voluntary act. But why might the law have such a requirement?

5.1   WHY MIGHT THE LAW HAVE A VOLUNTARY ACT REQUIREMENT?

One reason the law may require an act is the argument that the criminal law should not punish evil thoughts alone. But why not? Several reasons could be advanced for this:[115]

(1)   Those who fantasize about crime have not done anything which is sufficiently harmful to society to justify criminalization. We do not punish people for being bad, but for doing bad things.[116]

---

[113] Hart (1968: 91–2).

[114] See Finkelstein (2002a) for a discussion of defendants who voluntarily put themselves in a position where they act involuntarily.

[115] P. Robinson (1993) usefully summarizes the debate.   [116] M. Moore (1993: 51).

(2) There would be enormous difficulties of proof if an offence were directed towards the thoughts of the defendant alone. Requiring an act lessens the chance of a wrongful conviction by demanding some outward manifestation of the wrongful thoughts.

(3) The requirement limits government power. Punishing people for their thoughts is normally associated with the most authoritarian of governments and is too open to manipulation by corrupt governments or officials who wish to punish those they perceive to be a threat to their power.[117]

Why must the act be voluntary? As indicated in our consideration of Alfred and Chau, an involuntary action is one for which not only is the defendant not responsible, it is not even properly described as *his* act. It would clearly be unjust to punish a defendant for something he could not have avoided 'doing', even if he had tried his best.

5.2 WHAT IS THE 'VOLUNTARY ACT REQUIREMENT'?

The obvious meaning of the requirement is that any offence must involve proof that the defendant did something. But Donald Husak has argued that the requirement must mean more than that. His point is that an offence of 'thinking evil thoughts while knitting' is objectionable even though it involves proof of an act (namely knitting). The offence is still objectionable because it is the evil thoughts and not the act of knitting which the offence is actually seeking to prevent. Hence Husak argues that criminal liability must be imposed '*for* an act'.[118] ←2 (p.73)

To understand the requirement further we need to consider what we mean by a 'voluntary act'.

The traditional view: acts as 'willed voluntary movements'

The traditional view is that actions are 'willed bodily movements'.[119] Although the traditional view has in recent years rather fallen into disrespect, interest in it has been revitalized by an impressive and complex book in support, namely *Act and Crime* by Michael Moore.[120] In this passage, he summarizes the traditional view:

M. Moore, *Act and Crime* (Oxford: OUP, 1993), 44–6

1. Preliminary Overview of the Act Requirement

As I would unpack it, there are four theses to this theory, as it was propounded by Bentham, (John) Austin, Holmes, and Walter Cook, and carried on into our own time by the American Law Institute's Model Penal Code. The four theses are as follows. First, what I shall call the identity thesis holds that the acts required for criminal liability are partially identical to events of a certain kind, namely, bodily movements like moving one's finger or tongue. Such bodily movements on which the act requirement focuses are the simplest things one knows how to do as a means to achieving some end. Raising one's arm, for example, is usually such a

---

[117] In *Robinson v California* 370 US 660 (1962) the US Supreme Court held that a criminal offence of being addicted to drugs infringed the American constitution.

[118] Husak (1995a). [119] M. Moore (1993: 28).

[120] M. Moore (1993). See also M. Moore (1994 and 1997), who places his theories of acts in a wider context.

simple act because one doesn't do (or know how to do) some even more simple act in order to do it. If, however, one raises one's arm by moving one's foot on a pulley arrangement attached to the arm, then raising the arm on that occasion is not the act focused on by the act requirement of criminal law. *A fortiori*, if one's raising one's arm on some occasion is to signal the start of a race, so that in moving one's arm one was starting a race, the latter act is also not the act focused on by the criminal law's act requirement; for starting a race is far removed from the simplest act one knows how to do.

Secondly, the only acts that exist are the simple acts on which the act requirement focuses. Although there are complex acts of killing, hitting, scaring, telephoning, and the like, and although criminal codes invariably use these complex action descriptions in their substantive prohibitions, these acts in reality are never anything but some acts of bodily movement. I shall call this the exclusivity thesis.

Thirdly, not just any bodily movements (that are the simplest things one knows how to do) are acts satisfying the act requirement. A reflex movement of the leg, for example, is not an act no matter how identical it is behaviourally to simple leg movements that are acts. Thus, the third thesis—what I shall call the mental cause thesis—requires that such bodily movements must be caused by a certain mental event or state. Such event or state is variously styled as an act of willing, a volition, a desire, a simple intention, or a choice. Because all of these ordinary expressions have connotations inappropriate to this third thesis when it is most favourably construed, I shall use the least ordinary of the terms, 'volition'.

The three theses thus far, taken together, assert that the criminal law's act requirement requires that there be a simple bodily movement that is caused by a volition before criminal liability attaches, and that such a movement is all the action a person ever performs. This is the positive core of the orthodox view of the criminal law's act requirement. The fourth thesis seeks to accommodate this univocal act requirement of the general part of the criminal law to the multiple, complex action descriptions used in the various prohibitions of the special part. Statutes almost never use simple action descriptions like 'moving one's finger'; they prohibit actions described as 'starting a race without a permit', 'killing', 'disfiguring', 'removing another's property', etc. For the act requirement just described to fit the criminal law as we know it, something must be said about how such diverse, complex action prohibitions are related to the univocal, simple act requirement. This is the burden of the fourth thesis.

This thesis asserts that any complex action description used in the special part of the criminal law is equivalent to (and thus can be replaced by) a description of some simple act (as defined above) of the accused causing a prohibited state of affairs. Murder statutes prohibit the complex action of killing another, for example. The fourth thesis—what I shall call the equivalence thesis—asserts that such a prohibition is equivalent to a prohibition that forbids 'any simple act that causes the death of another'.

Three objections to that traditional view will now be summarized:

(1) Defining an act as a willed voluntary movement can produce an artificial view of the world.[121] It would describe as 'moving a hand to the right' both a person doing an aerobic exercise and a person punching another. In other words by describing an action simply in terms of what movement was done without considering the context or consequences of that movement gives a misleading (or at least not very useful) description of what was done.[122] Indeed in our day-to-day lives we understand ourselves to be doing certain activities; for

---

[121] Husak (1995a) suggests that although the traditional view may have some merit for the purpose of philosophical discussion, it is not a useful one for criminal lawyers.

[122] Shapira (1998).

example, eating, walking, or talking; and not doing the separate bodily movements that make up those activities.[123]

In reply to such arguments, Moore[124] has suggested that his definition of an act describes what it is in our power to do. I can intend to move my arm to the left; whether it hits the person next to me is not something over which I have direct control. Therefore, we should not, he insists, include consequences in the definition of an action.

(2) A second objection is that the traditional view would not answer the point that people sometimes act on 'automatic pilot' when engaging in some routine act (e.g. shaving or eating) where it would be artificial to talk about such acts being willed. But it might be said that in such cases there is an 'unconscious will'[125] which is operating or that such actions *could have been* guided by decisions of the actor if he or she had wished, even if in fact they were not.[126]

(3) It can be argued that the traditional definition of an act may be too narrow, in that it excludes some omissions which would be quite properly described as 'acts'. Consider a meeting at which it was said that if anyone objected to a proposal they should raise their hand and everyone remained still. It would then be generally accepted that by not raising their hands those attending were supporting the motion, even if they had not moved: their non-movement would be regarded as an act of support for the motion.[127] Yet Moore, in requiring a movement, would say that they had not acted.

Alternatives to the traditional view

If we decide that the traditional view of the voluntary act requirement is not accepted, what alternatives are there? The most popular has become known as 'the control principle': that it would be unjust to impose criminal liability for a state of affairs over which the defendant had no control.[128] Although Susan Dimock has preferred the 'agency principle'—'that liability be imposed for conduct that is expressive of the defendant's agency'[129]—she is willing to accept that a person may have no control over their behaviour, but have chosen to put themselves into that position (e.g. through intoxication). In such a case their behaviour may express their agency, even if uncontrolled.

In the following passage, Andrew Simester summarizes the 'control principle' and then considers some of its practical implications. Notice that the 'control principle' makes it far easier to punish omissions than the 'voluntary act requirement' does:[130]

A.P. Simester, 'On the So-called Requirement for Voluntary Action' (1998) 1 *Buffalo Criminal Law Review* 403 at 414–18

The indispensable minimum, then, is to establish that D is responsible for the explicit or implicit behavior element of the actus reus, regardless of whether the behavior is named as

---

[123] Hart (1968).   [124] M. Moore (1994).

[125] Fletcher (1978: 434–9) is willing to include within the definition of a voluntary act defendants who have a conscious or subconscious reason for acting as they did.

[126] Duff and von Hirsch (1997).

[127] Some supporters of the traditional view argue that flexing muscles to stay still (e.g. a gymnast holding a position) can be regarded as movements.

[128] Husak (1999b); Simester (1998).   [129] Dimock (2012).

[130] Note, however, the argument in J. Gardner (1994b: 499) that the voluntary act requirement and the issue of whether liability should attach to omissions should be seen as quite distinct.

an act or omission, and of whether D was an agent in respect of that behavior. This requirement is met when D's behavior is voluntary. Recall our opening case scenario. [One fine September morning, Jim is discovered dead in his home. His skull has been crushed by a blow inflicted with a heavy object. The police are called. Upon further investigation, they establish that he was murdered by his daughter, Alice, who killed him in order to receive her inheritance under his will.] Suppose that Alice did in fact cause Jim's death, but that she did so while suffering an epileptic seizure, during which her movements caused a heavy object to fall and crush Jim. Alice's behavior, which causes Jim's death, is not voluntary. She is not morally responsible for his death, and cannot be convicted of murder.

Very often, acquittal in these circumstances need not be based upon involuntariness. Crimes such as murder require proof of some form of mens rea on the part of the defendant. In most jurisdictions, murder itself cannot be committed unless D intends or is reckless about the victim's death. Thus, even though Alice's behavior may have caused death, she lacks the mental element required to be guilty of murder.

But involuntariness is not merely a denial of intention, or of other forms of mens rea, or even a denial of fault in general. Alice does not claim that she killed Jim by accident. Her denial is much more profound. It is a claim that the movements of her body which caused Jim's death do not belong to Alice as a reasoning person.

As part of our conception of what it is to be a human being, we draw a distinction between a deliberative or reasoning person and her body. Not all movements of one's body can be identified with the person whose body it is that moves. When the doctor tests Simon's reflexes by tapping him on the knee, the swinging of his leg cannot be attributed to Simon. It is merely an event in the history of his body, rather like the lurching of passengers standing in a crowded bus. These are not actions that a person is answerable for doing; they are things that happen to him, over which he has no control, and for which he is not responsible. So it is with Alice. Her behavior is part of her body's history, but is not traceable to her as a reasoning person. It is not produced by any exercise of the capacities which mark Alice out as a moral agent. In the words of H.L.A. Hart:

> 'What is missing in these cases appears to most people as a vital link between mind and body; and both the ordinary man and the lawyer might well insist on this by saying that in these cases there is not "really" a human action at all and certainly nothing for which anyone should be made criminally responsible however "strict" legal responsibility may be.'

QUESTIONS

1. Is it wrong to assume that an act is either voluntary or involuntary? Would it be better to accept that there is a scale of voluntariness? Would doing so render the law too uncertain? (See Denno (2002).)

2. Is it possible to distinguish 'moral voluntariness' (where a defendant is under intense moral pressure, e.g. duress) and 'physical voluntariness' (where a defendant is physically unable to act otherwise than he did)? (See Norrie (2002: ch. 6).)

FURTHER READING

Hart, H. (1968) 'Acts of Will and Responsibility' in H. Hart, *Punishment and Responsibility: Essays in the Philosophy of Law* (Oxford: OUP).

Husak, D. (1999b) 'Does Criminal Liability Require an Act?' in R.A. Duff (ed.) *Philosophy and the Criminal Law* (Cambridge: Cambridge University Press).

Moore, M. (1993) *Act and Crime* (Oxford: OUP).

Moore, M. (2009) *Causation and Responsibility: An Essay in Law, Morals, and Metaphysics* (Oxford: OUP).

Simester, A. (1998) 'On the So-called Requirement for Voluntary Action' *Buffalo Criminal Law Review* 1: 403.

6 OMISSIONS

As we saw in Part I of this chapter, the criminal law is generally reluctant to impose criminal liability on a defendant who failed to act. It will do so only if there is a legal duty on the defendant to act.

6.1 SHOULD THE CRIMINAL LAW PUNISH OMISSIONS?

Despite the bitter arguments over the punishment of omissions, in fact there is less disagreement than appears at first sight. Few people suggest that we should be guilty for every omission, nor do many suggest that omissions should never be punished.[131] The debate is really over which omissions should be punished. ←3 (p.74)

Arguments against criminalizing omissions

It is argued by some that it cannot be said that an omission causes a result.[132] If a person walks past a drowning child in a pond can it be said that that person caused the child's death? Using but for causation it can be argued that had the defendant not been there the child would still have died at the same time and in the same place. The omission failed to alter the status quo. Further it could be argued that the person's failure to save the child was as significant as anyone else's failure to rescue. Another point is that it is often difficult to know for sure what would have happened if the defendant had acted. Even if he had tried to save the drowning child he may not have been able to.[133]

Those who support liability for omission have struggled to overcome this argument. Hart and Honoré[134] explain that omissions liability can be supported by their distinction between normal and abnormal events (discussed further in Section 8.2). They suggest that if someone is under a duty to act and fails to do so this will be regarded as 'abnormal' and hence a cause of the result. For example, if several people walk past a child drowning in the pond, including the child's father, the fact that the father is under a duty to save the child in English law means that it is abnormal for him to walk past, while it would be 'normal' for others to walk past. This explanation is, however, problematic. It concerns an ambiguity over the meaning of 'normal'. If 'normal' means that an action is statistically likely, it is far from clear that statistically it is abnormal for people to help children in peril.[135] If normal means what

---

[131] e.g. even Michael Moore (1993: 32), who is generally reluctant to punish omissions, accepts that a parent who fails to feed his or her child deserves to be convicted.

[132] M. Moore (1993: 267). [133] W. Wilson (2010). [134] Hart and Honoré (1995: 31–2).

[135] Benyon (1987).

'ought' to occur then the argument simply becomes that people are punished for omissions because they ought to be.[136]

It is crucial to realize that this causation argument is not a 'knockout argument' for those who do not wish to punish omissions. The argument is simply stating that one cannot sensibly argue that an omission causes a result. That does not mean that the law cannot seek to punish omissions. The causation argument could not be used against a statute which stated that it was a criminal offence not to offer aid to someone you could reasonably be expected to help. Such a statute does not claim that the omission has caused anything—it punishes for the failure to act itself. In the following extract, Joshua Dressler considers such laws, which are often known as 'Bad Samaritan laws'.[137] You should note that in this passage 'BS laws' is Dressler's (rather unfortunate!) abbreviation for Bad Samaritan laws:[138]

J. Dressler, 'Some Brief Thoughts (Mostly Negative) about "Bad Samaritan" Laws' [2000] *Santa Clara Law Review* 971 at 981–9

2. Refuting the Justifications for Bad Samaritan Laws

. . .

Criticisms of BS laws begin with legalist concerns with retributive overtones. First, why is the offense called a 'Bad Samaritan' law? The name suggests, I think, that we punish the bystander for being a bad person, i.e., for his 'selfishness, callousness, or whatever it was' that caused him not to come to the aid of a person in need. However, the criminal law should not be (and, ordinarily, is not) used that way: criminal law punishes individuals for their culpable acts (or, perhaps here, culpable non-acts), but not generally for bad character. As mortals, we lack the capacity to evaluate another's soul. It is wrongful conduct, and not an individual's status as a bad person or even an individual's bad thoughts, that justify criminal intervention. BS laws may violate this principle. At a minimum, there is a serious risk that juries will inadvertently punish people for being (or seeming to be) evil or 'soulless,' rather than for what occurred on a specific occasion. One need only consider David Cash and the public's intense feelings of disgust and anger toward him to appreciate why jurors might convict Bad Samaritans less on the basis of the 'technicalities' of a statute, and more on the basis of character evaluation.

Second, for retributivists, punishment of an innocent person is always morally wrong, and the risk of false positives—punishing an innocent person—is especially high with BS laws. Consider, for example, the Vermont BS law. To be guilty of this crime the bystander must 'know' that another is at risk of 'grave physical harm,' and must give 'reasonable assistance' if he can do so 'without danger or peril to himself.' If any one of these elements is lacking, the bystander is innocent and, therefore, in a society committed to the principle of legality, does not deserve punishment.

Notice the inherent problem of punishing people for not-doings rather than wrongdoings. When a person points a loaded gun at another and intentionally pulls the trigger, it is reasonable to infer that the actor intended to cause harm. His *mens rea* is obvious. It is far harder to

---

[136] See M. Smith (2001) for further argument.

[137] The reference is to the parable of the Good Samaritan found in the *Bible* (Luke 10:30–7) in which two people walked past a man who had been mugged and left for dead, but the Good Samaritan stopped to help him.

[138] Dingwall and Gillespie (2008).

determine why a person does not act. Return to the Bystander and Blind Person example. The facts stated that Bystander knew what was going on and wanted harm to occur. In the real world, however, it would be exceedingly difficult to reliably determine Bystander's potential guilt. How do we know Bystander realized what was about to happen? Did he see BP? Did he realize BP was about to walk into the street? Did Bystander see the truck? Did he realize the truck driver was not paying attention? Beyond that, why did Bystander not act? Maybe he froze up, maybe he didn't think fast enough, or maybe (reasonably or unreasonably) he believed that helping BP would jeopardize his own safety.

For that matter, why did the Genovese bystanders[139] hear the woman scream but fail to act, if in fact that was the case? Is it at least possible that some of the bystanders did not know she was in dire jeopardy? A person who wakes up from a sleep often fails to appreciate her surroundings. Also, perhaps some of them—even all of them—believed that someone else had already called the police. It may be that, despite the condemnation directed at the Genovese bystanders, few, if any, of them were guilty of Bad Samaritanism. In view of the inherent ambiguities in such circumstances, if juries take their duties seriously—including the presumption of innocence—few, if any, BS convictions will result. If emotions and bad character attributions rule the day, however, innocent persons will be improperly convicted.

Third, the threat of convicting innocent persons points to a related danger. BS statutes are so rubbery in their drafting that they grant police and prosecutors too much discretion to determine whether and whom to prosecute. The due process clause prohibits the enforcement of penal laws that 'fail to establish guidelines to prevent "arbitrary and discriminatory enforcement" of the law.' However, even if the issue is seen as a non-constitutional matter, it is difficult to see how a prosecutor can fairly determine when charges are proper.

Again, the distinction between actions and non-actions demonstrates the vagueness problem. BS laws compel people to make the world (or, at least, a small part of it) better, rather than punish actors for actively making it worse. In the latter case, the identifiable conduct of the accused, and the demonstrable harm caused by those actions, serve to single out the actor as a plausible candidate for prosecution. With laws that punish for nothing, rather than something, there is a need for alternative objective criteria. At least with commission-by-omission liability, there are identifiable criteria, such as the status relationship of the parties, contractual understandings, or the suspect's personal connection to the emergency by having created the initial risk. In contrast, with BS laws, which impose a duty to aid strangers (potentially, anyone), criminal responsibility is based on imprecise factors (e.g. the duty to provide 'reasonable assistance') and nearly unknowable circumstances (e.g. that the stranger is exposed to 'grave' physical harm, and that assistance can be rendered without any 'danger or peril' to the actor or others).

As the Genovese case demonstrates, these omission criteria are far less helpful in determining whether and against whom a prosecution should be initiated than are identifiable acts of commission. There is a significant risk with BS laws that the decision to prosecute will be based on a prosecutor's perceived need to respond to public outrage, which in turn, may be based less on the merits of the case and more on media coverage (which, in turn, may be founded on inappropriate factors, such as race, background, or even the physical

---

[139] The reference is to the following incident referred to earlier in the article: 'Kitty Genovese—a young Queens, New York woman—cried for help for more than half an hour outside an apartment building as her assailant attacked her, fled, and then returned to kill her. According to reports at the time, as many as thirty-eight persons heard her pleas from the safety of their residences, but did nothing to help her.'

attractiveness of the victim and/or the supposed poor character of the bystander). Not only may persons guilty of Bad Samaritanism avoid conviction because of selective enforcement, but the process may result in prosecution of persons who, upon cooler reflection, we might realize are innocent of wrongful not-doing.

There are also utilitarian reasons to question the wisdom of BS legislation. First, if such laws are taken seriously, the costs of investigating and potentially prosecuting bystanders might be prohibitive. Imagine the investigation necessary to decide whether to prosecute any of the Genovese bystanders and, if the decision were to proceed, to determine which of them to prosecute. Second, to the extent that BS statutes are narrowly drafted to reduce the risk of unfairness, prosecutions are likely to be rare (and convictions even rarer). Therefore, it is unlikely that the threat of punishment will have the desired effect of inducing bystanders to help persons in peril. The muted threat of a misdemeanor conviction is less likely to promote good behavior than the threat of public scorn that follows the publicity of such cases, or a Samaritan's own conscience.

Third, to the extent that such laws do, in fact, compel 'Good Samaritanism,' there is a risk that the Samaritan will hurt the person she is trying to assist, hurt others in the process, or unforeseeably harm herself. Fourth, since BS statutes are not linked to any prevention-of-harm causal requirement (i.e., it is not necessary to successfully prevent the threatened harm from occurring; it is enough to give it 'the old college try'), the costs of such laws may easily outweigh their limited practical benefits. Even supporters of BS legislation concede that the law only helps at the boundaries.

There is one final reason to question the wisdom of BS statutes. Not only are positive duties morally less powerful than negative ones, but they also restrict human liberty to a greater degree. A penal law that prohibits a person from doing X (e.g. unjustifiably killing another person) permits that individual to do anything other than X (assuming no other negative duty). In contrast, a law that requires a person to do Y (e.g. help a bystander) bars that person from doing anything other than Y. The edict that 'no student may laugh aloud at a fellow student's silly answers to a professor's questions' only marginally restricts a student's autonomy—she can silently laugh at her colleague, sleep through the answer, or walk out of the room to protest the student's stupidity, just to name a few examples. However, a rule requiring a student to 'provide reasonable assistance to a fellow student in jeopardy of offering a silly answer to a professor's question,' not only is less precise, but also prevents students from doing anything other than help.

Arguments in favour of punishing omissions

There are two main arguments in favour of punishing omissions. The first is that the line between an act and an omission is too fine a line on which to place any great weight. Consider a person who drops a vase: is this an act ('dropping the vase') or an omission ('not holding on to it')? We saw in Part I of this chapter that this argument has received some judicial support.[140] In reply those who support the distinction accept that cases on the borderline are complex, but that is often true when one seeks to draw a distinction between two concepts. They argue that the distinction is a basic one in morality: taking food away from a starving person is not the same as failing to provide food to such a person. To these kinds of arguments William Wilson has replied: 'What is morally worse/causally more significant: shooting a child to prevent the agony of her burning to

---

[140] e.g. Lord Mustill in *Bland* [1993] AC 789.

death in a flaming inferno one is powerless to prevent, or failing to save a similar child from a similar fate by the simple mechanism of unlocking the door behind which she is trapped?'[141]

The second argument in favour of punishing omissions is based on the concept of social responsibility. This draws attention to the need for cooperation in social life. Ashworth and Horder explain the principle further in this passage:[142]

A. Ashworth and J. Horder, *Principles of Criminal Law* (7th edn, Oxford: OUP, 2013) 54–5

[The social responsibility principle] adopts the welfare-based proposition that society requires a certain level of co-operation and mutual assistance between citizens. There are powerful arguments of welfare which support certain duties to act to protect others in dire situations. Many other European countries criminalize the failure to render assistance to another citizen who is in peril, so long as that assistance can be given without danger to oneself. Three arguments are often raised against such 'extensions' of the criminal law. First, it is objected that it will inevitably be unclear what is expected of the citizen: such laws often use the word 'reasonable', and this fails to give fair warning of what would be done and when. A second and consequential objection is that the exercise of prosecutorial discretion then becomes a major determinant of criminal liability. This may be criticized as weakening the rule of law, by transferring effective power to officials. Thirdly, it is argued that omissions liability calls for much greater justification than the imposition of liability for acts. It is said that this reflects a widely felt moral distinction: 'we do much more wrong when we kill than when we fail to save, even when such a failure violates a positive duty to prevent death.' But even if there is such a distinction, it would only establish that omissions are viewed less seriously than acts, not that they are unsuitable for criminalization—and research into public attitudes suggests otherwise. So long as proper attention is paid to 'rule of law' protections such as the principle of fair warning, there may be good arguments for criminal liability for omissions, but the requirements of and boundaries of omissions liability need further debate and elucidation.

The recognition of some social duties is therefore essential if all individuals are to have a proper capacity for autonomy, and further the imposition of duties backed up by the criminal sanction may be justifiable to safeguard vital interests (such as life and physical integrity), if this can be done without risk or hardship to the citizen. This principle of social responsibility would therefore support, for example, an offence of failing to render assistance to a citizen in peril, where that assistance can be accomplished without danger to the rescuer. The critical element here is the danger to human life and the (qualified) duty to take certain action: it is not a prescription for making all citizens into their fellow citizens' keepers, nor need it render D liable for all the consequences.

In the following passage Neil Cobb warns of the assumptions that can underpin the current law on liability for omission. He critically examines the decision of *Stone and Dobinson*.[143]
←4 (p.77)

---

[141] W. Wilson (2003: 81).

[142] For the arguments against Ashworth's views, see G. Williams (1991a). See Ashworth (2013) for a fuller explanation.

[143] [1977] QB 354 (CA).

N. Cobb, 'Compulsory Care-giving: Some Thoughts on Relational Feminism, the Ethics of Care and Omissions Liability' (2008) 39 *Cambrian Law Review* 11 at 21–4

(a) "Special" relationships of care: judging motherhood

Perhaps the most well-established omission duties derive from the special set of obligations imposed by the criminal law upon particular human relationships. These status relationships are clearly signifiers of law's own hierarchy of the responsibilities human beings owe to one another. Intrinsic relationships of care-giving are those founded upon conjugality between spouses, the dependency of a child upon his or her parent and other proximate blood relationships. To a certain extent, this approach to compulsory care-giving must pose difficulties for some feminists. Considered against the backdrop of the refusal to impose duties towards strangers, these rules reinforce a traditional normative model of kinship and interdependency organised around conjugality and blood ties. In turn, they provide another reminder of the historic heteronormative preoccupations of the common law.

On the other hand, one might expect relational feminists to support the significance given here to the care of children. Recognition of the value of the nurturing of the young, and the depth of the interrelationship between mother and child, is central to relational theories. As noted earlier, many such scholars derived their ethical framework from the practical reality of women's care-giving arising from their role as mothers. For instance, Martha Fineman proposes a normative hierarchy of care-giving that places the mother-child dyad at the heart of care. One might conclude, then, that at the very least the criminal law's claim about the intrinsic responsibilities of care-giving incumbent on a parent is indisputable from a feminist relational perspective. Yet what must still remain troubling for feminists in this context is the role of judgement intrinsic to a disciplinary, and materially punitive, system like the criminal law, and how invariably this judgement has gendered implications.

Moral judgment by the legal system upon child-rearing is likely to affect women disproportionately because they remain predominantly responsible for the care of young people. One of the classic liberal arguments against omissions duties is that, unlike offences of action defined clearly in terms of the prohibited behaviour, the criminal law provides no guide to the steps required to satisfy their duties of care-giving. Yet there is unlikely to exist the same jurisprudential concern about lack of clarity in the context of parenting, as caring duties of parenthood tend to be presented as self-evident. More particularly, contemporary discourses tend to glorify motherhood. Society continues to shore up powerful standards upon women and this gives rise to the general concern that an ethics of care, when associated with women specifically, has dangerous implications. Indeed, this fear seems to be borne out by the recent spate of 'failure to protect' statutes. The reality of many women's lived experiences, in which harm to children in contexts of domestic violence by violent male partners, seems to carry little weight in the face of an apparent expectation that mothers can and should do everything in their power to protect their children from harm. Moreover, the process of punishment of mothers in contexts of domestic violence also ensures discursive constructions that position mother and child in opposition to one another. In such circumstances, law fails to adequately recognise the extent to which punishment of the mother ultimately harms the child and that they are both the victims of the violence meted out most often by a man.

In light of these observations, the decision in *Stone and Dobinson* is perhaps revealing when considered again from a relational feminist perspective (as long as one remains aware of the provisos raised earlier about the contribution a single case can make to our conclusions about the care-giving experiences of women). Generally (and most obviously) what the decision seems to reinforce is the broader claim that women more often than not find themselves

primary care-givers in domestic relationships. Though the victim was Stone's blood relative it was Dobinson who took on all care-giving responsibilities. There is the suggestion of
even greater illustrative potential, however, when one considers the short paragraph, entirely
ignored by the Court of Appeal itself in reaching its judgment on the case, in which the leading judge describing in passing Dobinson's interrogation by the police:

> When asked, "You are a woman and you go into the bedroom. Your own common
> sense would tell you that she needed attention?" She is said to have replied "She
> never complained so I didn't bother."

The specific, explicit reference to Dobinson's sex, and the particular common sense of
caring apparently available to her as a woman, provides a fleeting glimpse, perhaps, of
deeper gendered conclusions about her conduct. In the context of care-giving there is
seemingly nothing more damning than a woman's inability (or refusal) to satisfy the social
expectations of her gender.

(b) Voluntary undertaking of responsibility: of choice and coercion

One might well conclude that the rule that an omissions duty will arise if a defendant has
voluntarily undertaken responsibility for another provides a more attractive model for compulsory care-giving than the imposed status offences. There are two components to the
justification for criminal liability in this context. First, in undertaking responsibility for another
you are identified as primary carer and, accordingly, others that might seek to take on caring
responsibilities would be deterred from interfering in the welfare of the dependent individual. Second, the requirement of voluntariness appears to reflect again the prioritisation
placed by the criminal law upon individual autonomy. Beyond the expectation of the law
that you care for those within the (constructed) family unit, care is entirely in your gift, to be
entered into in a quasi-contractual fashion. Drawing once more from my previous argument,
while responsibilities to others are subject, then, to the prior value of the individual, this
could in fact be viewed as necessary, in certain circumstances, to enable the realisation of
prior care-giving responsibilities. Rather than treating such an approach as an indication of a
selfish legal order it might be seen instead to provide individuals with a space within which
they can ensure that they satisfy their responsibilities to those dependent upon them. If one
wishes to care for another then one should be able to take on that responsibility voluntarily,
bringing oneself within the ambit of the criminal law.

Yet I am also concerned by the broader implications of the notion of a voluntary undertaking of responsibility. Underpinning the interpretation of the duty as I have presented it here
is a construction of care-giving that appears once again to be based upon a masculine model
of care. Voluntary undertaking of responsibility for others as an ethical basis for criminal
liability, because one has actively claimed a duty for another's care, assumes that individuals are empowered to negotiate these responsibilities freely. However, as noted above, the
experience of womanhood promulgated by relational feminists asserts that connection is too
often the result of economic, social or psychological coercion. Put another way, the notion
of voluntary undertaking of responsibility fails to consider the possibility that care-giving
might not always be freely negotiated (with all the implications carefully evaluated) from a
position of separation and therefore power, but may be imposed when contexts and circumstances position individuals within relationships of care-giving and dependency. One particular problem with such coercion is that individuals often find themselves subject to care-giving
responsibilities that they are unable to effectively satisfy. More importantly, however, it is
men who are usually most free to negotiate in and out of these relationships of care.

My concern extends beyond the parenting role to all relationships in which one finds systemic coercion over the care-giving roles of individuals. For instance, a well-established basis for omissions liability, deriving from the broader liability arising from voluntary undertaking of responsibility, is the contract. Alan Norrie has suggested that the development of this contractual model reflected the need to find a basis for the increasing interconnectedness of capitalism in late nineteenth century England. But with capitalism comes also the role economic power plays in shaping the process of undertaking, again challenging the model of free negotiation of care-giving responsibilities (available to the white, middle class male) that the criminal law presumes.

I want to return, finally, to the case of *Stone* and a further excerpt from the overlooked police interview with Mrs Dobinson. Once again, I am wary of drawing specific conclusions about the nature of law from this case. It involves one story, one particular era, and one particular woman. Yet what seems [so] peculiar to me is the absence of any consideration of the explicitly gendered implications of the context in which Dobinson's care-giving seems to have taken place. As the Court of Appeal noted:

> The appellant [Dobinson] said she kept telling Ted (the other appellant), but that he would not do anything. He just told her, "Leave it while tomorrow." She was asked why she did not get help and she replied, "I asked him to get a doctor. He said he had tried to, but because the deceased was not on his panel the doctor wouldn't come." When asked why she did not speak to the lady next door or to Mrs. Wilson's daughter, who was a nurse, she is said to have replied, "I daren't. He is boss down there. I daren't do anything unless he tells me. She is not my sister, so I left it to him."

This excerpt serves as an illustration of the reality that care-giving by women often takes place in the absence of the kind of empowerment predominantly experienced by men, and assumed by the notion of voluntary undertaking.

Finally, the decision in *Stone and Dobinson* is useful for relational feminists beyond the insight it provides into women's experience of compulsory care-giving because it suggests the rule on voluntary undertaking of responsibility potentially remains structurally gendered. As Alan Norrie has previously noted, closer consideration of the case suggests some problematic reasoning:

> The argument rests on a play on the concept of an undertaking. Dobinson had, as a matter of fact, 'undertaken' certain actions on the deceased's behalf, but there was no evidence that she had made an undertaking to perform such tasks as she performed. There is a slide in the judgment between 'undertaking' in a practical and in a 'contractual' sense.[144]

Norrie argues that the concept of undertaking was deliberately "manipulated into action" in this way by the judges of the Court, who appreciated "they had no real basis in law for establishing a duty to act in the case of [the] defendant", in order to ensure a conviction in the face of the harrowing death of the victim. However, from a relational feminist perspective I want to pose a further alternative interpretation of this apparent slippage in meaning. Could it be said instead that the judges of the Court, acculturated themselves according to a masculine vision of empowered negotiation of care-giving responsibilities, actually believed that evidence of Dobinson's practical care-giving presupposed that her responsibility was voluntarily undertaken? If so, it is perhaps time the reality of coercive care-giving (not just among women) was confronted explicitly within the rules on criminal liability for omissions.

[144] Norrie (2001: 127).

QUESTIONS

1. In *Brock and Wyner* [2001] 2 Cr App R 31 (discussed in Padfield (2000) and Glazebrook (2001)) two project workers at a hostel for homeless people were convicted under section 8 of the Misuse of Drugs Act 1971 for not preventing drug selling in the hostel. Is such a conviction appropriate?

2. Is it a greater infringement of your liberty to be required to act in a particular way or to be forbidden to act in a particular way?

3. If a celebrity were seriously injured in a car crash and a photographer took photographs, rather than summoning help, should the photographer be guilty of an offence?

FURTHER READING

Alexander, L. (2002) 'Criminal Liability for Omissions' in A. Simester and S. Shute (eds) *Criminal Law Theory* (Oxford: OUP).

Ashworth, A. (1989) 'The Scope of Criminal Liability for Omissions' *Law Quarterly Review* 105: 424.

Ashworth, A. (2013) *Positive Obligations in Criminal Law* (Oxford: Hart), ch. 2.

Ashworth, A. (2015) 'Manslaughter by Omission and the Rule of Law' *Criminal Law Review* 563.

Dingwall, G. and Gillespie, A. (2008) 'Reconsidering the Good Samaritan: A Duty to Rescue?' *Cambrian Law Review* 39: 26.

du Bois-Pedain, A. (2014) 'The Duty to Preserve Life and Its Limits in English Criminal Law' in D. Baker and J. Horder (eds) *The Sanctity of Life and the Criminal Law* (Cambridge: Cambridge University Press).

Elliott, T. and Ormerod, D. (2008) 'Acts and Omissions—A Distinction Without a Defence?' *Cambrian Law Review* 39: 40.

Fletcher, G. (1994) 'On the Moral Irrelevance of Bodily Movements' *University of Pennsylvania Law Review* 142: 1443.

Glazebrook, P. (1978) 'Situational Liability' in P. Glazebrook (ed.) *Reshaping the Criminal Law* (London: Sweet & Maxwell).

Kamm, M. (1994) 'Action, Omission, and the Stringency of Duties' *University of Pennsylvania Law Review* 142: 1493.

McGee, A. (2011) 'Ending the Life of the Act/Omission Dispute: Causation in Withholding and Withdrawing Life-Sustaining Measures' *Legal Studies* 31: 478.

Simester, A. (1995) 'Why Omissions are Special' *Legal Theory* 1: 311.

Williams, G. (1991a) 'Criminal Omissions—The Conventional View' *Law Quarterly Review* 107: 86.

Wilson, W. (2010) 'Murder by Omission: Some Observations on a Mismatch between the General and Special Parts' *New Criminal Law Review* 13: 1.

7 CAUSATION: SHOULD CONSEQUENCES MATTER?

There has been much academic debate over whether the law should hold people criminally responsible for their actions. This is a debate to which we will return several times in this book, but we will outline the arguments now.

7.1 ARGUMENTS AGAINST HOLDING PEOPLE RESPONSIBLE FOR THE CONSEQUENCES OF THEIR ACTIONS

Although students often assume that criminal law must concern itself with causation, it would be possible to construct a system of criminal law where issues of causation were irrelevant. Supporters of such a system argue that the consequences of our acts are beyond our control and a matter of luck. One way of putting the argument is this: Alf, Bertha, and Charles all throw a punch at someone, intending to give her a black eye. Alf's victim jumps out of the way at the last moment and escapes unhurt. Bertha's punch lands on target and gives the victim the hoped-for black eye. Charles's victim tries to jump out of the way of the punch, but falls over, bangs her head, and dies. Did not Alf, Bertha, and Charles all do the same thing? The different consequences were out of their control. Charles was 'unlucky' that his victim died; it was just luck that Alf's escaped. It is therefore only fair, the argument goes, to punish people for what is within their control, that is, what they do, and to ignore the things which are outside their control, such as what happens as a result of their actions. The criminal law should therefore only penalize acts and ignore the consequences of those acts. In practical terms the law would punish acts which endangered others; whether any harm actually resulted being a matter of chance.[145] Many leading figures in the academic world are sympathetic to the force of this argument: Joel Feinberg,[146] Andrew Ashworth,[147] and Sanford Kadish,[148] to name but a few.[149] A recent powerful example of this argument can be found in Larry Alexander and Kimberly Kessler Ferzan's book, *Crime and Culpability*:

L. Alexander and K. Kessler Ferzan, *Crime and Culpability* (Cambridge: Cambridge University Press, 2009), 172–3

Consider the following thought experiment. Assume that you are watching a DVD in which an actor decides that he wishes to kill his victim. He buys the gun. He lies in wait until she arrives home. He fires the gun. *Now, press stop on the remote control.* At this point, the actor has revealed his willingness to harm the victim. He has shown that he does not respect her life. He has acted with the purpose of killing her. *Now, hit play.* The bullet hits the victim, and the victim dies.

---

[145] Ashworth (1987). Although whether the harm did or did not result would be useful evidentially in indicating whether the conduct was dangerous.

[146] Feinberg (1970 and 1995).   [147] Ashworth (1988).   [148] Kadish (1994).

[149] Parker (1984). Many supporters draw on the writing of Kant (see the discussions in A. Moore (1990) and Nagel (1979)). For a rejection, see Johnson (2010) and Wallen (2010).

What have these later frames told you about what the actor deserves? We submit that they tell you nothing. These later frames speak neither to the influence that the law and morality can have over the actor nor to the influence that the actor can have over the harm that occurs. Choice is a desert basis. Causation is not. . . .

Consider the following claim by Michael Moore (2010) " 'Causation matters' seems a pretty good candidate for a first principle of morality". Really? It seems to us that "you break it, you buy it" is not a first principle of the criminal law. Rather, the first principle is "treat others with sufficient concern". Now, whatever the actor is going to *do*, the criminal law can influence the actor only by guiding the choice he makes. It is at this point that law and morality guide action, and it through his choice that the agent controls his action and the results of his action. If the agent does not foresee harm, he is not held responsible for harm just because he caused it. In other words, causation without choice does not matter. So, if the criminal law's power and the agent's power over results occur at the point in time that the actor chooses to act, from where does the result itself derive additional moral power?

At first this sounds a thoroughly convincing argument, but, as Paul Robinson has pointed out, those who argue that consequence should not matter are 'a breed that exists (and will probably always exists) only in academia. I know of no jurisdiction that actually takes such a view'.[150] John Gardner has argued that it seeks to prove too much:

anyone who denies the existence of moral reasons to bring about results or consequences also denies the existence of (normal) moral reasons to *try to* bring about results or consequences. So if one will not assess actions morally according to their results or consequences, one should not assess them according to their intentions either. If our successes do not count, then neither do our endeavors. With no inputs or outputs, there is nothing left of us as moral agents.[151]

7.2 ARGUMENTS THAT CONSEQUENCES DO MATTER

The reactions of the actor and bystanders

The consequences of a person's actions affect the reaction of the actor and passers-by. If A is driving dangerously and kills a child, quite different emotions will be felt by all involved than if A just misses a child.[152] A will feel very guilty about the death of the child, but may soon forget the near miss. The fact that such reactions are near universal indicates that they reflect a moral truth that consequences do matter and people feel responsible for the consequences of what they do.[153] Even if there is not a 'logical'[154] argument that can explain why we should be responsible for the consequences of our actions, it is clearly fundamental to our common experience and the way our society works. Kimberly Kessler[155] suggests, however,

---

[150] P. Robinson (1997: 109).   [151] J. Gardner (2012).   [152] B. Williams (1981).

[153] Jareborg (1993) argues that deciding the appropriate public response to wrongdoing involves considerations that are not relevant in making a moral judgment about the behaviour.

[154] M. Moore (1997: 232) argues that the fact that a defendant is responsible for the consequences of his or her action is self-evident as a 'foundationalist principle'.

[155] Kessler (1994).

that such reactions reflect the distress at the harm suffered (or not suffered) by the victim, rather than judgments about the actor's responsibility.

Action reasons and outcome reasons

John Gardner[156] argues that there is an important difference between what he calls 'action reasons' and the 'outcome reasons' against doing something. An action reason is an argument for not performing a certain kind of action, whatever the consequences. An outcome reason sees the reason for not performing the action as the bad consequences that flow from that action. An example will clarify. A person tells a lie to a friend. Telling a lie could be described as wrong simply because lying is wrong (an action reason) but also because lying has bad consequences (it breaks down the trust in the friendship). The consequences of an action therefore do matter in that they provide another (outcome) reason for (or against) acting in a particular way.

The importance of consequences to our humanity

Tony Honoré[157] argues that it is part of treating people as human that both the good and bad consequences of their actions are taken into account. Who we are is defined by what we do. We are judged in exams by how we perform, not what we try to do. In sport there is all the difference in the world between the striker who tries to score a goal, but fails, and one who tries but succeeds. Results matter.

Part of our response to when people are in fact injured by the defendant's action is an acknowledgement that the victim has been harmed. A major complaint about the Alexander/Kessler Ferzan view is that it fails to adequately acknowledge the harm done to the victim by the defendant. A defendant who kills a victim has not just done 'an act which is likely to endanger life', he or she has actually killed someone. Although their theory is very persuasive if criminal law were just about assessing a defendant's blameworthiness, the criminal law also has an important role in recognizing the wrong done to victims. That the Alexander/Kessler Ferzan view fails to do.

Of course, the choice is not just between saying you are not responsible for any of the consequences of your actions and saying you are responsible for all of the consequences. Most commentators take the view that you are responsible for some but not all of them. It is the rules of causation in the criminal law that seek to take this middle path and define for which of the consequences of an accused's actions you are responsible.[158]

FURTHER READING

Alexander, L. and Kessler Ferzan, K. (2009) *Crime and Culpability* (Cambridge: Cambridge University Press).

Ashworth, A. (1988) 'Criminal Attempts and the Role of Resulting Harm under the Code, and in the Common Law' *Rutgers Law Journal* 19: 725.

Gobert, J. (1993) 'The Fortuity of Consequences' *Criminal Law Forum* 4: 1.

---

[156] J. Gardner (1998).   [157] Honoré (1988).
[158] For a wider discussion, see Cane (2003: ch. 4) and Morse (2000).

Honoré, A. (1988) 'Responsibility and Luck' *Law Quarterly Review* 104: 530.

Morse, S. (2004) 'Reason, Results and Criminal Responsibility' *University of Illinois Law Review* 363.

Westen, P. (2010) 'Resulting Harms and Objective Risks as Constraints on Punishment' *Law and Philosophy* 401.

8 SEEKING A COHERENT APPROACH TO CAUSATION

One key question about causation in the law is: 'To what extent is causation a question or fact and to what extent is it a question of judgment?' In other words, in causation cases are we asking 'Did the defendant cause this result?' or 'Should the defendant be held responsible for this consequence?'[159] To some, causation should not be regarded as a quasi-scientific question but rather a question about whether it is fair to impute this consequence to the defendant.[160] To others the questions of culpability and causation should be kept quite distinct.[161]

It has become common for those examining the case law on causation to conclude that, rather than applying any general principles, the judge simply considers what he or she considers to be the common sense answer on causation and declares that to be the legal position.[162] In other words it is not possible to set out any guiding rules of causation. This section will consider attempts by those who reject such an argument and seek to develop some general principles governing the law on causation. ←6 (p.89)

8.1 'CAUSAL MINIMALISM'

This view is that factual causation (but for) causation (as explained in Section 3.1 at p.88) should be the guiding rule for the criminal law. Opponents point out that it could throw the net of potential liability very widely: the stabber's grandmother could be said to be a 'but for' cause of the stabbing. Supporters reply that such concerns are easily dealt with by the law on *mens rea*, which would acquit the grandmother because she clearly lacked it. However, this reply is not available in relation to crimes of strict liability, which do not require proof of *mens rea*.[163]

8.2 HART AND HONORÉ

In their important work, *Causation in the Law*,[164] Hart and Honoré suggest an alternative approach. They place much weight on giving causation its ordinary meaning. They focus on the difference between normal and abnormal effects. Only abnormal conditions can be causes; normal conditions cannot. Normal conditions 'are those conditions which are present as part of the usual state or mode of operation of the things under inquiry'.[165] They give

---

[159] Fumerton and Kress (2001).   [160] Brudner (1998).   [161] e.g. M. Moore (1999).

[162] As seen in Part I of this chapter, the legal principles relied upon by the courts, such as the operating and substantial cause test, are so vague that they leave the judiciary open to such charges.

[163] For criticism of causal minimalism, see R. Wright (1985 and 1988).

[164] Hart and Honoré (1985).   [165] *Ibid*, 35.

an example of a person who lights a match by a haystack, setting it ablaze. The fact that there is oxygen in the air will be a normal condition and so not a cause. The lighting of the match will be abnormal and so can be regarded as a cause. In the following passage, they explain that the free, voluntary, and informed act of a human being will be regarded as an abnormal act that 'breaks the chain of causation' and takes over responsibility for resulting harms, rendering earlier actions no longer causes:

H.L.A. Hart and A. Honoré, *Causation in the Law* (2nd edn, Oxford: OUP, 1985), 42–4

If unusual quantities of arsenic are found in a dead man's body, this is up to a point an explanation of his death and so the cause of it: but we usually press for a further and more satisfying explanation and may find that someone deliberately put arsenic in the victim's food. This is a fuller explanation in terms of human agency; and of course we speak of the poisoner's action as the cause of the death; though we do not withdraw the title of cause from the presence of arsenic in the body—this is now thought of as an ancillary, the 'mere way' in which the poisoner produced the effect. Once we have reached this point, however, we have something which has a special *finality* at the level of common sense: for though we may look for and find an explanation of why the poisoner did what he did in terms of motives like greed or revenge, we do not regard his motive or speak of it as the cause of the *death* into which we are inquiring, even if we do (as is perhaps rare) call the poisoner's motive the 'cause' of his action. The causal explanation of the particular occurrence is brought to a stop when the death has been explained by the deliberate act, in the sense that none of the antecedents of that deliberate act will count as the cause of death. This is not to say that causal inquiries may not be pursued further. We may, for example, discover that someone provided a reason or opportunity for the poisoner to do the deed, e.g. by persuading him not to hesitate or by supplying an appropriate dose of poison. In that case a causal relationship *of some sort* may indeed be established between the conduct of the person who supplies the advice or means and the death of the victim. The latter can properly be described as a consequence of the persuasion or the provision of poison. But the fact that what is here unearthed is not the central type of causal relationship but something more tenuous is marked by the fact that we would not happily say that the accomplice had either 'caused' the death or 'caused' the poisoner to kill. We do not therefore trace the *central type* of causal inquiry *through* a deliberate act.

Although Hart and Honoré's approach has received much judicial and academic support it has its critics. Michael Moore, for example, is concerned about their premise that causation should take its meaning from the normal usage of the word.[166] He is not convinced that there is a 'normal usage', at least in difficult cases of causation. Other concerns surround their emphasis on the distinction between 'normal' and 'abnormal' events or conditions.[167] It can be argued that these terms are vague and too easily permit a judge to smuggle in value judgments when considering whether a cause is abnormal or not.[168] In the extract from Alan Norrie's book at the end of this chapter, further objections are made to Hart and Honoré's analysis.

---

[166] See also Cane (2002: 118).   [167] Christlieb (1993).

[168] An interesting example is Chamallas and Kerber (1990), who (writing from a feminist perspective) criticize the courts' approach to women who die in attempts to escape from threatening circumstances.

8.3 REASONABLE FORESEEABILITY

Some commentators and courts have sought to argue that defendants cause the reasonably foreseeable consequences of their actions.[169] Such a test has a refreshing simplicity. In the following passage, Dennis Klimchuk sets out its moral justification: ←7 (p.99)

D. Klimchuk, 'Causation, Thin Skulls and Equality' (1998) 11 *Canadian Journal of Law and Jurisprudence* 115 at 129–35

The standard of reasonable foreseeability gives expression to a powerful moral intuition, namely, that it is unfair to ask others to answer for those consequences of their actions which we could not reasonably have expected them to consider in deciding what actions to perform or to refrain from performing. This suggests that the fact that extraordinary operations of nature would break the causal chain between the actions of a wrongdoer and the victim's eventual injury follows from the fact that to extend my actions through the intervention of such extraordinary operations would in some sense be unfair. The reasonable foreseeability test makes explicit the reliance of the doctrine of causation on a sense of fairness only implicit in the substantial or operating cause test.

On what does this sense of fairness rely? The key to the answer I defend lies in giving attention to the work done by the concept of reasonableness in the standard of reasonable foreseeability. I want to borrow an idea that John Rawls develops in *Political Liberalism*, namely that reasonableness and equality are correlative: to act rationally is to act so as to further one's own ends; to act reasonably is to interact with others on terms of equality. Thus, the intuition of fairness to which I appealed above relies on the idea that the reasonable foreseeability standard gives expression to what I called the principle of equality, namely the principle that the law should treat persons as equals.

We have to give some content to the principle of equality. What equality requires in a given legal context will be in part a function of the sorts of interests the law protects in that context. As a part of public law, the primary relationship in terms of which criminal law is typically conceptualized is that between the state and citizen. Indeed, this suggests a common means by which the contrast between public and private law is drawn: tort law, for example, may be understood as having as its domain those aspects of wrongful conduct in which the state has no direct interest, but the pursuit of whose remedy is rather left to the private parties involved.

However, along with the relationship between the citizen and the state—most clearly at issue when the question is whether some *type* of action ought to attract the state's interest—criminal law has as its object, no less than tort law, the relationship citizens have as among themselves—most clearly at issue when the question is whether some *particular* action constitutes a violation of the sort of rights the criminal law protects. Thus to ask, for example, whether self-defence should be recognized as a defence at all is to ask whether the state should ever permit persons the right to self-help when the state's agents are not there to protect them, and this is a question of the relationship between the state's interests and the interests of the individual. To ask whether this particular assault was an act of self-defence is to inquire into the structure of the interaction between two individuals at the time of their violent confrontation. At stake here are not the interests of the state versus those of the individual but rather the protection of an individual's interests as against their interference

---

[169] See e.g. Yeo (2000).

by another. Following Arthur Ripstein, I would suggest that the relevant interests here are liberty and security. The link to equality is provided by an idea—Kantian in spirit—on which I will here rely: to treat persons as equals is to permit them as much exercise of their liberty and security interests as is compatible with everyone else doing the same.

My suggestion, then, is that the reasonable foreseeability test alone among the options I have considered succeeds in doing so. It will be easiest to see this if we begin by seeing how the other options fail to. Along with the substantial or operating cause test, I considered earlier two criteria by which we might answer the question of which of his consequences a wrongdoer must answer for, namely (1) the wrongdoer must answer for all of those consequences which would not have occurred but for his actions, and (2) the wrongdoer must answer for only those consequences which he acted so as to bring about. I suggested above that both of these can be dismissed on grounds of unfairness; now I want to give some content to the intuition to which I there appealed. Then I will return to the substantial or operating cause and reasonable foreseeability tests.

Let's call the view that the wrongdoer must answer for all of those consequences which would not have occurred but for his actions the *objective view* and the view that the wrongdoer must answer for only those consequences which he acted so as to bring about the *subjective view*. As I suggested above, the contrast between these two views can be captured in terms of the degree to which an agent has authority over the question of which consequences of his actions will count as his doings. On the objective view, the agent has no such authority; on the subjective view, he has the final say. This contrast can also be captured in terms of who must bear the costs of the agent's intervention into the causal chains in which he acts and is acted upon. On the objective view, the agent, we might say, acts at his own peril; on the subjective view he acts at the peril of others.

The second way of making the contrast most clearly illustrates the extent to which the principle of equality, interpreted in the terms I introduced above, is at issue here. To say that on the objective view, A acts at his own peril, is to say that (supposing A wishes not to do wrong) A cannot act even when the foreseeable consequences of his action do not include harm to others, because if harm were to occur, A would have to answer for it anyway. That is to say, the security of those who might be harmed if A acted is purchased at the cost of his liberty. To say that, on the subjective view, A acts at the peril of others is to say that A will not have to consider as reasons against acting a broad range of the consequences of his actions—all those other than those he acted so as to bring about, including consequences which will consist in harms to others. That is to say, our security is purchased at the cost of A's liberty.

Above I suggested that we think of the substantial or operating cause test and the reasonable foreseeability test as attempts to chart a middle ground between the extremes represented by what I am here calling the objective and subjective views. But note that the substantial or operating cause test shares the shortcomings of the objective view on the terms of analysis just introduced. This follows from the fact that the difference between causes *sine qua non* and substantial or operating causes is one of degree. No less than on the objective view, on the substantial or operating cause test the agent is deprived of any say over which of the consequences of his actions will count as his doings. No less than on the objective view, on the substantial or operating cause test the agent acts at his own peril. Thus on the substantial or operating cause test, our security is purchased at the expense of the agent's liberty, and so the substantial or operating cause test violates the principle of equality.

The reasonable foreseeability test splits the difference, as it were, between the objective view and the substantial or operating cause test on the one hand, and the subjective view on the other. On the one hand, by tying the test concerning which consequences a wrongdoer must answer for to foresight, the reasonable foreseeability standard does not deprive the agent of all say whatsoever over which of the consequences of his actions will count as his doings. On the other hand, by tying the answer to what the agent could have *reasonably* foreseen, the reasonable foreseeability standard prevents the agent from having final authority over which of the consequences of his actions will count as his doings. In this sense, the standard of reasonable foreseeability is both public and objective. It is public to the extent that it can operate as a rule which guides conduct (unlike the objective view and the substantial or operating cause test, which both leave the question of which consequences count as my doings to fortune). It is objective to the extent that it prevents the wrongdoer from measuring the rights of others in terms of his judgment (unlike the subjective view, which leaves the question of which of my consequences count as my doings to my say): and the law treats us as equals, in part, precisely by denying us the privilege of so doing.

Critics of reasonable foreseeability claim that it does not operate fairly in thin skull rule cases, and notably Klimchuk goes on in his article to support the existence of the thin skull test in certain cases as an exception to the reasonable foreseeability test.[170] Klimchuk justifies the thin skull rule because it prevents the defendant claiming that the victim must take legal responsibility for her physical weakness or 'protected beliefs'.[171]

8.4 NATURAL CONSEQUENCES

The 'natural consequence' approach claims that the defendant is responsible for the natural consequences of his actions. It may be thought that there is little difference between the reasonable foreseeability test and the natural consequence test. The key difference seems to be this:[172] the reasonable foreseeability test looks at the issue from the defendant's point of view at the time when he or she acted (could he or she have foreseen the result?), while the natural consequence test looks back from the injury inflicted on the victim and attempts to find out which cause or causes were the most legally significant. Michael Moore supports a version of this theory, arguing that a defendant should be responsible for proximate cause (those things caused in the normal routine) but not for 'freakish' results. Critics might reply that the terms 'natural' or 'proximate' are too vague to be useful.

In the following passage, Victor Tadros makes a different objection and that is that when making causation assessments the courts do (and should) take into account normative issues (i.e. questions of how people should have behaved). He makes the point here using the example of third party interventions:

V. Tadros, *Criminal Responsibility* (Oxford: OUP, 2005), 173–5

It is commonly argued that the actions of third parties at least sometimes break the chain of causation even where those actions would not have happened but for the action of the

---

[170] Of course, other supporters of the reasonable foreseeability test would not permit such an exception.

[171] Klimchuk (1998) argues that in *Blaue* the right to hold religious views (except in so far as they might harm others) means that the victim had the right to exercise her religious beliefs in refusing the blood transfusion and so it should not be said that her decision broke the chain of causation.

[172] Shute (1992).

defendant. If D acts which then gives rise to an action by D2, it is at least sometimes the case that D is not legally responsible for consequences of the action by D2. That normative considerations are significant in assessing whether the activities of third parties break the chain of causation should be relatively familiar to legal scholars. However, the issue is a complex one and it seems implausible that a general test can be developed to determine when actions of third parties break the chain of causation.

The basic issue can be illuminated by a consideration of the facts of *R v Williams and Davis*. In that case the two defendants gave a lift to a hitch-hiker who they allegedly attempted to rob. The hitch-hiker jumped out of the car and died from head injuries sustained by falling into the road. Two considerations might be thought important in assessing whether the defendants caused the death of the hitch-hiker. The first is the factual question of whether the actions of the hitch-hiker were foreseeable. The second is an assessment of the reasonableness (or rightness, or some other normative assessment) of the acts of the hitch-hiker.

Foreseeability is often thought to be an important element of the law of causation. If a consequence is not foreseeable, it is said, it is not caused. There is a general problem with this idea. Due to lack of knowledge, it may not have been foreseeable in 1900 that cancer would result from smoking, but that does not entail that in 1900 smoking was not a cause of cancer. Whether or not D caused E, then, is not sensitive to the knowledge that we have, or could be expected to have, about E. It is quite possible that we do everything that could be done to establish whether D caused E and still be wrong about the answer because there is something about the world that we do not, and even could not, know. This is a sense in which questions of causation are questions of fact.

Whether the actions of the hitch-hiker were reasonable, on the other hand, might well properly be a determining factor in assessing whether the chain of causation was broken by his jumping from the car. Suppose that the actions of the hitch-hiker were spectacularly unreasonable. Suppose that the threat was very trivial, say because the force threatened was only a slap. In that case surely it would be wrong to say that the death was caused by the actions of the defendants. On the other hand, suppose that the hitch-hiker reasonably thought that he would be killed whether or not he gave over his money, perhaps because the defendants were known to the hitch-hiker to be convicted serial killers on the run. Then it seems quite right to say that the death of the hitch-hiker was caused by the actions of the defendants. Normative considerations, then, clearly play a role in the assessment of whether intervening acts of third parties break the chain of causation.

Wilson [(2002: 181)] is critical of basing accounts of causation on the idea of reasonableness later in the chapter on causation. He suggests that the difficulty here is that even unreasonable intervening acts of third parties may not break the chain of causation. He considers the case of *R v Cheshire*, in which D shot the victim in the leg and abdomen which induced respiratory problems. In attempting to alleviate this, the doctors performed a tracheotomy. It was negligently performed and the victim died. The chain of causation was held not to have been broken. Wilson approves and thinks that this shows that it is strictly not the 'reasonableness' of the response of the third party that is relevant, but rather the 'reactive nature' of the third party's action. The third party, in such cases, the argument goes, is reacting to a state of affairs created by the defendant. Reactive acts do not, it is claimed, break the chain of causation.

Relevant to deciding the case, Wilson rightly argues, is the fact that doctors 'who have emergency surgery thrust upon them cannot be expected to get it right all the time'. There is a difference between what is right and what is reasonable, of course, but that cannot decide the case. Not only can we not expect doctors to get it right all the time, we cannot always expect them to behave reasonably, or at least even if we do expect them to behave reasonably, unreasonable actions of doctors ought not always to break the chain of causation. Holding the defendant criminally responsible for the death in *R v Cheshire* ought not to preclude at least civil liability for the doctor. And for this reason we should not think that the 'reasonableness' test is very strict. But that is not to say that reasonableness is not the right concept to apply here. It is just that the intervening action must have fallen very far below the level of reasonableness to break the chain of causation in these cases. For, if the action of the doctors is bad enough, the chain of causation will be broken, despite the fact that they are reacting to circumstances created by the defendant.

This explains the decision not to attribute liability in another case that Wilson considers: that of *State v Preslar*. In that case, a husband forced his wife out of their home by his violent acts. She died due to the cold close to her father's house, the explanation being that she didn't want to disturb her father to let her in. Presumably it is because her reason for staying outside was so weak that the defendant could not be held criminally liable. Had there been some, albeit insufficient, good reason for her not to disturb her father (perhaps he had a heart condition, or would likely have attempted to shoot the defendant) then, presumably, the chain of causation would not have been broken. In such cases, much depends upon the reasonableness of the action of the third party, albeit that it is only very unreasonable acts that break the chain of causation.

It is hard to see anything but a specifically legal explanation of this idea. Surely the reason why only very unreasonable acts break the chain of causation is that the scope of legal liability ought not to be restricted by unrealistic expectations of medical professionals and others to behave rightly. In the natural world, on the other hand, we may be inclined to suggest that the chain of causation is broken more easily. For example, suppose that there is a medical condition which always requires an operation. Some operations of this kind will cause scarring and others will not. In establishing whether the disease was the cause of the scarring in a particular case, it may well be appropriate to suggest that the chain of causation was broken if the doctors conducted the operation negligently.

There are good reasons for the law to be more restrictive about how unreasonable the conduct must be for the chain of causation to be broken. The general requirement that reasonableness is the appropriate concept to determine whether the chain of causation is broken applies in legal and in scientific investigations. But it is plausible that the concept applies differently depending on the purpose of the enquiry.

8.5 NARROWNESS OF CAUSATION APPROACH

Critical scholars have argued that the criminal law with its assumption that individuals are responsible for their actions is placing undue focus on one individual and is ignoring the wider exercise of powers within society. Power structures within society, political assumptions, economic inequality, and cultural and social factors all play a role in influencing people to commit crime. The law's approach enables the problem of crime to be seen as the results of the actions of a few evil people, rather than recognizing it as a product of an unequal and excluding society.[173] In the following extract, Alan Norrie develops several of these points in criticizing the approach to causation developed by Hart and Honoré (which was summarized at Section 8.2): ←5 (p.87)

---

[173] See the interesting discussion of metaphysics and causation in Morse (2000).

A. Norrie, *Crime, Reason and History* (Cambridge: Cambridge University Press, 2014), 175–6

Liberal Principles for the Imputation of Causation

. . .

Hart and Honoré's position is most plausible where they draw their examples from situations in which an individual, isolated and alone, acts to bring about some effect in nature, for example, the lighting of a match which sets a forest on fire. Here, the person lighting the match is the cause of the fire, and its necessary conditions (eg oxygen, dry materials) are distinguishable underlying conditions which do not cause the first, though they are necessary for it to occur. But this is a simple example and, particularly in social settings, what is the cause and what the condition is harder to determine.

This becomes clear in the crucial distinction they draw between abnormal and normal conditions, where the former have the power to disrupt or relocate causal attributions—to become the cause. An individual is only the moral/legal cause of those events in the world that are accompanied by the normal range of attendant conditions. Where an abnormal condition ensues, it becomes the cause in place of the human intervention, which in turn becomes an antecedent condition to the abnormal element. The problem is that what is normal and what is abnormal, what is cause and what is condition, is a matter of judgment and perspective. To use one of the authors' own (slightly modified) examples . . ., the effect of a famine in a developing country might appear to a peasant as caused by drought, and to a relief agency as the result of the inefficiency and corruption of government. To a charity activist, it would be seen as the product of the meanness of the industrialised countries, and to a radical as the effect of economic underdevelopment resulting from neo-liberal economics. All these different factors could be singled out as the cause, with the others regarded as the background conditions; each could be presented as the factor which 'makes the difference', but it depends on one's standpoint. . . .

A good illustration is provided by Lord Scarman . . . in his report into English inner city riots in the early 1980s. Speaking of the events leading to a particular riot, he stated that

Deeper causes undoubtedly existed, and must be probed: but the immediate cause of Saturday's events was a spontaneous combustion set off by the spark of one particular incident. (1981, 37)

Which factor 'makes the difference', the 'deeper causes' or the 'immediate cause'? . . . Elsewhere in his report, Lord Scarman did draw a distinction between the 'causes' and the 'conditions' of the riots (1981, 16). This was shortly before he argued that the *conditions* of young black people cannot exclude their guilt for grave criminal offences which, as causal agents, they have committed (1981, 14). If Hart and Honoré are correct to say it is all a matter of perspective, competing views as to the essential cause of the riot would be established. . . .

Second, there is the question of the law's use of the concept of voluntariness. On the face of it, the idea of a new intervening voluntary act by a third party possesses a measure of solidity that the distinction between the normal and the abnormal condition does not. However, this is illusory since it all depends on how one defines 'voluntary'. Only a voluntary act will break the causal chain, so the act of a third party may not break the chain if it is adjudged 'involuntary'. The problem is that Hart and Honoré concede that there are narrower and broader uses of the terminology (1985, 138). Much hinges upon their notion of what constitutes a 'fair choice', without which an act cannot be said to be voluntary. This, they say, 'depends in part on what conduct is regarded from a moral or legal point of view as reasonable in the circumstances', an issue that 'raises questions of legal policy'...

What is voluntary may be subject to a more or less individualistic interpretation. If it is a matter of looking at whether an individual was conscious when he acted, this is a narrow focus on the individual and his mental state. If, on the other hand, it is a question of examining social or legal obligations, or questions of fairness, this locates the individual in a network of social relations and understandings, and presents a broad view of the voluntary/ involuntary line. From this latter, more social view, rooting the individual in a context of interpersonal relations, it is questionable just what significance the voluntariness of human agency should have...

Hart and Honoré's argument is that voluntary human agency has a special finality about it. While we may look for reasons why a poisoner did what he did in terms of motives like greed or revenge, we do not regard his motive as the cause of death, although we may consider it the cause of his action.... A good counter-example is provided by J B Priestley's play, *An Inspector Calls*. The author persuades us to look behind the 'voluntary' act of the young woman's suicide to the conduct of the various members of the well-to-do family, who each in their own way have contributed to the girl's decision to take her life. Priestley forces the family to see that each of its members has in his or her own way caused the girl's death. They cannot conceal behind the girl's 'voluntary' act their own causal roles stemming from the interconnectedness of relations in their house and, beyond that, between a family and its servants, and between rich and poor. It is this which ensures that any focus on individual agency can only be falsely narrow. The girl's suicide is 'voluntary', but it is still caused by the acts of the family, so that no special finality is given to her actions. 'Voluntariness' loses its special character when a broader view of events and actions is taken.

QUESTIONS

1. Which of these approaches would (a) make most sense to a jury and (b) be most desirable in theory?

2. Do you think there is a difference in thin skull cases where because of the physical infirmity the victim suffers a worse injury than would otherwise occur, and cases where an action which otherwise would be harmless causes a serious injury? (This question is discussed in Gobert (1993).)

3. If Norrie's argument were accepted, would it be possible to have any kind of criminal law that took appropriate account of the political and social forces that influence the commission of crime?

FURTHER READING

Brudner, A. (1998) 'Owning Outcomes: On Intervening Causes, Thin Skulls and Fault-undifferentiated Crimes' *Canadian Journal of Law and Jurisprudence* 11: 90.

Hart, H. and Honoré, A. (1985) *Causation in the Law* (2nd edn, Oxford: OUP).

Hassett, P. (1987) 'Absolutism in Causation' *Syracuse Law Review* 38: 683.

Klimchuk, D. (1998) 'Causation, Thin Skulls and Equality' *Canadian Journal of Law and Jurisprudence* 11: 115.

Mead, G. (1991) 'Contracting into Crime' *Oxford Journal of Legal Studies* 11: 147.

Moore, M. (2011) 'Causation in the Criminal Law' in J. Deigh and D. Dolinko (eds) *The Oxford Handbook of Philosophy of Criminal Law* (Oxford: OUP).

Norrie, A. (1991) 'A Critique of Criminal Causation' *Modern Law Review* 54: 685.

Sullivan, G.R. and Simester, A. (2012) 'Causation without Limits: Causing Death while Driving without a Licence, while Disqualified, or without Insurance' *Criminal Law Review* 753.

Tadros, V. (2005a) *Criminal Responsibility* (Oxford: OUP), ch. 6.

Wilson, W. (2008b) 'Dealing with Drug-Induced Homicide' in C. Clarkson and S. Cunningham (eds) *Criminal Liability for Non-Aggressive Death* (Aldershot: Ashgate).

9 CONCLUDING THOUGHTS

The *actus reus* is a central aspect of criminal law. It defines the harm done to the victim and the wrong performed by the defendant. In many cases this involves proof that the defendant caused a particular result. That is often an easy question, but not always. The courts have struggled to produce a set of principles for causation that are consistently applied. This, in part, reflects the wide range of complex moral, political, and theoretical issues that questions of causation throw up. It is notable that the courts have been reluctant to open up a can of worms and consider the extent to which any of us are responsible for our actions. The criminal law proceeds on the great fiction that we are all fully responsible for our actions, in the absence of one of the recognized defences. While it is difficult to imagine how the criminal law could do otherwise, the fact that much of criminal law is based on a possibly unfounded assumption cannot be comfortable for criminal lawyers.

3

MENS REA:
THE MENTAL ELEMENT

CENTRAL ISSUES

1. A defendant is taken to have intended a result if it was her or his aim or purpose. If the result was foreseen as virtually certain to occur as a result of the defendant's actions, and the defendant realized this, then the jury are entitled to find that the defendant intended the result.

2. Defendants will be found to be reckless if they appreciated that because of their actions there was a chance that the result might occur, and it was unreasonable for them to act as they did.

3. A defendant will be negligent if he or she behaved in a way that a reasonable person would not. It is rare for negligence to be sufficient *mens rea* for a serious criminal offence.

4. If a defendant is voluntarily intoxicated when committing an offence, then generally he or she will be found to have been reckless. If the defendant, even though intoxicated, intended the result, then the jury should find that there was intention.

PART I: THE LAW

1   THE MEANING OF *MENS REA*

Mens rea[1] is the legal term used to describe the element of a criminal offence that relates to the defendant's mental state. Those who suffer from Latin-phobia may prefer the phrase 'the mental element of the crime'. Different crimes have different *mentes reae*:[2] some require intention, others recklessness, negligence, or knowledge. Some crimes do not require proof of any mental state of the defendant. These are known as strict liability offences and will be discussed in Chapter 4.

---

[1] This Latin phrase means 'guilty mind'.   [2] *Mentes reae* is the plural of *mens rea*.

It has often been suggested that *mens rea* plays the crucial role of ensuring that only blame-worthy defendants are punished for their crimes. Someone who causes another's death by an unforeseeable accident does not deserve punishment; someone who causes another's death intentionally does. However, in assessing a defendant's blameworthiness his or her state of mind is only part of the picture. A mercy killer and a contract killer may both intend to kill, but most people would not regard their actions as equally wicked. Indeed, the existence of defences such as duress or self-defence demonstrate that *mens rea* is not by any means the law's sole criterion for determining blameworthiness. Indeed, the courts have made it quite clear that *mens rea* is not equivalent to moral guilt. In *Yip Chiu-Cheung*[3] a police officer, as part of an undercover operation, pretended to be a drug dealer and agreed with a drug baron to import drugs. The Privy Council confirmed that the police officer had the *mens rea* for a conspiracy to import drugs. In moral terms his behaviour was not blameworthy (some would even say it was commendable), but in the eyes of the law he had the *mens rea* for the conspiracy because he agreed to import drugs.[4]

This chapter will consider the following concepts that are used throughout criminal law: (a) intention, (b) recklessness, (c) negligence, and (d) knowledge. These are not the only kinds of *mens rea*. Others will be discussed elsewhere in the book in the context of specific offences. For example, dishonesty will be discussed when we consider property offences. Which *mens rea* is required depends on the particular offence. For example, murder requires proof that the defendant intended death or grievous bodily harm, while criminal damage requires proof that the defendant was reckless as to whether the property belonging to another would be damaged. Occasionally an offence will have a different *mens rea* in respect of different aspects of the *actus reus*. For example, in rape the defendant must intend to sexually penetrate the victim, but need only be reckless as to whether the victim was not consenting.

As a general rule intention is seen as the worst kind of *mens rea*, recklessness the next worst, and negligence the least serious. Therefore these concepts will be discussed in that order.

2 INTENTION

> **DEFINITION**
>
> Intention is to be given its normal meaning: purpose or aim. In the majority of cases the judge should just ask the jury to give intention its everyday meaning. In exceptional borderline cases the jury can be directed that they are entitled to find intention if a result was virtually certain to occur and the defendant realized it was virtually certain to occur.

In the criminal law the concept of intention is the most blameworthy state of mind: it is usually worse to kill someone intentionally than to kill someone recklessly or negligently. Despite it being such an important concept, the meaning of intention has caused problems for the courts.[5] The core meaning of intention is fairly straightforward. What have caused

---

[3] [1995] 1 AC 111 (HL).   [4] Although, not surprisingly, he was never charged with the offence.

[5] *DPP v Smith* [1961] AC 290 (HL); *Hyam v DPP* [1975] AC 55 (HL); *Moloney* [1985] AC 905 (HL); *Hancock and Shankland* [1986] AC 455 (HL); *Woollin* [1999] 1 AC 82 (HL).

difficulties are cases on the borderline of intention and recklessness. We shall first look at the basic meaning of intention, before moving on to consider such problematic cases.

2.1 THE CORE MEANING OF INTENTION

The House of Lords made it clear that the legal meaning of the word 'intention' is the ordinary meaning of the word. This led Lord Bridge in the House of Lords in *R v Moloney*[6] to explain:

> The golden rule should be that, when directing a jury on the mental element necessary in a crime of specific intent, the judge should avoid any elaboration or paraphrase of what is meant by intent, and leave it to the jury's good sense to decide whether the accused acted with the necessary intent, unless the judge is convinced that, on the facts and having regard to the way the case has been presented to the jury in evidence and argument, some further explanation or elaboration is strictly necessary to avoid misunderstanding.

So the 'golden rule' is that judges normally avoid defining intention by telling the jury to give it its ordinary meaning. The Court of Appeal has praised a trial judge who simply asked the jury in a murder trial to consider whether the defendant intended to kill the victim and avoided 'chameleon-like concepts of purpose, foresight of consequence and awareness of risk'.[7] In *Hales*[8] the Court of Appeal indicated that only in rare cases will the judge need to give further directions to the jury on intention. In *Ogunbowale*[9] the defendant gave the victim a karate-style strike against the neck. It was said in such a case there was no need to give a complex direction on intention.[10] Presumably that was because there was no other purpose the defendant could have had other than causing harm, and so the only real issue was whether it was serious harm that was intended. →1 (p.173)

But what is the ordinary meaning of intention? The courts have not told us because (presumably) they think it is obvious. The widely accepted view is that the defendant intends a consequence of his action if he acts with the aim or purpose of producing that consequence. Lord Asquith in *Cunliffe v Goodman*[11] explained that intention 'connotes a state of affairs which the party intending . . . does more than merely contemplate: it connotes a state of affairs which, on the contrary, he decides, so far as in him lies, to bring about.'

It should be remembered that the jury will need to be persuaded beyond reasonable doubt that the defendant intended the result. In *Haigh*[12] there was clear evidence that the defendant had smothered her child. However, there was no evidence as to how or in what circumstances she had done this. In such a case the Court of Appeal held the jury could not have been persuaded beyond reasonable doubt that the mother had intentionally killed the child. She could therefore be guilty of manslaughter, but not murder.

A useful test for seeing whether a result was the purpose of the defendant is to rely on Antony Duff's *test of failure*:[13] had the result not occurred would the defendant regard himself as having failed in his plan? Consider the following case. David throws a burning rag into Veronica's house, wanting to frighten her by causing a fire. The rag in fact sets fire to

---

[6] [1985] AC 905, 926. [7] *R v Wright* The Times, 17 May 2000 (CA).
[8] [2005] EWCA Crim 1118. [9] *R v Ogunbowale* [2007] EWCA Crim 2739.
[10] i.e. to give a direction based on *Woollin* [1999] 1 AC 82. [11] [1950] 2 KB 237, 253.
[12] [2010] EWCA Crim 90. [13] Duff (1990 and 1996: ch. 1).

the house and Veronica is killed. Here, had the rag not caused a fire and so Veronica had not been frightened, David would have regarded his enterprise as a failure. David therefore intended to cause the fire. However, had Veronica lived, David would not have regarded the enterprise as a failure (he wanted to frighten her, not kill her) and therefore he did not intend to kill Veronica.[14]

Although Duff's test is a very useful one there is one set of cases where it has to be treated with caution. That is where a result is a means to achieve a desired end. Imagine Martin kills his great aunt Alfreda in order to get his inheritance. The purpose of Martin's action was to get the inheritance. Using Duff's test of failure we could say that Martin would be delighted if Alfreda had lived, but he had somehow got hold of her money. However, it is generally agreed that Martin would be said to intend his great aunt Alfreda's death. This is because under his plan the desired result (obtaining the inheritance) will be achieved through the means of killing her. So when we consider the purpose of the defendant this includes not only the aim, but also the means he wants to use to achieve that end.

To further clarify the core notion of intention, it is useful to distinguish it from other concepts.

Distinguishing intention and foresight

In relation to the core meaning of intention, whether the defendant's act was likely to produce the consequence is irrelevant. If Neil sees Mary a long way away and shoots at her, hoping to kill her, but realizing that because Mary is so far away he is unlikely to succeed, Neil will still be found to have intended to kill Mary. That is because it was his purpose to kill her. However, many commentators accept that if the defendant believes that it is impossible for his action to cause the result, he cannot be said to intend it, however much he may have wanted the result to occur.[15] This is because he cannot be said to act with the purpose of producing a result if he did not believe that the result could possibly be caused by his act.

The House of Lords in several cases made it clear that foresight of a consequence is not the same as intention, but it is evidence from which a jury may infer or find intention.[16] The defendant may foresee that there is a risk that he will hit a fellow golf player by hitting the ball towards the green when there are people still on it, but that does not mean he intends to hit them. However, the degree of likelihood is evidence from which a jury may infer that a defendant intended a result. As Lord Scarman put it in *Hancock and Shankland*:[17]

> the greater the probability of a consequence the more likely it is that the consequence was foreseen and . . . if that consequence was foreseen the greater the probability is that the consequence was also intended . . . [T]he probability, however high, of a consequence is only a factor.

In other words the jury may reason that, given all the evidence of the case and the fact that the consequence was so likely to occur following the defendant's actions, the consequence must have been the purpose of his actions and therefore he intended the result. If Charlotte points a gun at Emily, fires and thereby kills Emily, Charlotte may say to the jury 'I did not want to kill Emily, my purpose was to see how loud the bang was when the gun went off.'

---

[14] Duff (1990a).   [15] *Ibid*, 58.
[16] *Hyam v DPP* [1975] AC 55; *Moloney* [1985] AC 905; *Hancock and Shankland* [1986] AC 455.
[17] [1986] AC 455, 473.

The jury in such a case is likely to disbelieve Charlotte and decide that she must have wanted to kill Emily.

Distinguishing intention and motive

The courts have consistently stated that 'intention is something quite different from motive or desire'.[18] In other words it is possible to intend a consequence without wanting it to happen. In *Hales*[19] the defendant ran over a police officer in his car in attempting to escape from an arrest. It was not his motive to kill the police officer, but he was, Keene LJ explained, 'prepared to kill in order to escape' and therefore intended to kill. That said, of course, proving that someone had a motive to kill the victim is strong evidence that that person intended to kill the victim. Imagine that Dorothy cooks Agatha a meal and puts rat poison in the food, killing her. If the jury hears evidence that Agatha had recently made a will leaving Dorothy a large legacy, the jury are less likely to believe Dorothy if she claims this was an absent-minded mistake and more likely to decide that Dorothy intended to kill Agatha. →2 (p.200)

Distinguishing intention and premeditation

A person may act instinctively in the heat of the moment and yet intend to kill.[20] It should not be thought that a person can intend a result only if he has carefully formulated a plan as to how he is going to produce the result. The person who kills in the heat of an argument wanting to kill the victim can be said to intend to kill as much as the premeditated killer.

Most of what has been said so far is uncontroversial and cases of this kind have not greatly troubled the courts. Far more problematic are cases of so-called indirect intention or oblique intention: where it is not the defendant's purpose to produce the result, but the result was a virtually certain consequence of the defendant's actions.

2.2 BORDERLINE CASES OF INTENTION

As we have seen, in the majority of cases it is enough for the judge to direct the jury that they are to give intention its normal meaning and there is no need to give further direction to the jury.[21] Indeed in *MD* it was held to be inappropriate to give further direction in a normal case.[22] Further direction is only necessary in 'very rare'[23] or exceptional'[24] cases where, even though it is very likely that the result will occur following the defendant's actions, the result was not the defendant's purpose.[25] In many cases, for example where the defendant shoots the victim, it will be unbelievable that the defendant could have any other purpose in mind other than to kill or cause serious injury. But it is not impossible to think of cases where although the defendant's act was very likely to cause death, that was not the defendant's purpose. For example, a further direction was appropriate in *Royle*,[26] where the defendant killed an elderly woman during a robbery. Although his purpose in attacking

---

[18] *Moloney* [1985] AC 905, 926.   [19] [2005] EWCA Crim 1118.
[20] See Cane (2000) for a discussion of 'fleeting' states of mind.
[21] Lord Bridge in *Moloney* [1985] AC 905, 926 thought it would be necessary to give a further direction only in 'rare' and 'exceptional' cases.
[22] [2004] EWCA Crim 1391.   [23] *McNamara (Richard)* [2009] EWCA Crim 2530.
[24] *Allen* [2005] EWCA Crim 1344, para. 63; *Phillips* [2004] EWCA Crim 112.
[25] *Hayes* [2002] All ER (D) 6 (Aug).   [26] [2013] EWCA Crim 1461.

her was to get her handbag, it was certain he would cause her serious harm. Another, oft-quoted, example is where a person plants a bomb on an aeroplane, hoping to destroy items on board which he has insured. Although he does not want the pilot of the plane to die he knows that this will inevitably occur if the bomb goes off in mid-flight. In such cases, it is necessary for the judge to give a further direction to the jury. *Woollin*, the leading case of the House of Lords, is the latest in a long line of cases discussing the correct direction to give a jury in these borderline cases. It represents the present law.[27] The key question for the House of Lords was the appropriateness of a direction proposed by Lord Lane CJ in the Court of Appeal case of *Nedrick*:[28]

> Where the charge is murder and in the rare cases where the simple direction is not enough, the jury should be directed that they are not entitled to infer the necessary intention, unless they feel sure that death or serious bodily harm was a virtual certainty (barring some unforeseen intervention) as a result of the defendant's actions and that the defendant appreciated that such was the case.

R v Woollin
[1999] AC 82

Stephen Woollin (the appellant) killed his 3-month-old son after throwing him onto a hard surface in a fit of temper. At one point in his summing up the judge directed the jury that if they were satisfied that the appellant had realized that there was a substantial risk that the child would suffer serious harm, they could convict him of murder. The appellant appealed unsuccessfully to the Court of Appeal. He then appealed to the House of Lords.

Lord Steyn

The Court of Appeal certified the following questions as of general importance:

'1. In murder, where there is no direct evidence that the purpose of a defendant was to kill or to inflict serious injury on the victim, is it necessary to direct the jury that they may only infer an intent to do serious injury, if they are satisfied (a) that serious bodily harm was a virtually certain consequence of the defendant's voluntary act and (b) that the defendant appreciated that fact?

2. If the answer to question 1 is "yes," is such a direction necessary in all cases or is it only necessary in cases where the sole evidence of the defendant's intention is to be found in his actions and their consequence to the victim?'

On appeal to your Lordships' House the terrain of the debate covered the correctness in law of the direction recommended by Lord Lane CJ in *Nedrick* and, if that direction is sound, whether it should be used only in the limited category of cases envisaged by the Court of Appeal. And counsel for the appellant renewed his submission that by directing the jury in terms of substantial risk the judge illegitimately widened the mental element of murder.

---

[27] See Coffey (2009) for a summary of the current law.   [28] [1986] 1 WLR 1025.

[Having quoted extensively from Lord Lane's direction in *Nedrick*, **Lord Steyn** concluded:]

The effect of the critical direction is that a result foreseen as virtually certain is an intended result.

. . .

The Crown did not argue that as a matter of policy foresight of a virtual certainty is too narrow a test in murder. Subject to minor qualifications, the decision in *Nedrick* was widely welcomed by distinguished academic writers: see Professor JC Smith QC's commentary on *Nedrick* [1986] Crim LR 742, 743–744; Glanville Williams, 'The *Mens Rea* for Murder: Leave it Alone' (1989) 105 LQR 387; JR Spencer, 'Murder in the Dark: A Glimmer of Light?' [1986] CLJ 366–367; Ashworth, *Principles of Criminal Law*, 2nd ed (1995), p 172. It is also of interest that it is very similar to the threshold of being aware 'that it will occur in the ordinary course of events' in the Law Commission's draft Criminal Code (see *Criminal Law: Legislating the Criminal Code: Offences against the Person and General Principles*, Law Com No 218 (1993) (Cm 2370), App A (Draft Criminal Law Bill with Explanatory Notes), pp 90–91): compare also Professor JC Smith QC, 'A Note on "Intention"' [1990] Crim LR 85, 86. Moreover, over a period of twelve years since *Nedrick* the test of foresight of virtual certainty has apparently caused no practical difficulties. It is simple and clear. It is true that it may exclude a conviction of murder in the often cited terrorist example where a member of the bomb disposal team is killed. In such a case it may realistically be said that the terrorist did not foresee the killing of a member of the bomb disposal team as a virtual certainty. That may be a consequence of not framing the principle in terms of risk taking. Such cases ought to cause no substantial difficulty since immediately below murder there is available a verdict of manslaughter which may attract in the discretion of the court a life sentence. In any event, as Lord Lane eloquently argued in a debate in the House of Lords, to frame a principle for particular difficulties regarding terrorism 'would produce corresponding injustices which would be very hard to eradicate': Hansard (HL Debates), 6 November 1989, col 480. I am satisfied that the *Nedrick* test, which was squarely based on the decision of the House in *Moloney*, is pitched at the right level of foresight.

. . . It may be appropriate to give a direction in accordance with *Nedrick* in any case in which the defendant may not have desired the result of his act. But I accept the trial judge is best placed to decide what direction is required by the circumstances of the case.

The disposal of the present appeal

It follows that the judge should not have departed from the *Nedrick* direction. By using the phrase 'substantial risk' the judge blurred the line between intention and recklessness, and hence between murder and manslaughter. The misdirection enlarged the scope of the mental element required for murder. It was a material misdirection. . . .

The status of *Nedrick*

In my view Lord Lane CJ's judgment in *Nedrick* provided valuable assistance to trial judges. The model direction is by now a tried-and-tested formula. Trial judges ought to continue to use it. On matters of detail I have three observations, which can best be understood if I set out again the relevant part of Lord Lane's judgment. It was as follows:

'(A) When determining whether the defendant had the necessary intent, it may therefore be helpful for a jury to ask themselves two questions. (1) How probable was the consequence which resulted from the defendant's voluntary act? (2) Did he foresee that consequence?

If he did not appreciate that death or serious harm was likely to result from his act, he cannot have intended to bring it about. If he did, but thought that the risk to which he was exposing the person killed was only slight, then it may be easy for the jury to conclude that he did not intend to bring about that result. On the other hand, if the jury are satisfied that at the material time the defendant recognised that death or serious harm would be virtually certain (barring some unforeseen intervention) to result from his voluntary act, then that is a fact from which they may find it easy to infer that he intended to kill or do serious bodily harm, even though he may not have had any desire to achieve that result. . . .

(B) Where the charge is murder and in the rare cases where the simple direction is not enough, the jury should be directed that they are not entitled to infer the necessary intention, unless they feel sure that death or serious bodily harm was a virtual certainty (barring some unforeseen intervention) as a result of the defendant's actions and that the defendant appreciated that such was the case.

(C) Where a man realises that it is for all practical purposes inevitable that his actions will result in death or serious harm, the inference may be irresistible that he intended that result, however little he may have desired or wished it to happen. The decision is one for the jury to be reached upon a consideration of all the evidence.' (Lettering added)

First, I am persuaded by the speech of my noble and learned friend, Lord Hope of Craighead, that it is unlikely, if ever, to be helpful to direct the jury in terms of the two questions set out in (A). I agree that these questions may detract from the clarity of the critical direction in (B). Secondly, in their writings previously cited Glanville Williams, Professor Smith and Andrew Ashworth observed that the use of the words 'to infer' in (B) may detract from the clarity of the model direction. I agree. I would substitute the words 'to find.' Thirdly, the first sentence of (C) does not form part of the model direction. But it would always be right for the judge to say, as Lord Lane CJ put it, that the decision is for the jury upon a consideration of all the evidence in the case.

Appeal allowed; conviction of murder quashed; conviction of manslaughter substituted.

This decision makes it clear that in a murder case the jury should usually just be told to give intent its normal meaning. Where it is not the purpose of the defendant to cause death or grievous bodily harm only rarely will the defendant be found to have the *mens rea* for murder (an intention to kill or cause grievous bodily harm). Only if the death or grievous bodily harm was a virtually certain consequence of the defendant's actions and the defendant realized this was so, can the jury find that the defendant intended death or grievous bodily harm.

Parliament has made it clear that just because a defendant foresaw death was a likely result of his actions does not mean that he necessarily intended death.[29] Section 8 of the Criminal Justice Act 1967 states that a jury

shall not be bound in law to infer that he intended or foresaw a result of his actions by reason only of its being a natural and probable consequence of those actions; but shall decide whether he did intend or foresee that result by reference to all the evidence, drawing such inferences from the evidence as appear proper in the circumstances.

→3 (p.178)

[29] *Moloney* [1985] AC 905.

EXAMINATION TIP

The following provides a useful chart for deciding whether a defendant has intention:

Was it the result of the defendant's purpose?	YES: he intended it. NO: ask the next question:
Was the result a virtually certain result of his actions and did the defendant realize that the result was a virtually certain result of his actions?	YES: then the jury is entitled to find that he intended the result. NO: he did not intend the result.

The *Woollin* virtual certainty test at first sight appears straightforward, but there are a number of uncertainties about its interpretation: →4 (p.176)

(1) What does 'virtually certain' mean? It means that the result will occur unless something completely unexpected occurs.[30] For example, if George pushes Edward off the top of a high cliff, it is conceivable that despite the fall Edward will not suffer death or serious injury. Just occasionally there are stories of people falling great heights without serious injury, but it is virtually certain that Edward will suffer death or serious injury. In other words, 'virtually certain' means as certain as we can be about anything.

(2) If it is shown that the event was virtually certain to result from the defendant's acts and the defendant appreciates this, *must* the jury find intent or *may* the jury find intention? There has been much academic debate on this question.[31] It was considered by the Court of Appeal in *Matthews*[32] who after a careful analysis of the authorities made it clear that it was a misdirection for a judge to tell a jury that if a result was foreseen as virtually certain then they *must* find intention. However, the Court of Appeal felt that there were cases, including *Matthews* itself, where, having answered the *Nedrick* questions affirmatively, a finding of intent would be 'irresistible' for the jury.[33]

(3) How should the jury decide whether or not to find intention? What factors are the jury to take into account? The answer is that they may take into account any factors they wish. It is likely that a jury would consider the motives of the defendant and the circumstances of his actions. Compare these cases:

(a) Alice plants a bomb on an aeroplane intending to blow up the plane so that she can claim money for goods on board which she has insured. She knows it is virtually certain that the bomb will cause the death of those on the plane.

(b) Ben is at the top of a burning building with his baby. As the flames grow closer he is convinced he and the baby are about to be burnt to death. He throws the baby from the rooftop, even though he knows the baby is almost bound to die because he believes that that is the only way the baby's life may be spared.

Although the matter is entirely in the hands of the jury it is likely that the jury would find that Alice, but not Ben, intended to kill. A jury is likely to be sympathetic to a person who is acting from a good motive (like Ben) rather than a person acting from a disreputable motive (like Alice). In fact case (b) is particularly striking because Ben's purpose was to save the life of the baby. Therefore to find that he intended to kill the baby seems almost perverse.[34]

---

[30] *Moloney* [1985] AC 905, 925.   [31] e.g. Mirfield (1999).   [32] [2003] EWCA Crim 192.
[33] See also *Stringer* [2008] EWCA Crim 1222.
[34] It should be added that in many cases where a defendant had a good motive for acting as he or she did, a defence will be available.

(4) There is some doubt whether, using the *Woollin* test, it is necessary to show that the result was actually virtually certain, as well as showing that the defendant believed it was. It appears from the approved *Nedrick* direction that both must be shown. So the bomber who placed the bomb on the plane may not, under the *Woollin* test, be said to intend the result if (unknown to the bomber) the plane was fitted with a special device which meant that it could normally land safely even if a bomb went off in its cargo hold. This is a little odd, in that it suggests that the structure of the plane can affect the legal classification of the defendant's state of mind. Those seeking to avoid that conclusion might refer to Lord Steyn's *dicta*: '[A] result foreseen as virtually certain is an intended result', which implies that all that needs to be shown is that the defendant foresaw the result as virtually certain. However, that is not what the recommended direction for the jury in *Woollin* states and the Court of Appeal in *Hayes*[35] and *Matthews*,[36] admittedly without discussing the issue in detail, assumed that the *Woollin* direction required both that the result was in fact virtually certain to occur and that the defendant realized this.

(5) What is the significance of Lord Steyn changing the word 'infer' in the *Nedrick* direction to the word 'find'? Unfortunately Lord Steyn did not explain the reason for the change. Here are two possible explanations:

(a) He may simply have thought that 'find' was an easier word for juries to understand than 'infer'. This view, then, is that Lord Steyn did not mean to change the meaning of the direction, just to use more everyday language. If this view is correct then it is not surprising that he offers no explanation for the change.

(b) He may have meant to suggest that foresight of virtual certainty is not just evidence from which one could infer intention, but actually is intention (in the legal sense). The word 'infer' is used when we use one fact to presume the existence of another fact. For example, you infer from the fact that someone is wearing a wedding ring that he or she is married. Being married and wearing a wedding ring are not the same thing, but one is evidence of the other. Therefore talk about inferring intent from foresight of virtual certainty indicates that foresight of virtual certainty and intent are different, but that one is evidence of the other. By contrast, saying that you can find intent from foresight of virtual certainty might suggest that a jury is entitled to conclude that foresight of virtual certainty is intention. The main argument in favour of this view is that Lord Steyn refers to an article of Professor Smith who was critical of the courts' use of the word 'inference' and argued that foresight of virtual certainty actually is intention.

(6) Is the *Woollin* test just to be used in cases of murder, or does it apply to other crimes which require proof of intention? Notably Lord Steyn expressly restricted his discussion to murder. Therefore, whenever a crime requires proof of intent the court must consider whether the intention is restricted to its core meaning or whether the *Woollin* direction also applies. Findlay Stark[37] has, for example, argued that where the word intention is used in section 44 of the Serious Crime Act 2007 it does not include cases involving foresight of virtual certainty and only applies in cases of direct intent.

(7) In *R (Nicklinson) v Ministry of Justice*[38] Lord Neuberger, following a well-established line of authority, stated that 'a doctor commits no offence when treating a patient in a way which hastens death, if the purpose of the treatment is to relieve pain and suffering', even in cases where the treatment will inevitably cause death. It seems this is an exception to the general rule in *Woollin*, that in cases of virtual certainty the jury has a discretion to decide whether to find intent. Where doctors are appropriately giving pain relief, the jury cannot find intent.

---

[35] [2002] All ER (D) 6 (Aug). [36] [2003] EWCA Crim 192.
[37] Stark (2013a). [38] [2014] UKSC 38.

QUESTION

Bill is suffering from a terminal illness and is in great pain. His doctor gives him a large dose of painkillers which cause Bill's death within 24 hours. Consider the following states of mind the doctor could have. Which would lead to a conviction of murder?

1. The doctor wants to lessen Bill's pain by the pills, although she knows that the pills will hasten Bill's death.

2. The doctor believes Bill has suffered enough and wants to end his pain by killing him.

3. The doctor wants Bill to die because she knows Bill has left her a large sum of money in his will.

For guidance on answering this question, please visit the Online Resource Centre that accompanies this book: www.oxfordtextbooks.co.uk/orc/herringcriminal7e.

Read accounts of the trial of Dr Moor (P. Arlidge, 'The Trial of Dr David Moor' [2000] *Criminal Law Review* 31; J. Smith, 'A Comment on Moor's Case' [2000] *Criminal Law Review* 41) for a discussion of a case involving a doctor alleged to have 'mercy killed' his patient.

FURTHER READING

For further reading on the correct interpretation of the *Woollin* decision, read:

Norrie, A. (1999) 'After *Woollin*' *Criminal Law Review* 532.

Norrie, A. (2000) *Punishment, Responsibility, and Justice* (Oxford: OUP), ch. 8.

Pedain, A. (2003) 'Intention and the Terrorist Example' *Criminal Law Review* 579.

Simester, A. and Shute, S. (1999) 'Letter' *Criminal Law Review* 41.

Smith, J.C. (1998) 'Commentary on *R v Woollin*' *Criminal Law Review* 890.

Wilson, W. (1999) 'Doctrinal Rationality after *Woollin*' *Modern Law Review* 62: 448.

See Part II for reading on the theoretical approaches to intention.

2.3 INTOXICATION AND INTENT

What about a case where a defendant is charged with an offence which requires proof of intent, but at the time of the offence he was intoxicated through alcohol or drugs? Where the defendant is intoxicated (involuntarily or voluntarily)[39] the jury or magistrates should consider the intoxication as part of the evidence in deciding whether the result was the defendant's purpose or whether he foresaw the result as virtually certain:[40]

(1) If the drunken defendant had as his purpose the result he intended it: a 'drunken intent is still an intent'.[41]

---

[39] See Section 7.1 at p.155.

[40] The question for the jury or magistrates is whether or not the defendant had the intention, not whether or not the defendant, in his drunken state, was capable of forming an intention (*Hayes* [2002] All ER (D) 6 (CA)).

[41] *Majewski* [1977] AC 443 (HL).

(2) If the drunken defendant lacked intent he is not guilty of an intent-based crime, although he may be guilty of a recklessness-based offence.

A good example of how intent and intoxication can interrelate is *Moloney*.[42] There the defendant and his stepfather had engaged on a long drinking spree. They then decided to engage in a shooting competition to see who could load and fire a gun the fastest. The defendant won, but in so doing shot his stepfather dead. His evidence was that he had fired the gun with the purpose of winning the shooting competition. His story would, no doubt, have been disbelieved by the jury had he been sober, but the fact he was intoxicated made his version of events more believable. Note here though that his defence is not the intoxication, but the fact that he lacked *mens rea*. His intoxication was evidence from which the jury could conclude he lacked intent.[43]

Moloney can be contrasted with *Bunch*,[44] where a very drunk man killed his wife. The Court of Appeal held that the 'nature of the attack and the level of force used in the stabbing plainly pointed to an intention to kill, or at least to cause really serious injury'. His drunkenness and the fact he could not remember what he had done were not relevant as it was clear he had acted at the time with an intent to kill or cause grievous bodily harm.

3   RECKLESSNESS

If purpose is at the heart of intention, risk-taking is at the heart of recklessness. For many years the law on recklessness was confusing because there were two definitions of recklessness, which have become known as *Cunningham* recklessness and *Caldwell* recklessness. Some crimes used one and some the other. However, the House of Lords has abolished *Caldwell* recklessness and so now there is only one kind of recklessness used. For once a change in the law has made it easier for students to understand rather than harder!

3.1   *CUNNINGHAM* RECKLESSNESS

> **DEFINITION**
>
> There are two elements that need to be shown for *Cunningham* recklessness:
>
> (1) The defendant was aware that there was a risk that his or her conduct would cause a particular result.
>
> (2) The risk was an unreasonable one for the defendant to take.

The taking of a risk

In *Cunningham*[45] Byrne J explained that recklessness meant that 'the accused has foreseen that the particular kind of harm might be done and yet has gone on to take the risk of it'. Two points in particular need to be stressed about this definition. First, it is necessary to show

---

[42] [1985] AC 905 (HL).   [43] He was still guilty of manslaughter.
[44] [2013] EWCA Crim 2498.   [45] [1957] 2 QB 396, 399.

only that the accused foresaw that there was *a* risk. It does not have to be foreseen as highly likely to occur. Second, the question is whether the accused foresaw the risk, not whether the risk was obvious or would have been foreseen by a reasonable person. This point is demonstrated in *Stephenson*,[46] where the defendant (who suffered from schizophrenia) lit a fire in a haystack and destroyed it. Because of his illness he did not realize that in lighting a match there was a risk to the haystack. Although the risk to the haystack was obvious and most people would have foreseen the risk, the defendant did not, and so he was not *Cunningham* reckless. →5 (p.183) Indeed as the court emphasized the question was not even whether the defendant could have foreseen the risk. The simple point was he did not foresee it and so was not reckless.

This requirement that the defendant consciously took a risk caused problems in the following case:

R v Parker
[1977] 2 All ER 37

Daryl Parker was fined £10 plus 75p compensation to the Post Office after causing criminal damage to a telephone kiosk. He had had a terrible evening. He had overslept on the train home after a function in London and missed his station. He was charged an excess fare for travelling further than his ticket permitted. He tried to telephone for a taxi but the telephone did not work. He was seen by the police to 'smash down' a telephone handset onto the dialling box of the public telephone and thereby damage it.

Lord Justice Geoffrey Lane

What was in dispute was, first of all, whether it was the appellant who had caused the damage to the telephone receiver; he said it was not he who had caused the damage; and, secondly, the degree of force which he had used when bringing the handset down on to the receiver. The way in which the appellant himself when giving evidence described the situation was this:

'I went to the telephone box to call a taxi. I put two pence on the slot—not in, but on— I picked up the headset [that must have been the handset]; I heard a tone . . . I did not know it was necessary to put two pence in before dialling. I dialled two or three times without success. I put the headset down, hard. It did not fit on to the cradle so I put it down hard again. I did not lift it before putting it down the first time. I must have missed the cradle the first time. I did not intend to damage it nor was I reckless as to whether I damaged it or not. It did not occur to me that what I was doing might damage it. I was simply reacting to the frustration which I felt. As I put the telephone down hard for the second time there were the police opening the door.' . . .

The complaint made by counsel for the appellant is that the learned judge misdirected the jury in regard to the necessary mental element on which the jury had to be satisfied before convicting. . . .

[Counsel for the appellant] draws support from a decision of this court, *R v Briggs* [1977] 1 All ER 475. That was a case where the facts were very different from those in the instant

---

[46] [1979] QB 695.

case. In the course of the judgment the following passage is to be found ([1977] 1 All ER 475 at 477, 478):

> 'A man is reckless in the sense required [and that is dealing, of course, with s 1 of the Criminal Damage Act 1971] when he carries out a deliberate act knowing that there is some risk of damage resulting from that act but nevertheless continues in the performance of that act. That being so, it is clear from the three passages to which I have in particular referred that the judge did not give a correct direction to the jury on this aspect of the case. Using the words which he did, he might have cured the defect by explaining to the jury in clear terms that the test to be applied was the test of the state of the appellant's mind, but he did not put that anywhere in his summing-up.'

We are bound by that decision and, indeed, at least so far as the first sentence which I have read is concerned, we would not for one moment wish to disagree even were we able to so do. The test is the test of the defendant's state of mind. But, and in the facts of the instant case it is a substantial 'but', the circumstances of this case are that the appellant was plainly fully aware of all the circumstances of the case. He was fully aware that what he was handling was a telephone handset made of Bakelite or some such material. He was well aware that the cradle on to which he admittedly brought down the handset was made of similar material. He was well aware, of course, of the degree of force which he was using—a degree described by counsel for the appellant before us as slamming the receiver down and—demonstration by counsel whether wittingly or not, was given of a hand brought down from head-height on to whatever the receiving object was.

In those circumstances, it seems to this court that if he did not know, as he said he did not, that there was some risk of damage, he was, in effect, deliberately closing his mind to the obvious—the obvious being that damage in these circumstances was inevitable.

In the view of this court, that type of action, that type of deliberate closing of the mind, is the equivalent of knowledge and a man certainly cannot escape the consequences of his action in this particular set of circumstances by saying, 'I never directed my mind to the obvious consequences because I was in a self-induced state of temper.'

We, accordingly, do not differ from the views expressed in *R v Briggs* [1977] 1 All ER 475 with the exception of adding to the definition these words: 'A man is reckless in the sense required when he carries out a deliberate act knowing or closing his mind to the obvious fact that there is some risk of damage resulting from that act but nevertheless continuing in the performance of that act.'

Appeal dismissed.

What is noticeable here is that the Court of Appeal was willing to stretch recklessness to its limits in order to convict the defendant whom it regarded as blameworthy. Having a risk in the back of your mind is not the same as consciously taking a risk, although the Court of Appeal was willing to accept that it was sufficient to amount to *Cunningham* recklessness.[47] However, in *Foster v CPS*[48] it was emphasized that to be reckless it was not enough to show that had the defendant stopped to think about the risk, he would have seen it. It was emphasized that recklessness requires that the defendant actually saw the risk.

In *Brady*[49] the Court of Appeal rejected an argument that after *G and R* a defendant would only be reckless if he foresaw an obvious and significant risk. It was enough if the defendant

---

[47] See Part II of this chapter for further discussion.　[48] [2013] EWHC 3885 (Admin).
[49] [2007] EWCA Crim 2413.

foresaw a risk. In that case the defendant had perched on some railings above a dance floor and then by accident fallen onto the crowds below causing a woman a serious injury. The Court of Appeal suggested one way of looking at the case would be to say that by getting onto the railings he had realized there was a danger he would fall and hurt someone. Therefore even if the falling off was entirely accidental, in getting onto the railings he had taken the risk he would cause an injury and that could be enough to render him reckless.

The risk was unreasonable

This requirement is rarely in dispute. It will be unusual for there to be a case where it is reasonable for the defendant to take a risk that a person will be injured. However, there will be some cases where it is. If the defendant is driving and a child runs out in front of his car and he swerves out of the way, the swerve may pose a risk to other road users, but to swerve would often be regarded as reasonable. It should be stressed that this requirement is objective. In other words that whether the risk was a reasonable one to take is to be decided by the standards of the ordinary and reasonable person.[50] Whether the defendant thought it was or was not reasonable to take the risk is irrelevant.

Intoxication and recklessness

Defendants who were voluntarily intoxicated at the time of the offence and therefore failed to foresee a risk which they would have foreseen if they had been sober, will be treated as having foreseen the risk.[51] This means that defendants will not be able to claim that they failed to foresee an obvious risk because they were drunk.[52] If defendants are involuntarily intoxicated then there are no special rules, and defendants will be reckless if they foresaw the risk, but if they did not foresee the risk they will not be reckless.[53]

QUESTIONS

1. If a psychologist gave evidence that Mr Parker was so angry that he was not aware of a risk, would he deserve to be acquitted? Is there a clear difference between (a) consciously being aware of a risk, (b) putting a risk to the back of your mind, and (c) not being aware of a risk?

2. Thousands of deaths and injuries occur each year in cars. Anyone driving a car is aware that in driving a car there is a risk they will injure someone. Is it beyond doubt that it is still reasonable to drive cars? What about skiing?

3. Is it justifiable to describe as 'reckless' people who are so drunk that they do not see an obvious risk, but not people who are so angry that they do not see an obvious risk? (We will return to this question in Part II.)

---

[50] One important issue will be whether the defendant's behaviour was socially useful. A defendant who harms another while carrying out medical treatment is likely to be acting reasonably, while a defendant who harms another while shooting birds for fun will find it harder to persuade a jury his behaviour was reasonable.

[51] It is sometimes said that a defendant who is voluntarily intoxicated is prevented from introducing evidence that he did not see a risk because he was intoxicated. However, as Simester (2009) argues that seems to require the courts to proceed on the basis of a fiction.

[52] *Bennett* [1995] Crim LR 877.   [53] *Kingston* [1995] 2 AC 355.

3.2 *CALDWELL* RECKLESSNESS

As already mentioned *Caldwell* recklessness has now been abolished. However, it is useful to know in outline what it was and why the House of Lords decided to abolish it.

DEFINITION

Defendants were *Caldwell* reckless if:

(1) they are aware of a risk; OR

(2) there was an obvious and serious risk AND they failed to consider whether or not there was a risk.

Caldwell recklessness was different from *Cunningham* recklessness because it included defendants who were not aware of an obvious risk. *Caldwell* recklessness fell into disrepute because it punished defendants for failing to notice a risk which would have been obvious to a reasonable person. The issue was considered in *Elliott v C*,[54] where a 14-year-old girl with learning difficulties set fire to a shed by lighting white spirit. The court stated that Lord Diplock in *Caldwell* had made it clear that the test was whether a reasonable person would have realized that the lighting of the spirit would create a risk of damage to the shed, not whether the risk was obvious to the defendant or obvious to a reasonable person of the defendant's age and mental abilities.[55] As she had failed to consider the risk and it would have been obvious to a reasonable person, she was guilty of criminal damage. The decision caused an outcry amongst academic commentators. Had they been tabloid writers it would have been given the title 'the most hated case in Britain'. The reason for the outrage is this: it can lead to the punishment of a defendant who fails to appreciate a risk that she was incapable of foreseeing. C was liable for failing to foresee a risk that because of her mental condition she may have been incapable of foreseeing. The harshness of this approach is revealed by the following example: a blind person is walking down the pavement and walks into a bicycle left lying on the pavement, damaging it. As the risk would be obvious to an ordinary (sighted) person he would be *Caldwell* reckless as he failed to foresee the risk. This is extraordinary. With this in mind it was not surprising that the House of Lords in *G and R* decided that *Caldwell* recklessness had to go: →6 (p.184)

R v G and R
[2004] 1 AC 1034[56]

One night two boys, aged 11 and 12, went camping without their parents' permission. In the early hours of the morning they set fire to some newspapers under a wheelie bin they found outside a supermarket. The fire spread and ultimately burned down the supermarket and adjoining buildings. They were convicted on the basis that it would have been obvious to a reasonable person that what they were doing was posing a risk to property. They unsuccessfully appealed to the Court of Appeal, and then on to the House of Lords.

---

54 [1983] 2 All ER 1005 (DC).
55 *Elliott v C* was followed in *Stephen (Malcolm R)* (1984) 79 Cr App R 334.
56 [2003] UKHL 50, [2003] 3 WLR 1060, [2003] 4 All ER 765, [2004] 1 Cr App R 21, [2004] Crim LR 369.

Lord Bingham of Cornhill

1. The point of law of general public importance certified by the Court of Appeal to be involved in its decision in the present case is expressed in this way:

'Can a defendant properly be convicted under section 1 of the Criminal Damage Act 1971 on the basis that he was reckless as to whether property was destroyed or damaged when he gave no thought to the risk but, by reason of his age and/or personal characteristics the risk would not have been obvious to him, even if he had thought about it?'

The appeal turns on the meaning of 'reckless' in that section. This is a question on which the House ruled in *R v Caldwell* [1982] AC 341, a ruling affirmed by the House in later decisions. The House is again asked to reconsider that ruling. . . .

28. The task confronting the House in this appeal is, first of all, one of statutory construction: what did Parliament mean when it used the word 'reckless' in section 1(1) and (2) of the 1971 Act? In so expressing the question I mean to make it as plain as I can that I am not addressing the meaning of 'reckless' in any other statutory or common law context. In particular, but perhaps needlessly since 'recklessly' has now been banished from the lexicon of driving offences, I would wish to throw no doubt on the decisions of the House in *R v Lawrence* [1982] AC 510 and *R v Reid* [1992] 1 WLR 793.

29. Since a statute is always speaking, the context or application of a statutory expression may change over time, but the meaning of the expression itself cannot change. So the starting point is to ascertain what Parliament meant by 'reckless' in 1971. As noted above in paragraph 13, section 1 as enacted followed, subject to an immaterial addition, the draft proposed by the Law Commission. It cannot be supposed that by 'reckless' Parliament meant anything different from the Law Commission. The Law Commission's meaning was made plain both in its Report (Law Com No 29) and in Working Paper No 23 which preceded it. These materials (not, it would seem, placed before the House in *R v Caldwell*) reveal a very plain intention to replace the old-fashioned and misleading expression 'maliciously' by the more familiar expression 'reckless' but to give the latter expression the meaning which *R v Cunningham* [1957] 2 QB 396 and Professor Kenny had given to the former. In treating this authority as irrelevant to the construction of 'reckless' the majority fell into understandable but clearly demonstrable error. No relevant change in the mens rea necessary for proof of the offence was intended, and in holding otherwise the majority misconstrued section 1 of the Act.

30. That conclusion is by no means determinative of this appeal. For the decision in *R v Caldwell* was made more than 20 years ago. Its essential reasoning was unanimously approved by the House in *R v Lawrence* [1982] AC 510. Invitations to reconsider that reasoning have been rejected. The principles laid down have been applied on many occasions, by Crown Court judges and, even more frequently, by justices. In the submission of the Crown, the ruling of the House works well and causes no injustice in practice. If Parliament had wished to give effect to the intention of the Law Commission it has had many opportunities, which it has not taken, to do so. Despite its power under *Practice Statement (Judicial Precedent)* [1966] 1 WLR 1234 to depart from its earlier decisions, the House should be very slow to do so, not least in a context such as this.

31. These are formidable arguments, deployed by Mr Perry [counsel for the Crown] with his habitual skill and erudition. But I am persuaded by Mr Newman QC for the appellants that they should be rejected. I reach this conclusion for four reasons, taken together.

32. First, it is a salutary principle that conviction of serious crime should depend on proof not simply that the defendant caused (by act or omission) an injurious result to another but that his state of mind when so acting was culpable. This, after all, is the meaning of the

familiar rule *actus non facit reum nisi mens sit rea*. The most obviously culpable state of mind is no doubt an intention to cause the injurious result, but knowing disregard of an appreciated and unacceptable risk of causing an injurious result or a deliberate closing of the mind to such risk would be readily accepted as culpable also. It is clearly blameworthy to take an obvious and significant risk of causing injury to another. But it is not clearly blameworthy to do something involving a risk of injury to another if (for reasons other than self-induced intoxication: *R v Majewski* [1977] AC 443) one genuinely does not perceive the risk. Such a person may fairly be accused of stupidity or lack of imagination, but neither of those failings should expose him to conviction of serious crime or the risk of punishment.

33. Secondly, the present case shows, more clearly than any other reported case since *R v Caldwell*, that the model direction formulated by Lord Diplock (see paragraph 18 above) is capable of leading to obvious unfairness. As the excerpts quoted in paragraphs 6–7 reveal, the trial judge regretted the direction he (quite rightly) felt compelled to give, and it is evident that this direction offended the jury's sense of fairness. The sense of fairness of 12 representative citizens sitting as a jury (or of a smaller group of lay justices sitting as a bench of magistrates) is the bedrock on which the administration of criminal justice in this country is built. A law which runs counter to that sense must cause concern. Here, the appellants could have been charged under section 1(1) with recklessly damaging one or both of the wheelie-bins, and they would have had little defence. As it was, the jury might have inferred that boys of the appellants' age would have appreciated the risk to the building of what they did, but it seems clear that such was not their conclusion (nor, it would appear, the judge's either). On that basis the jury thought it unfair to convict them. I share their sense of unease. It is neither moral nor just to convict a defendant (least of all a child) on the strength of what someone else would have apprehended if the defendant himself had no such apprehension. Nor, the defendant having been convicted, is the problem cured by imposition of a nominal penalty.

34. Thirdly, I do not think the criticism of *R v Caldwell* expressed by academics, judges and practitioners should be ignored. A decision is not, of course, to be overruled or departed from simply because it meets with disfavour in the learned journals. But a decision which attracts reasoned and outspoken criticism by the leading scholars of the day, respected as authorities in the field, must command attention. One need only cite (among many other examples) the observations of Professor John Smith ([1981] Crim LR 392, 393–396) and Professor Glanville Williams ('Recklessness Redefined' (1981) 40 CLJ 252). This criticism carries greater weight when voiced also by judges as authoritative as Lord Edmund-Davies and Lord Wilberforce in *R v Caldwell* itself, Robert Goff LJ in *Elliott v C* [1983] 1 WLR 939 and Ackner LJ in *R v Stephen Malcolm R* (1984) 79 Cr App R 334. . . .

35. Fourthly, the majority's interpretation of 'recklessly' in section 1 of the 1971 Act was, as already shown, a misinterpretation. If it were a misinterpretation that offended no principle and gave rise to no injustice there would be strong grounds for adhering to the misinterpretation and leaving Parliament to correct it if it chose. But this misinterpretation is offensive to principle and is apt to cause injustice. That being so, the need to correct the misinterpretation is compelling.

. . .

37. In the course of argument before the House it was suggested that the rule in *R v Caldwell* might be modified, in cases involving children, by requiring comparison not with normal reasonable adults but with normal reasonable children of the same age. This is a suggestion with some attractions but it is open to four compelling objections. First, even this modification would offend the principle that conviction should depend on proving the state of mind of the individual defendant to be culpable. Second, if the rule were modified in relation to children on grounds of their immaturity it would be anomalous if it were not also modified in relation to the mentally handicapped on grounds of their limited understanding. Third, any

modification along these lines would open the door to difficult and contentious argument concerning the qualities and characteristics to be taken into account for purposes of the comparison. Fourth, to adopt this modification would be to substitute one misinterpretation of section 1 for another. There is no warrant in the Act or in the *travaux préparatoires* which preceded it for such an interpretation.

. 38. A further refinement, advanced by Professor Glanville Williams in his article 'Reckless-ness Redefined' (1981) 40 CLJ 252, 270–271, adopted by the justices in *Elliott v C* [1983] 1 WLR 939 and commented upon by Robert Goff LJ in that case is that a defendant should only be regarded as having acted recklessly by virtue of his failure to give any thought to an obvious risk that property would be destroyed or damaged, where such risk would have been obvious to him if he had given any thought to the matter. This refinement also has attractions, although it does not meet the objection of principle and does not represent a correct interpret-ation of the section. It is, in my opinion, open to the further objection of over-complicating the task of the jury (or bench of justices). It is one thing to decide whether a defendant can be believed when he says that the thought of a given risk never crossed his mind. It is another, and much more speculative, task to decide whether the risk would have been obvious to him if the thought had crossed his mind. The simpler the jury's task, the more likely is its verdict to be reliable. Robert Goff LJ's reason for rejecting this refinement was somewhat similar (*Elliott v C*, page 950).

39. I cannot accept that restoration of the law as understood before *R v Caldwell* would lead to the acquittal of those whom public policy would require to be convicted. There is nothing to suggest that this was seen as a problem before *R v Caldwell*, or (as noted above in paragraphs 12 and 13) before the 1971 Act. There is no reason to doubt the common sense which tribunals of fact bring to their task. In a contested case based on intention, the defendant rarely admits intending the injurious result in question, but the tribunal of fact will readily infer such an intention, in a proper case, from all the circumstances and probabilities and evidence of what the defendant did and said at the time. Similarly with recklessness: it is not to be supposed that the tribunal of fact will accept a defendant's assertion that he never thought of a certain risk when all the circumstances and probabilities and evidence of what he did and said at the time show that he did or must have done . . .

41. For the reasons I have given I would allow this appeal and quash the appellants' convictions. I would answer the certified question obliquely, basing myself on clause 18(c) of the Criminal Code Bill annexed by the Law Commission to its Report 'A Criminal Code for England and Wales Volume 1: Report and Draft Criminal Code Bill' (Law Com No 177, April 1989):

> 'A person acts recklessly within the meaning of section 1 of the Criminal Damage Act 1971 with respect to—
>
> (i)   a circumstance when he is aware of a risk that it exists or will exist;
>
> (ii) a result when he is aware of a risk that it will occur; and it is, in the circumstances known to him, unreasonable to take the risk.'

[**Lords Rodger** and **Steyn** gave speeches agreeing that the appeal should be allowed. **Lord Hutton** and **Lord Browne-Wilkinson** agreed with **Lord Bingham**.]

Appeal allowed.

R v G, then, confirms that for criminal damage *Caldwell* recklessness should not be used and instead a defendant will be reckless if he or she realizes that there is a risk of the harm arising and decides to take that risk, when to do so is unreasonable. In *Attorney-General's Reference (No. 3 of 2003)*[57] the Court of Appeal confirmed that *R v G* has abolished *Caldwell* recklessness not just for criminal damage, but for all crimes which had used *Caldwell* recklessness.

To many *G and R* is a welcome decision removing the unfairness that resulted from using the *Caldwell* test in cases like *Elliott v C*. The decision, however, is certainly not without its critics. One major source of disappointment was the failure of the House of Lords to consider an alternative to either *Caldwell* or *Cunningham* recklessness. Here are two alternatives that their Lordships might have considered:

(1) Defendants would be reckless if they were aware of a risk or failed to consider a risk which should have been obvious to a reasonable person of their age and mental abilities.

(2) Defendants would be reckless if they were aware of a risk or failed to consider an obvious risk, without a good explanation.[58] This would lead to the acquittal of those who failed to see a risk due to an illness or emergency, but lead to the conviction of those who failed to see the risk due to drunkenness or anger.

As a result of *G and R* critics are concerned that it will be too easy for a defendant to claim that they did not consider a risk to others and so be entitled to acquittal. Indeed if a defendant can persuade the jury that he is an utterly selfish person who gives no thought to other people's welfare then he should be acquitted if he does a dangerous act without thinking about its consequences. It may be that in such cases the jury will simply disbelieve a defendant or convict regardless of the judge's direction. Alternatively it is likely that we will see in the future much weight being placed on the decision in *Parker* (excerpted at The taking of a risk, p.144) and the idea of a risk being 'in the back of a defendant's mind'. You should also note that although the House of Lords in *G and R* proudly asserted the importance of proving a subjective *mens rea* (i.e. an actual awareness of risk), they also confirmed the rules relating to intoxication whereby a defendant who is voluntary intoxicated can be convicted without awareness of the risk. The House of Lords presented the intoxication rules as a special exception to the normal requirement of having to prove a subjective state of mind, but given the number of crimes committed by intoxicated people it is not clear whether in courtrooms the intoxication rules are in fact the normal rule, rather than an exception. →7 (p.196)

FURTHER READING

Child, J. (2009) 'Drink, Drugs and Law Reform: A Review of Law Commission Report No. 314' *Criminal Law Review* 488.

Crosby, C. (2008) 'Recklessness—The Continuing Search for a Definition' *Journal of Criminal Law* 72: 313.

Field, S. and Lynn, M. (1993) 'Capacity, Recklessness and the House of Lords' *Criminal Law Review* 127.

Gardner, S. (1993b) 'Recklessness Refined' *Law Quarterly Review* 109: 21 (a very useful commentary on *Reid*).

---

[57] [2004] 2 Cr App R 367.
[58] This kind of approach was indicated by the House of Lords in *Reid* [1992] 3 All ER 673.

Kimel, D. (2004) 'Inadvertent Recklessness in the Criminal Law' *Law Quarterly Review* 20: 548.

Norrie, A. (1996) 'The Limits of Justice: Finding Fault in the Criminal Law' *Modern Law Review* 59: 540.

Simester, A. (2009) 'Intoxication is Never a Defence' *Criminal Law Review* 3.

4 NEGLIGENCE

DEFINITION

If the defendant has behaved in the way in which a reasonable person would not, then he or she is negligent.

There are a large number of crimes for which the *mens rea* is negligence,[59] although most of them are minor crimes of a regulatory nature. There are therefore few reported cases which discuss its meaning. Negligence uses an objective test. In other words the defendant's state of mind is not relevant in deciding whether the defendant is negligent. There is no need to show that the defendant intended or foresaw a risk. What matters is the conduct of the defendant: did the defendant behave in a way which was reasonable in the circumstances? If the defendant behaves in the way in which a reasonable person would not then he or she is negligent. To give a practical example, if a defendant while driving crashes into the car in front, to decide whether or not he or she was negligent you simply ask: would a reasonable person in D's shoes have crashed the car or not? If even a reasonable driver would have crashed then the defendant is not negligent. If the reasonable person would not have been travelling as fast as the defendant or would have braked earlier and avoided the accident then the defendant is negligent. →8 (p.191)

There are a number of disputes over the meaning of negligence:

(1) What if the defendant has acted as a result of panic or fear? Consider a case where a person is driving a car when suddenly a child runs out in front of her and she swerves to the right and hits an oncoming car. We might say that in fact it would have been better and reasonable to swerve to the left, where the driver would have hit no one.[60] Is the driver negligent? The answer seems to be that a defendant is expected to act only as a reasonable driver would do. Even reasonable people reacting to an emergency would not necessarily respond in the way that in retrospect would have been the ideal way of acting. As long as he or she responded in a way that a reasonable person might have done when faced with a similar emergency the defendant will not be negligent.

(2) Is the standard expected of the person 'reasonable' or 'ordinary'? Does negligence require people to live up to the standard of behaviour which we think people *ought* to abide by, or the standard of behaviour that is the norm? In many cases these will be identical tests. But not always. We know that drivers ought always to keep strictly to the speed limits.

---

[59] As we shall see in Part II, some commentators argue that negligence should not be regarded as a form of *mens rea*.

[60] *Simpson v Peat* [1952] 2 QB 24, 28 (CA) considers a similar example.

However, we also know that most drivers do on occasion exceed them. If the driver was driving at 35mph in a 30mph speed zone could he or she claim not to be driving negligently if it could be demonstrated that on that stretch of road most drivers exceeded 30mph?[61] There is no definitive ruling on this question by the courts.

(3) What if the defendant is unable to act in accordance with the standard of the reasonable person? Simester, Spencer, Sullivan, and Virgo[62] argue that the defendant should be expected to live up only to the standard expected of a reasonable person with the defendant's physical characteristics, including age, sight, and hearing. So, for example, a blind defendant would be expected to act only as a reasonable blind person would. There is, however, limited case law to support this proposition.[63] Indeed it has been rejected in relation to negligence in the law of tort.[64] It is well established that a learner driver can be convicted of careless driving if he or she is driving at the standard below that expected of the reasonable driver, even if he or she is not doing too badly for the first ever effort at driving.[65] Also the cases of *Elliot v C* and *G and R*[66] suggest that the standard in *Caldwell* recklessness is strictly objective and the defendant is not to be judged by the standard expected of a reasonable person with his or her characteristics. If this was so for recklessness it might also to be true of negligence, however unacceptable that is.

(4) Is it possible to expect the defendant to show a higher standard of behaviour than that expected of the reasonable person? It is clear that if a person is purporting to act in a professional capacity he or she is expected to act as a reasonable professional. For example, a doctor is expected to exercise the skill expected of a reasonable doctor, not just the standard of an ordinary person.[67]

5 GROSS NEGLIGENCE

In relation to manslaughter a defendant's negligence must be labelled gross negligence (in essence really bad negligence) if there is to be a conviction.[68] It must be shown that the defendant killed negligently and that this negligence was so bad as to justify a criminal conviction. Manslaughter is the only offence which requires the negligence to be gross. We will discuss this in detail in Chapter 5.

6 DISTINGUISHING BETWEEN INTENTION, RECKLESSNESS, AND NEGLIGENCE

We are now in a position to define more precisely the difference between intention and recklessness and between recklessness and negligence. The precise boundary between intention and recklessness is that point at which the *Woollin* direction applies: cases where a result was not the defendant's purpose but it was foreseen as virtually certain. It is clear that if the result was the defendant's purpose then the result is intended. If the result is not the defendant's purpose but is foreseen as a possible result of his actions then the defendant is reckless.

---

61 Such an argument could not, of course, defeat a charge that he or she was breaking the speed limit.
62 Simester, Spencer, Sullivan, and Virgo (2013: 154–5).
63 *Hudson* [1966] 1 QB 448, 455 provides an *obiter dictum* that might support their argument.
64 *Dunnage v Randall* [2015] EWCA Civ 673.   65 *McCrone v Riding* [1938] 1 All ER 721.
66 [2002] EWCA Crim 1992.   67 *Adomako* [1995] 1 AC 171.   68 *Ibid.*

The borderline between intent and recklessness is where the defendant foresees the result as virtually certain. After *Woollin* it is for the jury to decide whether a person who falls into this hinterland intends or is reckless.

The difference between recklessness and negligence is fairly straightforward. To be reckless the defendant must foresee the result, while for negligence the only question is whether the defendant acted as a reasonable person would. However, the division between the two becomes more complex when *Parker*[69] is raised. There a defendant was found reckless because the knowledge of the risk was in the 'back of his mind'. There is a temptation to conclude that because a risk is one a reasonable person would have known about, the defendant must have known about it really, somewhere in his or her brain. If this argument is used too readily the division between recklessness and negligence becomes blurred. Further it should be recalled that a defendant who is voluntarily intoxicated can be convicted of a recklessness-based crime if the risk was one he would have known about if sober. This can be regarded as a form of negligence-based liability.

7   INTOXICATION

At various points so far we have discussed the impact of intoxication upon intention and recklessness. It is useful now to bring these threads together.[70] Intoxication can be relevant in a criminal case in three ways:

(1) The defendant may for some crimes seek to rely on his intoxication as evidence that he lacked *mens rea*.

(2) The prosecution may in some crimes seek to rely on the defendant's intoxication to establish the defendant's *mens rea*.

(3) There are certain crimes that specifically refer to being intoxicated. For example, it is an offence to drive a vehicle while under the influence of drink or drugs.[71] These offences will not be discussed in this book.

To understand the law on intoxication it is necessary to make two important distinctions: between voluntary and involuntary intoxication and between offences of basic and specific intent.

DEFINITION

A summary of the law on intoxication:

Defendants who are involuntarily intoxicated can introduce evidence of their intoxication to persuade the jury that they lacked the *mens rea* of the crime. If, however, the jury finds they had the *mens rea* they will be guilty. If they did not, they are not guilty.

Defendants who are voluntarily intoxicated can introduce evidence of their intoxication to prove that they lacked the *mens rea* in crimes of specific intent and are therefore not guilty. In crimes of basic intent the fact that they were intoxicated when they committed the crime will provide the evidence that they had the necessary *mens rea*. →9 (p.196)

---

[69] [1977] 2 All ER 760.   [70] For a very helpful discussion, see Simester (2009).
[71] Road Traffic Act 1988, s. 4(2).

7.1 INVOLUNTARY AND VOLUNTARY INTOXICATION

In simple terms someone is voluntarily intoxicated if he or she chooses to take substances which he or she knows or ought to know are intoxicating. In fact it is a little more complicated than this. It is necessary to distinguish a case where the defendant has taken alcohol or illegal drugs from those where the defendant has taken lawful substances, such as medicines prescribed by a doctor.

Alcohol and illegal drugs

Where the defendant has voluntarily taken a substance and is aware that the substance is alcohol or an illegal drug then he or she is voluntarily intoxicated. This rule even applies where the defendant thought he or she was taking a low-alcohol drink. This was made clear in *Allen*,[72] where the defendant was drinking his friend's home-made wine, which he believed had only a little alcohol in it. In fact it contained a high level of alcohol. He was held to be voluntarily intoxicated. It would be quite different if he had thought that what he was drinking was a non-alcoholic fruit punch, which in fact had alcohol (or drugs) in it. In such a case the defendant would be involuntarily intoxicated. Similarly, a person who was forced to drink alcohol or take drugs against his or her will would be involuntarily intoxicated. A person who is addicted to drugs or alcohol is treated as voluntarily taking the substances, unless they can show they had no control at all over taking them.[73]

Legal substances

If the defendant is taking a lawful substance, he is voluntarily intoxicated if he is aware that the substance would have this effect on him. In the case of medicine prescribed by a doctor the defendant will be voluntarily intoxicated if he took the medicine in a way not prescribed by the doctor (e.g. by exceeding the stated dose).[74] In *Hardie*[75] the defendant was given some out-of-date valium tablets. He was told that the tablets would calm his nerves and do him no harm. In fact he became intoxicated and caused a fire. He was held to be involuntarily intoxicated. The judgment does not make it clear whether the test is that the defendant is voluntarily intoxicated if he *knew* the substance was intoxicating, or whether the defendant *ought to have known* that the substance was intoxicating.

7.2 OFFENCES OF BASIC AND SPECIFIC INTENT

As is clear from the previous summary of the law the distinction between crimes of basic and specific intent is important.[76] Unfortunately the House of Lords' decision which emphasized the distinction (*Majewski*) failed to explain precisely what was meant by it. Subsequently courts, academics, and students have struggled to explain the distinction. The most popular view appears to be that offences of specific intent are those which have intention as their *mens rea*; whereas crimes of basic intent are those for which the *mens rea*

---

[72] [1988] Crim LR 698.

[73] It is possible that a drug addict or alcoholic could rely on a defence of insanity or diminished responsibility (on a charge of murder) (see the discussion in Chapter 12).

[74] *Quick* [1973] QB 910.   [75] [1984] 3 All ER 848.

[76] It is discussed in detail in Horder (2005b).

element can be satisfied by recklessness.[77] Greater uncertainty surrounds crimes which contain elements of intent and elements of recklessness. For example, rape, where the *mens rea* is an intent to engage in sexual intercourse with negligence as to whether the victim consented. Commentators are divided on such crimes. Some suggest that the court will decide whether a crime is predominantly one of recklessness or intent and label it one of specific or basic intent accordingly.[78] Others argue that it is simply a case of applying the specific intent rule to the intent part of the crime, but the basic intent rules to the basic intent part. So a defendant who is drunk and therefore believes the victim is consenting is guilty of rape, but a defendant who is so drunk that he does not intend sexual intercourse[79] would have a defence. The Court of Appeal addressed the issue in the following case:

R v Heard
[2007] EWCA Crim 125

The appellant was convicted of a sexual assault. This offence is defined in section 3(1) of the Sexual Offences Act 2003:

> (1) A person (A) commits an offence if—
>
>   (a) he intentionally touches another person (B),
>
>   (b) the touching is sexual,
>
>   (c) B does not consent to the touching, and
>
>   (d) A does not believe that B consents.

The appellant while very drunk exposed his penis and rubbed it against the thigh of a police officer. Due to his intoxication he had no recollection of the incident. He claimed that he lacked the intention necessary under section 3(1)(a). The trial judge ruled that the intentional requirement was one of basic intent and so therefore voluntary intoxication was no defence.

Lord Justice Hughes

14. The first thing to say is that it should not be supposed that every offence can be categorised simply as either one of specific intent or of basic intent. So to categorise an offence may conceal the truth that different elements of it may require proof of different states of mind. . . .

15. The offence of sexual assault, with which this case is concerned, is an example. The different elements of the offence, identified in paragraphs (a) to (d) of section 3, do not call for proof of the same state of mind. . . . It is accordingly of very limited help to attempt to label the offence of sexual assault, as a whole, one of either basic or specific intent, because the state of mind which must be proved varies with the issue. For this reason also, it is unsafe to reason (as at one point the Crown does) directly from the state of mind required in relation to consent to the solution to the present question.

---

[77] *Caldwell* [1982] AC 341.   [78] Simester, Spencer, Sullivan, and Virgo (2013: 697).
[79] It would be hard to imagine a jury ever believing a defendant who made such a claim.

16. Since it is only the touching which must be intentional, whilst the sexual character of the touching is, unless equivocal, to be judged objectively, and a belief in consent must be objectively reasonable, we think that it will only be in cases of some rarity that the question which we are posed in this appeal will in the end be determinative of the outcome.

17. We do not think that it determines this appeal. On the evidence the Appellant plainly did intend to touch the policeman with his penis. That he was drunk may have meant either:

i) that he was disinhibited and did something which he would not have done if sober; and/or

ii) that he did not remember it afterwards.

But neither of those matters (if true) would destroy the intentional character of his touching. In the homely language employed daily in directions to juries in cases of violence and sexual misbehaviour, "a drunken intent is still an intent." And for the memory to blot out what was intentionally done is common, if not perhaps quite as common as is the assertion by offenders that it has done so. In the present case, what the appellant did and said at the time, and said in interview afterwards, made it perfectly clear that this was a case of drunken intentional touching . . .

18. We do not attempt the notoriously unrealistic task of foreseeing every possible permutation of human behaviour which the future may reveal. But it nevertheless seems to us that in the great majority of cases of alleged sexual assault, or of comparable sexual crimes, as in the present case, the mind will have gone with the touching, penetration or other prohibited act, albeit in some cases a drunken mind.

19. It is, however, possible to envisage the exceptional case in which there is a real possibility that the intoxication was such that the mind did not go with the physical act. In *R v Lipman* (1969) 55 Cr App R 600 the defendant contended that when he killed his victim by stuffing bedclothes down her throat he was under the illusion, induced by hallucinatory drugs voluntarily taken, that he was fighting for his life against snakes. If an equivalent state of mind were (assumedly genuinely) to exist in someone who committed an act of sexual touching or penetration, the question which arises in this appeal would be directly in point.

20. A different situation was also put to us in the course of argument. Its formulation probably owes much to Professor Ormerod's current edition of *Smith and Hogan's Criminal Law* (11th edition, page 624). It is that of the intoxicated person whose control of his limbs is uncoordinated or impaired, so that in consequence he stumbles or flails about against another person, touching him or her in a way which, objectively viewed, is sexual for example because he touches a woman on her private parts. Can such a person be heard to say that what happened was other than deliberate when, if he had been sober, it would not have happened?

21. In the present case the Judge directed the jury that drunkenness was not a defence, although coupling with it the direction that the touching must be deliberate. Whether or not the jury's decision was likely to be that the appellant had acted intentionally (albeit drunkenly), the Judge had to determine whether or not it was necessary for the jury to investigate the suggestion that the appellant was so drunk that his mind did not go with his act. That question may also face judges and juries, as it seems to us, in many cases where a defendant wishes to contend that he was thus intoxicated, and scientific or medical evidence can say no more than that in an extreme case drink or drugs are capable of inducing a state of mind in which a person believes that what he is doing is something different to what he in fact does. In those circumstances, and in deference to the full argument which we have heard, we have concluded that we should address the issue, rather than confine ourselves to saying that this conviction is safe.

22. We are in the present case concerned with element (a), the touching. The Act says that it must be intentional. We regard it as clear that a reckless touching will not do. The Act plainly

proceeds upon the basis that there is a difference between 'intentionally' and 'recklessly'. Where it wishes to speak in terms of recklessness, the Act does so: see for example sections 63(1), 69(1)(c) & (2)(c) and 70(1)(c). It is not necessary to decide whether or not it is possible to conceive of a reckless, but unintentional, sexual touching. Like their Lordships in *R v Court* [1989] 1 AC 28, we think that such a possibility is a remote one, but we are unable wholly to rule it out. One theoretical possible example might be a Defendant who intends to avoid (just) actual physical contact, but realises that he may touch and is reckless whether he will.

23. Because the offence is committed only by intentional touching, we agree that the Judge's direction that the touching must be deliberate was correct. To flail about, stumble or barge around in an unco-ordinated manner which results in an unintended touching, objectively sexual, is not this offence. If to do so when sober is not this offence, then nor is it this offence to do so when intoxicated. It is also possible that such an action would not be judged by the jury to be objectively sexual, on the basis that it was clearly accidental, but whether that is so or not, we are satisfied that in such a case this offence is not committed. The intoxication, in such a situation, has not impacted on intention. Intention is simply not in question. What is in question is impairment of control of the limbs. . . . We would expect that in some cases where this was in issue the Judge might well find it useful to add to the previously-mentioned direction that 'a drunken intent is still an intent', the corollary that 'a drunken accident is still an accident'. To the limited, and largely theoretical, extent that a reckless sexual touching is possible the same would apply to that case also. Whether, when a defendant claims accident, he is doing so truthfully, or as a means of disguising the reality that he intended to touch, will be what the jury has to decide on the facts of each such case.

24. The remaining question is whether the Judge was also correct to direct the jury that drunkenness was not a defence.

25. We do not agree with [counsel for the appellant's] submission for the appellant that the fact that reckless touching will not suffice means that voluntary intoxication can be relied upon as defeating intentional touching. We do not read the cases, including *DPP v Majewski*, as establishing any such rule. As we shall show, we would hold that it is not open to a defendant charged with sexual assault to contend that his voluntary intoxication prevented him from intending to touch. The Judge was accordingly correct, not only to direct the jury that the touching must be deliberate, but also to direct it that the defence that voluntary drunkenness rendered him unable to form the intent to touch was not open to him.

30. There are a number of difficulties about extracting Mr Stern's proposition [that *Majewski* decides that it is only where recklessness suffices that voluntary intoxication cannot be relied upon] from the passages cited.

i) Lord Elwyn-Jones was addressing the submission made on behalf of the appellant in *Majewski* that it was unprincipled or unethical to distinguish between the effect of drink upon the mind in some crimes and its effect upon the mind in others. In rejecting that submission, and upholding the distinction between crimes of basic and of specific intent, he was drawing attention to the fact that a man who has got himself into a state of voluntary intoxication is not, by ordinary standards, blameless. Both the Lord Chancellor and others of their Lordships made clear their view that to get oneself into such a state is, viewed broadly, as culpable as is any sober defendant convicted of a crime of basic intent, whether because he has the basic intent or because he is reckless as to the relevant consequence or circumstance. Throughout *Majewski* it is clear that their Lordships regarded those latter two states of mind as equivalent to one another for these purposes. It therefore does not follow from the references to recklessness that the same rule (that voluntary intoxication cannot be relied upon) does not apply also to basic intent; on the contrary, it seems to us clear that their Lordships were treating the two the same.

ii) The new analysis of recklessness in *Caldwell* may have led readily to the proposition that voluntary intoxication is broadly equivalent to recklessness, thus defined. But that analysis and definition of recklessness have now been reversed by the House of Lords in *R v G* [2004] 1 AC 1034. As now understood, recklessness requires actual foresight of the risk.

iii) Since the majority in *Caldwell* held that it was enough for recklessness that the risk was obvious objectively (thus, to the sober man) no question of drink providing a defence could arise; it follows that the explanation of *Majewski* which was advanced was plainly obiter.

iv) Lord Diplock's proposition in *Caldwell* attracted a vigorous dissent from Lord Edmund-Davies, who, like Lord Diplock, had been a party to *Majewski*, and with whom Lord Wilberforce agreed. They dissented not only from the new definition of recklessness, but also from the analysis of *Majewski*. Their view was that arson being reckless as to the endangering of life is an offence of specific, not of basic, intent; that would seem to have been because the state of mind went to an ulterior or purposive element of the offence, rather than to the basic element of causing damage by fire.

v) There were, moreover, many difficulties in the proposition that voluntary intoxication actually supplies the mens rea, whether on the basis of recklessness as re-defined in *Caldwell* or on the basis of recklessness as now understood; if that were so the drunken man might be guilty simply by becoming drunk and whether or not the risk would be obvious to a sober person, himself or anyone else. That reinforces our opinion that the proposition being advanced was one of broadly equivalent culpability, rather than of drink by itself supplying the mens rea.

31. It is necessary to go back to *Majewski* in order to see the basis for the distinction there upheld between crimes of basic and of specific intent. It is to be found most clearly in the speech of Lord Simon, at pages 478B to 479B. Lord Simon's analysis had been fore-shadowed in his speech in *DPP v Morgan* [1976] AC 182, 216 (dissenting in the result), which analysis was cited and approved in *Majewski* by Lord Elwyn-Jones (at 471). It was that crimes of specific intent are those where the offence requires proof of purpose or consequence, which are not confined to, but amongst which are included, those where the purpose goes beyond the actus reus (sometimes referred to as cases of 'ulterior intent'). Lord Simon put it in this way at 478H:

> 'The best description of "specific intent" in this sense that I know is contained in the judgment of Fauteux J in *Reg v George* (1960) 128 Can CC 289, 301 "In considering the question of mens rea, a distinction is to be made between (i) intention as applied to acts considered in relation to their purposes and (ii) intention as applied to acts apart from their purposes. A general intent attending the commission of an act is, in some cases, the only intent required to constitute the crime while, in others, there must be, in addition to that general intent, a specific intent attending the purpose for the commission of the act." '

That explanation of the difference is consistent with the view of Lord Edmund-Davies that an offence contrary to s 1(2)(b) Criminal Damage Act is one of specific intent in this sense, even though it involves no more than recklessness as to the endangering of life; the offence requires proof of a state of mind addressing something beyond the prohibited act itself, namely its consequences. We regard this as the best explanation of the sometimes elusive distinction between specific and basic intent in the sense used in *Majewski*, and it seems to us that this is the distinction which the Judge in the present case was applying when he referred to the concept of a 'bolted-on' intent. By that test, element (a) (the touching) in sexual assault contrary to s 3 Sexual Offences Act 2003 is an element requiring no more than basic intent. It follows that voluntary intoxication cannot be relied upon to negate that intent.

. . .

33. For all these reasons, this conviction is in no sense unsafe. Further, our view is that the Judge's directions were substantially correct. Sexual touching must be intentional, that is to say deliberate. But voluntary intoxication cannot be relied upon as negating the necessary intention. If, whether the Defendant is intoxicated or otherwise, the touching is unintentional, this offence is not committed.

Appeal dismissed.

As already mentioned, prior to this case many academics had suggested that the difference between basic and specific intent offences lay in whether or not intention or knowledge was an aspect of the *mens rea* from the crime. If it was the offence was one of specific intent; whereas crimes of recklessness, negligence, or strict liability were basic. However, that appears not to have been the approach accepted in *Heard*. If it had been then subsection (a) of this offence would have been regarded as involving specific intent. Instead the court took the 'radical'[80] approach of saying that an offence of specific intent is one that requires an 'ulterior intent' (para. 31). That is an intent to do more than simply the act; but an intent to produce a further consequence. So here the requirement that the touching be intentional did not carry an ulterior intent. The only intent required related to the act itself. Therefore it was not an offence of specific intent, but basic intent. This reasoning, which was *obiter*, has not been well received by commentators.[81] It would raise a question over whether murder is a crime of specific or basic intent because there is no ulterior intent required there. Yet murder has long been regarded as a crime of specific intent and it is very unlikely the courts will change their mind on that.[82]

Particular difficulty comes from the use in *Heard* of the concept of an accidental touch. Hughes LJ gives an example of a drunken dancer who grabs a woman's 'private parts' while flailing around. It might be thought that as he is drunk and the offence is one of basic intent that therefore he is to be convicted. However, Hughes LJ disagrees, saying, as the touching was accidental, he has a defence. It is unclear why this is not regarded reckless. If he had been sober he would have seen the risk. It is not quite clear how Hughes LJ's hypothetical dancer differs from the appellant in the case. True it seems in that case his touching of his penis was not accidental, but was the dancing? One can only hope that the Supreme Court is asked soon to look at this issue and produce some clearer guidance.[83] Interestingly, the Law Commission[84] has suggested the case is wrongly decided.

It may be that *Heard* is best understood as a rather special exception to the general rule that basic intent refers to where intent is required for the *mens rea*. There were two aspects of *Heard* which were special. First, unusually, there was no lesser recklessness-based crime for which the defendant could be convicted of. Normally if a drunken defendant lacks intention, there is a lesser recklessness-based crime for which they are still liable. That was not the case here and so his drunken lack of intention would have meant he could escape all liability had the Court of Appeal not decided that the offence should be treated as one of basic intent.[85] Second, it might be argued that drunken sexual assaults are particularly harmful and common in our society and so protection of the public justifies a departure from the normal approach. The

---

[80] Ormerod (2007b: 656).
[81] e.g. Simester, Spencer, Sullivan, and Virgo (2013: 697); R. Williams (2007).
[82] See e.g. *Moloney* [1985] AC 905.
[83] For further discussion of this case, see R. Williams (2007).
[84] Law Commission Report No. 314 (2009a: para. 2.8).
[85] See the discussion in Simester (2009).

argument that public policy can provide an exception from the normal rules on intoxication can be found in *Magee v CPS*.[86] There public policy was referred to as a reason why a person could be convicted of the offence of failing to stop after a traffic accident in section 170(4) of the Road Traffic Act 1988, even if they drunkenly believed no accident had taken place.

7.3 STATING THE PRESENT LAW

Given the state of confusion following *Heard* it is difficult to summarize the current law with certainty. The following is the best summary of the current law, albeit one that is inconsistent with the *obiter* statements in *Heard*.

A voluntarily or involuntarily intoxicated defendant who has *mens rea* for the offence

A defendant who is voluntarily or involuntarily intoxicated but has the *mens rea* required for the offence is guilty.[87] This is true for all crimes. As is often said, 'a drunken intent is still an intent', and we can add 'drunken recklessness is still recklessness'. It is not a defence for intoxicated defendants to claim that they would not have committed the offence had they been sober.[88]

The defendant is involuntarily intoxicated and lacks the *mens rea* for the offence

In such a case the defendant must be acquitted.[89] So if Barbara asks for an orange juice and is (unknown to her) given an orange juice spiked with a large amount of vodka, and she then becomes so intoxicated that she is unaware of what she is doing and attacks someone, then she is not guilty of an assault. It should be stressed that she will be acquitted because of her lack of *mens rea* and not because of the intoxication itself.

The defendant is voluntarily intoxicated and lacks the *mens rea* for the offence

If the defendant is voluntarily intoxicated and lacks the *mens rea* then the effect of the law is that such a defendant will be deemed reckless, but the defendant will be acquitted of an offence requiring intention.[90] It should be noted that in most cases where the defendant is acquitted of an offence requiring intent (e.g. murder) he may be convicted of a lesser offence which requires recklessness (e.g. manslaughter).

Intoxication to enable the commission of a crime

If the defendant has taken drink for the purpose of giving herself the courage to commit the crime she is still guilty, even if at the time she lacks the *mens rea*.[91]

---

86 [2014] EWHC 4089 (Admin).   87 Simester (2009).   88 *Bowden* [1993] Crim LR 379 (CA).

89 The question is whether or not the defendant had the *mens rea*, not whether the accused was capable of forming it (*Sheehan and Moore* (1974) 60 Cr App R 308 (CA)).

90 *Sheehan and Moore* (1974) 60 Cr App R 308 (CA).

91 *Attorney-General of Northern Ireland v Gallagher* [1963] AC 349.

FURTHER READING

Simester, A. (2009) 'Intoxication is Never a Defence' *Criminal Law Review* 3.

Williams, R. (2013) 'Voluntary Intoxication—A Lost Cause?' *Law Quarterly Review* 126: 264.

8 KNOWLEDGE AND BELIEF

DEFINITION

Knowledge involves a positive belief that a state of affairs exists. A defendant who fears that circumstances may exist and deliberately decides not to make any further inquiries in case his or her suspicions prove well founded will be said to know the circumstances.

For some offences it must be shown that the defendant did an act knowing or believing that a certain state of affairs existed. It should be noted that in cases where the *mens rea* is knowledge, careful consideration should be given to which aspects of the *actus reus* need to be known.[92] For example, the offence of handling stolen goods requires proof that the defendant knew or believed that the goods were stolen.[93] The difference between knowledge and belief appears simply to be based on whether the facts known or believed turned out to be true. If they were true then the defendant knew them to be true, if they were false the defendant believed them to be true.[94] Knowledge requires a positive belief. A suspicion may not be enough.[95] The court in *Reader*[96] makes it clear that belief that property might be stolen is not enough for a belief that it is stolen. This does not mean that the defendant must be absolutely certain that the circumstances exist. If he or she assumes a set of facts to be true and has no serious doubt about them, then that state of mind amounts to knowledge.[97]

If the court decides that the defendant was aware that there was a risk that the circumstances existed, and deliberately decided not to make any further enquiries to find out whether his or her fears are true, then in effect the defendant is presumed to know the facts. This is sometimes known as the doctrine of 'wilful blindness'. The House of Lords in *Westminster CC v Croyalgrange Ltd*[98] explained:

> it is always open to the tribunal of fact, when knowledge on the part of a defendant is required to be proved, to base a finding of knowledge on evidence that the defendant had deliberately shut his eyes to the obvious or refrained from enquiry because he suspected the truth but did not want to have his suspicion confirmed.

An example of wilful blindness is if Margaret has a friend, William, whom she knows is a regular burglar and William offers Margaret a television for £10. Margaret may decide to buy the cheap television and not to ask William where he got the television from for fear

---

[92] *Forbes (Giles)* [2001] UKHL 40.

[93] As Shute (2002a) points out, statutes involving knowledge rely on a variety of formulations.

[94] Shute (2002a).　　[95] *Grainge* [1974] 1 All ER 928; *Forsyth* [1997] 2 Cr App R 299, 320.

[96] (1977) 66 Cr App R 33.　　[97] *Griffiths* (1974) 60 Cr App R 14; *Woods* [1969] 1 QB 447.

[98] [1986] 2 All ER 353, 359.

of hearing that it has been stolen. The court may be willing to find that Margaret knew the goods were stolen and hence could be guilty of knowingly handling stolen goods.[99]

It should be emphasized that knowledge and belief are subjective concepts. The question concerns what the defendant knew, not what a reasonable person would have known.[100] Although knowledge is a subjective concept occasionally a statute specifically asks the jury or magistrates to consider what the defendant ought to have known. For example, a defendant is guilty of an offence under the Protection from Harassment Act 1997 if he ought to know that his behaviour would harass the victim.

9 TRANSFERRED *MENS REA*

The doctrine of transferred *mens rea* is often called the doctrine of transferred malice. That is a misleading label as the doctrine does not apply just to malice, but to any *mens rea*. The doctrine applies where a person aims to harm one person or piece of property but misses and harms another.[101] The classic example of the application is where A shoots at B, but misses and instead kills C.[102] Contrast the following examples:

(1) Darren shoots at Marjorie, intending to kill her, but the bullet misses and kills Anna. If Darren is charged with the murder of Anna, is the intention to kill Marjorie sufficient *mens rea*? The answer is 'yes'. The *mens rea* (intention to kill Marjorie) can be 'transferred' to the *actus reus* (the killing of Anna) to create the offence of murder.

(2) Craig shoots at Nick, misses and damages Narinda's property. If Craig is charged with criminal damage to Narinda's property the doctrine of transferred *mens rea* does not lead to a conviction. This is because adding together the intention to kill Nick and the damage to Narinda's property does not create an offence.[103] The *actus reus* and *mens rea* are those of different kinds of offences (murder and criminal damage). Although transferred *mens rea* might not assist in this context, this does not mean that Craig has not committed an offence. Craig will be guilty of attempting to kill Nick. Indeed Craig may be guilty of criminal damage, not using transferred *mens rea*, but because he has been reckless as to damaging Narinda's property.

(3) Brian is being attacked by Josh and in order to defend himself throws a brick at Josh. Josh ducks and the brick hits Elizabeth. Brian's intent to injure Josh can be transferred to Elizabeth, and so too can his defence of self-defence. So Brian would be able to use self-defence to any charge relating to Elizabeth's injuries.[104]

(4) Paul shoots dead someone whom he believes to be Helen, his enemy. To his horror he discovers he has shot Jade, who looks like Helen. Here Paul is guilty of Jade's murder. There is no need to rely on the doctrine of transferred *mens rea*. Paul intended to shoot dead the person in front of him and that person did die. Although Paul was mistaken as to that person's identity that mistake is irrelevant to his *mens rea*.

---

[99] See Hellman (2009) who argues that there can be cases where one is justified in being wilfully blind. She has in mind professionals acting in accordance with good practice or a parent respecting a child's autonomy.

[100] Although the concept of wilful blindness blurs these concepts.

[101] A good example of the application of the doctrine is *Mitchell* [1983] 2 All ER 427 (CA).

[102] *Gnango* [2011] UKSC 59.

[103] *Pembliton* (1874) LR 2 CCR 119. If Craig attempted to damage Nick's property and in fact damaged Narinda's the offence would be made out.

[104] *Gross* (1913) 77 JP 352.

(5) Devina shoots into a crowd, not caring who is killed, and Tanya dies from the shot. Here the law relies on 'general malice': where a defendant does an act intending to kill anyone in the way then the defendant is guilty of murder if he kills someone.[105]

(6) Evan shoots at Una, intending to kill her. He misses and badly injures Vera. Evan can be guilty of intentionally causing grievous bodily harm to Una (section 18 of the Offences Against the Person Act 1861). Although the harm he did to Vera was less than what he intended to do to Una, an intention to kill can be taken to include an intent to do serious harm.[106] →10 (p.206)

EXAMINATION TIP

When answering a problem question always remember that whenever the doctrine of transferred *mens rea* applies there are always two offences to consider:

(1) an attempt to commit the intended offence; and

(2) the full offence involving the harm that occurred.

One particularly difficult case on transferred *mens rea* was *Attorney-General's Reference (No. 3 of 1994)*,[107] where the accused stabbed his pregnant girlfriend. As a result of the wound the child was born early and died from the wound. One key issue was whether the defendant could be charged with murder. You might at first think that this case could be resolved by a straightforward application of the doctrine of transferred *mens rea*. The accused's intention to cause grievous bodily harm to the girlfriend can be transferred to the killing of the baby to create the offence of murder. The difficulty with this reasoning is that at the time of the stabbing the foetus was not a person in the eyes of the law. The House of Lords held that it was not possible to transfer the intent to kill from the mother to the child who (at the time of the stabbing) did not yet exist as a legal person.[108] What about arguing that the defendant's intention to kill or cause grievous bodily harm to the girlfriend could be transferred to the child who actually died? The House of Lords described the argument as involving an impermissible 'double transfer': from the mother to the unborn child; from the unborn child to the person it would become in the future. The House of Lords was still able to hold that the defendant was guilty of manslaughter because (as we shall see in Chapter 5) for that offence there was no need to show an intent to injure any particular person.

FURTHER READING

Bohlander, M. (2010) 'Transferred Malice and Transferred Defenses: A Critique of the Traditional Doctrine and Arguments for a Change in Paradigm' *New Criminal Law Review* 13: 555.

Horder, J. (2006) 'Transferred Malice and the Remoteness of Unexpected Outcomes from Intentions' *Criminal Law Review* 383.

---

[105] *Attorney-General's Reference (No. 3 of 1994)* [1998] AC 245. See the useful discussion in Horder (2006: 386–8).

[106] *Grant* [2014] EWCA Crim 143.   [107] [1998] AC 245.

[108] Although the foetus is not regarded as a person, it can still be a criminal offence to kill a foetus: see e.g. the offence of procuring a miscarriage contrary to the Offences Against the Person Act 1861, s. 58.

10 COINCIDENCE OF *ACTUS REUS* AND *MENS REA*

It is a general principle of criminal law that the requirements of *mens rea* and *actus reus* should coincide in time. So, for example, in a murder case the defendant must intend to kill or cause grievous bodily harm by doing an act which causes the death of the victim. Consider these examples:

(1) One evening Adele decides to kill Sandy at some point in the future and spends the whole night deciding how to do so. The next morning, driving to work, Adele falls asleep at the wheel of her car and drives into a pedestrian killing him. The pedestrian happens to be Sandy. Adele is not guilty of murder. Although the evening before Adele had the *mens rea* for murder and Adele did actually kill Sandy, the *mens rea* and *actus reus* did not coincide at the same time[109] and so Adele should not be convicted of murder.[110]

(2) Spencer is driving along uttering murderous words about Alison whom he hopes to kill as soon as an opportunity arises. Spencer is not paying attention to his driving and crashes into a bus shelter, killing someone who happens to be Alison. Although you may think that the *actus reus* (the causing of the death of Alison) and the *mens rea* (an intention to kill Alison) existed at the same time, this is not a case of murder. Spencer did not intend to kill *by that act*. In other words, he did not intend to kill Alison with the act that caused her death.

(3) Alex stabs Kate intending to kill her and Kate collapses. Alex repents of his actions and desperately tries to save Kate's life. But despite his best efforts she dies. Although it could be argued that at the time of Kate's death Alex did not intend her to die this is in fact irrelevant in the criminal law. The key question is whether at the time Alex did the act which caused the death he had the *mens rea*. At the time of the stabbing Alex had the *mens rea* and so he is guilty of murder.

(4) Johnny is driving his car and begins to feel sleepy. He decides to drive on rather than to stop for a rest. He falls asleep at the wheel and kills a pedestrian. Although at the time when he drove into the pedestrian he was acting involuntarily and so technically 'not driving',[111] his careless driving (in deciding not to stop for a rest and to continue) caused him to fall into an involuntary state, which, in turn, caused the pedestrian's injuries.[112] He is guilty of causing death by dangerous driving.

10.1 'EXCEPTIONS' TO THE COINCIDENCE REQUIREMENT

Despite the requirement that the *mens rea* and *actus reus* coincide the courts have developed ways of flexibly interpreting it, or some would say creating exceptions to it. The case law can be divided into three kinds of cases.

---

109 At the time of the killing she was asleep and was not intending anything.
110 She may be guilty of causing death by dangerous driving.   111 He was an automaton.
112 *Kay v Butterworth* (1945) 173 LT 191.

The defendant may have the *mens rea* at one point in time and then later (without *mens rea*) perform the *actus reus*

A good example of this kind of case is *Meli v R*.[113] The appellants as part of a preconceived plan struck a man over the head. They thought he was dead and threw what they thought was his corpse over a cliff. In fact medical evidence established that the blow to the head had not killed the victim, but being thrown over the cliff had. The difficulty was that at the time of the *actus reus* (throwing the body over the cliff) the appellants lacked *mens rea*, although they had had the *mens rea* earlier when they hit the victim. The Privy Council held that they could properly be convicted of murder as their acts were part of a plan and so could be described as 'one transaction'. As long as the act performed with *mens rea* and the act which constituted the *actus reus* could be described as part of one transaction then the defendant could be convicted.[114] The Court of Appeal in *Le Brun*[115] extended this reasoning to a case where there was no preconceived plan. In that case the defendant hit his wife and she collapsed. He then picked her body up to take it inside. He dropped her and she died. It was held that he could be convicted of manslaughter as the hitting and the carrying of the body could be regarded as one transaction or a single 'sequence of events'. Key to this case was the fact that the defendant was carrying his wife inside to hide what he had done. Had he been taking her to a doctor the court might well have decided that there was not one sequence of events.[116]

The approach to cases of this kind was approved by Lord Mustill in *Attorney-General's Reference (No. 3 of 1994)*,[117] where he summarized the position:

> The existence of an interval of time between the doing of an act by the defendant with the necessary wrongful intent and its impact on the victim in a manner which leads to death does not in itself prevent the intent, the act and the death from together amounting to murder, so long as there is an unbroken causal connection between the act and the death.

Whether the series of events is part of the same sequence of events or part of an 'unbroken causal connection' is a question of fact for the jury.

The defendant committed the *actus reus* at one point in time (without the necessary *mens rea*), but at a later point in time he has the *mens rea*

An example of such a case is where the defendant while asleep starts a fire, then afterwards realizes what he has done and runs off. The courts have dealt with such cases in two ways:

(1) The prosecution could argue that the defendant's initial act should be seen as a continuing act which is still continuing at the point in time when the *mens rea* arises.

(2) An alternative way of considering such cases is to argue that the defendant's failure to stop the harm he was causing amounted to a criminal omission for which the defendant could be convicted. The most significant case discussing this approach is *Miller* (which is excerpted at Chapter 2, Creation of the danger, p.78).[118] There it will be recalled that once the defendant has set off a chain of events which poses a danger

---

[113] [1954] 1 WLR 228.   [114] See also *Moore* [1975] Crim LR 229 and *Church* [1966] 1 QB 59.
[115] [1991] 4 All ER 673.
[116] An alternative line of reasoning the court adopted was that the original hit was an operating cause of the death in the sense that the attempt to carry her away did not break the chain of causation.
[117] [1998] AC 245, 265.   [118] [1983] 2 AC 161.

he is under a duty to act to prevent the danger arising. Once the defendant is aware of the danger, but fails to prevent it materializing or mitigate it, the *mens rea* and the *actus reus* (the failure to act) coincide.

These arguments were considered in the following case:

Fagan v Metropolitan Police Commissioner
[1969] 1 QB 439 (QBD)

The appellant, who was driving his car, was asked by a police officer to pull over. The appellant did so, but ended up on the policeman's foot. The police officer apparently then said: 'Get off, you are on my foot.' The appellant did not move the car. When the police officer repeated the request the appellant eventually did so.

Mr Justice James

The justices at quarter sessions on those facts were left in doubt whether the mounting of the wheel on to the officer's foot was deliberate or accidental. They were satisfied, however, beyond all reasonable doubt that the appellant 'knowingly, provocatively and unnecessarily' allowed the wheel to remain on the foot after the officer said 'Get off, you are on my foot'. They found that, on these facts, an assault was proved.

Counsel for the appellant relied on the passage in *Stone's Justices' Manual* (1968 Edn.), Vol. 1, p. 651, where assault is defined (Viz., 'An assault is an attempt by force, or violence, to do bodily injury to another. It is an act of aggression done against or upon the person of another without his consent; not necessarily against his will, if by that is implied an actual resistance or expression of objection made at the time . . .'). He contends that, on the finding of the justices, the initial mounting of the wheel could not be an assault, and that the act of the wheel mounting the foot came to an end without there being any *mens rea*. It is argued that thereafter there was no act on the part of the appellant which could constitute an *actus reus*, but only the omission or failure to remove the wheel as soon as he was asked. That failure, it is said, could not in law be an assault, nor could it in law provide the necessary *mens rea* to convert the original act of mounting the foot into an assault. Counsel for the respondent argues that the first mounting of the foot was an *actus reus*, which act continued until the moment of time at which the wheel was removed. During that continuing act, it is said, the appellant formed the necessary intention to constitute the element of *mens rea* and, once that element was added to the continuing act, an assault took place. In the alternative, counsel argues, that there can be situations in which there is a duty to act and that, in such situations, an omission to act in breach of duty would in law amount to an assault. It is unnecessary to formulate any concluded views on this alternative.

. . .

To constitute this offence, some intentional act must have been performed; a mere omission to act cannot amount to an assault. Without going into the question whether words alone can constitute an assault, it is clear that the words spoken by the appellant could not alone amount to an assault; they can only shed a light on the appellant's action. For our part, we think that the crucial question is whether, in this case, the act of the appellant can be said to be complete and spent at the moment of time when the car wheel came to rest on the foot, or whether his act is to be regarded as a continuing act operating until the wheel was removed. In our judgment, a distinction is to be drawn between acts which are complete—though results may continue to flow—and those acts which are continuing. Once the act is complete, it cannot thereafter be said to be a threat to inflict unlawful force on the victim. If the act, as distinct from the results thereof, is a continuing act, there is a continuing threat to inflict unlawful force. If the assault involves a battery and that battery continues, there is a continuing act of assault. For an assault to be committed, both the elements of *actus reus* and *mens rea* must be present at the same time. The '*actus reus*' is the action causing the effect on the victim's mind: see the observations of Parke, B., in *R. v. St. George* (1840), 9 C. & P. 483 at pp. 490, 493. The '*mens rea*' is the intention to cause that effect. It is not necessary that *mens rea* should be present at the inception of the *actus reus*; it can be superimposed on an existing act. On the other hand, the subsequent inception of *mens rea* cannot convert an act which has been completed without *mens rea* into an assault.

In our judgment, the justices at Willesden and quarter sessions were right in law. On the facts found, the action of the appellant may have been initially unintentional, but the time came when, knowing that the wheel was on the officer's foot, the appellant (i) remained seated in the car so that his body through the medium of the car was in contact with the officer, (ii) switched off the ignition of the car, (iii) maintained the wheel of the car on the foot, and (iv) used words indicating the intention of keeping the wheel in that position. For our part, we cannot regard such conduct as mere omission or inactivity. There was an act constituting a battery which at its inception was not criminal because there was no element of intention, but which became criminal from the moment the intention was formed to produce the apprehension which was flowing from the continuing act. The fallacy of the appellant's argument is that it seeks to equate the facts of this case with such a case as where a motorist has accidentally run over a person and, that action having been completed, fails to assist the victim with the intent that the victim should suffer.

We would dismiss this appeal.

[**Lord Justice Parker** agreed with **Mr Justice James**'s judgment.]

[**Mr Justice Bridge** handed down a dissenting judgment.]

Appeal dismissed.

It is unclear when the *actus reus* occurred

An example of this difficulty is revealed in the rather grizzly facts of *Attorney-General's Reference (No. 4 of 1980)*.[119] Here the defendant slapped his girlfriend, pushed her down the stairs, put a rope around her neck, dragged her back up the stairs, cut her throat and cut her body into pieces. It was unclear which of these acts had caused her death, although it was clear one of them had! The Court of Appeal held that as long as the defendant had the necessary *mens rea* at the time of each of the possible acts that caused the death he could be properly convicted of murder or manslaughter.

> **REVISION TIP**
>
> When you come to revise specific criminal offences you will need to learn both the *actus reus* and *mens rea* for those offences. But remember with the *mens rea* that you will need to learn not only whether intention, recklessness, or negligence is required, but for what. So do not just say the *mens rea* for murder is intention. You need to say that the *mens rea* for murder is an intention to kill or cause grievous bodily harm to the victim.

[119] [1981] 1 WLR 705.

QUESTIONS

1. Peter believes that his enemy, Olive, may possibly be allergic to peanuts. He puts peanut oil on Olive's toothbrush, hoping to kill her. It turns out that Olive is allergic to the oil and after brushing her teeth suffers an allergic reaction and dies. Bob, Olive's friend, wants to terrify Peter to teach him a lesson. He sets fire to Peter's house. Peter dies in the fire. Did Peter intend to kill Olive? Did Bob intend to kill Peter?

For guidance on answering this question, please visit the Online Resource Centre that accompanies this book: www.oxfordtextbooks.co.uk/orc/herringcriminal7e/.

2. Steve is rollerblading down a pavement. Someone steps out in front of him. Without thinking, he jumps to one side. He crashes into a car and scratches the paintwork. Was Steve reckless as to damaging the car? Was he negligent?

FURTHER READING

Sullivan, G.R. (1993b) 'Cause and the Contemporaneity of *Actus Reus* and *Mens Rea*' *Criminal Law Journal* 487.

PART II: *MENS REA* THEORY

11 GENERAL DISCUSSION ON *MENS REA*

Sanford Kadish has suggested that the existence of *mens rea* shows that the criminal law regards people as autonomous agents who are responsible for the choices they make rather than robots which have malfunctioned and need to be mended.[120] Indeed commentators see *mens rea* as being at the heart of the criminal law, fulfilling several important roles:[121]

(1) It ensures that censure correctly attaches to a criminal conviction. If a criminal conviction is to signify that society censures an individual for his or her actions then it is not enough just to show that the defendant harmed the victim. He or she must have done so in a blameworthy way.

(2) *Mens rea* is not just about ensuring that only blameworthy people are convicted, but also that they are convicted of the right offence.[122] Many people would draw a clear moral distinction between, for example, an intentional killer and a negligent one. Such distinctions, it is said, should be reflected in the criminal law. Hence we distinguish between murder and manslaughter.

(3) *Mens rea* may also help to define the wrong done to the victim. If you are out shopping and are pushed over your reaction will be different depending on whether you were deliberately or accidentally pushed over. If it was deliberate you will feel you have been attacked; if it was accidental you are likely to find the incident far less

---

[120] Kadish (1987b: 3). [121] See Chan and Simester (2011) and M. Moore (2011).
[122] Brudner (2008).

traumatic. The intention behind the action in part defines the kind of harm the victim has suffered.

(4) *Mens rea* ensures that the victim is given fair warning of what is criminal.[123] Citizens can be confident in knowing whether or not what they plan to do will be a crime if they are only liable if they intend or foresee a harm to another. A law which made it a crime even though the defendant had no *mens rea* would mean even a citizen trying very hard to comply with the law may unwittingly commit a crime.

(5) Chan and Simester[124] argue that the requirement of *mens rea* also helps restrict the ambit of the criminal law so that it does not cover too many people. They argue it helps protect freedoms and helps in the fight against over-criminalization.

It is interesting to consider what a criminal law would be like if it contained no *mens rea* requirements. Baroness Wootton[125] proposed such a legal system. At the heart of her thinking was the view that the criminal court was not in a position to assess the blameworthiness of a defendant. We would need to know far more about human psychology and courts would have to be told far more about defendants' personal history if they were truly to assess blameworthiness.[126] Wootton proposed that offences should simply require proof that the defendant harmed the victim. At the sentencing stage the judge would be free to take into account the defendant's state of mind along with other relevant considerations. Opponents of proposals such as Wootton's point out that under them we would then have to accept that a person could be guilty of a crime even though he or she was entirely blameless for his or her actions. It is true that such a defendant may receive no punishment, but the censuring effect of a conviction itself would be lost. We could not assume that a person found guilty of a crime was morally blameworthy. A person who deliberately killed the victim and a person who killed another through no fault of his or her own would both be guilty of murder.[127] There are, however, benefits to Wootton's approach. It does acknowledge the harm done to the victim. Imagine the trauma a rape victim feels when her assailant is acquitted because he was not aware that she was not consenting. Her perception is understandably that the criminal law has failed to acknowledge that from her perspective she was raped, whatever the defendant's state of mind. A further important point is Wootton's argument that we must not be overconfident in the law's ability to assess the moral blameworthiness of a defendant.

Most commentators reject the notion of a criminal law system without *mens rea* and insist that serious criminal offences must require proof of *mens rea*. Professor Williams has argued that the requirement of *mens rea* is 'a mark of advancing civilisation'.[128] Indeed, as we shall see in Chapter 4, the House of Lords[129] has stated that there is a presumption that offences require proof of *mens rea* unless there is clear evidence rebutting that presumption. But before English and Welsh lawyers get too puffed up with pride on the humanity and moral subtlety demonstrated by their criminal legal system's use of *mens rea* three points should be emphasized:

(1) As William Wilson has pointed out, we pride ourselves in not punishing animals, infants, or the insane on the basis that they are not responsible agents. Yet animals

---

[123] Chan and Simester (2011).   [124] *Ibid.*   [125] Wootton (1981).

[126] Some would say that only an omniscient, good God would be in a position to make such a judgment.

[127] Although one could give them markedly different sentences. Indeed, if blameworthiness became irrelevant such a system logically could return to the practice (common in medieval law) of sentencing animals for criminal offences (Evans 1987)!

[128] G. Williams (1983: 70).   [129] *B v DPP* [2000] 2 AC 428.

that attack other animals or people are liable to be put down, children who commit serious crimes are likely to be taken into state care, and the insane are hospitalized. As Wilson notes, 'The rhetoric says that such a response is not a mark of blame and such treatment is not punishment. The reality is that those concerned would hardly know the difference.'[130]

(2) A point which will be made several times in this chapter is that the extent to which criminal law seeks to examine the moral blameworthiness of a defendant's actions is limited. For example, a defendant who argues that his criminal behaviour has more to do with his socio-economic background than personal blameworthiness will have little chance of success before a court.[131]

(3) Although *mens rea* is seen as an important principle, in fact many crimes do not require proof of the defendant's state of mind.[132] The large majority of crimes are negligence-based or are offences of strict liability, which require only proof that the defendant acted in a particular way. Andrew Ashworth suggests that there are thousands of strict liability offences.[133] Even if we consider just the more serious offences which cannot be heard by magistrates and must be tried in the Crown Court, over half of these are offences of strict or objective liability.[134]

Despite these important points the judiciary and many academics place much weight on the significance of *mens rea* and much academic and judicial ink has been spilt trying to define the key *mens rea* terms discussed in Part I.

12 CHOICE/CAPACITY/CHARACTER THEORY

The debate over the correct definition of the *mens rea* terms reflects the disputes over the choice, capacity, and character theories. These were mentioned in Chapter 1 and will be discussed in more detail in Chapter 12, so will be mentioned only briefly here:

(1) The *choice theory* centres on an argument that people are responsible for the things they chose to do. People should be guilty of a crime only if they chose effectively to do the *actus reus*.[135]

(2) The *capacity theory* is similar to the choice theory in that it accepts the argument that people are responsible for what they chose to do. But it also accepts that it is proper to punish those who *could* have effectively chosen to act lawfully, but did not.

(3) The *character theory* focuses on the argument that the defendant is responsible for his or her character. If his or her criminal actions reveal character traits that are opposed by the criminal law he or she should be punished.

These different theories suggest alternative understandings of *mens rea*. The choice theory supports crimes based on intention and *Cunningham* recklessness, but would not support offences based on *Caldwell* recklessness, negligence, or strict liability, where the defendant did not necessarily choose to commit a crime. The capacity theory would also support intention and *Cunningham* recklessness, but would also be willing to support criminal liability

---

130 W. Wilson (2003: 120).   131 Kymlicka, Lernestedt, and Matravers (2014).
132 Ashworth and Blake (1996).   133 Ashworth (2009: 96).
134 Lacey, Wells, and Quick (2003: 23–8).   135 G. Williams (1997).

for inadvertence, at least in so far as the defendant *could* have appreciated the risk. The capacity theory would therefore support the acquittal of *Stephenson*,[136] but deplore the conviction of C in *Elliott v C*.[137] The capacity theory would also be happy for some convictions to be based on negligence, but only where the defendant had the capability of acting non-negligently.[138] The character theory would be less obsessed with the defendant's foresight or intention than the other theories. Although, usually, an intentional or *Cunningham* reckless act would indicate bad character, it need not always. The character theory could distinguish between a deliberate killing and a mercy killing, in that arguably the former but not the latter indicates a bad character. Some negligence or strict liability could be supported on the basis that the defendant's actions revealed that he did not care enough about other people. Other commentators have rejected an approach for *mens rea* which focuses on grand overarching theories. John Gardner argues:

> the question of what should be the mens rea for a particular crime is a question which calls, in the first instance, for a local answer specific to that crime. For it depends . . . on what exactly is wrong, or is supposed to be wrong, with perpetrating that particular crime.[139]

13 SUBJECTIVE/OBJECTIVE

As we have already seen in Chapter 1, another way of looking at the disputes over *mens rea* terms is to see them as a disagreement between the objectivists and subjectivists.[140] Subjectivists focus on what was going on inside the defendant's mind when he or she committed the crime: what did he or she intend, foresee, know, or believe? Objectivists tend to focus more on the defendant's actions: is what the defendant did unreasonable? Objectivists may consider what a reasonable person in the defendant's shoes would have intended, foreseen, known, or believed.

Although there is sometimes talk of a battle between subjectivism and objectivism it is perfectly sensible to take the view that some offences should be drafted in objective terms and others in subjective terms.[141] Generally subjectivists support liability for intention and *Cunningham* recklessness and reject *Caldwell* recklessness, negligence, and strict liability as objectivist, although, as we shall see, it is in fact far more complicated than this.

QUESTIONS

1. Is 'inadvertence' or 'indifference' to a risk a state of mind or an absence of a state of mind?

2. Read R. Tur, 'Subjectivism and Objectivism: Towards Synthesis' in S. Shute, J. Gardner, and J. Horder (eds) *Action and Value in Criminal Law* (Oxford: OUP, 1993). Do you think it is possible to synthesize subjectivism and objectivism?

---

[136] [1979] QB 695.   [137] [1983] 1 WLR 939 (QBD).

[138] M. Moore (2000: ch. 7) suggests that liability for negligence could be supported on the basis of un-exercised capacity.

[139] J. Gardner (2008: 27).

[140] See Tur (1993) for a further discussion on subjectivism and objectivism.

[141] Sullivan (2002b: 222–3).

14 NORMAL MEANING

One theme that has run through many of the judicial decisions is that *mens rea* words like 'intention' and 'recklessness' should carry their normal, everyday meaning.[142] At first this seems uncontroversial. After all, it is far easier for a jury to give words their normal meaning than some technical, legal meaning which they may misunderstand.[143] Further, giving such words their normal meaning helps to make the law predictable and readily understandable to ordinary people. For example, if dishonesty in theft was given a highly technical, outdated meaning a defendant might justly complain 'How on earth was I meant to know that dishonesty meant that?' Also, giving such words their ordinary meaning enables the law to keep abreast of changes in the moral and cultural climate. Defining dishonesty in terms of the standards expected of the ordinary, honest person is said by some to mean that the legal concept of dishonesty is kept in line with current standards of morality. ←1 (p.134)

However, some commentators reject any assumption that the legal meanings and normal meanings of words should be the same.[144] Does the word 'intention', for example, have an everyday meaning? Even if it does is it precise enough to assist in borderline cases?

Behind this debate on whether words should have their normal meaning is a debate over how much power a jury should have. If the judge provides a precise legal definition of the concept the judge (in theory) retains control over the definition of the term.[145] If the jury are to give the term its normal meaning then they retain a degree of discretion in deciding, for example, what the current standards of morality are. The hidden use of references to ordinary language is brought out in the following passage by Nicola Lacey. She has just considered those scholars who seek to clarify the notion of intention using 'conceptual analysis', who, she suggests, appear to believe that if only we could come up with a morally sophisticated definition of intention the difficulties in the law would be resolved. She rejects this because:

> the real source of uncertainty and disagreement in the application of criminal law concepts such as intention is not ultimately to do with the concept, but with practical, moral and political issues. Should this person be convicted, and of what offence?

She then turns to those who believe that giving intention its normal meaning will resolve the problems over the definition of intention:

N. Lacey, 'A Clear Concept of Intention: Elusive or Illusory?' (1993) 56 *Modern Law Review* 621

Ordinary Usage

At the other end of the spectrum, we have the resort in the face of difficulties of definition to 'ordinary usage.' It should be noted that ordinary usage is itself something of a chimera. For just as 'legal usage' is arguably a relatively specific and autonomous area of discourse, many other areas of linguistic usage develop particular, local and technical meanings for 'ordinary' words. And even within these local areas, usage is fluid and often contested. This

---

[142] *Brutus v Cozens* [1973] AC 854 (HL).   [143] Buxton (1988).
[144] G. Williams (1987).   [145] Lacey (1993a).

notwithstanding, the resort to the 'common usage' or the 'ordinary person's understanding' of a particular term is a familiar technique in criminal law—perhaps most famously debated in recent years in the context of the concept of dishonesty under the Theft Act 1968. On the view which appeals to 'ordinary usage,' the attempt to articulate and fix particular conceptual analyses in legislative or judicial form is both unnecessary and misguided. It is unnecessary because, in the case of concepts such as intention, dishonesty, violence and so on, 'ordinary people' have a clear if unarticulated sense of what these terms mean. So it can simply be left to the jury or the lay magistrate to apply those ordinary understandings to the case at hand. And it is misguided, because part of the function of criminal laws which employ those terms is precisely to bring to bear on the alleged offender the standards of judgment thought to be buried within and reflected by 'ordinary usage': the thought behind the legal proscription in question is the application of a general rather than a technical standard in this respect. The 'ordinary language' view is therefore motivated by at least two concerns: the investment of *mens rea* terms with 'ordinary' or 'common sense' meanings, and the delegation of decision making power in Crown Court cases to jury rather than judge. In some sense, on this view, the framers of criminal laws articulate definitions of offences in terms of a combination of legal and factual questions. The line between questions of law and those of fact is notoriously hard to draw, but the approach based on 'ordinary language' does appear to make conviction depend, in a wide range of cases, on questions of fact—or what might more accurately be called 'lay evaluation.' We should note the attractions to law makers of the rhetorical force which attaches to legislation framed in terms of 'ordinary' terms which resonate with citizens' pre-legal ideas of wrongdoing.

To set out the view which appeals to 'ordinary language' is already to suggest its main weakness as a tool of legal practice. This lies in its assumption that a settled, widely shared understanding underpins the usage of all or most such terms employed by criminal law. It seems only reasonable to observe that this assumption is undermined by recent case law history. Even giving due weight to the opacity of the trial judges' directions in recent murder cases such as *Moloney, Hancock and Shankland*, and *Nedrick*, it is hardly to be doubted that the return of the jury for further advice about the meaning of 'intention' must be put down not just to bewilderment in the face of legal 'guidelines' but also to uncertainty and disagreement over 'ordinary language.' On all the evidence, and in ordinary terms, could Moloney be said to have intended to kill his stepfather; could Hancock and Shankland be said to have intended to kill or seriously injure the drivers and occupants of the vehicles coming up the motorway? Can at least some 'core' notion of intention be identified, in relation to which 'penumbral' cases can easily be incorporated within 'ordinary' usage?

In the face of this kind of problem, judges and commentators have often favoured an intermediate position in which the resort to ordinary language is buttressed by recourse to conceptual analysis and stipulation. Typically, this has consisted in the incomplete and often negative delineation of the term in question, either in terms of a partial definition, or of judicial guidelines, or both. A good example would be dishonesty under the Theft Act 1968, of which section 2 partially defines dishonesty by excluding three specific instances and including another. This is supplemented at the judicial level by guidelines which set out two questions which the jury has to ask itself in determining whether the defendant is dishonest. These questions mark out the concept without supplying the ultimate standard to be applied. A similar compromise strategy is being worked out in the case of intention, and the recent cases will now be analysed in more depth. My aim is to suggest that the strategy entails a fundamental tension, widely present in criminal law cases. This tension is interesting, because it undermines the traditional doctrinal insistence on the importance and (at least relative) possibility of coherence and consistency of principle in criminal law.

15 INTENT

Although academics have written an enormous amount about intent and its meaning has been a matter of heated debate, in practice intent is rarely relevant in criminal trials.[146] Very few offences require proof that the defendant intended a result. Recklessness or negligence is normally sufficient. Nevertheless intent is an important concept in the criminal law because it is widely regarded as the 'worst' kind of *mens rea*.

But what makes intent the most serious form of *mens rea*? That is considered in the following passage:

T. Weigend, 'Subjective Elements of Criminal Liability' in M. Dubber and
T. Hörnle (eds) *The Oxford Handbook of Criminal Law* (Oxford: OUP, 2014), 493

It is generally assumed that intentional fault is of greater gravity than non-intentional (negligent) fault. Yet, a negligent person can do as much harm as someone who commits an intentional offense, and a negligent person likewise fails in his obligation to take other persons' legitimate interests into account when he acts. Why, then, do most legal systems impose greater punishment on intentional offenders, and why do they limit criminal responsibility for merely negligent conduct to a small number of offenses? Several explanations have been given for the claim that more severe consequences should be imposed on an intentional offender: he has taken a conscious decision to violate the interest protected by the law; his conduct is indicative of an attitude that consciously ignores the commands of the law; his knowledge of all relevant facts makes it easier for him to avoid the criminal conduct; and intentional violations of the law do more harm to the public feeling of security and therefore require harsher sanctions in order to restore the confidence of the public in the rule of law. With regard to preventive purposes of the criminal law, one might say that intentional conduct lends itself to being deterred more than mere inadvertence, and a person showing anti-legal tendencies may be in greater need of reform than someone who just does not pay attention.

Before we look at some of the controversial theoretical issues surrounding intention, there is an important point to make. Much of the discussion of the meaning of intention has occurred in the context of the law of murder. It is all too easy in discussing this topic to confuse the issue 'Did D intend to kill V?' with the question 'Should D be convicted of murder?' But these are separate questions.

We must now turn to some of the most controversial issues surrounding the concept of intention.

15.1 DISTINGUISHING INDIRECT INTENTION AND DIRECT INTENTION

As you will have gathered from the summary of the law in Part I, the greatest area of dispute is over the extent to which a result which is not the actor's purpose, but which was foreseen by him, can be said to be intended by him. There is widespread agreement that if it was the

---

[146] Lacey (1993b: 621).

defendant's purpose to cause a result or the defendant wanted the result to occur in order to achieve his purpose then he intended it.[147] We called this the 'core meaning of intention' in Part I of this chapter.[148] As mentioned there, the courts have been troubled by cases of indirect or oblique intention. Commentators have equally been divided on the issue. To assist in understanding the different views taken we will consider four hypothetical cases:

(1) **The desperate surgeon** D, a surgeon, has a wife who is in desperate need of a heart transplant. D removes a heart from a healthy patient (V) and transplants it into his wife. D does not want V to die (his purpose is to save his wife's life), but is aware that if he removes V's heart V will die.

(2) **The aeroplane bomber** D puts a bomb on an aeroplane which carries goods which D has insured. His plan is to blow up the plane in mid-flight and claim the insurance money on the destroyed goods. He knows that if the bomb goes off it is virtually certain that the pilot will die. In due course the bomb goes off, killing the pilot.

(3) **The burning father** D is holding his baby on the top of a burning building. As the flames get very close he throws the baby from the building in a last-ditch attempt to save the baby's life, but aware that the baby is almost bound to die as a result of the fall. Unfortunately the baby does indeed die, but miraculously the father is rescued by a helicopter.

(4) **The revengeful wife** D, on discovering that her husband is having an affair with V, sets fire to V's house. Her purpose is to scare V away from her husband, although she knows it is likely that V or her family will be inside and may therefore die.

Four views will be sketched in outline here,[149] but there are nearly as many views on what intention is as there are people who have written on the issue: ←4 (p.140)

The 'pure intention' view

This view[150] is promoted by those who argue that intention should mean purpose, nothing more and nothing less.[151] Supporters point out that it is quite possible to foresee a result as virtually certain but not intend it. You may foresee that by drinking ten dry sherries in the bar you will get a hangover the next morning, but that does not mean that you intend to get a hangover when you drink.[152] John Finnis has written that he may foresee that his lecture will confuse half those attending, but that does not mean he intends them to be confused.[153] As Wilson points out: 'If I pull my child's loose tooth out, knowing this cannot be done without him suffering significant pain, only a passing spaceman from Mars could reach the conclusion that I intended to hurt him.' Although if Wilson is correct in saying this quite a few lecturers in criminal law are Martians!

Looking at our scenarios there is no doubt that under the 'pure intention view' the plane bomber, the burning father, and the revengeful wife did not intend the death of V.[154] More

---

[147] e.g. Finnis (1991: 36).

[148] See the discussion of whether purpose is preferable to want or desire in Kugler (2002: ch. 1).

[149] The names I have given to these theories are mine.   [150] Finnis (1991: 32).

[151] M. Moore (1999). This narrow view of intention is popular with those who take the view that it is never justifiable intentionally to take someone's life. See e.g. Finnis (1991).

[152] Duff (1990a: 61).   [153] Finnis (1991: 64).

[154] Supporters of this view suggest that if we do not like this conclusion in respect of, say, the plane bomber, then we should change the law on what the *mens rea* for murder is, rather than artificially stretch the law on intention.

problematic is the desperate surgeon. You might think that the pure intention view would hold that the surgeon's purpose was to save his wife's life and so he did not intend to kill V. However, the argument 'I intended to take V's heart out, but did not intend to kill her' is very unattractive. One possible escape route for supporters of the pure intent view is to say that intending to take someone's heart out simply is intending to kill them: the two consequences are inseparable.[155] There is, in our world, no difference between taking out someone's heart and killing them.

Supporters of the pure intention view often support the 'ethical doctrine of double effect', which has been defined by John Keown in the following extract:

J. Keown, *Euthanasia, Ethics and Public Policy* (Cambridge: Cambridge University Press, 2003), 20

According to this ethical tradition, it is permissible to allow a bad consequence to result from one's actions, even if it is foreseen as certain to follow, provided certain conditions are satisfied. Those conditions are identified by the principle of 'double effect.' According to this ethical principle, it is permissible to produce a bad consequence if:

- the act one is engaged in is not itself bad;
- the bad consequence is not a means to the good consequence;
- the bad consequence is foreseen but not intended; and
- there is a sufficiently serious reason for allowing the bad consequence to occur.

It should be noted that Keown's explanation of the doctrine of double effect is more than a description of *mens rea*. The fourth factor requires the jury to make a moral assessment of what the defendant did.[156]

The 'moral elbow room' view

The 'moral elbow room' view[157] is that intention is purpose, but that where a defendant is aware that a result is virtually certain to follow from his actions the jury should be given a discretion to decide whether the mental state is wicked enough to be called intention. This would enable supporters of this view to reach what many people would regard as intuitively the correct result: the plane bomber and the desperate surgeon intended to kill V; the burning father and the revengeful wife did not. In these cases some argue that the defendant's wicked recklessness was tantamount to intention and should therefore be treated as such.[158]

Opponents argue that such a test would produce too much uncertainty. Should the case of the desperate surgeon be left to the jury's deliberation: should we not be clear that that is intention? Leaving cases such as that of the plane bomber to the jury means that there is a danger that different juries may reach different conclusions on different facts, leading to the injustice of inconsistent verdicts. It should be the law, not the whim of the jury, which decides whether a person's state of mind constitutes intention.

---

[155] R. Cross (1967: 224) gives an example of a head-hunter who removes someone's head for his collection, but denying that he intended to kill the 'owner' of the head. For further discussion, see Simester (1996a and 1996b).

[156] For further discussion, see Foster, Herring, Hope, and Melham (2011 and 2013).

[157] The phrase appears in Horder (1995a: 687).   [158] Horder (2005b: 38).

The 'oblique intention' view

This view is that a result which is foreseen as virtually certain is simply intended. If a person knows that a result will occur as a result of his acts he intended it. Or at least that state of mind is more appropriately classified as intention than recklessness, even if, strictly speaking, it is not intention.[159] Therefore the desperate surgeon, the plane bomber, and the burning father intended to kill V, but the vengeful wife did not (she saw V's death as likely, not virtually certain). The problem scenario for this view is the burning father. Supporters simply reply that although he intended V's death he should be given a defence to ensure he is not guilty of murder. To opponents of this view, to say that the father intended to kill the child when he had the opposite purpose (to save the baby's life) is unsupportable.[160]

The 'Hyam' view

This view suggests that if a result is foreseen as likely then it is intended. Although it has the support of the majority of the House of Lords in *Hyam*, it in fact has few supporters nowadays. Supporters of this view would decide that in all four of our scenarios the defendants intend to kill. Opponents of the view argue that if foresight of a result is intention then the boundary between intention and recklessness becomes hopelessly blurred. ←3 (p.139)

In the following passage, Glanville Williams expresses his support for the oblique intention view:

G. Williams, 'Oblique Intention' (1987) 46 *Cambridge Law Journal* 417 at 424–5

Arguments for recognising oblique intent

That cases of the types mentioned should be treated in the same way as ordinary cases of intention is obvious, but opinions differ between two methods of carrying out the policy. One method would be that already proposed: to relax the definition of intent sufficiently to allow oblique intent as a kind of intent. The other would be to redefine all crimes of intention, when it is desired to bring in oblique intent, by making express provision for it.

The second alternative would involve defining murder, for example, as causing death (i) with intent to cause death or serious injury, or (ii) with knowledge that such death or injury is virtually certain. This would make the law perfectly clear, but the definitions of the relevant crimes would become slightly more cumbrous. There appears to be no possibility that Parliament would now revise the law of murder to make specific provision for this additional mental state (upon which the prosecution would rarely need to rely), and any attempt to do so would reopen the whole thorny issue of risk-taking and murder. And not only murder but also various other crimes requiring intention would need the extended definition.

The first alternative would avoid this drawback. As was shown before, there are solid reasons for saying that oblique intent is recognised in the law as it stands, and if the courts accept this opinion no legislative departures are needed.

The case for taking a broad view of intention is particularly strong where the desired consequence is inseparably bound up with the foreseen though undesired consequence. (i) Consider *Arrowsmith* v. *Jenkins*. A political campaigner commenced to address people on the highway, and continued to do so although she knew that she was causing the highway to be blocked, to a degree that (whether she knew it or not) the law regarded as unreasonable.

---

[159] Simester (1996a). [160] Duff (1990a: 98); Norrie (1999).

She was convicted of wilfully obstructing the highway, even though her purpose was to hold a meeting, not to obstruct the highway. In the circumstances, holding the meeting was the same thing as obstructing the highway; they were simply two sides of the same coin. (ii) The following were the facts of a notorious Brighton case of 1871. A woman inserted strychnine into a chocolate and attempted to administer it to V. The chocolate she gave having been found to be poisoned, the woman said that she did not know it, and tried to prove her innocence by showing that poisoned chocolates were circulating in the locality. She did this by introducing strychnine into a confectioner's stock of chocolates; and the buyer of some chocolates died. The poisoner was held guilty of murder; yet her primary intent was to dispel the suspicion against her. She did not want anyone other than V to die, and would not have felt frustrated if, by chance, no one died. In those days the crime of murder was much wider than now; but if the poisoner felt sure that her poisoned chocolates would kill someone, would she not still be rightly convicted of murder on the ground that she intended to kill, notwithstanding that she did not desire to do so?

A peculiar group of cases are those where the law theoretically requires proof of fact *y* but the courts regard it as readily satisfied by proof of *x*. A publisher may be convicted of conspiracy to corrupt public morals, obscenity, or blasphemy, on account of an assumed intent to commit these crimes, if he knowingly publishes matter which the jury find to have a tendency to corrupt public morals, to deprave and corrupt those to whom it is published, etc.; and no evidence is needed to support the jury's conclusion. Strict proof of the purported conclusion would be practically impossible, requiring a large sociological enquiry and a consensus on disputed values. The courts simplify the matter by making the equation $x=y$, x being the physical event that the defendant intends (the publication) and y being the jury's determination that it amounts to y.

15.2 IS INTENTION AN ISSUE OF FACT OR AN ISSUE OF MORAL RESPONSIBILITY?

Is intention a factual concept or is it one that involves a judgment?[161] In other words is intention a psychological fact: if we could see everything that was going on inside the defendant's mind would we know if there was intent? Or is intention in the nature of a moral judgment: is the defendant's state of mind bad enough to deserve the label 'intention'?[162] In the following passage, Alan Norrie discusses these different approaches to intention:

A. Norrie, *Crime, Reason and History* (Cambridge: Cambridge University Press, 2014), 57–60

(i) **Two approaches to intention**

It will be helpful if we begin by exploring the meaning of the concept of intention. This is not straightforward for we can identify not one but two conceptions, both of which are

---

[161] Linked to this issue is a debate over the extent to which defences, such as necessity, become merged with the notion of intention.

[162] See Horder (1995a). It should be noted that other *mens rea* terms do involve an element of moral judgment. A person is reckless only if he takes an unjustifiable risk; a person is negligent only if he behaves unreasonably. It would not, therefore, be extremely radical to suggest that intention carries an element of moral judgment. For further discussion of this point, see Simester and Chan (1997).

relevant to the law. The first is the one that is favoured by the 'orthodox subjectivists' such as Williams and Smith and Hogan, and which has a prominent position in the law itself. It is a formal, 'factual', psychological definition. The second is a more morally substantive, less factual and psychological, account which is reflected in the work, for example, of Anthony Duff (1990), John Gardner (1998) and Jeremy Horder (2000). Here, the emphasis is not on whether the individual as a matter of fact conceived an intention, revealing psychological control of the ensuing action, but rather whether that person's intention was *in its intrinsic quality* morally good or bad. I argue that this latter understanding is also to be found in or behind the law, often in conflict with the first approach, which appears on the surface to predominate. We need to understand this interlacing of conflicting views.

(a) The formal psychological ('orthodox subjectivist') approach

In this approach, the paradigm case is the easiest. To talk of intending to do something is to talk of 'meaning' or 'aiming' to do it. It concerns applying one's mind to a particular task and directing one's action to a particular 'aim', 'end' or (the standard lawyer's synonym) 'purpose' (Smith and Hogan, 2011, 111). Our 'purpose' is what we intend to bring about through our actions.

In perhaps most situations it will be relatively clear that an outcome was the direct product of an individual's purpose. A punch on the nose will normally (though not always) be brought about by an intention to punch someone on the nose, so that outcome and intention are directly linked. But there are other situations in which an outcome will not be directly linked to an intention or purpose (end) but will be either a means to a particular end or a by-product or side-effect of such an end. The outcome is not the product of a direct intention, but emerges *obliquely*, as the consequence of the achievement of a desired end (Williams, 1987). Where the outcome is indirectly achieved as a means to an end or as a side-effect (which may not be desired in itself), can one be said to intend it?

Where the means are *necessary* to the desired end, and knowingly undertaken in that light, it is argued that the individual intends the means as well as the end, even if he does not desire (or like) the means themselves. Where the side-effect is known to be a *certain* by-product of achieving one's purpose, it is also argued that one intends the side-effect in addition to the purpose. This analysis conforms with that of Lord Hailsham in *Hyam* ((1974) at 52) where he stated that 'intention' must 'include the means as well as the end and the inseparable consequences of the end as well as the means . . .' For the 'orthodox subjectivist', this linking of what was intended to matters that were strictly not intended involves no element of artificiality: it is quite acceptable to talk of intentions as being either direct or indirect (oblique) (cf Williams, 1987; Goff, 1988, 45–7; Smith and Hogan, 2011, 106–16). Where artificiality would enter the analysis would be if the means or side-effect were not a *necessary* consequence but a consequence about which there was a degree of chance or probability of its occurrence. Where a side-effect was known to be likely, possible, or probable, one could say that the person *took the risk* that the consequence would occur, but not that he intended it to occur. In other words, he was *reckless* as to its occurrence . . ., rather than intending it.

Finally, an important point of qualification. In the last paragraph, we spoke of *necessary* means and *certain* side-effects of one's actions. But the world is such that we can never act with one hundred per cent certainty that a particular means will be necessary or that a by-product is bound to be created. The world is full of unanticipatable and unanticipated effects which alter or wreck the best-made calculation. I intend to injure my enemy standing behind a closed window by throwing a stone. In 999 cases out of 1000, I must break the window in order to achieve my purpose. On the occasion in question, by a fluke, the window is thrown open as the stone leaves my hand. Or, I intend to collect the insurance on a parcel on a plane by timing a bomb to explode in mid-air. I know it to be a plane without parachutes or eject-or seats. It is as certain as can be that the pilot will be killed but, by a freak, he falls from a great height and lives. Could the stone thrower or the bomb planter claim that the possibility of a fluke or freak stopping the means or side-effect occurring meant that he did not intend it, since it was not *absolutely bound* to happen? Could he rely on the chance in a thousand to say that the means or side-effect was not intended since it was not *genuinely* certain to occur? Could he claim that he very much hoped that the window would be thrown open or the pilot would be saved, and that given the possibility of the outside chance, he therefore did not intend the side-effect?

The answer on this analysis is that our actions and plans are always subject to the intervention of the unexpected and this is as true of our direct purposes as of the means to our ends or side-effects of our purposes. The unexpected may defeat the achievement of our purpose or render our calculation of means and side-effects wrong, but it does not cancel our intentions or purposes whether those are either direct or indirect. We need therefore to qualify the argument about the certainty of means or side-effects by talking of certainty 'for all practical purposes'. Judges have used the phrases 'moral' or 'virtual' certainty to denote a situation where an event will occur 'barring some unforeseen inter-vention' (*Nedrick* (1986)). The important point to note is that 'virtual certainty' *is* a kind of certainty (the only kind in fact that ever exists) and not a kind of high probability or chance.

(b) The morally substantive approach

Duff's critique of the foregoing approach is that it fails to reflect the way in which we under-stand wrongdoing. Orthodox subjectivism splits one moral judgment, whether a person directed his moral energies into doing something wrong, into two (subjective and object-ive) components. The 'objective' component is the harm that constitutes the wrong or the crime, which is measured in terms of the bad consequences it produces. The 'subjective' element is the fault of the wrongdoer, which is judged by whether the objective conse-quences were *as a matter of fact* known, foreseen or intended. For Duff, this approach is inadequate for it fails to reflect the nature of our moral judgments, in which 'objective' wrongdoing and 'subjective' fault are always combined. Thus to judge harm, we need to know about the *moral* quality of what was intended:

> 'Both the murder victim and the victim of natural causes suffer death: but the charac-ter of the harm that they suffer surely also depends on the way in which they die. One who tries to kill me . . . *attacks* my life and my most basic rights; and the harm which I suffer in being murdered . . . essentially involves this wrongful attack on me . . . The "harm" at which the law of murder is aimed is thus not just the *consequential* harm of death, but the harm which is *intrinsic* to an attack on another's life'. (Duff, 1990, 113)

And to judge intention, we need to know its moral quality:

> 'Human actions are purposive: they are done for reasons, in order to bring something about; their direction and their basic structure is formed by the intentions with which their agents act. It is through the intentions with which I act that I engage in the world as an agent, and relate myself most closely to the actual and potential effects of my actions; and the central or fundamental kind of wrong-doing is to *direct* my actions towards evil—to *intend* and to *try* to do what is evil.' (Duff, 1990, 112–13)

The intention to do wrong is not a crime because a person has a psychological intention to do a criminal act, but because that intention manifests moral wrong-doing. The idea that intentions reveal bad moral attitudes leads to less emphasis on the precise forms of intention and more on what they reveal about the wrongdoer's motives. For the orthodox subjectivist, a person is guilty of murder where he intends to kill or cause serious ('grievous bodily') harm, or foresees death or serious injury as a virtual certainty, but not where he foresees death or serious injury as a probability. These are the law's requirements too. For the orthodox subjectivist, there is doubt as to whether intending to cause serious harm ('implied malice') is a sufficient alternative mental state to a direct intention to kill. Even foreseeing death as a virtual certainty (indirect intention) smacks to some of a false constructivism because there is no direct link between what was intended and the outcome of death. Only an intention actually to kill truly links with the result. Certainly foreseeing death or serious injury as a probable consequence (reckless killing) does not link what was intended sufficiently to the outcome of death to count as murder.

For Duff, the killer in all these situations may legitimately be convicted of murder. Where there is foresight of virtual certainty of death or serious injury, the killer displays 'an utter indifference to [the victim's] rights or interests' (Duff, 1990, 114). Further, where a person foresees the probability of death by exposing his victim to its serious risk (which English law does not see as murder), Duff argues that it is legitimately charged as murder. Such a person is 'wickedly reckless' and guilty of murder, for death 'is an integral aspect of his intended attack' (Duff, 1990, 177). On the orthodox subjectivist approach, as with the law of murder, such a person is guilty only of reckless manslaughter. With the morally substantive approach, this is not so. The moral quality in the act is more important than a precise distinguishing of different psychological states.

QUESTIONS

1. Larry Alexander and Kimberly Fessler Kerzan (2009) have argued that we should not draw a distinction between intention and recklessness. They both indicate essentially the same vice: insufficient concern for others. He sees the justifiability of the risk as more important than the difference between foresight (recklessness) and purpose (intent). Distinguishing in moral terms the mercy killer and the terrorist risking people's lives in terms of the justifiability of the risk taken is more persuasive than considering the cases in terms of purpose or foresight. Do you agree?

2. The Law Commission (2006b: para. 9.10) has suggested the following definition of intention:

   '(1) A person should be taken to intend a result if he or she acts in order to bring it about.

   (2) In cases where the judge believes that justice may not be done unless an expanded understanding of intention is given, the jury should be directed as follows: an intention to bring about a result may be found if it is shown that the defendant thought that the result was a virtually certain consequence of his or her action.'[163]

3. Would this result in a change in the law?

---

[163] See Norrie (2006) for a discussion of the Law Commission's thinking on intention.

FURTHER READING

Chan, W. and Simester, A. (2011) 'Four Functions of *Mens Rea*' *Cambridge Law Journal* 70: 381.

Crosby, C. (2010) 'Culpability, *Kingston* and the Law Commission' *Journal of Criminal Law* 74: 434.

Duff, R.A. (1990a) *Intention, Agency and Criminal Liability* (Oxford: Blackwell).

Duff, R.A. (2014) 'Intention Revisited' in D. Baker and J. Horder (eds) *The Sanctity of Life and the Criminal Law* (Cambridge: Cambridge University Press).

Finnis, J. (1991) 'Intention and Side-Effects' in R. Frey and C. Morris (eds) *Liability and Responsibility* (Oxford: OUP).

Gorr, M. (1996) 'Should the Law Distinguish between Intention and (Mere) Foresight' *Legal Theory* 2: 359.

Horder, J. (1995a) 'Intention in the Criminal Law—A Rejoinder' *Modern Law Review* 58: 678.

Kaveny, C. (2004) 'Inferring Intention from Foresight' *Law Quarterly Review* 120: 81.

Kugler, I. (2002) *Direct and Oblique Intention in the Criminal Law* (Aldershot: Ashgate).

Kugler, I. (2004) 'Conditional Oblique Intention' *Criminal Law Review* 284.

Lacey, N. (1993a) 'A Clear Concept of Intention: Elusive or Illusory?' *Modern Law Review* 56: 621.

Lacey, N. (1995b) 'In(de)terminable Intentions' *Modern Law Review* 58: 592.

Pedain, A. (2003) 'Intention and the Terrorist Example' *Criminal Law Review* 579.

Simester, A. (1996a) 'Moral Certainty and the Boundaries of Intention' *Oxford Journal of Legal Studies* 16: 445.

Tadros, V. (2005a) *Criminal Responsibility* (Oxford: OUP), ch. 8.

Weigend, T. (2014) 'Subjective Elements of Criminal Liability' in M. Dubber and T. Hörnle (eds) *The Oxford Handbook of Criminal Law* (Oxford: OUP).

Williams, G. (1987) 'Oblique Intention' *Cambridge Law Journal* 46: 417.

16 RECKLESSNESS

16.1 SUBJECTIVE AND OBJECTIVE FORMS OF RECKLESSNESS AND INADVERTENCE

As shown in Part I of this chapter there were until relatively recently two kinds of recklessness in English and Welsh criminal law: *Cunningham* recklessness and *Caldwell* recklessness. Neither form of recklessness has escaped criticism. ←5 (p.144)

Criticisms of *Cunningham* recklessness

Cunningham recklessness is too narrow, say some commentators. Can it be right that a defendant who cares so little about other people that he does not consider whether his actions might harm them deserves to be acquitted? Should defendants who are so angry or self-absorbed that they do not notice the risks they are posing to others be acquitted?[164] Indeed, critics point out, it is noticeable that if a defendant fails to notice a risk because he is drunk he is still *Cunningham* reckless: why restrict this to drunkenness? Why not include other blameworthy reasons for failing to see an obvious risk? Critics add that attempts by the courts to include 'putting awareness to the back of your mind'[165] within the concept of recklessness demonstrate that pure *Cunningham* recklessness is too narrow. And does *Cunningham* recklessness presuppose that we can draw a clear line between our conscious and subconscious awareness?[166]

Supporters of *Cunningham* recklessness are often supporters of the choice theory. They argue that a defendant cannot be said to have chosen to undertake a risk of which he was unaware. Indeed he cannot be blamed for being indifferent to other people's welfare if he was not aware that they were at risk of being harmed.[167] We can only guess what the defendant's attitude would have been had he been aware of the risk. Michael Moore[168] concludes that there is a fundamental difference between a choice (advertent risk) and an unexercised capacity (inadvertent risk). John Gardner, however, argues that part of having good moral judgment is making good assessments about the consequences of your action: '[G]ood moral judgment depends very extensively on good causal judgment'.[169]

Some supporters of *Cunningham* recklessness are willing to accept that a person may be blameworthy for failing to notice an obvious risk, but argue that such a person is not as blameworthy as the person who sees the risk and nevertheless takes it. Inadvertent defendants may deserve blame, but they do not deserve to be classified as reckless.[170]

Criticisms of *Caldwell* recklessness

Caldwell recklessness has many critics. The decision enraged some commentators so much that ordinary standards of etiquette when commenting on judicial decisions were put aside, with Professor Smith calling Lord Diplock's reasoning in the case 'pathetically inadequate'.[171] One particular ground of criticism is based around the decisions in *Elliott v C*[172] and *Coles*.[173] By convicting these defendants on the basis of failing to see a risk which would have been obvious to a reasonable person (even if it would not have been obvious to a reasonable person of those defendants' mental abilities), they are said to go against fundamental principles of justice. Even accepting the moral thrust of *Caldwell* recklessness (we blame a defendant for failing to see a risk which he *should* have seen) such an argument is legitimate only where the defendant could have foreseen the risk. To punish someone for failing to do something he or she was incapable of doing seems manifestly unjust.[174] It is hard to mount a defence of the reasoning in these cases except on the basis that it is more important to protect victims from harm from others than to achieve justice in every case. ←6 (p.147)

Although there is hardly a consensus amongst commentators, it seems that a majority would accept that *Cunningham* recklessness is too narrow, while *Caldwell* recklessness is too wide. Is there a middle way between the two forms? Some commentators have suggested

---

164 S. Gardner (1993).   165 e.g. *Parker* [1977] 1 WLR 600 (CA).
166 See Bandes (2010).   167 White (1991: ch. 7).   168 M. Moore (1996: ch. 1).
169 J. Gardner (2012).   170 Kessler Ferzan (2001).
171 J.C. Smith (1981).   172 [1983] 2 All ER 1005 (DC).   173 [1995] 1 Cr App R 157 (CA).
174 Whether on the detailed facts of the particular case C deserved to be punished is discussed in Field and Lynn (1992).

that the decision of the House of Lords in *Reid*[175] hinted at one.[176] In cases of inadvertence we should ask why the defendant failed to see an obvious risk. If the defendant has a good reason (e.g. a sudden emergency) he is not reckless. But if he does not have a good reason (e.g. he is angry) then he is reckless.

We will now consider the writings of two theorists who have sought to develop a middle way between *Cunningham* and *Caldwell* recklessness.

16.2   AN INSUFFICIENT REGARD FOR THE INTERESTS OF OTHERS: VICTOR TADROS

Victor Tadros describes the vice of recklessness as an insufficient regard for the interests of others. In the following passage, he explains why he thinks that people can be responsible for the way they form their belief that their actions are or are not risky:

V. Tadros, 'Recklessness and the Duty to Take Care' in S. Shute and A. Simester (eds) *Criminal Law Theory* (Oxford: OUP, 2002), 248–50

We are responsible for our beliefs. That idea, it seems to me, is part of the motivation of many of those who argue for objective recklessness. Some who argue for a very strong form of objective recklessness seem to think that it is the falsity of the defendant's belief that provides the target for criminal liability. But, as we have seen, that one has all of the virtues associated with belief formation in proper balance does not guarantee that one's beliefs will all be true. One can have all of the virtues associated with believing and yet hold false beliefs, even beliefs that most ordinary reasonable people would not hold. For this reason, our responsibility for our beliefs is not sufficient ground for imposing criminal liability in cases where the defendant had a false belief that there was no risk involved in the action that she performed. Consequently, our attention turns from the nature of the belief that is held to the process of belief formation.

To see this, let us return to example (6). [I am driving home to watch the football and I come to a junction. I am about to rush out, not caring that a pedestrian might be killed. However, I suddenly realize that I might damage my lovely new car and consequently look either way, just as a responsible driver would. I form the belief that there is no danger but I fail to notice a pedestrian who unexpectedly dashes in front of my car, and run her over.] In that example, I formed a belief that there was no danger to pedestrians, but that was not a response to my concern for pedestrians but rather my concern for my car. However, I did all that was required of me to ensure that the way was clear; I fulfilled my responsibility. In that case it is wrong to make me criminally liable for the death of the pedestrian. I had *done* as much as could be expected of a truly virtuous person, even though I was not truly virtuous. That I was indifferent to the fate of the pedestrian is not sufficient reason to hold me criminally liable. Fulfilling my responsibility to ensure that the way was clear ought to absolve me of criminal liability even if false beliefs are formed. The falsity of the belief itself is not sufficient evidence of fault. If we are to find fault, we must find it in the process of belief formation. Furthermore, it may be that the defendant has not formed his belief in the way that he ought and yet criminal liability may still be inappropriate. For it must be shown that, in holding a false belief, the defendant manifests the appropriate kind of vice.

---

[175] [1992] 3 All ER 673 (HL).   [176] Field and Lynn (1993).

It might be thought that the appropriate kind of vice is displayed whenever the defendant has formed an irrational or unreasonable belief about the risks. If that were the case, irrationality or unreasonableness would not simply be descriptions of the nature of the belief itself, regardless of who holds it, but descriptions of the way in which the belief was formed. Such a view might be supported by Joseph Raz's recent analysis of irrational beliefs. 'A belief is irrational', Raz writes, 'if and only if holding it displays lack of care and diligence in one's epistemic conduct'. Showing lack of care and diligence, it might be argued, displays a vice that is central to the imposition of criminal liability. After all, that one fails to take care or be diligent also shows that one is insufficiently motivated by the interests of the individuals who might suffer from one's lack of care and diligence.

However, it is not at all clear that the fact that one holds an irrational belief necessarily shows a vice of this kind. That one holds an irrational belief is not itself evidence of a lack of care on the part of the believer. A number of other vices might result in the formation of an irrational belief. It might be that the defendant is merely stupid or illogical; vices which, whilst in themselves warranting blame, do not give rise to the kind and degree of blame that the imposition of criminal liability expresses. If one has such vices, one can take all the care that is required and yet fail to form rational beliefs. In fact, this argument might even be stretched to include some other failings, such as some instances of arrogance.

Consider *R v Shimmen*, in which a martial arts expert attempted to perform a kick near to a window without breaking it. Suppose that he formed the belief that there was no risk involved at all due to an arrogant belief in his own ability. We might conclude that he had manifested a vice in breaking the window, and consequently attribute responsibility to him for breaking the window. But is it correct to attribute criminal liability to him? The difficulty in doing so is that the criminal law should not be interested in the kinds of vice that Shimmen manifested. That Shimmen was arrogant does not show clearly that Shimmen was 'insufficiently different' to the interests of others. It may be that he cared deeply about the shopkeeper and his window, and was sincerely mortified at having broken it (and not because of a change of heart, motivation, or perspective), but truly (though arrogantly) believed that he was doing nothing to put the window at risk. Shimmen may have been responsible for breaking the window but, at least on this presentation of the facts, he did not display an appropriate vice in breaking the window and consequently he ought not to be made criminally liable for it. He did not show an insufficient regard for the interests of others. And that, as I argued above, is central to the concerns of the criminal law.

These considerations militate against many popular constructions of objective recklessness. For example, accounts that rely on the risks that the defendant ought to have recognized, even those such as Hart's that restrict liability to the capacity of the accused to recognize the risks involved in performing a particular action, are too broad. Defendants such as Shimmen, on my construction of the facts, ought to recognize the risks and have the capacity to recognize the risks. Nevertheless, they ought not to be made criminally liable.

This should help to guide us in formulating an appropriate definition of objective recklessness. An appropriate definition of objective recklessness would focus on the process of belief formation. And it would be required to distinguish between cases of mere irrationality, stupidity, or arrogance and cases where the formation of an irrational belief shows that the defendant was not adequately motivated by the interests of others. In an earlier part of the discussion, I suggested that our responsibility for our beliefs is grounded on two facts. The first fact is that belief formation is governed by norms. There are norms that govern the ways in which we ought to see the world, and to interpret what we see. One important aspect of the intellectual virtues has to do with the system of norms that we ought to apply to the formation of beliefs. The second fact is that we have some control over which evidence we are presented with. There are also norms that apply to evidence-gathering; the intellectual virtues relate to the system of norms we apply to evidence-gathering as well. Might these two facts provide grounds upon which we can construct a test for objective recklessness? It will be no surprise that I think that they can.

However, one caveat is in order. My claim is not that these are the only ways in which belief formation is sufficiently vicious to warrant criminal liability. It may be that the test of objective recklessness can be extended to include other cases, in particular cases where the offending belief is derived from a further belief that was viciously formed. Space does not permit me fully to discuss such cases here, though I will try to illuminate some potential problems for assessing liability in such cases. The two cases that I will concentrate on here are, I think, the central cases. The first is where the individual has sufficient information at his fingertips to form the belief that there is a significant risk of a wrong being done to another but, due to a motivational reason of a particular kind, fails to form the belief that such a wrong will be brought about. The second is where an individual knows that a situation that he is in, or the activity that he is performing, might give rise to particular risks and fails to investigate whether there are such risks. In the next section I will show how these two cases might be appropriate targets for the imposition of criminal liability.

. . .

D. Conclusions

From this discussion, we can derive a test of recklessness that can be applied where the agent has failed to realize the risks that his action created. The agent will be reckless if the following conditions are fulfilled:

(a) the action was of a kind that might carry risks with it according to the beliefs of the individual; and either:

(bi) given those beliefs the agent failed to fulfil his duty of investigating the risks; or

(bii) the agent wilfully blinded himself to the existence of the risks.

Where these conditions are not fulfilled it might well be appropriate to make the defendant civilly liable for any harm that is caused through his risky action. But, for the most part at least, criminal liability is inappropriate. This is because the criminal law, unlike the civil law, is concerned not with distributing losses but with punishing the defendant for harms both for which he is responsible and which manifest the appropriate kind of vice.

The test proposed marks a middle way between purely objective and purely subjective accounts. In favour of objective accounts, there are at least some cases where one can attribute *mens rea* to the defendant despite the fact that she does not recognize the risks involved in what she is doing. If her background beliefs are such that she ought to investigate the risks and she does not perform that investigation adequately, or if she forms a belief that there is no risk for a non-evidential reason, it is appropriate to regard her as reckless for the purposes of the criminal law. On the other hand, the test is sensitive to considerations of the rule of law that subjectivists are concerned with. Citizens are given a fair opportunity to know when they are and are not breaching the criminal law, without being required to go far beyond the call of duty in investigating the risks involved in acting day-to-day. It is only those actions that are already recognized by the defendant as risky that have attached to them burdens of investigation, at least as far as the criminal law is concerned. Furthermore, the central purpose of the criminal law, of punishing those who manifest vices such as cruelty or indifference, is achieved without also making criminals of the stupid, the ignorant, or the clumsy.

16.3 PRACTICAL INDIFFERENCE: ANTONY DUFF

Antony Duff[177] has proposed an understanding of recklessness based on the concept of practical indifference:[178]

> An appropriate general test of recklessness would be—did the agent's conduct (including any conscious risk-taking, any failure to notice an obvious risk created by her action, and any unreasonable belief on which she acted) display a seriously culpable practical indifference to the interests which her action in fact threatened?

This proposal is an attempt to develop a form of recklessness which is in between *Caldwell* and *Cunningham* recklessness. It is wider than *Cunningham* recklessness but narrower than *Caldwell*. It captures both those who see a risk and take it and those who fail to see a risk because they are practically indifferent to the needs of others.[179] The significance of the term 'practically indifferent' is that Duff is able to argue that inadvertence caused by practical indifference is a subjective state of mind: an attitude of the defendant. Whether or not a defendant notices a risk indicates what his or her attitude towards such risks is. The failure to notice an obvious risk might indicate that the defendant could not care less whether the risk materialized. He gives as an example a bridegroom who is found drinking in a pub at the time of his wedding and explains that he completely forgot about his big day. Quite simply this is the kind of thing one should not forget about and we can properly assume that he did not regard the wedding as sufficiently important.[180] Duff argues that what we do reflects what we care about. Others reject the argument that an action can encapsulate inadvertence.[181] Kessler Ferzan discusses eating an ice-cream cone.[182] Does this show an indifference to whether I gain weight, she asks? It might, or it might in fact be that I debated long and hard within myself whether or not to eat the cone, given its weight-inducing possibility. In the latter case it could hardly be said that I was indifferent to putting on weight, she argues.[183] Another way of considering practical indifference is to ask how would the defendant have acted if he or she had been aware of the risk. If he or she would have acted in the same way then that demonstrates that he or she has the same lack of concern for others as a person who deliberately takes a risk of harming others.[184]

Although Duff's proposal is attractive it has received its critics. Alan Norrie[185] focuses on the example of rape, which Duff discusses. Duff argues that a man who does not ask a woman whether she consents to sexual intercourse and just assumes that she does is practically indifferent to the woman's interests and can therefore be classified as reckless. Norrie argues that although any right-thinking person would blame such a man, we cannot say that he is necessarily indifferent to the woman's interest. He may hold outrageous views on women's consent to sexual intercourse (e.g. that any woman would want to have sexual intercourse with him), but it does not follow that he is *indifferent* to the woman.[186] He may

---

[177] Duff (1990a: 172).   [178] See also Simons (1992) who uses the term 'culpable indifference'.

[179] Gardner and Jung (1991) take the view that advertence to a risk can be described as an example of indifference.

[180] Although if the defendant had simply forgotten about the risk, would that suggest a lack of consideration? See for discussion of forgetting risks Husak (2011).

[181] Kessler Ferzan (2001).   [182] *Ibid*, 618.

[183] A further difficulty is how the law should deal with a defendant who fails to see a risk due to his racist or sexist beliefs.

[184] Simons (1992).   [185] Norrie (2001: ch. 4).   [186] See also Brady (1996).

genuinely care whether or not she consents but believe she consents because he is irresistibly attractive, for example. Norrie argues that Duff is classifying such a man as 'practically indifferent' not because that is actually his state of mind, but because 'we' are appalled at his attitude towards women. Norrie is happy to blame such a defendant, but he says Duff cannot claim that doing so is a subjective test. Norrie argues that Duff moves from the notion that the defendant ought to have realized this risk to the notion that the defendant was indifferent to the risk too quickly. Duff's response to this argument is that he does not accept the argument that we can consider states of mind divorced from actions.[187] In other words the actions of the defendant are the actions of an indifferent person, and hence the defendant is classified as indifferent. This reply will convince only those who agree with Duff's understanding of the meanings of actions. However, most subjectivists do not.[188]

More supportive critics may agree with Duff that the practically indifferent people are blameworthy, but argue that he needs to demonstrate that they are sufficiently blameworthy to be classified along with the advertent as reckless. Brady[189] picks up on Duff's example of the groom in the pub at the time of the wedding and argues that we may blame him, but surely he is not in the same class of blameworthiness as the groom who is drinking while fully aware that the bride and all the guests are waiting for him. In other words, even if inadvertence may be blameworthy, it is not as blameworthy as advertence.[190] Perhaps the truth is that some inadvertence, but not all, is blameworthy. Donald Husak[191] gives the example of a person texting while driving and so failing to notice a danger and crashing into another car. Is texting while driving any more or less blameworthy than a driver who decides to speed?

By contrast Alexander and Kessler Ferzan focusing on insufficient concern for others focus on a subjective test. Notice that their approach has relevance for them not only to *mens rea* issues, but also the law on causation:

L. Alexander and K. Kessler Ferzan, 'Beyond the Special Part' in S. Green and R.A. Duff (eds) *Philosophical Foundations of Criminal Law* (Oxford: OUP, 2011), 232–5

In *Crime and Culpability*, we analyse what it would mean for the criminal law to take retributive justice seriously. How would we formulate crimes if they were designed to give individuals what they deserve? In our view, individuals deserve punishment when they act culpably, and an actor is culpable when he exhibits insufficient concern for others. (Culpability as insufficient concern for others is a view not only of criminal culpability but also of moral culpability more generally; for us, culpability is a univocal notion.) Actors demonstrate insufficient concern for others when they (irrevocably) decide to harm or risk harming other people (or their legally protected interests) for insufficient reasons—that is, when they act in a way that they believe will increase others' risk of harm without and regardless of any further action on their part, and their reasons for unleashing this risk fail to justify doing so. If Alex decides to drive 100 miles an hour on the highway, whether we deem Alex culpable and deserving of blame and punishment will depend upon whether he has chosen to impose this risk to impress his friends with how fast his car can drive or, alternatively, to transport a critically injured friend to the hospital.

---

[187] Duff (1996: ch. 1).   [188] See further Kessler Ferzan (2002).   [189] Brady (1996).
[190] For an alternative analysis based on the notion of 'acceptance', see Michaels (1998).
[191] Husak (2012c).

As criteria for insufficient concern, the criminal law need not employ the Model Penal Code's four mental states—purpose, knowledge, recklessness, and negligence. The same type of assessment is involved whether we are judging purpose, knowledge, or recklessness—a weighing of the risks the actor believes he is imposing and his reasons for doing so. When an actor purposefully aims to injure another—injuring is his conscious object for acting—his reasons are presumptively culpable. When an actor knowingly harms another—believes to a practical certainty that his act will harm—the degree of risk is presumptively culpable. But, in instances of both purpose and knowledge, these presumptions may be rebutted by showing that the actor was justified in imposing the risk that he did. In contrast, as formulated, recklessness requires the risk to be unjustified, thus building lack of justification into the mental state itself. In all of these cases, however, for a defendant ultimately to be deserving of punishment, the risks he takes must be unjustified. The current approach of separating this single criterion for culpability into three discrete mental states creates doctrinal difficulties as well as the false impression that these three mental states neatly line up in a culpability hierarchy.

Negligence, on the other hand, is not culpable. There is no principled and rationally defensible way to construct the 'reasonable person' against whom we judge the actor and who we are to presume would have adverted to the risk to which the actor failed to advert. Infinite possible constructs exist between full omniscience and the actor's own subjective beliefs, but there is no reason to privilege any of these constructs as the appropriate normative standard against which to judge the actor. Moreover, even if we could construct such a perspective, the negligent actor lacks the requisite control over this 'risk'. Risk is a matter of epistemic perspective, and a 'negligent' actor who assesses a risk as lower than others would is not culpable for his epistemic shortcomings. It is the risk that the actor estimates—not the risk an actor possessed of more information, a better perspective, or superior inferential ability would have estimated—that determines culpability.

QUESTIONS

1. Anne finds a gun in a park and for a joke, assuming that it has no bullets in it, fires it at her friend Bertha. In fact there are bullets in the gun, and Bertha's eye is seriously injured. Anne is not guilty of assaulting Bertha (she did not intend and was not *Cunningham* reckless as to the injury). If Bertha were later to die from her injuries Anne might be guilty of manslaughter (she may be grossly negligent). Is this the law being an ass?

2. Is it arguable that for minor crimes such as criminal damage the law is entitled to use a more objective test so that cases can be dealt with more quickly in the courts, while for more serious offences, such as an assault, the law should take more time to ensure that the defendant really is blameworthy and hence a subjective test should be used? Is it more justifiable to punish a defendant for indifference when he is doing something which he knows to be particularly dangerous (e.g. driving)?

FURTHER READING

Alexander, L. (2000) 'Insufficient Concern: A Unified Conception of Criminal Culpability' *California Law Review* 88: 931.

Alexander, L. and Kessler Ferzan, K. (2011) 'Beyond the Special Part' in S. Green and R.A. Duff (eds) *Philosophical Foundations of Criminal Law* (Oxford: OUP), 232–5.

Brudner, A. (2008) 'Subjective Fault for Crime: A Reinterpretation' *Legal Theory* 14: 1.

Duff, R.A. (1990a) *Intention, Agency and Criminal Liability* (Oxford: Blackwell).

Husak, D. (2011) 'Negligence, Belief, Blame and Criminal Liability: The Special Case of Forgetting' *Criminal Law and Philosophy* 5: 199.

Husak, D. (2012c) 'Distraction and Negligence' in L. Zedner and J. Roberts (eds) *Principles and Values in Criminal Law and Justice: Essays in Honour of Andrew Ashworth* (Oxford: OUP).

Kessler Ferzan, K. (2002) 'Don't Abandon the Model Penal Code Yet! Thinking Through Simons's *Rethinking*' *Buffalo Criminal Law Review* 6: 185.

Norrie, A. (1992) 'Subjectivism, Objectivism and the Limits of Criminal Recklessness' *Oxford Journal of Legal Studies* 12: 45.

Nourse, V. (2008) 'After the Reasonable Man: Getting Over the Subjectivity/Objectivity Question' *New Criminal Law Review* 11: 34.

Simons, K. (2002) 'Does Punishment for "Culpable Indifference" Simply Punish for "Bad Character"?' *Buffalo Criminal Law Review* 6: 219.

Staihar, J. (2010) 'Culpability and the Relevance of Substantial Risks, Motivations, and Lesser Harms' *Law and Philosophy* 385.

Tadros, V. (2002a) 'Recklessness and the Duty to Take Care' in S. Shute and A. Simester (eds) *Criminal Law Theory* (Oxford: OUP).

Tadros, V. (2005a) *Criminal Responsibility* (Oxford: OUP), ch. 9.

17 NEGLIGENCE

Although many crimes are based on negligence, nearly all of them concern minor offences which carry a slight stigma, such as motoring offences. As noted in Part I of this chapter liability for negligence does not depend on the state of mind of the defendant but rather what the defendant did: did he or she act in a way in which a reasonable person would not have acted? This has led some commentators to argue that negligence should not be classified as a *mens rea*, a state of mind.[192] Of greater importance is the fact that many commentators feel that it is improper for the criminal law to use negligence.[193] ←8 (p.152)

17.1 OPPOSITION TO THE USE OF NEGLIGENCE IN CRIMINAL LAW

Clearly those who support the choice theory will object to liability based on negligence.[194] A negligent actor has not chosen to risk the harm to others. Character theorists will find it easier to support the doctrine because a negligent act may indicate a blameworthy

---

[192] e.g. G. Williams (1982).   [193] e.g. Kenny (1978).
[194] e.g. M. Moore (2000); Brady (1980); Mackie (1977: 210).

characteristic (e.g. a lack of concern for others). However, Michael Moore argues that a single negligent act does not manifest a careless disposition.[195] A single act of negligence might simply be an accident or forgetfulness. It is only once a pattern of negligent acts develops that we may conclude that the defendant's character is in fact indifference to others. Moore concludes that the character theory cannot explain why an isolated act of negligence is punished. Indeed most of us take risks of causing harm to others at times, it is very hard not to.[196]

David Archard[197] argues that we need to consider the social usefulness of the activity the defendant is doing in assessing whether negligence liability is appropriate. We might, he suggests, decide that negligent doctors should not be subject to criminal sanctions, because their activities are socially beneficial. We might take a different attitude towards those who harm others negligently while having a fun time.

17.2 SUPPORT FOR THE USE OF NEGLIGENCE IN CRIMINAL LAW

We will now consider the writings of those who seek to support liability for negligence, at least in some cases. Professor Herbert Hart has sought to justify a modified form of negligence. The defendant should be liable if, given his or her mental and physical capabilities, he or she had the capacity to see the risk:

H.L.A. Hart, 'Negligence, *Mens Rea* and the Elimination of Responsibility' in H.L.A. Hart, *Punishment and Responsibility* (Oxford: OUP, 1968), 152–7

What is crucial is that those whom we punish should have had, when they acted, the normal capacities, physical and mental, for doing what the law requires and abstaining from what it forbids, and a fair opportunity to exercise these capacities. Where these capacities and opportunities are absent, as they are in different ways in the varied cases of accident, mistake, paralysis, reflex action, coercion, insanity, etc., the moral protest is that it is morally wrong to punish because 'he could not have helped it' or 'he could not have done otherwise' or 'he had no real choice.' But . . . there is no reason (unless we are to reject the whole business of responsibility and punishment) *always* to make this protest when someone who 'just didn't think' is punished for carelessness. For in some cases at least we may say 'he could have thought about what he was doing' with just as much rational confidence as one can say of any intentional wrong-doing 'he could have done otherwise.'

Of course, the law compromises with competing values over this matter of the subjective element in responsibility. . . .

The most important compromise which legal systems make over the subjective element consists in its adoption of what has been unhappily termed the 'objective standard.' This may lead to an individual being treated for the purposes of conviction and punishment as if he possessed capacities for control of his conduct which he did not possess, but which an ordinary or reasonable man possesses and would have exercised. The expression 'objective' and its partner 'subjective' are unhappy because, as far as negligence is concerned, they obscure

---

[195] M. Moore (1997: 241).
[196] See further Alexander and Kessler Ferzan (2009). Although see Leipold (2011), who emphasizes that negligence only captures those who take unreasonable risks.
[197] Archard (2013).

the real issue. We may be tempted to say with Dr Turner that just because the negligent man does not have 'the thought of harm in his mind,' to hold him responsible for negligence is *necessarily* to adopt an objective standard and to abandon the 'subjective' element in responsibility. It then becomes vital to distinguish this (mistaken) thesis from the position brought about by the use of objective standards in the application of laws which make negligence criminally punishable. For, when negligence is made criminally punishable, this itself leaves open the question: whether, before we punish, both or only the first of the following two questions must be answered affirmatively.

(i) Did the accused fail to take those precautions which any reasonable man with normal capacities would in the circumstances have taken?

(ii) Could the accused, given his mental and physical capacities, have taken those precautions?

. . . If our conditions of liability are invariant and not flexible, *i.e.* if they are not adjusted to the capacities of the accused, then some individuals will be held liable for negligence though they could not have helped their failure to comply with the standard. In *such* cases, indeed, criminal responsibility will be made independent of any 'subjective element,' since the accused could not have conformed to the required standard. But this result is nothing to do with negligence being taken as a basis for criminal liability; precisely the same result will be reached if, in considering whether a person acted intentionally, we were to attribute to him foresight of consequences which a reasonable man would have foreseen but which he did not. 'Absolute liability' results, not from the admission of the principle that one who has been grossly negligent is criminally responsible for the consequent harm even if 'he had no idea in his mind of harm to anyone,' but from the refusal in the application of this principle to consider the capacities of an individual who has fallen below the standard of care.

It is of course quite arguable that no legal system could afford to individualise the conditions of liability so far as to discover and excuse all those who could not attain the average or reasonable man's standard. It may, in practice, be impossible to do more than excuse those who suffer from gross forms of incapacity, viz. infants, or the insane, or those afflicted with recognisably inadequate powers of control over their movements, or who are clearly unable to detect, or extricate themselves, from situations in which their disability may work harm. Some confusion is, however, engendered by certain inappropriate ways of describing these excusable cases, which we are tempted to use in a system which, like our own, defines negligence in terms of what the reasonable man would do. We may find ourselves asking whether the infant, the insane, or those suffering from paralysis did all that a reasonable man would *in the circumstances* do, taking 'circumstances' (most queerly) to include personal qualities like being an infant, insane or paralysed. This paradoxical approach leads to many difficulties. To avoid them we need to hold apart the primary question (1) What *would* the reasonable man with ordinary capacities have done in these circumstances? from the second question (2), *Could* the accused with *his* capacities have done that? Reference to such factors as lunacy or disease should be made in answering only the second of these questions. This simple, and surely realistic, approach avoids difficulties which the notion of individualising the standard of care has presented for certain writers; for these difficulties are usually created by the mistaken assumption that the only way of allowing for individual incapacities is to treat them as part of the 'circumstances' in which the reasonable man is supposed to be acting. Thus Dr Glanville Williams said that if 'regard must be had to the make-up and circumstances of the particular offender, one would seem on a determinist view of conduct to be pushed to the conclusion that there is no standard of conduct at all. For if every characteristic of the individual is taken into account, including his heredity the conclusion is that he could not help doing as he did.' (The General Part (1st Ed.) p. 82.)

But 'determinism' presents no special difficulty here. The question is whether that individual had the capacity (inherited or not) to act otherwise than he did, and 'determinism' has no relevance to the case of one who is accused of negligence which it does not have to one accused of intentionally killing.

QUESTIONS

1. Is punishing negligence punishing someone for an omission: for failing to act as a reasonable person would have done? Is this legitimate, given the law's general reluctance to punish omissions?

2. Is it more legitimate to punish for negligence when the defendant is doing an activity which is known to be dangerous (e.g. driving, carrying out an operation) than where the defendant is doing something that is not especially risky?

FURTHER READING

Horder, J. (1997c) 'Gross Negligence and Criminal Culpability' *University of Toronto Law Journal* 47: 495.

Huigens, K. (1998) 'Virtue and Criminal Negligence' *Buffalo Criminal Law Review* 1: 431.

Leipold, A. (2010) 'A Case for Criminal Negligence' *Law and Philosophy* 455.

Simester, A. (2000) 'Can Negligence be Culpable?' in J. Horder (ed.) *Oxford Essays in Jurisprudence* (Oxford: OUP).

Stark, F. (2013a) 'It's Only Words: On Meaning and *Mens Rea*' *Cambridge Law Journal* 155.

Tadros, V. (2008a) 'The Scope and Grounds of Responsibility' *New Criminal Law Review* 11: 191.

18 INTOXICATION

18.1 INTOXICATION AND CRIME

Alcohol

Many commentators accept that there is a link between alcohol and crime.[198] But the strength of that link is a matter of debate. The following comment summarizes the general opinion: '[A]lcohol may be neither a necessary nor sufficient *cause* of crime, but may nevertheless *affect* crime'.[199] Consider these statistics, which may yet persuade you to take a vow of temperance(!):

(1) In 2013, 15 per cent of adults questioned admitted 'binge drinking' (drinking at least eight units in one drinking session) in the previous week. Although it is worth

---

[198] Marsh *et al* (2001).   [199] Raistrick *et al* (1999: 54).

noting that they are outnumbered by the 21 per cent of adults who never drink alcohol.[200]

(2) According to the 2013/14 Crime Survey for England and Wales, there were 1,327,000 violent incidents, of which 53 per cent were cases where the victim believed the offender(s) to be under the influence of alcohol. Although 70 per cent of violence at weekends was related to alcohol.[201]

(3) An estimated 8,320 people were casualties of reported drink-driving accidents in the UK in 2013 including 240 who were killed and 1,100 who suffered serious injury.[202]

(4) In 2013/14, there were an estimated 1,105,210 admissions to English hospitals related to alcohol consumption where an alcohol-related disease, injury, or condition was the primary reason for hospital admission or a secondary diagnosis.[203] There were 6,592 alcohol-related deaths.

(5) Alcohol misuse *costs* England approximately £21 billion per year in health care, crime, and lost productivity costs.[204]

Although these statistics may indicate a strong connection between alcohol and crime, at least one commentator has expressed the view that given the number of people intoxicated at any given time among the general population, it is not surprising that so many offenders are drunk![205] It may be added that many victims of violent offences were drunk at the time.[206]

Drug misuse

Of course alcohol is a kind of drug, but it is a legal one. There is a well-established link between illegal drug use and crime, although there is some dispute whether serious drug users are usually involved in crime before starting their drug misuse.[207] The link between drug crime and property offences committed to finance a drug habit is well established. A recent study suggested that 30 per cent of those arrested were addicted to drugs.[208]

18.2 ALCOHOLISM AND DRUG DEPENDENCY: ILLNESS OR WEAKNESS?

There is much debate over the correct understanding of alcohol and drug dependency. On the one hand there are some who see alcoholism (properly known as alcohol dependency syndrome) and drug addiction as a kind of illness or disease which should be treated as a medical condition.[209] Others see them as a major social problem caused by people's own character weaknesses (drunkenness being an 'odious and loathsome sin')[210] requiring a tough response from the criminal justice system.[211] In the terms of a criminal trial there is a debate whether intoxication should be regarded as an aggravating or mitigating factor.[212]

---

[200] Health and Social Care Information Service (2015).
[201] Office for National Statistics (2015d).   [202] Department of Transport (2015).
[203] Health and Social Care Information Service (2015).   [204] Alcohol Concern (2013).
[205] South (1999: 948).   [206] Home Office (2000).   [207] Hough (1996).
[208] Travis (2001).
[209] See the discussion in Bogg and Herring (2012).
[210] See the discussion of the history of the law's response towards intoxication in Horder (1997a).
[211] See the excellent discussion in Tomlie (2002).   [212] *Bradley* (1980) 2 Cr App R (S) 12.

It may be that attitudes towards drugs are changing, with at least one commentator controversially suggesting that young people now regard drug misuse as 'normal' behaviour.[213] Certainly alcohol misuse is widespread. ←7 (p.151)

18.3 EXPLAINING THE PRESENT LAW ON INTOXICATION

As was seen in Part I, the law's approach to intoxication can be regarded as confusing. In relation to crimes involving intention (specific intent offences) intoxication is simply regarded as part of the evidence the jury can take into account in deciding whether the defendant intended the result. Similarly for recklessness (basic intent offences) and involuntary intoxication the question is simply whether the defendant foresaw the risk, and the involuntary intoxication is simply part of the evidence concerning what the defendant foresaw. The only special legal rule concerns crimes of recklessness where the defendant was voluntarily intoxicated. One explanation is that the defendant is treated as having foreseen the risk (whether or not in fact he did) and therefore reckless. How can we explain the law? ←9 (p.154)

This 'presumption of recklessness' could be explained in this way: a person who takes alcohol or drugs is aware there is a risk that he may behave in an unpredictable way. Behaving in an unpredictable way must include committing a crime. Therefore by drinking or taking drugs the defendant is aware that he or she runs the risk of carrying out an offence.[214] He or she is therefore reckless. This reasoning has been criticized on several grounds:

(1) Section 8 of the Criminal Justice Act 1967 requires a jury to consider all the evidence before deciding whether the accused foresaw a result. This could mean that the jury should not rely on presumptions of foresight flowing from intoxication.

(2) Even if it is accepted that there is recklessness at the time of the drinking there is no coincidence of the *actus reus* and *mens rea*, as is normally required in the criminal law.[215]

(3) The foresight, as explained in the previous argument, is that the defendant is aware that he may commit some crime after drinking. However, normally in offences requiring recklessness it is necessary to show that the defendant foresaw a specific kind of harm (e.g. that she would injure someone).

(4) Some argue that the explanation of the law is unconvincing where the defendant has never drunk alcohol before and is unaware of its potential effects. There are similar problems where the defendant is an experienced drinker who, for example, has had two dry sherries before dinner all his life, without ever committing an offence, but on one night the sherries intoxicate him and he commits a crime.[216] In such cases these defendants may justifiably claim that they did not foresee that they might commit an offence.

In the light of these objections some fall back on the view that the law here is based on public policy. What the law is really doing is deterring drunkenness and protecting people from

---

[213] H. Parker (1997). See Herring, Regan, Weinberg, and Withington (2012) for a broader discussion.

[214] See e.g. *Bennett* [1995] Crim LR 877. This explanation appears to have been explicitly rejected in *Heard* [2007] EWCA Crim 125, para. 30.

[215] Weight was placed on this argument by the High Court of Australia in *O'Connor* (1980) 54 ALJR 349.

[216] Orchard (1993).

those who become violent when drunk. Indeed Lord Salmon in *Majewski* explained that the decision was not based on logic, but on 'justice, ethics and common sense'.

An alternative explanation of the present law is that it concerns only the law of evidence. The defendant is prevented from introducing evidence of his intoxication to demonstrate that he did not foresee a risk.[217] If the risk was an obvious one and the defendant is not able to introduce evidence that he did not foresee because he was drunk then the jury will almost inevitably find that he foresaw the risk. But why does this 'rule of evidence' apply to recklessness but not intention (remember the defendant *can* introduce evidence of intoxication to rebut intention)? Jeremy Horder's explanation is that where a crime involves intention that intention is an aspect of the wrong done to the victim.[218] Where that is lacking the kind of wrong done to the victim is missing.[219] Opponents of Horder's analysis argue that in the criminal law it is inappropriate to reject relevant evidence. To do so is to base the law on what we know to be a fiction. Of course there is little problem in dealing with intoxication for those who see recklessness in a more objective way. For Husak, the intoxicated defendant has shown 'too little care for the interests of others' and so is liable to be found reckless.[220]

18.4 ALTERNATIVES TO *MAJEWSKI*

The opposition to *Majewski* inevitably gives rise to the question whether there are alternative approaches the law could take towards intoxication. Rebecca Williams has summarized the challenges for those seeking to reform the law:

R. Williams, 'Voluntary Intoxication—A Lost Cause?' (2013) 126 *Law Quarterly Review* 264 at 265–6

It is well known that the law concerning voluntary intoxication presents three important challenges.

First, those who are intoxicated are *in general* more likely to do more harm, but in each case the defendant's *individual* culpability may be less than if he or she had been sober. It is true that a drunken individual poses a threat to himself and to others, and that in some cases the defendant's intoxicated conduct may have posed a risk of even greater harm than that which actually occurred. However, at the same time it is also arguable that the individual culpability of drunken stupidity is less than that of sober and deliberate calculation. This dilemma is further sharpened by evidence from a Cardiff study that more than half of those arrested for alcohol-related crime are first-time offenders. Either we can protect society from those who take intoxicants and then do harm, or we can follow the logic and principle of criminal law by acquitting those who lack the relevant mens rea for the offences with which they are charged. We cannot, apparently, do both.

Secondly, wherever law reform is attempted, to some extent a choice must be made between justice and simplicity. On the one hand, the more varied degrees of culpability the law is able to represent, the more accurately it will label the convicted defendant and the more fully it will be able to realise its goal of achieving justice. On the other, the more complex the law becomes in order to take account of these varying degrees of culpability, the more

---

[217] Wells (1982).
[218] Many people would regard a deliberate push as a different kind of wrong from an accidental push.
[219] For further discussion, see Gough (1996).   [220] Husak (2012c).

difficult it becomes for juries and courts to understand and operate. Nowhere is this more true than in relation to proposed reforms of the law relating to intoxication.

Thirdly, not only will more varied degrees of culpability take longer to explain and understand within each trial, they may also lead to greater difficulty for a particular jury in reaching a verdict. On the one hand, it is clearly important and helpful for juries to be able to signal to judges precisely why they have chosen to convict a particular defendant so that the judge can then give effect to that reasoning at the stage of sentencing. On the other hand, the greater the number of options open to the deliberating jury, the greater the risk that they will not be able to reach a unanimous verdict.

Here are some proposed reforms:[221]

(1) There should be no special legal regulations governing intoxication. It would be possible simply to treat intoxication as one piece of evidence that a jury considers to decide whether a defendant had intention or recklessness. So, a drunken defendant who did not foresee a risk would not be reckless. This approach has been adopted by the courts in Australia and New Zealand.[222] In fact, in very few cases in those jurisdictions have intoxicated defendants been able successfully to plead that they lacked *mens rea*.[223] It appears that an intoxicated defendant who claims he did not foresee a risk is often disbelieved by the jury. An alternative interpretation is that Australian juries are unwilling to acquit intoxicated defendants and convict them regardless of the judge's direction.

(2) Some who argue that the criminal law should penalize drunkenness could argue that drunkenness should constitute the *mens rea* for any offence.[224] Such a view might be supported on the basis of an individual's 'responsibility . . . to stay sober if his intoxication will jeopardise the lives and safety of others'.[225] Few support this view. Even taking a hostile view of intoxication, convicting a defendant of an intent-based offence, rather than a recklessness-based offence, seems unnecessary.

(3) There should be a new offence of 'causing harm while intoxicated'.[226] The Law Commission Consultation Paper proposed an offence of causing certain kinds of harm while intoxicated to a significant extent.[227] Law Commission Report No. 229 rejected this on the basis of fierce opposition from many respondents to the Consultation Paper. Opponents of the Consultation Paper's approach might argue that such an approach draws an inappropriate distinction between drunken and sober vandals who lack concern towards others.[228]

(4) An argument can be made for a crime of public intoxication.[229] A Home Office report has stated: 'Public drunkenness can give rise to serious problems of disorderly conduct, nuisance, criminal damage and alcohol-related assaults, particularly in the proximity of licensed premises at closing time. In addition, it can create a fear of alcohol-related violence, which impacts on the quality of life for many. The government is determined to tackle these issues.'[230] However, one study suggested that less than 1 per cent of intoxicated people commit serious criminal offences.[231]

---

[221] Law Commission Report No. 314 (2009a).
[222] Orchard (1993). Australia, South Africa, and Canada have all abandoned the *Majewski* rule.
[223] Orchard (1993).   [224] Keiter (1997).
[225] Justice David Souter in *State v Dufield* 549 A 2d 1205, 1208 (NH, 1988).
[226] Law Commission Consultation Paper No. 127 (1993a). The Butler Committee (1975) proposed an offence of dangerous intoxication.
[227] Virgo (1993) is generally supportive.   [228] Gough (1996).
[229] Ashworth (1980).   [230] Home Office (2000).   [231] Mitchell (1988).

(5) An alternative approach is to see the 'problem' as not with intoxication, but with our understanding of intoxication. If our legal system was not so in thrall to subjective recklessness and was willing to include within recklessness a concept of failing to foresee an obvious risk for some blameworthy reason, then there would be no difficulty in classifying voluntarily intoxicated defendants who fail to foresee an obvious risk as reckless.[232]

FURTHER READING

Bogg, A. and Herring, J. (2012) 'Addiction and Responsibility' in J. Herring, C. Regan, D. Weinberg, and P. Withington (eds) *Intoxication and Society* (Basingstoke: Palgrave Macmillan).

Child, J. (2009) 'Drink, Drugs and Law Reform: A Review of Law Commission Report No. 314' *Criminal Law Review* 488.

Husak, D. (2012a) 'Intoxication and Culpability' *Criminal Law and Philosophy* 6: 363.

Mackay, R. (1995) *Mental Condition Defences in the Criminal Law* (Oxford: OUP), ch. 8.

Simester, A. (2009) 'Intoxication is Never a Defence' *Criminal Law Review* 3.

Sullivan, G.R. (1996a) 'Making Excuses' in A. Simester and A. Smith (eds) *Harm and Culpability* (Oxford: OUP).

Tolmie, J. (2001) 'Alcoholism and Criminal Liability' *Modern Law Review* 64: 688.

Williams, R. (2013) 'Voluntary Intoxication—A Lost Cause?' *Law Quarterly Review* 126: 264.

---

19 MOTIVE

19.1 IS MOTIVE RELEVANT IN THE CRIMINAL LAW?

The courts have been consistent in stating that motive and intention are separate. Indeed it is often said that motive is irrelevant in the criminal law.[233] In *Lynch v DPP*[234] the defendant was told by a group of terrorists that he would be killed if he did not assist in a killing. The House of Lords held that he intended to assist in the killing, even though his motive was to avoid being killed by the terrorists. However, the position is not this straightforward. It seems that in some cases the courts do attach significance to the defendant's motives. Here are three examples:

(1) In *Steane*[235] a defendant who, during the war, assisted the enemy[236] because he feared that otherwise his family would be sent to a concentration camp was held not to have intended to assist the enemy.

(2) In *Adams*[237] it was held that a doctor who gave pain-relieving drugs to a patient, aware that these may slightly shorten the patient's life span, did not intend to kill the patient, because his purpose was to relieve pain, not kill.

---

[232] J. Gardner (1994). [233] J.C. Smith (2002: 95). *Contra* W. Wilson (2002: ch. 5).
[234] [1975] AC 653 (HL). [235] [1947] KB 997 (CA).
[236] This was an offence under special wartime regulations.
[237] *Bodkin Adams* [1957] Crim LR 365.

(3) In *Gillick v West Norfolk and Wisbech AHA*[238] the House of Lords held that a doctor who gave a girl aged under 16 contraceptive advice and pills would not necessarily be committing the offence of aiding and abetting unlawful (underage) sexual intercourse. Even though the doctor might know that as a result of the advice a girl might therefore engage in sexual intercourse, he did not intend to assist her. ←2 (p.136)

It seems that in fact it is misleading to describe motive as irrelevant. There are many ways that motive may in fact be relevant in the criminal law:

(1) Motive may help in establishing what the defendant's purpose is. Often a person's motive is to produce a particular result, in which his or her motive and intention are the same. Indeed Norrie[239] argues that it is difficult to imagine someone having an intention to do something without having a motive. Motive, he suggests, is the driving force behind the intention.

(2) Motive may be relevant in deciding, in cases of oblique intention, whether the jury will find from virtual certainty and foresight of that virtual certainty that there was intention.[240]

(3) Some offences specifically require proof of motive, for example racially aggravated assaults.[241]

(4) In relation to defences it is important to know whether what motivated the defendant's actions was the justifying reason.[242] For example, in order to plead self-defence defendants must use force in order to defend themselves and not out of revenge.

(5) It is impossible to assess whether the defendant was acting dishonestly for the purpose of property offences without considering the motive of the defendant.

(6) Motive can be relevant at the sentencing stage. As Norrie tersely remarks, 'Having insisted upon a strict legal code so as to protect the liberty of the individual, it transpires that the individual's liberty is ultimately dependent not upon the rule of law at all but on a group of men operating with a wide discretion at the sentencing stage.'[243]

(7) There have been cases where it is widely thought that the jury has acquitted the defendant because they have believed he acted from the best of motives, despite a clear direction from the judge that he is guilty in the eyes of the law.[244]

19.2 ARGUMENTS IN FAVOUR OF TAKING MOTIVE INTO ACCOUNT

It seems odd that if *mens rea* is all about ascertaining the blameworthiness of the defendant that motive is not taken into account. Most people would see a clear difference in moral terms between a contract killer and a mercy killer, but the difference lies in their motivation (not their intention).[245] Even so under the law of murder they are treated identically. Indeed, as hinted at in Part I, motive may be an even better guide to blameworthiness than intention or recklessness.

---

[238] [1985] 3 All ER 402 (HL).   [239] Norrie (2001: 36).
[240] Ashworth and Horder (2013: 170–3).   [241] Crime and Disorder Act 1998, s. 28(1)(b).
[242] See J. Gardner (1998).   [243] Norrie (2002: 200).
[244] e.g. *Ponting* (Central Criminal Court, 11 February 1985).   [245] Kessler Ferzan (2008).

Alan Norrie[246] has argued that the line between motives and intention is in fact almost impossible to draw. He argues that once we look at what causes intentions and start looking at motive we inevitably bring in complex social and political explanations for people's actions. For example, once we start to consider greed as a motivation we inevitably have to consider the unequal distribution of goods in our society which nurtures feelings of greed. Norrie argues that the legal system, in not wanting to challenge the social and political status quo, avoids entering such treacherous waters by generally refusing to consider motives. However, he argues, where it is convenient to do so motive can suddenly become relevant again, for example in permitting the doctors in *Gillick* to prescribe contraception to under-16-year-olds.[247]

19.3 ARGUMENTS AGAINST TAKING MOTIVE INTO ACCOUNT

Antony Duff[248] justifies the statement that motive is irrelevant to the criminal law by redefining what commentators mean by such a statement: motive is relevant only when Parliament has declared it to be relevant as part of the definition of an offence. If Parliament has not so declared it the courts cannot permit the defendant to raise his good motive as a defence. For example, if the government had decided to permit trials of genetically modified crops, but a defendant, opposing the growing of such crops, destroyed them, to permit him a defence to a charge of criminal damage on the basis that the jury or magistrates believed that the defendant was acting from good motives would be to undermine the authority of Parliament. If the defendant objects to the law the way to raise it is through political channels and not by committing crimes and raising the issue by way of a defence. A similar point could be made in relation to euthanasia. The legal response to euthanasia should be decided by Parliament, not by juries deciding on individual cases whether the defendant's motives were good. Duff accepts that such an argument is appropriate only as long as there are suitable channels for individuals to raise their points of view. In relation to those in desperate poverty who steal, the solution to their difficulties is to seek the assistance of welfare provision: that is the 'forum' for dealing with dire poverty, not by committing theft and raising poverty as an issue. Although it should be emphasized that Duff accepts that his argument has legitimacy only providing that the welfare provisions are adequate.

FURTHER READING

Motive

Ashworth, A. (1996) 'The Treatment of Good Intentions' in A. Simester and A. Smith (eds) *Harm and Culpability* (Oxford: OUP).

Binder, G. (2002) 'The Rhetoric of Motive and Intent' *Buffalo Criminal Law Review* 6: 1.

Duff, R.A. (1998b) 'Principle and Contradiction in the Criminal Law: Motives and Criminal Liability' in R.A. Duff (ed.) *Philosophy and the Criminal Law* (Cambridge: Cambridge University Press).

Horder, J. (2000) 'On the Irrelevance of Motive in Criminal Law' in J. Horder (ed.) *Oxford Essays in Jurisprudence* (Oxford: OUP).

---

246 Norrie (2002: 170–81).   247 See further Gardner and Jung (1991).   248 Duff (1998b).

Husak, D. (1989) 'Motive and Criminal Liability' *Criminal Justice Ethics* 1: 3.

Kessler Ferzan, K. (2008) 'Beyond Intention' *Cardozo Law Review* 26.

Norrie, A. (2002) *Punishment, Responsibility, and Justice* (Oxford: OUP), 170–81.

Tadros, V. (2011) 'Wrongdoing and Motivation' in S. Green and R.A. Duff (eds) *Philosophical Foundations of Criminal Law* (Oxford: OUP).

Knowledge and belief

Callender, D. (1994) 'Wilful Ignorance, Knowledge and the Equality Culpability Thesis' *Wisconsin Law Review* 129.

Shute, S. (2002a) 'Knowledge and Belief in the Criminal Law' in S. Shute and A. Simester (eds) *Criminal Law Theory* (Oxford: OUP).

Sullivan, G.R. (2002b) 'Knowledge, Belief, and Culpability' in S. Shute and A. Simester (eds) *Criminal Law Theory* (Oxford: OUP).

Wasik, M. and Thompson, M. (1981) ' "Turning a Blind Eye" as Constituting *Mens Rea*' *Northern Ireland Law Quarterly* 32: 328.

20 THE 'CORRESPONDENCE PRINCIPLE'

At the end of Part I of this chapter it was emphasized that when you learn what the *mens rea* of a crime is it is not enough just to learn that intention or recklessness is required, but you should learn what must be intended or foreseen. However, this raises the so-called correspondence principle, which is one of the most controversial issues in criminal law. Imagine an offence of causing grievous bodily harm. If we assume that the offence involves recklessness, what exactly must D foresee: grievous bodily harm, at least actual bodily harm, or any harm however minor? These possibilities reflect three views that could be taken:

(1) **The correspondence principle** The principle requires the *mens rea* of a crime to match the *actus reus*. In other words the defendant must intend or be *Cunningham* reckless as to the *actus reus*. So in this case the defendant must foresee grievous bodily harm. Anything less will be inadequate.

(2) **The 'proportionality' principle** The defendant need foresee only an injury which is proportionate to the *actus reus*.[249] It does not matter if the injury is slightly more than that foreseen, but if the injury is in a different league from that foreseen (it is not proportionate) the defendant should not be responsible for it. In our example actual bodily harm is close to grievous bodily harm. If the defendant had only foreseen a touching he should not be guilty of an offence involving grievous bodily harm because that would be of a different degree of seriousness.

(3) **The 'moral threshold' principle** Supporters of this view simply require that the defendant foresaw some kind of harm. Once the defendant acts, foreseeing that he will injure the victim, he loses the sympathy of the law and is responsible for the harm caused.[250]

There are two questions that may be asked here:

---

[249] Tadros (2002b).   [250] See Ashworth (2008b) for a powerful critique of this view.

20.1 WHICH PRINCIPLE BEST REFLECTS THE LAW?

Although there may be some fine historical precedent for the correspondence principle,[251] it is in fact honoured far more in the breach than in the observance in current criminal law. Of course all strict liability offences infringe it; even murder (which accepts intention to do grievous bodily harm for the *mens rea*) does not observe it. Of the significant offences against the person only section 18 of the Offences Against the Person Act 1861 (inflicting grievous bodily harm with intent to cause grievous bodily harm) complies with it.

20.2 WHICH PRINCIPLE IS MOST JUSTIFIABLE IN THEORY?

Underlying the debate behind these theories is the notion of 'moral luck', which we will discuss in detail in Chapter 14.[252] Imagine that the defendant picks up a stick and throws it at the victim. What happens next may be described as a matter of luck: the stick may hit the victim, the victim may jump out of the way, a sudden gust of wind may blow the stick out of the way, a passer-by may push the victim out of the way. It is then argued that what the defendant can control is his action and his state of mind, but what happens beyond that is just chance that should not affect his liability. If you are persuaded by this argument a number of consequences follow which we shall discuss at various points in this book (e.g. the argument that attempted crimes and complete crimes should be treated identically[253]). However, the argument is relevant in relation to the correspondence principle because it holds that a defendant who throws the stick intending actual bodily harm is equally blameworthy whether it causes actual bodily harm or grievous bodily harm. The level of harm the stick throwing causes is just luck. Therefore the defendant should be guilty only of intentionally causing actual bodily harm. He should not be responsible for the higher level of harm that occurred because of his action: that was just bad luck.[254] Michael Moore in his book has gone so far as to say that 'a majority of respectable criminal law theoreticians' take this view.[255]

Those who reject the argument tend to raise a number of arguments:

(1) Most people do not regard the consequences of people's actions as just 'bad luck'. It was not just bad luck that the victim suffered grievous bodily harm; it was because the defendant threw a stick at him! Had he or she not thrown the stick the chance factors (the wind, the movements of the victim) would not have had a role to play. Jeremy Horder[256] has talked of a defendant 'making his own bad luck'. Many people have sympathy for a defendant who genuinely causes an injury by bad luck (e.g. when he or she trips over a paving stone and bumps into someone). However, where a person has set out to cause an injury to someone he or she cannot claim it is an accident, he or she loses the sympathy of the law, and is now liable for the consequences of his or her actions. In response Mitchell has stated while the defendant 'cannot claim that his victim's death was simply bad luck, the prosecution cannot deny that luck did play a part in it'.[257]

251 Although J. Gardner (1994) denies that the correspondence principle has ever been part of the law.
252 Duff (2008); Enoch and Marmor (2007); Nagel (1979); Mandil (1987); Schulhofer (1974); B. Williams (1981); Honoré (1989); J.C. Smith (1971); Fletcher (1998).
253 Ashworth (1988).   254 For a theological perspective, see Stern (1999).
255 The impressive list includes Kadish (1994); Gobert (1993); Becker (1974); Jarvis Thomson (1986); Ashworth (1988); Gross (1979); Schulhofer (1974); Feinberg (1970).
256 Horder (1995c).   257 Mitchell (2009: 504).

(2) Surveys of public opinion indicate that the majority of people questioned do support making people liable for the harms they cause, even if that harm is greater than they foresaw or intended.[258]

(3) Consequences matter to onlookers and to the perpetrator. Nagel,[259] in a famous example, discusses a person who leaves a child in the bath with the tap running to answer the door and chats, forgetting the child. If the child manages to survive we dismiss the action as careless; if the child dies this transforms our judgment and the action becomes appalling.[260] We expect different reactions from onlookers and the defendant depending on the consequence of the act (e.g. relief rather than outrage). The fact that the consequences do affect our emotional reaction could be said to indicate that a moral difference exists between the two.

Simester and Sullivan argue that it is important to distinguish between acts where the luck (the risk of harm) is extrinsic or intrinsic to the nature of the act.[261] For those actions which are inherently dangerous the defendant cannot claim that it is just bad luck if someone is injured. For those actions which are not inherently dangerous then it may be regarded as luck whether or not the victim is injured. An example of an intrinsically dangerous act is dangerous driving. Other acts are not inherently dangerous. Simester and Sullivan consider the hypothetical scenario of a secretary who is told to collect blood samples as part of a staff survey, but fails to do so. When a worker later falls ill and a blood transfusion cannot be provided because the worker's blood group is not known this is bad luck: she could not have known that her failure to collect the samples for the survey would have fatal consequences.

In the following extract, Michael Moore stresses that we have two reasons for blaming people: culpability and wrongdoing. He admits that culpability is the poorer relation as it is both necessary and sufficient as the basis for punishment, but wrongdoing is neither:

M. Moore, *Placing Blame* (Oxford: OUP, 1997), 213–16

The problem of moral luck, as Nagel frames it, is how we can justify holding people more responsible for causing harm than for merely intending or risking harm when they lack that *control* (over whether the harm occurs or not) we generally require for responsibility.

Moral luck is good when an actor fails to cause the harm he has intended or risked, for the actor gets moral credit for something over which he lacked control; moral luck is bad when the actor does cause the harm he intended or risked, because he gets moral demerits for something over which he lacked control. Nagel's question is how such luck could be justified in the face of our control requirement for responsibility.

The question as Nagel poses it arises only if we think that there is such a thing as moral luck. By this, I do not mean to join Kant *et al.* in denying that wrongdoing has any independent moral significance. I mean that an anti-Kantian here might deny that there is any *luck* involved in being held more responsible for successful wrongdoing than for intended or risked wrongdoing that does not materialize. There undoubtedly is some luck involved in whether we cause the harms we intend or risk, but there will be *moral luck* only *vis-à-vis* some moral baseline of the normal that places all such luck on the side of the extraordinary.

We do have a criminal law doctrine that explicitly deals with the question of luck with regard to consequences. This is the doctrine of proximate causation. The proximate cause

---

258 Robinson and Darley (1995 and 1998).   259 T. Nagel (1979).
260 For a rejection of attaching weight to these arguments, see J. Gardner (2011).
261 See further Tadros (2008a).

tests in criminal law have as their function the separation of harms in fact caused by a defend-ant's voluntary act into two camps: those freakishly so caused, in which event the actor is liable only for lesser crimes of attempt, specific intent, or risk-imposition; and those more normally so caused, in which event the actor is liable for the more serious punishments reserved for completed crimes. Sometimes these tests are explicit about their being tests of luck. The Model Penal Code, for example, provides that an act is the cause of a harm when the harm would not have happened but for the act, and (with complications here ignored) the 'actual result is not too remote or accidental in its occurrence to have a just bearing on the actor's liability or on the gravity of his offense'. Even when the proximate cause tests are not explicitly directed to this freakishness or luck question, they implicitly aim at just this factor. The foreseeability test of proximate causation, for example, seems to be aimed at an actor's culpability: could he have foreseen that such a harm would result from his action? In reality, given the well-known conundrum about specifying the details of the harm about which to ask foreseeability questions, what the test really asks is whether the 'freakishness of the facts refuses to be drowned' or not.

Consider some examples of Hart and Honoré's: (1) A defendant culpably throws a lighted cigarette onto some bushes; the bushes catch fire, but would burn themselves out if it were not for a normal evening breeze that comes up, carrying the fire to the forest and burning it down. (2) Same as (1), except that the breeze that comes up is a gale force wind never before seen at this time of year, which wind uproots the burning bushes and carries them to a distant forest, which ignites and burns. (3) Same as (1), except no breeze, normal or abnormal, arises; rather, a would-be extinguisher of the fire in the bushes himself catches fire, and in his agony he runs to the forest, which burns. (4) Same as (1), except a second culpable defendant is the vehicle for transferring the fire from the bushes to the forest: he sees that the fire in the bushes is about to go out, so he pours a gasoline trail from the forest to the burning bushes, in order to burn down the forest, which then occurs.

On the direct cause notion of proximate causation that Hart and Honoré so elegantly explore the initial defendant in (1) and (3) is criminally liable for burning down the forest, whereas in variations (2) and (4) the causal routes from defendant's act to the ultimate harm are too accidental, too fortuitous, too much a matter of chance or luck, for the defendant to be liable for such harm; at most, he can be held only for attempted destruction of the forest, or for risking its destruction.

Notice that the normal breeze in (1), the gale in (2), the movements of the clumsy would-be fire extinguisher in (3), and the actions of the arsonist in (4), are all equally outside the control of the initial fire-starter. In Nagel's sense of 'luck', thus, all cases involve moral luck: bad moral luck in (1) and (3) where the fire-starter is held liable, and good moral luck in (2) and (4), where he is not. Nagel's sense of 'luck' is thus obviously not the same as that employed in the criminal law doctrines of proximate causation and the morality that underlies them, for those doctrines use a different notion of luck to distinguish some as matters of luck and others not.

The notion of luck always involves some baseline of comparison. As the proximate cause tests of the criminal law use the notion, the baseline is the normal way things come about. When a defendant negligently operates a train too fast, so that he cannot stop it before it hits another's railroad car, there is no luck involved in his injuring the second car because that is how such things normally happen. When, however, the same negligently speeding defend-ant causes the same damage to the same car, but does so because a first collision (which does no damage) throws the defendant against the reverse throttle of his engine, thereby knocking him unconscious, whereupon his engine goes in reverse around a circular track, colliding with the other's car and then causing it damage, there is luck involved because of the abnormal conjunction of events taking place between the defendant's act and the harm.

Moral luck, on this concept of luck, would exist whenever the consequence of moral blame or credit is brought on one in an abnormal, freakish, or chance way. If one were truly to blame for someone else's actions over whom one had no control, for example, that would be a case of (bad) moral luck. But if one's blameworthiness only comes about in the normal, non-freakish, not-by-chance way, there is no *moral* luck involved in such blameworthiness, wherever it exists, even if there is luck involved. The crucial question, of course, is to spell out when blameworthiness attaches in a normal, as opposed to an abnormal, way. Nagel thinks that this notion of normalcy is to be fleshed out with his idea of control: blameworthiness for a harm would attach in a normal way only if the agent was in control of all factors causally contributing to that harm. Yet this is surely not the notion of normalcy presupposed by the criminal law's notion of luck. And this last observation is not the observation that Nagel requires *complete* control (of *all* factors) while the criminal law and the morality that underlies it only requires control of *some* factors; rather, the observation is that the notion of control is alien to the criminal law's idea of luck. The baseline is freakishness of causal route, not degree of control by the agent of the intervening factors. For notice again: the actors equally lack any control of the breezes or second agents whose interventions were necessary for the destruction of the forest in scenarios (1) to (4) above. It is the normalcy of causal route that decides the normalcy of moral blameworthiness in such cases, ideas of normalcy to which control is simply irrelevant.

In the following extract, Jeremy Horder applies some of this theoretical material to the issue of transferred *mens rea*: ←10 (p.164)

J. Horder, 'Transferred Malice and the Remoteness of Unexpected Outcomes from Intentions' [2006] *Criminal Law Review* 383 at 384–6, 390–1, 398

[H]ow D causes the actual V's death is of no legal importance . . . So long as D acts with the fault element of murder, and kills in consequence, they may be convicted of murder (other things being equal). . . . The justification for convicting of murder in such cases is the assumed moral insignificance of the way someone is killed, as well as of the identity of the person killed (the central issue according to the impersonality doctrine), when death has been intentionally caused. In that regard, the transferred malice doctrine is really better understood as an application of what I will call the "prohibited outcome" doctrine. So long as the prohibited outcome comes about (intentional killing), it matters not how or respecting whom.

. . .

There has been an understandable difference of opinion amongst scholars over whether a murder conviction is ever appropriate when D killed someone they did not attempt to kill, even though D's attempt to kill did in fact end in a killing. I will assume that, at least in some instances, it can be appropriate to convict D of murder in these circumstances. I will argue, however, that the range of instances in which this is appropriate is now rightly coming to be circumscribed by what I will be calling the "remoteness" principle. The remoteness principle may serve to prevent conviction in the following kinds of example:

Example 1: D fires a gun at V1, intending to kill V1. D misses, but the noise of the gun being fired startles a bystander, V2, who consequently dies of a heart attack.

Example 2: D shoots V1, intending to kill V1. V1 is wounded and taken to hospital. Whilst waiting for treatment, V1 is seen by his father, V2. V2 is so aghast at the sight of V1 covered in blood that the shock kills him. V1 survives.

Example 3: D shoots at V1, intending to kill V1. The bullet misses, but enters a munitions factory behind V1. The bullet sets off an explosion that kills a large number of people.

Broadly speaking, Andrew Ashworth is right to argue that the appropriate charges, on facts such as these, are attempted murder in relation to the intended victim, and (where appropriate) manslaughter in relation to actual victim(s). A conviction for murder—a crime of specific intent—would often fail to label D's crime in a "morally representative" way in any of these kinds of instances. Sensible use of prosecutorial discretion is, though, probably the best way to ensure that this unrepresentative labelling is avoided, rather than creating a legal barrier to conviction for murder. In part, this is because one should not, in fact, completely bar murder convictions in such cases.

For Glanville Williams, a murder conviction in relation to the actual victim would be appropriate as long as, "the consequence was brought about by negligence in relation to the actual victim". I share Williams' instinct that a murder conviction should not be completely ruled out in such cases. Williams purports to give legal effect to this instinct through the inclusion of a specific further fault element of negligence in relation to the actual death, alongside the intention to kill. I believe, however, that this—the presence or absence of negligence—does not adequately conceptualise the basis for determining whether a murder conviction is or is not appropriate in the three examples. What should matter in these examples is not only that the actual victims were unintended victims, but also that they died in an unanticipated way. This double element of deviation from D's plan is what, in principle, may make the deaths too "remote" from what D intended for murder to be a representative label. This idea of "remoteness" provides a better way of understanding when a murder conviction would or would not be justified, in terms of representative labelling . . .

The transferring of malice is really the application of a doctrine in particular circumstances, rather than a doctrine in itself. I am calling the doctrine of which it is an application the "prohibited outcome" doctrine. The prohibited outcome doctrine is "permissive", in that it allows liability when a particular kind of interest has been culpably invaded or destroyed, even when the victim was not the intended victim, or the interest was not invaded or destroyed in the way intended. By way of contrast with the prohibited outcome doctrine, the remoteness doctrine is a restrictive doctrine. It constrains the reach of liability that would otherwise be justified by the prohibited outcome doctrine, by factoring in consideration of how the remoteness of outcome from intention (or foresight) affects the representative character of conviction for a particular offence. The remoteness doctrine is, in turn, related to but distinct from a separate rule that restricts the reach of the prohibited outcome doctrine in justifying criminal liability. This is the rule that a fault element for one offence cannot be "translated" into the fault element for another offence.

So, in explaining the legal concept of transferred intent, we need to concern ourselves with four doctrines, principles or rules (terminology, in this respect, is not so very important):

(a) prohibited outcome doctrine (the transferring of malice being a warranted application);

(b) the labelling principle (conviction must constitute a representative label for D's wrong);

(c) the remoteness doctrine (transfers of intent must not compromise the labelling principle);

(d) the 'no-translation' rule (different fault elements cannot be transferred between crimes).

The so-called doctrine of transferred malice operates as a residual example of a "common law doctrine" within the criminal law. That is to say, it must be grasped through an appreciation of the examples in which it has been held to apply, or not to apply, rather than through the application of a general rule.

. . .

The persistence of the prohibited outcome doctrine is one manifestation of the law's hostility to the view that all elements of "bad luck" in bringing about a consequence must be eliminated, before one can begin proper moral assessment of the agent's action in bringing it about. This is most obvious in the doctrines of causation. Consider an example in which D stabs V with intent to kill, and V only dies after negligent treatment at the hospital. There is little doubt that D may be guilty of murder, even if proper treatment might have saved V, unless the treatment was grossly in itself, criminally-negligent. What will matter is whether the jury regard the stab wound as still an operating, albeit perhaps a now more minor, cause of death, or just the setting in which another cause—the negligent treatment—is operating. If the jury do regard the stab wound as a still operating cause, D's "bad luck" in actually causing V's death, as things turn out, will not affect his liability for murder. Like the causal doctrines that operate to draw these distinctions, the remoteness doctrine is meant to ensure that, whilst bad luck need not be eliminated before moral responsibility can adequately be judged, what happened as a result of D's conduct must not be *almost solely* a matter of bad luck. The burden is, then, on those who oppose the transfer of malice under the prohibited outcome doctrine to say why luck should favourably affect D's responsibility in such cases, but not in the cases (other than those in which D's involvement is relegated to mere historical background) where the causal chain takes a preventable turn.

FURTHER READING

Simons, K. (2012) 'Is Strict Criminal Liability in the Grading of Offences Consistent with Retributive Desert? Strict Liability in Grading' *Oxford Journal of Legal Studies* 32: 445.

---

21 INDIVIDUALISM AND *MENS REA*

An interesting critique of the current approach to *mens rea* is that it is over-individualistic. In other words our notions of culpability focus on what the defendant intended or foresaw, rather than considering the defendant within his or her community and society.[262] The argument is developed by Victoria Nourse in the following extract:

V. Nourse, 'Heart and Minds: Understanding the New Culpability' (2002) 8 *Buffalo Criminal Law Review* 361

My second fear is that all this emphasis on the proper 'state of mind' occludes an important assumption shared by most of the participants in this debate—the assumption that it is the individual who is the proper focus of the debate. The common law was, I believe, quite a bit more sensitive to this assumption than are we moderns. When the [American] Model Penal Code drafters eschewed common law formulations, they not only got rid of ambiguous terms, they got rid of an entire structure of culpability. Whether we are looking for desire or acceptance or indifference, the modern debate has followed this trend. It has located culpability in the hearts and minds and capacities of individual defendants. We ask whether we should judge the defendant by his choices or his character or his desires. This focus on the individual must be false or at least incomplete; we don't live in bubbles or on islands. People

---

[262] See Deigh (2011) for further discussion.

commit crimes against others; and it is the relation between the 'other' and the 'defendant' that informs most of our judgments about the relative blameworthiness of the parties. We know this, in a sense. We know that for all our focus on individuality, all our attempts to describe defendants more and more particularly, whether it be in terms of their choice or their character or their virtue, that this has only led to reaction—to cries of hyperindividualism and abuse excuse and loss of agency.

It is time to reconsider more actively the assumption that the best way to protect individuals is to describe their hearts or minds, rather than to judge their relations to each other. This, by the way, has nothing to do with communitarianism or antiliberalism; it is simply a call for a 'relational individualism,' a call for the consideration of a different, and more direct (in my view), means to protect individuals. Even those who aim toward radical individuation, those who study mind for a living, recognize that the question of protecting individuals is in determining how an 'individual can stand in a healthy relation to his society,' precisely because the very notion that an individual exists at all depends upon a social world of relations.

A final comment (whose implications await elaboration elsewhere): In the end, crime is about power. Power is a relation, a relation that implies not only our regard for each other but the relation between citizens and state. This is why a criminal code will always be susceptible to public, majoritarian sentiment about culpability and blameworthiness even if drafted with the best intentions to protect individuals from unthinking minoritarian norms. Criminal law scholarship must stop hiding the ball in positivism and descriptivism, pretending to be a science, rather than a set of contingent norms. It must openly navigate the risks to the few and the many, to majorities and minorities, rather than deny that they exist. This navigation is impossible in a state of denial: if all the norms are buried in places that look like they are facts of nature, like passion and time and risk, then normativity will continue to be denied. That doesn't mean that the norms go away, it simply means that they will have more force, propelling us back and forth between apparent lenience and vengeance, abuse excuse and legal moralism, more a victim of a crude and unthinking politics than we ever hoped or desired.

It is not enough, any longer, in my view, to imagine culpability either in the image of a lonely cunning self or a cruel deterministic world. The man on an island needs no criminal law for he is fundamentally alone. The man with no government needs no criminal law since he may simply 'take the law into his own hands.' The criminal law helps to constitute our relation to each other as well as the nation in which we live. Conduct an intellectual experiment: Eliminate mens rea entirely from the criminal law and what do you have? A criminal law used to punish the innocent or the accidental is a hallmark of totalitarian regimes. History, if nothing else, tells us that when rulers seek to oppress their people, they repair easily to the criminal law. There is more at stake in a criminal code than individuals, state of mind, or particular words. The criminal law poses important questions about, quite literally, how we govern each other.

QUESTION

Read Dillof (1998), who poses the following hypothetical:

Andre is undertaking shooting practice at a firing range. His enemy Brett wanders into the range close to the target. Andre fires two shots in quick succession: one at Brett and then one at the target. Evidence later shows that the shot Andre aimed at Brett in fact hit the target and the shot he aimed at the target hit Brett.

Is this a case of murder? If not, how is it different from a transferred malice case?

FURTHER READING

Ashworth, A. (1978) 'Transferred Malice and Punishment for Unforeseen Consequences' in P. Glazebrook (ed.) *Reshaping the Criminal Law* (London: Sweet & Maxwell).

Ashworth, A. (2008b) 'A Change of Normative Position: Determining the Contours of Culpability in Criminal Law' *New Criminal Law Review* 11: 232.

Bohlander, M. (2010) 'Transferred Malice and Transferred Defenses: A Critique of the Traditional Doctrine and Arguments for a Change in Paradigm' *New Criminal Law Review* 13: 555.

Dillof, A. (1998) 'Transferred Intent: An Inquiry into the Nature of Criminal Culpability' *Buffalo Criminal Law Review* 1: 501.

Duff, R.A. (2008) 'Whose Luck is it Anyway' in C. Clarkson and S. Cunningham (eds) *Criminal Liability for Non-Aggressive Death* (Aldershot: Ashgate).

Eldar, S. (2012) 'The Limits of Transferred Malice' *Oxford Journal of Legal Studies* 32: 633.

Horder, J. (1995c) 'A Critique of the Correspondence Principle' *Criminal Law Review* 759.

Horder, J. (1997b) 'Questioning the Correspondence Principle—A Reply' *Criminal Law Review* 206.

Horder, J. (2006) 'Transferred Malice and the Remoteness of Unexpected Outcomes from Intentions' *Criminal Law Review* 383.

Mitchell, B. (1999) 'In Defence of the Correspondence Principle' *Criminal Law Review* 195.

Mitchell, B. (2009) 'More Thoughts about Unlawful and Dangerous Act Manslaughter and the One-Punch Killer' *Criminal Law Review* 502.

Morse, S. (2000) 'The Moral Metaphysics of Causation and Results' *California Law Review* 88: 879.

Nourse, V. (2002) 'Heart and Minds: Understanding the New Culpability' *Buffalo Criminal Law Review* 8: 361.

Westen, P. (2013) 'The Significance of Transferred Intent' *Criminal Law and Philosophy* 7: 321.

22 CONCLUDING THOUGHTS

Most serious crimes require proof that the defendant had a particular state of mind. These requirements play an important role in determining the extent of the defendant's blameworthiness. However, as this chapter shows, it can be a difficult job for the jury to decide what was going on inside someone's mind. Even if it is possible to do that, it is far from easy to know how to assess their blameworthiness. While the House of Lords have declared that the criminal law requires a subjective *mens rea* for criminal offences, this has proved a difficult requirement to implement. Defendants who should have seen a risk are, in some cases, blameworthy and some defendants who have seen a risk are not. Further, although the terms intention, recklessness, and negligence are readily distinguishable at a broad level, drawing the precise boundaries between them has proved troublesome.

STRICT LIABILITY

CENTRAL ISSUES

1. An offence of strict liability is one where it is not necessary to prove any mental state of the defendant. All that needs to be shown is that the defendant caused a particular result or carried out a particular act.

2. The courts will only interpret the offence to be one of strict liability where Parliament has made it quite clear that there is no *mens rea* requirement for the offence.

3. There are some offences which just require proof that the defendant possessed a prohibited item.

PART I: THE LAW

DEFINITION

A defendant is guilty of a strict liability offence if by a voluntary act he or she causes the prohibited result or state of affairs. There is no need to prove that the defendant had a particular state of mind.

1 WHAT IS A STRICT LIABILITY OFFENCE?

Offences of strict liability require proof that the defendant performed the prohibited conduct, but do not require proof that the defendant was blameworthy.[1] For example, in *Harrow London BC v Shah*[2] the defendant was convicted of selling a lottery ticket to a person under the age of 16, even though he was not aware that the purchaser was under 16 nor was it

---

[1] e.g. *Callow v Tillstone* (1900) 83 LT 411. For a detailed discussion of the meaning of strict liability, see Green (2005).

[2] [2000] Crim LR 692.

obvious that the person was under that age. In fact nearly half of all criminal offences are offences of strict liability.[3]

Most strict liability offences are minor offences. The criminal law covers a wide range of crimes, from murder at one end to parking tickets at the other. At the lower end such offences are often regarded by the general public as 'not really' criminal. These 'less serious' offences play the role of regulating people's behaviour so that society can work effectively, rather than indicating that the defendant has behaved in a morally reprehensible way.[4] These regulatory offences often do not require proof of *mens rea* because they do not carry the weight of moral censure that more serious crimes carry. It should be added that it is possible for an offence to be one of strict liability for some aspects of the *actus reus*, but not others.[5] →1 (p.225)

Strict liability offences should be distinguished from negligence-based offences where the prosecution must demonstrate that the defendant acted unreasonably. As already indicated for strict liability offences, if the defendant has committed the *actus reus* he or she is guilty even if he or she was acting reasonably.[6] The line between a strict liability offence and a negligence-based offence is somewhat blurred where a statute does not require proof that defendants acted unreasonably, but the defendants will have a defence if they can prove they acted with 'due diligence'[7] in avoiding the prohibited harm. These are distinct from negligence offences because the burden of proof lies with the defendants to prove that they were acting reasonably, rather than the prosecution proving they were acting negligently. Even where an offence is one of strict liability defences such as duress or self-defence may still apply.[8]

2 WHICH OFFENCES ARE STRICT LIABILITY?

The vast majority of strict liability offences are found in statutes, although there may be a few common law strict liability offences.[9] For statutes, the key question for a court is how to interpret a statutory offence if Parliament has not included a *mens rea* requirement. In such a case the court has to decide whether to interpret the crime as one of strict liability or to read in a *mens rea* requirement. If Parliament made it absolutely clear for every offence what the *mens rea* requirement (if any) was the courts' job would be easier. Unfortunately Parliament has not.

The following case has reinforced the common law that in construing statutory offences there is a presumption against strict liability and in favour of *mens rea*: →2 (p.226)

---

[3] Ashworth and Blake (1996).

[4] A distinction is sometimes drawn between crimes that are *male in se* (the activity is in itself harmful (e.g. killing)) and crimes that are *male prohibita* (where the activity is wrong only because it has been prohibited (e.g. driving on the right-hand side of the road)).

[5] *Hibbert* (1869) LR 1 CCR 184.

[6] As acknowledged, e.g. by Maurice Kay J in *Barnfather v Islington London BC* [2003] EWHC 418 (Admin), at para. 30.

[7] Ashworth and Horder (2013: 161–2) suggest that such statutes might not, strictly speaking, be strict liability offences.

[8] *R v Gregory* [2011] EWCA Crim 1712.

[9] e.g. criminal libel or public nuisance. However, these are rarely charged and there is some debate whether these are strict liability offences or not.

R v K
[2002] 1 AC 462

K, aged 26, was charged with indecently assaulting a 14-year-old girl, contrary to section 14 of the Sexual Offences Act 1956. He claimed that the sexual activity between them was consensual and that he believed the girl was 16 as she had told him. The judge indicated that the prosecution would be required to prove that at the time of the incident the defendant did not honestly believe that the girl was 16 or over. The prosecution argued that this direction was wrong and appealed. The Court of Appeal allowed the appeal, but granted leave to appeal to the House of Lords, certified that the following points of law of general public importance were involved in the decision:

(a) Is a defendant entitled to be acquitted of the offence of indecent assault on a complainant under the age of 16 years, contrary to section 14(1) of the Sexual Offences Act 1956, if he may hold an honest belief that the complainant in question was aged 16 years or over?

(b) If yes, must the belief be held on reasonable grounds?

Section 14 of the 1956 Act reads:

(1) It is an offence, subject to the exception mentioned in subsection (3) of this section, for a person to make an indecent assault on a woman.

(2) A girl under the age of 16 cannot in law give any consent which would prevent an act being an assault for the purposes of this section.

(3) Where a marriage is invalid under section two of the Marriage Act 1949, or section one of the Age of Marriage Act 1929 (the wife being a girl under the age of 16), the invalidity does not make the husband guilty of any offence under this section by reason of her incapacity to consent while under that age, if he believes her to be his wife and has reasonable cause for the belief.

(4) A woman who is a defective cannot in law give any consent which would prevent an act being an assault for the purposes of this section, but a person is only to be treated as guilty of an indecent assault on a defective by reason of that incapacity to consent, if that person knew or had reason to suspect her to be a defective.

Lord Steyn

33. It is now possible to face directly the question whether section 14(1) makes it compellingly clear that the supplementation of the text by the presumption is ruled out. The actual decision of the House in *B (A Minor)* [sub nom. *B (A Child) v DPP*] *v Director of Public Prosecutions* [2000] 2 AC 428 on the meaning of section 1(1) of the Indecency with Children Act 1960 springs to mind. The House concluded that on the statutory provision involved in that case the presumption was not displaced. But the particular wording of section 14(1) gives greater scope for the Crown's argument in the present case. Thus it is noteworthy that subsection (4) of section 14, but not subsection (2), makes specific provision,

in the context of consent, for a defence of absence of *mens rea*. Nevertheless, I would hold that in the present case a compellingly clear implication can only be established if the supplementation of the text by reading in words appropriate to require *mens rea* results in an internal inconsistency of the text. Approaching the problem in this way, one can readily accept that section 14(2) could naturally have provided that a genuine belief by the accused that the girl was over 16 was no defence. Conversely, section 14(2) could have provided that a genuine belief that the girl was under 16 was a defence. In my view a provision of the latter type would not have been conceptually inconsistent with any part of section 14. By contrast, the terms of sections 5 and 6 of the 1956 Act namely offences of having sexual intercourse with girls under 13 (section 5) and with girls under 16 (section 6) are inconsistent with the application of the presumption. The 'young man's defence' under section 6(3) makes clear that it is not available to anybody else. The linked provision in section 5, dealing with intercourse with younger girls, must therefore also impose absolute liability. There is nothing in section 14(1) as clearly indicative of the displacement of the presumption. In these circumstances it cannot in my view be said that there is a compellingly clear implication ruling out the application of the presumption.

34. This is a result which serves the public interest. It would have been a strange result to conclude that Parliament created by section 14(1) offences of strict liability where any heterosexual or homosexual contact takes place between two teenagers of whom one is under 16. Fortunately, the strong presumption of *mens rea* enabled the House to avoid such a result.

35. For these reasons, as well as the reasons given by Lord Bingham of Cornhill, I would allow the appeal.

Lord Millett

40. My Lords, I have had the advantage of reading in draft the speech of my noble and learned friend Lord Bingham of Cornhill, with which I agree. For the reasons he gives I would allow the appeal and answer the certified questions as he proposes.

41. I do so without reluctance but with some misgiving, for I have little doubt that we shall be failing to give effect to the intention of Parliament and will reduce section 14 of the Sexual Offences Act 1956 to incoherence. . . .

44. . . . [T]he age of consent has long since ceased to reflect ordinary life, and in this respect Parliament has signally failed to discharge its responsibility for keeping the criminal law in touch with the needs of society. I am persuaded that the piecemeal introduction of the various elements of section 14, coupled with the persistent failure of Parliament to rationalise this branch of the law even to the extent of removing absurdities which the courts have identified, means that we ought not to strain after internal coherence even in a single offence. Injustice is too high a price to pay for consistency.

[**Lord Bingham of Cornhill**, **Lord Nicholls of Birkenhead**, and **Lord Hobhouse of Woodborough** gave speeches allowing the appeal.]

Appeal allowed.

In *R v K* and *B (A Child) v DPP*[10] the House of Lords strengthened the presumption in favour of *mens rea*, and all cases decided prior to these decisions have to be read in the

---

[10] [2000] 2 AC 428.

light of them.[11] As a result of these decisions the court will read *mens rea* into a statute unless either:

(1) there is clear wording in the statute indicating that the offence is to be one of strict liability;[12] or

(2) there is a 'compellingly clear' inference that the offence is to be one of strict liability.[13]

3 WHEN WILL A COURT NOT PRESUME *MENS REA*?

The factors which a court will take into account in deciding whether there is a 'compellingly clear' inference that the offence is to be one of strict liability include the following:

(1) If some sections of a statute refer explicitly to a *mens rea* requirement and others do not that may indicate that those sections which do not are meant to be strict liability.[14] However, this will not be a conclusive factor,[15] as is clear from the decision in *K* itself.

(2) The court will examine not only the statute in question, but also other statutes which cover analogous offences,[16] in an attempt to ascertain the will of Parliament.

(3) The court will consider the social context of the offence.[17] In some cases it has been suggested that the court will consider whether the offence is intended to be 'truly criminal'. If it is intended not to be 'truly criminal' and more in the nature of a regulatory offence then that may be a factor indicating that the offence is to be one of strict liability. In deciding whether an offence is 'truly criminal' the court will look at the following factors:

   (a) The severity of the punishment[18] and the level of stigma that attaches to a conviction for that offence.[19] The lower the maximum sentence the more likely it is that the offence is regulatory. However, in *Howells*[20] the fact that the offence[21] carried five years' imprisonment did not prevent the imposition of strict liability. Even more dramatically in *G*[22] the rape of a child under 13 was seen as a strict liability offence, even though it carries a life sentence.

   (b) Whether the offence is aimed at preventing a very serious danger. Where an activity involves a potentially grave social harm (e.g. a potentially polluting activity) it is more likely to be an offence of strict liability.[23] Where there is no public danger the offence is less likely to be one of strict liability.

---

[11] *Kumar* [2005] 1 Cr App R 34. Although see *R v Doring* [2002] EWCA Crim 1695, where the Court of Appeal declined to alter the interpretation of the strict liability offence in the Insolvency Act 1986, s. 216.

[12] For a recent case where it was felt that the statutory words made it clear that the offence was to be one of strict liability, see *R v G* [2008] UKHL 37.

[13] Although it should be noted that in *R v K* [2001] UKHL 41 Lord Steyn seemed to suggest that the presumption could be rebutted only by specific language. However, this is not consistent with his *obiter* refusal to apply the presumption of *mens rea* to s. 5 of the Sexual Offences Act 1956 in *B v DPP* ([2000] 1 All ER 833 at 843g–h) even though there was nothing in the wording of that section that would exclude it.

[14] *Cundy v Le Cocq* (1884) 13 QBD 207; *Pharmaceutical Society of Great Britain v Storkwain Ltd* [1986] 1 WLR 903; *R v Muhamad* [2002] EWCA Crim 1856; *R v Matudi* [2003] EWCA Crim 697.

[15] *Sherras v De Rutzen* [1895] 1 QB 918.   [16] *B v DPP* [2000] 2 WLR 452.

[17] *Gammon (Hong Kong) Ltd v Attorney-General of Hong Kong* [1985] AC 1.

[18] *B v DPP* [2000] 2 WLR 452.   [19] *Barnfather v Islington London BC* [2003] EWHC 418 (Admin).

[20] [1977] QB 614.   [21] Firearms Act 1968, s. 1(1)(a).   [22] [2006] EWCA Crim 821.

[23] e.g. *McCrudden* [2005] EWCA Crim 466; *Alphacell Ltd v Woodward* [1972] AC 824.

(c) Whether rendering the offence one of strict liability will assist in discouraging the activity.[24] An argument that being strict liability will make it easier to prove and so easier to enforce will not of itself be sufficient to persuade a court to interpret the offence to be one of strict liability.[25] But if rendering the offence one of strict liability could be said to persuade potential defendants to change their behaviour this would be an argument in favour of strict liability.

(d) Whether the offence applies generally to members of the public or if it is addressed to a group of professionals or to those who engage in a particular kind of activity.[26] It is less likely to be one of strict liability if the offence is addressed to members of the public at large.

4 WHAT *MENS REA* WILL BE PRESUMED?

If there is no clear evidence that the statute is to be one of strict liability the court will presume *mens rea*. The presumed *mens rea* will be that the defendant will have a defence if the defendant believed (even if unreasonably) that an aspect of the *actus reus* did not exist. This can be made clearer by considering the facts of *B v DPP* where the defendant was charged with the offence of inciting a girl under the age of 14 to commit an act of gross indecency, into which the court decided to presume *mens rea*.[27] Contrast the following states of mind:

(1) D believes the victim is 16. Here he will be not guilty. This is so even if his belief as to her age was unreasonable.

(2) D has not thought about the age of the victim. D will be guilty. He has a defence only if he honestly believes that the victim is over 14.

(3) D knows the victim is under 14 but believes that she is Tina (his friend's sister) when it is in fact Becca (who looks like Tina). Here his mistaken belief does not relate to an aspect of the *actus reus*, and so he is guilty.

5 THE HUMAN RIGHTS ACT AND STRICT LIABILITY OFFENCES

The courts have so far not accepted an argument[28] that Article 6 of the European Convention on Human Rights (ECHR) prohibits the existence of strict liability offences.[29] The fact that a defendant can be convicted without proof of his or her *mens rea* does not infringe the right to a fair trial. Article 6 requires that the trial procedures will be fair, but cannot be used to challenge the substance of the law.[30] However, in *R v G*[31] the Court of Appeal suggested that

---

[24] *R v Matudi* [2003] EWCA Crim 697. See also *Lim Chin Aik v R* [1963] AC 160.

[25] *Barnfather v Islington London BC* [2003] EWHC 418 (Admin).

[26] *Sweet v Parsley* [1970] AC 132.

[27] It is important to realize that the age of the girl was here an aspect of the *actus reus*.

[28] Arden (1999).

[29] *Muhamad* [2002] EWCA Crim 1856; *Barnfather v Islington London BC* [2003] EWHC 418 (Admin); *R v G* [2006] EWCA Crim 821; *Williams (Orette)* [2012] EWCA Crim 2162.

[30] See Sullivan (2005) and Salako (2006) for a detailed argument on the potential impact of the Human Rights Act on strict liability offences.

[31] [2006] EWCA Crim 821.

where the defendant was not blameworthy, although technically guilty of a strict liability offence, a prosecution for that offence might interfere with the defendant's rights under Article 8 of the Convention. That case was taken to the House of Lords:

R v G
[2008] 1 WLR 1379

The defendant, aged 15, had sex with a girl under the age of 13. He was convicted of the offence of rape of a child under the age of 13, contrary to section 5 of the Sexual Offences Act 2003. The case proceeded on the basis that the victim had told the defendant that she was 15 and that she had consented to the act. The defendant pleaded guilty and was sentenced to a twelve month detention and training order. He appealed on the basis that because the offence was one of strict liability his ECHR Article 6 rights to a fair trial had been interfered with. Further it violated his right to respect for his private life under Article 8 of the ECHR because he was not charged with the lesser offence under section 13 of the Sexual Offences Act 2003. The Court of Appeal dismissed his appeal and he appealed to the House of Lords.

Lord Hoffmann

3. The mental element of the offence under section 5, as the language and structure of the section makes clear, is that penetration must be intentional but there is no requirement that the accused must have known that the other person was under 13. The policy of the legislation is to protect children. If you have sex with someone who is on any view a child or young person, you take your chance on exactly how old they are. To that extent the offence is one of strict liability and it is no defence that the accused believed the other person to be 13 or over.

4. Article 6(1) provides that in the determination of his civil rights or any criminal charge, everyone is entitled to a "fair and public hearing" and article 6(2) provides that everyone charged with a criminal offence "shall be presumed innocent until proved guilty according to law". It is settled law that Article 6(1) guarantees fair procedure and the observance of the principle of the separation of powers but not that either the civil or criminal law will have any particular substantive content: see *Matthews v Ministry of Defence* [2003] UKHL 4; [2003] 1 AC 1163. Likewise, article 6(2) requires him to be presumed innocent of the offence but does not say anything about what the mental or other elements of the offence should be. In the case of civil law, this was established (after a moment of aberration) by *Z v United Kingdom* (2001) 34 EHRR 97. There is no reason why the reasoning should not apply equally to the substantive content of the criminal law. In *R v Gemmell* [2002] EWCA Crim 1992; [2003] 1 Cr App R 343, 356, para 33 Dyson LJ said:

> "The position is quite clear. So far as Article 6 is concerned, the fairness of the provisions of the substantive law of the Contracting States is not a matter for investigation. The content and interpretation of domestic substantive law is not engaged by Article 6."

5. The only authority which is said to cast any doubt upon this proposition is the decision of the Strasbourg court in *Salabiaku v France* (1988) 13 EHRR 379 and in particular a statement in paragraph 28 (at p.388) that "presumptions of fact or of law" in criminal proceedings should be confined "within reasonable limits". No one has yet discovered what this paragraph means but your Lordships were referred to a wealth of academic learning which tries to solve the riddle.

6. My Lords, I think that judges and academic writers have picked over the carcass of this unfortunate case so many times in attempts to find some intelligible meat on its bones that the time has come to call a halt. The Strasbourg court, uninhibited by a doctrine of precedent or the need to find a ratio decidendi, seems to have ignored it. It is not mentioned in *Z v United Kingdom* (2001) 34 EHRR 97. I would recommend your Lordships to do likewise. For my part, I would simply endorse the remarks of Dyson LJ in *R v Gemmell* [2003] 1 Cr App R 343, 356.

7. The other ground of appeal is that the conviction violated the appellant's right of privacy under article 8. This is, on the face of it, an astonishing proposition. Is it really being suggested that a young person under 18 has a human right to have undisturbed sexual intercourse with a child under 13? If anything is likely to bring human rights into disrepute, it is such a claim.

8. When one examines the argument of Mr Owen QC for the appellant, however, he is not saying any such thing. He does not claim that sexual intercourse with children under 13, even in the privacy of the appellant's home, ought not to be prohibited. But he says that, as he was only 15 at the time of the offence, the Crown acted unduly harshly by prosecuting him under section 5 rather than under section 13, which deals with sexual offences committed by persons under 18 and carries a maximum penalty of imprisonment for 5 years.

9. Assuming this to be right, the case has in my opinion nothing to do with article 8 or human rights. Article 8 confers a qualified right that the state shall not interfere with what you do in your private or family life. Any interference with your conduct by the state must be necessary and proportionate for one of the purposes mentioned in article 8.2. But you either have such a right or you do not. If the state is justified in treating your conduct as unlawful, for example, because you are beating your wife or sexually abusing children, article 8 does not generate an additional right that the state shall not be too hard on you for whatever you have done because it happens to have been done at home.

10. Prosecutorial policy and sentencing do not fall under article 8. If the offence in question is a justifiable interference with private life, that is an end of the matter. If the prosecution has been unduly heavy handed, that may be unfair and unjust, but not an infringement of human rights. It is a matter for the ordinary system of criminal justice. It would be remarkable if article 8 gave Strasbourg jurisdiction over sentencing for all offences which happen to have been committed at home. This case is another example of the regrettable tendency to try to convert the whole system of justice into questions of human rights.

12. . . . That leaves only the question of whether in the particular circumstances of this case, it was an abuse of process for the Crown to prosecute under section 5. That is not a question which has been certified. For what it is worth, I agree with the Court of Appeal that the Crown was not obliged to withdraw the charge under section 5 when they found themselves having to accept the appellant's version of events. "Rape of a child under 13" still accurately described what the appellant had done. Parliament decided to use this description because children under 13 cannot validly or even meaningfully consent to sexual intercourse. So far as the basis of plea provided mitigation, they were entitled to leave the judge to take it into account. I would dismiss the appeal.

Lord Hope

34. Article 8(1) guarantees to everyone the right to respect for his private life, and a teenager has as much to [right] respect for his private life as any other individual. It is unlawful for a prosecutor to act in a way which is inconsistent with a Convention right. So I cannot accept Lord Hoffmann's proposition that the Convention rights have nothing to do with prosecutorial policy. How an offence is described and the range of sentences that apply to it are

matters for the contracting state. But where choices are left to the prosecutor they must be exercised compatibly with the Convention rights. The questions then are whether the appellant's continued prosecution for rape under section 5 was necessary in a democratic society for the protection of any of the interests referred to in article 8(2), and whether it was proportionate. Account must be taken in this assessment of the alternative courses that were open to the prosecutor, including proceeding under section 13 instead of section 5, as well as the sentencing options that are available to the court in the event of a conviction under either alternative and the labels which each of them would attract.

. . .

36. I would not go so far as to say that it was disproportionate for a child under 15 to be prosecuted for committing a sexual act with a child under 13 just because it was consensual. The offences which the 2003 Act has created are expressed in very broad terms. They recognise that the circumstances in which mutual sexual activity may take place between children of the same or the opposite sex, and the acts that they may perform on one another as fashions change, will inevitably vary greatly for case to case. But there is great force in the point that McLachlin J made in *R v Hess; R v Nguyen* [1990] 2 SCR 906 about the need for children to be protected. Their need to be protected against themselves is as obvious as is their need to be protected from each other. There is much to be said for the view that where acts are perpetrated on children under 13 by children of a similar age intervention of some kind is necessary for the protection of their physical and moral health. My noble and learned friend Baroness Hale of Richmond offers a unique insight into these issues, and I agree with all she says about the dangers of under age sexual activity. The fact that there was consent is to this extent simply irrelevant.

[**Baroness Hale**, **Lords Carswell**, and **Mance** gave speeches agreeing that the appeals should be dismissed and agreeing with **Lord Hope** on the Article 8 point.]

Following this decision a court will not find a strict liability offence will infringe Article 6 of the ECHR.

6 COMMON LAW DEFENCES AND STRICT LIABILITY OFFENCES

As is clear from the definition of a strict liability offence there can be no defence of no *mens rea* because *mens rea* is not required. But what about other common law defences such as self-defence, duress of circumstances, or insanity? The Court of Appeal in *Backshall*[32] has confirmed that duress is available as a defence to a strict liability offence. Presumably, therefore, so would be self-defence, necessity, or automatism.[33] There seems, however, to be some doubt over insanity. In *DPP v H*[34] McCowan LJ stated:

The [insanity] defence is based on the absence of *mens rea*, but none is required for the offence of driving with an excess of alcohol. Hence the defence of insanity has no relevance to such a charge as it is an offence of strict liability.

---

[32] [1999] Crim LR 662 (CA).   [33] *Hennessey* [1989] 2 All ER 9 (CA); *Isitt* [1978] RTR 211 (CA).
[34] The Times, 2 May 1997; discussed in Ward (1997).

This reasoning has been strongly criticized.[35] Insanity is not an absence of *mens rea*. It is quite possible for a defendant to be insane and yet intend to kill, for example.

7 POSSESSION OFFENCES

Several statutory offences involve possession of, for example, offensive weapons,[36] drugs,[37] and articles for use in burglary, theft, or deception.[38] Strictly speaking these are not strict liability offences, but their *mens rea* requirement can be minimal and so are analogous to them. Possession offences, from a theoretical point of view, are problematic. There are two particular difficulties:

(1) Does possession involve an act? The difficulty may be that at the time when the person is arrested in possession of the prohibited thing, she may not be doing anything. This may infringe the so-called 'voluntary act principle' discussed in Chapter 3. It could be argued that possession involves an initial act of taking into possession, followed by failure to divest of possession. An analogy could be drawn with the decision in *Fagan*[39] (excerpted at Chapter 3, The defendant committed the *actus reus* at one point in time (without the necessary *mens rea*), but at a later point in time he has the *mens rea*, p.167), where the defendant (accidentally) parked his car on the victim's foot and then refused to move it off. That explanation might be supported by the fact that momentarily holding an item will not amount to possession.[40]

(2) Does the word 'possess' include any *mens rea* element? In *Warner v Metropolitan Police Commissioner*[41] the defendant picked up two boxes which he thought contained perfume. In fact they contained drugs and the defendant was charged with possession of drugs. The House of Lords held that if a person possesses a container he possesses the items in the container.[42] There are two exceptions to this:[43]

(a) If the item has been placed in the defendant's bag or pocket without his or her knowledge and without an opportunity to discover that the item has been placed there then it is not possessed by the defendant.

(b) If the accused believed that the container had something in it which was completely different from what was actually there then the defendant does not possess the item. However, the width of this exception is not as wide as may appear because in *Warner* it was held that perfume was not wholly different from drugs and in *McNamara*[44] it was suggested that pornography was not radically different from cannabis resin, both of which are rather surprising findings.

---

[35] Simester, Spencer, Sullivan, and Virgo (2013: 186–7).   [36] Prevention of Crime Act 1953.
[37] Misuse of Drugs Act 1971.   [38] Theft Act 1968, s. 25.
[39] [1969] 1 QB 439.   [40] *T* [2011] EWCA Crim 1646.   [41] [1969] 2 AC 256.
[42] The leading case where drugs are found on or in something which is not a container is *Marriot* [1971] 1 All ER 595, where the defendant possessed a penknife. Unknown to him, the penknife had cannabis attaching to the blade. It was held that unless he was aware that there were substances attaching to the penknife he could not be convicted of possession of the cannabis.
[43] The defendant bears the evidential burden in respect of these exceptions (*McNamara* (1988) 87 Cr App R 270 (CA)).
[44] (1988) 87 Cr App R 246.

The approach taken by the courts towards possession has been found to be consistent with the ECHR in *Deyemi*.[45] The House of Lords has confirmed the definition of possession in *Warner* in the following decision:

R v Lambert
[2001] UKHL 37[46]

The appellant was charged with possession of a class A drug with intent to supply contrary to section 5(3) of the Misuse of Drugs Act 1971. He had picked up a duffel bag containing 2 kilograms of cocaine at a railway station. His defence, based on section 28 of the Misuse of Drugs Act 1971, was that although he had been in possession of the bag he did not know or suspect, or have reason to suspect, the nature of the contents of the bag. He was convicted and appealed on the basis that he should not have been required to establish his defence on a balance of probabilities. (The case involved a discussion of the impact of the Human Rights Act on the burden of proof, which was discussed in Chapter 1.)

Lord Slynn of Hadley

16. The first question asks whether it is an essential element of the offence of possession of a controlled drug under section 5 of the Misuse of Drugs Act 1971 that the accused knows that he has a controlled drug in his possession. Bearing fully in mind the importance of the principle that the onus is on the prosecution to prove the elements of an offence and that the provisions of an Act which transfer or limit that burden of proof should be carefully scrutinised, it seems to me that the Court of Appeal in *R v McNamara* (1988) 87 Cr App R 246 rightly identified the elements of the offence which the prosecution must prove. I refer in particular to the judgment of Lord Lane CJ, at p 252. This means in a case like the present that the prosecution must prove that the accused had a bag with something in it in his custody or control; and that the something in the bag was a controlled drug. It is not necessary for the prosecution to prove that the accused knew that the thing was a controlled drug let alone a particular controlled drug. The defendant may then seek to establish one of the defences provided in section 5(4) or section 28 of the 1971 Act.

Lord Hope

61. . . . I consider the settled law to be correct on this point. As far as the 1971 Act is concerned, there are two elements to possession. There is the physical element, and there is the mental element. The physical element involves proof that the thing is in the custody of the defendant or subject to his control. The mental element involves proof of knowledge that the thing exists and that it is in his possession. Proof of knowledge that the thing is an article of a particular kind, quality or description is not required. It is not necessary for the prosecution to prove that the defendant knew that the thing was a controlled drug which the law makes it an offence to possess. I observe that Mr Owen did not submit that it was necessary for the prosecution to prove that the defendant was aware that the thing was a class A, B or C drug, as the case may be, although the class into which the drug falls will usually be relevant to any sentence he may receive.

Appeal dismissed.

---

[45] [2007] EWCA Crim 2060.   [46] [2001] 3 WLR 206.

8 CONSTRUCTIVE LIABILITY

Constructive liability arises where the defendant has committed a crime, with the *mens rea* for that, but the defendant is then held liable for a much more serious wrong. A good example is manslaughter, which is discussed in Chapter 5. This is not strict liability because some *mens rea* is required. However, it is linked to the law on strict liability as the defendant need have no *mens rea* in relation to the harm he or she is held to account for. The following case is a good example of the issue:

R v Hughes
[2013] 1 WLR 2461

The defendant was convicted of the offence under section 3ZB of the Road Traffic Act 1988 of causing death by driving while being an unlicensed, disqualified, or uninsured driver. Hughes was driving while uninsured. He was involved in a collision with Mr Dickinson. Dickinson had taken heroin and had been driving erratically and narrowly missed various vehicles and was driving on the wrong side of the road when he crashed into the defendant. It was accepted that the defendant was driving in a faultless way and that the victim was responsible for the accident. Nevertheless, he was charged and convicted under section 3ZB based on authorities that to be guilty of that offence it was not necessary that there should be anything wrong with the driving. All that needed to be shown was that he was driving without insurance and while driving he had an accident which caused death. The issue for the Supreme Court was whether that approach was correct.

Lord Hughes and Lord Toulson [delivered the judgment of the court]

9. The difficulty, however, exposed by the present case and others like it is that instead of Mr Hughes being punished for what he did wrong, namely for failing to pay his share of the cost of compensation for injuries to innocent persons, he is indicted and liable to be punished for an offence of homicide, when the deceased, Mr Dickinson, was not an innocent victim and could never have recovered any compensation if he had survived injured. A further difficulty is that since using a car uninsured is an offence of strict liability, it is an offence which may well be committed not only by the likes of Mr Hughes, who deliberately fail to take out insurance, but also by those who overlook a renewal notice, or who find themselves uninsured because of an office mistake by brokers, or because they have driven someone else's car when both they and the owner believed there was valid insurance but in fact there was not, for example because a condition in the policy had been overlooked. If the ruling in the present case is correct, all such persons will be guilty of a very serious offence of causing death by driving if a fatal collision ensues, even if they could have done nothing to avoid it. Has Parliament used language which unambiguously has such far reaching effects?

. . .

17. It may readily be accepted that the intention [of Parliament] was to create an aggravated form of the offence of having no insurance [etc.], but that only begs the question whether the intention was to attach criminal responsibility for a death to those whose driving had nothing to do with that death beyond being available on the road to be struck. It is certainly true that an uninsured person ought not to be driving at all, although there is no general prohibition

on his driving and if he paid for insurance he could drive perfectly lawfully, but this too begs the question whether the intention was to make him criminally responsible as a killer for an offence of homicide in the absence of any act or omission on his part which contributed to the death other than his presence as a motorist capable of being hit. To say that he is responsible because he ought not to have been on the road is to confuse criminal responsibility for the serious offence of being uninsured with criminal responsibility for the infinitely more serious offence of killing another person. The criminal law is well used to offences of which there are aggravated forms carrying additional punishment where greater harm has been done. The escalating offences of common assault, assault occasioning actual bodily harm, and causing grievous bodily harm are but simple examples; there are many more. But ordinarily, the greater punishment is linked to additional harm which is caused by a culpable act on the part of the defendant. In the case of section 3ZB, it is not. On the contrary, the present offence, if construed in the manner for which the Crown contends, represents a rare example of double strict liability, where both the underlying or qualifying condition is an offence (in the cases of unlicensed or uninsured driving) which can be committed unwittingly as well as deliberately, and also the aggravating element can be constituted by an event for which the defendant is not culpable.

. . .

26. This is a statute creating a penal provision, and one of very considerable severity. The offence created is a form of homicide. To label a person a criminal killer of another is of the greatest gravity. The defendant is at risk of imprisonment for a substantial term. Even if, at least in a case of inadvertent lack of insurance or venial lack of licence, a sentence of imprisonment were not to follow, the defendant would be left with a lifelong conviction for homicide which would require disclosure in the multiple situations in which one's history must be volunteered, such as the obtaining of employment, or of insurance of any kind. Nor should the personal burden or the public obloquy be underestimated; to carry the stigma of criminal conviction for killing someone else, perhaps a close relative, perhaps as in the kind of situation referred to in para 19 an innocent child, is no small thing. A penal statute falls to be construed with a degree of strictness in favour of the accused. It is undoubtedly open to Parliament to legislate to create a harsh offence or penalty, just as it is open to it to take away fundamental rights, but it is not to be assumed to have done so unless that interpretation of its statute is compelled, and compelled by the language of the statute itself. The rule of construction which applies to penal legislation, and a fortiori to legislation which carries the penalty of imprisonment, is not identical to, but is somewhat analogous to, the principle of statutory interpretation known as the principle of legality.

27. Lord Hoffmann described that principle in this way in *R v Secretary of State for the Home Department Ex p Simms and O'Brien* [2000] 2 AC 115, 131E:

"Parliamentary sovereignty means that Parliament can, if it chooses, legislate contrary to fundamental principles of human rights. . . . But the principle of legality means that Parliament must squarely confront what it is doing and accept the political cost. Fundamental rights cannot be overridden by general or ambiguous words. This is because there is too great a risk that the full implications of their unqualified meaning may have passed unnoticed in the democratic process. In the absence of express language or necessary implication to the contrary, the courts therefore presume that even the most general words were intended to be subject to the basic rights of the individual."

This is not a case of fundamental human rights. However, the gravity of a conviction for homicide, for which the sentence may be a term of imprisonment, is such that if

Parliament wishes to displace the normal approach to causation recognised by the common law, and substitute a different rule, it must do so unambiguously. Where, as here, Parliament has plainly chosen not to adopt unequivocal language which was readily available, it follows that an intention to create the meaning contended for by the Crown cannot be attributed to it.

28. It follows that in order to give effect to the expression "causes . . . death . . . by driving" a defendant charged with the offence under section 3ZB must be shown to have done something other than simply putting his vehicle on the road so that it is there to be struck. It must be proved that there was something which he did or omitted to do by way of driving it which contributed in a more than minimal way to the death. The question therefore remains what can or cannot amount to such act or omission in the manner of driving.

. . .

36. For the reasons set out, enquiry into apportionment of liability in civil terms is not appropriate to a criminal trial. But it must follow from the use of the expression "causes . . . death . . . by driving" that section 3ZB requires at least some act or omission in the control of the car, which involves some element of fault, whether amounting to careless/inconsiderate driving or not, and which contributes in some more than minimal way to the death. It is not necessary that such act or omission be the principal cause of the death. In which circumstances the offence under section 3ZB will then add to the other offences of causing death by driving must remain to be worked out as factual scenarios are presented to the courts. In the present case the agreed facts are that there was nothing which Mr Hughes did in the manner of his driving which contributed in any way to the death. It follows that the Recorder of Newcastle was correct to rule that he had not in law caused the death by his driving. The appeal should be allowed and that ruling restored.

PART II: THE THEORY OF STRICT LIABILITY OFFENCES

9 THE ARGUMENTS FOR AND AGAINST STRICT LIABILITY

We will shortly consider the arguments that can be made for and against a strict liability offence. But first it is important to appreciate the wide range of alternatives available to a legal system which wishes to restrict the need to prove *mens rea*. Here are some:

(1) To require that the defendant was negligent as to the *actus reus*.

(2) To provide a defence for a defendant who can prove that he was not negligent.

(3) To establish special defences based on a legal or evidential burden on the defendant.

(4) Only to require that the defendant caused the *actus reus*.

As these alternatives show, if it is decided that the prosecution should not be required to prove any *mens rea* on the defendant's part, strict liability is not the only option by any means.

9.1 ARGUMENTS FOR STRICT LIABILITY OFFENCES

The following are some of the main arguments in favour of strict liability offences:

Protection of the public

The main justification in favour of strict liability offences is that they protect the general public.[47] Most strict liability offences are found in those areas of life which pose a risk to others; for example, the sale of food, medical drugs, and alcohol; the prevention of pollution.[48] The argument is that where a person or company is about to engage in an activity which is potentially dangerous (e.g. an industrial activity that may cause pollution) we want the company not just to take 'reasonable steps' to prevent the harm, but to do everything it possibly can.[49] The imposition of strict liability, rather than negligence, may encourage the company to pull out every stop to prevent pollution. The difficulty with this argument is that it suggests that the law expects people to take unreasonable steps to prevent harm.

Ease of proof

Strict liability offences are easier for the prosecution to prove because there is no need to prove the defendant's state of mind. Imagine, for example, that a motorist could be convicted of speeding only if he or she knew that he or she was speeding. It would become almost impossible then to succeed in a prosecution for speeding and court cases would take far longer.

Risk-creating activities

It can be argued that if someone chooses to undertake a dangerous activity the law is justified in requiring him or her to ensure that he or she does not harm others. A person performing a dangerous activity should not escape criminal punishment by saying that he or she did not foresee that the act might harm someone. ←1 (p.212)

Difficulties in convicting corporations

Many strict liability offences involve commercial activities. This means that for many statutory offences the defendant is likely to be a company. As we shall see in Chapter 13 there are real difficulties in demonstrating that a company has *mens rea*. By making such offences strict liability it is far easier to convict companies. However, negligence liability could also be used to assist in the conviction of companies.

9.2 ARGUMENTS AGAINST STRICT LIABILITY OFFENCES

Many opponents of strict liability accept that there is some merit in the points just made, but argue that they do not demonstrate why the law must require strict liability rather than a negligence-based offence or at least one where there is a defence of 'due diligence'.[50]

---

[47] Levenson (1993). See Wootton (1963), who argues that strict liability should be the norm for all criminal offences.

[48] Bergelson (2011). [49] See *Alphacell Ltd v Woodward* [1972] AC 824 and Wootton (1981).

[50] See Horder (2005c) for a detailed argument in favour of a 'due diligence defence'.

They point out that there is no evidence that strict liability is more effective than negligence-based offences at preventing harmful activities.[51] Opponents argue further that it is unjust to convict defendants who have acted in an entirely reasonable way but unpredictably caused a harm. To convict such defendants weakens the stigma that attaches to a criminal conviction and endangers the distinction between criminal and civil law.[52] Such draconian criminal laws may also have the effect of discouraging people from engaging in socially beneficial commercial activities.

Supporters of strict liability suggest that such concerns are overreactions. Where a defendant is genuinely blameless he or she will not be prosecuted or, if he or she is, only a lower sentence will be imposed.[53] Indeed there is evidence that regulatory agencies charged with enforcing some strict liability offences exercise considerable discretion in deciding whether or not to prosecute.[54] Further, supporters of strict liability offences reply that many of the objections overlook the fact that these offences are not, as the courts have put it, 'truly criminal', to which Professor Smith[55] has replied 'this is a peculiar notion of truth. The truth is that it is a crime.' ←2 (p.212)

In the following extract, Andrew Simester considers the moral case against strict liability offences:

A. Simester, 'Is Strict Liability Always Wrong?' in A. Simester (ed.) *Appraising Strict Liability* (Oxford: OUP, 2005), 33–7

Intrinsic Objections to Strict Liability

It is, in short, arguable that there are instrumental benefits to be gained from the device of strict liability, although their scope and extent is uncertain. However, assuming they exist, those benefits must be weighed against the intrinsic moral objections to strict liability set out below. In the context of stigmatic crimes, it seems to me that these objections are decisive.

Objections Specific to Paradigm (Stigmatic) Crimes

Suppose that the state were to create a crime of 'homicide', defined as a strict liability offence of causing death. Objections to crimes of this type depend, in turn, on the nature of the criminal law. Without dwelling on the familiar analysis, there seem to me to be certain paradigm features associated with the criminalization of μing. *Ex ante*, μing is prohibited and declared to be wrong: citizens are not merely requested but instructed not to. *Ex post*, where D is found to have transgressed, he is convicted of μing and liable to punishment which may be substantial, perhaps including imprisonment. The conviction and the punishment also express censure, to D, Y, and the public at large. As well as suffering hard treatment, D is labelled as a particular sort of criminal (a 'μer'), a labelling that conveys a public implication of culpable wrongdoing.

---

[51] Jackson (1991); Richardson (1987); Baldwin (1990); Packer (1962: 109).
[52] P. Robinson (1996a).   [53] *Smedleys Ltd v Breed* [1974] AC 839.
[54] There are concerns that the agencies are underfunded and unable to enforce the strict liability offences effectively (Ashworth 2009: 162–3).
[55] J.C. Smith (2002: 125).

These paradigm features of the criminal law imply certain objections to making μing a strict liability crime, at least where strict liability leads to conviction of blameless defendants . . .

Wrongful Censure

The main objection to strict liability in stigmatic crimes law is that it involves the conviction and punishment of persons who are not at fault. Morally speaking, it is wrong to convict the innocent. If a person does not deserve to be convicted then he has a right not to be; and his conviction cannot be justified by such consequential considerations as deterrence.

Since both are censorious, this objection applies to both conviction and punishment. The imposition of punishment is, *qua* punishment, justified only when D deserves it, in virtue of culpably having done wrong. Indeed, the imposition of hard treatment cannot count as punishment unless it conveys this message. But in the context of strict liability, the state does not rely on the proposition that D is culpable as a precondition of imposing punishment. So the state cannot claim to be punishing D in accordance with D's desert; it is simply imposing hard treatment in virtue of the fact that μing (an *actus reus*) has occurred.

This criticism may be evaded, in part. Even if μing is a strict liability offence, the quantum of punishment imposed for transgressions might still be related to desert in a criminal legal system that required *sentences* to take account of D's level of culpability, with fault being a post-conviction matter for consideration during sentencing.

However, the same get-out is not available with regard to the conviction itself. Independently of the sanction imposed, the conviction also conveys censure. A conviction for μing has the effect of naming D a criminal (in respect of that particular offence), a branding which is communicated to society as well as to D. Assuming that, if imposed on a strict liability basis, the label 'criminal-μ' continues to retain its stigmatic quality, this amounts to systematic moral defamation by the state. Given the public understanding of that designation, when it labels him a criminal the state is no longer telling the public the truth about D. People have a right not to be censured falsely as criminals, a right that is violated when one is convicted and punished for a stigmatic crime without proof of culpable wrongdoing.

That falsehood is no ordinary lie. There is something especially troubling when wrongful censure is imposed by the state. In ordinary defamation cases, the attack is characteristically private; it may affect D, and even harm D's interests, but it lacks the authoritative voice of the state and normally does not undermine his membership of the community. An act of defamation may bring D into conflict with P, but it normally does not alienate D from society. By contrast, convictions are official. They condemn D on behalf of society as a whole. To say that D has a criminal record is to say that he has been labelled as a reprehensible wrongdoer; that the state has made a formal adverse statement about *him*. Moreover, the statement marks D out in such a way that it becomes appropriate, within the community, for the regard in which he is held to be affected. Certain exclusions, both social and professional, may legitimately follow. As such, the criminal record becomes part of the material that frames D's engagement with his community, with adverse implications for D's ability to live his life—a life that is, in part, defined in terms of D's interactions within, and membership of, his society. The conviction (and indeed the punishment, in its censorious facet) tends not only to censure D for the particular act that is proscribed, but also to undermine D's participation in the society itself.

Censure and Stigma

We can elaborate this concern by distinguishing between censure, which the state expresses through its action of convicting (and punishing) the defendant, and the *effect* of that action, in terms of the stigma that attaches to D and his conduct. Of course, as the foregoing discussion has suggested, one reason why the state ought not falsely to censure D for a serious crime is supplied by the consequences for D's life. But the two do not always go together, and D has a right to be neither falsely censured *nor* falsely stigmatized. Even if D suffers no stigma, the state should not purport to censure him without believing him to be culpable. Telling lies is wrong in itself and not merely because of the consequences.

Consider, on the other hand, an argument that the state is not *really* censuring D, since both the state and D know that fault has not been proved when D is convicted of a strict liability offence. The problem with this 'private colloquy' reasoning is that the state should not ignore the significance of its actions for others. When labelling D guilty of a stigmatic crime, the state is bound by the public meaning of the words it uses. Thus, for example, Parliament cannot legitimately enact an offence of 'paedophilia', defined as 'parking for more than one hour on a central London street'. It cannot do so because that is not what paedophilia means. Even if D understands that the label is a technical usage, the state may not disregard the rest of its audience, and the effect that such a label will have on D's life.

Treating a conviction for 'paedophilia' as highly stigmatic is, of course, a reasonable public response. A more difficult case would arise if the reaction of the public, in terms of stigmatizing D, is unreasonable and far exceeds what is deserved in light of the state's censure. Suppose that, in the public mind, parking offenders (labelled as such) came to be regarded like paedophiles. In that event, a strict liability parking conviction, although not intended as censorious, would be highly stigmatic. Even in this sort of case, at least where the stigma is predictable, it seems to me that the state should take account of the consequences of a conviction for defendants. The offence should no longer involve strict liability.

Rights and Instrumental Reason

Of course, some error in the criminal justice system is unavoidable. When the state convicts a person of a stigmatic offence, it generally requires that guilt be proved beyond reasonable doubt. Inevitably, this leaves open the possibility that a particular defendant, properly convicted on that standard of proof, is not in fact guilty. The defamation and wrongful punishment of such persons is none the less justified. Moreover, it is justified by consequential reasons: in particular, by the need to set an achievable standard of proof if society is to have a practicable criminal justice system at all. It might be thought that an analogy can be drawn between these instrumental considerations, which permit wrongful convictions whenever the criminal proof standard is met, and those set out [earlier in the essay], which support convictions on the basis of strict liability.

But the analogy strikes me as false. Where guilt is proved beyond reasonable doubt in stigmatic crimes, the state convicts in good faith—D is believed to be culpable. Further, although error is systemic it remains unsystematic: the distribution of error is unknown, and we cannot predict the likelihood that any particular conviction is a mistake. By contrast, where strict liability is employed in a stigmatic crime, the state consistently labels D as a culpable wrongdoer without believing this to be true. Moreover, defamation is predictable—there are reasons for thinking that the state is particularly likely to censure and punish D wrongly in that class of cases. Hence, while instrumental considerations of an institutional nature may sometimes be relied upon to justify the risk of good-faith erroneous convictions, arguments of this type seem inadequate to justify strict liability for stigmatic crimes.

QUESTIONS

1. In what circumstances, if any, is the imposition of strict liability justifiable?

2. Jeremy Horder (2002b) has suggested that criminal offences which regulate activities which have intrinsic value for participants (e.g. they are aspects of an individual's vision of the good life) should not normally be strict liability offences. But offences which regulate activities which have instrumental value (i.e. the activities are not valuable in themselves, but are only a means to another end (e.g. in Horder's view transport)) are more appropriate as being interpreted as strict liability. Do you think this is a helpful distinction?

For guidance on answering this question, please visit the Online Resource Centre that accompanies this book: www.oxfordtextbooks.co.uk/orc/herringcriminal7e/.

FURTHER READING

Bergelson, V. (2011) 'A Fair Punishment For Humbert Humbert: Strict Liability and Affirmative Defenses' *New Criminal Law Review* 14: 55.

Duff, R. A. (2009) 'Strict Responsibility, Moral and Criminal' *Journal of Value Inquiry* 43: 295.

Gardner, J. (2005) 'Wrongs and Faults' in A. Simester (ed.) *Appraising Strict Liability* (Oxford: OUP).

Green, S. (2005) 'Six Senses of Strict Liability: A Plea for Formalism' in A. Simester (ed.) *Appraising Strict Liability* (Oxford: OUP).

Horder, J. (2001) 'How Culpability Can, and Cannot, be Denied in Under-age Sex Crimes' *Criminal Law Review* 15.

Horder, J. (2002b) 'Strict Liability, Statutory Construction and the Spirit of Liberty' *Law Quarterly Review* 118: 459.

Horder, J. (2004) *Excusing Crime* (Oxford: OUP), ch. 6.

Horder, J. (2005c) 'Whose Values Should Determine When Liability is Strict?' in A. Simester (ed.) *Appraising Strict Liability* (Oxford: OUP).

Husak, D. (1995c) 'Varieties of Strict Liability' *Canadian Journal of Law and Jurisprudence* 8: 189.

Husak, D. (2005) 'Strict Liability, Justice, and Proportionality' in A. Simester (ed.) *Appraising Strict Liability* (Oxford: OUP).

Jackson, B. (1991) '*Storkwain*: A Case Study in Strict Liability and Self-regulation' *Criminal Law Review* 892.

Levenson, L. (1993) 'Good Faith Defenses: Reshaping Strict Liability Crimes' *Cornell Law Review* 78: 401.

Simester, A. (2005) 'Is Strict Liability Always Wrong?' in A. Simester (ed.) *Appraising Strict Liability* (Oxford: OUP).

Simons, K. (1997) 'Criminal Law: When is Strict Criminal Liability Just?' *Journal of Criminal Law and Criminology* 87: 1075.

Simons, K. (2012) 'Is Strict Criminal Liability in the Grading of Offences Consistent with Retributive Desert? Strict Liability in Grading' *Oxford Journal of Legal Studies* 32: 445.

Stanton-Ife, J. (2007) 'Strict Liability: Stigma and Regret' *Oxford Journal of Legal Studies* 27: 151.

Sullivan, G.R. (2005) 'Strict Liability for Criminal Offences in England and Wales Following Incorporation into English Law of the European Convention on Human Rights' in A. Simester (ed.) *Appraising Strict Liability* (Oxford: OUP).

10 CONCLUDING THOUGHTS

In this chapter we have been looking at strict liability offences. These may, at first, seem to be capable of producing injustice because they do not require proof of any *mens rea*. However, they have proved an effective tool, especially in the area of regulatory offences. Whether the benefits of these offences in terms of deterrence and ease of prosecution are sufficient to justify the occasional case of injustice is very much a matter of debate. What the existence of these offences shows is that there are times that protection of the public trumps a desire to ensure that defendants are proved to be blameworthy.

5

HOMICIDE

CENTRAL ISSUES

1. The offence of murder is committed where the defendant caused the death of the victim and intended to kill or cause serious bodily harm.

2. There is a defence of loss of control to a charge of murder. To succeed the defendant must show that, at the time of killing, she had lost her self-control as a result of a 'qualifying trigger' and that a person with a normal degree of tolerance and self-restraint would have responded in the same way. A qualifying trigger is a fear of serious violence or a justifiable sense of being seriously wronged. If the defence is successful the defendant is not guilty of murder, but guilty of manslaughter.

3. Diminished responsibility is only a defence to a charge of murder and if successful reduces the charge to manslaughter. To use it, a defendant needs to show that she had an abnormality of mental functioning which substantially impaired her ability to understand the nature of her conduct, form a rational judgment, or exercise self-control.

4. If a person kills another in the course of a suicide pact they will not be guilty of murder, but manslaughter.

5. A woman who kills a child under the age of one, while the 'balance of her mind was disturbed' following the birth, will commit the offence of infanticide and will not be guilty of murder or manslaughter.

6. Constructive manslaughter is committed where a defendant has carried out an unlawful and dangerous act which has caused the death of the victim.

7. Gross negligence manslaughter occurs where the defendant has killed the victim through a negligent act or omission which the jury believes to be sufficiently serious to justify a criminal conviction.

8. The Law Commission has recommended a restructuring of the law on murder and manslaughter. However, the government has only implemented some of these reforms.

PART I: THE LAW

1 GENERAL

Homicide in the criminal law can be divided into the following categories:

(1) murder;

(2) manslaughter;

(3) infanticide;

(4) a number of specific offences concerned with causing death while driving.

The first two categories are by far the most important and so they will be discussed in the greatest detail. The topic of corporate homicide will be discussed in Chapter 13. There are a number of specific offences connected with death, such as causing death by dangerous driving. These will not be discussed in this chapter.

2 MURDER

> **DEFINITION**
>
> *Actus reus*: the unlawful killing of another person in the Queen's peace.
>
> *Mens rea*: an intention to cause death or grievous bodily harm to the victim.
>
> A person convicted of murder must be given a sentence of life imprisonment.

2.1 *ACTUS REUS*

The *actus reus* of murder is the unlawful killing of another person in the Queen's peace.[1] These terms need a little more elucidation.

A person

The victim of homicide must be a person.[2] There are two controversial issues which need to be considered here:

(1) When does life begin? According to the law human life begins at birth.[3] Foetuses or unborn children cannot be the victims of murder or manslaughter because they are not yet people.[4] However, the *actus reus* of murder or manslaughter is made out if the child is injured while in the womb, is then born alive, but dies shortly afterwards from the injuries.[5]

---

[1] Coke 3 Inst 47.   [2] See Davis (2011) for a detailed discussion of this issue.

[3] In *Vo v France* (2005) 40 EHRR 259 it was not accepted that a foetus necessarily had a right to life under the European Convention on Human Rights (ECHR).

[4] Although the foetus is not regarded as a person, it can still be a criminal offence to kill a foetus; see e.g. the offence of procuring a miscarriage contrary to the Offences Against the Person Act 1861, s. 58.

[5] *Senior* (1832) 1 Mood CC 346.

The crucial moment at which the foetus becomes a human being is when the child is born alive and is completely outside the mother.[6] The child must be capable of breathing, although need not actually have begun to breathe.[7] Although foetuses are not people, this is not to say that unborn children are not protected by the criminal law until they are born.[8] They are protected by the offences of causing or procuring a miscarriage[9] or child destruction,[10] both of which carry the maximum sentence of life imprisonment.[11]

(2) When does life end? If the victim was already dead when he or she was shot by the defendant, the defendant cannot be guilty of murder.[12] The law accepts the medical definition of death.[13] The basic position is that a person dies once the brain ceases to function: in other words 'brain death'.[14]

Unlawfully

If the defendant is able to rely on the defence of self-defence he or she has not killed unlawfully.[15] Self-defence will be discussed further in Chapter 12.

Queen's peace

It must be shown that the killing took place in the Queen's peace.[16] What this means is that the killing of enemy aliens during war and under battle conditions is not a criminal homicide.[17] An English court can try a British citizen for murder or manslaughter committed in any country.[18]

Killed

It must be shown that the defendant caused the death of the victim. The law on causation is discussed in Chapter 2. In the context of murder it is necessary to show that the defendant accelerated the victim's death by more than a negligible amount.[19] This is interpreted fairly generously in cases of doctors providing pain-relieving drugs to terminally ill patients. A doctor who provides a dying patient with drugs to ease his

---

6 *Poulton* (1832) 5 C & P 329. There is no need for the umbilical cord to have been cut.

7 *Enoch* (1830) 5 C & P 539; *Brain* (1834) 6 C & P 349.

8 See Herring (2011a) for further discussion.

9 Offences Against the Person Act 1861, ss. 58, 59. For a detailed discussion of these offences, see *R (Smeaton) v Secretary of State for Health* [2002] Crim LR 664 (which held that prescription and supply of the 'morning after pill' did not constitute a criminal offence) and *R v Ahmed* [2010] EWCA 1949 (which held the offences did not apply to a case where a husband sought to arrange an abortion for his wife without her consent).

10 Infant Life (Preservation) Act 1929. This Act applies when the child is capable of being born alive. The Human Fertilisation and Embryology Act 1990, s. 37(1)(a), explains that if a pregnancy has lasted 24 weeks, it is presumed that the child is capable of being born alive.

11 There is no offence if the procedure is permitted by the Abortion Act 1967.

12 Although a charge of attempted murder may lie (see Chapter 14).

13 *Re A (A Minor)* [1992] 3 Med LR 303. See Chau and Herring (2007) for a detailed discussion of the definitions of death.

14 *Malcherek and Steel* [1981] 1 WLR 690 (CA).   15 *Beckford* [1988] AC 130 (PC).

16 Hirst (2008).   17 The example is given by Hale, 1 PC 433.

18 Offences Against the Person Act 1861, s. 9.

19 *Adams* [1957] Crim LR 365; *Cox* [1992] BMLR 38.

or her pain will not have committed the *actus reus* of murder if the drugs shorten the patient's life by a few minutes, although the doctor would if the time involved was days or weeks.[20] →1 (p.266)

It used to be the law that a defendant was liable for murder only if the victim died within a year and a day of the defendant's actions. The rule gave rise to difficulties, especially where victims were kept alive on life support machines, and was abolished in the Law Reform (Year and a Day Rule) Act 1996.

2.2 MENS REA

The *mens rea* of murder is an intention to kill or cause grievous bodily harm. This was established by *Cunningham*,[21] where the House of Lords upheld the conviction of a defendant who killed a victim by hitting him on the head with a chair. Even though there was no intent to kill, the defendant intended to cause grievous bodily harm, and that was sufficient for a murder conviction. Historically the *mens rea* for murder has been described as 'malice aforethought', although this is a misleading phrase because there is no need to show any kind of malice or ill-will. For example, a mercy killing (where a defendant kills the victim out of compassion) could still involve malice aforethought.[22] There are three issues about the *mens rea* for murder that need elaboration:

Intention

Intention is given the meaning that was discussed in detail in Chapter 3. You should reread that chapter to obtain a detailed discussion of the law, but it will be summarized again here. Intention is to be given its ordinary meaning or purpose. In most cases it will not be necessary for the judge to give any special direction to the jury on the meaning of intent. In difficult cases where the defendant may not have acted with the purpose of killing or causing grievous bodily harm, but that was an extremely likely result of the defendant's actions, then the jury should be given the *Woollin*[23] direction. That is that the jury may find intention only if the death or grievous bodily harm was a virtually certain result of the defendant's actions and the defendant realized this was so.

Kill or cause grievous bodily harm to the victim

Grievous bodily harm here means really serious harm.[24] A harm can be a grievous bodily harm even though it would not pose a risk to the life of the victim.[25] The fact that an intention to cause grievous bodily harm is sufficient *mens rea* for murder is controversial. Some commentators think that nothing less than an intention to kill should suffice. We shall discuss this further in Part II.

Although the *mens rea* for murder requires the defendant to intend to kill or cause grievous bodily harm *to the victim*, there is no difficulty in establishing a murder conviction if the defendant intends to kill one person, but in fact kills another. This is because the doctrine of transferred *mens rea* operates and the defendant can be guilty of murder.[26]

---

[20] *Adams* [1957] Crim LR 365.   [21] [1982] AC 566.   [22] *Inglis* [2010] EWCA Crim 2637.
[23] [1999] 1 AC 82 (HL).   [24] *DPP v Smith* [1961] AC 290 (HL).
[25] *Bollom* [2003] EWCA Crim 2846.
[26] The doctrine of transferred *mens rea* is discussed at Chapter 3, Section 9.

However, the doctrine of transferred *mens rea* cannot apply in murder if the defendant intended to kill an animal or damage a piece of property, but in fact killed the victim. In such a case there is no murder, although there may be manslaughter. →2 (p.284)

The *mens rea* of murder, as outlined previously, is a product of common law. The most important statutory provision is section 1 of the Homicide Act 1957, which states:

> Where a person kills in the course or furtherance of some other offence, the killing shall not amount to murder unless done with the same malice aforethought (express or implied) as is required for a killing to amount to murder when not done in the course or furtherance of another offence.
>
> For the purposes of the foregoing subsection, a killing done in the course or for the purpose of resisting an officer of justice, or of resisting or avoiding or preventing a lawful arrest, or of effecting or assisting an escape or rescue from legal custody, shall be treated as a killing in the course or furtherance of another offence.

As section 1 makes clear, it is no longer sufficient for a murder conviction to show that the defendant killed while committing some other crime. Only an intention to kill or cause grievous bodily harm will do.[27]

QUESTIONS

1. Ralph punches Kirsten, intending to give her a nose bleed. She falls over and bangs her head. Because she has a thin skull she dies. Has Ralph murdered Kirsten?

2. Ewan in a fit of spite forces his former girlfriend, Cameron, who is pregnant, to drink a vile substance. He hopes that the substance will cause the baby to be born seriously disabled. In fact the substance causes Cameron to miscarry. Cameron, overcome with grief, commits suicide. What offences have been committed? (Do not forget to consider here whether the doctrine of transferred *mens rea* could apply.)

For guidance on answering this question, please visit the Online Resource Centre that accompanies this book: www.oxfordtextbooks.co.uk/orc/herringcriminal7e/.

---

3 MANSLAUGHTER: AN INTRODUCTION

Manslaughter is a less serious form of homicide than murder. There are two main kinds of manslaughter:

(1) **Voluntary manslaughter** These are killings which would be murder but for the existence of defined extenuating circumstances. Here the law is acknowledging that in certain circumstances even though the defendant had the *mens rea* and *actus reus* of murder he or she does not deserve the label 'murderer'.

(2) **Involuntary manslaughter** These are killings where the defendant does not intend to kill or cause grievous bodily harm but there is sufficient fault to justify criminal liability. The difficulty the courts have found is in defining how little fault is sufficient to justify a manslaughter conviction.

---

[27] *R v Vickers* [1957] 2 QB 664 (CA).

These labels are in fact most misleading. For example, 'involuntary manslaughter' has nothing to do with the concept of involuntariness. Nevertheless the terminology is very widely used.

The following is a complete list of the kinds of manslaughter. The first three are examples of voluntary manslaughter and the last three of involuntary manslaughter:

(1) A defendant who successfully pleads loss of control to a charge of murder.

(2) A defendant who successfully pleads diminished responsibility to a charge of murder.

(3) A defendant who successfully pleads suicide pact to a charge of murder.

(4) A defendant convicted of reckless manslaughter.

(5) A defendant convicted of gross negligence manslaughter.

(6) A defendant convicted of constructive (or unlawful act) manslaughter.

EXAMINATION TIP

When answering a problem question on homicide, start by considering whether the defendant has caused the death of the victim. If they have, discuss whether the defendant has the *mens rea* of murder. If they have, then consider whether the defendant can rely on a general defence (see Chapter 12) or the defence of loss of control or diminished responsibility. If the defendant does not have the *mens rea* of murder examine whether the defendant is guilty of reckless, constructive, or gross negligence manslaughter.

---

4 LOSS OF CONTROL

DEFINITION

Loss of control is a defence only to murder, and if successful the defendant will still be guilty of manslaughter.

The defendant must show:

(1) he or she had lost self-control;

(2) the loss of self-control was caused by a 'qualifying trigger'; and

(3) a person of the defendant's age and sex with a normal degree of tolerance and self-restraint would have reacted in the same way.

EXAMINATION TIP

Mean examiners have been known to set problem questions which appear to raise issues about the defence of loss of control, but the victim is not killed. Remember, loss of control is a defence only in a case of murder. If you have a problem question where the defendant could not be guilty of murder you should *not* discuss loss of control.

Loss of control is a defence only to murder.[28] If the defence is successful then the defendant is still guilty of manslaughter.[29] For other offences, such as assaults, the fact that the defendant was provoked into attacking the victim may be relevant in deciding the appropriate sentence, but it does *not* provide a defence.[30] Even in a case of homicide it is crucial to appreciate that loss of control should be considered only if the jury is sure that the defendant is otherwise guilty of murder. If there is sufficient evidence to raise an issue[31] that the defendant could rely on the defence of loss of control, then the prosecution carries the burden of proving that the defence is not made out beyond all reasonable doubt.[32] A judge is entitled not to leave the defence of loss of control to the jury if there is no evidence that the defendant lost their self-control.[33]

The defence of loss of control is found in section 54 of the Coroners and Justice Act 2009. That legislation replaced the defence of provocation which had previously dealt with some of the cases now dealt with by the defence of loss of control.[34]

(1) Where a person ("D") kills or is a party to the killing of another ("V"), D is not to be convicted of murder if—

   (a) D's acts and omissions in doing or being a party to the killing resulted from D's loss of self-control,

   (b) the loss of self-control had a qualifying trigger, and

   (c) a person of D's sex and age, with a normal degree of tolerance and self-restraint and in the circumstances of D, might have reacted in the same or in a similar way to D.

(2) For the purposes of subsection (1)(a), it does not matter whether or not the loss of control was sudden.

(3) In subsection (1)(c) the reference to "the circumstances of D" is a reference to all of D's circumstances other than those whose only relevance to D's conduct is that they bear on D's general capacity for tolerance or self-restraint.

(4) Subsection (1) does not apply if, in doing or being a party to the killing, D acted in a considered desire for revenge.

(5) On a charge of murder, if sufficient evidence is adduced to raise an issue with respect to the defence under subsection (1), the jury must assume that the defence is satisfied unless the prosecution proves beyond reasonable doubt that it is not.

(6) For the purposes of subsection (5), sufficient evidence is adduced to raise an issue with respect to the defence if evidence is adduced on which, in the opinion of the trial judge, a jury, properly directed, could reasonably conclude that the defence might apply.

(7) A person who, but for this section, would be liable to be convicted of murder is liable instead to be convicted of manslaughter.

[28] Loss of control is not a defence to attempted murder. For criticism of this, see Bohlander (2011). It is a defence to those charged as accomplices to murder (Coroners and Justice Act 2009, s. 54(1)).

[29] Coroners and Justice Act 2009, s. 54(7). However, this gives the judge a wide discretion on sentencing, including handing down a non-custodial sentence.

[30] *R v Hussain and Hussain* [2010] EWCA Crim 94.

[31] Coroners and Justice Act 2009, s. 54(6) explains that 'sufficient evidence is adduced to raise an issue with respect to the defence if evidence is adduced on which, in the opinion of the trial judge, a jury, properly directed, could reasonably conclude that the defence might apply.'

[32] Coroners and Justice Act 2009, s. 54(5).   [33] *R v Barnsdale-Quean* [2014] EWCA Crim 1418.

[34] Coroners and Justice Act 2009, s. 56.

> (8) The fact that one party to a killing is by virtue of this section not liable to be convicted of murder does not affect the question whether the killing amounted to murder in the case of any other party to it.

As is indicated by section 54, there are three limbs to the defence:

(1) the defendant must show that his or her acts or omissions resulted from a loss of self-control;

(2) the loss of self-control must result from a 'qualifying trigger'; and that

(3) a person of the defendant's age and sex, with normal powers of tolerance and self-control, in the defendant's circumstances would have responded to the trigger in the same or a similar way.[35]

It is important to appreciate that all of these requirements must be satisfied. If an unusually calm defendant facing a qualifying trigger did not in fact lose self-control, even though a reasonable person would have done, the defence is not available.

The three limbs of the loss of control defence need to be discussed in more detail.

4.1 THE DEFENDANT LOST SELF-CONTROL

The need to show that the defendant lost self-control is a subjective question. The jury must look into the mind of the defendant and ask whether the defendant actually lost his self-control, rather than considering whether a reasonable person would have lost his self-control.[36]

In *Gurpiner*[37] Lord Thomas CJ declined to speculate on whether 'the loss of self-control had to be a total loss or whether some loss of self-control was sufficient'. The courts will need to answer that question at some point. In doing so it is important to recall that to be guilty of murder the defendant must have intended to kill or cause grievous bodily harm.[38] This means that loss of self-control cannot require that the defendant has completely lost control of her actions or was so angry that she was not aware of what she was doing, because if either of these were true, then the defendant would not have the *mens rea* or *actus reus* of murder.

The better interpretation of the loss of control requirement is that a defendant knows what they are doing, but has severely impaired powers to restrain themselves from acting. In *Jewell*[39] loss of control was said to involve 'loss of the ability to act in accordance with considered judgment or a loss of normal powers of reasoning'. Where, therefore, the evidence suggests a sustained and calculated attack it is unlikely the defendant will be able to rely on this defence.[40] Indeed section 54(4) explicitly says that if a defendant acts out of a desire for revenge the defence will not be available.[41]
→3 (p.297)

---

[35] *Dawes* [2013] EWCA Crim 322.

[36] See Fontaine (2009) for a discussion of how emotional disturbance can affect cognitive capacity as well as levels of self-control.

[37] [2015] EWCA Crim 178, para. 20.

[38] For an examination of the nature of loss of control, see Mitchell (2011).

[39] [2014] EWCA Crim 414.   [40] *Serrano* [2006] EWCA Crim 3182.

[41] For further discussion on the nature of self-control, see Holton and Shute (2007).

Under the law prior to the 2009 Act it had to be shown that the loss of self-control was 'sudden and temporary'. However, section 54(2) makes it clear that there is no need for the loss of self-control to be sudden. In *Dawes*[42] Lord Judge CJ explained:

> Provided there was a loss of control, it does not matter whether the loss was sudden or not. A reaction to circumstances of extreme gravity may be delayed. Different individuals in different situations do not react identically, nor respond immediately.
>
> The defendant may therefore be able to rely on loss of control even though the qualifying trigger occurred some time previously. So, if V says something gravely provocative to D, and D thinks about it, gradually getting more and more upset, and then some time later D loses self-control and kills V, then the defence could be used. However, do not forget section 54(4), which makes it clear that if D acted out of a desire for revenge he or she cannot rely on the defence of loss of self-control. The longer the time after the trigger the more likely it is that the jury will decide that the trigger did not cause the loss of control.

While traditionally the law on provocation/loss of control has been focused on cases where the defendant has been extremely angry there is, in fact, nothing in the requirements of loss of control that requires the defendant to be acting out of anger. Indeed one of the qualifying triggers, as we shall see, is that the defendant was facing serious violence and so a loss of control through fear is certainly possible. Presumably a loss of control through grief, despair, moral outrage, or depression is also possible. Notably when someone loses self-control through these emotions this may not exhibit itself in the same way as angry loss of control would.

It has been suggested[43] that under the new law the loss of control requirement will play a minor role. Once it is shown that the defendant was acting in response to a qualifying trigger the court might readily infer a loss of control. The primary role of loss of control is to ensure the defendant was not acting out of revenge. It remains to be seen whether the courts will take this looser approach to the requirement.

4.2 THE LOSS OF CONTROL WAS A RESULT OF A QUALIFYING TRIGGER

It is not enough for the defendant just to show she lost self-control. She must show she was provoked by a qualifying trigger into losing self-control. In *Acott*[44] the defendant killed his mother in a frenzied attack. There was clear evidence that he had lost his self-control and killed, but there was no evidence of why that had happened. It appears he had just suddenly 'flipped'. It was held that as there was no evidence of a provoking incident the judge was right not to leave the defence of provocation to the jury. Although decided under the old law of provocation, the case would be decided the same way under the new law on loss of control. Under the old law provocation was available if the defendant lost self-control as a result of something 'said or done'. The new law has greatly narrowed the law. To be a qualifying trigger the thing said or done must fall within one of the three categories in section 55. In brief these are:

(1) Fear of serious violence.

(2) An extremely provocative act.

(3) A combination of a fear of violence and an extremely provocative act.

---

[42] [2013] EWCA Crim 322.   [43] This argument is developed in Herring (2011b).
[44] [1997] 1 All ER 706 (HL).

The definition of a 'qualifying trigger'

Section 55 of the Coroners and Justice Act 2009 defines a 'qualifying trigger':

> (2) A loss of self-control had a qualifying trigger if subsection (3), (4) or (5) applies.
>
> (3) This subsection applies if D's loss of self-control was attributable to D's fear of serious violence from V against D or another identified person.
>
> (4) This subsection applies if D's loss of self-control was attributable to a thing or things done or said (or both) which—
>
>   (a) constituted circumstances of an extremely grave character, and
>
>   (b) caused D to have a justifiable sense of being seriously wronged.
>
> (5) This subsection applies if D's loss of self-control was attributable to a combination of the matters mentioned in subsections (3) and (4).
>
> (6) In determining whether a loss of self-control had a qualifying trigger—
>
>   (a) D's fear of serious violence is to be disregarded to the extent that it was caused by a thing which D incited to be done or said for the purpose of providing an excuse to use violence;
>
>   (b) a sense of being seriously wronged by a thing done or said is not justifiable if D incited the thing to be done or said for the purpose of providing an excuse to use violence;
>
>   (c) the fact that a thing done or said constituted sexual infidelity is to be disregarded.

Fear of serious violence as a qualifying trigger

There are several things to notice about this trigger. First, there only needs to be a fear of violence, it does not need to be shown that there was violence. The trigger would apply even where the defendant incorrectly believed that violence was to be used against him or her.

Second, the fear must be of *serious* violence. This suggests that fear of damage to property, or fear of minor acts of violence would not be enough.

Third, the threat of violence can be to D or another person. So if D kills V having lost self-control because V is threatening serious violence against his or her child, the defence will be available.

Fourth, it appears that the trigger only applies in cases where D kills the person who is posing the threat of serious violence. So, if D, in the face of violence from V, kills X, it appears the defence of loss of control will not be available.[45]

Fifth, according to section 55(6)(a) D cannot rely on this trigger if what caused the fear of violence was 'a thing which D incited to be done or said for the purpose of providing an excuse to use violence'. This restriction is designed to prevent a defendant who deliberately tries to get V to attack him or her so that he or she can use violence against V. So if D were to say to V, 'Go on, punch me in the face', hoping that V would do so, so he or she could use serious violence against V, he or she could not rely on loss of control. Notice, however, that the restriction only applies if D incited the attack for the purpose of providing an excuse. So if D was insulting V for the fun of it and as a result V attacked him or her, the loss of control defence would still be available.[46]

---

[45] If D is facing violence from V and tries to kill V, but misses, and kills X, it should be possible to 'transfer' the defence.

[46] *Clinton* [2012] EWCA Crim 2.

Sixth, remember that there must be a loss of self-control. So, if D saw that V was going to attack him, and calmly concluded that the only way to prevent the attack would be to kill V, the defence of loss of control would not be available because D would not have lost self-control. In such a case D may be able to rely on self-defence.

That last point leads to an important issue. In most cases where D, facing a fear of serious violence, kills V, he or she will be able to rely on the defence of self-defence. That is a complete defence to murder. So where the defendant has a choice he or she should use self-defence rather than loss of control.[47] With that in mind, when will a defendant want to use loss of self-control under the fear of violence trigger?

The answer is where the killing was not reasonable in the circumstances of the case. As we shall see when we discuss self-defence in Chapter 10, self-defence is only available where the degree of forced used is reasonable. So loss of control may be appropriate where there was a way of escaping from the violence which made it reasonable for D to escape rather than kill V, but that in the face of the violence D lost self-control and killed. In such a case self-defence may not be available (it was not reasonable to kill), but loss of control might be. There may also be cases where D could have prevented the threat by using a less force than killing. Again in such a case D may not be able to rely on self-defence, but might be able to rely on loss of control. The government has set out the two circumstances in which it believes that the trigger may be relevant:

(1) where a victim of sustained abuse kills his or her abuser in order to thwart an attack which is anticipated but not immediately imminent; and

(2) where someone overreacts to what they perceive as an imminent threat.[48]

When the legislation was prepared the government of the time accepted that the trigger will rarely be relied upon:

> The Law Commission's proposal for a new partial defence of killing in response to a fear of serious violence is intended to plug what they see as a loophole in circumstances when the defendant, fearing serious violence from an aggressor, overreacts by killing the aggressor in order to prevent the feared attack. We do not think that there is much of a loophole in practice, partly because the scope of the complete defence of self-defence is so wide and partly because of the way that the courts have over the years extended the application of the partial defence of provocation. Our analysis of cases from 2005 did not reveal anywhere a murder conviction appeared to have resulted inappropriately as a result of the absence of such a partial defence.[49]

Being seriously wronged as a qualifying trigger

The second form of qualifying trigger is where the defendant is facing circumstances of an extremely grave character and the defendant has a justifiable sense of being seriously wronged. →4 (p.300) Note the following important points about this trigger:

(1) The defendant must have been facing circumstances of an 'extremely grave character'. The statute does not really explain what these words mean. It is suggested that the best interpretation is that the circumstances facing the defendant must have been unusual, and not part of the normal trials and disappointments of life. So, being jostled in a

---

[47] S. Edwards (2010).   [48] Ministry of Justice (2009: para. 27).   [49] *Ibid*, para. 26.

supermarket, having someone queue jump in front of you, or being sworn at would not amount, in themselves, to grave circumstances. For that reason in *Dawes*[50] the Court of Appeal explained that the ending of a relationship would not itself normally amount to a qualifying trigger.

(2) The defendant must have a justifiable sense of being seriously wronged. Just because the defendant feels he was wronged does not mean that in fact he was. This involves an objective test.[51] So a man who kills a traffic warden who has just put a ticket on his car, could not rely on loss of control. However, badly he might think the traffic warden has behaved, the injury would not be regarded as a serious wrong. In a decision under the old law, *Doughty*,[52] it was assumed that the crying of a baby could constitute a provocative act. That decision would not be followed under the new provisions. However annoying the crying might be, it would not create a justifiable sense of being seriously wronged. The legislation seems designed to restrict this defence to a very narrow range of cases. Minor insults and upsets will be insufficient. The government gave the example of a victim of rape who killed her attacker as being the kind of case where the defence might be available.[53] That again suggests that only rarely will the trigger be available. One issue which the courts will need to address is a case where the victim did something that would not be a serious wrong to most people, but was to the defendant. For example, throwing a piece of bacon at someone might not be a grave wrong to most people, but it might be to a Muslim.

(3) The act must be a serious wrong *to the defendant*. If, therefore, the defendant came across someone uttering terrible insults to her friend, she could probably not argue that they were a grave wrong *to her*. This is not straightforward, however. Has someone who has sexually abused a child, committed a grave wrong to the child's parents? Can racial insults uttered to one person be seen as insults to all people of that race, allowing a passer-by who hears them and loses self-control and kill to rely on the defence?

(4) The trigger can only be used where there is something said or done. So circumstances alone could not amount to a qualifying trigger. The fact that a defendant's shares have collapsed in value or that there is a terrible traffic jam would not amount to something 'done or said'.

(5) In *Clinton*[54] it was held that the defendant must feel gravely wronged to rely on the trigger. This suggests that if the defendant was seriously insulted, but was not upset by what was said, they cannot rely on it as a trigger. This makes sense because if they were not upset by the remarks it is hard to see how they could cause them to lose self-control.

(6) Section 55(6)(b) makes it clear that D cannot rely on something said or done if he or she incited it for the purpose of providing an excuse. So if D asked V to say the most insulting thing that V could think of in order to provide him or her with an excuse for killing V, he or she could not rely on this as a qualifying trigger for the purposes of the defence.

(7) Section 55(6)(c) specifically provides that sexual infidelity is not a thing said or done that can amount to a qualifying trigger. This provision was introduced because it was

---

[50] [2013] EWCA Crim 322.   [51] *Dawes* [2013] EWCA Crim 322.   [52] (1986) 83 Cr App R 319.
[53] Ministry of Justice (2009: para. 34).   [54] [2012] EWCA Crim 2, para. 12.

felt that juries were being too sympathetic to men who killed their partners when discovering their partners were being unfaithful. Of course, there could be a case where D killed V after she was unfaithful to him, but he could point to some other trigger which justified him having the defence. The government at the time explained:

> It is quite unacceptable for a defendant who has killed an unfaithful partner to seek to blame the victim for what occurred. We want to make it absolutely clear that sexual infidelity on the part of the victim can never justify reducing a murder charge to manslaughter. This should be the case even if sexual infidelity is present in combination with a range of other trivial and commonplace factors.[55]

The provision has proved problematic and has been considered by the Court of Appeal in the following decision:[56]

R v Clinton
[2012] EWCA Crim 2

Jon-Jacques Clinton's wife, Dawn, admitted to him that she had been having an affair and described in detail various sexual encounters she had had. He told his wife he was going to commit suicide and she replied that he had not got the 'balls' to do it. He killed his wife after beating her around the head with a baton and strangling her. The trial judge did not allow him to rely on the evidence relating to sexual infidelity. He appealed against his conviction.

Lord Bingham of Cornhill CJ

35. We have examined the legislative structure as a whole. The legislation was designed to prohibit the misuse of sexual infidelity as a potential trigger for loss of control in circumstances in which it was thought to have been misused in the former defence of provocation. Where there is no other potential trigger, the prohibition must, notwithstanding the difficulties identified earlier in the judgment, be applied.

36. The starting point is that it has been recognised for centuries that sexual infidelity may produce a loss of control in men, and, more recently in women as well as men who are confronted with sexual infidelity. The exclusion created by section 55(6) cannot and does not eradicate the fact that on occasions sexual infidelity and loss of control are linked, often with the one followed immediately by the other. Indeed on one view if it did not recognise the existence of this link, the policy decision expressly to exclude sexual infidelity as a qualifying trigger would be unnecessary.

37. In section 54(1)(c) and (3) the legislation further acknowledges the impact of sexual infidelity as a potential ingredient of the third component of the defence, when all the defendant's circumstances fall for consideration, and when, although express provision is made for the exclusion of some features of the defendant's situation, the fact that he/she has been sexually betrayed is not. In short, sexual infidelity is not subject to a blanket exclusion when the loss of control defence is under consideration. Evidence of these matters may be

---

[55] Ministry of Justice (2009: para. 32).
[56] See Clough (2012) and Baker and Zhao (2012) for helpful discussions.

deployed by the defendant and therefore the legislation proceeds on the basis that sexual infidelity is a permissible feature of the loss of control defence.

38. The ambit of section 55(3) and (4)—the second component, the qualifying triggers—is clearly defined. Any qualifying trigger is subject to clear statutory criteria. Dealing with it broadly, to qualify as a trigger for the defendant's loss of control, the circumstances must be extremely grave and the defendant must be subject to a justifiable sense of having been seriously wronged. These are fact specific questions requiring careful assessment, not least to ensure that the loss of control defence does not have the effect of minimising the seriousness of the infliction of fatal injury. Objective evaluation is required and a judgment must be made about the gravity of the circumstances and the extent to which the defendant was seriously wronged, and whether he had a justifiable sense that he had been seriously wronged.

39. Our approach has, as the judgment shows, been influenced by the simple reality that in relation to the day to day working of the criminal justice system events cannot be isolated from their context. We have provided a number of examples in the judgment. Perhaps expressed most simply, the man who admits, "I killed him accidentally", is never to be treated as if he had said "I killed him". That would be absurd. It may not be unduly burdensome to compartmentalise sexual infidelity where it is the only element relied on in support of a qualifying trigger, and, having compartmentalised it in this way, to disregard it. Whether this is so or not, the legislation imposes that exclusionary obligation on the court. However, to seek to compartmentalise sexual infidelity and exclude it when it is integral to the facts as a whole is not only much more difficult, but is unrealistic and carries with it the potential for injustice. In the examples we have given earlier in this judgment, we do not see how any sensible evaluation of the gravity of the circumstances or their impact on the defendant could be made if the jury, having, in accordance with the legislation, heard the evidence, were then to be directed to excise from their evaluation of the qualifying trigger the matters said to constitute sexual infidelity, and to put them into distinct compartments to be disregarded. In our judgment, where sexual infidelity is integral to and forms an essential part of the context in which to make a just evaluation whether a qualifying trigger properly falls within the ambit of subsections 55(3) and (4), the prohibition in section 55(6)(c) does not operate to exclude it.

40. We have proceeded on the assumption that legislation is not enacted with the intent or purpose that the criminal justice system should operate so as to create injustice. We are fortified in this view by the fact that, although the material did not assist in the construction of section 55(6)(c), our conclusion is consistent not only with the views expressed in Parliament by those who were opposed in principle to the enactment of section 55(6)(c) but also with the observations of ministers who supported this limb of the legislation.

. . .

The responsibilities of the judge

(a) at the conclusion of the evidence

45. One of the responsibilities the trial judge in the context of the new defence is defined. Unless there is evidence sufficient to raise the issue of loss of control it should be withdrawn from consideration by the jury. If there is, then the prosecution must disprove it. In this context "sufficient evidence" is explained by reference to well understood principles, that is, that a properly directed jury could "reasonably conclude that the defence might apply". In reaching this decision the judge is required to address the ingredients of the defence, as defined in section 54 and further amplified in section 55. There must be sufficient evidence to establish each of the ingredients defined in subsections 54(1)(a), (b) and

(c), and this carries with it, evidence which satisfies the test in subsections 55(4)(a) and (b). In making the decision in accordance with the principles identified in this judgment the judge must exclude the specific matters which might otherwise be regarded as constituting possible justification in section 55(c)(b) and the express conditions to be disregarded in accordance with section 55(6)(a) and (c). In the end however, although the judge must bear these different features in mind when deciding whether the case should be left to the jury, and the task is far from straightforward, these statutory provisions reflect well established principles summarised in the phrase "the evidential burden". Sufficient evidence must be adduced to enable the judgment to be made that a jury could reasonably decide that the prosecution had failed to negate the defence of loss of control.

46. This requires a common sense judgment based on an analysis of all the evidence. To the extent that the evidence may be in dispute, the judge has to recognise that the jury may accept the evidence which is most favourable to the defendant, and reject that which is most favourable to the prosecution, and so tailor the ruling accordingly. That is merely another way of saying that in discharging this responsibility the judge should not reject disputed evidence which the jury might choose to believe. Guiding himself or herself in this way, the more difficult question which follows is the judgment whether the circumstances were sufficiently grave and whether the defendant had a justifiable grievance because he had been seriously wronged. These are value judgments. They are left to the jury when the judge concludes that the evidential burden has been satisfied.

. . .

(b) The Summing Up

49. Confining ourselves to the second component (the qualifying trigger or triggers under section 55), for the reasons already given, if the only potential qualifying trigger is sexual infidelity, effect must be given to the legislation. There will then be no qualifying trigger, and the judge must act accordingly. The more problematic situations will arise when the defendant relies on an admissible trigger (or triggers) for which sexual infidelity is said to provide an appropriate context (as explained in this judgment) for evaluating whether the trigger relied on is a qualifying trigger for the purposes of subsection 55(3) and (4). When this situation arises the jury should be directed:

a) as to the statutory ingredients required of the qualifying trigger or triggers;

b) as to the statutory prohibition against sexual infidelity on its own constituting a qualifying trigger;

c) as to the features identified by the defence (or which are apparent to the trial judge) which are said to constitute a permissible trigger or triggers;

d) that, if these are rejected by the jury, in accordance with (b) above sexual infidelity must then be disregarded;

e) that if, however, an admissible trigger may be present, the evidence relating to sexual infidelity arises for consideration as part of the context in which to evaluate that trigger and whether the statutory ingredients identified in (a) above may be established.

. . .

76. At the conclusion of the evidence Judge Smith directed herself that there was no evidence that the loss of self-control necessary for the purposes of this defence was due to one of the qualifying triggers identified in the statute. She was required "specifically" to disregard anything said or done that constituted sexual infidelity. The remarks allegedly made by the wife, challenged about her infidelity, to the effect that she had intercourse with five men were to be ignored. Removing that element of that evidence, what was left was the evidence when the wife saw that the appellant had visited the suicide site on the internet,

she commented that he had "not the balls to commit suicide" and that she also said, so far as the future was concerned, that he could have the children who were then currently living with him at their home. The judge observed that she could not see that the circumstances were of an extremely grave character or that they would cause the defendant to have a justifiable sense of being seriously wrong[ed]. On this issue no sufficient evidence had been adduced. She could not find that a jury properly directed could reasonably conclude that the defence might apply. In due course she proceeded to her summing up, leaving diminished responsibility for the consideration of the jury.

77. In addressing these problems, Judge Smith did not have the advantage of the careful and detailed submissions made to us by leading counsel on behalf of the appellant and the Crown. On the basis that the remarks made by the wife had to be disregarded, her conclusion that the defence should be withdrawn from the jury was unassailable. In context, it was a characteristically courageous decision. For the reasons we have endeavoured to explain in this judgment, we have concluded that she misdirected herself about the possible relevance of the wife's infidelity. We have reflected whether the totality of the matters relied on as a qualifying trigger, evaluated in the context of the evidence relating to the wife's sexual infidelity, and examined as a cohesive whole, were of sufficient weight to leave to the jury. In our judgment they were. Accordingly the appeal against conviction will be allowed.

78. In the circumstances of this case, we shall order a new trial. The issues should be examined by a jury.

It is clear in this decision that the Court of Appeal was not keen on section 55(6)(c), which excludes sexual infidelity from being a qualifying trigger. Lord Judge CJ pointed out that it had the potential to 'produce surprising results'[57] and 'anomalies'.[58] The problems they highlighted include the following:

- The definition of sexual infidelity is unclear. Is flirting sexual infidelity? Is viewing pornography?[59] *Clinton* does not provide much guidance on the definition of sexual infidelity. Although Judge CJ did state that infidelity assumed that there was a continuing relationship. So a stalker who killed his prey's partner out of sexual jealousy would not be covered. Of course he would find it difficult to show that there was a justifiable sense of being seriously wronged in such a case.

- Section 55(6)(c) could mean that a defendant who is facing a less serious wrong is better able to present the defence. For example, a defendant who came home and found his partner in bed with another man and kills her, has clearly been provoked by sexual infidelity and could not rely on that as a qualifying trigger. But if he came home and found her laughing with a man and killed her in jealousy he might be able to use that provocation as it would not be 'sexual' infidelity.[60]

- Sexual infidelity is well known to produce loss of control. Is it artificial to pretend it does not or exclude evidence of it when it clearly was central to the case? The jury will not understand in a case like *Clinton* being told that the sexual infidelity is not a qualifying trigger when they might think it obviously a serious wrong.

- Sexual infidelity can be considered as a factor when considering the defence of diminished responsibility. Where, as in *Clinton* itself, the defendant is pleading provocation

---

[57] *Clinton*, para. 2.   [58] *Ibid*, para. 20.   [59] See Reed and Wake (2011).
[60] Although it would be hard to show that there was a serious wrong here.

and diminished responsibility it will *be con*fusing for the jury to be told that they can consider sexual infidelity for one defence but not another.

- Often allegations of sexual infidelity are aspects of the provocative circumstances. If, for example, a husband came home and found his wife in bed with another man and she then uttered a string of insults at the husband, who killed the other man, it will be difficult for the jury to separate out which aspects of what happened were sexual infidelity and which were not.

This last point led to the approach promoted by the Court of Appeal, which is captured in the following comment:

> where sexual infidelity is integral to and forms an essential part of the context in which to make a just evaluation whether a qualifying trigger properly falls within the ambit of subsections 55(3) and (4), the prohibition in section 55(6)(c) does not operate to exclude it.[61]

This suggests that in a future case a distinction should be made from a situation which involves 'pure' sexual infidelity, in which case it cannot amount to a qualifying trigger. So if the sole provocation is that the defendant sees his partner in a sexual act with someone else that cannot be used. However, in a 'mixed case': where there is sexual infidelity *plus* other facts then the sexual infidelity can be used to give the other factors their context. So in the *Clinton* case, arguably, the severity of the wrong when the wife said Clinton did not 'have the balls' to commit suicide can only be understood in the context of her earlier admission to sexual infidelity. In cases like that the sexual infidelity can be taken into account because otherwise the legitimate potential qualifying trigger cannot be considered. However, the sexual infidelity can be used only to provide the context for a permitted trigger and not itself become the trigger.

In truth, it will be rare that a case will be seen as pure sexual infidelity and so rare for section 55(6)(c) to be raised. Any barrister worth their salt will be able to point to another legitimate trigger (e.g. a comment made), which can then be said to only be appreciated if understood in the context of sexual infidelity. The distinction between sexual infidelity being a trigger itself (which is forbidden) and being the context for a permitted trigger (which is not forbidden) may escape most juries. Further as Stark notes: '[G]iven the heated circumstances in which killings usually take place, it might not be clear what triggered the defendant's loss of self-control: was the victim's infidelity a context for the defendant's loss of control, or the cause of it?'[62]

Supporters of the decision in *Clinton* will say that since the Court of Appeal was faced with a provision which could not be sensibly interpreted, they have found a neat way of sidelining it. Critics of the Court of Appeal will claim that the decision has bypassed Parliament's clear wishes. The section could have been read as a clear bar to relying on sexual infidelity as constituting a grave wrong. It could have been interpreted to forbid all reference to sexual infidelity when considering whether a serious wrong qualifying trigger existed.[63]

The debate in part centres on one's response to those who kill on discovering sexual infidelity.[64] Supporters of the provision say such killers are revealing outdated views on ownership and possessiveness over sexual partners, which should never be permitted to

---

[61] *Clinton*, para. 39.　　[62] Stark (2012).　　[63] Baker and Zhao (2012).
[64] See Horder and Fitz-Gibbon (2015) for a fascinating discussion of sentencing in cases of killing following suspected infidelity.

form a basis of a defence in criminal law.[65] Notably the Court of Appeal in *Clinton* was not convinced by that claim:

> Meanwhile experience over many generations has shown that, however it may become apparent, when it does, sexual infidelity has the potential to create a highly emotional situation or to exacerbate a fraught situation, and to produce a completely unpredictable, and sometimes violent response. This may have nothing to do with any notional "rights" that the one may believe that he or she has over the other, and often stems from a sense of betrayal and heartbreak, and crushed dreams.[66]

4.3 WOULD A PERSON WITH NORMAL TOLERANCE AND SELF-RESTRAINT HAVE ACTED AS D DID?

In order to rely successfully on the defence of loss of control it is not enough for the defendant just to show that he or she lost his or her self-control as a result of a qualifying trigger. It must also be shown that a 'person of D's sex and age, with a normal degree of tolerance and self-restraint and in the circumstances of D, might have reacted in the same or in a similar way to D.'[67] This objective[68] question is entirely one for the jury.

This objective limb of the test proved highly problematic for the old law on provocation and a number of issues need to be addressed:

The normal degree of tolerance and self-restraint

The reference to a normal degree of tolerance is designed to prevent a defendant from using the defence who loses self-control because he or she is intolerant or has low levels of self-restraint. If a person with normal powers of tolerance and self-restraint would not have responded to the qualifying trigger by killing the victim, then the defendant cannot rely on the defence. The test here operates in a strict way. Even if the defendant has lower levels of tolerance and self-restraint through no fault of their own, for example because they have a mental illness, they are still required to show the levels of tolerance and self-restraint of an ordinary person of their age and sex. Such a defendant would be better off relying on the defence of diminished responsibility. Only age and sex can be used to impact upon the degree of self-restraint or tolerance expected.

The reference to tolerance is designed to deal with cases where the defendant regards actions as particularly provocative because of his or her intolerant belief. If, for example, a son informed his homophobic father that he was gay and the father then flew into a rage and killed the son, the father would not be able to rely on the loss of control defence. That would be for two main reasons. First, the information about the son's sexuality could not be regarded as giving D a 'justifiable sense of being seriously wronged'. It could not, therefore, be a qualifying trigger. Second, because a person with a normal degree of tolerance would not react by killing his or her son. His response indicates he was unusually intolerant. By the same reasoning, if a defendant is intoxicated he or she must show the level of self-control of a sober person.[69]

---

[65] Howe (2014).   [66] *Clinton*, para. 16.   [67] See Taylor (2011) for a detailed discussion.
[68] For the difference between an objective and subjective question, see Chapter 1, Section 7.1.
[69] *R v Asmelash* [2013] EWCA Crim 157.

The reference to self-restraint is an acknowledgement that the law expects people to show self-control. Even if a person is gravely insulting, the defendant should show restraint. However, the defence acknowledges that there are circumstances where, even armed with the self-restraint of an ordinary person, someone might kill in the face of grave wrong. An important point to notice is that all the defendant needs to show is that the person of normal tolerance and restraint *might* have reacted in the way he or she did. If the jury are not sure whether or not the normal person would have responded in that way they should allow the defendant to use the defence.

It is clear from the wording of section 54(1)(c) that the defendant's age is a factor in deciding how much tolerance or self-restraint can be expected. Under the old law on provocation Lord Diplock, in the case of *Camplin*,[70] had concluded that the courts could not expect an 'old head on young shoulders' and therefore required the jury to consider whether the defendant had demonstrated the level of self-control *expected of a person of his or her age*. The reference to sex in the section is rather odd. It implies that different degrees of tolerance and self-restraint might be expected from men and women.[71] While it is arguable that a particular insult or circumstance might be graver for a woman than a man, or vice versa, there is no good reason why the level of tolerance or self-restraint should be any different.

The reference to the defendant's circumstances

Section 54(1)(c) states that the jury should consider how the person of D's age and sex and in the circumstances of D would have reacted. The significance of this is that it allows the jury to take into account the circumstances the defendant was in. One consequence of this is that the nature of the trigger must be seen in the light of the defendant's history.[72] This means that what might appear to be a minor wrong, when seen in the light of the history of the event, is in fact a grave wrong. For example, if Alf has repeatedly sexually abused his daughter, Bertha, and one day calls her 'a whore', this is a far graver wrong to Bertha, in the context of their relationship, than it would be if he said those words to a stranger. Sometimes the courts have referred to the concept of 'cumulative provocation' or 'cumulative impact',[73] where a long series of incidents, each minor in itself, cause the defendant to lose his or her self-control after being provoked by the 'last straw'.

In *Clinton*[74] it was pointed out that although sexual infidelity alone cannot be relied upon as a trigger it will amount to part of the circumstances in determining how a person with the normal degree of self-restraint will respond. Judge CJ accepted that this was 'counter-intuitive' but was required by the wording of the statute. So if a man comes home and finds his wife and her lover in bed, and that during their love making they have broken his favourite vase, only the breaking of the vase can be considered in determining whether a qualifying trigger has been established, but the sexual infidelity can be considered in deciding how a normal person would have reacted.

The defendant, then, can rely on their circumstances or characteristics to show that a particular wrong was particularly serious for them. But they cannot use their circumstances or characteristics to affect the level of self-control. So, to use an example from an Australian case, an Italian man might be allowed to suggest that imputations about his masculinity

---

[70] [1978] AC 705 (HL).   [71] For an excellent discussion, see Cobb and Gausden (2011).

[72] See *Hill* [2008] EWCA Crim 76, where it was accepted that a person who had suffered sexual abuse as a child might find a sexual assault more provoking than another defendant.

[73] *Dawes* [2013] EWCA Crim 322, para. 54.   [74] [2012] EWCA Crim 2.

were a particularly serious insult because he was Italian, he could not suggest that because he was Italian he was hot-blooded and so had less powers of self-restraint.[75]

The reaction of the hypothetical person

Section 54 requires the jury to consider whether the person of D's age and sex might have reacted in the same or in a similar way to D. This requires the jury to consider not just whether the person would have lost self-control and killed, but also whether they would have done so in the way the defendant did. Imagine, for example, a defendant who when gravely wronged loses self-control and kills in a particularly barbaric way. Then a jury might conclude that although a normal person might have lost self-control as a result of the wrong, they would not have acted so savagely, and so the defendant could not use the defence. In *van Dongen*,[76] a case heard under the old law, the court held that even if a reasonable person might have reacted violently, he or she would not have given the victim fifteen head wounds; most of them while the victim was defenceless on the ground.[77] If the case was heard under the new law, even if a jury were persuaded that a reasonable person would have lost control they might not be persuaded that the reasonable person would have attacked the victim in such a prolonged way.

4.4 LOSS OF CONTROL AND VICTIMS OF DOMESTIC VIOLENCE

One issue which greatly troubled the courts in the old law of provocation were cases where a victim of domestic violence had killed their abusive spouse. The following is an example of how such cases were dealt with under the old law:

R v Ahluwalia
[1992] 4 All ER 889 (CA)[78]

Kiranjit Ahluwalia was an Asian woman who had entered an arranged marriage with her husband. She had suffered many years of violence and abuse from him. This included an attempt to kill her. One evening the husband threatened to attack her. That night, while he was asleep, Ahluwalia poured petrol over him and set it alight. The husband died from the burns he received. At her trial the judge directed the jury that it had to be shown that Ahluwalia had suffered a sudden and temporary loss of self-control. She appealed, inter alia, on the ground that such a direction was incorrect.

Lord Taylor of Gosforth CJ

The phrase 'sudden and temporary loss of self-control' encapsulates an essential ingredient of the defence of provocation in a clear and readily understandable phrase. It serves to underline that the defence is concerned with the actions of an individual who is not, at

---

[75] *R v Masciantonio* (1994–5) 183 CLR 58 (Austral. HC).   [76] [2005] Crim LR 971 (CA).

[77] See Fontaine (2009) for a discussion of how emotional disturbance can affect cognitive capacity as well as levels of self-control.

[78] (1993) 96 Cr App R 133, [1993] Crim LR 63.

the moment when he or she acts violently, master of his or her own mind. Mr Robertson suggested that the phrase might lead the jury to think provocation could not arise for consideration unless the defendant's act followed immediately upon the acts or words which constituted the alleged provocation. He submits a direction to this effect would have been inappropriate and inconsistent with a number of authorities (see, for example, *R v Hall* (1928) 21 Cr App R 48, *Lee Chun-Chuen v R* [1963] AC 220 and *Parker v R* [1964] AC 1369).

Nevertheless, it is open to the judge, when deciding whether there is any evidence of provocation to be left to the jury, and open to the jury when considering such evidence, to take account of the interval between the provocative conduct and the reaction of the defendant to it. Time for reflection may show that after the provocative conduct made its impact on the mind of the defendant, he or she kept or regained self-control. The passage of time following the provocation may also show that the subsequent attack was planned or based on motives, such as revenge or punishment, inconsistent with the loss of self-control and therefore with the defence of provocation. In some cases, such an interval may wholly undermine the defence of provocation; that, however, depends entirely on the facts of the individual case and is not a principle of law.

Mr Robertson referred to the phrase 'cooling off period' which has sometimes been applied to an interval of time between the provocation relied upon and the fatal act. He suggests that although in many cases such an interval may indeed be a time for cooling and regaining self-control so as to forfeit the protection of the defence, in others the time lapse has an opposite effect. He submits, relying on expert evidence not before the trial judge, that women who have been subjected frequently over a period to violent treatment may react to the final act or words by what he calls a 'slow-burn' reaction rather than by an immediate loss of self-control.

We accept that the subjective element in the defence of provocation would not as a matter of law be negatived simply because of the delayed reaction in such cases, provided that there was at the time of the killing a 'sudden and temporary loss of self-control' caused by the alleged provocation. However, the longer the delay and the stronger the evidence of deliberation on the part of the defendant, the more likely it will be that the prosecution will negative provocation.

In the present case, despite the delay after the last provocative act or words by the deceased, and despite the appellant's apparent deliberation in seeking and lighting the petrol, the trial judge nevertheless left the issue of provocation to the jury. His references to 'sudden and temporary loss of self-control' were correct in law. He did not suggest to the jury that they should or might reject the defence of provocation because the last provocative act or word of the deceased was not followed immediately by the appellant's fatal acts.

We consider that the learned judge's direction was in accordance with the well established law and cannot be faulted.

[The Court of Appeal went on to decide that a retrial should be ordered because evidence concerning diminished responsibility was not properly left for consideration by the jury.]

Appeal allowed. Conviction quashed. Retrial ordered.

It is not clear whether or not under the new law Mrs Ahluwalia would be able to rely on the defence of loss of control. She would almost certainly be able to show that she was facing circumstances of a grave character. She would also be able to show that she had a justifiable sense of being seriously wronged. Indeed she would also be able to show she had a fear of serious violence from the defendant. So, she would have no difficulty in showing that there was a qualifying trigger.

A more difficult issue would be whether she could show that she had lost her self-control as a result of the qualifying trigger. The prosecution might argue that her acts before the killing reveal that she was acting in a calm and deliberate way, rather than in the way one would expect a person who had lost self-control. Indeed they might even suggest she was acting out of revenge. The defence was that she had lost her self-control through the despair and abasement suffered during the violence. While 'angry loss of self-control' might reveal itself in shouting and stamping, loss of self-control following sustained abuse might manifest itself differently.

The jury would also need to consider whether a person of Ahluwalia's age and in her circumstances, but with a normal degree of tolerance and self-restraint, would have acted as she did. The defence might try and introduce evidence from an expert in the experience of abused women who could give evidence about the impact of abuse.

QUESTIONS

1. Following a brain injury suffered in a car crash Mick finds that he suffers from moments of intense irritability. One day Paul calls him a 'short tempered idiot', following which Mick flies into a terrible rage and kills Paul. Is Mick guilty of murder?

For guidance on answering this question, please visit the Online Resource Centre that accompanies this book: www.oxfordtextbooks.co.uk/orc/herringcriminal7e/.

2. Professor Bach is a psychologist who specializes in techniques to control anger. A colleague describes his latest book as 'utter rubbish', Bach loses his temper and kills him. Can the jury expect Bach to exhibit a higher level of self-control than ordinary self-control?

3. Why should gender affect the level of self-control expected?

4. Withey (2011) quotes Baroness Mallalieu's observations:

    'I have had people turn to me, look at me in disbelief and say, "How on earth did you let that pass through the House of Lords?" . . . [H]owever, if these clauses on provocation go through I shall not be able to show my face again there at all. The phrase "dog's breakfast" would be a kindness.'

    Is that a fair summary of the new law on loss of control?

FURTHER READING

Edwards, S. (2010) 'Anger and Fear as Justifiable Preludes for Loss of Self-control' *Journal of Criminal Law* 74: 223.

Herring, J. (2011b) 'The Serious Wrong of Domestic Abuse and the Loss of Control Defence' in A. Reed and M. Bohlander (eds) *Loss of Control and Diminished Responsibility: Domestic, Comparative and International Perspectives* (Aldershot: Ashgate).

Morgan, C. (2013) 'Loss of Self-Control: Back to the Good Old Days' *Journal of Criminal Law* 77: 119.

Norrie, A. (2010) 'The Coroners and Justice Act 2009—Partial Defences to Murder (1) Loss of Control' *Criminal Law Review* 275.

Taylor, R. (2011) 'The Model of Tolerance of Self-Restraint' in A. Reed and M. Bohlander (eds) *Loss of Control and Diminished Responsibility* (Aldershot: Ashgate).

Withey, C. (2011) 'Loss of Control, Loss of Opportunity?' *Criminal Law Review* 263.

5 DIMINISHED RESPONSIBILITY

DEFINITION

Diminished responsibility is a defence only to murder and, if successful, reduces the charge to manslaughter.

Diminished responsibility: the defendant must show that he or she suffered from an abnormality of mental functioning, arising from a recognized medical condition, which provides an explanation for committing the killing. It must be shown that the abnormality substantially impaired his or her ability to understand the nature of his or her conduct, form a rational judgment, and exercise self-control.

Diminished responsibility is a defence only to murder.[79] Even then it is only a partial defence. If successfully raised the accused will be acquitted of murder, but convicted of manslaughter.[80] The significance of this is that on sentencing for manslaughter the judge has a discretion as to the appropriate sentence, while for murder only the life sentence can be imposed.

Diminished responsibility is defined in section 2(1) of the Homicide Act 1957, as amended by the Coroners and Justice Act 2009:

(1) A person ("D") who kills or is a party to the killing of another is not to be convicted of murder if D was suffering from an abnormality of mental functioning which—

(a) arose from a recognised medical condition,

(b) substantially impaired D's ability to do one or more of the things mentioned in subsection (1A), and

(c) provides an explanation for D's acts and omissions in doing or being a party to the killing.

(1A) Those things are—

(a) to understand the nature of D's conduct;

(b) to form a rational judgment;

(c) to exercise self-control.

(1B) For the purposes of subsection (1)(c), an abnormality of mental functioning provides an explanation for D's conduct if it causes, or is a significant contributory factor in causing, D to carry out that conduct.

---

[79] Diminished responsibility is not a defence to attempted murder (*Campbell* [1997] Crim LR 495). Diminished responsibility cannot be relied upon if the defendant has been found unfit to plead under the Criminal Procedure (Insanity and Unfitness to Plead) Act 1991 (*R v Antoine* [2000] 2 All ER 208).

[80] Homicide Act 1957, s. 2(3).

It should be stressed that if the defendant wishes to raise the defence of diminished respon-sibility the burden of proof of establishing the defence is on him or her, but only on a balance of probabilities.[81] This has been held to be consistent with Article 6(2) of the ECHR because the prosecution is required to prove the elements of murder, and the burden on the defend-ants of raising the defence of diminished responsibility rests on them only if they wish to raise it.[82] Indeed the judge should not instruct the jury about diminished responsibility unless the defendant has consented to it being raised.[83]

In practice if the defendant pleads guilty to manslaughter on the ground of diminished responsibility the prosecution will often accept such a plea and not seek to disprove it. However, the Court of Appeal in *Vinagre*[84] has stated that the prosecution should do this only where there is clear evidence of the defendant's mental abnormality. If there is not, the jury should be presented with the evidence and be left to decide whether there is suf-ficient evidence of diminished responsibility or whether the defendant must be convicted of murder.

There are four requirements that must be met if a defendant wishes to rely on diminished responsibility:

(1) He or she was suffering from an abnormality of mental functioning.

(2) The abnormality of mental functioning was caused by a recognized medical condition.

(3) As a result of the abnormality the defendant's ability to understand the nature of his or her conduct, form a rational judgment, or exercise self-control, was substantially impaired.

(4) That the abnormality of mental functioning provided an explanation for the defend-ant's conduct, in that it was a significant contributory factor in carrying it out.

Section 2(1) of the Homicide Act 1957 was significantly reformed by the Coroners and Justice Act 2009. The case law on the old law therefore needs to be treated with great care. It is noticeable that in the old law the defence had been interpreted flexibly to ensure that those thought deserving of a defence by doctors or lawyers were provided with one. The new definition of the defence is notably tighter and may well prove more difficult to establish.

5.1 'ABNORMALITY OF MENTAL FUNCTIONING'

Under the old law it was only necessary to prove an abnormality of mind. In *Byrne*[85] it was held that it was enough that the defendant's mind was sufficiently different from a normal mind to be classified as abnormal. The new law is much stricter than that. It must be shown that the defendant has a 'recognised medical condition'. Under the old law the defendant in *Vinagre*[86] was found to have killed his wife while suffering from 'Othello syn-drome', defined as 'morbid jealousy for which there was no cause', and entitled to rely on the defence of diminished responsibility. Cynics might believe the syndrome was invented by the defendant's lawyers to enable him to use the defence. Such a decision could not be reached under the new law, unless the defendant was able to show 'Othello syndrome' was

---

[81] Homicide Act 1957, s. 2(2).   [82] *Foye* [2013] EWCA Crim 475.
[83] *Campbell* (1986) 84 Cr App R 255.   [84] (1979) 69 Cr App R 104 (CA).
[85] [1960] 2 QB 396.   [86] (1979) 69 Cr App R 104.

a recognized medical condition. The government, in proposing the reforms explained that they would bring the

terminology up-to-date in a way which would accommodate future developments in diagnostic practice and encourage defences to be grounded in a valid medical diagnosis linked to the accepted classificatory systems which together encompass the recognised physical, psychiatric and psychological conditions.[87]

Although the condition must be a recognized mental condition, it does not have to be a serious mental illness. A mild depression would be sufficient, although a defendant suffering from that might not be able to satisfy the other elements of the defence.

The defendant must introduce evidence from an expert witness to establish the defence. But that might be thought to create a problem. If the expert says that the defendant suffers from a recognized medical condition and the elements of the defence are made out, does that mean the jury have to accept that view. That question was considered in the following case, which states that the expert evidence must be accepted if there is no contradictory evidence, but if there is other contradictory evidence, the jury are entitled to reject the view of the expert:

R v Brennan
[2014] EWCA Crim 2387

Michael Brennan killed Paul Simons. The only issue at trial was whether Brennan could rely on the partial defence of diminished responsibility. He had had a very troubled childhood and had mental health issues. He introduced evidence from an experienced consultant forensic psychiatrist, which supported the defence, stating he suffered from Schizotypal Disorder and Emotionally Unstable Personality Disorder, both recognized medical conditions. The Crown introduced no expert evidence at all. The jury convicted of murder and Brennan appealed, arguing that in the light of the unchallenged medical evidence the jury had to accept the defence.

Davis LJ

43. The problem that a case of this kind throws up derives from the fact that there are two relevant but potentially conflicting principles that are brought into play. The first principle is the general principle that in criminal trials cases are decided by juries, not by experts. Indeed experts are permitted by reason of their expertise to express *opinions* by way of evidence: but cases ultimately fall to be decided by juries, and they decide on the *entirety* of the evidence. The second principle, however, is that juries must base their conclusions on the *evidence*. That fundamental principle finds reflection, for example, in directions conventionally given to juries not to speculate and not to allow their views to be swayed by feelings of distaste or emotion.

44. There can, as we see it, be no room for departure from so fundamental a principle as the second principle. It reflects the very essence of the jury system and of a just and fair trial. But the first principle, whilst most important and undoubtedly descriptive of the general position, is also capable, as it seems to us, of admitting of degree of qualification in a suitably exceptional case. Clearly no difficulty arises (normally) where there is a dispute as

---

[87] Ministry of Justice (2008: para. 49).

to the expert evidence. The jury decides. But suppose, for example, a matter arises falling exclusively within the domain of scientific expertise; suppose, too, that all the well qualified experts instructed on that particular matter are agreed as to the correct conclusion and no challenge is made to such conclusion. Can it really be said that the jury nevertheless can properly depart from the experts as to that conclusion on that particular matter: simply on the basis that it is to be said, by way of mantra, that the ultimate conclusion is always for the jury? We would suggest not. Where there simply is no rational or proper basis for departing from uncontradicted and unchallenged expert evidence then juries may not do so.

48....[W]e think it important to draw attention to the significant differences between the statutory provisions as contained in s.2 of the 1957 Act and the statutory provisions contained in s.2 after its amendment by s.52 of the 2009 Act....

49. The original provisions of the 1957 Act are broadly phrased and rather more obviously couched in terms of a value judgment, by the references to *substantial* impairment of mental *responsibility*. But the provisions as substituted by the 2009 Act are altogether more tightly structured: for example by removing the (undefined) reference to mental responsibility, even while retaining the concept of substantial impairment. As stated by Lord Judge LCJ in *Brown* [2012] 2 CAR(S) 27 (at paragraph 23 of the judgment) it appears that one purpose of the amendments was to ensure "a greater equilibrium between the law and medical science". The new wording gives significantly more scope to the importance of expert psychiatric evidence....

50. That this is so is borne out by consideration of the actual provisions of the amended section. There are essentially four stages:

i) Was the defendant suffering from an abnormality of mental functioning? If so:

ii) Did it arise from a recognised medical condition? If so:

iii) Did it substantially impair the defendant's ability *either* to understand the nature of his conduct *or* to form a rational judgment *or* to exercise self-control (or any combination)? If so:

iv) Did it provide an explanation for the defendant's conduct?

51. The third stage involves, as did the former version of the section, reference to "substantial impairment". That does, we accept, involve a degree of evaluation potentially indicative of being a jury question (what the phrase actually connotes has recently been the subject of further discussion by a constitution of this court in *Golds* [20141 EWCA Crim 748). But overall the provisions of s.2 as amended are altogether significantly more structured than the former provisions, in particular by reference to "substantial impairment of mental responsibility" as contained in the original version of s.2 of the 1957 Act. As we see it, most, if not all, of the aspects of the new provisions relate entirely to psychiatric matters. In our view it is both legitimate and helpful, given the structure of the new provisions, for an expert psychiatrist to include in his or her evidence a view on all four stages, including a view as to whether there was substantial impairment. As Professor Ormerod explains in his paper: "Since the question of whether there is impairment of ability is a purely psychiatric question, it would also seem appropriate for the expert to offer an opinion on whether there is 'substantial' impairment". We agree. Moreover where the expert is able to and does express a view on all four matters we can see no legal or other objection to such expert, if willing and prepared to do so (as here), making explicit in evidence his or her opinion on what is called the "ultimate issue": the more so when such view will in any event probably have been implicit from his or her stated opinion on the four matters. It is difficult to see how the expression by an expert of such a view in a given case could contravene any principle of deference to the jury as the ultimate decision makers. It is therefore, in a diminished responsibility case where the expert evidence is uncontradicted, to be left to the evaluation by the trial judge of all the

circumstances of the case, where an application to withdraw the case of murder is made at the close of evidence. The judge will assess the position in the light of the uncontradicted expert evidence and in the light of any other evidence. It at all events seems unprincipled in cases of this type, where an application to withdraw is made, that murder should be left to the jury simply and solely because the prosecution wants it to be. A charge of murder should not be left to the jury if the trial judge's considered view is that on the evidence taken as a whole no properly directed jury could properly convict of murder.

Appeal against murder conviction allowed and conviction for manslaughter substituted.

5.2 THE EFFECT OF THE ABNORMALITY OF MENTAL FUNCTIONING

It must be shown that the effect of the abnormality of mental functioning was to substantially impair one of the following: the defendant's ability to understand the nature of his conduct, to form a rational judgment, or to exercise self-control. We shall consider these separately.

A failure to understand the nature of the conduct could mean that the defendant does not know what he or she is doing or did not understand the nature of his or her acts. It is difficult to imagine a case where this could apply. Remember that we are dealing with cases which would otherwise be murder. It cannot, therefore, be relevant in a case where the defendant did not know what he or she was doing. The defendant is only guilty of murder if he or she intended to kill or cause grievous bodily harm. So, if the defendant believed he was killing a garden gnome when in fact he was killing his neighbour he would not be guilty of murder because he did not intend to kill a person.[88] Rarely will a defendant not understand the nature of his or her acts, but still have the necessary intent. Further, a defendant who is suffering a disease of the mind which means they do not know the nature and quality of their acts can use the defence of insanity, which is a complete defence. So in most cases where a defendant's mental abnormality means they do not understand the nature of their conduct, they will not have the necessary intention to be guilty of murder or they will use the defence of insanity.[89] The Law Commission gives the following example of a case where this version of the defence might apply:

a boy aged 10 who has been left to play very violent video games for hours on end for much of his life, loses his temper and kills another child when the child attempts to take a game from him. When interviewed, he shows no real understanding that, when a person is killed they cannot simply be later revived, as happens in the games he has been continually playing.[90]

An alternative ground for the defence is to argue that the abnormality substantially impaired the defendant's ability to form a rational judgment. The Law Commission gives the following as an example:

a mentally sub-normal boy believes that he must follow his older brother's instructions, even when they involve taking part in a killing. He says, 'I wouldn't dream of disobeying my brother and he would never tell me to do something if it was really wrong'.[91]

---

[88] And, no, a gnome is not a person, however strongly you may feel about them!
[89] The defence of insanity is discussed further in Chapter 12.
[90] Law Commission Report No. 304 (2006b: para. 5.121).   [91] *Ibid.*

The defendant relying on this ground will need to show that his or her ability to make an assessment of what is the right thing to do has been substantially impaired by the mental abnormality.

The final possible impact of the abnormality is that it affects the defendant's ability to exercise self-control. As we shall see shortly there is the defence of loss of control which is available in some cases where the defendant has lost self-control. Although there may be some overlap between the two defences it is important to appreciate the differences. First, for diminished responsibility it is necessary to show there was an abnormality of mental functioning; there is no need to show that for loss of control. Second, for loss of control the defendant must have shown a normal degree of tolerance and self-restraint, while diminished responsibility has no such requirement. So, diminished responsibility is appropriate in a case where a defendant suffering from a mental abnormality has lost self-control and killed. The Law Commission uses the following example of the kind of loss of self-control in question:

> a man says that sometimes the devil takes control of him and implants in him a desire to kill, a desire that must be acted on before the devil will go away.[92]

An important point to notice about the defence is that all that needs to be shown is that there is a substantial impairment in the defendant's ability to do one of the three things we have just discussed. This suggests a complete impairment is not required. So a defendant may still have some ability to exercise self-control or form a rational judgment, but still suffer a substantial impairment if his or her abilities have been limited to a notable extent.[93] On the other hand, in *Osborne*[94] the fact the defendant suffered from attention deficit hyperactivity disorder did not necessarily mean that the impairment of responsibility was substantial.

The leading case on the meaning of substantial is the following:[95]

R v Mark Richard Golds
[2014] EWCA Crim 748

Mark Golds was convicted of murder. He admitted killing his partner Claire Parish, at a family barbecue. The only question for the jury was whether it was murder or manslaughter by virtue of diminished responsibility. At the trial there was expert evidence he had psychosis and depression, for which he received medication. Also one expert suggested he had personality disorder. He was convicted of murder and appealed on several grounds. One was that the judge had not adequately directed the jury on the meaning of the word substantial for the purposes of the defence of diminished responsibility.

Elias LJ

55. At the heart of this submission is the contention that the word "substantial" is capable of having two different meanings. One possible meaning is that the abnormality of mental functioning substantially impairs if it does so to more than a trivial or minimal extent; it then has substance and the impairment is substantial. A second meaning is that the abnormality

---

[92] Law Commission Report No. 304 (2006b: para. 5.121).
[93] *Brown (Robert)* [2011] EWCA Crim 2796.
[94] [2010] EWCA Crim 547.   [95] See Wake (2011) for further discussion.

of mental functioning only substantially impairs where, whilst not wholly impairing the defendant's ability to do the things specified in section 2(1A), it significantly or appreciably impairs that ability, beyond something that is merely more than trivial or minimal. For example, if a salary is described as substantial, that would not convey the meaning that it is something a little more than minimal; on the contrary, it suggests that it is significantly more than that.

[The court explored the previous authorities which disagreed on the meaning of substantial.]

71. We are concerned if the position is—as we believe it might be—that different judges are in fact directing juries in different ways with respect to this important principle. If the substantial test is met once something more than trivial or minimal is shown, that is very different from a test which requires the jury to determine its meaning by applying their common sense in the range from trivial or minimal to total. No doubt the concept must derive its meaning from its context, but there is at least a respectable case for saying that Parliament may have intended that any material impairment would be substantial if it has substance i.e. is more than trivial, and that this ought to be sufficient to reduce the offence from murder to manslaughter. The extent of the impairment thereafter would be relevant only to sentence....

72.... The jurisprudence is very clear. Judges ought not to adopt the narrower meaning. This requires that they should either refuse to provide any further explanation of the term, as in *Mitchell* and in this case, on the arguably optimistic premise that the meaning is obvious; or if asked for further help, they should be given a direction of the kind adopted in *Simcox*.

["'Do we think, looking at it broadly as common-sense people, there was a substantial impairment of his mental responsibility in what he did?' If the answer is 'no', there may be some impairment, but we do not think it was substantial, we do not think it was something that really made any great difference, although it may have made it harder to control himself, to refrain from crime, then you would find him guilty."]

73. It follows that although we grant permission on this ground we find that the judge was not in error in failing to direct the jury in accordance with the narrower meaning, nor was he obliged to give the jury any fuller direction than he did.

Appeal dismissed.

5.3 EXPLANATION FOR THE ACTS

Section 2(1)(c) requires proof that the defendant's abnormality of mental functioning 'provides an explanation for D's acts and omissions in doing or being a party to the killing'. This is a rather strangely worded provision. Presumably it is designed to ensure that not only does the defendant suffer an abnormality of mental functioning, but that it is a cause of the killing. Without this provision a defendant might have killed while suffering from a mental abnormality, but the abnormality not, in fact, have anything to do with the killing. So, even if the defence produces evidence that the defendant suffered from an abnormality of mind, the jury still need to determine that its impact was such as to cause the substantial impairment.[96] The requirement is explored further in this passage:

---

[96] *Khan* [2009] EWCA Crim 1569.

R. Mackay, 'The Coroners and Justice Act 2009—Partial Defences to Murder (2) The New Diminished Responsibility Plea' [2010] *Criminal Law Review* 290 at 297–300

Provides an explanation for D's acts and omissions in doing or being a party to the killing

This provision follows the recommendation of the Law Commission. Initially the Commission recommended a stronger causal provision which was as follows,

> "the abnormality was a significant cause of the defendant's conduct in carrying out or taking part in the killing".

However, after consultation the Commission decided that such a requirement might be problematical and instead opted for the provision (which now appears in subs.(1)(c) of the 1957 Act as amended) stating,

> "we have framed the issue in these terms: the abnormality of mind, or developmental immaturity, or both, must be shown to be 'an explanation' for D's conduct. This ensures that there is an appropriate connection (that is, one that grounds a case for mitigation of the offence) between the abnormality of mental functioning or developmental immaturity and the killing. It leaves open the possibility, however, that other causes or explanations (like provocation) may be admitted to have been at work, without prejudicing the case for mitigation."

Both the MOJ and government ministers have repeatedly opined that a stronger causal requirement is necessary. As a result subs.(1B) of the 1957 Act as amended provides:

> "For the purposes of subsection (1)(c), an abnormality of mental functioning provides an explanation for D's conduct if it causes, or is a significant contributory factor in causing, D to carry out that conduct."

The MOJ has been adamant that, "there must be some connection between the condition and the killing for the partial defence to be justified". In its response to its consultation exercise the MOJ further opined:

> "With regard to the link between the impairment and the defendant's conduct, we have carefully thought through the various comments made but have concluded that it is right to maintain the position set out in the consultation paper. We are satisfied that it is right that, while it need not be the sole cause of the defendant's behaviour, it should be a significant contributory factor in causing the conduct—that is, more than a merely trivial factor. The partial defence should certainly not succeed where the jury believes that the impairment made no difference to the defendant's behaviour—he would have killed anyway."

The Attorney General explained this further during debate on the Bill in the House of Lords saying:

> "The Government consider it is necessary to spell out what connection between the abnormality of mental functioning and the killing is required for the partial defence to succeed. Otherwise a random coincidence would suffice. It need not be the sole cause or even the most important factor in causing the behaviour but it must be more than merely a trivial factor. We believe this gets the balance about right."

The reference to "random coincidence" seems strange. How—it may be asked—can this be possible if the defendant is able to prove that his abnormality of mental functioning gave rise to a substantial impairment of one or more of the abilities specified in subs.(1A) of the 1957 Act as amended? Surely, if such is the case then the killing cannot have been a "random coincidence". In any event, why, if the defendant proves that this is so, is this not enough? One possible line of argument is that subs.(1B) of the 1957 Act as amended is merely making express provision for what is already impliedly provided for in the original s.2(1). Two sources might be used to support this approach. The first is the following remark made by Lord Hutton in *Dietschmann*:

"I think that in referring to substantial impairment of mental responsibility the subsection does not require the abnormality of mind to be the *sole cause* of the defendant's acts in doing the killing. In my opinion, even if the defendant would not have killed if he had not taken drink, the *causative effect of the drink* does not necessarily prevent an abnormality of mind suffered by the defendant from substantially impairing his mental responsibility for his fatal acts."

The second is the Judicial Studies Board Specimen Direction on diminished responsibility which states:

"Substantially impaired means just that. You must conclude that his abnormality of mind was *a real cause* of the defendant's conduct. The defendant need not prove that his condition was the sole cause of it, but he must show that it was more than merely a trivial one [which did not make any real/appreciable difference to his ability to control himself]."

The following points can be made about these sources. First, Lord Hutton's reference to "sole cause" has to be read in the context of the facts of the case, namely the causative relationship between the effect of alcohol and abnormality of mind. There is no suggestion in *Dietschmann* that his Lordship was seeking to express an opinion on the need for some more general causal requirement in s.2(1) of the 1957 Act. Secondly, the reference in the Specimen Direction to "real cause" is nowhere to be found in Lord Hutton's judgment. Despite this the Specimen Direction was used by Maria Eagle MP, the Parliamentary Under-Secretary of State, to support her conclusion that:

"While there is no reference to causation in [the] statute, we believe that the existing requirement that the abnormality substantially impairs mental responsibility for the killing implies a causative connection and that in practice the law is applied in this way. We therefore do not consider that the approach we are taking here represents any real departure from current law and practice or indeed from the Law Commission proposal."

However, such a conclusion seems highly contentious for, as is mentioned above, there is no real support for such a strict causal requirement within the original s.2(1) of the 1957 Act. Not only that, no other diminished responsibility plea contains any such express requirement. In particular, none is to be found in the New South Wales revised plea upon which s.52 of the 2009 Act is modelled. Finally, it seems worth in this connection turning to the insanity defence. The *M'Naghten Rules* do not contain any such similar causal requirement. All the Rules require is "a defect of reason, from disease of the mind". What is necessary is that a "disease of the mind" cause "a defect of reason". There is no additional need to prove that the "disease of the mind" *caused or was a significant contributory factor in causing, D to carry out his conduct*. As a result one is compelled to ask whether it will not now be easier for a defendant whose mental state at the time of the offence satisfies all the elements of both pleas (with the exception of this causal requirement) to prove insanity within the *M'Naghten Rules* rather than the new diminished responsibility plea.

5.4 DIMINISHED RESPONSIBILITY AND INTOXICATION

How should a jury deal with a case when at the time of the killing the defendant was both suffering from an abnormality of mind and intoxicated?[97] It is necessary to distinguish between two categories of cases:

(1) Where the defendant does not suffer from alcohol dependency syndrome but suffers an abnormality of mental functioning due to a disease or inherent condition (e.g. depression) and is intoxicated. In such a case the jury must consider whether the impact of the abnormality of mind (and not the intoxication) was sufficient to substantially diminish his or her responsibility at the time of the killing, in the ways referred to in section 2(1A).[98] If it was, he or she can rely on the defence of diminished responsibility. The fact that he or she was also drunk at the time does not rob him or her of the availability of the defence. Section 2(1B) makes it clear that as long as the defendant's abnormality of mental functioning was a 'significant contributory factor in causing, [the defendant] to carry out that conduct', a defendant can rely on diminished responsibility even if drunk at the time of the killing, as long as the abnormality of mental functioning was a significant cause of the killing.

(2) Where the defendant suffers from alcohol dependency syndrome then that will be treated as an abnormality of mental functioning for the purposes of the defence, if it is a severe case. If the jury decides that the syndrome has caused involuntary drinking (i.e. the defendant is unable to resist the impulse to drink) then the impact of the involuntary intoxication can be included as an abnormality of mental functioning.[99] In such a case the jury can take into account any other abnormality of mental functioning (e.g. any depression), the alcohol dependency syndrome, and the impact of the involuntary intoxication, and consider whether these substantially impaired the defendant's responsibility in the way required for his or her actions.[100]

The issue has been addressed by the Court of Appeal:

R v Dowds
[2012] EWCA Crim 281

Stephen Dowds consumed a vast amount of alcohol and killed his partner. He asserted that he had no recollection of the events, but accepted that he must have caused her death. He did not claim to be an alcoholic, but rather a heavy but elective drinker. On appeal the key question was whether the judge had been correct to rule that transient acute intoxication was insufficient to raise the defence of the partial defence. He relied on the fact that the World Health Organization's International Statistical Classification of Diseases and Related Health Problems (ICD) lists acute intoxication as a recognized mental condition.

---

[97] Gibson (2011).   [98] *Dietschmann* [2003] UKHL 10 adopted this approach under the old law.
[99] Medical evidence will be needed to establish this: *Bunch* [2013] EWCA Crim 2498.
[100] *Wood* [2008] EWCA Crim 1305; *Stewart* [2009] EWCA Crim 593.

Lord Justice Hughes

34. We are here concerned only with intoxication which is (a) voluntary and (b) uncomplicated by any alcoholism or dependence. Whilst we are concerned with alcohol, our conclusions must be the same in relation to the effects of the voluntary ingestion of other drugs or substances.

35. The deceptively simple argument for the appellant by-passes the very clear general law against the background of which this new amendment to section 2 of the Homicide Act was enacted. For the reasons which we have explained, the exception which prevents a defendant from relying on his voluntary intoxication, save upon the limited question of whether a 'specific intent' has been formed, is well entrenched and formed the unspoken backdrop for the new statutory formula. There had been no hint of any dissatisfaction with that rule of law. If Parliament had meant to alter it, or to depart from it, it would undoubtedly have made its intention explicit. Such an intention cannot be inferred from the adoption in the new formulation of the expression "recognised medical condition" because the origins of that were clearly explained by the Law Commission. They explicitly did not include writing the terms of ICD-10 and/or DSM-IV into the legislation, for which purpose those terms are demonstrably unsuited. . . .

. . .

39. In the present case, Judge Wait relied in refusing to leave diminished responsibility to the jury on the additional factor that the condition of the defendant was a transitory or temporary one. That, he was disposed to hold, was not capable of amounting to a 'recognised medical condition' for the purposes of the new section 2 of the Homicide Act. We prefer not to rest our conclusion on this consideration, although it is clearly a relevant factor. We do not think that we should rule out the possibility that there may be genuine mental conditions, in no sense the fault of the defendant and well recognised by doctors, which although temporary may indeed be within the ambit of the Act. Whether concussion, for example, is such a condition is a question which does not arise for decision in this case.

40. Nor do we attempt to resolve the many questions which may arise as to other conditions listed in either ICD-10 or DSM-IV. It is enough to say that it is quite clear that the re-formulation of the statutory conditions for diminished responsibility was not intended to reverse the well established rule that voluntary acute intoxication is not capable of being relied upon to found diminished responsibility. That remains the law. The presence of a 'recognised medical condition' is a necessary, but not always a sufficient, condition to raise the issue of diminished responsibility.

41. If we had concluded that the defence of diminished responsibility ought to have been left to the jury, we should have been unable to accept the Crown's invitation to hold that it could not have succeeded in any event because of what must have been the findings of the jury. We agree that the jury must have rejected the defendant's assertion that he had been so drunk as to be unable to form the intention to kill or to do serious bodily harm. We agree that his use of the telephone in the immediate aftermath of the killing tends quite strongly to suggest that he was in much better control of himself than was suggested. We agree that there were good grounds on which it may well be that the jury rejected also his assertion that he had no recollection of events. We agree that the jury rejected the argument that he had lost self-control in circumstances in which a reasonable man might have done as he did. But if it had been the law that voluntary acute intoxication could found diminished responsibility, the level of drunkenness involved would not necessarily have to reach inability to form an intent, nor would the loss of self-control necessarily have to be such as might have led a reasonable man to do as the defendant did. On our very clear conclusions, however, these

considerations do not arise. Voluntary acute intoxication, whether from alcohol or other substance, is not capable of founding diminished responsibility.

42. It follows that this appeal must be dismissed.

FURTHER READING

Fortson, R. (2011) 'The Modern Partial Defence of Diminished Responsibility' in A. Reed and M. Bohlander (eds) *Loss of Control and Diminished Responsibility* (Aldershot: Ashgate).

Gibson, M. (2011) 'Intoxicants and Diminished Responsibility: The Impact of the Coroners and Justice Act 2009' *Criminal Law Review* 909.

Griew, E. (1988) 'The Future of Diminished Responsibility' *Criminal Law Review* 75.

Kennefick, L. (2011) 'Introducing a New Diminished Responsibility Defence' *Modern Law Review* 74: 750.

Mackay, R. (1995) *Mental Condition Defences in the Criminal Law* (Oxford: OUP).

Mackay, R. (2000) 'Diminished Responsibility and Mentally Disordered Killers' in A. Ashworth and B. Mitchell (eds) *Rethinking English Homicide Law* (Oxford: OUP).

Mackay, R. (2010) 'The Coroners and Justice Act 2009—Partial Defences to Murder (2) The New Diminished Responsibility Plea' *Criminal Law Review* 290.

Sparks, R. (1964) ' "Diminished Responsibility" in Theory and Practice' *Modern Law Review* 27: 9.

Sullivan, G.R. (1994) 'Intoxicants and Diminished Responsibility' *Criminal Law Review* 156.

6 SUICIDE PACT

Section 4 of the Homicide Act 1957 provides that if the defendant kills another in pursuance of a suicide pact he or she is guilty of manslaughter, not murder. The definition of a suicide pact is found in section 4(3):

a common agreement between two or more persons having for its object the death of all of them, whether or not each is to take his own life, but nothing done by a person who enters into a suicide pact shall be treated as done by him in pursuance of the pact unless it is done while he has the settled intention of dying in pursuance of the pact.

An example of a suicide pact is where a husband and wife agree that they will die together. The plan is that the husband will shoot his wife and then turn the gun on himself. He kills his wife, but a passer-by stops the husband killing himself, or he loses his nerve and cannot do it.[101] In such a case the husband could face a charge of murdering his wife. If he could show that he shot his wife in pursuance of a suicide pact, as defined above, then his charge

---

[101] The cases tend to be very sad. See BBC News Online (2008b), where a husband and wife in their 80s tried to commit suicide together after being told the wife had to be taken to a care home.

would be reduced to manslaughter.[102] It should be noted that under section 2(1) of the Suicide Act 1961 there is an offence of encouraging or assisting the suicide of another, and this carries a maximum penalty of 14 years.[103] So a person who helps another commit suicide as part of a suicide pact will simply be convicted of this offence: suicide pact being a defence only to a charge of murder. The Law Commission has recommended the abolition of the defence of suicide pact as part of their reform of the law of homicide.[104]

FURTHER READING

Wheat, K. (2000) 'The Law's Treatment of the Suicidal' *Medical Law Review* 8: 182.

---

7 MERCY KILLING AND EUTHANASIA

Mercy killing and euthanasia are widely used terms to describe situations where the defendant kills a person who is suffering from a terminal illness. The ethical issues are very different where the victim is consenting to the killing and where the victim is not.[105] However, the law is straightforward: there is no defence of mercy killing in English criminal law. It is murder to do an act which significantly shortens a person's life, even if that person is in agony and asks to be killed.[106] Lord Neuberger in *R (Nicklinson) v Ministry of Justice*[107] was clear:

> Mercy killing is a term which means killing another person for motives which appear, at least to the perpetrator, to be well-intentioned, namely for the benefit of that person, very often at that person's request. Nonetheless, mercy killing involves the perpetrator intentionally killing another person, and therefore, even where that person wished to die, or the killing was purely out of compassion and love, the current state of the law is that the killing will amount to murder or (if one or more of the mitigating circumstances are present) manslaughter.

As Lord Neuberger indicates, people who have killed terminally ill relatives have been able to use diminished responsibility.[108]

The law on end-of-life issues in the medical context is complex and controversial, but Lord Sumption has helpfully provided a summary of the current law:

R (Nicklinson) v Ministry of Justice
[2015] AC 657

Lord Sumption

255. The current position may fairly be summarised as follows:

(1) In law, the state is not entitled to intervene to prevent a person of full capacity who has arrived at a settled decision to take his own life from doing so. However, such a person does not have a right to call on a third party to help him to end his life.

---

102 The burden of proof is on the accused (Homicide Act 1957, s. 4(2)).
103 It is also an offence to attempt to commit this offence (*McShane* (1977) 66 Cr App R 97).
104 Law Commission Consultation Paper No. 177 (2005: para. 5.69).
105 See Herring (2014c: ch. 8) for further discussion.   106 *Inglis* [2010] EWCA Crim 2637.
107 [2014] UKSC 38.   108 e.g. *Inglis* [2010] EWCA Crim 2637.

(2) A person who is legally and mentally competent is entitled to refuse food and water, and to reject any invasive manipulation of his body or other form of treatment, including artificial feeding, even though without it he will die. If he refuses, medical practitioners must comply with his wishes: *Sidaway v. Board of Governors of the Bethlem Royal Hospital and the Maudsley Hospital* [1985] A.C. 871, 904–905; *In re F (Mental Patient: Sterilisation)* [1990] 2 A.C. 1; *Airedale NHS Trust v Bland* [1993] AC 789. A patient (or prospective patient) may express his wishes on these points by an advance decision (or "living will").

(3) A doctor may not advise a patient how to kill himself. But a doctor may give objective advice about the clinical options (such as sedation and other palliative care) which would be available if a patient were to reach a settled decision to kill himself. The doctor is in no danger of incurring criminal liability merely because he agrees in advance to palliate the pain and discomfort involved should the need for it arise. This kind of advice is no more or less than his duty. The law does not countenance assisted suicide, but it does not require medical practitioners to keep a patient in ignorance of the truth lest the truth should encourage him to kill himself. The right to give and receive information is guaranteed by article 10 of the Convention. If the law were not as I have summarised it, I have difficulty in seeing how it could comply.

(4) Medical treatment intended to palliate pain and discomfort is not unlawful only because it has the incidental consequence, however foreseeable, of shortening the patient's life: *Airedale NHS Trust v Bland* [1993] AC 789, 867D (Lord Goff), 892 (Lord Mustill), *R (Pretty) v Director of Public Prosecutions* [2002] 1 AC 800, 831H–832A (Lord Steyn).

(5) Whatever may be said about the clarity or lack of it in the Director's published policy, the fact is that prosecutions for encouraging or assisting suicide are rare. Between 1998 and 2011, a total of 215 British citizens appear to have committed suicide with medical assistance at the Dignitas clinic in Switzerland. Not one case has given rise to prosecution. Although cases of assisted suicide or euthanasia are periodically reported to the police (85, we were told, between 1 April 2009 and 1 October 2013) there has been only one recent prosecution for assisting suicide, and that was a particularly serious case.

In *R (Nicklinson) v Ministry of Justice* the Supreme Court went on to consider whether the current law was consistent with the European Convention on Human Rights. They declined to make a final ruling on this, determining the matter was, at least for the moment, determined by Parliament. The issues raised involve complex ones of constitutional, human rights, and medical law and will not be considered further in this book.[109] ←1 (p.234)

FURTHER READING

Greasley, K. (2010) '*R (Purdy) v DPP* and the Case for Wilful Blindness' *Oxford Journal of Legal Studies* 30: 301.

[109] See Herring (2014a) for a fuller discussion.

Herring, J. (2014) *Medical Law and Ethics* (Oxford: OUP), ch. 8.

Norrie, A. (2012) 'Legal Form and Moral Judgement: Euthanasia and Assisted Suicide' in R.A. Duff, L. Farmer, S. Marshall, M. Renzo, and V. Tadros (eds) *The Structures of the Criminal Law* (Oxford: OUP).

8 INFANTICIDE

The legal term 'infanticide' is a little odd because it is the name of both an offence and a defence. The prosecution may choose to charge the defendant with infanticide.[110] But if it charges the defendant with murder or manslaughter[111] she can raise infanticide as a defence. If successful, she will be guilty of the offence of infanticide (rather than manslaughter). It is possible for a defendant to be convicted of attempted infanticide.[112]

The offence or defence is described in section 1(1) of the Infanticide Act 1938:

Where a woman by any wilful act or omission causes the death of her child being a child under the age of twelve months, but at the time of the act or omission the balance of her mind was disturbed by reason of her not having fully recovered from the effect of giving birth to the child or by reason of the effect of lactation consequent upon the birth to the child, then, if the circumstances were such that but for this Act the offence would have amounted to murder or manslaughter, she shall be guilty of . . . infanticide, and may for such an offence be dealt with and punished as if she had been guilty of the offence of the manslaughter of the child.

The offence concerns the voluntary killing of a child under the age of one year by her mother. It is most often used where the defendant kills her child while suffering from post-natal depression.[113] Although section 1(1) talks about the disturbance being caused by the birth of the child, in fact, post-natal depression is rarely caused by the birth per se, but this is often overlooked by the courts.[114] However, in *Kai-Whitewind*[115] the Court of Appeal was strongly critical of the defence of infanticide because it was restricted to issues relating to the birth or lactation. The maximum sentence for the offence is life imprisonment, although most cases are dealt with by a probation order.[116] The defence is available only to mothers. Fathers who kill, suffering from the stresses of parenthood, will need to rely on the defence of diminished responsibility. It should also be noted that the defence is available only if the child killed is under the age of 12 months.

---

[110] Where it is charged as an offence there is no need to show that there was an intention to kill or cause grievous bodily harm, but rather simply that the relevant act or omission was wilful (*Gore* [2008] Crim LR 388).

[111] The Coroners and Justice Act 2009 amended the Infanticide Act 1938 to allow the defence to apply to manslaughter.

[112] *Smith* [1983] Crim LR 739.   [113] Mackay (1995: 207–14).

[114] Maier-Katkin and Ogle (1993). See Loughnan (2012b) for a helpful discussion.

[115] [2006] Crim LR 348.   [116] e.g. *Sainsbury and Lewis* [1990] Crim LR 903.

9 CONSTRUCTIVE MANSLAUGHTER

DEFINITION

To be guilty of constructive manslaughter the defendant must be proved to have performed an act which was:

(1) unlawful;

(2) dangerous; and

(3) caused the death of the victim.

The term 'constructive manslaughter' indicates that the crime is constructed from liability for a lesser crime. It is based on the theory that if a person kills in the course of committing a crime then he or she deserves to be guilty of manslaughter. This kind of manslaughter is sometimes known as 'unlawful act manslaughter'.

The House of Lords undertook a thorough examination of constructive manslaughter in the following case:

Attorney-General's Reference (No. 3 of 1994)
[1998] AC 245 (HL)

B stabbed his girlfriend (M) whom he knew was pregnant. Sixteen days after the stabbing M went into labour. The child, born grossly premature, managed to survive for 121 days in intensive care but eventually died. B was charged with the murder of the child. The House of Lords held that he could not be convicted of murder (see Chapter 3, Section 9 at p.164 for a discussion of that aspect of the case). In this extract Lord Hope considers whether B could be convicted of constructive manslaughter.

Lord Hope of Craighead

The *actus reus*

I have no difficulty in finding in the facts of this case all the elements which were needed to establish the *actus reus* both of murder and manslaughter. The *actus reus* of a crime is not confined to the initial deliberate and unlawful act which is done by the perpetrator. It includes all the consequences of that act, which may not emerge until many hours, days or even months afterwards. In the case of murder by poisoning, for example, there is likely to be an interval between the introduction of the victim to the poison and the victim's death. There may be various stages in the process between each of which time will elapse. The length of the interval is not now important: Law Reform (Year and A Day Rule) Act 1996. What is needed in order to complete the proof of the crime is evidence of an unbroken chain of causation between the defendant's act and the victim's death. Although we cannot now know, as the Court of Appeal have pointed out, whether the jury would have been satisfied on the issue of causation, there was clearly a sufficient case to go to the jury on this matter. There was a respectable body of medical evidence that the child was born prematurely as a result of the stabbing, and that it was as a result of the prematurity of her birth that she died. It was not disputed that injury to a foetus before birth which results in harm to the child when it is born can give rise to criminal responsibility for that injury. So the fact that the child was not yet born when the stabbing took place does not prevent the requirements for the *actus reus* from being satisfied in this case, both for murder and for manslaughter, in regard to her subsequent death.

The *mens rea*

The difficult issues all relate to the question whether B had the *mens rea* which would be required for him to be guilty of the child's murder or manslaughter. . . .

Murder

I have had the advantage of reading in draft the speech which has been prepared by my noble and learned friend, Lord Mustill. I gratefully adopt his analysis of the rules for the crime of murder and of their historical origin, and I agree entirely with the conclusion which he has reached that the *mens rea* for murder was not present in this case. . . .

Manslaughter

Criminal homicide is divided by common law into two separate crimes of murder and manslaughter. Manslaughter itself can be divided into various categories, depending on the context for the exercise. In regard to *mens rea* it is usually convenient to distinguish between (1) cases where the defendant intended to injure the deceased and (2) cases where the defendant had no such intention. Within the first category there are the cases (a) where he intended to cause grievous bodily harm to his victim but his criminal responsibility is reduced on the ground of provocation at the time of the act; and (b) where he intended to cause only minor harm to the victim but death ensues as a result of his act unexpectedly. Within the second category there are the cases (a) where the defendant's act was not unlawful but the death of the victim was the result of negligence of such a gross nature as to be categorised as criminal; and (b) where the defendant's act was both unlawful and dangerous because it was likely to cause harm to some person. The present case is an example of unlawful act manslaughter. But the placing of it into this category does no more than touch the surface of the problem where the ultimate victim of that act was not the intended victim and, moreover, was not even alive when the unlawful act was perpetrated.

. . .

So far as *mens rea* for the common law crime of manslaughter is concerned, I consider that it is sufficient that at the time of the stabbing B had the *mens rea* which was needed to convict him of an assault on the child's mother. That was an unlawful act, and it was also an act which was dangerous in the sense indicated by Humphreys J in *Rex v Larkin* (1943) 29 Cr App R 18, 23 in the passage which was quoted with approval by Lord Salmon in *Director of Public Prosecutions v Newbury* [1977] AC 500, 506–507. Dangerousness in this context is not a high standard. All it requires is that it was an act which was likely to injure another person. As 'injury' in this sense means 'harm,' the other person must also be a living person. A person who is already dead cannot be harmed any longer, so injury of the kind which is required is no longer possible. That is why it was held in *Reg v Church* [1966] 1 QB 59 that it was a misdirection for the jury to be told simply that it was irrelevant to manslaughter whether or not the appellant believed that the woman whom he threw into the river was already dead. But in this case injury to another living person—the child's mother—was the inevitable result of B's deliberate and unlawful act. Such was the character of the *mens rea* which B possessed when he committed the initial act in the series of events which resulted in the death of the child.

. . . Nor is it necessary, in order to constitute manslaughter, that the death resulted from an unlawful and dangerous act which was done with the intention to cause the victim to sustain harm. This is because it is clear from the authorities that, although the defendant must be proved to have intended to do what he did, it is not necessary to prove that he knew that his act was unlawful or dangerous. So it must follow that it is unnecessary to prove that he knew that his act was likely to injure the person who died as a result of it. All that need be proved is that he intentionally did what he did, that the death was caused by it and that, applying an objective test, all sober and reasonable people would recognise the risk that some harm would result.

. . .

The only questions which need to be addressed are (1) whether the act was done intentionally, (2) whether it was unlawful, (3) whether it was also dangerous because it was likely to cause harm to somebody and (4) whether that unlawful and dangerous act caused the death.

I think, then, that the position can be summarised in this way. The intention which must be discovered is an intention to do an act which is unlawful and dangerous. In this case the act which had to be shown to be an unlawful and dangerous act was the stabbing of the child's mother. There can be no doubt that all sober and reasonable people would regard that act, within the appropriate meaning of this term, as dangerous. It is plain that it was unlawful as it was done with the intention of causing her injury. As B intended to commit that act, all the ingredients necessary for *mens rea* in regard to the crime of manslaughter were established, irrespective of who was the ultimate victim of it. The fact that the child whom the mother was carrying at the time was born alive and then died as a result of the stabbing is all that was needed for the offence of manslaughter when *actus reus* for that crime was completed by the child's death. The question, once all the other elements are satisfied, is simply one of causation. The defendant must accept all the consequences of his act, so long as the jury are satisfied that he did what he did intentionally, that what he did was unlawful and that, applying the correct test, it was also dangerous. The death of the child was unintentional, but the nature and quality of the act which caused it was such that it was criminal and therefore punishable. In my opinion that is sufficient for the offence of manslaughter. There is no need to look to the doctrine of transferred malice for a solution to the problem raised by this case so far as manslaughter is concerned.

As Lord Hope's speech indicates, there are three elements of constructive manslaughter:

(1) The defendant must have done an unlawful act.

(2) The unlawful act must have been dangerous.

(3) The unlawful and dangerous act must have caused the death of the victim.

These will now be considered separately:

9.1 AN UNLAWFUL ACT

It is necessary to show that there is a criminal act. The prosecution in a case of constructive manslaughter should make it clear which criminal offence is being relied upon. It is not enough for the act to be a tort or a breach of contract; the act must be criminal, but not necessarily an act of violence.[117] The defendant must be shown to have committed both

---

[117] *DPP v Andrews* [1937] AC 576 (HL). In *Goodfellow* (1986) 83 Cr App R 23 (CA), criminal damage was the unlawful act.

the *actus reus* and the *mens rea* and not have a defence to the crime.[118] In *Dhaliwal*[119] a husband was abusive to his wife, causing her severe emotional trauma, which lead to her taking her own life. His prosecution for constructive manslaughter failed because it was found that reducing her to an emotional wreck was not an unlawful act. In Chapter 6 it will be explained why doing that was not an assault. Although the court was willing to accept he had caused her death, as there was no unlawful act there could be no conviction for constructive manslaughter. The prosecution would have done better to rely on gross negligence manslaughter.[120]

To be guilty of unlawful act manslaughter it does not need to be shown that the defendant intended or foresaw death or even an injury to the victim. The only *mens rea* required is that needed for the unlawful act. So, if the unlawful act is criminal damage, it need only be shown the defendant intended or was reckless as to damaging property belonging to another.[121]

In *Andrews v DPP* a driver killed a pedestrian while overtaking another car. It was accepted that the defendant was guilty of the offence of dangerous driving. The House of Lords stated that for constructive manslaughter an act which was intrinsically criminal was required and not just 'a lawful act with a degree of carelessness which the legislature makes criminal'.[122] This *dictum* is hard to interpret, but the generally accepted view seems to be that a strict liability offence[123] or an offence of negligence (e.g. dangerous driving) cannot form the basis of constructive manslaughter.[124] However, *obiter*, in *Meeking*[125] the Court of Appeal suggested that a negligent act could form the basis of a constructive manslaughter charge. The issue needs a clear ruling from the Court of Appeal.

There is some debate whether constructive manslaughter could arise from a criminal omission. There is no clear view. In *Senior*[126] the defendant failed to summon medical help for his child, who later died, and this was accepted as manslaughter. However, subsequently, in *Lowe*[127] the defendant also failed to call for medical assistance for a dying child, but the Court of Appeal suggested that constructive manslaughter could not be based on an omission. In practice if the case does involve an omission the prosecution may choose to present the case as one of gross negligence manslaughter, which undoubtedly can be committed by omission.[128] →5 (p.293)

9.2 DANGEROUS ACT

The unlawful act must be dangerous. This means that the act constitutes a risk of some physical injury.[129] A risk of an emotional harm (e.g. fear or panic) is insufficient,[130] unless it is likely that that emotional distress will lead to a physical injury, for example

---

[118] *Slingsby* [1995] Crim LR 570.   [119] [2006] EWCA Crim 1139.
[120] Horder and McGowan (2006).   [121] *R v JF and NE* [2015] EWCA Crim 351.
[122] [1937] AC 576, 584.
[123] Although in *Andrews* [2003] Crim LR 477 (CA) the Court of Appeal upheld a conviction for unlawful act manslaughter on the basis of a strict liability issue. The issue was not raised before the court.
[124] *Lamb* [1967] 2 QB 981 (CA). Negligent acts could, in an extreme case, amount to gross negligence manslaughter, which will be discussed later.
[125] [2012] EWCA Crim 641.   [126] [1899] 1 QB 283.   [127] [1973] QB 702.
[128] *Khan and Khan* [1998] Crim LR 830.   [129] *Carey* [2006] Crim LR 842.
[130] Although this represents the law on the present authorities, it might be arguable that following the acceptance by the House of Lords in *Ireland* [1998] AC 147 that actual bodily harm could include psychiatric injuries, it is not impossible that the issue could be open to re-examination.

by causing a heart attack. The understanding of dangerousness was stretched in *Carey*,[131] where it was suggested that shock could be included within the concept of physical harm. In *Johnston*[132] it was held that spitting and insulting an apparently healthy victim could not be regarded as dangerous, even if they in fact led to a cardiac arrest and death. The spitting was not 'likely' to cause death, even though in fact it did.

The jury should consider whether there is a risk that the act might cause an injury. In *Bristow*[133] a burglary from an isolated vehicle repair shop was held to be dangerous because if the burglars were interrupted they planned to escape by driving away at speed and that posed a risk of harm to the person who intervened. This is a somewhat controversial conclusion because it was not the criminal act (burglary) which itself caused the risk of the harm, but rather what the defendants might do if someone interfered.

Dangerousness is to be judged objectively. This means that there is no need to show that the defendant was aware that his act was dangerous; the question is whether a reasonable person in the defendant's shoes would appreciate that it was dangerous.[134] This is demonstrated by *Dawson*.[135] The defendant approached a petrol station which was staffed by a 50-year-old man. The defendant was armed with an imitation gun and the victim suffered a heart attack and died. The jury should have been asked whether a reasonable person in the defendant's shoes would have realized that his actions were likely to create a risk of physical injury.[136] The test is not quite a straightforward objective test. The jury should consider whether a reasonable person in the defendant's shoes *with any special knowledge that the defendant has* would have realized that the victim might suffer a physical injury. So, if the facts in *Dawson* had been different and the defendant had known that the petrol station attendant had a weak heart, then the court would certainly have found the act dangerous.[137]

Dawson can be contrasted with *JM and SM*[138] where the defendants got into a fight with a group of bouncers outside a club. One of the bouncers (who was not directly involved in the fight but had offered to help) suffered a heart aneurism and died. The conviction for constructive manslaughter was upheld. The fighting did create a risk of some harm and so was dangerous. It did not matter that the harm risked was not harm of the kind that actually occurred.[139]

In *R v JF and NE*[140] the Court of Appeal confirmed the law as set out in *Dawson*, but did suggest Parliament might consider whether reform of the law was needed. It might be argued, for example, that the offence should require the defendant foresaw a risk of death or serious harm to the victim. However, that is clearly not the current law.

An important case in this area is *Lamb*.[141] The accused and his friend were playing with a loaded gun. The accused checked that there was no bullet opposite the firing pin, and pulled the trigger. He had not appreciated that the chamber revolves when shot and so the chamber with a bullet moved to opposite the pin and the gun went off and his friend was shot. It was confirmed that although the act was dangerous (a reasonable person would have known that

---

[131] [2006] Crim LR 843.   [132] [2007] EWCA Crim 3133.   [133] [2013] EWCA Crim 1540.
[134] *R v JF and NE* [2015] EWCA Crim 351.   [135] (1985) 81 Cr App R 150 (CA).
[136] *Watson* [1989] 2 All ER 865 (CA).
[137] However, the unreasonable mistaken beliefs of the defendant are not to be attributable to the reasonable person in the defendant's shoes (*Ball* [1989] Crim LR 730).
[138] [2012] EWCA Crim 2293.   [139] *R v Bristow* [2013] EWCA Crim 1540.
[140] [2015] EWCA Crim 351.   [141] [1967] 2 QB 981 (CA).

the gun might go off) there was no unlawful act (he lacked *mens rea*) and so he could not be convicted of manslaughter.[142]

Where the defendant did a number of acts to the victim, it must be shown that the act that caused the death of the victim was unlawful and dangerous. In *R v Carey*[143] the defendant had punched the victim. This was unlawful and dangerous to the victim. But it was not that act which caused the victim's death, it was rather the defendant's aggressive behaviour (an affray) which caused the victim to run away, suffer a ventricular fibrillation and die. The affray was not dangerous in the sense that it was not likely to cause physical harm. Hence the defendant could not be convicted for unlawful act manslaughter.

9.3 CAUSATION

It is necessary to show that the unlawful and dangerous act caused the death of the victim. The normal rules of causation apply, for which see Chapter 2.

At one time it was suggested that the defendant's unlawful and dangerous act had to be 'aimed at' the victim.[144] This was rejected by Lord Hope in *Attorney-General's Reference (No. 3 of 1994)*,[145] where he confirmed that as long as there is an unlawful and dangerous act which causes the victim's death it does not matter if the act was directed towards someone else. So if the defendant pushes one person who falls over and knocks into someone else who also falls over and dies, constructive manslaughter is available.[146]

It must be shown that it was the unlawful and dangerous act of the accused that caused the death of the victim, and not simply that the victim died while the defendant was committing an unlawful and dangerous act. This appears to have been overlooked in *Cato*[147] where the defendant supplied unlawful drugs to the victim and then injected the victim with the drugs as a result of which the victim died. The Court of Appeal suggested that the unlawful act could be seen as the possession. With respect, this is hard to support. The possession did not cause the death. The better basis for a manslaughter conviction, which the Court of Appeal suggested as an alternative analysis, was that the injection by the accused was the offence of poisoning contrary to section 23 of the Offences Against the Person Act 1861. This unlawful and dangerous act was the act that caused the death.[148] The issue is particularly significant where there were a number of actions of the defendant which may have caused the death, some of which were unlawful and some of which were not. Then it must be proved that it was the unlawful and dangerous acts of the defendant which were a substantial and operating cause of death.[149]

We shall now turn to gross negligence manslaughter, but before doing so note that the concepts of constructive manslaughter and gross negligence manslaughter are not mutually exclusive.[150] In other words it is possible for a person to be guilty of manslaughter of both kinds at the same time.

---

[142] There was no assault because both boys were playing and there was no intention to frighten or cause harm.

[143] [2006] EWCA Crim 17.   [144] *Dalby* [1982] 1 All ER 916.   [145] [1997] 3 All ER 936.

[146] This actually happened in *Mitchell* (1983) 76 Cr App R 293 (CA), as a result of which the defendant was convicted of manslaughter.

[147] [1976] 1 WLR 110 (CA).   [148] See also *Kennedy* [2007] UKHL 38.

[149] *Johnston* [2007] EWCA Crim 3133.   [150] *Willoughby* [2004] EWCA Crim 3365.

10 GROSS NEGLIGENCE MANSLAUGHTER

> **DEFINITION**
>
> For gross negligence manslaughter it must be shown that:
>
> (1) The defendant owed the victim a duty of care.
> (2) The defendant breached that duty of care.
> (3) The breach of the duty caused the death of the victim.
> (4) The breach was so gross as to justify a criminal conviction.

The leading case on gross negligence manslaughter is the House of Lords' decision in *Adomako*:

R v Adomako
[1995] 1 AC 171 (HL)

Adomako was an anaesthetist who failed to notice for six minutes that a tube that supplied oxygen to his patient had become disconnected from the ventilator. As a result, the patient died. He was convicted of gross negligence manslaughter, but appealed on the basis that the judge had misdirected the jury.

Lord Mackay of Clashfern LC

The jury convicted the appellant of manslaughter by a majority of 11 to 1. The Court of Appeal, Criminal Division dismissed the appellant's appeal against conviction but certified that a point of law of general public importance was involved in the decision to dismiss the appeal, namely:

> 'In cases of manslaughter by criminal negligence not involving driving but involving a breach of duty is it a sufficient direction to the jury to adopt the gross negligence test set out by the Court of Appeal in the present case following *R v Bateman* (1925) 19 Cr App R 8 and *Andrews v DPP* [1937] AC 576 without reference to the test of recklessness as defined in *R v Lawrence* [1982] AC 510 or as adapted to the circumstances?'

[Having quoted from *R v Bateman* (1925) 19 Cr App R 8 and *Andrews v DPP* [1937] AC 576 **Lord Mackay** continued:]

In my opinion the law as stated in these two authorities is satisfactory as providing a proper basis for describing the crime of involuntary manslaughter. . . . On this basis in my opinion the ordinary principles of the law of negligence apply to ascertain whether or not the defendant has been in breach of a duty of care towards the victim who has died. If such breach of duty is established the next question is whether that breach of duty caused the death of the victim. If so, the jury must go on to consider whether that breach of duty should be characterised as gross negligence and therefore as a crime. This will depend on the seriousness of the breach of duty committed by the defendant in all the circumstances in which the defendant was placed when it occurred. The jury will have to consider whether the extent to which the defendant's conduct departed from the proper standard of care incumbent upon him, involving as it must have done a risk of death to the patient, was such that it should be judged criminal.

It is true that to a certain extent this involves an element of circularity, but in this branch of the law I do not believe that is fatal to its being correct as a test of how far conduct must depart from accepted standards to be characterised as criminal. This is necessarily a question of degree and an attempt to specify that degree more closely is I think likely to achieve only a spurious precision. The essence of the matter, which is supremely a jury question, is whether, having regard to the risk of death involved, the conduct of the defendant was so bad in all the circumstances as to amount in their judgment to a criminal act or omission.

. . . I am of the opinion that this appeal should be dismissed and that the certified question should be answered by saying:

'In cases of manslaughter by criminal negligence involving a breach of duty, it is a sufficient direction to the jury to adopt the gross negligence test set out by the Court of Appeal in the present case following *R v Bateman* (1925) 19 Cr App R 8 and *Andrews v DPP* [1937] AC 576 and it is not necessary to refer to the definition of recklessness in *R v Lawrence* [1982] AC 510, although it is perfectly open to the trial judge to use the word "reckless" in its ordinary meaning as part of his exposition of the law if he deems it appropriate in the circumstances of the particular case.'

. . .

Personally I would not wish to state the law more elaborately than I have done. In particular I think it is difficult to take expressions used in particular cases out of the context of the cases in which they were used and enunciate them as if applying generally. This can I think lead to ambiguity and perhaps unnecessary complexity. The task of trial judges in setting out for the jury the issues of fact and the relevant law in cases of this class is a difficult and demanding one. I believe that the supreme test that should be satisfied in such directions is that they are comprehensible to an ordinary member of the public who is called to sit on a jury and who has no particular prior acquaintance with the law. To make it obligatory on trial judges to give directions in law which are so elaborate that the ordinary member of the jury will have great difficulty in following them, and even greater difficulty in retaining them in his memory for the purpose of application in the jury room, is no service to the cause of justice. The experienced counsel who assisted your Lordships in this appeal indicated that as a practical matter there was a danger in over-elaboration of definition of the word 'reckless'. While therefore I have said in my view it is perfectly open to a trial judge to use the word 'reckless' if it appears appropriate in the circumstances of a particular case as indicating the extent to which a defendant's conduct must deviate from that of a proper standard of care, I do not think it right to require that this should be done and certainly not right that it should incorporate the full detail required in *R v Lawrence* [1982] AC 510.

Appeal dismissed.

The ruling in *Adomako* was challenged before the Court of Appeal in *Misra*[151] on two grounds. First, it was said to be inconsistent with the House of Lords' decision in *R v G and R*. Second, it was argued that it was inconsistent with the ECHR. The Court of Appeal rejected both challenges and confirmed that *Adomako* represents the current law on gross negligence manslaughter.

---

[151] [2004] EWCA Crim 2375.

It is clear from Lord Mackay's speech in *Adomako* that there are four elements of gross negligence manslaughter, which will be considered separately:

10.1   A DUTY

It must be shown that the defendant owed the victim a duty of care.[152] The Court of Appeal in *Wacker*[153] and *Evans (Gemma)*[154] confirmed that the 'duty of care' is usually to be given the meaning it has in the tort of negligence.[155] It is not possible to provide a complete analysis of when a duty of care arises under tort law. Much simplified, you owe a duty of care towards anyone who may foreseeably be harmed by your actions. Hence a driver owes a duty of care to other road users, a doctor owes a duty of care to a patient,[156] the captain of a boat owes a duty of care to the crew,[157] and an electrician owes a duty of care to the homeowner whose house he is rewiring.[158] The Court of Appeal in *Evans*[159] has confirmed that whether or not there is a duty of care on a given set of facts is a question of law for the judge to decide. Therefore the judge should direct the jury in terms: 'If you find the facts to be X then there is a duty of care, while if you find they are Y there is not.'[160]

EXAMINATION TIP

The law can get rather confusing where it is claimed that it was a defendant's failure to act which was grossly negligent. In that case the normal rules on omissions in criminal law apply and it is necessary to show that the defendant was under a duty to act (see Chapter 2), as well as demonstrating that the defendant was under the tort law duty of care. Fortunately wherever a criminal duty to act arises there will also be a duty of care in tort.

10.2   A BREACH OF A DUTY

It must be shown that the defendant breached his or her duty of care to the victim. In order to decide whether there is a breach of duty the jury must ask whether the defendant's action fell below the standard expected of the reasonable person. Where the defendant is purporting to exercise a special skill, the test is whether the defendant was exercising the skill expected of a reasonable person possessing that skill. So in *Adomako* the accused had to act as a reasonable anaesthetist. In that case the accused had raised arguments that he was exhausted after a long work shift and was inadequately trained. These did not affect the standard: the jury was not to consider whether it was reasonable for Adomako himself to

---

[152] The *Adomako* test is to be applied whether the case is about an act or an omission of the defendant (*Litchfield* [1998] Crim LR 507).

[153] [2003] Crim LR 108 (CA). However, on the particular facts of that case (the defendant killed many immigrants while illegally bringing them into the country) there was no liability in tort because of the doctrine of *ex turpi causa*, which prevents one criminal from suing another criminal for harm caused while pursuing a criminal enterprise together. The Court of Appeal explained that the public policy behind that rule did not bar a criminal conviction.

[154] [2009] EWCA Crim 650.   [155] See Herring and Palser (2007) for a detailed discussion.

[156] *Adomako* [1995] 1 AC 171 (HL).   [157] *Litchfield* [1998] Crim LR 507 (CA).

[158] *Prentice* [1993] 4 All ER 935 (CA).   [159] *R v Evans (Gemma)* [2009] EWCA Crim 650.

[160] Herring and Palser (2007) and Elliott (2010).

act as he did; but to consider whether he fell below the standard expected of a reasonable anaesthetist.[161]

10.3 CAUSING THE DEATH

It must be shown that the defendant's breach of the duty caused the victim's death. This is a straightforward application of the rules of causation. The point made in *Hayward*[162] is important. There the defendant was driving a horse and cart without holding the reins when he hit a young girl, killing her. Although he clearly caused the death of the girl, the court found that *his negligence* did not. It was found that even if he had been driving with all due care he would not have avoided hitting her: she ran out in front of him without warning. The simplest way for the jury to consider the question would be to ask: if the defendant had acted reasonably would the victim have been killed?

10.4 GROSS NEGLIGENCE

It must be shown that the defendant's breach of duty was gross. Lord Mackay in *Adomako* explained that the jury should ask themselves whether the defendant's actions or omissions were so bad as to deserve a criminal conviction. The point is that establishing that the defendant was negligent will mean that the defendant could be required to pay compensation to the victim (or his or her family). The jury must ask whether the law should go further and in addition require punishment for the wrong.

Adomako leaves the jury a wide discretion to decide whether to convict the accused. The jury can take all the facts into account and it is hard to predict how a jury will decide a particular case. It is likely that the jury will consider questions such as: did the defendant foresee that his or her actions or omissions would cause death? What were the motives influencing the defendant's actions or omissions? Was the defendant indifferent to the well-being of the victim? Were there any good explanations for why the defendant acted or failed to act as he or she did? In summary the jury will consider the 'badness' of the defendant's actions.[163]

The Court of Appeal in *Attorney-General's Reference (No. 2 of 1999)*[164] made it clear that it is *not* necessary to demonstrate that a defendant foresaw a risk of death before he or she can be convicted of gross negligence manslaughter. However, if the defendant did foresee death it is more likely that the jury will find the negligence to be gross than if he or she did not.

A slightly different question is whether it is possible to convict a person of gross negligence manslaughter if the risk of death was not foreseeable. In *Adomako* itself it is unclear whether Lord Mackay required that a risk of death be foreseeable. At one point he talked about gross negligence involving consideration of 'the risk of death involved', however, he also approved *dicta* in *Stone and Dobinson*[165] and *R v West London Coroner, ex p Gray*[166] which seemed to suggest that a risk to the health and safety of the victim

---

[161] The fact that the victim consented to the activity does not prevent a conviction for gross negligence manslaughter (*Wacker* [2003] Crim LR 108).

[162] (1908) 21 Cox CC 692.

[163] *R (Brenda Rowley) v DPP* [2003] EWHC 693 (Admin) approved of the use of 'badness' here.

[164] [2000] QB 796 (CA).   [165] [1977] QB 354.   [166] [1988] QB 467.

was sufficient, even if death itself was not foreseeable. In *Singh (Gurphal)*[167] the Court of Appeal approved the trial judge's direction that a risk of death must have been foreseeable by a reasonably prudent person. However, there was no real discussion of the issue in that case, so it may still be open to debate. Whatever the position is, it would be a most unusual case where death was not foreseeable but the jury decided that the negligence was gross. →6 (p.295)

11   SUBJECTIVE RECKLESS MANSLAUGHTER

DEFINITION

Subjective reckless manslaughter: the defendant killed the victim foreseeing a risk of death or serious injury.

If the defendant killed the victim, foreseeing a risk of death or serious injury, then he or she can be convicted of subjective reckless manslaughter.[168] It is, in fact, rare for a case explicitly to rely on subjective reckless manslaughter[169] because whenever there is subjective reckless manslaughter it will be possible to charge constructive or gross negligence manslaughter and these will be easier to prove. Therefore, although it is generally accepted to exist as a form of manslaughter,[170] there are no cases which discuss its exact definition.

QUESTIONS

1. Charles, a fierce opponent of European Monetary Union, throws paint at the Prime Minister. The Prime Minister pushes his bodyguard, Evander, in the way. Evander is covered in paint and as a result suffers a nasty rash. Evander is interested in alternative medicine and takes a herb recommended by Hu, a local herbalist. Evander suffers an allergic reaction to the herb and dies. Research just published indicates that one in two million people are known to be allergic to this herb. What offences, if any, have been committed? (Some causation issues are raised in this problem. Remember to consider the potential criminal liability of all 'suspects': Charles, the Prime Minister, and Hu all need to be considered.)

2. One Saturday, Thomas, the President of the International Pogo Stick Society, was travelling down the pavement of a crowded street on his pogo stick. He was jumping carefully when his attention was grabbed momentarily by a striking poster advertising colourful knitwear. When he looked back to where he was going, he realized that he was about to crash into Clare. He decided to attempt a highly complex manoeuvre which he thought would avert the accident. Unfortunately it failed and he landed on top of Clare, killing her and breaking her valuable watch.

---

[167] [1999] Crim LR 582.

[168] I use the term 'subjective reckless manslaughter' to avoid confusion with *Caldwell* reckless manslaughter, which was thought to exist at one time, but has now been replaced with gross negligence manslaughter.

[169] For a rare example, see *R v Lidar* [2000] 4 Archbold News 3.

[170] Law Commission Report No. 237 (1996: para. 2.26); Clarkson (2000).

> For guidance on answering this question, please visit the Online Resource Centre that accompanies this book: www.oxfordtextbooks.co.uk/orc/herringcriminal7e/.
>
> 3. Clare's fiancé, Michael, who has a mental age of nine and has difficulties in controlling his temper, had been walking beside Clare. He was so upset at what had happened that he picked up a traffic cone and threw it at Thomas, intending to cause him an unpleasant injury. Thomas parried the cone with his pogo stick, but the cone landed on the head of Alfred, a young child who was passing by. Alfred fell to the ground. Thomas immediately rushed over and attempted to give Alfred mouth-to-mouth resuscitation. Unfortunately it had been a long time since he had attended his first-aid classes, and his efforts resulted in asphyxiating Alfred, who died. What offences, if any, have been committed?

12 CAUSING OR ALLOWING THE DEATH OR SERIOUS PHYSICAL HARM OF A CHILD OR VULNERABLE ADULT

Section 5 of the Domestic Violence, Crime and Victims Act 2004 created the offence of causing or allowing the death of a child or vulnerable adult.[171] It is useful particularly where a child has died while in the care of adults and it is clear one of the adults killed the child, but it is not clear which one. The section 5 offence is committed if the following are proved:

(1) V (the child or vulnerable adult) has died as a result of an unlawful act of a person who was in the same household as the victim and had frequent contact with him or her;

(2) there was a significant risk of serious physical harm being caused to V by the unlawful act;

(3) either:

(a) D was the person whose act caused V's death or serious physical harm;[172] or

(b) D was or ought to have been aware that there was a significant risk of serious physical harm being carried out to V by an unlawful act and D failed to take such steps as he or she could reasonably have been expected to have taken to protect V from the risk;

(4) the killing or serious physical harm of V occurred in circumstances which D foresaw or ought to have foreseen.

The offence carries a maximum sentence of 14 years. It is to be noted that its *mens rea* is negligence. The test focuses on what D knew or ought to know and what D could reasonably be expected to have done to protect the victim.[173] The offence was justified as a means of protecting children's rights to protection from abuse.[174] In a case where there has been domestic violence the courts will bear in mind that it might be extremely dangerous for a mother, say, to contact the police about fears over what her abusive partner will do to their child.[175]

---

[171] For a detailed analysis of this offence, see Hoyano and Keenan (2007: 158–77); Herring (2008), Morrison (2013), and Clayton-Helm (2014).

[172] The reference to serious physical harm was added by the Domestic Violence, Crime and Victims (Amendment) Act 2012. See Clayton-Helm (2014) for discussion.

[173] *R v Khan (Uzma)* [2009] EWCA Crim 2.   [174] Hayes (2006).

[175] *R v Khan (Uzma)* [2009] EWCA Crim 2. See Herring (2007c).

PART II: THEORETICAL ISSUES IN HOMICIDE LAW

13 HOMICIDE: THE STATISTICS

Be prepared to be surprised by the statistics on homicide. The popular perception of homicide in England and Wales which is usually created by popular television dramas and 'who-done-it' detective books is far from the reality. Consider the following facts:

(1) In 2014/15 there were 534 recorded homicides in England and Wales.[176] The rate of homicide has fallen by almost half between the year ending March 2004 and the year ending March 2015, from 17 homicides per million population to 9 homicides per million population.

(2) The most likely victim of homicide is under the age of one. The least likely age group to be murdered are the 5–16-year-olds.[177]

(3) Female victims were more likely than male victims to be killed by someone they knew. Over three-quarters (80 per cent) of female victims knew the main suspect, compared with 50 per cent of male victims. In most of these cases, female victims were killed by a current or ex-partner (46 per cent of all female victims) while male victims were most likely to be killed by a friend or acquaintance (40 per cent). Of victims aged under 16, only 9 per cent were killed by a stranger.

(4) More men than women are victims of homicide: 65 per cent of homicide victims are men.[178]

(5) The vast majority of killers are men.[179]

The last statistic is perhaps the least surprising, but should be the most shocking. The causes of the link between masculinity and killing are outside the scope of this book, but they must dominate any understanding of homicide in practice.[180] It should be stressed that these statistics are based on the law's definition of homicide. As we shall see later, deaths on roads or in workplace 'accidents' are not described as homicides and so not included in the statistics.

14 THE STRUCTURE OF HOMICIDE

Different countries around the world structure their laws on homicide in a variety of ways the English criminal law recognizing basically two kinds of general homicide: murder and manslaughter.[181] The most serious offence is murder; the next is manslaughter. Then we move on to civil liability, where there is no criminal punishment. The defendant may be

---

[176] Office for National Statistics (2015a).   [177] Office for National Statistics (2015b).
[178] Office for National Statistics (2015a).   [179] *Ibid*.   [180] Chan (2001: ch. 1).
[181] Infanticide could be included as a third category, but this is rare and can be seen as a defence.

required to pay compensation (damages) for the loss caused, but does not suffer the censure attached to a criminal conviction or any form of punishment. At the end of the spectrum is a killing for which the defendant is neither criminally nor civilly liable. Cases where the killing was a pure accident and for which the defendant was not to blame fall within this category.

Under English and Welsh law, because there are only two kinds of homicide, each category has to be fairly broad. Lord Hailsham in *Howe*[182] explained:

> Murder, as every practitioner of the law knows, though often described as one of the utmost heinousness, is not in fact necessarily so, but consists of a whole bundle of offences of vastly differing degrees of culpability, ranging from brutal cynical and repeated offences like the so-called Moors murders to the almost venial, if objectively immoral, 'mercy killing' of a beloved partner.

Similarly, into the category of manslaughter will fall a whole range of killings: from an act just short of murder to a case where a person gently pushes the victim who falls over, bangs his or her head and dies.

The Law Commission following a review of the law concluded that the 'present law of murder in England and Wales is a mess'.[183] This has led to a wide ranging review of the current law. However, the government has, to date, only sought to implement some of their proposals relating to provocation and diminished responsibility, through the Coroners and Justice Act 2009. It has no plans to implement the more wide ranging proposals of the Law Commission in relation to homicide.

The way that homicide is structured in English and Welsh law is only one of a number of ways in which the law could be organized.[184] Before considering the alternatives it should be noted that there are two main reasons why the law may seek to distinguish killings by using different labels (e.g. murder and manslaughter).[185] This may be done in order to differentiate between serious and less serious killings so that the appropriate level of censure is attached to a conviction. Alternatively, the different categories may be used to manage the sentencing stage. For example, in English law a person convicted of murder *must* be given a life sentence, whereas if a defendant is convicted of manslaughter the judge has a wide discretion to decide the appropriate sentence.

Here are some of the alternative ways of structuring the law on homicide:[186]

14.1 CREATING A WIDE RANGE OF KINDS OF HOMICIDE

It would be possible to develop a far more complex structure, for example, by distinguishing between murders in the first degree, second degree, and third degree, and then having various levels of manslaughter. The degree of murder would depend on the moral blameworthiness of the defendant's state of mind. There could also be a range of partial defences to ensure as accurate a description as possible of the crime committed by the defendant. The advantage would be to have a more finely tuned system, although

---

[182] [1987] 2 WLR 568, 581.   [183] Law Commission (2004: para. 2.74).
[184] See Pillsbury (1998).   [185] See the discussion in Lacey (2000a).
[186] These suggestions are not necessarily mutually exclusive.

there would be problems in defining the exact distinction between the different grades of murder.

14.2 LEAVING DISTINCTIONS TO SENTENCING

Rather than widening the range of homicides it could be argued that we should have a single offence of homicide, which would replace murder and manslaughter.[187] The proposal would be that the differences between killings would be dealt with at the sentencing stage, rather than by seeking to distinguish them with different labels. The proposal raises the arguments over the 'fair labelling principle', which was discussed in Chapter 1: Is it justifiable to use the same label for offences which differ so much in their level of culpability? Also there is the question whether there is a special stigma attached to a murder conviction, which the law should utilize to signify that these are particularly heinous killings.

14.3 DISTINGUISHING ON THE BASIS OF THE VICTIMS

The law could also seek to distinguish between killings involving particular kinds of victims. For example, there could be special offences of murdering children or police officers. The argument in favour of this proposal is that public opinion regards such killings as more serious than other killings.[188] Others strongly oppose this proposal, arguing that the life of a child or a police officer is no more valuable than the life of anyone else. Therefore, whatever the public opinion is, as a matter of principle it would be improper to treat the deaths of some victims as worse than those of others.[189] In reply it could be argued that in the case of children the child's whole lifespan is destroyed, which makes the killing worse than that of an adult, or that the killing of a vulnerable person such as a child indicates a particular viciousness, which deserves a particular stigma.[190]

14.4 LABELLING THE METHOD OF KILLING USED

A murder or manslaughter conviction tells us nothing about the form of the killing. Murder could be by poisoning, shooting, or torture. Some jurisdictions take a different approach and distinguish between homicide based on the method of killing, for example seeing killing with guns as being particularly serious.[191] The difficulty with such an approach is that the kind of weapon does not necessarily reveal the blameworthiness of the conduct. A stabbing, for example, could be a vicious attack or an accident involving a knife.[192]

---

[187] Lord Kilbrandon in *Hyam v DPP* [1975] AC 55, 98.

[188] Although whether this is a reflection of public opinion (as opposed to what the tabloid press would say the public opinion is) is a matter of debate (see Mitchell (2000)). See also Elliot and de Than (2009), who argue that there is a case for treating cases of homicide involving domestic violence or racial aggravation more seriously than other homicides.

[189] Clarkson (2000).   [190] *Ibid.*

[191] Mitchell (2000) suggests that the general public do see the method of killing as relevant in assessing its seriousness. The Home Secretary has indicated that cases of murder using a firearm or explosive should be regarded as particularly serious and requiring a sentence of at least 30 years (Home Office 2003).

[192] *Larkin* (1943) 29 Cr App R 18.

15 THE *ACTUS REUS* OF HOMICIDE

Causation is discussed in Chapter 2. The *actus reus* of homicide also raises controversial issues in relation to abortion, euthanasia, or the medical treatment of neonates which will not be considered in this book.

> **FURTHER READING**
>
> Horder, J. (2012) *Homicide and the Politics of Law Reform* (Oxford: OUP).

16 NON-HOMICIDAL KILLINGS

There are many more people killed in road accidents or as a result of suicide than are murdered or are the victims of manslaughter. For example, in 2013 there were 6,708 deaths recorded by suicide in the UK and 1,713 people died in road accidents.[193]

Critics of the present approach argue that industrial and road killings may involve individuals showing a similar lack of regard for others' lives as those convicted for murder or manslaughter. Indeed it could be argued that if the law wanted to protect people from being killed it would do far better to enforce, or increase the regulation of, driving and safety at work than fine tuning the criminal law on homicide. It is not difficult to see why some critical scholars have argued that the law is concerned about protecting lives only if doing so does not involve interfering with the lifestyles of those who enjoy driving fast cars or engaging in dangerous business practices: there is one law for the poor killers and another for the rich ones. That said, the evidence suggests that juries are very reluctant to convict people who kill while driving.[194] So if there is prejudice here it seems to be a prejudice shared by the general public. Juries may well feel in driving cases, 'There but for the grace of God go I'.[195] Those who support the present law's approach argue that control of driving and industry through regulatory agencies can be more effective in protecting people's lives than the criminal law. Some of these issues and the appropriate form of regulation for corporations are discussed in greater detail in Chapters 4 and 13.

17 THE *MENS REA* FOR MURDER

As is clear from Part I of this chapter, the *mens rea* for murder is an intention to kill or cause grievous bodily harm. There are three main theoretical issues here:

17.1 THE MEANING OF INTENTION

This is discussed in detail in Chapter 3. One point worth emphasizing here is that at the exact borderline between murder and manslaughter (that is between intention and recklessness) the *Woollin* test applies and the jury is given an element of discretion to decide whether or not to find intention from evidence of foresight of virtual certainty.[196] Supporters of the

---

[193] Department for Transport (2014).   [194] Cunningham (2008).
[195] *Ibid.*   [196] Horder (1995a).

present law argue that this provides the jury with 'moral elbow room'[197] to decide whether the defendant deserves to be called a murderer. However, others such as William Wilson have been concerned about the discretion this gives to juries and have argued that 'Whether someone has committed murder is not a matter of opinion'.[198]

17.2 IS INTENTION THE APPROPRIATE *MENS REA*?

Some have argued that intention is not the most appropriate form of *mens rea* for murder. Relying on intent means that the present law on murder is both under- and over-inclusive.[199] Consider these two examples:

(1) A rogue plants a bomb on an aeroplane, having insured the goods on board. His plan is that the plane will explode, the goods be destroyed, and then he will claim money from the insurance company. However, the bomb has only a 90 per cent chance of working. He may not be able to be convicted of murder. Death or grievous bodily harm was not his purpose and he did not foresee that as virtually certain. However, such a bomber would be regarded by many people as deserving a murder conviction.

(2) A terminally ill woman pleads with her husband to kill her for months on end. The husband finally gives way to her wishes and kills her. He intends to kill her and faces a murder conviction, with its mandatory life sentence.

Do such examples indicate that intention is not the most suitable form of *mens rea* for murder?

Some suggest that, rather than looking at intention, the key question should be the attitude of the defendant.[200] Did he demonstrate a callous contempt for the value of other people's lives? Did the defendant show 'wicked recklessness'?[201] Did the defendant have a 'depraved heart, devoid of social duty, and fatally bent on mischief'?[202] Those who prefer to ask such questions argue that merely looking at intention or recklessness is too narrow and does not take into account all the moral and social evaluations that would be considered in making a full assessment of the defendant's blameworthiness.[203] Some people suggest that considering the defendant's attitude towards other people's lives is a better indication of his blameworthiness than considering how likely his action was to cause death.[204] ←2 (p.235)

QUESTIONS

1. What factors do you think the jury really take into account in deciding whether a defendant is guilty of murder or manslaughter?

2. Would asking juries to consider whether the defendant's attitude was 'wicked' or 'callous' focus the jury's mind on the really important question or would it lead to injustice, with different juries reaching different conclusions on cases involving similar facts?

---

[197] Horder (1995a).   [198] W. Wilson (2000: 28).   [199] Tadros (2006b).   [200] Pillsbury (1998).
[201] Goff (1988). The phrase comes from Scots law.   [202] W. Wilson (2000: 29).
[203] Ashworth and Horder (2013: 271–3).   [204] Gobert (1995).

3. If a husband, say, kills his terminally ill wife at her request because he cannot bear to see her suffer any more, should he be guilty of murder? If not, should this be because he lacked the *mens rea* for murder or should the law create a special defence?

17.3 THE FACT THAT INTENTION TO CAUSE GRIEVOUS BODILY HARM IS SUFFICIENT

The fact that an intention to cause grievous bodily harm is sufficient *mens rea* for murder is controversial. Lord Mustill[205] and Lord Steyn[206] have indicated that they would be willing to reconsider the law if an appropriate case was brought before the House of Lords. Lord Mustill in *Attorney-General's Reference (No. 3 of 1994)* stated 'the grievous harm rule is an outcropping of old law from which the surrounding strata of rationalisations have weathered away'.[207] In many ways this is a dispute over the application of the so-called correspondence principle, which is discussed in Chapter 3. Most commentators seem to fall within one of three camps:

(1) A strict understanding of the correspondence principle requires that the *mens rea* should always match the *actus reus*. Those who take this view argue that for murder the only appropriate *mens rea* is an intent to kill. To them the present law is clearly unacceptable.[208]

(2) Those who would be willing to take a more flexible interpretation to the correspondence principle might be happy if the law required the defendant to intend to kill or do a life-threatening act. For example, Lord Steyn in *Powell* recommended that the *mens rea* for murder should be an 'intention to kill or an intention to cause really serious harm coupled with awareness of the risk of death.'[209] Supporters of this view may be concerned that the phrase 'grievous bodily harm' in the present law is too wide—it is possible to cause grievous bodily harm which would be most unlikely to threaten life. For example, if D stabbed P in the leg, but P died because (unknown to D) she was a haemophiliac, D could be convicted of murder, as a stab in the leg could well be regarded as serious harm by a jury. The argument here is that if the defendant is aware that his or her action might endanger the victim's life, he or she has taken the victim's life into his or her hands and cannot complain if he or she is held fully responsible if death results.

(3) Those who reject the correspondence principle would see an intention to cause serious harm as crossing a moral threshold, at which point the defendant is responsible for creating his own bad luck. This might be used to support the present grievous bodily harm requirement, or could be used to support a wider rule, whereby it is sufficient that the defendant intended to commit an attack against the victim.[210]

---

[205] *Attorney-General's Reference (No. 3 of 1994)* [1997] 3 All ER 936, 945–6 (HL).
[206] *Powell* [1997] 4 All ER 545 (HL).   [207] [1998] AC 245, 258.
[208] Although note as Tadros (2006b) points out, you might argue that some very serious grievous bodily harms would be worse than death (e.g. where the victim was left for a long time in an agonizing condition).
[209] [1999] AC 1, echoing the Criminal Law Revision Committee, Fourteenth Report (1980).
[210] J. Gardner (1994a).

The Law Commission has undertaken a major review of the law of homicide.[211] The following is the summary of their proposals:[212]

Law Commission Report No. 304, *Murder, Manslaughter and Infanticide*
(London: TSO, 2006), paras 1.63–1.68

1.63 We recommend that there should be a new Homicide Act for England and Wales. The new Act should replace the Homicide Act 1957. The new Act should, for the first time, provide clear and comprehensive definitions of the homicide offences and the partial defences. In addition, the new Act should extend the full defence of duress to the offences of first degree and second degree murder and attempted murder, and improve the procedure for dealing with infanticide cases.

1.64 In structuring the general homicide offences we have been guided by a key principle: the 'ladder' principle. Individual offences of homicide should exist within a graduated system or hierarchy of offences. This system or hierarchy should reflect the offence's degree of seriousness, without too much overlap between individual offences. The main reason for adopting the 'ladder' principle is as Lord Bingham has recently put it (in a slightly different context):

> The interests of justice are not served if a defendant who has committed a lesser offence is either convicted of a greater offence, exposing him to greater punishment than his crime deserves, or acquitted altogether, enabling him to escape the measure of punishment which his crime deserves. The objective must be that defendants are neither over-convicted nor under-convicted . . .

1.65 The 'ladder' principle also applies to sentencing. The mandatory life sentence should be confined to the most serious kinds of killing. A discretionary life sentence should be available for less serious (but still highly blameworthy) killings.

1.66 Partial defences currently only affect the verdict of murder. This is because a verdict of murder carries a mandatory sentence. That sentence is not appropriate where there are exceptional mitigating circumstances of the kind involved in the partial defences. These mitigating circumstances necessitate a greater degree of judicial discretion in sentencing. The law creates this discretion by means of the partial defences which reduce what would otherwise be a verdict of murder, which carries a mandatory sentence, to manslaughter, which does not. Therefore, our recommended scheme does not extend the application of the partial defences to second degree murder or manslaughter. These offences would permit the trial judge discretion in sentencing and they therefore lack the primary justification for having partial defences.

The structure of offences

1.67 We believe that the following structure would make the law of homicide more coherent and comprehensible, whilst respecting the principles just set out above:

(1) First degree murder (mandatory life penalty)

    (a) Killing intentionally.

    (b) Killing where there was an intention to do serious injury, coupled with an awareness of a serious risk of causing death.

(2) Second degree murder (discretionary life maximum penalty)

    (a) Killing where the offender intended to do serious injury.

---

[211] For an excellent discussion of the issues surrounding reform of homicide law, see Horder (2008 and 2013).
[212] For detailed discussion of these, see Horder (2013), Ashworth (2007), W. Wilson (2006), and Taylor (2007).

(b) Killing where the offender intended to cause some injury or a fear or risk of injury, and was aware of a serious risk of causing death.

(c) Killing in which there is a partial defence to what would otherwise be first degree murder.

(3) Manslaughter (discretionary life maximum penalty)

(a) Killing through gross negligence as to a risk of causing death.

(b) Killing through a criminal act:

(i) intended to cause injury; or

(ii) where there was an awareness that the act involved a serious risk of causing injury.

(c) Participating in a joint criminal venture in the course of which another participant commits first or second degree murder, in circumstances where it should have been obvious that first or second degree murder might be committed by another participant.

Partial defences reducing first degree murder to second degree murder

1.68 The following partial defences would reduce first degree murder to second degree murder:

(1) provocation (gross provocation or fear of serious violence);

(2) diminished responsibility;

(3) participation in a suicide pact.

In the following passage, Professor Ashworth sets out some of his concerns about the Law Commission's proposed definition of murder:

A. Ashworth, 'Principles, Pragmatism and the Law Commission's Recommendations on Homicide Law Reform' [2007] *Criminal Law Review* 333 at 334–5

(a) Intention. The concept of intention will be relevant to the new murder 1 in both its forms, either intent to kill or intent to do serious injury. The Commission favours a definition along the lines of the existing law, rather than one that purports to make provision for a wider range of possibilities. Thus the simple definition should be "acting in order to bring a result about", a definition based on purpose but without the element of deliberation sometimes implied by that term. The extended definition, applicable where "the judge believes that justice may not be done unless an expanded understanding of intention is given", is the *Nedrick-Woollin* formula:

"an intention to bring about a result may be found if it is shown that the defendant thought that the result was a virtually certain consequence of his or her action."

Whatever position one holds on whether this extended definition should be regarded as a species of intention or as a separate culpability requirement, it is unfortunate that the Commission leaves open the possibility that a jury may decide that D thought the act was virtually certain to cause death and then go on to decide—for some unarticulated reason—that this does not amount to intention and therefore not to murder. In other words, D's foresight that the consequence is virtually certain allows the jury to "infer intention" or to "find intention" but does not *require* them to do so. The Commission defends giving this latitude to juries as "the price of avoiding complexity." The implication is that leaving juries with this "moral elbow-room" removes the need to make specific provision for possible scenarios such as Lord Goff's example of the man who throws his children from a burning building, believing it is virtually certain that they will die or suffer serious injury as a result but also believing that they are virtually certain to die if they remain in the building. However, for an offence as serious as murder, the aim should be to produce a tighter definition that *requires* juries to bracket foresight of virtual certainty with intention proper, leaving these unusual cases to be dealt with by (partial) defences or otherwise.

(b) Serious injury. Three issues may be raised here. First, the Commission is surely right to adopt "injury" in preference to "bodily harm", in the hope that "injury" will more easily encompass psychiatric illnesses. Secondly, the Commission decides against recommending that "serious injury" should be defined. This decision is not discussed in relation to murder 1, perhaps because it is assumed that the question whether or not an intended injury was "serious" will be overshadowed, in murder 1, by the question whether D was aware of the serious risk of causing death. The Commission merely states that juries "will not bring in a murder verdict unless the harm intended was very serious indeed." However, there is no reference to "very serious injury" in the recommended formula for murder 1, and one assumes that the prevailing reason for this is that the adjective "serious" has not caused problems in the past, when juries have been instructed in murder cases that the harm intended must have been "really serious harm." Thirdly, account must be taken of the likelihood that this head of liability for murder 1 will be much relied upon. Under existing law, the minimum task for the prosecution is to prove an intent to cause really serious harm. Under the recommended law, the minimum task for the prosecution would be to prove an intent to do "serious injury" combined with awareness of a serious risk of causing death. It is likely that many cases will turn on this head of liability, and, if so, this suggests some need for precision in the law. After all, where the prosecution prove that D intended only non-serious injury, coupled with awareness of a serious risk of causing death, that is a form of murder 2. So the difference between that category of murder 2 and the second head of murder 1 lies only in the distinction between injury and serious injury. It may well be concluded that any definition of "serious injury" would have to be so complex as to be counter-productive, since it would confuse juries and give rise to frequent appeals. But, given the vital boundary that it marks, one might have expected more exploration of the possibilities of a definition or partial definition.

(c) Serious risk. In its consultation paper the Commission argued that cases of an intent to cause serious injury should be classified as murder 2, rather than murder 1, largely on the ground that it is possible to intend serious harm without risking danger to another person's life. This is a widely-held criticism of the present GBH rule, that it fails to mark out a category of the most heinous killings. In its Report the Commission partly recants, as we have just noted, concluding that killings based on an intent to do serious injury do warrant classification as murder 1 if an awareness of a serious risk of causing death is also proved. The main argument for this is discussed in (d) below, but we must pause here on the term "serious". What is a "serious risk" of causing death? Risks may be ranged, theoretically, on a probability scale from 0 to 100. Nobody expects a criminal statute to specify a particular degree of probability, but it ought to indicate the approximate level of risk required. The Commission asserts that "serious risk" is one of those concepts that juries "can safely be left to apply to the facts of a case with a minimum amount of embellishment", and that minimum is found in the recommendation "that a risk is to be regarded as serious if it is more than insignificant or remote."

There are two weaknesses in this approach. The first is that the word "serious" is already used in a different sense in the same clause—intent to cause serious injury coupled with awareness of a serious risk of causing death. It is surely best to avoid that, especially when there are other statutes that use a phrase such as "a significant risk of serious harm", thereby avoiding the use of "serious" as indicating a degree of risk. If the Commission really wants to have "serious" rather than "significant", it needs to say much more about the difference. The second weakness is the Commission's suggestion that the term "serious" is preferred because it is not just a question of probability, but also one of "whether the risk ought to be taken seriously." Degree of risk is merely "one factor" in the assessment. Does this indicate a further evaluative element? Does it suggest that juries should be free to evaluate whether taking this degree of risk with someone's life might render the offence unworthy of the murder 2 label and sufficient only for manslaughter? If so, the Commission must explain the proper parameters of such crucial judgements. If not, the use of the word "serious" here should be reconsidered.

(d) *The moral equivalence thesis*. It is widely accepted that causing death with intent to kill is a paradigm case of murder, but the Commission now moves away from its previous position that this should be the only form of murder 1 and seeks to bring in killings where there is an intent to cause serious injury coupled with an awareness of a serious risk of causing death. Leaving aside the detailed comments above, is this a convincing move? The Commission justifies this change by arguing that in cases where these two features are united—the intent to do serious injury, and awareness of a significant risk of causing death— the killing is morally equivalent to causing death with intent to kill, the other form of murder 1. This approach avoids one objection to the current law, which is that a mere intent to cause GBH might amount to nothing more than an intent to break someone's arm or leg, which is not normally life-threatening. But it is hardly necessary for the Commission to go so far as to assert moral equivalence between the two heads of the new murder 1, and thereby to challenge the ingenious. It is enough to argue that such cases are morally closer to other cases of murder 1 than to other cases of murder 2. The Commission is recommending in effect that the two main forms of (what were formerly) murder 2 be top-sliced: the worst cases of killing with intent to do serious injury are those where D is also aware that a significant risk of death is being created, and the worst cases of killing by intentionally injuring someone in the knowledge that this creates a significant risk of death are those where D also intends to do serious injury. Where an offence is at the top of both categories of murder 2, as it were, it warrants inclusion within murder 1.

FURTHER READING

Blom-Cooper, L. and Morris, T. (2004) *With Malice Aforethought* (Oxford: Hart).

Goff, Lord (1988) 'The Mental Element in the Crime of Murder' *Law Quarterly Review* 104: 30.

Horder, J. (2008) 'Homicide Reform and the Changing Character of Legal Thought' in C. Clarkson and S. Cunningham (eds) *Criminal Liability for Non-Aggressive Death* (Aldershot: Ashgate).

Horder, J. (2012) *Homicide and the Politics of Law Reform* (Oxford: OUP).

Law Commission (2006b) Report No. 304, *Murder, Manslaughter and Infanticide* (London: TSO).

Loughnan, A. (2012b) 'The "Strange" Case of the Infanticide Doctrine' *Oxford Journal of Legal Studies* 32: 685.

Mitchell, B. (2009) 'More Thoughts about Unlawful and Dangerous Act Manslaughter and the One-Punch Killer' *Criminal Law Review* 502.

Norrie, A. (1999) 'After *Woollin*' *Criminal Law Review* 532.

Simester, A. (1999) 'Murder, *Mens Rea*, and the House of Lords—Again' *Law Quarterly Review* 115: 17.

Wilson, W. (2007) 'What's Wrong with Murder?' *Criminal Law and Philosophy* 1: 157.

18 DEFINING THE *MENS REA* FOR MANSLAUGHTER

We have just been discussing the exact boundary between murder and manslaughter, that is, the difference between the least serious kind of murder and the most serious kind of manslaughter. This section will discuss the debate at the other end of manslaughter: where the boundary should be drawn between the criminal offence of manslaughter and conduct which is not criminal, but which might attach civil liability (i.e. liability to pay compensation). Is it fair to convict people of manslaughter if they have not foreseen death or serious harm? Consider this scenario: Kian gives Shane a gentle shove. Surprisingly Shane falls over, bangs his head and dies. Having been shoved, 999 times out of a 1,000, Shane would just have stepped back. At the most Kian might have expected a conviction for assault, with a maximum sentence of six months. However, because Shane has died, Kian could be convicted of constructive manslaughter, one of the most serious of criminal offences, carrying a maximum sentence of life imprisonment. Some would say mere 'bad luck' should not affect someone's criminal liability to such an extent. Others argue that by the fact that the victim has been killed, 'an irrevocable evil has occurred',[213] and this was caused by the defendant's aggressive act, and that this should be acknowledged by a conviction for manslaughter.[214]

In the following passage, the Law Commission considers whether the offence of unlawful act manslaughter should be retained:

Law Commission Report No. 237, *Legislating the Criminal Code: Involuntary Manslaughter* (London: HMSO, 1996), paras 4.35–4.43

Part IV

. . .

4.35 As we saw in Part II, the present law provides that a person is guilty of 'unlawful act manslaughter' if she causes death by committing an act which is a crime in itself, and which carries a foreseeable risk of causing *some* injury to another person. A person who commits a relatively minor assault which unexpectedly causes death is thus guilty of manslaughter.

4.36 Our respondents were divided on the question whether this type of manslaughter, or something very close to it, should continue to exist. A number of different reasons were

---

[213] Duff (1990a).   [214] See Simons (2012).

given. For example, the Law Society, in its response to our consultation paper, was of the view that 'those who commit crimes involving, albeit slight, violence should take the consequences if the results turn out to be more catastrophic than they expected.' Mr Justice Rix agreed: 'It seems to me that once a person undertakes a violent act he sets himself deliberately . . . on a road which is not only seriously antisocial, . . . but potentially leading to calamitous results . . . [H]e has deliberately embarked on an act of criminal violence, which it is, or ought to be, well known, leads to incalculable consequences.' It is interesting that Rix J described the accused's culpability in terms of failing to advert to a 'well known' risk of causing serious harm: this is similar to the first criterion upon which we insisted in our discussion of 'culpable inadvertence' above.

4.37 Dr John Gardner, in his response, argued that the starting point in assessing criminal liability ought to be *what the actor did and the consequences of her action*:

> The first question, in all cases of culpability, is 'what did the defendant do?', the answer to which will be some concrete action with results and circumstances incorporated into it already, e.g. 'kill' . . . Then we must ask, naturally, to what extent the culpability is mitigated or moderated by the conditions under which the act was performed, including the accidental nature of the result etc . . . It is not 'why does the mere fact that someone happens to die add to one's crime, or make a major crime out of an otherwise venal act?', but rather, 'how does the mere fact that one kills accidentally serve to mitigate or otherwise intercede in the wrongness of killing?'

4.38 He did not, however, maintain that *all* killings should be subject to criminal sanction. First, he argued, the defendant must be *culpable in some way*, even if this culpability does not extend to the causing of death. Secondly, principles of justice and the rule of law require that the killer must have some *forewarning that her act will incur some criminal liability*. On his view, then, unlawful act manslaughter is, in principle, perfectly acceptable:

> . . . since the act was plainly dangerous, culpability is not eliminated, and this was still a wrongful killing. Then it is asked 'what protections are required to make sure that the defendant has not been taken totally unawares by the law?'—to which the answer is that the act must have been criminal under some other heading *as well as* dangerous, so as to put the defendant on legal notice.

4.39 Unless one accepts moral luck arguments, it is not clear *why* a person ought to be held criminally responsible for causing death if death or serious injury were the *unforeseeable* consequences of her conduct, just because she foresaw, or it was foreseeable, that *some* harm would result. Surely a person who, for example, pushes roughly into a queue is morally to blame for the foreseeable consequences of her actions—that a few people might get jostled, possibly even lightly bruised, and that people might get annoyed—but not for causing a death if, quite unexpectedly, she sets in train a series of events which leads to such an outcome. We consider that the criminal law should properly be concerned with questions of moral culpability, and we do not think that an accused who is culpable for causing *some harm* is sufficiently blameworthy to be held liable for the unforeseeable consequence of death.

4.40 One final argument in favour of recommending that a person ought to be liable for causing death, even if death or serious injury were not foreseeable consequences of her action, would be that this would be necessary for the protection of the public. This argument was considered by the Royal Commission on Capital Punishment which, in 1953, recommended the abolition of the doctrine of constructive malice in murder:

> We think it would be generally agreed that any liability for constructive crime offends against modern feeling, and that any departure from a subjective test of criminal

liability can be justified, if at all, only if it is clearly established that it is essential for the protection of the public.

The Royal Commission concluded that the public would be adequately protected by the existence of other criminal offences—principally, it has to be said, manslaughter.

. . .

4.42 Since, in the cases here under discussion, the risk of causing death or serious injury was neither foreseen by the accused, nor foreseeable by her, it is difficult to see what deterrent effect would be achieved by imposing criminal liability for causing death which would not be achieved equally by imposing liability for the appropriate non-fatal offence.

Conclusion

4.43 In conclusion, we consider, as a matter of principle, that the criminal law ought to hold a person responsible for unintentionally causing death only in the following circumstances:

(1) when she unreasonably and *advertently* takes a risk of causing death or serious injury; or

(2) when she unreasonably and inadvertently takes a risk of causing death or serious injury, where her failure to advert to the risk is culpable because

(a) the risk is obviously foreseeable, and

(b) she has the capacity to advert to the risk.

The Home Office published a Consultation Paper in 2000[215] which accepted the proposals of the Law Commission, but also sought consultation on whether a person who killed someone while intentionally committing another offence should be convicted of manslaughter. There is no sign yet of legislation putting any of this into force. In the 2006 Law Commission Report the following offence was proposed to replace constructive manslaughter:

Killing another person:

(a) through the commission of a criminal act intended by the defendant to cause injury, or

(b) through the commission of a criminal act that the defendant was aware involved a serious risk of causing some injury.[216]

It should be clear from this discussion that subjectivists in particular are unhappy with the present state of the law. To them it is objectionable that a defendant can be guilty of manslaughter, even though he or she did not intend or foresee the death of the victim. The present law on the *mens rea* for constructive manslaughter is well short of the subjectivists' ideal. In relation to constructive manslaughter the defendant needs the *mens rea* only for a criminal offence, which could just be the *mens rea* required for criminal damage, for example.[217] It is even worse in the case of gross negligence, where it is not necessary to show that the defendant foresaw anything. Even objectivists may take the view that the present law is too wide because for constructive manslaughter it is not even necessary to show that

---

[215] Home Office (2000).   [216] Law Commission Report No. 304 (2006b: para. 2.163).

[217] Mitchell (2000) suggests that a conviction in such a case would not accord with the views of the general public.

a reasonable person would have foreseen the risk of death or serious harm. All that needs to be shown is that *some* harm was *foreseeable*. ←5 (p.271)

In the following extract Victor Tadros sets out some of his concerns about the law on gross negligence manslaughter:

V. Tadros, 'The Limits of Manslaughter' in C. Clarkson and S. Cunningham (eds) *Criminal Liability for Non-Aggressive Death* (Aldershot: Ashgate, 2008), 49–52

The *Adomako* test has been criticised for its circularity: it defines what is criminal by referring to what should be criminal. But I don't think that this circularity is vicious, in principle at least. We should expect coherence at the outer limits of the criminal law; the distinction between criminal and non-criminal behaviour should be set by comparable levels of fault. Given that, there is nothing wrong in principle with comparing putative gross negligence cases to the line that is drawn between criminal and non-criminal conduct more generally to determine whether the defendant's fault was sufficient to warrant the imposition of criminal responsibility. If the appropriate fault level in other offence contexts is easier to draw precisely, there is nothing wrong with a test that fixes less precise concepts by inviting comparison with the fault level in those contexts. The problems with the test are otherwise.

First, the criminal law includes a number of offences of strict liability, where there is no fault requirement, as well as a number of offences with 'due diligence' defences. In England and Wales there is no formal distinction between 'true' criminal law and regulatory offences. Manslaughter is obviously a 'true' criminal offence, but in determining the scope of gross negligence what other offences provide appropriate comparisons for determining whether the defendant's conduct was criminal? The criminal law as it stands doesn't provide an appropriate set of standards of criminality in other offence contexts against which gross negligence cases can be compared.

. . .

Secondly, juries have the role of determining whether the defendant was grossly negligent. But they lack the knowledge of the relevant standards in other contexts to do the comparison in the appropriate way. So they are likely to fall back on their own understanding of what should count as criminal. But the scope of the criminal law is to be determined by public reason, and decisions by juries cannot provide the appropriate kind of public reason for these purposes. In fact, given that juries play a silent and passive role in trials, it is questionable whether their decisions can be regarded as part of public reason at all. If the test in *Adomako* is intended to reflect personal decisions by the jury about the proper scope of the criminal law rather than setting the fault standard by reference to other parts of the criminal law, it will not achieve the desired coherence, and it will not be subject to the appropriate constraints of a public system of law . . .

Thirdly, including the duty of care as part of a *mens rea* concept is confusing and unhelpful. There is an important question about the circumstances in which liability might be imposed with respect to outcomes which are caused as a consequence of a failure on the part of the defendant to act where he has a duty to do so. But that question is not obviously dependent on the particular nature of the outcome. There is no obvious reason why the question should be asked in cases where death is caused, rather than cases where the victim suffers grievous bodily harm (GBH) for example. But as gross negligence is the *mens rea* only of manslaughter, and not for assault occasioning GBH, for example, the law is only likely to become incoherent on this issue. The better approach is to treat the question of omissions liability in the general part of the criminal law, and that is so even if there is some variation about how it should apply across offence contexts.

Fourthly . . ., in inviting the defendant to be convicted in respect of the standard of conduct shown rather than by reference to any awareness of the risk or failure with respect to his attitude towards others, the test invites convictions in cases where the defendant did not display the kind of vice appropriate to ground criminal responsibility. Arguably *Adomako* was one such case, in that the defendant in the case did everything that he believed to be appropriate to ensure that the victim did not come to harm. He could not be criticised for lack of care for the victim, only for lack of ability as an anaesthetist. A person's lack of ability provides an inappropriate basis on which to convict him, particularly in those institutional settings such as hospitals where others have the responsibility to ensure that workers have the appropriate training and capabilities.

Fifthly, why is gross negligence the appropriate *mens rea* of manslaughter at all? The lower limit of manslaughter should be set by recklessness, and recklessness should be defined in a way that is neither purely subjective (as it has recently been in the context of criminal damage) nor purely objective (which would make it similar to gross negligence). It is not clear that having different concepts of gross negligence and recklessness in different offence concepts helps to ensure that the law is clear and consistent or that convictions are imposed only in deserved cases. Why should recklessness be the appropriate concept to use in criminal damage, for example, but not in manslaughter?

QUESTIONS

1. Do you agree with the view that the criminal law should start with the fact that the defendant killed the victim and then consider whether there is a reason why the defendant should not be held responsible for the victim's death, or should we focus on the defendant and ask whether there is any reason why the defendant should be held responsible for the victim's death (see the two quotations in the Law Commission Report excerpt from J. Gardner (1998))? Read again the material in Chapter 3 on the correspondence principle before answering this.

2. Had Dr Adomako's (see Section 10 at p.274) negligent actions left the victim in a seriously disabled condition, but not killed him, there would have been no criminal liability for any offence. Is it right that the fact that death has been caused means we are more ready to convict a defendant?

Particular controversy surrounds gross negligence manslaughter. Is it appropriate to hold a person criminally responsible when he or she is not even aware that his or her actions are liable to cause harm to another?[218] You should reread the parts of Chapter 3 on when, if at all, it is appropriate to punish people for negligence.

There are some particular concerns about the use of gross negligence manslaughter in *Adomako*:

(1) It is said that the *Adomako* test is circular. This is because if the jury asked a judge: 'How do we know if the defendant's negligence was bad enough to be criminal?', they would have to be told, 'It is if you think it is.' The jury is given no guidance on what factors they

---

[218] See e.g. Alexander (2000).

should take into account in reaching their decision. To supporters of *Adomako* this gives the jury a wide discretion to decide whether the defendant deserves a criminal conviction, using the standards of the community. To opponents it too readily leads to inconsistent verdicts being reached on cases of similar facts. Consider the case of a junior doctor, exhausted after working a ridiculously long shift, who negligently causes the death of a patient. It is not difficult to imagine some juries being very sympathetic to such a defendant and deciding that his negligence is not gross, but other juries being less sympathetic and convicting. As Simon Gardner[219] points out, asking the jury to decide whether a person is tall produces uncertainty because we do not have an agreed idea of at exactly what height someone becomes tall. But, he suggests, the uncertainty in the *Adomako* test is worse than the uncertainty in the 'tall person' case. This is because with tallness we are agreed on what we are measuring (i.e. height), even if it is unclear exactly where the boundary is between being tall and being short. However, with the *Adomako* test the jury is not given guidance on what criminality is.

(2) Many cases of gross negligence involve people acting in a professional capacity, and some argue that punishing such cases is inappropriate.[220] The point can be made that people such as doctors, managers, or electricians are normally acting for good reasons and are doing things that are socially useful, even if doing them incompetently.[221] Contrast one person shoving another in a queue who is doing nothing of social benefit. To other people this involves treating professional, middle class killers more leniently than others. There is another issue here and that is the concern that punishing the individual in question might disguise the fact that the defendant's employer is in fact the person who really deserves blame. Take the facts of *Adomako*. Adomako claimed he had never been properly trained and that he was exhausted after working extremely long hours. Was not the proper blame in that case to attach to a health system which employs under-trained people and works them to the bone, rather than to the individual himself? By focusing on Adomako's liability such questions can be neatly avoided.

(3) The Crown Prosecution Service has complained that it is particularly difficult for it to decide whether or not to prosecute someone for gross negligence following an 'accident'. In part this is because it is so difficult to predict how a jury will respond to a particular case.[222] ←6 (p.278)

In response to these and other criticisms, the Law Commission has recommended a reform of gross negligence manslaughter. Their proposed definition is as follows:[223]

> We recommend the adoption of the definition of causing death by gross negligence given in our earlier report on manslaughter:
>
> (1) a person by his or her conduct causes the death of another;
>
> (2) a risk that his or her conduct will cause death . . . would be obvious to a reasonable person in his or her position;
>
> (3) he or she is capable of appreciating that risk at the material time; and
>
> (4) . . . his or her conduct falls far below what can reasonably be expected of him or her in the circumstances . . .

---

[219] S. Gardner (1995b).   [220] Quick (2010).   [221] Clarkson (2000); Quick (2006).
[222] See Quick (2006) for a discussion of the lack of guidance for prosecutors. See also *R (Stephens) v DPP* (QBD, 19 October 2000), where the Crown Prosecution Service's decision not to prosecute for gross negligence manslaughter was challenged by way of judicial review.
[223] Law Commission Report No. 304 (2006b: para. 3.60).

QUESTIONS

1. Imagine you are working for the Crown Prosecution Service. You are handed a file about two teachers who were in charge of a group of children doing a mountain climbing expedition. The teachers failed to check the weather forecast before they went out and an appalling storm set in. In the terrible conditions a child was separated from the group and died. Should there be a prosecution for gross negligence manslaughter? Is it a relevant consideration that teachers may decide not to volunteer to take school trips if there is a prosecution? Would it be relevant whether the local education authority had failed to issue guidance on school trips?

2. Shriver (2003: 157) writes through a character in a novel: 'I'm tremendously sympathetic with the sort of diligent mother who turns her back for an eye blink—who leaves a child in the bath to answer the door and sign for a package, to scurry back only to discover that her little girl has hit her head on the faucet and drowned in two inches of water. Two inches. Does anyone ever give the woman credit for the twenty-four-hours-minus-three-minutes a day that she has watched that child like a hawk? . . . Oh, no. We prosecute these people, we call it, "criminal parental negligence" and drag them to court through the snot and salty tears of their own grief. Because only the three minutes count, those three miserable minutes that were just enough.' In the light of this, is it right to punish people who are normally dedicated to the concerns of others for a moment's inadvertence?

3. Mitchell (2007) argues that in practice whether a defendant is found guilty of murder or manslaughter depends less on the legal definitions and more on the behaviour and attitudes of those who investigate, prosecute, and defend homicides, not to mention the vagaries of the jury. Does this suggest criminal lawyers should not become too obsessed about the precise definitions of murder and manslaughter?

FURTHER READING

Ashworth, A. and Mitchell, B. (eds) (2000) *Rethinking English Homicide Law* (Oxford: OUP).

Horder, J. (ed.) (2007) *Homicide in Comparative Perspective* (Oxford: Hart).

Horder, J. (2013) *Homicide and the Politics of Law Reform* (Oxford: OUP).

Keating, H. (1996) 'The Restatement of a Serious Crime' *Criminal Law Review* 535.

Mitchell, B. (2007) 'Distinguishing between Murder and Manslaughter in Practice' *Criminal Law Journal* 30: 318.

Mitchell, B. (2009) 'More Thoughts about Unlawful and Dangerous Act Manslaughter and the One-Punch Killer' *Criminal Law Review* 502.

Quick, O. (2006) 'Prosecuting Gross Medical Negligence Manslaughter, Discretion, and the Crown Prosecution Service' *Journal of Law and Society* 33: 421.

Quick, O. (2010) 'Medicine, Mistakes and Manslaughter: A Criminal Combination?' *Cambridge Law Journal* 69: 161.

Simons, K. (2012) 'Is Strict Criminal Liability in the Grading of Offences Consistent with Retributive Desert? Strict Liability in Grading' *Oxford Journal of Legal Studies* 32: 445.

Tadros, V. (2006b) 'The Homicide Ladder' *Modern Law Review* 69: 601.

Tadros, V. (2008b) 'The Limits of Manslaughter' in C. Clarkson and S. Cunningham (eds) *Criminal Liability for Non-Aggressive Death* (Aldershot: Ashgate).

19 LOSS OF CONTROL

19.1 THEORY

The loss of control defence (provocation, as it used to be) is one of the most controversial defences in English and Welsh law and has received an enormous amount of academic attention. At the heart of much of the debate is a discussion about what is the theoretical basis of the defence. To simplify matters three versions will be presented here:

The 'pure excuse' view

This view[224] is based on the argument that a defendant who acts having lost self-control is not fully responsible for his actions.[225] Provoked defendants are far less to blame, having killed in the heat of the moment, than those who kill in cold blood.[226] It might be said that defendants who lost self-control did not calmly choose to act in the way they did, or did not have a fair opportunity to act otherwise. However, because defendants in loss of control cases had *some* control over their actions they are not granted a complete excuse and are still guilty of manslaughter.[227] This version of the defence of loss of control sees it as almost a form of diminished responsibility.

Those who oppose this view might ask, as Andrew Ashworth[228] has done, whether it is right to provide a defence to a person who loses his or her self-control and kills on being arrested by a police officer. If there is to be no assessment of whether it was right or appropriate to lose self-control such a person would be entitled to a defence. Those who take the pure excuse view might reply that they would be happy to allow a defence in such a case, pointing out that a manslaughter conviction can carry a life sentence. The loss of control defence in such a case acknowledges that the killing was not as serious as a callous, premeditated killing of the police officer in similar circumstances would be. ←3 (p.238)

The 'justification' view

This approach argues that loss of control should be available as a defence when the defendant was partially justified in doing what he or she did. In other words that there was something reasonable about what the defendant did, even if it was not fully justifiable.[229] It is this that distinguishes loss of control from diminished responsibility. (See the Horder extract later

---

[224] The differences between an excuse and a justification are explained in detail in Chapter 12.

[225] Uniacke (2007) provides a sophisticated development of this view.

[226] Mousourakis (1998a).   [227] Smith and Wilson (1993).   [228] Ashworth (1976).

[229] Dressler (2002b: 972) doubts that it is possible to be partially justified: 'Either a person has a right to act in a certain manner or he does not.'

in this chapter which develops this point.) There are two main ways in which commentators have suggested that a loss of control killing could be regarded as partially justified:

(1) The victim caused his or her own death by either threatening or wronging the defendant. In other words both the victim and the defendant must share responsibility for the death.[230]

(2) In the light of the qualifying trigger some display of righteous anger was appropriate. If a man confesses to parents that he has molested their child some display of anger or outrage is expected from the parents. Indeed to remain unperturbed in the face of such a confession could be regarded as immoral. It is true that killing may be an over-reaction in the face of such provocation, but that is reflected in the fact that the defendant is still convicted of manslaughter and not given a complete defence. The defence acknowledges that there was something good about what the defendant did (he was right to display indignation) even though in killing he used an inappropriate way of demonstrating his anger.[231]

The 'reasonable excuse' view

A middle approach between these two views accepts that the basis of the defence is an excuse, namely that the defendant was not in full control of his or her behaviour and therefore it does not necessarily reveal bad character, but that this can provide an excuse only if it was appropriate for the defendant to recognize the wrong and suffer the loss of self-control.[232] A central part of the loss of control defence is therefore an assessment of whether the defendant had a good reason for responding to the wrong or fear of violence as he or she did. In other words the defendant must show not only that he or she lost self-control, but also that he or she ought to have displayed his or her indignation at the wrong in that way.

In the following passage Alan Norrie considers whether the new loss of control defence has a different theoretical basis from the old law on provocation:

A. Norrie, 'The Coroners and Justice Act 2009—Partial Defences to Murder (1) Loss of Control' [2010] *Criminal Law Review* 275 at 277–9

The Underlying Philosophy

If this is a bare summary of what has happened, consideration of the nature of the reform and the likely issues to which it will give rise depend on understanding the underlying philosophy of the changes proposed. Here a significant change occurred. In their first report, the Law Commission distinguished two approaches to provocation, one with a justificatory, the other with an excusatory basis. While acknowledging that this was problematic, the Commission felt it did produce helpful arguments, and the distinction between the two operates to identify two different philosophies of provocation. What are these? The first is that of what I shall call *imperfect justification*, and it is this which informs the Law Commission's own thinking. In this view, anger is not a morally impermissible emotion, for it reveals a normal and, at one level, appropriate, even perhaps virtuous, response to certain forms of words or action. How this insight fits with the law is complex and operates at two

---

[230] McAuley (1987).   [231] For a critique of the concept of loss of control, see Mitchell (2011).
[232] J. Gardner (1998b).

different levels. Some would argue that "anger cannot ethically afford any ground for miti-gating the gravity of deliberately violent action", but the counter-argument is that it "can be an ethically appropriate emotion and that . . . it may be a sign of moral weakness or human coldness not to feel strong anger". Even in this view, however, anger cannot justify outright a violent response, certainly not a killing. Nevertheless,

> "a killing in anger produced by serious wrongdoing is ethically less wicked, and there-fore deserving of a lesser punishment, than, say, killing out of greed, lust, jealousy or for political reasons".

Where a

> "belief that the provoked [person] has been wronged by the provoker . . . is justified, it does not justify the provoked person in giving vent to his or her emotions by resort-ing to unlawful violence, however great the provocation. Two wrongs do not make a right. However, . . . there is a distinction in moral blameworthiness between over reaction to grave provocation and unprovoked use of violence."

This idea of responding by way of an action that requires a nuanced and complex judgment of *both* its particular rightfulness *and* its overall wrongness I seek to catch by the term "imperfect justification". Note that in this approach, no reference need be made to a loss of self-control, for on this account, it is the way that anger righteously informs action, albeit in a context of overall wrongness, that provides the element of justification to set against the overall sense of a wrongdoing. On this model, it would be inappropriate to require a loss of self-control as a part of the defence. The defendant need not be out of control, though he or she acted when the "blood was up". Indeed to be out of control might take the moral edge off what has been done in righteous, but sanctionable, anger. Note also that what is true of anger is also true of fear, for fear too may be an appropriate and justified, if overall wrong-ful, emotional response. With both anger and fear, "there is a common element namely a response to unjust conduct".

If this is the approach of the Law Commission, how does it compare with the previous law and its underlying theoretical approach? As the Law Commission point out, the approach informing the 1957 Act was not one of justification but one based on excuse. Though they do not elaborate it, I would call it one of *compassionate excuse*. This reflects the fact that the person is held to have lost self-control, so that their act is intrinsically marked from the first as wrong. It is (arguably) one thing to act out of morally appropriate anger, remaining in control of one's actions, the new approach. It can never be right at any level to lose one's control, for this entails a defect in one's rationality, the sine qua non of moral action. Loss of self-control, hijacking reason, is a problem from the start. At the same time, it can in appropriate circum-stances be understood, sympathised with, and therefore be partially condoned or excused. The law condemns the act both for the wrong done *and* the loss of control, but still extends a compassionate hand to the actor. This is the basis for the idea that provocation is a conces-sion to human frailty, for the loss of self-control and its consequence is condemned, but the weakness it represents is viewed with sympathy. Note in this, by the way, the crucial rider "in appropriate circumstances", for it is not every loss of self-control that will produce sympathy. Much will depend on the moral quality of the provocation to which there was a reaction, as well as to the particular human circumstances of the defendant. What was it about both the provocation and the provoked defendant that caused her to lose self-control, and is the "ordi-nary person" sympathetic to their plight? Is their weakness something that can be condoned on a "there but for the grace of God go I" basis? In sum, if the moral mark of the new Law Commission approach is that conduct is imperfectly rightful, and therefore both condemned

> and partially vindicated, the mark of the old law was that conduct was partially excused, both wrongful and partially condoned on ground of compassion. This, as we shall see, marks out two different territories for the old law of provocation and the new law of loss of control. I now return to the core problems that led to change in the law.

Many of the disputes over the elements of loss of control in fact reflect a dispute over the correct understanding of the defence.[233] We will consider some of the most controversial issues:

19.2 THERE MUST BE A QUALIFYING TRIGGER

As noted in Part I, the present law requires that there must be something said or done which amounts to a qualifying trigger and which caused the defendant to lose his or her self-control. Some who take the pure excuse view argue that this aspect of the present law is unsatisfactory because as long as the defendant lost his or her self-control it should not matter what caused it.[234] However, those who take the justification or reasonable excuse view require there to be a sufficiently serious triggering event if the defendant's action or loss of control is to be justified. They therefore support the approach of the present law.[235] ←4 (p.241)

19.3 THE OBJECTIVE REQUIREMENT

Under the old law of provocation, the courts struggled with the question of to what extent the defendant's characteristics should be relevant in assessing the gravity of the provocation or the level of self-control expected. The new loss of control defence appears to make it clear that only age and sex can affect the degree of tolerance and self-restraint expected. However, other characteristics can be taken into account when considering how a person with a normal degree of tolerance and self-restraint would respond. The debates over the objective requirement reflect a dispute over the role it should play in the defence:

An evidentiary role

The role of the objective test is no more than a 'double check' to provide evidence that the defendant really lost his or her self-control. If there is evidence that the defendant had lost his or her self-control and that a normal person would have, then we can be confident that the defendant did truly lose his or her self-control. Those taking such an approach would be happy to consider how a reasonable person with all of the defendant's characteristics would react because this would provide the most accurate evidence of the defendant's state of mind.

Although this could be an approach a legal system could take, it does not seem to explain the way in which the new defence of loss of control applies in England and Wales. If the jury is convinced that the defendant did lose his or her self-control, but also decide that a person

---

[233] Dressler (1988b).　　[234] J.C. Smith (2002: 366).　　[235] Gardner and Macklem (2001b).

with normal powers of tolerance and self-restraint would not have done so, then the defendant must be convicted of murder. This indicates that the reasonable person test is doing more than playing an evidential role.

Justificatory

Those who see loss of control as a justification see the objective test as the key part of the defence, in that it ensures that the defendant's acts were partially justified. If this approach is taken then the defendant's characteristics are relevant only in assessing the gravity of the wrong done to the defendant and are not relevant in assessing the level of self-restraint expected. So, for example, if a racial insult is hurled, the jury must ask what is an appropriate reaction to that insult. The person's racial background may explain why the insult was aggravating, but it is not relevant in deciding the morally appropriate response to a provocation of that gravity.[236] As John Gardner and Timothy Macklem[237] argue, if we do not allow a defendant who 'suffers' from a dishonest personality to have a defence, why should we allow it to someone who is short-tempered? In other words just as we require all defendants to live up to the same standards of honesty should we not expect all defendants to live up to the same standards of self-control?

Ensuring the defendant is not at prior fault

As shall be seen in Chapter 12, there is a general principle in the law on defences that an individual cannot rely on a defence which is self-induced. In this context the defence of loss of control is available only if the defendant is not to blame for losing his self-control. This approach may be more sympathetic to the use of characteristics for which the defendant is not to blame, for example, age or mental disability, but not characteristics for which the defendant is responsible, for example being an irritable person.[238] Lord Clyde in *Morgan Smith*,[239] a case under the old law of provocation, suggests that we should be asking whether the accused had made a reasonable effort to control him or herself, bearing in mind the limits of what he or she can reasonably be expected to do. The difficulty with such an approach is that it requires a distinction to be drawn between characteristics for which a defendant is responsible and those for which he or she is not. Such a distinction is not an easy one to make.

Policy level constraint

Dennis Klimchuk[240] has argued that the objective requirement can be seen as a policy-based constraint. It is there to protect the general public. Although we may be sympathetic to a defendant whose psychological make-up means that it is difficult to control his or her behaviour, in order to protect the public it is necessary to convict of murder those who kill in the face of minor wrongs, even if in moral terms they may be less blameworthy than other killers. There is some difficulty with this explanation in that it is possible to impose a life sentence on a person who successfully pleads loss of control if he or she poses a danger to the public.

---

[236] See Herring (1996).   [237] Gardner and Macklem (2001a).   [238] See Herring (1996).
[239] [2000] 3 WLR 654, 684.   [240] Klimchuk (1994).

QUESTIONS

1. Giovanni, an Italian, is called 'a wimp' by John. Giovanni flies into a rage and kills John. To which of the following arguments, if any, should the law be sympathetic?

   (a) Italian men are well known to be hot-blooded and so Giovanni should be expected to demonstrate only the level of self-control expected of the reasonable Italian man.

   (b) Italian men are macho and so insults about their masculinity are far more insulting than such insults to English men, and the jury should be instructed to bear this in mind.

   When considering this, note the criticism in the following question that the loss of control defence tends to encourage racial and gender stereotyping!

2. McHugh J in *Masciantonio* (1994–5) 183 CLR 58 (High Court of Australia) questioned whether it is right to judge a person by the standard expected of 'a white middle class Australian of Anglo-Saxon-Celtic heritage'. Do you agree with the statement? Should people from certain educational, ethnic, cultural, or socio-economic backgrounds be expected to have lower (or higher) levels of self-control than others?

For guidance on answering this question, please visit the Online Resource Centre that accompanies this book: www.oxfordtextbooks.co.uk/orc/herringcriminal7e/.

3. Jeremy Horder (1992: 126) gives this example: 'Consider the case of a South African defendant brought up in England as a die-hard Afrikaner (let us call him Terreblanche) who fervently believes that coloured people should never speak to a white man on any matter whatsoever unless spoken to first, and that it is the highest form of insult to a white man for coloured people to break this rule of social intercourse. The "provocation" put in evidence by Terreblanche is that the coloured person he passed in the street, let us say, said "Good morning" to him before Terreblanche had said anything to him.' Should the law regard Terreblanche as being provoked?

4. Lord Goff in *Morhall* thought that the jury should be asked to consider how an ordinary person would react to the provocation, whereas the majority in *Morgan Smith* preferred to refer to the reasonable man. The new defence of loss of control refers to normal degrees of tolerance and self-restraint. What is the difference between an ordinary person, a reasonable person, and a normal one? Which is the more appropriate test for self-control?

19.4 THE GENDERED NATURE OF THE DEFENCE

There has been a substantial amount written claiming that the old defence of provocation is based on a male ideal of anger: it too easily provides men who kill with a defence, and is too hard to invoke as a defence for women who kill, especially women who kill partners who have been abusing them.[241] It will be interesting to see if the new defence of loss of control makes it easier or harder for defendants who kill following domestic violence to raise a defence. It might help victims of domestic abuse who kill in fear of future violence

---

[241] For a discussion on the rates of domestic violence and potential causes, see Miles (2001) and Kaganas (2002).

because they can rely on the violence trigger.[242] However, that will not be available to victims who have suffered emotional abuse, but do not fear violence. Some commentators have argued that if the courts are able to appreciate that using domestic abuse against someone is a grave wrong against them, then the new loss of control defence may be easier for victims of domestic violence to rely on.[243] We will be returning to the question of what defence should be available to a battered woman who kills in Chapter 12 (see Chapter 12, Section 23.2 at pp.738–42).

The defence is too readily available to men

It is clear that the origins of the provocation defence were gendered. The classic examples of provocations in the nineteenth century included a man finding another man in the act of committing adultery with his wife and the sight of an Englishman being unlawfully deprived of his liberty.[244] More recently there have been cases where men have been able to use the defence claiming that their wife's constant 'nagging' or unfaithfulness has caused them to lose their self-control.[245] In such cases the resulting sentence can be surprisingly low.[246] Some commentators argue that such decisions can reinforce male possessiveness and control of women. The new defence of loss of control seeks to tackle these concerns in three ways. First, it makes it clear the defence is only available if the defendant has a 'justifiable sense of being seriously wronged'.[247] It is unlikely that 'nagging' would amount to this. Second, there must be 'circumstances of an extremely grave character'[248] a phrase which requires something much more serious than 'nagging'. Third, section 55(6) of the Coroners and Justice Act 2009 makes it clear that sexual infidelity cannot amount to a 'qualifying trigger'.

Loss of control is difficult for battered women to use

There is clear statistical evidence that the majority of women who kill their partners have been abused by them. Such cases must be considered in the light of the social background and in particular the problem of domestic violence.[249] Government statistics indicate that one woman in four will experience domestic violence at some stage in her life, and that domestic violence accounts for one-quarter of all violent crime.[250]

Women who have killed their partners following months of abuse have not readily found a defence in the criminal law.[251] As self-defence is not available if the defendant is not facing an imminent threat, many such defendants previously sought to rely on provocation, but have faced a number of difficulties in doing so, including the following:[252]

(1) Battered women are sometimes said to exhibit a 'slow-burn reaction'. That is, rather than the defendant lashing out in anger in response to a provocation, her anger slowly increases until violence is exhibited some time after the provocative incident. The law appears more sympathetic to men 'snapping' at discovering their wife having an affair, but not with women driven to killing after years of abuse. In recent years the law on this area

---

[242] S. Edwards (2010).   [243] Herring (2011c).   [244] Wells (2000).
[245] *Singh* (1992) 13 Cr App R (S) 123 (CA); McColgan (2000a).
[246] Horder and Fitz-Gibbon (2015).   [247] Coroners and Justice Act 2009, s. 55(4).
[248] *Ibid.*   [249] Chan (2001).   [250] Home Office (1999).
[251] S. Edwards (1999); O'Donovan (1993); Chan (1994); Nicolson (1995); Bridgeman and Millns (1998); McColgan (1993).
[252] McColgan (1993).

has become more accessible to battered women following *Ahluwalia*, where it was accepted that even if there is a gap in time between the provocative act and the killing, the jury may still be persuaded that the defendant suffered a sudden and temporary loss of self-control. It is notable that this greater flexibility in the law was achieved only after the court accepted expert medical evidence of a condition known as battered woman syndrome (BWS), one of the symptoms of which is 'slow-burn reaction'. In other words the 'slow' reaction of women is seen by the courts not as normal under the circumstances, but as a result of a special medical condition.[253]

The 'slow-burn problem' is likely to be less of a problem with the new loss of control defence. There is no need to show that there was a sudden loss of control.[254]

(2) Sometimes in cases of battered women the defendant has finally snapped after what appears to be a relatively minor incident. It has therefore been difficult to show that the killing was a reasonable response to the provocation. Under the new law, the objective test must be applied when considering all of the circumstances of the defendant. This should mean that the wrongful act must be seen in the light of the defendant's whole history and, hence, what might appear to be a minor wrong, is in fact a very grave one and can be seen as the 'last straw' following years of abuse.[255] The courts may also be open to arguments that a sustained campaign of coercive control by a man of his partner will amount to the commission of a grave wrong against her.[256]

(3) Under the old law there was difficulty in establishing the loss of self-control requirement. Take the facts of *Ahluwalia*[257] (excerpted in Part I of this chapter). The defendant waited until her abusive husband was asleep, found some petrol, poured it over him, and set him alight, killing him. It may be thought that these acts, far from showing a loss of self-control, reveal a carefully thought-out plan. The cases on loss of self-control[258] suggest that the law presently takes a rather narrow view of loss of self-control, requiring a wild flailing around in anger. If loss of self-control could include a loss of self-restraint or loss of moral self-control, battered women may more easily be able to use the defence.[259] Think of it this way. No doubt Ahluwalia must have wanted to kill her husband on many previous occasions, but managed to control her desires. On this night that 'moral check' was lost. Could this not be regarded as a form of loss of self-control?[260] It will be interesting to see if the courts will be more or less flexible about how loss of self-control is understood when interpreting the new loss of control defence.

(4) Under the old law there were difficulties in showing that the defendant responded to the provocation in a reasonable way. For example, the trial judge argued in *Thornton*:[261]

> There are . . . many unhappy, indeed miserable, husbands and wives . . . But on the whole it is hardly reasonable, you may think, to stab them fatally when there are other alternatives available, like walking out or going upstairs.

[253] For a sceptical look at BWS, see Loveless (2014).   [254] Coroners and Justice Act 2009, s. 54(2).
[255] *Thornton (No. 2)* [1996] 1 WLR 1174 (CA).   [256] Herring (2011b).
[257] [1992] 4 All ER 889 (CA).   [258] e.g. *Cocker* [1989] Crim LR 740 (CA).
[259] See Garvey (2009) for a philosophical discussion of those defendants who know they should not act in a particular way and try not to, but fail.
[260] See the proposed 'self-preservation defence' in Griffiths (2000: 148).
[261] Quoted in *Thornton* [1992] 1 All ER 306, 312 (CA).

In response to such an argument it could be replied that the defendant acted as a reasonable woman suffering from BWS.[262]

It will have been noted that some of the difficulties facing battered women who kill, who sought then to rely on provocation, have been overcome by the courts' willingness to receive evidence that they suffer from BWS.[263] Nicholson and Sanghvi explain that sufferers of BWS 'develop a number of common characteristics, such as low self-esteem, self-blame for the violence, anxiety, depression, fear, general suspiciousness, and the belief that only they can change their predicament.'[264] It is also claimed that the effect of this syndrome is that women suffer 'learned helplessness' such that they see no escape from the violence apart from killing.

Despite the fact that recognition of BWS has meant that battered women have more easily been able to find a defence, some commentators have been very concerned about its use in these cases.[265] The concerns include the following:

(1) Regarding BWS as the cause for the killing disguises other reasons why battered women stay in violent relationships (e.g. the lack of refuges available for battered women or the absence of effective legal responses to domestic violence).[266] Also it is arguable that staying in the violent relationship, far from indicating a mental abnormality, may even be a sensible decision. There is evidence that women who leave an abusive partner may be at even greater risk of violence than they would have been had they stayed with him.[267] The emphasis placed on the syndrome also 'individualizes' the problem in that it fails to see domestic violence as part of the wider picture of a society within which violence and oppression against women are permitted, if not encouraged.[268]

(2) Commentators argue that women who kill having suffered long periods of violence and facing the prospect of even more violence are responding reasonably and not acting while suffering from some form of mental abnormality.[269] Indeed many commentators have argued that the law should permit battered women to rely on self-defence rather than loss of control[270] (the availability of self-defence for battered women will be discussed in Chapter 12).

(3) Focusing the jury's mind on BWS leads the jury to concentrate on the evidence of the expert, rather than the evidence of the woman herself, who is seen as unreliable because she suffers from an abnormality. This can lead to claims that battered women's experiences are being rewritten in a medical discourse in criminal cases.[271] This in turn can lead to subsequent problems for battered women, for example applications that their children be taken into care.[272]

Other commentators have responded differently and argued that killing an abusive partner, rather than leaving him, is a clearly disproportionate response and that too readily permitting defences to such conduct could be seen as condoning, or even encouraging, it.

---

262 *Thornton (No. 2)* [1996] 2 All ER 1023 (CA).   263 Walker (1989); Kaganas (2002).
264 Nicolson and Sanghvi (1993).
265 See e.g. Wells (1993) and Sheehy, Stubbs, and Tolmie (1992).   266 *Ibid.*
267 Wilson and Daly (1993).   268 Hanmer (2000).   269 Kaganas (2002: 106).
270 Canadian courts are more willing to use self-defence (*Lavallee* [1990] 1 SCR 852). See also Wells (1994); Norse (1997); Rosen (1986).
271 Kaganas (2002).   272 Raitt and Zeedyk (2000).

19.5 THE CASE FOR THE ABOLITION OF THE DEFENCE

Some commentators take the view that the loss of control defence should be abolished. Indeed when the government considered the reform of the law on provocation it considered the option of abolition seriously. These are some of the arguments that have been used:

(1) Jeremy Horder[273] has engaged in a sustained attack on the loss of control defence. He argues that killing in anger is no more worthy of a defence than killing while overcome by greed or envy. In the light of a provocation a display of righteous indignation may be appropriate, but a killing after a loss of self-control is so far in excess of an appropriate response that there is no moral warrant for it. There is, in other words, no good reason for killing in anger, and so it should not provide a defence.

(2) Asking what is a reasonable response for a person with the defendant's characteristics encourages the jury to rely on racial and sexual stereotypes.[274] In *Masciantonio*,[275] an Australian case, the defendant attempted to argue that in considering how a reasonable person would react the jury should consider the fact that he was Italian and was therefore hot-blooded and more prone to lose his self-control. This clearly indicates the ways in which loss of control can lead to stereotyping.

(3) The loss of control defence invites the defendant to defame the deceased.[276] It encourages the defendant to put forward evidence of insulting behaviour by the deceased. For example, a husband who has killed his wife wanting to use the defence of loss of control might seek to introduce evidence that he was continually insulted and demeaned by his wife to such a point that he lost his self-control. Of course, the deceased in such a case is unable to respond to such allegations.

(4) The gender bias in the operation of the defence means that it should be abolished.[277] Horder points out that on average 52.5 per cent of women who kill their male partners are able to rely on the defence of loss of control, while 30 per cent of men who kill their female partners are able to do so.[278] At first sight these figures might suggest, if anything, that the defence operates in a way that is pro-women. However, this would be misconceived. It must be recalled that the vast majority of women who have killed their partners have been subject to sustained physical abuse, while the number of men who will have been subjected to violence by their partners will be tiny. In the light of this the percentage figures for women look very low and the figures for men look surprisingly high. Although these statistics do provide a strong basis for an argument that loss of control be abolished, it must be asked, if the defence is removed, upon what defence will the 52.5 per cent of women who kill their abusive partners and currently use loss of control be able to rely?[279]

In the following passage, having criticized the way in which the old law on provocation too easily provided a defence for a man who killed his wife who had announced she was leaving him, but found it hard to provide a defence for a woman who killed a man

---

[273] Wells (2000) and Horder (1992).   [274] Wells (2000).

[275] (1994–5) 183 CLR 58 (Austral. HC).   [276] Wells (2000).

[277] Yeo (1999) argues that it is the operation of the defence, rather than the substantive law, which operates in a gendered way.

[278] Horder (1992: 187).   [279] Sullivan (1993a).

some time after the attack in which he had raped her, Victoria Norse goes on to consider whether a preferable form of the defence can be developed:[280]

V. Norse, 'Passion's Progress: Modern Law Reform and the Provocation Defense' (1997) 106 *Yale Law Journal* 1331 at 1389–92

Advocates of abolition face an obvious question: If we abolish the defense, what becomes of the woman who, distraught and enraged, kills her stalker, her rapist, or her batterer? I suspect that many would say that these women deserve our compassion. The most persuasive scholarly defenses of provocation have all invoked examples, like these, in which the defendant's emotion reflects the outrage of one responding to a grave wrong that the law otherwise punishes. Commentators frequently use examples of men killing their wives' rapists or children who kill abusive parents as clear cases of provoked murder. . . .

The problem comes when we focus on cases in which the emotion is based on less compelling 'reasons'—when women kill their departing husbands or men kill their complaining wives. Under conventional liberal theory, if extreme emotion is shown, these cases should be handled no differently from cases where victims kill their rapists and stalkers and batterers. The quantity or intensity of the emotion provides the excuse, not the reasons for the emotion. This focus on emotion, to the exclusion of reason, reflects a very important assumption made by liberal theories of the defense, that emotion obscures reason. When we distinguish the rapist killer from the departing wife killer, we acknowledge a very different view of emotion, one in which emotion is imbued with meaning. Both the departing wife killer and the rapist killer may be upset, but the meanings embodied in their claims for emotional understanding are quite different. In distinguishing these cases based on the reasons for the claimed emotion, we acknowledge a view of emotion in which emotion is not the enemy of reason but, instead, its embodiment.

. . .

Where does this understanding of emotion lead us? It helps us to see why we might distinguish intuitively the rapist killer from the departing wife killer. In the first case, we feel 'with' the killer because she is expressing outrage in ways that communicate an emotional judgment (about the wrongfulness of rape) that is uncontroversially shared, indeed, that the law itself recognizes. Such claims resonate because we cannot distinguish the defendant's sense of emotional wrongfulness from the law's own sense of appropriate retribution. The defendant's emotional judgments are the law's own. In this sense, the defendant is us. By contrast, the departing wife killer cannot make such a claim. He asks us to share in the idea that leaving merits outrage, a claim that finds no reflection in the law's mirror. In fact, the law tells us quite the opposite: that departure, unlike rape and battery and robbery, merits protection rather than punishment.

This understanding finally allows us to suggest an answer to the paradox with which we continually confront our law students: How can it be that a reasonable person kills in these circumstances and, if a reasonable person would, why not completely exonerate him? The short answer is that 'reasonable men and women' do not kill in these circumstances, but reasonable men and women may well possess emotions that the law needs to protect. Without protecting some emotions, the criminal law contradicts itself. It punishes the very emotions implicit in the law's own judgments that killing and raping and robbing are both wrong and merit retribution. At the same time, protecting emotion does not require us to protect the

---

[280] For a rejection of her view, see Dressler (2002b).

deed. If we protect the act of killing, the criminal law commits itself to a different contradiction, one in which the State embraces or at least tolerates vigilantism.

We can now see why the provocation defense has always stood on the fence, partially condoning, yet partially exculpating. In every provoked murder case the law risks the embrace of revenge. To maintain its monopoly on violence, the State must condemn, at least partially, those who take the law in their own hands. At the same time, however, some provoked murder cases temper our feelings of revenge with the recognition of tragedy. Some defendants who take the law in their own hands respond with a rage shared by the law. In such cases, we 'understand' the defendant's emotions because these are the very emotions to which the law itself appeals for the legitimacy of its own use of violence. At the same time, we continue to condemn the act because the defendant has claimed a right to use violence that is not his own.

The important point to see here is that the provoked killer's claim for our compassion is not simply a claim for sympathy; it is a claim of authority and a demand for our concurrence. The defendant who asks for our compassion, that we feel 'with him,' asks that we 'share the state of mind that [he] expresses.' He asks that we share his judgments of emotional blame. Precisely because he asks us to embrace those emotional judgments, he asks us to embrace him as legislator, as one who rightly sets the emotional terms of blame and wrongdoing vis-a-vis his victim. When a defendant responds with outrage to wrongs the society otherwise punishes, he asks us to believe that he has legislated nothing. However, when a defendant responds with outrage to conduct society protects, he seeks to supplant the State's normative judgment, to impose his individual vision of blame and wrongdoing not only on the victim, but also on the rest of us.

As should be obvious by now, my theory of the defense is based as much on equality as it is on autonomy. All defendants who kill, with good reason or no reason at all, assert superiority over their victims, the superiority that comes from using the victim as a means rather than an end. But in provoked murder cases we also risk allowing the defendant to assert an emotional and normative superiority. The danger is not only that the defendant will 'use' the victim but also that he will rationalize the 'use' of the victim by claiming that we share in his distribution of emotional blame. When we are sure that the victim would not have shared the killer's emotional judgments (where she left because she was beaten) or when we know that the victim would not have expected punishment for the acts triggering the defendant's outrage (bad cooking, complaints, and messy houses), we see that the defendant's claim for compassion is false. It is a claim that we share in a set of emotional judgments vis-a-vis the victim that are not shared. To embrace such claims is to permit the defendant to sit on a higher normative plane.

. . .

Conventional understandings of criminal law place defenses in two mutually exclusive categories: as excuse or justification. In the excuse category are defenses, such as insanity, that focus on state of mind; these defenses do not embody judgments that what the defendant did was 'right' or 'justified,' but that the defendant was less blameworthy. In the 'justification' category are defenses, such as self-defense or necessity, which assume that what the defendant has done, overall, was 'right' or 'warranted.' Traditionally, 'excuse' and 'justification' have been viewed as mutually exclusive categories: A defendant cannot be both excused and justified because an excused action presupposes that the action was wrong and therefore unjustified. This assumes, however, a crucial feature of the inquiry—that we are evaluating acts and acts alone. To say that an act cannot be both justified and excused is to say something about acts, not emotions. It is perfectly consistent to say that one's emotions are justified or warranted even when one's acts are not. Indeed, as I have noted above, we may easily say that passionate killings are not justified even if we believe that the emotions causing some killings are, in some sense, the 'right' emotion.

It is by focusing on the emotion, rather than the act, that my proposal distinguishes itself quite easily (both in theory and practice) from the traditional model of provocation as partial justification. My proposal does not depend upon the theory that the victim deserves to be punished. Instead, I propose that the law should see the defendant's state of mind (his emotion) as something that, in some cases, it should protect. Unlike a partial justification model, my approach allows the defense to retain many features associated with excuse. The law need not impose an 'objective' standard. It may continue to focus on the defendant's perception of the triggering act, rather than its quality in the abstract—something that the partial justification model rejects. Thus, a defendant who believes she is being stalked, even if she is not, could properly claim her emotion was warranted, based on her perception of the situation. The law may also keep a liberal regard for the defendant's characteristics when they are relevant to the underlying defense—again, something irrelevant to the partial justification model. Thus, a defendant who claims that she killed when enraged by a hate crime obviously raises an issue to which racial, gender, or other characteristics may be relevant, if not crucial. Finally, the law may provide for cases in which emotion builds over time—a position that traditional models typically reject. A defendant who claims that he was sodomized and later outraged by taunts will be allowed to pursue the defense, as would a battered woman who claimed that her outrage and fear developed over time.

. . .

If accepted, this theory should bar many, if not most, provocation claims in intimate homicide cases. It would not be enough for a defendant to claim that a divorce or a protective order or moving out caused her rage. Defendants who ask us for compassion in these cases can point to neither law nor social norm that would punish leaving. My proposal would also bar the defense in cases in which the defendant claimed rage inspired by infidelity. Society is no longer willing to punish adultery. In the absence of such a willingness, the adulterer killer has no claim that his emotions were no different from the emotions to which the law itself appeals to rationalize punishment. This does not mean that infidelity is not emotionally painful. It does mean that those who urge compassion based on infidelity can point to nothing in the law itself that would demand that we have compassion for their violent outrage. The law only suffers contradiction when it refuses to embrace a sense of outrage which is necessary to the law's rationalization of its own use of violence. When the law refuses to jail adulterers, the contradiction operates the other way: We are compelled to ask why it is that private parties may enforce a sense of outrage that society has refused itself.

. . .

To adopt this theory, of course, requires us to reject the idea upon which almost all contemporary theories of the defense are predicated: that we partially excuse because the defendant lacks a full or fair capacity for self-control. Let me be clear about what we reject here: We do not reject self-control to embrace judgment; we reject a disguised judgment for one that is acknowledged. No matter how much we try to tie the defense to behavior, no matter how insistent the rhetoric of subjectivity, decisions applying this defense express judgments about when defendants 'should' exercise self-control. The law can continue to deny this if it chooses, to bury it within the qualities of a reasonable person, but it pays a heavy price—one not only of incoherence, but of intellectual passivity and circularity. To say that we partially excuse provoked murderers to increase men's freedom but that their freedom is a condition of granting the excuse is to indulge in tautology. In this circularity resides a space in which we find ourselves committed to beliefs about men and women and their relationships that the law itself long ago abandoned.

FURTHER READING

Ashworth, A. (1976) 'The Doctrine of Provocation' *Cambridge Law Journal* 35: 292.

Chan, W. (2001) *Women, Murder and Justice* (Basingstoke: Palgrave).

Cobb, N. and Gaudsden, A. (2011) 'Feminism, "Typical" Women, and Losing Control' in A. Reed and M. Bohlander (eds) *Loss of Control and Diminished Responsibility* (Aldershot: Ashgate).

Dressler, J. (1988b) 'Provocation: Partial Justification or Partial Excuse?' *Modern Law Review* 51: 467.

Dressler, J. (2002b) 'Why Keep the Provocation Defense? Some Reflections on a Difficult Subject' *Minnesota Law Review* 86: 959.

Dressler, J. (2006) 'Descent into Murder: Provocation's Stricture—The Prognosis for Women Who Kill Men Who Abuse Them' *Journal of Criminal Law* 29: 342.

Edwards, S. (2011) 'Loss of Self-Control: When His Anger is Worth More Than Her Fear' in A. Reed and M. Bohlander (eds) *Loss of Control and Diminished Responsibility* (Aldershot: Ashgate).

Gardner, J. and Macklem, T. (2001a) 'Compassion without Respect? Nine Fallacies in *R v Smith*' *Criminal Law Review* 623.

Gardner, J. and Macklem, T. (2001b) 'Provocation and Pluralism' *Modern Law Review* 64: 815.

Gardner, J. and Macklem, T. (2004) 'No Provocation without Responsibility' *Criminal Law Review* 213.

Garvey, S. (2005) 'Passion's Puzzle' *Iowa Law Review* 90: 1677.

Herring, J. (2011b) 'The Serious Wrong of Domestic Abuse and the Loss of Control Defence' in A. Reed and M. Bohlander (eds) *Loss of Control and Diminished Responsibility: Domestic, Comparative and International Perspectives* (London: Ashgate).

Holton, R. and Shute, S. (2007) 'Self-Control in the Modern Provocation Defence' *Oxford Journal of Legal Studies* 27: 49.

Horder, J. (1992) *Provocation and Responsibility* (Oxford: OUP).

Horder, J. (2005a) 'Reshaping the Subjective Element in the Provocation Defence' *Oxford Journal of Legal Studies* 25: 123.

Kaganas, F. (2002) 'Domestic Violence, Gender and the Expert' in A. Bainham, S. Day Sclater, and M. Richards (eds) *Body Lore and Laws* (Oxford: Hart).

Mackay, R. and Mitchell, B. (2003) 'Provoking Diminished Responsibility: Two Pleas Merging into One' *Criminal Law Review* 745.

Mackay, R. and Mitchell, B. (2004) 'Replacing Provocation' *Criminal Law Review* 219.

Mackay, R. and Mitchell, B. (2005) 'But is This Provocation? Some Thought on the Law Commission Report on Partial Defences to Murder' *Criminal Law Review* 44.

McColgan, A. (1993) 'In Defence of Battered Women Who Kill' *Oxford Journal of Legal Studies* 15: 508.

Mitchell, B. (2011) 'Loss of Self-Control under the Coroners and Justice Act 2009: Oh No!' in A. Reed and M. Bohlander (eds) *Loss of Control and Diminished Responsibility* (Aldershot: Ashgate).

Mitchell, B., Mackay, R., and Brookbanks, W. (2008) 'Pleading for Provoked Killers: In Defence of *Morgan Smith*' *Law Quarterly Review* 124: 675.

Mousourakis, G. (1998a) *Criminal Responsibility and Partial Excuse* (Aldershot: Ashgate).

Norrie, A. (2002) 'From Criminal Law to Legal Theory: The Mysterious Case of the Reasonable Glue Sniffer' *Modern Law Review* 65: 538.

Norrie, A. (2010) 'The Coroners and Justice Act 2009—Partial Defences to Murder (1) Loss of Control' *Criminal Law Review* 275.

Uniacke, S. (2007) 'Emotional Excuses' *Law and Philosophy* 26: 95.

Wells, C. (2000) 'Provocation: The Case for Abolition' in A. Ashworth and B. Mitchell (eds) *Rethinking English Homicide Law* (Oxford: OUP).

20 DIMINISHED RESPONSIBILITY

In order to understand the theoretical basis for diminished responsibility it is important to remember some of the other defences available to a charge of murder. In particular there are the defences of no *mens rea*, automatism, and insanity. So diminished responsibility is not intended for those whose mental abnormality is so severe that they are insane or are non-insane automatons. Indeed it should be emphasized that diminished responsibility is a partial defence: the defendant who successfully raises the defence is still guilty of manslaughter, with the potential for a life sentence. So a defendant who successfully raises the defence is not blameless, it is rather that his level of blame is not sufficient to justify a murder conviction. This is not to mean that he is unable to act voluntarily and intentionally, but rather that his moral character is so distorted that he is unable critically to evaluate his conduct.[281]

Peter Sparks[282] has argued that there is a fundamental flaw in the notion of diminished responsibility. He suggests that we ask whether the defendant would have killed had he or she not suffered from the abnormality of mental functioning. If we decide that the defendant would not, Sparks argues that the defendant should have a complete defence, because it was the abnormality which caused the defendant to commit the crime. However, if we decide that even without the abnormality the defendant would still have killed then he or she deserves no defence. In other words the defendant's abnormality of mental functioning might justify a complete defence or no defence, but not a partial defence. Supporters of diminished responsibility might argue that this overlooks the possibility that the abnormality of mental functioning made it very difficult, but not impossible, to avoid killing.

---

[281] For further discussion, see Mackay (2000); Horder (1999a); Morse (1993).   [282] Sparks (1964).

The old diminished responsibility plea was successful in 90 per cent of cases in which the defendant raises it.[283] This was because in 80 per cent of cases the prosecution does not dispute the defendant's evidence of his mental abnormality. Where the prosecution does challenge, the defence succeeded in 64 per cent of cases.[284] It will be interesting to see whether the new rules on diminished responsibility reduce its success rate. The amendments require that the defendant's abnormality of mental functioning be a 'recognised medical condition'. That may mean some of the more bizarre abnormalities relied upon under the old law would not be available. However, if experts are willing to be generous in their diagnoses it is likely that if a doctor is convinced that a defendant was not sufficiently responsible for his or her actions, then it will be found that he falls within some kind of recognized mental condition.

Key to the successful plea of diminished responsibility is finding medical evidence to support it. However, the emphasis on medical evidence is problematic.[285] Doctors and others have complained that they are expected to give evidence on the basis of the law, but that terminology is not medical. Although medical evidence might be able to establish whether the defendant suffered from an abnormality of mental functioning, it is far harder to give evidence about whether the defendant was suffering a substantial impairment of responsibility. The question of the defendant's responsibility is not a question of medical fact, but rather a moral judgment.[286] It is therefore not properly an issue upon which a doctor can give expert advice.

Often the flexibility of the terminology can work to show compassion for a defendant in an unhappy situation.[287] For example, some cases of mercy killing are brought within diminished responsibility, even though there is not technically an abnormality of mental functioning The operation of the defence involves what has been described as a 'benevolent conspiracy' between lawyers and doctors to ensure that defendants who do not deserve the stigma of a murder conviction are able to avoid it.[288] The difficulty is that there appears to be inconsistent practice among psychiatrists.[289]

QUESTIONS

1. In the light of the Horder extract, consider whether battered women should use the defence of loss of control or diminished responsibility.

2. Do you think a person who kills while suffering diminished responsibility is more or less blameworthy than a person who kills under loss of control?

FURTHER READING

Griew, E. (1988) 'The Future of Diminished Responsibility' *Criminal Law Review* 75.

Kennefick, L. (2011) 'Introducing a New Diminished Responsibility Defence' *Modern Law Review* 74: 750.

Mackay, R. (1995) *Mental Condition Defences in the Criminal Law* (Oxford: OUP).

---

[283] Mackay (1995).   [284] Mackay and Machin (2000).

[285] Mackay (1999) questions whether the Human Rights Act 1998 and Art. 6 of the ECHR require that a defendant's plea of diminished responsibility should be assessed by a group of experts, rather than the jury.

[286] Mackay (2000).   [287] Mackay (1995: 185).   [288] Bluglass (1867: 10).   [289] Griew (1988).

Mackay, R. (2000) 'Diminished Responsibility and Mentally Disordered Killers' in A. Ashworth and B. Mitchell (eds) *Rethinking English Homicide Law* (Oxford: OUP).

Sparks, R. (1964) 'Diminished Responsibility in Theory and Practice' *Modern Law Review* 27: 9.

21 CONCLUDING THOUGHTS

It is remarkable that so much academic and political energy is put into homicide law, given the relatively few homicide offences that take place each year. What this reveals is that the law's approach to homicide has great symbolic importance in both political and legal terms. You can tell much about a legal system from the way it structures its homicide law. Politics is never far away too. Indeed the government's failure to abolish the mandatory life sentence for murder has had a lasting effect on the structure of homicide law. It has required the expansion of the partial defences, partly to ensure that the mandatory life sentence is not applied in inappropriate cases. Indeed, arguably, the refusal to abolish the life sentence has produced a skewed and unprincipled set of laws.

It will be interesting to see how the courts go about interpreting the Coroners and Justice Act 2009. In particular, all eyes will be open to see if the courts will be able to interpret the loss of control defence in a way which enables victims of domestic violence who kill their abusers to use the defence. It will also be intriguing to see if the amendments to the defence of diminished responsibility will mean that fewer defendants will be able to rely on it, especially in cases of so-called mercy killing.

6

NON-FATAL NON-SEXUAL
OFFENCES AGAINST THE PERSON

CENTRAL ISSUES

1. An assault occurs when the defendant causes the victim to apprehend an imminent use of force. A battery requires the defendant to touch or apply force against the victim. Both offences can be committed if the defendant is reckless as to the result.

2. It is an offence to cause the victim actual bodily harm as a result of an assault or a battery.

3. There are two offences of causing grievous bodily harm to the victim. The more serious requires proof that the defendant intended to cause grievous bodily harm. The less serious only requires that the defendant foresaw that some harm would result from his or her actions.

4. There are several offences connected to poisoning.

5. There are specific offences where violence is motivated by the defendant's reaction to the victim's race or religion.

6. There are offences in the Protection from Harassment Act 1997 which were designed to deal with stalking, but which, in fact, cover a series of acts which cause harassment to the victim.

7. The current law states that if a person passes on a sexually transmitted disease, they can be guilty of an offence if they knew there was a risk they would transmit the disease, and they did not have the victim's consent to run the risk of acquiring the disease. The current law has led to some criticism by some academics.

8. If the harm done to the victim is actual bodily harm or worse, then the fact the victim consented to the harm provides no defence unless the case falls within one of the exceptional categories recognized in the law (e.g. surgery, sports). Many commentators believe that the law should be willing to recognize that the victim's consent is a defence in a wider range of circumstances.

PART I: THE LAW

1 INTRODUCTION

This chapter will cover a wide range of offences: from an unwanted touching on an arm to a life-threatening attack. Key to the law is the right to bodily integrity: a person should not be touched against his or her wishes. This right is protected under the common law[1] and Article 8 of the European Convention on Human Rights. The significance the law attaches to this right is revealed by these two cases:

(1) In *Thomas*[2] it was held that the unwanted touching of the bottom of a girl's skirt amounted to a battery. The rubbing of someone's clothing might appear to some to be too trivial a harm to justify the intervention of the criminal law, but it reveals the weight attached to the right not to be touched without one's consent.

(2) The decision of the Court of Appeal in *St George's Healthcare NHS Trust v S*[3] reveals that the right to bodily integrity is protected, even if there may be some very good reasons for infringing it. There, a woman in the late stages of labour was advised that she should have a Caesarean section operation, without which her life and that of her unborn child were in danger. She refused to consent to the operation, wanting a natural delivery. The hospital authorities, having obtained a court order permitting them to do so, carried out the operation against her will. The Court of Appeal held that the court order should not have been granted. The woman's right to bodily integrity was held to be preciously guarded by the law. Even if her decision might appear to be irrational to others, and even if abiding by her decision might lead to her own death and that of her child, it had to be respected by doctors, as long as the woman was competent.

This chapter will consider how the criminal law protects the right to bodily integrity, although it will not consider sexual offences, which will be examined in Chapter 7.

There are five key offences against the person which will be considered in this chapter:

(1) assault;

(2) battery;

(3) assault occasioning actual bodily harm;

(4) malicious wounding or inflicting grievous bodily harm;

(5) wounding or causing grievous bodily harm with intent.

Some commentators[4] see these as a 'ladder' of offences, starting with the least serious offence of assault, rising to the most serious offence of wounding with intent.

The chapter will then look at some of the other offences against the person which address particular forms of assaults. These include poisoning offences, racially aggravated assaults, and harassment offences.

---

[1] *St George's Healthcare NHS Trust v S* [1999] Fam 26 (CA).   [2] (1985) 81 Cr App R 331 (CA).
[3] [1998] 3 All ER 673, discussed in Herring (1998a).   [4] Ashworth and Horder (2013: 321).

2 ASSAULT AND BATTERY

Under section 39 of the Criminal Justice Act 1988:

> Common assault and battery shall be summary offences and a person guilty of either of them shall be liable to a fine not exceeding level 5 on the standard scale, to imprisonment for a term not exceeding six months or to both.

Technically assault and battery are two separate crimes.[5] In brief, a battery involves an unlawful and unwanted contact with the body of another, while an assault involves causing another to apprehend the possibility of imminent unlawful contact.

In *R (Kracher) v Leicester Magistrates' Court*[6] the defendant was charged with assault by battery. The magistrates convicted because although they were not sure he had hit the victim, they were convinced he had threatened him. An appeal against the conviction was allowed. He had been charged with a battery and so could not be convicted of the different offence of common assault. Of course, often both crimes can be committed in the same incident. Imagine that the defendant approached a victim and then hit her. There would be an assault when the defendant approached the victim and the victim feared some imminent unlawful touching. There would be a battery when the defendant actually hit her. It should be seen from this brief summary that 'assault' in the legal sense does not correspond to its everyday meaning of an attack.

2.1 ASSAULT

The definition of an assault is as follows:

> **DEFINITION**
>
> *Actus reus*: the defendant caused the victim to apprehend imminent unlawful force.
>
> *Mens rea*: the defendant intended or was reckless that the victim would apprehend imminent unlawful force. Although the basic meaning of 'assault' is straightforward, the courts have struggled with the precise parameters of the offence.

The following are some of the questions which have troubled the courts:

Can words alone amount to an assault?

The key decision on this question is the House of Lords' decision in *R v Ireland*,[7] in the following excerpt. The decision makes it clear that words can constitute an assault. In that case silent telephone calls were held to be assaults. It is clear from Lord Steyn's judgment that what matters is that the defendant has caused the victim to apprehend imminent harm. Exactly how that fear was created is immaterial (be it by acts, silence, writing,[8] or words). In the following extract, Lord Steyn also considers precisely what is meant by the term 'imminent' in

---

[5] *Nelson* [2013] EWCA Crim 30.   [6] [2013] EWHC 4627 (Admin).

[7] [1998] AC 147, discussed in S. Gardner (1998c) and Herring (1999).

[8] *Constanza* [1997] 2 Cr App R 492.

the definition of an assault. The case concerned a charge of assault occasioning actual bodily harm, but Lord Steyn held that in order to convict someone of that offence it first had to be established that an assault or a battery had been committed. →1 (p.374)

R v Ireland
[1998] AC 147 (HL)

Robert Ireland made a large number of telephone calls to three women. When they answered he remained silent. The women as a result suffered psychological harm. He pleaded guilty to a charge of assault occasioning actual bodily harm, contrary to section 47 of the Offences Against the Person Act 1861, following the direction of the trial judge that the facts of the case could justify such a conviction. He appealed on the basis that the admitted facts were incapable of amounting to the offence.

Lord Steyn

My Lords, it is easy to understand the terrifying effect of a campaign of telephone calls at night by a silent caller to a woman living on her own. It would be natural for the victim to regard the calls as menacing. What may heighten her fear is that she will not know what the caller may do next. The spectre of the caller arriving at her doorstep bent on inflicting personal violence on her may come to dominate her thinking. After all, as a matter of common sense, what else would she be terrified about? The victim may suffer psychiatric illness such as anxiety neurosis or acute depression. Harassment of women by repeated silent telephone calls, accompanied on occasions by heavy breathing, is apparently a significant social problem. That the criminal law should be able to deal with this problem, and so far as is practicable, afford effective protection to victims is self-evident.

. . .

Reg v Ireland: Was there an assault?

It is now necessary to consider whether the making of silent telephone calls causing psychiatric injury is capable of constituting an assault under section 47. The Court of Appeal, as constituted in the *Reg v Ireland* case, answered that question in the affirmative. There has been substantial academic criticism of the conclusion and reasoning in *Reg v Ireland* . . . Counsel's arguments, broadly speaking, challenged the decision in *Reg v Ireland* on very similar lines. Having carefully considered the literature and counsel's arguments, I have come to the conclusion that the appeal ought to be dismissed.

   The starting point must be that an assault is an ingredient of the offence under section 47. It is necessary to consider the two forms which an assault may take. The first is battery, which involves the unlawful application of force by the defendant upon the victim. Usually, section 47 is used to prosecute in cases of this kind. The second form of assault is an act causing the victim to apprehend an imminent application of force upon her: see *Fagan v Metropolitan Police Commissioner* [1969] 1 QB 439, 444D–E.

   One point can be disposed of, quite briefly. The Court of Appeal was not asked to consider whether silent telephone calls resulting in psychiatric injury is capable of constituting a battery. But encouraged by some academic comment it was raised before your Lordships' House. Counsel for Ireland was most economical in his argument on the point. I will try to match his economy of words. In my view it is not feasible to enlarge the generally accepted legal meaning of what is a battery to include the circumstances of a silent caller who causes psychiatric injury.

It is to assault in the form of an act causing the victim to fear an immediate application of force to her that I must turn. Counsel argued that as a matter of law an assault can never be committed by words alone and therefore it cannot be committed by silence. The premise depends on the slenderest authority, namely, an observation by Holroyd J to a jury that 'no words or singing are equivalent to an assault': *Rex v Meade and Belt* (1823) 1 Lew 184. The proposition that a gesture may amount to an assault, but that words can never suffice, is unrealistic and indefensible. A thing said is also a thing done. There is no reason why something said should be incapable of causing an apprehension of immediate personal violence, e.g. a man accosting a woman in a dark alley saying, 'Come with me or I will stab you.' I would, therefore, reject the proposition that an assault can never be committed by words.

That brings me to the critical question whether a silent caller may be guilty of an assault. The answer to this question seems to me to be 'Yes, depending on the facts.' It involves questions of fact within the province of the jury. After all, there is no reason why a telephone caller who says to a woman in a menacing way 'I will be at your door in a minute or two' may not be guilty of an assault if he causes his victim to apprehend immediate personal violence. Take now the case of the silent caller. He intends by his silence to cause fear and he is so understood. The victim is assailed by uncertainty about his intentions. Fear may dominate her emotions, and it may be the fear that the caller's arrival at her door may be imminent. She may fear the possibility of immediate personal violence. As a matter of law the caller may be guilty of an assault: whether he is or not will depend on the circumstance and in particular on the impact of the caller's potentially menacing call or calls on the victim. Such a prosecution case under section 47 may be fit to leave to the jury. And a trial judge may, depending on the circumstances, put a common sense consideration before the jury, namely what, if not the possibility of imminent personal violence, was the victim terrified about? I conclude that an assault may be committed in the particular factual circumstances which I have envisaged. For this reason I reject the submission that as a matter of law a silent telephone caller cannot ever be guilty of an offence under section 47. In these circumstances no useful purpose would be served by answering the vague certified question in *Reg v Ireland*.

Having concluded that the legal arguments advanced on behalf of Ireland on section 47 must fail, I nevertheless accept that the concept of an assault involving immediate personal violence as an ingredient of the section 47 offence is a considerable complicating factor in bringing prosecutions under it in respect of silent telephone callers and stalkers. That the least serious of the ladder of offences is difficult to apply in such cases is unfortunate.

Appeals dismissed.

Apprehension of force

If the victim suffers no apprehension there can be no assault. So if the defendant utters vile threats against the victim, which do not perturb the victim at all (e.g. because he or she does not believe for a moment that the defendant will carry them out) there can be no assault.[9]

Does the victim of an assault have to apprehend violence, or is the apprehension of a touching sufficient? Although the House of Lords in *Savage and Parmenter* and in *Burstow and Ireland* defined an assault as involving the apprehension of violence, it is well established

---

[9] Further, because assault is a summary offence there is no offence of attempting to assault.

in the case law that an apprehension that one is about to be stroked or kissed can amount to an assault.[10] What if the threat was not to do something that was actually a touching, but was to cause harm? For example, if the defendant threatened to pour away a victim's medicine, which the victim needed, would this amount to an assault? It appears that this would not, because the victim did not foresee that the defendant would be touching him or her.[11] It is arguable that in the light of the acceptance that actual bodily harm can include a psychological harm (see Section 3), apprehension that one might suffer a psychological injury caused by the defendant should be sufficient for an assault.[12]

What does 'imminent' mean?

The victim's apprehension must be of imminent harm. It is well established that a threat to be violent in the distant future (e.g. 'I will beat you up next week') is not an assault.[13] But what about a threat to cause violence in the near future? Lord Steyn in *Ireland* indicated that a fear of violence 'within a minute or two' might be sufficient to constitute an assault.[14] This leaves open the question of exactly where the line is to be drawn: is fear of violence in ten minutes enough, an hour, a day? We can know only when we have further guidance from the courts.

The decision in *Ireland* does not mean that every silent telephone call will amount to an assault. It is not enough just to show that the victim was frightened: it must be shown that the victim apprehended an imminent attack. That said, as Lord Steyn pointed out, if the victim of a silent telephone call gives evidence that she was frightened the jury may ask themselves 'What, if not the possibility of imminent personal violence, was the victim terrified about?' Simester, Spencer, Sullivan, and Virgo[15] have questioned this reasoning, arguing that a person may be terrified without that fear having a particular focus. They point out that a person watching a horror film may feel terror, without that amounting to terror of imminent violence. The difficulty in proving that the victim feared imminent violence in cases involving abusive telephone calls or letters may lead prosecutors to rely on the offences under the Communications Act 2003[16] or the Protection from Harassment Act 1997, which are easier to prove.

EXAMINATION TIP

A warning of a common misunderstanding: for an assault it is necessary to show that the victim had an apprehension of imminent harm. It is not enough to show that as a result of the defendant's actions the victim immediately feared that he or she might be harmed a long time in the future. In other words there must be a fear of imminent harm not an imminent fear of harm in the future.

---

[10] Horder (1998a).

[11] The closest the courts have come to recognizing that this may be an assault was the argument of the Court of Appeal in *Ireland* ([1996] 3 WLR 650) that there was an assault because the victim foresaw that she would suffer psychological harm as a result of the telephone calls. For criticism of the reasoning in the Court of Appeal in *Ireland*, see Herring (1997).

[12] Wells (1997).

[13] But there are some specific offences that relate to threats to harm in the future, e.g. there is an offence of threatening to kill in the Offences Against the Person Act 1861, s. 16.

[14] See also *Smith v Superintendent of Woking Police Station* (1983) 76 Cr App R 234.

[15] Simester, Spencer, Sullivan, and Virgo (2013: 435).

[16] See e.g. *DPP v Collins* [2005] Crim LR 794.

Is it enough for the victim to fear there may be violence?

Lord Steyn stated that an assault would occur if the victim feared the defendant *might* come round within a minute or two. The significance of this was revealed in *Constanza*[17] where the defendant sent over 800 letters to the victim, repeatedly drove past her home, and on three occasions wrote offensive words on her front door. On 4 and 12 June she received two letters which she interpreted as threatening. It was accepted that when she opened the letters and read them she feared that the defendant might harm her 'at some time not excluding the immediate future'.[18] This was sufficient to amount to an assault because among her fears was that the defendant might inflict some force imminently.

Must the threat be of a touching from the defendant?

What if the defendant threatens to ask someone else to cause harm to the victim? Could this be an assault? The issue has not been addressed directly by the courts, but the answer is likely to be yes. It is an assault for a defendant to threaten to set an animal on the victim.[19] By analogy, threatening to set a boyfriend on the victim should also be an assault. But it would seem unlikely for there to be an offence where the defendant simply tells the victim that she is being followed by someone. This is not an assault because, although as a result of what the defendant has said the victim may apprehend imminent force, there is nothing in the nature of a threat in what the defendant has said.

Does the defendant have to intend to carry out the threat?

The fact that the defendant does not intend to carry out the attack does not mean that an act cannot constitute an assault. In *Logdon v DPP*[20] the defendant showed the victim a gun and announced he would keep the victim hostage. The defendant argued that he did not intend to carry out his threat, and indeed because the gun was a fake he was not able to and therefore he could not be guilty of an assault. His conviction for assault was upheld because he had created fear of violence in the victim. The fact that he did not intend to carry out the threat and was incapable of doing so provided no defence.

What if the threat is conditional?

What is the position if the defendant says 'Unless you retract that insult I will punch you'? The argument could be made that this is not an assault because the victim has it in his or her power to avoid the violence by acting as requested and so cannot apprehend imminent force.[21] However, there are also arguments that the victim is still placed at risk of violence because by acting in a lawful way (e.g. keeping silent) she will still be liable to violence and this should amount to an assault.[22] The courts have not provided clear guidance on this issue. In *R (Kracher) v Leicester Magistrates' Court*[23] the words 'Fuck off. If you come round the back I will beat you up'[24] were held to be an assault, although arguably they only threaten to beat up the defendant if he 'comes round the back'.

---

[17] [1997] Crim LR 576.   [18] [1997] Cr App R 492, 494.
[19] This was assumed to be the law by the Court of Appeal in *Dume* The Times, 16 October 1986 (CA).
[20] [1976] Crim LR 121.   [21] *Blake v Barnard* (1840) 9 C & P 626, 173 ER 985.
[22] *Read v Coker* (1853) 138 ER 1437.   [23] [2013] EWHC 4627 (Admin).
[24] They were having an argument over parking outside some flats.

It is important to distinguish a conditional threat from words which negate a threat. For example, in *Tuberville v Savage*,[25] while holding a sword the defendant stated: 'If it were not assize time, I would not take such language.' Here the defendant was making it clear he was not going to attack the victim. The case has been widely interpreted[26] as one where the defendant's words negated what would otherwise be an assault (the holding of the sword). Jeremy Horder[27] has argued that in some cases there can be an assault even if the defendant's words negative the threat: if the defendant said to the victim 'If we were alone I would attack you' this might be seen as an implied threat that the moment the other people left an attack would be carried out.

Does an assault require an act?

In *Fagan v Metropolitan Police Commissioner*[28] it was suggested by the Divisional Court that an assault requires proof of a positive act and cannot be committed merely by an omission. Consider the following: a man is looking up at a house when he sees a woman come to the window, notice him, and appear frightened. Is it an assault if he remains standing where he is and does not move? The *dicta* in *Fagan* imply that he could not be guilty. However, a strong case can be made for saying that an omission can amount to an assault if the defendant is acting unlawfully.[29] So if a trespasser is suddenly aware that his presence in the victim's garden is startling the victim, he may be committing an offence by remaining there.

What does it mean that the apprehension must be of unlawful force?

The force which the victim apprehends must be unlawful. So if the apprehended touching would not be a criminal offence, for example because it would be done lawfully in self-defence, then there would be no assault.

What is the *mens rea* for an assault?

The defendant must be shown to intend or be reckless[30] as to the creation of apprehension of imminent unlawful violence. This was made clear in the Court of Appeal's decision in *Venna*,[31] which was approved *obiter* by the House of Lords in *Savage and Parmenter*.[32]

2.2 BATTERY

> **DEFINITION**
>
> *Actus reus*: the defendant touched or applied force to the victim.
>
> *Mens rea*: the defendant intended or was reckless as to touching or applying force to the victim.

---

[25] (1669) 1 Mod Rep 3, 86 ER 684.

[26] Although in fact the court did not resolve the question whether or not there was an assault.

[27] Horder (1998a: 402).   [28] [1969] 1 QB 439 (QBD).

[29] *Smith v Superintendent of Woking Police Station* (1983) 76 Cr App R 234 (DC).

[30] As explained in Chapter 3, this means that the defendant actually foresaw the result (i.e. that the victim would apprehend the imminent harm).

[31] [1975] 3 All ER 788.   [32] [1992] 1 AC 699, 736, per Lord Ackner.

A battery can be committed without the victim suffering any kind of injury. So a touching can constitute a battery.[33] Indeed even touching the clothes that someone is wearing can be.[34] So the offence of battery does not necessarily involve a harming of the body (as the more serious offences against the person do); it includes an invasion of 'personal space'.[35] This is shown by the fact that a battery can take place even if the victim did not feel the touching.[36]

Again we will consider some of the questions about the meaning of battery which have troubled the courts.

Can the battery be carried out via an object?

There seems little doubt that a battery can be carried out through an object. In *Fagan* the defendant committed a battery by placing his car on the victim's foot and leaving it there. By virtue of similar reasoning it has been well established that spitting on someone[37] or throwing beer on them[38] constitutes a battery.

Can the battery be carried out by omission?

It is clear from *Fagan* that the courts are willing to find a battery, even if in a sense the case involved an omission. There, by placing the car on the policeman's foot and not removing it, the defendant was continually committing a battery. However, it is unclear whether the courts would find a battery in a hypothetical case like this: Brian is sitting in a dark ally. He hears someone running towards him and is aware they probably will not see him and decides not to move. Sure enough Penny, who is out for a jog, falls over his leg.

This is different from *Fagan* where there was an initial act of touching the victim (driving onto the foot) and the omission involving the failure to move. In our hypothetical example, it might be argued that the victim walked into the defendant, rather than the defendant touched the victim. In *DPP v Santa-Bermudez*[39] the defendant was asked by a police officer who was planning to search his clothing whether he had on him any sharp objects. He said he did not, but when the officer put her hand in the pocket she was cut by a needle. The Divisional Court had no difficulty in finding a battery, holding that 'where someone (by act or word or a combination of the two) creates a danger and thereby exposes another to a reasonably foreseeable risk of injury which materialises, there is an evidential basis for the *actus reus* of an assault occasioning actual bodily harm.'[40]

Does a battery require the application of force?

Must a battery involve the application of force or can a battery be committed indirectly, for example where a person sets a booby trap which the victim falls into or someone shouts 'fire' in a crowded theatre, having blocked the exits, causing people to be crushed in an attempt to escape?[41] The decisions to date suggest these are batteries.[42] *Obiter* in *Savage* Lord Ackner appeared to suggest otherwise, giving an example of a person who interfered with the braking mechanism of a car so that the driver subsequently had a car accident and was injured.[43]

---

[33] *Collins v Wilcock* [1984] 3 All ER 374.   [34] *Thomas* (1985) 81 Cr App R 331.
[35] J. Gardner (1994a: 508).   [36] *Thomas* (1985) 81 Cr App R 331.
[37] *Smith* (1866) 176 ER 910.   [38] *Savage* [1992] 1 AC 699.
[39] [2003] EWHC 2908.   [40] *Ibid*, para. 10.   [41] Hirst (1999).
[42] *Martin* (1891) 8 QBD 54.   [43] [1992] 1 AC 699, 725.

He suggested that that might not amount to a battery (although it could be a wounding). However, later cases have not followed the implication that a battery must involve the direct application of force. In *DPP v K*[44] a schoolboy had placed some acid he had stolen from the science laboratory in a hand-drier. Another pupil used the hand-drier and acid was splashed upon him. It was held that this amounted to a battery, even though the schoolboy had not directly applied the acid. In *Haystead v Chief Constable of Derbyshire*[45] the defendant struck a woman who was holding her baby. As a result of the blows she dropped the baby. The defendant was charged with battering the baby. It was held that he was properly convicted because he had caused unlawful force to be applied to the baby when the baby hit the floor.

These decisions, it is submitted, are correct adapting the reasoning in *Ireland* that in cases of assault it does not matter what means the defendant uses to create the apprehension of violence; similarly it should not matter what technique the defendant uses to apply force to a person's body in cases of battery. Throwing a pint of beer at someone and placing a pint of beer on the top of a door so that it falls on them when they open the door seem equally blameworthy and it would be artificial to distinguish between them. There must, however, be something that touches the victim. Lord Steyn in *Ireland* rejected the argument that the silent telephone call constituted a battery; if anything it was an assault. He argued that to hold otherwise would mean that there would be too great a separation between the legal meaning of battery and its ordinary meaning.

Can everyday touchings amount to a battery?

If you were to board a tube train in London during the rush hour, inevitably you would touch others and they would touch you. Indeed some touchings are part of everyday life. The law would not regard such touchings as batteries, as the following case demonstrates:

Collins v Wilcock
[1984] 3 All ER 374 (QBD)

Two police officers suspected that two women were soliciting for the purpose of prostitution. They approached the women, but one (the appellant) refused to answer questions and walked away. One police officer took hold of her arm. The appellant responded by scratching the officer, and for that she was later convicted of assaulting a police officer in the execution of her duty, contrary to section 51(1) of the Police Act 1964. She appealed against the conviction on the basis that when the assault occurred the police officer was not acting in the execution of her duty. The key question on appeal was whether in grabbing hold of the appellant the police officer was committing a battery.

Lord Justice Robert Goff

The fundamental principle, plain and incontestable, is that every person's body is inviolate. It has long been established that any touching of another person, however slight, may amount to a battery. So Holt CJ held in 1704 that 'the least touching of another in anger is a battery': see *Cole v Turner* 6 Mod Rep 149, 90 ER 958. The breadth of the principle reflects the fundamental nature of the interest so protected as Blackstone wrote in his Commentaries,

---

[44] [1990] 1 All ER 331.   [45] [2000] 3 All ER 890.

'the law cannot draw the line between different degrees of violence, and therefore totally prohibits the first and lowest stage of it every man's person being sacred, and no other having a right to meddle with it, in any the slightest manner' (see 3 Bl Com 120). The effect is that everybody is protected not only against physical injury but against any form of physical molestation.

But so widely drawn a principle must inevitably be subject to exceptions. For example, children may be subjected to reasonable punishment, people may be subjected to the lawful exercise of the power of arrest and reasonable force may be used in self-defence or for the prevention of crime. But, apart from these special instances where the control or constraint is lawful, a broader exception has been created to allow for the exigencies of everyday life. Generally speaking, consent is a defence to battery and most of the physical contacts of ordinary life are not actionable because they are impliedly consented to by all who move in society and so expose themselves to the risk of bodily contact. So nobody can complain of the jostling which is inevitable from his presence in, for example, a supermarket, an underground station or a busy street nor can a person who attends a party complain if his hand is seized in friendship, or even if his back is (within reason) slapped (see *Tuberville v Savage* (1669) 1 Mod Rep 3, 86 ER 684). Although such cases are regarded as examples of implied consent, it is more common nowadays to treat them as falling within a general exception embracing all physical contact which is generally acceptable in the ordinary conduct of daily life. We observe that, although in the past it has sometimes been stated that a battery is only committed where the action is 'angry, or revengeful, or rude, or insolent' (see 1 Hawk PC c 62, s 2), we think that nowadays it is more realistic, and indeed more accurate, to state the broad underlying principle, subject to the broad exception.

Among such forms of conduct, long held to be acceptable, is touching a person for the purpose of engaging his attention, though of course using no greater degree of physical contact than is reasonably necessary in the circumstances for that purpose. So, for example, it was held by the Court of Common Pleas in 1807 that a touch by a constable's staff on the shoulder of a man who had climbed on a gentleman's railing to gain a better view of a mad ox, the touch being only to engage the man's attention, did not amount to a battery (see *Wiffin v Kincard* (1807) 2 Bos & PNR 471, 127 ER 713; for another example, see *Coward v Baddeley* (1859) 4 H & N 478, 157 ER 927). But a distinction is drawn between a touch to draw a man's attention, which is generally acceptable, and a physical restraint, which is not. So we find Parke B observing in *Rawlings v Till* (1837) 3 M & W 28 at 29, 150 ER 1042, with reference to *Wiffin v Kincard*, that 'There the touch was merely to engage a man's attention, not to put a restraint on his person.' Furthermore, persistent touching to gain attention in the face of obvious disregard may transcend the norms of acceptable behaviour, and so be outside the exception. We do not say that more than one touch is never permitted for example, the lost or distressed may surely be permitted a second touch, or possibly even more, on a reluctant or impervious sleeve or shoulder, as may a person who is acting reasonably in the exercise of a duty. In each case, the test must be whether the physical contact so persisted in has in the circumstances gone beyond generally acceptable standards of conduct and the answer to that question will depend on the facts of the particular case.

. . . The fact is that the respondent took hold of the appellant by the left arm to restrain her. In so acting, she was not proceeding to arrest the appellant and since her action went beyond the generally acceptable conduct of touching a person to engage his or her attention, it must follow, in our judgment, that her action constituted a battery on the appellant, and was therefore unlawful. It follows that the appellant's appeal must be allowed, and her conviction quashed.

Appeal allowed. Conviction quashed.

Although the decision makes it clear that everyday touchings are not batteries, it is not clear why this is so. There are two possible explanations:

(1) **Implied consent** When entering crowded places or attending events when touchings are common, a person impliedly consents to the physical contact that results.

(2) **Necessity** Some everyday touchings are an essential part of life.[46] Modern life would not be possible if it were illegal to touch anyone without their consent. So it is necessary to create a general exception to the offence of battery to cover 'all physical contact which is generally acceptable in the ordinary conduct of everyday life'.[47]

It may be important which explanation is true. If a man wanting to board a tube train can enter only by squeezing in next to his former wife from whom he is acrimoniously divorced can this be a battery on the basis that, although she may have impliedly consented to touching people when entering the tube, her implied consent cannot extend to him? On the other hand if such touchings are simply not batteries based on public policy, then the lack of implied consent may not be a defence.

Must the battery be hostile?

There has been some debate whether a battery must involve a hostile act. The view with the most support in the case law is that there is no need for the touching to be hostile, rude, or aggressive.[48] A person who lovingly strokes another's hair without that person's consent is guilty of a battery. The issue is in doubt, in part because Lord Jauncey in *Brown*[49] suggested that a battery must involve hostility. However, he seems to have understood hostility to mean that the act was not consented to, rather than to require the act to be aggressive.

What is the *mens rea* of battery?

The *mens rea* of battery is that the defendant must intend or be reckless as to the application of force or touching of the victim.

Are the *mentes reae* of assault and battery interchangeable?

What if the defendant intends to commit a battery, but in fact commits an assault? Consider this scenario: Tom approached Sean, who was asleep, intending to touch his hair and Sean suddenly awoke and saw Tom close to him and, terrified, ran away before Tom touched him. Here Tom had the *mens rea* for battery, but committed only the *actus reus* of an assault. But does that matter? The courts are yet to provide a clear answer. One argument is that, as the offences are so closely linked, it is possible to use the *actus reus* of an assault and the *mens rea* of the battery to establish the offence. Another view is that *Nelson*[50] states that the offences are separate and that this distinction needs to be taken seriously. Normally it is not possible to combine the *mens rea* of one offence with the *actus reus* of a different offence.

---

[46] Try running London Underground after forbidding passengers to touch each other!
[47] Lord Goff in *F v West Berkshire Health Authority* [1990] 2 AC 1, 25 (HL).
[48] *Faulkner v Talbot* [1981] 3 All ER 468, 471.   [49] [1994] 1 AC 212.
[50] [2013] EWCA Crim 30.

3 ASSAULT OCCASIONING ACTUAL BODILY HARM

Section 47 of the Offences Against the Person Act 1861 states:

> Whosoever shall be convicted upon an indictment of any assault occasioning actual bodily harm shall be liable . . . to be imprisoned for any term not exceeding five years.

DEFINITION

Actus reus: the defendant must commit an assault or battery which causes the victim to suffer actual bodily harm.

Mens rea: the defendant must intend or be reckless as to the assault or battery. (NB: There is no need to show that the defendant intended or foresaw actual bodily harm.)

This offence can be broken down into three elements:

(1) **It must be shown that there was an assault** This means either an assault or a battery. Both the *mens rea* and *actus reus* of the assault or battery must be shown.

(2) **The victim must suffer actual bodily harm** The phrase 'actual bodily harm' is used to indicate a level of harm which is greater than a mere touching (a battery).[51] Actual bodily harm has been defined as 'any hurt or injury calculated to interfere with the health or comfort' of the victim.[52] The harm need not be permanent, but it should 'not be so trivial as to be wholly insignificant'.[53] Bruisings, grazes, the causing of tenderness,[54] temporary loss of consciousness,[55] or breaking teeth could be included within actual bodily harm. The Guidance issued to Prosecutors recommends that 'the fact that there has been significant medical intervention and/or permanent effects have resulted' is taken into account in deciding whether the injuries amount to actual bodily harm.[56] In *DPP v Smith*[57] the defendant cut off a woman's pony tail. This was held to be actual bodily harm. There was no need to show pain because 'harm' included hurt or damage. Hair was included as part of the body, as would be the nervous system or brain of a victim. The court did emphasize that hair was intrinsic to the identity of the individual. Cresswell J said that 'to a woman her hair is a vitally important part of her body'. Surely this is true of some men too. No doubt if only a small piece of hair had been cut off this would have been just a battery.

The House of Lords in *Ireland*[58] held that psychological injuries could be included in the term 'actual bodily harm', but only if they were medically recognized conditions which involved more than fear, panic, or distress.[59] Although it might be thought to be stretching the meaning of 'bodily' to include psychological, the House of Lords accepted the argument that

---

[51] The fact that the maximum sentence for a s. 47 offence is five years indicates that it can cover some reasonably serious incidents.

[52] *Donovan* [1934] 2 KB 498.   [53] Hobhouse LJ in *Chan-Fook* [1994] 1 WLR 689, 696.

[54] *R v Reigate Justices, ex p Counsell* [1984] 148 JP 193.   [55] *T v DPP* [2003] Crim LR 622.

[56] Crown Prosecution Service (2013a).   [57] [2006] EWHC 94 (Admin).

[58] [1998] AC 147.   [59] *Burstow* [1998] AC 147; *Chan-Fook* [1994] 1 WLR 689.

'the body' includes all the organs, including the brain.[60] In *Dhaliwal*[61] it was clear that through a campaign of domestic violence the defendant had caused the victim severe psychological harm, but experts were not able to conclude it was an actual recognized illness. The Court of Appeal held that this could not therefore amount to actual bodily harm. It would be stretching the law too far, they held, to extend the meaning of bodily harm to psychological harms which were not recognized illnesses. It is important to remember at this point that the offence is not committed if there is no assault. If a man breaks off his engagement, causing his fiancée to suffer depression, there will be no offence under section 47 because he did not commit an assault.

(3) **It must be shown that the actual bodily harm was occasioned by the common assault or battery of the defendant** 'Occasioned' has been interpreted as meaning the same as caused.[62] In the case of battery this is normally straightforward. If A hits B in the face, that is a battery; if that leaves B with a bruise then clearly there has been an assault (i.e. a battery) which has occasioned actual bodily harm. It is also possible for the offence to involve an assault. A good example is *Roberts*,[63] where the Court of Appeal convicted a defendant who made indecent proposals to a woman in his car; she was so frightened that she jumped out of the car. Here he assaulted her and this assault caused her to jump out of the car and suffer actual bodily harm. In a case like *Ireland*[64] it may be hard to show that the psychological harm was caused by the apprehension of imminent harm rather than by something else.

It should be stressed that the only *mens rea* requirement for an assault occasioning actual bodily harm is intent or recklessness that the victim will suffer an assault or battery. There is no need to show that the defendant foresaw the actual bodily harm. This was made clear in the House of Lords' decision in *Savage and Parmenter*.[65] This offence therefore infringes 'the correspondence principle'. →2 (p.377)

QUESTION

Alf sends Bertha several threatening text messages, following which Bertha suffers depression. What offences has Alf committed?

Alf will be charged with an assault occasioning actual bodily harm (Offences Against the Person Act 1861, section 47). Clearly the prosecution will want to rely on *Ireland* to show that words can amount to assault, and that the depression can be regarded as actual bodily harm. But the prosecution will face three difficult tasks:

(1) The prosecution must show that Bertha, as the result of the text messages, apprehended an imminent use of force. It would not be enough if she was just afraid in a general sense.

(2) It must be shown that Alf intended or foresaw that Bertha would apprehend an imminent use of force.

(3) It must be shown that Bertha suffered the depression because of the apprehension of imminent force.

---

[60] In *Morris* [1998] 1 Cr App R 386 (CA) there was evidence that the victim suffered anxiety, fear, and sleeplessness. But it was held that this was insufficient to amount to actual bodily harm because it did not involve a recognized medical condition.
[61] [2006] EWCA Crim 1139.
[62] *Roberts* (1972) 56 Cr App R 95.   [63] *Ibid.*
[64] [1997] 4 All ER 225.   [65] [1992] 1 AC 699.

4 MALICIOUS WOUNDING

The Offences Against the Person Act 1861, section 20 states:

> Whosoever shall unlawfully and maliciously wound or inflict any grievous bodily harm upon any other person, either with or without any weapon or instrument, shall be liable . . . to imprisonment for a term not exceeding five years.

DEFINITION

Actus reus: the defendant unlawfully either:

(1) wounded the victim; or

(2) inflicted grievous bodily harm to the victim.

Mens rea: the defendant foresaw that the victim might suffer some harm. (NB: It is not necessary to show that the defendant intended or foresaw that the victim would suffer grievous bodily harm.)

The following terms need to be defined in greater detail:

(1) **Unlawfully** This means that the defendant acted without lawful justification. An example of a lawful justification is where the defendant was acting in self-defence. This will be discussed further in Chapter 12.

(2) **Wound** This has been interpreted in *C v Eisenhower*[66] to mean a break in the continuity of the whole of the skin.[67] A rupture of an internal blood vessel is not a wound.[68] However, the breaking of an inner membrane which is analogous to skin may constitute a wound. So it is generally accepted that an injury to the inside of a mouth was a wound.[69] The requirement that the whole of the continuation of the skin be broken means that a scratch may draw blood but may not be deep enough for a wound if it only disturbs the outer layer of the skin.

William Wilson has argued that the normal meaning of the word 'wound' is that a wound can occur only if there is a direct application of force.[70] If his argument is correct it would mean that if the defendant terrified the victim into running away and the victim fell over and cut herself, there was no wound. In such a case the defendant caused the victim to suffer a wound, but did not wound the victim.[71] Against Wilson's view is the argument that the use of the words 'either with or without any weapon' in section 20 suggests that the courts should not be too concerned with the way the wound is caused. We await a clear decision from the courts on this issue.

---

[66] [1984] QB 331 (DC).

[67] The breaking of just the outer skin is insufficient (*M'Loughlin* (1838) 173 ER 651). The skin comprises two layers: dermis and epidermis. Both must be broken for there to be a wound.

[68] *JCC (A Minor) v Eisenhower* (1984) 78 Cr App R 48 (DC). This means that there may be bleeding without there being a wound.

[69] In *Waltham* (1849) 3 Cox CC 442 a policeman was kicked in the genitals in such a way that the lining membrane of the urethra was ruptured, leading to bleeding. The urethra was held to be, in effect, a continuation of the external skin and so there was a wound.

[70] W. Wilson (2003: 308).

[71] It should be noted that s. 20 does not include the phrase 'by any means whatsoever', which is found in s. 18.

(3) **Grievous bodily harm** Grievous bodily harm (gbh) means 'really serious bodily harm'.[72] It is for the jury to decide whether the injuries amount to gbh[73] using 'contemporary social standards'.[74] That is, perhaps, surprising; you might think that expert evidence could be useful, especially in cases of lesser known harms. In deciding whether the harm is really serious it is necessary to consider the totality of the injuries inflicted on the victim. So if the defendant punched a victim a large number of times, leaving him bruised all over his body, the totality of the bruising could constitute grievous bodily harm, even if each individual bruise would only constitute actual bodily harm.[75] In *Brown and Stratton*[76] the Court of Appeal allowed an appeal after a judge had directed the jury to consider whether the victim regarded the injuries as serious. This was said to be wrong: whether the injuries were really serious was an objective test. It is not quite clear what this means. Clearly, just because the victim regards the injuries as serious does not mean that the jury must find them serious. But what is not clear is whether the jury in assessing the seriousness of the harm can take into account the characteristics of the victim. For example, if the defendant injured a concert pianist's finger, which meant that she could not play the piano, could the jury decide that this injury *for this victim* was a serious injury, even if for most people it would not be? In *Bollom*[77] the Court of Appeal held that in assessing whether the injuries were really serious, the impact of them on the particular victim should be taken into account. So what might not be a serious injury to an adult might be to a baby. Further, injuries may be regarded as really serious even if they do not cause the victim great pain.[78]

Grievous bodily harm can include very serious psychological harm.[79] To amount to grievous bodily harm there must be more than serious distress or upset: there must be a serious identifiable clinical condition.[80] For example, a very serious depression could amount to grievous bodily harm.

It is important to note that the statute requires that the injury either be a wound or the infliction of grievous bodily harm. Breaking a collar bone would not be a wound,[81] but may well constitute grievous bodily harm. On the other hand some wounds may not amount to grievous bodily harm. A pinprick may be a wound, but not amount to grievous bodily harm.

(4) **Infliction of grievous bodily harm** It is necessary to show that the defendant *inflicted* the grievous bodily harm. There is much debate over what inflicted means in section 20, and particularly how it differs from the word 'cause' in section 18. What has been established beyond doubt is that there is no need to demonstrate that there has been an assault in order to establish a conviction under section 20. It used to be thought that inflict had a narrower meaning than cause, in that inflict required the direct application of force, whereas cause meant to bring about in any way.[82] However, in *Burstow*,[83] Lord Steyn explained that although the words cause and inflict were not synonymous, 'in the context of the Act of 1861 there is no radical divergence between the meaning of the two words'.[84] As to the argument

---

[72] *DPP v Smith* [1961] AC 290. But it has been suggested that sometimes it is permissible for the judge simply to define it as 'serious harm' (*Janjua* [1999] 1 CAR 91).

[73] *Hill* [2015] EWCA Crim 1292. [74] *Golding* [2014] EWCA Crim 889.

[75] *Grundy* [1977] Crim LR 543. [76] [1998] Crim LR 484. [77] [2003] EWCA Crim 2846.

[78] *Meachen* [2009] EWCA Crim 1701. [79] *Burstow* [1998] AC 147.

[80] Hobhouse LJ in *Chan-Fook* (1994) 99 Cr App R 147, 152. [81] *Wood* (1830) 1 Mood CC 278.

[82] *Clarence* (1888) 22 QBD 23. [83] [1998] AC 147.

[84] The House of Lords in *Wilson* [1984] AC 242 and *Mandair* [1995] 1 AC 208 had already made it clear that an infliction does not require proof of an assault or a battery.

that infliction required an application of force to the body, Lord Steyn called this 'absurd'.[85] Having decided that for the purposes of the Act inflict and cause are synonymous, their Lordships were able to hold that a serious psychological condition could be inflicted by a defendant pursuing a campaign of harassment against the victim.[86] So the judgments in *Burstow* indicate that inflict now means the same as cause.[87]

(5) **The *mens rea* requirement** The *mens rea* for section 20 is that the defendant must intend or foresee (*Cunningham* recklessness) that he or she may cause some kind of harm, albeit minor harm. So it is *not* necessary for the prosecution to show that the defendant intended or foresaw grievous bodily harm. It is not even necessary to show that the defendant believed that he or she *would* cause some harm: it is enough if it is proved that the defendant believed he or she *might*.[88]

Quite what harm means in this context is not clear. It clearly covers physical injuries to bodies, but what about psychological injuries? It seems likely that a court would follow *Burstow and Ireland*[89] and hold that a recognizable psychological condition would constitute a harm, but that fear on its own would not.[90] This would mean that a defendant will be guilty if he makes a silent telephone call, foreseeing that the victim may suffer a psychological illness as a result, but the victim, in terror, runs down the stairs of her house and falls, suffering grievous bodily harm. He is guilty because his foresight that the victim would suffer a psychological illness would constitute the *mens rea* for a section 20 charge.

The *mens rea* of malicious wounding was established in the following important decision of the House of Lords:

R v Savage; R v Parmenter
[1992] 1 AC 699 (HL)

Susan Savage was convicted of unlawful wounding contrary to section 20 of the Offences Against the Person Act 1861. The charge resulted from an incident when Ms Savage approached Ms Beal in a pub and said 'Nice to meet you, darling'. Ms Savage had in her hand a pint of beer. She threw the beer over Ms Beal, the glass slipped out of her hand, broke, and Ms Beal was cut. Philip Parmenter caused injuries to his baby son while playing with him in a vigorous way. He explained that he did not realize that what he was doing would cause injury. He was convicted under section 20 of the Offences Against the Person Act 1861.

Lord Ackner

I. Is a verdict of guilty of assault occasioning actual bodily harm a permissible alternative verdict on a count alleging unlawful wounding contrary to s 20 of the 1861 Act?

The critical question remained: do the allegations in a s 20 charge 'include either expressly or by implication' allegations of assault occasioning actual bodily harm? As to this, Lord Roskill concluded (*R v Wilson (Clarence)* [1984] AC 242 at 261):

---

[85] [1997] 3 WLR 534, 545.   [86] *Burstow* [1998] AC 147.
[87] This was applied in *Dica* [2004] EWCA Crim 1103.
[88] This was stressed in *Rushmore* (1992) 95 Cr App R 252 and *DPP v A* [2001] Crim LR 140.
[89] [1998] AC 147.   [90] *Sullivan* [1981] Crim LR 46.

'If "inflicting" can, as the cases show, include "inflicting by assault", then, even though such a charge may not necessarily do so, I do not for myself see why on a fair reading of s 6(3) these allegations do not at least impliedly include "inflicting by assault". That is sufficient for present purposes, though I also regard it as also a possible view that those former allegations expressly include the other allegations.' (Lord Roskill's emphasis)

I respectfully agree with this reasoning and accordingly reject the submission that *R v Wilson (Clarence)* was wrongly decided. I would therefore answer the first of the certified questions in *R v Savage* [whether a verdict of guilty of assault occasioning actual bodily harm is a permissible alternative verdict on a count alleging unlawful wounding contrary to section 20 of the Offences Against the Person Act 1861] in the affirmative. A verdict of guilty of assault occasioning actual bodily harm is a permissible alternative verdict on a count alleging unlawful wounding contrary to s 20 of the 1861 Act.

II. Can a verdict of assault occasioning actual bodily harm be returned upon proof of an assault together with proof of the fact that actual bodily harm was occasioned by the assault, or must the prosecution also prove that the defendant intended to cause some actual bodily harm or was reckless as to whether such harm would be caused?

Your Lordships are concerned with the mental element of a particular kind of assault, an assault 'occasioning actual bodily harm'. It is common ground that the mental element of assault is an intention to cause the victim to apprehend immediate and unlawful violence or recklessness whether such apprehension be caused (see *R v Venna* [1976] QB 421). It is of course common ground that Mrs Savage committed an assault upon Miss Beal when she threw the contents of her glass of beer over her. It is also common ground that however the glass came to be broken and Miss Beal's wrist thereby cut, it was, on the finding of the jury, Mrs Savage's handling of the glass which caused Miss Beal 'actual bodily harm'. Was the offence thus established or is there a further mental state that has to be established in relation to the bodily harm element of the offence? Clearly the section, by its terms, expressly imposes no such a requirement. Does it do so by necessary implication? It uses neither the word 'intentionally' nor the word 'maliciously'. The words 'occasioning actual bodily harm' are descriptive of the word 'assault', by reference to a particular kind of consequence.

In neither *R v Savage* not *R v Spratt* nor in *R v Parmenter* was the court's attention invited to the decision of the Court of Appeal in *R v Roberts* (1972) 56 Cr App R 95. This is perhaps explicable on the basis that this case is not referred to in the index to Archbold's *Criminal Pleading, Evidence and Practice* (43rd edn, 1988). The relevant text, states (para 20-117): 'The mens rea required [for actual bodily harm] is that required for common assault', without any authority being provided for this proposition.

It is in fact *R v Roberts* which provides authority for this proposition. Roberts was tried on an indictment which alleged that he indecently assaulted a young woman. He was acquitted on that charge, but convicted of assault occasioning actual bodily harm to her. The girl's complaint was that while travelling in the defendant's car he sought to make advances towards her and then tried to take her coat off. This was the last straw and, although the car was travelling at some speed, she jumped out and sustained injuries. The defendant denied he had touched the girl. He had had an argument with her and in the course of that argument she suddenly opened the door and jumped out. In his direction to the jury the chairman of quarter sessions stated: 'If you are satisfied that he tried to pull off her coat and as a result she jumped out of the moving car then your verdict is guilty.'

It was contended on behalf of the appellant that this direction was wrong since the chairman had failed to tell the jury that they must be satisfied that the appellant foresaw that she might jump out of the car as a result of his touching her before they could convict . . . Thus, once the assault was established, the only remaining question was whether the victim's conduct was the natural consequence of that assault. The words 'occasioning' raised solely a question of causation, an objective question which does not involve inquiring into the accused's state of mind.

. . . The decision in *R v Roberts* (1972) 56 Cr App R 95 was correct. The verdict of assault occasioning actual bodily harm may be returned upon proof of an assault together with proof of the fact that actual bodily harm was occasioned by the assault. The prosecution are not obliged to prove that the defendant intended to cause some actual bodily harm or was reckless as to whether such harm would be caused.

III. In order to establish an offence under s 20 of the 1861 Act, must the prosecution prove that the defendant actually foresaw that his act would cause harm, or is it sufficient to prove that he ought so to have foreseen?

Although your Lordships' attention has been invited to a plethora of decided cases, the issue is a narrow one. Is the decision of the Court of Criminal Appeal in *R v Cunningham* [1957] 2 All ER 412, [1957] 2 QB 396 still good law, subject only to a gloss placed upon it by the Court of Appeal, Criminal Division in *R v Mowatt* [1968] 1 QB 421, or does the later decision of your Lordships' House in *R v Caldwell* [1982] AC 341 provide the answer to this question?

[Having surveyed the case law **Lord Ackner** concluded:]

[I]n order to establish an offence under s 20 the prosecution must prove either that the defendant intended or that he actually foresaw that his act would cause harm.

IV. In order to establish an offence under s 20 is it sufficient to prove that the defendant intended or foresaw the risk of some physical harm or must he intend or foresee either wounding or grievous bodily harm?

It is convenient to set out once again the relevant part of the judgment of Diplock LJ in *R v Mowatt* [1967] 3 All ER 47 at 50, [1968] 1 QB 421 at 426. Having considered Professor Kenny's statement, which I have quoted above, he then said: 'In the offence under s 20 . . . for . . . which [no] specific intent is required—the word "maliciously" does import . . . an *awareness* that his act may have the consequence of causing some physical harm to some other person. That is what is meant by the "particular kind of harm" in the citation from Professor Kenny's *Outlines Of Criminal Law* (18th edn, 1962, para 158a, p 202). It is quite unnecessary that the accused should have foreseen that his unlawful act might cause physical harm of the gravity described in the section, i.e. a wound or serious physical injury. It is enough that he should have foreseen that some physical harm to some person, albeit of a minor character, might result.' (My emphasis.)

Mr Sedley submits that this statement of the law is wrong. He contends that, properly construed, the section requires foresight of a wounding or grievous bodily harm. He drew your Lordships' attention to criticisms of *R v Mowatt* made by Professor Glanville Williams and by Professor JC Smith in their textbooks and in articles or commentaries. They argue that a person should not be criminally liable for consequences of his conduct unless he foresaw a consequence falling into the same legal category as that set out in the indictment.

Such a general principle runs contrary to the decision in *R v Roberts* (1972) 56 Cr App R 95, which I have already stated to be, in my opinion, correct. The contention is apparently based on the proposition that, as the *actus reus* of a s 20 offence is the wounding or the infliction of grievous bodily harm, the *mens rea* must consist of foreseeing such wounding or grievous bodily harm. But there is no such hard and fast principle. To take but two examples, the *actus reus* of murder is the killing of the victim, but foresight of grievous bodily harm is sufficient and, indeed, such bodily harm need not be such as to be dangerous to life. Again, in the case of manslaughter death is frequently the unforeseen consequence of the violence used.

The argument that, as ss 20 and 47 have both the same penalty, this somehow supports the proposition that the foreseen consequences must coincide with the harm actually done, overlooks the oft-repeated statement that this is the irrational result of this piecemeal legislation. The Act 'is a rag-bag of offences brought together from a wide variety of sources with no attempt, as the draftsman frankly acknowledged, to introduce consistency as to substance or as to form' (see Professor JC Smith in his commentary on *R v Parmenter* ([1991] Crim LR 43)).

If s 20 was to be limited to cases where the accused does not desire but does foresee wounding or grievous bodily harm, it would have a very limited scope. The *mens rea* in a s 20 crime is comprised in the word 'maliciously'. As was pointed out by Lord Lane CJ, giving the judgment of the Court of Appeal in *R v Sullivan* [1981] Crim LR 46, the 'particular kind of harm' in the citation from Professor Kenny was directed to 'harm to the person' as opposed to 'harm to property'. Thus it was not concerned with the degree of the harm foreseen. It is accordingly in my judgment wrong to look upon the decision in *R v Mowatt* [1968] 1 QB 421 as being in any way inconsistent with the decision in *R v Cunningham* [1957] 2 QB 396.

My Lords, I am satisfied that the decision in *R v Mowatt* was correct and that it is quite unnecessary that the accused should either have intended or have foreseen that his unlawful act might cause physical harm of the gravity described in s 20, i.e. a wound or serious physical injury. It is enough that he should have foreseen that some physical harm to some person, albeit of a minor character, might result.

In the result I would dismiss the appeal in Savage's case but allow the appeal in Parmenter's case, but only to the extent of substituting, in accordance with the provisions of s 3(2) of the Criminal Appeal Act 1968, verdicts of guilty of assault occasioning actual bodily harm contrary to s 47 of the 1861 Act for the four s 20 offences of which he was convicted.

Savage's appeal dismissed. Parmenter's appeal allowed.

QUESTION

An unintended consequence of *Burstow and Ireland*?

If a husband tells his wife that he has had an affair and therefore she suffers serious depression would the husband be guilty of an offence under section 20?

It would be most surprising if he could be convicted of an offence in such a case. But it seems he can. If the husband realizes that his wife may suffer depression in these circumstances, he has the *mens rea* for the section 20 offence. Further, in the light of *Burstow* he can be said to have inflicted the harm (if inflict means the same as cause). There are three possible ways of avoiding this conclusion. First, it could be argued that the conduct of the defendant was not unlawful. However, unlawful in this context simply means that the defendant successfully pleads one of the law's recognized defences (e.g. duress or self-defence). The husband here cannot plead one of these defences. A second argument is to recall that a defendant is *Cunningham* reckless only if the risk of harm taken was an unreasonable one to take. The husband in admitting adultery could be said to be acting reasonably. A third response is to point out that it is not unusual for offences to be very broadly defined and then leave the prosecution to use the offence sensibly. No sensible officer of the Crown Prosecution Service would charge the husband in this example, even if technically he could be convicted of the offence.

5   WOUNDING WITH INTENT

Section 18 of the Offences Against the Person Act 1861 states:

> Whosoever shall unlawfully and maliciously by any means whatsoever wound or cause any grievous bodily harm to any person . . . with intent . . . to do some grievous bodily harm to any person, or with intent to resist or prevent the lawful apprehension or detainer of any person, shall be guilty of an offence and being convicted thereof shall be liable, . . . to imprisonment for life.

DEFINITION

Actus reus: the defendant unlawfully wounded or caused grievous bodily harm to any person.

Mens rea: either: (a) the defendant intended to cause grievous bodily harm; or (b) the defendant intended to resist or prevent the lawful apprehension or detention of any person.

The wording of section 18 is very similar to that of section 20, and the meaning of many of the terms used in section 18 has already been discussed. There are four key differences between the section 18 and section 20 offences:

(1)   The most important difference is the *mens rea*. The core *mens rea* for section 18 is that the defendant intended to do some grievous bodily harm. Intention here is to be given the same meaning as that discussed in Chapter 3. The *mens rea* requirement for section 18 is, then, more stringent than that required for section 20. Section 18 requires proof of intention, while recklessness is enough for section 20; section 18 requires proof that grievous bodily harm was intended, while section 20 requires that some harm was foreseen. Notice that the *mens rea* for section 18 is an intent to cause grievous bodily harm, an intent to wound will not be sufficient.[91]

Even if the defendant did not intend grievous bodily harm he can still be convicted under section 18 if he was intending to prevent or resist an arrest. It is necessary to show both:

(a)   the defendant was *Cunningham* reckless (which is how the courts have interpreted maliciously) probably to causing grievous bodily (but possibly just some) harm;[92] and

(b)   that he intended to resist or prevent the lawful apprehension or detention of any person.

---

[91]   *O'Donnell* [2010] EWCA Crim 1480.
[92]   The question was left open in *Morrison* (1989) 89 Cr App R 17 (CA).

As regards (b) it is no defence to show that the defendant thought the arrest was unlawful.[93] What must be shown is that the defendant intended to resist or prevent an apprehension, which was in fact a lawful apprehension. If in fact the arrest was not lawful then the offence would not be committed.

(2) Section 20 states that the wound or cause of grievous bodily harm can be 'with or without any weapon or instrument', whereas section 18 states that it can be 'by any means whatsoever'. It is submitted that the best view is that there is no significance in this difference in the wording. If there is any difference it could be argued that section 20 requires some kind of direct blow, whereas section 18 requires only proof that the defendant caused the injuries in any way.[94]

(3) The third difference in the wording of the two sections is that section 20 states that the defendant must cause injury to 'any other person', while in section 18 the injury must be caused to 'any person'. It could therefore be argued that if a defendant caused him or herself grievous bodily harm intentionally he or she committed an offence contrary to section 18; but if he or she did so recklessly there would be no offence contrary to section 20. However, no reported prosecution has been brought under section 18 on the basis that the defendant caused him or herself grievous bodily harm.

(4) We have already discussed the fact that section 18 requires the defendant to have caused grievous bodily harm, while section 20 requires proof that the defendant inflicted grievous bodily harm. After *Burstow and Ireland* and *Dica*[95] it is clear that inflict and cause mean the same thing. →3 (p.377)

6 MIXING AND MATCHING THE OFFENCES

If a defendant is charged with one of these assaults, but the jury acquits him or her of that offence, the jury can nevertheless convict the defendant of a lesser assault.[96] So if the defendant is charged with a section 18 offence the jury can still convict him or her of an offence under section 20 or 47; if charged with a section 20 offence he or she can still be convicted of an offence under section 47.

7 POISONING

Two poisoning offences will be considered in detail:[97]

(1) Offences Against the Person Act 1861, section 23, which says:

> Whosoever shall unlawfully and maliciously administer to or cause to be administered to or taken by any other person any poison or other destructive or noxious thing, so as thereby to endanger the life of such person, or so as thereby to inflict upon such person any grievous bodily harm shall be guilty of [an offence], and being convicted thereof shall be liable . . . to imprisonment for any term not exceeding ten years.

---

[93] *Bentley* (1850) 4 Cox CC 406.   [94] J. Gardner (1994a).   [95] [2004] EWCA Crim 1103.
[96] Although in practical terms this is highly convenient, there are theoretical problems with it (see Hare (1993)).
[97] You should also be aware of the Sexual Offences Act 2003, s. 61, which makes it an offence to administer a substance to stupefy a victim to enable the sexual activity with them to take place.

> **DEFINITION**
>
> Section 23 of the Offences Against the Person Act 1861:
>
> *Actus reus*: the defendant administered to or caused to be administered to or taken by the victim a poison, noxious, or destructive thing. As a result, he or she (a) endangered the life of the victim or (b) inflicted upon the victim any grievous bodily harm.
>
> *Mens rea*: the defendant was *Cunningham* recklessness as to the administration of a poison, noxious, or destructive thing. (NB: It does not need to be shown that the defendant intended or foresaw that the victim's life would be endangered or that the victim would suffer any grievous bodily harm.)

(2) Offences Against the Person Act 1861, section 24, which states:

> Whosoever shall unlawfully and maliciously administer to or cause to be administered to or taken by any other person any poison or other destructive or noxious thing, with intent to injure, aggrieve, or annoy such person, shall be guilty of an offence, and being . . . convicted thereof shall be liable to imprisonment for a term not exceeding five years.

> **DEFINITION**
>
> Section 24 of the Offences Against the Person Act 1861:
>
> *Actus reus*: the defendant administered or caused to be administered to or taken by the victim a poison, noxious, or destructive thing.
>
> *Mens rea*: the defendant was reckless to the administration of the poison or noxious thing *and* intended to injure, aggrieve, or annoy the victim.

Although both sections 23 and 24 have the same basic element (unlawfully and maliciously administering or causing to be administered or be taken by a person any poison or other destructive or noxious thing), they have different aggravating features:

(1) In section 23 it is the effect of the poisoning: there must be the infliction of grievous bodily harm or an endangerment of the victim's life. All that needs to be foreseen is the administration of the poison or noxious thing.

(2) In section 24 it is the intent of the defendant which is the aggravating feature: there must be an intent to injure, aggrieve, or annoy the victim.

7.1 THE MEANING OF 'POISON' OR 'NOXIOUS SUBSTANCE'

'Poison' has been widely interpreted by the courts. It is necessary to distinguish between:

(1) Substances which are in their nature poisoning or noxious (e.g. cyanide, sulphuric acid, or heroin). Such substances are poisons or noxious substances whatever quantity is used. To put arsenic in someone's tea is to administer poison to them, even if it is harmless in the amount administered.[98] In *Cato*[99] it was confirmed that heroin is noxious even if taken by a regular user who suffers no direct harm.[100]

---

[98] *Cramp* (1880) 5 QBD 307 (a case considering the meaning of 'poison' under the Offences Against the Person Act 1861, s. 58 (administration of poison to procure an abortion)).

[99] *Cato* [1976] 1 All ER 260 (CA).   [100] This view was also adopted in *Cramp* (1880) 5 QBD 307.

(2) Substances which are not in their nature harmful. For such substances it must be shown that the substance was administered in a quantity sufficient to be harmful.[101] So placing a large amount of cod liver oil in someone's cappuccino could poison them, even though a very small amount would not.

A noxious substance is a substance which is hurtful, unwholesome, or objectionable.[102] If the substance is not in its nature noxious, it can become noxious if administered in such large doses that it becomes so. In *Marcus*[103] a sedative administered in large quantities became noxious, even though, had it been administered in small quantities, it would not have been harmful (and so not noxious).

7.2 THE MEANING OF 'ADMINISTER'

'Administration' is widely defined in the statute. It includes the defendant administering the poison, as well as causing the victim to take the poison him or herself. This seems certainly to cover the situation where the defendant secretly poisoned the victim's drink.[104] In *Kennedy*[105] it was held that supplying a drug at the request of the victim who then took it himself could not constitute administration.[106] In *Gillard*[107] it was accepted that spraying CS gas onto the victim would amount to administering poison. It was confirmed by McNeill J that administration of a poison did not require the substance to enter the victim's body, although it would require contact with the body. So simply putting poison in an enemy's food would not in itself be an administration, until someone ate the food.

7.3 THE MEANING OF 'MALICIOUSLY'

This has been interpreted to mean recklessness. That means that the defendant must foresee that his or her act will cause the poison to be administered. For example, in *Cunningham*[108] the defendant broke a gas pipe in a basement. It was confirmed that the prosecution had to prove that the defendant foresaw that the gas would escape and be administered to the victim. One issue which is left unresolved by the case law is whether the defendant has to foresee that the gas will be noxious. In other words is it enough that the defendant foresaw the administration of a substance or must it be shown that the defendant foresaw the administration of a poison or noxious substance?

---

101 *Marlow* (1964) 49 Cr App R 49.
102 *Marcus* [1981] 2 All ER 833. In one case a woman put dog excrement in her husband's curry. No doubt this would be deemed unwholesome (BBC News Online 2007a).
103 [1981] 2 All ER 833.
104 *Harley* (1830) 4 C & P 396; *Dale* (1852) 6 Cox CC 14.
105 *Kennedy* [2007] UKHL 38.
106 This is on the basis that the victim, if acting in a free, voluntary, and informed way, was breaking the chain of causation by administering the drugs themselves.
107 (1988) 87 Cr App R 189.   108 [1957] 2 QB 396.

7.4 THE MEANING OF 'ENDANGERMENT OF LIFE' OR 'CAUSE GRIEVOUS BODILY HARM'

For section 23 it is not necessary to show that the defendant intended or foresaw that the victim would suffer grievous bodily harm or endangerment of life. There is some debate whether the causation of grievous bodily harm or endangerment of life in section 23 must be caused directly by the poisoning. Imagine this: the defendant poisons the victim who then feels drowsy, falls down, and suffers grievous bodily harm. It might be argued that in such a case the offence would not be made out because it would not be the poison itself which caused the harm. However, if 'cause' in this section were to be given its ordinary meaning, there seems little doubt that the causation would be established.

7.5 THE MEANING OF 'WITH INTENT TO INJURE, AGGRIEVE OR ANNOY'

'Intent' in section 24 is to be given its normal meaning within the criminal law, as set out in Chapter 3. The words 'injure', 'aggrieve', or 'annoy' should be given their ordinary meaning. However, there was some debate over whether it is necessary to show that the intent was to injure, aggrieve, or annoy as a direct result of the poisoning or whether it was sufficient to poison with the intent of injuring, aggrieving, or annoying in some other way. The issue was raised in *Hill*.[109] The defendant gave some tablets to boys aged 11 and 13. They were slimming tablets which had the side effect of causing sleeplessness. The prosecution argued that Hill's plan was that the tablets would mean the boys would stay up late and would therefore be more susceptible to his sexual advances. In fact the defendant made no sexual advances and the boys suffered diarrhoea and vomiting. The House of Lords held that the defendant could properly be convicted of an offence under section 24. An intention of keeping boys awake in order to abuse them could constitute an intention to 'injure, aggrieve or annoy' for the purposes of section 24. Lord Griffiths[110] suggested that if a mother gave her children a tablet to keep them awake so that they could welcome their father home this would not amount to the requisite intention. So in deciding whether there was an intent to injure, aggrieve, or annoy the jury should consider not only the intended effects of the substance, but the overall plan of the defendant.

FURTHER READING

Bell, B. and Harrison, K. (1993) '*R v Savage, DPP v Parmenter* and the Law of Assault' *Modern Law Review* 56: 83.

Chalmers, J. (2014) 'Offenses against the Person' in M. Dubber and T. Hörnle (eds) *The Oxford Handbook of Criminal Law* (Oxford: OUP).

Gardner, S. (1998c) 'Stalking' *Law Quarterly Review* 114: 33.

Hare, I. (1993) '*R v Savage, DPP v Parmenter*—A Compelling Case for the Code' *Modern Law Review* 56: 74.

Herring, J. (1998b) 'The Criminalisation of Harassment' *Cambridge Law Journal* 57: 10.

Hirst, M. (1999) 'Assault, Battery and Indirect Violence' *Criminal Law Review* 557.

Horder, J. (1998a) 'Reconsidering Psychic Assault' *Criminal Law Review* 392.

---

[109] (1986) 83 CAR 386.   [110] *Ibid*, 390.

8 OTHER ASSAULT CRIMES

There are a number of other assault offences which will not be covered in this book[111] including assaulting an officer of the court,[112] assaulting a clergyman in the discharge of his duties in a place of worship or burial place,[113] assaulting with intent to rob,[114] assaulting with intent to commit a sexual offence,[115] assaulting with intent to resist arrest, and assaulting a police officer.[116] There are also some important public order criminal offences which are not dealt with here, for example, riot; violent disorder; affray; causing harassment, alarm, or distress.

9 RACIALLY AND RELIGIOUSLY AGGRAVATED CRIMES

There has been increasing concern over racially or religiously motivated crimes.[117]

In 2013/14, there were 44,480 hate crimes recorded by the police in England and Wales. Of these:

- 37,484 (84 per cent) were race hate crimes;
- 4,622 (10 per cent) were sexual orientation hate crimes;
- 2,273 (5 per cent) were religion hate crimes;
- 1,985 (4 per cent) were disability hate crimes; and
- 555 (1 per cent) were transgender hate crimes.[118]

Those are figures of reported incidents, of course many go unreported.[119] In creating these offences the government decided that crimes with a racial element should be given higher sentences and be specifically labelled as such. The justification for this is that:

> The Government recognises that racist crime does not simply injure the victim or their property, it affects the whole family and it erodes the standards of decency of the wider community. Trust and understanding built up over many years between communities can be eroded by the climate of fear and anxiety which can surround a racist incident.[120]

Baroness Hale in *Rogers*[121] explained the offences in this way:

> The mischiefs attacked by the aggravated versions of these offences are racism and xenophobia. Their essence is the denial of equal respect and dignity to people who are seen

---

111 See *R v Cockburn* [2008] Crim LR 802 for an example of how some of these unusual assaults are still occasionally used.

112 County Courts Act 1984, s. 14(1)(b).   113 Offences Against the Person Act 1861, s. 36.

114 Theft Act 1968, s. 8.   115 Sexual Offences Act 2003, s. 62.   116 Police Act 1996, s. 89.

117 Home Office (1997). For a discussion of whether gender-based hate offences should be created, see Walters and Tumath (2014).

118 Home Office (2014a). The percentages do not add up to 100 as sometimes hatred was shown based on several characteristics.

119 See Owusu-Bempah (2015) for a helpful discussion of the difficulties in prosecuting these offences in practice.

120 Home Office (1998a: para. 1.1).   121 *Rogers* [2007] UKHL 8, para. 12.

as 'other'. This is more deeply hurtful, damaging and disrespectful to the victims than the simple versions of these offences. It is also more damaging to the community as a whole, by denying acceptance to members of certain groups not for their own sake but for the sake of something they can do nothing about.

Sections 28 to 32 of the Crime and Disorder Act 1998 created a new category of racially or religiously aggravated crimes.[122]

DEFINITION

1. The defendant has committed one of the following offences:
   (a) common assault;
   (b) section 47 of the Offences Against the Person Act;
   (c) section 20 of the Offences Against the Person Act;
   (d) section 2 of the Protection from Harassment Act 1997;
   (e) section 4 of the Protection from Harassment Act 1997;
   (f) criminal damage;
   (g) sections 4, 4A, and 5 of the Public Order Act 1986.
2. The offence was racially or religiously aggravated.

A person commits an offence under section 29 of the Act[123] if he or she commits one of the offences listed in the previous box, which is 'racially or religiously aggravated'.[124]

DEFINITION

(1) An offence is racially or religiously aggravated . . . if—
   (a) at the time of committing the offence, or immediately before or after doing so, the offender demonstrates towards the victim of the offence hostility based on the victim's membership (or presumed membership) of a racial or religious group; or
   (b) the offence is motivated (wholly or partly) by hostility towards members of a racial group based on their membership of that group.

(2) In subsection (1)(a) above—
   'membership' in relation to a racial or religious group includes association with members of that group;
   'presumed' means presumed by the offender.

(3) It is immaterial for the purpose of paragraph (a) or (b) of subsection (1) above whether or not the offender's hostility is also based, to any extent, on any factor not mentioned in that paragraph.

(4) In this section 'racial group' means a group of persons defined by reference to race, colour, nationality (including citizenship) or ethnic or national origins.

(5) In this section 'religious group' means a group of persons defined by reference to religious belief or lack of religious belief.

---

[122] Burney (2003) and Burney and Rose (2002) provide useful discussions of the Act's operation.

[123] As amended by the Anti-terrorism, Crime and Security Act 2001.

[124] There is no racially aggravated version of s. 18 of the Offences Against the Person Act 1861 because that offence has a maximum sentence of life imprisonment, and so it cannot be given a higher sentence.

There are therefore two ways of showing the offence is racially or religiously aggravated:[125]

(1) that under section 28(1)(a) racial or religious hostility was demonstrated during the commission of the offence; or

(2) under section 28(1)(b) that the offence was motivated by D's hostility to V.

Section 28(1)(a) will be relied upon where some racial or religious insult was uttered during the attack. It should be noted that, under this subsection, as long as racial or religious hostility is demonstrated, there is no need to show that the attack was motivated by racial or religious hostility.[126] The subsection can be relied upon where hostility is demonstrated immediately before or immediately after the attack. The victim need not be aware that the hostility has been demonstrated.[127] Indeed a conviction could be found even though there was no victim present of the race referred to by the defendant.[128] Where no insulting words are spoken it may be easier in many cases to rely on section 28(1)(b) if it can be shown that the attack was motivated by race or religion. For this offence the motivation of the defendant is key.[129] How easily this can be proved may depend on how ready a jury will be to assume that an attack is racially or religiously motivated from the fact that the attacker and victim are of a different race or religion and there is no other apparent reason for the attack. There is no need to show that race was the sole motivation for the offence.[130]

In *Rogers*[131] the defendant assaulted a group of women calling them 'bloody foreigners'. This was held by the House of Lords to be hostility based on a racial group. It was held that the notion of race should be defined widely and included groups defined by their colour, race, ethnic origin, nationality, and national origins. Their Lordships held that race in this context was not intended to be a technical term. In *Attorney-General's Reference (No. 4 of 2004)*[132] it was held that the phrase 'immigrant doctor' could be thought by the jury to be a demonstration of racial hostility. Ultimately it is for the jury to decide whether a particular phrase is racial hostility or is simply general abuse. In *R v SH*[133] the Court of Appeal suggested that repeatedly calling a Nigerian national 'a monkey' created a strong prima facie case of racial hostility.

It should not be assumed that because a racial insult was uttered prior to the attack race was the motivation for the attack. In *DPP v Pal*[134] a caretaker at a community centre, described as being of Asian appearance, ejected the defendant (an Asian youth) from the building. The defendant called the caretaker a 'brown Englishman' and uttered other racial insults, and later attacked him. It was held by the Divisional Court that this was not a racially aggravated assault because the assault was motivated by the defendant's anger at having to leave the centre and at what he regarded as the victim's close relationships with whites, rather than his race as such. The court, however, emphasized that simply that the defendant and victim were of the same race did not prevent the assault being racially aggravated. The court gave the example of a white man attacking another white man because he was going out with a black woman. However, in *DPP v McFarlane*[135] *Pal* was said to be heavily

---

[125] The courts have indicated that they are willing to give 'race' a wide interpretation (*White* [2001] EWCA Crim 216, [2001] 1 WLR 1352 (CA)).

[126] *DPP v Woods* [2002] EWHC 85 (Admin); *Jones v DPP* [2010] EWHC 523 (Admin).

[127] *Parry v DPP* [2004] EWHC 3112 (Admin).

[128] *R (DPP) v Dykes* [2008] EWHC 2775 (Admin).

[129] *Jones v DPP* [2010] EWHC 523 (Admin).   [130] *Johnson v DPP* [2008] EWHC 509 (Admin).

[131] [2007] UKHL 8.   [132] [2005] Crim LR 799.   [133] [2010] EWCA Crim 1931.

[134] [2000] Crim LR 756.   [135] [2002] EWHC 485 (Admin).

dependent on the facts of the case and that normally where a racial insult was uttered during a crime it would be regarded as racially aggravated.[136] In *Johnson v DPP*[137] it was accepted that racially aggravated offences can be committed against majority white populations, as well as minority group members.

FURTHER READING

Burney, E. (2003) 'Using the Law on Racially Aggravated Offences' *Criminal Law Review* 28.

Burney, E. and Rose, G. (2002) *Racially Aggravated Offences: How is the Law Working?*, Home Office Research Study No. 244 (London: Home Office).

Home Office (1997) *Racial Violence and Harassment: A Consultation Document* (London: Home Office).

Malik, S. (1998) 'Racist Crime: Racially Aggravated Offences in the Crime and Disorder Act 1998, Part II' *Modern Law Review* 62: 409.

---

10 PROTECTION FROM HARASSMENT ACT 1997

10.1 SECTION 1: HARASSMENT

Under section 1 of the Protection from Harassment Act 1997:

(1) A person must not pursue a course of conduct—

    (a) which amounts to harassment of another; and

    (b) which he knows or ought to know amounts to harassment of the other.

(2) For the purposes of this section the person whose course of conduct is in question ought to know that it amounts to harassment of another if a reasonable person in possession of the same information would think the course of conduct amounted to harassment of the other.

(3) Subsection (1) does not apply to a course of conduct if the person who pursued it shows—

    (a) that it was pursued for the purpose of preventing or detecting crime;

    (b) that it was pursued under any enactment or rule of law or to comply with any condition or requirement imposed by any person under any enactment; or

    (c) that in the particular circumstances, the pursuit of the course of conduct was reasonable.

DEFINITION

Actus reus: the defendant engaged in a course of conduct which amounted to harassment.

Mens rea: the defendant knew or ought to have known that that conduct amounted to harassment.

---

[136] See also *Rogers* [2005] EWCA Crim 2863. [137] [2008] EWHC 509 (Admin).

The offence can be broken down into the following four elements:[138]

(1) **A course of conduct** A course of conduct[139] must involve at least two incidents.[140] A single incident, however disturbing, will not constitute the offence.[141] In order to amount to a course of conduct, the two or more incidents must be linked: there must be some *nexus* between them.[142] The fewer the number of incidents and the further apart in time they are the stronger the linking theme must be before the court will find a course of conduct. The following four cases provide a flavour of how the courts decide whether there is a course of conduct:

(a) In *Lau v DPP*[143] the defendant slapped the victim and then four months later he threatened the victim's new boyfriend with violence. This was held not to constitute a course of conduct. The incidents were too far apart in time and were different in nature.

(b) In *Hills*[144] the defendant was violent to his partner twice in the course of six months. It was held not to be a course of conduct because the couple had reconciled and cohabited between the two incidents, thereby severing the link between them.[145]

(c) In *Kelly v DPP*[146] the defendant left three messages on the victim's voice mail facility in the space of five minutes. The victim listened to them all at the same time. The Divisional Court held that the magistrates were entitled to take the view that each call was separate and distinct and therefore could amount to a course of conduct.

(d) In *R v Curtis*[147] there were a series of violent incidents between a cohabiting couple in a volatile relationship. The court held that 'The spontaneous outbursts of ill-temper and bad behaviour, with aggression on both sides, which are the hallmarks of the present case, interspersed as those outbursts were with considerable periods of affectionate life, cannot be described as such a course of conduct.'[148]

(2) **The course of conduct must amount to harassment** Harassment is said in section 7(2) to include causing the victim alarm or distress. However, because the statute uses the word 'includes' it is clear that it is possible to harass a victim who has not been alarmed or distressed.[149] The Supreme Court in *Hayes v Willoughby*[150] stated that 'Harassment is a persistent and deliberate course of unreasonable and oppressive conduct, targeted at another person, which is calculated to and does cause that person alarm, fear or distress.'

Inevitably the courts have had to draw fine lines between acts of legitimate courting and acts of harassment.[151] In *King v DPP*[152] it was explained that offering a plant to the victim as a gift and writing one letter to the victim asking her whether she was interested in a

---

[138] Six months is the maximum sentence of imprisonment.

[139] Conduct is said in s. 7(4) to include speech.

[140] Protection from Harassment Act 1997, s. 7(3).

[141] Although in *Wass v DPP* (QBD, 11 May 2000) the Divisional Court was willing to treat two occurrences within a few minutes of each other as a course of conduct.

[142] *Lau v DPP* [2000] 1 FLR 799.   [143] [2000] Crim LR 586.   [144] [2001] Crim LR 318.

[145] See also *Widdows* [2011] EWCA Crim 1500, where it was held that the Act was not meant to cover cases where the parties were generally in a close and mainly affectionate relationship, but occasionally behaved badly towards each other.

[146] [2003] Crim LR 43.   [147] [2010] EWCA Crim 123.   [148] *Ibid*, para. 32.

[149] *DPP v Ramsdale* [2001] EWHC Admin 106.   [150] [2013] UKSC 17.

[151] There are also, of course, difficulties in distinguishing between legitimate and illegitimate expressions of complaint (*Baron v CPS* (QBD, 13 June 2000)) or points of view (*Thomas v News Group Newspapers Ltd* [2001] EWCA Civ 1233).

[152] QBD, 20 June 2000.

relationship would not amount to harassment. But in *James*[153] it was held that offering a very valuable gift to a person the defendant hardly knew could be harassment.

It should be noted that the partial definition of harassment in section 7(2) focuses on the effect of the defendant's conduct, rather than describing the conduct itself. So if the conduct causes alarm or distress to the victim, it can amount to harassment, even though most people would not be bothered by the conduct. This approach to the definition of harassment nearly caused problems in *King v DPP*[154] where the defendant (inter alia) had been secretly filming the victim. It was held that although the conduct could be described as harassment because, although the victim was not aware of the filming at the time, when she was told by the police what the defendant had been doing she was alarmed and distressed.

(3) **The defendant must know or ought to know that the conduct is harassing** The section 1 offence contains alternatives of either a subjective or an objective *mens rea*. The defendant is guilty if he or she knew or ought to know that his or her conduct amounted to harassment. This is significant. It means that it is no defence for a defendant to claim, 'I thought I was expressing my love for the victim; I did not realize she would find this distressing' if it would have been obvious to a reasonable person that the conduct was harassing. Further, if the defendant was acting in a way which he or she knew was harassing the victim he or she can be guilty, even if a reasonable person would not realize that the conduct was harassing. In the following case, the Court of Appeal considered whether the reasonable person should be endowed with the characteristics of the defendant (e.g. as is done in the defence of loss of control). They decided not.

R v Colohan
[2001] EWCA Crim 1251

The appellant suffered from schizophrenia. He wrote a number of incoherent, abusive, and threatening letters to his Member of Parliament. The appellant was, as a result, charged with an offence under sections 1 and 2 of the Protection from Harassment Act 1997. The appellant argued that in considering whether he ought to know that his conduct amounted to harassment, the jury should be told to consider what a reasonable person suffering from schizophrenia would have known (by analogy with the defences of provocation and duress). He also argued that his illness rendered his conduct reasonable under section 1(3)(c).

Mr Justice Hughes

. . .

17. The question raised by these submissions [the arguments of the appellant's counsel] is one of the proper construction of the Protection from Harassment Act 1997. As the first word of that title suggests, this is an Act whose purpose is significantly protective and preventative. The long title is 'An act to make provision for protecting persons from harassment and similar conduct'.

18. . . . As is well known, the 1997 Act was passed with the phenomenon of 'stalking' particularly, although not exclusively, in mind. The conduct at which the 1997 Act is aimed, and from which it seeks to provide protection, is particularly likely to be conduct pursued by those of obsessive or otherwise unusual psychological make-up and very frequently by

---

[153] [2006] Crim LR 629.   [154] QBD, 20 June 2000.

those suffering from an identifiable mental illness. Schizophrenia is only one such condition which is obviously very likely to give rise to conduct of this sort.

19. We are satisfied that to give the 1997 Act the construction for which Mr Butterfield [counsel for the appellant] contends would be to remove from its protection a very large number of victims and indeed to run the risk of significantly thwarting the purpose of the Act. If such a construction is correct it would prevent the conduct in question from being a breach of s 1 and thus exclude not only suitable punishment for the perpetrator, but also damages, and, more especially, an injunction or restraining order for the protection of the victim. We do not believe that Parliament can have meant the provisions in question to have the meaning for which Mr Butterfield contends. Moreover, as it seems to us, if Mr Butterfield's submission were correct then s 1(2) would have been inserted unnecessarily into the Act.

20. We agree accordingly with the judge that, except insofar as it requires the jury to consider the information actually in the possession of this defendant, s 1(2) requires the jury to answer the question whether he ought to have known that what he was doing amounts to harassment by the objective test of what a reasonable person would think. Its words, we are satisfied, are abundantly clear.

21. As to s 1(3)(c), that, we are satisfied, poses even more clearly an objective test, namely whether the conduct is in the judgment of the jury reasonable. There is no warrant for attaching to the word 'reasonable' or via the words 'particular circumstances' the standards or characteristics of the defendant himself.

Appeal dismissed.

(4) **Defences to harassment** Section 1(3) sets out the statutory defences available to the defendant. The one that is likely to be relied upon the most is subsection (c): that the conduct of the defendant is reasonable. The courts have made it clear that unlawful conduct (e.g. actions in breach of an injunction) will not be regarded as reasonable.[155] In *Colohan*, discussed earlier in this section, the defendant sought to argue that his conduct was reasonable, given that he was schizophrenic. The Court of Appeal held that his mental illness did not render his conduct reasonable. In *Hayes v Willoughby*[156] the Supreme Court held that if a harasser was relying on the defence of prevention of crime they had to show that their belief was reasonable. Lord Sumption explained what that meant:

Before an alleged harasser can be said to have had the purpose of preventing or detecting crime, he must have sufficiently applied his mind to the matter. He must have thought rationally about the material suggesting the possibility of criminality and formed the view that the conduct said to constitute harassment was appropriate for the purpose of preventing or detecting it.[157]

10.2 SECTION 4 OF THE PROTECTION FROM HARASSMENT ACT 1997

Section 4 of the Protection from Harassment Act 1997 states:

(1) A person whose course of conduct causes another to fear, on at least two occasions, that violence will be used against him is guilty of an offence if he knows or ought to know that his course of conduct will cause the other so to fear on each of those occasions.

---

[155] *R v DPP, ex p Moseley* (QBD, 23 June 1999).   [156] [2013] UKSC 17.   [157] *Ibid*, para. 15.

(2) For the purposes of this section, the person whose course of conduct is in question ought to know that it will cause another to fear that violence will be used against him on any occasion if a reasonable person in possession of the same information would think the course of conduct would cause the other so to fear on that occasion.

(3) It is a defence for a person charged with an offence under this section to show that—

(a) his course of conduct was pursued for the purpose of preventing or detecting crime,

(b) his course of conduct was pursued under any enactment or rule of law or to comply with any condition or requirement imposed by any person under any enactment, or

(c) the pursuit of his course of conduct was reasonable for the protection of himself or another or for the protection of his or another's property.

To establish a conviction under section 4[158] it has to be shown that the accused has undertaken a course of conduct which on at least two occasions led the victim to fear that violence would be used against him or her. It is not enough to show that the victim is 'seriously frightened' in a general way; there must be a specific fear that violence will be used.[159] It does not need to be shown that the threat was issued against the victim: an ostensible threat to a victim's dog could be interpreted by the victim as a threat of violence against the victim.[160] But, as emphasized in *Henley*,[161] it is not enough for the victim to fear that violence will be used against his family.[162] Although section 4 does not state this, in *Haque*[163] it was confirmed that it must be shown the course of conduct in question was harassment and that it was intended to harass the other person. Further, it needed to be shown that the conduct was targeted at an individual. These are important limitations because they mean that a person who is generally being aggressive (e.g. because they are drunk) and causing fear of violence might escape liability under section 4 on the basis that their behaviour was not targeted at individuals.

10.3 STALKING

The Protection of Freedoms Act 2012 created a new offence of stalking in section 2A of the Protection from Harassment Act.[164]

Protection from Harassment Act 1997, section 2A

2A Offence of stalking

(1) A person is guilty of an offence if—

(a) the person pursues a course of conduct in breach of section 1(1), and

(b) the course of conduct amounts to stalking.

---

[158] The maximum sentence of imprisonment is five years.
[159] *Henley* [2000] Crim LR 582.   [160] *R v DPP* [2001] Crim LR 397.
[161] [2000] Crim LR 582.   [162] *Caurti v DPP* [2002] Crim LR 131.
[163] [2011] EWCA Crim 1871; following, with some reluctance, *R v Widdows* [2011] EWCA Crim 1500.
[164] See MacEwan (2012) and Gowland (2013) for a helpful discussion.

(2) For the purposes of subsection (1)(b) (and section 4A(1)(a)) a person's course of conduct amounts to stalking of another person if—

(a) it amounts to harassment of that person,

(b) the acts or omissions involved are ones associated with stalking, and

(c) the person whose course of conduct it is knows or ought to know that the course of conduct amounts to harassment of the other person.

(3) The following are examples of acts or omissions which, in particular circumstances, are ones associated with stalking—

(a) following a person,

(b) contacting, or attempting to contact, a person by any means,

(c) publishing any statement or other material—

(i) relating or purporting to relate to a person, or

(ii) purporting to originate from a person,

(d) monitoring the use by a person of the internet, email or any other form of electronic communication,

(e) loitering in any place (whether public or private),

(f) interfering with any property in the possession of a person,

(g) watching or spying on a person.

There is also an offence of stalking involving fear of violence or serious alarm or distress, which is found in section 4A of the Protection from Harassment Act 1997.

FURTHER READING

Finch, E. (2001) *The Criminalisation of Stalking* (London: Cavendish).

Finch, E. (2002) 'Stalking the Perfect Stalking Law: An Evaluation of the Efficacy of the Protection from Harassment Act 1997' *Criminal Law Review* 703.

MacEwan, N. (2012) 'The New Stalking Offences in English Law: Will They Provide Effective Protection from Cyberstalking?' *Criminal Law Review* 767.

Wells, C. (1997) 'Stalking: The Criminal Law Response' *Criminal Law Review* 463.

---

11 CONTROLLING OR COERCIVE BEHAVIOUR

A new offence of 'controlling or coercive behaviour in an intimate or family relationship' has been created in section 76 of the Serious Crime Act 2015:

(1) A person (A) commits an offence if—

(a) A repeatedly or continuously engages in behaviour towards another person (B) that is controlling or coercive,

(b) at the time of the behaviour, A and B are personally connected,

(c) the behaviour has a serious effect on B, and

(d) A knows or ought to know that the behaviour will have a serious effect on B.

(2) A and B are "personally connected" if—

   (a) A is in an intimate personal relationship with B, or

   (b) A and B live together and—

      (i) they are members of the same family, or

      (ii) they have previously been in an intimate personal relationship with each other.

(3) But A does not commit an offence under this section if at the time of the behaviour in question—

   (a) A has responsibility for B, for the purposes of Part 1 of the Children and Young Persons Act 1933 (see section 17 of that Act), and

   (b) B is under 16.

(4) A's behaviour has a "serious effect" on B if—

   (a) it causes B to fear, on at least two occasions, that violence will be used against B, or

   (b) it causes B serious alarm or distress which has a substantial adverse effect on B's usual day-to-day activities.

(5) For the purposes of subsection (1)(d) A "ought to know" that which a reasonable person in possession of the same information would know.

(6) For the purposes of subsection (2)(b)(i) A and B are members of the same family if—

   (a) they are, or have been, married to each other;

   (b) they are, or have been, civil partners of each other;

   (c) they are relatives;

   (d) they have agreed to marry one another (whether or not the agreement has been terminated);

   (e) they have entered into a civil partnership agreement (whether or not the agreement has been terminated);

   (f) they are both parents of the same child;

   (g) they have, or have had, parental responsibility for the same child.

(7) In subsection (6)—

"civil partnership agreement" has the meaning given by section 73 of the Civil Partnership Act 2004;

"child" means a person under the age of 18 years;

"parental responsibility" has the same meaning as in the Children Act 1989;

"relative" has the meaning given by section 63(1) of the Family Law Act 1996.

(8) In proceedings for an offence under this section it is a defence for A to show that—

   (a) in engaging in the behaviour in question, A believed that he or she was acting in B's best interests, and

   (b) the behaviour was in all the circumstances reasonable.

(9) A is to be taken to have shown the facts mentioned in subsection (8) if—

   (a) sufficient evidence of the facts is adduced to raise an issue with respect to them, and

   (b) the contrary is not proved beyond reasonable doubt.

(10) The defence in subsection (8) is not available to A in relation to behaviour that causes B to fear that violence will be used against B.

(11) A person guilty of an offence under this section is liable—

   (a) on conviction on indictment, to imprisonment for a term not exceeding five years, or a fine, or both;

   (b) on summary conviction, to imprisonment for a term not exceeding 12 months, or a fine, or both.

This offence was designed to deal with the fact that although domestic abuse often involves acts of violence, seen individually they may not capture the true nature of the abuse. Domestic abuse is best understood as a programme of 'coercive control' where one party seeks to dominate the other. This is typically by cycles of increasingly demanding behaviour designed to get the other partner to follow their commands. This may be through violence, but can also be through threats, emotional abuse, psychological abuse, and sulking.[165] Psychologist Mary Ann Dutton[166] explains:

> Abusive behaviour does not occur as a series of discrete events. Although a set of discrete abusive incidents can typically be identified within an abusive relationship, an understanding of the dynamic of power and control within an intimate relationship goes beyond these discrete incidents. To negate the impact of the time period between discrete episodes of serious violence—a time period during which the woman may never know when the next incident will occur, and may continue to live with on-going psychological abuse—is to fail to recognize what some battered woman experience as a continuing 'state of siege'.

As one victim put it:[167]

> He always found something wrong with what I did, even if I did what he asked. No matter what it was. It was never the way he wanted it. I was either too fat, didn't cook the food right....I think he wanted to hurt me. To hurt me in the sense...to make me feel like I was a nothing.

There are several things to highlight about the new offence:

(1) The offence can only be committed if the parties are in an intimate personal relationship or live together as a family.

(2) The offence is committed only if the defendant 'repeatedly or continuously' behaved in a controlling or coercive way. A single piece of controlling behaviour or even just a couple of incidents will not amount to the new offence, although it could amount to an assault or an offence under the Protection from Harassment Act 1997.

(3) The behaviour must have a 'serious effect' on the victim. This is a rather vague phrase. Subsection 4 defines a serious effect as a case where the victim fears violence on two occasions or where the victim suffers 'serious alarm or distress which has a substantial adverse effect on B's usual day-to-day activities'. This means that if there is a controlling relationship but the victim is perfectly happy with the relationship there is no offence. Arguably if the parties were members of a religion which taught that wives must obey their husbands, the relationship may be controlling, but the wife is happy with that. If she is not suffering a 'serious effect' there may be no offence.

The *mens rea* is objective. The defendant must either know or ought to know his behaviour will have a serious effect on the victim. Interestingly it is not necessary to show the defendant realized they were controlling or coercive.

Subsection 4 makes it clear that a parent cannot be convicted of this offence in relation to a child. There are other offences, such as child cruelty, which could apply in such cases.[168]

---

[165] For a more detailed discussion, see Herring (2011b). [166] Dutton (2003: 1204).
[167] Quoted by Tuerkheimer (2004: 962). [168] Children and Young Persons Act 1933, s. 1.

12 THREATS OFFENCES

Generally it is not an offence to threaten someone. However, statutes have created some specific offences:

(1) threat to kill;[169]

(2) threat to damage or destroy property belonging to another;[170]

(3) blackmail: making an unwarranted demand with menaces;[171]

(4) threatening violence for the purpose of securing unlawful entry to occupied premises;[172]

(5) menacing over a public electronic communications network;[173]

(6) bomb hoax;[174]

(7) various kinds of threatening behaviour in public places.[175]

There are many others.

13 TRANSMITTING DISEASE

There has been much discussion over whether a defendant who passes on a disease can be convicted of an offence.[176] This is now governed by the following two decisions: →4 (p.400)

R v Dica
[2004] QB 1257 (CA)

Mohammed Dica was aware that he was HIV positive. Nevertheless he had unprotected sexual intercourse with two women who were subsequently diagnosed as HIV positive. He was charged with inflicting grievous bodily harm upon them contrary to section 20 of the Offences Against the Person Act 1861. At his trial the judge ruled that the jury could convict the defendant even if he was able to show that the women were aware of his condition. In other words the consent of the victims to running the risk of becoming HIV positive provided him with no defence. He was convicted and appealed.

Before the Court of Appeal there were two main questions. First, whether the defendant could be said to have inflicted grievous bodily harm and, second, in what circumstances, if any, the consent of the victims were relevant to the charge he faced. As to the first, the Court of Appeal, following the House of Lords' decision in *R v Burstow* concluded that the word 'inflict' in section 20 of the Offences Against the Person Act carried the same meaning as the word 'cause'. Any suggestion in the case of *Clarence* that a harm could not be 'inflicted' in the course of consensual sexual intercourse was rejected.

---

[169] Offences Against the Person Act 1861, s. 16.   [170] Criminal Damage Act 1971, s. 2.
[171] Theft Act 1968, s. 21.   [172] Criminal Law Act 1977, s. 6.
[173] Communications Act 2003, s. 127.   [174] Criminal Law Act 1977, s. 51(1).
[175] Public Order Act 1986, ss. 1–5.   [176] See e.g. Burris and Weait (2014) and Cowan (2014).

Lord Justice Judge

37. The present case is concerned with and confined to section 20 offences alone, without the burdensome fiction of deemed consent to sexual intercourse. The question for decision is whether the victims' consent to sexual intercourse, which as a result of his alleged concealment was given in ignorance of the facts of the defendant's condition, necessarily amounted to consent to the risk of being infected by him. If that question must be answered 'Yes', the concept of consent in relation to section 20 is devoid of real meaning.

38. The position here is analogous to that considered in *R v Tabassum* [2000] 2 Cr App R 328. The appellant was convicted of indecently assaulting women who allowed him to examine their breasts in the mistaken belief that he was medically qualified. Rose LJ considered *Clarence*, and pointed out that in relation to the infection suffered by the wife, this was an additional, unexpected, consequence of sexual intercourse, which was irrelevant to her consent to sexual intercourse with her husband. Rejecting the argument that an 'undoubted consent' could only be negatived if the victim had been deceived or mistaken about the nature and quality of the act, and that consent was not negatived 'merely because the victim would not have agreed to the act if he or she had known all the facts', Rose LJ observed, in forthright terms, at p 337, 'there was no true consent'. Again, in *R v Cort* [2004] QB 388, a case of kidnapping, the complainants had consented to taking a ride in a motor car, but not to being kidnapped. They wanted transport, not kidnapping. Kidnapping may be established by carrying away by fraud:

> 'it is difficult to see how one could ever consent to that once fraud was indeed established. The "nature" of the act here is therefore taking the complainant away by fraud. The complainant did not consent to that event. All that she consented to is a ride in the car, which in itself is irrelevant to the offence and a different thing from that with which Mr Cort is charged.' (p 393)

39. In our view, on the assumed fact now being considered, the answer is entirely straightforward. These victims consented to sexual intercourse. Accordingly, the defendant was not guilty of rape. Given the long-term nature of the relationships, if the defendant concealed the truth about his condition from them, and therefore kept them in ignorance of it, there was no reason for them to think that they were running any risk of infection, and they were not consenting to it. On this basis, there would be no consent sufficient in law to provide the defendant with a defence to the charge under section 20.

. . .

40. We must now address the consequences if, contrary to their own assertions, the complainants knew of the state of the defendant's health, and notwithstanding the risks to their own, consented to sexual intercourse. Following Judge Philpot's second ruling, this issue was not considered by the jury. In effect the judge ruled that in law such consent (if any) was irrelevant. Having listened to the exchanges on this topic between Mr Carter-Manning, for the defendant, and the court, and on further reflection, Mr Gadsden for the Crown accepted that this issue should not have been withdrawn from the jury. Although we can take the issue relatively briefly, we must explain why this concession was right.

41. As a general rule, unless the activity is lawful, the consent of the victim to the deliberate infliction of serious bodily injury on him or her does not provide the perpetrator with any defence. Different categories of activity are regarded as lawful. Thus no one doubts that necessary major surgery with the patient's consent, even if likely to result in severe disability (eg an amputation) would be lawful. However the categories of activity regarded as lawful are not closed, and equally, they are not immutable. . . .

42. The present policy of the law is that, whether or not the violent activity takes place in private, and even if the victim agrees to it, serious violence is not lawful merely because it enables the perpetrator (or the victim) to achieve sexual gratification. Judge Philpot was impressed with the conclusions to be drawn from the well-known decision in *R v Brown (Anthony)* [1994] 1 AC 212. Sado-masochistic activity of an extreme, indeed horrific kind, which caused grievous bodily harm, was held to be unlawful, notwithstanding that those who suffered the cruelty positively welcomed it. This decision of the House of Lords was supported in the European Court of Human Rights on the basis that although the prosecution may have constituted an interference with the private lives of those involved, it was justified for the protection of public health: *Laskey, Jaggard and Brown v United Kingdom* (1997) 24 EHRR 39. . . .

[**Judge LJ** then referred to *R v Donovan* [1934] 2 KB 498; *R v Boyea* (1992) 156 JP 505; *R v Emmett* The Times, 15 October 1999.]

46. These authorities demonstrate that violent conduct involving the deliberate and intentional infliction of bodily harm is and remains unlawful notwithstanding that its purpose is the sexual gratification of one or both participants. Notwithstanding their sexual overtones, these cases were concerned with violent crime, and the sexual overtones did not alter the fact that both parties were consenting to the deliberate infliction of serious harm or bodily injury on one participant by the other. To date, as a matter of public policy, it has not been thought appropriate for such violent conduct to be excused merely because there is a private consensual sexual element to it. The same public policy reason would prohibit the deliberate spreading of disease, including sexual disease.

47. In our judgment the impact of the authorities dealing with sexual gratification can too readily be misunderstood. It does not follow from them, and they do not suggest, that consensual acts of sexual intercourse are unlawful merely because there may be a known risk to the health of one or other participant. These participants are not intent on spreading or becoming infected with disease through sexual intercourse. They are not indulging in serious violence for the purposes of sexual gratification. They are simply prepared, knowingly, to run the risk—not the certainty—of infection, as well as all the other risks inherent in and possible consequences of sexual intercourse, such as, and despite the most careful precautions, an unintended pregnancy. At one extreme there is casual sex between complete strangers, sometimes protected, sometimes not, when the attendant risks are known to be higher, and at the other, there is sexual intercourse between couples in a long-term and loving, and trusting relationship, which may from time to time also carry risks.

48. The first of these categories is self-explanatory and needs no amplification. By way of illustration we shall provide two examples of cases which would fall within the second.

49. In the first, one of a couple suffers from HIV. It may be the man: it may be the woman. The circumstances in which HIV was contracted are irrelevant. They could result from a contaminated blood transfusion, or an earlier relationship with a previous sexual partner, who unknown to the sufferer with whom we are concerned, was himself or herself infected with HIV. The parties are Roman Catholics. They are conscientiously unable to use artificial contraception. They both know of the risk that the healthy partner may become infected with HIV. Our second example is that of a young couple, desperate for a family, who are advised that if the wife were to become pregnant and give birth, her long-term health, indeed her life itself, would be at risk. Together the couple decide to run that risk, and she becomes pregnant. She may be advised that the foetus should be aborted, on the grounds of her health, yet, nevertheless, decide to bring her baby to term. If she does, and suffers ill health, is the male partner to be criminally liable for having sexual intercourse with her, notwithstanding that he knew of the risk to her health? If he is liable to be prosecuted, was she not a party

to whatever crime was committed? And should the law interfere with the Roman Catholic couple, and require them, at the peril of criminal sanctions, to choose between bringing their sexual relationship to an end or violating their consciences by using contraception?

50. These, and similar risks, have always been taken by adults consenting to sexual intercourse. Different situations, no less potentially fraught, have to be addressed by them. Modern society has not thought to criminalise those who have willingly accepted the risks, and we know of no cases where one or other of the consenting adults has been prosecuted, let alone convicted, for the consequences of doing so.

51. The problems of criminalising the consensual taking of risks like these include the sheer impracticability of enforcement and the haphazard nature of its impact. The process would undermine the general understanding of the community that sexual relationships are pre-eminently private and essentially personal to the individuals involved in them. And if adults were to be liable to prosecution for the consequences of taking known risks with their health, it would seem odd that this should be confined to risks taken in the context of sexual intercourse, while they are nevertheless permitted to take the risks inherent in so many other aspects of everyday life, including, again for example, the mother or father of a child suffering a serious contagious illness, who holds the child's hand, and comforts or kisses him or her goodnight.

52. In our judgment, interference of this kind with personal autonomy, and its level and extent, may only be made by Parliament.

. . .

54. We have taken note of the various points made by the interested organisations. These include the complexity of bedroom and sex negotiations, and the lack of realism if the law were to expect people to be paragons of sexual behaviour at such a time, or to set about informing each other in advance of the risks or to counsel the use of condoms. It is also suggested that there are significant negative consequences of disclosure of HIV, and that the imposition of criminal liability could have an adverse impact on public health because those who ought to take advice, might be discouraged from doing so. If the criminal law was to become involved at all, this should be confined to cases where the offender deliberately inflicted others with a serious disease.

. . .

Conclusion

58. We repeat that the Crown did not allege, and we therefore are not considering the deliberate infection, or spreading of HIV with intent to cause grievous bodily harm. In such circumstances, the application of what we may describe as the principle in *Brown* [1994] 1 AC 212 means that the agreement of the participants would provide no defence to a charge under section 18 of the 1861 Act.

59. The effect of this judgment in relation to section 20 is to remove some of the outdated restrictions against the successful prosecution of those who, knowing that they are suffering HIV or some other serious sexual disease, recklessly transmit it through consensual sexual intercourse, and inflict grievous bodily harm on a person from whom the risk is concealed and who is not consenting to it. In this context, *Clarence* has no continuing relevance. Moreover, to the extent that *Clarence* suggested that consensual sexual intercourse of itself was to be regarded as consent to the risk of consequent disease, again, it is no longer authoritative. If however, the victim consents to the risk, this continues to provide a defence under section 20. Although the two are inevitably linked, the ultimate question is not knowledge, but consent. We shall confine ourselves to reflecting that unless you are prepared to take

whatever risk of sexually transmitted infection there may be, it is unlikely that you would consent to a risk of major consequent illness if you were ignorant of it. That said, in every case where these issues arise, the question whether the defendant was or was not reckless, and whether the victim did or did not consent to the risk of a sexually transmitted disease is one of fact, and case specific.

Conviction quashed. Retrial ordered.

R v Konzani
[2005] EWCA Crim 706

Feston Konzani was convicted of inflicting grievous bodily harm on three different women, contrary to section 20 of the Offences Against the Person Act 1861. He had been warned that he was HIV positive and was aware of the risk that by having unprotected sexual intercourse he could infect his partners. Nevertheless he had sexual relations with three women without informing them of his HIV status.

Lord Justice Judge

41. We are concerned with the risk of and the actual transmission of a potentially fatal disease through or in the course of consensual sexual relations which did not in themselves involve unlawful violence of the kind prohibited in *R v Brown*. The prosecution did not seek to prove that the disease was deliberately transmitted, with the intention required by s 18 of the 1861 Act. The allegation was that the appellant behaved recklessly on the basis that knowing that he was suffering from the HIV virus, and its consequences, and knowing the risks of its transmission to a sexual partner, he concealed his condition from the complainants, leaving them ignorant of it. When sexual intercourse occurred these complainants were ignorant of his condition. So although they consented to sexual intercourse, they did not consent to the transmission of the HIV virus. *Dica* analysed two different sets of assumed facts arising from the issue of the complainants' consent, by distinguishing between the legal consequences if, as they alleged, the truth of his condition was concealed from his sexual partners by *Dica*, and the case that he would have developed at trial if he had not been prevented from doing so by the judge's ruling, that far from concealing his condition from the complainants, he expressly informed them of it, and they, knowing of his condition because he had told them of it, consented to unprotected sexual intercourse with him. There is a critical distinction between taking a risk of the various, potentially adverse and possibly problematic consequences of sexual intercourse, and giving an informed consent to the risk of infection with a fatal disease. For the complainant's consent to the risks of contracting the HIV virus to provide a defence, it is at least implicit from the reasoning in *R v Dica*, and the observations of Lord Woolf CJ in *R v Barnes* confirm, that her consent must be an informed consent. If that proposition is in doubt, we take this opportunity to emphasise it. We must therefore examine its implications for this appeal.

42. The recognition in *R v Dica* of informed consent as a defence was based on but limited by potentially conflicting public policy considerations. In the public interest, so far as possible, the spread of catastrophic illness must be avoided or prevented. On the other hand, the public interest also requires that the principle of personal autonomy in the context of adult non-violent sexual relationships should be maintained. If an individual who knows that he is

suffering from the HIV virus conceals this stark fact from his sexual partner, the principle of her personal autonomy is not enhanced if he is exculpated when he recklessly transmits the HIV virus to her through consensual sexual intercourse. On any view, the concealment of this fact from her almost inevitably means that she is deceived. Her consent is not properly informed, and she cannot give an informed consent to something of which she is ignorant. Equally, her personal autonomy is not normally protected by allowing a defendant who knows that he is suffering from the HIV virus which he deliberately conceals, to assert an honest belief in his partner's informed consent to the risk of the transmission of the HIV virus. Silence in these circumstances is incongruous with honesty, or with a genuine belief that there is an informed consent. Accordingly, in such circumstances the issue either of informed consent, or honest belief in it will only rarely arise: in reality, in most cases, the contention would be wholly artificial.

43. This is not unduly burdensome. The defendant is not to be convicted of this offence unless it is proved that he was reckless. If so, the necessary mens rea will be established. Recklessness is a question of fact, to be proved by the prosecution. Equally the defendant is not to be convicted if there was, or may have been an informed consent by his sexual partner to the risk that he would transfer the HIV virus to her. In many cases, as in *Dica* itself, provided recklessness is established, the critical factual area of dispute will address what, if anything, was said between the two individuals involved, one of whom knows, and the other of whom does not know, that one of them is suffering the HIV virus. In the final analysis, the question of consent, like the issue of recklessness is fact-specific.

44. In deference to Mr Roberts' submission, we accept that there may be circumstances in which it would be open to the jury to infer that, notwithstanding that the defendant was reckless and concealed his condition from the complainant, she may nevertheless have given an informed consent to the risk of contracting the HIV virus. By way of example, an individual with HIV may develop a sexual relationship with someone who knew him while he was in hospital, receiving treatment for the condition. If so, her informed consent, if it were indeed informed, would remain a defence, to be disproved by the prosecution, even if the defendant had not personally informed her of his condition. Even if she did not in fact consent, this example would illustrate the basis for an argument that he honestly believed in her informed consent. Alternatively, he may honestly believe that his new sexual partner was told of his condition by someone known to them both. Cases like these, not too remote to be fanciful, may arise. If they do, no doubt they will be explored with the complainant in cross examination. Her answers may demonstrate an informed consent. Nothing remotely like that was suggested here. In a different case, perhaps supported by the defendant's own evidence, material like this may provide a basis for suggesting that he honestly believed that she was giving an informed consent. He may provide an account of the incident, or the affair, which leads the jury to conclude that even if she did not give an informed consent, he may honestly have believed that she did. Acknowledging these possibilities in different cases does not, we believe, conflict with the public policy considerations identified in *R v Dica*. That said, they did not arise in the present case.

45. Why not? In essence because the jury found that the complainants did not give a willing or informed consent to the risks of contracting the HIV virus from the appellant. We recognise that where consent does provide a defence to an offence against the person, it is generally speaking correct that the defendant's honest belief in the alleged victim's consent would also provide a defence. However for this purpose, the defendant's honest belief must be concomitant with the consent which provides a defence. Unless the consent would provide a defence, an honest belief in it would not assist the defendant. This follows logically from *R v Brown*. For it to do so here, what was required was some evidence of an honest

belief that the complainants, or any one of them, were consenting to the risk that they might be infected with the HIV virus by him. There is not the slightest evidence, direct or indirect, from which a jury could begin to infer that the appellant honestly believed that any complainant consented to that specific risk. As there was no such evidence, the judge's ruling about 'honest belief' was correct. In fact, the honest truth was that the appellant deceived them.

46. In our judgment, the judge's directions to the jury sufficiently explained the proper implications to the case of the consensual participation by each of the complainants to sexual intercourse with the appellant. The jury concluded, in the case of each complainant, that she did not willingly or consciously consent to the risk of suffering the HIV virus. Accordingly the appeal against conviction will be dismissed.

Appeal dismissed.

DEFINITION

To summarize the ruling in *R v Dica* and *R v Konzani*:[177] if D is HIV positive and has sexual relations with another person and causes that person to become HIV positive, then D is guilty:

(1) of an offence under section 20 of the Offences Against the Person Act 1861 if:

    (a) D is aware that there is a risk that by having sexual relations he or she might cause the other person to suffer some harm (e.g. by becoming HIV positive);

    (b) the victim has not given consent to run the risk of becoming HIV positive;

(2) of an offence under section 18 of the Offences Against the Person Act 1861 if D intends to cause the victim to suffer grievous bodily harm as a result of the sexual intercourse. In such a case even if the victim consents to running the risk of acquiring the HIV virus there would be no defence.

The cases still leave quite a number of issues unsettled. It is clear that the defendant who is aware they may be infectious and transmits a disease can be guilty of an offence. They can have a defence if the victim explicitly consents to run the risk of catching a disease.[178] However, the law is unclear in several areas:

(1) A defendant is only guilty if they are reckless; in other words they realize there is a risk that they are infectious and might transmit the disease. In *Dica* and *Konzani* this was unproblematic because the defendants had been informed by their doctors they were positive and told of the risks of passing on the disease. But what of a defendant who has engaged in unsafe sex, and so is aware that they might possibly be infected with an STD but has not been tested. Should they be treated as reckless? Or what if an HIV-positive person used a condom and therefore greatly reduced the chance of transmitting the virus?[179]

---

[177] Crown Prosecution Service (2013b) sets out the factors the CPS will take into account when considering whether to prosecute cases of this kind.

[178] In *Golding* [2014] EWCA Crim 889 the defendant was convicted under s. 18 for transmitting the herpes virus.

[179] Hughes (2013). The risk of passing on HIV during unprotected sexual intercourse is disputed, but the figures are generally somewhere between 1 in 50 and 1 in 2,000: Gurnham (2013).

(2) Defendants can have a defence if the victim consents to run the risk of catching a disease,[180] but it is not quite clear what that consent involves. What, for example, if the victim knew that her partner was HIV positive, but falsely believed that if she had a shower after sexual intercourse there was no risk of her being infected? Also what if the victim knew the defendant was promiscuous and therefore knew there was a risk of him being infectious; is that sufficient to be consent for the purposes of a section 20 charge? If so, it might be argued that we all know that having unprotected sex carries a risk of acquiring an infection and so there is always consent to running the risk of harm.

(3) What of a defendant who transmits a disease by means other than sexual intercourse? In *Marangwanda*[181] a defendant was convicted on the basis he had passed on gonorrhoea through a shaving towel. Could a person be charged after sneezing on someone and passing on the common cold, or passing on a verruca at a swimming pool? What about a mother who passes on the HIV virus to her baby through breastfeeding?[182]

(4) Following on from the previous point, what kind of diseases are we talking about? The case law has been applied to HIV and to herpes.[183] Does it apply to chlamydia, the common cold, verrucas, or head lice?

13.1 CLARIFICATION

Some students get confused by the fact that although the cases of *Dica* and *Konzani* appear to say the same thing about the law Dica's appeal was allowed, while Konzani's was not. The explanation is this. Remember that when the Court of Appeal allows an appeal it is not saying that it thinks the defendant was not guilty, but rather that there was a flaw in the trial process. In *Dica* the judge had told that jury that even if the victim consented the defendant would be guilty. That was incorrect and so the appeal had to be allowed. In fact there was a retrial and Dica was convicted on his second trial. In *Konzani* the judge gave the jury the correct direction.

> ### QUESTION
>
> Martin is told by his doctor that he may be suffering from an STD and is warned that he should not engage in sexual relations. He ignores the advice and has sexual intercourse with Steve, not telling Steve that he may be infectious. Steve subsequently discovers that he has caught an STD from Martin, and suffers depression as a result. What offences has Martin committed? Would your answer be any different if Martin had warned Steve that he may be infectious? (To answer the second question you will need to read the next section of this chapter on consent and assault.)
>
> For guidance on answering this question, please visit the Online Resource Centre that accompanies this book: www.oxfordtextbooks.co.uk/orc/herringcriminal7e/.

---

[180] In *Golding* [2014] EWCA Crim 889 the defendant was convicted under s. 18 for transmitting the herpes virus.
[181] [2009] EWCA Crim 60.   [182] Bennett (2013).   [183] *Golding* [2014] EWCA Crim 889.

FURTHER READING

Harris, J. and Holm, S.(1995) 'Is There a Moral Obligation Not to Infect Others?' *British Medical Journal* 311: 1215.

Hughes, D. (2013) 'Condom Use, Viral Load and the Type of Sexual Activity as Defences to the Sexual Transmission of HIV' *Journal of Criminal Law* 77: 136.

Loveless, J. (2013) 'Criminalising Failure to Disclose HIV to Sexual Partners: A Short Note on Recent Lessons from the Canadian Supreme Court' *Criminal Law Review* 213.

Munro, V. (2007a) 'On Responsible Relationships and Irresponsible Sex—Criminalising the Reckless Transmission of HIV' *Child and Family Law Quarterly* 19: 112.

Slater, J. (2011) 'HIV, Trust and the Criminal Law' *Journal of Criminal Law* 75: 309.

Weait, M. (2005a) 'Harm, Consent and the Limits of Privacy' *Feminist Legal Studies* 13: 97.

Weait, M. (2005b) 'Knowledge, Autonomy and Consent: *R v Konzani*' *Criminal Law Review* 763.

Weait, M. (2005c) 'Criminal Law and the Sexual Transmission of HIV' *Modern Law Review* 68: 121.

Weait, M. (2007) 'On Being Responsible' in V. Munro and C. Stychin (eds) *Sexuality and the Law* (London: Cavendish).

Weait, M. (2013) 'Unsafe Law: Health, Rights and the Legal Response to HIV' *International Journal of Law in Context* 9: 535.

14 CONSENT AND ASSAULT

Can a defendant be guilty of a non-fatal assault against the person if the victim consented to the force being used against them? As we shall see in Part II of this chapter there has been much debate over whether consent should be regarded as a defence to a charge of assault or whether lack of consent should be regarded as a defence. For now it will be assumed that consent is a defence to a charge of assault because that was the view of the majority of the House of Lords in *Brown*.[184]

14.1 TO WHAT OFFENCES AGAINST THE PERSON IS CONSENT A DEFENCE?

This question has been considered by the House of Lords in one of the most controversial judgments of recent years:

---

[184] [1994] 1 AC 212 (HL).

R v Brown (Anthony); Lucas; Jaggard; Laskey; Carter
[1994] 1 AC 212 (HL)

The appellants were a group of sadomasochists who engaged in consensual acts of violence against each other for sexual gratification. Some of the group found pleasure in inflicting the pain, others in receiving it. The appellants were convicted of offences under sections 20 and 47 of the Offences Against the Person Act 1861. The appellants sought to rely on the consent of the 'victims' of these offences as a defence to the charges, but the trial judge ruled that the prosecution was not required to prove that the 'victims' did not consent. The appellants appealed unsuccessfully to the Court of Appeal and then on to the House of Lords.

Lord Templeman

The Court of Appeal upheld the convictions and certified the following point of law of general public importance:

> 'Where A wounds or assaults B occasioning him actual bodily harm in the course of a sadomasochistic encounter, does the prosecution have to prove lack of consent on the part of B before they can establish A's guilt under section 20 or section 47 of the Offences against the Person Act 1861?'

. . .

In the present case each of the appellants intentionally inflicted violence upon another (to whom I refer as 'the victim') with the consent of the victim and thereby occasioned actual bodily harm or in some cases wounding or grievous bodily harm. Each appellant was therefore guilty of an offence under section 47 or section 20 of the Act of 1861 unless the consent of the victim was effective to prevent the commission of the offence or effective to constitute a defence to the charge. In some circumstances violence is not punishable under the criminal law. When no actual bodily harm is caused, the consent of the person affected precludes him from complaining. There can be no conviction for the summary offence of common assault if the victim has consented to the assault. Even when violence is intentionally inflicted and results in actual bodily harm, wounding or serious bodily harm the accused is entitled to be acquitted if the injury was a foreseeable incident of a lawful activity in which the person injured was participating. Surgery involves intentional violence resulting in actual or sometimes serious bodily harm but surgery is a lawful activity. Other activities carried on with consent by or on behalf of the injured person have been accepted as lawful notwithstanding that they involve actual bodily harm or may cause serious bodily harm. Ritual circumcision, tattooing, ear-piercing and violent sports including boxing are lawful activities.

[Having considered the previous case law **Lord Templeman** continued:]

My Lords, the authorities dealing with the intentional infliction of bodily harm do not establish that consent is a defence to a charge under the Act of 1861. They establish that the courts have accepted that consent is a defence to the infliction of bodily harm in the course of some lawful activities. The question is whether the defence should be extended to the infliction of bodily harm in the course of sado-masochistic encounters. . . .

The question whether the defence of consent should be extended to the consequences of sado-masochistic encounters can only be decided by consideration of policy and public interest. Parliament can call on the advice of doctors, psychiatrists, criminologists, sociologists and other experts and can also sound and take into account public opinion. But the question must at this stage be decided by this House in its judicial capacity in order to determine whether the convictions of the appellants should be upheld or quashed.

Counsel for some of the appellants argued that the defence of consent should be extended to the offence of occasioning actual bodily harm under section 47 of the Act of 1861 but should not be available to charges of serious wounding and the infliction of serious bodily harm under section 20. I do not consider that this solution is practicable. Sado-masochistic participants have no way of foretelling the degree of bodily harm which will result from their encounters. The differences between actual bodily harm and serious bodily harm cannot be satisfactorily applied by a jury in order to determine acquittal or conviction. Counsel for the appellants argued that consent should provide a defence to charges under both section 20 and section 47 because, it was said, every person has a right to deal with his body as he pleases. I do not consider that this slogan provides a sufficient guide to the policy decision which must now be made. It is an offence for a person to abuse his own body and mind by taking drugs. Although the law is often broken, the criminal law restrains a practice which is regarded as dangerous and injurious to individuals and which if allowed and extended is harmful to society generally. In any event the appellants in this case did not mutilate their own bodies. They inflicted bodily harm on willing victims. Suicide is no longer an offence but a person who assists another to commit suicide is guilty of murder or manslaughter.

The assertion was made on behalf of the appellants that the sexual appetites of sadists and masochists can only be satisfied by the infliction of bodily harm and that the law should not punish the consensual achievement of sexual satisfaction. There was no evidence to support the assertion that sado-masochist activities are essential to the happiness of the appellants or any other participants but the argument would be acceptable if sado-masochism were only concerned with sex, as the appellants contend. In my opinion sado-masochism is not only concerned with sex. Sado-masochism is also concerned with violence. The evidence discloses that the practices of the appellants were unpredictably dangerous and degrading to body and mind and were developed with increasing barbarity and taught to persons whose consents were dubious or worthless.

. . . The dangers involved in administering violence must have been appreciated by the appellants because, so it was said by their counsel, each victim was given a code word which he could pronounce when excessive harm or pain was caused. The efficiency of this precaution, when taken, depends on the circumstances and on the personalities involved. No one can feel the pain of another. The charges against the appellants were based on genital torture and violence to the buttocks, anus, penis, testicles and nipples. The victims were degraded and humiliated sometimes beaten, sometimes wounded with instruments and sometimes branded. Bloodletting and the smearing of human blood produced excitement. There were obvious dangers of serious personal injury and blood infection. Prosecuting counsel informed the trial judge against the protests of defence counsel, that although the appellants had not contracted AIDS, two members of the group had died from AIDS and one other had contracted an HIV infection although not necessarily from the practices of the group. Some activities involved excrement. The assertion that the instruments employed by the sadists were clean and sterilised could not have removed the danger of infection, and the assertion that care was taken demonstrates the possibility of infection. Cruelty to human beings was on occasions supplemented by cruelty to animals in the form of bestiality. It is fortunate that there were no permanent injuries to a victim though no one knows the extent of harm inflicted in other cases. It is not surprising that a victim does not complain to the police when the complaint would involve him in giving details of acts in which he participated. Doctors of course are subject to a code of confidentiality.

In principle there is a difference between violence which is incidental and violence which is inflicted for the indulgence of cruelty. The violence of sado-masochistic encounters involves the indulgence of cruelty by sadists and the degradation of victims. Such violence is injurious to the participants and unpredictably dangerous. I am not prepared to invent a defence of consent for sado-masochistic encounters which breed and glorify cruelty and result in offences under sections 47 and 20 of the Act of 1861.

. . .

Society is entitled and bound to protect itself against a cult of violence. Pleasure derived from the infliction of pain is an evil thing. Cruelty is uncivilised. I would answer the certified question in the negative and dismiss the appeals of the appellants against conviction.

Lord Jauncey of Tullichettle

In my view the line properly falls to be drawn between assault at common law and the offence of assault occasioning actual bodily harm created by section 47 of the Offences against the Person Act 1861, with the result that consent of the victim is no answer to anyone charged with the latter offence or with a contravention of section 20 unless the circumstances fall within one of the well known exceptions such as organised sporting contests and games, parental chastisement or reasonable surgery. There is nothing in sections 20 and 47 of the Act of 1861 to suggest that consent is either an essential ingredient of the offences or a defence thereto. If consent is to be an answer to a charge under section 47 but not to one under section 20, considerable practical problems would arise. It was held in *Reg v Parmenter* [1992] 1 AC 699 that a verdict of guilty of assault occasioning actual bodily harm is a permissible alternative verdict on a count alleging unlawful wounding contrary to section 20: Lord Ackner, at p 740D. A judge charging a jury in a section 20 case would therefore not only have to direct them as to the alternative verdict available under section 47, but also as to the consequences of consent in relation to that alternative only. Such direction would be more complex if consent was an answer to wounding under section 20 but not to the infliction of grievous bodily harm under the same section. These problems would not arise if consent is an answer only to common assault. I would therefore dispose of these appeals on the basis that the infliction of actual or more serious bodily harm is an unlawful activity to which consent is no answer. . . .

. . . [I]n considering the public interest it would be wrong to look only at the activities of the appellants alone, there being no suggestion that they and their associates are the only practitioners of homosexual sado-masochism in England and Wales. This House must therefore consider the possibility that these activities are practised by others and by others who are not so controlled or responsible as the appellants are claimed to be. Without going into details of all the rather curious activities in which the appellants engaged it would appear to be good luck rather than good judgment which has prevented serious injury from occurring. Wounds can easily become septic if not properly treated, the free flow of blood from a person who is HIV positive or who has AIDS can infect another and an inflicter who is carried away by sexual excitement or by drink or drugs could very easily inflict pain and injury beyond the level to which the receiver had consented. Your Lordships have no information as to whether such situations have occurred in relation to other sado-masochistic practitioners. . . .

My Lords I have no doubt that it would not be in the public interest that deliberate infliction of actual bodily harm during the course of homosexual sado-masochistic activities should be held to be lawful. . . . If it is to be decided that such activities as the nailing by A of B's foreskin or scrotum to a board or the insertion of hot wax into C's urethra followed by the burning of his penis with a candle or the incising of D's scrotum with a scalpel to the effusion of blood are injurious neither to B, C and D nor to the public interest then it is for Parliament with its accumulated wisdom and sources of information to declare them to be lawful.

[**Lord Lowry** gave a speech dismissing the appeal.]

Lord Mustill [dissenting]

My Lords, this is a case about the criminal law of violence. In my opinion it should be a case about the criminal law of private sexual relations, if about anything at all. Right or wrong, the point is easily made. The speeches already delivered contain summaries of the conduct giving rise to the charges under the Offences against the Person Act 1861 now before the House, together with other charges in respect of which the appellants have been sentenced, and no longer appeal. Fortunately for the reader my Lords have not gone on to describe other aspects of the appellants' behaviour of a similar but more extreme kind which was not the subject of any charge on the indictment. It is sufficient to say that whatever the outsider might feel about the subject matter of the prosecutions—perhaps horror, amazement or incomprehension, perhaps sadness—very few could read even a summary of the other activities without disgust. The House has been spared the video tapes, which must have been horrible. If the criminality of sexual deviation is the true ground of these proceedings, one would have expected that these above all would have been the subject of attack. Yet the picture is quite different.

[**Lord Mustill** considered the case law and potential relevance of the European Convention on Human Rights and continued:]

IV. Public Policy

The purpose of this long discussion has been to suggest that the decks are clear for the House to tackle completely anew the question whether the public interest requires section 47 of the Act of 1861 to be interpreted as penalising an infliction of harm which is at the level of actual bodily harm, but not grievous bodily harm; which is inflicted in private (by which I mean that it is exposed to the view only of those who have chosen to view it); which takes place not only with the consent of the recipient but with his willing and glad co-operation; which is inflicted for the gratification of sexual desire, and not in a spirit of animosity or rage; and which is not engaged in for profit.

My Lords, I have stated the issue in these terms to stress two considerations of cardinal importance. Lawyers will need no reminding of the first, but since this prosecution has been widely noticed it must be emphasised that the issue before the House is not whether the appellants' conduct is morally right, but whether it is properly charged under the Act of 1861. When proposing that the conduct is not rightly so charged I do not invite your Lordships' House to endorse it as morally acceptable. Nor do I pronounce in favour of a libertarian doctrine specifically related to sexual matters. Nor in the least do I suggest that ethical pronouncements are meaningless, that there is no difference between right and wrong, that sadism is praiseworthy, or that new opinions on sexual morality are necessarily superior to the old, or anything else of the same kind. What I do say is that these are questions of private morality; that the standards by which they fall to be judged are not those of the criminal law; and that if these standards are to be upheld the individual must enforce them upon himself according to his own moral standards, or have them enforced against him by moral pressures exerted by whatever religious or other community to whose ethical ideals he responds. The point from which I invite your Lordships to depart is simply this, that the state should interfere with the rights of an individual to live his or her life as he or she may choose no more than is necessary to ensure a proper balance between the special interests of the individual and the general interests of the individuals who together comprise the populace at large. Thus, whilst acknowledging that very many people, if asked whether the appellants' conduct was wrong, would reply 'Yes, repulsively wrong,' I would at the same time assert that this does not in itself mean that the prosecution of the appellants under sections 20 and 47 of the Offences against the Person Act 1861 is well founded.

This point leads directly to the second. As I have ventured to formulate the crucial question, it asks whether there is good reason to impress upon section 47 an interpretation which penalises the relevant level of harm irrespective of consent, i.e., to recognise sadomasochistic activities as falling into a special category of acts, such as duelling and prize-fighting, which 'the law says shall not be done.' This is very important, for if the question were differently stated it might well yield a different answer. In particular, if it were to be held that as a matter of law all infliction of bodily harm above the level of common assault is incapable of being legitimated by consent, except in special circumstances, then we would have to consider whether the public interest required the recognition of private sexual activities as being in a specially exempt category. This would be an altogether more difficult question and one which I would not be prepared to answer in favour of the appellants, not because I do not have my own opinions upon it but because I regard the task as one which the courts are not suited to perform, and which should be carried out, if at all, by Parliament after a thorough review of all the medical, social, moral and political issues, such as was performed by the Wolfenden Committee. Thus, if I had begun from the same point of departure as my noble and learned friend, Lord Jauncey of Tullichettle, I would have arrived at a similar conclusion; but differing from him on the present state of the law, I venture to differ.

. . .

V. Conclusion

Accordingly I would allow these appeals and quash such of the convictions as are now before the House.

Lord Slynn of Hadley [dissenting]

The determination of the appeal, however, does not depend on bewilderment or revulsion or whether the right approach for the House in the appeal ought to be liberal or otherwise. The sole question is whether when a charge of assault is laid under the two sections in question, consent is relevant in the sense either that the prosecution must prove a lack of consent on the part of the person to whom the act is done or that the existence of consent by such person constitutes a defence for the person charged.

. . .

My conclusion is thus that as the law stands, adults can consent to acts done in private which do not result in serious bodily harm, so that such acts do not constitute criminal assaults for the purposes of the Act of 1861. My conclusion is not based on the alternative argument that for the criminal law to encompass consensual acts done in private would in itself be an unlawful invasion of privacy. If these acts between consenting adults in private did constitute criminal offences under the Act of 1861, there would clearly be an invasion of privacy. Whether that invasion would be justified and in particular whether it would be within the derogations permitted by article 8(2) of the European Convention on Human Rights, it is not necessary, on the conclusion to which I have come, to decide, despite the interesting arguments addressed to your Lordships on that question and even on the basis that English law includes a principle parallel to that set out in the European Convention on Human Rights.

. . .

If Parliament considers that the behaviour revealed here should be made specifically criminal, then the Offences against the Person Act 1861 or, perhaps more appropriately, the Sexual Offences Act 1967 can be amended specifically to define it. Alternatively, if it is intended that this sort of conduct should be lawful as between two persons but not between more than two persons as falling within the offence of gross indecency, then the limitation period for prosecution can be extended and the penalties increased where sado-masochistic acts are involved. That is obviously a possible course; whether it is a desirable way of changing the law is a different question.

. . .

Accordingly I consider that these appeals should be allowed and the convictions set aside.

Appeals dismissed.

The appellants took their decision to the European Court of Human Rights in *Laskey v UK*.[185] While the court found that the law prohibiting consensual sadomasochistic activity did violate the right to respect for one's private life under Article 8(1), the interference was justified as necessary in a democratic society for the protection of health and the interests of others.[186]

DEFINITION

Summary of the law following *Brown*:

The consent of the victim is a defence to an assault or battery. But is not a defence to an offence involving actual bodily harm or more serious injury, unless the case falls within one of the following recognized exceptional categories:

(1) sporting activities;

(2) dangerous exhibitions and bravado;

(3) rough and undisciplined horseplay;

(4) surgery;

(5) tattooing and body piercing;

(6) religious flagellation;

(7) consensual intimate acts in the course of which one party is infected with a medical condition, where the victim had consented to run the risk of acquiring the infection.

Consent can never be a defence in cases where the victim has died.[187] If the court is persuaded that the defendant's conduct is beneficial to society a court may be persuaded to create a new exceptional category. →5 (p.385) As will be suggested shortly, it may be that following *Dica*, an exceptional category need only be proved if the defendant is intending to cause harm.

In the following case, the Court of Appeal returned to the question of when the consent of the victim provided a defence to the charge. The decision has led to much debate as to how it can be reconciled with the House of Lords' decision in *Brown*:

---

[185] [1997] 24 EHRR 39.
[186] The European Court has confirmed this stance in *KA and AD v Belgium* App Nos 42758/98 and 45558/99, 17 February 2005.
[187] *Wacker* [2002] EWCA Crim 1944.

R v Wilson (Alan)
[1997] QB 47 (CA)

Alan Wilson was convicted of an assault occasioning actual bodily harm on his wife. He had branded his initials on her buttocks with a hot knife, apparently at her request. He appealed against his conviction on the basis that his wife's consent provided him with a defence to the charge.

Lord Justice Russell [read the following judgment of the court]

At the conclusion of the evidence called by the prosecution, defence counsel submitted that his client had no case to answer. The judge, in a ruling of which we have a transcript, after reviewing the facts and authority, concluded as follows:

'The reality that I have to deal with is that on the face of it the majority in the House of Lords in *Reg v Brown* (*Anthony*) [1994] 1 AC 212 approved of the dicta in *Rex v Donovan* [1934] 2 KB 498 and that accordingly until such time as the legislature or the European Court do something about it we are now saddled with a law that means that anyone who injures his partner, spouse, or whatever, in the course of some consensual activity is at risk of having his or her private life dragged before the public to no good purpose. Sadly, I take the view that I am bound by the majority in *Reg v Brown* and that I would have to, in those circumstances, direct this jury to convict.'

Counsel for the defendant, in the light of that ruling, did not call his client and did not make any submissions to the jury, who in due course convicted the appellant. The judge conditionally discharged him for a period of twelve months.

It is effectively against that ruling of the judge that the appeal is brought to this court. In the court below, and before us, reference was predictably made to *Rex v Donovan* [1934] 2 KB 498, a decision of the Court of Criminal Appeal, and to *Reg v Brown* (*Anthony*) [1994] 1 AC 212, a decision of the House of Lords. They are the two authorities to which the trial judge referred in the observations we have cited.

In *Rex v Donovan* [1934] 2 KB 498 the appellant, in private, beat a girl of 17 years of age for the purposes of sexual gratification, with her consent. The act had about it an aggressive element. The court held that consent was immaterial. In *Reg v Brown* [1994] 1 AC 212 the appellants engaged in sado-masochism of the grossest kind, involving inter alia, physical torture, and as Lord Templeman pointed out, at p 236D: 'obvious dangers of serious personal injury and blood infection.' The facts of the case were truly extreme.

We are abundantly satisfied that there is no factual comparison to be made between the instant case and the facts of either *Rex v Donovan* [1934] 2 KB 498 or *Reg v Brown* [1994] 1 AC 212: Mrs Wilson not only consented to that which the appellant did, she instigated it. There was no aggressive intent on the part of the appellant. On the contrary, far from wishing to cause injury to his wife, the appellant's desire was to assist her in what she regarded as the acquisition of a desirable piece of personal adornment, perhaps in this day and age no less understandable than the piercing of nostrils or even tongues for the purposes of inserting decorative jewellery.

In our judgment *Reg v Brown* is not authority for the proposition that consent is no defence to a charge under section 47 of the Act of 1861, in all circumstances where actual bodily harm is deliberately inflicted. It is to be observed that the question certified for their Lordships in *Reg v Brown* related only to a 'sado-masochistic encounter.' However, their Lordships recognised in the course of their speeches, that it is necessary that there must be exceptions to what is no more than a general proposition. The speeches of Lord Templeman, at p 231, Lord Jauncey of Tullichettle, at p 245, and the dissenting speech of Lord Slynn of Hadley, at p 277, all refer to tattooing as being an activity which, if carried out with the consent of an adult, does not involve an offence under section 47, albeit that actual bodily harm is deliberately inflicted.

For our part, we cannot detect any logical difference between what the appellant did and what he might have done in the way of tattooing. The latter activity apparently requires no state authorisation, and the appellant was as free to engage in it as anyone else. We do not think that we are entitled to assume that the method adopted by the appellant and his wife was any more dangerous or painful than tattooing. There was simply no evidence to assist the court on this aspect of the matter.

Does public policy or the public interest demand that the appellant's activity should be visited by the sanctions of the criminal law? The majority in *Reg v Brown* clearly took the view that such considerations were relevant. If that is so, then we are firmly of the opinion that it is not in the public interest that activities such as the appellant's in this appeal should amount to criminal behaviour. Consensual activity between husband and wife, in the privacy of the matrimonial home, is not, in our judgment, normally a proper matter for criminal investigation, let alone criminal prosecution. Accordingly we take the view that the judge failed to have full regard to the facts of this case and misdirected himself in saying that *Rex v Donovan* [1934] 2 KB 498 and *Reg v Brown* [1994] 1 AC 212 constrained him to rule that consent was no defence.

In this field, in our judgment, the law should develop upon a case by case basis rather than upon general propositions to which, in the changing times in which we live, exceptions may arise from time to time not expressly covered by authority.

We shall allow the appeal and quash the conviction. We conclude this judgment by commenting that we share the judge's disquiet that the prosecuting authority thought it fit to bring these proceedings. In our view they serve no useful purpose at considerable public expense. We gave the appellant leave to appeal against his sentence. Had it been necessary for us to consider sentence we would have granted the appellant an absolute discharge.

Appeal allowed. Conviction quashed.

There has been much dispute over the correct interpretation of this case and how it can be reconciled with *Brown*. To some commentators the difference in the approach of the Court of Appeal in *Wilson* and the House of Lords in *Brown* lies in the fact that the Wilsons were a married couple and that therefore their conduct was more 'acceptable' to the Court of Appeal than the group homosexual behaviour of the appellants in *Brown*. However, the Court of Appeal in *Emmett*[188] rejected such an analysis in convicting a man who had seriously injured his fiancée in the course of alleged sadomasochistic behaviour. The explanation of the difference between the two cases provided by the Court of Appeal in *Emmett* was that in *Wilson* the activity was analogous to the exception that exists for tattooing, whereas the behaviour in *Brown* (and *Emmett* itself) did not fall into one of the exceptional categories of cases. We will discuss this further in Part II.

So now let us consider what the categories of exceptional cases are where consent will provide a defence to an offence involving actual bodily harm or a more serious level of injury:

(1) **Sports** Consent is usually a defence to injuries received in the course of a sporting event, even if those injuries involve actual bodily harm.[189] It is presumed that by deciding

---

[188] *Emmett* (CA, 18 June 1999).

[189] See Anderson (2008), Livings (2006 and 2007), and Fafinksi (2005) for a discussion of criminal offences and sport.

to play the sport the victim has consented to the infliction of the kind of force normally involved in the game.[190] So a rugby player cannot claim that when tackled with the ball he was being unlawfully battered. Even if the injury is committed in the course of a foul the court may well feel that when playing a sport you accept that you will be fouled. However, there comes a point where the kind of force used will not be regarded as the kind of foul you consent to by playing that sport. In *R v Barnes*[191] the Court of Appeal held that if there was a foul 'quite outside what could be expected to occur in the course of a football game'[192] that could be a criminal offence. This requires the court to distinguish 'normal fouls', which are consented to and are not criminal offences, and 'over-the-top fouls', which are beyond what might be expected and are not consented to and can amount to a criminal offence. A jury would probably be willing to convict a player who deliberately fouled the other team's best player in an attempt to injure him. In 2007 a rugby player who stamped on another player's head was convicted of unlawful wounding.[193]

This exceptional category applies only to organized and regulated sports. Two people who got into a fight with each other in a street would both be convicted of assault: they could not claim they were engaged in a boxing match![194] Some unorganized games could fall within the category of 'rough and undisciplined horseplay', which will be discussed in paragraph (3).[195]

(2) **Dangerous exhibitions and bravado** Under this heading fall activities such as circus acts and stunts (e.g. being a human cannonball, bungee jumping).[196] In the Canadian Supreme Court decision of *Jobidon*[197] it was suggested that stuntmen agreeing to perform daredevil activities are engaged 'for the good of the people involved, and often for a wider group of people as well'. Within the 'bravado' heading might be a case where the victim says to the defendant 'my stomach is iron, hit me as hard as you like and it won't hurt' and is then injured by the defendant's punch. No offence would be committed if the court as willing to regard this as an act of bravado by the victim.

(3) **Rough and undisciplined horseplay** A good example of this exceptional category is *Jones*[198] where the defendant (a schoolboy) and other children were playing around and throwing the victim up in the air. The victim was dropped and suffered a broken arm and ruptured spleen. The defendant's appeal against a conviction for an assault occasioning actual bodily harm was allowed. The Court of Appeal held that the victim had consented (or at least the defendant believed the victim had consented) to the rough horseplay,[199] and that consent to rough horseplay provided a defence to offences involving actual bodily harm. The decision could be based on two justifications. First, that otherwise all around the country there would be thousands of offences taking place in school playgrounds. Rough games are part of childhood and it would be unrealistic to punish them. Second, more positively, that such games are beneficial: being an important part of growing up and encouraging exercise. It should, however, be borne in mind that a line has to be carefully drawn between rough horseplay and bullying.

---

[190] Ormerod and Gunn (1995) provide a useful discussion of the law's response to boxing.

[191] [2005] 1 WLR 910.   [192] *Ibid*, para. 28.   [193] BBC News Online (2007c).

[194] *Attorney-General's Reference (No. 6 of 1980)* [1981] QB 715.

[195] In *Erisman* [1988] 1 Hong Kong Law Reports 370 the Hong Kong High Court suggested that injuries caused in a war game involving firing pellets at each other were covered by the rough and undisciplined horseplay exception.

[196] See Cooper and James (2012) for a discussion of whether injuries in TV shows such as *Jackass* are covered by the defence of consent.

[197] [1991] 2 SCR 714, discussed in Kell (1994).   [198] (1986) 83 Cr App R 375.

[199] Although not to the injuries.

Jones was extended in *Aitken*,[200] where the defendants were members of the Air Force who set fire to the victim after a party. It was held that such conduct could fall within the rough horseplay exception, and so the victim's consent[201] could provide a defence. Similarly students throwing each other off balconies were found to be engaged in rough horseplay and the victim's consent (or the defendant's belief in the victim's consent) provided a defence to a criminal charge.[202]

(4) **Surgery** This has long been recognized as an activity where a person's consent to the injury renders the act lawful. No one would deny that if an operation is required to improve a patient's health it should be permitted. Even operations which are perhaps more controversial and less obviously beneficial (e.g. cosmetic surgery) are generally accepted to be lawful based on the victim's consent. Statute has made it clear that certain operations (e.g. female genital mutilation) are illegal.[203]

(5) **Tattooing and body piercing** Tattooing and body piercing for the purpose of personal adornment are permitted. In *Wilson*[204] the Court of Appeal held that 'do it yourself' tattooing, where the husband using a hot knife branded his initials onto his wife's buttocks was included within the exception.

(6) **Religious flagellation** Lord Mustill in *Brown* indicated that there is an exception for those who use flagellation to express feelings of penitence as part of religious practices. In 2008, a man who encouraged two boys to flagellate themselves with knives as part of a Shia religious ceremony was convicted of child cruelty.[205] The court as not convinced the boys were mature enough to consent.

(7) **Infectious intimate relations** In *Dica*[206] (excerpted at Section 13) the Court of Appeal accepted that if the victim agreed to have sexual relations with the defendant, aware that he was infectious and that therefore there was a risk that the infection would be passed on, this consent provided a defence to a charge under section 20 of the Offences Against the Person Act 1861.

(8) **Where the harm is not caused intentionally** Whether this category exists or not is unclear. In an *obiter* discussion the Court of Appeal in *Dica*[207] emphasized that in *Brown* the injuries were caused intentionally and that was regarded as central to their Lordships' reasoning. So, the Court of Appeal in *Dica*[208] was willing to allow consent to apply in cases of reckless transmission of HIV, but not in cases of intentional transmission. A wide reading of *Dica*[209] would suggest that only in cases of intentional causing of actual bodily harm or worse, will a court require a defendant to prove his or her behaviour fell into one of the exceptional categories. Such an approach would not, however, sit well with the decision in *Wacker*[210] where the consent of the illegal immigrants to being put into a van with limited ventilation was not a defence to the charge of gross negligence manslaughter that followed their death. A better approach might be to say that following *Dica*[211] the courts will be particularly willing to find new exceptional categories in cases where the harm is caused recklessly. Indeed it may well be correct to say that rarely will consent not provide a defence if the harm is caused recklessly.[212]

---

[200] (1992) 95 Cr App R 304.

[201] In *Aitken*, controversially, the Court of Appeal seemed willing to assume the consent of the victim to the horseplay from the fact he had been present at the party where such conduct took place.

[202] *Richardson and Irwin* [1999] 1 Cr App R 392.   [203] Female Genital Mutilation Act 2003.

[204] [1996] 3 WLR 125.   [205] BBC News Online (2008c).   [206] [2004] EWCA Crim 1103.

[207] *Ibid.*   [208] *Ibid.*   [209] *Ibid.*

[210] [2003] QB 1207.   [211] [2004] EWCA Crim 1103.

[212] I am very grateful to Alan Bogg for suggesting these ways of looking at the case law.

In *Brown* their Lordships indicated that this was not a closed list and that if they were persuaded that it was appropriate to do so they would add in a new category. On the facts of that case they declined to add sadomasochistic activity to the list of exceptions.

14.2 WHAT IS CONSENT?

The meaning of 'consent' will be discussed in detail in Chapter 7, and will only be summarized here.

Express or implied consent

Consent can be express or implied. A wife who kisses her husband first thing in the morning can rely on the husband's implied consent. Even two strangers may be able to rely on implied consent if the touching is seen as part of the normal touchings of everyday life.[213] Lack of consent may be implied where the victim has been subjected to violence.[214] In *H v CPS*[215] the Divisional Court rejected an argument that teachers at a school for children with special educational needs could be implied to have consented to violence from the pupils. They may have foreseen that by taking up the job they would be exposed to violence, but foresight of violence is not the same thing as consent to it.

Capacity

Consent can be given only by a person with capacity. An adult is presumed to have capacity to consent.[216] Sections 2(1) and 3(1) of the Mental Capacity Act 2005 explain when a person will be deemed to lack capacity:

> a person lacks capacity in relation to a matter if at the material time he is unable to make a decision for himself in relation to the matter because of an impairment of, or a disturbance in the functioning of, the mind or brain. . . .
>
>   . . . [A] person is unable to make a decision for himself if he is unable—
>
> (a) to understand the information relevant to the decision,
>
> (b) to retain that information,
>
> (c) to use or weigh that information as part of the process of making the decision, or
>
> (d) to communicate his decision (whether by talking, using sign language or any other means).

This test is issue-specific. In other words, a person may have capacity to decide some issues, but not others.[217] Where the victim is a child or an adult with learning difficulties the court will be particularly wary of finding that they had the capacity to consent.[218] Children are not presumed to have capacity, however, in the case of older children the court may be willing to find that they had sufficient maturity to be able to give effective consent.[219]

---

[213] *Collins v Wilcock* [1984] 3 All ER 374.   [214] *CPS v Shabbir* [2009] EWHC 2754 (Admin).
[215] [2010] EWHC 1374 (Admin).   [216] Mental Capacity Act 2005, s. 1.
[217] See Herring (2015b) for a detailed discussion.   [218] *Burrell v Harmer* [1967] Crim LR 169.
[219] *Gillick v West Norfolk and Wisbech AHA* [1986] AC 112.

Consent given in cases where the victim was 'consenting' due to fear or mistake

The law accepts that even though a victim may appear to consent to the force being used by the defendant, that consent may not be true consent. That may be so in the following circumstances:

(1) The 'consent' was given by a victim who was mistaken as to the identity of the defendant.

(2) The 'consent' was given by a victim who was mistaken as to the nature of the proposed act.

(3) The 'consent' was given by a defendant who was so fearful that the 'consent' should be regarded as submission and so ineffective.

We will be discussing consent further in Chapter 7 in the context of rape and will explore these issues more fully there.

What if consent is given to actual bodily harm but less harm is caused?

What if a masochist asked a sadist to cause him or her actual bodily harm or grievous bodily harm, but in fact the sadist inflicted only a battery? Could the sadist be convicted of a battery or would the masochist's consent provide a defence? One view is that *dicta* in *Donovan*[220] and *Boyea*[221] suggest that consent to actual bodily harm is not lawful consent and therefore is invalid. Therefore in our scenario the sadist is guilty of a battery. On the other hand the majority in *Brown* accepted without adding any qualifications that consent was a defence to a battery. That would suggest the sadist is not guilty of an offence.

Consent where the extent of harm is not foreseen

What if a defendant believes he or she is committing a battery, to which the victim has consented but in fact what he or she is doing causes actual bodily harm or grievous bodily harm? Is the victim's consent a defence to such an offence? There are three views that have been expressed:

(1) No. In *Attorney-General's Reference (No. 6 of 1980)*[222] it was suggested that if actual bodily harm or more serious injury was caused the victim's consent would not provide a defence.[223]

(2) Not if actual bodily harm was foreseeable. In *Boyea*[224] it was suggested that if actual bodily harm was a foreseeable result of the defendant's actions then the victim's consent would not provide a defence. However, if actual bodily harm was not a foreseeable result the victim's consent could provide a defence, even if actual bodily harm (or a more serious injury) resulted.

---

[220] [1934] 2 KB 498.   [221] [1992] Crim LR 574.   [222] [1981] 1 WLR 705.

[223] This approach appears to have been approved in *Andrews* [2003] Crim LR 477, but without a detailed consideration of the issue.

[224] [1992] Crim LR 574.

(3) Not if actual bodily harm was foreseen by the defendant as a result of his actions. In *Slingsby*[225] Judge J held that if the defendant thought he was committing a battery and had not *foreseen* a more serious injury the victim's consent would still provide a defence to any charge involving a more serious injury. However, if the defendant was aware that there was a risk that the victim would suffer a more serious injury than a battery or an assault then he or she cannot rely on the consent of the victim.

We need an authoritative ruling on the question, but the *Slingsby* ruling is most in line with the general approach on *mens rea* in offences against the person, which relies on *Cunningham* recklessness. In *Meachen*[226] the Court of Appeal appeared to accept this, following the *Slingsby* approach.

14.3 WHAT IF THERE IS NO CONSENT BUT THE DEFENDANT BELIEVES THAT THERE IS CONSENT?

The Court of Appeal in *Jones*[227] confirmed that, in a case where the victim's consent would provide a defence, the defendant will also have a defence if he or she honestly believes that the victim is consenting, even if in fact the victim is not. This is so even if the defendant's belief was unreasonable. Bizarrely, in *Richardson and Irwin*[228] it was held that a drunken belief that the victim had consented to the injury as part of rough horseplay was held to provide a defence. Normally in the criminal law a drunken belief that the victim consented does not provide a defence (e.g. in the context of rape).[229] Many commentators therefore assume that *Richardson and Irwin* is incorrect on this point.[230]

QUESTIONS

1. Simone has sexual intercourse with Bill. She knows she has not recently cut her toenails and that she may therefore scratch Bill during the intercourse. She does indeed give an unpleasant scratch. What offences has Simone committed? (Consider here the *Boyea* and *Slingsby* cases and also whether the scratch may be a wound.)

2. Tom (a tattooist) gives Viv an intimate body piercing. Tom does not normally perform piercings, but found Viv attractive and so agreed to do it. What offences (if any) has Tom committed? (Is this more like *Brown* or *Wilson*?)

For guidance on answering this question, please visit the Online Resource Centre that accompanies this book: www.oxfordtextbooks.co.uk/orc/herringcriminal7e/.

FURTHER READING

Giles, M. (1994) '*R v Brown*: Consensual Harm and the Public Interest' *Modern Law Review* 57: 101.

Roberts, P. (1997a) 'Consent to Injury: How Far Can You Go?' *Law Quarterly Review* 113: 27.

---

[225] [1995] Crim LR 570.   [226] [2006] EWCA Crim 2414.   [227] (1986) 83 Cr App R 375.
[228] [1999] 1 Cr App R 392, 397, although the judgment is, with respect, rather ambiguous.
[229] *Fotheringham* (1989) 88 Cr App R 206.
[230] See e.g. Simester, Spencer, Sullivan, and Virgo (2013: 704).

PART II: THEORETICAL ISSUES ON ASSAULTS

15 THE TRUE NATURE AND EXTENT OF VIOLENT CRIME

In 2014/15, 779,027 offences of violence against the person in England and Wales were recorded.[231] But looking at such bald statistics is not particularly useful in assessing the level of violent offending. First, of course, there are many more violent incidents which are not reported. The Crime Survey for England and Wales findings estimated that in the same period there were 1,321,000 incidents of violence.[232] Second, the harm for which a person is convicted may not reflect the actual offence done to the victim. The process from committal of the crime to conviction is not a straightforward one.[233] A procedure known as down-charging is common. This is where a defendant is ultimately convicted in court for an offence which is lower than the wrong which the victim has alleged. Imagine a case where the victim has been stabbed by the defendant. One might expect this to result in a charge under section 18 or 20 of the Offences Against the Person Act 1861. However, if the prosecution is not confident that it can establish the necessary *mens rea*, it may prefer to charge under section 47 where the *mens rea* is easier to prove. Alternatively there may be a plea bargain where the defendant offers to plead guilty to section 47, but will plead not guilty to section 20. In both these cases the prosecution may, in order to save time and resources, prosecute for the lower offence.

The popular image of an assault in the newspapers is probably an attack in a dark alley, but this is only part of the picture. Incidents of violence are in fact common in the home.[234] In 2013/14 there were 1.1 million female victims and 500,000 male victims of abuse from their partners.[235] In that year 6.8 per cent of women and 3 per cent of men had experienced domestic abuse. Also 28.3 per cent of women and 14.7 per cent of men reported experiencing domestic abuse since their sixteenth birthday. These figures are the tip of the iceberg. Only around one in ten incidents of domestic abuse are reported to the police.[236] Around one in five violent crimes reported to the police are domestic violence, and many incidents go unreported.[237] As Anthony Giddens has written:

> The home is, in fact, the most dangerous place in modern society. In statistical terms, a person of any age or of either sex is far more likely to be subject to physical attack in the home than on the street at night.[238]

In the following extract, Shazia Choudhry and I reject arguments that the state should not be involved in cases of domestic violence because they are a private matter:

---

[231] Office for National Statistics (2015a).   [232] *Ibid.*   [233] Clarkson *et al* (1994).
[234] See Herring (2015b: ch. 7) for a general discussion of the law's response to domestic violence.
[235] Office for National Statistics (2015c).   [236] *Ibid.*   [237] *Ibid.*   [238] Giddens (1989).

S. Choudhry and J. Herring, 'Righting Domestic Violence' (2006) 20 *International Journal of Law, Policy and the Family* **95**

There has been much written on the concept of privacy. The traditional liberal approach is that respect of private life is all about protecting the individual from improper state intrusion. This has had two consequences. The first is that the right of privacy was one held against the state. The right inhibited state intrusion into personal life. It was not relevant where one citizen was interfering in the private life of another. Second, what is private is not the state's business and should be free from government interference. As is well known, the notion of privacy has historically been used as the basis of government non-intervention in issues of domestic violence. State authorities should not, it is said, intrude into the nation's bedrooms and seek to control the behaviour that occurs there. Violence in the home is less serious than violence in public because it causes less disturbance to the 'public peace'. Such an approach has been powerfully critiqued by feminist commentators. MacKinnon (1987: 32) characterized the ideology of privacy as 'a right of men "to be let alone" to oppress women one at a time'. In place of the traditional notion of privacy work has been done to rethink the meaning of the concept.

A good starting point for rethinking the nature of privacy is to ask: Why should the state respect the private life of its citizens? One popular answer lies in the concept of autonomy. Each person should be entitled to develop her/his own understanding of the 'good life'. We could have a state that attempted to enforce a beneficial lifestyle on each citizen, telling her/him what to read, eat and do, but most people would find such a society repellent. Not least because living in a society of 'clones' would be boring indeed. So, the notion of privacy plays a role in allowing us to develop our lives and intimate relations in the ways we wish. This produces a wide range of different personalities and lifestyles which provide part of the enjoyment of life. But, so understood, privacy is not necessarily a negative concept about state non-intervention, but rather about an enabling of each individual to flourish as a person. For those with power that may be possible with little intervention from the state. However, for the less powerful, state intervention may be necessary to enable a person (or groups of people) to live their lives fully . . .

Adopting such an approach means that privacy is not a concept which prevents state intervention in incidents of domestic violence but which in fact requires it. Without state intervention a victim of domestic violence will be prevented from pursuing her vision of the good life. To quote just one statistic to support that: over 50 percent of women in touch with mental health services in England and Wales had suffered in violent and abusive relationships. So, then, if the state wishes to promote privacy in this sense the ability to thrive in one's attempt to do what they wish with their lives then protection from violence is required. To leave a person in an abusive relationship which is restricting her ability to develop her life as she wishes is not respecting her privacy, quite the opposite.

Other reasons we give for rejecting the argument that domestic abuse is a private matter is that where children are present it can cause them serious harm and that domestic abuse harms the state's interests in promoting a more equal society.

A strong case can be made for saying that we should not only reject the argument that domestic violence is less serious than violence in the street, but we should go further and argue that domestic violence should be seen as more serious than violence between strangers.[239] As it

---

[239] Herring (2013b).

takes place within an ongoing relationship which is marked by 'coercive control' it can have a far more significant impact on the victim's sense of self and well-being than a mugging in the street. Further, its impact on children and society's wish to promote greater gender equality mean domestic abuse can be seen as a major social issue.

FURTHER READING

Bessant, C. (2014) 'Protecting Victims of Domestic Violence—Have We Got the Balance Right?' *Journal of Criminal Law* 79: 102.

Choudhry, S. and Herring, J. (2006) 'Righting Domestic Violence' *International Journal of Law Policy and the Family* 20: 95.

Clarkson, C. *et al* (1994) 'Assaults: The Relationship between Seriousness, Criminalisation and Punishment' *Criminal Law Review* 4.

Cretney, A. and Davis, G. (1997) 'Prosecuting "Domestic" Assault' *The Howard Journal* 36: 146.

Herring, J. (2011b) 'The Serious Wrong of Domestic Abuse and the Loss of Control Defence' in A. Reed and M. Bohlander (eds) *Loss of Control and Diminished Responsibility: Domestic, Comparative and International Perspectives* (Aldershot: Ashgate).

Levi, M. (2002) 'Violent Crime' in M. Maguire, R. Morgan, and R. Reiner (eds) *The Oxford Handbook of Criminology* (Oxford: OUP).

Madden Dempsey, M. (2009a) *Prosecuting Domestic Violence* (Oxford: OUP).

Tadros, V. (2005b) 'The Distinctiveness of Domestic Abuse' in R.A. Duff and S. Green (eds) *Defining Crimes* (Oxford: OUP), 121–5.

Van Brunschot, T. (2003) 'Freedom and Integrity: Relationships and Assault' *British Journal of Criminology* 43: 122.

---

16 THE NATURE OF AN ASSAULT

There has been some debate over the correct understanding of the essence of the offence of assault. Is the offence about the creation of fear (if so why must the fear be of imminent force?) or is it closer to an attempted battery (if so why can words amount to an assault?)? In the following passage, Jeremy Horder suggests that the best way to understand the nature of the assault is as a threatening confrontation: ←1 (p.317)

J. Horder, 'Reconsidering Psychic Assault' [1998] *Criminal Law Review* 392 at 399–402

Assaults as threatening confrontations

It is odd that fear remains comparatively under-analysed by criminal lawyers, as a possible species of harm, as compared with bodily and psychiatric injury (of great concern both to criminal and civil lawyers) or with 'moral offence' (of great concern to liberal political thinkers). As a species of harm, fear has a relatively transitory character inconsistent with its recognition as a kind of 'bodily' harm for the purposes of the Offences Against the Person Act 1861. None the less, some kinds of fear—perhaps especially the fear of physical mistreatment—unacceptably detract from the kind of 'moral environment' in which people can be expected to flourish in both their public and their private lives. In this, the kind of set-back to one's interests that it constitutes, fear shares something with the much-discussed notion of 'offence to others': moral offence. But (crucially), fear of physical interference is not generated by the largely moral disapproval of others' activities that gives rise to the notion of 'offensiveness', and which makes the latter so controversial as a basis for criminal-isation. That does not mean, however, that, even if it were permissible, it would necessarily be appropriate to seek to criminalise every means by which an unjustified fear of physical interference is induced in another. So, what is morally significant about the wrong in psychic assault, if not the mere causing (by whatever means) of apprehension?

For Williams, an assault is just one kind of 'unlawful interference with another', but the notion of an 'interference' is, without more, too abstract to be imbued with much of moral significance. Closer to the mark is Gardner's contention that '[i]ts [assault's] essential quality lies in the invasion by one person of another's body space'. This contention suggests some-thing of moral significance in assault other than simply causing fear, namely the invasion of body space, but the problem is that it is difficult to square with cases in which unusual physical proximity (such as 'eyeball-to-eyeball' hostilities) is clearly absent, but where there is nevertheless an undoubted assault, as in *Smith v. Newsam* or *Ireland*.

I suggest that what should be regarded as morally significant about the *actus reus* of a psy-chic assault is that it is experienced as a threatening *confrontation* by the victim. The victims in, for example, *Smith v. Newsam*, *Ireland*, *Thomas v. NUM* and *Smith v. Superintendent of Woking Police Station* were all confronted by a threat. What is, in this regard, to be regarded as a 'confrontation'? To be confronted by a threat, for the purposes of the law of assault, should be to perceive it as it is being made. There is something approaching an analogy here with the importance (albeit now somewhat diminished) still attributed, in limiting claims in tort for damage due to nervous shock, to the fact that the shock resulted from 'the sensory and contemporaneous' observance of the accident or its immediate aftermath. What matters is not physical propinquity to what is happening, but actual perception of what is happening or has just happened: sensory and contemporaneous awareness, involving what Lord Ackner vividly describes as, 'the sudden appreciation by sight or sound of a horrifying event, which violently agitates the mind'. My claim is not, of course, that it is necessarily *worse* to perceive a threat as it is made, to be confronted with the making of it, than it is to receive notification of it (say) by letter. Distinctions of moral significance between offences do not necessarily bear on their relative gravity, just as similar distinctions between defences do not necessar-ily alter their effect on liability. Consider this analogy. The legal effect of having acted under duress *per minas* is, for most purposes, much the same as having acted under duress of circumstances or conditions of necessity. But the experience of being threatened by another is not the same kind of experience as that of responding to a natural emergency, and different evaluative considerations may be involved in each. My claims are that (i) a psychic assault is the sensory and contemporaneous experience of being threatened, being 'confronted' with a threat, an experience that induces a fear of physical interference—whether or not to be inflicted immediately—being done by the threatener and (ii) that this experience is morally distinct as a form of harm, albeit not necessarily more serious, from receiving a threatening letter or the like.

Understanding psychic assault in this way, we can confidently assert that there was an assault in *Ireland*, just as there was in *Smith v. Newsam* and in *Smith v. Superintendent of Woking Police Station*. For, in *Ireland*, the threat was perceived by the victim as it was made by the defendant (*i.e.* there was 'sensory and contemporaneous' perception: Lord Ackner's 'sudden appreciation by sight or sound of a horrifying event'), inducing a fear of physical interference (Lord Ackner's notion of a violent agitation of the mind) in the former. This morally distinctive element of a fear of physical interference, induced through a confrontation, renders irrelevant the fact that the defendant, in *Ireland*, was clearly unable to implement his implied threat immediately. As explained above, moreover, the emphasis on V's perception of D's words as threatening, as the *actus reus*, also allows us confidently to defend the view that there was an assault in *Light*, as there was in *Tuberville v. Savage*. Following a quarrel, Tuberville laid his hand on his sword and said to Savage: 'If it were not assize-time I would not take such language from you'. It is commonly supposed that the Court held that this was not an assault because (in my terms) Tuberville was setting out a defeating condition: 'the declaration of [Tuberville] was, that he would not assault him, the judges being in town'. The argument I have put forward suggests that the supposed ruling ought now to be questioned. Tuberville's words can only be regarded as a defeating condition if one assumes that threats in assault cases must be of immediate violence. But if one abandons this assumption, Savage had every reason to think Tuberville was setting out a mere suspensory condition: he (Tuberville) might well have been saying that he would attack Savage when the judges left town. If Savage thought this (if he was led by Tuberville's words to fear that Tuberville would attack him at some time in the future), then Savage *was* psychically assaulted when Tuberville uttered his now famous words, because of his 'sensory and contemporaneous' observance of the threat, his 'sudden appreciation by sight or sound of a horrifying event, which violently agitates the mind'.

17 OBJECTIONS TO AND REFORM OF THE OFFENCES AGAINST THE PERSON ACT 1861

There is much unhappiness with the law of offences against the person, particularly the Offences Against the Person Act 1861.[240] After all it is hardly surprising that an 1861 Act has had difficulty dealing with our 'modern' problems of email harassment, racially motivated assaults, stalking, and HIV infection. Professor Ashworth has referred to the Act being 'unprincipled' and 'expressed in language whose sense is difficult to convey to juries'. He is concerned that 'it may lead judges to perpetrate manifest distortions in order to secure convictions in cases where there is "obvious" guilt but where the Act falls down.'[241] Lord Ackner has referred to the 'irrational result of this piecemeal legislation'.[242]

The most common areas of complaint about the 1861 Act are as follows:

(1) **Maximum sentences** The maximum penalty for the section 20 offence (wounding or inflicting grievous bodily harm) is five years, which is the same as that for the section 47 one (assault occasioning actual bodily harm). It seems odd that they should have the same maximum sentence, given that the section 20 offence requires proof of a more serious *actus reus* (grievous, rather than actual bodily harm) and a graver *mens rea* (foresight of some harm, rather than foresight of an assault or battery). In practice, section 20 is treated by prosecutors and the judiciary as more serious than section 47. It appears then that both theory and practice would be better reflected if section 20 had a higher maximum sentence than section 47.

---

[240] Jefferson (2012) provides a helpful summary of the issues.   [241] Ashworth (2009: 322).
[242] *Savage and Parmenter* [1992] 1 AC 699, 723.

It is also notable that there is a large jump in sentencing from section 20 (five years) to section 18 (life). Andrew Ashworth suggests it should be questioned whether the distinction between intention and recklessness (at least in the context of offences which often involve acts of instinctive violence) is sufficient to warrant the difference.[243]

(2) **Correspondence principle** The correspondence principle has been discussed in detail in Chapter 3. In brief its adherents claim that it is wrong to have an offence where the defendant is guilty even though he or she did not intend or foresee the *actus reus*. For example, a defendant under section 20 should be guilty of causing grievous bodily harm only if he intended or foresaw that his act would produce such a result. As we have seen, the Offences Against the Person Act 1861 does not accord with the correspondence principle in respect of section 47 (there is no need to intend or foresee actual bodily harm) and section 20 (there is no need to intend or foresee grievous bodily harm). However, as noted in Chapter 3, other commentators reject the correspondence principle (see e.g. the extract from John Gardner in the following extract). ←2 (p.327)

(3) **'Wound or grievous bodily harm'** The *actus reus* of sections 18 and 20 involves wounding *or* causing grievous bodily harm.[244] The complaint is that wounding can involve a minor cut which may essentially heal in minutes, and that it is wrong to group it together with grievous bodily harm. It can be argued that there was some justification in 1861 for treating wounding and grievous bodily harm similarly because a cut could (at that time) all too easily turn septic and endanger the victim's life. Therefore treating a break in the skin as equivalent to a life-threatening harm was reasonable. Nowadays those who support the 1861 Act tend to rely on one of two arguments. The first is that a cut, a breaking of the skin, involves a significant invasion of the person. It is not just because of the pain that people dread injections. Thus, although not as painful as a broken arm (say), the invasion of the person's sense of self in a wounding case is significantly worse. The second is that the inclusion of wounding in the offence could be justified as a deterrent to those who use knives or sharp implements in an attack.

(4) **Inflict/cause** As we saw in Part I there is some dispute over the meaning of the words 'inflict' in section 20 and 'cause' in section 18. Probably the position the law has reached is that inflict means the same as cause, in which case it must be asked why the word 'caused' was not used in both sections. It is certainly confusing that two closely linked sections contain two different words with apparently the same meaning. ←3 (p.335)

(5) **Archaic language** Some commentators and members of the judiciary feel that the language of the Offences Against the Person Act 1861 is archaic and does not describe the offences covered in accessible and clear language. This has meant, they suggest, that the courts have had to give a strained interpretation of the meaning of the sections' words on occasions. One example might be the inclusion of psychological illnesses within the term 'bodily harm'.

(6) **The need for an assault in section 47** Why is there a requirement in section 47 of an assault? Why should it not be sufficient simply to prove that the defendant caused the victim actual bodily harm? Horder gives the example of someone who puts acid in another's bath, causing actual bodily harm. In such a case should there be any doubt that there has been an

---

[243] Ashworth (2009: 323).
[244] The complaint is weaker in relation to s. 18, where the defendant must intend grievous bodily harm (even if in fact he wounded).

offence under section 47 because it may not be easy to demonstrate that there was a battery or an assault?[245]

Although the Law Commission[246] and many commentators are convinced by these arguments there are few commentators who are willing to stand up for the Offences Against the Person Act 1861. One of the strongest defences of the Act is provided by John Gardner. In the following extract, he replies to some of the objections mentioned previously. He starts by challenging the claim that the Act is irrational:

J. Gardner, 'Rationality and the Rule of Law in Offences Against the Person' (1994) 53 *Cambridge Law Journal* 502 at 503–11

The rationality argument figures less prominently in the Law Commission's latest report than it does in the consultation paper which preceded it. One can only speculate as to the causes of its demotion, but its spirit certainly lives on in the draft Bill. The spirit of the argument is captured in the Commission's comment that 'sections 18, 20 and 47 of the 1861 Act . . . were not drafted with a view to setting out the various offences with which they deal in a logical or graded manner'. The assumption is that the three offences can, in substance, be graded, and that this would be the logical way to define and organise them. Between them they deal with matters which would most naturally be dealt with in a hierarchy of more and less serious offences all conforming to a standard definitional pattern. The irrationality of the 1861 Act lies in its failure to take this natural path, its failure to carry the underlying hierarchy of seriousness over into the actual definition and organisation of the offences. Thus, section 18 should be regarded, in substance, as an aggravated version of section 20; and yet there are miscellaneous differences between the two sections which do not appear to bear any rational relation to the aggravation. Likewise, section 20 should be regarded, in substance, as the more serious cousin of section 47; and yet the two offences are drafted in quite different terms, so that the essential difference in point of seriousness is obscured by a mass of other, utterly irrelevant differences. If the sections were properly graded in definition as they are in substance, then section 18 would surely cover a narrower class of cases than section 20 which would cover a narrower class of cases than section 47; and yet section 47 is, in at least one respect, the narrowest offence of the three, while section 18 is, in at least one respect, broader than section 20. That is surely irrational. The law on such matters should be thoroughly governed, in the Law Commission's words, 'by clear distinctions . . . between serious and less serious cases'.

That a section 18 offence should be regarded, in substance, as a more serious version of a section 20 offence is easy enough to understand. Section 20 covers malicious wounding and the malicious infliction of grievous bodily harm. Section 18 covers malicious wounding and maliciously causing grievous bodily harm, when these things are done with intention to do grievous bodily harm or to prevent or resist arrest. The extra element of intention required for a section 18 offence obviously accounts for the difference between the sentencing maxima (five years' imprisonment under section 20 and life under section 18), and marks a difference in point of seriousness (or potential seriousness) which the Law Commission is rightly anxious to retain in its hierarchy of replacement offences. The Commission has not even felt the need to explain its decision, however, to eliminate the difference in the *causal* elements of sections 18 and 20. Section 20 requires that grievous bodily harm be *inflicted*, whereas for section 18 it need only be *caused*. The law at present tells us that infliction requires

---

[245] In fact, in the light of *DPP v K* [1990] 1 All ER 331 there is likely to be a battery.
[246] Law Commission (2014).

violent force. One may cause grievous bodily harm by, for example, passing on an infection or poisoning. But one may not inflict grievous bodily harm in that way. If that is right, one may commit a section 18 offence without using violent means, but a section 20 offence requires such means. This the Commission apparently holds to be a self-evidently irrational point of distinction between the two offences. One may glean the reasons. In the first place the distinction between 'causing' and 'inflicting', as the law presents it, fails the test which the Commission uses to determine what factors may affect the seriousness of a crime in this area of the law. For the Commission, seriousness varies only 'according to the type of injury that [the defendant] intended or was aware that he might cause'. In the second place, and more straightforwardly, the distinction we are looking at appears to operate back to front. The extra element of violence is required for the less serious offence, not the more serious. The distinction is not merely irrational, it may be said, but perverse. Not so. The distinction is easy enough to understand. One must begin by thinking of section 20 as the basic offence, and infliction as the basic mode of causation with which the two offences together are concerned. That is not hard to do. Only someone who mistakes the *harm* in section 20 for the *wrong* in section 20 would think it irrelevant how the harm came about. For the wrong is that of bringing the harm about in that way. In morality, as in law, it matters how one brings things about. It matters, first and foremost, in deciding which wrong one committed. You have not been mugged, although you have been conned, if I trick you into handing over your money by spinning some yarn. You have not been coerced, although you have been manipulated, if I get you to do something by making you think you wanted to do it all along. You have not been killed, although you have been left to die, if a doctor fails to prescribe life-saving drugs. These are matters of intrinsic moral significance. The fact that one inflicted harm rather than merely causing it can be, likewise, a matter of intrinsic moral significance. It is this, among other things, which distinguishes the torturer, who continues to enjoy a distinctive offence all of his own in the Law Commission's proposals, and an offence, moreover, which is still explicitly defined in terms of 'infliction'. The old section 20 builds on the same moral significance, although without restricting attention to the special case of the torturer. Under section 20, that is to say, one does not merely end up grievously harmed. One is a victim of violence. This is the common factor, moreover, which unites the infliction of grievous bodily harm with wounding, accounting for the fact that these sit side by side in a single offence. Thus section 20 is correctly regarded, not merely as a core offence against the person, but as a core crime of violence. Violence is the basic section 20 theme which has to be adapted for the purposes of the more heinous offence under section 18.

That the process of adaptation involves extending the crime to cases where grievous bodily harm comes about other than by violence—cases where it is caused without being inflicted—may sound paradoxical, but it is in fact a natural move to make. The move is connected with the familiar maxim that intended consequences are never too remote. That maxim paints a somewhat exaggerated picture, but to the extent that it speaks the truth it proceeds from the thought that those who intend some result could otherwise enjoy a bizarre kind of mastery over their own normative situation. They could evade a moral or legal rule which is means-specific simply by adopting different means. Since the very fact that one adopts means to some result *entails* that one intends it, this kind of evasion is by definition unavailable to those who do not intend the result. So there is good reason, other things being equal, to withdraw some or all of the means-specificity from a moral or legal rule where its violation consists in the intentional pursuit or achievement of some result. That is precisely what section 18 does. Lest the fact that it does this be summarily dismissed as mere slip of the draftsman's pen, it is worth noting that section 18 explicitly confirms the profound importance of the point by including the words 'by any means whatsoever' in its definition, words which contrast neatly with section 20's infliction-oriented proviso 'with or without any weapon or instrument'. So whether or not one believes that there should be specific crimes of violence among the most basic offences against the person, as soon as one appreciates that section 20 creates such a crime, one can at once grasp the rational explanation for the differences between it and section 18.

None of this contradicts the Commission's view that section 18 should be regarded as the more serious version of section 20. On the contrary, it confirms that view. It merely casts doubt on the Commission's reductive assumption about the kind of variations one should expect to find between the definitions of more serious offences and those of less serious offences. These need not be restricted, as a matter of principle, to variations in the configuration of *mens rea* and resulting harm. That is the clear message of the relationship between sections 18 and 20. When we come to relate sections 18 and 20 to section 47, however, the message is quite different. What needs to be uprooted here is the assumption that the former relate to the latter, in substance, as more serious offences to less serious. That assumption needs to be replaced with a sensitivity to the essential qualitative differences between section 47 offences and those covered by sections 18 and 20. They are incomparably different types of offences, with different basic themes. Looking at the 1861 Act one might have thought this obvious. In the first place, section 47 has the same maximum sentence as section 20. That instantly alerts one to the possibility that offences under sections 20 and 47 should be regarded like those under sections 1 and 17 of the Theft Act 1968 (*i.e.* theft and false accounting), as offences which are, in essence, neither more serious nor less serious than each other. In the second place section 47 belongs clearly to its own family of offences, namely those of assault (sections 38 to 47). Since the rest of that family is not treated as having some simple scalar relation to section 18 and 20 offences, one may ask why section 47 should be thought to be any different.

The answer lies, once again, in mistaking the harm for the wrong. Section 47 prohibits assault occasioning actual bodily harm. Because actual bodily harm is plainly a less serious variant of grievous bodily harm, too much focus on the harm can lead one to think that section 47 is, in substance, a less serious variant of section 20. And the harm is obviously where one focuses, at the outset, if one adopts the Law Commission's view that seriousness varies in this context only 'according to the type of injury that [the defendant] intended or was aware that he might cause'. But in fact one should pay attention first, in section 47, to the assault, not the harm. Here we find a major point of distinction between section 47 and section 20. For in spite of the fact that most assaults do involve violence, assault is not a crime of violence. Its essential quality lies in the invasion by one person of another's body space. As every law student knows, such an invasion may take one of two forms. It may take the form of a *mere* assault, an invasion of body space without bodily contact but with the apprehension of its imminence, or it may take the form of a battery, when the contact between the two bodies actually takes place. The Law Commission's own proposed redefinition of assault makes it sound as if the contact, apprehended or actual, must be violent. Their draft provisions speak of 'force' and 'impact'. But this has never been the common law's emphasis, and it distorts the substance of the offence. One may assault someone without violence: by removing their coat or shoes, by sitting too close to them, by stroking their hair, etc. Conversely, one may subject another to violence without assaulting them: by luring someone into the path of an express train, for example, or by leaving a brick where it will fall on someone's head. These are not peripheral but central cases. They reveal how far the subject-matter of sections 38 to 47 of the 1861 Act differs, in substance as well as in detail, from that of section 20. The accident of drafting is not so much that the assault crimes in sections 38 to 47 diverge from the crimes of violence in sections 18 and 20. The accident, on the contrary, is that they ever coincide.

It is, of course, no accident that section 47 adds a harm requirement to the element of assault. That is precisely what distinguishes a section 47 assault from an assault *simpliciter*, and from the various other special categories of assault specified in the 1861 Act and elsewhere. It would be a mistake to jump to the conclusion, however, that the harm plays the same logical role in section 47 that it plays in sections 18 and 20. In common with other aggravated assault provisions, but quite unlike sections 18 and 20, section 47 creates a crime of constructive liability, *i.e.* a crime which one commits by committing another crime. Committing a certain crime, *e.g.* assault or dangerous driving, may always carry the risk of harm, or other primary risks. But in a constructive liability context, it also exposes one to secondary risks, risks of additional liability, which one would not have faced but for one's commission of the original crime. Under section 47, those who commit the crime of assault take the risk, not only that it will occasion harm (the primary risk), but also that, if it does, they will have committed a more serious crime (the secondary risk). They likewise take the risk, under section 51 of the Police Act 1964, that their assault will be upon a police officer in the execution of his duty (the primary risk), and that, if it is, they will again have committed the more serious crime of assaulting a police officer in the execution of his duty (the secondary risk). And so on. By committing an assault one changes one's own normative position, so that certain adverse consequences and circumstances which would not have counted against one but for one's original assault now count against one automatically, and add to one's crime.

Constructive offences, although common enough even in modern legislation, are not easily accommodated within the criminal law principles espoused by many contemporary criminal lawyers, and taken for granted by the Law Commission. In particular, such offences violate what Andrew Ashworth calls the 'correspondence principle', whereby every element of the *actus reus* must carry with it a corresponding element of *mens rea*. Fortunately, this 'correspondence principle' is not and never has been a principle of English law. The relevant principle of English law is *actus non facit reum nisi mens sit rea*; no guilty act without a guilty mind. Constructive offences, when they are properly conceived and designed, do not violate this principle. The more basic offences with which they are associated require *mens rea*, and that *mens rea* is naturally carried over into the constructive offence. The guilty act must therefore still be attended by a guilty mind, in line with *actus non facit reum nisi mens sit rea*. What need not be attended by any *mens rea* are the consequences and circumstances, the risk of which one bears because one committed the original crime. For if these were attended by *mens rea*, that would make a nonsense of the idea, at the heart of all constructive liability, that those who embark on crimes, or at least certain risky crimes, change in the process their own normative positions regarding the risks they take. That is why there is no grand departure from principle in the House of Lords' recent, and I would say overdue, confirmation that section 47 of the 1861 Act has no *mens rea* requirement apart from the *mens rea* of assault. It also explains the causal element in section 47, the element of 'occasioning'. The chain of 'occasioning' should be regarded as very elastic, stretching to harms rather more remote than any which are caused or inflicted. You lunge towards me, I step backwards, someone's umbrella trips me up, I fall backwards, a cyclist runs me over. The assault occasions the resulting harm even though it does not cause it. Section 47 liability may therefore arise even though the actual bodily harm comes about by a very indirect route, perhaps involving successive coincidences. In committing an assault, on this view, one bears not only the risk that harm will come about, but also, up to a point, the risk of *how* it will come about. In respect of the harm, then, some of the protection of the doctrine of *novus actus interveniens* is forfeited by the assaulter, along with some of the protection of the doctrine of *mens rea*.

In line with its general principle of offence seriousness, the Law Commission would restore both of these protections. In the process it would remove the section 47 offence from the assault family, drop its constructive elements, and replace it with an offence in the same family as those offences which would serve as replacements for sections 18 and 20. Yet this move is not a replacement of less rational organisation with more, as we can now see, but a choice between two possible rational arrangements in the law of non-sexual and non-fatal offences against the person. After all, we have just supplied a perfectly rational explanation for the main features of the section 47 offence, understood as a variation on the assault theme. There are also, as the Law Commission shows, rational explanations for the features of the proposed replacement for section 47, understood as a variation on the theme of sections 18 and 20. The point is, however, that one cannot have it both ways, since the assault theme (invasion of body space) is not the same as the theme of sections 18 and 20 (personal violence). The Law Commission can make their proposed arrangements seem to have it both ways only by diluting the two themes so that they become harder to distinguish. The violence theme is weakened in the replacements for sections 18 and 20 by the eradication of the 'infliction' paradigm. At the same time the spatial invasion theme is weakened in the restatement of assault by concentration on 'force' and 'impact'. But this two-way *rapprochement* generates a regrettable loss of discrimination in the law of offences against the person which no amount of rational reordering can compensate. It represents a triumph of reductive thinking. Codification need not be like this. In the law of offences against property, excellently codified during the 1960s and 1970s, we find many different offences involving much the same harms. Whether one is a victim of theft, deception, criminal damage or making off, one is harmed by being deprived of one's belongings. Yet this codification did not seek to eradicate the different themes of the different offences, and turn out some general scale of seriousness. On the contrary, it went out of its way to capture these different themes in precise and differentiated language. That is because, in the realm of property offences, the harm does not capture all that is interesting, or rationally significant, about the wrong. Nor are things any different in the law of offences against the person. In substance, the wrong of an assault crime is different from the wrong of a section 20 crime much as the wrong of theft is different from the wrong of fraud. The two may happen to overlap, even across a large proportion of their terrain, but one cannot in principle unify them into a neatly scaled family of crimes. Indeed the Law Commission recognises this, in spite of its own inclinations, by preserving distinct offences of poisoning and torture, and by hiving off the sexual offences to a different corner of the codification agenda. One may ask why the basic thematic separation of sections 18 and 20 from section 47 does not also deserve preservation. Certainly the rationality argument does not supply the answer, for there is nothing irrational, to speak of, in either section 47 or sections 18 and 20.

18 PROPOSED REFORMS TO THE OFFENCES AGAINST THE PERSON ACT

The Home Office has proposed replacement of the offences with a more coherent pattern of offences:[247]

(i) A person is guilty of an offence if he intentionally causes serious injury to another.

(ii) A person is guilty of an offence if he recklessly causes serious injury to another.

---

[247] Home Office (1998b). The proposals were made in 1998, but there have been no signs of the proposals being legislated in the near future. The Law Commission (2014) is undertaking consultation on further proposals.

(iii)   A person is guilty of an offence if he intentionally or recklessly causes injury to another.

(iv)   A person acts intentionally with respect to a result if—

   (a) it is his purpose to cause it, or

   (b) although it is not his purpose to cause it, he knows that it would occur in the ordinary course of events if he were to succeed in his purpose of causing some other result.

(v)   A person acts recklessly with respect to a result if he is aware of a risk that it will occur and it is unreasonable to take that risk having regard to the circumstances as he knows or believes them to be.

(vi)   Injury means physical injury or mental injury.

(vii)   [Save for the offence of intentionally causing serious injury] physical injury does not include anything caused by disease but (subject to that) it includes pain, unconsciousness and any other impairment of a person's physical condition.

(viii)   A person is guilty of an offence if—

   (a) he intentionally or recklessly applies force to or causes an impact on the body of another, or

   (b) he intentionally or recklessly causes the other to believe that any such force or impact is imminent.

There are two points of particular note about these proposals. The first is that they largely accord with the correspondence principle: a person is only responsible for the degree of injury he foresaw or intended.[248] The second is that the language used is simple and readily comprehensible.

But such praises are, however, exactly the reasons why others oppose the proposals. Jeremy Horder sees the simplicity of the language as a vice.[249] He would prefer a statute which defined precisely the wrong that the defendant had done to the victim (e.g. that it would be an offence if the defendant 'castrates, disables, disfigures, or dismembers . . . or removes an internal body part' of a victim). He argues that such a statute would comply with labelling theory (described in Chapter 1, Section 4.5) by accurately and precisely defining the wrong done to the victim.

The strongest objection to Horder's proposals would be the possibility of a defendant appealing unmeritoriously against a conviction, on the basis that he was not charged with precisely the correct kind of assault. For example, using Horder's suggestion, much court time and effort might be spent by a defendant claiming 'I did not disable, I disfigured'. In contrast, by adopting the broader definition 'causing serious injury' in the Home Office's proposals such arguments could be avoided.

QUESTIONS

1. Is it more important to have an offence which accurately describes what the defendant has done to the victim, or to have offences which broadly define the defendant's harm and can be speedily prosecuted?

2. Do you find the distinction John Gardner draws (in the passage in Section 17) between the harm done to the victim and the wrong done to the victim a useful one?

---

[248] They are perhaps not in perfect accord with the correspondence principle because there is no distinction drawn in (iii) between intentionally and recklessly causing injury.

[249] Horder (1994b).

FURTHER READING

Clarkson, C. (1994) 'Law Commission Report on Offences against the Person and General Principles: (1) Violence and the Law Commission' *Criminal Law Reform* 324.

Gardner, J. (1994a) 'Rationality and the Rule of Law in Offences against the Person' *Cambridge Law Journal* 53: 661.

Genders, E. (1999) 'Reform of the Offences against the Person Act: Lessons from the Law in Action' *Criminal Law Review* 689.

Home Office (1998b) *Violence: Reforming the Offences against the Person Act 1861* (London: Home Office).

Horder, J. (1994b) 'Rethinking Non-Fatal Offences against the Person' *Oxford Journal of Legal Studies* 14: 335.

Jefferson, M. (2012) 'Offences against the Person: Into the 21st Century' *Journal of Criminal Law* 472.

Smith, J.C. (1998b) 'Offences against the Person: the Home Office Consultation Paper' *Criminal Law Review* 317.

19 CONSENT

19.1 DEFENCE OR *ACTUS REUS*?

Is it better to regard the consent of the victim as a defence or its absence as an aspect of *actus reus*? In Part I we noted that the House of Lords in *Brown*[250] regarded consent as a defence to a charge of assault. In the following passage, Vera Bergelson argues that in some cases consent operates as a defence and in other cases lack of consent is part of the *actus reus*:

V. Bergelson, 'The Defense of Consent' in M. Dubber and T. Hörnle (eds)
The Oxford Handbook of Criminal Law (Oxford: OUP, 2014), 651–2

What distinguishes cases of theft, rape, or kidnapping, on the one hand, from cases of killing or maiming on the other? One obvious answer is that, in the first group of cases, the consent of the participants bars criminal conviction, whereas in the second group it does not. But why?

I have argued elsewhere that the moral difference between the two groups of cases has to do with the character of the act in question and the message criminal law wants to send to the community. In the case of theft, rape, or kidnapping, the act itself does not violate a prohibitory norm. Having sex, transporting someone to a different location, or taking other people's property is not bad in itself. It becomes bad only due to the absence of consent. In other words, using George Fletcher's terminology, in the case of theft, rape, or kidnapping, non-consent is a part of the definition of the offense regardless of how a particular criminal statute is drafted. Its role is inculpatory. Therefore, the mere presence of consent defeats the charge against the defendant—the prosecutor simply would not be able to establish all the required elements of the offense.

---

[250] [1994] 1 AC 212.

In contrast, causing pain, injury, or death is not morally neutral—it is regrettable. Bringing about a regrettable state of events is bad and should be avoided. Therefore, we would want a conduct rule that prohibits the very act of killing or hurting, providing, of course, for the necessary exceptions such as self-defense. However, the fact that a person may be legally justified in killing an aggressor in self-defense does not make the killing as morally neutral as borrowing a book—it is still regrettable. Similarly, consensual killing or hurting is regrettable and prima facie prohibited. In certain circumstances consent may be able to overcome this presumption against killing and hurting. Accordingly, the role of consent here is exculpatory; it may only serve as an affirmative defense. Unlike the failure of proof, the affirmative defense shields the defendant from punishment only if there are special circumstances that may excuse or justify the prima facie prohibited act. We, therefore, need two distinct sets of consent rules—one, for offenses like rape, theft, or kidnapping, in which the mere presence of consent defeats the charge; and the other for offenses involving physical harm (e.g. homicide or battery) for which consent may only serve as an affirmative defense.

Not everyone will agree with Bergelson's analysis. Why does she say that pain is regrettable? Some people enjoy spicy food or a scary movie, even if in one sense they may be said to cause pain. Further, when she says that 'non-consent' is part of the offence of kidnapping or rape, that seems odd because 'non-consent' is a nothing, it is the absence of something, so how can it turn a good thing into a bad thing?

19.2 THE DISPUTE OVER *BROWN*

The decision of the House of Lords in *Brown*[251] is one of the most controversial in recent years. It has been greatly criticized, and even the few who are sympathetic to the conclusions reached by the majority are not impressed by the reasoning used. For example, Lord Jauncey's argument that holding the defendants' actions to be lawful would be to give 'judicial imprimatur' to the actions cannot, with respect, be correct. To hold an action lawful does not indicate that the law approves of it. Adultery is not illegal, but this does not mean that it is approved of by the law; indeed adultery is a ground of divorce. ←5 (p.364)

Key to the differences between the speeches of the majority and minority are their starting points:

(1) The majority saw the case as involving violence. One person should not inflict violence upon another unless there are very good reasons for doing so. The provision of sexual pleasure is not sufficient.[252] Indeed the majority went further than they needed in saying that not only does sadomasochistic sex not benefit society, it in fact has the potential to cause serious harms.

(2) The minority saw the case as involving consensual private sexual activity. They argued that unless there are strong reasons to render such conduct unlawful it should be permitted. No reasons had been produced to justify rendering the defendants' conduct unlawful.[253]

---

[251] *Ibid*. For useful discussions, see Giles (1994) and Bix (1993).
[252] Indeed the majority thought there were very good reasons why the activity should not be allowed.
[253] For a very useful article expounding the approach of the minority, see Kell (1994).

The arguments in favour of *Brown*

The arguments in favour of the approach of the majority can be summarized as follows:

Concerns about the participants in sadomasochism

The majority expressed the following ways in which they believed permitting sadomaso-chistic sexual activities could harm the participants:

(1) The majority expressed concerns that groups of sadomasochists may be insufficiently organized, leading to non-consensual injuries being caused. For example, if in the middle of the activity one person withdraws his consent,[254] the other, caught up in the sexual excitement of the moment, may continue. There was no evidence that this had occurred with the group in *Brown*, but the majority presumably feared that other groups would be less well run. Lord Jauncey feared that there were particular concerns that this might occur if members of the group had taken alcohol or illegal drugs.[255]

(2) Lord Templeman was concerned that the results of the appellants' actions were 'unpredictably dangerous'. So because the 'victims' could not be aware of the potential consequences of the activity their consent should be regarded as suspect.

(3) Lord Templeman suggested that the consent of some participants to sadomasochistic group sex should be regarded as dubious. He had in mind particularly the fact that many of the 'victims' in *Brown* were aged about 21, while the appellants were middle-aged men.

The response of the minority to these concerns is that it might be better to prosecute whenever the victims did not truly consent rather than to outlaw all sadomasochistic activities.

Concerns that the activities would harm others

The majority indicated that they were concerned that the activities might lead to harms to members outside the group. Lord Templeman suggested that to permit sadomasochistic activities would 'breed and glorify violence'. It was feared that the activities could overspill into illegal activities against non-consenting victims who were not members of the group. The minority found there was no evidence to suggest that such fears were well founded.

Moral outrage at what the defendants did

It was clear that the majority of their Lordships felt moral outrage at what the appellants had done. Lord Templeman described the activities as an 'indulgence of cruelty'. He explained that 'infliction of pain is an evil thing'. Lord Lowry referred to the 'perverted and depraved sexual desire' of the appellants.

Human dignity

An argument, not made explicitly by the majority but which could be used to support their approach, is that there is an important taboo in society against deliberately inflicting harm

---

[254] Kaplan (2014) states that in sadomasochistic groups it is common to rely on a special word or phrase which when uttered indicates that the individual no longer consents to the harm being caused.

[255] Although it might be added that the horseplay exception is far more open to misuse in cases of bullying than permitting sadomasochism would be (Padfield 1992).

on another. The protection of this taboo is crucial if society is not to show a lack of respect for human dignity.[256] However, as William Wilson suggests, 'As things now stand, no threat to society's moral integrity is likely to result from the esoteric practices of a group of homosexuals, beyond the odd burst blood vessel suffered by "Outraged of Tunbridge Wells".'[257] But he goes on to suggest that there is 'one fundamental residual moral value' which forms a building block of society and that is that 'hurting people is wrong'.[258] To others in our multicultural, multi-faith society we have so many different notions of right and wrong that it is not possible to talk of key moral principles that form the cement of our society.

Dennis Baker has argued that 'A person can waive his right not to be harmed, but he cannot waive his right to maintain a certain level of dignity as a human being.'[259] In the following passage, Antony Duff develops a similar argument: that it is permissible for the state to prohibit dehumanizing behaviour. He starts discussing the point made by Irving Kristol,[260] that we would not be happy to permit a gladiatorial contest which spectators paid to witness:

R.A. Duff, 'Harms and Wrongs' (2001) 5 *Buffalo Criminal Law Review* 13 at 39–41

If we tried to explain what is so disturbing about the gladiatorial example (apart from the likely further effects of such activities), we might talk not just of 'the objective regretability of millions deriving pleasure from brutal bloodshed', but of the dehumanization or degradation perpetrated by the gladiators on each other, and by the spectators on the gladiators and on themselves. We might talk in similar terms, though with less emphatic insistence, about the sadomasochism of *R v Brown*. Whilst there were no spectators to degrade or be degraded, we might still say that the participants were degrading or dehumanizing themselves and each other. This would involve an appeal, in both cases, to a normative conception of 'humanity'—of what it is to be human and to recognize the humanity of others, and of what it is to deny or fail to respect that humanity in others or in oneself.

What makes Kristol's gladiatorial combat dehumanizing and degrading is not just the fact that the participants are trying to kill each other. Though radical pacifists might argue that a proper respect for the humanity of others absolutely precludes trying to kill them, most who take humanity seriously allow that we can respect the humanity even of those whom we try to kill, for instance in a just war. Nor need we think that every kind of individual combat (outside war) in which the participants try to kill each other must be dehumanizing. We might be able to recognize a social practice of dueling or of jousting as one in which the participants can respect each other's humanity. Whether such a practice could be consistent with a mutual recognition of, and respect for, the humanity of the participants would depend on the structure of values and conceptions which forms its social context and which provides the participants (and spectators, if any) with their expected motivations. Can we, for instance, see the practice of jousting as one in which citizens can display those martial virtues on which the defense of their families and country depend? Can we see the practice of dueling as one in which honor can be vindicated and restored between gentlemen? If we can, we can also see these practices as at least consistent with a respect for the humanity of the participants. The participants can respect each other as participants in a noble enterprise. Spectators can watch with admiration these displays of appropriate human excellences.

---

[256] See e.g. Devlin (1965). [257] W. Wilson (1992: 392). [258] W. Wilson (2002: ch. 1).
[259] Baker (2008). [260] Kristol (1971).

I do not say that we should see any actual historical practice of jousting or dueling in this light. My point is only that combats to the death are not necessarily inconsistent with a mutual respect for each other's humanity amongst the combatants, or with a due recognition amongst the spectators of the humanity of the participants. Kristol's gladiatorial combats, however, are inconsistent with such respect. They are commercial events. What motivates both promoters and gladiators is the prospect of making money from paying spectators. What the gladiators must do, to earn their pay, is to give the customers what they want; and what they want is not the display of martial virtues that can be admired for their civic worth, but 'brutal bloodshed' that they encourage by 'their bloodthirsty screams'. But the 'brutality' that the spectators are paying to see, and that the gladiators must aim to provide, is (one might say 'by definition') a denial of the humanity of those involved. They are reduced to 'brutes' who must try to maim and kill each other for the amusement of a paying and baying crowd.

The defendants in *R v. Brown* were not performing for paying spectators. But they were (on one reading of sadomasochism), trying precisely to degrade and humiliate each other. They were enacting rituals of torture, which treat the person tortured as, or try to reduce him to, a humiliated and degraded animal. This conduct was, no doubt, set in a larger context in which they treated and respected each other as human equals, and they degraded each other in this way only because each freely consented to it. Nonetheless, what they consented to and sought was treatment that, in itself, denied their humanity.

Of course, much more work is needed to flesh out the normative conception of humanity on which these comments about Kristol's gladiators and *R v. Brown* depend. But I hope I have said enough to make such appeals to 'humanity' familiar and plausible.

It should be noted that in later writing Duff appears to have taken a different view to that expounded in the previous extract. He has written 'the argument is that the *Brown* defendants' conduct is worthy of at least our moral respect: it is orientated toward morally legitimate ends (mutual sexual pleasure); it is informed by morally admirable values (love and respect); even if the means by which those ends are pursued and those values are expressed are unusual, and to others' eyes shocking, when understood in their particular context they lose their morally shocking character.'[261]

The wrongful intent of the sadist

That conclusion may be contrasted with Madden Dempsey's sophisticated analysis[262] which locates the wrong of the sadist in the reasons for their actions. They perform 'violent acts (at least in part) for the very reason that doing so will cause pain and suffering to the masochist', distinguishing them from surgeons who are acting to promote the well-being of the 'victim', she argues. The sadist is producing pain so that they will gain pleasure from that.[263] It would seem from her analysis that there would be less objection to someone harming a masochist simply to give the masochist pleasure because they would be promoting the masochist's well-being, as understood by the masochist. The problem with the sadist is that they are not harming for reasons grounded in any understanding of the well-being of the masochist. Some practitioners of SM will disagree with this analysis and argue that mutual pleasure is central to their appreciation of what is happening. Margo Kaplan has argued that in sadomasochistic encounters 'Violence is only celebrated to the extent that another

---

[261] Duff (2007: 112).   [262] Madden Dempsey (2013).
[263] Although see Cowan (2012b), who sees SM in more mutual terms.

individual derives pleasure from it'. She insists that the purpose is not to inflict harm but to cause sexual pleasure and that should be regarded as a good, rather than a bad, thing.[264] By contrast Matthew Kramer[265] accepts that the sadist, who is aiming to derive sexual gratification 'from the thrill of knowing that he is causing intense pain to the victim', is acting morally wrongfully, but he thinks this is insufficient to justify criminal punishment. An act may be morally wrong but the criminal law is not appropriate where the wrongfulness 'is due exclusively to the outlook with which that conduct has been undertaken'.

Feminist concerns

These concerns are also found in the writings of some feminist commentators: that sadomasochism may in fact disguise incidents of domestic violence or the abuse of vulnerable people.[266] Indeed there are grave concerns this may have happened in the cases of *Wilson* and *Emmett* described earlier. In both these cases the defendants claimed the harms they had inflicted had been consented to by the victims and this formed the basis of their defences. However, neither victim was willing to give evidence to support their partner's claims. Both had sought medical help, following which their doctors decided the cases should be reported to the police.[267] The fact both of these cases are commonly presented in textbooks as cases of sadomasochism shows the ease with which a case of domestic abuse can be presented as sadomasochism. Cases of the most serious domestic abuse where the victim becomes completely subservient to the abuser and accepts the violence as appropriate punishment for their wrong doing, look chillingly like cases where couples adopt BDSM (bondage, dominance and submission, and sadomasochism) roles.[268] At the least this shows great caution needs to be exercised before accepting an argument that the case is one of consensual BDSM.

The arguments against *Brown*

The arguments for the approach of the minority were in part rejecting the approach of the majority, as already mentioned previously. The minority's view is based on the principle that private consensual activities should be rendered illegal only if it can be shown that such conduct harms society. One point strongly in favour of the minority's approach is that the list of exceptional circumstances in which consent can provide a defence (e.g. surgery, sports) is more easily explained by the approach of the minority than the majority. For example, it is easier to explain that the rough and tumble horseplay, tattooing, and religious flagellation exceptions form the minority's perspective (such actions do not harm society) than it is to explain them from the majority's point of view (such actions are beneficial to society and so the violence is justified). The best response for supporters of *Brown* may be to suggest that what the majority objected to in *Brown* was the *intentional* infliction of harm.[269] The exceptional cases, on this explanation, are explained on the basis that they involve situations where the defendant does not intend to cause the harm but rather to play a sport, take part in rough games, give a tattoo, etc. By contrast, in *Brown* the defendants intended to inflict pain because if there had been no pain their activities would have been a flop for all concerned.[270]

---

264 Kaplan (2014).   265 Kramer (2013).

266 Hanna (2001). Other feminist writers do not share these concerns (Pa 2001; Kaplan 2014).

267 This would appear to breach medical confidentiality, which would be justified if the doctor believed their patient needed protection from domestic abuse.

268 See Herring (2016).   269 Herring (2014b).

270 See Weait (2005b: 108–10) for some powerful criticism of this way of reading the case.

This would also explain the decision in *Wilson*[271] because in that case it was not part of Mr Wilson's purpose that Mrs Wilson suffer pain.

Some opponents of the decision in *Brown* have seen prejudicial attitudes in the courts' decisions in this area. In particular they reveal what the courts see as appropriately 'manly' behaviour.[272] Real men may set each other alight as part of a prank (*Aitken*), but do not wound each other for sexual pleasure (*Brown*). Indeed it has been suggested that public attitudes towards sexual matters have moved on so much from *Brown* that courts should feel free to depart from it.[273]

Julia Tolmie[274] has criticized the use by the majority in *Brown* of categories of behaviours to which consent is or is not permitted. This can require artificial distinctions to define the categories, for example she suggests the line between the DIY tattoo in *Wilson* and the sado-masochism in *Emmett* is blurry. More significantly she argues:

> because any dilution of free choice results from factors personal to the participants, rather than being a result of the type of activity undertaken, making decisions based on generic categories of activity tends to ultimately overlook any vulnerability on the part of the person harmed, and any exploitative circumstances in which consent to that harm was obtained, when finally deciding whether the defence of consent is available.

Adopting her point we may focus less on the nature of the activity and more on the relationship between the parties and the extent to which the behaviour is, or is not, exploitative.

In the following passage, Paul Roberts approaches the question of the relevance of the victim's consent in a criminal case from a philosophical perspective. He outlines three approaches that could be taken: liberalism, paternalism, and legal moralism:

P. Roberts, 'Appendix C' in Law Commission Consultation Paper No. 139, *Consent in the Criminal Law* (London: HMSO, 1995), C.39–C.72

Liberalism and Criminalisation

C.39 The centrality of autonomy in the liberal's scheme of values gives him a preference for minimal state intervention in people's lives. The liberal is particularly hostile to state intervention through the mechanism of criminal prohibition and regulation, for the obvious reason that criminalisation is the state's most coercive form of social control. What could be more invasive of personal autonomy than a system of prohibitions backed by sanctions, including fines, community service and incarceration, administered and enforced by full-time professional investigators, prosecutors, judges and prison officers? As Raz observes:

> '[C]oercion by criminal penalties is a global and indiscriminate invasion of autonomy. Imprisoning a person prevents him from almost all autonomous pursuits. Other forms of coercion may be less severe, but they all invade autonomy, and they all, at least in this world, do it in a fairly indiscriminate way. That is, there is no practical way of ensuring that the coercion will restrict the victims' choice of repugnant options but will not interfere with their other choices.'

---

[271] [1996] 2 Cr App R 241.   [272] Bibbings (2001).   [273] Murphy (2011).
[274] Tolmie (2012).

C.40 The criminal law places direct limits on individual freedom which the liberal wants to keep to a minimum. But that there *must be* limits to individual freedom is implicit in the liberal's own position, for the absolute autonomy of one is incompatible with the autonomy of any others. Brown's freedom to punch Green in the face is clearly at odds with Green's freedom to go about his business without suffering violent assault. The liberal does not value absolute liberty ('licence'), but rather the maximum individual liberty that is compatible with similar liberty for all. That is, the liberal supports the harm and offence principles, as elaborated and augmented for example by Feinberg, but she cannot countenance criminalisation on any other basis. For the liberal the harm and offence principles exhaust the moral limits of the criminal law.

C.41 The criminalisation of harm to others has a strong intuitive appeal, as was noted above, but it is necessary to say something more at this point about the criminalisation of offence. Liberals support the offence principle because some forms of offence can be so extreme and protracted that they unacceptably infringe the autonomy of unwilling observers and are therefore, on liberal principles, legitimate candidates for criminalisation. The liberal is, however, extremely cautious in using the criminal law to this end and will only endorse an offence principle that is properly qualified and carefully circumscribed. The reason is clear: since just about every conceivable activity might give offence to *somebody*, *everybody's* autonomy would be severely and unacceptably curtailed if the criminal law routinely targeted offensive conduct. This point is deployed with particular force in response to the argument that conduct should be criminalised solely on the basis that people are repelled by the mere thought of it going on in private. In most cases, people who use this argument are not really claiming that they are *offended* by the conduct, but rather that it is evil and should be stopped. This is a legal moralist argument, to which no liberal would subscribe. But suppose that someone really was offended by the mere thought of, say, consensual 'unnatural sexual intercourse' taking place behind locked doors and closed shutters, to such an extent that his obsession with the thought of it dominated and disrupted his life to a seriously detrimental extent. How would the liberal (or anybody else) deal with this situation? We would surely say that the cause of that person's malady is his own abnormal sensitivity. We might set about helping him to deal with his illness, but we would not pass criminal laws which indiscriminately restrict the freedom of other people with normal sensibilities. The liberal, at any rate, will only countenance criminalising offence which is extreme and unavoidable, and this can never be said of activity which takes place in private.

Consent and the Harm Principle

C.42 It follows from the fact that liberalism will only countenance interference with individual liberty in order to prevent harm or serious offence to others that it is inconsistent with liberal principles to criminalise self-injury. Self-injury may be in the actor's interests and contribute to his well-being overall, as where a man cuts off his finger to prevent the spread of infection, but the liberal will not interfere with his determination to injure himself even where injury is not in his interests. This man chooses, perversely we may think, to set back his own interests, but he does not wrong himself. From the liberal perspective, his conduct is not within the legitimate province of the criminal law. Moreover, a person who genuinely consents to being harmed by another cannot be said to be wronged in the relevant sense either, as Feinberg explains:

'The harm principle will not justify the prohibition of consensual activities even when they are likely to harm the interests of the consenting parties; its aim is to prevent only those harms that are wrongs.'

C.43 Feinberg poses the question whether a person can ever be wronged by conduct to which he has fully consented, and then proceeds to answer it:

'There is a principle of law which emphatically answers this question in the negative: *Volenti non fit injuria* ("To one who has consented no wrong is done"). This ancient maxim is found in the Roman Law and has a central place in all modern legal systems. Perhaps the earliest arguments for it are found in Aristotle's *Nicomachean Ethics*. One person wrongs another, according to Aristotle, when he inflicts harm on him voluntarily, and a harmful infliction is voluntary when it is not the result of compulsion, and is performed in full awareness of all the relevant circumstances including the fact that the action is contrary to the wish of the person acted upon. Therefore it is impossible for a person to consent to being treated unjustly (wronged) by another, for this would be to consent to being-treated-contrary-to-one's-wishes, which is absurd.'

C.44 The liberal position on criminalisation and the effect of consent can be derived directly from the principles contained in the last quotation:

'It follows from these premises that no one can rightly intervene to prevent a responsible adult from voluntarily doing something that will harm only himself (for such a harm is not a "wrong"), and also that one person cannot properly be prevented from doing something that will harm another when the latter has voluntarily assumed the risk of harm himself through his free and informed consent.

'[F]ully valid consent ought to be a defense to all the crimes that are defined in terms of individuals acting on other individuals, including battery, [serious injury] and murder. . . . Collaborative behaviour ought never to be criminal when the collaboration is fully voluntary on both sides and no interests other than those of the collaborative parties are directly or substantially affected. (The latter position excludes as proper crimes sodomy, bigamy, adult incest, prostitution, and mutual fighting, among other things.)'

Paternalism

C.58 As applied to the proper scope and content of the criminal law, 'legal paternalism' may be defined thus:

Legal Paternalism: It is always a good reason in support of a prohibition that it is probably necessary to prevent harm (physical, psychological, or economic) to the actor himself.

C.59 The legal paternalist advocates just what the liberal denies: that the state may be justified in using its most coercive powers to force a person to act or forbear to act against his will in order to promote his own self-interest and well-being.

Paternalism Ideals and Values

C.60 Legal paternalism coheres with those philosophies which place a greater value on the attainment of some objective or end-state than on the ideal of autonomy. The defining feature of legal paternalism is that it justifies criminal prohibitions exclusively on the grounds that they promote an actor's own welfare; that is, it endorses state interference with one's freedom of choice and action *for one's own good.* . . .

Paternalism and Criminalisation

C.61 The challenge for the legal paternalist in marking out the moral limits of the criminal law is to explain *why* the promotion of an individual's welfare should take precedence over the liberal preference for respecting his or her autonomy. The paternalist faces an up-hill battle because the ideal of liberty/autonomy is greatly treasured by, and deeply ingrained in, the (political) culture of this country. Its effects on public and private thought and action are pervasive and diffuse. Nevertheless, the perfectly familiar notion of a man being mistaken about what is in his own best interests, and consequently acting in a way that is detrimental to his own well-being, lends to the paternalist's argument a degree of plausibility. Suppose a person is about to do something—say, give away all her earthly belongings to a religious sect—which is manifestly against her interests and which she will soon come to regret. Her proposed action will greatly diminish her well-being by effectively closing off most of the valuable options and projects which she might otherwise have used her wealth to pursue. Her decision to divest herself of her property will make her destitute and thoroughly miserable. Is the state impotent in this situation? Is not the liberal's insistence that such people should be left to their fate lofty, detached or even callous? The paternalist seems to have the answer: we should legislate to save people from themselves, to prevent them from doing grave harm to their own welfare. People should therefore be prohibited from assigning all their property to religious sects, and such transactions should be declared null and void for the purposes of the civil law of property.

C.62 The paternalist argument for criminalisation has a certain plausibility when it is applied to this kind of scenario, and over the years it has attracted some illustrious supporters. One of these was J S Mill, who held that nobody was free to sell himself into permanent slavery, since that would be to relinquish irrevocably the very freedom that he saw as each person's inalienable birth-right. On closer inspection, however, the paternalist argument is not as attractive as it may at first appear. When one tries to evaluate paternalistic justifications for criminal prohibitions there are three points that must be borne firmly in mind.

C.63 First, the paternalist argues from a philosophical slippery slope and is at constant risk of taking a tumble. The fact is that many of us make life-style choices which do not promote our immediate or long-term interests. Smoking certainly falls into this category of choices: for the paternalist it should be a clear target for criminalisation. But the point goes much further. If (as seems plausible) a balanced, healthy diet and regular exercise would be in every person's interests the paternalist has a reason for criminalising fatty foods and sedentary life-styles. Risk-taking without good reason would also be ruled out. Sky-diving, mountaineering and most contact sports would have to be criminalised. In principle, the paternalist seems to be committed to using the criminal law to turn us all into super-fit, clean-living 'spartans,' whether we like it or not. Paternalism seems less attractive when its implications are made apparent.

C.64 Secondly, some criminal prohibitions which have intuitive appeal and which are often justified by paternalist arguments are in fact best explained in terms of the harm principle and are therefore perfectly consistent with liberalism. Professor Glanville Williams gave an example of one such prohibition when he explained the rationale behind the criminalisation of duelling. At first sight this appears to be a paternalistic measure: (presumably) men who wanted to defend their honour in the traditional way were prevented from doing so *for their own good*. We are told, however, that many people were in fact hounded into duels against their will because prevailing social expectations effectively robbed them of any say in the matter. Once a man was slighted he was bound to offer a duel and his tormentor was bound to accept the challenge, even if neither wanted to fight. The duelling statute was therefore an exemplar of the harm principle. Far from interfering with people's choices in order to promote their welfare, by 'setting men free from the tyranny of custom' the statute gave effect to their authentic desires not to be injured at the hands of another. The liberal can and does support this type of statute without appealing to paternalistic arguments.

C.65 And thirdly, the liberal need not be as austere or uncompassionate as the paternalist paints her, because situations in which people might foolishly impair their own welfare do not present a straight choice between criminalisation and inaction. Modern-day liberals follow Mill in pointing out that the state can do a great deal to assist people to make the right choice without resorting to the coercion of criminal sanctions. The liberal state can educate, inform, remonstrate, persuade and exhort, and provided that it stops short of outright coercion it retains its liberal credentials. If, however, a man should freely and voluntarily consent to placing himself in permanent servitude, the consistent liberal will let him have his head. Although the paternalist's solution is apparently attractive in these extreme circumstances, it is purchased only with the sacrifice of autonomy, and that is too high a price for the liberal to pay.

...

Legal Moralism

C.70 The final group of arguments can be grouped under the rubric 'legal moralism'. It will be useful to distinguish two different versions:

(1) *Strict legal moralism:* It can be morally legitimate to prohibit conduct on the ground that it is *inherently immoral*, even though it causes neither harm nor offence to the actor or to others.

(2) *Moral conservatism:* It can be morally legitimate to prohibit conduct on the ground that it will lead to *drastic change in traditional ways of life*, even though it causes neither harm nor offence to the actor or to others.

C.71 Legal moralism provides justifications for criminalising what Feinberg calls 'free-floating non-grievance evils'. These are evils that do not directly harm or offend anyone. They do not infringe people's rights and therefore do not give any particular individual a legitimate ground for grievance or complaint. Criminal prohibition is aimed directly at what is intrinsically evil, evils that, as it were, 'float free' of human interests. Such evils might include:

(1) violation of social or religious taboos;

(2) sexual immorality, such as fornication or adultery;

(3) moral corruption of character (one's own or that of another);

(4) evil or impure thoughts;

(5) false beliefs;

(6) wanton killing of a spider or fly;

(7) extinction of a species of animal;

(8) extinction of cultural identity through assimilation to another culture;

(9) drastic change in the moral or aesthetic climate;

(10) diminishing good manners, etiquette and social grace;

(11) increasing environmental ugliness or drabness;

(12) diminishing standards of architectural good taste.

C.72 As we have seen, liberalism is not the view that morality can never be enforced by means of criminal prohibition, for the injunctions against causing harm or serious offence to others are surely moral rules. The distinction between liberalism and legal moralism is not that the moralist enforces morals whilst the liberal does not, but that the liberal will only use the criminal law to enforce that part of morality constituted by the harm principles. By contrast, the moralist will in principle use the criminal law to proscribe *any* immorality, even if it causes no harm or offence to anybody.

The Law Commission[275] in its report produced after the decision in *Brown* chose not to adopt wholeheartedly any of the three positions outlined in Roberts's paper.[276] They preferred to take what they described as a pragmatic approach. At the heart of their proposals is the concept of a 'serious disabling injury'. This is defined as:

any injury or injuries which—

(1) cause serious distress, and

(2) involve the loss of a bodily member or organ or permanent bodily injury, or permanent functional impairment, or serious or permanent disfigurement, or severe and prolonged pain, or serious impairment of mental health, or prolonged unconsciousness;

and in determining whether an effect is permanent, no account should be taken of the fact that it may be remediable by surgery.

The Law Commission's basic approach was that a person should not be able to provide effective consent for a 'serious disabling injury'[277] but could for a lesser injury.[278] But there are three exceptional situations where that basic approach does not apply:

(1) A person may consent to a non-fatal injury which is a seriously disabling injury if it is caused during the course of proper medical treatment or care or approved medical research.

(2) Injuries (even if not seriously disabling injuries) caused in the course of a fight (unless the fight is a boxing match or a recognized sport) will be an offence.

(3) The consent of a person under 18 to injuries intentionally caused for sexual, religious, or spiritual purposes should not be valid consent.[279]

QUESTIONS

1. Why should people not be allowed to do anything they like with their bodies?

2. Should the law draw any distinction between a case where a person deliberately injures himself and where he asks someone else to injure him?[280]

3. Can you think of any categories that should be added to the list of exceptional cases where the consent of the victim is a defence to a charge of actual bodily harm?

---

[275] The work of the Law Commission in this area is discussed in Leng (1994); Shute (1996); Ormerod and Gunn (1996).

[276] Law Commission Report No. 139 (1995: para. 2.13). See Roberts (1997) for further discussion.

[277] Law Commission Report No. 139 (1995: para. 4.47).

[278] If the victim does not actually consent the defendant can have a defence if he believed that the victim was consenting unless it would be obvious to a reasonable person that the victim was not.

[279] Law Commission Report No. 139 (1995: paras 10.52–10.55).

[280] BBC News Online (2006a) reports that some treatment centres permit patients to harm themselves as part of treatment for self-harming behaviour. See Herring (2013c) for a discussion on self-harm.

4. Duff may find sadomasochism dehumanizing, but how could he respond to a participant who claimed he or she found such conduct life enhancing?[281]

5. In 2000 Armin Meiwes, a German computer technician, posted an internet message seeking a 'well built man, 18–30 years old for slaughter'. Bernd Brandes replied 'I offer myself to you and will let you dine from my live body. Not butchery, dining!!' They eventually met and first Meiwes cut off part of Brandes's body and they had that as a snack. Meiwes then killed Brandes and ate 20kg of him with a South African Red. His conviction of murder was upheld in the German courts. Should it have been? See Bergelson (2007) for further discussion of this case.[282]

FURTHER READING

Baker, D. (2008b) 'The Moral Limits of Consent in Criminal Law' *New Criminal Law Review* 12: 93.

Bamforth, N. (1994) 'Sado-Masochism and Consent' *Criminal Law Review* 661.

Bergelson, V. (2007b) 'The Right to be Hurt: Testing the Boundaries of Consent' *George Washington Law Review* 75: 165.

Bergelson, V. (2014) 'The Defense of Consent' in M. Dubber and T. Hörnle (eds) *The Oxford Handbook of Criminal Law* (Oxford: OUP).

Cowan, S. (2012a) 'To Buy or Not to Buy? Vulnerability and the Criminalisation of Commercial BDSM' *Feminist Legal Studies* 20: 263.

Cowan, S. (2012b) 'Criminalizing SM: Disavowing the Erotic, Instantiating Violence' in R.A. Duff, L. Farmer, S. Marshall, M. Renzo, and V. Tadros (eds) *The Structures of the Criminal Law* (Oxford: OUP).

Cowan, S. (2014) 'Offenses of Sex or Violence? Consent, Fraud, and HIV Transmission' *New Criminal Law Review* 17: 135.

Elliot, C. and De Than, C. (2007) 'The Case for a Rational Reconstruction of Consent in Criminal Law' *Modern Law Review* 70: 225.

Kell, D. (1994) 'Social Disutility and Consent' *Oxford Journal of Legal Studies* 14: 121.

Madden Dempsey, M. (2013) 'Victimless Conduct and the Volenti Maxim: How Consent Works' *Criminal Law and Philosophy* 7: 11.

Ormerod, D. and Gunn, M. (1996b) 'The Second Law Commission Consultation Paper on Consent: Consent—A Second Bash' *Criminal Law Review* 694.

Roberts, P. (1997b) 'The Philosophical Foundations of Consent in the Criminal Law' *Oxford Journal of Legal Studies* 14: 389.

Shute, S. (1996) 'Something Old, Something New, Something Borrowed . . .' *Criminal Law Review* 684.

Tolmie, J. (2012) 'Consent to Harmful Assaults: The Case for Moving Away from Category Based Decision Making' *Criminal Law Review* 656.

Wilson, W. (1995) 'Consenting to Personal Injury: How Far Can You Go?' *Contemporary Issues in Law* 1: 45.

---

[281] See Cowan (2012a).

[282] See BBC News Online (2012) for a less dramatic example of someone consenting to be stabbed who died as a result.

20 EMOTIONAL HARM

One striking feature of the current law is that while physical injuries are clearly covered, the causing of emotional harm rarely amounts to a criminal offence. It is if it amounts to a recognized psychological injury, harassment, or the creation of fear of imminent violence, but otherwise it is not.[283] The case of *Dhaliwal*[284] where the husband reduced his wife to an emotional wreck, but that was not a crime, is a particularly striking example. In the following passage John Stannard considers, and rejects, the arguments that are normally used to explain why the law does not penalize the causing of emotional harm:

J. Stannard, 'Sticks, Stones and Words: Emotional Harm and the English Criminal Law' (2010) 74 *Journal of Criminal Law* 533 at 543–5

First of all, there is the argument from certainty. This was put forward most forcefully by Sir Igor Judge P in *Dhaliwal* itself. Commenting that to allow emotional harm to fall within the ambit of s. 47 of the Offences Against the Person Act would involve a blurring of the line between such harm and recognised psychiatric injury, he said that this would in his opinion introduce unnecessary uncertainty into the law. In his own words:

> In any event, however, the extension sought by the prosecution would introduce a significant element of uncertainty about the true ambit of the relevant legal principles to which the concept of 'bodily harm' in the 1861 Act applies, which would be compounded by the inevitable problems of conflicting medical opinion in this constantly developing area of expertise. By adhering to the principle of recognisable psychiatric illness, although some medical experts may be concerned with the way in which the definitions are arrived at, the issue which requires to be addressed can be clearly understood and those responsible for advising the prosecution and defendants can approach their cases with an appropriate degree of certainty.

It is, however, hard to see how allowing emotional harm to count for these purposes would introduce any more uncertainty to the criminal law than already exists under the present test. As for the problems of conflicting medical opinion, these exist already, as *Dhaliwal* itself shows. One suspects that what the courts are doing in this situation is not so much establishing a principled distinction as handing over the decision to the expert witnesses: emotional harm will qualify provided the psychiatrists can put a medical label of some sort on it.

The second argument is put forward by Roscoe Pound, and is based on the subjectivity of emotion and on difficulties of proof. Writing in 1915, Pound said that courts were naturally slow and cautious in developing the law in this area. In his words:

> A nervous derangement manifested objectively is like any bodily illness. But our law does not protect against purely subjective mental suffering except as it accompanies or is incident to some other form of injury and within certain disputed limits. There are

---

[283] *Hussein v Secretary of State for Defence* [2014] EWCA Civ 1087 confirmed just shouting at someone was not an assault.
[284] [2006] EWCA Crim 1139.

obvious difficulties of proof in such cases, so that false testimony as to mental suffering may be adduced easily and is very hard to detect. Hence this individual interest has to be balanced carefully with a social interest against the use of the law to further imposture. For these reasons courts, thinking more of the practical problem of proof than of the logical situation, have looked to see whether there has been some bodily impact or some wrong infringing some other interest, which is objectively demonstrable, and have put nervous injuries which leave no physical record and purely mental injuries in the same category.

However, it has been argued that the fear of fabricated evidence in this context has been exaggerated, and that similar difficulties exist even under the law as it stands. The courts are well used to dealing with the evidence of witnesses testifying to matters peculiarly within their own range of knowledge, and about which it is therefore easy for them to lie. The criminal law requires that the prosecution prove its case beyond reasonable doubt, and there would be no harm in a reluctance to convict a defendant for inflicting emotional injury merely on the word of the victim. But it is a different matter where the emotional injury, as in *Dhaliwal*, is plain for all to see. The essence of Pound's argument is that since it is easy to lie about 'nervous injury', the courts will not take account of it even where it is quite clear that the witness is telling the truth!

The third argument is the argument expressed by Lord Bridge that grief and distress are 'normal human emotions' and should therefore not give rise to recovery. It is not clear what he means by 'normal' in this context, and why in any event the fact that something is 'normal' should prevent it being a recognised category of criminal or civil harm. Cuts, grazes and other injuries are part of everyday life, but nobody suggests that it is therefore not a crime to inflict such injuries. Death is the universal lot of man, but does this mean that murder should not be a crime? What Lord Bridge may however be doing here is to make not an empirical but a normative statement; grief and distress are the sort of emotions that we all ought to put up with on a day-to-day basis, and therefore should not result in civil or criminal sanctions. This is a rather stronger argument, and it has parallels elsewhere in the criminal law. Thus for instance though any unwanted physical contact amounts in principle to a battery, no offence is committed in the general physical contacts of ordinary life such as jostling in a bus queue or supermarket. Traditionally these cases have been regarded as examples of implied consent, but as Robert Goff LJ said it might be better to regard them as within a general exception embracing all physical contact which is generally acceptable in the ordinary conduct of daily life. And what goes for physical contact surely applies with even greater force to emotional harm.

The fourth argument is a version of the traditional 'floodgates' argument. In *Hicks v Chief Constable of South Yorkshire*, as we have seen, the House of Lords refused to allow the relatives of those who died in the Hillsborough football disaster to recover in respect of the terror experienced in the minutes leading up to their death, saying that to do so would mean that all the survivors would have to recover in the same way, and similar concerns can be expressed in relation to the criminal law. But Teff has argued that here as in other contexts these dangers have been greatly exaggerated, and what he says applies with even greater force to criminal liability than it does to tort, given the public control over the conduct of prosecutions. Of course, it can still be argued that emotional harm is not limited in its potential scope in the same way as is physical harm or even psychiatric injury; a single word or action on the part of a person can cause emotional harm to a very large number of people. This certainly provides a good argument for both the criminal and the civil law being sparing in taking account of this sort of harm. What it does not justify is the rigidity of the law's present approach.

21 STALKING

Several of the recent developments in the law on offences against the person have been a response to the problem of stalking,[285] in particular the Protection from Harassment Act 1997 and the decision of the House of Lords in *Ireland*.[286] In one survey 23 per cent of women stated that they had suffered stalking at some point since their sixteenth birthday.[287] Emily Finch, in the leading work on stalking in English and Welsh law, suggests that although it is not possible to provide a definition of stalking it is possible to identify three central characteristics of stalking: '[R]epeated conduct that is unwanted and which provokes an adverse reaction in the recipient'.[288] One critique of the literature on stalking claims that women have to daily put up with harassment and unwanted attention. The literature on stalking sometimes presents it as unusual, psychologically disturbed behaviour. However, it is an experience of everyday life for many women.[289]

QUESTIONS

1. Do you think it would be better to define harassment in terms of what the defendant does or in terms of the effect of the defendant's conduct on the victim?

2. How can the law draw the line between acceptable standards of 'courtship' and harassment or stalking?

FURTHER READING

Budd, T. and Mattinson, J. (2000) *The Extent and Nature of Stalking: Findings from the 1998 British Crime Survey* (London: HMSO).

Harris, J. (2000) *Evaluation of the Use and Effectiveness of the Protection from Harassment Act 1997* (London: HMSO).

McAnaney, K., Curliss, L., and Abeyta-Price, C. (1993) 'From Imprudence to Crime: Anti-stalking Laws' *Notre Dame Law Review* 68: 819 (discussing the American responses to stalking).

Reece, H. (2011) '"Unpalatable Messages"? Feminist Analysis of United Kingdom Legislative Discourse on Stalking 1996–1997' *Feminist Legal Studies* 19: 205.

Walby, J. and Allen, H. (2004) *Assault and Stalking: Findings from the British Crime Survey*, Home Office Research Study 276 (London: Home Office).

---

[285] See Finch (2001); S. Gardner (1998); C. Wells (1997); Herring (1998b). For a discussion of the psychological aspects of stalking, see Davis, Frieze, and Maiuro (2000).

[286] [1998] AC 147.   [287] Home Office (2007).

[288] Finch (2001: 80). For a useful discussion of the problems in defining stalking, see McAnaney, Curliss, and Abeyta-Price (1993).

[289] Kelly and Humphreys (2000), questioned in Reece (2011).

22 TRANSMITTING DISEASE AND THE CRIMINAL LAW

As we have seen in Part I, the courts have been dealing with cases where a defendant has infected his or her[290] partner in the course of sexual relations. There has also been much debate over what the law should be.[291] On the one hand there are those who suggest a person who recklessly or intentionally causes another harm should be convicted of a criminal offence, and that should be so even if the means used is disease.[292] While accepting that the law puts a burden of disclosure on HIV patients which will interfere with their private life, George Mawhinney is clear the balancing of rights should fall in favour of disclosure:[293]

> The right not to be harmed, the right to life, must take precedence over social awkwardness every time in any morally sound person's mind. There is always another option, and that is to refrain from unprotected intercourse, if an honest confession as to the risk D poses to V should they have unsafe sex is too onerous for D.

He goes on to object to proposals that the offence should only be committed if the victim has asked the defendant if he is infected and he denies it. Mawhinney objects as it would mean 'the onus is on V to stop the crime's successful commission, rather than on D not to commit it in the first place'.[294]

However, others argue that the criminalization of infection might work contrary to public health strategies. If a person believes he or she may be suffering from a sexually transmitted disease we wish him or her to seek treatment, and not be discouraged from doing so for fear of a criminal prosecution. Nor do we want people to be deterred from taking tests to see if they have a sexually transmitted disease for fear of its potential impact on their sex life. Around a third of those with HIV are unaware of their status.[295] In the context of HIV there are specific fears that the offence may operate as (or be perceived as) an attack on the gay community.[296] Although in 2006, 60 per cent of newly diagnosed cases were among heterosexual men.[297] There is also the issue of why the same law (or prosecution practice) does not apply to other communicable diseases, such as influenza or even the common cold.[298] Similarly HIV-positive mothers who pass on the virus during pregnancy or breastfeed their babies are never prosecuted.[299]

Indeed it has been argued that efforts to prevent the spread of HIV and other conditions would be better focused on behaviours which are closely associated with the spread of HIV, such as human trafficking and organ selling, than prosecuting individuals.[300] ←4 (p.350)

In the following passage, Matthew Weait challenges the way in which the courts have examined this issue. He suggests that sexual activity can be regarded as a joint activity, with each participant being responsible for the potential consequences:[301]

---

[290] See BBC News Online (2006c) for a report of a case where a woman was convicted of recklessly passing on the HIV virus.

[291] Strickland (2001a and 2001b).

[292] See the useful discussion in the Canadian Supreme Court case of *Cuerrier* [1998] 2 SCR 371.

[293] Mawhinney (2013).   [294] *Ibid.*   [295] Medical Research Council (2008).

[296] Ormerod and Gunn (1996) and Home Office (1998c: para. 3.16).

[297] Medical Research Council (2008).   [298] Verweij (2005).

[299] Bennett (2013).   [300] Francis and Francis (2012).

[301] See also Weait (2007) and Herring (2012b: ch. 4).

M. Weait, 'Knowledge, Autonomy and Consent: *R v Konzani*' [2005]
Criminal Law Review 763 at 768–71

Given the importance of the principles at stake, the judgment of the Court of Appeal in *Konzani* is disappointing in its exploration of the justifications for the conclusion reached. Such principled justification as exists is to be found in one critical passage, referred to above, where it explains that a complainant's 'personal autonomy is not enhanced if [the defendant] is exculpated when he recklessly transmits the HIV virus to her through consensual sexual intercourse'. What might this mean, and what merit does it have as a justification for imposing criminal liability via the denial of a defence based on honest belief in consent?

Autonomy means, literally, self-government. In the context of law generally, and in the context of the law as it relates to sexual offences and offences against the person in particular, it suggests the right of a person to be free from unwarranted and unwanted physical interference. Thus the essence of rape law, in which the absence of consent is definitional of the actus reus, is that no legal wrong is done if consent exists, because the partner with whom a person has sexual intercourse is exercising his or her autonomy rather than having it infringed or violated; and where consent operates as a defence to a charge of assault, or causing bodily harm, it reflects the law's recognition that there exists a sphere (albeit one circumscribed by public policy considerations) in which people should be entitled to freedom from liability because to hold otherwise would result in a significant and unjustified diminution of essential human freedoms. It is of critical importance to recognise the distinction. In the former (rape) example the reason why the law does not criminalise the putative defendant is that there is no legally recognised harm committed. However in the latter (assault) example the law protects a putative defendant from criminal liability not on the basis that no recognisable harm has been caused, but because of the context in which it has taken place. It follows that in such circumstances the law is not, at least prima facie, concerned with protecting, or indeed 'enhancing' the autonomy of the person harmed, but rather with protecting the person who harms from the imposition of unjustified liability. Put simply, it is his autonomy (in the sense of his right to be free from unwarranted interference and condemnation by the state) that the law is concerned to protect.

If the principles underpinning this argument are sound then any departure from them demands strong and careful justification. With respect, the Court of Appeal in *Konzani* not only departs from them but fails to provide any such justification. The court indicates that a complainant's autonomy is not enhanced by exculpating a person who recklessly harms her by transmitting HIV (and, by implication, that it is enhanced by denying such a defendant the right to assert an honest belief in her consent to the risk of such harm). In so doing it starts from the premise that, in the context of non-fatal offences against the person at least, it is the autonomy of the person harmed that it is the law's function to protect. However, if this were so then those who recklessly harm people should be denied the defence of consent on the basis of honest belief or otherwise, irrespective of the context in which such harm occurs; and yet case law demonstrates that this is not the case. Without explicitly acknowledging this difficulty, the court identifies the failure of a person to disclose his known HIV positive status, and the deception that is thereby practised on a partner to whom he transmits HIV, as the basis for making the distinction. The nondiscloser may not assert an honest belief in his partner's consent, because the fact of non-disclosure renders her 'consent' uninformed, legally nugatory, and therefore not one on which he is, or should be, entitled to rely. This line of reasoning is emphasised in the court's second reference to the autonomy of a complainant, when it states that this is:

'not normally protected by allowing a defendant who knows that he is suffering from the HIV virus which he deliberately conceals, to assert an honest belief in his partner's informed consent to the risk of the transmission of the HIV virus. Silence in these circumstances is incongruous with honesty, or with a genuine belief that there is an informed consent. Accordingly, in such circumstances the issue either of informed consent, or honest belief in it will only rarely arise: in reality, in most cases, the contention would be wholly artificial.'

What is to be made of the court's deployment of autonomy in this way? While it no doubt has a certain intuitive appeal, it is submitted that the consequences of this line of reasoning are such that it should be rejected.

The court recognised in *Dica* that people should be entitled in principle to consent to the risks associated with sexual intercourse because to deny them this right (and the correlative defence such a right provides to those who expose them to such risks) would amount to an infringement of autonomy that only Parliament should sanction. In *Konzani*, however, the court has made clear that only an informed consent, grounded in knowledge gained from direct or indirect disclosure of a partner's HIV positive status, amounts to consent for these purposes. In effect, therefore, the cumulative ratio of the two cases is not that a person should be entitled to consent to the risks associated with sexual intercourse, but that she should be entitled to consent to such risks as have been directly or indirectly disclosed to her. It is only in the latter context that a defendant's claim of honest belief in consent can, and should, be legally recognised. If this is indeed the ratio, a number of consequences follow.

First, in emphasising that it is only in the most exceptional of cases that nondisclosure to a sexual partner by an HIV positive person will be 'congruent' with an honest belief, the court has, in effect, imposed a standard of reasonable belief in cases where there has been an absence of disclosure. This may be consistent with legislative developments in the law of rape, but if such is the trajectory the law should follow then it is submitted that this should be for Parliament to decide, not—with respect—the Court of Appeal. Secondly, the court has also, in effect, imposed a positive duty of disclosure on people who know they are HIV positive (and who wish to avoid potential criminal liability) before they have sex which carries the risk of transmission. Since there is no reason in principle why this positive duty should be limited to HIV (which is, for those able to access treatment at least, a manageable if life limiting condition), it should be assumed that it applies to all those who are aware that they are suffering from a serious STI. Given that chlamydia may, if untreated in a woman, lead to infertility, that hepatitis B can lead to severe liver damage, and that syphilis—if untreated—can result in significant mental and physical impairment, it is presumably safer to assume that this positive duty now applies to all those who have been diagnosed with these, and other potentially serious, diseases who wish to avoid the possibility of prosecution and imprisonment. Thirdly, in the absence of any indication to the contrary by the court, disclosure as a precautionary principle ought presumably to be adopted by those that are infected with serious or potentially serious contagious diseases. A passenger with SARS or 'flu' may very well be aware that on a transatlantic 747 flight there could be elderly people or others with impaired immune systems (including people living with HIV). Such people's autonomy is certainly not 'enhanced' if the passenger is able to assert that he honestly believed they would consent to being infected by a virus that results in their developing pneumonia; nor is it 'normally protected', where, knowing that he is suffering from a condition that can cause such an effect, he conceals this information.

These consequences of the court's reasoning may be thought more or less fanciful; but the point is, surely, that in using the language of autonomy so loosely, and in failing to specify precisely what the justification for, and scope of, the decision in *Konzani* is, the Court of

Appeal has delivered a judgment that fails abjectly to deal with the core issues which its subject matter raises.

Concluding remarks: public health and criminal law

It is a perfectly legitimate question to ask whether, and if so in what circumstances, a person should be held criminally liable for the transmission of serious disease. The problem is that our answer to that question will inevitably depend on the assumptions we make about the role of the criminal law and the values and principles that inform it. If we start, as is commonplace, within the liberal legal tradition that emphasises autonomy, choice, individual responsibility and rationality, which treats causation as unidirectional and a matter of 'common sense', and which resorts to 'public policy' when confronted with hard cases, it is no wonder that the transmission of HIV by people who fail to disclose their HIV positive status to partners who are subsequently infected is constructed as a wrong that should be punished. It is also inevitable, given that criminal trials are concerned only with the finding of facts in, and the application of existing law to, the individual case, and that criminal appeals deal only with the discrete point(s) of law at issue, that the broader context of transmission is occluded and the wider social and epidemiological implications of criminalisation ignored.

Some concrete examples should serve to illustrate why the current approach of the law to the transmission of HIV is a problem. As a result of *Dica* and *Konzani* a person who, knowing his own HIV positive status, recklessly transmits HIV to a sexual partner, commits a criminal offence. He may only escape liability where the person to whom he transmits the virus gave an informed consent to the risk of transmission. The Court of Appeal in *Konzani* has indicated that such consent will, essentially, arise only where there has been prior disclosure. A number of potentially adverse consequences for public health may follow from this. First, by treating recklessness in this context simply as conscious unjustifiable risk-taking, but without clarifying whether the appropriate use of condoms negates recklessness as a matter of law, the Court of Appeal has provided no clear guidance as to whether their use will preclude the possibility of a conviction. It would be useful if such clarification could be provided so that people living with HIV understand the scope of any duty they might have. Secondly, the requirement that a person knows his HIV positive status before he can be treated as reckless may have the effect of dissuading some people from having an HIV test and so accessing available medical care, advice and treatment. While it is to be welcomed that, as a matter of general principle, no liability should be incurred by people who are in fact unaware that they may transmit HIV to their partner(s), and that the alternative (of imposing liability on those who are aware (or ought to be aware) that they may be HIV positive) would cast the net of liability too widely, the courts should recognise, and deal explicitly with, the potential public health consequences of applying the mens rea requirement in this way. Third, by in effect imposing a duty to disclose known HIV status prior to sex which carries the risk of transmission (which, even if prophylaxis is used, remains a possibility) the courts appear to be working on the assumption, implicitly at least, that those who are HIV positive and know this will in fact (if they behave in the rational manner upon which criminal law and the justification for punishment are premised) disclose their status to partners in order to avoid criminal liability. Moreover, as a direct result of this people may assume that sexual partners who do not disclose their HIV positive status are in fact HIV negative—why would they risk a criminal conviction for a serious offence by not doing so? Finally, where an HIV positive person has not disclosed prior to sex, and where transmission may have occurred, that person may be dissuaded from informing his partner of the possibility thereby preventing that partner from accessing post-exposure prophylaxis (i.e.

intensive drug treatment that may prevent the virus taking hold) because to do so would in effect amount to confessing the commission of a serious criminal offence.

These consequences demonstrate that if we start from a set of a priori assumptions about the function(s) of criminal law in this context, and treat incidents of HIV transmission simply as an opportunity to apply the principles which have traditionally informed the law relating to non-fatal offences against the person, we risk doing more harm than good. UNAIDS, and many other national and international organisations have—since the early years of the HIV/AIDS pandemic—emphasised the importance of dealing with the spread of HIV as first and foremost a public health issue in which we are all implicated, and for which we are all ultimately responsible. If legislators, courts, prosecutors and police, resisted the immediate temptation to treat alleged cases of HIV transmission as individualised, momentary and (potentially) blameworthy incidents; if they were willing to acknowledge and treat seriously the mass of sound empirical research which explains the reasons why people fail to disclose their HIV positive status to significant others; and if they were to recognise that the use of the criminal law may serve not only to perpetuate people's anxieties about HIV, but also, critically, to have a negative public health impact, this would—I believe—better serve the public interest in the longer term.

Contrast Weait's approach with Dennis Baker's, who, in the following passage, argues that an HIV positive person should not be able to rely on consent to justify risking transmission of the condition:

D. Baker, 'The Moral Limits of Consent in Criminal Law' (2008) 12 *New Criminal Law Review* 93 at 107–9

I assert that the Court was wrong to hold that informed consent would have been sufficient to provide the defendant in *Konzani* with a defense. A person should not be able to rely on consent as a defense when he *knows* that there is a very real risk that the consenter will suffer grave harm. Of course, it is important that there be a real risk of harm. If a person has full knowledge that her partner has HIV but freely chooses to have unprotected sexual intercourse, then she is consenting to more than a remote risk of grave harm. It is not easy to draw a clear line, as surely those who engage in unprotected casual sex are also risking their human dignity. The mental element for criminalization in this context would require that the harmdoer knew that there was a real risk (i.e., a high degree of endangerment as opposed to low-level endangerment) of harm transpiring. A consenter should be able to take remote chances, as this preserves her personal autonomy. Thus, promiscuous people (swingers) who risk infection by having unprotected sexual relations with strangers could not be criminalized for infecting others for merely knowing their sexual practices make it likely that they are carriers of the virus. This would be too great an extension of criminal responsibility.

. . .

The HIV cases pose some problems as the consenter is only consenting to a risk of harm, and it is not certain what that harm might be. Nonetheless, we are able to turn to other straightforward examples to strengthen the case for limiting consent as a defense. For instance, if a person intentionally amputates a consenter's arms and legs with a chainsaw, or intentionally pokes the consenter's eyes out so as to blind her, or intentionally kills and eats the consenter for the sake of achieving sexual gratification, then the consenter will suffer irreversible harm of an extraordinary grave kind. The difference with these examples is that the violence is intentional and the harm easy to measure. There is no reason why *recklessness* cannot take the place of *intention*, or why serious endangerment cannot substitute for actual harm. For example, when *x* drives an automobile at 160 miles per hour in a 30-mile-per-hour speed zone whilst intoxicated, she does not aim to harm anyone, but her recklessness poses a real risk of harm to others. There is no need to be able to identify the exact *ex post facto* harm at the *ex ante* criminalization stage, so long as the reckless behavior generally poses a real risk of grave harm.

QUESTIONS

1. Do you agree with Weait's suggestion that a person infected with HIV has no cause for complaint under the criminal law against his or her infector? Does Weait's argument work only where the sexual encounter is a 'casual' one or does it also apply in a relationship where the parties have promised to be monogamous?[302] Would you treat a case where a husband failed to disclose to his wife that he had become HIV positive after an adulterous affair differently from a case where a female sex worker failed to disclose the fact that she was HIV positive to her clients? (Weait 2005b).

2. Should those who support criminal sanctions against those who recklessly transmit HIV also support liability for those who go out in public even if they are suffering from a cold, and may therefore infect others?

3. Spencer (2004) writes 'To infect an unsuspecting person with a grave disease you know you have, or may have, by behaviour that you know involves a risk of transmission, and that you know you could easily modify to reduce or eliminate the risk, is to harm another in [a] way that is both needless and callous. For that reason, criminal liability is justified unless there are strong countervailing reasons. In my view there are not.' Do you agree?

4. Harris and Holm (1995) argue that society is entitled to impose obligations upon those who are infectious, but only if society offers adequate care, support, and treatment for them. Does the inadequacy of society's response to AIDS mean that it loses its entitlement to impose obligations upon those who are HIV positive?

5. Research (e.g. Francis and Francis (2013)) suggests that criminalizing the transmission of HIV does not affect people's risky sexual behaviour. Indeed Weait (2013) claims 'the extensive use of punitive laws has a negative impact on HIV prevention and contributes to the stigmatisation of, and discrimination against, people living with HIV'. How does this impact on the issue of criminalizing HIV transmission?

FURTHER READING

Ashford, C. (2010) 'Barebacking and the "Cult of Violence": Queering the Criminal Law' *Journal of Criminal Law* 74: 339.

Burris, S. and Weait, M. (2014) *Criminalisation and the Moral Responsibility for Sexual Transmission of HIV* (New York: Global Commission on HIV and the Law).

---

302 See Slater (2011) who thinks the distinction between committed and casual relationships is key.

Francis, L.P and Francis, J. (2012) 'Criminalizing Health-Related Behaviors Dangerous to Others? Disease Transmission, Transmission-Facilitation, and the Importance of Trust' *Criminal Law and Philosophy* 6: 47.

Francis, J. and Francis, L.P. (2013) 'HIV Treatment as Prevention: Not an Argument for Continuing Criminalization of HIV Transmission' *International Journal of Law in Context* 9: 520.

Harris, J. and Holm, S. (1995) 'Is there a Moral Obligation Not to Infect Others?' *British Medical Journal* 311: 1215.

Slater, J. (2011) 'HIV, Trust and the Criminal Law' *Journal of Criminal Law* 75: 309.

Strickland, C. (2001a) *HIV/AIDS and the Criminal Law in England and Wales: A Comparative Analysis* (London: Cavendish).

Strickland, C. (2001b) 'Why Parliament should Create HIV Specific Offences' *Web Journal of Current Legal Issues*.

Weait, M. (2001) 'Taking the Blame: Criminal Law, Social Responsibility and the Sexual Transmission of HIV' *Journal of Social Welfare and Family Law* 23: 441.

Weait, M. (2005a) 'Harm, Consent and the Limits of Privacy' *Feminist Legal Studies* 13: 97.

Weait, M. (2007) 'On Being Responsible' in V. Munro and C. Stychin (eds) *Sexuality and the Law* (London: Cavendish).

Weait, M. (2013) 'Unsafe Law: Health, Rights and the Legal Response to HIV' *International Journal of Law in Context* 9: 535.

23   CONCLUDING THOUGHTS

It is remarkable that the law on assaults is based on an Act which is nearly 150 years old. Few, if any, commentators would draft their ideal law on assaults with the language that appears in the 1861 Act. Nevertheless, the courts have, with some imaginative statutory interpretation, been able to use the 1861 Act to provide an effective response to a wide range of contemporary problems: from transmission of HIV to stalking. The law on assaults reflects wider social attitudes about what counts as harm to a person and what a person may or may not do with their bodies. This has meant that several of the topics discussed in this chapter, especially sadomasochism and HIV transmission, have led to heated debates. In part these reflect wider issues about the place of the body in modern society and the significance of concepts such as dignity and autonomy.

7

SEXUAL OFFENCES

CENTRAL ISSUES

1. The offence of rape requires proof that the defendant penetrated the vagina, anus, or mouth of the victim with his penis, without the consent of the victim. To be guilty it must be shown that he knew or ought to have known that the victim did not consent to the penetration. There has been much debate over the meaning of consent in this context.

2. There are a range of other offences concerning non-consensual sexual activity.

These include sexual penetration (where the penetration is with something other than a penis), sexual assault (where there is a sexual touching), and causing another person to engage in a sexual activity.

3. There are a broad range of sexual offences which are designed to protect children and those with mental disorders from sexual abuse.

PART I: THE LAW ON SEXUAL OFFENCES

This chapter will primarily focus on the offences of rape and sexual assault. Other sexual offences will be discussed in outline. This topic can be one of the most difficult to study. Anyone who has experienced the horror of a sexual assault will find the judicial and academic writings unbearably dry. How can such a horrific crime be discussed in such clinical terms? Yet the seriousness of the offences requires them to be subject to careful, but sensitive, analysis.

The law on sexual offences has been transformed by the Sexual Offences Act 2003. That Act changed the previous law set out in the Sexual Offences Act 1956, which was described by the government as 'archaic, incoherent and discriminatory'.[1]

---

[1] Home Office (2002: 1).

1 RAPE

Rape is defined in section 1 of the Sexual Offences Act 2003 thus:

> (1) A person (A) commits an offence if—
>   (a) he intentionally penetrates the vagina, anus or mouth of another person (B) with his penis,
>   (b) B does not consent to the penetration, and
>   (c) A does not reasonably believe that B consents.
> (2) Whether a belief is reasonable is to be determined having regard to all the circumstances, including any steps A has taken to ascertain whether B consents.[2]

DEFINITION

Actus reus: the defendant penetrated the vagina, anus, or mouth of the victim with his penis and the victim did not consent to the penetration.

Mens rea:

(1) the defendant intended to penetrate the vagina, anus, or mouth of the victim with his penis; *and*

(2) the defendant did not reasonably believe that the victim consented to the penetration.

1.1 WHO CAN COMMIT RAPE?

Who can rape?

Only someone with a penis can commit rape. This is because the offence requires penetration with a penis.[3] If a woman forces a man to engage in sexual intercourse against his will this can amount to a sexual assault[4] or the offence of causing another person to perform a sexual act without consent,[5] but will not be rape. It is possible for a woman to be an accessory to the crime of rape (i.e. to aid, abet, counsel, or procure rape).[6]

Can a husband rape a wife?

A husband can be convicted of raping his wife. This was clear only after the 1994 amendments to the Sexual Offences Act 1956, which put into statutory effect the decision of the House of Lords in *R v R*.[7] The House of Lords rejected the outdated view that on marriage a wife gave irrevocable consent to sexual relations at any time during the marriage and therefore marital intercourse could not be unlawful.[8] The shocking fact that marital rape

---

[2] The offence carries a maximum sentence of life.

[3] This includes a surgically created penis (Sexual Offences Act 2003, s. 79(3)).

[4] Sexual Offences Act 2003, s. 3. If she penetrates his anus or mouth she can be guilty of assault by penetration (s. 2).

[5] *Ibid*, s. 4.

[6] In *Cogan and Leak* [1976] QB 217 it had been suggested a woman can be guilty of rape as the principal if she uses an innocent agent to have sexual intercourse with a woman. However, the case has been heavily criticized and subsequent cases have suggested that it is better in such cases to charge the woman with procuring rape (*DPP v R and B* [1997] 1 Cr App R 36).

[7] [1991] 4 All ER 481.   [8] Hale, 1 PC 29.

could not be prosecuted until 1991 is seen by many to be indicative of the slowness of the law to intervene to protect women from sexual assault. Of course, the fact that the parties were married will be relevant as a matter of evidence. For example, a husband may more easily persuade the jury that he believed that his wife was consenting to sexual intercourse than if the victim were a stranger.[9]

At what age can a man commit rape?

There used to be a rule under common law that a boy under 14 was incapable of committing sexual intercourse. This was abolished for acts after 20 September 1993 by section 1 of the Sexual Offences Act 2003. Of course, to be guilty of rape a boy must be above the age of criminal responsibility (i.e. over the age of 10).

1.2 WHO CAN BE THE VICTIM OF RAPE?

A man or woman can be the victim of rape because anal or oral rape is included within section 1. Section 79(3) of the Sexual Offences Act 2003 makes it clear that a surgically constructed vagina is included within the definition of a vagina. This means that a transgender woman who has undergone sex reassignment surgery can be vaginally raped.

1.3 WHAT IS PENETRATION?

To amount to rape the only act that is sufficient is penetration of the anus, vagina,[10] or mouth by the defendant's penis. Penetration with objects or other parts of the body apart from the penis against the victim's consent will not amount to rape, although it would amount to the offence of assault by penetration contrary to section 2 of the 2003 Act. →1 (p.489)

The definition of rape in the 2003 Act requires only penetration.[11] This makes it clear that there can be rape even if there is no ejaculation. If the defendant tries to penetrate but fails to do so this may amount to attempted rape.[12]

One important issue is whether the *actus reus* of rape is complete once penetration takes place or whether it continues as long as there is penetration. The issue is important in cases where the victim consents to the initial penetration, but then asks the man to withdraw, but he refuses.[13] The Sexual Offences Act 2003 provides a clear answer in section 79(2): 'Penetration is a continuing act from entry to withdrawal.' This means that if the victim withdraws his or her consent after the initial penetration, but the defendant does not withdraw within a reasonable length of time, this can be rape. What exactly is a reasonable time may cause difficulties in some cases and will be left to the 'common sense' of the jury.

---

9 Herring (2011c). See Rumney (1999) and Warner (2000) for a discussion of differences in sentencing practice in cases of 'marital rape'.

10 'Vagina includes vulva' (Sexual Offences Act 2003, s. 79(9)).

11 What exactly will amount to penetration is an issue which is likely to be left to the jury, giving penetration its normal meaning.

12 See Chapter 14.   13 See e.g. the facts in *Kaitamaki* [1985] AC 147.

1.4 WHAT IS CONSENT?

It is important to appreciate that questions over the victim's consent arise in two contexts in relation to rape. First, as a matter of the *actus reus* it must be shown that the victim did not consent to the penetration. Second, as a matter of the *mens rea* it must be shown that the defendant did not reasonably believe that the victim consented. These two questions must be dealt with separately. First, we will be looking at the *actus reus* issues: did the victim consent?

EXAMINATION TIP

When answering problem questions in relation to rape it is very easy to merge together the questions: (a) did the victim consent? and (b) did the defendant think the victim was consenting? These must be treated as two separate questions: the first is a matter of the *actus reus* and the second is to do with the *mens rea* of rape.

The 2003 Act defines consent in the following way in section 74:

> a person consents if he agrees by choice, and has the freedom and capacity to make that choice.

This leaves unanswered a lot of questions about the meaning of consent and we will now address these. After the 2003 Act the law is a little complicated because there are circumstances under which consent is presumed to be lacking. Where the presumption does not apply or when deciding whether the presumption has been rebutted the courts will turn back to the basic meaning of consent.

So in deciding whether or not the victim has consented the following approach is recommended:

EXAMINATION TIP

To decide whether the victim consented ask:

(1) Is this a case in which the victim is conclusively presumed to have not consented?

If YES: The victim did not consent.

If NO: Consider question 2.

(2) Is this a case in which there is an evidential presumption that the victim did not consent?

If YES: Then you must consider whether or not the presumption is rebutted. If it is: consider question 3; If it is not: The victim did not consent.

If NO: Consider question 3.

(3) Did the victim consent under the basic meaning of consent in section 74?

If YES: The victim did consent.

If NO: The victim did not consent.

Conclusive presumptions: deception as to the nature or purpose of the act

As suggested by the previous box, the place to start is to consider whether this is a case where the conclusive presumptions operate. These are found in section 76:

76. Conclusive presumptions about consent

(1) If in proceedings for an offence to which this section applies it is proved that the defendant did the relevant act and that any of the circumstances specified in subsection (2) existed, it is to be conclusively presumed—

    (a) that the complainant did not consent to the relevant act, and

    (b) that the defendant did not believe that the complainant consented to the relevant act.

(2) The circumstances are that—

    (a) the defendant intentionally deceived the complainant as to the nature or purpose of the relevant act;

    (b) the defendant intentionally induced the complainant to consent to the relevant act by impersonating a person known personally to the complainant.

It should be noted that these are conclusive presumptions. So, for example, once it is shown that the defendant intentionally deceived the complainant as to the nature of the act he will be guilty of rape. There is no way that he can rebut the presumption. Note also that when the presumption applies both the *mens rea* and *actus reus* of rape are proved.[14]

We will first consider further the circumstances in which it will be presumed that a victim who is mistaken as to the nature of the act does not consent under section 76(2)(a). The following need to be shown:

(1) **There must be a deception** If the victim is mistaken as to the nature or purpose of the act but not because of any deception of the defendant's then the statutory presumption does not apply. However, the jury would, no doubt, find there was not consent in its general meaning. Another interesting point to note is that a literal reading of the subsection does not require the deception to have caused the consent. So, for example, if Dec tells Carol that he needs to have sexual intercourse with her in order to cure her of an illness, whereas in fact this is a complete fabrication, this could fall into section 76(2)(a) even if in fact Carol would have been quite happy to have sex with Dec, even without his deception. However, it must be shown that the victim was deceived. So in the example just given if Carol realized Dec was lying and had sex with him because she fancied him, that would not fall under the presumption.

(2) **The deception must be intentional** The statutory presumption of no consent applies only if the defendant's deception was intentional. →2 (p.473)

(3) **There must be a deception as to the nature or purpose of the act** If the victim is mistaken as to the nature of the act there is no true consent. Perhaps the best known example is that in *Williams*[15] in which a singing teacher persuaded his pupil (aged 16)

---

14 As Tadros (2006a) points out it is odd that these are seen as cases where there is conclusive evidence of no consent; rather than simply constituting no consent. Where V has been deceived as to the nature of the act this means there is no consent, not just that there is good evidence of no consent.

15 [1923] 1 KB 340. There have also been cases where women have been persuaded to agree to acts said to be 'medical treatment', but which were in fact sexual intercourse (see e.g. *Case* (1850) 4 Cox CC 220).

to agree to let him do something that would improve her breathing. She was unaware that in fact he was engaging in sexual intercourse with her. He was convicted of rape. The act she consented to (the assistance in breathing technique) was different in nature from the act the defendant did. The case would have been less straightforward if the victim had understood that they were to have sexual intercourse, but the defendant had persuaded the victim that having sexual intercourse would make her sing better. Although she would then not have been mistaken as to the nature of the act she may have been deceived as to the purpose of the act.[16]

The interpretation of the phrase 'nature and purpose' in the presumption has proved problematic. The three leading cases on deceptions and consent in the Sexual Offences Act 2003 are as follows:

R v Jheeta
[2007] EWCA Crim 1699

Harvinda Jheeta and the complainant had been going out together and having sexual relations. When the relationship cooled the defendant anonymously sent various threatening text messages to the complainant. She consulted the defendant and he suggested he contact the police. He then, over several years, sent her text messages purporting to be from the police, and further threatening messages. In some of the messages purporting to come from the police, she was told she should keep having sexual relations with the defendant otherwise she may have to pay a fine for causing him distress. She said she had sex with the defendant on about 50 occasions, only because of the 'police advice'. When interviewed the defendant said he realized that the victim had not been consenting to sexual intercourse with him and had sex because of his deceptions.

Lord Justice Judge

23. The starting point in our analysis is to acknowledge that in most cases, the absence of consent, and the appropriate state of the defendant's mind, will be proved without reference to evidential or conclusive presumptions. When they do apply, section 75 and section 76 are directed to the process of proving the absence of consent to whichever sexual act is alleged. They are concerned with presumptions about rather than the definition of consent. . . .

24. In our judgment the ambit of section 76 is limited to the "act" to which it is said to apply. In rape cases the "act" is vaginal, anal or oral intercourse. Provided this consideration is constantly borne in mind, it will be seen that section 76(2)(a) is relevant only to the comparatively rare cases where the defendant deliberately deceives the complainant about the *nature or purpose* of one or other form of intercourse. No conclusive presumptions arise merely because the complainant was deceived in some way or other by disingenuous blandishments of or common or garden lies by the defendant. These may well be deceptive and persuasive, but they will rarely go to the nature or purpose of intercourse. Beyond this limited type of case, and assuming that, as here, section 75 has no application, the issue of consent must be addressed in the context of section 74.

25. It may be helpful to reinforce these observations by reference to a number of cases at common law which provide examples of deceptions as to the nature or purpose of the act of

---

[16] Presuming that Williams's purposes were sexual.

intercourse. As to the nature of the relevant act, in *R v Flattery* [1877] 2 QBD 410 the Court of Crown Cases Reserved upheld a conviction for rape where intercourse took place after the complainant, a girl of 19, was persuaded that the defendant was performing a surgical operation which would break "nature's string" and provide a remedy for the fits to which she was subject. In *R v Williams* [1923] 1 KB 340 the conviction for rape was upheld where the defendant deceived a girl of 16 into having sexual intercourse with him to cure a problem with her breathing which prevented her from singing properly. . . .

26. Deception as to purpose is sometimes said to be exemplified in *R v Tabassum* [2000] 2 CAR 328, a decision described by the late Professor Sir John Smith as a "doubtful case". A number of women agreed to participate in a breast cancer research programme at the behest of the appellant when, as a result of what he said or did, or both, they wrongly believed that he was medically qualified or trained. They consented to a medical examination, not to sexual touching by a stranger. "There was consent to the nature of the act, but not to its quality". However section 76(2)(a) does not address the "quality" of the act, but confines itself to its "purpose". In the latest edition of *Smith and Hogan Criminal Law*, (11th edition) Professor David Ormerod identifies a better example, *R v Green* [2002] EWCA Crim 1501. Bogus medical examinations of young men were carried out by a qualified doctor, in the course of which they were wired up to monitors while they masturbated. The purported object was to assess their potential for impotence. Although the experiment did not involve any form of intercourse, it illustrates the practice of a deception as to the "purpose" of the physical act.

27. These examples demonstrate the likely rarity of occasions when the conclusive presumption in section 76(2)(a) will apply. For example, *R v Linekar* [1995] 2 CAR 49 would not fall within its ambit. The appellant promised to pay a prostitute £25 if she had intercourse with him. It was a promise he never intended to keep. On this aspect of the case, that is, that the defendant tricked the prostitute into having intercourse with him, the judge left it to the jury to consider whether his fraud vitiated her consent which was given on the basis that he would pay. The conviction was quashed. The consent given by the complainant was a real consent, which was not destroyed by the appellant's false pretence. If anything, he was guilty of an offence under section 3 of the 1956 Act, that is an offence identical to the offence alleged in counts one and two of the present indictment. *Linekar* deceived the prostitute about his intentions. He undoubtedly lied to her. However she was undeceived about either the nature or the purpose of the act, that is intercourse. Accordingly the conclusive presumptions in section 76 would have no application.

28. With these considerations in mind, we must return to the present case. On the written basis of plea the appellant undoubtedly deceived the complainant. He created a bizarre and fictitious fantasy which, because it was real enough to her, pressurised her to have intercourse with him more frequently than she otherwise would have done. She was not deceived as to the nature or purpose of intercourse, but deceived as to the situation in which she found herself. In our judgment the conclusive presumption in section 76(2)(a) had no application, and counsel for the appellant below were wrong to advise on the basis that it did. However that is not an end of the matter.

29. We are being asked to examine the safety of convictions for rape where the appellant pleaded guilty. He did so on the basis of plea which accepted the accuracy of his admissions in interview with the police, and in particular did not question his unequivocal admission that there were occasions when sexual intercourse took place when the complainant was not truly consenting. This is entirely consistent with his acknowledgement that he persuaded the complainant to have intercourse with him more frequently than otherwise, and the persuasion took the form of the pressures imposed on her by the complicated and unpleasant scheme which he had fabricated. This was not a free choice, or consent for the purposes of the Act. In these circumstances we entertain no reservations that on some occasions at least

the complainant was not consenting to intercourse for the purposes of section 74, and that the appellant was perfectly well aware of it. His guilty plea reflected these undisputed facts. Accordingly the appeal against conviction is dismissed.

R v Devonald
[2008] EWCA Crim 527

Stephen Devonald posed on the internet as a 20-year-old woman named 'Cassey'. He deliberately set out to meet the victim, a 16-year-old boy who was his daughter's ex-boyfriend. Pretending to be Cassey he persuaded the victim to masturbate on the web-cam. Devonald's plan, it appears, was to put film of this on the internet, causing the victim embarrassment and thereby exact revenge for what he regarded as the bad way he had treated his daughter. Devonald was charged with causing a sexual activity (the mastur-bation) without consent, contrary to section 4 of the Sexual Offences Act. A key issue was whether the victim consented. The prosecution argued that under section 76(2)(a), because the victim had been deceived as to the nature or purpose of the act, there was no consent.

Lord Justice Leveson

The learned judge ruled that it was open to the jury to conclude that the complainant was deceived as to the purpose of the act of masturbation. We agree. On the facts, as we have described them, it is difficult to see how the jury could have concluded otherwise that the complainant was deceived into believing that he was indulging in sexual acts with, and for the sexual gratification of, a 20-year-old girl with whom he was having an on line relation-ship. That is why he agreed to masturbate over the sex cam. In fact, he was doing so for the father of his ex-girlfriend who was anxious to teach him a lesson doubtless by later embar-rassing him or exposing what he had done.

It is an inevitable inference that it is for that reason that the applicant changed his plea to guilty when the judge so ruled. Miss Howell [counsel for the appellant] has over focused on the phrase "nature of the act", which undoubtedly was sexual but not on its purpose, which encompasses rather more than the specific purpose of sexual gratification by the defendant in the Act of mas-turbation. In our judgment, this ruling was correct and there is no grounds for challenging the basis on which the applicant changed his plea. This application is therefore refused.

Although the *Devonald* case concerned the offence of causing the victim to perform a sexual act, the law on consent in that case is based on the same principles that apply to rape.

R v B
[2013] EWCA Crim 823

The defendant contacted his girlfriend (X) on a social networking site, using a false name (Grant). She sent Grant topless photographs of herself, not realizing that she was sending them to the defendant. 'Grant' then told X to perform sexual acts in front of a webcam, threatening to otherwise publish the photographs of her on the internet. She obeyed. She told her boyfriend (the defendant) what had happened. He later told her he had found Grant and killed him. The defendant then again used the networking site, this time pretending to be Chad. He contacted X and told her that he had got the photographs from Grant and again threatened to publish them unless X performed sex acts, which she did. The judge, relying on *Devonald* directed the jury that if they were persuaded that there was a deception as to the defendant's purpose they could presume a lack of consent. He appealed against the conviction on the basis that the direction was wrong.

Lord Justice Hallett

19. There is no definition of the word *purpose* in the Act. It is a perfectly ordinary English word and one might have hoped it would not be necessary to provide a definition. It has been left to the courts and academics to struggle with its meaning in the context of a sexual act. We say "struggle" advisedly because it may not be straightforward to ascertain the *purpose* of a sexual act. Those engaging in a sexual act may have a number of reasons or objectives and each party may have a different objective or reason. The Act does not specify whose *purpose* is under consideration. There is, therefore, a great danger in attempting any definition of the word *purpose* and in defining it too widely. A wide definition could bring within the remit of section 76 situations never contemplated by Parliament.

20. We shall, therefore, simply apply the normal rules of statutory construction and echo what was said in *Jheeta*. Where, as here, a statutory provision effectively removes from an accused his only line of defence to a serious criminal charge it must be strictly construed. We respectfully adopt the approach of the court in *Jheeta*. If there is any conflict between the decisions in *Jheeta* and *Devonald*, we would unhesitatingly follow *Jheeta*. Thus, it will be a rare case in which section 76 should be applied.

21. Is this one of those rare cases? Miss Kidd reminded the court of the extent of the deception and the affect upon the complainant. It was not unlike the extent and effect of the deception in *Jheeta*. Just as in *Jheeta*, this appellant undoubtedly deceived his girlfriend in a cruel and despicable way. However, the fact that there was a catalogue of deception of an unpleasant kind begs the question as to whether it was deception as to *purpose* so as to trigger the operation of section 76. We have our doubts.

22. The complainant was never asked what her purpose or understanding of the purpose of the act was and the appellant's purpose seems far from clear. His accounts varied but the most likely explanation, as the prosecution argued, was some kind of perverted sexual gratification. The complainant knew full well what she was being asked to do and what she did in fact do, namely perform a sexual act for the benefit of the camera. She could have been in no doubt that the motive was at least in part sexual gratification. If so, on one view, even if one were to extend the definition of *purpose* to include the appellant's intention, as has been suggested, there is here no evidence going to the issue of deceit as to his purpose.

23. Further, we see force in Mr Bindloss's submission that if reliance was to be placed on section 76, which effectively withdrew the accused's only line of defence, it was incumbent upon the judge to identify the evidence which went to the issue of "deceit as to purpose". Here there was no such analysis, and the jury were never directed that the word had a restricted meaning—see *Jheeta*. They were not informed that deceit as to what some commentators have called "peripheral matters" was not enough.

24. For those reasons we are troubled by the way in which the prosecution put their case and by the way in which it was left to the jury. We understand how prosecuting counsel and the judge may have thought that the decision in *Devonald* applied and appeared to support reliance on section 76. However, as we have indicated, reliance upon section 76 in this case,

on these facts and this evidence, was misplaced. The prosecution needed to look no further than the provisions of section 74. It provides that "a person consents if he agrees by choice and has the freedom and capacity to make that choice". If the complainant only complied because she was being blackmailed, the prosecution might argue forcefully she did not agree by choice.

Retrial ordered.

While we are a long way from being able to offer a definitive analysis of what constitutes a deception as to the nature or purpose of the act under section 76, it seems the following points have been established:

- A deception might be relevant to consent in two ways. If the deception is as to 'nature or purpose' it can fall under the conclusive presumption and negate consent. If the deception is not as to 'nature or purpose' it might still mean that the victim did not consent, considering the general meaning of consent under section 74. Notably in both *Jheeta* and *B* the deception was held not to negate consent under the conclusive presumption but to potentially mean there was no consent under the general meaning.[17]

- A deception as to a 'peripheral matter' will not amount to a deception as to 'nature or purpose'. So a defendant who tells a woman he meets at a party that he is a lawyer and as a result she agrees to sleep with him, will not have been deceived in a matter which affects the nature or purpose of the act. Indeed, only in rare cases will a case involve a deception which falls within the conclusive presumption.

- It seems from *B* that if the victim is aware of some of the defendant's purposes she will not be deceived as to the purpose of the act even though she is not aware of all the defendant's purposes. In that case she knew the act was for sexual gratification, even if his motivations seem a little more complex than that. By contrast in *Devonald* where the victim was completely unaware of the motivations of the defendant there may be a deception as to purpose. That would suggest the courts would follow the pre-2003 Act case of *Tabassum*.[18] There, it was found that women who agreed to examination of their breasts after the defendant had untruthfully said he was medically qualified and wished to examine them as part of a research project, were found not to have consented. They were completely deceived as to the nature of the acts.[19]

- Cases of deception as to nature of the act involving sexual intercourse will be limited, it seems, to cases where the victim is unaware the act is sexual intercourse. In *Assange v Swedish Prosecution Authority*[20] it was held that if the woman had agreed to have sex if the man wore a condom, but he penetrated her without one, that would not fall within section 76. It would not affect the nature of the act. However, it could still be rape because the woman would not have consented to the act in the general meaning of consent in section 74. In *R v EB*[21] a defendant who did not disclose he was HIV positive was held not to have deceived as to the nature or purpose of the act.

---

[17] Rogers (2013) argues that only the deceptions listed in s. 76 negate consent, but that view is not supported in the case law.

[18] [2000] 2 Cr App R 328. [19] See also *Green* [2002] EWCA Crim 1501.

[20] [2011] EWHC 2849 (Admin). [21] [2006] EWCA Crim 2945 (CA).

Conclusive presumption: cases of impersonation

Section 76(2) also creates a conclusive presumption in cases of impersonation. The following points can be made about this subsection:

(1) **There must be an impersonation** In *Elbekkay*,[22] at night time, the defendant entered the victim's bedroom. She assumed that he was her boyfriend and so consented to sexual intercourse. The defendant realized his mistake, but had sexual intercourse with her. The presumption does not apply in such a case because the defendant had not impersonated the boyfriend (he had said nothing to suggest he was the boyfriend). However, he will still be guilty of rape because under the general meaning of consent the victim did not consent.[23]

(2) **The impersonation must be of a person known personally to the complainant** Clearly the presumption would apply where the defendant impersonated the victim's husband, partner, or even friend. But, it seems, the presumption would not apply where the defendant impersonated the victim's favourite film star or pop star. Similarly, if the defendant simply claimed an attribute which he did not have (e.g. that he was rich or was a qualified lawyer) this would not negate consent.

(3) **Rather oddly, the subsection seems to apply even if the victim is not taken in by the impersonation** Consider this: Dave fancies his best friend Mick, but Mick is not interested. Pete (whom Dave does not know) fancies Dave and, learning of Dave's liking of Mick, decides to try to impersonate Mick. When Dave sees Pete he realizes that Pete is not Mick, but agrees to sexual intercourse with him because Pete looks so like Mick he can live out a fantasy. It seems that if section 76 were interpreted literally this would be rape. But that is absurd; the subsection (although it does not say so) is surely meant to apply only where the victim is taken in by the impersonation.

There are two kinds of cases where the statutory presumption of non-consent does not apply, but the jury may still decide that the victim does not consent under the general meaning of consent:

(1) **Where there is no deception** In *Elbekkay*[24] (a case under the old law, summarized previously) the Court of Appeal found that the victim had not consented to sexual intercourse with the defendant, even though the defendant had not in fact impersonated the boyfriend. The victim had consented to sexual relations with her partner, not the defendant. There was therefore no consent.

(2) **Where the mistake is as to the identity of a person not known to the victim** As already mentioned the statutory presumption applies only where the defendant impersonates someone the victim knew personally. For a long time the common law view was that impersonation only of a spouse could negate consent. However, this was extended to unmarried partners in *Elbekkay*.[25] *Obiter*, McCowan LJ, giving the judgment of the court, explained that 'The vital point about rape is that it involves the absence of consent. That absence is equally crucial whether the woman believes that the man she is having sexual intercourse with is her husband or another.' The phrase 'or another' may suggest the common law is even wider than the statutory presumption and includes cases of impersonation of anyone.

---

[22] [1995] Crim LR 163 (CA). [23] [2007] EWCA Crim 1699.
[24] [1995] Crim LR 163 (CA). [25] *Ibid*.

What we know for sure is that if the victim is mistaken as to an attribute of the defendant, rather than the identity of the person, then that will not create a conclusive presumption of no consent. So if the victim met a man at a party who simply claimed to be a well-known actor that mistake would not vitiate the victim's consent. That is because his or her mistake would simply be over an attribute (the man's occupation) rather than his identity. In *Richardson*[26] the defendant purported to be a legitimate dentist when in fact she had been struck off the register of dentists. Patients who received treatment from her were said not to be mistaken as to her identity: she was the very Diane Richardson they thought she was; they were, however, mistaken as to her attributes (she was not a registered dentist). So there was consent to the dentistry work.

Evidential presumptions

The evidential presumptions are set out in section 75:

75. Evidential presumptions about consent

(1) If in proceedings for an offence to which this section applies it is proved—

    (a) that the defendant did the relevant act,

    (b) that any of the circumstances specified in subsection (2) existed, and

    (c) that the defendant knew that those circumstances existed, the complainant is to be taken not to have consented to the relevant act unless sufficient evidence is adduced to raise an issue as to whether he consented, and the defendant is to be taken not to have reasonably believed that the complainant consented unless sufficient evidence is adduced to raise an issue as to whether he reasonably believed it.

(2) The circumstances are that—

    (a) any person was, at the time of the relevant act or immediately before it began, using violence against the complainant or causing the complainant to fear that immediate violence would be used against him;

    (b) any person was, at the time of the relevant act or immediately before it began, causing the complainant to fear that violence was being used, or that immediate violence would be used, against another person;

    (c) the complainant was, and the defendant was not, unlawfully detained at the time of the relevant act;

    (d) the complainant was asleep or otherwise unconscious at the time of the relevant act;

    (e) use of the complainant's physical disability, the complainant would not have been able at the time of the relevant act to communicate to the defendant whether the complainant consented;

    (f) person had administered to or caused to be taken by the complainant, without the complainant's consent, a substance which, having regard to when it was administered or taken, was capable of causing or enabling the complainant to be stupefied or overpowered at the time of the relevant act.

(3) In subsection (2)(a) and (b), the reference to the time immediately before the relevant act began is, in the case of an act which is one of a continuous series of sexual activities, a reference to the time immediately before the first sexual activity began.

---

[26] [1999] QB 444 (CA).

Where it is proved by the prosecution that one of the sets of facts listed in section 75(2) existed and the defendant was aware they existed, then there is a presumption that the *actus reus* and *mens rea* of rape are established. But this is only an evidential presumption and it is open to the defendant to introduce evidence that in fact the *mens rea* or *actus reus* of rape did not exist.[27] Where the defendant produces 'sufficient evidence to raise an issue' as to whether the *actus reus* or *mens rea* of rape existed then the presumption is rebutted. The prosecution must then prove beyond reasonable doubt that the *actus reus* and *mens rea* of rape existed. This is all a bit confusing, but the following example may assist:

> The prosecution prove that a minute before D and V had sexual intercourse that D intentionally had hit V. Under section 75(2)(a) this creates a presumption that D is guilty of rape. If the defence introduces no evidence the jury should convict D. However, D may try and introduce evidence to rebut the presumption. He might argue, for example, that after he hit V he immediately apologized, she forgave him and they then had sexual intercourse. If he introduces sufficient evidence to raise an issue about this then the presumption is rebutted. The prosecution must then persuade the jury beyond reasonable doubt that the *actus reus* and *mens rea* of rape existed.[28]

A key issue is what 'introduces sufficient evidence to raise an issue' means. In the previous example, if D just gave evidence to the effect that they had made up and had consensual sex, would that be enough? If the answer is 'yes' then that means that it would be very easy to rebut the presumption: the defendant just has to say there was in fact consent, in which case it might well be wondered whether these presumptions are worth having. They are going to be very complicated to explain to a jury, which may well be confused by them. On the other hand, if the answer is 'no', what more evidence could D introduce in a case like this, apart from his own eyewitness account? Court guidance on the meaning of 'sufficient evidence is adduced to raise' is eagerly awaited. In *Ciccarelli*[29] it was emphasized that the defendant, to rebut the presumption of *mens rea*, had to introduce evidence that he reasonably believed the victim consented. It was not enough just to say he did so believe.

The Judicial Studies Board has suggested that it is for the judge to decide whether the defendant has introduced sufficient evidence to raise an issue. The judge only needs to give a direction on the presumptions if there is no such evidence. It seems that in practice the presumptions are so confusing that they are not often relied upon by barristers in courts.[30]

Section 75(2)(a)–(c) deals with cases where there is a threat of violence or unlawful detention. The following points can be made:

(1) Notice that under section 75(2)(b) it does not need to be shown that the defendant used or threatened violence against the victim. So if the defendant's friend threatens to beat up the victim unless she 'agrees' to sexual intercourse with the defendant the presumption will apply. Similarly, the threat of violence need not be to the victim, but can be to another. So if the defendant threatened to beat up the victim's friend unless she agreed to sexual intercourse, the presumption could also apply.

(2) The presumption applies only if the threat is of violence. If the threat is to destroy property, for example, then the presumption does not apply. Also, it seems that threats to cause an emotional harm (e.g. to end a relationship) are not included.

---

[27] *Lewis MBA* [2012] EWCA Crim 2773.

[28] Tadros (2006a) argues that where there has been the use of threat of violence this is not just evidence of a lack of consent, but constitutes a lack of free choice and so not consent.

[29] [2011] EWCA Crim 2665.   [30] Gunby, Carline, and Beynon (2010).

(3) The presumption applies only if the threat is of immediate violence. So the presumption will not apply if the threat is that the victim will be beaten up next week.

Section 75(2)(d)–(e) deals with cases where the victim is incapable of consenting, either because they are asleep, unconscious, or unable to communicate their consent. It must be said that in these cases it is hard to imagine how the presumption could be rebutted. Perhaps it is plausible that V might ask D to have sex with him while he is asleep. A strong case can be made for saying that where V is unconscious then there cannot be consent, not just that there is a presumption of no consent. It opens the door too easily for a defendant to have sexual intercourse with a sleeping or unconscious woman then to argue that had she been awake she would have consented. In *R v Ciccarelli*[31] the Court of Appeal had no difficulty in upholding the conviction of a man who had sexually assaulted a woman who was asleep. The defendant had sought to rebut the presumption of no consent and lack of reasonable belief in consent by referring to an incident earlier in the evening when she had been friendly towards him. The Court of Appeal said that could not count as evidence that she had consented or he reasonably believed she had and so he had not raised an issue and the presumption of no consent and *mens rea* stood.

Under section 75(2)(f) there is an evidential presumption of no consent where 'any person had administered to or caused to be taken by the complainant, without the complainant's consent, a substance which, having regard to when it was administered or taken, was capable of causing or enabling the complainant to be stupefied or overpowered at the time of the relevant act.' This provision clearly deals with cases of drug-assisted rape.[32] It is, however, problematic.[33] The first point to make is that it is very surprising that this is an evidential rather than conclusive presumption. Could there be a scenario in which a defendant gave the victim stupefying drugs without her consent and then had sexual intercourse with her in which it could be said that the victim consented? Maybe yes, where the victim was given a drug which could have been stupefying, but in fact had no effect. However, the fact that the presumption is evidential means that the defendant can seek to claim that the effect of the drug on the victim's consent was negligible and this might involve the jury in difficult questions about the impact of the drug on the victim's mental state. A second concern is that the evidential presumption only arises where the drug is capable of stupefying or overpowering the victim. The problem here is that the drugs used in this kind of offence can have a range of different effects. Some drugs can have the effect of stupefying the victim, but as Emily Finch and Vanessa Munro point out:

> the drugs may reduce the victim's ability to resist sexual advances, render her unable to communicate her wishes regarding intercourse, or engender an uncharacteristic inclination to participate in sexual activity . . . it seems that victims may be induced to agree to intercourse with virtual strangers however uncharacteristic this would be in the absence of the drugs. Moreover, it is likely that they will not appreciate that such behaviour is uncharacteristic, thus, whatever their sober preferences in such matters, they will believe that their consent to intercourse represents their genuine wishes regarding sexual activity at the time.[34]

---

[31] [2011] EWCA Crim 2665.

[32] Despite the press attention to the issue, a study by the Association of Chief Police Officers (2007) found no evidence of widespread use of Rohypnol and very little evidence of use of GBH.

[33] Finch and Munro (2003, 2004, and 2005).

[34] Finch and Munro (2003: 775).

A third issue, and one which may be of the greatest practical significance, is whether alcohol is included within this evidential presumption. It is submitted it certainly should be included. It is a substance which is 'capable of causing or enabling the complainant to be stupefied or overpowered'. Some would be concerned that this throws the net of the presumption too widely. But it should be recalled that the presumption would only apply where the victim is given alcohol without her consent. This leaves open the question of where a victim knows she is drinking alcohol, but the defendant has spiked her drunk to make it more alcoholic than she realizes. Surely this is to administer the extra substance without her consent, but the point might be thought debatable. A fourth point worth emphasizing is that the presumption applies even if it was not the defendant who administered the drugs. Finally, it is worth noting that the presumption applies where the substance is capable of stupefying the victim, it does not need to be shown that the substance actually had that effect.

EXAMINATION TIP

A warning:

Do not think that just because the presumption of no consent in section 75 or 76 does not apply the court must decide that there is consent. For example, if the defendant threatens to burn down the victim's house unless she agrees to sexual intercourse, as a result of which the victim submits to sexual intercourse, there is no threat of violence and so there is no presumption of lack of consent under section 75, but it is still open to the jury to decide that the victim did not consent. All sections 75 and 76 are doing is setting out circumstances under which it will be presumed that there is no consent. It is *not* setting out the only circumstances under which a jury can find there is no consent.

Consent in its general meaning: introduction

If consent is not found using one of the conclusive or evidential presumptions the jury will need to consider whether there is consent under the general meaning. Section 74 states that a person 'consents if he agrees by choice, and has the freedom and capacity to make that choice'. This makes it clear that even if the victim said 'yes', if this was not the result of a free choice then it will not count as consent. →3 (p.468)

Consent in its general meaning: positive consent required

The victim must actively agree to the penetration if it is not to amount to rape.[35] It does not need to be shown that the victim resisted the penetration, or even opposed it. The point is demonstrated by the following cases, decided before the 2003 Act, but which would have been decided in the same way after it:

(1) In *Lartner*[36] the victim was asleep throughout the act of intercourse. Although she had not actively opposed or resisted the sexual intercourse she had not positively consented to it and so the *actus reus* of rape was made out.

---

[35] *R v Malone* [1998] 2 Cr App R 447 (CA).   [36] [1995] Crim LR 75 (CA).

(2) In *Malone*[37] the victim was so drunk she was unaware that the defendant was having sexual intercourse with her, still the *actus reus* of the offence was made out.

Although the fact that consent requires agreement, not just lack of resistance, is important, it should be recalled that the jury must be persuaded beyond reasonable doubt that the victim was not consenting, and so where there is no apparent resistance the prosecution will face a harder job persuading the jury that there was no consent than in a case where the victim made her objections obvious. However, it would be wrong to say that there must be resistance if lack of consent is to be proved.

It is also crucial to appreciate that the consent question is about the victim's state of mind. In *McFall*[38] (a case decided before the 2003 Act came into force), the victim had been kidnapped by the accused, who then indicated that he wished to have sexual intercourse with her. The victim was so terrified he would kill her that she pretended to consent to the intercourse and even 'faked an orgasm'. Even though she may have appeared to an onlooker to consent, the Court of Appeal was able to find the *actus reus* of rape established because it was clear that subjectively (in her mind) the victim did not consent. Of course, whether the victim appeared to consent will be an important question in relation to the *mens rea* question: whether the defendant believed the victim was consenting.

Consent in its general meaning: capacity to consent?

Section 74 makes it clear that in order to be able to consent the victim must have sufficient capacity to consent. For example, a child or an adult suffering from mental illness or learning difficulty may not have the capacity to consent. Several groups of people need to be considered separately:

(1) **Children** The law does not presume that at a particular age a child becomes old enough to be able to consent to sexual penetration. If the child has sufficient maturity and understanding she may be competent to consent. In a case concerning whether an under-16-year-old could validly consent to being given contraceptive advice and treatment[39] the House of Lords held that she could if she was mature enough to understand the issues involved, including the moral ones.[40] The courts are likely to take the same approach in relation to sexual intercourse. It should be noted that even if a child is sufficiently competent to be able to consent, and hence the defendant is not guilty of rape, he may be guilty of one of the other offences under the 2003 Act, such as the rape of a child under the age of 13 under section 5, or one of the abuse of a position of trust offences in sections 16 to 24, which do not require the activities to be without the consent of the victim.[41] Notably the section 5 offence (rape of a child under the age of 13) is committed even if the victim consents and even if the defendant reasonably believes the child to be over 16.[42]

(2) **Mental disorder or learning difficulties** There is a presumption that an adult does have the mental capacity to consent.

---

[37] [1998] 2 CAR 447 (CA).   [38] [1994] Crim LR 226.

[39] *Gillick v West Norfolk and Wisbech Area Health Authority* [1986] AC 112 (HL).

[40] This has become known as *Gillick* competence.

[41] The consent of the victim may be relevant in sentencing (*Attorney-General's Reference (No. 29 of 2008)* [2008] EWCA Crim 2026).

[42] *R v G* [2006] EWCA Crim 821. See Stevenson (2012) for a discussion of the age of consent.

7 SEXUAL OFFENCES | 423

Section 3 of the Mental Capacity Act 2005 states:

(1) . . . a person is unable to make a decision for himself if he is unable—

   (a) to understand the information relevant to the decision,

   (b) to retain that information,

   (c) to use or weigh that information as part of the process of making the decision, or

   (d) to communicate his decision (whether by talking, using sign language or any other means).

A person with a mental disorder (P) might lack capacity to consent to sexual relations either generally because they do not understand what sex is or in the particular circumstances of the case.[43] For example, they might suffer a panic attack, a delusion, or impaired awareness at a particular moment which means they lack the capacity at that point in time.

In *A Local Authority v H*[44] Hedley J listed the following factors a person would need to understand and weigh up in order to be able to consent.

- The 'mechanics of the physical acts'.

- 'That vaginal intercourse may lead to pregnancy'.

- 'Some grasp of sexual health', although that only need be rudimentary and it would 'suffice if a person understands that sexual relations may lead to significant ill-health and that those risks can be reduced by precautions like a condom'.

- Understanding that she does have a choice and that she can refuse.

In *GA*[45] it was accepted this is not a high hurdle, but that is because even for people with capacity, the decision to have sex was 'largely visceral rather than cerebral, and owes more to instinct and emotion rather than to analysis'. It was not appropriate to require those with learning difficulties to make decisions about sex based on a sophisticated intellectual understanding of the issues, when people without capacity issues do not make decisions related to sex on that basis.

Hedley J rejected an argument that the individual had to understand the moral issues involved because there is no societal consensus on what those are. Further he said that the courts would be very wary of finding that because it is thought that P's partner is an inappropriate individual, that P lacked consent.[46] Just because a person with a mental disorder is found to have capacity to consent, it does not, of course, follow they did in fact consent. So the jury should keep separate the questions: did the complainant have the capacity to consent and did the complainant in fact consent? Indeed there is ample abuse of those with psychosocial difficulties and it is important they are protected from sexual exploitation.[47]

(3) **Others who lack capacity** What about other people who may lack capacity? Perhaps the most controversial cases will involve victims who are drunk. There is little difficulty with the victim who is so drunk he or she is unaware of what is happening; clearly such a victim does not consent. What of the victim who is drunk and loudly consents to sexual

43 *D CC v LS* [2010] EWHC 1544 (Fam).

44 [2012] EWHC 49 (COP), criticized in Herring (2013a).   45 [2014] EWCA Crim 299.

46 See Herring (2013a) for a critique of this approach.   47 Benedet and Grant (2014).

intercourse, but whose intoxicated judgment is severely clouded? There is no clear guidance from the case law on this, but presumably the jury would be asked whether the victim's state of mind was sufficiently clear to understand what was happening, consider the issue, and reach a decision.[48] It should be noted that if the defendant has administered a substance to the victim without her consent and this 'stupefies' the victim, then there is an evidential presumption that the victim did not consent under section 75(2)(f). →4 (p.481)

R v Bree
[2007] EWCA Crim 804

Benjamin Bree, a 25-year-old man, went to visit his brother who was a student at University in Bournemouth. There he had an evening with his brother and his brother's friends, including the complainant. They all drank a considerable amount of alcohol. The complainant says she remembers little about walking home with the appellant. Once home she was sick and the appellant and his brother washed her hair. The complainant's evidence was that she remembers nothing after this until regaining consciousness with the appellant engaging in sexual activity with her and there was sexual penetration. She agreed she had not said 'no' but said she had never consented. When interviewed, the appellant accepted that the complainant was intoxicated but said that she was lucid enough to consent. He said she seemed keen and had undressed herself. The jury convicted the appellant and he appealed on the basis that the judge had not made it clear that even though a person is intoxicated she can still consent to sexual activity.

Lord Justice Judge

22. . . . Arguments about consent abound just because consent to sexual intercourse extends from passionate enthusiasm to reluctant or bored acquiescence, and its absence includes quiet submission or surrender as well as determined physical resistance against an attacker which might expose the victim to injury, and sometimes death. The declared objective of the White Paper, *Protecting the Public* (Cm. 5668, 2002) was to produce statutory provisions relating to consent which would be "clear and unambiguous". As enacted, the legislation on this topic has not commanded totally uncritical enthusiasm. For some it goes too far, and for others not far enough. The law in the area, and our decision, must be governed by the definition of consent in section 74.

23. Neither "freedom", nor "capacity", are further defined or explained within section 74 itself, nor indeed in sections 75 and 76, which create evidential presumptions relating to consent. . . .

24. Section 75 and section 76 of the 2003 Act address the issue of consent in practical situations which arise from time to time in cases of alleged sexual offences including rape. They are not, however, exhaustive. The presumptions in section 75 are evidential and rebuttable, whereas those in section 76 are irrebuttable and conclusive. In this appeal we are not concerned with either of the conclusive presumptions relating to consent specified in section 76. The common characteristic of the particular situations covered by the evidential presumptions in section 75 is that they are concerned with situations in which the complainant is involuntarily at a disadvantage. Section 75(2)(f) is plainly adequate to deal with the situation when a drink is "spiked", but unless productive of a state of near unconsciousness, or incapacity,

---

[48] *Lang* (1976) 62 Cr App R 50 (CA).

this paragraph does not address seductive blandishments to have "just one more" drink. Section 75(2)(d) repeats well established common law principles, and acknowledges plain good sense, that, if the complainant is unconscious as a result of her voluntary consumption of alcohol, the starting point is to presume that she is not consenting to intercourse. Beyond that, the Act is silent about the impact of excessive but voluntary alcohol consumption on the ability to give consent to intercourse, or indeed to consent generally.

25. It is perhaps helpful to identify a number of features of the law relating to consent which although obvious are sometimes overlooked. On any view, both parties to the act of sexual intercourse with which this case is concerned were the worse for drink. Both were adults. Neither acted unlawfully in drinking to excess. They were both free to choose how much to drink, and with whom. Both were free, if they wished, to have intercourse with each other. There is nothing abnormal, surprising, or even unusual about men and women having consensual intercourse when one, or other, or both have voluntarily consumed a great deal of alcohol. Provided intercourse is indeed consensual, it is not rape.

26. In cases which are said to arise after voluntary consumption of alcohol the question is not whether the alcohol made either or both less inhibited than they would have been if sober, nor whether either or both might afterwards have regretted what had happened, and indeed wished that it had not. If the complainant consents, her consent cannot be revoked. Moreover it is not a question whether either or both may have had very poor recollection of precisely what had happened. That may be relevant to the reliability of their evidence. Finally, and certainly, it is not a question whether either or both was behaving irresponsibly. As they were both autonomous adults, the essential question for decision is, as it always is, whether the evidence proved that the appellant had sexual intercourse with the complainant without her consent.

. . .

30. We are not aware of any reported decisions which deal with this aspect of the new legislation. We should however refer to the much publicised case of *R v Dougal*, heard in Swansea Crown Court, in November 2005. Having heard the evidence of the complainant, the Crown decided to offer no further evidence. Before the jury counsel for the Crown explained:

> "the prosecution are conscious of the fact that a drunken consent is still a consent and that in the answer, in cross examination, she said, in terms, that she could not remember giving her consent and that is fatal to the prosecution's case. In those circumstances the prosecution will have no further evidence on the issue of consent. This is a case of the word of the defendant against that of the complainant on that feature It is fatal to the prosecution's case . . ."

31. The judge (Roderick Evans J) directed the jury that as the prosecution was no longer seeking a guilty verdict, there was only one verdict which could be returned, and that was an acquittal. He added that he agreed with the course the prosecution had taken.

32. Without knowing all the details of the case, and focusing exclusively on the observations of counsel for the Crown in *Dougal*, it would be open to question whether the inability of the complainant to remember whether she gave her consent or not might on further reflection be approached rather differently. Prosecuting counsel may wish he had expressed himself more felicitously. That said, one of the most familiar directions of law provided to juries who are being asked to conclude that the voluntary consumption of alcohol by a defendant should lead to the conclusion that he was too drunk to form the intention required for proof of the crime alleged against him, is that a drunken intent is still an intent. (*R v Sheehan and Moore* [1975] 60 CAR 308 at 312). So it is, and that we suspect is the source of the phrase

that a "drunken consent is still consent". In the context of consent to intercourse, the phrase lacks delicacy, but, properly understood, it provides a useful shorthand accurately encapsulating the legal position. We note in passing that it also acts as a reminder that a drunken man who intends to commit rape, and does so, is not excused by the fact that his intention is a drunken intention.

33. Some of the hugely critical discussion arising after *Dougal* missed the essential point. Neither counsel for the Crown, nor for that matter the judge, was saying or coming anywhere near saying, either that a complainant who through drink is incapable of consenting to intercourse must nevertheless be deemed to have consented to it, or that a man is at liberty to have sexual intercourse with a woman who happens to be drunk, on the basis that her drunkenness deprives her of her right to choose whether to have intercourse or not. Such ideas are wrong in law, and indeed, offensive. All that was being said in *Dougal* was that when someone who has had a lot to drink is in fact consenting to intercourse, then that is what she is doing, consenting: equally, if after taking drink, she is not consenting, then by definition intercourse is taking place without her consent. This is unexceptionable.

34. In our judgment, the proper construction of section 74 of the 2003 Act, as applied to the problem now under discussion, leads to clear conclusions. If, through drink (or for any other reason) the complainant has temporarily lost her capacity to choose whether to have intercourse on the relevant occasion, she is not consenting, and subject to questions about the defendant's state of mind, if intercourse takes place, this would be rape. However, where the complainant has voluntarily consumed even substantial quantities of alcohol, but nevertheless remains capable of choosing whether or not to have intercourse, and in drink agrees to do so, this would not be rape. We should perhaps underline that, as a matter of practical reality, capacity to consent may evaporate well before a complainant becomes unconscious. Whether this is so or not, however, is fact specific, or more accurately, depends on the actual state of mind of the individuals involved on the particular occasion.

35. Considerations like these underline the fact that it would be unrealistic to endeavour to create some kind of grid system which would enable the answer to these questions to be related to some prescribed level of alcohol consumption. Experience shows that different individuals have a greater or lesser capacity to cope with alcohol than others, and indeed the ability of a single individual to do so may vary from day to day. The practical reality is that there are some areas of human behaviour which are inapt for detailed legislative structures. In this context, provisions intended to protect women from sexual assaults might very well be conflated into a system which would provide patronising interference with the right of autonomous adults to make personal decisions for themselves.

36. For these reasons, notwithstanding criticisms of the statutory provisions, in our view the 2003 Act provides a clear definition of "consent" for the purposes of the law of rape, and by defining it with reference to "capacity to make that choice", sufficiently addresses the issue of consent in the context of voluntary consumption of alcohol by the complainant. The problems do not arise from the legal principles. They lie with infinite circumstances of human behaviour, usually taking place in private without independent evidence, and the consequent difficulties of proving this very serious offence.

. . .

42. In short, the only specific feature of the complainant's alcohol consumption identified by the judge was its possible relevance to her reliability as a witness. Beyond that, if the jury were able to derive anything from what the judge said, it was vague in the extreme. The context, after all, was that although the appellant conceded that the complainant had been drunk, it was a fundamental part of his defence that she was conscious throughout and did in fact consent to sexual activities and intercourse with him. From the defence point of view,

the drink she had consumed was a factor which may have led her to behave in a way which, if sober, she would not. She had drunk far more that she was accustomed to. This critical aspect of the case was not sufficiently addressed in the summing up, indeed it was not addressed at all. The questions whether she might have behaved differently drunk than she would have done sober, and whether, although and perhaps because drunk, she might have behaved as the appellant contended, and the way in which the jury should consider these important issues, were not mentioned at all.

Appeal allowed.

As a result of this decision it is for the jury to decide whether or not the victim consented to the sexual penetration, even though she was drunk.[49] The court clearly accepts that a person can be pretty intoxicated, but still have sufficient capacity to consent to sexual penetration. However, it should not be thought that, as a result of this case, if the victim is so intoxicated she cannot remember what happened that she should be taken to consent. In *R v H*[50] a judge stopped a trial after the prosecution evidence showed that the victim was extremely intoxicated at the time of the intercourse. She had little recollection of what had happened, but was clear she would not have consented to sexual intercourse with a stranger. There was clear medical evidence that the defendant had had sexual intercourse with the victim (despite his initial denials). The judge held that there was insufficient evidence that the victim had not consented. The Court of Appeal (on an appeal by the prosecution) held that the trial should not have stopped:

Issues of consent and capacity to consent to intercourse in cases of alleged rape should normally be left to the jury to determine. It would be a rare case indeed where it would be appropriate for a judge to stop a case in which, on one view, a 16 year old girl, alone at night and vulnerable through drink, is picked up by a stranger who has sex with her within minutes of meeting her and she says repeatedly she would not have consented to sex in these circumstances.[51]

The Court of Appeal emphasized that *Bree*[52] had not held that where a victim could not remember what had happened a prosecution could not take place. In *Wright*,[53] the complainant's evidence was that she was so intoxicated she was unconscious. The Court of Appeal held that the judge was entitled not to give a detailed direction on consent because if her evidence was accepted there was no doubt that there was no consent.[54] A final point to remember is that just because the jury conclude that the victim was not so intoxicated that she was unable to consent, does not mean that the victim did in fact consent.

Consent in its general meaning: consent provided through pressure

What if the victim has appeared to agree to sexual intercourse, but only out of fear? Many cases of consent provided through fear will be dealt with under the evidential presumption under section 75(2). But if the case is not, the general meaning of consent must be considered. In section 74 it is emphasized that the agreement must be by choice and the choice must be a free one.

---

[49] See the discussion in Wallerstein (2009).   [50] [2007] EWCA Crim 2056.
[51] *Ibid*, para. 34.   [52] [2007] EWCA Crim 804.   [53] *R v Wright* [2007] EWCA Crim 3473.
[54] *R v Kamki* [2013] EWCA Crim 2335.

The leading case under the law on 'consent', prior to the 2003 Act, after threats is the following. It is likely that the courts in interpreting section 74 will follow its approach:

R v Olugboja
[1982] QB 320 (CA)

The defendant and the co-accused L met the complainant and K at a discotheque and offered to take them home. In fact they drove them to L's bungalow. The complainants refused to go in and began to walk away. The defendant went into the bungalow but L followed the girls and raped the complainant in the car. The three returned to the bungalow where L dragged K into a bedroom. The defendant then told the complainant that he was going to have intercourse with her. She told him what had happened in the car and asked him to leave her alone. He told her to take off her trousers. She did and he had intercourse with her. The defendant, who admitted having sexual intercourse with the complainant, was charged with rape. The judge directed the jury that, although the complainant had neither screamed nor struggled, and no direct threat had been made towards her, it was open to them to decide that she had submitted, rather than consented, to the sexual intercourse. The defendant was convicted and appealed.

Lord Justice Dunn [reading the judgment of the court]

The question of law raised by this appeal is whether to constitute the offence of rape it is necessary for the consent of the victim of sexual intercourse to be vitiated by force, the fear of force, or fraud; or whether it is sufficient to prove that in fact the victim did not consent.

. . .

Mrs. Trewella [counsel for the defendant] accepted that submission by the victim did not necessarily involve consent, but the submission must be induced because of fear of violence: see *Reg. v. Day*, 9 C. & P. 722. She submitted that moral or economic pressure or even blackmail causing a woman to submit to sexual intercourse could never be enough to found a charge of rape. Otherwise she said the film producer who induced an actress to have sexual intercourse by telling her she would not get a part in his new film if she did not, or the man who induced a woman to have sexual intercourse by telling her that if she did not he would tell her fiancé that she had been a prostitute, would be guilty of rape. . . .

Mrs. Trewella submitted that just as the law limits the circumstances in which any person may say he has acted involuntarily owing to duress, which involves threats of death or violence to that person or a close relative, so it is consistent that the common law has limited the circumstances in which a woman who has had sexual intercourse may say that the act was not consensual.

Mrs. Trewella submitted finally that to say, as the judge did, that any constraint upon Jayne's will could negative consent constituted a misdirection. The word 'constraint' includes moral as well as physical pressure and moral pressure is not enough. Even to tell a girl that she would not be taken home until she had sexual intercourse, in the absence of any threat of violence expressed or implied, would not vitiate her consent.

[**Dunn LJ** went on to consider some earlier cases and the history of the Sexual Offences Act 1956.]

Accordingly in so far as the *actus reus* is concerned the question now is simply: 'At the time of the sexual intercourse did the woman consent to it?' It is not necessary for the prosecution to prove that what might otherwise appear to have been consent was in reality merely submission induced by force, fear or fraud, although one or more of these factors will no doubt be present in the majority of cases of rape.

We do not agree, as was suggested by Mrs. Trewella, that once this is fully realised there will be a large increase in prosecutions for rape. Nor, on the other hand, do we agree with Mr. Brent's submission, on behalf of the Crown, that it is sufficient for a trial judge merely to leave the issue of consent to a jury in a similar way to that in which the issue of dishonesty is left in trials for offences under the Theft Act 1968. In such cases it is sufficient to direct the jury that 'dishonest' is an easily understood English word and it is for them to say whether a particular transaction is properly so described or not. Although 'consent' is an equally common word it covers a wide range of states of mind in the context of intercourse between a man and a woman, ranging from actual desire on the one hand to reluctant acquiescence on the other. We do not think that the issue of consent should be left to a jury without some further direction. What this should be will depend on the circumstances of each case. The jury will have been reminded of the burden and standard of proof required to establish each ingredient, including lack of consent, of the offence. They should be directed that consent, or the absence of it, is to be given its ordinary meaning and if need be, by way of example, that there is a difference between consent and submission; every consent involves a submission, but it by no means follows that a mere submission involves consent: per Coleridge J. in *Reg. v. Day*, 9 C. & P. 722, 724. In the majority of cases, where the allegation is that the intercourse was had by force or the fear of force, such a direction coupled with specific references to, and comments on, the evidence relevant to the absence of real consent will clearly suffice. In the less common type of case where intercourse takes place after threats not involving violence or the fear of it, as in the examples given by Mrs. Trewella to which we have referred earlier in this judgment, we think that an appropriate direction to a jury will have to be fuller. They should be directed to concentrate on the state of mind of the victim immediately before the act of sexual intercourse, having regard to all the relevant circumstances; and in particular, the events leading up to the act and her reaction to them showing their impact on her mind. Apparent acquiescence after penetration does not necessarily involve consent, which must have occurred before the act takes place. In addition to the general direction about consent which we have outlined, the jury will probably be helped in such cases by being reminded that in this context consent does comprehend the wide spectrum of states of mind to which we earlier referred, and that the dividing line in such circumstances between real consent on the one hand and mere submission on the other may not be easy to draw. Where it is to be drawn in a given case is for the jury to decide, applying their combined good sense, experience and knowledge of human nature and modern behaviour to all the relevant facts of that case.

Looked at in this way we find no misdirection by the judge in this case.

Appeal dismissed.

It is crucial to appreciate the width of the decision. It is clear that a victim's apparent consent can be negated by a threat, even if the threat is not of death or serious injury. What the jury must focus on is not the nature of the threat (how much violence was threatened) but the effect of the threat (how great was its effect). The jury must decide, given the effect of the threat, whether the victim was consenting to the penetration. Reluctant acquiescence amounts to consent; submission does not. The distinction is not always easy to draw. In *Doyle*,[55] Pitchford LJ stated:

---

[55] [2010] EWCA Crim 119.

> there are circumstances in which the jury may well require assistance as to the distinction to be drawn between reluctant but free exercise of choice on the one hand, especially in the context of a long term and loving relationship, and unwilling submission to demand in fear of more adverse consequences from refusal on the other.[56]

It should be re-emphasized that the question is subjective to the victim. The focus is not on what the defendant did or threatened, but, rather, the state of mind of the victim.[57] In *Olugboja* the defendant did not actually utter any threat: what was crucial was that the victim regarded his conduct as threatening; such that she did not truly consent. In fact, a victim could interpret a defendant's actions to be so threatening that she was not truly consenting, even though the defendant did not mean to be threatening.[58]

In *R v W*[59] the trial judge had directed the jury to consider: 'Was the complainant freely consenting to sexual intercourse or was she submitting to a demand that she felt unable to resist.' This, Burnett LJ held, was not consistent with the law because:

> It is possible for a person to submit to a demand which he or she feels unable to resist, but without lacking the capacity or freedom to make a choice. That is an example of reluctant consent.

This is a surprising comment and it is not explained further in the judgment. If someone feels they are unable to resist, it is not obvious they have the 'freedom to make the choice' which is required to have consent under section 74. Perhaps the best reading of the *dicta* is that Burnett LJ was saying that a person may *feel* compelled to make a choice, but in fact they have freedom. Just as a person who says 'I have just got to have some ice cream', does not mean they really do not have a choice.

As we shall see in Part II there has been much academic discussion whether a threat not to provide a benefit (as opposed to a threat to cause harm) can vitiate consent. Some commentators take the view that consent following an offer can, in unusual circumstances, be an invalid consent. They reject the view that a sharp distinction between threats and offers can be drawn. Many commentators have discussed whether the film director has committed rape if he has sexual intercourse with an out-of-work actress to whom he has said 'I will only give you a leading role if you agree to sexual intercourse with me.' →5 (p.479) The following case gives some indication of how the courts will deal with such situations:

R v Kirk
[2008] EWCA Crim 434

The victim, aged 14, had run away from home and was sleeping rough. She was tired, dirty, hungry, and had nowhere to go. She went to the appellant's minicab office seeking help. Although the appellant had previously abused her she hoped he would help her.

---

[56] [2010] EWCA Crim 119, para. 21.

[57] See the discussion in *Wellard* (1978) 67 Cr App R 364, 368 of a case where a man was convicted of rape after pretending to be a security officer and pressuring a girl into having sexual intercourse with him. He threatened to tell the girl's parents that she had been having sexual intercourse with her boyfriend.

[58] In such a case the *mens rea* may be hard to prove.   [59] [2015] EWCA Crim 559.

The appellant offered to give her £3.25 if she agreed to sexual intercourse. She agreed and later used the money to buy food. He was convicted of rape and appealed.

Lord Justice Pill

91. We have considered the judge's use of the expression "willing submission" on two occasions. He stated:

> "Just where the line is to be drawn between real consent and submission, albeit willing submission, may not be easy to draw, but the law leaves it to juries who have heard all the evidence of the witnesses to say where the line is to be drawn and whether in any case lack of consent is proved".

That was followed by the further direction:

> "Therefore, I will leave it to you to draw that line. Was it consent or was it submission and therefore not consent?"

92. The expression "willing submission" is not an easy one in this context. Willingness is usually associated with consent. However, we are satisfied that the jury would not, in the context of this very full direction, have been misled by the use of the word "willing". This was not a case where it was alleged that submission had been achieved by physical force. It was willing in the sense that there was no attempt at physical resistance by the complainant and the judge used it in that sense. That leaves open the possibility that the circumstances were such that the complainant submitted to sexual intercourse rather than consented to it. That was the overall effect of the direction. We are satisfied that, having regard to the full direction given, the jury would not have been misled or distracted, by the use of the expression "willing submission", from the question they were told they had to answer. It is not, however, an expression we would commend for use on other occasions.

Appeal dismissed.

This case suggests that the courts are willing to accept that there can be circumstances in which 'an offer' to have sexual intercourse in exchange for some benefit will be regarded as such that there is no genuine consent. The jury should look at all of the pressures facing the victim and the broad circumstances in deciding whether there could be said to be freedom to make a choice.

Consent in its general meaning: consent provided through grooming

There is increasing acknowledgement that vulnerable people have been sexually exploited through grooming.

In *R v Robinson*[60] Elias LJ stated:

> Grooming is not a term of art, but it suggests cynical and manipulative behaviour designed to achieve a particular sexual objective. Not all relationships with underage children can fairly be characterised as involving grooming, although many will. But even where they can, the fact of grooming plainly does not necessarily vitiate consent. Many a seducer achieves his objectives with the liberal and cynical employment of gifts, insincere compliments and false

---

[60] *R v Robinson* [2011] EWCA Crim 916, para. 21.

promises. But such manipulative and deceitful methods could not be relied upon to establish a lack of consent whenever the seduction was successful. The situation will often be no different where the complainant is under age. But where the exploitation is of a girl who is of an age where she does not, or may not, have the capacity to understand the full significance of what she is doing, and in particular, where, as here, there was evidence of acquiescence or acceptance rather than positive consent, we think that, as the judge found, it would be open to the jury to conclude that the complainant, perhaps out of embarrassment or some other reason, had in reality unwillingly gone along with the acts which she did not in fact wish to engage in.

There are particular offences which are designed to tackle the problem. However, the courts have also considered cases of rape, where it is said the victim consented, but as a result of grooming. In *Ali*[61] the Court of Appeal explained 'where there is evidence of exploitation of a young and immature person who may not understand the full significance of what he or she is doing, that is a factor the jury can take into account in deciding whether or not there was genuine consent.' They went on to say in such a case the victim might appear to comply with a request for sex, but that might 'mask the lack of true consent'.

In *Ali*[62] Fulford LJ explained further when grooming may negate consent:

One of the consequences of grooming is that it has a tendency to limit or subvert the alleged victim's capacity to make free decisions, and it creates the risk that he or she simply submitted because of the environment of dependency created by those responsible for treating the alleged victim in this way. Indeed, the individual may have been manipulated to the extent that he or she is unaware of, or confused about, the distinction between acquiescence and genuine agreement at the time the incident occurred.

Consent in its general meaning: conditional consent

In some cases the victim will have given conditional consent to sex. They consent to sex, but only if X. In such a case if X is not present there is no consent. For example, in *Assange v Swedish Prosecution Authority*[63] it was accepted that if a woman agreed to have sex if the man wore a condom and the man then deliberately penetrated her without a condom, the jury could decide this was done without consent. Quite simply he had done an act to which she had not consented. One can readily imagine other examples of where this line of reasoning may apply: the victim consents to sex with the man, on condition he is not infected with an STD or is unmarried. In such cases the infected man or married man who has sex with the woman would, following *Assange*, be guilty of rape.

Consent in its general meaning: mistaken consent

Where the defendant has deceived the victim as to the nature and purpose of the act the conclusive presumption under section 76 will apply. As we have seen the recent cases have interpreted that provision strictly. So cases involving mistakes and deceptions will most likely be considered under section 74. In particular where the victim is mistaken about the

---

[61] [2015] EWCA Crim 1279.   [62] *Ibid.*   [63] [2011] EWHC 2849 (Admin).

act it may be questioned whether or not she had the freedom or capacity to consent to the act, or indeed whether she had consented to the act the defendant did at all.

One important issue is that under section 74 the question is about the victim's state of mind, not what the defendant did. So the question is whether the mistake of the victim is such as to mean there was no proper consent. It does not matter whether the victim's mistake was as a result of what the defendant did or something else.

The cases to date have made it clear that a jury may decide that the victim did not consent under the general meaning even if the mistake is not one as to the 'nature or purpose of the act'. Indeed in *Jheeta*[64] and *B*[65] the courts were clear that the deceptions could negate consent under section 74, even though they did not fall into section 76. So, it is clear even if the mistake does not relate to the 'nature or purpose' of the act, as understood in section 76, the mistake may still mean the victim did not have the freedom and capacity to consent.

It seems the central question is how important the mistake was to the decision for the victim in question. If, for them, this issue was central to their decision to have sex, then being deceived about it or mistaken about it would mean they lacked consent.

The following cases are two controversial examples:

R (F) v Director of Public Prosecutions
[2013] EWHC 945 (Admin)

A woman sought judicial review of the decision of the DPP not to prosecute her former partner for rape or sexual assault. The woman claimed that her partner had agreed not to ejaculate inside her during intercourse, but in fact he did. The CPS and DPP refused to prosecute on the basis that even if her evidence was entirely accepted by the jury it did not constitute rape or sexual assault.

The Lord Chief Justice

24. We must emphasise that we are not addressing the situation in which sexual intercourse occurs consensually when the man, intending to withdraw in accordance with his partner's wishes, or their understanding, nevertheless ejaculates prematurely, or accidentally, within rather than outside his partner's vagina. These things happen. They always have and they always will, and no offence is committed when they do. They underline why withdrawal is not a safe method of contraception. Equally we are not addressing the many fluctuating ways in which sexual relationships may develop, as couples discover and renew their own levels of understanding and tolerance, their codes of communication, express or understood, and mutual give and take, experimentation and excitement. These are intensely private matters, personal to the couple in question.

. . .

26. In law, the question which arises is whether this factual structure can give rise to a conviction for rape. Did the claimant consent to this penetration? She did so, provided, in the language of s.74 of the 2003 Act, she agreed by choice, when she had the freedom and capacity to make the choice. What *Assange* underlines is that "choice" is crucial to the issue of "consent", and indeed we underline that the statutory definition of consent provided in s.74 applies equally to s.1(1)(c) as it does to s.1(1)(b). The evidence relating to "choice" and the "freedom" to make any particular choice must be approached in a broad commonsense way.

---

[64] [2007] EWCA Crim 1699.   [65] [2013] EWCA Crim 823.

If before penetration began the intervener had made up his mind that he would penetrate and ejaculate within the claimant's vagina, or even, because "penetration is a continuing act from entry to withdrawal" (see s.79(2) of the 2003 Act) he decided that he would not withdraw at all, just because he deemed the claimant subservient to his control, she was deprived of choice relating to the crucial feature on which her original consent to sexual intercourse was based. Accordingly her consent was negated. Contrary to her wishes, and knowing that she would not have consented, and did not consent to penetration or the continuation of penetration if she had any inkling of his intention, he deliberately ejaculated within her vagina. In law, this combination of circumstances falls within the statutory definition of rape.

27. The entire body of evidence, both in relation to the nature and history of the relationship between these two people, and as it applies to each of the individual, specific occasions of complaint, requires re-examination in the light of these observations. This decision should be reviewed in the light of the legal principles explained in this judgment. This is an appropriate case in which to order a judicial review.

R v McNally
[2013] EWCA Crim 1051

The defendant was convicted of assault by penetration. The defendant met the victim (X) online when the victim was 12 and the defendant 13. The defendant claimed to be a boy. The relationship developed and X believed the defendant to be her boyfriend. The defendant orally and digitally penetrated X. When X discovered that the defendant was a girl she notified the police and was prosecuted for assault by penetration. The pre-sentence report disclosed that the defendant had a history of confusion around her gender identity. Three years' detention was imposed as the sentence. She appealed primarily on the basis that a deception as to identity could not negate consent. The case was not argued on the basis of a conclusive presumption but simply on whether or not there was consent for the purpose of section 74.

Lord Justice Leveson

23. The case for the Crown was that M's consent was obtained by fraudulent deception that the appellant was a male and that had she known the truth, she would not have consented to acts of vaginal penetration. Mr Wainwright argues that deception as to gender cannot vitiate consent; in the same way deception as to age, marital status, wealth or, following EB, HIV status being deceptions as to qualities or attributes cannot vitiate consent. Thus, he submits that Assange and R(F) can be distinguished as the deceptions in those cases were not deceptions as to qualities or attributes but as to the features of the act itself.

24. We reject this analysis. First and foremost, EB was not saying that HIV status could not vitiate consent if, for example, the complainant had been positively assured that the defendant was not HIV positive: it left the issue open. As Mr McGuinness for the Crown contends, the argument that in Assange and R(F) the deceptions were as to the features of the act is not sustainable: the wearing of a condom and ejaculation are irrelevant to the definition of rape and are not 'features' of the offence and no such rationale is suggested. In the last two cases, it was alleged that the victim had consented on the basis of a premise that, at the time of the consent, was false (namely, in one case, that her partner would wear a condom and, in the second, that he would ejaculate outside her body).

25. In reality, some deceptions (such as, for example, in relation to wealth) will obviously not be sufficient to vitiate consent. In our judgment, Lord Judge's observation that "the evidence relating to 'choice' and the 'freedom' to make any particular choice must be approached in a broad commonsense way" identifies the route through the dilemma.

26. Thus while, in a physical sense, the acts of assault by penetration of the vagina are the same whether perpetrated by a male or a female, the sexual nature of the acts is, on any common sense view, different where the complainant is deliberately deceived by a defendant into believing that the latter is a male. Assuming the facts to be proved as alleged, M chose to have sexual encounters with a boy and her preference (her freedom to choose whether or not to have a sexual encounter with a girl) was removed by the appellant's deception.

27. It follows from the foregoing analysis that we conclude that, depending on the circumstances, deception as to gender can vitiate consent.

Two issues in particular are worth emphasizing about these decisions. The first is that the question is not whether the mistake related to an issue which most people would think was important, but rather whether the mistake was important to the victim. Many people would not mind about the birth sex of their partner or do not mind if their partner ejaculates inside them. For such people mistakes as to these matters will not negate consent. In these two cases those matters were said to be important to the victims and the courts accepted that to be mistaken as to them meant there was no consent. This means we cannot answer the abstract question 'what kinds of mistake negate consent' because it all depends on what issues were important for the victim themselves. Where the issue is so important that they would not have consented had they known the truth, they were not giving informed consent to the sex.

The second is that the *mens rea* is key in these cases. One can imagine a case where a victim was mistaken about an important issue, say the religion of her partner, but he was not aware that religion mattered to her. In such a case the defendant would not be guilty of rape, because he would lack the *mens rea*. It is interesting to note in *R (F) v DPP*[66] that the court emphasized that the defendant knew the victim would not have allowed him to penetrate her had she known he planned to ejaculate. He clearly had the *mens rea*.

A third point relates to *McNally*, which is a problematic case. The presentation of the facts by the court is questionable. Was McNally male or female? It was assumed that McNally deceived the victim, but it is not clear how. It was also assumed that the victim minded what birth sex McNally was, although there was no clear evidence as to that.

QUESTIONS

1. The Court of Appeal in *McAllister* [1997] Crim LR 233 suggests that only if improper pressure is used by the defendant may it negate the victim's consent. Can it ever be proper to put pressure on another to engage in sexual intercourse? Would the law have greater certainty if, rather than considering the effect of the threat on the victim, it considered the propriety of the defendant's actions?

2. Max knows that his girlfriend Bertha is emotionally unstable. She does not want to have sexual intercourse until they are married. He threatens to end the relationship

---

[66] [2013] EWHC 945 (Admin).

> unless Bertha agrees to sexual intercourse. Bertha, terrified at the possibility of the ending of the relationship, agrees to sexual intercourse. Is Max guilty of rape?
>
> 3. Tricia suggests to her boyfriend Simon that they have sexual intercourse as an expression of their undying love. Simon agrees, even though he has fallen in love with someone else and is simply engaging in sex for carnal pleasure. Is this rape?

1.5 *MENS REA*: AN INTENT TO PENETRATE

As we saw earlier, section 1 of the Sexual Offences Act 2003 sets out the *mens rea* for rape. There are two elements. First, we will discuss the requirement that the defendant must intend to penetrate. Section 1 opens:

> (1) A person (A) commits an offence if—
>
> (a) he intentionally penetrates the vagina, anus or mouth of another person (B) with his penis, . . .

The *mens rea* aspect of this will only rarely arise in a rape case. If the defendant claims that he did not intend to penetrate the victim it is unlikely that this will be believed. Sexual penetration is not something that is done by accident.[67] Although it seems there have been cases where a defendant has persuaded a jury that he had sexual intercourse with the victim while he was asleep.[68] One case which is perhaps in doubt is where the defendant intended to engage in vaginal intercourse, but in fact engaged in anal intercourse.[69] It is submitted that as both are the form of *actus reus* of the offence, an intent to penetrate either orifice is sufficient.

1.6 *MENS REA*: THE DEFENDANT DOES NOT REASONABLY BELIEVE THAT THE VICTIM CONSENTS

Section 1 of the Sexual Offences Act 2003 goes on to state the second element of the *mens rea*:

> (1)(c) A does not reasonably believe that B consents.
>
> (2) Whether a belief is reasonable is to be determined having regard to all the circumstances, including any steps A has taken to ascertain whether B consents.

Section 1 makes it clear that the defendant will have the *mens rea* if he has any state of mind apart from one in which he reasonably believes that the victim consents. This includes any of the following three states of mind:

(1) He knows the victim does not consent.

---

[67] If a couple agreed to have a naked cuddle, but not engage in sexual intercourse, it might be possible for there to be accidental penetration.

[68] BBC News Online (2008d).

[69] It seems this is not that uncommon (Norfolk (2005) found 10 per cent of women in a survey said it had happened to them).

(2) He gives no thought to whether the victim consented. This would cover a case where the defendant had decided to engage in sexual penetration of the victim whatever her wishes and therefore gave no thought to whether the victim consented.

(3) He otherwise does not reasonably believe the victim consents. This may cover a case where the defendant does consider whether the victim consents, but simply does not care whether or not she does. Or he believes the victim is consenting but does not have reasonable grounds for his belief.

The Sexual Offences Act 2003 sets out certain circumstances in which it will be presumed that the defendant knew that the victim did not consent. We have come across these already in considering the meaning of consent:

(1) Under section 75(1) if the defendant knew that any of the circumstances listed in section 75(2) were present then 'the defendant is taken not to have reasonably believed that the complainant consented unless sufficient evidence is adduced to raise an issue as to whether to reasonably believe it.'[70] Section 75(2) includes where the victim was asleep at the time of the act or where violence had been used against the victim. It should be noted that these are evidentiary presumptions. It is therefore open to the defendant to show that he did reasonably believe that the victim consented. For example, he could try to argue that even though he knew the victim had been subjected to violence immediately before the penetration he reasonably believed that she was consenting.

(2) Under section 76 if the defendant had intentionally deceived the victim as to the nature or purpose of the act, or had impersonated a person known to the victim, then he is presumed not to believe that the victim consented to the act. This is a conclusive presumption.

Section 1 invites the jury to consider whether a reasonable person would believe that the victim was consenting. This asks the jury to imagine a reasonable person in the defendant's shoes: would he believe that the victim is consenting? If the reasonable person would not believe that the victim is consenting the defendant cannot claim to have a reasonable belief that the victim is consenting. In some cases (e.g. where the victim is ferociously resisting) it will be obvious that a reasonable person would not believe that the victim is consenting. Other cases may be more ambiguous (e.g. where the victim is being simply passive in the face of the defendant's 'advances') or the victim appears to keep changing his or her mind on the issue of consent to sexual activity. It should be noted that the question is not 'would the reasonable person think the victim might be consenting', but rather 'would the reasonable person believe the victim is consenting'. So if the reasonable person would conclude, 'I think the victim is consenting, but I am not at all sure' then arguably the defendant cannot have a reasonable *belief* that the victim consented.

Under section 1(2), in deciding whether a belief is reasonable, the jury should consider all the circumstances including any steps the defendant has taken in ascertaining whether the victim consents. *Protecting the Public*, the government White Paper which preceded the Act, suggests that in deciding whether a reasonable person would have a doubt:

> The jury would . . . have to take into account the actions of both parties, the circumstances in which they have placed themselves and the level of responsibility exercised by both.[71]

---

[70] Sexual Offences Act 2003, s. 75(1).   [71] Home Office (2002: 17).

The jury is also likely to consider issues such as: How long have the defendant and victim known each other? Have they had a sexual relationship in the past? Have they discussed the possibility of sexual relations? Of course, the jury will be careful not to assume that because someone consented to sexual relations in the past that this means they have consented to sexual relations in the future.

The statute asks the jury to consider whether the defendant had reasonable grounds to believe the victim consented. A case could arise where the defendant was having sex with A, believing the person to be B. If the defendant had reasonable grounds to believe that B would consent, but did not have reasonable grounds to believe that A would consent, would the defendant be guilty of rape?[72] It is submitted that the correct question would be whether the defendant had reasonable grounds to believe that A was B, he would then reasonably believe that the victim was consenting, but if he did not have reasonable grounds for his mistake then he would have reasonable grounds to believe that there was consent.

One issue which the courts will need in due course to resolve is whether in deciding whether the defendant's belief that the victim consented was reasonable the jury should take into account the characteristics of the defendant and, if so, which characteristics. *Protecting the Public* states, ' "Reasonable" will be judged by reference to what an objective third party would think in the circumstances.' The Court of Appeal in the following case has provided strong, albeit *obiter*, support for that view:

R v B
[2013] EWCA Crim 3

B was convicted of raping his partner. Expert evidence suggested B was a paranoid schizophrenic. This caused him to have delusional beliefs. In particular he believed he had 'sexual healing powers', meaning that by having sex with someone he could make them better. On the occasion in question he told the victim he would make her better by having sexual intercourse with her. The victim objected, but he persisted. The central question was whether in deciding whether his belief in consent was reasonable the jury should take into account the defendant's mental condition and beliefs.

Lord Justice Hughes

34. On the facts of this case, we do not think that in the end the issue arises. The evidence of Dr Volkanskaia was that the defendant's illness did *not* affect his ability to understand whether or not his partner was saying no. This was not a case where the issue was whether he might, through illness, have misunderstood subtle social signals which a man without his illness would not have misunderstood. The fact that Mr Spence skilfully elicited the evidence that he had an impaired ability to interpret events normally does not alter that position. He clearly did, at the very least at the time of these events, have such an impaired ability; his delusions that he was a healer with special powers and that he was being poisoned, and perhaps that his partner was taking an improper interest in other men, were all examples of his not interpreting events normally. Dr Volkanskaia's evidence, assuming it were accepted, certainly left it as a possibility that he believed that he had good reason to

---

[72] The issue was raised but not resolved in *Attorney-General's Reference (No. 79 of 2006)* [2007] 1 Cr App R (S) 752.

oblige his partner to have intercourse with him, either because he believed it would heal her or because he believed she had been consorting with other men and he was irrationally jealous of her. But what Dr Volkanskaia was *not* saying was that his illness would or might have led him to think that his partner was consenting when she was not. She was saying the reverse. In the face of that evidence, and in the absence of any account from the defendant suggesting misunderstanding, Mr Spence's submission to us that he may not have understood that the complainant was frightened and thus thought that her submission was consent can only be mere speculation. For these reasons alone, the convictions for rape in the present case cannot be considered to be unsafe.

35. If, however, we are wrong about that, and the defendant's delusional beliefs could have led him to believe that his partner consented when she did not, we take the clear view that such delusional beliefs cannot in law render reasonable a belief that his partner was consenting when in fact she was not. The Act does not ask whether it was reasonable (in the sense of being understandable or not his fault) for the defendant to suffer from the mental condition which he did. Normally no doubt, absent at least fault such as self-induced intoxication by drink or drugs, the answer to that in the case of acute illness such as this defendant seems to have suffered will be that it is reasonable. What the answer would be if the condition were an anti-social, borderline or psychopathic personality disorder may be more problematic. But the Act asks a different question: whether the belief in consent was a reasonable one. A delusional belief in consent, if entertained, would be by definition irrational and thus *un*reasonable, not reasonable. If such delusional beliefs were capable of being described as reasonable, then the more irrational the belief of the defendant the better would be its prospects of being held reasonable. The possible condition of the defendant in *MM* (supra at [27]) may afford an example. It seems that he may have been suffering from a bi-polar affective disorder which disinhibited him and made him grossly impulsive. He apparently believed that he was entitled to have intercourse with his former girlfriend despite her objections because those objections were, to him, invalid. If, instead, he had believed, for the same reason, that she consented, the question would have arisen whether his belief was reasonable. Similarly, the beliefs of a sexual predator that all to whom he is sexually attracted welcome his attentions may be attributable to mental disorder, whether correctly labelled a personality disorder or otherwise, and whether susceptible to any form of treatment or not. So may the beliefs of those who excessively idealise or excessively devalue their partners—sometimes swinging abruptly from the one to the other.

36. Both the common law and statute law are well used to a rule which judges a defendant by his subjective state of mind. So, for example, in a case where self defence is at issue, the defendant is to be judged according to the facts as he genuinely believed them to be, whether his belief was reasonable or not, at least unless it was attributable to voluntary intoxication. Criminal damage, which arises also in the present case, is not committed if the defendant honestly believes he had (or would have had) the consent of the owner of the property damaged to do what he did, even if that belief was unreasonable. But the decisive indication as to the law of rape is, we think, that the Sexual Offences Act 2003 deliberately departs from this model. It deliberately does not make genuine belief in consent enough. The belief must not only be genuinely held; it must also be reasonable in all the circumstances. This was a conscious departure from the former law. Under the former law, a genuine belief in consent (reasonable or not) was a complete defence to rape; the reasonableness of the belief was material only as a factor to be considered *en route* to the decision whether it was genuinely held: see the Sexual Offences (Amendment) Act 1976.

...

40. We conclude that unless and until the state of mind amounts to insanity in law, then under the rule enacted in the Sexual Offences Act beliefs in consent arising from conditions such as delusional psychotic illness or personality disorders must be judged by objective standards of reasonableness and not by taking into account a mental disorder which induced a belief which could not reasonably arise without it. The defendant's mental condition, and its impact on his behaviour, is of course extremely relevant to sentence. If punishment is inappropriate, a non-custodial sentence may result when otherwise there would have been a substantial sentence of imprisonment, and whether a hospital order is needed by the time of trial or not. In other cases it may significantly mitigate the punishment required. In yet others, it may result in a substantial custodial sentence recognising the danger which the defendant presents.

41. It does not follow that there will not be cases in which the personality or abilities of the defendant may be relevant to whether his positive belief in consent was reasonable. It may be that cases could arise in which the reasonableness of such belief depends on the reading by the defendant of subtle social signals, and in which his impaired ability to do so is relevant to the reasonableness of his belief. We do not attempt exhaustively to foresee the circumstances which might arise in which a belief might be held which is not in any sense irrational, even though most people would not have held it. Whether (for example) a particular defendant of less than ordinary intelligence or with demonstrated inability to recognise behavioural cues might be such a case, or whether his belief ought properly to be characterised as unreasonable, must await a decision on specific facts. It is possible, we think, that beliefs generated by such factors may not properly be described as irrational and might be judged by a jury not to be unreasonable on their particular facts. But once a belief could be judged reasonable only by a process which labelled a plainly irrational belief as reasonable, it is clear that it cannot be open to the jury so to determine without stepping outside the Act.

42. For those reasons, even if we are wrong about the import of the psychiatric evidence in this case, and even if there was, contrary to our view, any room for the possibility that the defendant (a) genuinely believed that his partner was consenting and (b) did so because of a delusional state consequent upon his mental illness, the judge was correct, on the evidence in this case, in his direction to the jury.

Section 1(2) deals with the situation where a reasonable person would be unsure whether the victim consented. The defendant must act reasonably in ascertaining whether the victim consented in doubtful cases. The most obvious way of resolving a doubt would be for the defendant to ask the victim whether or not she was consenting. But there may be other ways where the couple know each other well.[73]

Presumably a defendant would not reasonably believe that a victim was consenting if he was relying on what someone else has told him. In *DPP v Morgan*[74] the victim's husband told some men that they should have sexual intercourse with his wife. He warned them that she might appear to resist, but that she would be doing this only to heighten her sexual enjoyment. The men went ahead and had intercourse with the wife despite her evident protests. There is no doubt that such men would now be convicted of rape because they did not *reasonably* believe that the victim consented. →6 (p.484) Similarly a defendant who unreasonably believed the victim was consenting because he was drunk can be convicted.

---

[73] e.g. the couple could have developed a way of communicating concerning sexual matters with certain touches or noises indicating a keenness to engage in sexual intercourse.

[74] [1976] AC 182.

> **QUESTIONS**
>
> 1. Lord Lloyd in the debates on the Sexual Offences Bill suggested that rather than section 1 leading to a larger number of convictions it will lead to a larger number of appeals due to its complexity (HL Debs, col. 860, 13 February 2003). Do you agree?
> 2. Brian has a low IQ and is sexually inexperienced. He meets Dawn who appears to be very friendly and accepts an invitation for a cup of tea in his flat. He decides that she must be willing to have intercourse with him. Dawn resists his advances but Brian decides that she must be consenting. Has Brian committed rape?
>
> For guidance on answering this question, please visit the Online Resource Centre that accompanies this book: www.oxfordtextbooks.co.uk/orc/herringcriminal7e/.

2 ASSAULT BY PENETRATION

Under section 2 of the Sexual Offences Act 2003:

2. Assault by penetration

(1) A person (A) commits an offence if—

    (a) he intentionally penetrates the vagina or anus of another person (B) with a part of his body or anything else,

    (b) the penetration is sexual,

    (c) B does not consent to the penetration, and

    (d) A does not reasonably believe that B consents.

(2) Whether a belief is reasonable is to be determined having regard to all the circumstances, including any steps A has taken to ascertain whether B consents.

(3) Sections 75 and 76 apply to an offence under this section.

Much of this offence is self-explanatory and has much in common with the offence of rape, just discussed. It is worth noting that the penetration must be sexual. This means that if a doctor inserts a medical instrument into a patient's vagina or anus as part of medical treatment, without getting the patient's consent, he or she will not be committing this offence.[75]

3 SEXUAL ASSAULT

Section 3 of the Sexual Offences Act 2003 states:

3. Sexual assault

(1) A person (A) commits an offence if—

    (a) he intentionally touches another person (B),

    (b) the touching is sexual,

    (c) B does not consent to the touching, and

    (d) A does not reasonably believe that B consents.

---

[75] Although he or she may be committing a battery.

(2) Whether a belief is reasonable is to be determined having regard to all the circumstances, including any steps A has taken to ascertain whether B consents.

(3) Sections 75 and 76 apply to an offence under this section.

DEFINITION

Actus reus: the defendant touches the victim sexually and the victim does not consent to the touching.

Mens rea: the defendant does not reasonably believe that the victim consents.

A number of points need to be made about this offence:

(1) There must be some touching for there to be a sexual assault. Touching is defined in section 79(8) as including: '[T]ouching (a) with any part of the body, (b) with anything else, (c) through anything'.[76] This means that, for example, if the defendant forced the victim to undress by threatening violence, but did not touch the victim, the offence would not be committed. However, it has been held that grabbing hold of the victim's trousers was touching them.[77]

(2) The touching must be sexual. Section 78 explains:

> penetration, touching or any other activity is sexual if a reasonable person would consider that—
>
> (a) whatever its circumstances or any person's purpose in relation to it, it is because of its nature sexual, or
>
> (b) because of its nature it may be sexual and because of its circumstances or the purpose of any person in relation to it (or both) it is sexual.

This definition of sexual is notably objective. In other words whether or not an act is sexual does not depend on whether the defendant found it to be sexual. What matters is whether a reasonable person would consider it sexual. However, as section 78(b) makes clear, a reasonable person could take into account the purposes of the defendant in deciding whether or not it is sexual.[78] Contrast these three cases:

(1) A defendant forcibly removes the victim's clothing in public. He does this in order to humiliate her and is not sexually motivated. This *could* still be a sexual assault. The jury might think that the act, looked at as a whole, is sexual, even though the defendant was not acting for sexual purposes.[79]

(2) An underground train becomes very crowded and a man stands against a woman whom he finds very attractive. His touching of her may be to him very sexually provocative, but this is *not* a sexual assault, as under section 78(a) standing next to someone on

---

[76] Section 79(8) also makes it clear that just because a touching is also a penetration does not prevent it from being a touching.

[77] *R v H* [2005] EWCA Crim 732.   [78] See the discussion in Bantekas (2008).

[79] It is unclear whether this means that an intimate medical examination, even if properly conducted, will automatically be sexual (see *Kumar* [2006] EWCA Crim 1946); of course, if it does, agreement will often provide a consent.

a crowded tube is not sexual in its nature. Under section 78(b) a touching which in its nature is not sexual cannot be regarded as sexual because of the defendant's purposes.

(3) A shopkeeper is found hitting a girl on her shorts.[80] This might be regarded as 'objectively' an ambiguous case. This may be sexual or it may not. If the shopkeeper admits that he was sexually motivated then the reasonable person looking at all the circumstances (including the defendant's sexual purposes) probably would regard the spanking as sexual. However, if the shopkeeper gave evidence that he was punishing the girl as he had caught her shoplifting, then the reasonable person might conclude that it was not sexual.[81]

It must be admitted that perhaps inevitably the meaning of sexual is ambiguous and it is not difficult to think of cases where it might be hard to predict whether the jury will think that the reasonable person would regard the act as sexual.

The *mens rea* provisions are identical to those used in relation to rape.

QUESTIONS

1. In *George* [1956] Crim LR 52 a man had a foot fetish and removed the victim's shoes without her consent. Would this now be a sexual assault?

2. George visits his doctor, Steve. Steve finds George very attractive and says (untruthfully) that for medical reasons he needs to conduct an intimate examination of George, to which George consents. Is this a sexual assault?

3. Sam visits her doctor, Cynthia. Cynthia conducts an intimate examination which is medically necessary. However, Cynthia has invited her friend Brian to hide in the surgery so that he can watch such examinations for sexual purposes. Has Brian committed a sexual assault? Has he committed any offence? (You will need to read the rest of the chapter to consider this. Do not forget to consider the issue of Cynthia's consent.)

---

4 CAUSING SEXUAL ACTIVITY WITHOUT CONSENT

Section 4 of the Sexual Offences Act states:

(1) A person (A) commits an offence if—

    (a) he intentionally causes another person (B) to engage in an activity,

    (b) the activity is sexual,

    (c) B does not consent to engaging in the activity, and

    (d) A does not reasonably believe that B consents.

(2) Whether a belief is reasonable is to be determined having regard to all the circumstances, including any steps A has taken to ascertain whether B consents.

---

[80] These were the facts in the case of *Court* [1989] AC 28.
[81] He might still be guilty of a battery.

This is similar to sexual assault, but does not require the defendant to have touched the victim. Indeed the requirement is that the victim engages in a sexual activity, but the defendant does not need to engage in a sexual activity. In *Abdullahi*[82] the defendant caused a child to watch a pornographic film. He was guilty of the section 4 offence, even though he had not touched the child. Further, it was held that he was guilty even though the defendant was not seeking to obtain sexual gratification by watching the film, he was hoping that as a result of watching the film the child would engage in sexual activity with him. In *Grout*[83] the Court of Appeal suggested that even a conversation or exchange of texts could amount to a sexual activity.

5 PREPARATORY OFFENCES

The Act prohibits certain activities done with intent to enable the defendant to commit a sexual offence. For example, under section 61 it is an offence for the defendant to administer a substance to the victim 'with the intention of stupefying or overpowering [him or her], so as to enable any person to engage in a sexual activity that involves [the victim]' without the consent of the victim. Also if a person is a trespasser[84] in any structure, part of a structure, or any land and intends to commit a sexual offence or does commit any sexual offence he or she commits an offence.[85]

6 SEXUAL OFFENCES DESIGNED TO PROTECT CHILDREN

The Sexual Offences Act 2003 produces a large range of offences which are designed to protect children from harmful sexual acts. It is not possible to discuss them all but here is a summary:

6.1 OFFENCES WHICH ARE VERSIONS OF THE GENERAL OFFENCES

The following are versions of the general sexual offences specifically designed to protect children under the age of 13:

(1) Section 5: rape of a child under 13.

(2) Section 6: assault of a child under 13 by penetration.

(3) Section 7: sexual assault of a child under 13.

(4) Section 8: causing or inciting a child under 13 to engage in a sexual activity.[86]

All of these offences are equivalent to the adult version of the offences, but with two key modifications. First, there is no *mens rea* requirement, except the intent to penetrate, touch,

---

[82] [2007] Cr App R 14.

[83] [2011] EWCA Crim 299.   [84] Sexual Offences Act 2003, s. 63.   [85] *Ibid.*

[86] *Jones* [2007] EWCA Crim 1118 makes it clear it is not necessary to identify a particular child who was incited.

incite, or cause the victim to engage in an activity. There is no need to show that the defendant was aware that the victim was 13.[87] Second, it is no defence to prove that the victim consented to the activity. Where the victim is under 13 his or her consent is irrelevant to these offences. It is not even a defence if the defendant reasonably believed the victim to be over the age of 13 and to have consented.[88]

The government White Paper suggests that where the parties are close in age (e.g. a 13-year-old having sexual relations with a 12-year-old), although the 13-year-old could in theory be convicted of one of these offences, it may be more appropriate for the matter to be treated as an issue of child protection for the social services, rather than being appropriate for the ministrations of the criminal courts.[89] In *R (E) v DPP*[90] the court quashed the decision of the DPP to prosecute a 14-year-old girl who when 12 had been involved in the abuse of her sisters.

In the following case Baroness Hale set out the reasons why there are special offences designed to protect children:

R v G
[2009] AC 92

See Chapter 4, Section 5 for the facts of this case and a discussion of other issues raised.

Baroness Hale

44. Section 5 of the 2003 Act has three main features. First, it singles out penetration by the male penis as one of the most serious sorts of sexual behaviour towards a child under 13; secondly, it applies to such penetration of a child under 13 of either sex; and thirdly it calls this "rape". This is its novel feature but it is scarcely a new idea. The offences of unlawful sexual intercourse under sections 5 and 6 of the 1956 Act were often colloquially known as "statutory rape". This is because the law regards the attitude of the victim of this behaviour as irrelevant to the commission of the offence (although it may, of course, be relevant to the appropriate sentence). Even if a child is fully capable of understanding and freely agreeing to such sexual activity, which may often be doubted, especially with a child under 13, the law says that it makes no difference. He or she is legally disabled from consenting.

45. There are a great many good reasons for this: see, eg, *R v Hess; R v Nguyen* [1990] 2 SCR 906, per McLachlin J. It is important to stress that the object is not only to protect such children from predatory adult paedophiles but also to protect them from premature sexual activity of all kinds. They are protected in two ways: first, by the fact that it is irrelevant whether or not they want or appear to want it; and secondly, by the fact that in the case of children under 13 it is irrelevant whether or not the possessor of the penis in question knows the age of the child he is penetrating.

46. Thus there is not strict liability in relation to the conduct involved. The perpetrator has to intend to penetrate. Every male has a choice about where he puts his penis. It may be

---

[87] *R v G* [2006] EWCA Crim 821. There the Court of Appeal rejected a claim that the offence interfered with the defendant's human rights.

[88] See Raitt (2010) for a discussion of producing evidence in child abuse cases.

[89] Home Office (2002: 17). But they argued that if a child has a history of abusing other children the criminal law may well be suitable.

[90] [2011] EWHC 1465 (Admin).

difficult for him to restrain himself when aroused but he has a choice. There is nothing unjust or irrational about a law which says that if he chooses to put his penis inside a child who turns out to be under 13 he has committed an offence (although the state of his mind may again be relevant to sentence). He also commits an offence if he behaves in the same way towards a child of 13 but under 16, albeit only if he does not reasonably believe that the child is 16 or over. So in principle sex with a child under 16 is not allowed. When the child is under 13, three years younger than that, he takes the risk that she may be younger than he thinks she is. The object is to make him take responsibility for what he chooses to do with what is capable of being, not only an instrument of great pleasure, but also a weapon of great danger.

47. I venture to think that none of this would be at all controversial if the possessor of the penis in question were over the age of 16, certainly if he were an adult. Much has been made of the overlap between the offence of "rape of a child under 13" under section 5 of the 2003 Act and the offence of "sexual activity with a child" under section 9. The section 9 offence distinguishes, in the maximum sentences prescribed, between penetration and other kinds of sexual touching, between victims under and over 13, and, through a combination of sections 9 and 13, between perpetrators aged under and over 18. But it is not suggested that it would be disproportionate to charge the section 5 offence against a man who had sexual intercourse with a girl under 13 simply because the same conduct would also be covered by the section 9 offence which carries a lesser (although still severe) penalty.

48. What difference can it make that the possessor of the penis is himself under 16? There was a great deal of anxiety in Parliament about criminalising precocious sexual activity between children. The offences covered by section 13 in combination with section 9 cover any sort of sexual touching however mild and however truly consensual. As sexual touching is usually a mutual activity, both the children involved might in theory be prosecuted. Indeed, section 9 expressly contemplates that the person penetrated may be the offender. Obviously, therefore, there will be wide variations in the blameworthiness of the behaviour caught by sections 9 and 13. Both prosecutors and sentencers will have to make careful judgments about who should be prosecuted and what punishment, if any, is appropriate. In many cases, there will be no reason to take any official action at all. In others, protective action by the children's services, whether in respect of the perpetrator or the victim or both, may be more appropriate. But the message of sections 9 and 13 is that any sort of sexual activity with a child under 16 is an offence, unless in the case of a child who has reached 13 the perpetrator reasonably believed that the child was aged 16 or over. There are many good policy reasons for the law to convey that message, not only to adults but also to the children themselves.

6.2 OFFENCES DESIGNED SPECIFICALLY TO PROTECT CHILDREN FROM SEXUAL ABUSE

The following are offences designed to protect children from sexual abuse:

(1) Section 9: sexual activity with a child.

(2) Section 10: causing or inciting a child to engage in a sexual activity.

(3) Section 11: engaging in sexual activity in the presence of a child.

(4) Section 12: causing a child to watch a sexual act.[91]

---

[91] The requirements of this offence are discussed in *R v Abdullahi* [2007] Crim LR 184.

(5) Section 13: child sex offences committed by children or young persons.

(6) Section 14: arranging or facilitating commission of a child sex offence.

(7) Section 15: meeting a child following sexual grooming etc.

Most of these offences are self-explanatory. But two will now be briefly defined:

9. Sexual activity with a child

(1) A person aged 18 or over (A) commits an offence if—

    (a) he intentionally touches another person (B),

    (b) the touching is sexual, and

    (c) either—

        (i) B is under 16 and A does not reasonably believe that B is 16 or over, or

        (ii) B is under 13.

The section 9 offence is therefore designed to cover sexual touchings even where the victim[92] consents to the touching.[93] The defendant is not guilty if he reasonably believes that the victim is 16 or over unless the victim is under 13. The defendant can be guilty only if he himself is over 18. If the defendant is under 18 he can still be charged under section 13. This means that even consensual touchings between teenagers who are consenting will be criminal offences. The government White Paper explained that although many such touchings will be 'experimental' and so 'the intervention of the criminal law may not be appropriate', it was useful to create such an offence to deal with cases where the touchings were consented to but there was 'manipulation'.[94]

15. Meeting a child following sexual grooming etc.

(1) A person aged 18 or over (A) commits an offence if—

    (a) A has met or communicated with another person (B) on at least two occasions and subsequently—

        (i) A intentionally meets B,

        (ii) A travels with the intention of meeting B in any part of the world or arranges to meet B in any part of the world, or

        (iii) B travels with the intention of meeting A in any part of the world,

    (b) A intends to do anything to or in respect of B, during or after the meeting mentioned in paragraph (a)(i) to (iii) and in any part of the world, which if done will involve the commission by A of a relevant offence,

    (c) B is under 16, and

    (d) A does not reasonably believe that B is 16 or over.

---

[92] If the victim were under 13 the offence would be committed under s. 7.

[93] If the victim consented then there may also be offences contrary to s. 5, 6, or 7.

[94] Home Office (2002: 25).

This is the offence described in the statute as 'sexual grooming'.[95] There is no requirement for the communications prior to the meeting to be sexual. However, there must be at least two communications between the defendant and victim to establish the offence. It was enough to prove the defendant had developed a relationship from which they intended to 'launch sexual offending'.[96] However, the offence is only committed if there is an intentional meeting. It does not arise if the offender merely takes advantage of a situation to commit an offence. It needed to be shown that either A had travelled to B, or that B had travelled to A and that A intended to commit the sexual offence. The relevant offences are listed in section 15(2) and include any of the offences in the Sexual Offences Act 2003.

6.3 ABUSE OF POSITION OF TRUST OFFENCES

The Sexual Offences Act 2003 contains a number of offences which involve sexual abuse by a person who is in a position of trust:

(1) Section 16: abuse of position of trust: sexual activity with a child.

(2) Section 17: abuse of position of trust: causing or inciting a child to engage in sexual activity.

(3) Section 18: abuse of position of trust: sexual activity in the presence of a child.

(4) Section 19: abuse of position of trust: causing a child to watch a sexual act.

Typical of these offences is section 16(1):

(1) A person aged 18 or over (A) commits an offence if—

    (a) he intentionally touches another person (B),

    (b) the touching is sexual,

    (c) A is in a position of trust in relation to B,

    (d) where subsection (2) applies, A knows or could reasonably be expected to know of the circumstances by virtue of which he is in a position of trust in relation to B, and

    (e) either—

        (i) B is under 18 and A does not reasonably believe that B is 18 or over, or

        (ii) B is under 13.

The term 'position of trust' is extensively defined in sections 22 and 23. It covers the situation where an adult is looking after people under the age of 18 in certain circumstances. 'Looks after' means being 'regularly involved in caring for, training, supervising, or being in sole charge of such persons.'[97] There is a long list of circumstances which this definition includes. It includes, by way of example, the following:

(1) This subsection applies if A looks after persons under 18 who are accommodated and cared for in one of the following institutions—

    (a) a hospital,

    (b) an independent clinic,

    (c) a care home, residential care home or private hospital,

---

[95] The government was particularly concerned about the use of the internet for grooming purposes (Home Office 2002: 25). For further discussion of grooming, see Gillespie (2006).

[96] *R v G* [2010] EWCA Crim 1693.   [97] Sexual Offences Act 2003, s. 22(2).

(d) a community home, voluntary home or children's home,

(e) a home provided under section 82(5) of the Children Act 1989, or

(f) a residential family centre, and B is accommodated and cared for in that institution.

(5) This subsection applies if A looks after persons under 18 who are receiving education at an educational institution and B is receiving, and A is not receiving, education at that institution.

The defendant to a charge under one of the abuse of trust offences will have a defence in any of the following circumstances:

(1) The defendant proves that he reasonably believed the victim was over 18.[98]

(2) The defendant could not reasonably be expected to know that he was in a position of trust in respect of the victim.[99]

(3) If the defendant is lawfully married to the victim at the time of the offence.[100]

(4) If, immediately before the position of trust arose, a sexual relationship[101] existed between the defendant and the victim.[102]

6.4 FAMILIAL CHILD SEX OFFENCES

The 2003 Act also creates a number of offences which are designed to protect children from abuse by family members:

(1) Section 25: sexual activity with a family member.

(2) Section 26: inciting a child family member to engage in sexual activity.[103]

Family relationships are defined in section 27:

(1) The relation of one person (A) to another (B) is within this section if—

(a) it is within any of subsections (2) to (4), or

(b) it would be within one of those subsections but for section 67 of the Adoption and Children Act 2002 (c. 38) (status conferred by adoption).

(2) The relation of A to B is within this subsection if—

(a) one of them is the other's parent, grandparent, brother, sister, half-brother, half-sister, aunt or uncle,

(b) A is or has been B's foster parent.

(3) The relation of A to B is within this subsection if A and B live or have lived in the same household, or A is or has been regularly involved in caring for, training, supervising or being in sole charge of B, and—

(a) one of them is or has been the partner of the other's step-parent,

(b) A and B are cousins, or

[98] *Ibid*, ss 16(1), 17(1), and 18(1). But the defendant is guilty if the victim was in fact under 13.
[99] But only if that is one of the positions of trust defined in s. 21(2)–(5).
[100] Sexual Offences Act 2003, s. 23.
[101] This defence cannot be relied upon if the relationship involved unlawful sexual intercourse.
[102] Sexual Offences Act 2003, s. 24.   [103] *Ibid*, s. 64 contains an offence of incest.

(c) one of them is or has been the other's stepbrother or stepsister, or

(d) the parent or present or former foster parent or one of them is or has been the other's foster parent.

(4) The relation of A to B is within this subsection if—

(a) A and B live in the same household, and

(b) A is regularly involved in caring for, training, supervising or being in sole charge of B.

(5) For the purposes of this section—

(a) 'aunt' means the sister or half-sister of a person's parent, and 'uncle' has a corresponding meaning;

(b) 'cousin' means the child of an aunt or uncle;

(c) a person is a child's foster parent if—

(i) he is a person with whom the child has been placed under section 23(2)(a) or 59(1)(a) of the Children Act 1989 (c. 41) (fostering for local authority or voluntary organisation), or

(ii) he fosters the child privately, within the meaning given by section 66(1)(b) of that Act;

(d) a person is another's partner (whether they are of different sexes or the same sex) if they live together as partners in an enduring family relationship;

(e) 'step-parent' includes a parent's partner and 'stepbrother' and 'stepsister' include the child of a parent's partner.

6.5 CHILD PROSTITUTION AND CHILD PORNOGRAPHY

The Act also includes provisions which are designed to render illegal the payment for sex with a child,[104] or causing, inciting, controlling, arranging, or facilitating child prostitution or pornography.[105] This book does not cover these issues.[106]

7 OFFENCES AGAINST THOSE WITH A MENTAL DISORDER

There is in the 2003 Act a raft of offences designed to protect those with a mental disorder:[107]

(1) Section 30: sexual activity with a person with a mental disorder impeding choice.

(2) Section 31: causing or inciting a person with a mental disorder impeding choice to engage in sexual activity.

---

[104] Sexual Offences Act 2003, s. 47.   [105] *Ibid*, ss 47, 48, 49, 52, and 53.

[106] See e.g. Madden Dempsey (2011) and Munro (2010).

[107] 'Mental disorder' is given the definition in the Mental Health Act 1983, s. 1 (Sexual Offences Act 2003, s. 79(6)). Learning disability is not defined in the Act. For an example of the evidential difficulties facing prosecutors in these kinds of cases, see *R v Watts* [2010] EWCA Crim 1824.

(3) Section 32: engaging in sexual activity in the presence of a person with a mental disorder impeding choice.

(4) Section 33: causing a person with a mental disorder impeding choice to watch a sexual act.

(5) Section 34: inducement, threat, or deception to procure sexual activity with a person with a mental disorder.

(6) Section 35: causing a person with a mental disorder to engage in or agree to engage in sexual activity by inducement, threat, or deception.

(7) Section 36: engaging in sexual activity in the presence, procured by inducement, threat, or deception, of a person with a mental disorder.

(8) Section 37: causing a person with a mental disorder to watch a sexual act by inducement, threat, or deception.

(9) Section 38: care workers: sexual activity with a person with a mental disorder.

(10) Section 39: care workers: causing or inciting sexual activity.

(11) Section 40: care workers: sexual activity in the presence of a person with a mental disorder.

(12) Section 41: care workers: causing a person with a mental disorder to watch a sexual act.

The defendant will be guilty of these offences if he or she knew, or could reasonably be expected to know, that the victim had a mental disorder and that because of it the victim was unable to refuse (be that because he or she lacked the capacity to make a choice whether to consent or because he or she was unable to communicate the decision). In *R v C*[108] the House of Lords held that whether a complainant suffered from a relevant mental disorder was to be determined by considering the particular time at which the touching or activity took place. So, a complainant might usually be able to refuse, but if at the time of the act their mental disorder meant they were unable to refuse, the defendant could be guilty.[109]

8   PROSTITUTION AND TRAFFICKING

There are a variety of provisions which are designed to deal with prostitution. Sections 52 and 53 prohibit the causing, inciting, or controlling of prostitution for gain. Section 59A creates offences prohibiting the trafficking into, within, or out of the UK of people for sexual exploitation.

9   MISCELLANEOUS OFFENCES

The Act also includes a number of miscellaneous offences. These include exposure,[110] voyeurism,[111] intercourse with an animal,[112] and sexual penetration of a corpse.[113] The Bill

---

[108] [2009] UKHL 42.

[109] See further Herring (2010). See Benedet and Grant (2014) for a powerful discussion of the abuse of women with mental disabilities.

[110] Sexual Offences Act 2003, s. 66.

[111] *Ibid*, s. 67. See Gillespie (2008) for a further discussion of this offence. See also *R v Bassett* [2008] EWCA Crim 1174, which includes a fascinating discussion on whether 'Moobs' (male breasts) are breasts for the purposes of the 2003 Act.

[112] Sexual Offences Act 2003, s. 69. For further discussion, see Jones (2011).

[113] Sexual Offences Act 2003, s. 70. For further discussion, see Herring (2007d).

originally had an offence of sexual activity in public.[114] The last had attracted much comment. The government White Paper reassuringly stated: '[I]t is not our intention to interfere in everyday behaviour that does not cause offence to the vast majority of people such as kissing or cuddling';[115] nor did the Bill intend to criminalize sexual activity[116] in 'an isolated place where one would reasonably expect not to be observed'. However, such reassurance did not persuade Parliament, which rejected the proposed offence. That said, the offence of outraging public decency was used to prosecute a couple who had oral sex in the ATM lobby of a bank.[117] A woman who sunbathed naked in her garden was prosecuted for indecent exposure.[118] She was acquitted even though the court was offered video footage of her shot by a 'shaken' neighbour.

QUESTIONS

1. Lord Thomas of Gresford in his speech at the second reading of the Bill stated:

   '[I]t is important to set out a principle at the beginning: that sex between two consenting adults and, in our culture, in private is a healthy, life-enhancing, pleasurable activity. [It] should be recognised as in my view [that] a great amount of deviant behaviour takes place because it is not recognised due to guilt, inadequacy and immaturity' (HL Debs, col. 779, 13 February 2003).

   Do you think the 2003 Act recognizes such a principle?

2. The Act at several points uses the term 'reasonable'. Do you think in sexual matters there is a community consensus which the jury can rely upon when considering what a reasonable person would do or think?

3. In *Leather* (1993) 14 Cr App R (S) 736 the defendant grabbed the testicles of a police officer to stop him making an arrest. This was held to be an indecent assault. Would it be an offence under the 2003 Act?

4. Schulhofer (1998: 90) writes: 'In rape law, flexibility almost inevitably means *under*-enforcement and *non*-compliance'. With this in mind is the Sexual Offences Act 2003 too vague?

FURTHER READING

Cowan, S. (2007) '"Freedom and Capacity to Make a Choice": A Feminist Analysis of Consent in the Criminal Law of Rape' in V. Munro and C. Stychin (eds) *Sexuality and the Law* (London: Routledge).

Finch, E. and Munro, V. (2003) 'Intoxicated Consent and the Boundaries of Drug Assisted Rape' *Criminal Law Review* 773.

Finch, E. and Munro, V. (2004) 'Intoxicated Consent and Drug Assisted Rape Revisited' *Criminal Law Review* 789.

---

114 Sexual Offences Bill 2003, cl. 74.   115 Home Office (2002: 32).   116 *Ibid.*
117 *Rose v DPP* [2006] Crim LR 993.   118 BBC News Online (2006b).

Herring, J. (2011d) 'No More Having and Holding: The Abolition of the Marital Rape Exemption' in S. Gilmore, J. Herring, and S. Gilmore (eds) *Landmark Cases in Family Law* (Oxford: Hart).

Herring, J. (2014b) 'Rape and the Definition of Consent' *National Law School of India Review* 16: 62.

Laird, K. (2014) 'Rapist or Rogue? Deception, Consent and the Sexual Offences Act 2003' *Criminal Law Review* 492.

Munro, V. (2007b) 'Dev'l-in Disguise? Harm, Privacy and the Sexual Offences Act 2003' in V. Munro and C. Stychin (eds) *Sexuality and the Law* (London: Routledge).

Sjölin, C. (2015) 'Ten Years On: Consent under the Sexual Offences Act 2003' *Journal of Criminal Law* 79: 20.

Spencer, J. (2004b) 'Child and Family Offences' *Criminal Law Review* 347.

Tadros, V. (2006a) 'Rape without Consent' *Oxford Journal of Legal Studies* 26: 515.

Temkin, J. (2002) *Rape and the Legal Process* (2nd edn, Oxford: OUP).

Temkin, J. and Ashworth, A. (2004) 'Rape, Sexual Assaults and the Problems of Consent' *Criminal Law Review* 328.

Wallerstein, S. (2009) '"A Drunken Consent is Still Consent"—or Is It? A Critical Analysis of the Law on Drunken Consent to Sex Following *Bree*' *Journal of Criminal Law* 73: 318.

PART II: THE THEORY OF SEXUAL OFFENCES

10 BACKGROUND OF SEXUAL CRIMES

For many people sexual touchings represent not only some of the most wonderful, but also the worst, moments of their lives. This highlights a key dilemma in relation to sexual offences: people need to be protected from the unwanted sexual activity which infringes their right to bodily integrity and sexual autonomy,[119] but at the same time people wish to be free to express themselves sexually without government intrusion.[120] Unfortunately, the history of sexual offences shows a failure to protect victims of rape and sexual assault and a willingness to intervene to prohibit what is regarded as immoral sexual activity (especially in cases of same-sex sexual activity).[121]

In the following extract, the experiences of victims of sexual crimes are described in an attempt to identify the wrong of forced sex:

---

[119] Sexual autonomy is protected under Art. 8 of the European Convention on Human Rights (*ADT v UK* [2000] Crim LR 1009).

[120] Munro (2005); Brants (2001); Coughlin (1998).   [121] Selfe and Burke (2001: chs 1 and 2).

S.H. Pillsbury, 'Crimes against the Heart: Recognizing the Wrongs of Forced Sex' (2002) 35 *Loyola at Los Angeles Law Review* 845 at 893–5

The victims speak about self-identity: who they are to themselves. They speak of a basic change in their idea of themselves as a unique person, constituted of particular experiences, tendencies and abilities, particular thoughts and feelings. They report that sexual violation does such violence to these aspects of identity that their own thoughts and feelings become alien to themselves.

These accounts point us to an important and insidious aspect of the injury of sexual aggression. They reveal that, in some unexpected fashion, the aggressor overcomes psychic defenses to invade the inner person. Normally we can defend ourselves against hostile physical attacks, and even if we cannot, we can separate harm to the body from harm to the inner self. We can keep our minds intact. Indeed rape victims frequently do this by mentally separating from their bodies during the attack. They watch their bodies being used, becoming observers to themselves. But this works only for a time. Eventually the victim's self, her spirit, must rejoin the body and this requires the spirit's acceptance of what the body has suffered.

The victims' accounts remind us that regardless of the power of our minds, we remain embodied beings, inextricably linked to our physical existences. Our bodily and psychic lives are absolutely intertwined, and more closely than we sometimes realize in this age of virtual exploration and fantasy. A meaningful life requires a joining of body and mind, and when their connection is torn, it takes long and hard work to rebuild. The sometimes overwhelming temptation for victims—to treat the body as tainted, as separate from the self—just prolongs the rapist's act of disregard for personal integrity.

The same point can be made another way. The victim accounts remind us of the importance of sex to gender and personal identity. Whether sexually active or inactive, adults generally see themselves as individuals with a particular sexual identity, which implies certain kinds of relationships with others. An important part of every life story is the individual's development of a particular sexual identity through chosen interactions with others. Among the most powerful influences on that development can be physical sexual contact. When that contact is unwanted, it can wreak havoc on the individual's sense of self and future direction.

Although this injury is internal and individual, it has important social repercussions. Because of the perpetrator's invasion of the victim's self and disruption of identity, because of his disregard for her value, many survivors of rape feel socially devastated. Victims feel the attack has dragged them from a place of social order and comfort to one of indifference and cruelty, where ordinary human bonds do not function. They feel abandoned in a place of utter loneliness:

> 'It's as though the moment I was hit . . . I was cut off from myself—as though all my connections to the world were slashed.'

. . . To summarize: By forcibly using the other's body sexually, the rapist intrudes not just into the body but into the mind, and not just temporarily, but in many cases permanently. A crude and in many ways stupid physical act can violate the individual's sense of self and security, crippling the victim's ability to connect to others. Because the injury is sexual it goes deep into the self; because it goes deep, we should consider it a harm, a crime to the soul.

But it would be wrong to consider sexual crimes just from the perspective of the individual victim. The impact of sexual assaults is not limited to the direct victims, but has a severe impact on the wider female population and the children of victims.[122] One study found that rape is the crime women fear more than any other.[123] *Protecting the Public* opens with the statement:

> Sexual crime, and the fear of sexual crime, has a profound and damaging effect on the social fabric of communities, and the fight against it is of the highest priority to the Government.[124]

It cannot be ignored that the majority of sexual offences are perpetrated against women.[125] The law's protection of people from sexual assault therefore also exists as part of the wider programme to promote equality of men and women. As Cory J wrote in the Canadian decision of *Osolin*, sexual assault 'is an assault upon human dignity and constitutes a denial of any concept of equality for women'.[126]

11 STATISTICS ON RAPE

There were a total 58,954 reported sexual assaults and 29,267 recorded rapes of women in England and Wales in 2014/15 (of which just under 5,000 involved girls under the age of 16). There were increases of 41 per cent and 36 per cent respectively. There were 1,553 rapes of males (of which around two-thirds involved boys under the age of 16).[127] One study found that 19.7 per cent of women and 2.3 per cent of men had suffered a sexual assault or attempted sexual assault since their sixteenth birthday. Also, 2.3 per cent of women and 0.5 per cent of men questioned had suffered an actual or attempted sexual assault in the previous year.[128] Serious sexual assault was most likely to be committed by someone known to the victim (54 per cent of female and 51 per cent of male victims).[129] All of these figures need to be treated with caution because according to Home Office estimates 90 per cent of rape cases go unreported and in 38 per cent of cases the victim does not tell anyone.[130] The government estimates that in any given year 2.5 per cent of females and 0.4 per cent of males will be the victim of a sexual offence.[131] Each year 0.5 per cent of all women will be raped. That is 85,000 women a year. One in five of all adult women report they have been the victim of a sexual assault since their eighteenth birthday.[132] In an NUS survey one in seven female students at university reported a sexual or physical assault while at university.[133]

It should be clear from these statistics that the popular image that rape is committed by a stranger is in fact not the most common form of rape. It is more likely that a victim of rape knows the rapist than she does not.[134] Indeed, the Ministry of Justice states: 'Around 90 per cent of victims of the most serious sexual offences in the previous year knew the perpetrator.'[135] As Morrison Torrey puts it:[136] 'It is a horrifying reality for women; we have more to fear from those who say they love us than from strangers.'

The conviction rate for rape is appallingly low.[137] In 2013/14, 5,850 rape complaints were handed on by the police to the CPS. Given what we know from surveys of the public, this is

---

[122] Morgan and Zedner (1992: ch. 3).   [123] Myhill and Allen (2002: 1).
[124] Home Office (2002: 1).   [125] Selfe and Burke (2001: 61).
[126] *R v Osolin* [1993] 4 SCR 595, 669.
[127] Office for National Statistics (2015b).   [128] Home Office (2011a).
[129] Home Office (2011a).   [130] Home Office (2011b).   [131] Ministry of Justice (2013).
[132] Ministry of Justice (2013).   [133] NUS (2012).
[134] For further discussion, see Home Office (2011a).   [135] Ministry of Justice (2013).
[136] Torrey (1995: 35).   [137] Larcombe (2011).

a tiny proportion of the number of rapes that have occurred. In 2013/14, there were 3,891 prosecutions for rape and 2,348 convictions.[138] Given that at least 85,000 rapes take place each year,[139] the proportion of convictions is tiny (around 2.7 per cent). There are a range of reasons for this, including: the attitude of the police towards complaints of rape, the *mens rea* requirement, the law on evidence at rape trials, and the atmosphere of rape trials themselves.[140] One of the aims of the Sexual Offences Act 2003 was to increase the rate of rape convictions. It is far from clear whether it has succeeded in doing that.[141]

A shocking survey in 2005 demonstrated attitudes towards victims of rape which one might have thought would be rarely held nowadays. The ICM poll found that 34 per cent of those questioned in the UK thought that a woman is partially or totally responsible for being raped if she has behaved in a flirtatious manner[142] and 26 per cent said the same where a woman was wearing 'sexy or revealing clothing'.

12 THE NATURE OF RAPE

The government has declared that rape is 'one of the most serious and abhorrent crimes a person can commit'.[143] But exactly what is the wrong that is at the heart of rape?[144] This is a controversial issue and it is one which has a significant impact on many of the hotly debated topics in the law of rape.[145] Here are some of the alternatives:[146]

12.1 THE HISTORICAL EXPLANATION

In the past rape was seen as a wrong against the victim's husband, father, or brother.[147] Rape thereby protected the husband's interest in ensuring a legitimate family line. It is unlikely anyone would seriously propose this understanding of rape in modern times.

12.2 THE AUTONOMY EXPLANATION

This view argues that at the heart of the law is the principle that people have the right to decide with whom to have sexual relations: the right of sexual autonomy.[148] This is why the issue of the consent of the victim plays such an important role in rape trials.

---

[138] CPS (2014). Around 60 per cent of successful prosecutions resulted from a guilty plea from defendants.
[139] Rape Crisis (2015).
[140] Temkin and Krahé (2008); Kelly, Lovett, and Regan (2005). Lacey (2001) emphasizes that the full legal position of rape cannot be understood without consideration of the law of evidence and the procedure governing rape trials.
[141] See Withey (2007b) for an excellent discussion of the attempts to improve reporting and conviction rates for rape. See Ellison, Munro, Hohl, and Wallan (2015) for concerns over the police response to victims with psychosocial disability who have been raped.
[142] Amnesty International (2005).   [143] Home Office (2002: 21).   [144] Cahill (2001).
[145] See McGlynn (2011b) calling for the use of restorative justice in rape.
[146] A significant omission from this list is economic theories of rape (see Posner (1992), criticized in West (1993a)).
[147] Burgess-Jackson (1996: ch. 1).
[148] The leading proponent of this view is Schulhofer (1998). See also Larson (1993).

John Gardner and Stephen Shute,[149] supporting this view, posit the example of a defendant who has sex with an unconscious victim who suffers no physical or emotional harm. Such a victim is clearly still raped. This indicates that it is not the physical or emotional consequences of rape which are key to the offence, but the lack of respect shown to the victim's sexual autonomy. As they put it, rape is 'the sheer use of another person'.[150]

Other commentators disagree. Victims speaking of their experiences of rape focus on the tangible physical and psychological harms rather than the intangible notion of sexual autonomy. To focus primarily on autonomy overlooks the bodily violation that occurs in rape.[151]

The concept of consent is at the heart of the sexual autonomy approach. The concept is, however, problematic as Vanessa Munro explains in this extract:

V. Munro, 'Sexual Autonomy' in M. Dubber and T. Hörnle (eds) *The Oxford Handbook of Criminal Law* (Oxford: OUP, 2014), 765–7

At the heart of the criminal law's regulation of sexual autonomy—in the contexts outlined previously and beyond—lies the concept of consent. Indeed, so engrained is the language and ideology of consent that it is almost impossible to construct a regime for the regulation of sexuality that does not invoke or rely upon it, as the efforts in some jurisdictions to de-center consent from rape laws have demonstrated. Though superficially appealing as a binary mechanism by which to token agency, a wealth of critical commentary has highlighted the shortcomings of the consent threshold, at least as it has been conceptualized and operationalized within dominant liberal (and neoliberal) frameworks. Consent as currently understood has been criticized for inappropriately presuming the existence of detached, unencumbered, unconditioned, and free human agency, in a world in which—as was observed at the outset of this chapter—we are all inevitably constructed and constrained in our choices by relationships, expectations, and sociocultural environments, with some identity groups (including women) being particularly restricted and curtailed. It has also been criticized precisely for its binary nature, which obscures a diversity of levels of submission, acquiescence, and wantedness, and for its ambiguity as to whether consent is a state of mind to be discerned by would-be partners or a status that must be verbally articulated.

Efforts to rescue the consent threshold from these limiting tendencies have been undertaken—arguments have been lodged about the need to adopt "consent-plus" standards that reflect underlying levels of desire that accord with a narrative sense of one's self, distinctions have been drawn between episodic and programmatic choices that merit more careful scrutiny, and calls have been made in general for more nuanced, contextualized, and circumspect evaluations of agency. Though such initiatives are, in my view, to be commended, more needs to be done in order to rescue and rehabilitate consent as a model by which progressively to regulate sexual autonomy. More specifically, greater attention also needs to be paid to the . . . ways in which the contours and parameters of consent are often at the mercy of a diversity of other sociopolitical forces. The problems with consent that critical commentators have identified do not arise simply from reliance on an abstract notion of the liberal person, too often presumed as a disembodied and detached male. They arise also from the malleability of the notion of consent itself, and its perpetual porosity to the influence of alternative frameworks grounded in equally problematic and abstract imperatives, such

---

[149] Gardner and Shute (2000).   [150] *Ibid*, 205.   [151] Tadros (2006a); Cahill (2001).

as the need to protect "the vulnerable," to prevent "exploitation," to promote "responsibility," and to ensure "practical expediency" and "cost-effectiveness" in the criminal law's enforcement.

It is a truism of the human condition that we are all vulnerable to some degree, and yet the labeling of some individuals or groups as peculiarly "vulnerable" (often without a clear designation of to what exactly) has become an increasingly prominent lever in ratcheting up the levels of sexual protectionism countenanced by the criminal law. On the one hand, women who are intoxicated have, for example, been increasingly depicted as vulnerable to sexual abuse, with much media and policy attention focused on their plight, and yet it remains doubtful how far this approach has either heightened the moral censure upon men who "take advantage" of that intoxication or ensured greater justice for women who cannot recall whether, in an inebriated state, they directly said no to their assailant's sexual advances. Similarly, the tendency in much policy rhetoric to depict all sex workers as infantilized and inherently vulnerable has bolstered the legitimacy of calls to criminalize clients, but has done little to explore the reality of the complex intersections of survival and sex. The concept of vulnerability operates in these, and other, arenas in close association, moreover, with the concept of exploitation. Amongst the things to which the "vulnerable" are most at risk is "exploitation"—but delineating the contours of condemnation are similarly complex in this frame, since we are all subject to exploitation to some degree, and often in ways that we do not consider morally blameworthy. The questions of what makes a form of exploitation unacceptable, of what role the criminal law has to play in its regulation, and of whether the presence of consent or harm on the part of the "victim" hold any relevance continue to be hotly contested and rarely amenable to a straightforward resolution. Despite this, the language of exploitation has crept into the regulation of sexual autonomy, restricting the types of conduct that can be consented to (including, e.g., commercial sex work or BDSM activity) and reflecting a vigorous commitment to limiting a person's engagement in debasing or degrading (sexual) activities undertaken for another's gratification or benefit.

But whilst the intersection of consent frameworks with burgeoning agendas around vulnerability and exploitation can be seen, on the one hand, to justify the increased encroachment of the criminal law on the regulation of sexual autonomy, on the other hand, it has assisted in a classic neoliberal sleight of hand whereby the role of the state has been sidelined. The root causes of vulnerability and exploitation are rarely connected to fiscal or social policies of the state that generate hardship and exclusion; and, ultimately, the responsibility for redressing the situation lies with the individual. In the case of rape, the message that is consistently reinforced ensures that women act as sexual gatekeepers—they must not place themselves in positions of increased risk from the uncontrollable sexual urges of men, and where sex is unwanted, they must communicate this unequivocally and ideally forcefully, with resistance and physical injuries being sustained.

The notion of sexual autonomy has been recently criticized by Professor Jed Rubenfeld.[152] He argues that:

guaranteeing everyone a right to sexual 'self-determination' is quite impossible. First, one person's sexual self-determination will inevitably conflict with others': John's will require that he sleep with Jane, but Jane's will require otherwise.

[152] Rubenfeld (2013).

This argument shows the dangers of talking loosely about 'sexual autonomy'. Rubenfeld assumes that John's autonomous wish to sleep with Jane deserves as much protection as Jane's autonomous decision to sleep with John. If Jane refuses to sleep with John, his autonomous wish will not be fulfilled. If John forces sex with Jane, her autonomous wish is not fulfilled. But this argument is misconceived.

Respect for autonomy gives us a reason to leave someone alone so that they can live the life they wish. It does not require us to fulfil everyone else's desires. That would be an impossibly onerous expectation. You would be giving all your money away in minutes for a start! The law in fact treats rights to bodily integrity as key to this dilemma. If John has sex with Jane without her consent not only has he interfered with a decision she has made, he has imposed his wishes on her body. If Jane refuses to sleep with John she has imposed nothing on his body and has not interfered in his rights.[153]

Professor Rubenfeld has a second point. He notes we do not normally allow exercises of autonomy that harm others. Yet, he says: 'Paradigmatic exercises of sexual autonomy routinely do serious harm to others. A's refusal to have sex with B can cause B acute suffering.'

Again he misstates the principle of autonomy. You must not exercise your autonomy in a way which *unjustifiably* harms another. Jane, in refusing to sleep with John, is hardly unjustified. She has no obligation to do so. People do not need to provide a good reason for not having sex with someone.

12.3 RAPE AS VIOLENCE

To some, rape should be regarded as a form of violence.[154] Two reasons are often used to support this view. First, it is claimed that what motivates rape is not sexual desire but a wish to express domination over and hatred of women.[155] Describing rape as a crime of violence, rather than a sex crime, emphasizes this. Second, by recognizing rape to be an offence of violence the focus of the crime is moved away from the victim's consent. In rape trials there is always a danger that the victim becomes the person on trial because the key question becomes whether or not she consented.[156] By focusing on the violence done by the defendant, rather than the state of mind of the victim, rape trials may be less traumatic for victims.[157]

Against this view is the argument that such an approach trivializes rapes where there is no violence, but threats of force or deceptions are used to manipulate the victim into sexual intercourse.[158] In reply, some supporters of the 'rape as violence' view have replied that rapes which involve force are different from rapes where there is no force (which may sometimes deserve to be criminal offences, but not of the same kind as violent rape).[159] In a controversial comment Donald Dripps has argued that the use of force is an essential element in rape. He sees unwanted sex (sex where there is no violence) as not particularly serious:

---

[153] *Ibid.*

[154] Brownmiller (1975). See Tadros (2012: 75–8) for a helpful discussion of the significance of the different understandings of violence.

[155] Schwartz and Clear (1980). For views that rape is about sexual desire, see Posner (1992) and Baker (1999b).

[156] MacKinnon (1989: 245).   [157] Cahill (2001: 20).

[158] Tong (1984).   [159] Duncan (2007).

People generally, male and female, would rather be subjected to unwanted sex than be shot, slashed, or beaten with a tire iron. . . . Whether measured by the welfare or by the dignity of the victim, as a general matter unwanted sex is not as bad as violence. I think it follows that those who press sexual advances in the face of refusal act less wickedly than those who shoot, or slash, or batter.[160]

This generalization is one that has been widely rejected, especially by commentators who have themselves been raped or sexually abused. However, his suggestion that the law should recognize two kind of sexual offences: forcible rape (rape with the use of force) and expropriation of sexual services (sexual intercourse following deceptions or where the defendant has intercourse with a victim who is saying no but no force is used)[161] has received some support.[162]

12.4 RAPE AS INVASION OF INTEGRITY

This view seeks to combine the best parts of the two theories just discussed.[163] It argues that the harm of rape is not the violence exactly, but rather an invasion of an embodied person.[164] This view is explained further in the following extract by Nicola Lacey:

N. Lacey, 'Unspeakable Subjects, Impossible Rights: Sexuality, Integrity and Criminal Law' (1998) 11 *Canadian Journal of Law and Jurisprudence* 47 at 62–6

Reinserting the corporeal: from autonomy to integrity?

I have suggested that the primary good which a liberal theory of criminal law would expect the sexual offences to respect is that of sexual autonomy. As usually understood, this idea of what is at issue in the area of sexual harm is one which expresses precisely the elevation of mind over body to which feminist criticism has drawn our attention. In focusing on an individualised notion of consent, rather than the conditions under which choices can be meaningful, the prevailing idea of sexual autonomy *assumes* the mind to be dominant and controlling, irrespective of material circumstances. Furthermore, the liberal discourse of autonomy appears to leave no space for the articulation of the affective and corporeal dimensions of *certain* violations of autonomy—in other words, it closes off the possibility of developing a sophisticated conception of sexual harms. While the idea of autonomy as independence seems directly relevant to the wrong of rape, it dominates at the expense of the development of a positive conception of what kinds of sexual relationships matter to personhood.

Might it be possible to reconstruct the idea of autonomy or to find an alternative analytic and normative framework within which to rethink the sexual offences—one which would allow repressed corporeality to be thought and spoken, which would contextualise the victim's and the defendant's encounter more adequately, and which would accord the embodied aspects of human existence their proper place? I should like to suggest that we can draw on the work of two feminist legal theorists, Drucilla Cornell and Jennifer Nedelsky, to make significant progress in just this direction.

---

[160] Dripps (1992: 1792).   [161] Dripps (1992).
[162] See also Schulhofer (1992: 75). For criticism, see e.g. Fairstein (1994) and West (1994).
[163] Gibson (1993).   [164] West (1988: 70); Childs (2001); Cornell (1995).

In her most recent work, Drucilla Cornell has argued for the importance of what she calls the 'imaginary domain'. The imaginary domain generates the psychic and political space within which sexual equality might be realised. Taking one step back from the quasi-contractual starting point of much recent political theory, Cornell focuses on those conditions under which a human being can pursue her life project of becoming a person. These conditions, Cornell asserts, include a fantasy dimension: the psychic space in which each of us can imagine ourselves as whole persons. The core of a substantial liberalism, in Cornell's view, is the political and legal guarantee that this space will be equally open to all.

Cornell's imaginary domain consists in three elements: bodily integrity, access to symbolic forms sufficient to achieve linguistic skills permitting the differentiation of oneself from others, and the protection of the imaginary domain itself. Central to each of these elements is the fact that a crucial part of existence for all humans is our status as sexed and embodied beings, and our sexual desire: without access to the means of expressing one's desire, and of having one's sexuality accorded such respect as is consistent with a similar respect for others, one can never have the psychic space to pursue the project of personhood. For one is barred from the identification with one's sexual imago which is central to the possibility of imagining oneself as a whole being, worthy of respect and capable of self-esteem.

Might the notion of sexual integrity which we can derive from Cornell's argument constitute a better analytic peg on which to hang our framing of sexual offences than the mentalist conception of autonomy? Certainly, the idea of integrity, as developed by Cornell, puts the bodily and affective aspects of sexual life more directly in issue, quite simply because the body is implicated in the relationships which are central to human integrity. Within the language of integrity, the real damage of rape might be expressed more fully, recognising the way in which rape violates its victims' capacity to integrate psychic and bodily experiences. Understood in this way, respect for victims' integrity seems an eminently worthy ideal for rape law and its enforcement. But it is also worth thinking carefully about the potential for reconstructing the ideal of autonomy so as to escape its dualistic implications. Many critics of atomistic versions of liberalism, from Marx to the present day, have shown that the idea of autonomy can be reconstructed in positive terms. Autonomy, in this sense, focuses on the capability of persons to realise their life plans as much as on formal choice and the negative freedom not to be interfered with. But even among those who embrace the positive conception of freedom, the emphasis has tended to be on the provision of goods and resources external to the person. Because of its close association with the dominant image of the abstract, choosing subject, the history of the concept of autonomy conduces to the body's concealment.

More recently, however, Jennifer Nedelsky's important work on the concepts of autonomy and rights has demonstrated that these ideas can be reconstructed so as to encompass the body. The core of Nedelsky's argument is that human autonomy is fundamentally premised upon the relational aspects of life—our bodily and psychic dependence upon others. This inevitable relational interdependence renders the very idea of atomistic autonomy nonsensical. Without sustaining and respectful relationships, we cannot realise our personhood; and relationships inevitably implicate the corporeal. Hence the connection between autonomy and the repression of the body, and the supposed opposition between the feminist prioritising of the body and the liberal value of autonomy, begins to unravel. Embodied autonomy becomes, by contrast, a precondition for the pursuit of personal integrity. In Marilyn Friedman's terms, recent liberal conceptions do recognise the importance of relationships as *external* conditions necessary to the realisation of autonomy, but they fail to acknowledge that certain kinds of relationship may be conditions *internal* to autonomy itself. This is not to deny the importance of autonomy as, on occasion, the power to exclude others or to maintain separateness and privacy, nor is it to deny the importance of distinguishing between connections which are valuable in the sense of fostering personhood and those which may be oppressive. It is, rather, to affirm the need to locate our assessments of autonomy in the context of the relational conditions which obtain between human subjects.

The interdependence of autonomy and integrity may easily be demonstrated. In Cornell's sense, integrity embraces both physical integrity and the affective sense in which access to bodily or sexual integrity also depends on a host of social and psychic conditions. These range from external conditions such as adequate sustenance and medical care through to the conditions of respect for differently embodied subjects, different sexualities—respectful relationships as conditions internal to human integrity. A recognition of the value of integrity invites the incorporation of implications of sexual abuse such as shame, loss of self-esteem, objectification, dehumanisation. These are, of course, features central to the emerging social understandings of the wrong of sexual assault, and ones which have led feminist legal scholars such as Robin West to equate rape with 'murder of the spirit'. When combined with the emphasis on personhood as project—as a process of becoming which has an imaginary dimension and no definite end—the idea of integrity promises to escape the dangers both of essentialising a particular conception of the body and of propagating a vision of feminine empowerment which is premised, paradoxically, on a victim status which accords access to 'truth'. It conduces rather to reflection on the conditions under which a multiplicity of bodies and sexualities can be lived by full citizens, and to the opening up of a political debate about the nature of those conditions.

The right to bodily integrity which Cornell advocates is, in one important sense, impossible: it is not something which can be realised or determined institutionally; rather, it operates as a vision which generates both individual ideals and critical standards for the assessment of existing legal and political arrangements. There is an asymmetry in the imaginary domain: it cannot be captured or realised by institutions, but it can be killed or closed off by them. The vision of sexual integrity is at once a necessary condition for the ongoing project of personhood and an impossible ideal which forms a motivating horizon in political rhetoric.

It is interesting to consider, nonetheless, what a rape law framed around the ideal of sexual integrity and relational autonomy as opposed to proprietary autonomy would look like. I would argue that an analysis in terms of sexual integrity and relational autonomy has implications for each of the features of rape law discussed in this paper; for the definition of rape; for evidential and other aspects of the trial process; and for a rethinking of the symbolic role of the criminalisation of rape. As far as the definition of rape is concerned, the most obvious change would be a move away from the emphasis on lack of consent understood in abstract and asymmetrical terms as the central determinant of sexual abuse. Rather, it conduces to a more complex sexual assault law which articulates a distinctive conception of sexual as opposed to proprietary autonomy, specifying particular conditions under which coercive, violent or degrading sexual encounters should be prohibited. In rethinking the idea of autonomy as integrity, we are led to a rethinking of consent itself in both broader terms and ones which assume a mutuality of relationship and responsibility between victim and defendant. The argument, for example, would unambiguously support the proposal currently being advanced by the British pressure group, Women Against Rape, which calls for a legislative definition of consent in the following terms: 'A person shall not be deemed or presumed to have consented to sexual intercourse if that person agreed to it under coercion, including the use of threat or physical violence . . . economic deprivation, abuse of authority, deception, or threat to the welfare or security of a child.' Even this broad statement of the conditions which may undermine the 'reality' of consent, however, does not address the question of mutuality. This, I would argue, could best be dealt with by moving towards some form of 'positive consent' standard: for example, by the institution of a negligence-based fault standard supplemented by a 'no-negligence' defence. While no such reform is a panacea, it would express far more nearly than does the current law in England and Wales a vision of the parties as presumptively equal partners in sexual encounters, adjusted to account for the asymmetry of possible harms arising out of misunderstandings about mutual willingness.

Even more directly, the analysis of rape in terms of relational autonomy and integrity would necessitate the reform of rules of evidence so as to allow victims more fully to express their own narrative in the court room setting, as well as ensuring that they are able to do so without having the rape trial turned into an at large examination of their sexual history. . . .

Finally, however, it should be noted that the value of sexual integrity would not direct a very great reliance on criminalisation as a mode of protecting the imaginary domain. On the contrary, criminal law is likely to be an effective defender of the imaginary domain at a symbolic rather than an instrumental level: what matters is that the criminal law of rape should express an unambiguous commitment to the positive integrity as well as the full humanity of both rape victims and men accused of rape. In my view, this militates towards the maintenance of a distinctive offence rather than a subsumption of the law of rape within the general law of assault. Though lawyers are inclined to lose sight of this obvious fact, the most important conditions for sexual equality and integrity lie in cultural attitudes rather than coercive legal rules. Nonetheless, as I have argued throughout this paper, legal rules may be inimical to these ideals, and the need to avoid this situation is among the most pressing reasons for rape reform in Britain as elsewhere.

12.5 RAPE AS MORAL INJURY

Another view is that rape should be seen as a crime which causes a particular kind of moral injury: it involves a disrespect for the value of the victim.[165] The act of rape expresses the view that the victim is of an inferior status.[166] Rape involves using another person for one's own ends. It involves treating the other person as an object. Joan McGregor argues that rape 'sends the message that this woman is for his enjoyment, an object to be used for his pleasure.' She goes on to claim that the message of rape is sent to all women: 'The message of inferiority, of what women are for, is received by all women, not merely by the woman who experiences the rape.' She is keen to emphasize she is not downplaying the impact of the rape on the particular woman, but believes it is important to understand the message that rape, and the response to rape by the law and society, sends to all women.

12.6 THE RADICAL FEMINIST EXPLANATION OF RAPE

It is sometimes said that the radical feminist explanation is that all male–female sexual relations are a form of rape.[167] This is not quite accurate. The argument is that all heterosexual sexual relationships are on a continuum of subordination. As Catherine MacKinnon puts it:

The wrong of rape has proved so difficult to define because the unquestionable starting point has been that rape is defined as distinct from intercourse, while for women it is difficult to distinguish between the two under conditions of male dominance.[168]

---

[165] Hampton (1999).   [166] McGregor (2005).
[167] Bevacqua (2000) discusses the influence of feminist thinking on reform of rape law.
[168] MacKinnon (1989: 174).

Robin Morgan, suggesting much, if not all, heterosexual sex can be regarded as involuntary, puts it this way:

> Rape exists any time sexual intercourse occurs when it has not been initiated by the woman out of her own genuine affection and desire. . . . Because the pressure is there, and it need not be a knife blade against the throat; it's in his body language, his threat of sulking, his clenched or trembling hand, his self-deprecating humor or angry put-down or silent self-pity at being rejected. How many millions of times have women had sex 'willingly' with men they did not want to have sex with?[169]

The argument is not that every man who engages in heterosexual sexual intercourse should be arrested and charged with rape.[170] Rather, the argument is that we cannot pretend there is a neat division between 'bad rape' and 'good sexual intercourse'. Certainly one study found that 26 per cent of men and 50 per cent of women reported having engaged in unwanted sexual activity within the two-week period of the study.[171]

Even among feminists this approach has not met with unanimous support. Lynn Henderson argues that a victim of rape knows the difference between rape and consensual intercourse, and that to deny a distinction is liable to fail to recognize the rape victim's trauma.[172] Other feminists are concerned that the approach may portray women as weak and incapable of giving true consent.[173]

In the following passage, Catherine MacKinnon sets out her views:

C.A. Mackinnon, 'Feminism, Marxism, Method and the State: Toward Feminist Jurisprudence' (1983) 8 *Signs* 635 at 646–7, 649–50

> The more feminist view to me, one which derives from victims' experiences, sees sexuality as a social sphere of male power of which forced sex is paradigmatic. Rape is not less sexual for being violent; to the extent that coercion has become integral to male sexuality rape may be sexual to the degree that, and because, it is violent.
>
> The point of defining rape as 'violence not sex' or 'violence against women' has been to separate sexuality from gender in order to affirm sex (heterosexuality) while rejecting violence (rape). The problem remains what it has always been: telling the difference. The convergence of sexuality with violence, long used at law to deny the reality of women's violation, is recognized by rape survivors, with a difference: where the legal system has seen the intercourse in rape, victims see the rape in intercourse. The uncoerced context for sexual expression becomes as elusive as the physical acts come to feel indistinguishable. Instead of asking, what is the violation of rape, explain what is right about sex. If this, in turn, is difficult, the difficulty is as instructive as the difficulty men have in telling the difference when women see one. Perhaps the wrong of rape has proven so difficult to articulate because the unquestionable starting point has been that rape is definable as distinct from intercourse, when for women it is difficult to distinguish them under conditions of male dominance. . . .
>
> Having defined rape in male sexual terms, the law's problem, which becomes the victim's problem, is distinguishing rape from sex in specific cases. The law does this by adjudicating the

---

[169] Morgan (1980: 134–5).   [170] Schulhofer (1992: 56).

[171] See O'Sullivan and Rice Allgeier (1998: 239) and Muehlenhard and Cook (1988: 69). For a general discussion of the evidence, see Thomas III (2000).

[172] Henderson (1988: 226).   [173] Naffine (1997: 102); Lacey (1998c: 49).

level of acceptable force starting just above the level set by what is seen as normal male sexual behaviour, rather than at the victim's or woman's point of violation. Rape cases finding insufficient force reveal that acceptable sex, in the legal perspective, can entail a lot of force. This is not only because of the way the injury itself is defined as illegal. Rape is a sex crime that is not a crime when it looks like sex. To seek to define rape as violent, not sexual, is understandable in this context, and often seems strategic. But assault that is consented to is still assault; rape consented to is intercourse. The substantive reference point implicit in existing legal standards is the sexually normative level of force. Until this norm is confronted as such, no distinction between violence and sexuality will prohibit more instances of women's experienced violation than does the existing definition. The question is what is *seen as* force, hence as violence, in the sexual arena. Most rapes, as women live them, will not be seen to violate women until sex and violence are confronted as mutually definitive. It is not only men convicted of rape who believe that the thing they did different from what men do all the time is get caught.

Michelle Madden Dempsey and I have argued not that all sexual intercourse is rape, but rather that a sexual penetration is a prima facie wrong.[174] In other words it is an act which requires the penetrator to have a good reason for the act of penetration. We offer three reasons for this.[175] The first is that the act of penetration requires the use of force and it is a prima facie wrong to use force against another. The second is that the act of penetration carries with it the risk of a variety of harms, such as STDs, pregnancy, or psychological harms. Again, risking harm to another is a prima facie wrong. Third, the act of sexual penetration carries a negative social meaning about women. We explain that in this passage:

M. Madden Dempsey and J. Herring, 'Why Sexual Penetration Requires Justification' (2007) 27 *Oxford Journal of Legal Studies* 467 at 485–6

One current social meaning of penile penetration of a woman's vagina or anus is that such conduct constitutes a violation of the woman: it is an act through which she is rendered less powerful, less human, whilst the male is rendered more powerful and more human. The language we use to describe the act of sexual penetration betrays this social meaning: fuck, bang, screw, rail, drill, smash, hit it, hump, let her have it, poke, shaft, slay, etc. The grammatical structure of our language is such that these verbs feature in sentences which take the form: 'subject-verb-object'. Notably, it is typically the person who plays the male role who is assigned as subject and the person who plays the female role who is assigned as object. Thus, as MacKinnon has observed, the language of sexual penetration follows a familiar and illuminating grammatical pattern: 'man fucks woman: subject-verb-object.' Moreover, as Robert Baker has explained, the passive constructions of verbs indicating penile sexual penetration are also typically used to indicate that a person is being harmed. The lexical meaning of words such as 'fucked', 'screwed', 'shafted', etc. in sentences such as 'Bobbie fucked Marion' or 'Bobbie screwed Marion' are equivocal as between at least two possible meanings: (i) the literal meaning that Bobbie sexually penetrated Marion (who played the female role during penetration), or (ii) the metaphorical meaning that Marion was deceived, hurt, or taken advantage of by Bobbie. Thus, Baker observes, 'we say such things as 'I've

[174] See also Wall (2015), who agrees with this conclusion, but for different reasons.
[175] For a different analysis see Thorburn (2012), who argues that 'Conduct that is undertaken with consent is not an interference with another's sovereignty (because it is simply carrying out the wishes of the person who is sovereign over his own body) and therefore it is not in need of justification.'

been screwed' ('fucked', 'had', 'taken', and so on) when we have been treated unfairly, been sold shoddy merchandise, or conned out of valuables'. Given the meaning and gendered construction of our language regarding sexual penetration, Baker correctly concludes that 'we conceive of a person who plays the female sexual role as someone who is being harmed'.

The devaluing and disrespecting of women through sexual penetration is a consistent theme in our language, as well as in our literature, film, advertising, television, pornography and internet depictions of sexual penetration. In recent years, this social meaning is perhaps conveyed most clearly in the way penile sexual penetration of the vagina and/or anus are discussed through spam email.

The credibility principle, when applied to interpret the meaning of the words we use to describe sexual penetration, their gendered function in our language and the depictions of sexual penetration in our literature, film, advertising, television, pornography and internet discourse, supports the conclusion that at least one of the social meanings of penile sexual penetration can only credibly be interpreted as a devaluation of women *qua* women and a disrespecting of women's humanity. The meaning becomes clear: that the penetrated woman is not an equal to the penetrating man, but is instead less of a person in virtue of having been fucked by him. It is important to recall that our observations regarding the social meaning of sexual penetration do not imply that men have any conscious purpose to devalue or disrespect women through sexual penetration (although presumably some do). Rather, our point is simply that any credible interpretation of the practices of, language regarding, and depictions of sexual penetration in our culture betray a social meaning of sexual penetration which devalues women *qua* women and disrespects women's humanity to an extent which renders such conduct prima facie wrong.

Note that we emphasize that a sexual penetration can be justified and so this negative meaning may be outweighed by many positive meanings attached to a particular act of sexual penetration. The view expressed in our article is certainly a minority one. For most commentators who have written on the issue there is no wrong in sexual penetration per se; it is only sexual penetration without consent which is wrongful. The difference of opinion is more than merely theoretical. It matters enormously when we look at how to understand consent/lack of consent. For the majority view we are looking for circumstances which are bad enough to justify rendering the act of sexual penetration criminal. On the Madden Dempsey/Herring view we are looking for circumstances which justify an otherwise wrongful act.

FURTHER READING

Cowan, S. (2007) '"Freedom and Capacity to Make a Choice": A Feminist Analysis of Consent in the Criminal Law of Rape' in V. Munro and C. Stychin (eds) *Sexuality and the Law* (London: Routledge).

Dripps, D. (1992) 'Beyond Rape: An Essay on the Difference between the Presence of Force and the Absence of Consent' *Columbia Law Review* 92: 1780.

Gardner, J. and Shute, S. (2000) 'The Wrongness of Rape' in J. Horder (ed.) *Oxford Essays in Jurisprudence* (Oxford: OUP).

Herring, J. and Madden Dempsey, M. (2010) 'Rethinking the Criminal Law's Response to Sexual Penetration: On Theory and Context' in C. McGlynn and V. Munro (eds) *Rethinking Rape Law* (Abingdon: Routledge).

Knight, S. (2012) 'Libertarian Critiques of Consent in Sexual Offences' *UCL Journal of Law and Jurisprudence* 137.

Lacey, N. (1998c) 'Unspeakable Subjects, Impossible Rights: Sexuality, Integrity and Criminal Law' *Canadian Journal of Law and Jurisprudence* 11: 47.

McGlynn, C. (2011) 'Feminism, Rape and the Search for Justice' *Oxford Journal of Legal Studies* 31: 825.

Madden Dempsey, M. and Herring, J. (2007) 'Why Sexual Penetration Requires Justification' *Oxford Journal of Legal Studies* 27: 467.

Naffine, N. (1994) 'Possession: Erotic Love in the Law of Rape' *Modern Law Review* 57: 10.

Wall, J. (2015) 'Sexual Offences and General Reasons Not to Have Sex' *Oxford Journal of Legal Studies* 35: 777.

West, R. (1996) 'A Comment on Consent, Sex and Rape' *Legal Theory* 2: 233.

13 CONSENT AND SEXUAL ACTIVITY

In the English and Welsh law on sexual offences it is the notion of consent which has become central.[176] Some commentators suggest that lack of consent can transform a 'loving act of sexual intercourse' into 'rape'.[177] But, as will be clear from Part I, there are many difficulties over the meaning of consent.

13.1 WHAT IS CONSENT: IS IT OBJECTIVE OR SUBJECTIVE?

Imagine this: Bill and Ben meet at a night club. Ben has had a lot to drink. Bill soon asks whether Ben would be interested in sexual intercourse. Ben is so drunk he does not understand what is happening, but says 'yes'. Sexual intercourse follows. Did Ben consent?[178] Subjectively (looking at his mind) he did not, but objectively (looking at what he said) he did. This is a topic over which there has been much legal and philosophical disagreement.[179] Three main views can be found in the literature:[180]

(1) The 'subjective view' of consent. This sees consent as a state of mind of the victim.[181]

(2) The 'objective view' which sees consent as an outward manifestation by the victim in words or acts which indicate permission is granted to the defendant to do the act. As Nathan Brett[182] puts it: 'To consent is to *act* in a way that has conventional significance in communicating permission'.

(3) The third view is a combination of these views and requires *both* a subjective state of mind of the victim and the expression of that state of mind.

As seen in Part I, English and Welsh law has adopted the 'subjective view'.

---

[176] For an excellent discussion on the use of consent, see Cowan (2007).   [177] Hurd (1996).
[178] Finch and Munro (2003 and 2004) and Falk (2002) discuss cases where a defendant uses drink or drugs deliberately to enable him to have sexual intercourse with the victim.
[179] Hurd (1996) and Alexander (1996).   [180] Wertheimer (2000).
[181] e.g. the discussion in Bryant (1989).   [182] Brett (1998: 70).

13.2 WHAT IS CONSENT: TO WAIVE OR INTEND?

What precisely does it mean to consent? One view is that to consent is to forgo one's complaint against the other's action,[183] while another is that consent requires one to intend the other to act in the particular way.[184] The difference between these views can be revealed by the example of a wife whose husband would like to have sexual intercourse. The wife is reluctant to agree, but does so because she does not want to have a row. Although she may have forgone her complaint, it might be said that she does not intend him to have sexual intercourse. Both of these views reinforce the point that it is difficult to draw a sharp distinction between consent and no consent.[185] ←3 (p.421)

13.3 WHAT IS CONSENT: IS A FAILURE TO VOICE OPPOSITION CONSENT?

As we have seen in Part I, the English and Welsh courts have been consistent in holding that the *actus reus* of rape is made out if a man has sexual intercourse with a woman who is asleep or too drunk to resist. They have stressed that the *actus reus* requires the absence of consent, not the absence of resistance or opposition. However, this is not an uncontroversial approach to take. It is not, for example, adopted in parts of the United States where, if the victim fails to voice any complaint about sexual intercourse, there can be no rape.[186]

Donald Husak and George Thomas III take the objective view of consent. They argue that to appreciate what consent is we have to understand the social understandings that surround the event. Therefore, when you put your hand out to stop a taxi, get inside, and ask to be taken somewhere, although you do not explicitly agree to pay, that is the social convention that surrounds that activity.[187] They argue that many women feel uncomfortable asking for sex. This is seen as being too forward or distasteful. Various conventions have therefore been developed under which consent may be assumed, even if it is not made explicit.[188] In the light of these conventions they argue that if a woman behaves in a way which would normally be taken to indicate consent, that behaviour should be taken as consent, even if in fact that was not her intention and even if she never explicitly said she wanted to have sex. David Bryden provides an example:

> A woman who after being propositioned, walks into her host's bedroom and disrobes, may not have given verbal consent. But she has 'affirmatively' manifested her intentions, and that should suffice.[189]

Husak and Thomas III are quick to add that they hope these conventions change so that men and women can more openly and explicitly discuss sexual matters, but until then it

---

[183] Alexander (1996). For further discussion, see Archard (1998).   [184] Hurd (1996).

[185] Dripps (1992).

[186] Bryden (2000: 319). Many scholars reject this: Schulhofer (1992); Chamallas (1988); Mandhane (2001); and Kasubhai (1996), e.g., argue strongly for a requirement that there is a positive act of consent.

[187] Thomas III and Edelman (2000).

[188] One study of Texan undergraduates claimed that 39.3 per cent, including most of those with sexual experience, had sometimes pretended that they did not want sex when in fact they wanted it, while 60.7 per cent stated they had never said no when they wanted sex (Muehlenhard and Hollabaugh 1988: 872).

[189] Bryden (2000: 397).

is unfair to punish a man who assumes the normal conventions apply when the woman does not mean them to. They go on to add that if the law were to be changed to require that each party to a sexual encounter must explicitly consent to it, that could have unintended consequences:

> A proposal designed to make it more difficult for men to get away with rape might have the unanticipated effect of making it harder for some women to get what they want.[190]

Making a wider point Joshua Dressler argues:

> Men should be taught in our culture to seek permission, but women should also be taught in our culture to express their wishes, whether it is to invite or reject sexual contact.[191]

In *Protecting the Public* the government sought to adopt a view somewhere between Schulhofer's and Husak and Thomas III's views:

> Human beings have devised a complex set of messages to convey agreement or lack of it. Agreement or lack of agreement is not necessarily verbal, but both parties should understand it. Each must respect the right of the other to demonstrate or say 'no' and mean it. We do not of course wish to formalise such understanding into an unnecessary or semi-contractual agreement; it is not the role of Government or the law to prescribe how consent should be sought and given. It is, however, the role of the law to make it unambiguously clear that intimate sexual acts should only take place with the agreement of both parties.[192]

It might be useful to return to the hypothetical scenario at the start of the Schulhofer extract concerning the athlete and the surgeon. To some commentators this is a convincing analogy, but others disagree.

Some argue that the case for convicting a man who proceeds with sexual intercourse without an explicit consent is stronger than the case of the surgeon. The doctor may have a good reason for engaging in the treatment (it is in the patient's best interests) and the doctor could legitimately start with a presumption that the patient will consent (the doctor could presume that the patient will want his doctor to do what is in his best interests). But until a person who is about to engage in sexual contact with another knows what the wishes of the other person are, he does not have a good reason for engaging in the activity nor for assuming that the other consents.[193]

Others argue that the analogy is misleading. Thomas III argues that conventionally patients do not give consent by acquiescence, whereas silence is an established way of granting consent to sexual activity.[194] Another point is made by David Bryden who argues that sex is characterized by spontaneity and that therefore it is different from surgery where all decisions are to be carefully thought out and considered. We can expect a doctor to act professionally and follow reasonable rules; parties engaging in sexual intercourse cannot be expected so to behave.[195]

---

[190] Husak and Thomas III (1992: 112).
[191] Dressler (1998: 428). For a full development of such an argument, see Panichas (2006).
[192] Home Office (2002: para. 29).   [193] Herring (2002: 192–3).
[194] Thomas III (2000: 530).   [195] Bryden (2000).

One of the difficulties in relying on consent is that juries inevitably use general social understandings of consent. Widespread attitudes towards women and sexual penetration are built on 'rape myths'.[196] The myths that women 'like it rough' and that 'unless they say no they mean yes' and 'any woman who is drunk wants to have sex'[197] are myths barely beneath the surface of many commonly expressed attitudes to sex.[198] There are also myths about how victims are expected to react to being raped[199] and how they ought to perform in the courtroom.[200] These myths can particularly impact on a victim who claims she has been raped by a former or current partner, with common perceptions being that a woman who has agreed to sex with a man in the past may have agreed on this occasion (or at least the man may have thought she did).[201] A survey by Amnesty International[202] found that 30 per cent of people believed that if a woman had behaved flirtatiously she was partly or completely responsible for a rape, and 26 per cent thought the same if she wore revealing clothing or had been drunk. Astonishingly 6 per cent thought a woman wearing revealing clothing was totally responsible if she was raped and 8 per cent that a woman who was known to have had several sexual partners was again totally responsible. This leads some to suggest that only 'good victims' can hope to receive protection from the criminal law.[203] In a study by Ellison and Munro[204] it was found that even people who reject the myths at a general level, use them when faced with a specific scenario. This suggests that the use of rape myths may be even higher than suggested by studies such as the Amnesty International one.

It certainly appears that some people seem to believe that women can generally be taken to agree to sex at any time with any man, unless she dresses in very baggy clothing, stays indoors, is rude and unfriendly, and fights any man who attempts to have sex with her.

As this discussion has shown there can be considerable uncertainty over what constitutes consent. Consider this policy from one US college which seeks to encourage clearer communication:

Goucher College, *Policy on Sexual Misconduct, Relationship Violence and Stalking* (Towson, MD: Goucher College, 2015)

Consent

Sexual misconduct sometimes involves the absence of consent. Consent means willingly and knowingly agreeing to engage in mutually understood sexual conduct. Consent must be mutual and ongoing, offered freely and knowingly, and cannot be given by a person who is incapacitated, as described below.

Relying solely on non-verbal communication often leads to misunderstandings about consent. For this reason and for the purposes of this policy, **consent to sexual activity must be expressed in explicit words**. For a sexual encounter to be consensual, each participant is expected to obtain or give verbal consent to each act of sexual activity. Consent to engage

---

196 Vandervort (2013); Temkin (2010); Temkin and Krahé (2008); Chapleau, Oswald, and Russell (2007). See Baker (2008) for a general discussion on assumptions about female victims of crime. But note Reece (2013) for a more sceptical consideration of the literature, questioning how many people really believe in the 'myths'. Her article has produced a powerful response in Conaghan and Russell (2014).

197 Gunby, Carline, and Beynon (2010).

198 On the myth that false allegations are regularly made, see McGlynn (2011); Burton (2013).

199 Ellison and Munro (2009).   200 Schuller, McKimmie, Masser, and Klippenstine (2010).

201 Ellison and Munro (2013).   202 Amnesty International (2005).

203 West (1996).   204 Ellison and Munro (2010).

in one form of sexual activity does not constitute consent to engage in other forms of sexual activity, and either party may withdraw consent at any time.

Consent may not be inferred from silence, passivity, lack of resistance, or lack of an active response. Non-communication or silence constitutes lack of consent. A verbal "no" constitutes lack of consent, even if it sounds insincere or indecisive. Incapacitation also constitutes lack of consent. If at any time during a sexual interaction any confusion or ambiguity should arise about consent, it is the responsibility of the person initiating the activity to stop and clarify the other's willingness to continue. If at any time consent is withdrawn, the activity must stop immediately.

Consumption of drugs or alcohol, in and of itself, does not relieve a party of responsibility to obtain ongoing consent.

In order for consent to be valid, all parties must be capable of making a rational, reasonable decision about the sexual act and must have a shared understanding of the nature of the act to which they are consenting. Under this policy, a person is considered incapable of giving consent, or "incapacitated," if her or his judgment is substantially impaired by drugs, alcohol, or some other physical or mental condition; or if incapacitated by being threatened, intimidated, or coerced into giving consent. Indications of consent are irrelevant if the person is incapacitated. Engaging in sexual activity with someone who is incapacitated constitutes sexual misconduct and violates this policy.

Examples of incapacitation include, but are not limited to, being passed out, asleep, unable to communicate, subjected to violence or threat of violence, or intoxicated at a level that substantially impairs judgment. Physical indicators of incapacitation may include:

- Slurred speech
- Unsteady gait or stumbling
- Vomiting
- Unfocused or bloodshot eyes
- Outrageous or unusual behavior
- Expressed memory loss
- Disorientation
- Unresponsiveness
- Being asleep

QUESTIONS

1. A wife in order to please her husband on his birthday agrees to sexual intercourse. She does not really want to have sex, but is willing to put up with it. Her husband knows that this is her state of mind but they have sexual relations. Should this be rape? Does this example suggest requiring a positive desire for sexual intercourse is too strict?

2. Look again at the Goucher College policy (for other examples, see e.g. Harrison, Downes, and Williams (1991)). Would such a regime be a good idea as a national law? Some claim it would rob sexual activity of its spontaneity and passion. Would it? Even if it did, would it be worth it if it reduced the incidence of unwanted sex?

For guidance on answering this question, please visit the Online Resource Centre that accompanies this book: www.oxfordtextbooks.co.uk/orc/herringcriminal7e/.

13.4 CONSENT: WHAT IS THE STATUS OF A MISTAKEN CONSENT?

The traditional common law position, as explained in Part I, is that only a mistake of identity (e.g. where the victim incorrectly assumes that the defendant is her boyfriend) or as to the nature of the act (e.g. where the victim consents to a medical operation, but the defendant engages in sexual intercourse) will be sufficient to negate the consent of the victim. To some commentators the courts have been asking the wrong question: rather than asking whether the mistake is sufficiently serious to negate consent, the courts should ask a simpler question: 'Is what the defendant did the act which the victim consented to?'[205]

Whatever the question asked the topic has excited much debate. Here are three of the hypotheticals which have attracted much comment:

(1) A girlfriend agrees to sexual intercourse with her boyfriend after he tells her that he loves her. In fact he does not, and plans to leave her as soon as they have had sex.

(2) A woman has sex with a man, who tells her that he is not married. She has moral objections to committing adultery and when she discovers that he is married she is deeply distressed.

(3) A man tells a woman that he has been recently tested for HIV and was found not to be positive. She agrees to have sex with him, but she would not have done so if she had known the truth, which was that he had tested positive.

In all of these cases there is no doubt that the man has behaved in a morally reprehensible way, but should he be convicted of a criminal offence? If the criminal law should intervene should these situations be classified as rape or as some kind of lesser sexual offence (e.g. procuring sexual intercourse by deception)? Here are some views:

(1) At one extreme is the view that '[i]f at the time of the sexual activity a person would not have consented to it had they known all the facts at that time (including the defendant's state of mind) then there is no consent.'[206] Such a view would readily convict all three of these defendants. Supporters of such an approach tend to emphasize that sexual relationships involve intimacy and trust, and therefore there are heightened obligations of a fiduciary nature.[207] This means that the standards of honesty and probity expected between lovers should be higher than those expected between two business people, for example. Some commentators argue that as having sex with someone can potentially cause them serious harm, the defendant has a responsibility to ensure there is full consent.[208]

Objectors to this view argue that the use of deceptions is common in 'chatting up'. If the view became law, it would lead to the criminalization of an extraordinary amount of sexual activity. Some have argued that protestations of love are known to be analogous to 'commercial puffing'[209] and are not to be taken seriously.[210] The use of ruses and lies to obtain sexual

---

[205] Herring (2002: 194–5).

[206] Herring (2002); see also Alldridge (1993a); Estrich (1987: 96).

[207] Herring (2014c); Balos and Fellows (1991); Larson (1993).

[208] Herring (2014c).   [209] Bryden (2000: 462).

[210] Jeremy Horder has described as 'trivial' a case where one partner deceives another as to whether he loves her in order to persuade her to consent to sexual intercourse (1999b: 108). For an article warning of the dangers of over-criminalization in the arena of sexual offences, see Bronitt (1991). For a strong rejection of the view that all deceptions are fair 'in love and war', see Larsen (1993: 444).

intercourse is all part of the 'sexual game',[211] although such replies may overlook the evidence of serious psychological harm caused to those who have been tricked into agreeing to sexual intercourse.[212] There is also an argument that to use this rule would create enormous evidential problems. How do we know if 'I love you' is a lie? What exactly does the phrase mean anyway? How can anyone know if the victim would or would not have agreed to sexual intercourse had she known the truth?[213] At the very least there is often 'confusion and messiness' surrounding the party's expectations, particularly in casual sexual liaisons, and so it is inappropriate to probe too deeply into what may or may not have motivated someone to engage in sex.[214] Further, if the sexual intercourse is enjoyed at the time, can it be said that the act was harmful when the victim later discovers the truth?[215]

Even those who would be willing to accept that the law should criminalize the use of deceptions to obtain consent to sexual intercourse might argue that to label it rape belittles that offence.[216] A man lying about his emotional feelings is so far removed from the violent assault that accompanies the 'normal' understanding of rape that it should be labelled differently.[217] Others argue that rights to sexual autonomy are infringed where deception is used as much as where force is used to enable sexual intercourse to take place.[218]

(2) A more moderate view is to argue that we should consider whether the matter about which the victim has made a mistake played 'such a compelling role [in her decision to have sexual relations] that she should be dissociated from her decision on account of it.'[219] This requires the jury to consider how important the lied-about matter was to the victim in reaching his or her decision to engage in sexual intercourse.[220] The difficulty with such a view despite its theoretical attractions is its usability. If it is to be distinguished from view (1), it must be possible to imagine a case where, even though a victim would not have agreed to sexual intercourse without knowing a particular fact, that fact is not regarded as compelling. There is a danger that this will slip into a moral assessment of the victim's reasons for deciding to engage in sexual intercourse.

(3) The common law approach restricts 'rape by deception' to only the most serious cases: those where there is a deception as to the nature of the act or the identity of the person. It might be claimed that this is to impose the law's values as to what is regarded as a fundamental mistake upon the victim. In *Papadimitropoulos*[221] the defendant deceived the victim into believing they had been through a ceremony of marriage and she therefore agreed to engage in sexual intercourse. The Australian High Court held that there was no rape because the victim was not mistaken as to the nature of the act: she knew that they were to engage in sexual intercourse. But to some with religious views (for example) there may be the world of difference between marital sexual intercourse and extra-marital sexual intercourse. ←2 (p.411)

---

[211] Alldridge (1993a) considers, but rejects, such arguments. Schulhofer (1992) talks about the importance of fantasy in sexual matters.

[212] Hecht Schafran (1993).   [213] Schulhofer (1992: 93).

[214] Childs (2001); Bryden (2000). Larsen (1993) and Subotnik (1995) suggest that sexual fraud should be regarded as a tort.

[215] Bohlander (2008).   [216] Dripps (1992).   [217] Thomas III (2000).

[218] Balos and Fellows (1991); Estrich (1987); Boyle (2000).   [219] Larsen (1993: 288).

[220] S. Gardner (1996).   [221] (1957) 98 CLR 249 (Austral. HC).

In the following extract, I criticize the traditional approach of the law and support the first view, although it is an approach which very few commentators have been willing to adopt.[222] Indeed some leading academics have described it as 'preposterous':[223]

J. Herring, 'Mistaken Sex' [2005] *Criminal Law Review* 511 at 513–15, 523–4

There are four specific criticisms of the common law:

The meaning of an act

The meaning of an act depends very much on the cultural understandings surrounding it. The raising of a finger at a person has multiple meanings, depending on its context. It will be appreciated as an insult, a vote or a greeting, depending on its social significance. Such an act can be described simply in mechanical terms (the lifting of a finger), but such a description is one only used by the most erudite of philosophers. In normal life an act gains its meaning from its context and surrounding circumstances. Take sexual intercourse. This can have a wide variety of meanings for different people which may include the following:

1. It may have special religious significance indicating that the parties are embarking on a spiritual union.
2. The act may simply be an expression and conformation of the love the parties have for each other.
3. The act may simply be one which is entered into for physical pleasure.
4. The act of sexual intercourse may be regarded as solely a procreative act.

The same sexual act will have a different meaning for many people depending on the identity of the partner and the time in their lives. A prostitute may well regard sexual activities with her client as completely different from sexual relations with her partner. Similarly a religious person may regard marital intercourse as an expression of spiritual union blessed by God, while an extra-marital union as an odious sin. Yet, as we saw in *Linekar* and *Papadimitropoulos* the traditional common law would not recognise such distinctions which for these people are of fundamental importance.

Defendant-based approach

The traditional approach asks whether the victim's mistake is sufficient to negate her consent. The proper question should be: is the defendant's act that to which the victim has consented? As argued above once the question is asked in that way the victim's response is unlikely to be: 'I consented to X putting his penis inside my vagina/anus/mouth.' It is likely to be much more complicated than this; more complicated in two ways. First, the act is likely to be understood in the context of what it represents: be that 'a moment of mad fun' or 'an affirmation of our love for each other'. Secondly, the act is likely to be understood in the context of the relationship between the parties. The act will be sited in the individuals' understanding of what has happened in the past and what will happen in the future. In other words we need to move away from the simplistic question, 'did the victim say yes or no'. Instead we should be asking how the victim understood the act that she was consenting to. Nicola Lacey puts the point in this way:

---

[222] Although see Knight (2012), who takes a similar view.
[223] Simester, Spencer, Sullivan, and Virgo (2013: 755); Rubenfeld (2013).

'The victim's consent responds to power by conferring legitimacy, rather than shaping power in its own terms: consent is currently understood not in terms of mutuality but rather in relation to a set of arrangements initiated, by implication, by the defendant, in an asymmetric structure which reflects the stereotypes of active masculinity and passive femininity . . .'

The assumption that sexual conduct is good

A further challenge to the traditional approach is that it starts with an assumption that sexual intimacy is a good thing and that we need to identify and criminalise those aspects of sexual intimacy which are harmful. But we could look at this another way and start by seeking to describe the forms of acceptable sexual connection and criminalise the others as harmful. This might particularly have attraction for those sympathetic to the view which casts doubt on whether a woman can ever be said to consent to sexual intercourse with a man, given the oppression under which women live, particularly in the context of sexual relations. Attempting to define what might be regarded as an acceptable form of sexual intimacy would be an interesting task and there is not space to deal with it here. But it is likely that such relations would involve ideas of reciprocity, integration, responsibility, and mutuality. As the Home Office suggests: 'it is important for society as a whole for sexual relationships to be based on mutual respect and understanding.' Unlike commercial transactions, in sexual relations, people are entitled to expect their partners not to consider solely their own interests but rather engage in a cooperative and mutually beneficial relationship. We are therefore entitled to expect sexual partners to owe each other heightened standards of obligation of a fiduciary nature. It hardly seems onerous to expect lovers to behave in a conscionable way with each other.

Deceit negates free choice

Deceit, as much as force and threats, can 'negate consent'. Deceit, like violence, manipulates people into acting against their will. Like threats deceit restricts the options available to another. It does this by making the other unaware of the options the other has available. For example, a man who deceives his partner as to his identity prevents a partner making a decision about whether to have sex with him. Restricting the information on which a person makes a choice can be as inhibiting of a free choice as making an option unattractive through a threat. Indeed in one sense a deception can be regarded as worse than a threat in that the deception uses the victim's own decision-making powers against herself: rendering her an instrument of harm against herself.

. . .

In the past it was said:

[A] male [may] make promises that will not be kept, . . . indulge in exaggeration and hyperbole, or . . . assure any trusting female that . . . the ugly frog is really the handsome prince. Every man is free, under the law, to be a gentleman or a cad.

But we should no longer be in an age when the 'gentle art of seduction' is revered and praised; when women or men are sexual objects to be prised open by whatever means comes to hand. It should no longer be enough just to ask did the complainant say 'yes' in relation to the proposed sexual activity. Now the values that should underpin our sexual offences law are those of mutual respect, reciprocity, connection and honesty. If we respect sexual integrity and the importance of being able to choose with whom to have sexual partners then the choice must be one that is free from coercion and fraud. A man who has sexual intercourse with another knowing that that person would not be agreeing to the activity if s/he knew the truth is using that person for his own ends. It is the 'sheer use of another person'. It should be rape.

Critics of my approach might question whether it is correct that the law should encourage sexual partners to be honest with each other. James Slater argues 'individuals who engage in casual sex should either ensure the trustworthiness of their partners or, if not, minimise or accept the risks that flow from that activity.'[224] He offers an explanation of why fraud to obtain property is different from fraud to obtain sex: while the law needs to encourage people to engage in financial transactions and so protects them from the property fraud offences, there is no social good in casual sexual encounters and so people do need protecting from fraud in relation to them. Can it really be expected that before a casual relationship a partner is expected to reveal every aspect of their history and character which might affect their partner's decision on whether to have sex? From a different perspective Alex Sharpe has mounted a strong objection that my proposal would require a transperson to disclose their gender history to a new partner, which would infringe the transperson's human rights.[225]

Contrast my approach with the following by Rebecca Williams, who suggests that we should focus on the category of mistakes victims make. The benefit of her approach is that a defendant can clearly know in advance what kind of mistakes will mean that the apparent consent of a victim will not be regarded as consent in the law. The disadvantage is that it means that the law, rather than the views of the victim, determine how important different kinds of mistake are.

R. Williams, 'Deception, Mistake and Vitiation of the Victim's Consent' (2007) 124 *Law Quarterly Review* 132 at 156–8

Perhaps, then, instead of trying to find a single test capable of providing all the answers, we should instead return to the "categories" approach to mistake cases with which we began. This existing approach has been found to have two major problems; first that it is out of line with the wholly subjective approach used in cases of pressure and secondly that it is currently based on unarticulated and unjustifiable assumptions. However, it is submitted that neither of these problems is insoluble.

First, it is true that *Olugboja* seeks to establish a spectrum of pressure, on which the key line is to be drawn between "reluctant acquiescence" (consent) and "mere submission" (non-consent), but that line is notoriously difficult to draw. The interesting point is that in order to help juries to find the line, s.75 of the SOA [Sexual Offences Act] 2003 has itself adopted a "categories" approach, listing certain circumstances in which evidential presumptions will be raised against the defendant. Whether or not the particular categories listed there are desirable in their own terms, their existence in the pressure context means that if they were to be introduced to cope with instances of mistake the difference between the two areas would no longer be so great.

If this is accepted, then the first objection falls away and we are left with the second. The real problem here, however, is not the use of categories per se, but the use of finite, rigid, conclusive categories based on unarticulated and unjustifiable assumptions. Unlike the existing categories of mistake, any new categories must therefore fulfil three requirements. First, they must be rational. It must be possible to describe the categories in such a way that the

224 Slater (2011).   225 Sharpe (2012 and 2014).

reason for their existence can be easily understood. Thus, for example, we might include "*non est factum*" mistakes as one category on the basis that, as explained above, a person cannot be said to be consenting to an activity if they do not even know that it is taking place. Secondly, they must be predictable in the sense that it must be possible to ascertain in advance whether a particular case will fall into a given category or not. Thus at present one cannot, in the light of *Tabassum* and *Richardson* predict whether qualifications will be seen as going to "the nature of the act" or "the identity of the defendant". However, it is possible to predict that if V knew she was having sex with D but did not know he was HIV positive she would not fall into the *non est factum* category (though she may fall into another, such as the "physical difference" category). Thirdly, the lines drawn must produce acceptable results in policy terms. Thus we may reject a category of all "but-for" mistakes on the basis that it produces undesirable results in the case of anti-Semitic victims, or we may create a category of "qualification mistakes" on the basis that we wish to protect the institution of marriage or the requirements of professional training. Of course, there will be differences of opinion about whether or not the categories chosen *do* strike the right balance in practice, but the key point is that this discussion must take place openly and not be hidden behind apparently self-applying concepts such as "nature and quality of the act".

In case this conclusion is thought to be too open-ended, my opening bid is that we might wish to regard consent as inoperative where any of the following three kinds of mistakes have been made:

(a) *Non est factum* mistakes

While it may very well be undesirable to confine vitiating mistakes to this category alone, that does not mean that its identification as a category is useless. It can simply form one category of relevant mistakes that is readily identifiable, distinguishable and justifiable. It is likely that mistakes of this kind will only be negative, "condition" mistakes in the sense that if the victims were to be asked why they were consenting to the supposed "operations" they would not reply "because it is not sexual intercourse", rather they would never have consented if they had known that it was. But as explained earlier, since both kinds of mistakes are capable of undermining autonomous consent there is no reason in principle to distinguish between them.

(b) Physical difference mistakes

Again, while this test cannot do all the work alone it is useful as far as it goes and mistakes of this kind should prevent consent from operating. This would include cases of disease transmission and also "whole identity" cases, where the victim mistakes the defendant for another person altogether, real or fictional, known personally or not. It would not, however, include qualification cases, or cases where the victim mistakenly believes the defendant has one particular attribute which would not make a physical difference to the action or transaction itself. Again, there is no reason in this category to distinguish between positive "reason" mistakes and negative "condition" mistakes; either kind should remove consent.

(c) Legal qualification cases

This may be an instance in which a particular categorical line does have to be drawn so that only cases of legal characteristics (such as marriage, entitlements to use credit cards or to practise) are included. It would not then matter whether the qualification in question was the defining characteristic or positive reason for the interchange (I do not care who my dentist is, or about any of his other characteristics, as long as he is a trained dentist) or simply a negative condition placed upon it (I go to my dentist because I have been pleased with his treatment of me in the past but would stop going were I to discover that he was not qualified to treat me). In policy terms, as mentioned above, such a category would support the protection given to such institutions elsewhere in law.

QUESTIONS

1. Alf agrees to have sex with Angie after:

   (a) Angie impersonates Bertha, Alf's girlfriend, who left him five years ago and whom he has never forgotten;

   (b) Angie impersonates Cecile, a family friend whom Alf vaguely knows;

   (c) Angie impersonates Drew, Alf's favourite film star, about whom he knows everything there is to know;

   (d) Angie pretends to be a devout Christian, Alf agreeing to have sexual relations with Angie only because she shares his religion.

   Should any of these be criminal offences? Can any distinction be drawn between them?

2. Fred agrees to sexual relations with Gloria in the following situations:

   (a) Fred suggests they have sex as a religious act, expressing their spiritual union. Gloria has no idea what he is talking about, but agrees to sex as she fancies Fred.

   (b) Gloria agrees to sexual intercourse after Fred tells her he is sterile. In fact he is not and Gloria becomes pregnant as a result.

   (c) Fred suggests they have sex as a demonstration of their mutual adoration. In fact Fred does not love Gloria.

   Should any of these be criminal offences?

3. A newspaper report (*Daily Telegraph*, 2015) records a case of a woman who met a man online who claimed to be a 'male model' who she met for blindfolded BDSM sexual encounters in the dark. He turned out to be a balding 68-year-old man. Should that be rape?

4. 'A woman who consents to have sex with a man after he assures her that he is unmarried has the same state of mind whether his representation turns out to be true or merely a credible lie' (Dripps 1996: 114). Is this a convincing argument for saying that a mistake should never negate consent?

5. 'A man befriends a woman and untruthfully says he loves her. As a result of his declaration she gives him substantial gifts and engages in sexual intercourse. If the facts can be proved there would be little difficulty in obtaining a conviction for obtaining the property (the gifts) by deception. She consented to handing over the property, but the consent was acquired by deception and so provides no defence. Many commentators, however, would deny that he is guilty of rape. But is the right to decide with whom to have sexual contact to be ranked somewhere below the right not to be deprived improperly of one's property?' (Herring 2005: 200). Discuss.

6. Hyman Gross (2007: 225) complains that some writers (e.g. Herring (2005)) are seeking to use criminal law 'to bring about moral improvement in the way men and women relate to each other sexually'. Such moralism he sees as interfering in people's human rights because the criminal law should only be used where there is a serious

offence. I have replied: 'A man meets a woman to whom he is attracted. Their relationship progresses and one night he is keen to have sex. Despite his charms it is clear she is not interested. Without the use of threats, force or lies he will be disappointed. My proposed version of the law would require him to zip up and accept that he is not going to get any tonight. Does such a law infringe his human rights? Hardly. Does it protect the woman's right to sexual autonomy? Exactly' (Herring 2007: 231).

Whose view do you prefer? Is there a danger with my view that any 'bad' sex will become criminal?

7. Michael Bohlander (2008: 414) writes: 'In a society where the secular and liberal section of society, men *and* women, condescendingly smirks at suggestions that they should employ more caution about whom they go to bed with and how soon, that they should "save themselves for Mr. or Ms. Right" or maybe even, *horribile dictu*, marriage, when even some educated university law students make a sporting event of "sleeping around", is there such a thing as a woman who blindly believes what her Romeo tells her? Will she even want to know? Will he even wonder whether she really cares? Are female decisions about engaging in sex always a merely responsive accessory to the principal motivation and initiative of the male? What an antiquated and deeply chauvinist concept!' Is there a danger of the law being over-protective of women?

13.5 CONSENT AND PRESSURE

What if the victim consents to sexual acts as a result of pressure? Few would disagree that a victim who says 'yes' to sexual intercourse in the face of a threat of death or serious harm cannot be properly said to have consented. But what about lesser threats? What about a threat to cause only a minor physical harm (e.g. a slap); or what about a threat to cause emotional harm (e.g. 'I will break off our engagement'); or a financial loss ('I will fire you')? Also, as we have seen with mistake cases, there is a debate over whether or not sexual intercourse procured by the use of illegitimate threats should be regarded as rape[226] or be criminalized using a different label.[227]

Where should the line be drawn?

To some commentators nothing less than a threat of death or serious injury should do. In all kinds of areas of life people reluctantly do things under pressure. Many people do a job only because they need the income to live a certain lifestyle. The fact that the employer threatens not to pay them if they do not work should not be said to undermine their consent to work.[228] As Donald Dripps puts it: 'Any woman who says "yes" because of the pressures of an unjust world deserves our efforts to make the pressures of the world less unjust. But she also deserves our respect for whatever she chooses.'[229] ←5 (p.430)

To other commentators the key question is not so much the nature of the threat, but the appropriateness of the pressure.[230] Although it is permissible (to say the least) for an employer to threaten not to pay a worker who does not work, it is not for an employer to threaten not to pay a worker who does not engage in sexual intercourse with him or her. This

---

[226] McGregor (1996); Estrich (1987).
[227] Schulhofer (1992) discusses civil remedies that could be relied upon.
[228] Bryan (2000).   [229] Dripps (1994: 142–3).   [230] Waye (1992).

view would require a moral assessment of the pressure used. But it is by no means clear that there are generally accepted moral standards of the kinds of 'seduction techniques' that are permissible.

One response advocated by Susan Leahy[231] is to create a particular offence of procuring consent to sex by threats. This would avoid the problem of deciding which threats negate consent. It might, however, be taken to imply that rape by threats is less serious than other rapes.

Should a line be drawn between a threat and an offer?

Some commentators have suggested that it is useful to distinguish cases where the defendant has threatened harm to the victim unless she agrees to sexual activity (where the threat may invalidate the 'consent') and cases where the defendant has made an offer to the victim (where an offer will never invalidate a 'consent').[232] Such commentators therefore see a significant difference between these two cases:

(1) An aspiring actress is told by a director that he will give her the leading role in his new film if she agrees to have sexual intercourse. The 'consent' is induced by an offer and therefore it cannot be rape.

(2) An actress is told by a director that he will replace her in the leading role she has been given in his new film unless she agrees to have sexual intercourse with him. The 'consent' is induced by a threat. This could amount to rape if the threat was considered sufficiently serious to negate the effectiveness of the consent.

Other commentators reject such a distinction, arguing that in both cases the level of pressure on the victim will be the same, and it is artificial to consider the distinction between them.[233] Such commentators often take the view that the law should focus on the effect of the threat or offer on the victim, rather than the classification of the threat as an offer or a threat.[234] The difficulty with such a position is that it produces (at least from the defendant's point of view) uncertainty in the law. He may put some pressure on a woman (e.g. 'I will end our relationship unless you agree to sexual intercourse'), and unknown to him the effect of such a threat may be very severe. For example, some commentators have suggested that repeated requests for sexual intimacy can be regarded as intimidatory. Some men would be surprised to hear that. To some extent these concerns can be dealt with by the *mens rea* requirement which we will examine later.

Social pressures

One of the claims that is commonly made by feminist commentators is that we live in a culture where there are strong social expectations that men should be allowed to have sex with women as they wish. A recent study for the Children's Commissioner found that girls under 16 felt that it was expected a girl would consent to sex with her boyfriend and that something was wrong if they did not consent. As one girl commented:

---

[231] Leahy (2014).

[232] Wertheimer (2012). See Hirshman and Larson (1998) for a discussion of 'sexual bargaining'.

[233] Chamallas (1998: 820–30).

[234] Schulhofer (1998: 120). Tadros (1999), e.g., suggests that the issue should be whether or not the victim had a fair opportunity to exercise her will.

> I think it's a given now that you are expected if you ever go out with a guy or whatever, it's expected that you are supposed to be having sex with him. Even when you are little [young].

The survey also found considerable pressure on young men to have sex and thereby gain 'man points'.[235] The issue must also be seen in the broader culture of casual sexism. As an NUS survey[236] found:

> Campus cultures were also defined as gendered, and strongly connected with if not insep-arable from 'lad culture'. 'Lad culture' was seen as a 'pack' mentality evident in activities such as sport and heavy alcohol consumption, and 'banter' which was often sexist, misogynist and homophobic. It was also thought to be sexualized and to involve the objectification of women, and at its extremes rape supportive attitudes and sexual harassment and violence.

Some commentators have gone so far as to claim we live in a 'rape culture'.[237]

This is a tricky issue. The danger is if taken too far it may lead to a conclusion that in a patriarchal culture no woman consents to sex, which would harm women's sexual auton-omy and seem to deny the possibility of consensual pleasurable sex.[238] On the other hand we cannot take the issue of consent to sex out of its particular cultural and social setting.[239]

13.6 CONSENT: INTOXICATED MISTAKE

In the following passage, Alan Wertheimer summarizes the views that could be taken in a case where the victim of rape was intoxicated at the time of sexual intercourse:[240] ←4 (p.424)

A. Wertheimer, 'Intoxicated Consent to Sexual Relations' (2001) 20 *Law and Philosophy* 373

> To facilitate the analysis, let us distinguish among five claims that appear in discussions of this issue . . . First, it may be argued that if B consents to sexual relations while voluntarily intoxicated, we should regard it as impermissible for A to have sexual relations with B. Call this the *impermissibility claim*. The impermissibility claim represents our all things consid-ered judgment as to whether we should treat B's intoxicated consent as valid. Second, it may be argued that if a woman consents while intoxicated, her consent is *necessarily* invalid because intoxication always undermines the capacity requirements of valid consent, whether or not B's intoxication is voluntary. Call this the *intoxication claim*. The intoxication claim says that intoxication *entails* invalidity, and so it also entails that we should accept the impermissibility claim. Third, it may be argued that if B's intoxication is itself voluntary or self-induced, then we should treat B as responsible for her intoxicated behavior. Call this the *responsibility claim*. By itself, the responsibility claim says nothing about the validity of B's consent. It is a general claim about one's responsibility for one's intoxicated behavior.

---

[235] Coy, Kelly, Elvine, Garner, and Kanyeredzi (2013).   [236] NUS (2012).

[237] Madden Dempsey and Herring (2007), but see Gittos (2015).   [238] Kaplan (2014).

[239] Baker (2015) argues we should not expect the criminal law to outlaw all rape because we cannot cap-ture all rapes in a legal definition.

[240] For contrary views, see Cowan (2008). See Finch and Munro (2006) for differing views among mem-bers of the public over the impact of intoxication on consent.

The fourth claim connects the responsibility claim to consent. It might be argued that if a woman is responsible for her intoxicated behavior, it follows that her intoxicated consent must be treated as valid. Call this the *responsibility entails validity claim*, or, more briefly, the *validity claim*. If we accept the responsibility claim and the validity claim, then we must treat B's consent as valid, that is, we must say that it is permissible for A to have sexual relations with B if B consents while voluntarily intoxicated. A fifth claim supports the position that we should reject the impermissibility claim by drawing an analogy between intoxicated consent and intoxicated criminal behavior. On this view, if people should be held responsible for wrongful acts committed while intoxicated (including acts of violence against women), then we should also treat B's consent as valid. Call this the *consistency claim*.

It seems among the general public there is a common view that if a couple have sex while equally intoxicated, this may be an unpleasant experience, but should not be regarded as rape.[241] That may explain why it has proved so difficult to obtain a conviction in cases where the victim has been intoxicated. At the very least it can be difficult for a jury to be sure beyond reasonable doubt what happened if neither party to the incident has a clear recollection of what happened. That said, generally the law does not regard intoxication as a defence for a defendant who harms another. Why should rape be treated any differently from a case of where a defendant, for example, drunkenly injures someone?

QUESTIONS

1. How should the law deal with cases where, although there has been no direct threat, there is a 'power imbalance' between the parties? In the United States there has been much discussion over sexual relationships between university lecturers and their students or between attorneys and doctors and their clients. Should there be a presumption of non-consent in such cases? Should this be dealt with as a breach of professional ethics, rather than a criminal matter?

2. Do the difficulties over the definition of consent indicate that it would be better to formulate the law on sexual offences without reference to consent? Chamallas (1988) suggests asking whether the sexual activity reveals 'mutuality' (see also Pineau (1989)). Is that a useful alternative to consent?

13.7 SHOULD CONSENT BE ENOUGH?

So far most of the discussion has assumed that if there is consent, then the sexual penetration should not be criminal. However, some commentators have argued that consent should not be seen as the touchstone of whether or not sex is lawful. Catherine MacKinnon (2003)[242] argues:

The problem with consent-only approaches to criminal law reform is that sex, under conditions of inequality, can look consensual when it is not wanted, at times because women know that sex that women want is the sex men want from women. Men in positions of

---

[241] Gunby, Carline, and Beynon (2015).   [242] MacKinnon (2003).

> power over women can thus secure sex that looks, even is, consensual without that sex ever being freely chosen, far less desired.

Not only may it be argued that the consent approach fails to take account of wider social pressures, it may also be argued that it is too narrow in its approach. The story is structured by the 'consent question' as construed by the law: the man wanted to engage in penile penetration, so the question for the jury is did the complainant agree or not? Such a picture reflects images of an active masculinity and passive femininity, but it also closes out the story of what happened before and what was intended to happen after: of how the act was to be understood. Nicola Lacey[243] has written:

> The victim's consent responds to power by conferring legitimacy, rather than shaping power in its own terms: consent is currently understood not in terms of mutuality but rather in relation to a set of arrangements initiated, by implication, by the defendant, in an asymmetric structure which reflects the stereotypes of active masculinity and passive femininity.

It may also be argued that the consent approach overlooks the responsibilities that sexual partners owe each other. Respecting a person's sexual autonomy may require more than the other has said 'yes', but also that their humanity is respected and dignity upheld.

Although it is easy to find problems with consent of the kind just mentioned, it is far harder to find an alternative to it, which can distinguish rape and other sexual penetration. It may be that concepts of mutuality, communicative sexuality, and sexual responsibilities can be developed to create such an approach. However, they may lack the simplicity and practical benefits of a consent-based approach.[244]

This leads to a more profound question. What moral work does consent do? How, exactly, does consent distinguish rape from permissible sex? Relying on the writing of Michelle Madden Dempsey, I give one answer and explain the consequences of that approach:

J. Herring, 'Rape and the Defence of Consent' (2014) 16 *National Law School of India Review* 62 at 68–9

> When the victim (V) gives effective consent, this provides the defendant (D) a justifying reason for having sex with V. It gives D a reason to assume that the act is in the V's well-being and so allows D to set aside reasons against penetration which rest in the well-being of V. Broadly understood, this is because D, in this context, is permitted to rely on V's assessment that the act is overall in the V's best interests. In effect, where consent is effective Madden Dempsey [2013] claims that D is entitled to say:
>
>> "This is [V]'s decision. He's an adult and can decide for himself whether he thinks the risk is worth it. In considering what to do, I will assume that his decision is the right one for him. After all, he is in a better position than I to judge his own well-being. And so, I will not take it upon myself to reconsider those reasons. Instead, I will base my decision of whether to [harm] him on the other relevant reasons."

---

[243] Lacey (1998b: 114).
[244] See Anderson (2005) for further discussion.

Applying that in the context of opposite sex sexual intercourse, where the woman gives effective consent the man is entitled to say: "She has made the decision to agree to sex and decided that is what she wants to do. I will assume she has determined that the sex is in her best interests. I do not therefore need to worry about arguments that it might not be in her best interests for her to have sex with me."

This approach assists us in determining a range of questions which have troubled criminal lawyers in their understanding of consent in this context. To be effective consent it must provide D with sufficient grounds to be able to conclude that V has made an appropriate assessment of whether the penetration is in her best interests. Some of the issues that have troubled academics and courts in understanding consent will now be explored from that starting point....

One appealing feature of the Madden Dempsey model of consent is that it emphasises the notion of responsibility. When D has sex with V, because he is committing a prima facie wrong, he has responsibilities to ensure that the act is justified and he has good reasons for doing what he did.

... As will be clear by now, the approach advocated in this article means that more is expected of D than simply listening to whether V says "yes" or "no". A proper respect for sexual integrity should allow the telling of a V's story of what happened before the incident, and the context within which it took place. D should be listening to what V is saying about the proposed act as it is likely to require appreciating how V understands the act within its wider relational and social meaning; so that D can be assured that the act is one which V has properly assessed as promoting her well-being.

14 *MENS REA* FOR RAPE

Great controversy surrounds the *mens rea* for rape. We will now consider some of the views that have been taken: ←6 (p.440)

14.1 THE INTENT-BASED VIEW

It could be argued that it is only rape if the defendant intends that the victim did not consent. This is almost impossible to prove. Very rarely would it be said to be the defendant's purpose that the victim did not consent.[245] It is unlikely that the defendant would regard his enterprise to be a failure if it turned out that the victim consented. This view has received very little support in the academic commentary.

14.2 THE SUBJECTIVE RECKLESSNESS VIEW

This view requires proof that the defendant knew or believed that the victim did not consent; in other words that the defendant was *Cunningham* reckless as to the victim's lack of consent. This view would acquit a defendant who unreasonably took the view that the victim consented, for example because he believed he was irresistible to all women.

---

[245] *Khan* [1990] 2 All ER 783 (CA).

14.3 THE *MORGAN* VIEW

This view, developed by the House of Lords' decision in *Morgan*,[246] holds that the defendant is guilty unless he positively believes that the victim consented. This is slightly different from the subjective recklessness view because it includes not only the state of mind where the defendant knows that the victim is not consenting, it also includes the defendant who does not consider whether the victim consents[247] or not, or 'could not care less'; indeed any state of mind except a clear belief that the victim consents is sufficient.

The *Morgan* decision was controversial.[248] The objection to it is straightforward: it is easy for a man to have reasonable grounds for his belief as to whether the victim consents if he is in any doubt: he just has to ask.[249] If the man gets it wrong he causes the victim an enormous level of harm, so surely requiring him to take such a simple step when risking such a serious harm is not too onerous a duty.[250] As Huigens puts the defendants in *Morgan*, if they believed that Mrs Morgan consented they did so out of 'callousness, immaturity, self-absorption, and stupidity' and those should not provide the basis of a defence.[251] Such arguments tend to lead one to support a negligence-based test for rape.

One of *Morgan*'s few academic supporters, although a very notable one, is Professor John Smith.[252] His view is that a person who has chosen to have intercourse with the victim without her consent is not at the same level of blame as a person who has carelessly not checked whether the victim is consenting. Further, negligence is no longer used for offences against the person and it would be anomalous to introduce it just for the offence of rape.[253]

14.4 THE NEGLIGENCE VIEW: 'UNREASONABLE BELIEF'

This view asks simply whether the defendant's view of the victim's consent was reasonable or not. In other words the question is whether a reasonable person in the defendant's shoes would have reached the decision that the victim was consenting.[254] If the reasonable person would have known that the victim was not consenting then the *mens rea* of rape is made out. This is close to the position reached in the definition of rape in the Sexual Offences Act 2003.

Benefits claimed for the negligence approach are that it may increase the conviction rate for rape, which is so low at present.[255] The argument is that it is difficult under the *Morgan* test for the jury to be sure that the defendant did not think that the victim was consenting. Another alleged benefit is that it would mean that the focus would not be so much on what was actually going on in the victim's mind, but rather what a reasonable person would think

---

[246] [1976] AC 182 (HL).

[247] Bryden (2000: 342) argues that it is impossible for a man engaging in sexual intercourse not to avert to the issue of whether the victim consented.

[248] Duncan (1994) deconstructs the judgments in *Morgan*. The government of the day took the issue so seriously that they set up a special committee to examine the decision and its ramifications: the Heilbron Committee (1976).

[249] If the victim expresses consent, then the defendant will have reasonable grounds for his belief.

[250] Pickard (1980); Wells (1982); Charlow (2002).   [251] Huigens (2005: 202).

[252] J.C. Smith (1975). See also Bohlander (2008).   [253] Bohlander (2008).

[254] See Taslitz (2005), who suggests that many men who have unreasonable beliefs that women are consenting to sex are 'wilfully blind' to the truth (i.e. they have deliberately deceived themselves as to what the woman is thinking).

[255] Home Office (2002).

was the victim's attitude to the proposed sexual activity.[256] This might lead to the prevention of distressing lines of cross-examination in rape trials where the defence seeks to show that in fact the victim was enjoying what was happening.

In the following extract, Victor Tadros sets out some concerns about the *mens rea* for rape as set out in the Sexual Offences Act 2003, based on reasonable belief:

V. Tadros, 'Rape without Consent' (2006) 26 *Oxford Journal of Legal Studies* 515 at 534–6

C. The Mens Rea of Rape

Pure objective tests do not adequately discriminate between defendants whose beliefs show insufficient regard for the interests of others and defendants who are stupid, naïve or ignorant. It may be that the Parliamentary twist to section 1 [requiring the jury to consider all the circumstances of the case] helps to do the relevant work in this regard, but it is unclear how that twist will be interpreted. In general, as I have noted, vague standards tend to lead to under-enforcement of the law of rape. However, this may be different with regard to defendants who may be the victims of other kinds of discrimination in the courts. For example, in the US there has been concern that black defendants, particularly in cases where there are white complainants, tend to be treated particularly harshly by vague and ambiguous provisions. The occurrence of a similar problem in England and Wales cannot be discounted. At any rate, it will clearly be much simpler to appreciate the significance of the debate between subjectivists and objectivists in this context by considering different types of rape. It will immediately become much clearer what the limitations of subjectivism are as well as the potential risks involved in objectivism regarding defendants of whom we have lower expectations with regard to their knowledge or their cognitive capacities.

Furthermore, at least some of the worries that have led to a rejection of subjectivism in the law of rape begin to evaporate once the *actus reus* of the offence is properly differentiated. Consider a defendant who has broken into the complainant's home. He has intercourse with the complainant and she is too terrified to offer any resistance. If the jury are asked to consider whether the defendant honestly believed that she consented, it may be difficult to provide an answer. The defendant may have a distorted appreciation of what consent *really is*. Ideally, of course, the jury ought not to take the defendant's interpretation of what consent is as relevant, just as, in the interpretation of the offence of wounding with intent to cause grievous bodily harm, the defendant's interpretation of what counts as grievous is not relevant in answering the question. However, it is very difficult to direct the jury in a way that ensures that the defendant's interpretation of what consent is does not distort the judgement of the jury. In contrast, this problem would not be faced if there was a provision built precisely around the fear of the complainant. Suppose that part of the definition of rape was as follows: a person commits the offence of rape if he penetrates another person, B, and she submits to that penetration as a consequence of fear. A subjectivist definition of the *mens rea* of that part of rape would be as follows: the defendant is not guilty of the offence of rape if he honestly believed that the victim was not submitting to penetration as a consequence of fear. It is consistent with subjectivism for the jury to convict if the defendant thought that there was any risk that the complainant was submitting due to fear. That only leaves rare cases where the defendant honestly believed that the victim was definitely not submitting because she was afraid. At least some such cases ought to result in rape convictions. But whether that is accepted or not, redefinition of the *actus reus* of the offence in a differentiated way prevents decision-makers becoming distracted by different interpretations of what consent is in assessing whether the defendant fulfilled the *mens rea* of the offence.

Casting the provision evidentially seems a poor second to properly outlining the conditions under which the accused displays a sufficient disregard for the sexual autonomy of the victim to constitute rape. This is true in four respects. First, the evidential provisions of the SOA leave far too much open to 'interpretation' by the courts, or rather to manipulation and under-enforcement. The evidential provisions indicate that the legislature takes seriously some of the conditions under which sexual autonomy might be undermined by an accused in a rape case even where the complainant has said 'yes' to intercourse. But they fail to define the different ways in which sexual autonomy might be undermined with sufficient accuracy.

Second, in treating the relevant circumstances as evidence of a lack of consent rather than as constitutive of the offence, the Act fails to recognize the proper significance of, for example, violence or involuntary intoxication. In the proper circumstances these constitute a failure to respect the sexual autonomy of the complainant rather than providing evidence of such a failure.

Third, the SOA still retains the multiply ambiguous concept of consent as the central idea around which the law of rape is constructed. This problematically supposes that a single concept is capable of capturing all of the different ways in which the sexual autonomy of the complainant might be undermined by the defendant. The ambiguity in the concept of consent, which is manifest in the drafting of the SOA, and its vagueness, are open to exploitation throughout the criminal process.

Fourth, the definition of the *actus reus* of rape introduces substantial confusion into the *mens rea* of rape, obfuscating the important questions that are relevant to deciding whether the defendant ought to be convicted of the offence. Hence, although the SOA is a step forward in the definition of the offence of rape, at least in some respects, it is insufficient to meet the central concerns that ought to motivate rape reform.

14.5 THE NEGLIGENCE VIEW: 'UNREASONABLE FORMATION OF BELIEF'

This approach is similar to the one just described, but asks whether the defendant acted reasonably in forming his belief that the victim consented. In other words it looks at his reasoning process, rather than the decision actually reached.[257] Simon Gardner suggests that such an approach may be useful in ensuring that defendants who suffer from mild learning difficulties or who are sexually inexperienced and try their very best to ascertain whether the victim is consenting, but reach the wrong conclusion, are not convicted on the basis that a reasonable person would have known that the victim did not consent.[258] The main difficulty with this approach is that juries in rape trials seem to find it hard enough to decide whether or not the defendant thought the victim consented; they will find it even harder to work out the reasoning process the defendant used in reaching that conclusion.

---

[257] S. Gardner (1991).   [258] Brett (1998).

14.6 STRICT LIABILITY APPROACH TO RAPE

It would be possible to argue that rape should be a strict liability offence. In other words, once it is proved that there was penetration without the victim's consent the offence is made out. This would of course be very harsh on defendants who, on perfectly reasonable grounds, believe the victim consents, but in fact it is proved that she did not.[259] Therefore, few commentators are willing to suggest that rape generally should be a strict liability offence. But some commentators suggest that under certain circumstances it is fair to impose strict liability.

Balos and Fellows[260] suggest that if there is a pre-existing relationship there is a heightened duty on the man to ascertain accurately whether the woman consents to sex. Where the defendant fails to obtain her consent, he is guilty even if he was acting reasonably or in good faith. They go further and claim that where the relationship has been characterized by violence, any consent given by a woman in such a relationship will be presumed to be invalid.[261]

David Bryden rejects the analogy drawn by Balos and Fellows between the relationship of lovers and other relationships where the law presumes undue influence (e.g. solicitor–client relationships).[262] He argues that it is wrong to assume that women are weak and powerless in their sexual relations. There is a danger that the Balos and Fellows approach portrays woman as feeble. Their critics might also argue that strict liability is normally restricted to minor offences.[263]

An alternative version of a strict liability approach is that a man who had sexual intercourse with a woman who had manifested some kind of opposition to it (be it verbal or physical) has committed rape. This is so even if at the time of sexual intercourse she appeared to be consenting and he reasonably believed that she was consenting.[264] This approach is controversial, especially in cases where there is a significant gap in time between the 'no' and the subsequent 'yes': may not the woman change her mind as the defendant's seductive techniques take effect?[265] However, what to some are 'seduction techniques' are from another perspective coercive. Susan Estrich, for example, argues that repeated requests for sex are inherently coercive.[266] This reveals a major difficulty in this area. What by some men are regarded as 'normal seduction techniques' appear to some women to be threatening behaviour.[267] It is perhaps the lack of open communication and understanding between the genders which is a key difficulty in tackling the issue of unwanted sex.[268]

15 THE *ACTUS REUS* OF RAPE

There has been some debate over the *actus reus* of rape. Should it be restricted to penetration of the vagina or should it include penetration of the anus and mouth, as the Sexual Offences Act 2003 states? And should rape be restricted to penetration by a penis or should it include penetration with objects or other parts of the body? To some rape has a well-established meaning (penile penetration) which is known to the public and it would cause unnecessary confusion to extend it. Another argument that has been used in favour of the

---

[259] Husak and Thomas III (1992). [260] Balos and Fellows (1991: 603–4).
[261] See also Basile (1999). [262] Bryden (2000: 349). [263] *Ibid*, 364.
[264] Henderson (1992: 158); Estrich (1987: 102–3). [265] Bryden (2000: 391).
[266] Estrich (1987: 105). [267] Kinports (2001). [268] Weiner (1983).

traditional understanding of rape as penile penetration is that it uniquely includes the risk of pregnancy.[269] However, some argue that the public needs to be educated that the definition of rape is phallo-centric[270] and male-dominated: that from a male point of view whether he is penetrating the victim with his finger or his penis is of great significance. However, from the victim's point of view it is not. Further the public may need to be made more aware of the reality of the rape of men by men[271] or arguably the rape of men by women.[272] ←1 (p.409)

Jennifer Temkin has suggested that we could adopt the Canadian approach, suggesting that first-degree sexual assault should be defined to include penetration involving the penis, vagina, or anus, together with the threat or infliction of serious injury. Second-degree assaults would involve penetration involving the penis, vagina, or anus, following a threat or infliction of injury. Third-degree assaults would cover all other sexual assaults involving penetrations, and fourth-degree assaults cover indecent assault not involving penetration.[273]

In the following passage, John Gardner and Stephen Shute seek to support a narrower definition of rape:

J. Gardner and S. Shute, 'The Wrongness of Rape' in J. Horder (ed.) *Oxford Essays in Jurisprudence* (Oxford: OUP, 2000), 209–12

In many jurisdictions, including ours, what counts as sexual intercourse for the purposes of the crime of rape is limited to (one or another kind of) penetrative violation. Why is penetration so special? Does it count as a special way of using another person? The natural answer, of course, is that it counts as an especially humiliating way of using them. But again the special humiliation seems epiphenomenal. There was no special humiliation in the pure case because there was no humiliation at all in the pure case: the rape was never discovered. If, in more everyday cases, penetrative violations *are* particularly humiliating (or terrifying, confidence-sapping, etc.) in the eyes of those who experience them, then as usual we want to know the reason why. Why do violations of *this* kind have such special import for those who suffer them? One might say, of course, that the law itself contributes something to the special significance of penetration by historically reserving the name of 'rape' for that class of violations. Certainly there is something in that: the historic legal names of some criminal offences have gathered moral import with age, and often do contribute to structuring people's moral thinking. The thinking here goes: rape is (particularly) terrible; rape is non-consensual penetration; so non-consensual penetration is (particularly) terrible. But this cannot serve *by itself* to justify the law's maintaining its insistence on penetration. Perhaps the old focus on penetration was superstitious or corrupt and the modern law should now be doing its utmost to change the confused moral thinking which that old focus left in its wake. Some aspects of the law of rape or the practice of rape prosecution, such as the marital rape exemption and the institutional blindness to date-rape, as well as the accompanying interest in evidence of the victim's sexual history, are now widely acknowledged to have left a false trail, and hence a false understanding of rape, in public consciousness. Is not the penetration condition, with its crude phallocentrism, in the same camp? Does it not hang over from an era of obsession with female virginity and overbearing preoccupation with

---

[269] Naffine (1994) is concerned about any definition of rape which disguises the fact that the victims of rape are predominantly female.

[270] Duncan (1995).

[271] For a discussion of the treatment in the courtrooms of male rape, see Rumney (2001b).

[272] Rumney (2001a).   [273] Temkin (2002: 95–109).

the sin of bearing illegitimate children, an era in which women were *officially* regarded as objects (chattels of their fathers and husbands) rather than subjects? So maybe we should dump this condition now? We do not think that the answer is quite so simple.

What is true is that the justification of the penetration condition in the modern law of rape does involve some attention to social meaning. Some associate the Kantian argument we adopted above with a view of morality as a body of eternal verities which one abandons on pain of self-contradiction. In places this was how Kant himself presented the applications of the argument. But in fact the applications of the argument depend on many contingencies, including the social meaning of many actions. Which actions count as paradigms of sheer use-and-abuse of human beings varies, even though the Kantian argument against the sheer use-and-abuse of human beings has enduring force. Often the special symbolism of a particular act or class of acts is tied to the particular symbolism of acts which are regarded as their moral opposites. The special symbolism of penetrative violation is closely associated, in our culture, with the special symbolism of penetrative sexual activity. That latter symbolism may be over-romanticized. It may come of an aspiration to an impossible perfect union of two selves through two bodies, by making the two bodies, in a sense, just one (recall Shakespeare's 'beast with two backs'). Be that as it may, the fact that penetrative sex is regarded as having that significance actually endows it with that significance by changing its social meaning. The social meaning of the subversion of penetrative sex—its subversion in rape—tends to mirror the social meaning of penetrative sex. If the latter is thought of as a perfection of subject–subject relations—through the most complete and literal intertwining of selves—then the former may well come to represent a paradigm of subject–object relations. This is relevant to explaining and justifying the reactions even of those who do not share the aspiration to intertwine selves in this literal way (e.g. those who eschew or avoid penetrative sexual relationships, or those who see them as purely functional). The use of penetration can be a special weapon even against these people, perhaps *especially* against these people. It can become a peculiarly dramatic way of objectifying them, of turning them into mere things to be used, mere means to another's ends. That being so, there is reason for all those who suffer such violations to feel humiliated, whether or not they see particular value, or any value, in consensual penetrative sexual activity. The social meaning of consensual sexual penetration is not necessarily the meaning it has for them, and it is the social meaning of consensual sexual penetration which the rapist exploits by subverting it.

This is not a case against expanding the legal definition of rape to include some kinds of non-penetrative violations, or for discriminating among various kinds of penetration. In fact, it is not an argument for any particular legal definition of rape. It merely points out that the reactions of those who attach particular significance to penetrative violations, or to certain penetrative violations, need not be irrational. They may be supported by symbolic values. Much is left to lawmakers and law-interpreters in deciding how best to embody and reflect such symbolic values in a given legal system. Social meanings are often ambiguous, and always have grey areas. Rarely do they set definite boundaries to moral wrongdoing without additional instrumental arguments, and instrumental argument also introduces many contingencies which can affect legal classifications. We showed this already in discussing the 'lack of consent' requirement. The instrumental question of what system of sexual relations would lead to the least use-and-abuse of human beings was an element of the argument. No doubt similar instrumental issues arise in the case of the penetration condition. The point is that although the mere use of people is a timeless evil, the elevation of penetrative nonconsensual sexual violation to the status of special paradigm is a longstanding, but culturally conditioned application.

These remarks on the importance of social meaning merit the attention of those who are uneasy about the tendency to associate rape with sex, and in particular the tendency to think of it as a 'sexual offence'. Many campaigners and social researchers tell us that rape typically has nothing to do with sexual desire, and everything to do with a male desire for power over women. Surely it should be regarded as a crime of misogynist aggression, a hate-crime, rather than a sexual offence? We are uneasy about the essentialist view of sexual desire which this critique seems to harbour: Why, we wonder, cannot a misogynist desire to subordinate women be a sexual desire? (Is it because sex is wonderful and misogyny is vile?) But even if we grant the integrity of the assumed contrast between sexual desire and other kinds of desire, the main objection to this line of thought is that it assumes that 'sexual offences' are those offences which are differentiated by the offender's motivations. In our view, the real reason for thinking of rape as a sexual offence has nothing to do with the offender's motivations. It is that rape is a weapon against its victim which trades on the social meaning of sexual penetration. It is a way of taking a paradigm subject–subject relationship—a possibly over-romanticized conception of sexual intimacy—and turning it against someone to make a mere object of her. This does not rule out, and indeed may well suggest, that the perpetrator hates the victim, or what she represents. It is not necessary to deny the connection between rape and sex in order to make this clear. On the contrary, if the connection with sex is dropped and rape is simply labelled as, say, 'aggravated assault', then it seems to us that (for better or worse) we have decided no longer to recognize in law what is *particularly* wrong with rape. True, a rape can *accurately* be labelled as a kind of assault (as the police often label it when conducting their investigations) since the unifying theme of assault crimes is invasion by one of another's personal space, and the rapist clearly does invade his victim's personal space. But this is a wrong incidental to, and usually rather trivial when placed alongside, the most fundamental element of wrongdoing in rape. So the description of rape as an assault, though accurate, is reductive and unrevealing? That most fundamental element of wrongdoing in rape, which differentiates rape from (most) assaults and gives rape a separate theme from the family of assault crimes, is the *sheer use* of the person raped, whether that is how the rapist saw what he was doing or otherwise. To understand how rape counts as sheer use, the social meaning of sexual penetration has to be kept in focus.

Whatever the offender means by it, and indeed whatever it means to its victim, rape is a crime of sexual violation according to its social meaning; and that social meaning is the meaning which is at the heart of rape's wrongness. One may still insist that 'violence' would be a better word here than 'violation'. Would it not at least have more political bite? We doubt whether even this is true. Assimilation of rape to the category of 'violent crime' in the media and in public discussion of crime has, in our view, done more than almost anything else to maintain the public myth that rapists are strangers waiting in dark alleys who subdue their victims by force. But rapists work by many more insidious methods than this and they still wrong their victims by non-consensual objectification of them. As our pure case of rape serves to remind us, and many more common kinds of case amply illustrate, the violation that is rape need not be associated with any kind of violence. Nor are the worst rapes necessarily the most violent rapes. Rapes in breach of trust using subtle threats or surreptitiously administered drugs to forestall any resistance can, in some cases, represent an even more egregious abuse of the person raped and can therefore be worse *qua* rapes (and this still remains true, on our analysis, whether or not these are the rapes that involve the worst experiences for the person raped).

QUESTIONS

1. One survey found that 26 per cent of men and 50 per cent of women in dating relationships reported having engaged in unwanted sexual activity within the two-week

period of the study (O'Sullivan and Rice Allgeier 1998). See also Muehlenhard and Cook (1988). Does this suggest that the law on sexual assault is failing badly?

2. Is there much the criminal law can do to change people's behaviour in sexual matters? Does that mean the law should not try?

3. A survey published in 2005 (BBC News Online 2005c) found 1 in 10 men said that they had used a prostitute. A similar survey in 1990 had found the figure to be 1 in 20. Does this tell us anything about attitudes towards sexual relations and sexual crimes?

4. Jeffrie Murphy (1994) suggested rape was analogous to forcing someone to eat sushi or taking something that is normally pleasurable and forcing it upon someone. How can people say such things?

5. Is sex that is unwanted the same as sex that is not consented to? Robin West (2012) argues that consensual sex can be harmful. She gives this example: 'It may also be emotionally abusive; repetitive sex wanted by one party but undesired by the other, night after night for months, years, or an entire adulthood, carries with it the message that her subjective hedonic life—her pleasures, pains, and interests—are of no consequence. They don't figure into the equation of what to do. That is damaging to a person's self-sovereignty as well as one's sense of self-sovereignty: A woman who endures unpleasant invasive sex over time has implanted in her body, so to speak, the truth that her subjective pleasures and interests don't matter.' Do you agree?

6. Joan McGregor (2005: 183) writes: '[T]he problem with fraud in the inducement is that exaggeration and puffery are part and parcel of romantic or sexual relationships. People make themselves sound and appear better in order to impress their partner and entice them into sex. Men drive more expensive cars than they can afford and women wear push-up bras to entice and influence men's choices.' Does this mean we should be reluctant to find deceptions negate consent to sexual relations?

7. There is much debate over the extent and nature of 'false allegations' of rape (see Rumney (2006); Burton (2013)). Do you think concerns over false allegations should affect the legal definitions of rape?

8. Does the fact we have an 'age of consent' reveal that the current law on consent is unsatisfactory? Consider this comment from Janine Benedet (2010):

> 'Age of consent laws are only really necessary where the judicial understanding of nonconsent is so thin and impoverished that the power imbalances between a girl and an older man cannot be recognized for what they are—proof that no consent was in fact present. Reliance on presumptions based on age or other factors may make us lazy about developing a definition of coercion or nonconsent that reflects the reality of male sexual violence as practiced.'

9. Meredith Duncan (2007) has argued that it should only be rape where force has been used by the man and that 'at least' recklessness is shown. He argues this is necessary in order to ensure that a clear line is drawn between non-consensual sex and rape. He explains:

> 'I am not suggesting that a woman is to blame when she is the victim of nonconsensual sex. Not at all. Rape is a very serious crime. My intent is not to belittle or minimize the injury to rape victims. However, I am suggesting that in a society where morals have loosened to the point that premarital sex is not considered as immoral as it once was (or dare I say, is not considered immoral at all), and

sex outside of marriage often appears to be and is encouraged as the norm in society, we should be very careful about convicting less culpable individuals for forcible rape. We should be very careful when convicting men and boys of rape in uncertain circumstances. As our society moves more toward treating women as equals, women should bear some of the responsibility for sexual misunderstandings as part of that equality. The old adage that even a dog can tell the difference between being kicked and being tripped over does not necessarily hold true in the acquaintance rape context.'

Should the law do more to restrict rape to the clearest cases of the offence?

FURTHER READING

Archard, D. (1998) *Sexual Consent* (Boulder, CO: Westview).

Benedet, J. and Grant, I. (2014) 'Sexual Assault and the Meaning of Power and Authority for Women with Mental Disabilities' *Feminist Legal Studies* 22: 131.

Bohlander, M. (2008) 'Mistaken Consent to Sex, Political Correctness and Correct Policy' *Journal of Criminal Law* 71: 412.

Bryden, D. (2000) 'Redefining Rape' *Buffalo Criminal Law Review* 3: 317.

Cowan, S. (2008) 'The Trouble with Drink: Intoxication, (In)capacity, and the Evaporation of Consent to Sex' *Akron Law Review* 41: 899.

Dripps, D. (1992) 'Beyond Rape: An Essay on the Difference between the Presence of Force and the Absence of Consent' *Columbia Law Review* 92: 1780.

Duncan, M. (2007) 'Sex Crimes and Sexual Miscues: The Need for a Clearer Line between Forcible Rape and Nonconsensual Sex' *Wake Forest Law Review* 42: 1087.

Gardner, S. (1996) 'Appreciating *Olugboja*' *Legal Studies* 16: 275.

Green, L. (2013) 'Should Law Improve Morality?' *Criminal Law and Philosophy* 7: 473.

Henderson, L. (1992) 'Rape and Responsibility' *Law and Philosophy* 11: 127.

Herring, J. (2005a) 'Mistaken Sex' *Criminal Law Review* 511.

Herring, J. (2009a) 'Relational Autonomy and Rape' in S. Day Sclater *et al* (eds) *Regulating Autonomy* (Oxford: Hart).

Herring, J. (2014a) 'Consent in the Criminal Law: The Importance of Relationality and Responsibility' in A. Reed and M. Bohlander (eds) *General Defences in Criminal Law* (Aldershot: Ashgate).

Herring, J. (2014b) 'Rape and the Definition of Consent' *National Law School of India Review* 16: 62.

Huigens, K. (2005) 'Is Strict Liability Rape Defensible?' in R.A. Duff and S. Green (eds) *Defining Crimes* (Oxford: OUP).

Leahy, S. (2014) '"No Means No", But Where's the Force? Addressing the Challenges of Formally Recognising Non-Violent Sexual Coercion as a Serious Criminal Offence' *Journal of Criminal Law* 78: 309.

McGregor, J. (2005) *Is It Rape?* (Aldershot: Ashgate).

Madden Dempsey, M. (2013) 'Victimless Conduct and the *Volenti* Maxim: How Consent Works' *Criminal Law and Philosophy* 7: 11.

Madden Dempsey, M. and Herring, J. (2007) 'Why Sexual Penetration Requires Justification' *Oxford Journal of Legal Studies* 27: 467.

Munro, V. (2008) 'Constructing Consent: Legislating Freedom and Legitimating Constraint in the Expression of Sexual Autonomy' *Akron Law Review* 41: 923.

Munro, V. (2010) 'An Unholy Trinity? Non-Consent, Coercion and Exploitation in Contemporary Legal Responses to Sexual Violence in England and Wales' *Current Legal Problems* 45.

Rubenfeld, J. (2013) 'The Riddle of Rape-by-Deception and the Myth of Sexual Autonomy' *Yale Law Journal* 122: 1372.

Schulhofer, S. (1998) *Unwanted Sex: The Culture of Intimidation and the Failure of Law* (Cambridge, MA: Harvard University Press).

Tadros, V. (2006a) 'Rape without Consent' *Oxford Journal of Legal Studies* 26: 515.

Temkin, J. (2010) '"And Always Keep A-hold of Nurse, for Fear of Finding Something Worse": Challenging Rape Myths in the Courtroom' *New Criminal Law Review* 13: 719.

Temkin, J. and Krahé, B. (2008) *Sexual Assault and the Justice Gap: A Question of Attitude* (Oxford: Hart).

Wertheimer, A. (2003) *Consent to Sexual Relations* (Cambridge: Cambridge University Press).

West, R. (1993b) 'Legitimating the Illegitimate: A Comment on Beyond Rape' *Columbia Law Review* 93: 1442.

West, R. (2012) 'Sex, Law, and Consent' in F. Miller and A. Wertheimer (eds) *The Ethics of Consent: Theory and Practice* (Oxford: OUP).

Williams, R. (2009) 'Deception, Mistake and Vitiation of the Victim's Consent' *Law Quarterly Review* 124: 132.

16 CONCLUDING THOUGHTS

There are few more controversial topics in criminal law than the area of sexual offences. As we have seen in this chapter there are some who are concerned that the current law has dangerously crossed a line so that behaviour which does not live up to the highest moral standards is labelled rape. They believe that the concept of rape has been extended far beyond its natural meaning of forced intercourse by a defendant who is aware the victim is not consenting. There are others who believe that the law does not go far enough in adequately protecting women from sexual abuse. There can be little doubt that attitudes towards sexual matters and what can reasonably be expected of a sexual partner are changing rapidly. One thing that can be agreed upon is that the issues raised by this chapter are extremely important and it is crucial than an effective law on sexual offences is developed.

8

THEFT, HANDLING, AND ROBBERY

CENTRAL ISSUES

1. Theft is committed where the defendant has dishonestly appropriated property belonging to another with intention to deprive the other of it permanently.

2. The offence of robbery involves the defendant using force at the time of or immediately before a theft. The offence is also committed where the defendant causes the victim to fear that force will be used, but does not actually use force.

3. If a defendant is involved in the retention, removal, disposal, or realization of stolen goods which he or she knows or believes to be stolen goods, then an offence is committed.

PART I: THE LAW

1 THEFT

Section 1 of the Theft Act 1968 defines theft:

A person is guilty of theft if he dishonestly appropriates property belonging to another with the intention of permanently depriving the other of it.

The offence can be broken down into five elements:

DEFINITION
The defendant is guilty of theft if he or she:

(1) appropriates;

(2) property;

(3) belonging to another;

(4) dishonestly;

(5) with an intention permanently to deprive.

The *actus reus* of theft is, therefore, appropriating property belonging to another.

The *mens rea* is dishonesty and an intention permanently to deprive.

We will now consider these five elements. In order to understand appropriation it is necessary first to understand the meaning of 'property'.

1.1 PROPERTY

Section 4(1) of the Theft Act 1968 defines property as follows:

'Property' includes money and all other property, real or personal, including things in action and other intangible property.

This is a wide definition which includes most things that would normally be regarded as property, ranging from cars to pieces of paper. Even illegal drugs have been held to be property.[1] Before we look at things on the borderline of the concept of property, some of the phrases in section 4(1) may need explaining:

(1) Real property is land.

(2) Personal property is property which is not land.

(3) A thing in action (sometimes known as 'a chose in action') means a property right that can be claimed in a court action. A common example of 'a thing in action' is a debt. If someone owes you £50 you do not own £50, but under the law of theft you do have a piece of property in the right to sue the other person for that money.

(4) Intangible property' includes patents and copyrights.[2] So a person who purports to sell another's rights under a patent is committing theft.[3]

We will now consider cases on the borderline of what is property for the purposes of theft:[4]

Land

Land cannot be stolen. So moving a garden fence to add an extra foot to your garden will not amount to theft of the land. This straightforward proposition needs clarification in three particular situations:

---

[1] *R v Smith (Michael Andrew)* [2011] EWCA Crim 66.

[2] *Mensah-Lartey and Relevy* [1996] Cr App R 143 (CA).

[3] A person who infringes a copyright (e.g. by illegally copying a CD) is not committing theft. This is because he does not appropriate the copyright (he does not act as the copyright holder); he simply infringes the copyright. He may, then, be liable to pay damages in a civil case, but there is no theft.

[4] It is notable that some things are not property under the general law of property and so cannot be stolen. Others things are property under the general law, but s. 4 specifically excludes them from the definition of property for the purposes of the law of theft.

(1) Where the defendant is acting as a trustee or personal representative. Under section 4(2)(a) there can be theft of land by the defendant:

> when he is a trustee or personal representative, or is authorised by power of attorney, or as liquidator of a company, or otherwise, to sell or dispose of land belonging to another, and he appropriates the land or anything forming part of it by dealing with it in breach of the confidence reposed in him.

This means that if the defendant is a trustee and is authorized to sell some land he can be convicted of theft if he sells more land than he is authorized to do.

(2) Things found on a piece of land (e.g. a tree, a piece of garden furniture) fall into one of two categories: they either do or do not form part of the land. Something is part of the land if it is growing on the land (e.g. a rose bush), is a permanent structure (e.g. a garden shed), or is an integral part of such a structure or a fixture (e.g. a roof tile). Things that are moveable (e.g. a piece of garden furniture) are not part of the land. Things that do not form part of the land are property for the purpose of theft.

The law is more complex for things that form part of the land. To understand the law in this area it is necessary to distinguish between those who are in possession of the land, those who are tenants and those who are not in possession of the land:

(a) Those who are in possession of the land. This includes the owners of the land. For them, not surprisingly, it is no offence to take property which forms part of the land or to sever the property from the land. Therefore (of course) an owner of a house does not commit theft if he or she picks flowers from his or her garden.[5]

(b) Those who are not in possession of the land (e.g. a trespasser or a person invited onto the land by the owner). Such people are dealt with under section 4(2)(b). There can be theft by a defendant of things forming part of the land: '[W]hen he is not in possession of the land and appropriates anything forming part of the land by severing it or causing it to be severed, or after it has been severed.' So if a trespasser removed something that formed part of the land (e.g. a garden shed) this would be theft.

(c) Tenants in possession. It would not be an offence for a tenant to remove something that formed part of the land he was renting unless what he removed was a 'fixture or structure'.[6] A fixture is anything permanently attached to the land. It includes a staircase or a wall, but not a plant or gravel.

(3) Special rules relate to fruits and plants from the land. Section 4(3) of the Theft Act 1968 states:

> A person who picks mushrooms growing on any land, or who picks flowers, fruit or foliage from a plant growing wild on any land, does not (although not in possession of the land) steal what he picks, unless he does it for reward or for sale or other commercial purposes.

These rules apply only to those who are not in possession of the land. In essence picking wild mushrooms, fruit, or flowers from land is not theft unless it is done for commercial reasons (section 4(3)). There are three important restrictions here. First, it should be noted

---

[5] This is true even if the seeds were planted by the previous owner. [6] Theft Act 1968, s. 4(2)(c).

that the section refers specifically to 'picking' and so does not apply to people who dig up whole plants, or cut parts of plants, who are guilty of theft.[7] Second, it applies only to wild mushrooms and plants, and so a person who picks cultivated flowers commits an offence. Third, a defendant who is picking wild flowers etc. for commercial purposes is guilty of an offence. This provision means that someone out for a walk in the countryside who picks a blackberry for a little snack is not committing an offence. Someone who picks the black-berries to sell at a market stall is.

Wild creatures

These are dealt with by section 4(4) of the Theft Act 1968, which provides:

> Wild creatures, tamed or untamed, shall be regarded as property; but a person cannot steal a wild creature not tamed nor ordinarily kept in captivity, or the carcase of any such creature, unless either it has been reduced into possession by or on behalf of another person and possession of it has not since been lost or abandoned, or another, or another person is in course or reducing it into possession.

The key distinction drawn in this section is between tamed creatures (e.g. pets), wild creatures kept in captivity (e.g. wild animals kept in a zoo) or reduced into possession (e.g. wild animals which have been trapped), and wild creatures not kept in captivity. Tame animals are treated as property and can be stolen. Similarly, wild animals kept in captivity or reduced into possession can be stolen.[8] However, wild animals not kept in captivity are not property and cannot be stolen.

Information

Information is not property. In *Oxford v Moss*[9] a civil engineering student copied an examination paper and then returned it.[10] The Court of Appeal quashed a conviction for theft as confidential information cannot be stolen.[11] The protection of confidential information is found in civil law where injunctions can be obtained to prevent its revelation. It should be noted that the Computer Misuse Act 1990 creates special offences which deal with people accessing confidential information held on computers. →1 (p.535)

Electricity

It seems that electricity is not property, although there is a specific offence under section 13:[12]

> A person who dishonestly uses without due authority, or dishonestly causes to be wasted or diverted, any electricity shall on conviction on indictment be liable to imprisonment for a term not exceeding five years.

---

[7] Unless they are in possession of the land.

[8] *Cresswell v DPP* [2006] EWHC 3379 (Admin) held that wild badgers were not property.

[9] (1979) 68 Cr App R 183 (CA).   [10] Do not get any ideas!

[11] Law Commission Consultation Paper No. 150 (1997) suggested the creation of an offence of disclosing trade secrets.

[12] Theft Act 1968, s. 13, discussed in *Low v Blease* [1975] Crim LR 513.

Gas[13] and water in an artificial retainer[14] are property and can be stolen. Water in a stream or a pond is treated as part of the land on which it lies and is dealt with under the rules governing land described previously.

Bodies

The traditional view is that bodies, parts of bodies, bodily products, and corpses are not property.[15] However, this view is coming under challenge, and it is now accepted that sometimes these can be property. At present, it appears that there are three circumstances in which bodily matter could amount to property for the purposes of the law of theft:

(1) If a corpse is reduced to another's possession or control it becomes property. So a buried corpse is not property, but if the corpse has been taken into the possession or control of a hospital then it is regarded as property that can be stolen.

(2) Bodily products (such as blood, urine, semen) become property if they are taken into someone's control. In *Welsh*[16] a man gave a urine sample to the police, and then ran off with it. He was convicted of theft of the urine. So blood stored at a blood bank or sperm stored at an infertility clinic can be regarded as property. But bodily products left lying around or disposed of in the normal way are not regarded as theft. So a hairdresser who took hair cut from a pop star and sold it would probably not be committing theft.

(3) If someone has exercised special skills in relation to a corpse or part of a body then that corpse or body part may be transformed into property.[17]

In *Yearworth v North Bristol NHS Trust*[18] the Court of Appeal held that the traditional approach to ownership of bodies was outdated. In that case the court held that men who gave sperm to a hospital for storage, in case they should need it in the future for fertility treatment, had a property interest in the sperm. The court did not go into detail about when precisely ownership in bodily products is retained. The court in that case emphasized the statutory duties on the hospital to store the sperm subject to the men's consent and the importance of the sperm to the men. Later cases will give further clarity to the law. It may be we are gradually moving to the position that a person will retain ownership of bodily parts and products where there is a good reason to do so.[19]

In some areas Parliament has passed legislation to tackle dishonest dealings with things that are not property for the purposes of theft. For example, the Computer Misuse Act 1990 was passed to protect confidential information on computers and the Human Tissue Act 2004 governs body parts.[20]

---

[13] *White* (1853) 169 ER 696.   [14] *Ferens v O'Brien* (1883) 11 QBD 21.

[15] *Sharpe* (1857) D & B 160. For a detailed discussion of this issue, see J.W. Harris (1996b) and Herring and Chau (2007).

[16] [1974] RTR 550. See also *Rothery* [1976] RTR 550. In *Herbert* The Times, 22 December 1960 a man was convicted of theft after cutting off someone's hair.

[17] *R v Kelly* [1999] QB 621.   [18] [2009] EWCA Civ 37.

[19] See Goold, Greasley, Herring, and Skene (2015) and Herring (2012c) for more detail.

[20] Services cannot be stolen. A person who takes a taxi journey and then runs away without paying does not steal the journey, although such conduct is covered in the Fraud Act 2006, s. 11.

> **QUESTION**
>
> Anne picks some wild blackberries to use in her crumble for her boyfriend. When he arrives at dinner that night he announces that he does not like blackberries. Anne decides to sell the blackberry crumble at her shop the next day. Has she committed theft?

1.2 BELONGING TO ANOTHER

It is normally straightforward whether the property belongs to another.[21] If there is any doubt the law of property normally readily provides an answer.[22] Sometimes property is deemed to belong to no one. This occurs most obviously where property has been abandoned by the owner, with no interest in its return or treatment.[23] However, there are some borderline cases and these are dealt with by the four subsections in section 5 of the Theft Act 1968:

Section 5(1)

Section 5(1) states:

> Property shall be regarded as belonging to any person having possession or control of it, or having in it any proprietary right or interest (not being an equitable interest arising only from an agreement to transfer or grant an interest).

This means that property does not just belong to the person who owns it, but also belongs to any person who has possession or control of it,[24] or has a proprietary interest in it.[25] In *R (Ricketts) v Basildon Magistrates' Court*[26] a defendant's conviction of theft of property left outside a charity shop was upheld. There were two counts. For the second, bags of clothes had been left in a storage bin at the back of the shop. It was held that the items left there were within the possession or control of the shop and so the conviction should stand. The first charge related to bags left on the pavement outside the shop. These could not be said to be in the possession or control of the shop.[27] The donor of the bags had not abandoned them, as they intended them to be a gift to the shop, rather than a gift to anyone passing by. In relation

---

[21] Although see *Sullivan and Ballion* [2002] Crim LR 758 (CA), where the money had been taken from a dead person.

[22] See *Marshall* [1998] 2 Cr App R 282, excerpted in Section 1.4.

[23] So a miss-hit golf ball which the player decides she cannot be bothered to look for is abandoned by her (although the ball may then 'belong to' the owner of the golf course for the purposes of the Theft Act as he or she has 'possession and control' over the ball (*Hibbert v McKiernan* [1948] 2 KB 142)). *Williams v Phillips* (1957) 41 Cr App R 5 held (perhaps surprisingly) that property put in a rubbish bin was not abandoned, in that the owner intended it to be removed by the council refuse collectors and not any passer-by.

[24] Generally a person who owns land controls any property on it, even if he or she does not know of the property's existence (*Woodman* [1974] QB 754 (CA)).

[25] It is beyond the scope of this book to discuss all the circumstances in which someone may acquire a legal or equitable interest in the property.

[26] [2010] EWHC 2358 (Admin).

[27] So although the bags were intended to come into the shop's possession and control, at the time of the appropriation they had not been.

to the first charge, the defendant should have been charged with theft from the unknown person who left the bags, rather than the shop.[28]

It should be added that the possession or control does not have to be lawful possession or control.[29] In other words, if Tim steals property and then Sam takes the property from Tim, this can still be theft by Sam. The fact that he was taking the property from Tim who did not have lawful possession of it is no defence. Similarly in *Smith (Michael Andrew)*[30] the defendant was convicted of stealing illegal drugs from a drug dealer, even though the drug dealer would not have been able to enforce his legal rights of possession in a court of law.

A further significance of this is that the owner can be convicted of theft of his own property. At first sight this seems a most peculiar idea, but is quite appropriate in some cases. One example was *Turner (No. 2)*[31] where a defendant drove his car away from a garage where he had left it to be repaired, without paying the bill. He was convicted of theft of his car. The car belonged to another because the garage had lawful control of it.[32]

Section 5(2)

Section 5(2) states:

> Where property is subject to a trust, the persons to whom it belongs shall be regarded as including any person having a right to enforce the trust, and an intention to defeat the trust shall be regarded accordingly as an intention to deprive of the property any person having that right.

Normally, if property is held on trust it is owned by the beneficiaries. However, this subsection deals with the property of trusts which do not have beneficiaries (e.g. charitable trusts). In such a case the property shall be regarded as belonging to those entitled to enforce the trust (e.g. the Attorney General in the case of charitable trusts).

Section 5(3)

Section 5(3) states:

> Where a person receives property from or on account of another, and is under an obligation to the other to retain and deal with that property or its proceeds in a particular way, the property or proceeds shall be regarded (as against him) as belonging to the other.

This subsection deals with the situation where a defendant is given property and is under an obligation to deal with that property in a particular way.[33] Although the defendant is in civil law the owner of the property, if he is under an obligation to the victim to deal with that property in a particular way then the property is treated as belonging to the victim for the

---

[28] See Thomas (2011) for a discussion of whether 'freegans' commit theft when taking out-of-date produce from supermarket bins.

[29] *Kelly* [1998] 3 All ER 741 (CA).   [30] [2011] EWCA Crim 66.

[31] (1971) 55 Cr App R 336 (CA).   [32] See also *Bonner* [1970] 2 All ER 97 (CA).

[33] Sometimes giving property to people and placing them under an obligation to deal with it in a particular way will create a trust and therefore s. 5(1) or (2) can be relied upon as an alternative to s. 5(3). A court will not be sympathetic to arguments that the prosecution case should have been based on s. 5(1), rather than 5(3) or vice versa (see *Hallam and Blackburn* [1995] Crim LR 323).

purposes of the law of theft. The obligation must be a legal obligation: a moral obligation is not enough.[34]

In the following case, the Court of Appeal emphasized that it must be shown that the defendant was obliged to deal with *that property* in a particular way:

R v Hall
[1973] 1 QB 126 (CA)

Geoffrey Hall, a travel agent, received money from some clients by way of deposits for air flights to America. He paid the money into the firm's general account. In fact none of the flights materialized and the money was not refunded. He was convicted of theft, but appealed, arguing that the money did not belong to another and section 5(3) did not apply.

Lord Justice Edmund Davies [reading the judgment of the court]

Point (1) turns on the application of s 5(3) of the Theft Act 1968, which provides:

> 'Where a person receives property from or on account of another, and is under an obliga-tion to the other to retain and deal with that property or its proceeds in a particular way, the property or proceeds shall be regarded (as against him) as belonging to the other.'

Counsel for the appellant submitted that in the circumstances arising in these seven cases there arose no such 'obligation' on the appellant. He referred us to a passage in the Eighth Report of the Criminal Law Revision Committee (*Theft and Related Offences*, Cmnd 2977 (1966), p 127) which reads as follows:

> 'Subsection (3) [of cl. 5 "Belonging to Another"] provides for the special case where property is transferred to a person to retain and deal with for a particular purpose and he misapplies it or its proceeds. An example would be the treasurer of a holiday fund. The person in question is in law the owner of the property; but the subsection treats the property, as against him, as belonging to the persons to whom he owes the duty to retain and deal with the property as agreed. He will therefore be guilty of stealing from them if he misapplies the property or its proceeds.'

Counsel for the appellant . . . submits that the position of a treasurer of a solitary fund is quite different from that of a person like the appellant, who was in general (and genuine) business as a travel agent, and to whom people pay money in order to achieve a certain object—in the present cases, to obtain charter flights to America. It is true, he concedes, that thereby the travel agent undertakes a contractual obligation in relation to arranging flights and at the proper time paying the airline and any other expenses. Indeed, the appel-lant throughout acknowledged that this was so, although contending that in some of the seven cases it was the other party who was in breach. But what counsel for the appellant resists is that in such circumstances the travel agent 'is under an obligation' to the client 'to retain and deal with . . . in a particular way' sums paid to him in such circumstances. . . .

Nevertheless, when a client goes to a firm carrying on the business of travel agents and pays them money, he expects that in return he will, in due course, receive the tickets and

---

[34] *Gilks* (1972) 56 Cr App R 734 (CA). It is for the judge to direct the jury on facts they must find before a legal obligation will arise (*Dunbar* [1995] 1 Cr App R 280 (CA)). Whether the obligation is legal or moral is a question of law, not a matter of the defendant's belief (*Dyke and Munro* [2001] EWCA Crim 2184, [2002] 1 Cr App R 30 (CA)). Although if the obligation was in fact legal but the defendant believed it to be moral, this might be a relevant issue for the purposes of dishonesty.

other documents necessary for him to accomplish the trip for which he is paying, and the firm are 'under an obligation' to perform their part to fulfil his expectation and are liable to pay him damages if they do not. But, in our judgment, what was not here established was that these clients expected them 'to retain and deal with that property or its proceeds in a particular way', and that an 'obligation' to do so was undertaken by the appellant. We must make clear, however, that each case turns on its own facts. Cases could, we suppose, conceivably arise where by some special arrangement (preferably evidenced by documents), the client could impose on the travel agent an 'obligation' falling within s 5(3). But no such special arrangement was made in any of the seven cases here being considered. It is true that in some of them documents were signed by the parties; thus, in respect of counts 1 and 3 incidents there was a clause to the effect that the People to People organisation [the appellant's firm] did not guarantee to refund deposits if withdrawals were made later than a certain date; and in respect of counts 6, 7 and 8 the appellant wrote promising 'a full refund' after the flights paid for failed to materialise. But neither in those nor in the remaining two cases (in relation to which there was no documentary evidence of any kind) was there, in our judgment, such a special arrangement as would give rise to an obligation within s 5(3).

It follows from this that, despite what on any view must be condemned as scandalous conduct by the appellant, in our judgment on this ground alone this appeal must be allowed and the convictions quashed.

Appeal allowed. Conviction quashed.

Key to the Court of Appeal's reasoning in this case was that the courts did not expect the travel agent to deal with the actual monies handed over in a particular way.[35] The customers expected the travel agent to buy tickets for them, but not using the particular monies they provided.

There are conflicting authorities on people who collect money on behalf of a charitable organization, but then keep the money for themselves. In the leading case of *Wain*[36] a defendant collected money for 'The Telethon Trust' (a charitable trust), but did not pass the proceeds on to a charity and transferred the money into his own account. It was held that the defendant was properly convicted because he was under an obligation to retain, if not the actual notes and coins collected, at least their proceeds.[37]

QUESTION

A mother visiting her son at university is concerned that he is not eating enough green vegetables or fresh fruit and gives him a £10 note, saying: 'You must spend this note on fresh fruit or vegetables and on nothing else.' He spends the money on beer. Has he committed theft?

For guidance on answering this question, please visit the Online Resource Centre that accompanies this book: www.oxfordtextbooks.co.uk/orc/herringcriminal7e/.

(In answering this question you will need to ask: Was this a legal or moral obligation? Was the obligation to deal with the particular note in a special way? Was there dishonesty? (See Section 1.5.).)

---

[35] Contrast *Klineberg and Marsden* [1999] 1 Cr App R 427.   [36] [1995] 2 Cr App R 660.
[37] Such cases often involve careful analysis of the legal obligations of the parties. In commercial contexts, this can become highly complex (see e.g. *Re Kumar* [2000] Crim LR 504).

Section 5(4)

Under section 5(4):

> Where a person gets property by another's mistake, and is under an obligation to make restoration (in whole or in part) of the property or its proceeds or of the value thereof, then to the extent of that obligation the property or its proceeds shall be regarded (as against him) as belonging to the person entitled to restoration, and an intention not to make restoration shall be regarded accordingly as an intention to deprive that person of the property or proceeds.

This subsection deals with the situation where the defendant has received property as a result of another's mistake and is under an obligation to restore the proceeds or their value. A good example of where section 5(4) operates is *Attorney-General's Reference (No. 1 of 1983)*,[38] where a police officer was overpaid her salary by the police force. She was under an obligation to return the money (once she was aware of the overpayment) and therefore the money could be treated as belonging to another (the police force).

DEFINITION

Where A hands to D property on the basis of a mistake, four situations need to be distinguished:

(1) The mistake is so fundamental that ownership does not pass. So although D possesses the property, in fact, it is still owned by A. There is therefore no difficulty in establishing the 'property belonging to another' requirement if D is charged with theft.

(2) The mistake is not so fundamental that ownership does not pass and so D owns the property. But the mistake is sufficient to mean that D is under an obligation to return the money or its proceeds. This means that, relying on section 5(4), the property belongs to A for the purposes of the law of theft and so D can be convicted.

(3) The mistake is one that means that D holds the property on trust for A. In such a case A has an equitable interest in the property and the property belongs to A under section 5(1) of the Theft Act, so D can be convicted of theft (see e.g. *Shadrokh-Cigari* [1988] Crim LR 465 (CA); *Hallam and Blackburn* [1995] Crim LR 323 (CA)).

(4) The mistake is not significant enough to give rise either to a claim that ownership did not pass, or to a claim that there is a legal obligation to make restoration. In that case the property will belong to D and no theft charge can lie, unless the transfer from A itself can be regarded as dishonest. In that case, after *Hinks* [2000] 3 WLR 1590 (HL), a charge of theft could be brought.

1.3 APPROPRIATION

Appropriation is a key element in the law of theft. Under section 3(1):

> Any assumption by a person of the rights of an owner amounts to an appropriation, and this includes, where he has come by the property (innocently or not) without stealing it, any later assumption of a right to it by keeping or dealing with it as owner.

---

[38] [1985] QB 182.

The House of Lords had to consider the interpretation of appropriation four times since the 1968 Act was passed. We will be quoting the two most recent and important cases shortly, but first we will summarize its conclusions on two key issues:

(1) There is an appropriation if the defendant has assumed *any* of the rights of the owner. This means that if the defendant has done something that an owner has the right to do then this is an appropriation. It is therefore appropriation to touch someone else's property, offer it for sale,[39] or destroy it. It must be shown that the act is something that only an owner has the right to do. Looking at something is therefore not appropriation because people other than the owner have the right to do that. Similarly, just making the defendant deal with his or her property in a particular way does not amount to appropriation.[40] There is no need to show that the victim has lost the property for there to be appropriation; indeed there is no need to show that the victim's property interests have been adversely interfered with. In *Morris* the defendant appropriated items by switching the sticky labels on items in a shop indicating their price.

This definition of appropriation does mean that theft takes place at an earlier point in time than would be assumed by most people. If a person walks into a supermarket and touches a tin of baked beans intending to steal it, theft is committed there and then. You might have thought that theft would not be committed until the defendant ran out of the store with it, but that is not the law.[41]

(2) Does an act of appropriation have to be one that was not consented to by the victim? The answer is simply no. A touching of a piece of property is an appropriation, whether the victim consented, requested, or objected to the act. The victim's state of mind is irrelevant to whether or not there is appropriation. This was confirmed in the *Gomez* decision. In *Hinks* the House of Lords held that even if the property was handed over by the victim to the defendant as part of a valid gift under the law of property this could amount to an appropriation.

The following decision of the House of Lords is the leading case on the interpretation of appropriation:

R v Gomez
[1993] AC 442 (HL)

Edwin Gomez was the assistant manager of a shop. A customer (an acquaintance of his) offered two stolen cheques as payment for some goods. Gomez was aware the cheques were stolen, but persuaded the manager of the shop to accept them by lying and saying that the cheques were 'as good as cash'. Gomez was charged with theft. At his trial he argued that there was no case to answer because the transfer of the goods had been consented to by the manager and there could therefore be no appropriation. He was convicted, the Court of Appeal allowed his appeal, and the prosecution appealed to the House of Lords.

---

[39] *Pitham and Hehl* (1976) 65 Cr App R 45.   [40] *Briggs* [2004] Crim LR 495.
[41] However, it will be difficult for a prosecution to prove that the defendant had the *mens rea* of theft if he is arrested before leaving the shop.

Lord Keith of Kinkel

The [Court of Appeal] granted a certificate under section 33(2) of the Criminal Appeal Act 1968 that a point of law of general public importance was involved in the decision, namely

'When theft is alleged and that which is alleged to be stolen passes to the defendant with the consent of the owner, but that has been obtained by a false representation, has (a) an appropriation within the meaning of section 1(1) of the Theft Act 1968 taken place, or (b) must such a passing of property necessarily involve an element of adverse [interference] with or usurpation of some right of the owner?'

[**Lord Keith** analysed the speeches in the House of Lords' decision in *Lawrence* [1972] AC 626 and continued:]

It will be seen that Viscount Dilhorne's speech contains two clear pronouncements, first that it is no longer an ingredient of the offence of theft that the taking should be without the owner's consent and second, that an appropriation may occur even though the owner has permitted or consented to the property being taken. . . .

[**Lord Keith** then considered the speech of Lord Roskill in the House of Lords in *Morris* [1984] AC 320 and concluded:]

In my opinion Lord Roskill was undoubtedly right when he said in the course of the passage quoted that the assumption by the defendant of any of the rights of an owner could amount to an appropriation within the meaning of section 3(1), and that the removal of an article from the shelf and the changing of the price label on it constituted the assumption of one of the rights of the owner and hence an appropriation within the meaning of the subsection. But there are observations in the passage which, with the greatest possible respect to my noble and learned friend Lord Roskill, I must regard as unnecessary for the decision of the case and as being incorrect. In the first place, it seems to me that the switching of price labels on the article is in itself an assumption of one of the rights of the owner, whether or not it is accompanied by some other act such as removing the article from the shelf and placing it in a basket or trolley. No one but the owner has the right to remove a price label from an article or to place a price label upon it. If anyone else does so, he does an act, as Lord Roskill puts it, by way of adverse interference with or usurpation of that right. This is no less so in the case of the practical joker figured by Lord Roskill than in the case of one who makes the switch with dishonest intent. The practical joker, of course, is not guilty of theft because he has not acted dishonestly and does not intend to deprive the owner permanently of the article. So the label switching in itself constitutes an appropriation and so to have held would have been sufficient for the dismissal of both appeals. On the facts of the two cases it was unnecessary to decide whether, as argued by Mr. Jeffreys, the mere taking of the article from the shelf and putting it in a trolley or other receptacle amounted to the assumption of one of the rights of the owner, and hence an appropriation. There was much to be said in favour of the view that it did, in respect that doing so gave the shopper control of the article and the capacity to exclude any other shopper from taking it. However, Lord Roskill expressed the opinion, at p. 332, that it did not, on the ground that the concept of appropriation in the context of section 3(1) 'involves not an act expressly or impliedly authorised by the owner but an act by way of adverse interference with or usurpation of those rights.'

While it is correct to say that appropriation for purposes of section 3(1) includes the latter sort of act, it does not necessarily follow that no other act can amount to an appropriation and in particular that no act expressly or impliedly authorised by the owner can in any circumstances do so. Indeed, *Reg. v. Lawrence* [1972] A.C. 626 is a clear decision to the contrary since it laid down unequivocally that an act may be an appropriation notwithstanding that it is done with the consent of the owner. It does not appear to me that any sensible distinction can be made in this context between consent and authorisation.

. . . *Lawrence* makes it clear that consent to or authorisation by the owner of the taking by the rogue is irrelevant. The taking amounted to an appropriation within the meaning of section 1(1) of the Act of 1968. *Lawrence* also makes it clear that it is no less irrelevant that what happened may also have constituted the offence of obtaining property by deception under section 15(1) of the Act.

. . .

My Lords, for the reasons which I have given I would answer branch (a) of the certified question in the affirmative and branch (b) in the negative, and allow the appeal.

Lord Browne-Wilkinson

My Lords, I have read the speech of my noble and learned friend, Lord Keith of Kinkel, with which I agree. I only add a few words of my own out of deference to the contrary view expressed by my noble and learned friend, Lord Lowry, and to consider the cases on thefts from companies to which we were referred in the course of argument.

. . .

The fact that Parliament used that composite phrase—'dishonest appropriation'—in my judgment casts light on what is meant by the word 'appropriation'. The views expressed (obiter) by this House in *Reg. v. Morris* [1984] A.C. 320 that 'appropriation' involves an act by way of adverse interference with or usurpation of the rights of the owner treats the word appropriation as being tantamount to 'misappropriation.' The concept of adverse interference with or usurpation of rights introduces into the word appropriation the mental state of both the owner and the accused. So far as concerns the mental state of the owner (did he consent?), the Act of 1968 expressly refers to such consent when it is a material factor: see sections 2(1)(b), 11(1), 12(1) and 13. So far as concerns the mental state of the accused, the composite phrase in section 1(1) itself indicates that the requirement is dishonesty.

For myself, therefore, I regard the word 'appropriation' in isolation as being an objective description of the act done irrespective of the mental state of either the owner or the accused. It is impossible to reconcile the decision in *Lawrence* (that the question of consent is irrelevant in considering whether there has been an appropriation) with the views expressed in *Morris*, which latter views in my judgment were incorrect.

[**Lord Slynn of Hadley** and **Lord Jauncey** concurred with the speeches of **Lord Keith** and **Lord Browne-Wilkinson**. **Lord Lowry** gave a dissenting judgment.]

Appeal allowed.

You may be puzzled why in *Gomez* the prosecution did not charge with the offence of obtaining property by deception (or the previous version of the fraud offence), which would arguably more accurately define the offence committed. There is no ready explanation for the prosecutors' course of action. →2 (p.539)

In the following case, the House of Lords had to decide whether *Gomez* meant that even where a transfer of property was one that was valid under civil law it could amount to an appropriation. To understand this case a few basic points on the law of property need to be understood. A transfer of money will be a valid one unless there is a 'vitiating factor'. This includes a misrepresentation, the use of undue influence, or the exercise of duress. The case proceeded on the basis that in this instance, although the defendant might have dishonestly acquired the money, there were no vitiating factors and so the transaction was a valid gift in civil law. →3 (p.536)

R v Hinks
[2001] 2 AC 241 (HL)

Karen Hinks made friends with John Dolphin, described as a naïve, trusting man of limited intelligence. Nearly every day for over six months Hinks accompanied Dolphin to his building society where he withdrew £300 (the maximum possible) and then handed over the money to her. The total received by Hinks was over £60,000. An expert psychiatrist gave evidence that it was unlikely that Dolphin had made the decision to hand over the money on his own. Hinks was convicted of theft. She appealed on the basis that the judge should have given the jury a clear direction that there could not be theft if the transfer had constituted a valid gift.

Lord Steyn

I

Since the enactment of the Theft Act 1968 the House of Lords has on three occasions considered the meaning of the word 'appropriates' in section 1(1) of the Act, namely in *Reg v Lawrence (Alan)* [1972] AC 626; in *Reg v Morris (David)* [1984] AC 320; and in *Reg v Gomez* [1993] AC 442. The law as explained in *Lawrence* and *Gomez*, and applied by the Court of Appeal in the present case (*Reg v Hinks* [2000] 1 Cr App R 1) has attracted strong criticism from distinguished academic lawyers . . . The academic criticism of *Gomez* provided in substantial measure the springboard for the present appeal. The certified question before the House is as follows:

> 'Whether the acquisition of an indefeasible title to property is capable of amounting to an appropriation of property belonging to another for the purposes of section 1(1) of the Theft Act 1968.'

In other words, the question is whether a person can 'appropriate' property belonging to another where the other person makes him an indefeasible gift of property, retaining no proprietary interest or any right to resume or recover any proprietary interest in the property.

Before the enactment of the Theft Act 1968 English law required a taking and carrying away of the property as the *actus reus* of the offence. In 1968 Parliament chose to broaden the reach of the law of theft by requiring merely an appropriation. . . .

VI

Counsel for the appellant submitted in the first place that the law as expounded in *Gomez* and *Lawrence* must be qualified to say that there can be no appropriation unless the other party (the owner) retains some proprietary interest, or the right to resume or recover some proprietary interest, in the property. Alternatively, counsel argued that 'appropriates' should be interpreted as if the word 'unlawfully' preceded it. Counsel said that the effect of the decisions in *Lawrence* and *Gomez* is to reduce the *actus reus* of theft to 'vanishing point' (see Smith & Hogan, *Criminal Law*, 9th ed (1999), p 505). He argued that the result is to bring the criminal law 'into conflict' with the civil law. Moreover, he argued that the decisions in *Lawrence* and *Gomez* may produce absurd and grotesque results. He argued that the mental requirements of dishonesty and intention of permanently depriving the owner of property are insufficient to filter out some cases of conduct which should not sensibly be regarded as theft. He did not suggest that the appellant's dishonest and repellent conduct came within such a category. Instead he deployed four examples for this purpose, namely:

(1) S makes a handsome gift to D because he believes that D has obtained a First. D has not and knows that S is acting under that misapprehension. He makes the gift. There is here a motivational mistake which, it is submitted, does not avoid the transaction. (Glanville Williams, *Textbook of Criminal Law*, 1st ed (1978), p 788.)

(2) P sees D's painting and, thinking he is getting a bargain, offers £100,000 for it. D realises that P thinks the painting is a Constable, but knows that it was painted by his sister and is worth no more than £100. He accepts P's offer. D has made an enforceable contract and is entitled to recover and retain the purchase price. (Smith & Hogan, *Criminal Law*, pp 507, 508.)

(3) A buys a roadside garage business from B, abutting on a public thoroughfare; unknown to A but known to B, it has already been decided to construct a bypass road which will divert substantially the whole of the traffic from passing A's garage. There is an enforceable contract and A is entitled to recover and retain the purchase price. The same would be true if B knew that A was unaware of the intended plan to construct a bypass road. (Compare Lord Atkin in *Bell v Lever Brothers Ltd* [1932] AC 161, 224.)

(4) An employee agrees to retire before the end of his contract of employment, receiving a sum of money by way of compensation from his employer. Unknown to the employer, the employee has committed serious breaches of contract which would have enabled the employer to dismiss him without compensation. Assuming that the employee's failure to reveal his defaults does not affect the validity of the contract, so that the employee is entitled to sue for the promised compensation, is the employee liable to be arrested for the theft the moment he receives the money? (Glanville Williams, 'Theft and Voidable Title' [1981] Crim LR 666, 672.)

My Lords, at first glance these are rather telling examples. They may conceivably have justified a more restricted meaning of section 3(1) than prevailed in *Lawrence* [1972] AC 626 and *Gomez* [1993] AC 442. The House ruled otherwise and I am quite unpersuaded that the House overlooked the consequences of its decision. On the facts set out in the examples a jury could possibly find that the acceptance of the transfer took place in the belief that the transferee had the right in law to deprive the other of it within the meaning of section 2(1)(a) of the Act. Moreover, in such cases a prosecution is hardly likely and if mounted, is likely to founder on the basis that the jury will not be persuaded that there was dishonesty in the required sense. And one must retain a sense of perspective. At the extremity of the application of legal rules there are sometimes results which may seem strange. A matter of judgment is then involved. The rule may have to be recast. Sir John Smith has eloquently argued that the rule in question ought to be recast. I am unpersuaded. If the law is restated by adopting a narrower definition of appropriation, the outcome is likely to place beyond the reach of the criminal law dishonest persons who should be found guilty of theft. The suggested revisions would unwarrantably restrict the scope of the law of theft and complicate the fair and effective prosecution of theft. In my view the law as settled in *Lawrence* and *Gomez* does not demand the suggested revision. Those decisions can be applied by judges and juries in a way which, absent human error, does not result in injustice.

Counsel for the appellant further pointed out that the law as stated in *Lawrence* [1972] AC 626 and *Gomez* [1993] AC 442 creates a tension between the civil and the criminal law. In other words, conduct which is not wrongful in a civil law sense may constitute the crime of theft. Undoubtedly, this is so. The question whether the civil claim to title by a convicted thief, who committed no civil wrong, may be defeated by the principle that nobody may benefit from his own civil or criminal wrong does not arise for decision. Nevertheless there is a more general point, namely that the interaction between criminal law and civil law can cause problems: compare J Beatson and AP Simester, 'Stealing One's Own Property' (1999) 115 LQR 372. The purposes of the civil law and the criminal law are somewhat different. In theory the two systems should be in perfect harmony. In a practical world there will sometimes be some disharmony between the two systems. In any event, it would be wrong to assume on a priori grounds that the criminal law rather than the civil law is defective. Given the jury's conclusions, one is entitled to observe that the appellant's conduct should constitute theft, the only available charge. The tension between the civil and the criminal law is therefore not in my view a factor which justifies a departure from the law as stated in *Lawrence* and *Gomez*. Moreover, these decisions of the House have a marked beneficial consequence. While in some contexts of the law of theft a judge cannot avoid explaining civil law concepts to a jury (e.g. in respect of section 2(1)(a)), the decisions of the House of Lords eliminate the need for such explanations in respect of appropriation. That is a great advantage in an overly complex corner of the law.

VII

My Lords, if it had been demonstrated that in practice *Lawrence* and *Gomez* were calculated to produce injustice that would have been a compelling reason to revisit the merits of the holdings in those decisions. That is however, not the case. In practice the mental requirements of theft are an adequate protection against injustice. In these circumstances I would not be willing to depart from the clear decisions of the House in *Lawrence* and *Gomez*. This brings me back to counsel's principal submission, namely that a person does not appropriate property unless the other (the owner) retains, beyond the instant of the alleged theft, some proprietary interest or the right to resume or recover some proprietary interest. This submission is directly contrary to the holdings in *Lawrence* and *Gomez*. It must be rejected. The alternative submission is that the word 'appropriates' should be interpreted as if the word 'unlawfully' preceded it so that only an act which is unlawful under the general law can be an appropriation. This submission is an invitation to interpolate a word in the carefully crafted language of the Act of 1968. It runs counter to the decisions in *Lawrence* and *Gomez* and must also be rejected. It follows that the certified question must be answered in the affirmative.

...

IX

My Lords, I would dismiss the appeal to the House.

Lord Hutton [dissenting]

In a criminal case this House is not confined to the certified question and can consider other points if it is necessary to do so in the interests of justice: see *Attorney-General for Northern Ireland v Gallagher* [1963] AC 349. Therefore the question arises whether it is appropriate in this case for the House to consider the element of dishonesty.

. . .

I therefore turn to consider dishonesty where the defendant contends, as in this case, that she received the money or property as a gift. My Lords, it appears contrary to common sense that a person who receives money or property as a gift could be said to act dishonestly, no matter how much ordinary and decent people would think it morally reprehensible for that person to accept the gift. Section 2(1)(b) of the Act recognises this common sense view by providing:

'(1) A person's appropriation of property belonging to another is not to be regarded as dishonest . . . (b) if he appropriates the property in the belief that he would have the other's consent if the other knew of the appropriation and the circumstances of it . . .'

It follows, *a fortiori*, that a person's appropriation of property belonging to another should not be regarded as dishonest if the other person actually gives the property to him.

. . . I think that in a case where the prosecution contends that the gift was invalid because of the mental incapacity of the donor it is necessary for the jury to consider that matter. I further consider that the judge must make it clear to the jury that they cannot convict unless they are satisfied (1) that the donor did not have the mental capacity to make a gift and (2) that the donee knew of this incapacity.

. . .

But in my opinion in a case where the defendant contends that he or she received a gift, a direction based only on *Ghosh* is inadequate because it fails to make clear to the jury that if there was a valid gift there cannot be dishonesty, and in the present case there is the danger that, if the gift was not void for want of mental capacity, the jury might nevertheless convict on the basis that ordinary and decent people would think it dishonest for a younger woman to accept very large sums of money which constituted his entire savings from a naive man of low intelligence, and that the woman would have realised this.

. . .

Accordingly, for the reasons which I have stated, I would allow the appeal and quash the convictions.

Lord Hobhouse of Woodborough [dissenting]

. . . The reasoning of the Court of Appeal therefore depends upon the disturbing acceptance that a criminal conviction and the imposition of custodial sanctions may be based upon conduct which involves no inherent illegality and may only be capable of being criticised on grounds of lack of morality. This approach itself raises fundamental questions. An essential function of the criminal law is to define the boundary between what conduct is criminal and what merely immoral. Both are the subject of the disapprobation of ordinary right-thinking citizens and the distinction is liable to be arbitrary or at least strongly influenced by considerations subjective to the individual members of the tribunal. To treat otherwise lawful conduct as criminal merely because it is open to such disapprobation would be contrary to principle and open to the objection that it fails to achieve the objective and transparent certainty required of the criminal law by the principles basic to human rights.

I stress once more that it is not my view that the resort to such reasoning was necessary for the decision of the present case. I would be reluctant to think that those of your Lordships who favour dismissing this appeal have fallen into the trap of believing that, without adopting the reasoning of the Court of Appeal in this case, otherwise guilty defendants will escape justice. The facts of the present case do not justify such a conclusion nor do the facts of any other case which has been cited on this appeal.

[**Lord Slynn of Hadley** and **Lord Jauncey of Tullichettle** agreed with the speech of **Lord Steyn**.]

Appeal dismissed.

These cases are, as we shall see in Part II, remarkably controversial. However, if nothing else, they make for an easy definition of appropriation. The assumption of any of the rights of an owner is appropriation, even if consented to by the victim and even if the transaction is a valid one under civil law. Whether or not the contract was void or voidable at common law is irrelevant to the question of appropriation. Indeed there can be an appropriation even if the victim does not lose out.[42] Of course, where the victim does not lose out it will be rare that there is dishonesty, but one could imagine a case where a victim is persuaded to sell something they did not really want to sell for a fair price in circumstances which were dishonest. →4 (p.541)

However, there are several issues which are still uncertain in the law:

Can an omission amount to an appropriation?

Consider these facts. Ann goes to a supermarket with her toddler. On returning home she notices that her toddler had grabbed a toy from the shelves, which she had not paid for, and has now thrown the toy into the garden. If Ann just leaves the toy lying in the garden could this amount to appropriation? The Court of Appeal is yet to address the issue in detail, but it is submitted that an omission can be an appropriation because section 3(1) describes an appropriation as including 'keeping . . . as owner'.[43] However, to amount to 'keeping . . . as owner' it may be necessary to show that the defendant has kept the property for a significant length of time. In *Broom v Crowther*[44] a defendant purchased a stolen theodolite. He later discovered it was stolen. He told the police, once he had found out that there was doubt over the origins of the theodolite, that he had not touched it, just kept it in his room. The Divisional Court quashed his conviction for theft on the basis that he had not appropriated it since discovering that it was stolen (and thereby becoming dishonest). The court held that he could not be said to be 'keeping . . . as owner' for the purposes of section 3 because he kept it only for a few days.

Can there be multiple appropriations?

A close reading of section 3 reveals the answer to be as follows. An individual can appropriate a piece of property any number of times until he or she steals it. So if a person leaving a restaurant picks up someone else's umbrella by mistake she will appropriate it every time she uses the umbrella, but once she has the *mens rea* for theft she commits theft just once and does not thereafter continue to steal the property every time she uses it. The significance of this tends to be in jurisdictional issues: in which country did the theft take place? In *Atakpu*[45] the defendants hired a car in Germany. The defendants decided to steal the car, drove it to England, and were arrested in Dover. The Court of Appeal held that the defendants had not committed theft in England. They had appropriated it the moment they dishonestly decided permanently to deprive the owner of the car (somewhere in Germany or Belgium), but once they had stolen the car they were not continuing to steal it wherever they drove it.

---

[42] *Wheatley and Penn v Commissioner of Police of the British Virgin Islands* [2006] UKPC 24.
[43] Indeed a conviction could be justified applying the normal laws relating to omissions.
[44] (1984) JP 592.
[45] [1994] QB 69. See also *Bowden* [2002] EWCA Crim 1279, suggesting that the time at which a theft was complete was a question for the jury.

Can there be appropriation by a bona fide purchaser?

If a person buys a piece of property, in good faith,[46] unaware that the property is stolen and then becomes aware that the property is stolen are they guilty of theft? This is dealt with by section 3(2):

> Where property or a right or interest in property is or purports to be transferred for value to a person acting in good faith, no later assumption by him of rights which he believed himself to be acquiring shall, by reason of any defect in the transferor's title, amount to theft of the property.

So a person who buys a piece of property in good faith will not become a thief on discovering that the property is stolen. If the purchaser is aware that the property may be stolen when they buy it they are not acting in good faith and so are guilty. It should be noted that section 3(2) applies only where the defendant has acquired the property by way of a purchase. It therefore does not apply in the case of gifts. A defendant who escapes liability for theft because of section 3(2) may still be guilty of handling stolen goods, an offence which we shall discuss shortly.

QUESTIONS

1. Matthew approaches some American tourists visiting London and offers to sell them Tower Bridge. Is this appropriation of the bridge? Can it therefore be theft?

2. Belinda and Catherine go into a supermarket and decide to steal a tube of toothpaste. They pick up a tube, but then notice that a security guard is close by, and so they return the tube to the shelf and make a quick getaway, empty-handed. Have they committed theft?

3. Davina knocks on the door of an elderly man and offers to mow his small lawn for £100. The man thinks the price sounds high but likes the look of Davina and so agrees. She mows the lawn and he gives her £100. Is this theft?

For guidance on answering this question, please visit the Online Resource Centre that accompanies this book: www.oxfordtextbooks.co.uk/orc/herringcriminal7e/.

1.4 INTENTION PERMANENTLY TO DEPRIVE

The core meaning of the requirement that the defendant must intend permanently to deprive is straightforward, but it has been extended by section 6 of the Theft Act 1968. →5 (p.546)

The core meaning of 'intentional deprivation'

The requirement of intentional deprivation means that borrowing does not normally amount to theft. Borrowing a friend's dress without her consent is not theft, even if the dress is stolen on the afternoon before a party at which she had intended to wear the dress. Perhaps more surprisingly, if a person walks into a video rental shop, takes a video without paying

---

[46] A 'bona fide' purchaser.

for it, intending to return it a week later, this does not amount to theft (although it amounts to another offence).[47] A few points should be stressed about the meaning of the requirement:

Intention

The defendant must *intend* permanently to deprive the victim of the item. So if Zhu, who is absent minded, borrows a friend's book, there can be no theft, even though Zhu realizes there is a risk that he may never be able to return the book, unless Zhu intends never to return it.

Deprivation

What needs to be shown is that the defendant intended to deprive the victim of the property. It does not need to be shown that the defendant intended to acquire the property. So snatching an item from a rail passenger and throwing it out of a train window can amount to theft because the act will deprive the owner of the item, even if there was no intention to gain. This point is backed up by section 1(2) of the Theft Act 1968 which states:

> It is immaterial whether the appropriation is made with a view to gain, or is made for the thief's own benefit.

Replacement of taken goods

What if the defendant took some property with the intention of replacing it with a similar item? For example, if the defendant took some bank notes from her employer's safe, intending to return the same sum of money in the future, this would still be theft (if the jury found it to be dishonest). The defendant intended to deprive the victim of the notes she took, even though she intended to return their equivalent value.[48] In cases where the defendant intends to provide a replacement for the item taken this will be very relevant in deciding whether there was dishonesty.

The defendant need not intend to deprive by the act of appropriation

It does not need to be shown that the defendant intended to deprive the owner of the property *by the act of appropriation*. If Ian moves a tin of baked beans to a shelf by the door of the supermarket so that he can run off with it a few minutes later this is theft, even though that moving is not intended to deprive the owner permanently. It is enough that Ian appropriates the property, while having an intention permanently to deprive the owner of it at some point in the future.

Conditional intention

The problem of conditional intention is best explained by an example. In *Easom*[49] the defendant picked up a handbag in a cinema. He looked through it, but decided that there was nothing worth stealing. He was charged with theft of 'one handbag, one purse, one notebook, a quantity of tissues, a quantity of cosmetics and one pen'. He was acquitted on the basis that he could not be said to intend permanently to deprive the victim of any of these items. What he intended was permanently to deprive the victim of whatever he found

---

[47] e.g. the Theft Act 1978, s. 3.   [48] *Velumyl* [1989] Crim LR 299.   [49] [1971] 2 QB 315.

of value. The general view is that the defendant could have been convicted if the charge had been carefully drafted. If he had been charged with theft of the contents of the handbag he could have been convicted on the basis that he intended permanently to deprive the victim of the contents (if he found them valuable). To avoid any possible difficulties an attempted theft charge may be best in cases of this kind.

Section 6 and the extension to the key meaning of 'permanent deprivation'

Section 6 provides an extended meaning to the phrase 'intending permanently to deprive'.[50] It states:

(1) A person appropriating property belonging to another without meaning the other permanently to lose the thing itself is nevertheless to be regarded as having the intention of permanently depriving the other of it if his intention is to treat the thing as his own to dispose of regardless of the other's rights; and a borrowing or lending of it may amount to so treating it if, but only if, the borrowing or lending is for a period and in circumstances making it equivalent to an outright taking or disposal.

(2) Without prejudice to the generality of subsection (1) above, where a person, having possession or control (lawful or not) of property belonging to another, parts with the property under a condition as to its return which he may not be able to perform, this (if done for purposes of his own and without the other's authority) amounts to treating the property as his own to dispose of regardless of the other's rights.

It must be admitted that the wording of this section is not clear. It appears that the section can apply in the following circumstances:

Throwing taken items away

If John snatches the victim's purse and runs off with it, later throwing it into a bin, he may argue that he did not intend to deprive the owner of it because he would have been happy if the victim had recovered the item. John can be convicted of theft relying on section 6(1) because he has 'treated the property as his own' and 'disposed' of it. In *Mitchell*[51] the defendants took the victim's car and abandoned it a few miles from the victim's house in a street with the hazard lights on. This was held not to amount to a disposal. It was emphasized that there was no attempt to conceal the car. It is important to remember that we are discussing the intention of the defendant here. So if a defendant intended to permanently deprive the victim of the bicycle, but on getting bored of walking it home decided to leave it in a street they could still be convicted of theft if, at the moment of taking it, they had intended a permanent deprivation.[52]

Selling the item back to the victim

If Tony takes Edward's property and tries to sell it back to him he may try to argue that he did not intend permanently to deprive Edward of it because Tony intended the victim to buy the property and so get it back. This argument is not available because of section 6(1);

---

[50] See Steel (2008) for a detailed analysis of s. 6.
[51] [2008] EWCA Crim 850.   [52] *R v Vinall* [2011] EWCA Crim 6252.

in offering the victim's property back to Edward, Tony is treating the property as his own and intending to 'dispose' of it.[53]

Ransoming property

If Simon takes a painting from Celia, but tells her he will return it to her if she pays a large sum of money, Simon may try to claim that he did not intend permanently to deprive the victim of the property because he intended Celia to pay the ransom and recover it. However, this situation is covered by section 6(1) and so is theft; Simon has treated the property as his 'own to dispose of'.[54]

Moving the defendant's property

Can moving property amount to disposing of or dealing in it? The natural meaning of the word dispose might lead you to think not, but in the surprising decision in *DPP v Lavender*[55] Tuckey J appeared willing to accept it could in a case where the defendant moved a door from one council flat to another. However, in *Mitchell*[56] the defendants took the victim's car and abandoned it a few miles from the victim's house in a street with the hazard lights on. This was held not to amount to a disposal. It was emphasized that there was no attempt to conceal the car. Unfortunately the Court of Appeal did not discuss *Lavender*, and it is hard to reconcile the two cases.[57]

Returning property in an impoverished state

What if the defendant borrowed the victim's season ticket for his local football team and returned it once the season was over? Could the defendant argue that he did not intend permanently to deprive the victim of the ticket? This is covered by section 6(1) which states that if the borrowing is 'equivalent to an outright taking or disposal' then this amounts to an intention permanently to deprive. So although the ticket is returned, it is useless as the season is over and so it is equivalent to it being permanently taken. The defendant can therefore be convicted of theft.

The subsection is not as wide as might at first appear because the borrowing must be equivalent to an outright taking. So if the season ticket was taken but returned with a few games left, it is arguable that those takings are not equivalent to an outright taking. In *DPP v SJ, PI, RC*[58] the defendants took the victim's headphones, snapped them, and returned them. It was held that this could amount to theft. It did not need to be shown that the goodness of the property had been 'completely exhausted' for section 6 to apply; it was enough that the property had lost its practical usefulness. The defendants could therefore be convicted of theft of the headphones.[59]

One question still unanswered is whether the goodness of value of the item is to be judged by the standards of the victim or objectively. If the defendant takes the victim's wedding dress and returns it the day after the wedding then it could be argued that the objective value of the dress is undiminished, even though *to the victim* the taking of the dress was equivalent to an outright taking.

---

[53] This is what happened in *Raphael* [2008] EWCA Crim 1014.   [54] *Ibid.*
[55] [1994] Crim LR 297.   [56] [2008] EWCA Crim 850.
[57] See also *Vinall* [2011] EWCA Crim 6252 where *Lavender* was not discussed.
[58] [2002] EWHC 291 (Admin).   [59] A charge of criminal damage would also lie in such a case.

Pawning the goods

If the defendant pawns or pledges goods, intending to pay back the debt and hence recover the item, this falls within section 6(2) and the defendant will be treated as intending permanently to deprive.

Risking the property

If the defendant gambles the victim's property or invests it in a risky investment the defendant will be treated as intending to deprive the victim of it.[60]

R v Marshall
[1998] 2 Cr App R 282 (CA)

The three appellants asked members of the public leaving Victoria underground station for their travel cards or underground tickets. They then resold the tickets on to other customers at a cheap price. They were convicted of theft of the tickets. They appealed on the basis that it could not be said that they intended permanently to deprive London Underground of the tickets.

Lord Justice Mantell [reading the judgment of the court]

[**Mantell LJ** quoted the summary prepared by the appellants' counsel of their argument:]

'It is submitted by the Appellants that in the circumstances although there was an assumption of the rights of the owner contrary to section 3 of the Theft Act 1968 which amounted to an appropriation there was nevertheless no intention on their part to deprive London Underground Limited of the said ticket. They intended either to return them directly to London Underground Limited or to do so through the third party buyer without resale to London Underground Limited and without any loss in the virtue of the ticket when returned.'

The argument proceeds:

'The ticket forms are pieces of paper printed over with information about the ticket. When returned to London Underground Limited they had no more and no less value than when they were originally purchased. The return to London Underground, notwithstanding these intervening transactions involved no loss of virtue to London Underground Limited's property.'

It was submitted s 6(1) of the Theft Act 1968 did not apply as that was only to be resorted to where there was a resale of the property to the original owner. It was further submitted that the issuing of a travel ticket was analogous to the drawing of a cheque and that as both were choses in action the reasoning in *R v Preddy* [1996] AC 815 was equally applicable.

It will be seen that the submission made on what is accepted to be the single issue in the appeal depends in part upon the misapprehension that the ticket forms would necessarily find their way back into the possession of London Underground. That was the factual basis upon which the learned judge ruled. As mentioned, we are content to deal with this appeal on a similar basis.

---

[60] *Fernandes* [1996] 1 Cr App R 175.

On this point the judge ruled as follows:

'I am satisfied that the essence of section 6 of the Theft Act 1968 is whether there was an intention to treat the tickets as their own regardless of the owner's rights. Mr Taylor has drawn my attention in particular to the cases of *R v Duru* [1972] 58 Cr App Rep 151 and *R v Preddy & Others* [1996] 3 WLR 255 and referred me to the commentary by Professor Smith to the case of *R v Mitchell* (1993) Crim LR p.788. I note that all these cases involved cheques and for my part I am not prepared to extend to the underground what the High Court have found in relation to cheques.'

For the reasons which follow we consider that the judge was right.

[**Lord Justice Mantell** then quoted section 6(1):]

On its face the subsection would seem apt to cover the facts of the present case. The ticket belongs to London Underground. It has been appropriated by an Appellant. It is the exclusive right of London Underground to sell tickets. By acquiring and re-selling the ticket the Appellant has an intention to treat the ticket as his own to dispose of regardless of London Underground's right. However Mr Taylor and Mr Simpson have reminded us of what was said by Lord Lane, Lord Chief Justice in the case of *R v Lloyd, Bhuee & Ali* [1985] QB 829, [1985] 2 All ER 661, at 666h–j of the latter report:

'Bearing in mind the observation of Edmund Davis LJ in *R v Warner* (1970) 55 Cr App Rep 93, we would try to interpret the section in such a way as to ensure that nothing is construed as an intention permanently to deprive which would not prior to the 1968 Act have been so construed. Thus the first part of section 6(1) seems to us to be aimed at the sort of case where a defendant takes things and then offers them back to the owner for the owner to buy if he wishes. If the taker intends to return them to the owner only upon such payment, then, on the wording of section 6(1) that is deemed to amount to the necessary intention permanently to deprive . . .'

It is submitted, therefore, that the subsection is to be construed narrowly and confined to the sort of case of which Lord Lane gave an example and of which the present is not one. . . .

The principal submission put forward on behalf of the Appellants is that the issuing of the ticket is analogous to the drawing of a cheque in that in each instance a chose in action is created which in the first case belongs to the customer and in the second to the payee. So by parity of reasoning with that advanced by Lord Goff in *R v Preddy & Others* [1996] AC 815 the property acquired belonged to the customer and not London Underground and there can have been no intention on the part of the Appellant to deprive London Underground of the ticket which would in due course be returned to the possession of London Underground. Attractive though the submission appears at first blush we do not think that it can possibly be correct.

'A "chose in action" is a known legal expression used to describe all personal rights of property which can only be claimed or enforced by action, and not by taking physical possession.' (See *Talkington v Magee* [1902] 2 KB 427 per Channell J at 430)

On the issuing of an underground ticket a contract is created between London Underground and the purchaser. Under that contract each party has rights and obligations. Theoretically those rights are enforceable by action. Therefore it is arguable, we suppose, that by the transaction each party has acquired a chose in action. On the side of the purchaser it is represented by a right to use the ticket to the extent which it allows travel on the underground system. On the side of London Underground it encompasses the right to insist that the ticket is used by no one other than the purchaser. It is that right which is disregarded when the ticket is acquired by the Appellant and sold on. But here the charges were in relation to the tickets and travel cards themselves and a ticket form or travel card and, dare we say, a cheque form is not a chose in action. The fact that the ticket form or travel card may find its way back into the possession of London Underground, albeit with its usefulness or 'virtue' exhausted, is nothing to the point. Section 6(1) prevails for the reasons we have given.

The Appellants by their pleas having acknowledged that they were acting dishonestly; it seems to us that there is no reason to consider the convictions unsafe and these appeals must be dismissed.

Appeals dismissed.

Offences involving temporary deprivation

Parliament has created some special offences to deal with temporary deprivations which are seen as sufficiently serious to justify a criminal conviction, even if they do not constitute theft. For example, it is an offence to remove property from places open to the public[61] (e.g. a museum, a church) or to take a conveyance (e.g. a car or motorcycle) without authority.[62]

1.5 DISHONESTY

The meaning of dishonesty is a mixture of statute and common law. The starting point is section 2 of the Theft Act 1968, which sets out various circumstances in which the defendant will not be dishonest. If the defendant is not dishonest under section 2 that is the end of the case. He or she must be acquitted. If, however, the defendant is not covered by section 2, then it is necessary to consider the common law definition of theft. →6 (p.548)

Section 2 of the Theft Act 1968

Section 2 states:

(1) A person's appropriation of property belonging to another is not to be regarded as dishonest—

  (a) if he appropriates the property in the belief that he has in law the right to deprive the other of it, on behalf of himself or a third person; or

  (b) if he appropriates the property in the belief that he would have the other's consent if the other knew of the appropriation and the circumstances of it; or

  (c) (except where the property came to him as trustee or personal representative) if he appropriates the property in the belief that the person to whom the property belongs cannot be discovered by taking reasonable steps.

(2) A person's appropriation of property belonging to another may be dishonest notwithstanding that he is willing to pay for the property.

---

[61] Theft Act 1968, s. 11(1).   [62] *Ibid*, s. 12(1).

This section defines three circumstances in which a person is *not* dishonest:

Section 2(1)(a): the defendant's belief that he has the right to deprive the owner of the property

If the defendant believes that he or she is legally entitled to deal with the property as he or she does then there is no dishonesty. This belief does not have to be reasonable, nor does it have to be based on an accurate understanding of the law.[63] The most obvious example of the section applying is where the defendant believes that the property is his or her own. For example, if Susan walks out of a restaurant taking someone else's umbrella, believing it to be her own, she is not dishonest. She believes that she is entitled to deal with the property in this way. However, the subsection is wider than this. In *Skivington*[64] a man held up a wages clerk, demanding his wife's wages. He believed that he was entitled to demand the money and so there was no theft.[65]

It should be stressed that the subsection applies only where the defendant has a belief (even an unreasonable one) that he or she has the right in law to deal with the property. A belief that morally the defendant is entitled to deal with the property is insufficient. Such a moral belief might possibly lead to a finding of not being dishonest on the basis of the common law definition of dishonesty.

Section 2(1)(b): belief that the owner would consent

A defendant is not dishonest if he or she believes that the owner would have consented to the taking. This subsection is most likely to apply where the defendant and the 'victim' are friends. Friends and relatives often use each other's property knowing or assuming that the other would consent. It should be stressed that the issue here is not whether the owner does in fact consent, but whether the defendant believes that the victim would consent. Again the belief need not be a reasonable one, but it must be a genuine belief.

Section 2(1)(c): belief that the owner could not be found

This section deals with the situation where a person finds property which he or she believes has been abandoned. The key question is whether the owner can be found by taking reasonable steps. If the defendant believes that the owner cannot be found then there is no theft. Again the belief must only be genuine; it does not have to be reasonable. Further, the defendant need believe only that *reasonable* steps would not identify the owner. If Elizabeth finds a wallet in a town square and keeps it, she may accept that if she spends the next three weeks knocking on the door of every single house in the town she may find the owner, but to do so would not be reasonable. One difficulty facing Elizabeth is that it may well be regarded as reasonable to hand the wallet in to the police. Another point worth noticing here is that even if Elizabeth is not dishonest when she first picks up the wallet (because she believes it to be abandoned) she may subsequently discover who the owner is (e.g. she sees a notice in a shop announcing that the owner has lost the wallet). If thereafter she appropriates the property she can be convicted of theft.

Section 2(2) reiterates that merely intending to pay for an item does not negate theft. To take a pint of milk delivered to your neighbour's door and leave the cash price for the milk

---

[63] *Small* (1987) 86 Cr App R 170; *Holden* [1991] Crim LR 478.   [64] [1968] 1 QB 166.
[65] And therefore no robbery.

can still be theft. Of course, leaving the money may be part of the defendant's belief that the owner would not object to the taking. Imagine this: D is walking in the countryside and comes across a village shop, but finds no shopkeeper. Desperate for a chocolate bar, D takes the bar, but leaves cash behind. The mere fact that he leaves cash does not mean he is not dishonest. However, he may well be able to persuade the jury that he believed the shopkeeper would have no objection as long as he paid for what he took and so he was not dishonest under section 2(1)(a).

The common law test for dishonesty

If the defendant is not acquitted on the basis of section 2(1) the jury will go on to consider the common law test for dishonesty, set out in *Ghosh*:

R v Ghosh
[1982] QB 1053 (CA)

Deb Baran Ghosh, a surgeon, claimed fees for carrying out operations in circumstances in which the prosecution said he should not have been paid. He was convicted of offences contrary to sections 15(1) and 20(2) of the Theft Act 1968. The judge directed the jury to consider whether the appellant had been dishonest according to contemporary standards of honesty and dishonesty. He appealed on the basis that the judge's direction on dishonesty had been wrong.

Lord Lane CJ [giving the judgment of the court]

This brings us to the heart of the problem. Is 'dishonestly' in section 1 of the Theft Act 1968 intended to characterise a course of conduct? Or is it intended to describe a state of mind? If the former, then we can well understand that it could be established independently of the knowledge or belief of the accused. But if, as we think, it is the latter, then the knowledge and belief of the accused are at the root of the problem.

Take for example a man who comes from a country where public transport is free. On his first day here he travels on a bus. He gets off without paying. He never had any intention of paying. His mind is clearly honest; but his conduct, judged objectively by what he has done, is dishonest. It seems to us that in using the word 'dishonestly' in the Theft Act 1968, Parliament cannot have intended to catch dishonest conduct in that sense, that is to say conduct to which no moral obloquy could possibly attach. This is sufficiently established by the partial definition in section 2 of the Theft Act itself. All the matters covered by section 2(1) relate to the belief of the accused. Section 2(2) relates to his willingness to pay. A man's belief and his willingness to pay are things which can only be established subjectively. It is difficult to see how a partially subjective definition can be made to work in harness with the test which in all other respects is wholly objective.

If we are right that dishonesty is something in the mind of the accused (what Professor Glanville Williams calls 'a special mental state'), then if the mind of the accused is honest, it cannot be deemed dishonest merely because members of the jury would have regarded it as dishonest to embark on that course of conduct.

So we would reject the simple uncomplicated approach that the test is purely objective, however attractive from the practical point of view that solution may be.

There remains the objection that to adopt a subjective test is to abandon all standards but that of the accused himself, and to bring about a state of affairs in which 'Robin Hood would be no robber': *Reg. v. Greenstein*. This objection misunderstands the nature of the subjective test. It is no defence for a man to say 'I knew that what I was doing is generally regarded as dishonest; but I do not regard it as dishonest myself. Therefore I am not guilty.' What he is however entitled to say is 'I did not know that anybody would regard what I was doing as dishonest.' He may not be believed; just as he may not be believed if he sets up 'a claim of right' under section 2(1) of the Theft Act 1968, or asserts that he believed in the truth of a misrepresentation under section 15 of the Act of 1968. But if he is believed, or raises a real doubt about the matter, the jury cannot be sure that he was dishonest.

In determining whether the prosecution has proved that the defendant was acting dishonestly, a jury must first of all decide whether according to the ordinary standards of reasonable and honest people what was done was dishonest. If it was not dishonest by those standards, that is the end of the matter and the prosecution fails.

If it was dishonest by those standards, then the jury must consider whether the defendant himself must have realised that what he was doing was by those standards dishonest. In most cases, where the actions are obviously dishonest by ordinary standards, there will be no doubt about it. It will be obvious that the defendant himself knew that he was acting dishonestly. It is dishonest for a defendant to act in a way which he knows ordinary people consider to be dishonest, even if he asserts or genuinely believes that he is morally justified in acting as he did. For example, Robin Hood or those ardent anti-vivisectionists who remove animals from vivisection laboratories are acting dishonestly, even though they may consider themselves to be morally justified in doing what they do, because they know that ordinary people would consider these actions to be dishonest.

Cases which might be described as borderline, such as *Boggeln v. Williams* [1978] 1 W.L.R. 873, will depend upon the view taken by the jury as to whether the defendant may have believed what he was doing was in accordance with the ordinary man's idea of honesty. A jury might have come to the conclusion that the defendant in that case was disobedient or impudent, but not dishonest in what he did.

So far as the present case is concerned, it seems to us that once the jury had rejected the defendant's account in respect of each count in the indictment (as they plainly did), the finding of dishonesty was inevitable, whichever of the tests of dishonesty was applied. If the judge had asked the jury to determine whether the defendant might have believed that what he did was in accordance with the ordinary man's idea of honesty, there could only been one answer—and that is no, once the jury had rejected the defendant's explanation of what happened.

In so far as there was a misdirection on the meaning of dishonesty, it is plainly a case for the application of the proviso to section 2(1) of the Criminal Appeal Act 1968.

Appeal dismissed.

So then, after *Ghosh*, when the jury has to decide whether or not the defendant is dishonest they must consider two separate questions:

(1) Was what the defendant did dishonest according to the standards of reasonable and honest people?

(2) Would the defendant realize that reasonable and honest people would regard what he did as dishonest?

If the answer to both these questions is 'yes' then the defendant is dishonest. If the answer to either question is 'no' then the defendant is not dishonest.[66]

Although this is the full test for dishonesty the courts have made it clear that it need not be used in every case.[67] Indeed only the first question needs to be asked unless the defendant gives evidence that he or she thought his or her conduct was honest according to the standards of ordinary people.[68] Also the *Ghosh* direction is not needed if the case is one of such obvious dishonesty that a jury could not believe a defendant who said he or she thought that the conduct was not dishonest.[69] Three points in particular should be made about this test:

(1) The standards of honesty of the ordinary person are a matter for the jury. It is not for the judge to tell the jury what is or is not dishonest: it is a question for the jury, applying their understanding of contemporary standards.[70] Further, jury members should not ask whether they themselves regard the conduct as dishonest, but consider whether ordinary people would regard it as dishonest.

(2) It is irrelevant whether the defendant believes that his conduct is dishonest: what matters is whether the defendant's conduct was dishonest according to the standards of reasonable and honest people and whether the defendant thought reasonable people would regard his conduct as dishonest. Consider these two examples:

(a) Theresa, a nun, picks up a newspaper left by a man on a train. Her high moral standards mean she feels that she is dishonest because she did not buy her own copy of the paper. The fact that she regards herself as dishonest is irrelevant because ordinary people would not (I suspect) regard such conduct as dishonest.

(b) Angelina, an ardent anti-fur protester, runs out of an exclusive clothes shop, taking some fur coats without paying for them. She regards this as honest, given the evils of fur trading, but she would probably have to admit that the majority of ordinary honest people would not be enlightened enough to see the goodness in her actions and would regard them as dishonest. She would therefore be dishonest under the *Ghosh* test.

(3) There may be a difference between conduct being praiseworthy and being dishonest. Imagine an anti-pornography protester who goes into a 'Private Shop' and runs out with hard-core pornography which he then burns. Although (maybe) the majority of people may be sympathetic to his cause, and may even be impressed by his actions, they could not call them honest.

There is one major difficulty in interpreting the *Ghosh* test: are the facts to be taken as those as understood by the defendant? At first the answer seems clear: yes. Lord Lane appeared to address the issue in *Ghosh*:

Take the man who comes from a country where public transport is free. On his first day here he travels on a bus. He gets off without paying. He never has any intention of paying. His mind is clearly honest; but his conduct, judged objectively by what he has done, is dishonest.

---

[66] In *Pattni, Dhunna, Soni and Poopalarajah* [2001] Crim LR 570 an argument that the *Ghosh* test was so uncertain that it infringed Art. 7 of the European Convention on Human Rights failed.

[67] *Squire* [1990] Crim LR 341; *Goodall* [2011] EWCA Crim 1887.

[68] *Brennan* [1990] Crim LR 118; *Buzalek and Schiffer* [1991] Crim LR 130.

[69] *Jouman* [2012] EWCA Crim 1850.

[70] *Feely* [1973] QB 530. But in a case involving a business person (*R v Goldman* [1997] Crim LR 894) it was suggested that the jury considers whether the conduct was dishonest by the standards of the ordinary business person.

Lord Lane concludes he is not dishonest because under the second limb he believes most people would regard his conduct as honest.[71] Of course, he cannot believe that most people would regard it as honest to leave a bus without paying in a country where one has to pay for public transport, but as he believes it is free then he is not dishonest. But consider an anti-abortion protester who believes that abortion is murder and so steals equipment from a clinic to prevent abortions. It may well be that most people would think it honest to take some equipment from a clinic in order to stop a person committing murder, but they would not think that abortion was murder. The answer, it seems, is that the facts must be taken as the defendant believes that most people would think them to be.

FURTHER READING

Griew, E. (1995) *The Theft Acts 1968 and 1978* (London: Sweet & Maxwell).

Harris, J.W. (1996b) 'Who Owns My Body?' *Oxford Journal of Legal Studies* 16: 55.

Ormerod, D. and Williams, D. (2007) *Smith's Law of Theft* (Oxford: OUP).

Spencer, J. (1977) 'The Metamorphosis of Section 6' *Criminal Law Review* 653.

---

2 ROBBERY

Section 8 of the Theft Act 1968:

(1) A person is guilty of robbery if he steals, and immediately before or at the time of doing so, and in order to do so, he uses force on any person or puts or seeks to put any person in fear of being then and there subjected to force.

(2) A person guilty of robbery, or of an assault with intent to rob, shall on conviction be liable to imprisonment for life.

In essence robbery is made up of two elements:

(1) It must be shown that the defendant has committed theft. The *mens rea* and *actus reus* of theft must be proved.[72]

(2) It must be shown that the defendant has used or threatened force at the time of the theft. Within this apparently simple requirement there are in fact three elements:

(a) There must be the use of force or threat of force. Force is to be given its ordinary meaning by the jury. However, the level of force need be of only a minimal kind. In *Dawson*[73] it was suggested that a nudge from the defendant while taking someone's wallet amounted to force. The force can be used against the person or against the property, but only if the touching of the property affects the victim's body.[74] There is a fine line to be drawn here: simply pulling property out of a bag would not of itself amount to force, but pulling the item out of the victim's grasp so that the victim's body was moved would amount to robbery.

---

[71] Griew (1985).

[72] *Forrester* [1992] Crim LR 793.   [73] [1976] Crim LR 692.

[74] *Clouden* [1987] Crim LR 56; *Corcoran v Anderton* (1980) 71 Cr App R 104.

In *P v DPP*[75] the defendant snatched a cigarette out of a person's hand. This was not robbery because force was not used against the victim's person. The force need not be used or threatened against the victim of theft. It would be robbery for the defendant to threaten to hit a baby if her father did not hand over his wallet. Also there is no need to show that the victim was afraid, as long as there was the use of force or threat of force.[76]

(b) The force must be used in order to steal and not for any other purpose. This means that the defendant must be aware that he or she is using force and intends to use that force in order to steal. The accidental use of force cannot therefore form the basis of a robbery charge.

(c) The force must be used at the time of the theft or immediately before it.[77] It is not robbery if the force is used simply in order to make a getaway from a scene of a theft. The following case demonstrates the significance of this point: →7 (p.555)

R v Hale
(1979) 68 Cr App R 415 (CA)[78]

Robert Hale was charged with robbery. He and McGuire knocked on the door of Mrs Carrett. Hale covered Mrs Carrett's mouth to prevent her screaming while McGuire went upstairs and took a jewellery box. They then tied her up before leaving the house. The trial judge had directed the jury that they could convict the appellant of robbery if they felt sure that by use of force or threats of force he had stolen her property. The appellant was convicted, but appealed on the basis that the direction could have indicated to the jury that they were permitted to convict if he had used force to enable him to escape and that was a misdirection.

Lord Justice Eveleigh

In the present case there can be little doubt that if the appellant had been interrupted after the seizure of the jewellery box the jury would have been entitled to find that the appellant and his accomplice were assuming the rights of an owner at the time when the jewellery box was seized. However, the act of appropriation does not suddenly cease. It is a continuous act and it is a matter for the jury to decide whether or not the act of appropriation has finished. Moreover, it is quite clear that the intention to deprive the owner permanently, which accompanied the assumption of the owner's rights was a continuing one at all material times. This Court therefore rejects the contention that the theft had ceased by the time the lady was tied up. As a matter of common-sense the appellant was in the course of committing theft; he was stealing.

There remains the question whether there was robbery. Quite clearly the jury were at liberty to find the appellant guilty of robbery relying upon the force used when he put his hand

---

[75] [2012] EWHC 1657 (Admin).

[76] In *B and R v DPP* [2007] EWHC 739 (Admin) convictions for robbery were upheld after the defendant threatened force and took the victim's property, even though the victim gave evidence that the threats had not made him fearful.

[77] This can require some careful consideration of when the theft has been completed (*Hale* (1978) 68 Cr App R 415).

[78] [1979] Crim LR 596.

over Mrs. Carrett's mouth to restrain her from calling for help. We also think that they were also entitled to rely upon the act of tying her up provided they were satisfied (and it is difficult to see how they could not be satisfied) that the force so used was to enable them to steal. If they were still engaged in the act of stealing the force was clearly used to enable them to continue to assume the rights of the owner and permanently to deprive Mrs. Carrett of her box, which is what they began to do when they first seized it.

Taking the summing-up as a whole, and in relation to the particular facts of this case, the jury could not have thought that they were entitled to convict if the force used was not at the time of the stealing and for the purpose of stealing. The learned judge said 'In order to be sure that the person is guilty of robbery you have to be sure they were stealing.' While the use of the words complained of would not serve as an alternative definition of robbery and could, if standing alone, be open to the criticism that the learned judge was arriving at a conclusion of fact which the jury had to decide, those words did not stand alone and this Court is satisfied that there was no misdirection. This appeal is accordingly dismissed.

Appeal dismissed.

3 ASSAULT WITH INTENT TO ROB

This offence was created by section 8(2) of the Theft Act 1968. It must be shown that the defendant committed an assault or battery with the intent to rob.

4 HANDLING STOLEN GOODS

The following are the key provisions of the Theft Act 1968 dealing with the offence of handling stolen goods:

Section 22 of the Theft Act 1968 states:

(1) A person handles stolen goods if (otherwise than in the course of the stealing) knowing or believing them to be stolen goods he dishonestly receives the goods, or dishonestly undertakes or assists in their retention, removal, disposal or realisation by or for the benefit of another person, or if he arranges to do so.

Goods are interpreted in section 34(2)(b):

'goods', except insofar as the context otherwise requires, includes money and every other description of property except land, and includes things severed from the land by stealing.

Section 24(2) of the Theft Act 1968 expands the scope of the offence:

(2) For purposes of these provisions references to stolen goods shall include, in addition to the goods originally stolen and parts of them (whether in their original state or not),

(a) any other goods which directly or indirectly represent or have at any time represented the stolen goods in the hands of the thief as being the proceeds of any disposal or

> realisation of the whole or part of the goods stolen or of goods so representing the stolen goods; and
>
> (b) any other goods which directly or indirectly represent or have at any time represented the stolen goods in the hands of a handler of the stolen goods or any part of them as being the proceeds of any disposal or realisation of the whole or part of the stolen goods handled by him or of goods so representing them.
>
> (3) But no goods shall be regarded as having continued to be stolen goods after they have been restored to the person from whom they were stolen or to other lawful possession or custody, or after that person and any other person claiming through him have otherwise ceased as regards those goods to have any right to restitution in respect of the theft.
>
> (4) For purposes of the provisions of this Act relating to goods which have been stolen (including subsections (1) to (3) above) goods obtained in England or Wales or elsewhere either by blackmail or in the circumstances described in section 15(1) of this Act shall be regarded as stolen; and 'steal', 'theft' and 'thief' shall be construed accordingly.

The maximum sentence is 14 years' imprisonment. At first this seems surprising as the maximum sentence for theft itself is only seven years. One explanation offered by the courts is that if there were no handlers willing to receive and distribute the goods there would be fewer thefts.[79]

This offence can be broken down into four elements:

4.1 IT MUST BE SHOWN THAT THE GOODS HAVE ALREADY BEEN STOLEN

It is not necessary for the prosecution to prove who stole[80] the goods, as long as it is clear the goods have been stolen by someone.[81] If the defendant believes the goods to be stolen, but in fact they are not, then the defendant may be guilty of an attempted handling offence.[82] The offence covers not only stolen goods, but also the proceeds of stolen goods. So if Robby steals a car and sells it for £1,000 and then passes the £1,000 to his friend, Lucy, then Lucy can be convicted of handling if she has the necessary *mens rea*. Section 24(3) (quoted in the previous extract) provides that goods will cease to be stolen in various situations: most notably where goods have been returned to the person from whom they were stolen or the goods have been recovered by the police.[83] So if a person took from a police car stolen property which had been found by the police the person would not be guilty of handling, but could, of course, be charged with theft.

---

[79] *Shelton* (1993) 15 Cr App R (S) 415; *Tokeley-Parry* [1999] Crim LR 578.

[80] As well as goods that are actually stolen, the offence covers handling goods obtained through robbery, burglary, blackmail, and by deception (Theft Act 1968, s. 24(4)).

[81] *Forsyth* [1997] 2 Cr App R 299. Goods would be stolen even if the 'thief' were able to rely on an excuse (e.g. duress) and so not be guilty of the offence of theft.

[82] Criminal Attempts Act 1981, s. 1(2). See *Haughton v Smith* [1975] AC 476 (HL).

[83] *Attorney-General's Reference (No. 1 of 1974)* (1974) 59 Cr App R 203 (CA); *Parker v British Airways Board* [1982] 1 All ER 834 (CA); and *Greater London Metropolitan Police Commissioner v Streeter* (1980) 71 Cr App R 113 (CA) provide detailed discussion of when property can be said to have entered the lawful possession or custody of the police.

4.2 IT MUST BE SHOWN THAT THE DEFENDANT HANDLED THE PROPERTY

DEFINITION

It must be shown that the defendant engaged in or arranged one of the following:

(1) receiving the property; or

(2) undertaking any of the following:

    (a) retention;

    (b) removal;

    (c) disposal;

    (d) realization

    of the goods either by another or for another's benefit; or

(3) assisting in any of the following:

    (a) retention;

    (b) removal;

    (c) disposal;

    (d) realization

    of the goods either by another or for another's benefit.

The terms used here are readily understandable and are to be given their normal meaning. But a few points of clarification may assist:

(1) Receiving involves taking goods into your possession or control. This means that the accused must be aware that he has possession or control of the items.[84] If the defendant is not aware when he or she receives the property that it is stolen, but later becomes aware that it is, then it is better to charge the defendant on the basis of retention, rather than receiving.[85] Merely touching the goods may be insufficient to amount to receiving. In *Hobson v Impett*[86] the defendant helped a thief unload stolen goods from a lorry. This was held not to amount to receiving them.

(2) Assisting has been held to involve help or encouragement and requires more than simply using property that someone else is retaining.[87] Lying to the police about whether there is stolen property on someone's premises is sufficient to amount to assisting another.[88] But in *Brown*[89] it was suggested that a failure to inform the police about where stolen goods were did not amount to assisting in the retention of goods.[90]

(3) The handling must be 'otherwise than in the course of stealing'. This is not to say that a thief cannot also be a handler, but that it must be shown that there was an act of handling which occurred after the theft had taken place.[91] Once all the elements of theft are established the defendant is guilty of theft and he or she does not continually

---

[84] *Hobson v Impett* (1957) 41 Cr App R 138.   [85] *Pitchley* (1973) 57 Cr App R 30.
[86] (1957) 41 Cr App R 138.   [87] *Sanders* (1982) 75 Cr App R 84.
[88] *Kanwar* (1982) 75 Cr App R 87.   [89] [1970] 1 QB 105.
[90] See also *Kanwar* (1982) 75 Cr App R 87.   [91] *Bosson* [1999] Crim LR 596.

steal each time he or she touches the item thereafter.[92] Further, appropriation, once the theft has occurred, can amount to handling.

(4) The defendant must have received the property 'by or for the benefit of another'. If the defendant is not alleged to have received the property, but one of the other forms of handling is being relied upon then it needs to be shown that the defendant acted for the benefit of another. The leading case is the following decision of the House of Lords which decided that the sale of a car to someone could not be said to be for the benefit of another:

R v Bloxham
[1983] AC 109 (HL)

Albert Bloxham agreed to buy a car for £1,300. At that time he did not know that the car had been stolen. He paid £500 on account and agreed to pay the balance once the registration documents were produced. They never were. Eleven months later he suspected that the car had been stolen and so he sold it to a third party for £200. He was charged with handling stolen goods. At his trial he argued that he had not disposed of or realized the car 'for the benefit of another'. The trial judge rejected this argument, holding that the purchaser had gained a benefit in that he had acquired use of the car, if not good legal title to it. He appealed to the Court of Appeal which upheld the trial judge's ruling.

Lord Bridge of Harwich [delivering a speech with which their other Lordships agreed]

The [Court of Appeal] certified the following point of law of general public importance as involved in their decision:

'Does a bona fide purchaser for value commit an offence of dishonestly undertaking the disposal or realisation of stolen property for the benefit of another if when he sells the goods on he knows or believes them to be stolen?'

The full text of s 22(1) of the Theft Act 1968 reads:

'A person handles stolen goods if (otherwise than in the course of the stealing) knowing or believing them to be stolen goods he dishonestly receives the goods, or dishonestly undertakes or assists in their retention, removal, disposal or realisation by or for the benefit of another person, or if he arranges to do so.'

It is, I think, now well settled that this subsection creates two distinct offences, but no more than two. The first is equivalent to the old offence of receiving under s 33 of the Larceny Act 1916. The second is a new offence designed to remedy defects in the old law and can be committed in any of the various ways indicated by the words from 'undertakes' to the end of the subsection . . .

The critical words to be construed are 'undertakes . . . their . . . disposal or realisation . . . for the benefit of another person'. Considering these words first in isolation, it seems to me that, if A sells his own goods to B, it is a somewhat strained use of language to describe this as a disposal or realisation of the goods for the benefit of B. True it is that B obtains a benefit from

[92] *Atakpu and Abrahams* [1994] QB 69.

the transaction, but it is surely more natural to say that the disposal or realisation is for A's benefit than for B's. It is the purchase, not the sale, that is for the benefit of B. It is only when A is selling as agent for a third party C that it would be entirely natural to describe the sale as a disposal or realisation for the benefit of another person.

But the words cannot, or course, be construed in isolation. They must be construed in their context, bearing in mind, as I have pointed out, that the second half of the section creates a single offence which can be committed in various ways. I can ignore for present purposes the concluding words 'or if he arranges to do so', which throw no light on the point at issue. The preceding words contemplate four activities (retention, removal, disposal, realisation). The offence can be committed in relation to any one of these activities in one or other of two ways. First, the offender may himself undertake the activity for the benefit of another person. Second, the activity may be undertaken by another person and the offender may assist him. Of course, if the thief or an original receiver and his friend act together in, say, removing the stolen goods, the friend may be committing the offence in both ways. But this does not invalidate the analysis, and if the analysis holds good it must follow, I think, that the category of other persons contemplated by the subsection is subject to the same limitations in whichever way the offence is committed. Accordingly, a purchaser, as such, of stolen goods cannot, in my opinion, be 'another person' within the subsection, since his act of purchase could not sensibly be described as a disposal or realisation of the stolen goods by him. Equally, therefore, even if the sale to him could be described as a disposal or realisation for his benefit, the transaction is not, in my view, within the ambit of the subsection.

Certified question answered in the negative. Order appealed from reversed. Conviction quashed.

4.3 IT MUST BE SHOWN THAT THE DEFENDANT KNEW OR BELIEVED THAT THE GOODS WERE STOLEN

It must be shown that at the time of the handling the defendant knew or believed that the goods were stolen.[93] The test is subjective. It does not matter whether a reasonable person would have known the goods were stolen. What matters is what the defendant knew.[94] The words knowledge and belief are to be given their normal meaning[95] and the matter should be left to the 'common sense of the jury'.[96]

It should be noted that the defendant must know *or* believe. Clearly, it will be rare for a defendant to *know* goods are stolen. The courts, however, have said that suspicion is not enough: the defendant must conclude that the goods are stolen.[97] The most difficult cases involve the concept of wilful blindness. This is where the defendant decides not to ask any questions and just assumes the goods are legitimate, while he or she is aware in the 'back of his mind' that there must be question marks over the origins of the goods. The courts have held that such wilful blindness does not amount to knowledge.[98]

---

[93] For an excellent discussion, see Shute (2002).   [94] *Atwal v Massey* [1971] 3 All ER 881.
[95] *Forsyth* [1997] 2 Cr App R 299.   [96] Waller LJ in *Reader* (1977) 66 Cr App R 33, 36.
[97] *Forsyth* [1997] 2 Cr App R 299.
[98] *Griffiths* (1974) 60 Cr App R 14. See also *Hall* (1985) 81 Cr App R 260. There is a special rule of evidence known as the doctrine of recent possession which enables the jury to infer knowledge or belief from the fact that the accused was in possession of goods which had been recently stolen.

4.4 THE DEFENDANT WAS DISHONEST

To convict the defendant of handling the jury must be persuaded that the defendant was dishonest. The *Ghosh* test for dishonesty will be used. However, it will be rare that someone who is handling what he or she knows or believes to be stolen goods will be able to claim successfully that he or she was acting honestly.[99] It may be that a defendant can claim that he or she was intending to return the goods to the original owner or the police.

FURTHER READING

Shute, S. (2002) 'Knowledge and Belief in the Criminal Law' in S. Shute and A. Simester (eds) *Criminal Law Theory* (Oxford: OUP).

Spencer, J. (1985) 'Handling, Theft and the Mala Fide Purchaser' *Criminal Law Review* 92.

Sullivan, G.R. (2002b) 'Knowledge, Belief and Culpability' in S. Shute and A. Simester (eds) *Criminal Law Theory* (Oxford: OUP).

Williams, G. (1985) 'Handling, Theft and the Purchaser Who Takes a Chance' *Criminal Law Review* 432.

---

5   MONEY LAUNDERING OFFENCES

Closely allied to handling offences are those involving money laundering. The Criminal Justice Act 1988, as amended by Part III of the Criminal Justice Act 1993 and the Money Laundering Regulations 1993 contain most of the important money laundering offences.

PART II: THEFT AND THEORY

6   INTRODUCTION TO PROPERTY OFFENCES

6.1   IN WHAT WAY DO PROPERTY OFFENCES HARM VICTIMS?

It is common when looking at the criminal law to distinguish between property offences and offences against the person. This is understandable as they appear to involve quite different kinds of harm. Indeed property offences are often said to be less serious than offences against the person. In part this is because often lost or damaged property (or at least its equivalent)[100] can be restored, but this is not true in the case of a physical injury.[101] However, it should not be forgotten that property offences can cause great emotional distress to the victim (burglary in particular). Further, the ownership and enjoyment of property are seen by some as an essential aspect of the expression and realization of human personality.[102]

---

[99] *Roberts* (1987) 84 Cr App R 117.   [100] But not always, e.g. a pet dog.
[101] Under the Powers of Criminal Courts (Sentencing) Act 2000 a court can order that stolen goods be returned by the defendant to the victim.
[102] Waldron (1988) and Dan-Cohen (2002: ch. 9).

In the following passage, John Gardner and Stephen Shute discuss why it would be wrong to dismiss property offences as being trivial wrongs and why property rights matter to individuals and society:

J. Gardner and S. Shute, 'The Wrongness of Rape' in J. Horder (ed.) *Oxford Essays in Jurisprudence* (Oxford: OUP, 2000), 199–203

What is our interest in property? Only some brief remarks are possible here. Those who focus on productivity are, fundamentally, on the right track so long as 'productivity' is construed widely enough to include the provision of shelter, security, comfort, amusement, and other benefits to the property-holder. The importance of property lies basically in the valuable things we can do with that property that we cannot so easily do without it. This we will call its *use-value*. Aspects of property rights other than the right to use property are basically derivative of the use-value of property. The value of being able to acquire and transfer property, for example, is basically the value of property's ending up where it can best be used. In conditions of global and indiscriminate abundance property rights may lose their basic moral purchase, because in these conditions everyone has more than they can use. The question whether something could best be used by a person other than the person who holds it is less prone to arise, for there is always plenty left to go round. But in times of scarcity or of merely local or discriminate abundance (i.e. abundance from which some are excluded, leaving them in conditions of scarcity) the question is always live: could this thing be better used by someone else? The idea of a property right to such things is that, up to a point, the question of where something is better used can least wastefully be settled by leaving the question to the person who already holds the thing. This means that, again up to a point, people are left free to hold property that they do not use. It is still theirs and cannot be taken without their say-so. If others were to take it away from them this might yield a better use for it, but the suboptimal use of a particular thing is justified, up to a point, by the general gains in use-value that are made from a co-ordinating system based on consensual transactions.

We say 'up to a point', but the question on everybody's lips is: up to which point? In the long history of property rights the point has been located in different places by different civilizations and regimes. Some things have been regarded at some times and in some places as incapable of being subject to property rights, or incapable of being subject to certain kinds of strong property rights such as ownership. The tendency to wastefulness by property-holders, their refusal to let things be put to their best use, has often been regarded (no doubt sometimes rightly) as too high a price to pay for the avoidance of the costs associated with alternative methods of distribution and allocation. Some things, the value of which is basically their use-value, have therefore on occasions been taken out of a fully-fledged property regime. Thus, at some times and in some places, housing has been publicly provided for tenancy but not for ownership, TV stations or take-off slots at airports have not been capable of being owned, etc. Meanwhile, some things have been owned but with special regulation inhibiting their use and disposal, such as rent control legislation, restrictions on inheritance, rules against predatory pricing or monopolization, and official scrutiny of hostile takeovers. Since the basic value of property is instrumental, different policies and practices may serve that value more or less effectively at different times and places, depending on other prevailing conditions—for instance, the extent of the public tendency towards decadence, the sluggishness of competition, the degree of scarcity, or the extent of globalization.

However, one observation that may be made regarding large parts of the inhabited world today is that property rights are tending to campaign, in a sense, for their own augmentation and deregulation. The rise of public faith in property-holding as a pat solution to the coordination problems associated with the use of things under conditions of scarcity, combined with people's increasing alienation from other human beings, leads people to attach great and ever-growing symbolic importance to the acquisition and holding of property. Increasingly, they come to identify with at least some things they hold as extensions of themselves, tokens of their own personality. The idea of 'sentimental value' has always highlighted this aspect of property holding. But it extends nowadays to much else besides the inherited keepsakes of the past or the gifts of friends and family. In fact, it is increasingly associated more with self-chosen than with other-chosen things. In so far as people regard themselves as autonomous beings, their own choice of property—which house to buy, which ties to wear, which CDs to collect—has an ever more important place in their self-expression. The result is the cultural condition which has come to be known as 'consumerism'. No doubt it has got wildly out of hand. But up to a point—and again the point cannot be settled out of local context—consumerism does effect the moral change which its participants seem to pre-suppose. They regard property as meaning more, as carrying more significance, than just the significance imported by its use-value. Their regarding it as carrying that significance actually endows it with that significance by changing its social meaning. People are increasingly identifying with what they have. So on top of its basic use-value, much more of what people hold now has what we might call *identification-value*. When property is taken away without the proper consensual process, it is not merely (or even) that the system of optimal use-value is disrupted. It is that people are metaphorically violated by the removal of a part of their extended selves.

Some think that identification-value, and particularly the value which comes of investing autonomous choice in property, suffices on its own to explain why property rights continue to reside in those who make suboptimal use of their property. But property rights can persist even when use-value and identification-value are both missing. Consider what might be regarded as the pure case of burglary. Suppose an estate agent who has keys to my house lets himself in while I am on holiday and takes a pile of my old clothes from the attic, passing them on to a charity shop. I had long since forgotten that the clothes were there, and I had no further use, anyway, for loon pants and kipper ties. The burglary goes forever undiscovered. (The estate agent, who told nobody of what he was doing, falls under a bus as he leaves the charity shop, as he would have done anyway even if my clothes had not been among those he delivered.) Yet my property right is violated. Why is this? After all, I have no interest in these old long-forgotten clothes that comes of either my use of them or my identification with them. But on top of that, as we already indicated, there is the co-ordinating value of property rights in securing use-value and identification-value at large (i.e. for people in general). My having this property right over my old clothes, which is violated by the intruding estate agent, does not come of any use-value or identification-value to me but of the contribution which my having such a property right makes to the perpetuation of a system of optimal use-value coupled, so far as possible, with optimal identification-value. So I have an interest in this property which is basically derivative of the public interest in my having such an interest.

In the last paragraph Gardner and Shute refer to the system of property rights which our society uses. Most members of the public probably assume that the form of ownership of property used in the UK is 'natural'. But it is not impossible to think of other property systems that England and Wales's legal system could adopt. They might emphasize communal ownership[103] of property to a far greater extent than we do,[104] or involve a system of property ownership

[103] Thompson (1989).

[104] J.W. Harris (1996) provides a fascinating discussion of alternative property structures that could be used.

based on the notion of stewardship which would emphasize the obligations as well as the rights of ownership.[105] Although the protection of property through the criminal law may appear a natural part of any liberal democracy it raises some complex issues. To name but a few:

(1) There is much dispute over what kinds of property should be protected by the criminal law. Lacey, Wells, and Quick have suggested: 'Criminal law defends not property at large, but certain kinds of—highly unevenly distributed—property. It thereby defends not only property, but the power of certain interests and the authority of the social order.'[106] Those sympathetic to such a point of view point out that interests in a clean environment, effective education, and healthy food are not protected by property offences, while 'commercial' interests generally are. From a different perspective others claim that the present law's understanding of property is out of touch with modern commercial practice in inadequately protecting 'new property', such as commercially valuable information or pension rights.

(2) It is significant that property offences, like the law of property generally, are concerned with the fair and effective transfer, control, and creation of property interests, but are not concerned with the fairness of the distribution of property that results.[107] In other words it would be theft for an impoverished person to pick the pocket of a rich one, but it is not theft for one person to own vast wealth while another has virtually nothing. To those of a Marxist persuasion by ensuring 'fair' transfers, but not fair distribution, the law on property offences reinforces and perpetuates the inequalities within society.[108] The law preventing taking works harshly on the destitute who have nothing, but protects the interests of those who are well provided for.[109] Hence Proudhon[110] famously declared that property was theft.[111] Of course, without any property offences it would not be the case that property was equally distributed, but rather the strongest would be able to take the property of the weak without punishment. But we could alter the purpose of property offences from ensuring that those who have can keep what they have to requiring those who have to give to those who have not.[112] One does not have to be a Marxist to make a strong case that theft can be regarded as morally wrong only if the basic framework of the property law is just.[113]

(3) There is a fine line to be drawn in the law on property offences between what is a civil wrong and what is a crime.[114] For example, if you were to decide to employ a builder and paid her in advance £500 to do some work on your flat, but she carried out only half the job and failed to return the money or complete the job, should your remedy be to sue her in the courts for breach of contract or should this be regarded as a criminal offence? This issue regularly arises in property offences. For example, should a temporary taking be regarded as theft or a matter for civil remedies?

(4) The criminal law is not the only way that society may tackle the problem of wrongful interference with property rights. It can certainly be argued that society's resources would be better spent trying to improve the designs of property such as homes, cars, or mobile phones to make them harder to steal, rather than pouring resources into the prosecution and punishment of thieves.

---

[105] Lucy and Mitchell (1996).   [106] Lacey, Wells, and Quick (2010: 341).
[107] Melissaris (2012).   [108] Marx and Engels (1967).
[109] L. Murphy (2001).   [110] Proudhon (1994).
[111] See also Christman (1994). Interestingly, there is evidence that property crimes increase at a faster rate when there is low economic growth (Barclay 1995: 5).
[112] No doubt taxation etc. would also be needed to ensure a more equal distribution.
[113] J.W. Harris (1996a: 14).
[114] Contrast the law on gross negligence manslaughter (*Wacker* [2003] Crim LR 108).

(5) How should we structure criminal offences? Should we distinguish between the value of property taken (e.g. have offences structured according to the value of the property lost) or by the means by which the property was acquired (e.g. distinguishing a robbery from a burglary)?

We shall start by examining the last of these issues, and the other points will be dealt with later on.

6.2 STRUCTURE OF PROPERTY OFFENCES

As a broad generalization, in relation to offences against the person, the law is structured according to the level of harm suffered by the victim. Hence the most serious offences involve death (murder and manslaughter), and then we move down to less serious offences involving rape, grievous bodily harm, and actual bodily harm, down to the least serious offences of assaults and batteries. For offences against the person the method used to cause the harm is largely immaterial. You are guilty of murder whether you kill the victim by drowning, strangling, or poisoning. However, property offences are different. They are less concerned with the value of property affected by the offence and instead focus on the method used by the defendant to acquire or deal with the property. Hence a distinction is drawn, for example, between theft, blackmail, robbery, burglary, and offences involving fraud. As we shall see, there is much debate over whether these should be seen as different kinds of wrong against a victim, or more or less serious forms of the same wrong.[115] Property offences also seek to protect particular kinds of property which are seen as particularly vulnerable to being abused. For example, there are statutory provisions to protect computers and cars from misuse.[116] ←1 (p.498)

6.3 THE CIVIL LAW–CRIMINAL LAW INTERFACE

At the heart of property offences is the definition of a property right. Inevitably criminal lawyers will turn to civil law to find out answers to questions such as: What is property? Who owns the property? Is the property held on trust? However, the need for the criminal law to interact with the civil law causes tensions. These came dramatically to a head in the House of Lords in *Hinks*, where it was held that a transaction which constituted a valid gift in civil law could be regarded as theft in the criminal law. To some this meant that the law was being two-faced, its criminal face labelling Hinks a thief, but its civil face declaring the transaction to be a valid gift. But there are other difficulties here too. If juries and magistrates are to be able to try cases the law needs to be relatively straightforward, and if the law of theft can be understood only by a complete understanding of English property law, juries and magistrates will be unable to do their job. There is also a danger that a criminal trial can get so tied up with the civil law issues that it loses sight of the key issue of the blameworthiness and harmfulness of what the defendant did.[117] Further, the definition of what is property for the purposes of civil law may not coincide with what kinds of activities the criminal law wants to prevent through property offences. Indeed just because the civil and criminal law disagree, it does not mean the criminal law is in the wrong.[118] These issues

---

115 That we shall look at in Chapter 9, Part II.
116 Computer Misuse Act 1990; Theft Act 1968, s. 12. See further Green (2014).
117 *Clowes (No. 2)* [1994] 2 All ER 316.   118 Sarah Green (2012).

in part reflect a difference in the aims of the criminal law and civil law in this area. For civil lawyers certainty of ownership is important; for criminal lawyers the prevention of dishonest conduct may be regarded as more important. The temptation may be for criminal lawyers to seek to free criminal law from the 'shackles of civil law'. But that would create all kinds of problems: if the property offences are not protecting the property interests as understood in civil law, what are they protecting? We shall return to this issue when we consider the case of *Hinks*. ←3 (p.508)

In the following passage, Andrew Simester and Bob Sullivan describe what they regard as the essence of theft: the protection of property interests. They, therefore, are strong opponents of the decision in *Hinks*:

A. Simester and G.R. Sullivan, 'The Nature and Rationale of Property Offences' in R.A. Duff and S. Green (eds) *Defining Crimes* (Oxford: OUP, 2005), 174–6

The essence of theft is to misappropriate, with intent to deprive, property to which one is not legally entitled, and to do so without justification or excuse. As such, theft is concerned directly and primarily with protecting the legal structure of proprietary entitlements. Imagine V, a misanthropic billionaire who has inherited and not created any of his wealth. He has withdrawn all his money from his investments, trusts, and bank accounts and stacked the cash away in cardboard boxes that litter the floors of his grim mansion. He is determined that noone shall have any use or pleasure from his wealth and has resolved that when his time is nigh, he will immolate himself and his cash. D is V's selfless home-carer, although paid a pittance by V, out of the goodness of her heart she ministers to V's needs beyond any call of duty. From time to time, she takes cash from one or other of the boxes, never for herself, but to ease the path of friends and acquaintances who are in dire economic straits. There is no profligacy in this: she takes enough, just enough, to stave off the worst consequences of the privations that afflict the people she helps. D is a thief; a thief despite the fact that V knows nothing of D's takings and is unharmed psychologically by what D has done, and despite the fact that, for him, the financial loss is *de minimis* in every conceivable sense. She has misappropriated V's property, usurped his property rights without his consent; no more is required. This conclusion follows, as we shall argue, even where D acts with a degree of selflessness and concern [that] would be vindicated as ethically correct under many versions of communitarian morality.

The example illustrates that the immediate victim of a theft may be harmed in a wholly conventional sense, without suffering any substantive disvalue or setback of human interests. Across a range of different cultures and circumstances, outcomes such as death, injury, physical and emotional pain, extreme discomfort, paralysing fear, bereavement, etc., are unequivocal—and pre-legal—harms. Although it does not follow that the infliction of such harms is always wrong, or that their categoric prohibition is justified, it may readily be agreed without reference to the law that a person who is badly physically or emotionally hurt is, while that condition endures, worse off than when her usual circumstances obtain. By contrast, and while D's conviction for theft may be justified in terms of protecting the proprietary regime itself, V is a victim only formally.

Violations of the ownership, control, or possession of property need not always set back the interests of an agent whose rights have been contravened. Of course, sometimes a loss of property may have devastating consequences for the nature and quality of an agent's life. Yet the accretion of property may have no beneficent effect on the quality of life or moral standing an agent. Take the misanthropic billionaire: no doubt from Aristotelian and communitarian perspectives his life and moral standing would improve immeasurably if, after some ghostly visitation, he were to give away the bulk of his fortune in well-judged and effective acts of philanthropy. Moreover, it may be argued from these moral perspectives that, absent any re-enactment of *The Christmas Carol*, D, his housekeeper, *should* have taken even more of V's money and redistributed it to the needy. It seems an inversion of sound moral judgment to castigate her as a thief. If she is to be criticised at all, it might be for her failure to take more of his money before he, his mansion, and the money went up in smoke.

6.4 THEFT: THE STATISTICS

The official figures

The 2013/14 Crime Survey for England and Wales found that theft was the most common offence in England and Wales.[119] There were around 1.8 million recorded theft offences.[120] People may be particularly likely to report property offences to the police if the property has been insured and they wish to make a claim on their insurance policies. The sums involved are not small. The most common forms of theft involve vehicles.

The reality?

Such official figures as those just quoted give perhaps a rather distorted picture of property wrongdoing. This is because it is clear that not all conduct which fulfils the legal requirements of a property offence is treated in the same way. It has been suggested that few people are entirely truthful with their tax returns.[121] Indeed a full, complete disclosure as technically required in the tax return would require some people to provide an extraordinarily lengthy return. Whether these are legitimate points, it is certainly true that if the tax authorities suspect that a person has not completed his or her tax return properly, criminal proceedings are rarely brought, and the matter is dealt with by 'negotiations' between the individual and HM Revenue & Customs, normally resulting in the individual paying an agreed sum to HM Revenue & Customs.[122] In recent years people on public transport who are found by a ticket inspector not to have bought a ticket normally have to buy a ticket with an extra surcharge, rather than the matter going through the courts. During the 2010 World Cup there were widespread press reports of employees not turning up for work and claiming to be sick, so that they could stay at home and watch the match. Few people suggested that this should be regarded as a criminal offence, but why not?

As these examples indicate, some property offences are dealt with in a way which in effect bypasses the criminal procedure. There is no criminal conviction, although sometimes a sum of money equivalent to a fine may have to be paid. These examples indicate that what is regarded as a property offence is not as straightforward as might at first appear. Our society has effectively licensed certain forms of conduct which technically fall within the definition of a property offence, but which are treated as non-criminal.[123] These points can be further considered with the following two examples:

(1) **Shoplifting** It has been estimated that there were 2,112,000 instances of shoplifting in 2014.[124] This indicates that the number of incidents reported to the police and dealt with

---

[119] Office for National Statistics (2015a).   [120] *Ibid.*   [121] Mears (1982).
[122] D. Cook (1989) contrasts the legal responses to tax evasion and benefit fraud.
[123] Lacey, Wells, and Quick (2010: ch. 11).   [124] Home Office (2015).

through the courts is tiny.[125] It is not that shoplifting is financially insignificant. The average value of goods shoplifted was £125. You will not be surprised to learn that for the year 2012/13 the cost of shoplifting was £3.8 billion.[126] You may well be surprised to learn about £1.6 billion of that is as a result of theft by members of staff.[127]

(2) 'White-collar crime'[128] Sutherland has defined a white-collar crime as 'a crime committed by a person of respectability and high social status in the course of his occupation'.[129] Property offences in the public imagination involve the sneaky pickpocket or the masked mugger, and not the suited executive arranging price fixing or malinvesting pension funds. Yet white-collar crimes can involve far larger sums than the traditional crime. Illegal tax evasion, for example, amounts to £14 billion a year.[130] Despite this, 'white-collar criminals' are less likely to be prosecuted or convicted, and if convicted their sentences may be lower than for analogous offences.[131] Some suggest that the explanation for the lack of prosecution for white-collar crime is the fine line in the business world that has to be drawn between criminal activity and sharp business practices.[132] Certainly the line between acceptable and unacceptable business practices can be said to be in a state of flux.[133] We will discuss business crime in greater detail in Chapter 13.

6.5 WHAT IS PROPERTY?

At the heart of property offences is the concept of property,[134] but how do we decide what things can be regarded as property and what cannot? The answer is not self-evident. Some things are held not to be property because of the antisocial consequences that may result (imagine what might happen if it were decided that the sun could be owned and people could be charged for using sunlight);[135] and other things cannot be property because it is not effectively possible to restrict or control access to them (e.g. to air). So, moral, practical, and legal arguments can operate to mean that something is declared not to be property for the purposes of the law. This means that whether something is regarded as capable of being property can change over time. It is arguable, for example, that bodies and body parts are undergoing a transition from being regarded as non-property to being regarded, in some cases at least, as property.[136]

> **FURTHER READING**
>
> Christie, A. (2006) 'Should the Law of Theft Extend to Information?' *Journal of Criminal Law* 69: 349.
>
> Gold, E. (1996) *Body Parts: Property Rights and the Ownership of Human Biological Matter* (Oxford: OUP).

---

[125] It is interesting that the offence is usually called shoplifting, rather than theft. A. Morris (1987) discusses the fact that shoplifting is one of the few crimes where women and men have similar rates of conviction.

[126] Centre for Retail Research (2013).   [127] BBC News Online (2010b).

[128] Nelken (2002).   [129] Sutherland (1983: 8).   [130] Starmer (2013).

[131] Lambiras (2003).

[132] Spalek (2001) discusses the impact of white-collar crimes on its victims.

[133] Hadden (1983).

[134] The leading works include Nozick (1974); Honoré (1961); Waldron (1988); Munzer (1990); Christman (1994); J.W. Harris (1996a); Penner (1996).

[135] Gray (1991).

[136] See further Reich (1964) and his discussion of 'new property', which includes things like pension entitlements and environmental interests.

Green, P. (2003) 'The Concept of White Collar Crime in Law and Legal Theory' *Buffalo Criminal Law Review* 8: 1.

Green, Sarah (2012) 'Theft and Conversion—Tangibly Different' *Law Quarterly Review* 128: 564.

Green, Stuart (2002) 'Plagiarism, Norms, and the Limits of Theft Law: Some Observations on the Use of Criminal Sanctions in Enforcing Intellectual Property Rights' *Hastings Law Journal* 54: 167.

Harris, J.W. (1996a) *Property and Justice* (Oxford: OUP), ch. 16.

Harris, J.W. (1996b) 'Who Owns My Body?' *Oxford Journal of Legal Studies* 16: 55.

Herring, J. (2002) 'Giving, Selling and Sharing Bodies' in A. Bainham, S. Day Sclater, and M. Richards (eds) *Body Lore and Laws* (Oxford: Hart).

Lipton, J. (2001) 'Protecting Valuable Commercial Information in the Digital Age: Law, Policy and Practice' *Journal of Technology Law and Policy* 6: 1.

Melissaris, E. (2007) 'The Concept of Appropriation and the Offence of Theft' *Modern Law Review* 70: 597.

Weinrib, A. (1988) 'Information and Property' *University of Toronto Law Journal* 38: 117.

Having considered some of the more general issues relating to property offences we now turn to theft and consider some of the controversial issues surrounding the definition of theft.

7 THE DEBATE OVER *GOMEZ*

It will be recalled that the House of Lords in *Gomez*[137] confirmed that an appropriation involved an act of interference with one of the rights of an owner, and that an act could amount to appropriation even if it was consented to or authorized by the victim. The decision was highly controversial. We will now summarize some of the arguments for and against the decision.[138] ←2 (p.507)

7.1 THE CASE FOR *GOMEZ*

In the following passage, Simon Gardner sets out his reasons for welcoming *Gomez*:

S. Gardner, 'Appropriation in Theft: The Last Word?' (1993) 109 *Law Quarterly Review* 194

[Having explained that the House of Lords in *Gomez* essentially decided the case by following *Lawrence*, Gardner continued:]

---

[137] [1993] AC 442 (HL).
[138] See also S. Gardner (1990 and 1998); Cooper and Allen (1993); Clarkson (1993).

In its own terms, this summary resolution is unimpeachable. The only question is whether the answer is desirable from first principles. It is suggested that it is. Most fundamentally, it is submitted that the quality of dishonest conduct is not necessarily altered by the victim's consent. Consider, above all, cases where the victim consents to the taking, but does so in a state of low-level, non-specific confusion. For example, elderly people are often exploited by rogues who dishonestly overcharge them for work, or underpay them for their treasures. The victim in such a case has consented to the taking, and her consent is not obviously vitiated, but it is very possible to sense that the rogue's conduct should be criminal. However, in such circumstances it is not easy to convict for anything except ordinary theft. There can be no conviction for obtaining by deception under section 15 of the Theft Act, for want of a clear deception (cf. R. v. Silverman (1988) 86 Cr. App. R. 213); nor for the special form of theft established under section 5(4), for want of a true mistake; nor for blackmail or robbery, for want of any pressure. If theft were negatived by the victim's consent, then, such cases would constitute no offence. By their Lordships' decision in Gomez, however, theft does lie here. That result is to be applauded.

Another argument in favour of Gomez is that, even were we attracted to a requirement of non-consent, we should reject it as making theft difficult of administration by the criminal courts, with their lay judges of fact. Consent is a problematic concept. Even if it simply meant 'saying yes,' difficulties would remain. As the facts in Lawrence show, the practical boundaries of 'saying yes' are not altogether clear. And making a victim say 'yes' at the point of a gun would apparently negate theft, and so too robbery. That would be absurd. The answer would have to be that consent means 'true consent'—that is, an owner's 'yes' would be subject to vitiation by such factors as mistake or pressure. This approach is familiar from other branches of the law, above all contract. To adopt it in theft, however, would require magistrates' benches and Crown Courts to handle notions which have been found elusive even in the higher courts on the civil side. Directions on the law would consequently be prone to error, and so to appeal; and even if a direction was sound (or even, perhaps, the more sound it was), the task of applying it might well baffle the lay judges of fact (cf. Whittaker v. Campbell [1984] Q.B. 318). Neither meaning of 'consent,' therefore, would leave the law of theft in a happy condition, if non-consent were a constituent of the offence.

7.2 THE CASE AGAINST *GOMEZ*

The following are some of the reasons why many commentators have opposed the *Gomez* decision:

(1) One of the reasons that has led to *Gomez* suffering such ferocious criticism is that as a result of the decision virtually every offence of obtaining property by deception contrary to section 15 of the Theft Act 1968 is theft.[139] The Fraud Act 2006 has abolished the section 15 offence and so this argument has less relevance than it once had. However, it is certainly true there is now a significant overlap between fraud and theft. That said, as the 2006 Act was passed after the decision in *Gomez* we can take Parliament to have intended there to be an overlap.

(2) Following *Gomez* an act can amount to an appropriation which is not 'manifestly theftuous', to use a phrase of George Fletcher's.[140] In other words an act which appears to be objectively innocent (e.g. picking a tin of baked beans from a supermarket shelf[141]) can become theft if accompanied by the necessary *mens rea*.[142] The argument is that there is a

---

[139] Stuart (1967) reviews the background to the Theft Act 1968. [140] Fletcher (1976).
[141] This would, after *Gomez*, be theft. [142] Giles and Uglow (1992).

danger that theft could become essentially a 'mind crime'.[143] In Chapter 14, when we will discuss the *actus reus* of attempted offences, we will see that the law is very reluctant to convict defendants unless they have clearly revealed that they intend to commit a crime. These concerns do not seem to have been given weight in the law's definition of appropriation.

(3) Lord Lowry in his dissenting judgment in *Gomez* placed much weight on the view that the decision of the majority is not in line with the view of the Criminal Law Revision Committee, whose report formed the basis of the Theft Act 1968.

8 THE *HINKS* DEBATE

Hinks has been deeply unpopular with many academic commentators, although it is by no means without its supporters.

8.1 THE ARGUMENTS AGAINST *HINKS*

Summarizing the main arguments against *Hinks* the following points can be made:

(1) The case sets up a conflict between the criminal and civil law. The law almost appears to be hypocritical, telling Karen Hinks that at the same time she received a valid gift (in civil law), she stole it (in criminal law). Lord Steyn, in the majority in *Hinks*, accepted that there appeared to be a conflict, but that this was acceptable, given the different aims that the civil and criminal laws have. The civil law will place great weight on the importance of certainty of ownership, while the criminal law will seek to penalize dishonest conduct. An alternative response is that if there is a conflict between civil law and criminal law in cases of this kind, it is civil law which has got it wrong. Elderly and vulnerable people need protection from being exploited by others.[144]

(2) There is much uncertainty following *Hinks*. Whether a transfer amounts to theft now very much depends on whether the action is thought by the jury to be dishonest.[145] Some commentators suggest that the law is challengeable as too uncertain for the purposes of Article 6 of the European Convention on Human Rights.[146] Notably the Law Commission Consultation Paper on Fraud and Deception decided that a general offence of dishonesty may be too vague to be compatible with Convention rights.[147]

(3) There is some difficulty in *Hinks* in explaining how it was that Hinks could be said to have appropriated property belonging to another. The difficulty is that the very act of appropriation (receiving the money) was the moment in time when the property ceased to belong to the victim and belonged to Hinks. In other words at exactly the same moment there was appropriation and ownership changed hands. The majority seemed happy to accept that this could still be regarded as appropriating property belonging to another.

These and other objections to the *Hinks* decision are explained in the following extract, although Stephen Shute does not find the objections as powerful as they might appear at first sight: ←4 (p.512)

---

[143] See Melissaris (2007) who accepts that appropriate is essentially a mental attitude which is harmful, but not harmful enough to warrant being criminal until it is manifested in an act.

[144] *Jouman* [2012] EWCA Crim 1850 provides a good example of this.

[145] *Jouman* [2012] EWCA Crim 1850.   [146] Phillips, Walsh, and Dobson (2001: 50).

[147] Law Commission Consultation Paper No. 155 (1999: para. 5.52).

S. Shute, 'Appropriation and the Law of Theft' [2002] *Criminal Law Review* 450–7

3. Arguments against *Hinks*

For many this enlargement of the scope of the criminal law to include cases where title passes as a result of an unimpeachable transaction is unjustified. One argument against such an expansion is that it rides roughshod over the intentions of the framers of the Theft Act 1968. . . .

A second objection to the decision in *Hinks* is that it opens the door to inappropriate prosecutions. Counsel for the appellant in *Hinks* offered four examples which, in his view, illustrated the 'absurd and grotesque results' that would follow if the appeal were to be dismissed. Once again Lord Steyn was not convinced. He pointed out that the House of Lords in *Gomez* could not have overlooked the consequences of its decision and he said that, in any event, a prosecution was hardly likely to be brought in such cases and, if it were brought, would be 'likely to founder' because the jury would not be persuaded that there was dishonesty in the required (*Ghosh*) sense of that term or would conclude that under section 2(1)(a) of the Theft Act 1968 the transferee believed that he had a legal right to deprive the transferor of the property.

A third objection to *Hinks* is that it pares down excessively the *actus reus* of theft: indeed, some have argued that the combined effect of *Hinks* and *Gomez* is to reduce the *actus reus* of theft to 'vanishing point'. Of course, as the *actus reus* of the crime shrinks, so the role played by the *mens rea* concept of dishonesty will necessarily increase: it will have to take much more of the strain of filtering out cases that ought not to be regarded as theft from those that are clearly theftuous. This, in turn, generates two interconnecting objections to the *Gomez/Hinks* position: one based on the rule of law; the other on the harm principle.

It is a foundational (although not an unqualified) principle of our criminal law that citizens ought to be able to predict in advance whether or not their actions or omissions will fall foul of criminal prohibitions. Honouring this principle enhances a number of significant rule of law values: it imposes constraints on the use of arbitrary power; it goes some way towards ensuring that state authorities show proper respect for human dignity and autonomy; it assists citizens who wish to plan for the future; and it increases human freedom by allowing citizens to choose effectively between various life options. Relying on dishonesty to take most of the definitional strain in the crime of theft is said to work against these values because it is far from easy to predict in advance whether one's actions will or will not be adjudged dishonest. This difficulty is compounded in English law by the fact that the Court of Appeal has held that dishonesty is a matter for the jury. Unless a trial judge can conclude that there is no evidence upon which the jury could properly regard the defendant as dishonest he must put the issue to them: he cannot direct the jury to convict, nor can he withdraw the issue of dishonesty from them on the basis that the defendant was patently dishonest. Where the jury does require some assistance they should be advised on the basis of the test laid out in *R v. Ghosh* which, if given at all, should be given *ipsissima verba*. . . .

Because different juries may take different views about what the ordinary standards of reasonable and honest people require, the *Ghosh* test is said to be too unpredictable in its outcome to do the work now required of it by *Gomez* and *Hinks*. There are, however, arguments that can be made in its support. Richard Tur, for example, has defended the legal role of 'standard-bearing concepts' like dishonesty on the basis that they help to 'guard against an academic tendency to convert questions of practical moral philosophy into technical questions exclusively determined by the law.' When assessing the strength of this argument much will turn on the empirical question of whether there is in fact an identifiable and vivid community norm of 'dishonesty'. If there is, then the benefits of relying on it to take much of the definitional strain in the crime of theft may be sufficient to outweigh the disadvantages of vagueness and unpredictability that may be inherent in a *Ghosh* direction. If there is not, then the rule of law argument against *Hinks* (and for that matter *Gomez*) may be conclusive, although it should also be remembered that incorporating a thicker concept of appropriation into the law of theft in an attempt to counter excessive reliance on dishonesty may not achieve the desired result of an overall reduction in vagueness and unpredictability: for it could be that a thicker concept of appropriation will throw up as many problems of interpretation for judges or juries as the ruling in *Hinks*.

A connected argument against *Hinks* derives from the role of the liberal 'harm principle'. This states that in a liberal society criminalisation is justified only if it serves to prevent harm. The principle operates as a principle of exclusion: it identifies activities that ought not to be criminalised because their criminalisation cannot be shown to serve the goal of preventing harm. The objection to *Hinks* is that it breaches the harm principle because it expands the scope of the offence of theft to include cases where no civil wrong has been committed. Consider, for example, the case of a shopper who, with theftuous intent, takes an incorrectly priced pair of shoes from a sale rack in the hope that when she reaches the checkout she will be charged the lower amount. What the shopper does, it is argued, is nothing more than a 'harmless preparatory activity'. Yet, following *Gomez* and *Hinks*, she will have committed the crime of theft.

Two points can be made in response to this argument; both are controversial. The first is that there are good grounds for thinking that the conditions of the harm principle are met not only where an activity is itself harmful but also where it is a member of a class of acts that *tend* to cause harm. Hence it is false to conclude that the actions of the dishonest shopper described in the preceding paragraph will not satisfy the requirements of the harm principle: for even if they were not directly harmful they were clearly members of a class of acts which have a propensity to cause harm. The second point is that, in any case, the harm principle does not say that only harmful wrongs may be criminalised. Rather, it states that even harmless wrongs may be criminalised if criminalisation diminishes their occurrence and if their wider occurrence would detract from other people's prospects—for example, by diminishing some public good, such as people's sense of ease with their living environment, or their ability to enjoy public spaces, or their use of commercial facilities, such as shops, or the degree of mutual respect that prevails in public culture at large. Once the harm principle is understood in this way it becomes possible to see why, even if the main reason for criminalising theft is to protect property rights, it may nonetheless be justifiable to extend the crime of theft to cases where no property right has been infringed. This is because a State's failure to criminalise wrongs that do not infringe property rights may itself undermine those rights or indeed some other public good.

A fourth objection to *Hinks* is that it brings the criminal law into conflict with the civil law. Lord Steyn gave this argument the same short shrift that he had given to arguments based on the possibility of inappropriate prosecutions and the intentions of the framers of the 1968 Act. He agreed that 'in theory the two systems should be in perfect harmony' but said that in 'a practical world' there will sometimes be some disharmony between them, especially as their purposes are 'somewhat different'. He added, moreover, (and in this he was influenced by a closely-argued article written by Simon Gardner) that 'it would be wrong to assume on *a priori* grounds' that if there was a disharmony it was the criminal law rather than the civil law that was defective. He concluded therefore that the tension between the civil and the criminal law was not a factor which justified a departure from the law as stated in *Lawrence* and *Gomez*.

But is this conclusion too quick? Professors Beatson and Simester certainly think that it is. In their view any extension of the law of theft to include unimpeachable transfers 'risks seriously distorting the law of property'. At the heart of their position is the claim that *Hinks* leaves the law on the horns of an uncomfortable dilemma. On the one hand the conflict between civil and criminal law could be resolved by requiring the civil law to yield: the existence of the criminal law wrong could, as it were, 'trump' the normal civil law rules, thus rendering an otherwise valid transaction voidable. But such a solution, Beatson and Simester assert, 'cannot be taken seriously'. Property offences are designed to protect property rights and if we were to allow the law governing property offences to trump civil law rules, that dependence would be broken and property crimes would be left with 'no rationale'. On the other hand if we attempt to avoid this apparently unpleasant consequence by leaving the civil law unchanged we will be impaled on the second horn of the dilemma, for we will have to accept that 'the principle that no-one may benefit by his wrong would [in these circumstances] have immediately to be abandoned'.

Beatson and Simester argue, in other words, that *Hinks* forces us to choose between abandoning a well-founded principle of civil law and divorcing property offences from their underlying rationale. Since each alternative is highly unattractive *Hinks* must, they conclude, have been wrongly decided. But, despite its ingenuity, this argument is mistaken. It is, as we have already seen, false to assume that, if the law allows a property offence to be committed without a property right having been infringed, then the link between property offences and property rights will necessarily have been broken. Beatson and Simester's error arises because they fail to see that even without breaching a recognised proprietary right the criminalised act may nonetheless have had a *tendency* to undermine property rights, either directly by attacking the interests that they protect, or indirectly by weakening an established system of property rights and so threatening the public good that that system represents. In either case the justification for criminalising the act may still be the protection of property rights, even though in this instance no property right has been violated.

For this reason there is no necessary threat to the underlying rationale of property offences if the law of theft is extended to cover otherwise unimpeachable transfers. Nor is there a threat to that rationale if a crime committed in these circumstances is able to 'trump' the normal civil law rules thus rendering an otherwise valid transfer voidable. In fact, the law of property has long since acknowledged such a possibility. It does so by giving legal effect to the principle that 'no-one may benefit from his own wrong'. The principle is both limited in its application and relatively weak: first, it applies only where there has been a 'wrong'; second, even where there has been a wrong, the principle is often redundant because the wrong itself will generate a cause of action that is, on its own, sufficient to strip the wrongdoer of his benefit; third, the principle is of limited weight and hence may easily be overridden or excluded by other considerations; fourth, even where operative, the principle usually works by estopping a wrongdoer from relying on the wrongful transaction rather than by creating a new cause of action in some other party; and, fifth, even when not outweighed, the principle need not require that the wrongdoer be stripped of all the benefits he obtained from his wrongdoing: a partial restitution may be all that is required to meet its demands. That said, however, the 'no benefit principle' comes into its own when a criminal wrong has been committed which is not based on a civil law wrong. In these circumstances, driven by a criminal law wrong but not by a civil law wrong, the principle can result in a thief such as Hinks being stripped of (at least some of) the benefits obtained through her wrongdoing. When this happens the civil law is, in a sense, required to 'yield' to the criminal law: if it had not been for the criminal wrong no restitution would have been possible. But this is not an indication of an unacceptable conflict between the civil and the criminal law. Nor is it an indication that there has been a 'serious distortion' of the law of property. Rather, it is an indication that both the criminal law and the law of property have (wisely) chosen to give legal effect to an important moral proposition.

In the following extract, Alan Bogg and John Stanton-Ife take up the argument in the last paragraph of the previous extract: that because the transfer was valid in civil law there was no harm to the victim. They suggest that even if a transfer were valid, it can be seen as harmful to the victim if it involves exploitation:

A.L. Bogg and J. Stanton-Ife, 'Theft as Exploitation' (2003) 23 *Legal Studies* **402 at 415–16**

The prosecution alleged that after having befriended the victim, Hinks manipulated or coerced him to donate his life savings and a television set to her. The victim . . . was a vulnerable individual of limited intelligence, said to be trusting, generous and exceptionally naïve. The defendant had taken unfair advantage of the victim's vulnerability, and abused his trust, in order to procure the transfer of his property. In taking unfair advantage of the victim and abusing his trust, the defendant had exploited the victim.[148] Exploitation is a wrong, though the degree of wrongfulness will depend on a number of features: the manner in which the victim is used, the characteristics that are utilised, and the way in which the exploitation allocates gains and losses. It is most wrongful if the manner of use involves coercion, deception or manipulation; if the characteristics used are moral virtues or particular vulnerabilities; and if the exploiter makes extensive gains at the expense of the victim's losses. All of these features were present in *Hinks*: the deployment of manipulation in a predatory and acquisitive manner, the taking advantage of the victim's trust and vulnerability, allowing the defendant to make huge financial gain at the expense of the victim's losses.

Critics may respond to Bogg and Stanton-Ife's arguments by claiming that *Hinks* might have engaged in exploitation and this should be criminal, but it is not the crime of theft.[149]

QUESTIONS

1. If you think the decision in *Hinks* is wrong, should Parliament nevertheless introduce special legislation to protect vulnerable people from financial exploitation (for evidence of the widespread financial abuse of elderly people, see Brogden and Nijhar (2000))? Or would such legislation be subject to many of the objections that *Hinks* is?

2. If a company's directors pay themselves such a high salary that it is regarded as dishonest, should they be guilty of theft?

---

9 TEMPORARY APPROPRIATION

As noted in Part I the present law requires there to be an intention of permanent deprivation for there to be theft. A taking intended to be a borrowing will not be a theft (unless it falls within section 6). The main justification for the law's approach is that borrowings are best dealt with under the civil law and are not sufficiently serious to justify the intervention of the criminal law.[150] Although the victim of a temporary appropriation may

---

[148] On the nature of exploitation, see Feinberg (1988: 176–210).

[149] Simester and Sullivan (2007).

[150] Tigar (1984), examining the history of the law of theft, has seen a shift from the protection of possession to the protection of property. This shift may explain why temporary interferences in possession are no longer seen as sufficient to justify the attentions of the criminal law.

have lost the ability to use the item for a period of time that is not as serious as an outright taking.[151] ←5 (p.513)

In the following passage, Glanville Williams sets out the case for stating that temporary appropriations should amount to theft:

G. Williams, 'Temporary Appropriation Should be Theft' [1981] *Criminal Law Review* 129 at 131–3, 137, 138

The general argument for changing the law

Suppose that a person removes a small piece of sculpture from a private exhibition, or a valuable book from a University library, and returns it after a year. During that time it has of course been lost to its owner; and both the owner and the police have been put to trouble. If the owner has made a claim upon an insurer or bailee, and been compensated on the basis of total loss, he may even find that the insurer or bailee claims the right to sell the article when it is recovered, so that the owner loses it. The taker of the article may use it in such a way as to put it at risk, or he may make a profit from it, or he may return it in an impaired condition; and if he is a person of no substance the owner's civil remedy against him will be an insufficient penalty.

The intent required by the present law of theft puts the jury or magistrates in a difficult situation. The taker may himself have no clear idea when he takes the things whether he is going to return it or not. I have recently seen a circular from the librarian of a library for undergraduates pointing out that in the last three years as many books have been lost to the library as have been bought for it. Most of these losses, he thinks, can be accounted for by 'careless borrowing which grows with time into theft. That is to say, people who borrow the books without signing them out, intending but in the end never bothering to return them.'

If a person has gone off with the property of another, and upon being apprehended and charged with theft swears that he meant to return it, is his statement to be accepted or not? To accept it too readily gives guilty defendants an easy line of escape; to reject it carries the risk of convicting people who are technically innocent, even though they are morally guilty because they have taken the article dishonestly. In 1953 an art student removed a bronze statuette of Psyche by Rodin from a picture gallery, but later returned it anonymously with a note saying: 'There was no mercenary intent behind my abduction of this exquisite creature. I merely wished to live with her for a while.' Had he been caught with the statuette, the jury might justifiably have disbelieved his explanation, even though, as the event showed, it was true. Technically, there would have been a miscarriage of justice, though not in the fullest sense of the expression. Why should not the dishonest taking be sufficient to constitute the offence of theft, thus relieving the prosecution of a very difficult burden of proof? . . .

In *Warner*,[152] a shop assistant, who had been annoyed by employees next door, took their tools and hid them in the shop. When asked by a policeman about the tools he denied all knowledge of them. When the tools were eventually discovered he explained that he had only meant to keep them for about an hour to get his own back. The jury convicted him of theft, but the conviction was quashed on appeal for misdirection, the Court of Appeal re-affirming the rule that theft required an intent to deprive the owner permanently. This was a

---

[151] W. Wilson (2002: 23).   [152] (1970) 55 Cr App R 93 (CA).

trivial case, and if the defendant had not lied to the police he would probably not have been prosecuted. It illustrates the point, however, that a person may take another's property by way of revenge without committing an offence; and he will not commit an offence even if he causes great loss and keeps the property a considerable time, if he intended to give it back in the end. . . .

The effect of changing the law

If the law is changed in the way here suggested, the result will be to simplify it and to preclude unmeritorious defences. It may also have some small effect upon public morality if it is brought home to people that any dishonest taking is theft. Just as supermarkets now exhibit notices saying that 'shoplifting is theft,' so libraries could announce that 'unauthorised removal of books is theft.' . . .

The objection of triviality

It may be that the reader, while accepting some of the arguments in this article, has throughout been afflicted by one other doubt. Is it seriously suggested that trivial cases of dishonestly using the property of another should be subject to prosecution as theft? The absurdity of this was an argument that appealed powerfully to the majority of the Criminal Law Revision Committee. It was elaborated by Lord Stonham, speaking for the government, in the debate on the Theft Bill in the House of Lords. He gave, as examples of trivial cases, using one's neighbour's lawn mower against his expressed wishes, taking a book from a public library beyond one's borrowing limit, and using a friend's dinner jacket without his consent.

The argument about trivial cases is frequently used to oppose extensions of the law, but it is never conclusive in itself, because practically every offence covers *some* trivial matters. If an offence is needed to deal with serious misconduct, that is sufficient to justify it. Even the present law could be abused by prosecuting for trivial thefts, but in practice a sensible discretion is generally exercised. The Canadian experience bears out the view that a law of *furtum usus* is unlikely to be used oppressively.

FURTHER READING

Bein, D. (1968) 'The Theft of Use and the Elements of "Intention to Deprive Permanently" in Larceny' *Israel Law Review* 3: 368.

Williams, G. (1981a) 'Temporary Appropriation Should be Theft' *Criminal Law Review* 129.

10 DISHONESTY

As has been indicated in our discussion on *Hinks*, after that decision many commentators feel that appropriation has been almost a token requirement, and that dishonesty has become the key notion in theft. To some this is all the more concerning because of the rather loose definition of dishonesty used by the law. In the following passage, Edward Griew sets out some of the arguments against the current law's definition of 'dishonest'.[153] He distinguishes between the *Feely* question: 'Was what was done dishonest according to the ordinary standards of reasonable and honest people?' and the *Ghosh* question: 'Must the defendant have realized that what he was doing was dishonest according to those standards?': ←6 (p.519)

E. Griew, 'Dishonesty: The Objections to *Feely* and *Ghosh*' [1985] *Criminal Law Review* 341

A. Objections to the *Feely* question

. . .

A1. More, longer and more difficult trials

If the law is right in principle, so be it; the fact that it tends to multiply and prolong trials cannot be a decisive objection. But as an addition to other objections it is of such practical importance that it should have pride of place. There are several distinct points.

(a) The question tends to increase the number of trials. Whereas a different approach to the dishonesty issue might make clear that given conduct was dishonest as a matter of law and therefore constituted an offence, the *Feely* question leaves the issue open. It may be worth a defendant's while to take the chance with the jury. . . .

(b) The question tends to complicate and lengthen contested cases. For it is difficult to say of any evidence relating to the defendant's state of mind or to the special circumstances in which he acted that is irrelevant to the *Feely* case. Moreover, it must be in the interests of some defendants to extend and complicate trials in order to obfuscate the issue. . . .

(c) At the end of a trial the jury may have to be asked not simply whether the defendant acted with the state of mind he claims to have had, or in other circumstances that, as he suggests, may have rendered his act not dishonest, but also (if he may have done so) whether his act with that state of mind, or in those circumstances, was dishonest, was dishonest according to ordinary standards. If these matters are not kept separate the jury may be seriously misled. But their careful separation shows the complexity of the direction that the *Feely* question will dictate in some cases. . . .

(d) The separate matters just referred to, that may need to figure in the judge's direction, must then be handled by the jury in their deliberations. They may find them hard to keep separate. The issues we present to juries should be as simple as possible; jury service, after all, imposes tasks on ordinary people that they are not accustomed to discharge. The *Feely* question involves complications that we are not justified in supposing that all jurors are competent to handle.

A2. Inconsistent decisions

The *Feely* question carries an unacceptable risk of inconsistency of decision. This objection has been voiced by many critics. The problem of inconsistency is likely, of course, to affect only a small proportion of cases. In most cases the issue is one as to the facts: what did D do? What was his state of mind? Once the facts are found there will usually be only one plausible answer to the *Feely* question. It is only a minority of cases that the matter will truly admit of argument. But within this crucial marginal group different juries as the presumptive embodiment of ordinary decent standards, may take different views of essentially indistinguishable cases. The law of the relevant offence will then vary as between different defendants. This must be unacceptable.

---

[153] Henry (1978) discusses the ambiguities amongst public opinion over what is dishonest or not.

A3. Fiction of community norms

The *Feely* question implies the existence of a relevant community norm. In doing so it glosses over difference of age, class and cultural background which combine to give the character of fiction to the idea of a generally shared sense of the boundary between honesty and dishonesty. This is the more obvious in a society with the range of cultural groups that ours now has; and it is the more relevant since jury service was extended to the generality of electors between 18 and 65. It is simply naïve to suppose—surely no one does suppose—that there is, in respect of the dishonesty question, any such single thing as 'the standards of ordinary decent people.' . . .

A4. 'Dishonesty' as an 'ordinary word'

The foregoing objection to the *Feely* question is closely related to another. The jury are to consult their sense of ordinary standards because the word 'dishonestly' is 'in common use.' Jurors in their own lives 'have to decide what is and what is not dishonest'; they do not 'require the help of a judge to tell them what amounts to dishonest.' . . . What must be expressed here is a doubt about the 'ordinary word.' It simply does not follow from the truth that a word such as 'dishonestly' is an ordinary word that all speakers of the language share the same sense of its application or non-application in particular contexts. . . .

A5. Specialised cases

The *Feely* question is in any case unsuitable where the context of the case is a specialised one, involving intricate financial activities or dealings in a specialised market. It is neither reasonable nor rational to expect ordinary people to judge as 'dishonest' or 'not dishonest' conduct of which, for want of relevant experience, they cannot appreciate the contextual flavour. . . .

A6. Ordinary dishonest jurors

The general understanding is that the jury may be taken to represent the 'ordinary decent people' to whom the *Feely* question refers. . . . Yet a vast number of what must surely be theft, handling and minor fraud offences are committed by 'ordinary' even 'ordinary decent' people such as serve upon juries: theft at work ('perks'), handling stolen goods being offered in the neighbourhood ('from off the back of a lorry'), inflation of expenses claims, inaccuracy or concealment in the income tax return. These ordinary people, as jurors, will either apply their own standards, as being the prevalent standards of which they know; or they will demand of their defendants higher standards than they themselves attain. To the extent (if at all) that the former occurs, the Court of Appeal in *Feely* and *Ghosh* will have achieved a reduction in the scope of dishonesty offences which it certainly did not intend. We ought not, on the other hand, to view the latter, presumably more common, occurrence, with complacency. It is perfectly acceptable for the law to require a jury to *apply* a standard higher than its own; it is not acceptable that the law should invite a jury to *impose* such a standard by an act of creative hypocrisy. The law in effect expects many jurors, in relation to very common kinds of offences, to have one conception of ordinary standards outside court and another conception inside. This is disreputable.

A7. 'Anarchic' verdicts

The *Feely* question, offered without qualification to the jury, is 'a question of moral estimation without guidelines' and permits ' "anarchic" verdicts which are not technically perverse.' A jury without stars or compass cannot be accused of bad navigation. The direction it takes may be deplorable, but cannot be wrong. A consequence of this, it has been pointed out, is that members of unpopular groups may receive inadequate protection from the law. . . .

A8. What is 'dishonest' should be a matter of law

Whether an individual defendant was dishonest is, of course, a question for the jury. But it should be so only in the sense that the jury will find the facts upon the strength of which, applying legal principles, they will be able to say whether the defendant acted dishonestly. Whether the facts that they find constitute a case of 'dishonesty' within the meaning of that word in the particular legal context is a matter of legal principle upon which they should be able to turn to the law for clear guidance.

How that guidance is achieved is not necessarily an easy question. But the fact that it is not easy does not justify a refusal to answer it—whether in general terms or case by case. A decision has to be made about the role that the word 'dishonestly' has in the specification of offences. It might have none except to exclude from the scope of offences cases of claim of right (as well as any, or any other, cases expressly excluded by statute as not cases of dishonesty). In addition to such excluded cases, however, might be those perceived by the judge as involving 'no moral obloquy'. In any such cases the judge would direct an acquittal, thereby making a precedent for the guidance of other courts. Another suggestion has been that in the case of theft 'dishonestly' might be interpreted to mean 'knowing that the appropriation will or may be detrimental to the interests of the owner in a significant practical way.'

. . .

A9. Dishonesty and defences

Leaving the dishonesty issue to the untutored application of community standards allows the issue a potentially unlimited function. The jury may be unwilling to condemn a defendant's conduct as 'dishonest' because they sympathise with his motive or are inclined to excuse what he did in the difficult circumstances in which he found himself; they may be still less willing if they are prepared to say that his conduct was justified in the circumstances. Thus the jury may create for their defendant a defence of necessity greater than any known to the law or a defence of pressure of circumstances where the law knows only a plea in mitigation. But the law of defences should develop in a disciplined way under judicial control, save indeed to the extent that it is statutorily defined.

. . .

A10. Inconsistency within the Theft Acts

The *Feely* question produces an inconsistency between theft and other offences in relation to a claim of right. One who appropriates property in the belief that he has in law the right to deprive the loser of it does not, as a matter of law, appropriate dishonestly. This principle is statutory. But no corresponding statutory principle is provided for any obtaining offence. The judges might have asserted such a principle, however, and could have been expected to do so but for *Feely* and *Ghosh*. As it is, they seem prepared to trust the jury to achieve the corresponding result for the individual in response to a *Ghosh* direction. The result is that it is *not* theft to obtain at the point of knife what you think you are entitled to, whereas it *may not* be an offence under section 15 of the 1968 Act to obtain the same property by telling a lie—it is up to the jury to say.

. . .

B. Objections to the *Ghosh* question

. . .

B1. More, longer and more difficult trials

Compare objection A1. The *Ghosh* question (a) creates an additional ground for contested trials; (b) justifies the introduction of additional evidence; (c) further complicates the judge's direction; and (d) adds further to the complexity of the jury's task. There is no need to labour these points.

. . .

B3. Inept correction of error

. . .

The confusion on this point in the *Ghosh* judgment is clear to see in the hypothetical treatment of the hypothetical visitor from a foreign country where public transport is free. He travels on a bus without paying. Does he do so dishonestly? The courts says that 'his conduct, judged objectively by what he has done, is dishonest.' The error enters the argument at this point. It cannot be right, as the structure of the court's argument plainly implies, that the visitor's conduct would be regarded as dishonest by ordinary decent standards. If the jury knew that he believed public transport to be free, they would say that, according to ordinary standards, he had not behaved dishonestly. There is no need to go further; his 'state of mind' has already been taken into account. But the court, having declared him dishonest when 'judged objectively,' has to introduce a further 'subjective' element to rescue him. This leads to the question: 'Did he know it was dishonest?'—an entirely unnecessary question.

B4. Mistake of law

The *Ghosh* question 'allows something like a mistake of law to be a defence.' The question is a mere addendum to the *Feely* question; it is the answer to the latter that determines the view to be taken of the defendant's conduct as in principle criminal. The jury's apprehension of current standards makes law for the case; the defendant's misapprehension of those standards is indeed 'something like a mistake of law.' It is not strictly one, of course; his failure to realise that ordinary people would call his conduct dishonest means (taking *Ghosh* literally) that it is not dishonest.

B5. The 'Robin Hood defence'

A person may defend his attack on another's property by reference to a moral or political conviction as passionately held that he believed (so he claims) that 'ordinary decent' members of society would regard his conduct as proper, even laudable. If the asserted belief is treated as a claim to have been ignorant that the conduct was 'dishonest' by ordinary standards (and it has been assumed that it might be so treated), and if the jury think (as exceptionally they might) that the belief may have been held, *Ghosh* produces an acquittal. The result is remarkable. Robin Hood must be a thief even if he thinks the whole of the right thinking world is on his side.

B6. A further threat to standards

A person reared or moving in an environment in which it is generally treated as legitimate to take advantage of certain classes of people—perhaps bookmakers or employers—may plausibly claim that he did not realise that his conduct of which a member of such a class was a victim, was generally regarded as dishonest. It is not acceptable that a claim of that sort should be capable even of being advanced. It has been said that 'the [*Ghosh*] question presents an even greater threat to the standard of honesty than the [*Feely*] question.'

In support of the view that there is no consensus on what amounts to dishonesty, Stuart Macdonald[154] refers to an online study by Stefan Fafinski and Emily Finch which asked the public whether they thought behaviour was dishonest. They found divergence on a range of issues. For example, 43 per cent of people thought it was dishonest for a carer to persuade an elderly person to leave them something after their death and 57 per cent of people did not. They have plenty of other examples too. However, they may not have asked the correct question. To simulate a jury situation it should be asked whether, beyond all reasonable doubt, there was dishonesty. That might generate far more consensus.

Those who support the present law can point to the fact that since *Ghosh* the meaning of dishonesty has not greatly troubled the courts.[155] Interestingly, when the Law Commission sought comments on whether the law on dishonesty needs to be reformed, the Magistrates' Association were in favour of retaining the present law.[156] Whatever its theoretical problems it seems therefore to have provided a workable definition.[157] What, of course, we do not know is whether juries and magistrates actually follow the *Ghosh* direction, or whether they give dishonesty its 'normal' meaning. What the *Ghosh* test is trying to do is to seek a compromise between having a purely objective test for dishonesty which would simply ask whether the conduct was dishonest by the standards of the ordinary person and a subjective approach which would ask whether the defendant regarded his or her conduct as dishonest.

One aspect of the debate over the meaning of property is whether theft can be justified in an unfair society. This is discussed in the following passage by Stuart Green:

S. Green, 'Property Offenses' in M. Dubber and T. Hörnle (eds) *The Oxford Handbook of Criminal Law* (Oxford: OUP, 2014), 784–5

[W]hat about societies in which property is distributed in a radically *unjust* manner? Some scholars have suggested that people who have suffered from severe societal injustice should be exempt from liability for a whole range of offenses—property crimes as well as violent crimes like murder and rape. A competing view is that the injustice of a given society should be viewed as more relevant with respect to judging the blameworthiness of offenses against property than it is with respect to offenses against the person. The reason is that the moral underpinnings of offenses such as murder and rape do not depend on background considerations of social justice. The moral obligations that D breaches when he commits a violent offense against another are obligations owed to his fellow human beings, as individuals, rather than to the government or to society generally, and they would likely exist even in a society without developed institutions of law.

---

[154] MacDonald (2014: 301).

[155] Although Glover (2010) claims it hindered the police's response to those who 'salvaged' cargo from a stricken ship.

[156] Law Commission Report No. 276 (2002: para. 5.14).

[157] *Ibid*, para. 5.15 stated that there was no evidence that juries were producing inconsistent verdicts on similar facts.

By contrast, the moral obligations that D breaches when he engages in violations of V's property rights by stealing his car or trespassing on his land are quite different. As Jim Harris put it:

> The background right [to property] is historically situated. It does not have the same ahistorical status as do rights not to be subjected to unprovoked violence to the person. There are no natural rights to full-blooded ownership of the world's resources.

Good faith implementation of the moral background right may or may not achieve a threshold of justice for a property institution. If it does, the trespassory rules of the institution are, *prima facie*, morally binding. Murder, assault, and rape are always moral wrongs. Theft is morally wrong only when this justice threshold is attained.

And when does a given property institution achieve a threshold of justice? That, of course, is an immensely complex and controversial question . . . [H]owever, it is safe to assume that the threshold would not be met by a regime under which a whole class of citizens was unjustly forbidden from owning property. In such a society, D, as a member of that class, would not be morally blameworthy for stealing property from V, at least to the extent that V helped to create or perpetuate the conditions that caused D's unjust impoverishment.

Emmanuel Melissaris has suggested in this context that we need to distinguish between societies in which injustice is "extreme" and those in which it is "partial." The former involve "cases of basic structural injustice, in which groups are denied the resources of liberties to which they are entitled by virtue of their status as participants in the political community and which are necessary for them to make the best of that status." The latter involve cases where "a fair scheme of distribution of resources and liberties is largely in place but there are imperfections, which means that some citizens are distributively short-changed." Where injustice is extreme, he says, the state can "make no demands of its citizens" and therefore is "not justified in criminalising interferences with property." Cases of partial injustice present a more complex issue. According to Melissaris, injustice of this sort sometimes causes excusing conditions, such as cognitive impairments and provocations, but it does not by itself justify D's acts.

In some cases . . . property lawbreaking serves a vital role in challenging moribund and unjust property regimes and creating a more just social order. They distinguish between two different kinds of what they call "property outlaws": "Expressive" outlaws seek to use their lawbreaking to send a message about the perceived injustice of existing property arrangements. A good example is the 1960s civil rights era lunch-counter protests, which targeted laws that prohibited African Americans from sitting at "whites-only" lunch counters and having access to other public accommodations. Like the more recent Occupy Wall Street movement, the civil rights protesters used trespass as a means of social advocacy. . . . By defying such laws, protesters sent a tangible message that such laws were unjust and harmful and that the interests they protected were illegitimate.

QUESTIONS

1. 'Once again the law of theft is in urgent need of simplification and modernization, so that a jury of 12 ordinary citizens do not have to grapple with concepts couched in the antiquated "franglais" of "choses in action", and scarce public resources in time and money are not devoted to hours of semantic argument divorced from the true merits of the case' (Beldam LJ in *Hallam* [1995] Crim LR 323). Do you agree? (In fairness it should be added, as Smith (1995) points out, that the Act uses the phrase 'things in action' not 'choses in action'.)

2. Do you think it possible to provide a better definition of dishonesty than that used in *Ghosh*?

3. Law Commission Report No. 276 (2002: para. 5.9) refers to a MORI poll in 1985 in which only 35 per cent of those questioned thought it dishonest to accept payment in cash to avoid payment of tax. But only 37 per cent of those questioned thought most people would regard it as honest. Does this indicate that it is sensible to leave questions of honesty to the jury?

4. In *DPP v Gohill* magistrates acquitted two employees who worked at a business which hired out machines. Where a customer wanted to borrow an item for a very short time they allowed customers to do this and falsified records. Customers often gave them a tip of £5 or £10. The employees said (with some justification) this created good customer relations and that they often refused the tips. The magistrates took the view that they could not be sure this was contrary to the standards of honesty of the reasonable person. On appeal the Divisional Court found this finding to be perverse and returned the case for a rehearing. Do you agree with the magistrates or the Divisional Court?

5. The 'dishonesty lab' at www.surrey.ac.uk/festivalofscience/honestylab gave people the chance to disclose their dishonest conduct and also comment on what was honest or not. What is the significance of the fact that people seem to have widely differing views on what is honest? Or is this only true of borderline cases? Do you think that, in fact, on clear cases there are clearly accepted standards of honesty?

FURTHER READING

Campbell, K. (1984) 'The Test of Dishonesty in *R v Ghosh*' *Cambridge Law Journal* 43: 349.

Elliott, D. (1982) 'Dishonesty in Theft: A Dispensable Concept' *Criminal Law Review* 395.

Elliott, D. (1991) 'Directors' Theft and Dishonesty' *Criminal Law Review* 732.

Glover, R. (2010) 'Can Dishonesty be Salvaged? Theft and the Grounding of the MSC Napoli' *Journal of Criminal Law* 74: 53.

Green, S. (2014), 'Property Offenses' in M. Dubber and T. Hörnle (eds) *The Oxford Handbook of Criminal Law* (Oxford: OUP).

Halpin, A. (1996) 'The Test for Dishonesty' *Criminal Law Review* 283.

Halpin, A. (2004) *Definition in the Criminal Law* (Oxford: Hart), ch. 4.

Thomas, S. (2010) 'Do Freegans Commit Theft?' *Legal Studies* 30: 98.

Tur, R. (1985) 'Dishonesty and the Jury' in A. Phillips Griffiths (ed.) *Philosophy and Practice* (Oxford: OUP).

Wasik, M. (1977b) '*Mens Rea*, Motive and the Problem of "Dishonesty" in the Law of Theft' *Criminal Law Review* 543.

11 ROBBERIES

The offence of robbery ranges from a carefully planned bank raid to a spur of the moment 'bag snatching'. In the popular imagination robbery has become synonymous with 'muggings', which have become a common part of urban life and cause much fear.[158] There is some justification for the fear: in 2014/15 there were 50,236 reported robberies.[159] Mobile phones have come to be closely linked with robberies. Around 2 per cent of people have their phones stolen every year.[160] For those aged 12–15 it rose to 5 per cent.

In the following passage, Andrew Ashworth outlines some of the difficulties with the legal definition of robbery: ←7 (p.525)

A. Ashworth, 'Robbery Re-assessed' [2002] *Criminal Law Review* 851 at 855–7

The Law on Robbery

Several features of the offence [of robbery] require comment.

First, there are three ways of committing robbery—using force, putting someone in fear, or seeking to put someone in fear. This leaves no doubt about the relevance of imitation weapons to the definition of robbery; but, on the other hand, the various ways of committing the offence are not ranked in order of relative seriousness.

Secondly, and echoing a point already made in relation to statistical classification, the dividing line between robbery and theft is anything but robust. This is not necessarily a criticism of the legal definition, since many offences inevitably have fuzzy edges. But the term 'uses force' has been interpreted so as to include relatively slight force, such as barging into someone or tugging at a handbag in such a way that the owner's hand is pulled downwards. The effect is to label such offences as robbery rather than theft, and to put them in a category which has life imprisonment as the maximum penalty.

And thirdly, robbery is a single offence: 'robbery with violence' and armed robbery are not legal terms of art, however often they may appear in crime novels. The single offence is also extraordinarily broad. The maximum penalty for theft is seven years' imprisonment; but, where force or the threat of force is used in order to steal, the category of robbery covers everything from a push or a raised hand in order to snatch a bag, to the most violent robbery of a security vehicle with guns fired and so forth. The single maximum penalty, life imprisonment, covers the whole range. The contrast with other offences involving violence is stark. Although English law remains in a rather antiquated state, the Offences Against the Person Act 1861 provides a ladder of non-fatal crimes—common assault, assault occasioning actual bodily harm, unlawful wounding or grievous bodily harm, and wounding or grievous bodily harm with intent. The structure is desperately in need of modernisation: most modern penal codes grade their offences of violence according to differences in the seriousness of the harm done and differences in culpability, but current English law does so only imperfectly. However, no one has been heard to suggest that we should have a single offence of violence, such as 'using force on another person', to replace everything from common assault to wounding with intent. That would be rejected on many grounds—sentencing would be at large rather than graduated according to different maxima, the label would fail to distinguish the serious from the not-so-serious, the label would be useless for classification purposes (*e.g.* when assessing an offender's criminal record), and so on.

If we (rightly) reject a single offence of violence, should we not also object to such a broad and undifferentiated offence as robbery, based on using or threatening force of any degree? I would argue that the offence of robbery is objectionable because it fails to mark in a public way the distinction between a mere push and serious violence, and because the label 'robbery' is therefore too vague and too liable to stereotypical interpretations—some may assume that serious violence, or a weapon, was involved when this was not necessarily the

---

[158] Hall (1978).   [159] Home Office (2010).   [160] BBC News Online (2010a).

case. It is often said that robbery is a serious offence, but that applies only to some robberies. There are some offences that involve a small theft with only slight violence that would not warrant more than a charge of assault or battery. Consideration must be given to dividing the offence, so as to mark out as particularly serious those robberies which involve the use or threat of significant violence.

Such an approach could also have a worthwhile practical and procedural consequence. At present all robberies are triable only on indictment. Again, this results in some offences being tried at a higher level than their separate elements (assault, theft) might warrant. Offences of assault occasioning actual bodily harm and section 20 wounding or grievous bodily harm are triable either way, as are offences of theft. If the essence of the offence would not otherwise justify a higher charge, it is surely questionable whether all robberies should go to the Crown Court if some offences against the person are summary only or triable either way.

FURTHER READING

Ashworth, A. (2002c) 'Robbery Re-assessed' *Criminal Law Review* 851.

Matthews, R. (2002) *Armed Robbery* (Cullompton: Willan).

Smith, J. (2003) *The Nature of Personal Robbery* (London: Home Office).

---

12 HANDLING STOLEN GOODS

There has been relatively little discussion on the moral basis for the offence of handling stolen goods. One view is that the offence is justified because people who handle or receive stolen goods are encouraging others to steal. If there was no one to sell property on to there would be much less incentive to steal. Another argument is that the handler is adding to the deprivation of the owners' property, by making it harder to locate and thereby less likely to be recovered. Perhaps the best argument is to conceive of the handler as complicit with the thief: they have joined together with the thief in the enterprise of removing the owners' property.

FURTHER READING

Green, Stuart (2011a) 'Thieving and Receiving: Overcriminalizing the Possession of Stolen Property' *New Criminal Law Review* 14: 35.

---

13 CONCLUDING THOUGHTS

The law on theft has proved surprisingly controversial. In part this is a result of the complex interaction between the civil law of property and the criminal law of property offences. The criminal courts have sought to avoid the complexities that would arise from fully integrating property law into the criminal law. However, in doing so, they have opened themselves up to objections that theft is punishing dishonesty, rather than an interference with property interests. Some commentators are happy with this shift in emphasis as it focuses on the morally significant issue (dishonesty) rather than more technical matters of property law. Others argue that it leaves the offence vague and lacking a clear justification.

9

FRAUD

CENTRAL ISSUES

1. The offence of fraud can be committed where the defendant dishonestly makes a false representation intending to make a gain for him or herself or a loss to another. The defendant is only guilty if he or she knows that the statement is, or might be, untrue or misleading.

2. Fraud is also committed where the defendant dishonestly fails to disclose information which he or she is under a duty to disclose, intending to make a gain for him or herself or cause a loss to another.

3. A third way of committing fraud is where the defendant misuses a position of trust in a dishonest way to make a gain or cause a loss.

4. There is an offence of obtaining services by a dishonest act and also of making off without payment from a place where payment is expected.

PART I: THE LAW ON FRAUD

In Chapter 8 we looked at theft, which, in simple terms, involves taking another's property. In this chapter we will look at the offence of fraud, where property has been obtained from the victim by other dishonest means. The Fraud Act 2006 came into force on 15 January 2007. It was passed following increasing dissatisfaction with the previous law on deception. The old offences had troubled courts, academics, and students for decades.

1 FRAUD

The Fraud Act 2006 creates a single offence of fraud which can be committed in three different ways: by false representation, failing to disclose information, and by abuse of position.

All of these offences are the crime of fraud so there is no need for the prosecution to prove which means was used as long as the jury is satisfied it was one of them. →1 (p.579)

1.1 FRAUD BY FALSE REPRESENTATION

Section 2(1) of the Fraud Act 2006 states:

> A person is in breach of this section if he—
>
> (a) dishonestly makes a false representation, and
>
> (b) intends, by making the representation—
>
>   (i) to make a gain for himself or another, or
>
>   (ii) to cause loss to another or to expose another to a risk of loss.

This form of committing the offence can be broken down into the following elements:

There must be a false representation

The representation can be made in any way. So it will include statements made orally, in writing, or on a website. In *Idrees v DPP*[1] the court had no difficulty in upholding the conviction of a person who had taken the written part of the driving test, impersonating someone else. By turning up at the test centre and presenting someone's identification they were impliedly claiming to be that person. Section 2(2) explains that a representation is to be regarded as false if it is 'untrue or misleading'. Section 2(3) makes it clear that the representation can be as to fact or law and it can include a representation as to someone's state of mind. Problematic cases will arise where a statement is literally true ('the car passed its MOT yesterday with no problems'), but is not the complete truth ('on the way back from the MOT the car broke down'). This might be regarded as a statement which is misleading for the purposes of section 2(2), especially if it is in response to a direct question about how well the car works. →2 (p.577)

It is well established in the case law that if a person uses a credit card they are representing not only that the card is theirs but also that they are authorized to use it.[2] If, therefore, a defendant has been told by his or her bank not to use a credit card or they have reached their credit limit and are longer authorized to use it they may be guilty of fraud. Note that the victim will be the shop because they have made a false statement to the shop that they are authorized to use the credit card.[3]

The false representation must be made by the defendant

Notice first that the representation must be made *by the defendant*. So if Michelle is aware that Liam has lied to Charlie and uses that lie to gain property, she will not have committed fraud by false representation. However, she may have committed one of the other versions of fraud (e.g. fraud by failing to disclose information). Notice also that the representation must

---

[1] [2011] EWHC 624 (Admin).   [2] *Lambie* [1982] AC 449.
[3] The same kind of reasoning applies if a defendant uses a cheque book when unauthorized to do so: *Gilmartin* [1983] QB 953.

be 'made'. This may indicate that representation cannot be made by silence. However, the matter is not straightforward. Section 2(4) explains that the representation can be express or implied. So acting in a way which impliedly makes a statement may be covered by this version of fraud. In the well-known case of *Barnard*,[4] a defendant went into a shop (in the 1830s) wearing an academic cap and gown of the kind typically worn by members of Oxford University at that time. The shopkeeper assumed he was a member of the University and therefore gave a discounted price. It was held that by wearing this garb the defendant was representing that he was a member of the University. As he was not, this amounted to a false representation. A more modern example is where a person walks through a staff entrance of a club (seeking to avoid payment of the entrance fee). She is representing that she is a member of staff and so this could be deceptive. Less obvious would be a case where a very high price tag was put on a copy of an old master painting: is the high price tag impliedly stating that the painting is an original?

A final point to notice is that there is no need to show that the false representation need be made to anyone. Most significantly section 2(5) states that the offence can be committed against a computer or other mechanical representation. Also it means that even if the victim was fully aware that the defendant was lying, the offence would be made out. It also means that if the prosecution can prove that a defendant sent out a fraudulent email, a conviction could be obtained, even if the email was never read by any of the would-be victims because it was caught in a spam-filter.

The defendant must know that the statement is or might be untrue or misleading

This is required by section 2(2)(b). Notice that it is sufficient if the defendant knows that what he or she is saying *might* be untrue. For example, if the defendant is selling his or her car and untruthfully says that the brakes work fine. If that is untrue, and he or she is aware that the brakes might have problems with them, he or she will have committed this offence.

In *Augunas*[5] the Court of Appeal emphasized that the test is a subjective one:

> What is required is that the accused person knows that the representation is, or might be, misleading. It is not enough that a reasonable person might have known this; what matters is the accused person's actual knowledge. In our judgment, it not good enough for the prosecutor to satisfy the jury that the accused ought to have appreciated that the representation made by him was or might be untrue or misleading, nor is it enough that the circumstances must have given rise to a reasonable suspicion that the representation was, or might be, untrue or misleading. Of course, if an accused person wilfully shuts his eyes to the obvious doubts as to the genuineness of the misrepresentation that he is making, then he knows that it might be untrue or misleading and he would be guilty of the offence.

The statement must be made with the intention to make a gain or a loss

It should be emphasized that it does not need to be shown that the defendant made any kind of gain or indeed that the victim suffers any kind of loss. So a defendant who made a false statement intending to obtain money would be guilty even if having made the statement the

---

[4] (1837) 173 ER 342.   [5] [2013] EWCA Crim 2046.

victim refused to hand over any money and instead called the police. In a way, therefore, fraud has the flavour of an attempted crime in that there is no need to show the victim actually suffered direct harm.

Notice that it must be shown that the defendant intended to make a gain by the representation.[6] Imagine Hugh, sitting on a street corner, untruthfully shouting out 'Please give me money. I have not eaten for seven days.' Hugh may be able to argue that although he hoped to get money, he did not actually think anyone would give him money as a result of the false representation. He thought people would know he was lying, but give him money anyway. If this is accepted that may mean he has a defence to a charge of fraud by false representation. Simon Gardner suggests that this kind of argument might provide a defence to a person in a market making wildly extravagant claims for goods they are selling.[7]

'Gain' or 'loss' must be in property or monetary terms. So using a false representation to injure someone's feelings or harm their reputation would not, on their own, amount to the offence. In *Gilbert*[8] the defendant lied in order to open a bank account. That was not a gain or loss in itself. It was true there were suspicions he would use the account to make gains, but that was too remote a gain for the offence to be made out. It should also be noted that a risk of a loss is sufficient. This would mean that if the defendant uses a false representation to obtain money which he or she hopes to repay to the victim soon, this could fall under this offence. If he or she is aware there is a risk he or she will not be able to pay back the money, he or she has committed the offence.

There must be dishonesty

There is no definition of dishonesty in the Fraud Act 2006. Presumably, therefore, the *Ghosh* test for dishonesty (see Chapter 8, Section 1.5 at p.521) will be used.[9] However, section 2 of the Theft Act 1968 will not apply. So the circumstances set down there for when a defendant will not be dishonest (e.g. where the defendant believes he or she has a legal right to the property) will not apply. Simester, Spencer, Sullivan, and Virgo describe the failure to replicate the section 2 defences as 'regrettable'.[10]

In the following extract, David Ormerod sets out some of the issues raised by fraud by false representation:

D. Ormerod, 'The Fraud Act 2006—Criminalising Lying?' [2007] *Criminal Law Review* 193 at 196–204

Section 2—fraud by false representation

Section 2 of the Act is the broadest form of the fraud offence and hence likely to be the most frequently charged. The *actus reus* requires only that a person made a false representation, and the *mens rea* is satisfied by proof that he knew the representation was or might be false, and that he acted dishonestly, with intent to gain or cause loss. Classic examples of conduct caught will be false representations on mortgage application forms,

---

[6] *R v Gilbert* [2012] EWCA 2392.   [7] S. Gardner (2008).   [8] [2012] EWCA Crim 2392.
[9] The government's explanatory notes concerning the Act say so (HM Government 2006: para. 10).
[10] Simester, Spencer, Sullivan, and Virgo (2013: 609).

life insurance forms, etc. The offence is also designed to criminalise dishonest "phishing" on the internet.

Before scrutinising individual elements, it is worth emphasising how dramatic is the shift from a result-based deception to a conduct-based representation offence. Under the old law D's conduct had to deceive V thereby causing V to do whatever act was appropriate to the charge—transferring property, executing a valuable security, etc. Under s.2, there is no need to prove a result of any kind or that an alleged victim or indeed any person believed any representation or acted on it; or, crucially, that the accused succeeded in making a gain or causing a loss by his representation. The effect is that D may be liable even though V knows that D's statement is false or V would have acted in the same way even if he had known of the falsity. The new offence has no requirement that V's property interests are damaged (temporarily or permanently), nor even that V's property interests are imperilled; it is sufficient that D intends to cause loss or make a gain. It is wider than conspiracy to defraud since a lone actor can be guilty without even prejudicing anyone's economic interests. This wholly inchoate offence appears to criminalise lying.

Should lying be a sufficient basis for criminal liability? What is the wrong which D performs which warrants the criminal sanction? It is not one derived from intentionally harming V's interests directly—there need be no such harm. Similarly, it is not one of potentially damaging V's interests. The wrong seems to be the act of lying or misleading with intent to gain or cause loss; the harm might be construed as one of destabilising society's processes of property and financial transfers. Even if this is sufficient to warrant criminalisation, is it properly called fraud? Classic definitions such as that from Stephen J. include, even at their widest, an element of intent to deceive which is much narrower than an intention to gain.

The absence of any loss direct *or* potential to V's interests may make the evaluation of the degree of blameworthiness and appropriate punishment very difficult. If D has typed an impressive high yield investment prospectus into his computer and emailed it, he seems to have breached s.2. What sentence is appropriate? The representation might have made millions of pounds from gullible investors, *or* been universally treated as irritating spam and deleted.

This shift has other serious practical implications. Obviously, the offence is complete earlier—on the making of the representation. In some instances s.2 might also catch conduct committed later in time—if, after D, a motorist, has with honest mind filled his fuel tank and the entire proprietary interest in the petrol has passed to him, he then falsely represents to V, the cashier, that it will be paid for by D's company, he breaches s.2. Although the "start" date of offending may be more difficult to specify when drafting particulars, this is unlikely to be material in most cases. A further effect is that V, formerly cast in a leading role in proving the causal effect of D's deception now becomes an optional extra. With liability complete on D's representation being made, no specific victim(s) need to be identified. No doubt prosecutors will still commonly prefer to call a victim to testify about the circumstances of the representation, but technically, all that matters is that D acted with the intention to gain *or* cause loss; the potential effect of the false representation need not be proved. As with the deception offences it replaced, there will be overlap with theft in cases in which the false representation enables D to "appropriate" V's property, even if with V's consent, as in *Gomez*. Of course, s.2 goes further by criminalising D who lies with the intent that V lend him property which D intends to return unaltered.

Making a representation. A representation must be "made", expressly *or* impliedly (s.2(4)). Most commonly this will be by words *or* conduct but as enacted, s.2 is not restricted to such behaviour. This prompts the question whether silent inaction will suffice. Section 3 criminalises fraud by failing to disclose, but is limited to circumstances where D is under a "legal duty" to disclose information; a broad reading of s.2 would not be so limited, but such an interpretation might be regarded as an undesirable extension of the criminal law. Four possibilities need considering. First, if D has made a false statement with *mens rea* he is guilty under s.2 irrespective of V's belief. Secondly, if he has not actively misled V, but realises that V is acting under a misconception he may be liable under s.3 if he is under a duty to correct V's error. Thirdly, if having not actively misled V, and not being under a duty to correct V's error, D could be construed as making an implied false representation, he may be liable under s.2. Fourthly, where, to D's knowledge, but not V's, circumstances have changed materially since D made a true representation, by continuing to act without correcting V's understanding D might be said to be "failing to 'undeceive'" by impliedly making a fresh and now false representation. If so he is liable under s.2.

Since s.2 is complete when the false representation is articulated, there may also be problems in identifying how many representations have been made. Are separate counts required for each representation? The broad nature of this element means that the scope for a charge of attempt is severely limited, except perhaps where D, having prepared documents containing false statements, is apprehended before having posted them, or where D unwittingly makes a true representation. With substantive offences this wide, who needs inchoates?

A "false" representation. The requirement that D's representation is false does little to limit the scope of s.2. Section 2(2) (a) provides that a representation is false by being either "untrue", or "misleading", and by subs. (3) "any representation as to fact or law, including a representation as to the state of mind of—(a) the person making the representation, or (b) any other person" will suffice. The Crown must establish that the representation is false or misleading in addition to proving D's knowledge as to its falsity. Falsity usually depends on the meaning intended or understood by the parties, and will usually be a question for the jury, even with documented representations. Exceptionally it may be for the judge to decide, as for example where the issue is as to a document's legal effect.

The concept of falsity is central to s.2, yet remains ill-defined, highlighting a recurring problem with the Act: Parliament was unwilling to define elements of the offences, being happy to acknowledge the (predictably) broad Home Office suggestions and leave matters to be resolved by the courts. This fails to promote certainty in an area where experience teaches us that it is vital. In this instance, the Home Office suggested that the term "misleading" meant "less than wholly true and capable of an interpretation to the detriment of the victim." That opens an astonishingly wide scope of liability. By advancing a very wide definition of "false", to include "misleading", the Home Office eschews the finer moral distinctions between lying (making untrue statements) and misleading (including making true statements which create a false impression). It is unclear whether the full practical implications have been realised.

If less than wholly true statements are caught, have "trade puffs" become criminal? Does s.2 criminalise street traders' repartee? The only defence to making false representations by selling a T-shirt "just like the one Beckham wears" may be a lack of dishonesty. Such arguments may sometimes be difficult to sustain in a courtroom remote in time and atmosphere from the theatre of a street market. If D's representation is untrue, D's claim that it was made for good reason, e.g. to recover property which (D believed) belonged to him, turns on the question of dishonesty. That element of the offence, which is left to shoulder so much of the burden of determining criminality, is also D's only safeguard where the falsity represented relates to a non-material particular. Beware the second-hand car salesman who habitually embellishes a series of honest statements as to the age, mileage, etc. of vehicles with the false and proverbial li(n)e "one careful lady owner." To what extent have we criminalised sharp practice—particularly bearing in mind that there need be no loss, nor imperilling of anyone's economic interests? If everything turns on the jury's perception of honesty, will stereotypically mistrusted trades and professions—estate agents, antique dealers, car salesmen—be exposed to conviction on prejudices?

Unless s.2 can be interpreted cautiously, it will trample on the principle of *caveat emptor*. We ought not to "indict one man for making a fool of another". For these reasons and the difficulties identified below, this commentator cannot give s.2 the "unequivocal welcome" extended by other commentators, nor agree that it will be free of difficulty in application, and certainly cannot subscribe to the view of the Home Office that "the law is not being widened in any significant way."

False representations and machines [Professor Ormerod explains that the new offence covers deception of machines which was a problem under the old law, although it is very widely drafted.]

Dishonesty. Dishonesty is the central *mens rea* for all three forms of fraud. The Law Commission and Home Office intend that the *Ghosh* definition should apply, and the Law Officers confirmed this in Parliament. The powerful criticisms of *Ghosh* need no repetition, but several issues do merit attention. Given the breadth of definition of other key elements of the offences, dishonesty will be the principal determinant of criminal liability. Dishonesty is based solely on *Ghosh*; as with deception there is no equivalent to s.2 of the 1968 Act and therefore, D's claims to be acting under a claim of right are no guarantee of acquittal. It is submitted that this is a fundamental flaw with the section. If D (genuinely believes he) has a claim of right to the property there should be no criminal liability. A fortiori, it seems that D qualifying his false representations with a disclaimer will not automatically lead to acquittal unless the qualification is judged sufficient to remove any degree of falsity. . . .

[Professor Ormerod then notes the objections that have been made concerning the *Ghosh* test for dishonesty.]

Knowing that the representation is or might be false. In addition to being dishonest, whatever that may mean, D must know either: that his representation is untrue or misleading; or that it might be untrue or misleading. Knowledge is a more onerous *mens rea* than "belief' and even "recklessness". Least difficult to establish, will be knowledge of the falsity of representations about existing facts. This will commonly be proved by inference. Greater difficulty lies in prov- ing D knew that present statements about future events *were* untrue or misleading. This prob- lem was anticipated and the alternative *mens rea*—that D knew that the representation *might* be false—seeks to avoid the problem. Proving that D knew that the representation *might* be untrue or misleading is also a more obvious route for the Crown when the allegation involves representations as to states of mind of those other than the accused; although D cannot easily be shown to know the state of another's mind, he may be shown to know what it might be.

Is the section rendered wider than anticipated by this alternative *mens rea?* D tells a cus- tomer that he has a Renoir for sale. D knows that there is a risk, as with all art, that the paint- ing might be a fake. Does D know that the statement *might be* misleading? He will only be guilty if the painting is not in fact a Renoir (he has to make a false statement), and he was dishonest. The element of dishonesty once again serves as the principal determinant of guilt. Interestingly, the Attorney-General had no difficulty with this example in Parliament:

> "If an art dealer said, 'This is a painting by Renoir', knowing that that statement can have a huge impact on the value of the painting—but not knowing whether it is true and thinking that it might be untrue—it would be for a jury to decide whether he was dishonest. If he was dishonest, I see no difficulty in saying that he is guilty of fraud in those circumstances."

Is this an oversimplification? The Attorney-General treats as synonymous *thinking* that a statement might be untrue or misleading and *knowing* that it might be untrue or mislead- ing. Is [the] difference between these degrees of D's cognisance or mental state sufficient to render him blameworthy? In this context it might be a distinction without a difference. It seems inevitable that in practice this *mens rea* element will blur unsatisfactorily into the element of dishonesty. A dealer who, while accepting that nothing can be certain in the art world, believes that his attribution in respect of this painting is true, acts honestly. The dealer who actually thinks it might be untrue, acts dishonestly. The courts need to be alert to guard against reckless representations being treated as sufficient dishonest acts when the section actually requires *both* dishonesty and knowledge. Perhaps the best that can be said is that at least both the *mens rea* requirements remain subjective.

The breadth of this fault element may extend even further if the courts demonstrate their customary willingness to interpret knowledge as including "shutting one's eyes to an obvious means of knowledge" or "deliberately refraining from making inquiries the results of which the person does not care to have." A precise definition of wilful blindness or connivance as it is sometimes known remains elusive, and could extend liability significantly in this context.

With intent to gain or cause loss. At face value, this is again a strict *mens rea* requirement. Intention as to consequences has to be proved. How remote can D's intentions be? Suppose that D makes false representations to induce V, a wealthy banker, to marry him. Is he guilty under s.2 if one intention is to enrich himself?

Intention should bear its ordinary meaning, and as elsewhere in the criminal law include foresight of a virtually certain consequence. In most cases V's loss will be D's gain, but the phrase, "intent to cause loss" is not superfluous as there may be circumstances in which D intends to cause a loss to V without any corresponding gain for himself. Again one might ask whether this is properly described as fraud. No gain or loss need actually occur, indeed, as noted no property of any person need actually be put in jeopardy by D's acts. D who starts a false rumour that his competitor V is going out of business, commits the offence if he does so with intent to lead customers away from V (and or to D) and is regarded as dishonest in doing so.

Although not a result-based offence, there is a causal link that *must* be established: it is "*by the*" false representation that D must intend to make the gain or cause the loss. What of the "sophisticated" fraudster who admits making the false representation but says that his only intent was to gain by subsequent dealings/trade and that the lie was not intended to cause gain/loss?

Section 5 defines "gain" and "loss" for the purposes of ss.2–4, in essentially the same terms as s.34(2)(a) of the Theft Act 1968. Thus, the offences extend only to (temporary or permanent) gain or loss in money or other property; and " 'property' means any property whether real or personal (including things in action and other intangible property)". "Gain" includes a gain by keeping what one has, as well as a gain by getting what one does not have. "Loss" includes a loss by not getting what one might get, as well as a loss by parting with what one has. The Government was keen to ensure that the definitions paralleled those in the Theft Act 1968. Arguably, adopting this definition renders the offence unduly wide by criminalising D who intends V not to get something which V might have gained, even though V was not entitled to it. Taking one of Professor Sullivan's early examples, if V asks D for a loan and D denies it him by saying falsely that he has no money to spare, D has made a false representation with intent to cause V to lose that which he might have obtained. V has at most suffered a loss of a chance. However, there may be a neat way around this: D might avoid liability by arguing that a simple refusal, however malicious or dishonest is not a "representation", and rather, it is the *explanation* for his refusal which is false, and it is not by the explanation "I have no money" that D intended to cause loss. D's additional/alternative saving grace is that he is probably not going to be regarded as dishonest in those circumstances. But, it is not an automatic defence that D believes he has a right to the gain he seeks/the loss he intends to cause. If he has such a belief, then he might not be dishonest under *Ghosh*. It could be argued that there is in fact no gain or loss where a person merely secures the repayment *of* that which he is owed. But the courts have held that if "gain in money or other property" means simply "acquisition", . . . D must still be caught.

1.2 FRAUD BY FAILING TO DISCLOSE INFORMATION

Section 3 of the Fraud Act 2006 states:

> A person is in breach of this section if he—
>
> (a) dishonestly fails to disclose to another person information which he is under a legal duty to disclose, and
>
> (b) intends, by failing to disclose the information—
>
> (i) to make a gain for himself or another, or
>
> (ii) to cause loss to another or to expose another to a risk of loss.

This offence has many of the elements we have already discussed. This offence deals with 'deception by silence'. However, the offence is only committed when the defendant is under a legal duty to disclose the information. The key issue will be when a person is under a legal duty to disclose information. The Act offers no guidance and so the issue must be one of general law. It will be a legal question and therefore one for the judge, rather than the jury. This might require a criminal trial to delve into some complex issues of civil law. However, the alternative of having one set of rules for disclosure at civil law and another at common law seems an even less attractive option. The government's explanatory notes[11] to the Act state that the following passage from the Law Commission Report explains how the legal duty should be understood:

Law Commission Report No. 276, *Fraud* (London: TSO, 2002), paras 7.28–7.29

> 7.28 . . . Such a duty may derive from statute (such as the provisions governing company prospectuses), from the fact that the transaction in question is one of the utmost good faith (such as a contract of insurance), from the express or implied terms of a contract, from the custom of a particular trade or market, or from the existence of a fiduciary relationship between the parties (such as that of agent and principal).
>
> 7.29 For this purpose there is a legal duty to disclose information not only if the defendant's failure to disclose it gives the victim a cause of action for damages, but also if the law gives the victim a right to set aside any change in his or her legal position to which he or she may consent as a result of the non-disclosure. For example, a person in a fiduciary position has a duty to disclose material information when entering into a contract with his or her beneficiary, in the sense that a failure to make such disclosure will entitle the beneficiary to rescind the contract and to reclaim any property transferred under it.

It remains to be seen how a court will deal with a case where there is clear dishonesty in failing to disclose, but technically under the civil law disclosure was not required. Remember in *Hinks*[12] in relation to theft the House of Lords were willing to find a criminal offence even where there was no civil wrong.

There appears to be considerable overlap between sections 2 and 3. Very often when D fails to disclose when he or she is legally required to disclose this could be an implied deception

---

[11] HM Government (2006: para. 18).   [12] [2001] 2 AC 241.

under section 2 or a failure to disclose under section 3. Where it is a clear failure to disclose, section 3 may be preferred as it will be clear to the jury what the prosecution's case is.

1.3 FRAUD BY ABUSE OF POSITION

Section 4(1) states:

A person is in breach of this section if he—

(a) occupies a position in which he is expected to safeguard, or not act against, the financial interests of another person,

(b) dishonestly abuses that position, and

(c) intends, by means of the abuse of that position—

(i) to make a gain for himself or another, or

(ii) to cause loss to another or to expose another to a risk of loss.

This is a rather broadly drafted offence. It will apply to trustees and those who owe a fiduciary relation to others. However, it is unclear whether it will apply more widely than this. Remarkably the Act fails to define 'a position in which he is expected to safeguard, or not act against, the financial interests of another person'. Jennifer Collins[13] notes the uncertainty over whose expectations are relevant in the definition: the expectation of the defendant, the victim, or the reasonable person? The government's explanatory notes to the Act refer to the following passage of a Law Commission Report as assisting in deciding whether or not there is the necessary position:

7.38 The necessary relationship will be present between trustee and beneficiary, director and company, professional person and client, agent and principal, employee and employer, or between partners. It may arise otherwise, for example within a family, or in the context of voluntary work, or in any context where the parties are not at arm's length. In nearly all cases where it arises, it will be recognised by the civil law as importing fiduciary duties, and any relationship that is so recognised will suffice. We see no reason, however, why the existence of such duties should be essential. This does not of course mean that it would be entirely a matter for the fact-finders whether the necessary relationship exists. The question whether the particular facts alleged can properly be described as giving rise to that relationship will be an issue capable of being ruled upon by the judge and, if the case goes to the jury, of being the subject of directions.

We do now have some guidance on what kind of relationships will be covered by section 4:

R v Valujevs
[2014] EWCA Crim 2888

Juris Valujevs and Ivars Mezals were charged with fraud by abuse of position contrary to section 4 of the Fraud Act 2006. It was claimed that they acted as unlicensed gangmasters

---

[13] Collins (2011).

who took illegitimate deductions from workers' earnings, charged excessive rental payments, and imposed unwarranted fines. The key issue at trial and on appeal was whether the gangmasters could be said to occupy 'a position in which he is expected to safeguard, or not act against, the financial interests of another person'.

Fulford LJ

34. The 2006 Act provides no definition of the person who "occupies a position in which he is expected to safeguard, or not to act against, the financial interests of another person". It is clear from the wording that Parliament did not intend to restrict the operation of the section to those situations in which the defendant owes a fiduciary duty to the alleged victim, not least because this result could readily have been secured by appropriate drafting.

. . .

37. In this case, the relevant acts of the gangmasters that are relied on by the prosecution have been set out in the draft amended count, namely that the defendants allegedly "withheld earnings, charged inflated rental payments and imposed unwarranted financial penalties". As described above, it is prohibited in the licensing standards to withhold or to threaten to withhold the whole or part of any payment due to a worker for any work they have done on account of "any matter within the control of the licence holder". In our view, at the very least, it is open to the jury on the evidence to decide that these defendants had gone beyond merely supplying workers and instead they had assumed control of and/or responsibility for collecting the wages of the workers or they controlled the amounts that the workers would be allowed to retain at the moment the wages were handed over. On either basis, the prosecution are able to contend that the defendants had taken on the obligation of paying the wages of the workers, and it is inherent in that commitment that the wages received by the workers will not be reduced by unwarranted financial penalties or deductions, unlawful demands for the repayment of suggested fines, or artificially inflated rental payments. (The prosecution does not rely on any other statutory/regulatory provision or any contractual term to establish an obligation by these defendants to pay the workers' wages without reductions.)

38. The duty not to withhold payment due to a worker has been imposed as part of an enforceable scheme to regulate the activities of gangmasters who provide labour, and in our judgment the prosecution is entitled to suggest that on this basis the relevant defendant "occupies a position in which he is expected to safeguard, or not to act against, the financial interests of another person" for the purposes of section 4. Put otherwise, having assumed responsibility for collecting the wages for a worker, or by exercising control over the wages that would be received by a worker at the point they are received, there is a clear expectation that the worker will receive them without a reduction in the form of (i) unwarranted financial penalties or deductions, (ii) unlawful demands for the repayment of suggested fines, or (iii) artificially inflated rental payments.

. . .

41. Although the statute does not provide any assistance on the issue, in our view the "expectation" in section 4 of the 2006 Act is an objective one. It is for the judge to assess whether the position held by the individual is capable of being one "in which he is expected to safeguard, or not to act against, the financial interests of another person". If it is so capable, it will be for the jury thereafter to determine whether or not they are sure that was the case. It would be untenable to suggest that the expectation should be that of either the potential victim (the test would, in all likelihood, be too low) or the defendant (the test

is likely to be set too high). Therefore, this is an objective test based on the position of the reasonable person.

42. We are unpersuaded by the defendants' contentions that unlicensed gangmasters are not caught by this "expectation". . . .

43. The prosecution has relied on other forms of questionable financial behaviour on the part of the defendants as part of its reliance on section 4 of the 2006 Act, such as the general device of charging excessive sums for rent, withholding work in order to ensure that the worker in question was indebted to the gangmaster, or lending money to workers for which claims are later made for repayment (as opposed to deducting sums from wages). In our judgment, potentially reprehensible behaviour of this kind falls outside the financial interests of a person the gangmaster could properly be expected to safeguard or not to act against. Individuals do not commit a criminal offence under section 4 of the 2006 Act if they seek rental payments in excess of the market rate and gangmasters are not under an obligation to provide employment for those seeking work. Gangmasters are entitled to ask for repayment of moneys that they have lent to workers. Although we recognise that these can be difficult situations, the individual is able to look for accommodation or employment elsewhere and we are unpersuaded that this suggested behaviour on the part of the defendants arguably provides the basis for inclusion as particulars of a section 4 2006 Act offence. In this critical sense we agree with the judge in the court below that to establish an abuse of position for the purposes of section 4 of the 2006 Act it is necessary for the prosecution to demonstrate a breach of a fiduciary duty, or a breach of an obligation that is akin to a fiduciary duty. This can conveniently be described, for instance, as a breach of trust or a breach of a privileged position in relation to the financial interests of another person. Section 4 does not apply to those who simply supply accommodation, goods, services or labour, whether on favourable or unfavourable terms and whether or not they have a stronger bargaining position. Therefore, the fact that an individual is a gangmaster who offers work or accommodation on particular terms, or lawfully requests the repayments of debts incurred by workers, does not ipso facto involve the abuse of a relevant position as regards the financial interests of another person.

44. We therefore concur with the conclusion of the judge that section 4 should not apply in "the general commercial area where individuals and businesses compete in markets of one kind or another, including labour markets, and are entitled to and expected to look after their own interests". We repeat, the critical factor in this case is that there is evidence that the defendants arguably assumed control of, and responsibility for, collecting the wages of the workers, or they controlled the wages at the moment that they were paid over, and the fact that they were acting as gangmasters merely provided the vital context relied on by the prosecution in which that role was assumed.

The Court of Appeal helpfully make it clear that when the jury are considering whether the defendant 'is expected to safeguard, or not act against, the financial interests of another person' the expectations in question are not those of the defendant, nor indeed the victim, but of the reasonable person. This approach was also adopted in *Pennock*,[14] which referred to the expectations of 'the reasonable member of the public as personified by the jury'. There may be concerns that this might disadvantage a defendant who unknowingly put themselves in a position where reasonable people would expect them to safeguard the financial interests of another. However, this concern need not be troubling because a defendant will only be liable if they are dishonest.

---

[14] [2014] EWCA Crim 958.

A surprising aspect of *Valujevs*[15] is Fulford LJ's suggestion that section 4 did not apply in 'the general commercial area where individuals and businesses compete in markets of one kind or another, including labour markets, and are entitled to and expected to look after their own interests'. What this approach overlooks is that some people are not able to look after their own interests. Is it appropriate that an employer or landlord who exploits a vulnerable worker or tenant can escape liability under the legislation? It should be recalled the offence only applies to dishonest defendants and so there should be no concerns that an employer or landlord who is using normal business practices will be convicted. It is suggested that Fulford LJ's *dicta* is misconceived and that an employer or landlord can be expected to not act against the financial interests of a tenant or employee, although it will be rare for the offence to apply. In both *Ousey*[16] and *Choi*[17] defendants were convicted of the section 4 offence on the basis of them being employees or ex-employees of the victim.

The notion of abuse is also rather unclear. In particular whether it is intended to apply just to cases where under civil law there is a breach of trust or fiduciary duty or whether or not it is intended to be wider than this. The concept of abuse may be particularly problematic where D's position is not technically a fiduciary one and so the exact standards of behaviour expected by the law are uncertain. This may be especially problematic where a person whose position of trust is informal (e.g. someone agrees to buy sandwiches for work colleagues and takes money from them).

The only real guidance we have on what it means to abuse a position is *Pennock*,[18] where it was said that abuse of position means ' "uses incorrectly" or "puts to improper use" the position held in a manner that is contrary to the expectation that arises because of that position.'

This offence is potentially very wide. Its coverage could include employees making an unlawful profit from their position, executors of wills improperly dealing with a deceased's assets, to directors of companies misbehaving. Its precise width is uncertain. Jennifer Collins, however, argues that it is not necessarily a bad thing because the moral basis of the offence is disloyalty:

J. Collins, 'Fraud by Abuse of Position: Theorising Section 4 of the Fraud Act 2006' [2011] *Criminal Law Review* 513 at 522

I argue that both the s.4 offence and the bribery offences exist to reaffirm the importance of loyalty of members to another or to a cause, in order to exist as a viable unit. Disloyalty, on this account, is criminalised because it has a corrosive effect on an important basic value held by society: the importance of trust relationships where an individual is entrusted with the oversight of financial affairs of another. The risk of harm to these trust relationships (in themselves a public good) passes the threshold for criminalisation. It is desirable that as citizens we can trust those who are entrusted with our financial affairs if the relevant expectation has arisen.

This, then, is the distinctive and much neglected advantage of the breadth of s.4. It is not necessarily a weakness that the offence includes the avaricious and predatory fiduciary alongside the recalcitrant employee. In fact, if the offence were not drafted in such broad terms it would not be able to uphold effectively the basic public good of protecting trust relationships in dealing with another's financial interests. We saw this to be true when we

---

[15] [2014] EWCA Crim 2888.   [16] [2015] EWCA Crim 984.
[17] [2015] EWCA Crim 1089.   [18] [2014] EWCA Crim 958.

examined the reasons for rejecting fiduciary duties as the theoretical rationale for s.4. We might want the offence to recognise the need for loyalty outside of the fiduciary paradigm. The parameters of the offence can then be narrowed down through prosecutorial policy which should aim to prevent "the criminal law being used as a debt collection agency or to protect the commercial interests of companies and organizations."

2 SECTION 6: FRAUD AND POSSESSION OFFENCES

Section 6(1) states:

A person is guilty of an offence if he has in his possession or under his control any article for use in the course of or in connection with any fraud.

David Ormerod says it is 'lamentable'[19] that no *mens rea* is required for this offence. As he points out, on its face, being in possession of a pen would fall under this section. Surely it must be shown that D intends the article to be used in fraud. This was the government's intention as it has said: 'The intention is to attract the case law on section 25 [Theft Act 1968], which has established that proof is required that the defendant had the article for the purpose or with the intention that it be used in the course of or in connection with the offence, and that a general intention to commit fraud will suffice.'[20]

Section 7 creates an offence of creating, adapting, supplying, or offering for supply any article knowing or intending it to be used in connection with fraud.

3 OBTAINING SERVICES DISHONESTLY

Section 11 creates an offence of obtaining services dishonestly. It states

(1) A person is guilty of an offence under this section if he obtains services for himself or another—

    (a) by a dishonest act, and

    (b) in breach of subsection (2).

(2) A person obtains services in breach of this subsection if—

    (a) they are made available on the basis that payment has been, is being or will be made for or in respect of them,

    (b) he obtains them without any payment having been made for or in respect of them or without payment having been made in full, and

    (c) when he obtains them, he knows—

        (i) that they are being made available on the basis described in paragraph (a), or

        (ii) that they may be,

   but intends that payment will not be made, or will not be made in full.

---

[19] Ormerod (2007a: 211).   [20] HM Government (2006: para. 25).

This offence will replace the offence in section 1 of the Theft Act 1978. It is specifically drafted to include obtaining services through dishonest electronic means. It is restricted to services which were provided on the basis that they would be paid for. It does not cover cases where by a deception D persuades V to provide gratuitous services. So if D were to persuade V to mow his lawn because D was suffering back pain, whereas in fact D was fine, just lazy, the offence would not be committed. The offence would also seem to cover illegally downloading music.[21]

Notice that unlike fraud, the offence requires the defendant to have actually obtained a service as a result of the dishonest act. It should be noted that the offence is only committed where it is the deception which has caused the obtaining. So if V would have provided the service even if D had told the truth then no offence would be committed. Also if D has paid for the service in full no offence is committed. So if D, aged 15, lies about his age and is able to buy a ticket to see an 18 rated film he will not commit the section 11 offence.

In the following extract, Carol Withey makes some observations on the section 11 offence:

C. Withey, 'The Fraud Act 2006—Some Early Observations and Comparisons with the Former Law' (2007) 30 *Journal of Criminal Law* 220 at 233–6

Under s. 11 of FA [Fraud Act] 2006, D commits the offence where he obtains services for himself or another by any dishonest act. This replaces the offence under s. 1 of the Theft Act 1978 of dishonestly obtaining services by deception.

A deception is no longer required and neither is a false representation. This means that D will be guilty where he dishonestly uses a foreign coin in a machine to obtain services. The fact that a machine can not be deceived is now irrelevant. All that is required is a dishonest act—for example, the conduct of inserting the coin into the machine. This will also allow conviction where services are gained through the provision of credit or debit card details, particularly on the internet. There appears to be overlap here with s. 2(1). By using the foreign coin D is guilty of s. 11, but it would seem that he also makes a representation, by his conduct of inserting the coin, that it is valid payment. By this representation he intends to gain, if gain includes keeping one's own money, and he intends to cause loss.

As was the case previously, an omission does not suffice, but what is the nature of an act? In *R v Rai* D applied to the council for a grant to renovate his disabled mother's bathroom. D's mother died, but he failed to tell the council of his changed circumstances. Under the Theft Act 1978, a false representation would be required. In *Rai*, D's true representation later became false. However, under s. 11 of FA 2006 a dishonest act is required. Does this include a false representation? If yes, then the previous law regarding continuing representation will apply, and D would be found guilty under s. 11. If representations are excluded, then the act will be the act of filling out the application form. However, the act must be dishonest and this will not be established unless it is the case that the original act continues to the point of dishonesty, just as it is the case that a true representation will become dishonest at the point that it later becomes false.

The meaning of 'service' is very similar to the old definition under s. 1 of the Theft Act 1978. Under s. 11(2) a person obtains a service where the service is made available on the basis that payment had been, is being, or will be made for or in respect of it. In addition,

---

[21] Ormerod (2007a: 214).

D obtains the service without having paid or paid in full, and where he knows that it is being made on the basis that it will be paid for, or might be, but intends that payment will not be made or made in full. A benefit provided gratuitously does not amount to a service.

Examples of acts amounting to services are: the provision of board and lodgings; the provision of entertainment (D attaches a decoder to his TV to enable him to access satellite TV where he has no intention of paying); the provision of social and sporting amenities (D climbs over a wall without paying to watch a football match); repairing and decorating; the provision of goods on hire; and the provision of transport.

The provision of a credit card, bank or building society account qualifies as a service. When the account is opened D is provided with a service. So a person who uses a false name to obtain such services would commit the offence. In *R* v *Nabina* D dishonestly lied about his personal details in order to obtain credit cards. This would now be a s. 11 offence.

In addition, the continued use of the card or account is a provision of a service as it represents the benefit of participating in the banking system, which is a service. *R* v *Sofroniou* held that although banks and credit card companies commonly make charges and charge interest, this can be avoided, thus charges cannot be incurred just by opening the account. However, in that case, there appeared to be an understanding that interest would be charged on overdrawn accounts. Whenever the card is used to obtain services, for example from the internet, this is also an offence.

. . .

D must obtain the service for himself or another, for example where D books a holiday for his mother with a card he obtained when using a false name. Under the previous law, it sufficed that P did not confer the benefit upon D himself but that he caused or permitted another to do so. This would include circumstances where the owner of a wedding car hire company allows his driver to take D to his wedding. The wording of s. 11 allows for such scenarios.

In contrast to s. 2 of FA 2006, under s. 11 there must be an obtaining (of services). Although there is no longer a requirement to show that a deception leads to the obtaining of the service, a causal link must still be established between the act and the obtaining of the service. This is because the statutory wording requires that the defendant *by* his dishonest act obtains the service. D will not be guilty of the offence where he obtains a service and *then* decides to decamp without paying: there is no dishonest act which brings about the obtaining. The dishonest act is the running off without paying, and even if 'act' includes false representations, this is subsequent to the obtaining. This dishonesty will have to be charged as making off without payment and is one reason why the offence is retained. The only time where D can be found guilty of obtaining the service dishonestly is where there is evidence that he was never going to pay, for example CCTV footage shows him bragging that he does not intend to pay before he enjoys the service. In *DPP* v *Ray* the services of a waiter in a restaurant were obtained before the deception was made. Under FA 2006 this cannot be a s. 11 offence as D's dishonest act precedes the obtaining. D, who registers as a guest at a hotel but who does not intend to pay, by his dishonest act of registering obtains the service. The problem is with proving the dishonesty at this stage. D may argue that he decided not to pay until *after* completing his stay. This therefore can only be the offence of making off without payment. Where D hails a taxi intending not to pay, he obtains a service by this dishonest conduct. Again the problem is proving the dishonest intent at the outset and D will have to be charged with making off without payment.

However, the new s. 11 offence can accommodate previous difficult examples of dishonest behaviour, such as where D uses his credit card or cheque book when he knows that he is overdrawn, and subsequently obtains a service, this service will be obtained by his dishonest act of proffering the card.

The *mens rea* of the offence is that D's act must be dishonest and D knows that the service is being made on the basis that it will be paid for, or might be, but intends that payment will not be made or made in full. This part of the *mens rea* is considered as part of the *actus reus*. In relation to dishonesty, *R* v *Ghosh* applies. The dishonesty must exist at the time of the act. As seen above, in *R* v *Rai* D was initially honest, but became dishonest at the point that the information on the application form became false.

4 CONSPIRACY TO DEFRAUD

There was much debate during the drafting of the Fraud Act 2006 over whether or not the offence of conspiracy to defraud should be abolished. The final decision was that it should not be. The main concern was that if it was abolished some forms of dishonest behaviour might end up not amounting to any offence. The offence of conspiracy to defraud is discussed in Chapter 14.

QUESTIONS

1. Bob is selling radios for £3 at a street market. He shouts out: 'These are the best radios in the world!' Cynthia, who is a touch naïve, hears this and believes him, and buys one. Has Bob committed fraud?

For guidance on answering this question, please visit the Online Resource Centre that accompanies this book: www.oxfordtextbooks.co.uk/orc/herringcriminal7e/.

2. Abby wants to sell her worn-out sofa on eBay. She takes a digital photograph of it, which she touches up to make the sofa look better than it is. On the website she says that it is a 'priceless sofa' and that she will not accept any offers less than £1,000. In fact the sofa is worth less than £80. Carlos, who is impressed by the photograph and the price tag assumes the sofa must be of very high quality and, as he likes the colour, bids £1,000. Abby accepts, but has she committed fraud?

For guidance on answering this question, please visit the Online Resource Centre that accompanies this book: www.oxfordtextbooks.co.uk/orc/herringcriminal7e/.

5 MAKING OFF WITHOUT PAYMENT: SECTION 3 OF THE THEFT ACT 1978

Section 3 of the 1978 Act states

(1) Subject to subsection (3) below, a person who, knowing that payment on the spot for any goods supplied or service done is required or expected from him, dishonestly makes off without having paid as required or expected and with intent to avoid payment of the amount due shall be guilty of an offence.

(2) For purposes of this section 'payment on the spot' includes payment at the time of collecting goods on which work has been done or in respect of which service has been provided.

(3) Subsection (1) above shall not apply where the supply of the goods or the doing of the service is contrary to law, or where the service done is such that payment is not legally enforceable.

(4) Any person may arrest without warrant anyone who is, or whom he, with reasonable cause, suspects to be, committing or attempting to commit an offence under this section.

DEFINITION

The key elements of the section 3 offence are:

(1) making off;

(2) dishonestly;

(3) without having paid as required or expected;

(4) knowledge that payment on the spot is required for goods or services;

(5) intent to avoid payment.

The *actus reus* is the making off without having paid as required or expected.

The *mens rea* is dishonesty: knowledge that payment on the spot is required for goods and services, and an intent to avoid payment.

NB: There is no need to prove a deception.

This offence carries a maximum sentence (on indictment) of two years' imprisonment. The offence is designed to deal with people who, for example, having eaten a meal at a restaurant run out without paying, or having taken a taxi ride disappear without paying the fare. Notably the Court of Appeal has stated that 'section 3(1) is indeed intended to create a simple and straightforward offence'.[22] The court indicated that it would not be sympathetic to interpretations of section 3 which would introduce unnecessary complexity.

The key elements of the offence are:

5.1 MAKING OFF FROM THE PLACE WHERE PAYMENT WAS EXPECTED

The term 'making off' simply means leaving. In *Brooks and Brooks*[23] the Court of Appeal rejected an argument that the term making off indicated that the defendant surreptitiously left. Boldly walking out of the front door of the restaurant is as much making off as leaving through a toilet window at the back. The defendant must make off from the place where payment was expected. This includes the door of a restaurant or even the side of an ice-cream van. In *McDavitt*[24] the defendant was apprehended while walking towards the door of a restaurant. Although it looked as if he was not going to pay it was held that the spot where he was expected to pay was the restaurant door, and so it was not until he walked out of the restaurant that he committed the offence, although he could be guilty of an attempted offence.[25] There does seem to be a gap in the section, in that if the defendant gives a taxi

---

[22] *Vincent* [2001] 1 WLR 1172, para. 11.   [23] (1982) 76 Cr App R 66.

[24] [1981] Crim LR 843.

[25] In *Moberley v Allen* The Times, 13 December 1991 it was stated that if there were two places where the defendant could pay then the offence was committed only when the defendant had passed them both.

driver some fake money and the taxi driver leaves then arguably the defendant has not made off; it is the victim who has left.[26]

There is some doubt whether a defendant can be said to be making off if the victim has given permission to the defendant to leave. *Hammond*,[27] a first instance decision, appears to suggest that if the owner has consented to the defendant's departure there is no making off. However, it is unclear whether this is so if the victim's consent was obtained by the defendant's deception. If, after a meal at a restaurant, the defendant (falsely) tells the owner that he has no money with him and gives the owner his name and address, saying he will pay later, and the owner therefore lets the defendant leave, can it be said he makes off?

John Spencer[28] argues that it is necessary to distinguish between two cases: where the defendant has left without it being possible to locate him in the future and where the defendant has left when it is possible to discover his whereabouts in the future (e.g. because the defendant has left a piece of paper with his name and address on it). He argues that in the latter case there is no making off as the situation is not the kind which the Act was meant to deal with, but the former is. However, as Sir John Smith argues, this may be to read too much into the phrase making off.[29]

5.2 GOODS SUPPLIED OR SERVICES DONE

The offence requires evidence that goods have been supplied[30] or services[31] done for the defendant. These terms are broadly interpreted to include a wide range of things people pay for, from petrol to parking spaces. However, the wording may provide some defendants with a loophole: if a defendant plays golf but runs away without paying, it may be argued that he has not been provided with services.[32] More significantly, however, there is also some dispute about where a defendant took goods from a self-service supermarket or restaurant: are such goods supplied? Griew argues not,[33] but Smith suggests that the goods are supplied, in that they are 'made available for sale'.[34] As theft is available in such cases it is perhaps not surprising that the courts have not been asked to resolve the dispute. In reality, in either case it would be unlikely that a court would take a restrictive interpretation of the offence.

Section 3(3) makes it clear that services or goods must be part of a legally enforceable contract. To make off from a brothel or run away from a café selling illegal drugs without paying for their illegal services would not involve the offence.

5.3 WITHOUT HAVING PAID AS REQUIRED OR EXPECTED

It must be shown that the defendant failed to pay as required or expected. This means that if the 'victim' has broken the contract with the defendant in such a way that the defendant is not obliged to pay for the service or goods the defendant commits no offence if he or she leaves without paying.[35] For example, if a restaurant serves inedible food and the customer

---

[26] Bennion (1983a).   [27] [1982] Crim LR 611.

[28] Spencer (1983). Contrast Bennion (1983a) and Bennion (1983b).   [29] J.C. Smith (2002: 5.78).

[30] Goods are defined in s. 34(2)(b) of the Theft Act 1968 as '"goods" except in so far as the context otherwise requires, includes money and every other description of property except land and includes things severed from the land by stealing.' This definition applies to the Theft Act 1978 (s. 5(2)).

[31] Services are defined in s. 1(2) of the Theft Act 1978.   [32] Griew (1995: 213).

[33] *Ibid*, 214.   [34] J.C. Smith (1997: para. 5.03).

[35] *Troughton v Metropolitan Police* [1987] Crim LR 138 (DC).

storms out without paying he or she may not be guilty of a section 3 offence on the basis that he or she was not required to pay for the food.[36]

There is much debate over the case where the defendant gives as payment a cheque which is subsequently dishonoured.[37] Is that payment as required or expected? In favour of finding the defendant not guilty in such a case is the argument that such conduct would be covered by section 2 of the Fraud Act 2006. Even if that argument fails, it could be suggested that the defendant, by paying with an ineffective cheque,[38] has not paid as 'expected or required'.

5.4 DISHONESTY

Dishonesty here has the same meaning as in the *Ghosh* case, discussed at The common law test for dishonesty, p.521. It must be shown that there was dishonesty at the time of the making off.

5.5 KNOWING THAT PAYMENT ON THE SPOT IS REQUIRED OR EXPECTED OF HIM

This requirement will be most relevant where the defendant is able to persuade the jury that he or she thought the goods and services were provided on the basis that he or she would pay at some point in the future or that another person would pay for the items. Imagine that Bill and Ben are dining at a restaurant, when Bill disappears. Ben is stopped as he walks out of the restaurant. He will have a defence to a charge under section 3 if he can prove that he believed Bill was going to pay for the meal. He did not know that payment was expected *of him*.[39] Ben will also have a defence to a section 3 charge if he lied to the manager and told him that he intended to pay the bill next week and that was why the owner of the restaurant let him leave.[40] This is because Ben was not being required or expected to pay as he made off. It might be different if Ben were allowed to leave the restaurant after saying that he needed to get his wallet from the car because in such a case he was still expected to pay on the spot.[41] His offence, if any, will be under section 2 of the Fraud Act 2006.

The fact that payment on the spot is required means that the defendant is expected to pay at that time and at that particular place. In *Aziz*[42] the defendant took a taxi ride, but refused to pay at the destination. The taxi driver decided to take the defendant back to the start of the journey. On the way back the defendant ran off. The defendant tried to argue that payment was expected at the destination, not when he ran off. However, the Court of Appeal rejected this argument: he had left the place where payment was expected (i.e. the taxi) at a time when he was liable to pay the full fare.

5.6 INTENT TO AVOID PAYMENT

Although the section does not specifically state that it must be shown that the defendant intended to avoid payment, this was established in *R v Allen*.[43]

---

[36] Such a person may also claim not to be dishonest (*Aziz* [1993] Crim LR 708 (CA)).
[37] Syrota (1980).
[38] If the cheque is backed up with a cheque guarantee card it may be an effective payment.
[39] *Brooks and Brooks* (1982) 76 Cr App R 66.   [40] *Vincent* [2001] 1 WLR 1172.
[41] *Ibid*, para. 11.   [42] [1993] Crim LR 708.   [43] [1985] 1 AC 1029.

PART II: THE THEORY OF FRAUD

6 THE EXTENT OF FRAUD

There were 230,630 reported cases of fraud in England and Wales in 2014/15.[44] However, the actual number is much higher. Victims often feel embarrassed and feel they are partly to blame for being duped. The National Fraud Authority estimates that £73 billion is lost as a result of fraud.[45]

7 THE NATURE OF FRAUD

In the following extract, Stuart Green suggests there is a need to distinguish between lying and other forms of deception: ←2 (p.558)

S.P. Green, 'Lying, Misleading, and Falsely Denying: How Moral Concepts Inform the Law of Perjury, Fraud, and False Statements' (2001) 53 *Hastings Law Journal* 157

I. Lying, Misleading, and Falsely Denying

Like many distinctions we make in our everyday moral thinking and discourse, the distinctions we make among the concepts of lying, misleading, and falsely denying are far from sharp. Nevertheless, these concepts are widely used, easily recognized, and generally understood. There are good reasons for thinking that the distinctions among them are based on genuine moral differences.

A. Conceptual Differences Between Lying and Other Forms of Deception

For purposes of this article, I shall use the term 'deception' to refer generally to the communication of a message with which the communicator, in communicating, intends to mislead—that is, the communication of a message that is intended to cause a person to believe something that is untrue. A few points about this definition are worth making.

The first is that there is no deception unless the communicator intends to deceive. Untrue statements made by mistake are not deceptive, although they might cause a listener to be misled. . . . Second, there is no requirement that the message itself be untrue, since 'literally true' statements (a concept that is discussed below) can obviously be deceptive. For example, if Bill is asked where he was on the night of February 3 and says he was 'either in Chappaqua or in the City,' while knowing for certain that he was in the City, he has deceived his questioner into believing that he is unsure about his whereabouts on that night, even though his statement is in fact true. Third, deception can come in a variety of different forms. One can deceive by making a statement, asking a question, issuing a command, stating an opinion, displaying a picture, making a facial expression or gesture, or engaging in various other forms of verbal and non-verbal behavior. Kant gives a famous example: A deceives B

---

44 Office for National Statistics (2015a).   45 National Fraud Authority (2012).

into believing that he is headed on a journey by conspicuously packing a suitcase, and hoping that B will draw the intended conclusion.

Lying constitutes a subset of deception, involving a much narrower range of behavior. As generally used, the term lying refers to (intentional) deception that (1) comes in the form of a verifiable assertion, and (2) is 'literally false.' By verifiable assertion, I refer to a statement that has a determinable truth value (i.e., is either true or false, although its truth value may not be known at the time the assertion is made). Because they have no truth value, questions, commands, statements of opinion, greetings, apologies, christenings, and so forth are not capable of being lies, although they can certainly be misleading. . . .

What does it mean for a statement to be 'literally false'? 'Assuming that a sentence is not ambiguous, [its] literal meaning is derived, roughly speaking, by determining the meaning of the individual words . . . and applying the grammatical rules of the language to those words.' The 'literal meaning' of the sentence is to be distinguished from what the speaker intends by the sentence when she utters it. A statement that is literally false is thus one that is false on its face, without reference to the speaker's meaning. . . .

The difference between lying and non-lying verbal deception (which I shall henceforth refer to simply as 'misleading') is, therefore, essentially the difference between (1) asserting what one believes is literally false, and (2) leading the listener to believe something false by saying something that is either true or has no truth value. . . .

B. Caveat Auditor: The Moral Distinction Between Lying and Merely Misleading

Assuming a formal distinction between lying and merely misleading, we need next to ask whether there exists any moral difference between the two concepts. Imagine that Bill, who was in Chappaqua from February 1–5, is asked about his whereabouts on February 3. Is there really any moral difference between his responding, 'no, I was not in Chappaqua on February 3' (a lie), and the statement, 'well, I was in Chappaqua on February 4' (a literally true statement that nevertheless creates the misleading impression that he was not in Chappaqua on February 3)? The fact is, people sometimes go to great lengths to avoid not only telling the truth, but also to avoid lying. If lying and merely misleading were morally equivalent, such behavior would be irrational. How can it be explained?

My claim is that, other things being equal, merely misleading is less wrongful than lying because what I call the principle of caveat auditor, or 'listener beware,' applies to merely misleading but does not apply to lying. Like the principle of caveat emptor, which says that a buyer is responsible for assessing the quality of a purchase before buying, the principle of caveat auditor says that, in certain circumstances, a listener is responsible for ascertaining that a statement is true before believing it.

Lying involves the creation, and simultaneous breach, of a relationship of trust between a speaker and listener. As Charles Fried has put it:

> 'Lying is wrong because when I lie I set up a relation which is essentially exploitative . . . . Lying violates respect and is wrong, as is any breach of trust. Every lie is a broken promise [which] is made and broken at the same moment. Every lie necessarily implies—as does every assertion—an assurance, a warranty of its truth.'

By making an assertion to B, A tells B that she herself believes what she is saying. As a result, B is justified in putting her faith in A; B need not be on her guard or question A's veracity. If A is mistaken about her assertion, then she is wholly responsible for B's false belief. And if A's untrue statement has been intentional, it is A who is wholly to blame.

Merely misleading involves a very different dynamic. When A merely misleads B without making an assertion, she has not told B that she believes what she is saying is true (since what she is saying is neither true nor false). There is thus no warranty of truth that B could rely on. Again, Kant's bag packer provides a good example. If the bag packer lies and asserts that he is going on vacation, then he will be wholly responsible for the spectator's false belief. But if the bag packer merely acts as if he is going on vacation, and his spectator draws the wrong conclusion from those actions, then the spectator will be partly responsible for his mistaken belief. . . .

Lying and merely misleading can also be distinguished on the grounds that each tends to elicit a different set of reactive emotions, and cause a different set of harms, in its victims. A victim who is deceived by a non-lie feels foolish and embarrassed, presumably because he believes he has contributed to his own harm by drawing unwarranted inferences from misleading premises. By contrast, a victim of lies is much more likely to feel 'brutalized' (in Adler's word) by some external force. . . .

In arguing that lying is distinguishable from other forms of deception, I do not of course mean to suggest either that lying is always wrong or that lying is always worse than other forms of deception. A lie told to avoid some greater harm is not likely to be viewed as wrongful. And non-lying deception about a matter of real importance will be viewed as more wrongful than an outright lie about some trivial concern. Moreover, in some unusual cases, a 'bald-faced' lie may actually seem less objectionable than other forms of deception—with all of their subterfuges, dissembling, and pretense. At this point, my claim is simply that there are real and articulable differences in moral content between lying and other forms of deception, and that, ceteris paribus, lying is more wrongful than merely misleading.

In the following extract, Professor Buell explains why he thinks it is so difficult to come up with a single definition of fraud or white-collar crime generally. As technology, business practice, and ethics change, so the concept of fraud changes too:[46] ←1 (p.558)

S. Buell, '"White Collar" Crimes' in M. Dubber and T. Hörnle (eds) *The Oxford Handbook of Criminal Law* (Oxford: OUP, 2014), 842–3, 861

The challenge of white-collar crime arises from, if you will, its embeddedness. Embeddedness is the extent to which an activity subject to criminal prohibition is enmeshed within, closely related to, and not readily distinguishable from socially acceptable or even welcome conduct. Think of murder. Only in rare cases does the law of homicide confront such problems—as, for example, when a doctor is challenged for discontinuing life-saving measures in a jurisdiction that has not settled its rules on the matter.

Criminally prohibited activities are arranged on a spectrum in this regard, with murder the easy case, assault a bit more likely to involve such difficulties, theft usually straightforward but sometimes not (as evident in the development of the common law of larceny), and so on. . . .

White-collar offenses tend to fall toward the end of this spectrum at which application of criminal prohibitions, as often as not, requires the legal system to make difficult determinations about when behaviors involving commercial transactions, political activity, adversarial litigation, and the like "cross the line" from "aggressive" or "sharp" to criminal. . . .

This feature of embeddedness in routine activities that are mostly conducted within legitimate and important social institutions—commerce in corporations, politics in government,

---

[46] See Green (2004), who highlights the moral ambiguities which can surround 'dubious' business practices.

dispute resolution in agencies and courts—produces acute problems of legal specification. It is difficult to articulate such close distinctions within generalized legal rules that must serve to address many and varied cases. This is true even if normative disagreements about precisely what kinds of behaviors should be criminalized in commercial, political, litigation, and like activities have been settled. Often they have not been. Making the problem more difficult, white-collar prohibitions deal with sectors of social activity in which technologies and norms evolve rapidly, potentially leaving each new move of legal regulation one step behind.

. . .

We thus arrive at explanations for two commonly observed features of white-collar criminal cases. The first is that white-collar cases, in contrast to cases of "street" crime, more often involve the question of whether conduct, the facts of which may not be in serious dispute, constitutes a crime than they do the question of whether someone was the true perpetrator or what happened at the scene of the crime. The second is that white-collar cases much more often turn on questions of *mens rea*—what precisely was in the defendant's mind at the relevant moment—than on questions of *actus reus*—what exactly did the defendant do.

A typical pattern in fraud cases, for example, is that the defendant's possession of a document or presence at a meeting will not be in dispute but the defense will vigorously contest that the defendant was aware, much less intended, that anyone would be misled by the document or the decision taken at the meeting. In the absence of the foolish "smoking gun" email to a colleague, which surprisingly continues to turn up in some cases at major financial institutions, arguments about lack of *mens rea* can be persuasive.

. . .

Two major influences likely perpetuate ambivalence towards white-collar crime, and thus contribute to boundary problems in crime definition and pendulum swings in sentencing law and practice. First, a capitalist economic system—and the United States is history's leading example—by definition requires citizens to believe in two conflicting ideas at once. Entrepreneurs must be unleashed to create wealth but penned in lest their pursuit of self-interest generate regrettable and harmful externalities. In the morally charged realm of criminal law, this makes likely a public belief that pursuit of wealth can be either worthy or repulsive, and difficulty in clearly understanding or seeing the difference between the two. Greed is both good and bad.

Secondly, robust U.S. discourse about the idea of equality plays out in complicated ways when it comes to white-collar crime. On the one hand, law should treat no one more favorably because of her social class. As the criminal justice system has grown . . . notoriously intrusive and punitive toward common criminals, the belief has grown that white-collar criminals ought not be treated any less severely than anyone else. This logic can lead to a kind of doubling-down on incarceration strategies. On the other hand, it can be difficult to ignore real differences that distinguish white-collar crimes—and often but not always the persons who commit them—from murders, rapes, robberies, burglaries, and assaults.

8 THE FRAUD ACT 2006

In 2002 the Law Commission produced its report on reform of fraud offences. It rejected a proposal that we should have a general offence of dishonesty or deception. Instead it proposed the new offence of fraud:

Law Commission Report No. 276, *Fraud* (London: TSO, 2002), paras 5.23–7.10

Would a general dishonesty offence be desirable?

The arguments for a general dishonesty offence

5.23 The Crown Prosecution Service favoured the creation of a general offence of fraud based on dishonesty 'because of the flexibility it would offer in prosecuting fraud cases' and 'because it would cover situations where deceit is not used to commit the fraud, or where it is difficult to establish a link between the deception and the outcome or intended outcome.' It argued that flexibility was crucial given the developments in financial markets and the increasing use of new technologies. It further argued that complicated and technical legal arguments could be avoided by a general offence and that clarifying issues might help to simplify complex fraud trials.

5.24 The Serious Fraud Office felt that the unresolved problems of internet fraud, where the fraud consisted of enjoyment of a service delivered over the internet which had legitimately been paid for by another, and fraud in financial markets, specifically Eurobond fraud, highlighted the complexity of modern financial practices. It felt that the speed at which such practices were changing and developing showed 'the need for extreme flexibility in the relevant criminal law'. The Department of Trade and Industry expressly agreed with the views of the CPS and the SFO.

The arguments against a general dishonesty offence

Legal certainty and fair warning

. . .

5.28 We continue to believe that a general dishonesty offence, by not requiring as an element some identifiable morally dubious conduct to which the test of dishonesty may be applied, would fail to provide any meaningful guidance on the scope of the criminal law and the conduct which may be lawfully pursued. We do not accept the argument that inherent uncertainty is satisfactorily cured by the promise of prosecutorial discretion. This cannot make a vague offence clear and, while it might ameliorate some of the risks, it does not excuse a law reform agency from formulating a justifiable and properly defined offence. . . .

Human rights

5.29 The principle of maximum certainty is now linked to the question of compatibility with the Human Rights Act 1998. [The Paper discusses potential compatibility with Article 7 of the European Convention on Human Rights and the views of respondents to their consultation paper.]

5.33 In the light of these responses, we take the view that general dishonesty offences (such as conspiracy to defraud) could perhaps be found to be compatible with the requirements of article 7. We nonetheless remain of the view that they offend against the principle of maximum certainty.

Fair labelling

. . .

5.35 We take the view that a general dishonesty offence would pay insufficient regard to the principle of fair labelling. It would not explain or reflect to society the nature of the wrongdoing or its scale of harm. The law in this area would lose its educative and declaratory functions.

Effect on other dishonesty offences

5.36 The practical consequence of the inroads into the principles of fair warning and fair labelling can be seen by the potential effect on other dishonesty offences. The widespread use of a general dishonesty offence would render largely academic the boundaries of all other offences of dishonesty. Where a person's conduct fell outside a particular offence because of the specific requirements that Parliament has thought appropriate for that offence, the prosecution would be able to circumvent the difficulty by charging the general dishonesty offence instead. For example, the receipt of stolen goods is not an offence under section 22 of the 1968 Act unless the receiver knows or believes them to be stolen. But some people would say it is dishonest to receive goods which one suspects to be stolen. The prosecution could therefore invite the fact-finders to convict a receiver of the general dishonesty offence without being satisfied of the knowledge or belief that the 1968 Act expressly requires. . . .

Is dishonesty criminal?

5.38 In Consultation Paper No 155, we argued that the case for a general dishonesty offence had to rest on the argument that all dishonest conduct should in principle be criminal. There would be no logical reason to attach criminal sanctions to every form of dishonesty for commercial gain, while giving complete licence to those who use dishonesty for political, emotional, social or sexual gains. On the other hand, if all dishonesty were to be criminalised, it would offend against the principle of minimum criminalisation. People across the jurisdiction tell small lies every day. This will often rightly result in social retribution, but such instances of dishonesty cannot be properly described as criminal. It is simply not appropriate to extend the scope of the criminal law to cover every minor social problem or instance of human frailty. A general dishonesty offence would be based on principles which, if taken to their logical conclusion, would trivialise the law and extend its scope too far.

. . .

A general deception offence

. . .

The concept of deception

6.10 Our informal discussion paper also discussed certain difficulties that currently exist in relation to the concept of deception, and would continue to exist if a new general offence were defined in terms of that concept.

6.11 First, as we explained in Part III above, there is a problem where the victim is indifferent to the truth of the proposition asserted by the defendant to be true, and it is therefore debatable whether he or she can be said to have been *deceived*—for example, where the fraud consists in the unauthorised use of a credit card or similar payment instrument. Our informal discussion paper suggested that this problem would be avoided if the law's focus were shifted away from the mind of the victim on to the conduct of the defendant, and to this end it proposed that the new general offence be defined in terms of 'false pretence' rather than deception. It would still have to be proved that the loss or gain *resulted* from the pretence. In order to meet the argument that a pretence has no effect unless it is believed, however, the paper proposed that it should be sufficient if the victim responded in some way to the actions of the defendant *as a whole* (as distinct from responding to the pretence in particular) even if that response were 'automatic' and not based on any positive belief in the truth of the pretence. This idea attracted only limited support: many respondents argued that it would be less artificial simply to recognise that the element of pretence is not essential in the first place. We are now persuaded by this argument. Misrepresentation is therefore one, but only one, of the ways in which the new fraud offence we recommend in Part VII could be committed.

6.12 Secondly, as we also pointed out in Part III, a requirement of deception cannot be satisfied where no human being is deceived because the defendant's false assertion was made only to a machine. It follows that, at present, it is not normally an offence to obtain services (as distinct from property, the dishonest acquisition of which is theft) by 'deceiving' a machine. Our informal discussion paper proposed to meet this problem by taking the idea of 'automatic' response by a human being and applying it to the literally automatic responses of machines. There was general agreement among respondents that the dishonest obtaining of services from machines should be brought within the criminal law, but again there was some opposition to the idea of doing this by stretching the concept of pretence. We are now persuaded that an offence designed to cover such conduct should be formulated simply in terms of the dishonest obtaining of services, rather than requiring that the services be obtained in a particular way which is analogous (but not identical) to deception . . .

. . .

A fresh approach

7.4 . . . We think it is possible to devise a general fraud offence which, without relying too heavily on the concept of dishonesty, would nevertheless be sufficiently broad and flexible to catch nearly every case that would today be likely to be charged as a conspiracy to defraud. Conspiracy to defraud would then be virtually redundant (in practice if not in theory), and could safely be abolished.

. . .

7.6 The difficulty that we have encountered in seeking to formulate a satisfactory fraud offence, we believe, results largely from the fact that the concept of fraud developed by the criminal courts has in some respects parted company from the word's ordinary meaning. This is not to say that the courts have overtly treated 'fraud' as a legal term of art. On the contrary, they have purported to analyse its ordinary meaning, and to apply that meaning for the purposes of conspiracy to defraud and of other offences defined as involving an element of fraud. It does not follow that they have always succeeded in accurately stating that meaning. According to the classic definition in *Scott*, for example, fraud includes any dishonest conduct which causes, or exposes another to the risk of, financial loss. This definition is wide enough to include conduct such as shoplifting, robbery or burglary, which a non-lawyer would hardly describe as fraud.

7.7 This divergence between the ordinary and legal meanings of fraud has laid a trap for law reformers. We have tended to assume that a fraud offence worthy of the name must inevitably embrace any conduct which the law currently regards as fraud, even if non-lawyers would not so regard it. Yet there is no need for a fraud offence to catch shoplifting, robbery or burglary, because these activities are adequately dealt with by existing statutory offences. To render conspiracy to defraud dispensable, a new fraud offence needs *only* to catch those kinds of dishonest conduct that an ordinary person would call fraud. The question is: what are the hallmarks of such conduct?

7.8 The classic statement of the nature of fraud is Stephen's:

'I shall not attempt to construct a definition which will meet every case which might be suggested, but there is little danger in saying that whenever the words "fraud" or "intent to defraud" or "fraudulently" occur in the definition of a crime two elements at least are essential to the commission of the crime: namely, first, deceit or an intention to deceive or in some cases mere secrecy; and, secondly, either actual injury or possible injury or an intent to expose some person either to actual injury or to a risk of possible injury by means of that deceit or secrecy.'

7.9 We note first that Stephen did not say these two elements are *sufficient* to constitute fraud: he said that they *at least* are essential. For reasons explained in Part V above, we are now persuaded, contrary to the view we provisionally expressed in Consultation Paper No 155, that the element of *dishonesty* should be essential to (though not sufficient for) criminal liability for fraud. With the addition of this element, Stephen's definition requires:

(1) deceit, intention to deceive or secrecy, *and*

(2) *either*

    (a) actual or possible injury to another *or*

    (b) an intent thereby to cause injury to another or to expose another to a risk of possible injury,

(3) *and* dishonesty.

Another issue surrounding fraud which has caused concern is the length and complexity of fraud trials. Famously the Jubilee Line trial lasted 21 months before being abandoned.[47] The defence still had a substantial amount of material they wished to introduce. Such cases inevitably give rise to concern.[48] The cost of the Jubilee Line trial was over £25 million.[49] The personal costs to the jurors who had to sit through such a long trial in some cases was significant.[50] A common concern is also that juries lack the abilities to deal with the sheer volume and complexities of the material involved, although the limited evidence we have suggests that the ability of juries to comprehend what is going on is often underestimated.[51] There are especial difficulties for jurors who have the task of determining the boundary between the hard-nosed business person, the exciting entrepreneur, and the dishonest criminal.[52]

QUESTIONS

1. Do you think the definition of fraud is too vague? Are you convinced by arguments that the definition needs to be vague?

2. Is there a clear distinction between theft and fraud? Does there need to be?

3. A woman who lied about where she lived in order to obtain a school place for her child faced prosecution for fraud (BBC News Online 2009a), although the case did not come to court. Is that the kind of issue which the criminal law should deal with?

---

[47] Lloyd-Bostock (2007).   [48] Wooler (2006).   [49] *Ibid*, v.
[50] Lloyd-Bostock (2007).   [51] See *ibid*.
[52] S. Wilson (2006) suggests insufficient weight has been placed on the psychology of juries when dealing with cases of this kind.

FURTHER READING

Buell, S. (2006) 'Novel Criminal Fraud' *New York University Law Review* 81: 1971.

Collins, J. (2011) 'Fraud by Abuse of Position: Theorising Section 4 of the Fraud Act 2006' *Criminal Law Review* 513.

Green, S. (2007) *Lying, Cheating, and Stealing* (Oxford: OUP).

Levi, M. and Burrows, J. (2008) 'Measuring the Impact of Fraud in the UK' *British Journal of Criminology* 48: 293.

MacEwan, N. (2013) 'A Tricky Situation: Deception in Cyberspace' *Journal of Criminal Law* 417.

Ormerod, D. (2007) 'The Fraud Act 2006—Criminalising Lying?' *Criminal Law Review* 193.

Ormerod, D. and Williams, D. (2007) *Smith's Law of Theft* (Oxford: OUP).

Withey, C. (2007) 'The Fraud Act 2006—Some Early Observations and Comparisons with the Former Law' *Journal of Criminal Law* 70: 220.

9 CONCLUDING THOUGHTS

The Fraud Act 2006 has significantly extended the law of fraud. In particular in stating that a fraud is committed even if there is in fact no gain for the defendant. It remains to be seen how broadly it will be used by prosecutors or interpreted by courts. Prosecutors are likely only to use it in cases where the defendant has made a gain or attempted to engage in a serious fraud. Even if it does get close to 'criminalizing lying', its use will probably be restricted to more serious cases. That said, the fact that it has such a potentially broad scope, means that it is, in principle, objectionable to many commentators.

10

BURGLARY AND BLACKMAIL

CENTRAL ISSUES

1. The offence of burglary is committed where a defendant enters a building as a trespasser with intent to commit one of the offences listed in section 9 of the Theft Act 1968. It is also committed where a defendant has entered a building as a trespasser and then committed one of a list of other offences.

2. To be guilty of blackmail, a defendant must make unwarranted demands with menaces with a view to making a gain for him or herself or a loss to another. The defendant will have a defence if he or she believed the demands were warranted and that the use of menaces was a proper means of enforcing payment.

PART I: THE LAW

1 BURGLARY

The 'person in the street' probably understands burglary to be the theft of property from someone's house. In fact, the offence is far more complicated than this. It is not limited to theft, but can involve the commission of other crimes inside a home. Further, burglary can involve entering someone's home with an intent to commit certain crimes, even without actually doing so. →1 (p.599)

Section 9 of the Theft Act 1968 defines the offence of burglary:

> (1) A person is guilty of burglary if—
>
>   (a) he enters any building or part of a building as a trespasser and with intent to commit any such offence as is mentioned in subsection (2) below; or
>
>   (b) having entered any building or part of a building as a trespasser he steals or attempts to steal anything in the building or that part of it or inflicts or attempts to inflict on any person therein any grievous bodily harm.

> (2) The offences referred to in subsection (1)(a) above are offences of stealing anything in the building or part of a building in question, of inflicting on any person therein any grievous bodily harm or raping any person therein, and of doing unlawful damage to the building or anything therein.

DEFINITION

It is important to appreciate that there are two kinds of burglary:

(1) section 9(1)(a): entering a building or part of a building as a trespasser with an intent to commit one of the following in the building:

 (a) theft;

 (b) criminal damage; or

 (c) infliction of grievous bodily harm;

(2) section 9(1)(b): having entered a building or part of a building as a trespasser, committing either:

 (a) theft or attempted theft; or

 (b) infliction or attempted infliction of grievous bodily harm.

The key difference between the two offences is the time at which the crime is committed:

(1) Section 9(1)(a) is committed when the defendant enters the building.

(2) Section 9(1)(b) is committed when, once inside the building, the defendant commits one of the listed crimes.

If a defendant enters as a trespasser, intending to steal property, and once inside does indeed steal property the defendant is guilty of both the forms of burglary. If the burglary is from domestic premises the maximum penalty is 14 years, whereas if the burglary is from a non-domestic building it is ten years.[1]

Several elements of the offence of burglary need further discussion:

1.1 BUILDING OR PART OF A BUILDING

A building must involve a permanent structure. A 25-feet-long freezer sitting in a farmyard for more than two years was held to be a building,[2] whereas a large container that formed the rear part of a lorry was not.[3] Section 9(4) states that an inhabited vehicle is included within the definition of a building. This is designed to cover houseboats and caravans which are permanently inhabited. To be a building there is no need for the structure to be occupied. A garden shed can therefore be a building.

If the defendant enters a building with the consent of the owner (and so is not a trespasser—see Section 1.3), but then enters a part of the building which he is not permitted to enter with intent to steal, he or she can be guilty of burglary. For example, Victor enters a shop, but

---

[1] Criminal Justice Act 1991.   [2] *B and S v Leathley* [1979] Crim LR 314.
[3] *Norfolk Constabulary v Seekings and Gould* [1986] Crim LR 167.

once inside walks into the manager's office. He can be charged with burglary when entering the manager's office as a trespasser: he has entered part of the building as a trespasser. To constitute a part of a building there must be some kind of physical mark or barrier. A separate room clearly constitutes a part of a building; less obviously a 'no entry' sign or rope could mark off a part of a room.[4]

1.2 ENTRY

What does 'enters' mean? The burglar must enter the building, but this does not mean that all of a burglar's body must enter the building. According to the Court of Appeal in *Brown*[5] there must be an 'effective entry'.[6] In *Brown* the defendant broke a shop window and stuck the top half of his body through it while investigating the inside of the shop. This was an effective entry and so the offence was made out. The Court of Appeal in *Ryan*[7] rejected an argument that the test should be whether there was a sufficient amount of the defendant's body inside to enable him or her to carry out one of the crimes. So if Tim enters a downstairs window he has still 'entered' for the purposes of burglary even if he is intending to steal a painting several floors up. If 'effective' does not mean 'effective to be able to commit one of the listed crimes' it is unclear what it means. It may be that all the phrase is doing is making clear that minimal entry (e.g. just a fingertip) would not be sufficient. The question will now be one for the jury to decide.

It is widely accepted that it is possible to commit burglary by using an object to enter the property, although there is no recent authority on the issue. So if a defendant put a pole through a window and pulled out an item this could be burglary. Further, if the defendant trained his or her young child[8] (or a dog) to enter other people's houses and steal property, the defendant would be guilty of burglary.[9]

1.3 TRESPASSER

To be guilty of burglary the defendant must enter as a trespasser, being aware that he or she is a trespasser. The term trespasser is in fact a term used in tort law. If someone enters a piece of land he or she does not own without legal authorization then prima facie he or she is a trespasser. The most common form of legal authorization is to have the consent of the owner of the land[10] or of the owner's family.[11]

In *Collins*[12] the key issue was whether the owner's daughter had invited the defendant into the house before he had entered. If she had he could not be convicted of burglary because he was not a trespasser.

---

[4] *Walkington* [1979] 2 All ER 716.

[5] It rejected the test in *Collins* [1973] QB 100 that there had to be 'an effective and substantial entry'.

[6] *Brown* [1985] Crim LR 212. [7] [1996] Crim LR 320.

[8] This would be to use an innocent agent. [9] *Wheelhouse* [1994] Crim LR 756.

[10] Other forms of legal authorization include police officers entering on the basis of a search warrant or a landlord distraining property for non-payment of rent.

[11] *Robson v Hallett* [1967] 2 QB 939 (CA): the son of the owner invited police officers into the house and so they were not trespassers.

[12] [1973] QB 100.

R v Collins
[1973] QB 100 (CA)

Stephen Collins had had a good deal to drink and was 'desirous of having sexual intercourse'. On passing the victim's house he noticed her light was on. He fetched a ladder, removed all of his clothes, apart from his socks, and climbed up the ladder. He pulled himself onto the window sill. The victim awoke and saw the outline of a naked male form. She assumed it must be her boyfriend and therefore beckoned him in. He joined her in bed and they had sexual intercourse. It was only when she switched on the light that she discovered he was not her boyfriend. He was charged with burglary with intent to rape. The appellant claimed that he would not have entered the room had the victim not beckoned him in. There was no clear evidence of where on the sill the defendant was when the victim welcomed him in. The judge directed the jury that they had to be satisfied that the appellant entered the room as a trespasser with intent to commit rape. Whether or not he was a trespasser depended on the question: was the entry intentional or reckless?

Lord Justice Edmund Davies [delivered the judgment of the court]

Under s 9 of the Theft Act 1968, which renders a person guilty of burglary if he enters any building or part of a building as a trespasser and with the intention of committing rape, the entry of the appellant into the building must first be proved. Well, there is no doubt about that, for it is common ground that he did enter this girl's bedroom. Secondly, it must be proved that he entered as a trespasser. We will develop that point a little later. Thirdly, it must be proved that he entered as a trespasser with intent at the time of entry to commit rape therein.

The second ingredient of the offence—the entry must be as a trespasser—is one which has not, to the best of our knowledge, been previously canvassed in the courts. Views as to its ambit have naturally been canvassed by the textbook writers, and it is perhaps not wholly irrelevant to recall that those who were advising the Home Secretary before the Theft Bill was presented to Parliament had it in mind to get rid of some of the frequently absurd technical rules which had been built up in relation to the old requirement in burglary of a 'breaking and entering'. The cases are legion as to what this did or did not amount to, and happily it is not now necessary for us to consider them. But it was in order to get rid of those technical rules that a new test was introduced, namely that the entry must be 'as a trespasser'.

What does that involve? According to the learned editors of Archbold (Criminal Pleading, Evidence and Practice (37th Edn 1969), p. 572, para 1505):

> 'Any intentional, reckless or negligent entry into a building will, it would appear, constitute a trespass if the building is in the possession of another person who does not consent to the entry. Nor will it make any difference that the entry was the result of a reasonable mistake on the part of the defendant, so far as trespass is concerned.'

If that be right, then it would be no defence for this man to say (and even were he believed in saying), 'Well, I honestly thought that this girl was welcoming me into the room and I therefore entered, fully believing that I had her consent to go in'. If Archbold is right, he would nevertheless be a trespasser, since the apparent consent of the girl was unreal, she being mistaken as to who was at her window. We disagree. . . .

In the judgment of this court, there cannot be a conviction for entering premises 'as a trespasser' within the meaning of s 9 of the Theft Act 1968 unless the person entering does so knowing that he is a trespasser and nevertheless deliberately enters, or, at the very least, is reckless whether or not he is entering the premises of another without the other party's consent.

Having so held, the pivotal point of this appeal is whether the Crown established that the appellant at the moment that he entered the bedroom knew perfectly well that he was not welcome there or, being reckless whether he was welcome or not, was nevertheless determined to enter. That in turn involves consideration as to where he was at the time that the complainant indicated that she was welcoming him into her bedroom. If, to take an example that was put in the course of argument, her bed had not been near the window but was on the other side of the bedroom, and he (being determined to have her sexually even against her will) climbed through the window and crossed the bedroom to reach her bed, then the offence charged would have been established. But in this case, as we have related, the layout of the room was different, and it became a point of nicety which had to be conclusively established by the Crown as to where he was when the girl made welcoming signs, as she unquestionably at some stage did.

. . .

[Having considered the trial judge's direction **Edmund Davies LJ** continued:]

We are compelled to say that we do not think the trial judge by these observations made it sufficiently clear to the jury the nature of the second test about which they had to be satisfied before the appellant could be convicted of the offence charged. There was no doubt that his entry into the bedroom was 'intentional'. But what the appellant had said was, 'She knelt on the bed, she put her arms around me and then I went in'. If the jury thought he might be truthful in that assertion, they would need to consider whether or not, although entirely surprised by such a reception being accorded to him, this young man might not have been entitled reasonably to regard her action as amounting to an invitation to him to enter. If she in fact appeared to be welcoming him, the Crown do not suggest that he should have realised or even suspected that she was so behaving because, despite the moonlight, she thought he was someone else. Unless the jury were entirely satisfied that the appellant made an effective and substantial entry into the bedroom without the complainant doing or saying anything to cause him to believe that she was consenting to his entering it, he ought not to be convicted of the offence charged. The point is a narrow one, as narrow maybe as the window sill which is crucial to this case. But this is a criminal charge of gravity and, even though one may suspect that his intention was to commit the offence charged, unless the facts show with clarity that he in fact committed it he ought not to remain convicted.

. . . One further matter that was canvassed ought perhaps to be mentioned. The point was raised that, the complainant not being the tenant or occupier of the dwelling-house and her mother being apparently in occupation, this girl herself could not in any event have extended an effective invitation to enter, so that even if she had expressly and with full knowledge of all material facts invited the appellant in, he would nevertheless be a trespasser. Whatever be the position in the law of tort, to regard such a proposition as acceptable in the criminal law would be unthinkable.

We have to say that this appeal must be allowed on the basis that the jury were never invited to consider the vital question whether this young man did enter the premises as a trespasser, that is to say knowing perfectly well that he had no invitation to enter or reckless of whether or not his entry was with permission.

Appeal allowed. Conviction quashed.

There are a number of difficulties with the trespasser requirement:

Withdrawal of permission

If Camilla has permission from Liz to enter her house, but that permission is later withdrawn and Liz asks Camilla to leave, Camilla is a trespasser unless she leaves within a reasonable length of time. However, to be guilty of burglary a person has to enter a building as a burglar. So if Camilla is invited into Liz's house, is then asked to leave, but does so very slowly, and on the way out steals some property there is no burglary (only theft). It should, however, be remembered that if a defendant enters a 'part' of a building as a trespasser that is sufficient for burglary. So if on her slow way out Camilla enters a new part of the building she can be convicted.

Acting in excess of permission

More difficult issues arise where the defendant has been given permission to enter a house for a particular purpose (e.g. to read a gas meter), but acts in excess of this permission (e.g. entering a bedroom). He or she is then trespassing and so can be convicted of burglary. This concept was explained in *Jones and Smith* (in the following extract).

Consent to enter based on a mistake

What if the defendant is given consent to enter a building on the basis of a fundamental mistake? An example was *Collins*, where the daughter gave consent to the defendant to enter on the assumption that he was her boyfriend. The position in civil law is that if the consent is provided following a fundamental mistake (such as to the identity of the individual) then the consent is invalid, but if the mistake is not fundamental (e.g. a mistake over an irrelevant matter) then the consent may still be valid. Presumably the criminal courts would take a similar approach. However, it should be recalled that it must be shown that the defendant knew he or she was a trespasser. So in the *Collins* case, even though the defendant was a trespasser because the daughter had made a fundamental mistake over his identity, if the defendant honestly believed that he was being invited in, he lacked the *mens rea* element because he did not know he was a trespasser.

The mens rea of a trespasser

As just mentioned, to be guilty of burglary defendants must know that they are trespassers or be reckless. This was emphasized by Edmund Davies LJ in *Collins*.[13] This does not require evidence that defendants understand the law of trespass and are aware that they may be committing trespass. Rather, it is enough if the defendants are aware of the facts that render them trespassers (e.g. that they entered a building without the permission of the owner). So if Edith, staying with a friend, goes out for a drink and on her return stupidly mistakes a neighbour's house for her friend's and enters it and carelessly breaks a chair she is not guilty of burglary because she believes (even if unreasonably) that she has permission to enter.

---

[13] [1973] QB 100.

R v Jones; R v Smith
[1976] 3 All ER 54 (CA)

John Jones and Christopher Smith were charged with burglary. They had entered Smith's father's house and stolen two television sets. At the trial Smith stated that his father had given him unreserved permission to enter his house. The appellants appealed against their conviction on the ground that Smith had not entered his father's house as a trespasser.

Lord Justice James [delivered the following judgment of the court]

The next ground of appeal relied on by counsel for the appellants in his argument is that which is put forward as the first ground in each of the appellant's grounds. It is the point on which counsel had laid the greatest stress in the course of his argument. The argument is based on the wording of the Theft Act 1968, s 9(1), which provides:

'A person is guilty of burglary if . . . (b) having entered any building or part of a building as a trespasser he steals or attempts to steal anything in the building or that part of it or inflicts or attempts to inflict on any person therein any grievous bodily harm.'

The important words from the point of view of the argument in this appeal are 'having entered any building . . . as a trespasser'.

It is a section of an Act of Parliament which introduces a novel concept. Entry as a trespasser was new in 1968 in relation to criminal offences of burglary. It was introduced in substitution for, as an improvement on, the old law, which required considerations of breaking and entering and involved distinctions of nicety which had bedevilled the law for some time.

Counsel for the appellants argues that a person who had a general permission to enter premises of another person cannot be a trespasser. His submission is as short and as simple as that. Related to this case he says that a son to whom a father has given permission generally to enter the father's house cannot be a trespasser if he enters it even though he had decided in his mind before making the entry to commit a criminal offence of theft against the father once he had got into the house and had entered that house solely for the purpose of committing that theft. . . .

The decision in *R v Collins* [1973] QB 100 in this court, a decision on the criminal law, added to the concept of trespass as a civil wrong only the mental element of *mens rea*, which is essential to the criminal offence. Taking the law as expressed in *Hillen and Pettigrew v ICI (Alkali) Ltd* [1936] AC 65 and in *R v Collins*, it is our view that a person is a trespasser for the purpose of s 9(1)(b) of the Theft Act 1968 if he enters premises of another knowing that he is entering in excess of the permission that has been given to him, or being reckless whether he is entering in excess of the permission that has been given to him to enter, providing the facts are known to the accused which enable him to realise that he is acting in excess of the permission given or that he is acting recklessly as to whether he exceeds that permission, then that is sufficient for the jury to decide that he is in fact a trespasser.

In this particular case it was a matter for the jury to consider whether, on all the facts, it was shown by the prosecution that the appellants entered with the knowledge that entry was being effected against the consent or in excess of the consent that had been given by Mr Alfred Smith to his son Christopher. The jury were, by their verdict, satisfied of that.

Appeals dismissed.

This was a controversial decision because it means that whether a person is a trespasser depends on his or her mental state (i.e. whether at the point of entering he or she intended to commit a crime). Taken to its logical conclusion the *Jones and Smith* rule would mean that every shoplifter was a burglar because when stealing in a shop the defendant was acting in excess of the permission of the shop owner (shop owners do not invite shoplifters into their shops).[14] It appears from *Walkington*,[15] heard after *Jones and Smith*, that the case will not be extended that far. There the Court of Appeal required proof that the defendant, having entered the shop intending to steal, entered a separate part of the shop he was not permitted to go into.

1.4 THE *MENS REA* FOR BURGLARY

The *mens rea* depends on which form of burglary is charged:

(1) Under section 9(1)(a) it must be shown that the defendant had an intention to commit one of the listed offences *at the time the defendant entered the building*. It should be stressed that if the defendant entered the building intending to steal, but once inside decided not to steal, the offence was still committed. Likewise if the defendant entered the building not intending to commit theft, but once inside decided to do so, there would be no burglary contrary to section 9(1)(a). What is yet to be decided by the courts is what would happen if the defendant intended to take property from the building and damage it outside. The question is whether the word 'therein' in section 9(1)(b) refers to the place where the property is found or the place where the damage takes place.

(2) Under section 9(1)(b) the *mens rea* of burglary under section 9(1)(b) is the *mens rea* for stealing. Less clear is where the relevant crime is the infliction of grievous bodily harm. Controversially the Court of Appeal in *Wilson and Jenkins*[16] suggested that it does not require the proof of any particular *mens rea*.[17] Many commentators have taken the view that this is incorrect and that at least *Cunningham* recklessness as to the infliction of grievous bodily harm is required.[18]

What if the defendant decides to enter property and see if there is anything that is going to be worth stealing? Such an intent is described as a conditional intent: the defendant has an intent to steal on condition that there is something that is worth stealing. Does such an intent amount to an intent to steal for the purposes of burglary? Yes, it does.[19]

2 AGGRAVATED BURGLARY

Section 10 of the Theft Act 1968 states:

(1) A person is guilty of aggravated burglary if he commits any burglary and at the time has with him any firearm or imitation firearm, any weapon of offence, or any explosive; and for this purpose—

(a) 'firearm' includes an airgun or air pistol, and 'imitation firearm' means anything which has the appearance of being a firearm, whether capable of being discharged or not; and

(b) 'weapon of offence' means any article made or adapted for use for causing injury to or incapacitating a person, or intended by the person having it with him for such use; and

---

[14] Pace (1985). [15] [1979] 1 WLR 1169.

[16] [1983] 1 All ER 1000, confirmed on other grounds in [1984] AC 242 (HL).

[17] There is no offence of simply inflicting grievous bodily harm under the Offences Against the Person Act 1861.

[18] e.g. Simester, Spencer, Sullivan, and Virgo (2013: 588).

[19] *Attorney-General's References (Nos 1 and 2 of 1979)* [1979] 3 All ER 143 (CA).

> (c) 'explosive' means any article manufactured for the purpose of producing a practical effect by explosion, or intended by the person having it with him for that purpose.

Aggravated burglary involves a defendant who has with him or her at the time of the burglary a firearm, imitation firearm, a weapon of offence, or an explosive.[20] If the burglary is under section 9(1)(a) then it must be shown that the defendant had the weapon at the time of entry;[21] under section 9(1)(b) it must be shown that the defendant had the weapon at the time of committing the further offence. In other words the defendant must possess the weapon at the time when the offence of burglary is committed.[22] The definition of a 'weapon of offence' is wide. It means that a screwdriver can be regarded as a weapon of offence if the defendant intends to use it to injure someone.[23] There is no need to show that the defendant intended to use the item at that particular burglary, as long as there was an intention to use the item against someone on some occasion.[24] However, it must be shown that the defendant was aware that he or she had the weapon with him or her at the time of the burglary.[25]

3 TRESPASS WITH INTENT TO COMMIT A SEXUAL OFFENCE

Under section 63 of the Sexual Offences Act 2003:

> (1) A person commits an offence if—
>   (a) he is a trespasser on any premises,
>   (b) he intends to commit a relevant sexual offence on the premises, and
>   (c) he knows that, or is reckless as to whether, he is a trespasser.

Notably, this offence refers to a structure (rather than a building). In section 63(2) it is explained that a structure 'includes a tent, vehicle or vessel or other temporary or movable structure'. The term 'sexual offence' is widely defined in section 62 and includes the sexual offences in the 2003 Act (which have been discussed in Chapter 7).

4 BLACKMAIL

> **DEFINITION**
>
> The *actus reus* is:
>
> (1) the defendant makes an unwarranted demand;
>
> (2) with menaces.

---

[20] Note also the Theft Act 1968, s. 25, on going equipped to steal.
[21] *Wiggins* [2012] EWCA Crim 885.
[22] *Francis* [1982] Crim LR 363; *O'Leary* (1986) 82 Cr App R 341.   [23] *Kelly* [1993] Crim LR 763.
[24] *Stones* (1989) 89 Cr App R 26; *Kelly* [1993] Crim LR 763.
[25] *Russell* (1985) 81 Cr App R 315; *Kelly* [1993] Crim LR 763.

The *mens rea* is:

(1) the defendant must act with a view to gain for himself or another or with intent to cause loss to another;

(2) the defendant either:

    (a) does not believe that he has reasonable grounds for making the demand; or

    (b) does not believe that the use of menaces is a proper means of reinforcing the demand.

At the heart of the offence of blackmail is the use of threats to acquire property or cause a loss to the victim. In a sense it is a combination of an offence against the person (the creation of fear of an unpleasant consequence) and a property offence (the financial gain to the defendant or loss to the victim). The offence of blackmail is defined in section 21 of the Theft Act 1968: →2 (p.601)

(1) A person is guilty of blackmail if, with a view to gain for himself or another or with intent to cause loss to another, he makes any unwarranted demand with menaces; and for this purpose a demand with menaces is unwarranted unless the person making it does so in the belief—

    (a) that he has reasonable grounds for making the demand; and

    (b) that the use of the menaces is a proper means of reinforcing the demand.

(2) The nature of the act or omission demanded is immaterial, and it is also immaterial whether the menaces relate to action to be taken by the person making the demand.

The key elements of the offence[26] are as follows:

4.1 A DEMAND

The demand can be either oral or written. In most cases of blackmail the demand will be explicit: 'Give me some money or else I'll . . .', but the demand can also be implicit.[27] If Oliver stopped Archie in a dark street, pointed a knife at him, and said 'Would you like to give some money to a good cause?', this could be regarded as much a demand as a cruder request for money. But if a victim voluntarily offers money without an express or implied demand from the defendant there is no blackmail. For example, if Peter catches Wendy red-handed in committing a theft and Wendy offers Peter £200 if he does not tell the police what he has seen, there is no blackmail.

The word 'demand' is to be given its ordinary meaning.[28] All that is necessary is that the demand is issued. There is no need for the victim to hear or receive the demand.[29] If a letter issuing a demand is put in a post box it is at that point that the offence is committed. Therefore, even if the letter is lost in the post and the victim never receives it, the defendant has still committed the offence.[30]

---

[26] The maximum sentence is 14 years.   [27] *Collister and Warhurst* (1955) 39 Cr App R 100.
[28] *Treacy v DPP* [1971] AC 537, 565, per Lord Diplock.   [29] *Ibid.*   [30] *Ibid.*

4.2 WITH A VIEW TO A GAIN OR LOSS

The demand must involve a financial gain to the defendant or a third party, or a financial loss to the victim.[31] This is clarified in section 34(2)(a) of the Theft Act 1968:

> . . . 'gain' and 'loss' are to be construed as extending only to gain or loss in money or other property, but as extending to any such gain or loss whether temporary or permanent; and—
>
> (i) 'gain' includes a gain by keeping what one has, as well as a gain by getting what one has not; and
>
> (ii) 'loss' includes a loss by not getting what one might get, as well as a loss by parting with what one has.

So a demand that the victim removes his or her clothes in public may involve a loss of dignity, but it cannot form the basis of a blackmail charge as there is no monetary loss.[32] In *Bevans*[33] the defendant demanded that a doctor give him some morphine, threatening to shoot him if he did not. The defendant could be convicted of blackmail because the morphine was of some monetary value.[34]

4.3 MENACES

The demand must be made with menaces. The Court of Appeal in *Lawrence and Pomroy*[35] suggested that a jury need be told only that 'menace' is to have its normal meaning and the judge need not explain the term further. The jury is likely to decide that the menace will involve a threat of 'any action detrimental to or unpleasant to the person addressed'.[36] The threat can be that something unpleasant will occur to the victim or a third party. It seems that the unpleasantness referred to here must not be of a minor nature. Sellers LJ in *Clear*[37] held that to amount to menaces the threats must be 'of such a nature and extent that the mind of an ordinary person of normal stability and courage might be influenced or made apprehensive so as to accede unwillingly to the demand'. In *Lambert*[38] the defendant phoned his grandmother and (untruthfully) said 'Nana, this is [x]. They've got me tied up. They want £5,000, Nana.' This it was held could amount to blackmail, even though the menace involved an unpleasant consequence for the defendant, rather than, as is more common, for the victim. As the court put it there were 'menacing pressures' and that was sufficient for the offence.

The hardest cases on menaces are those where the victim responds to the defendant's words in an unusual way. Contrast the following two situations:

(1) The defendant says something which most people would not regard as frightening, but because the victim is particularly timid he finds it menacing. That will be a menace if the defendant is aware of the effect of the words on the victim.[39]

---

[31] Theft Act 1968, s. 34.

[32] A sexual assault may be committed in such a case.   [33] (1987) 87 Cr App R 64.

[34] There is some dispute over whether being paid money legally due to you is 'a gain'. Such authority as there is suggests that it is (*Parkes* [1973] Crim LR 358).

[35] (1973) 57 Cr App R 64.

[36] Lord Wright in *Thorne v Motor Trade Association* [1937] AC 797, 817.

[37] [1968] 1 All ER 74, 80.   [38] [2009] EWCA Crim 2860.   [39] *Clear* [1968] 1 All ER 74.

(2) The defendant says something which most people would find menacing, but being particularly hard skinned the victim does not find it frightening. This would in law be regarded as a menace.

These points were emphasized in the following case:

R v Garwood
[1987] 1 All ER 1032 (CA)

Patrick Garwood believed a Mr Sayed had burgled his house. He asked Sayed for something 'to make it quits'. Sayed went home and got £10 to give to Garwood. Garwood was charged with blackmail. When considering their verdict the jury asked the judge whether menaces existed if the appellant appeared more menacing to a timid victim than he would have done to most people. The judge in his reply indicated that menaces can exist even though a person of normal stability would not have found what was said or done threatening, and even though the accused was unaware that the victim was unduly susceptible to threats.

Lord Lane CJ

In the judgment of this court [the judge's direction] might have led the jury to believe that the prosecution had proved the existence of menaces even though a person of normal ability would not have been influenced by the words or actions of the accused and the accused was not aware that the victim was thus unduly susceptible to threats. To that extent we think there was a misdirection.

In our judgment it is only rarely that a judge will need to enter upon a definition of the word menaces. It is an ordinary word of which the meaning will be clear to any jury. As Cairns LJ said in *Reg v Lawrence (Rodney)* (1973) 57 Cr App R 64, 72:

'In exceptional cases where because of special knowledge in special circumstances what would be a menace to an ordinary person is not a menace to the person to whom it is addressed, or where the converse may be true, it is no doubt necessary to spell out the meaning of the word.'

It seems to us that there are two possible occasions upon which a further direction on the meaning of the word menaces may be required. The first is where the threats might affect the mind of an ordinary person of normal stability but did not affect the person actually addressed. In such circumstances that would amount to a sufficient menace: see *Reg v Clear* [1968] 1 QB 670.

The second situation is where the threats in fact affected the mind of the victim, although they would not have affected the mind of a person of normal stability. In that case, in our judgment, the existence of menaces is proved providing that the accused man was aware of the likely effect of his actions upon the victim.

If the recorder had told the jury that Sayed's undue timidity did not prevent them from finding 'menaces' proved, providing that the appellant realised the effect his actions were having on Sayed, all would have been well. The issue before the jury was clear-cut. If they felt sure they thought that the appellant's version might be true, there were equally plainly no menaces. There was no need for the recorder to have embarked upon any definition of the word. It only served to confuse, as the jury's question showed.

> However, if he had given a proper and full answer to the jury's question in the terms which we suggested earlier, the jury could have been in no doubt at all that if Sayed's version was correct—which they must have felt that it was—the appellant must have realised from the moment that the conversation started the effect which his actions and words were having upon Sayed.
>
> This is accordingly eminently a case for the application of the proviso. The appeal against conviction is accordingly dismissed.
>
> *Appeal against conviction dismissed.*

4.4 THE DEMAND MUST BE UNWARRANTED

It is crucial that the demand be unwarranted. There are two stages to the test. First, the jury must decide whether or not they think the demand is unwarranted. It may be that the demand is perfectly reasonable. For example, most people would think that the threat 'unless you return the bicycle I lent you I will come round to your house and take it' was a warranted demand. However, even if the jury thinks it unwarranted they must still go on to consider section 21. Section 21(1) explains that the defendant's demand will be unwarranted unless it is made in the belief:

(1) that there are reasonable grounds for making it; and

(2) that the use of the menaces is a proper means of enforcing the demand.

If the defendant has the two beliefs mentioned the defendant cannot be guilty of blackmail because the demand will not be unwarranted. However, this is subject to an important caveat. If the defendant is aware that he or she is threatening to commit a crime, he or she cannot claim that the demand is reasonable.[40]

The Bribery Act 2010 creates an offence of bribery. This involves giving someone an inducement to encourage someone to perform an official function improperly. Like blackmail this involves seeking to manipulate another person to make a gain. That offence will not be discussed in detail in this book.[41]

QUESTIONS

1. In *Harry* [1974] Crim LR 32 a student organizing a 'rag event' wrote to shopkeepers offering immunity from the 'inconvenience' during rag events in return for a contribution to a charity. Could this amount to blackmail?

2. Bill (Angelina's gardener) has borrowed Angelina's bicycle, but he is refusing to return it. Angelina threatens not to pay Bill's salary unless he returns the bicycle. She has very high moral standards and feels that what she has done is in fact justifiable. Has she committed blackmail?

For guidance on answering this question, please visit the Online Resource Centre that accompanies this book: www.oxfordtextbooks.co.uk/orc/herringcriminal7e/.

3. Eliza tells Higgins that she will tell his wife that he has been committing adultery unless he redecorates her house for free. Is this blackmail?

---

[40] *R v Harvey, Ulyett and Plummer* (1981) 72 Cr App R 139.   [41] See Raphael (2010).

PART II: BURGLARY AND BLACKMAIL: THEORY

5 BURGLARY: THEORY

5.1 BURGLARY IN PRACTICE

England and Wales top the international league table for domestic burglary. They have a higher burglary rate than the United States and twice the rate of Germany.[42] In 2014/15, 3 in 100 households were the victims of burglary. The figure had been 9 in 100 in 1995, indicating a dramatic reduction in burglaries in the past 20 years. For the year 2014/15 there were 785,000 burglaries recorded by the Crime Survey for England and Wales,[43] although 197,021 burglaries were reported to the police.[44] The fear of burglary is high.[45] In fact the rate of burglaries depends very much on where in the country a person lives, their age, and lifestyle.[46] Also, as just mentioned, the number of burglaries has dramatically fallen in recent years. ←1 (p.586)

5.2 WHY IS BURGLARY AN OFFENCE?

Burglaries have a profound effect on the victims: both emotionally[47] and financially.[48]

This may demonstrate why victims regard burglary as a serious crime, but what is it that distinguishes burglary from theft?[49] And why should it be burglary to enter as a trespasser intending to steal, even if the defendant does not actually steal? It should be recalled that simple trespass is not a criminal offence, only a civil wrong.[50] Should the law regard the intent of the defendant as sufficient to transform a civil wrong into a serious criminal offence?

Here are some of the explanations for the offence:

(1) **Burglary as aggravated theft** In the same way that robbery can be classified as theft plus the use of force, burglary can be regarded as theft plus entry as a trespasser. The analogy is not exact because the force (in robbery) is itself a crime, while the aggravating factor in burglary (entering as a trespasser) is only a civil wrong. More significantly, although this explanation may be effective as an explanation of the section 9(1)(b) offence, it is less effective as an explanation of the section 9(1)(a) offence which does not require a theft actually to be committed.

(2) **Violation of the victim's private home** The wrong of burglary can be seen as the violation of the victim's home.[51] Many people's sense of identity is tied up with their

---

[42] European Commission (2013). [43] Office for National Statistics (2015a).
[44] *Ibid.* [45] *Ibid.* [46] *Ibid.*
[47] In one study Maguire and Kynch (2000) found that 20 per cent of victims were very much affected and 84 per cent suffered some kind of an emotional reaction. Also, 13 per cent reported difficulty sleeping.
[48] Tarling and Davison (2000).
[49] The maximum sentence for burglary is ten years; it is seven years for theft.
[50] There are some forms of trespass which can be criminal. These tend to be linked to public order offences, where a large group of people commit trespass (e.g. Criminal Justice and Public Order Act 1994, ss 61, 68, and 69).
[51] Maguire and Bennett (1982: 614).

home as a place of security and a private space. Most people would not feel deeply distressed if their garden sheds were broken into, but would if their homes were.[52] Homes are meant to be places of haven from the rigours of the outside world and so to have one's safe place invaded can be particularly disturbing.

(3) **Increased likelihood of harm** Burglary can be regarded as particularly serious for society because it is a form of theft which is particularly likely to lead to violence.[53] Quite simply, if a householder interrupts a burglary there is more likely to be violence on one side or the other than where a person discovers his pocket is being picked in a public place.

FURTHER READING

Anon (1951) 'A Rationale of the Law of Burglary' *Colorado Law Review* 51: 1009.

Budd, T. (1999) *Burglary of Domestic Dwellings* (London: Home Office).

Mawby, R. (2001) *Burglary* (Cullompton: Willan).

Pace, P. (1985) 'Burglarious Trespass' *Criminal Law Review* 716.

Simester, A. and Sullivan, G.R. (2005) 'The Nature and Rationale of Property Offences' in R.A. Duff and S. Green (eds) *Defining Crimes* (Oxford: OUP), 192–4.

Tarling, R. and Davison, T. (2000) *Victims of Domestic Burglary: A Review of the Literature* (London: Victim Support).

---

6 BLACKMAIL THEORY

6.1 THE INCIDENCE OF BLACKMAIL

Blackmail is not a crime which often reaches the courts, and only in the most obvious and serious of cases will the police charge the offence.[54] There were 3,524 recorded blackmail offences in the year 2014/15: a dramatic increase from the 1,497 reported in 2012/13.[55] The recent increase may include threats concerning photographs, including so-called 'revenge porn'.[56] Nowadays if someone has a secret about someone else they are more likely to sell their story to the press than to use it for blackmail. Despite its rarity in the law reports the crime is one that widely captures the imagination as a popular topic for film and books.[57] Lord Lane dramatically declared that 'in the calendar of criminal offences blackmail is one of the ugliest . . . because it involves what really amounts, so often, to attempted murder of the soul.'[58] The offence has also produced an impressive array of academic comment. It is this to which we must now turn.

---

[52] In *Brewster* [1998] 1 Cr App R 220, 225–7 Lord Bingham explained that the psychological harms to victims should be taken into account when sentencing.

[53] Cook and Ludwig (2002) argue that higher rates of gun possession among householders do not mean there are lower rates of burglary.

[54] Coarse (1988: 676) claims that the English law was deliberately drafted widely in order to leave prosecutors with a discretion to decide whether to prosecute. See also Lindgren (1989a).

[55] Office for National Statistics (2013).

[56] Criminal Justice and Court Act 2015, ss 33–35 create a new offence of disclosing private sexual photographs and films with intent to cause distress.

[57] McLaren (2002) provides a modern history of blackmail.

[58] Lord Lane in *R v Hadjou* (1989) 11 Cr App R (S) 29 (CA).

6.2 WHY IS BLACKMAIL A CRIME?

The paradox of blackmail

If Alan tells Samantha: 'I am planning to tell your husband that you have been committing adultery', this is not a criminal offence. If Alan says to Samantha: 'Would you like to give me £100?', this is not an offence. But if he says: 'I am going to tell your husband that you have been committing adultery. Would you like to give me £100?', this is an offence. Why should the combination of a threat which in itself is not an offence and a request which in itself is not an offence constitute a crime? In essence blackmail involves a threat to do a completely lawful activity. This then is the paradox of blackmail.

Some possible resolutions of the paradox

The resolution of this conflict has puzzled many commentators. Before we describe their solutions it should be admitted that the difficulty with some, if not all, of the theories is that under them some conduct which is blackmail in the eyes of the law is not explained by the theory, and some conduct which is not blackmail ought to be under the particular theory:[59] ←2 (p.595)

(1) The wrong of blackmail is the manipulation of the mind of the victim. An analogy could be drawn between obtaining property by deception and obtaining property by blackmail: both involve the acquisition of property through invalid coercion[60] of the victim. Leo Katz[61] suggests that blackmail is analogous to robbery: it is all about taking property from the victim using immoral means. The difficulty with these theories is that companies use all sorts of means to acquire property from people, for example through manipulative advertising and misleading claims for products, but these, even if regarded as immoral, are not normally criminal.[62]

(2) The wrong of blackmail is causing the victim to fear. Under this theory blackmail is seen as analogous to an assault. The threat in blackmail is to cause the victim serious emotional harm. The difficulty with this theory is that causing someone emotional harm (e.g. by ending a relationship) is not normally criminal, even if one is acting immorally in so doing.

(3) The offence could be seen as a means of protecting privacy.[63] Supporters of this view vigorously deny that one has a right to reveal private information.[64] Michael Gorr bases his explanation of the wrong of blackmail on the argument that it is wrong to reveal personal information.[65] The difficulty with this is that the moral principle is contestable. If you discover your best friend's boyfriend is cheating on her is it morally wrong to tell her?

(4) James Lindgren has suggested that the wrong in blackmail can be identified as the wrong to a third party.[66] His point can be made clearer by considering this hypothetical scenario. Anne is bringing a legal action against Bob. Cath has a document which would enable Bob to win the case. Cath tells Anne that she will destroy the document if Anne pays her some money. Here Cath is wronging Bob. She is using his legal rights to make a gain for herself.[67] The difficulty with this it that it runs counter to the common understanding that blackmail is very much a crime against the person who is threatened. Also other forms of blackmail will not necessarily involve a third party (e.g. 'I will publish nude photographs of you on the internet').[68]

---

[59] Lindgren (1989). [60] Lamond (1996). [61] Katz (1993). [62] Block and McGee (1999).
[63] Alldridge (1993b). [64] Scalise (2000). [65] Gorr (1992). [66] Lindgren (1993a).
[67] J. Brown (1993) argues that blackmail involves a kind of 'private justice'.
[68] See Rosenberg (2008), who sees the harm being to those whom the blackmail victim goes on to deal with.

(5) It could be argued that a blackmailer who suggests that he or she will keep quiet about some wrong if he or she is paid thereby becomes complicit in this way.[69] This is a persuasive explanation of some forms of blackmail, especially where the blackmailer is promising not to tell the police about a crime which the victim has committed. However, blackmail may not involve the revelation of an evil. If Jeffrey (who used to be a well-known politician) moves to a new town and wishes to keep his identity secret, and Margaret threatens to reveal his identity unless money is paid, it is hard to see what the evil is in which Margaret is complicit.

(6) George Fletcher sees the notion of domination as being at the heart of blackmail. The blackmailer manages to get in a position of great power over the victim, and what makes the offence serious is that that domination can continue for ever.[70] He suggests that blackmail can be seen as a form of moral slavery. This theory works less well where there has been a single incidence of blackmail (e.g. the defendant destroys the incriminating photographs after the victim has paid the requested sum and so has no hold over the victim).

(7) Mitchell Berman[71] proposes 'the evidentiary explanation of blackmail'. He argues that society may criminalize conduct that tends both to cause harm and to be undertaken with wrongful motives. We can assume that the revelation of private material for gain is done for morally unacceptable motives because if there were good motives the defendant would keep silent or reveal the information for free. What is being punished, then, is not the act of blackmail itself, but rather the morally unacceptable motive that normally undermines it. The danger with this argument is that there are all kinds of wrongly motivated conduct which are liable to cause harm but which we do not render illegal (e.g. adultery, lying).

(8) Some commentators argue that blackmail produces harmful results to society.[72] The victim may have to turn to crime to meet the demands of the blackmailer.[73] Imagine what a society which had no blackmail law might be like:[74] people would undertake intrusive investigations into the private life of others in the hope of making money from them.[75] But it has been argued that all kinds of things can lead to harmful effects. Fattening foods cause harm to people in society, but we do not outlaw them.[76]

(9) Scott Altman suggests that in fact, although no one of these theories can explain the present law on blackmail, together they provide a 'patchwork' explanation of the offence.[77]

Some commentators take the view that the difficulties in specifying the wrong of blackmail indicate that there is no good reason justifying the offence, and it should be legalized.[78]

In the following passage, Grant Lamond offers his reasons for the offence:

G. Lamond, 'Coercion, Threats and Blackmail' in A. Smith and A. Simester (eds) *Harm and Culpability* (Oxford: OUP, 1996), 230–4

The puzzle of blackmail, it will be recalled, rests in the impermissibility of demanding something in exchange for abstaining from what would otherwise be a permissible action. It will be apparent by now that an understanding of blackmail requires an appreciation of the normative role played by reasons for action. I will begin this section by drawing some

---

[69] See the discussion in Altman (1993: 1665).   [70] Fletcher (1993).   [71] Berman (1998).
[72] Murphy (1980); Hardin (1993).   [73] Epstein (1983: 564); Shavell (1993: 1092).
[74] Gordon (1993).   [75] Isenbergh (1993: 1911–15); Shavell (1993: 1092); DeLong (1993).
[76] Block (2000: 351).   [77] Altman (1993).   [78] Block (2000).

preliminary distinctions between the kinds of threats amounting to blackmail before going on to consider the nature of the wrong involved in the offence. As I indicated in the introduction, the discussion will range freely over actions which are immoral for the same reason as blackmail threats are criminal. Not all of these cases would, of course, be appropriate for criminalization. I will, in concluding, turn to the question of criminalization, and offer some observations on the compatibility of blackmail with the harm principle.

Blackmail threats can be divided into three categories. The first covers threats of actions which are impermissible *per se* (i.e., irrespective of the agent's reasons), such as physical violence, the destruction of property, and the publication of defamatory information. The second involves threats to perform actions which the maker is already duty-bound (to someone other than the recipient) to perform. A public official may, for example, threaten to revoke a licence where she is aware that conditions requiring revocation have already been fulfilled. Or an opposing party's witness in a civil suit may threaten to give her evidence truthfully unless she is bought off. Or an individual may threaten to report a crime committed against a third party unless her demand is satisfied. Thirdly, there is the category of threats where the action is permissible but not mandatory: the maker of the threat is not bound to take the action but may do so. This would cover cases such as threats to disclose having seen a person in a public place at a certain time, or to foreclose a mortgage which is in default, or to take one's business elsewhere.

The first two categories of blackmail threats are often regarded as unproblematic. The first category certainly is: it is clearly wrong to intend to commit an independent wrong against the recipient unless a demand is met. But the second category is itself puzzling. Why is the recipient of a blackmail demand regarded as the victim when the maker of the demand threatens to fulfil a duty to a third party, thereby proposing *not* to fulfil her duty if the demand is met? In many cases the recipient is better off for not having his licence revoked, or the testimony given, or the crime reported, and would prefer to do as demanded rather than see the duty to the third party discharged. I will return to this issue below. But it is the third category which is generally regarded as the genuinely puzzling one, for how can it be impermissible to threaten what it is permissible to do?

The first step towards elucidating the nature of blackmail is to appreciate that the actions proposed in the third category are not in fact permissible, because the permissibility of actions rests as much on the reasons her taking them as in their consequences. There is, for instance, nothing *per se* wrong in playing music at a reasonable volume or mowing the lawn on a weekend morning, even though a neighbour finds these activities annoying. Nor is there anything wrong in engaging in commercial competition with another, even if one knows that this will drive the competitor out of business. But to do these things *in order* to bring about the unwelcome effects upon another *is* impermissible. To undertake the actions for that reason is to adopt a course of conduct aimed at diminishing another's well-being rather than at pursuing some acceptable goal. The idea that there is a 'puzzle' of blackmail, therefore, rests on too limited a view of which actions are impermissible.

What is involved in blackmail (and in threats generally) is the intrinsic significance of actions—the fact that there are reasons for taking (or refraining from) an action other than the consequences it will bring about. To those with an instrumentalist or consequentialist cast of mind such reasons can seem inexplicable. But they are a pervasive feature of our lives: they account for why it is important not only that my children are cared for, but that they are cared for *by me*. The reasons for which we adopt a course of action are a constitutive part of the action—part of its internal aspect. It is not merely intentions which can contribute to the description under which an action is taken, it is also the reasons for so intending.

Many impermissible actions, of course, lie beyond legal regulation. There are limits to what can be rightly or practically regulated by law. Many immoralities, such as certain types of lies, are not the appropriate concern of the law. In addition, it is generally impractical for the law to adopt regulatory categories other than those based on the consequences of conduct and/or awareness of those consequences, rather than the reasons for bringing them about. Thus if an action is not sufficiently serious in its actual or potential consequences to warrant legal redress, it will be unusual for the actor's reasons to alter this assessment. This explains why many of the threatened actions involved in blackmail are not themselves subject to legal sanction, despite their impermissibility.

The wrong of blackmail, however, does not rest simply in the fact that what is threatened is impermissible. Instead it relates to the way in which the prospect of this action is used by the dominant party against the victim. Blackmail involves the attempt to obtain some advantage from the victim, whether in the form of financial advancement, sexual intimacy, or control over the victim's conduct. The dominant party thus seeks to secure an advantage which it is permissible to enjoy only with the victim's consent. It is the effect of such threats upon the validity of the consent so induced which is the key to understanding blackmail.

Consenting is a complex normative activity involving the manifestation of an intention to alter (or permit the alteration) of a normative situation. But a consent is effective only where it is the *valid* exercise of a normative power. Broadly speaking, a normative power exists where there are reasons for a person to be able to bring about an alteration in her own (and/or others') normative situation when she intends to do so. A person's normative situation is the set of her rights, duties, privileges, and immunities. Promises, for example, alter the promisor's normative situation by putting her under a duty to the promisee; the same act alters the promisee's normative situation by conferring on him a right to the performance of the promised act. Consent is a common way of granting permissions and transferring rights. There are a variety of reasons which justify normative powers, but a particularly important reason is that it enables individuals to exercise a degree of control over certain states of affairs. In some cases, such as the possession of personal property, the value of enjoying such control is regarded as outweighing the possibility of that control being used unwisely or incorrectly. In other cases the value of an activity is constituted by its being controlled by the participant: sexual intimacy, for example, has value only when participation is both willing and motivated for a particular range of reasons.

Whether a consent is valid depends upon whether the act manifesting the intention to consent is effective in those circumstances to bring about the normative change. One must distinguish, therefore, between the fact that a person intended to consent and the question whether it was valid. Whether a consent induced by a threat is valid is a matter of whether the circumstances are compatible with the purposes for which the power exists, *viz.* enabling the individual to control that state of affairs.

This is sometimes thought to be a matter of whether the consent is 'voluntary' or not, but such an approach does little more than restate the problem. It is of course a useful test where 'involuntariness' refers to physical or psychological compulsion: as consent is an intentional action it cannot he produced by physical compulsion, and it is unlikely that anything other than a fully intentional action would suffice, thereby ruling out psychological compulsion. But as most threats do not produce psychological compulsion this is beside the point. On the other hand, it is incorrect to say that consent must be voluntary in order to be valid if it suggests that the validity turns on the *degree* of pressure (either psychological or factual) under which the party acts. A person facing a hard choice, for example on the brink of bankruptcy, may be under immense pressure, but this does not in itself vitiate any transactions entered in those circumstances. Similarly, the fact that a country defeated in a war has no alternative but to surrender does not of itself affect the validity of that surrender. If 'voluntary' is not used to refer to compulsion, nor to the degree of pressure under which a person acts, it seems merely to describe those circumstances in which a consent will be effective in bringing about the purported normative consequences.

Where a party's consent is secured through his being presented with the choice of avoiding an impermissible action, that consent does not serve the purpose of allowing that party to control a state of affairs. Prima facie, therefore, such a consent is defective. There may be countervailing reasons in some cases (or classes of cases) which override this, but otherwise the consent will be invalid. This point is not limited to coercive threats: it also explains the (prima facie) invalidity of consents induced through (i) *offers* not to perform actions which are impermissible *per se* (i.e., irrespective of the offeror's reasons), and (ii) conditional *warnings* that an impermissible action will be taken if the recipient does not consent to something.

A coercive threat, I have argued, involves the maker of the threat committing herself to bringing about an unwelcome consequence because that consequence is unwelcome to the recipient. It follows that unless the threat is justifiable (or unless there are overriding countervailing reasons), any consent it induces is defective. The harm, then, which is involved in the crime of blackmail is the non-consensual obtaining of whatever is demanded from the victim. This explains why blackmail has traditionally been treated as a property crime and its analogues have been located with sexual offences and offences against the person.

QUESTIONS

1. Why should it be blackmail only if the defendant makes an economic gain or another suffers an economic loss? Should it not be blackmail if the defendant threatens to reveal a secret unless the victim takes his or her clothes off?

2. If the victim of blackmail has chosen not to seek the protection of the police before giving in to the threat, should he or she be protected by the criminal law?

3. Is it possible to distinguish these two cases:

   (a) Jane says to Tom: 'Unless you pay me £100 I will tell your employer about your criminal past'.

   (b) Jill says to Tim: 'I will give you £100 if you confess to your employer about your criminal past'?

FURTHER READING

Altman, S. (1993) 'A Patchwork Theory of Blackmail' *University of Pennsylvania Law Review* 141: 1639.

Berman, M. (1998) 'The Evidentiary Theory of Blackmail: Taking Motives Seriously' *University of Chicago Law Review* 65: 795.

Block, W. (2000) 'Threats, Blackmail, Extortion and Robbery and Other Bad Things' *Tulsa Law Journal* 35: 333.

Epstein, R. (1983) 'Blackmail, Inc' *University of Chicago Law Review* 50: 553.

Fletcher, G. (1993) 'Blackmail: The Paradigmatic Crime' *University of Pennsylvania Law Review* 141: 1617.

Gorr, M. (1992) 'Liberalism and the Paradox of Blackmail' *Philosophy and Public Affairs* 21: 43.

Katz, L. (1993) 'Blackmail and Other Forms of Arm-Twisting' *University of Pennsylvania Law Review* 141: 1567.

Lamond, G. (1996) 'Coercion, Threats and the Puzzle of Blackmail' in A.P. Simester and A.T.H. Smith (eds) *Harm and Culpability* (Oxford: OUP).

Robinson, P., Cahill, M., and Bartels, D. (2010) 'Competing Theories of Blackmail: An Empirical Research Critique of Criminal Law Theory' *Texas Law Review* 89: 291.

7 CONCLUDING THOUGHTS

While the offences of burglary and blackmail are usually regarded as property offences, it is their potential psychological impact on victims which is an important part of what makes them particularly serious. As we have seen, to many victims of burglary it is the violation of the home which is as significant, if not more so, than the loss of property. Further, with blackmail, it is the emotional turmoil caused which makes it a particularly unpleasant crime. The legal difficulties in defining these offences is in drawing the line between what are legitimate requests and what becomes a threat of blackmail; and between a non-criminal trespass and the offence of burglary.

CRIMINAL DAMAGE

PART I: THE LAW ON CRIMINAL DAMAGE

Four criminal damage offences are found in the Criminal Damage Act 1971: basic criminal damage, arson, aggravated criminal damage, and aggravated arson.[1] There is also an offence of racially aggravated criminal damage.

---

[1] There are also offences of threatening to damage property (Criminal Damage Act 1971, s. 2, explained in *Cakmak* [2002] Crim LR 581; *Ankerson* [2015] EWCA Crim 549) and possessing property with intent to cause criminal damage to another (Criminal Damage Act 1971, s. 3). There are specific offences involving damage to property under various pieces of legislation (e.g. causing an explosion likely to endanger life or to cause serious damage to property (Explosive Substances Act 1883) or placing wood on railway lines (Malicious Damage Act 1861, s. 2)).

1 BASIC CRIMINAL DAMAGE

> **DEFINITION**
>
> The *actus reus* is the destruction of or damage to property belonging to another without lawful excuse.
>
> The *mens rea* is that the defendant intended or was reckless (a) that his or her action would damage or destroy property and (b) that that property belonged to another.

Section 1 of the Criminal Damage Act 1971 states:

> (1) A person who without lawful excuse destroys or damages any property belonging to another intending to destroy or damage any such property or being reckless as to whether any such property would be destroyed or damaged shall be guilty of an offence.

The maximum punishment is ten years' imprisonment.[2] The offence contains the following elements:

1.1 DAMAGE

The statute uses the term 'destroy or damage'. The term 'destruction' indicates that following the acts of the defendant the item no longer exists. The term 'damage' therefore suggests that the acts have affected the property, but fall short of destruction. The idea of damage involves either:

(1) a reduction in the value of the item; or

(2) a reduction in the usefulness of the item.

Either of these will do. Denting the door of a car may not affect the car's usefulness, but it will affect the value of the car and so amount to damage. Removing a sandbag from a wall of sandbags may not affect the value of the sandbags but it will impair their usefulness and so will be damage. An act can constitute damage even if there is no visible effect. If a computer disk had a program removed this could constitute damage,[3] even though such damage would not be visible to the naked eye. There are a few issues on the meaning of damage over which there is some dispute:

(1) Is minimal damage excluded from the concept? The cases have not been consistent. In *A (A Juvenile) v R*[4] spitting on a police officer's raincoat was held not to amount to damage. It was argued that by simply wiping with a cloth the coat could be returned to its former state and therefore this could not constitute damage. However, other cases seem to take a broader view. Trampling grass on a field was regarded as damaging it[5] and graffiti on a cell wall

---

[2] Criminal Damage Act 1971, s. 4.

[3] *Cox v Riley* (1986) 83 Cr App R 54; *Whiteley* (1991) 93 Cr App R 25, although it should be noted that the Computer Misuse Act 1990 now deals with these offences.

[4] [1978] Crim LR 689.   [5] *Gayford v Chouler* [1898] 1 QB 316.

which could be removed easily with water was damage.[6] Of course, much depends on the nature of the property: scratching a painting is likely to be regarded as damage, but scratching a scaffolding pole may well not be.[7]

(2) Is adding to property damaging it?[8] Again, the courts have not taken a consistent approach. In *Lloyd v DPP*[9] and *Drake v DPP*[10] it was held that putting a wheel clamp on a car did not constitute criminal damage because it did not affect the integrity of the car; rather something is added to the car. However, these cases are controversial. It could be argued that the clamping of the car severely affects its usefulness. Contrast *Hardman v Chief Constable of Avon and Somerset Constabulary*[11] where it was confirmed that painting on a pavement was damage, although such painting did not infringe the 'integrity' of the pavement. Similarly, dumping rubbish on someone's land has been held to damage the land.[12]

(3) How significant is the opinion of the owner of property in deciding whether there was damage? While Lawrence was away on holiday Carol re-wallpapered his bedroom without his permission. If when Lawrence returned he was thrilled with the work one would certainly not say the room was damaged. However, if Lawrence was horrified could he claim that it was damaged? There is no case law directly addressing this issue, but it is interesting to note that the defendant's whitewashing over a National Front slogan that a third party had painted on the victim's property was not regarded as damage.[13]

1.2 PROPERTY

This is defined in section 10 of the Act:

> (1) In this Act 'property' means property of a tangible nature, whether real or personal, including money and—
>
> (a) including wild creatures which have been tamed or are ordinarily kept in captivity, and any other wild creatures or their carcasses if, but only if, they have been reduced into possession which has not been lost or abandoned or are in the course of being reduced into possession; but
>
> (b) not including mushrooms growing wild on any land or flowers, fruit or foliage of a plant growing wild on any land.
>
> For the purposes of this subsection 'mushroom' includes any fungus and 'plant' includes any shrub or tree.

The notion of property here is very similar to the notion of property in theft. However, property does not have the same meaning in both offences. For example, land can be damaged (e.g. by pollution), even though it cannot be stolen. By contrast intangible property, such as patents and copyrights, can be stolen, but not damaged.

---

[6] *Roe v Kingerlee* [1986] Crim LR 735.   [7] *Morphitis v Salmon* [1990] Crim LR 48.

[8] It is generally accepted that removing something from property (e.g. taking out an integral part of a machine so that it does not work) is damaging it (*Tacey* (1821) Russ & Ry 452; *Morphitis v Salmon* [1990] Crim LR 48).

[9] [1992] 1 All ER 982.   [10] [1994] RTR 411.   [11] [1986] Crim LR 330.

[12] *Henderson* (DC, 29 November 1984).   [13] *Fancy* [1980] Crim LR 171.

1.3 BELONGING TO ANOTHER

It should be stressed that it is not a criminal offence to damage your own property. →1 (p.622) The Act makes it quite clear that it is an offence under section 1 only to damage property which 'belongs to another'. However, it is an offence to damage your own property if the offence is one contrary to section 1(2) (see Section 3).

Section 10 states:

> (2) Property shall be treated for the purposes of this Act as belonging to any person—
>   (a) having the custody or control of it;
>   (b) having in it any proprietary right or interest (not being an equitable interest arising only from an agreement to transfer or grant an interest); or
>   (c) having a charge on it.
> (3) Where property is subject to a trust, the person to whom it belongs shall be so treated as including any person having a right to enforce the trust.
> (4) Property of a corporation sole shall be so treated as belonging to the corporation notwithstanding a vacancy in the corporation.

1.4 *MENS REA*

The *mens rea* for the offence is set out in section 1(1): it must be shown that the defendant intended or was reckless as to the damaging of property. The meaning of 'recklessness' was discussed in Chapter 3. It requires proof that the defendant foresaw that his or her act would damage property. This is a subjective test. So the man who tripped on his shoelaces in a museum in Cambridge and fell into vases worth hundreds of thousands of pounds, breaking them, was not prosecuted for criminal damage.[14] It should be noted that the *mens rea* applies to the damage *and* the fact that it belongs to another. This is most relevant in relation to intentional damage: a person who intentionally damages property believing it to be their own does not thereby intentionally damage property belonging to another.

In *Seray-Wurie v DPP*[15] a man wrote on some signs. He intended to write on the signs, but did not realize that doing so would constitute damage in the eyes of the law. His conviction was upheld because he intended to do the acts and produce the result, which was in the eyes of the law damage. The fact that he did not realize that the law would describe what he had done as damage was irrelevant.

1.5 DEFENCES

In addition to the general defences[16] (e.g. duress) there are some specific defences to criminal damage found in the Act. In section 5 a defendant has a lawful excuse:

> (2) . . .
>   (a) if at the time of the act or acts alleged to constitute the offence he believed that the person or persons whom he believed to be entitled to consent to the destruction of or

---

[14] BBC News Online (2006d).   [15] [2012] EWHC 208 (Admin).   [16] For which, see Chapter 12.

damage to the property in question had so consented, or would have so consented to it if he or they had known of the destruction or damage and its circumstances; or

(b) if he destroyed or damaged or threatened to destroy or damage the property in question . . . in order to protect property belonging to himself or another or a right or interest in property which was or which he believed to be vested in himself or another, and at the time of the act or acts alleged to constitute the offence he believed—

　　(i)　that the property, right or interest was in immediate need of protection; and

　　(ii)　that the means of protection adopted or proposed to be adopted were or would be reasonable having regard to all the circumstances.

(3) For the purpose of this section it is immaterial whether a belief is justified or not if it is honestly held.

(4) For the purposes of subsection (2) above a right or interest in property includes any right or privilege in or over land, whether created by grant, licence or otherwise.[17]

In brief, there is a defence for a defendant who honestly[18] believes that the victim was consenting or would consent to the damage.[19] It is also a defence to damage property in order to protect your own or another's property.[20] It is enough if you act because you believe that you were protecting the property,[21] even if in fact your property was not at risk or was not your own.[22] However, subsection (2)(b)(i) stresses that it must be shown that the defendant believed that property was in immediate need of protection and subsection (2)(b)(ii) that the protection would be reasonable in all the circumstances.[23] The defence in section 5(2) is, therefore, highly subjective: what matters is whether the defendant believed the actions were reasonable to protect property. Of course the more outrageous the defendant's alleged belief, the less likely the court is to believe they genuinely held the belief.[24]

The exact interpretation of these provisions is complex and was considered in the following case, which also summarizes the effect of the earlier decision of *Hunt*:[25]

R v Hill and Hall
(1989) 89 Cr App R 74 (CA)

Valerie Hill and Jennifer Hall were charged under section 3 of the Criminal Damage Act 1971 with having an article intending without lawful excuse to use it to destroy or

---

[17] See *Chamberlain v Lindon* [1998] 1 WLR 1252, where the defendant destroyed property to protect a right of way, showing the significance of subs. (4).

[18] As subs. (3) makes clear, the belief does not have to be reasonable. According to *Jaggard v Dickinson* [1980] 3 All ER 716 (DC) a defendant who has a drunken belief that the owner is consenting to the damage has a defence. However, the decision was doubted in *Magee v CPS* [2014] EWHC 4089 (Admin).

[19] This includes where the defendant believes X is the owner and consents, even though X is not the owner. But in *Blake v DPP* [1993] Crim LR 586 (DC) the Divisional Court rejected the defendant's argument that he believed God owned the property and had consented to the damage. Perhaps the best explanation was that the defendant did not believe that God was *in the eyes of the law* the owner.

[20] Section 5(2)(b) does not apply if the defendant is acting to protect a person and not property (*Baker and Wilkins* [1997] Crim LR 497).

[21] Property here is widely defined and can include an interest in property (e.g. a right of way) (*Chamberlain v Lindon* [1998] 1 WLR 1252).

[22] The jury is not therefore required to assess the legitimacy of the defendant's belief (*Jones* [2006] UKHL 16).

[23] *Unsworth v DPP* [2010] EWHC 3037 (Admin).　　　[24] *Ibid.*　　　[25] (1978) 66 Cr App R 105.

damage property belonging to another. They sought to rely on a defence under section 5 that they had a lawful excuse in that they were acting to protect property belonging to another. They were found in possession of a hacksaw blade, with which they intended to cut part of the perimeter fence of a United States naval facility in England. They were acting as part of a campaign organized by the Campaign for Nuclear Disarmament aimed at persuading the UK government to abandon nuclear weapons. They claimed that to do so would protect their and their neighbours' property.

Lord Lane CJ

The [trial judge], as I have already indicated, directed the jury to convict on two bases. The first basis was this, that what the applicant did or proposed to do could not, viewed objectively, be said to have been done to protect her own or anyone else's property under section 5(2)(b) which I have just read. It is simply, he concluded, part of a political campaign aimed at drawing attention to the base and to the risks as she described them raised by the presence of the base in Pembrokeshire. It aimed further at having the base removed. He came to the conclusion that the causative relationship between the acts which she intended to perform and the alleged protection was so tenuous, so nebulous, that the acts could not be said to be done to protect viewed objectively.

The second ground was with reference to the provision that the lawful excuse must be based upon an immediate need for protection. In each case the judge came to the same conclusion that on the applicant's own evidence the applicant could not be said to have believed under the provisions of section 5(2)(b)(i) that the property was in immediate need of protection.

. . .

The judge in each case relied upon a decision of this Court in *Hunt* (1978) 66 Cr App R 105 . . . We also have before us a more recent decision of this Court in *Ashford and Smith* (unreported) decided on May 26, 1988, in which very similar considerations were raised to those which exist in the present case. It also has the advantage of having set out the material findings of the Court in *Hunt* which were delivered by Roskill LJ. I am referring to p 4 of the transcript in *Ashford and Smith*, and it will help to set out the basis of the decision not only in *Ashford and Smith* but also in *Hunt* if I read the passage. It runs as follows:

> 'The judge relied very largely upon the decision of this Court in *Hunt* (1978) 66 Cr App R 105. That was a case in which the appellant set fire to a guest room in an old people's home. He did so, he said, to draw attention to the defective fire alarm system. He was charged with arson, contrary to section 1(1) of the Criminal Damage Act 1971. He sought to set up the statutory defence under section 5(2) by claiming to have had a lawful excuse in doing what he did and that he was not reckless whether any such property would be destroyed. The trial judge withdrew the defence of lawful excuse from the jury and left the issue of recklessness for them to determine. The jury by a majority verdict convicted the appellant. On appeal, held, that, applying the objective test, the trial judge had ruled correctly because what the appellant had done was not an act which in itself did protect or was capable of protecting property; but in order to draw attention to what in his view was an immediate need for protection by repairing the alarm system; thus the statutory defence under section 5(2) of the Act was not open to him; accordingly, the appeal would be dismissed.'

Giving the judgment of the Court Roskill LJ said, at p 108:

> 'Mr Marshall-Andrews' submission can be put thus: if this man honestly believed that that which he did was necessary in order to protect this property from the risk of fire and damage to the old people's home by reason of the absence of a working fire alarm,

he was entitled to set fire to that bed and so to claim the statutory defence accorded by section 5(2). I have said we will assume in his favour that he possessed the requisite honest belief. But in our view the question whether he was entitled to the benefit of the defence turns upon the meaning of the words "in order to protect property belonging to another". It was argued that those words were subjective in concept, just like the words in the latter part of section 5(2)(b) which are subjective. We do not think that is right. The question whether or not a particular act of destruction or damage or threat of destruction or damage was done or made in order to protect property belonging to another must be, on the true construction of the statute, an objective test. Therefore we have to ask ourselves whether, whatever the state of this man's mind and assuming an honest belief, that which he admittedly did was done in order to protect this particular property, namely the old people's home in Hertfordshire. If one formulates the question in that way, in the view of each member of this Court, for the reason Slynn J gave during the argument, it admits of only one answer: this was not done in order to protect property; it was done in order to draw attention to the defective state of the fire alarm. It was not an act which in itself did protect or was capable of protecting property.'

Then the judgment in *Ashford and Smith*, delivered by Glidewell LJ continued as follows:

'In our view that reasoning applies exactly in the present case. *Hunt* is, of course, binding upon us. But even if it were not, we agree with the reasoning contained in it.'

Now it is submitted by Mr Bowyer to us that the decision in *Hunt* and the decision in *Ashford and Smith* were wrong and that the test is a subjective test. In other words the submission is that it was a question of what the applicant believed, and accordingly, it should have been left to the jury as a matter of fact to decide what it was the applicant did believe.

. . .

That leaves us with the fact that we are bound by the decision in *Hunt*. But we add that we think that *Hunt* was correctly decided, for this reason. There are two aspects to this type of question. The first aspect is to decide what it was that the applicant, in this case Valerie Hill, in her own mind thought. The learned judge assumed, and so do we, for the purposes of this decision, that everything she said about her reasoning was true. I have already perhaps given a sufficient outline of what it was she believed to demonstrate what is meant by that. Up to that point the test was subjective. In other words one is examining what is going on in the applicant's mind.

Having done that, the judges in the present cases—and the judge particularly in the case of Valerie Hill—turned to the second aspect of the case, and that is this. He had to decide as a matter of law, which means objectively, whether it could be said that on those facts as believed by the applicant, snipping the strand of the wire, which she intended to do, could amount to something done to protect either the applicant's own home or the homes of her adjacent friends in Pembrokeshire.

He decided, again quite rightly in our view, that that proposed act on her part was far too remote from the eventual aim at which she was targeting her actions to satisfy the test.

It follows therefore, in our view, that the judges in the present two cases were absolutely right to come to the conclusion that they did so far as this aspect of the case is concerned, and to come to that conclusion as a matter of law, having decided the subjective test as the applicants wished them to be decided.

The second half of the question was that of the immediacy of the danger. Here the wording of the Act, one reminds oneself, is as follows: She believed that 'the property . . . was in immediate need of protection.'

> Once again the judge had to determine whether, on the facts as stated by the applicant, there was any evidence on which it could be said that she believed there was a need of protection from immediate danger. In our view that must mean evidence that she believed that immediate action had to be taken to do something which would otherwise be a crime in order to prevent the immediate risk of something worse happening. The answers which I have read in the evidence given by this woman (and the evidence given by the other applicant was very similar) drives this Court to the conclusion, as they drove the respective judges to the conclusion, that there was no evidence on which it could be said that there was that belief.
>
> *Applications refused.*

The decision is controversial because it takes a very narrow interpretation of 'acting in order to protect property'. Rather than seeing this test as being about the motive of the defendant (which might be thought to be the natural meaning of the words) the court interpreted it to be asking whether objectively (but on the facts as understood by the defendant) the act could be said to cause the protection of property.

2 ARSON

Arson is to be regarded as a species of criminal damage. Under section 1(3) of the Criminal Damage Act 1971:

> An offence committed under his section by destroying or damaging property by fire shall be charged as arson.

The requirements of arson are the same as criminal damage, the only difference being that it must be shown that the damage or destruction was caused by fire.[26]

3 AGGRAVATED CRIMINAL DAMAGE

Under section 1(2) of the Criminal Damage Act 1971:

> A person who without lawful excuse destroys or damages any property, whether belonging to himself or another—
>
> (a) intending to destroy or damage any property or being reckless as to whether any property would be destroyed or damaged; and
>
> (b) intending by the destruction or damage to endanger the life of another or being reckless as to whether the life of another would be thereby endangered shall be guilty of an offence.

---

[26] *Drayton* [2006] Crim LR 243. See Cahill (2008) and Kessler Ferzan (2009) for discussion of what is the wrong of arson: is it the endangerment of others or the harm to property?

The offence is punishable by life imprisonment.[27]

The *actus reus* of the offence involves destroying or damaging property without lawful excuse. This is similar to the *actus reus* of the basic offence except that the property does not have to belong to another. So the offence can be committed by the defendant damaging his own property.[28] For example, a defendant who decides to burn down his own house in an attempt to be rehoused, but recklessly forgets that there are still people inside could be guilty of this offence.

There is no need to show that the damage or destruction actually endangers the life of others.[29] In *Sangha*[30] the defendant was convicted of arson contrary to section 1(2)(b) by setting fire to some chairs in a flat with the result that the whole house was burnt down. He was convicted, even though in fact there was (unknown to the defendant) no one in the house, and so there was no risk to people. Because a reasonable person would have thought that there was a risk that people's lives would be endangered he could be convicted.

The *mens rea* is in two parts. First, it must be shown that the defendant intended to destroy or damage the property or was reckless whether or not he or she did so. This is the same as the *mens rea* requirement for simple criminal damage, discussed previously. Second, it must be shown that the defendant intended or was reckless to the endangerment of someone's life as a result of the criminal damage. Intention is to be given its usual meaning here, and recklessness refers to *Cunningham* recklessness. It should be stressed that the endangerment to life must result from the criminal damage. This was established in the following case:

R v Steer
[1988] AC 111 (HL)

Dennis Steer fired several shots at the windows of his former business partner's house. No injuries were caused to those inside. He was charged with damaging property being reckless whether the life of another would be endangered, contrary to section 1(2) of the Criminal Damage Act 1971. The certified question was: 'Whether, upon a true construction of section 1(2)(b) of the Criminal Damage Act 1971, the prosecution are required to prove that the danger to life resulted from the destruction of or damage to the property, or whether it is sufficient for the prosecution to prove that it resulted from the act of the defendant which caused the destruction or damage.'

Lord Bridge of Harwich

Under both limbs of s 1 of the 1971 Act it is the essence of the offence which the section creates that the defendant has destroyed or damaged property. For the purpose of analysis it may be convenient to omit reference to destruction and to concentrate on the references to damage, which was all that was here involved. To be guilty under sub-s (1) the defendant must have intended or been reckless as to the damage to property which he caused. To be guilty under sub-s (2) he must additionally have intended to endanger life or been reckless whether life would be endangered 'by the damage' to property which he caused. This is the context in which the words must be construed and it seems to me impossible to read the words 'by the damage' as meaning 'by the damage or by the act which caused the damage'.

---

[27] Criminal Damage Act 1971, s. 4.   [28] *Merrick* [1995] Crim LR 802.
[29] *Dudley* [1989] Crim LR 57.   [30] [1988] 2 All ER 385.

Moreover, if the language of the statute has the meaning for which the Crown contends, the words 'by the destruction or damage' and 'thereby' in sub-s (2)(b) are mere surplusage. If the Crown's submission is right, the only additional element necessary to convert a sub-s (1) offence into a sub-s (2) offence is an intent to endanger life or recklessness whether life would be endangered simpliciter. It would suffice as a ground for dismissing this appeal if the statute were ambiguous, since any such ambiguity in a criminal statute should be resolved in favour of the defence. But I can find no ambiguity. It seems to me that the meaning for which the respondent contends is the only meaning which the language can bear.

The contrary construction leads to anomalies which Parliament cannot have intended. If A and B both discharge firearms in a public place, being reckless whether life would be endangered, it would be absurd that A, who incidentally causes some trifling damage to property, should be guilty of an offence punishable with life imprisonment, but that B, who causes no damage, should be guilty of no offence. In the same circumstances, if A is merely reckless but B actually intends to endanger life, it is scarcely less absurd that A should be guilty of the graver offence under s 1(2) of the 1971 Act, B of the lesser offence under s 16 of the Firearms Act 1968.

Appeal dismissed.

This case, then, establishes that it must be shown that it is damage to property that endangers the victim's life, rather than, for example, the missile thrown by the defendant.[31] It does not need to be shown that the property which endangers the life of the other is the same as the property which is damaged. An example given in *Attorney-General's Reference (No. 3 of 1992)*[32] was where cutting the rope of a crane (property A) causes a load to fall onto the roof of a car (property B), which endangers life.

3.1 DEFENCES

The defences in section 5 do not apply to section 2: this is not surprising because it is rarely excusable to damage property being aware that doing so will endanger someone's life. However, the offence does use the phrase 'without lawful excuse', which implies the general defences, such as private defence, are available.

4 RACIALLY AGGRAVATED CRIMINAL DAMAGE

Section 30(1) of the Crime and Disorder Act 1998 states:

A person is guilty of an offence under this section if he commits an offence under section 1(1) of the Criminal Damage Act 1971 . . . which is racially or religiously aggravated for the purposes of this section.

The notion of racial or religious aggravation was discussed in Chapter 6.

---

[31] For an application of *Steer*, see *Webster* [1995] 2 All ER 168 (CA) and *Wenton* [2010] EWCA Crim 2361.
[32] (1994) 98 Cr App R 383.

QUESTIONS

1. Ivy places a leaf over part of a nude statue in her local park. At her trial she produces a petition which suggests that nearly 80 per cent of the inhabitants in her town think that the statue is now improved. Has she committed criminal damage? (Do not forget to consider the *mens rea* issues as well as the question of whether or not there is damage.)

For guidance on answering this question, please visit the Online Resource Centre that accompanies this book: www.oxfordtextbooks.co.uk/orc/herringcriminal7e/.

2. Janice is concerned that people are driving too quickly through her village. She puts some glass out in the road next to a sign warning that there is glass on the road. Several cars are not able to stop in time and their tyres are punctured. Has she committed criminal damage?

3. Brian is an organic farmer. His neighbour (Sid) decides to plant genetically modified (GM) crops as part of a government trial. Brian, having carefully researched the issue, believes that material from the GM crops is likely to come over onto his land and 'contaminate' his crops. One night, he sets fire to Sid's GM crops, destroying them. What offences have been committed?

FURTHER READING

Elliot, D. (1997) 'Endangering Life by Destroying or Damaging Property' *Criminal Law Review* 382.

Stalworthy, M. (2000) 'Damage to Crops' *New Law Journal* 150: 728 and 801.

5 COMPUTER CRIME: COMPUTER MISUSE ACT 1990

The Computer Misuse Act 1990 is designed to protect information kept on computers.[33] The term 'computer' is not defined in the Act. No doubt any attempted definition would rapidly become out of date. The courts appear to have taken a broad interpretation of the word 'computer', and it has been held to include electronic personal organizers, boxes attached to televisions which control access to cable television channels,[34] and cash registers.[35] →2 (p.623)

5.1 SECTION 1: UNAUTHORIZED ACCESS TO COMPUTER MATERIAL

This offence is designed to punish people who try to gain access to unauthorized data:

(1) A person is guilty of an offence if—
   (a) he causes a computer to perform any function with intent to secure access to any program or data held in any computer, or to enable any such access to be secured;

---

[33] The Act was amended by the Police and Justice Act 2006. See Fafinski (2008) and MacEwan (2008) for a discussion of the reforms.

[34] *Maxwell-King* [2001] 2 Cr App R (S) 136.

[35] *Attorney-General's Reference (No. 1 of 1991)* [1993] QB 94.

> (b) the access he intends to secure, or to enable to be secured is unauthorised; and
>
> (c) he knows at the time when he causes the computer to perform the function that that is the case.
>
> (2) The intent a person has to have to commit an offence under this section need not be directed at—
>
> (a) any particular program or data;
>
> (b) a program or data of any particular kind; or
>
> (c) a program or data held in any particular computer.

The *actus reus* of the offence is simply causing a computer to 'perform any function'. This could include switching a computer on.[36] It should be emphasized that there is no need to show that the defendant actually reached unauthorized material, only that he or she intended to do so. The *mens rea* requirement can be broken down into three elements:

An intention to secure or enable access to any program or data on any computer

The phrase 'secure access' is narrower than may be at first assumed. Section 17(2) states:

> A person secures access to any program or data held in a computer if by causing a computer to perform any function he—
>
> (a) alters or erases the program or data;
>
> (b) copies or moves it to any storage medium other than that in which it is held or to a different location in the storage medium in which it is held;
>
> (c) uses it; or
>
> (d) has it output from the computer in which it is held (whether by having it displayed or in any other manner);
>
> and references to access to a program or data (and to an intent to secure such access or to enable such access to be secured) shall be read accordingly.

This seems to mean that simply intending to look at unauthorized data on a computer does not infringe section 1. Once seeing the data the defendant must intend to do one of the four things listed in the section with the data, using a computer.[37] It is made clear in section 1(2) of the Computer Misuse Act that there is no need to prove an intent to obtain access to any particular program or data. In other words the offence is committed if a defendant is entering the computer just to see what he or she can find. Further, it does not matter whether the defendant is trying to reach data on the computer he

---

[36] Simply looking at a computer screen would not be enough.

[37] In *Zezev* [2002] EWHC Admin 589 it was held that sending an email that purported to come from one person but in fact came from another would cause a computer to record information that manifestly affected its reliability and therefore did fall within s. 17.

or she is using or attempting to reach data on another computer using his or her own computer.[38]

The intended access to the data must be unauthorized

To be authorized to access data it must be shown that the defendant was either entitled to control access to that data or had been given authority to access the information by a person who was able to control access to it.[39] It may be that a defendant is permitted access to some parts of a computer's database, but this is no defence if he or she is attempting to reach other parts of the database. For example, in *R v Bow Street Metropolitan Stipendiary Magistrate, ex p United States (No. 2)*[40] an employee of a credit card company was allotted certain customers and permitted to access data held about them on her company's computer. She accessed information about other customers. This constituted an offence under section 1 of the Act.

Similarly it may be that a defendant is authorized to access data for one purpose but not another.[41] So if a defendant is permitted access to data only for work purposes, but accesses the data for his or her own reasons then this will be seen as unauthorized access.[42] Further, a person may be entitled to view certain data, but not to amend it. Again, in such a case amending the data could infringe section 1.

The defendant knows that he or she is not authorized to access the program or data

It should be noted that this knowledge is based on a subjective test.

5.2 SECTION 2: UNAUTHORIZED ACCESS WITH INTENT

The offence in section 2 is a more serious one than that in section 1. It requires proof that a defendant committed an offence under section 1 and in addition that he or she intended to commit or facilitate the commission of a serious arrestable offence (e.g. theft).[43]

5.3 SECTION 3: UNAUTHORIZED ACTS

The *actus reus* of this offence, under section 3(1), is 'any unauthorised act in relation to a computer'; the *mens rea* is an intent to do the act and by so doing:

> (2) . . .
>
>   (a) to impair the operation of any computer;
>
>   (b) to prevent or hinder access to any program or data held in any computer;
>
>   (c) to impair the operation of any such program or the reliability of any such data; or
>
>   (d) to enable any of the things mentioned in paragraphs (a) to (c) above to be done.

---

[38] *Attorney-General's Reference (No. 1 of 1991)* [1993] QB 94 (CA).

[39] Computer Misuse Act 1990, s. 17(5).   [40] [2000] 2 AC 216.

[41] *Ellis v DPP (No. 1)* [2001] EWHC Admin 362 confirmed that a person may be authorized to use a computer, but not the program on the computer.

[42] *R v Bow Street Metropolitan Stipendiary Magistrate, ex p United States (No. 2)* [2000] 2 AC 216.

[43] e.g. theft.

It is also necessary to show that the defendant knew that the act was unauthorized. Thus a defendant has a defence if he or she was authorized to modify a program to some extent, but by mistake modified much more than he or she intended.

This section is clearly aimed at people who alter computer data with intent to corrupt a program or alter a database (e.g. by means of a virus).[44] The intent does not need to be directed towards any particular computer or data. As originally drafted the offence required proof that there was modification of data. This was amended because of its failure to convict a defendant whose actions impaired the operation of a computer system, without modifying it. In *DPP v Lennon*[45] the defendant had used a program to send over five million emails to his former employers over a weekend. Initially it was held there was no case to answer because, inter alia, the employers had consented to receive emails. On appeal by the prosecution it was held that although a person with an email address may generally be taken to accept emails, this does not mean they consent to an unlimited number of emails. No indication was given at which point the number of emails become unauthorized, although it was suggested that the court could ask whether the victim would have agreed to receiving that number of emails in advance.

The Serious Crime Act 2015 inserted a new offence in section 3Z of the Computer Misuse Act. This states:

(1) A person is guilty of an offence if—
   (a) the person does any unauthorised act in relation to a computer;
   (b) at the time of doing the act the person knows that it is unauthorised;
   (c) the act causes, or creates a significant risk of, serious damage of a material kind; and
   (d) the person intends by doing the act to cause serious damage of a material kind or is reckless as to whether such damage is caused.

(2) Damage is of a "material kind" for the purposes of this section if it is—
   (a) damage to human welfare in any place;
   (b) damage to the environment of any place;
   (c) damage to the economy of any country; or
   (d) damage to the national security of any country.

This offence is designed to deal with hacking which is intended to cause serious harm. Notably it can be used even if the harm is to occur in another country.

FURTHER READING

Fafinski, S. (2006) 'Access Denied: Computer Misuse in an Era of Technological Change' *Journal of Criminal Law* 70: 424.

Fafinski, S. (2008) 'Computer Misuse: The Implications of the Police and Justice Act 2006' *Journal of Criminal Law* 72: 53.

Law Commission (1989) Report No. 186, *Computer Misuse* (London: HMSO).

MacEwan, N. (2008) 'The Computer Misuse Act 1990: Lessons from Its Past and Predictions for Its Future' *Criminal Law Review* 955.

Wasik, M. (1991) *Crime and the Computer* (Oxford: OUP).

---

[44] Akdeniz (1996).   [45] [2006] EWHC 1201 (Admin).

PART II: THEORETICAL ISSUES ON CRIMINAL DAMAGE

6 CRIMINAL DAMAGE THEORY

We will briefly examine here some issues of particular theoretical interest in relation to criminal damage. Discussion of recklessness can be found in Chapter 3.

6.1 STATISTICS

The Crime Survey for England and Wales (interviewing members of the public) suggested that 4 per cent of all households suffered criminal damage in 2014/15,[46] with some 1.3 million incidents in total.[47]

6.2 WHAT IS SPECIAL ABOUT DAMAGING PROPERTY?

It might be argued that we should have a single offence of wrongful interference with property interests that could cover both theft and criminal damage. However, Simester and Sullivan have argued that criminal damage is different from theft or other offences involving property interests for two reasons. First, it is often linked with offences against the person. They explain that 'many typical instances of criminal damage involve forms of vandalism employing percussive force, fire or explosions, conduct that may well cause alarm and concern even to bystanders lacking any proprietary interest in the property being damaged.'[48] Second, criminal damage such as vandalism can contain an expressive dimension: communicating a contempt for society or the victim.[49]

6.3 SHOULD IT BE AN OFFENCE TO DAMAGE YOUR OWN PROPERTY?

At first it might be assumed that a fundamental aspect of ownership is that one is free to destroy one's own property. Some argue that an artist has creative rights in his or her property even once it has been sold.[50] For example, the American Visual Artists Rights Act 1990 disallows destruction of an original or limited edition and signed work where the artist is of recognized stature and his or her reputation would be harmed.[51] Thus, in *Martin v City of Indianapolis*[52] the artist obtained damages where the city council had purchased his sculpture, but later bulldozed it down in order to develop the land.

---

[46] In 1995 the figure had been 10 per cent (Office for National Statistics 2015a).
[47] Office for National Statistics (2015a).   [48] Simester, Spencer, Sullivan, and Virgo (2013: 536).
[49] *Ibid*.   [50] Halpern (1997).   [51] Discussed in Santilli (1997).
[52] 192 F 3d 608 (7th Cir, 1999).

6.4 THE DEFINITION OF DAMAGE

In our materialistic society the destruction or damaging of property can be seen as positively nihilistic. However, there are, as can be seen in Part I, several situations where it will be unclear whether property has been damaged. ←1 (p.610) One interesting example is graffiti:[53]

M.A. Gomez, 'The Writing on Our Walls: Finding Solutions through Distinguishing Graffiti Art from Graffiti Vandalism' (1993) 26 *University of Michigan Journal of Law Reform* 633 at 634–5, 650–3

Different motivations drive different types of graffiti, and graffiti cannot be understood or controlled without an understanding of the motivations behind its creation. Although they cannot capture fully the entire spectrum of graffiti, two particular classifications encompass most types of graffiti and the motivations behind it. First, 'graffiti art' describes graffiti-type works that exhibit many of the characteristics of pieces normally termed 'high art' or 'folk art.' The more intricate works of graffiti entitled 'pieces' belong in this category because they result from a desire to create artwork. Second, 'graffiti vandalism' describes those mere scrawlings that are motivated by a desire to mark territory, create notoriety, or show one's defiance of the law and society. Graffiti termed 'gang graffiti' or 'tags' belong in this category. These works are done most often without the permission of the property owner and possess few of the qualities of pieces normally deemed 'high art' or 'folk art.' Although graffiti possessing the characteristics of both art and vandalism is difficult to classify under the above scheme, the distinction is useful nonetheless because it recognizes that such works are stimulated by both types of motivations.

. . . From the viewpoint of many of those who consider graffiti to be vandalism, all graffiti is vandalism regardless of a piece's artistic value. For these opponents, there is no room for differentiation between mere scrawls or a mural. Graffiti is ugly, indicative of decay, invites crime and additional graffiti, and is done by criminals who should be punished. Graffiti should be eliminated even when it is on private property or was commissioned. Such a view leaves no room for the preservation of even the more intricate pieces of graffiti recognized as art. Opponents are against any encouragement of, or support for, graffiti and often claim that any write-up of graffiti incidents by the press encourages more vandalism. Opponents fail to appreciate what graffiti represents to the youth culture and what motivates the writer. Their only solution is to outlaw all graffiti and punish all writers.

Those who consider some graffiti to be art often differentiate more carefully between types of graffiti. Graffiti art proponents recognize that some pieces have extraordinary merit and deserve recognition. Proponents recognize that the motivation of many writers is not to deface property intentionally, but rather to express themselves or to gain respect by the only means that are accessible to them.

Graffiti's most ardent proponents often fail to acknowledge, however, that the art form often results in the defacing of property. At the same time, many proponents do recognize that defacing property is wrong. They therefore work to prevent writers from vandalizing public and private property by creating alternative outlets for writers' energies. Such alternatives include work on commissioned property or participation in sponsored exhibitions and programs which hone skills and can help writers find employment or win scholarships.

---

[53] See also I. Edwards (2009).

7 THE THEORY OF COMPUTER CRIMES

Given that the criminal law is generally rather reluctant to protect confidential information, the Computer Misuse Act looks anomalous. Why is it an offence to copy personal information without authority from a computer but not a filing cabinet?[54] There are four particular reasons suggested by the Law Commission[55] why it might be thought that information held on computers needs special protection by the criminal law. First, it is very hard to safeguard information stored on a computer, particularly as the information is often intended to be accessed by a number of authorized people. By contrast information on paper can be kept in a safe or other secure place. Second, the ease of destroying or corrupting data on a computer means it deserves protection, particularly as it is not always possible for the owner of the computer to realize that the data has been looked at. Third, the highly confidential nature of the kind of information kept on computers (often concerning many members of the public) is such that it needs particular protection. Fourth, it may be better to deter people from searching for confidential information because of the temptation to use it for fraudulent purposes once they have found it. Whether these are convincing or not is a matter for debate.[56] ←2 (p.617)

QUESTIONS

1. Do you think graffiti should be regarded as criminal damage or cultural expression?

2. Why are pollution and environmental offences not regarded as criminal damage?

3. Are there any good reasons why the temporary unauthorized use of a computer should be a criminal offence when it is not for other property?

FURTHER READING

All Party Parliamentary Internet Group (2004) *Revision of the Computer Misuse Act* (London: APIG).

Clough, J. (2011) 'Data Theft? Cybercrime and the Increasing Criminalization of Access to Data' *Criminal Law Forum* 22: 145.

Edwards, I. (2009) 'Banksy's Graffiti: A Not-So-Simple Case of Criminal Damage?' *Journal of Criminal Law* 73: 345.

Grabosky, P., Smith, R., and Dempsey, G. (2003) *Electronic Theft* (Cambridge: Cambridge University Press).

Katyal, N. (2001) 'Criminal Law in Cyberspace' *University of Pennsylvania Law Review* 149: 1003.

Walden, J. (2007) *Computer Crimes and Digital Investigations* (Oxford: OUP).

---

[54] See the discussion in Card and Ashworth (2000: 336–8).
[55] Law Commission Report No. 186 (1989). See also Fearon (2004).
[56] See further Essen (2002).

8 CONCLUDING THOUGHTS

This chapter has considered the protection of property interests from damage. It is notable that computers are given special protection in the law. In part this reflects the importance that computers and the information stored upon them has in our modern society. It also reflects their vulnerability to attack through viruses and cyber attacks. The law in this area is fast moving, and it has to be in order to keep up with the advances in technologies and the new interests which need protection and the new ways that computer data can be compromised.

12

DEFENCES

CENTRAL ISSUES

1. Even though the prosecution may have proved the *mens rea* and *actus reus* of the offence, the defendant may still be able to escape conviction if he or she can successfully raise a defence.

2. The defence of private defence is available where a defendant was responding reasonably to an unjust threat from the victim. This defence is also available where the defendant was responding reasonably to what he or she believed was an unjust threat, even if in fact the threat did not exist.

3. In very few cases have defendants successfully raised the defence of necessity, namely that the defendant was acting in a way which was 'the lesser of two evils'.

4. A defence of lawful chastisement can be raised where a parent uses force against a child, but only if the harm done to the child is less than actual bodily harm.

5. Duress is available as a defence to all crimes except murder and attempted murder. It can be used where the defendant responded reasonably to a threat of death or serious harm.

6. There is no general defence of entrapment. So a defendant who complains that she was tricked into committing an offence by an undercover police officer will still be guilty of a crime. However, under the law of evidence, bad police conduct may lead to some evidence being inadmissible at a trial.

7. Automatism is available as a defence where the defendant lost complete control over his or her conduct as a result of an external factor, in circumstances for which he or she was not responsible.

8. The defence of insanity can be used if the defendant is insane at the time at which he or she committed the offence, or is insane at the time of the trial. The definition of insanity is that the defendant suffered a disease of the mind which meant that he or she did not know what he or she was doing or did not know that what he or she was doing was wrong. Even if found not guilty due to insanity, a defendant can be detained under the civil law.

9. A child under the age of 10 cannot be guilty of a criminal offence.

10. A mistake will only provide a defence if, as a result of the mistake, the defendant lacked the *mens rea* required for the offence.

PART I: THE LAW

Even if the prosecution has been able to prove the *actus reus* and *mens rea* of an offence all is not lost for the defendant. He or she may still be able to rely on a defence. For example, even though the defendant is proved to have intentionally caused the victim grievous bodily harm he or she may still be acquitted if he or she was acting under duress. However, there is no straightforward definition of a defence. Criminal lawyers disagree on what should or should not be regarded as a defence, as we shall see in Part II of this chapter. In particular there is dispute whether some claims amount to a defence or in fact to a denial of the *actus reus* or *mens rea*. For example, one of the best known defences in criminal law, self-defence, has been held by the courts in fact to amount to a denial of the *actus reus*. In this chapter a wide definition of defences will be used to include any claim often said to be a defence.

There are also many different ways of classifying the defences, which we will outline in Part II. Not everyone, therefore, will agree with the classification used in this chapter, but one has to be chosen. This section will discuss the defences in the following order: →1 (p.693)

Defences based on the finding that the defendant acted in a permissible way

(1)   private defence;

(2)   necessity;

(3)   chastisement;

(4)   consent.

Defences based on the pressure exerted upon the defendant by another

(5)   duress;

(6)   entrapment;

(7)   superior orders.

Defences based on the defendant's mental condition

(8)   automatism;

(9)   insanity;

(10)   diminished responsibility;

(11)   loss of control;

(12)   children;

(13)   intoxication;

(14)   mistake.

1 PRIVATE DEFENCE AND THE PREVENTION OF CRIME

1.1 THE LEGAL SOURCE OF THE DEFENCE

> **DEFINITION**
>
> The requirements of private defence are:
>
> (1) The defendant was (or believed he or she was) facing a threat from the victim.
>
> (2) The defendant used a level of force against the threat (or the threat as it was believed to be) which was reasonable in the circumstances.

A complete defence is available to those who use force in order to defend themselves or another person from an unjustified attack.[1] Unfortunately there is no agreement over the correct name for this defence. Textbooks have used the terms self-defence, private defence, and lawful defence. Self-defence is probably the phrase most familiar to the person in the street, although it is misleading because the defence also applies if the defendant is protecting someone else from an attack. In this book the term private defence will be used. →2 (p.723)

Further confusion in English law results from the fact that the defence has two separate legal sources:[2]

(1) At common law a person has a defence if he or she is defending himself or another[3] from an attack.

(2) Under section 3 of the Criminal Law Act 1967:

> (1) A person may use such force as is reasonable in the circumstances in the prevention of crime, or in effecting or assisting in the lawful arrest of offenders or suspected offenders or of persons unlawfully at large.
>
> (2) Subsection (1) above shall replace the rules of the common law on the question when force used for a purpose mentioned in the subsection is justified by that purpose.

Fortunately the courts have held that the rules governing common law private defence and section 3 coexist.[4] In other words the legal rules are the same whichever form of the defence is used.[5] Therefore the courts and commentators usually talk about self-defence or private defence without saying whether they are talking about the statutory or common law version.

---

[1] In Part II an argument will be made that it is more accurate to say that self-defence arises when defendants defend themselves from unjustified threats, rather than attacks.

[2] There are also some statutes that provide a defence in a particular context (e.g. the Criminal Damage Act 1971: see Chapter 11).

[3] *Duffy* [1967] 1 QB 63 (CA).

[4] Technically the s. 3 defence is not available where the 'attacker' is not committing a crime (if, e.g., he or she is a child), although self-defence is.

[5] *Cousins* [1982] QB 526.

In section 76 of the Criminal Justice and Immigration Act 2008 Parliament sought to clarify some elements of both defences:[6]

(1) This section applies where in proceedings for an offence—

    (a) an issue arises as to whether a person charged with the offence ("D") is entitled to rely on a defence within subsection (2), and

    (b) the question arises whether the degree of force used by D against a person ("V") was reasonable in the circumstances.

(2) The defences are—

    (a) the common law defence of self-defence;

    (aa) the common law defence of defence of property; and

    (b) the defences provided by section 3(1) of the Criminal Law Act 1967 (c. 58) or section 3(1) of the Criminal Law Act (Northern Ireland) 1967 (c. 18 (N.I.)) (use of force in prevention of crime or making arrest).

(3) The question whether the degree of force used by D was reasonable in the circumstances is to be decided by reference to the circumstances as D believed them to be, and subsections (4) to (8) also apply in connection with deciding that question.

(4) If D claims to have held a particular belief as regards the existence of any circumstances—

    (a) the reasonableness or otherwise of that belief is relevant to the question whether D genuinely held it; but

    (b) if it is determined that D did genuinely hold it, D is entitled to rely on it for the purposes of subsection (3), whether or not—

        (i) it was mistaken, or

        (ii) (if it was mistaken) the mistake was a reasonable one to have made.

(5) But subsection (4)(b) does not enable D to rely on any mistaken belief attributable to intoxication that was voluntarily induced.

(5A) In a householder case, the degree of force used by D is not to be regarded as having been reasonable in the circumstances as D believed them to be if it was grossly disproportionate in those circumstances.

(6) In a case other than a householder case, the degree of force used by D is not to be regarded as having been reasonable in the circumstances as D believed them to be if it was disproportionate in those circumstances.

(6A) In deciding the question mentioned in subsection (3), a possibility that D could have retreated is to be considered (so far as relevant) as a factor to be taken into account, rather than as giving rise to a duty to retreat.

(7) In deciding the question mentioned in subsection (3) the following considerations are to be taken into account (so far as relevant in the circumstances of the case)—

    (a) that a person acting for a legitimate purpose may not be able to weigh to a nicety the exact measure of any necessary action; and

    (b) that evidence of a person's having only done what the person honestly and instinctively thought was necessary for a legitimate purpose constitutes strong evidence that only reasonable action was taken by that person for that purpose.

---

[6] The Crime and Courts Act 2013 made amendments relating to the householder cases.

(8) Subsections (6A) and (7) are not to be read as preventing other matters from being taken into account where they are relevant to deciding the question mentioned in subsection (3).

(8A) For the purposes of this section "a householder case" is a case where—

(a) the defence concerned is the common law defence of self-defence,

(b) the force concerned is force used by D while in or partly in a building, or part of a building, that is a dwelling or is forces accommodation (or is both),

(c) D is not a trespasser at the time the force is used, and

(d) at that time D believed V to be in, or entering, the building or part as a trespasser.

(8B) Where—

(a) a part of a building is a dwelling where D dwells,

(b) another part of the building is a place of work for D or another person who dwells in the first part, and

(c) that other part is internally accessible from the first part,

that other part, and any internal means of access between the two parts, are each treated for the purposes of subsection (8A) as a part of a building that is a dwelling.

(8C) Where—

(a) a part of a building is forces accommodation that is living or sleeping accommodation for D,

(b) another part of the building is a place of work for D or another person for whom the first part is living or sleeping accommodation, and

(c) that other part is internally accessible from the first part,

that other part, and any internal means of access between the two parts, are each treated for the purposes of subsection (8A) as a part of a building that is forces accommodation.

(8D) Subsections (4) and (5) apply for the purposes of subsection (8A)(d) as they apply for the purposes of subsection (3).

(8E) The fact that a person derives title from a trespasser, or has the permission of a trespasser, does not prevent the person from being a trespasser for the purposes of subsection (8A).

(8F) In subsections (8A) to (8C)—

"building" includes a vehicle or vessel, and

"forces accommodation" means service living accommodation for the purposes of Part 3 of the Armed Forces Act 2006 by virtue of section 96(1)(a) or (b) of that Act.

(9) This section, except so far as making different provision for householder cases, is intended to clarify the operation of the existing defences mentioned in subsection (2).

(10) In this section—

(a) "legitimate purpose" means—

(i) the purpose of self-defence under the common law,

(ia) the purpose of defence of property under the common law, or

(ii) the prevention of crime or effecting or assisting in the lawful arrest of persons mentioned in the provisions referred to in subsection (2)(b);

(b) references to self-defence include acting in defence of another person; and

(c) references to the degree of force used are to the type and amount of force used.

The Court of Appeal in *Keane*[7] explained that this section did not change the law but simply stated what the law had previously been.

1.2 TO WHAT CRIMES IS PRIVATE DEFENCE A DEFENCE?

Can a defendant seek to rely on private defence as a response to any charge or only a crime of violence? Although this has been a matter of debate in the past following *DPP v Bayer*[8] and *Morris*,[9] it is clear the defence can be relied upon in relation to any offence. In *Morris*[10] it was held a taxi driver could rely on section 3 of the Criminal Law Act 1967 when he engaged in dangerous driving in order to prevent a passenger running off without paying.[11]

1.3 WHAT NEEDS TO BE SHOWN TO ESTABLISH THE DEFENCE?

The key elements of the defence have been summarized in a notorious case. The defendant shot two young men who were burgling his house. The key issue was whether the question for the jury should have been whether the amount of force used was reasonable by the standards of the ordinary person, or whether it was sufficient to show that the defendant believed the level of force to be reasonable:

R v Martin (Anthony)
[2001] EWCA Crim 2245 (CA)[12]

Anthony Martin shot at two men who had entered his isolated house at night. He had been burgled several times in the past. Both men were wounded and one of the two died from his wounds. Martin was convicted of murder. On appeal his counsel sought to introduce new evidence that the appellant was suffering from a psychiatric condition which was relevant to show (a) Martin was suffering from diminished responsibility at the time of the killing and (b) because of his condition he was more likely genuinely to believe that he was about to be attacked than an ordinary person would be.

Lord Woolf CJ [handed down the following judgment of the court]

The law relating to self-defence

4. There was no dispute that Mr Martin had shot the two men. Mr Martin's defence to the principal offences with which he was charged was that he was acting in self-defence. When this defence is raised, the prosecution has the burden of satisfying the jury so that they are sure that the defendant was not acting in self-defence. A defendant is entitled to use reasonable force to protect himself, others for whom he is responsible and his property: see *Beckford v The Queen* [1988] AC 130.

---

[7] [2010] EWCA Crim 2514.   [8] [2004] Crim LR 663.   [9] [2013] EWCA Crim 436.
[10] *Ibid.*   [11] This would be the offence of making off without payment: Theft Act 1978, s. 3.
[12] [2002] 2 WLR 1.

5. In judging whether the defendant had only used reasonable force, the jury has to take into account all the circumstances, including the situation as the defendant honestly believes it to be at the time, when he was defending himself. It does not matter if the defendant was mistaken in his belief as long as his belief was genuine.

6. Accordingly, the jury could only convict Mr Martin if either they did not believe his evidence that he was acting in self-defence or they thought that Mr Martin had used an unreasonable amount of force. These were issues which were ideally suited to a decision of a jury.

7. As to the first issue, what Mr Martin believed, the jury heard his evidence and they could only reject that evidence if they were satisfied it was untrue. As to the second issue, as to what is a reasonable amount of force, obviously opinions can differ. It cannot be left to a defendant to decide what force it is reasonable to use because this would mean that even if a defendant used disproportionate force but be believed he was acting reasonably he would not be guilty of any offence. It is for this reason that it was for the jury, as the representative of the public, to decide the amount of force which it would be reasonable and the amount of force which it would be unreasonable to use in the circumstances in which they found that Mr Martin believed himself to be in. It is only if the jury are sure that the amount of force which was used was unreasonable that they are entitled to find a defendant guilty if he was acting in self-defence.

8. These features of the defence of self-defence are critical to the outcome of this appeal. They are difficult to criticise and mean that Mr Martin is faced with the fact that the jury must have decided that when he shot the two men, he was either not acting in self-defence or, if he was, he used excessive force.

9. What has been the subject of debate is whether a defendant to a murder charge should be convicted of murder if he was acting in self-defence but used excessive force in self-defence. It is suggested that such a defendant should be regarded as being guilty of manslaughter and not murder. He would not then have to be sentenced to life imprisonment but usually instead to a determinate sentence the length of which would be decided upon by the judge, having regard to the circumstances of the offence. If it is thought that this should be the law then the change would have to be made by Parliament. It was not even suggested on this appeal that it would be open to this court by judicial decision to bring about such a change. However, even in the case of a life sentence for murder the circumstances of the offence are taken into account. The Home Secretary, having considered the recommendations of the trial judge and the Lord Chief Justice of the day, fixes the tariff period, that is the period which has to elapse before a defendant can be recommended for parole by the Parole Board.

. . .

[**Lord Woolf** examined the new psychiatric evidence and continued:]

65. Mr Wolkind [counsel for Martin] relied on the recent decision of the House of Lords in *R v Smith (Morgan)* [2001] 1 AC 146. This was also a provocation case that Mr Wolkind contended could be applied to the similar issues which arise when a defendant relies on self-defence. In that case Smith was relying upon evidence that he suffered from clinical depression. There was no dispute that the evidence was admissible and relevant on the issue as to whether he was provoked, the subjective issue. The problem was as to whether the evidence was admissible as being relevant on the objective issue of loss of self-control. As to this the majority of their Lordships came to the conclusion that the jury were entitled to take into account some characteristic, whether temporary or permanent, which affected the degree of control which society could reasonably expect of a defendant and which it would be unjust not to take into account.

66. Is the same approach appropriate in the case of self-defence? There are policy reasons for distinguishing provocation from self-defence. Provocation only applies to murder but self-defence applies to all assaults. In addition, provocation does not provide a complete defence; it only reduces the offence from murder to manslaughter. There is also the undoubted fact that self-defence is raised in a great many cases resulting from minor assaults and it would be wholly disproportionate to encourage medical disputes in cases of that sort. Lord Hobhouse of Woodborough in his dissenting speech in *Smith* recognized that in relation to self-defence too generous an approach as to what is reasonable could result in an 'exorbitant defence' (p 195). Lord Hoffmann also appeared conscious of this. As a matter of principle we would reject the suggestion that the approach of the majority in *Smith* in relation to provocation should be applied directly to the different issue of self-defence.

67. We would accept that the jury are entitled to take into account in relation to self-defence the physical characteristics of the defendant. However, we would not agree that it is appropriate, except in exceptional circumstances which would make the evidence especially probative, in deciding whether excessive force has been used to take into account whether the defendant is suffering from some psychiatric condition.

. . .

[**Lord Woolf** also rejected an argument that the psychiatric evidence could have been relevant to the jury in assessing the reliability of Martin's evidence.]

74. For these reasons the fresh medical evidence has no bearing on the jury's rejection of Mr Martin's contention that he was entitled to be acquitted on the grounds that he was acting in self-defence. The position as to the fresh evidence relating to diminished responsibility is different. Here the evidence is admissible and relevant. The jury did not have the opportunity of considering this issue. Although the issue was never raised at the trial this was because the evidence was not then available to Mr Martin. Mr Martin is entitled to rely on the evidence for the purposes of his appeal (*R v Weekes (Stephen)* [1999] 2 Cr App R 520). The conviction for murder must therefore be quashed.

Conviction for murder quashed. Conviction for manslaughter substituted.

This case would now need to be read in the light of the 'householder' amendments to section 76 of the Criminal Justice and Immigration Act 2008, which we will discuss shortly.

The elements of private defence can be listed as follows:

(1) The victim must pose a threat.

(2) The threat must be unjustified.

(3) The use of force must be reasonable.

(4) The amount of force used must be reasonable.

(5) The defendant must be acting in order to defend himself or another or property.

These will be considered separately:

The victim must pose a threat

The victim must pose a risk to the defendant or someone else. Contrast these two examples:

(1) Brenda is in desperate need of a heart transplant. Her husband, Cyril, kills Edwin, a patient in the hospital where Brenda is staying, hoping that Edwin's heart can be transplanted to Brenda.

(2) Fred returns home to find Gavin, a burglar, about to shoot Fred's wife, Harriet. The only way to stop Gavin is to shoot him dead, which Fred does.

In these hypothetical cases both Cyril and Fred killed in order to save the lives of their wives. In both cases they believed that the only way to save their wives' lives was to do the killing. However, Fred, but not Cyril, can use private defence. This is because Gavin was posing a threat to Harriet, but Edwin was not posing a threat to Brenda.[13] →3 (p.742)

While this has long been assumed to be the law, the following case casts some doubt on it:

R v Hitchens
[2011] EWCA Crim 1626

Peter Craig Hitchens was charged with an assault on Kathleen Brown. His defence was that he acted in self-defence, in that he assaulted her in order to prevent her allowing a man into her flat, who Hitchens believed would assault him. The judge ruled that a defendant could not rely on self-defence in a case where the assault was against an innocent person in order to prevent an attack against a third party.

Lord Justice Gross

30. It is next convenient to focus on two separate strands. The first is whether self-defence at common law and section 3 Criminal Law Act 1967 is capable of extending to the use of force, against an innocent third party, to prevent a crime being committed by someone else. If and in so far as the judge thought that these defences were not capable of extending to the use of force against an innocent third party, we respectfully disagree and indeed Mr Wicks did not seek to contend otherwise. Although we suspect that the facts capable realistically of giving rise to such a defence will only rarely be encountered, examples can be adduced and two will suffice:

1. A police constable bundles a passer-by out of the way to get at a man he believes about to shoot with a firearm or detonate an explosive device.

2. Y seeks to give Z car keys with Z about to drive. X, believing Z to be unfit drive through drink, knocks the keys out of Y's hands and retains them.

As ever that the defence is capable of being advanced is of course a very different question from that of whether it would succeed.

Appeal allowed.

With respect, the Court of Appeal seem to have got this issue wrong. In the two hypothetical cases they discuss there is indeed a defence, but it is duress, not self-defence. This case threatens to undermine the distinction the law draws between duress and self-defence. The discussion in the court was brief and it is hard to believe it would survive a more sustained scrutiny.

---

[13] These were easy cases. In Part II we shall look at cases where it is far harder to tell whether or not the victim was posing a threat.

There is no doubt that the defence applies whether the threat is being posed to the defendant or to another person or to property.[14] Of course in cases in which property is involved the requirement of reasonableness will be key.[15]

The threat must be unjustified

Just because his or her attacker may not be committing an offence does not prevent a defendant relying on self-defence. A defendant can plead self-defence if he or she uses force against a child or sleepwalker who is attacking her, even though the child or sleepwalker was not committing a crime.[16] However, the threat must be unjust. If Mark attacks Jim and Jim defends himself by using force on Mark, Mark cannot then use further force against Jim and argue that this was in 'self-defence against Jim's attack'. Here, Jim's use of force was reasonable and justified in the eyes of the law, therefore Mark cannot use self-defence as a defence against it. In *Jones*[17] a crime committed in an attempt to stop the Iraq war could not be justified on the basis of private defence because the act of going to war in Iraq was not an offence under English law. An offence under international law was insufficient.

The use of force must be reasonable

This element means it must have been reasonable for the defendant to use force, rather than escape from the threat in some way. In other words if the defendant could have escaped from the threat peacefully but unreasonably failed to do so then he will not be able to use the defence.[18] This requirement can be easily misunderstood. We will now consider three points about this requirement:

(1) As section 76(6A) makes clear the defendant does not have a 'duty to retreat'.[19] So if a jury decided it was reasonable either to try and retreat or to stay and ward off the attack, the defendant could still rely on the defence. Nevertheless if the defendant had the opportunity to retreat, that will be a factor to consider in determining whether it was reasonable for the defendant to use force.[20] Clearly if the defendant tried unsuccessfully to escape from the threat and then used force to repel the attack the jury is particularly likely to find that the defendant was acting reasonably.[21]

(2) The law does permit the defendant to take 'a pre-emptive strike'[22] if to do so is reasonable.[23]

(3) It is not absolutely necessary to show that the attack is imminent or immediate.[24] If Kim is kidnapped by a violent terrorist gang she may use force to escape if she notices that all but one guard have fallen asleep even if she is not facing an imminent threat.

---

[14] See the discussion in Leverick (2006: ch. 7).   [15] *Morris* [2013] EWCA Crim 436.

[16] It is therefore inaccurate to suggest that there must be an unlawful attack.

[17] [2006] UKHL 16.

[18] See Simons (2008), who questions whether this is asking too much of a defendant. He suggests that in the face of an immediate threat all that can be expected is that the defendant exercised reasonable self-control.

[19] *Bird* [1985] 1 WLR 816 (CA). Although see Dsouza (2015) for when a duty to retreat might arise.

[20] Criminal Justice and Immigration Act 2008, s. 76(6A).   [21] *Bird* [1985] 1 WLR 816 (CA).

[22] *Beckford* [1988] AC 130, 414 (PC). Lanham (2005) points out some of the inconsistencies between the law of self-defence and the law prohibiting the possession of offensive weapons.

[23] In *Attorney-General's Reference (No. 2 of 1983)* [1984] QB 456 (CA) the defendant prepared some petrol bombs during a time of widespread rioting.

[24] *Attorney-General for Northern Ireland's Reference (No. 1 of 1975)* [1977] AC 105 (HL).

This is because her use of force was reasonable in that it would probably be her only chance to escape. That said, in the vast majority of cases it will be reasonable to use force only in the face of an imminent attack.

These examples show that the necessity requirement can be summarized with a simple question: 'Was it reasonable for the defendant to use force, rather than escape?'

The amount of force used must be reasonable

Following the amendments to section 76 of the Criminal Justice and Immigration Act 2008 created by the Crime and Courts Act 2013 it is necessary to distinguish 'householder' cases (where the defendant is using self-defence inside their home against a trespasser) and all other cases.

Non-householder cases

The defendant can successfully use the defence only if the level of force was reasonable in the face of the threat as perceived by the defendant.[25] The Court of Appeal in *Oye*[26] confirmed, in line with a long line of cases, that the question is whether a reasonable person would say that the level of force was reasonable, not whether the defendant thought the level of force used was reasonable.[27] Consider this example: Tony takes Ian's wallet. As Tony runs away, Ian pulls out a gun and shoots him dead. Ian thinks it is reasonable for him to shoot a pickpocket dead in order to protect his property. If Ian is charged with Tony's murder and he seeks to rely on private defence, the question is: was it reasonable for Ian to shoot Tony dead in these circumstances, *not* did Ian think it was reasonable for him to shoot Tony dead in these circumstances?

Sometimes it is suggested that the defendant must use a level of force which is proportionate to the threat. The concept of proportionality might suggest that the defendant should not use more force than he or she is threatened with. Indeed, section 76(6) states that 'the degree of force used by D is not to be regarded as having been reasonable in the circumstances as D believed them to be if it was disproportionate in those circumstances'. The use of proportionality is rather unfortunate here. The jury should remember that they are in the 'calm analytical atmosphere of the court room'[28] and that the defendant is reacting to a sudden attack and that 'a person acting for a legitimate purpose may not be able to weigh to a nicety the exact measure of any necessary action'.[29] The jury should also remember that the defendant is acting in the 'agony of the moment'.[30] The courts have preferred simply asking whether or not the use of force was reasonable, rather than considering whether the use of force was precisely proportionate.[31] Given that *Keane*[32] has said the legislation was not designed to change the law, it may be best to read proportionality as a synonym for reasonableness.

This would mean that, for example, a woman can use self-defence if she kills a person who is about to rape her.[33]

---

[25] *Yaman* [2012] EWCA Crim 1075. [26] [2013] EWCA Crim 1725.
[27] Including *Owino* [1995] Crim LR 743 (CA); *Martin* [2002] 2 WLR 1 (CA).
[28] *Attorney-General for Northern Ireland's Reference (No. 1 of 1975)* [1977] AC 105, 138, per Lord Diplock.
[29] Lord Morris in *Palmer* [1971] AC 814, 832 (PC).
[30] Criminal Justice and Immigration Act 2008, s. 76(7)(a). [31] *Keane* [2010] EWCA Crim 2514.
[32] *Ibid.* [33] See Leverick (2006: ch. 8).

Householder cases

Under section 76(5) of the Criminal Justice and Immigration Act 2008:

> In a householder case, the degree of force used by D is not to be regarded as having been reasonable in the circumstances as D believed them to be if it was grossly disproportionate in those circumstances.

A 'householder case' will be one where the victim is entering a building as a trespasser and the defendant is not a trespasser.[34] This will most obviously apply where D is at his or her home and a burglar is entering the property, who D attacks. The definition of householder is wide enough to cover a case where the defendant is staying with a friend and believes V to be a trespasser. In these cases the defendant's use of force will only be unreasonable if it is 'grossly disproportionate'. It may well be that this makes little change to the law because the jury would, even under the standard approach, take into account the emergency of the moment when considering whether a householder was acting reasonably and would be likely to only find a grossly disproportionate amount of force to be unreasonable.

The defendant must be acting in order to defend himself or another or property

A defendant who is acting not in order to defend him or herself or another, but solely out of revenge or retaliation will not be able to rely on the defence.[35] Similarly a defendant who has lost self-control cannot claim to be acting in self-defence.[36] This is part of what has become known as 'the *Dadson*[37] principle': the defendant cannot rely on the justifying circumstances of his or her actions of which he or she is not aware. The principle applies if Simone sees her enemy, Peter, and shoots him dead, but, unknown to Simone, Peter was about to attack her. Had Simone known she was about to be attacked she could have used self-defence, but as she did not know this she cannot rely on the defence. The requirement also meant that defendants in *Ayliffe v DPP*[38] who caused criminal damage while protesting against the Iraq war could not rely on private defence. Their actions were about protest not defending people or property.

1.4 WHAT ABOUT DEFENDANTS WHO THINK THEY ARE BEING ATTACKED BUT ARE NOT?

The position is that a defendant is to be judged on the facts as he or she genuinely believed them to be, as section 76(3) makes clear. There is no need to show the defendant had reasonable grounds for their belief. So if, for example, the defendant is approached by a person who is out for a jog and believes the jogger is in fact about to attack him or her and so pushes the jogger, he or she can rely on self-defence to an assault charge. The jury must ask whether, on the facts as perceived by the defendant, the level of force was reasonable.[39] Even if the

---

[34] For an excellent discussion, see Bleasdale-Hill (2015).

[35] *Bird* [1985] 1 WLR 816 (CA); *Hussain and Hussain* [2010] EWCA Crim 94.

[36] *Preston v CPS* [2013] EWHC 456 (Admin).

[37] *Dadson* (1850) 4 Cox CC 358; *Chapman* (1988) 89 Cr App R 190 (CA).   [38] [2005] 3 All ER 330.

[39] *Press and Thompson* [2013] EWCA Crim 2514; *Gladstone Williams* (1984) 78 Cr App R 276; *Beckford v R* [1988] AC 130.

belief they were being attacked was an absurd one, as long as it was the genuine belief of the defendant he could rely on the defence.[40] Of course the more absurd the belief the more reluctant the jury may be to believe that it was the genuine belief of the defendant.[41] As we shall see in Part II this is a controversial approach for the law to take, not least because it appears to provide a defence to a racist defendant who attacked a black man he believed was about to attack him simply because of his race. There is one exception to this rule and that is where the belief that he or she is being attacked is a voluntarily intoxicated one (section 76(5) of the Criminal Justice and Immigration Act 2008). So the person who is drunk and as a result mistakenly believes that they are being attacked cannot rely on private defence.[42] In the following case the Court of Appeal considered what should happen if the defendant believed he was being attacked as a result of insane delusions:

R v Oye
[2013] EWCA Crim 1725

Seun Oye had no previous convictions and held a respectable position in events management before the events that led to him appearing in court. He was found in the staff room of a coffee shop in the Westfield Shopping Centre in London in June 2011, 'twitching in a strange manner'. The police arrive and Oye tried to hide in a void in the ceiling. He threw crockery at the police and caused a minor injury. Later, when taken to a police cell, he made an attempt to escape and punched two police officers. He was convicted of affray and causing grievous bodily harm contrary to section 20 of the Offences Against the Person Act 1861. It the trial he claimed to have felt pursued by evil spirits and believed the police were evil. On appeal the key question was whether he should have been able to rely on self-defence based on the insane delusions that he was being attacked.

Lord Justice Davis

44. . . . . [Counsel for the appellant] submitted that *in the circumstances as the appellant believed them to be* the prosecution could not, on the evidence prove that the degree of force used was unreasonable or disproportionate in those circumstances. That his belief as to those circumstances derived from his insane delusion, it was submitted, was immaterial. The point was that that was his genuine, if insanely deluded, belief.

45. If this is right, the potential implications for other cases are most disconcerting. It could mean that the more insanely deluded a person may be in using violence in purported self-defence the more likely that an entire acquittal may result. It could mean that such an individual who for his own benefit and protection may require hospital treatment or supervision gets none. It could mean that the public is exposed to possible further violence from an individual with a propensity for suffering insane delusions, without any intervening preventative remedies being available to the courts in the form of hospital or supervision orders. Thus, whatever the purist force in the argument, there are strong policy objections to the approach advocated on behalf of the appellant.

---

[40] In *Press and Thompson* [2013] EWCA Crim 2514 the defendant relied on the fact he suffered from post-traumatic stress disorder following military service, to explain why he honestly believed he was under attack.

[41] Criminal Justice and Immigration Act 2008, s. 76(4)(a).

[42] *Hatton* [2005] EWCA Crim 2951. See Spencer and Dingwall (2006) for criticism of this case.

46. In our view it is not right.

47. The position remains, as we think plain from the provisions of s.76 of the 2008 Act, that the second limb of self-defence does include an objective element by reference to reasonableness, even if there may also be a subjective element: see in particular s.76(6) and see also the decision in *R v Keane & McGrath* [201[0]] EWCA Crim 2514. An insane person cannot set the standards of reasonableness as to the degree of force used by reference to his own insanity. In truth it makes as little sense to talk of the reasonable lunatic as it did, in the context of cases on provocation, to talk of the reasonable glue-sniffer.

48. . . . . [T]he appellant did not say that, in the coffee shop, the police were, in his mind, actually attacking or threatening immediately to attack him so as to warrant his violent response. As to the incident in the custody suite, whilst it may be that the police had (to him) demonic faces and he was trying to protect himself from them, it was very much in issue for example whether they either in fact or in his own belief "rushed" him—and he apparently conceded in any event (and as confirmed by the CCTV) that any "rushing" was after he had himself first struck Sergeant Watts. Overall there was no clear cut and irrefutable evidence that the danger actually perceived by him in his deluded state justified his actual responses. . . .

57. We thus reject the appellant's submissions on the issue of self-defence.

On other grounds a verdict of not guilty by reason of insanity was substituted for the conviction.

This decision needs to be read with care. Tony Storey[43] has suggested that the case states 'that a plea of self-defence will not be accepted where the defendant's own psychotic or otherwise insane delusions may have genuinely caused him to believe that he was under attack.' That seems too broad a reading. The appeal was lost because the evidence suggested that although he was suffering delusions he was not using force to defend himself or the amount of force used was in excess of what was reasonable on the facts as he believed them to be.[44] He attacked the evil spirits, but not to defend himself. Had his evidence been that he believed the police were evil spirits who were attacking him, then his case may have been successful if he had used a reasonable amount of force on the facts as he believed them to be. That said, one must sympathize with a jury who are asked to consider what is the reasonable amount of force to use against an evil spirit!

1.5 SELF-INDUCED PRIVATE DEFENCES

If the defendant caused the attack in the first place then he or she may not be able to rely on the defence.[45] The question for the jury is whether the defendant's use of force was reasonable in light of the fact that he or she had instigated the fight.[46] So if the defendant gravely insulted the victim who responded by poking the defendant it is unlikely the defendant would then be entitled to respond with violence back. If, on the other hand, in response to an insult the victim produced a gun, then it appears more likely a jury will think the defendant can reasonably defend him or herself against an attack. So a key issue in such cases is whether the victim's

---

[43] Storey (2014).   [44] Child and Sullivan (2014).
[45] Robinson (1985); Alexander (2013); Farrell (2013).   [46] *Rashford* [2006] EWCA Crim 3377.

response to the initial provocation or instigation of the defendant is reasonable.[47] This does not mean that the defence is unavailable simply because the defendant went to a place where he or she knew that he or she might be attacked and indeed was.[48]

R v Keane
[2010] EWCA Crim 2514

After a night visiting pubs Daniel Keane was being given a lift home by the victim and two women. Keane started to insult one of the women, including calling her a 'chav'. This led to a fight between Keane and the victim in which the victim suffered grievous bodily harm. On appeal a key question was whether the judge had correctly directed the jury on whether the defendant could rely on self-defence if he was the cause of the violence he was facing.

Lord Justice Hughes

17. . . . it is certainly true that it is not the law that the fact that a defendant either started the fight or entered it willingly is *always and inevitably* a bar to self-defence arising. The law is as stated by Lord Hope, then the Lord Justice General, in the Scottish case of *Burns* 1995 SLT 1090 at 1093H. The Lord Justice General said this:

> ". . . it is now clear that the propositions in Hume and Macdonald that the accused must not have started the trouble, or provoked the quarrel, are stated too broadly. It is not accurate to say that a person who kills someone in a quarrel which he himself started, by provoking it or entering into it willingly, cannot plead self defence if his victim then retaliates. The question whether the plea of self defence is available depends, in a case of that kind, on whether the retaliation is such that the accused is entitled then to defend himself. That depends upon whether the violence offered by the victim was so out of proportion to the accused's own actings as to give rise to the reasonable apprehension that he was in an immediate danger from which he had no other means of escape, and whether the violence which he then used was no more than was necessary to preserve his own life or protect himself from serious injury."

The Lord Justice General was dealing with a homicide case in which the issue was risk to life or limb, but of course the principle applies equally to lesser levels of violence. The key post of that formulation of the law is the proposition that self-defence may arise in the case of an original aggressor but only where the violence offered by the victim was so out of proportion to what the original aggressor did that in effect the roles were reversed. That statement of the law has been approved in this court in at least two cases and it may be more. They are *Balogun* [1999] EWCA Crim. 2120 and *Rashford* [2005] EWCA Crim. 3377, albeit that in neither case was the conviction unsafe despite the absence of such a direction.

18. As to its practical application, we would commend attention to the recent decision of this court in *Harvey* [2009] EWCA Crim. 469, which judgment we shall append to the present

---

[47] This led the court in *Marsh v DPP* [2015] EWHC 1022 (Admin) to conclude that the defendant could be convicted even though it was unclear who had started the fight. His response to the violence of the victim was excessive, whoever started it all.

[48] *Field* [1972] Crim LR 435 (CA).

judgment. We venture to suggest that practitioners will gain a good deal of help from Moses LJ's treatment in *Harvey* of the proper approach to cases when self-defence arises. In that case the court considered a direction given by the judge inviting the jury to consider whether "the tables had been turned". It seems to us that that kind of homely expression, like "the roles being reversed", can quite well encapsulate the question which may arise if an original aggressor claims the ability to rely on self-defence. We would commend it as suitable for a great many cases, subject only to this reminder. Lord Hope's formulation of the rule makes it clear that it is not enough to bring self-defence into issue that a defendant who started the fight is at some point during the fight for the time being getting the worst of it, merely because the victim is defending himself reasonably. In that event there has been no disproportionate act by the victim of the kind that Lord Hope is contemplating. The victim has not been turned into the aggressor. The tables have not been turned in that particular sense. The roles have not been reversed.

19. . . . It may well be true that if D provokes V to hit him, and succeeds so that V gives way to the invitation, V is acting unlawfully when he does so. It does not however follow that D thereby becomes entitled to rely on self-defence. There are many situations where two people are fighting and both are acting unlawfully, by which we mean other than in self-defence. It is true of every voluntary fight, challenge laid down and accepted. It is true of most fights in which one person deliberately incites and the other cheerfully responds with an unlawful use of force. We need to say as clearly as we may that it is not the law that if a defendant sets out to provoke another to punch him and succeeds, the defendant is then entitled to punch the other person. What that would do would be to legalise the common coin of the bully who confronts his victim with taunts which are deliberately designed to provide an excuse to hit him. The reason why it is not the law is that underlying the law of self-defence is the commonsense morality that what is not unlawful is force which is reasonably necessary. The force used by the bully in the situation postulated is not reasonably necessary. On the contrary, it has been engineered entirely unreasonably by the defendant. Exactly the same point emerges clearly from Lord Hope's formulation in Burns. In the situation postulated there has been no disproportionate reaction from the victim which removes from the defendant the quality of the aggressor and reverses the roles. Of course it might be different if the defendant set out to provoke a punch and the victim unexpectedly and disproportionately attacked him with a knife.

Appeal dismissed.

1.6 HAS THE HUMAN RIGHTS ACT 1998 CHANGED THE LAW?

Andrew Ashworth has suggested that the law on private defence may be challenged under the Human Rights Act, at least in the case of murder. He points to Article 2 of the European Convention on Human Rights (ECHR), which protects the right to life:

(1) Everyone's right to life shall be protected by law. No one shall be deprived of his life intentionally save in the execution of a sentence of a court following his conviction of a crime for which this penalty is provided by law.

(2) Deprivation of life shall not be regarded as inflicted in contravention of this Article when it results from the use of force which is no more than absolutely necessary:

(a) in the defence of any person from unlawful violence;

(b) in order to effect a lawful arrest[49] or to prevent the escape of a person lawfully detained;

(c) in action lawfully taken for the purpose of quelling a riot or insurrection.

Article 2 makes it clear in paragraph 2(a) that the taking of life is permissible if it is in the defence of a person. However, the European Court has interpreted paragraph 2(a) to mean that it can be relied upon only where the force is absolutely necessary and strictly proportionate.[50] The Court has accepted that paragraph 2(a) can apply in a case where a person mistakenly believes someone is in need of defence, but only if that mistaken belief is based on good reasons.[51] However, in deciding what constitutes a good reason the Court will take into account the fact that a decision to use force may have had to be made in the heat of the moment.[52] This suggests two ways in which the law on self-defence in English and Welsh law falls short of that expected in the ECHR:

(1) The level of force that may be used: the killing must be absolutely necessary and strictly proportionate according to the European Court, but only reasonable under the English and Welsh law.

(2) Whether the defence can be used if the defendant mistakenly believes he or she or another is being attacked: only if that mistake is based on a good reason according to the European Court, but as long as it is genuinely held under English and Welsh law.

In the following passage, Fiona Leverick summarizes her argument that the law on self-defence will need to be reconsidered in the light of the Human Rights Act:[53]

F. Leverick, 'Is English Self-defence Law Incompatible with Article 2 of the ECHR?' [2002] *Criminal Law Review* 347 at 361

The purpose of this paper was to assess the claim that in allowing an honest unreasonable mistake to ground an acquittal on the basis of self-defence, English law is contrary to Article 2 of the ECHR. The reason for this claim is that, in allowing the unreasonably mistaken defendant to escape punishment in this way, English law fails to respect the right to life of the person who, through no fault of their own, is mistaken for an attacker. An examination of relevant case law leads to the conclusion that the substance of English law does indeed contravene Article 2. It had been suggested that because killing in self-defence is not an intentional killing, Article 2 does not apply. Regardless of the theoretical merits of this suggestion, it can be dismissed as it has consistently

---

[49] As J.C. Smith (1994) points out, the suggestion that one can kill in order to arrest someone is bizarre. In 'the course of' rather than 'in order to' might have been better wording.

[50] *Andronicou and Constantinou v Cyprus* (1998) 25 EHRR 491 (ECtHR).

[51] *McCann v UK* (1996) 21 EHRR 97 (ECtHR) and *Andronicou and Constantinou v Cyprus* (1998) 25 EHRR 491 (ECtHR). In *McCann* the European Court of Human Rights explained that law enforcement operations must be organized so as to 'minimise to the greatest extent possible, recourse to lethal force'.

[52] *Andronicou and Constantinou v Cyprus* (1998) 25 EHRR 491 (ECtHR).

[53] For further development of this argument, see Leverick (2007: ch. 10).

been held that self-defensive killing *does* fall to be assessed under Article 2. Further, an examination of relevant cases shows that the court has consistently required that a mistaken belief in the need to use self-defensive force be based on good reasons. It is also clear, from cases such as *A v. United Kingdom* and *X and Y v. Netherlands*, that a violation of the Convention can take place when there has been a failure on the part of the State to provide a criminal law sanction that protects its citizens from the violent acts of other individuals, regardless of whether these individuals were State officials or private citizens. This is not to say that the Convention would necessarily require English law to convict the unreasonably mistaken self-defender of murder. It may be that a conviction for a lesser offence, such as manslaughter, is sufficient. Consideration of the degree of punishment appropriate in such circumstances is outside the scope of this paper. The point is that English law as it stands at present contains no sanctions *whatsoever* for the defendant who deprives another of her life in the unreasonable belief that she was an attacker.

The argument against this view is that the criminal law is simply stating that a defendant who kills believing him or herself to be under attack does not deserve punishment. It is not in any sense authorizing or permitting the defendant to take the victim's life. It is not, therefore, showing a lack of respect for the victim's life, but rather attempting to assess the blameworthiness of the defendant. The criminal law does not criminalize all negligent killings, and after all we do not say that the defence of insanity fails to protect the right to life of those who are killed by the insane.[54]

Of course Article 2 is not relevant in cases of non-deadly force. However, in non-fatal cases Article 3 or 8 may be relevant because they require protection of citizens from torture or inhuman or degrading treatment, and interferences with their physical or moral integrity.[55]

FURTHER READING

Ashworth, A. (1975) 'Self-Defence and the Right to Life' *Cambridge Law Journal* 34: 272.

Bleasdale-Hill, L. (2015) '"Our Home is Our Haven and Refuge—A Place Where We Have Every Right to Feel Safe": Justifying the Use of Up to "Grossly Disproportionate Force" in a Place of Residence' *Criminal Law Review* 407.

Leverick, F. (2002a) 'Is English Self-Defence Law Incompatible with Article 2 of the ECHR?' *Criminal Law Review* 347.

Leverick, F. (2002b) 'The Use of Force in Public or Private Defence and Article 2: A Reply to Professor Sir John Smith' *Criminal Law Review* 963.

Smith, J.C. (2002) 'The Use of Force in Public or Private Defence and Article 2' *Criminal Law Review* 958.

---

[54] Although one could reply that, while the law on self-defence might affect the way someone acted (and therefore offered greater or lesser protection of the right to life), the law on insanity clearly cannot affect how a defendant acts.

[55] *X and Y v Netherlands* (1986) 8 EHRR 235 (ECtHR).

2 NECESSITY

2.1 THE MEANING OF NECESSITY

Unfortunately there has been some confusion over the terminology used in relation to the defence of necessity in criminal law.[56] The term has been used in at least three different senses: →4 (p.731)

(1) The majority of the academic materials have used the term 'necessity' to refer to a defence that the defendant did 'the lesser of two evils': in other words that the defendant was in a situation which meant that whatever he or she did would result in harm being caused and the defendant chose the course of action which resulted in the least harm.

(2) Some cases have used the term 'necessity' to mean duress of circumstances.[57] In one case the Court of Appeal talked of 'necessity of circumstances'[58] which only increases the confusion.

(3) Sometimes necessity is used to describe an overarching doctrine which explains self-defence, duress, and the 'lesser of two evils';[59] the overarching theme being that the defendant was placed in an emergency of some kind and what the defendant did was necessary to avoid a harm.

In this book necessity will be used in the first sense (the lesser of two evils).

It should be stated immediately that the courts have not accepted a general defence of necessity. The straightforward claim, 'I broke the law but there would have been even worse consequences had I obeyed the law', will not in itself lead to an acquittal.[60] However, there are plenty of examples where the defence of necessity *in effect* is recognized, even if it is not called necessity or recognized as a general defence.

2.2 CASES DENYING THE EXISTENCE OF A GENERAL DEFENCE OF NECESSITY

The courts have been consistent in denying a general defence of necessity, most recently in *Nicklinson v Ministry of Justice*.[61] In *Southwark LBC v Williams*[62] the Court of Appeal held that homeless people seeking temporary refuge in empty accommodation had committed trespass. They could not rely on a defence that the trespass was a lesser wrong than their suffering. Lord Denning explained:

> if hunger were once allowed to be an excuse for stealing, it would open a door through which all kinds of lawlessness and disorder would pass. . . . If homelessness were once admitted as a defence to trespass, no one's house could be safe. Necessity would open a door which no man could shut.[63]

---

[56] Stark (2013c); S. Gardner (1991b).

[57] *Martin* (1989) 88 Cr App R 343 (CA); *Pipe v DPP* [2012] EWHC 1821 (Admin) but not all (see *Cichon v DPP* [1994] Crim LR 918).

[58] *Quayle* [2005] EWCA Crim 1415.

[59] Walker LJ in *Re A (Children) (Conjoined Twins: Surgical Separation)* [2001] 2 WLR 480.

[60] *Quayle* [2005] EWCA Crim 1415.

[61] [2013] EWCA Civ 961. See also *Pommell* [1995] 2 Cr App R 607 (CA) and *Shayler* [2001] 1 WLR 2206 (CA).

[62] [1971] 1 Ch 734 (CA).   [63] *Southwark LBC v Williams* [1971] 2 All ER 175, 179.

To similar effect, in *Kitson*[64] a drunk man who had fallen asleep in the back of his car awoke to find the car moving down a hill, and he steered the car to safety, avoiding any injury. He was still convicted of a drink-driving offence. The fact that the man was acting in a way society would have wanted him to act was welcomed. He was still guilty of the offence.

One of the most famous cases in English law is often used to stress that necessity is not a defence to murder: *Dudley and Stephens*.[65] There three men and a boy were shipwrecked in an open boat with no food or water. After several days the men killed the boy who was now very ill. They ate him and therefore managed to survive until they were rescued. In essence the three men claimed that had they not eaten the cabin boy all four of them would have died. Therefore the killing of the cabin boy was the lesser of two evils. Their defence failed and they were convicted of murder and sentenced to death, although their sentences were commuted to six months' imprisonment. The exact *ratio decidendi* of the case has been much debated, although in *Howe*[66] the House of Lords regarded the case as one setting down the general rule that necessity is not a defence to murder. As we shall see in *Re A (Children) (Conjoined Twins: Surgical Separation)*,[67] the majority of the Court of Appeal gave the decision a narrower interpretation.[68]

Despite the denial of a general defence of necessity, in fact a limited defence of necessity is recognized at common law and in some statutes.

2.3   THE LIMITED DEFENCE OF NECESSITY AT COMMON LAW

Despite the denial of a general defence of necessity the courts have been willing to accept a defence of necessity in special defined circumstances:

(1) Where the defendant damages or steals another's property in the public interest (e.g. in order to create a firebreak he or she pulls down someone's house).[69]

(2) Where the defendant damages the defendant's property or interferes with another's property in order to save his or her own person or property (e.g. where the defendant damages another's property to prevent the spread of fire onto his or her own land).[70]

(3) Where actions taken for the benefit of another person where that person is unable to consent. In *Re F (Mental Patient: Sterilisation)*[71] the doctrine was relied upon to authorize the sterilization of a mentally ill woman. The House of Lords found that the operation would be in her best interests and that she was unable to consent; necessity could therefore be relied upon.[72] Another example Lord Goff gave in that case was of a defendant who pushed a person out of the way of an oncoming vehicle. He was careful to limit this principle to cases where the 'victim could not consent' (e.g. was incompetent) or there was no time to obtain the victim's consent (e.g. the cases where a person was about to be run over).[73] Where the victim is competent and able to give consent and refuses to do so then it is unlawful to provide treatment to that patient, even if to do so would be in their best interests.[74]

---

[64] (1955) 39 Cr App R 66 (CA).   [65] (1884) 14 QBD 273.   [66] [1987] AC 417.

[67] [2001] 2 WLR 480.   [68] See further Bohlander (2006a).

[69] *Re F (Mental Patient: Sterilisation)* [1989] 2 All ER 545, 564–5 (HL).   [70] *Ibid.*

[71] [1990] 2 AC 1 (HL).

[72] Now such a case would be dealt with by the Mental Capacity Act 2005.

[73] See Herring (2009c) for a discussion of the use of necessity with vulnerable adults.

[74] *St George's Healthcare NHS Trust v S* [1999] Fam 26 (CA).

(4) It is permissible for a police constable to direct people to break traffic regulations if that is necessary and reasonable to protect life or property.[75] Further, obeying such a direction does not infringe the law.

(5) A very limited category of necessity as a defence to murder was recognized in *Re A (Children) (Conjoined Twins: Surgical Separation)*.[76] Although their Lordships were willing to recognize the availability of necessity on the highly unusual facts of that particular case, it is difficult to discover a general principle:

Re A (Children) (Conjoined Twins: Surgical Separation)
[2001] Fam 147 (CA)

Jodie and Mary were conjoined twins, born joined at the lower abdomen. Jodie was described as a bright and alert baby. Mary, however, had a 'primitive brain', no effective heart or lung function, and was alive only because a common artery enabled Jodie to circulate the blood for both of them. Jodie was capable of living independently of Mary, but Mary could not exist apart from Jodie. Doctors at the hospital wished to perform an operation which would separate the twins. If performed, the operation would lead to the death of Mary, but it was hoped it would save the life of Jodie. The parents of the twins refused to consent to the operation. The hospital applied to the court for a declaration that the operation would be lawful. The judge concluded that the operation would be in the best interests of both twins because Mary's continued existence was harmful to Jodie. The case was taken to the Court of Appeal. (This case raises complex issues of medical and family law. The extracts here will focus on the criminal law aspects, but they are only part of the Court's reasoning.)

Lord Justice Ward

[Having decided that if the doctors performed the operation and Mary were to die they would intentionally kill Mary, which would be murder, Ward LJ went on to consider whether there was any defence the doctors could rely on:]

7 Unlawfully

7.1 The search for settled principle
The search for settled principle is difficult where the law is as uncertain in this area as Brooke LJ's masterly analysis has shown it to be. Doing the best I can, I have come to these conclusions.

7.2 Necessity
Necessity in the *R v Dudley and Stephens* sense arises where A kills B to save his own life. The threat to A's life is posed by the circumstances, rather than an act of threat by B on A in conventional self-defence terms.

---

[75] *Johnson v Phillips* [1975] 3 All ER 682.   [76] [2001] 2 WLR 480.

7.3 Duress

Similar considerations apply to duress. There is, of course, a difference between them but as Lord Hailsham of St Marylebone LC said in *R v Howe* [1987] 1 AC 417 at 429:

'This, however, is, in my view a distinction without a relevant difference, since on this view duress is only that species of the genus of necessity which is caused by wrongful threat. I cannot see that there is any way in which a person of ordinary fortitude can be excused from one type of pressure on his will rather than the other.'

7.4 The policy of the law

The policy of the law is to prevent A being judge in his own cause of the value of his life over B's life or his loved one C's life, and then being executioner as well. The policy of the law was expressed in similar terms in Hale's *Pleas of the Crown* (1 Hale PC (1778) 51), and Blackstone's *Commentaries on the Laws of England* (4 Bl Com (1857 edn) 28). Blackstone wrote that a man under duress 'ought rather to die himself than escape by the murder of an innocent'. The sanctity of life and the inherent equality of all life prevails. . . .

[Ward LJ also quoted from *Howe* to support this proposition.]

7.5 A legal duty?

The first important feature is that the doctors cannot be denied a right of choice if they are under a duty to choose. They are under a duty to Mary not to operate because it will kill Mary, but they are under a duty to Jodie to operate because not to do so will kill her. . . .

7.6 The effect of a conflict of duty

. . .

What are the doctors to do if the law imposes upon them a duty which they cannot perform without being in breach of Mary's right to life if at the same time the respecting of her right puts them in breach of the equally serious duty of respecting Jodie's right to life? A resort to a sanctity of life argument does not enable both rights to receive the equal protection the doctrine is supposed to provide each of them equally. In those circumstances it seems to me that the law must allow an escape through choosing the lesser of the two evils. The law cannot say, 'heads I win, tails you lose'. Faced as they are with an apparently irreconcilable conflict, the doctors should be in no different position from that in which the court itself was placed in the performance of its duty to give paramount consideration to the welfare of each child. The doctors must be given the same freedom of choice as the court has given itself and the doctors must make that choice along the same lines as the court has done, giving the sanctity of life principle its place in the balancing exercise that has to be undertaken. The respect the law must have for the right to life of each must go in the scales and weigh equally but other factors have to go in the scales as well. For the same reasons that led to my concluding that consent should be given to operate so the conclusion has to be that the carrying out of the operation will be justified as the lesser evil and no unlawful act would be committed.

I should emphasise that the doctors do not cease to owe Mary a duty of care, they must continue to furnish such treatment and nursing care as may be appropriate to ensure that she suffers the least pain and distress and retains the greatest dignity until her life comes to an end.

7.7 Offending the sanctity of life principle

The second reason why the right of choice should be given to the doctors is that the proposed operation would not in any event offend the sanctity of life principle. That principle may be expressed in different ways but they all amount to the same thing. Some might say that it demands that each life is to be protected from unjust attack. Some might say as the joint statement by the Anglican and Roman Catholic bishops did in the aftermath of the Bland judgment that because human life is a gift from God to be preserved and cherished, the deliberate taking of human life is prohibited except in self-defence or the legitimate defence of others. The Archbishop defines it in terms that human life is sacred, that is inviolable, so that one should never aim to cause an innocent person's death by act or omission. I have added the emphases. The reality here—harsh as it is to state it, and unnatural as it is that it should be happening—is that Mary is killing Jodie. That is the effect of the incontrovertible medical evidence and it is common ground in the case. Mary uses Jodie's heart and lungs to receive and use Jodie's oxygenated blood. This will cause Jodie's heart to fail and cause Jodie's death as surely as a slow drip of poison. How can it be just that Jodie should be required to tolerate that state of affairs? One does not need to label Mary with the American terminology which would paint her to be 'an unjust aggressor', which I feel is wholly inappropriate language for the sad and helpless position in which Mary finds herself. I have no difficulty in agreeing that this unique happening cannot be said to be unlawful. But it does not have to be unlawful. The six-year-old boy indiscriminately shooting all and sundry in the school playground is not acting unlawfully for he is too young for his acts to be so classified. But is he 'innocent' within the moral meaning of that word as used by the Archbishop? I am not qualified to answer that moral question because, despite an assertion—or was it an aspersion—by a member of the Bar in a letter to The Times that we, the judges, are proclaiming some moral superiority in this case, I for my part would defer any opinion as to a child's innocence to the Archbishop for that is his territory. If I had to hazard a guess, I would venture the tentative view that the child is not morally innocent. What I am, however, competent to say is that in law killing that six-year-old boy in self-defence of others would be fully justified and the killing would not be unlawful. I can see no difference in essence between that resort to legitimate self-defence and the doctors coming to Jodie's defence and removing the threat of fatal harm to her presented by Mary's draining her life-blood. The availability of such a plea of quasi self-defence, modified to meet the quite exceptional circumstances nature has inflicted on the twins, makes intervention by the doctors lawful.

8 Conclusion

For these reasons, very shortly expressed, I conclude that the operation which I would permit can be lawfully carried out.

Lord Justice Brooke

Conclusion

I have considered very carefully the policy reasons for the decision in *R v Dudley and Stephens*, supported as it was by the House of Lords in *R v Howe*. These are, in short, that there were two insuperable objections to the proposition that necessity might be available as a defence for the Mignonette sailors. The first objection was evident in the court's questions: who is to be the judge of this sort of necessity? By what measure is the comparative value of lives to be measured? The second objection was that to permit such a defence would mark an absolute divorce of law from morality.

In my judgment, neither of these objections are dispositive of the present case. Mary is, sadly, self-designated for a very early death. Nobody can extend her life beyond a very short span. Because her heart, brain and lungs are for all practical purposes useless, nobody would have even tried to extend her life artificially if she had not, fortuitously, been deriving oxygen-ated blood from her sister's bloodstream.

It is true that there are those who believe most sincerely—and the Archbishop of Westminster is among them—that it would be an immoral act to save Jodie, if by saving Jodie one must end Mary's life before its brief allotted span is complete.

For those who share this philosophy, the law, recently approved by Parliament, which permits abortion at any time up to the time of birth if the conditions set out in s 1(1)(d) of the Abortion Act 1967 (as substituted) are satisfied, is equally repugnant. But there are also those who believe with equal sincerity that it would be immoral not to assist Jodie if there is a good prospect that she might live a happy and fulfilled life if this operation is performed. The court is not equipped to choose between these competing philosophies. All that a court can say is that it is not at all obvious that this is the sort of clear-cut case, marking an absolute divorce from law and morality, which was of such concern to Lord Coleridge and his fellow judges.

There are sound reasons for holding that the existence of an emergency in the normal sense of the word is not an essential prerequisite for the application of the doctrine of necessity. The principle is one of necessity, not emergency: see Lord Goff (in *Re F (mental patient: sterilisation)* [1990] 2 AC 1 at 75), the Law Commission in its recent report (Law Com No 218 (1993), paras 35.5 to 35.6), and Wilson J in *Perka v R* (1984) 13 DLR (4th) 1 at 33.

There are also sound reasons for holding that the threat which constitutes the harm to be avoided does not have to be equated with 'unjust aggression', as Professor Glanville Williams has made clear in s 26.3 of the 1983 edition of his book. None of the formulations of the doctrine of necessity which I have noted in this judgment make any such requirement: in this respect it is different from the doctrine of private defence.

If a sacrificial separation operation on conjoined twins were to be permitted in circum-stances like these, there need be no room for the concern felt by Sir James Stephen that people would be too ready to avail themselves of exceptions to the law which they might suppose to apply to their cases (at the risk of other people's lives). Such an operation is, and is always likely to be, an exceptionally rare event, and because the medical literature shows that it is an operation to be avoided at all costs in the neonatal stage, there will be in practic-ally every case the opportunity for the doctors to place the relevant facts before a court for approval (or otherwise) before the operation is attempted.

According to Sir James Stephen, there are three necessary requirements for the applica-tion of the doctrine of necessity: (i) the act is needed to avoid inevitable and irreparable evil; (ii) no more should be done than is reasonably necessary for the purpose to be achieved; and (iii) the evil inflicted must not be disproportionate to the evil avoided.

Given that the principles of modern family law point irresistibly to the conclusion that the interests of Jodie must be preferred to the conflicting interests of Mary, I consider that all three of these requirements are satisfied in this case.

Finally, the doctrine of the sanctity of life respects the integrity of the human body. The pro-posed operation would give these children's bodies the integrity which nature denied them.

For these reasons I, too, would dismiss this appeal.

Lord Justice Robert Walker

Of the many real and imagined examples put before the court it is worth mentioning two incidents which really did happen, although neither was the subject of a court deci-sion. One is the awful dilemma which faced the commander of an Australian warship, in peacetime, when a very serious fire occurred in the engine room. He ordered the engine room to be sealed off and flooded with inert gas, in order to save the ship and the rest of the crew, although the order meant certain death for anyone who was still alive in the engine room. The other is the equally awful dilemma of a mountaineer, Simon Yates, who held his fellow climber, Joe Simpson, after he had slipped and was dangling on a rope over a precipice at 19,000 feet in the Andes. Yates held Simpson for an hour, unable to recover him and becoming increasingly exhausted. Yates then cut the rope. Almost miraculously Simpson landed on a snowy ice bridge 100 feet below, and survived. When they met again Simpson said to Yates, 'You did right'. This incident is mentioned in Professor Smith's 1989 Hamlyn Lectures, *Justification and Excuse in the Criminal Law* (1989) (p 79).

The House of Lords has made clear that a doctrine of necessity does form part of the common law: see *Re F (mental patient: sterilisation)* [1990] 2 AC 1 (especially in the speech of Lord Goff ([1990] 2 AC 1 at 74–78) and *R v Bournewood Community and Mental Health NHS Trust, ex p L (Secretary of State for Health)* [1999] 1 AC 458. In the latter case Lord Goff said:

'The concept of necessity has its role to play in all branches of our law of obligations—in contract (see the cases on agency of necessity); in tort (see *Re F*); in restitution (see the sections on necessity in the standard books on the subject) and in our criminal law. It is therefore a concept of great importance. It is perhaps surprising, however, that the significant role it has to play in the law of torts has come to be recognized at so late a stage in the development of our law.' (See [1999] 1 AC 458 at 490.)

. . .

In truth there is no helpful analogy or parallel to the situation which the court has to consider in this case. It is unprecedented and paradoxical in that in law each twin has the right to life, but Mary's dependence on Jodie is severely detrimental to Jodie, and is expected to lead to the death of both twins within a few months. Each twin's right to life includes the right to physical integrity, that is the right to a whole body over which the individual will, on reaching an age of understanding, have autonomy and the right to self-determination: see the citations from Bland's case collected in *St George's Healthcare NHS Trust v S* [1999] Fam 26 at 43–45.

In the absence of Parliamentary intervention the law as to the defence of necessity is going to have to develop on a case by case basis, as Rose LJ said in *R v Abdul-Hussain*. I would extend it, if it needs to be extended, to cover this case. It is a case of doctors owing conflicting legal (and not merely social or moral) duties. It is a case where the test of proportionality is met, since it is a matter of life and death, and on the evidence Mary is bound to die soon in any event. It is not a case of evaluating the relative worth of two human lives, but of undertaking surgery without which neither life will have the bodily integrity (or wholeness) which is its due. It should not be regarded as a further step down a slippery slope because the case of conjoined twins presents an unique problem.

There is on the facts of this case some element of protecting Jodie against the unnatural invasion of her body through the physical burden imposed by her conjoined twin. That element must not be overstated. It would be absurd to suggest that Mary, a pitiful and innocent baby, is an unjust aggressor. Such language would be even less acceptable than dismissing Mary's death as a 'side-effect'. Nevertheless, the doctors' duty to protect and save Jodie's life if they can is of fundamental importance to the resolution of this appeal.

Declaration accordingly.

It will be noted that Brooke LJ quoted with approval three requirements for the defence of necessity:

(1) the act is needed to avoid inevitable and irreparable evil;

(2) no more should be done than is reasonably necessary for the purpose to be achieved; and

(3) the evil inflicted must not be disproportionate to the evil avoided.

The difficulty with these three requirements is that they would have provided a defence for the defendants in *Dudley and Stephens*, although all the members of the Court of Appeal were in agreement that that decision was correct. It may therefore be safest to state that the present approach of the courts is that necessity was available on the facts of *Re A*, and may be in analogous cases, but the courts will develop the law on a case-by-case basis. If one were to try to derive a general principle from *Re A*, the best may be the following suggestion of Nathan Tamblyn's:

> if a group of two or more people are virtually certain to suffer death imminently and together, from the same cause, but one or more could be saved only by killing a particular person in that group, then such killing would be lawful. (The killer does not have to be one of the group.)[77]

In *Nicklinson v Ministry of Justice*[78] the Court of Appeal refused to use the defence to permit euthanasia (see Chapter 5, Section 7). A major reason for not using the defence was that the Court believed it was for Parliament to decide whether or not to change the law on such a controversial issue, not for the courts. A discussion of how the courts might develop a more principled approach to necessity in these kinds of cases can be found in Part II of this chapter.

2.4 IMPLIED RECOGNITION OF NECESSITY

Although necessity is rarely recognized expressly, Peter Glazebrook has argued that there is 'concealed defence of necessity'. He argues that, even in cases where it is not openly recognized as a defence, the principle that a person should not be guilty of doing the lesser of two evils influences the courts' reasoning. Indeed there are very few cases where a defendant is convicted after doing an act which was the lesser of two evils.[79] In some cases where the defendant has done the lesser of two evils no prosecution is brought; in others the magistrates or jury acquit even if technically an offence was committed. Peter Glazebrook had argued that there is a general principle of statutory interpretation:

> that it requires clear and unambiguous language before the courts will hold that a statutory provision was intended to apply to cases in which more harm will, in all probability, be caused by complying with it than by contravening it.[80]

In fact this is probably part of the normal rule that a statute should be interpreted in such a way as to give effect to the purpose of the statute. An example may be *Bourne*[81] where the defendant (a surgeon) was charged under section 58 of the Offences Against the Person Act 1861 with unlawfully procuring a miscarriage. The surgeon had performed an abortion on a

---

[77] Tamblyn (2015).
[78] [2013] EWCA Civ 961. The argument was not pursued in the Supreme Court.
[79] *Kitson* (1955) 39 Cr App R 66 and *Dudley and Stephens* (1884) 14 QBD 273 are arguably two such cases.
[80] Glazebrook (1972: 93).   [81] [1938] 3 All ER 615.

suicidal 14-year-old who had been the victim of rape. MacNaughten J held that because the doctor had performed the operation in order to save the girl's life he had not acted unlawfully. Without saying so explicitly MacNaughten J appears to have been reading the defence of necessity into the word 'unlawful' in the statute.[82]

2.5 DURESS OF CIRCUMSTANCES

In some cases where the defendant does the lesser of two evils he or she will be able to rely on the defence of duress of circumstances. For example, in *Pipe v DPP*[83] a man was driving his ill son to hospital and broke the speed limit. Owen J held that the jury should have been allowed to consider whether he could rely on duress of circumstances (or necessity as he called it). As will be discussed in Section 5, duress provides a defence where the defendant reasonably believes that the circumstances are such that unless he or she commits a crime he or she or another will suffer death or serious injury and that a reasonable person in the same situation would have committed the crime. This defence clearly overlaps to some extent with necessity. Being faced with the threat of death which the defendant avoids by driving through a red light would fall under the defence of duress of circumstances, it would also be said to be the lesser of two evils. However, duress of circumstances is in some sense narrower and in some sense wider than necessity. It is narrower in that duress of circumstances is not available in order to avoid a threat less than death or grievous bodily harm. However, where it is available necessity may provide a defence even where the harm threatened is less than serious harm. Duress of circumstances is wider than a necessity defence would be, in that it covers the situation where the defendant reasonably believed there to be a threat of death or serious injury, even if there was in fact no such threat. A necessity defence would not cover such a situation.[84] Further, if the defendant was threatened with grievous bodily harm unless he or she caused grievous bodily harm, although the two kinds of harm may be the same and so he or she may not be able to rely on necessity, he or she may be able to rely on duress of circumstances and argue that a reasonable person would have given in to the threat.

FURTHER READING

Bohlander, M. (2006a) 'Of Shipwrecked Sailors, Unborn Children, Conjoined Twins and Hijacked Airplanes—Taking Human Life and the Defence of Necessity' *Journal of Criminal Law* 70: 147.

Bohlander, M. (2006b) 'In Extremis—Hijacked Airplanes, "Collateral Damage" and the Limits of Criminal Law' *Criminal Law Review* 579.

Gardner, S. (2005) 'Direct Action and the Defence of Necessity' *Criminal Law Review* 371.

Glazebrook, P. (1972) 'The Necessity Plea in English Criminal Law' *Cambridge Law Journal* 31: 87.

Stark, F. (2013c) 'Necessity and *Nicklinson*' *Criminal Law Review* 947.

Tamblyn, N. (2015) 'Necessity and Murder' *Journal of Criminal Law* 79: 46.

---

[82] See also *Cichon v DPP* [1994] Crim LR 918 and *Gillick v West Norfolk and Wisbech AHA* [1986] AC 112 (HL).

[83] [2012] EWHC 1821 (Admin).

[84] Unless the necessity defence was modified to cover the case where the defendant reasonably believed that he was acting in doing the lesser of two evils.

3 CHASTISEMENT

In the past the common law defence of lawful chastisement permitted one person to hit another over whom they exercised power. This covered the chastisement of apprentices, children, or servants. Nowadays the defence has been restricted to the chastisement of children and is available only to parents and those who have parental responsibility for the child.[85] Further it is not available if actual bodily harm or more serious injury has been caused. Section 58 of the Children Act 2004 now provides:

> (1) In relation to any offence specified under subsection (2), battery of a child cannot be justified on the ground that it constituted reasonable punishment.
>
> (2) The offences referred to in subsection (1) are—
>
> (a) an offence under section 18 or 20 of the Offences Against the Person Act 1861 (wounding and causing grievous bodily harm);
>
> (b) an offence under section 47 of that Act (assault occasioning actual bodily harm);
>
> (c) an offence under section 1 of the Children and Young Persons Act 1933.

In effect then, reasonable chastisement will only provide a defence to an assault or battery. Any punishment involving greater force than this will be unlawful. Critics of the new law may complain that it fails to give sufficient guidance to parents because the line between a battery and actual bodily harm is so unclear. Others might complain that the law still allows parents to hit children in a way which would be a criminal offence if done to an adult.

FURTHER READING

Choudhry, S. (2009) 'Parental Responsibility and Corporal Punishment' in R. Probert, S. Gilmore, and J. Herring (eds) *Responsible Parents and Parental Responsibility* (Oxford: Hart).

Department of Health (2000) *Protecting Children, Supporting Parents: A Consultation Document on the Physical Punishment of Children* (London: Department of Health).

Rogers, J. (2002) 'A Criminal Lawyer's Response to Chastisement' *Criminal Law Review* 98.

---

4 CONSENT

This defence was discussed in Chapter 6.

5 DURESS

DEFINITION

Duress is a defence to all crimes except murder, attempted murder, and certain forms of treason. To establish the defence a defendant must show that:

(1) he or she committed the crime because of threats of death or grievous bodily harm;

(2) a reasonable person would have acted as the defendant did.

---

[85] See Choudhry (2009) for an excellent discussion of the law.

5.1 TERMINOLOGY

There are two forms of duress that are recognized in the law: duress by threats and duress by circumstances. There is no difference in the legal requirements between them and the distinction is made to help clarify the law. Duress by threats occurs where one person commits a crime after another person has threatened to kill or injure someone if he or she does not commit a crime. For example, Alf is kidnapped by a terrorist and told he will be killed unless he sets fire to a building. If Alf does what he is told and is charged with arson he can plead the defence of duress by threats. Duress of circumstances arises where no one has specifically told the defendant to commit the crime but the circumstances are such that the defendant believes that unless he or she commits a crime he or she or others will suffer death or serious injury. For example, Brian while driving his car is approached by a man wielding a gun. He fears he is about to be shot and drives away breaking the speed limit. In such a case Brian may rely on the defence of duress of circumstances to a charge of dangerous driving. No one told him he must drive away at speed, but that is a reasonable way he can escape from the threat. Sometimes it can be difficult to decide whether a case was one of duress by circumstances or duress by threats,[86] but as the rules governing the two defences are identical[87] it does not matter in practice which it is. →5 (p.728)

5.2 TO WHAT CRIMES IS DURESS A DEFENCE?

It has been established[88] that duress is available to all crimes, except murder, attempted murder, and certain forms of treason.[89] The leading case establishing that duress is not a defence to murder is *Howe*:

R v Howe
[1987] AC 417 (HL)

The House of Lords heard a number of conjoined appeals. Michael Howe and John Bannister appealed against their convictions for murder. They claimed that they joined in two brutal assaults on young men which culminated in their deaths only because they had been told by an older man with a substantial criminal record that if they did not they would suffer violence. They understood him to mean they would be killed. Cornelius Burke and William Clarkson were convicted of murdering a man known as Button. Burke admitted he shot Button but said he did so only after Clarkson had threatened him with violence and that in any event the gun went off unintentionally. In both cases the key question was whether duress was a defence to murder.

---

86 See e.g. *Cole* [1994] Crim LR 582.

87 *Willer* (1986) 83 Cr App R 225; *Conway* (1988) 88 Cr App R 159; *Martin* (1989) 88 Cr App R 343.

88 The burden of proof is on the prosecution to disprove the defence once the defendant has introduced evidence that he acted under duress (*Giaquinto* [2001] EWCA Crim 2696). The significance of this is that if, e.g., the jury thought that a reasonable person in the defendant's shoes might possibly have acted as the defendant did they should acquit because the defence has not been disproved.

89 Although it seems that a statutory offence could make it clear that duress is not to be a defence (*New Forest Local Education Authority* [2007] EWHC 2584 (Admin)).

Lord Hailsham of St Marylebone LC

I begin by affirming that, while there can never be a direct correspondence between law and morality, an attempt to divorce the two entirely is and has always proved to be doomed to failure, and, in the present case, the overriding objects of the criminal law must be to protect innocent lives and to set a standard of conduct which ordinary men and women are expected to observe if they are to avoid criminal responsibility.

[**Lord Hailsham** then cited and discussed *Dudley and Stephens* (1884) 14 QBD 273.]

In general, I must say that I do not at all accept in relation to the defence of duress that it is either good morals, good policy or good law to suggest, as did the majority in *Lynch's* case and the minority in *Abbott v R*, that the ordinary man of reasonable fortitude is not to be supposed to be capable of heroism if he is asked to take an innocent life rather than sacrifice his own. Doubtless in actual practice many will succumb to temptation, as they did in *R v Dudley and Stephens*. But many will not, and I do not believe that as a 'concession to human frailty' (see Smith and Hogan *Criminal Law* (5th edn, 1983) p 215) the former should be exempt from liability to criminal sanctions if they do. I have known in my own lifetime of too many acts of heroism by ordinary human beings of no more than ordinary fortitude to regard a law as either 'just or humane' which withdraws the protection of the criminal law from the innocent victim and casts the cloak of its protection on the coward and the poltroon in the name of a 'concession to human frailty'.

I must not, however, underestimate the force of the arguments on the other side, advanced as they have been with such force and such persuasiveness by some of the most eminent legal minds, judicial and academic, in the country.

First, amongst these is, perhaps, the argument from logic and consistency. A long line of cases, it is said, carefully researched and closely analysed, establish duress as an available defence in a wide range of crimes, some at least, like wounding with intent to commit grievous bodily harm, carrying the heaviest penalties commensurate with their gravity. To cap this, it is pointed out that, at least in theory, a defendant accused of this crime under s 18 of the Offences against the Person Act 1861, but acquitted on the grounds of duress, will still be liable to a charge of murder if the victim dies within the traditional period of one year and a day. I am not, perhaps, persuaded of this last point as much as I should. It is not simply an anomaly based on the defence of duress. It is a product of the peculiar *mens rea* allowed on a charge of murder which is not confined to an intent to kill. More persuasive, perhaps, is the point based on the availability of the defence of duress on a charge of attempted murder, where the actual intent to kill is an essential prerequisite. It may be that we must meet this *casus omissus* in your Lordships' House when we come to it. It may require reconsideration of the availability of the defence in that case too.

I would, however, prefer to meet the case of alleged inconsistency head on. Consistency and logic, though inherently desirable, are not always prime characteristics of a penal code based like the common law on custom and precedent. Law so based is not an exact science. All the same, I feel I am required to give some answer to the question posed. If duress is available as a defence to some of the most grave crimes why, it may legitimately be asked, stop at murder, whether as accessory or principal and whether in the second or the first degree? But surely I am entitled, as in the view of the Common Serjeant in the instant case of Clarkson and Burke, to believe that some degree of proportionality between the threat and the offence must, at least to some extent, be a prerequisite of the defence under existing law. Few would resist threats to the life of a loved one if the alternative were driving across the red lights or in excess of 70mph on the motorway. But, to use the Common Serjeant's analogy, it would take rather more than the threat of a slap on the wrist or even moderate pain or injury to discharge the evidential burden even in the case of a fairly serious assault. In such a case the 'concession to human frailty' is no more than to say that in such circumstances a reasonable man of average courage is entitled to embrace as a matter of choice the alternative which a reasonable man could regard as the lesser of two evils. Other considerations necessarily arise where the choice is between the threat of death or *a fortiori* of serious injury and deliberately taking an innocent life. In such a case a reasonable man might reflect that one innocent human life is at least as valuable as his own or that of his loved one. In such a case a man cannot claim that he is choosing the lesser of two evils. Instead, he is embracing the cognate but morally disreputable principle that the end justifies the means.

I am not so shocked as some of the judicial opinions have been at the need, if this be the conclusion, to invoke the availability of administrative as distinct from purely judicial remedies for the hardships which might otherwise occur in the most agonising cases.

[**Lord Hailsham** went on to discuss *Dudley and Stephens*.]

Appeals dismissed.

This case then establishes that duress is not a defence to murder. By a majority of three to two the House of Lords in *Gotts*[90] decided that duress was not a defence to attempted murder. In *Ness* it was held that duress is available to a charge of conspiracy to murder.[91] In *Wilson (Ashlea)*[92] a 13-year-old boy helped his father kill a woman. He said he was terrified of his father. The Court of Appeal upheld his conviction for murder, noting that 'there may be grounds for criticising'[93] a law which stated that a 13-year-old could not rely on duress as a defence to murder. However, Lord Phillips confirmed that that was indeed the current state of the law.[94] The Law Commission has recommended that duress should be a complete defence to murder.

5.3 WHAT ARE THE ELEMENTS OF THE DEFENCE OF DURESS?

The two key elements of duress are set out by Lord Lane CJ in *Graham*, in a statement which was approved by the House of Lords in *Howe*:

Was [D], or may he have been, impelled to act as he did because, as a result of what he reasonably believed [E] had said or done, he had good cause to fear that if he did not so act [E] would kill him or . . . cause him serious physical injury?

If so, have the prosecution made the jury sure that a sober person of reasonable firmness, sharing the characteristics of [D], would not have responded to whatever he reasonably believed [E] said or did by [committing the crime]?

We will now look at these requirements in further detail:

The defendant must act because of a threat of death or serious injury

This requirement contains a number of separate elements:

The defendant must act because of the threats or the circumstances

The defendant must act because of the threats or circumstances and not for other reasons. It would be in only rather bizarre circumstances that the defendant would commit a crime following

---

[90] [1992] 2 AC 412. [91] [2011] Crim LR 645. [92] [2007] EWCA Crim 1251.
[93] *Ibid*, para. 17. [94] See Ashworth (2008a) for a critical discussion of this case.

threats of death or serious harm, but not because of the threats. The issue is most relevant in cases where the defendant is facing a variety of threats, only some of which are of death or serious harm. In *Valderrama-Vega*[95] the defendant was facing three pressures when he committed his offence: he had been threatened with disclosure of his homosexual tendencies, he was under severe financial pressures, and there were threats of death or serious injury. Only the threats of death or serious injury could form the basis of a defence of duress. The Court of Appeal held that he could still rely on the defence of duress as long as the threats of death or serious injury were for him a substantial reason for committing the crime. They did not have to be the only reason.

A case which raises a different aspect of this requirement is *DPP v Bell*,[96] where the defendant was in fear of his life and therefore drove off in a car, even though he had consumed excess alcohol. It was held that even if the defence had been available for his initial driving away he had to desist from the crime (the driving) once the threat was no longer potent. By continuing to drive having escaped from the danger area he was from then on not acting because of the threat and so could not rely on the defence of duress. A similar approach was taken in *DPP v Mullally*,[97] where two sisters were trying to escape from the violent husband of one of them, who was threatening them. They got into a car and drove off, even though they had consumed excess alcohol. They carried on driving even when they were over a mile away from the man and were being followed by a police car. The magistrate acquitted the driver of a drink-driving offence, as she explained that she did not stop because she was in her nightclothes and wanted to get home. On appeal the Divisional Court held that no reasonable person would have thought it reasonable to continue drunken driving once the threat had passed, due to what one was wearing. This makes it clear that an objective test is used in deciding when it was reasonable to stop committing the offence.

The threat must be one of death or grievous bodily harm

Duress is available only if the threat was of death or serious harm.[98] In *R v A*[99] the Court of Appeal explained, *obiter*, that rape could constitute serious harm in this context. A lesser kind of threat will not suffice.[100] So threats to property, reputation, or of minor injury cannot form the basis of a duress defence, even where the defendant has committed a very minor crime.[101] In *Dao*[102] the Court of Appeal expressed the provisional view that a threat of false imprisonment would not be sufficient to form the basis of the duress defence.

There is some doubt whether a threat to cause a serious psychological injury would be sufficient. The House of Lords in *Burstow* explained that the phrase 'grievous bodily harm' in the Offences Against the Person Act 1861 included serious psychological illnesses. In doing this they accepted that the law should not draw a line between physical and psychological injuries. However, in *Baker and Wilkins*[103] and *GAC*[104] it was suggested that for duress there had to be a threat of serious physical harm. This must be questioned, given the reluctance in the criminal law generally towards distinguishing physical and psychological injuries.[105]

---

[95] [1985] Crim LR 220.   [96] [1992] RTR 335.   [97] [2006] EWHC 3448 (Admin).

[98] *Graham* [1982] 1 All ER 801, approved by the House of Lords in *Howe* [1987] AC 417.

[99] [2012] EWCA Crim 434. See also *R v Hammond* [2013] EWCA Crim 2709, although that case suggested unwanted sexual touching would not amount to serious harm.

[100] A defendant who drove while intoxicated in order to acquire a painkiller for his daughter who was ill, but not seriously so, could not successfully rely on the defence of duress of circumstances (*DPP v Hicks* [2002] All ER (D) 285 (QBD)), although s. 5(2)(b) of the Criminal Damage Act 1971 provides a defence to a charge of criminal damage for lesser threats.

[101] For criticism of the law in this regard, see Herring (1999).   [102] [2012] EWCA Crim 1717.

[103] [1997] Crim LR 497 (CA).   [104] [2013] EWCA Crim 1472.   [105] Loveless (2014).

The point is particularly significant where a woman is in an abusive relationship and threatened with ongoing psychological abuse.

The threat can be of death or serious harm to anyone

At one time it was thought that for duress to provide a defence the threat must be directed towards the defendant or his close family.[106] It is now clear that the defence can be available if the defendant fears that anyone for whom the defendant reasonably regards himself responsible is under threat.[107] This might include a close friend or a child he was looking after. It can also include a pregnant woman's fears for her foetus.[108] Of course, the identity of the person who is in danger from the threat will be relevant when considering whether a reasonable person would give in to the threat.[109]

The threat must not come from the defendant himself

This point was stressed in *Rodger and Rose*,[110] where the defendants were charged with offences connected with escaping from prison. They sought to rely on the defence of duress. They argued that they had become so depressed because of the conditions in prison that they would have committed suicide had they not escaped. They were therefore facing a threat of death. The Court of Appeal held that duress was not available because the threat of death did not come from a source extraneous from the defendants.[111]

The defendant can rely on what he or she reasonably believed to be a threat

What if the defendant had thought that he or she was facing a threat, but in fact he or she was not? The direction in *Graham* makes it clear that the defendant must have reasonable grounds to believe that the threat had been made.[112] In *Cairns*[113] it was confirmed that if the defendant reasonably believed there was a threat of death or grievous bodily harm, the defence may be available, even if there is in fact no such threat.[114] Lord Bingham in *R v Z*[115] held that the defence of duress is only available if the defendant both genuinely and reasonably believes the threat to have been made.

> ### QUESTION
>
> It appears, then, that in cases of private defence if the defendant unreasonably believes that he or she is being attacked he or she can have a defence (*Williams*). But in cases of duress if the defendant unreasonably believes he or she is being threatened he or she cannot rely on the defence (*Graham*). Can you think of any reasons why this should be so?

---

[106] *Ortiz* (1986) 83 Cr App R 173 (CA).

[107] *R v Z* [2005] 2 AC 467 (HL), para. 19; *Abdul-Hussain* [1999] Crim LR 570 (CA).

[108] *R v GAC* [2013] EWCA Crim 1472.

[109] A vague threat to the general public will not be sufficient (see *Shayler* [2001] EWCA Crim 1977, [2001] 1 WLR 2206 (CA). The case went to the House of Lords ([2002] UKHL 11, [2002] 2 All ER 477), which did not discuss the duress issues).

[110] [1998] 1 Cr App R 143 (CA).

[111] The point was also applied in *R v Quayle* [2005] EWCA Crim 1415, where the defendants were committing a drug offence to avoid the pain of medical conditions.

[112] This was approved by Lord Bingham in *R v Z* [2005] UKHL 22, para. 23.

[113] [1999] 2 Cr App R 137.   [114] See also *Safi* [2003] Crim LR 721.

[115] [2005] UKHL 22, para. 23.

The reasonable person must have responded to the threat in the way the defendant did

In considering this issue there are various factors to be examined. These will be listed and then extracts from the leading cases discussing these issues will follow:

The jury must decide that the reasonable person must have responded to the threat as the defendant did

The jury, in deciding how a reasonable person would respond to the threat, is likely to consider how severe the threat was and how grave the required crime. In other words the jury is likely to consider whether the defendant responded in a way which was proportionate to the threat.[116] However, the jury will appreciate the terror felt by a person facing a threat of death or serious injury. The defendant is not expected to behave in an especially heroic way, but simply in a reasonable way.

What characteristics of the defendant should be attributed to the reasonable person?

The leading case is *Bowen* (in the following extract).

To clarify the implications of this judgment it is useful to distinguish two questions:

(1) Which characteristics can be taken into account?

(2) For what purposes are characteristics relevant?

As to question (1), *Bowen* provides a reasonably clear description of how a trial judge should decide whether a characteristic can be ascribed to the reasonable person. It must be shown:

(a) The characteristic provides a reason for failing to live up to the standards of the reasonable person. Hence low IQ was not relevant, but post-traumatic stress disorder may be.[117] There is no reason why those with a low IQ should be less brave than those with a higher IQ.[118] Contrast a person suffering with post-traumatic stress disorder who does have a good reason why they cannot be expected to be as brave as an ordinary person.

(b) The characteristic must not be self-induced (e.g. intoxication).[119]

As to question (2), although the Court of Appeal judgment in *Bowen* was ostensibly looking at characteristics which affect the level of firmness that can be expected, the court, in its list of potentially relevant characteristics, included pregnancy and physical disability. But surely these characteristics do not affect the level of bravery that can be demonstrated? What this may indicate is that characteristics may be ascribed to the reasonable person in duress for three different reasons:

(1) To affect the level of firmness expected.

(2) To affect the ability of the defendant to escape from the threat (e.g. physical disability).

(3) To affect the gravity of the threat (e.g. pregnancy).

Although the Court of Appeal did not say so explicitly it appears that characteristics may be relevant in any of these three ways. In *Bowen* the Court of Appeal perhaps did not give

---

[116] Lord Hailsham in *Howe* [1987] AC 417, 432.
[117] The criticisms of this are discussed in Part II of this chapter.
[118] Though see *Antar* [2004] EWCA Crim 2708 where the defendant's very low IQ and learning difficulties were held to be admissible characteristics.
[119] *Flatt* [1996] Crim LR 576.

as much consideration as it might have to the question whether the defendant's low IQ led him to think the threat was more serious than it was or to fail to see a way of escaping from the threat.

The defendant must take any reasonable opportunity to escape from the threat

The defendant must have taken any opportunity to escape from the threat that a reasonable person would have taken, for example by seeking police protection. In *Heath*[120] the defendant was threatened with violence unless he helped transport drugs in a few days' time. He was told that he could not rely on duress as a defence because he could have escaped from the threat by seeking assistance from the police or moving to relatives in Scotland.[121]

The threat must be of imminent harm

In *Abdul-Hussain*[122] the Court of Appeal stressed that the threat of death or serious injury had to be imminent. In *R v N*[123] the Court of Appeal upheld a direction that 'There has to be a belief that he reasonably and genuinely believed that he would be killed or seriously injured either immediately or almost immediately.'

The defendant must have good cause to believe that the threat could be carried out

The *Graham* direction makes it clear that the defendant must have good cause to believe that the threat could be carried out. If, therefore, Nick said he was going to kill the Queen unless Mary committed a robbery, the jury may require some convincing that Mary had good cause to believe that the threat would be carried out. Although, no doubt, in deciding whether or not Mary had good cause to believe the threat, the jury would take into account the pressurized position in which she found herself.

The defendant must not have put him or herself in a position in which he or she could have been threatened in this way

If defendants put themselves into a position where the threat could be made against them then the defence of duress is not available. So the defence is not available if the defendant associates with criminals in circumstances in which he or she knows or ought to know that he or she could become subject to compulsion to commit a crime. This was confirmed by the House of Lords in *R v Z* (extracted later in the section).

Internal duress cannot be relied upon

Defendants cannot rely on threats that come from within themselves. This was made clear in *Quayle* (extracted later in the section). In that case defendants who sought to use illegal drugs to provide pain relief from the effects of a medical condition were not entitled to rely on the defence of necessity. In *Altham*[124] the decision in *Quayle* was followed despite a claim by the defendant that the law infringed his human rights. He was in severe pain

---

120 [2000] Crim LR 109. See also *Harmer* [2002] Crim LR 401.

121 However, it seems that there are some cases in which the defendant may be able to persuade the jury that seeking police protection was not reasonable (e.g. if the gang is particularly vicious (see *Hudson* [1971] 2 All ER 244 (CA), although doubt was cast on that case in *R v Z* [2005] UKHL 22, para. 27, and it was held in *Batchelor* [2013] EWCA Crim 2638 to be incorrectly decided)).

122 [1999] Crim LR 570.   123 *R v N* [2007] EWCA Crim 3479.   124 [2006] Crim LR 633.

following an injury and used cannabis as a pain relief. He sought to argue that his right to protection from inhuman and degrading treatment in Article 3 of the ECHR gave him a right to use illegal drugs for pain relief purposes. The Court of Appeal held that Article 3 meant the state was obliged where reasonable to take steps to prevent him suffering ill treatment, but that did not mean the state had to allow him to use illegal substances as a remedy.

These issues were discussed in the following three leading cases:

R v Bowen
[1996] 4 All ER 837 (CA)

Cecil Bowen was convicted of obtaining services by deception. He accepted the key facts alleged by the prosecution but claimed that he had acted as he did only because two men had accosted him in a pub and threatened that he and his family would be petrol-bombed if he did not assist in the plan. He was also told that his family would be attacked if he sought the assistance of the police. There was some evidence that he had an IQ of 68 (which would be in the lowest 2 per cent of the population) and unusually suggestible. The question was whether the jury should have been directed to consider the response to the threat of a reasonable person with an IQ of 68.

Lord Justice Stuart-Smith [read the judgment of the court]

The classic statement of the law is to be found in the judgment of the Court of Appeal in *Graham* (1982) 74 Cr App R 235. At p 240 Lord Lane CJ, giving the judgment of the Court [stated]:

> 'Whether the words "in his situation" comprehend more than the surrounding circumstances, and extend to the characteristics of the defendant himself, it is difficult to say, and for that reason we would not recommend without qualification the adoption of that solution. We think that there should be an objective element in the requirements of the defence so that in the final event it will be for the jury to determine whether the threat was one which the defendant in question could not reasonably have been expected to resist. This will allow the jury to take into account the nature of the offence committed, its relationship to the threats which the defendant believed to exist, the threats themselves and the circumstances in which they were made, and the personal characteristics of the defendant. The last consideration is, we feel, a most important one. Threats directed against the weak, immature or disabled person, may well be much more compelling than the same threats directed against a normal healthy person.

> 'As a matter of public policy, it seems to us essential to limit the defence of duress by means of an objective criterion formulated in terms of reasonableness. Consistency of approach in defences to criminal liability is obviously desirable. Provocation and duress are analogous. In provocation the words or actions of one person break the self-control of another. In duress the words or actions of one person break the will of another. The law requires a defendant to have the self-control reasonably to be expected of the ordinary citizen in his situation. It should likewise require him to have the steadfastness reasonably to be expected of the ordinary citizen in his situation. So too with self-defence, in which the law permits the use of no more force than

is reasonable in the circumstances. And, in general, if a mistake is to excuse what would otherwise be criminal, the mistake must be a reasonable one.

'It follows that we accept Mr Sherrard's submission that the direction in this case was too favourable to the appellant. The Crown having conceded that the issue of duress was open to the appellant and was raised on the evidence, the correct approach on the facts of this case would have been as follows: (1) Was the defendant, or may he have been, impelled to act as he did because, as a result of what he reasonably believed King had said or done, he had good cause to fear that if he did not so act King would kill him or (if this is to be added) cause him serious physical injury? (2) If so, have the prosecution made the jury sure that a sober person of reasonable firmness, sharing the characteristics of the defendant, would not have responded to whatever he reasonably believed King said or did by taking part in the killing? The fact that a defendant's will to resist has been eroded by the voluntary consumption of drink or drugs or both is not relevant to this test.'

This formulation was approved by the House of Lords in *R v Howe* [1987] AC 417 (see per Lord Mackay of Clashfern at pp 65, 66 respectively).

But the question remains, what are the relevant characteristics of the accused to which the jury should have regard in considering the second objective test?

[**Lord Justice Stuart-Smith** reviewed the decisions in *Emery* (1993) 14 Cr App R (S) 394; *Hegarty* [1994] Crim LR 353; *Horne* [1994] Crim LR 584; *Hurst* [1995] 1 Cr App R 82; *Morhall* [1996] AC 90 and continued:]

What principles are to be derived from these authorities? We think they are as follows:

(1) The mere fact that the accused is more pliable, vulnerable, timid or susceptible to threats than a normal person are not characteristics with which it is legitimate to invest the reasonable/ordinary person for the purpose of considering the objective test.

(2) The defendant may be in a category of persons who the jury may think less able to resist pressure than people not within that category. Obvious examples are age, where a young person may well not be so robust as a mature one; possibly sex, though many women would doubtless consider they had as much moral courage to resist pressure as men; pregnancy, where there is added fear for the unborn child; serious physical disability, which may inhibit self protection; recognized mental illness or psychiatric condition, such as post traumatic stress disorder leading to learned helplessness.

(3) Characteristics which may be relevant in considering provocation, because they relate to the nature of the provocation, itself will not necessarily be relevant in cases of duress. Thus homosexuality may be relevant to provocation if the provocative words or conduct are related to this characteristic; it cannot be relevant in duress, since there is no reason to think that homosexuals are less robust in resisting threats of the kind that are relevant in duress cases.

(4) Characteristics due to self-induced abuse, such as alcohol, drugs or glue-sniffing, cannot be relevant.

(5) Psychiatric evidence may be admissible to show that the accused is suffering from some mental illness, mental impairment or recognized psychiatric condition provided persons generally suffering from such condition may be more susceptible to pressure and threats and thus to assist the jury in deciding whether a reasonable person suffering from such a condition might have been impelled to act as the defendant did. It is not admissible simply to show that in the doctor's opinion an accused, who is not suffering from such illness or condition, is especially timid, suggestible or vulnerable to pressure and threats. Nor is medical opinion admissible to bolster or support the credibility of the accused.

(6) Where counsel wishes to submit that the accused has some characteristic which falls within (2) above, this must be made plain to the judge. The question may arise in relation to the admissibility of medical evidence of the nature set out in (5). If so, the judge will have to rule at that stage. There may, however, be no medical evidence, or, as in this case, medical evidence may have been introduced for some other purpose, e.g. to challenge the admissibility or weight of a confession. In such a case counsel must raise the question before speeches in the absence of the jury, so that the judge can rule whether the alleged characteristic is capable of being relevant. If he rules that it is, then he must leave it to the jury.

(7) In the absence of some direction from the judge as to what characteristics are capable of being regarded as relevant, we think that the direction approved in Graham without more will not be as helpful as it might be, since the jury may be tempted, especially if there is evidence, as there was in this case, relating to suggestibility and vulnerability, to think that these are relevant. In most cases it is probably only the age and sex of the accused that is capable of being relevant. If so, the judge should, as he did in this case, confine the characteristics in question to these.

How are these principles to be applied in this case? Miss Levitt [counsel for Bowen], accepts rightly in our opinion, that the evidence that the appellant was abnormally suggestible and a vulnerable individual is irrelevant. But she submits that the fact that he had, or may have had, a low IQ of 68 is relevant since it might inhibit his ability to seek the protection of the police. We do not agree. We do not see how low IQ, short of mental impairment or mental defectiveness, can be said to be a characteristic that makes those who have it less courageous and less able to withstand threats and pressure. Moreover, we do not think that any such submission as is now made, based solely on the appellant's low IQ, was ever advanced at the trial. Furthermore, it is to be noted that in two places . . . the judge told the jury that if they thought the appellant passed the subjective test they should acquit him. We are quite satisfied that in the circumstances of this case the judge's direction was sufficient. He directed the jury to consider the only two relevant characteristics, namely age and sex. It would not have assisted them, and might well have confused them, if he had added, without qualification, that the person of reasonable firmness was one who shared the characteristics of the appellant.

For these reasons, the appeal will be dismissed.

Appeal dismissed.

R v Z (in some reports R v Hasan)
[2005] 2 AC 467

The defendant, Aytach Hasan, sought to rely on a defence of duress in response to a charge of burglary. It was alleged that he had entered the victim's house, claiming that the victim had telephoned for a prostitute. He produced a knife and took £4,000 from a safe. Hasan claimed that he had only done this in response to threats of violence from one Sullivan, for whom he worked and who had a reputation as a violent man. One issue considered by the House of Lords concerned the admissibility of various statements by the defendants. The issue of concern to substantive criminal law was the direction of the judge that the defendant could not rely on threats by a man known as S because he had associated with him and therefore put himself in a position in which he knew that he was likely to be subjected to threats. The defendant was convicted and appealed.

Lord Bingham of Cornhill

18. Where duress is established, it does not ordinarily operate to negative any legal ingredient of the crime which the defendant has committed. Nor is it now regarded as justifying the conduct of the defendant, as has in the past been suggested. . . . Duress is now properly to be regarded as a defence which, if established, excuses what would otherwise be criminal conduct: *Director of Public Prosecutions for Northern Ireland v Lynch* [1975] AC 653, 671, 680, 710–711 and *R v Hibbert* (1995) 99 CCC (3d) 193, 204, 213–214 and 219, paras 21, 38 and 47, per Lamer CJC.

19. Duress affords a defence which, if raised and not disproved, exonerates the defendant altogether. It does not, like the defence of provocation to a charge of murder, serve merely to reduce the seriousness of the crime which the defendant has committed. And the victim of a crime committed under duress is not, like a person against whom a defendant uses force to defend himself, a person who has threatened the defendant or been perceived by the defendant as doing so. The victim of a crime committed under duress may be assumed to be morally innocent, having shown no hostility or aggression towards the defendant. The only criminal defences which have any close affinity with duress are necessity, where the force or compulsion is exerted not by human threats but by extraneous circumstances, and, perhaps, marital coercion under section 47 of the Criminal Justice Act 1925.

. . .

21. Having regard to these features of duress, I find it unsurprising that the law in this and other jurisdictions should have been developed so as to confine the defence of duress within narrowly defined limits. Most of these are not in issue in this appeal, but it seems to me important that the issues the House is asked to resolve should be approached with understanding of how the defence has developed, and to that end I shall briefly identify the most important limitations.

(1) Duress does not afford a defence to charges of murder (*R v Howe* [1987] AC 417), attempted murder (*R v Gotts* [1992] 2 AC 412) and, perhaps, some forms of treason: Smith & Hogan, *Criminal Law*, 10th ed (2002), p 254. The Law Commission has in the past (eg in Criminal Law: Report on Defences of General Application (1977) (Law Com No 83; HC 556), paras 2.44–2.46) recommended that the defence should be available as a defence to all offences, including murder, and the logic of this argument is irresistible. But their recommendation has not been adopted, no doubt because it is felt that in the case of the gravest crimes no threat to the defendant, however extreme, should excuse commission of the crime. . . .

(2) To found a plea of duress the threat relied on must be to cause death or serious injury. . . .

(3) The threat must be directed against the defendant or his immediate family or someone close to him: Smith & Hogan, *Criminal Law*, 10th ed, p 258. In the light of recent Court of Appeal decisions such as *R v Conway* [1989] QB 290 and *R v Wright* [2000] Crim LR 510, the current (April 2003) specimen direction (no 49) of the Judicial Studies Board suggests that the threat must be directed, if not to the defendant or a member of his immediate family, to a person for whose safety the defendant would reasonably regard himself as responsible. The correctness of such a direction was not, and on the facts could not be, in issue on this appeal, but it appears to me, if strictly applied, to be consistent with the rationale of the duress exception.

(4) The relevant tests pertaining to duress have been largely stated objectively, with reference to the reasonableness of the defendant's perceptions and conduct and not, as is usual in many other areas of the criminal law, with primary reference to his subjective perceptions. It is necessary to return to this aspect, but in passing one may note the general observation

of Lord Morris of Borth-y-Gest in *Director of Public Prosecutions for Northern Ireland v Lynch* [1975] AC 653, 670:

> 'it is proper that any rational system of law should take fully into account the standards of honest and reasonable men. By those standards it is fair that actions and reactions may be tested.'

(5) The defence of duress is available only where the criminal conduct which it is sought to excuse has been directly caused by the threats which are relied upon.

(6) The defendant may excuse his criminal conduct on grounds of duress only if, placed as he was, there was no evasive action he could reasonably have been expected to take. It is necessary to return to this aspect also, but this is an important limitation of the duress defence and in recent years it has, as I shall suggest, been unduly weakened.

(7) The defendant may not rely on duress to which he has voluntarily laid himself open. The scope of this limitation raises the most significant issue on this part of this appeal, and I must return to it.

. . .

23. . . . It is evident that the judge, very properly, based himself on the Judicial Studies Board's specimen direction as promulgated in August 2000. That specimen direction included the words, adopted by the judge, 'he genuinely believed'. But the words used in *R v Graham (Paul)* and approved in *R v Howe* were 'he reasonably believed'. It is of course essential that the defendant should genuinely, ie actually, believe in the efficacy of the threat by which he claims to have been compelled. But there is no warrant for relaxing the requirement that the belief must be reasonable as well as genuine. There can of course be no complaint of this departure from authority, which was favourable to the defendant.

. . .

28. . . . It should . . . be made clear to juries that if the retribution threatened against the defendant or his family or a person for whom he reasonably feels responsible is not such as he reasonably expects to follow immediately or almost immediately on his failure to comply with the threat, there may be little if any room for doubt that he could have taken evasive action, whether by going to the police or in some other way, to avoid committing the crime with which he is charged.

29. . . . [T]he certified question on this part of the case . . . is: 'Whether the defence of duress is excluded when as a result of the accused's voluntary association with others: (i) he foresaw (or possibly should have foreseen) the risk of being subjected to any compulsion by threats of violence, or (ii) only when he foresaw (or should have foreseen) the risk of being subjected to compulsion to commit criminal offences, and, if the latter, (iii) only if the offences foreseen (or which should have been foreseen) were of the same type (or possibly of the same type and gravity) as that ultimately committed.' The Crown contend for answer (i) in its objective form. The defendant commends the third answer, omitting the first parenthesis.

. . .

37. The principal issue between the Crown on one side and the appellant and the Court of Appeal on the other is whether *R v Baker* correctly stated the law. To resolve that issue one must remind oneself of the considerations outlined in paras 18–22 above. The defendant is seeking to be wholly exonerated from the consequences of a crime deliberately committed. The prosecution must negative his defence of duress, if raised by the evidence, beyond reasonable doubt. The defendant is, ex hypothesi, a person who has voluntarily surrendered his will to the domination of another. Nothing should turn on foresight of the manner in which, in the event, the dominant party chooses to exploit the defendant's subservience. There need not be foresight of coercion to commit crimes, although it is not easy to envisage circumstances in which a party might be coerced to act lawfully. . . .

38. There remains the question, which the Court of Appeal left open . . . , whether the defendant's foresight must be judged by a subjective or an objective test: ie does the defendant lose the benefit of a defence based on duress only if he actually foresaw the risk of coercion or does he lose it if he ought reasonably to have foreseen the risk of coercion, whether he actually foresaw the risk or not? I do not think any decided case has addressed this question, and I am conscious that application of an objective reasonableness test to other ingredients of duress has attracted criticism: see, for example, D W Elliott, 'Necessity, Duress and Self-Defence' [1989] Crim LR 611, 614–615, and the commentary by Professor Ashworth on *R v Safi* [2003] Crim LR 721, 723. The practical importance of the distinction in this context may not be very great, since if a jury concluded that a person voluntarily associating with known criminals ought reasonably to have foreseen the risk of future coercion they would not, I think, be very likely to accept that he did not in fact do so. But since there is a choice to be made, policy in my view points towards an objective test of what the defendant, placed as he was and knowing what he did, ought reasonably to have foreseen. I am not persuaded otherwise by analogies based on self-defence or provocation for reasons I have already given. The policy of the law must be to discourage association with known criminals, and it should be slow to excuse the criminal conduct of those who do so. If a person voluntarily becomes or remains associated with others engaged in criminal activity in a situation where he knows or ought reasonably to know that he may be the subject of compulsion by them or their associates, he cannot rely on the defence of duress to excuse any act which he is thereafter compelled to do by them. It is not necessary in this case to decide whether or to what extent that principle applies if an undercover agent penetrates a criminal gang for bona fide law enforcement purposes and is compelled by the gang to commit criminal acts.

39. I would answer this certified question by saying that the defence of duress is excluded when as a result of the accused's voluntary association with others engaged in criminal activity he foresaw or ought reasonably to have foreseen the risk of being subjected to any compulsion by threats of violence.

. . .

Baroness Hale of Richmond

76. . . . The principle is that someone who voluntarily accepts the risk of being placed in the 'do it or else' dilemma should not be allowed to use that dilemma as an excuse (even if in some circumstances it might amount to mitigation). There are, however, two other questions.

77. The first is that the cases tend to talk about exposing oneself to the risk of 'unlawful violence'. That, it seems to me, is not enough. The foreseeable risk should be one of duress: that is, of threats of such severity, plausibility and immediacy that one might be compelled to do that which one would otherwise have chosen not to do. The battered wife knows that she is exposing herself to a risk of unlawful violence if she stays, but she may have no reason to believe that her husband will eventually use her broken will to force her to commit crimes. For the same reason, I would say that it must be foreseeable that duress will be used to compel the person to commit crimes of some sort. I have no difficulty envisaging circumstances in which a person may be coerced to act lawfully. The battered wife knows very well that she may be compelled to cook the dinner, wash the dishes, iron the shirts and submit to sexual intercourse. That should not deprive her of the defence of duress if she is obliged by the same threats to herself or her children to commit perjury or shoplift for food.

78. But this brings me to a concern which I have had throughout this case. It is one thing to deny the defence to people who choose to become members of illegal organisations, join criminal gangs, or engage with others in drug-related criminality. It

is another thing to deny it to someone who has a quite different reason for becoming associated with the duressor and then finds it difficult to escape. I do not believe that this limitation on the defence is aimed at battered wives at all, or at others in close personal or family relationships with their duressors and their associates, such as their mothers, brothers or children. The Law Commission's Bills all refer to a person who exposes himself to the risk 'without reasonable excuse'. The words were there to cater for the police infiltrator (see Law Com No 83, para 2.37) but they are also applicable to the sort of association I have in mind. The other elements of the defence, narrowly construed in accordance with existing authority, are more than adequate to keep it within bounds in such cases.

[**Lord Steyn**, **Lord Rodger of Earlsferry**, and **Lord Brown of Eaton-under-Heywood** gave speeches agreeing with Lord Bingham on the duress issue.]

R v Quayle
[2005] EWCA Crim 1415

Barry Quayle and two others were suffering various illnesses which caused them severe pain. They were arrested after it was found that they were growing cannabis for personal use. They were charged with possession of cannabis contrary to the Misuse of Drugs Act 1971. The defendants raised the defence of necessity. This was based on the argument that the use of cannabis was necessary to avoid serious injury and pain. Their defence was not left to the jury by the trial judge and an appeal was made to the Court of Appeal.

Lord Justice Mance

56. The necessitous medical use on an individual basis which is at the root of the defences suggested by all the appellants and Mr Ditchfield is in conflict with the purpose and effect of the legislative scheme. First, no such use is permitted under the present legislation, even on doctor's prescription, except in the context of the ongoing trials for medical research purposes. Secondly, the defences involve the proposition that it is lawful for unqualified individuals to prescribe cannabis to themselves as patients or to assume the role of unqualified doctors by obtaining it and prescribing and supplying it to other individual 'patients'. This is contrary not only to the legislative scheme, but also to any recommendation for its change made by the Select Committee and Runciman Reports. Further, it would involve obvious risks for the integrity and the prospects of any coherent enforcement of the legislative scheme. A parallel but lawful market in the importation, cultivation, prescription, supply, possession and use of cannabis would have to come into existence, which would not only be subject to no medical safeguards or constraints, but the scope and legitimacy of which would in all likelihood be extremely difficult to ascertain or control. . . . Neither judges nor juries are well equipped to resolve issues as to when and how far the deliberate policy of clear legislation should give way in a particular case to countervailing individual hardship, or as to what the overall effect of such derogations would be on the whole legislative scheme.

. . .

72. *Extraneous circumstances*. Lord Bingham spoke in *Hasan* of the need for 'a just and well-founded fear', while accepting that threats of death or serious injury will suffice. He noted that the relevant requirements had been defined objectively, and went on (with the majority of the House) to apply the same approach when he decided that the defence was not available if the defendant ought reasonably to have foreseen the risk of coercion. It is by 'the standards of honest and reasonable men' therefore that the existence or otherwise of such a fear or such threats falls to be decided. We have observed that Lord Bingham did not address or comment on the case of *Safi*, in which this court held that what matters is not whether there was actually a threat of torture, but whether there was a reasonable perception of such a threat. But that still involves an objective test based on external events, conduct or words about which evidence would have to be produced or given. It is also notable that Lord Bingham described the criminal defence which he thought had a close affinity with duress by threats as 'necessity . . . by extraneous circumstances'.

73. There is therefore considerable authority pointing towards a need for extraneous circumstances capable of objective scrutiny by judge and jury and as such, it may be added, more likely to be capable of being checked and, where appropriate, met by other evidence. . . .

76. *Pain*. It is, however, submitted on behalf of Messrs. Quayle . . . Wales and Kenny that any such test is satisfied in all their cases both because of the objectively ascertainable facts giving rise to the pain they suffer actually, or would suffer if they were not to use cannabis, whether from their afflictions or from taking alternative lawful medicaments, and because pain is capable of some degree of objective scrutiny and is not wholly subjective. In addressing this submission, we do not gain any real assistance from cases from other areas of the law, where distinctions may or may not have been drawn between injury and harm or pain.

77. The reason why we would not accept the submission is that the law has to draw a line at some point in the criteria which it accepts as sufficient to satisfy any defence of duress or necessity. Courts and juries have to work on evidence. If such defences were to be expanded in theory to cover every possible case in which it might be felt that it would be hard if the law treated the conduct in question as criminal, there would be likely to be arguments in considerable numbers of cases, where there was no clear objective basis by reference to which to test or determine such arguments. It is unlikely that this would lead overall to a more coherent result, or even necessarily to a more just disposition of any individual case. There is, on any view, a large element of subjectivity in the assessment of pain not directly associated with some current physical injury. The legal defences of duress by threats and necessity by circumstances should in our view be confined to cases where there is an imminent danger of physical injury. In reaching these conclusions, we recognise that hard cases can be postulated, but these, as Lord Bingham said, can and should commonly be capable of being dealt with in other ways. The nature of the sentences passed in the cases before us is consistent with this.

78. It is also submitted that the present cases involve not merely pain, but a risk of serious physical or psychological injury as a result of pain, or as a result of the alternative medicines which would have to be taken if cannabis was not. We have in the case of *Quayle* already given our reasons for rejecting on the facts Mr Fitzgerald's submission that there was any relevant risk of suicide in that case (paragraph 2(vi) above). In the case of *Wales*, the judge is criticised for failing to explain that serious pain could amount to serious injury because of its psychological consequences, but there does not appear to have been any evidence which could have justified such a case. Mr Wales did describe the pain he suffered as

'life-threatening' and the judge reminded the jury of this, although it does not appear to have been Mr Wales's case that there was an actual risk of suicide. His case on the facts was that cannabis helped him cope with the pain, without side effects, while the prescribed medicines had side-effects (stopping him eating) and, on the expert evidence that he called, also involved medical risks such as a general risk of peritonitis. We do not see in the evidence any basis on which a jury could be asked to conclude that Mr Wales faced any imminent risk of serious injury sufficient to justify him taking cannabis on a regular basis. Further, if there was such a case, it was left to the jury. Finally, in the case of *Kenny*, the evidence did not suggest any risk other than that of pain, and the criticism is that that risk should have been left to the jury.

79. *Imminence and immediacy.* We consider that these requirements represent another reason why, even at the detailed level, it is difficult to accept that there could be any successful defence of necessity in the cases of *Quayle, Wales* and *Kenny*. Their defences amount to saying that it is open to defendants on a continuous basis to plan for and justify breaches of the law. However, we need not express a view whether that would have alone justified a judge in refusing to leave their defences to a jury. The requirements of imminence and immediacy mean, in any event, in our view that the judge was right to refuse to leave any defence of necessity to the jury in *Taylor* and *Lee*, and that the defence should not have been left to the jury in *Ditchfield*. In each of these three cases, the defendant was taking a deliberately considered course of conduct over a substantial period of time, involving continuous or regular breaches of the law. In each case, the defendant was not the immediate sufferer and had every opportunity to reflect and to desist. The compassionate grounds which may well have motivated Mr Taylor and Ms Lee and which the jury evidently accepted did motivate Mr Ditchfield cannot avoid the fact that they deliberately chose to act contrary to the law on a continuous basis.

80. We note in passing that the court in *Southwark L.B.C. v. Williams* refused to recognise a defence of necessity raised by squatters in answer to a claim to recover possession of properties owned by the council. The evidence was that there were no homes for the squatters, they had been living in 'quite deplorable conditions' and the empty council properties in which they then squatted had been vandalised by the council to make them unfit for habitation, but that they had entered and lived there in an orderly way and repaired them after entry. Nevertheless, the court upheld summary possession orders, 'for the sake of law and order', as Lord Denning put it, and because the circumstances 'do not . . . constitute the sort of emergency to which the plea [of necessity] applies', as Edmund Davies LJ said. Megaw LJ agreed with both judgments on this aspect. The case is an old one, and the law has developed, so that we need not consider it further. But the underlying theme, that a continuous and deliberate course of otherwise unlawful self-help is unlikely to give rise to the defence has itself, in our view, continuing relevance.

81. The point made in paragraphs 79–80 may also be viewed in another way. Where there is no imminent or immediate threat or peril, but only a general assertion of an internal motivation to engage in prohibited activities in order to prevent or alleviate pain, it is also difficult to identify any extraneous or objective factors by reference to which a jury could be expected to measure whether the motivation was such as to override the defendant's will or to force him to act as he did. If the response is that the defendant was not forced, but chose to act as he did, then the considerations mentioned in the previous paragraph apply.

Appeal dismissed.

5.4 THE ABOLITION OF THE DEFENCE OF COERCION

The defence of marital coercion, which applied to wives who committed crimes in the presence of their husbands, was abolished by section 177 of the Anti-social Behaviour, Crime and Policing Act 2014.[125] Wives who are forced by husbands to commit crimes will now need to rely on the defence of duress. This is narrower than the abolished defence of coercion because coercion did not require proof of a threat to kill or cause serious harm, nor did it require proof of an overborne will.

FURTHER READING

Buchanan, A. and Virgo, G. (1999) 'Duress and Mental Abnormality' *Criminal Law Review* 517.

Edwards, S. (2013) '"The Straw Woman" at Law's Precipice: An Unwilling Party' in A. Reed and M. Bohlander (eds) *Participation in Crime* (Aldershot: Ashgate).

Horder, J. (1992) 'Autonomy, Provocation and Duress' *Criminal Law Review* 706.

Smith, K. (1999) 'Duress and Steadfastness: In Pursuit of the Unintelligible' *Criminal Law Review* 363.

---

6 ENTRAPMENT

DEFINITION

It is not a defence for the defendant to show that he or she committed the offence only because he or she was trapped by the police into committing it.

If a plain-clothes police officer poses as a person keen to acquire drugs and approaches a suspected drug dealer and the drug dealer supplies drugs can the alleged dealer be convicted of a drugs offence?[126] You may think the answer is obviously 'yes', but the defendant might not have supplied drugs unless requested to do so by the police officer. In *Sang*[127] the defendant claimed that he would not have committed the offence of dealing with counterfeit currency had he not suffered constant persuasion and insistence of an undercover police officer. The House of Lords rejected an argument that there was a defence of entrapment. However, their Lordships expressed their disapproval of using police officers as agents provocateurs.[128] Although entrapment does not provide a general defence, evidence obtained inappropriately can be excluded under the law on evidence[129] or even lead to a reduction in sentence.[130] In *Looseley*[131] the House of Lords held that it was appropriate to halt a trial for abuse of process where undercover officers had approached a person whom they had no

---

[125] Loveless (2010 and 2014).   [126] For a thorough discussion of the issue, see Ashworth (2002a).
[127] [1980] AC 402 (HL).   [128] Choo (1993) argues there should be a defence of entrapment.
[129] Section 78 of the Police and Criminal Evidence Act 1984 (see *Smurthwaite* [1998] Crim LR 751) and the common law (*Latif* [1996] 1 All ER 353 (HL)).
[130] *Springer* [1999] 1 Cr App R (S) 217 (CA).   [131] [2001] 4 All ER 897 (HL).

grounds for suspecting to be involved in drugs and given him cheap cigarettes, before asking him for drugs. However, their Lordships added that it would not be necessary to halt a trial for abuse of process where there were reasonable grounds to suspect that the defendant was a drug dealer and the officers had merely given the defendant an opportunity to commit the offence. The key test is 'whether the police conduct preceding the commission of the offence was no more than might be expected from others in the circumstances'.[132] In applying this test in *Jones (James)*[133] it was held that a drug dealer was only likely to sell to those asking for drugs and so an undercover police officer asking for drugs from a suspected drug dealer would not be engaging in entrapment.

Cases of entrapment must now be considered in the light of the Human Rights Act 1998. The issue of entrapment was considered by the European Court of Human Rights in *Teixeira de Castro v Portugal*.[134] The defendant, who had no criminal record, was introduced to two police officers. They asked him to buy heroin for them, which he did. He was sentenced to six years' imprisonment. The European Court held that the defendant's right to a fair trial under Article 6 was infringed by the police action. The distinction was drawn between where the undercover police officers were approached by a defendant (which was not illegitimate) and where the undercover police approached a defendant and proposed the commission of an offence (which was illegitimate).[135] This distinction appears to reflect that made in *Looseley*. In *Jones*[136] the defendant had left graffiti messages asking girls aged 13 or under to contact him to have sex. An undercover police officer, pretending to be under 13, texted him and arranged a meeting, where he was arrested. This was held not to amount to entrapment. It was not an abuse of power but an attempt to ensure children were not harmed. A key point here appears to have been the fact that the defendant had first sought to initiate contact by leaving the messages.

Occasionally a case arises where the claim is not that the police or the state entrapped the defendant, but another citizen, such as a journalist. There is relatively little authority on this question. It appears that this form of entrapment follows the same rules as apply to state entrapment.[137]

7 SUPERIOR ORDERS

Superior orders has never been recognized as a defence in English and Welsh law.[138] So a police officer or soldier who commits a crime has no defence by claiming 'I was only following orders.' Although it has never been directly in issue in an English or Welsh case there are *obiter* statements in the House of Lords and the Privy Council denying the existence of the defence in *Clegg*[139] and *Yip*.[140] Of course, the fact that the defendant was acting under superior orders could in extreme cases form the basis of a defence of duress or lack of *mens rea*.[141]

---

[132] For further discussion, see Squires (2006); Ashworth (2002b).
[133] [2010] EWCA Crim 925.   [134] [1998] Crim LR 751 (ECtHR).
[135] See also *Lewis* [2005] Crim LR 797.   [136] *Jones* [2007] EWCA Crim 1118.
[137] See *Morley and Hutton* [1994] Crim LR 919. For a detailed discussion, see Hofmeyr (2006).
[138] Brownlee (1989). For an excellent discussion of the issue, see Wallerstein (2010).
[139] [1995] 1 All ER 334 (HL).   [140] [1994] 2 All ER 924 (PC).
[141] *Hill v Baxter* [1958] 1 QB 277.

8 AUTOMATISM

> **DEFINITION**
>
> To plead automatism a defendant needs to show:
>
> (1) he had suffered a complete loss of voluntary control;
>
> (2) this was caused by an external factor;
>
> (3) he was not at fault in losing capacity.

Automatism occurs when a defendant suffers a complete loss of self-control caused by an external factor.[142] A popular example is a defendant who is hit on the head by a rock and then loses all awareness of what he or she is doing and injures someone. Such a defendant will be able to rely on the defence of automatism.

Automatism involves more than a claim that the individual lacked *mens rea* (which he or she did). It is a claim that he or she is not acting: it is a denial of the *actus reus*.[143] The significance of this is that automatism is a defence even to a crime of strict liability which has no *mens rea* requirement.

The three elements of automatism will be considered separately:

8.1 A COMPLETE LOSS OF VOLUNTARY CONTROL

The Court of Appeal in the following cases emphasizes that to rely on automatism there must be a *complete* loss of voluntary control:

Attorney-General's Reference (No. 2 of 1992)
[1994] QB 91 (CA)

The respondent was the driver of a heavy goods lorry. He had been driving six out of the preceding 12 hours and covered 343 miles when he steered onto the hard shoulder of a motorway. He crashed into a stationary white van. Two people were killed. The tyre marks indicated that the respondent's lorry had braked only at the very last minute. At his trial on a charge of causing death by reckless driving, the respondent produced evidence from a psychologist (Professor Brown) that he was suffering from a condition known as 'driving without awareness' caused by repetitive visual stimuli which created a trance-like state. The respondent claimed this amounted to automatism and that therefore he was not driving. He was acquitted by the jury, but the Attorney General referred the case to the Court of Appeal.

---

[142] If the defendant brings credible evidence raising the possibility of automatism the prosecution must show that beyond reasonable doubt the accused was not acting as an automaton.

[143] *Hill v Baxter* [1958] 1 QB 277.

Lord Taylor of Gosforth CJ

This is a reference pursuant to s 36 of the Criminal Justice Act 1972 whereby Her Majesty's Attorney General seeks the opinion of this court on a point of law following an acquittal on indictment. The point is defined in the reference as follows:

'Whether the state described as "driving without awareness" should, as a matter of law, be capable of founding a defence of automatism.'

This formulation relates to expert evidence given in the particular case. However, we take the point more generally to raise the question: 'What are the requirements and limits of the defence of automatism?'

. . .

[**Lord Taylor** referred to defence evidence of Professor Brown about the condition of driving without awareness and stated:]

Despite his phrase 'driving without awareness', Professor Brown agreed that the driver's body would still be controlling the vehicle, that there would be subconscious motivation to his steering and that, although 'largely unaware of what was happening ahead' and 'largely unaware of steering either', the unawareness was not total. Asked if nothing intrudes into the driver's consciousness when he is in this state, the professor said: 'I would not go so far as to say nothing, but very little.' There must, as a matter of common sense, be some awareness if, as Professor Brown accepted, the driver will usually be caused to 'snap out' of the condition by strong stimuli noticed by his eyes.

The contention on behalf of the Attorney General is that on the evidence given by Professor Brown, even taken at its highest, there was no basis for leaving the defence of automatism to the jury. Mr Jones QC [counsel for the Crown] submits that automatism as a defence in a driving case arises only where there is such total destruction of voluntary control that the defendant cannot be said to be driving at all. He cited *Hill v Baxter* [1958] 1 QB 277 at 283, in which Lord Goddard CJ said:

'I agree that there may be cases where the circumstances are such that the accused could not really be said to be driving at all. Suppose he had a stroke or an epileptic fit, both instances of what may properly be called Acts of God; he might well be in the driver's seat even with his hands on the wheel, but in such a state of unconsciousness that he could not be said to be driving.'

Pearson J gave as examples an epileptic fit, a coma, a blow on the head from a stone thrown up from the roadway and an attack by a swarm of bees so that the driver is—

'prevented from exercising any directional control over the vehicle and any movements of his arms and legs are solely caused by the action of the bees. In each of these cases it can be said that at the material time he is not driving and therefore not driving dangerously. Then suppose that the man in the driving seat falls asleep. After he has fallen asleep he is no longer driving, but there was an earlier time at which he was falling asleep and therefore failing to perform the driver's elementary and essential duty of keeping himself awake and therefore he was driving dangerously.' (See [1958] 1 QB 277 at 286.)

In *Bratty v A-G for Northern Ireland* [1963] AC 386 at 409 a defence of automatism due to an attack of psychomotor epilepsy was raised. Lord Denning said of the *actus reus*:

'No act is punishable if it is done involuntarily: and an involuntary act in this context— some people nowadays prefer to speak of it as "automatism"—means an act which is done by the muscles without any control by the mind such as a spasm, a reflex action or a convulsion; or an act done by a person who is not conscious of what he is doing such as an act done whilst suffering from concussion or whilst sleepwalking.'

The extent of the loss of control is crucial in the present case. Mr Jones referred to three other authorities in support of his proposition that automatism requires there to be total destruction of voluntary control and that impairment or reduction of voluntary control is insufficient.

[**Lord Taylor** then referred to *Watmore v Jenkins* [1962] 2 QB 572; *Roberts v Ramsbottom* [1980] 1 All ER 7; and *Broome v Perkins* [1987] RTR 321.]

. . .

We were referred to a number of decisions drawing a distinction between insane automatism and non-insane automatism: *R v Quick, R v Paddison* [1973] QB 910, *R v Sullivan* [1984] AC 156, *R v Hennessy* [1989] 2 All ER 9 and *R v Burgess* [1991] 2 QB 92. The effect of those decisions is that if the defence of automatism is said to arise from internal causes so as to bring the defendant within the M'Naghten Rules, then if it succeeds the verdict should be one of not guilty by reason of insanity (see *M'Naghten's Case* [1843–60] All ER Rep 229). An epileptic seizure (in *R v Sullivan*), a stress disorder, prone to recur and lacking the features of novelty or accident (in *R v Hennessy*) and sleepwalking (in *R v Burgess*) were all regarded as internal causes. If, however, automatism is said to arise from an external cause, for example a stone hitting the driver on the head, then a successful defendant is entitled to be acquitted.

Here, Mr Pert [counsel for the respondent] argues that the precipitating cause of the condition described by Professor Brown was the external factor of motorway conditions. However that may be, the proper approach is that prescribed by Lord Lane CJ in *R v Burgess* [1991] 2 QB 92 at 96 as follows:

'Where the defence of automatism is raised by a defendant two questions fall to be decided by the judge before the defence can be left to the jury. The first is whether a proper evidential foundation for the defence of automatism has been laid. The second is whether the evidence shows the case to be one of insane automatism, that is to say a case which falls within the M'Naghten Rules, or one of non-insane automatism.'

The first of those questions is the one raised by this reference. In our judgment, the 'proper evidential foundation' was not laid in this case by Professor Brown's evidence of 'driving without awareness'. As the authorities cited above show, the defence of automatism requires that there was a total destruction of voluntary control on the defendant's part. Impaired, reduced or partial control is not enough. Professor Brown accepted that someone 'driving without awareness' within his description, retains some control. He would be able to steer the vehicle and usually to react and return to full awareness when confronted by significant stimuli.

Accordingly, in our judgment the learned recorder ought not to have left the issue of automatism to the jury in this case and the answer to the point of law as formulated is No.

The requirement that there be a *complete* loss of voluntary control appears to be very harsh, but was confirmed recently in *Coley*.[144] Automatism does not arise simply because a person is acting irrationally: they need to have no physical control if they are to successfully use the defence.[145] Some commentators have suggested that this strict approach should be limited to driving offences or crimes of strict liability, and that for other crimes it is not necessary to

---

[144] [2013] EWCA Crim 223.   [145] *Coley* [2013] EWCA Crim 223.

show that there was a complete lack of control.[146] However, there is nothing in the judgment of the Court of Appeal in *Attorney-General's Reference (No. 2 of 1992)* that explicitly restricts their discussion to driving offences.

8.2 AN EXTERNAL FACTOR

If a person acts while unaware of what he is doing such a person may either be an automaton or insane.[147] The distinction between the two is whether the person's mental state was caused by an internal or external factor:

(1) If it is caused by an internal factor the person is classified as insane.

(2) If it is caused by an external factor the person has the complete defence of automatism.

It can be extremely difficult to tell whether a factor was an internal or external one. Examples of external factors are a blow to the head or the taking of prescribed medication. Internal factors include mental illnesses.[148] It used to be thought that sleepwalking was an external factor, but it was held by the Court of Appeal in *Burgess*[149] to be an example of insanity because it is a mental condition (an internal factor) which predisposes a person to sleepwalking.[150] It is clear that everyday tensions and pressure will not constitute external factors.[151]

Contrasting the following two cases may well illustrate the difference between internal and external factors:

(1) The Canadian Supreme Court in *Rabey*[152] held that a defendant who suffered a disassociated state and killed his former girlfriend was not an automaton. He sought to plead automatism, arguing that his lack of awareness was caused by an external factor (his girlfriend telling him she was leaving him). The Supreme Court held that this was a case of insanity; the reasoning being that many people have boy or girlfriends leaving them without it leading to complete lack of awareness, suggesting that it was the mental state of the defendant, rather than the girlfriend's actions which caused his mental state.

(2) In *R v T*[153] a woman had been raped and the rape was held to be an external factor. Rape could not be described as part of the 'ordinary stresses and disappointments of life'.

8.3 THE DEFENDANT WAS NOT AT FAULT IN CAUSING THE CONDITION

The defendant cannot plead automatism if he or she is responsible for causing his or her condition. So if the defendant's mental state is caused by taking alcohol or an illegal drug he or she cannot plead automatism.[154] There may be other ways in which the defendant is responsible for

---

[146] Simester, Spencer, Sullivan, and Virgo (2013).

[147] Some commentators use the terminology 'sane and insane automatism'.

[148] *Sullivan* [1983] 2 All ER 673.   [149] [1991] 2 QB 92.   [150] *Ibid*.

[151] For an argument that the requirement for an external factor should be abandoned, see Mackay and Mitchell (2006).

[152] (1980) 15 CR (3d) 225, a decision approved by the English Court of Appeal in *Burgess* [1991] 2 QB 92.

[153] [1990] Crim LR 256.   [154] *Lipman* [1970] 1 QB 152 (CA); *Coley* [2013] EWCA Crim 223.

his or her condition and so will not be able to rely on the defence.[155] For example, if the defendant is a diabetic and is aware that if he or she does not eat adequate food he or she may enter a state of lack of awareness, but refrains from eating when symptoms first appear, he or she may be held responsible for his or her condition.[156] It seems, although there is no definitive case law on the question, that the test is subjective: was the defendant aware that his or her actions or inactions would cause his or her mental condition, rather than asking whether the defendant *ought* to have been aware that his or her actions or inactions would cause his or her mental condition.

> **EXAMINATION TIP**
>
> A popular scenario for problem questions involves a defendant who is both intoxicated and suffers automatism (e.g. a drunk defendant who falls down, bangs his or her head and suffers concussion).
>
> *Stripp* indicates that the key question is whether the defendant's state was caused predominantly by his or her intoxication or by his or her concussion. If it was the concussion then he or she would be able to plead automatism; if the voluntary intoxication he or she would not (see also *Burns* and *Lipman*).

9 INSANITY

It is crucial to distinguish between two different claims in relation to insanity:

(1) A claim that a defendant was insane at the time he or she committed the offence.

(2) A claim that the defendant was insane at the time of the trial and so unable effectively to defend him or herself.

As we shall discuss in Part II there are many difficulties with the law's treatment of insanity. →6 (p.717)

9.1 INSANITY AT THE TIME OF THE ALLEGED OFFENCE

The definition of insanity

The issue of the defendant's insanity at the time of the crime can be raised in three ways:

(1) The defendant straightforwardly claims he or she was insane at the time of the offence.

(2) The defendant raises a defence of no *mens rea* or automatism, but the judge decides that the evidence discloses a defence of insanity. The judge may then instruct the jury to consider the issue of insanity.[157]

(3) If the defendant raises a plea of diminished responsibility then the prosecution is entitled to rebut the defence by producing evidence of insanity.[158]

---

[155] This has been particularly relevant in driving cases, e.g. *Broome v Perkins* (1987) 85 Cr App R 321; *Isitt* (1978) 67 Cr App R 44; *Marison* [1996] Crim LR 909.

[156] *Quick* [1973] QB 910.   [157] *Thomas* [1995] Crim LR 314.

[158] Section 6 of the Criminal Procedure (Insanity) Act 1964. In such a case the burden of proving insanity will be on the prosecution (*Bastian* [1958] 1 WLR 413).

> **DEFINITION**
>
> A defendant who wishes to plead that he or she was insane at the time of the offence must demonstrate that he or she was suffering from a defect of reason caused by a disease of the mind which meant that either:
>
> (1) he or she did not know the nature or quality of his or her actions; or
>
> (2) he or she did not know that what he or she was doing was wrong.
>
> If successful in his or her plea the defendant will be found 'not guilty, but insane'.

The following decision of the House of Lords is one of the leading (and most controversial) cases on the meaning of insanity.[159] The key issue was whether the defendant was to be labelled insane or whether he could rely on the defence of automatism. As we have seen, automatism is available only where the cause of the mental condition is an external one. This led the House of Lords in this case to conclude that an epileptic defendant could not rely on automatism and therefore was labelled insane:

R v Sullivan
[1984] 1 AC 156 (HL)

Patrick Sullivan was visiting an 80-year-old friend of his when he had an epileptic seizure, during which he kicked his friend in the head, inflicting grievous bodily harm. He admitted causing the injuries but sought to rely on the defence of automatism. The trial judge ruled that the facts revealed insanity, rather than automatism. In order to avoid being found not guilty by reason of insanity (and compulsory detention in a special hospital), Mr Sullivan pleaded guilty to an assault occasioning actual bodily harm. He was convicted and sentenced to probation under medical supervision. He appealed against the conviction on the basis that the judge's ruling was incorrect and he should have been able to plead the defence of automatism. The Court of Appeal dismissed his appeal and the case went to the House of Lords.

Lord Diplock

My Lords, the appellant, a man of blameless reputation, has the misfortune to have been a lifelong sufferer from epilepsy. There was a period when he was subject to major seizures known as grand mal but as a result of treatment which he was receiving as an out-patient of the Maudsley Hospital from 1976 onwards, these seizures had, by the use of drugs, been reduced by 1979 to seizures of less severity known as petit mal, or psychomotor epilepsy, though they continued to occur at a frequency of one or two per week.

. . .

Their expert evidence, which was not disputed by the prosecution, was that the appellant's acts in kicking Mr Payne had all the characteristics of epileptic automatism at the third or post-ictal stage of petit mal, and that, in view of his history of psychomotor epilepsy and the hospital records of his behaviour during previous seizures, the strong probability was that the appellant's acts of violence towards Mr Payne took place while he was going through that stage.

---

[159] For a very helpful discussion of the issues, see Child and Sullivan (2014).

The evidence as to the pathology of a seizure due to psychomotor epilepsy can be sufficiently stated for the purposes of this appeal by saying that after the first stage, the prodram, which precedes the fit itself, there is a second stage, the ictus, lasting a few seconds, during which there are electrical discharges into the temporal lobes of the brain of the sufferer. The effect of these discharges cause him in the post-ictal stage to make movements which he is not conscious that he is making, including, and this was a characteristic of previous seizures which the appellant had suffered, automatic movements of resistance to anyone trying to come to his aid. These movements of resistance might, though in practice they very rarely would, involve violence.

. . .

My Lords, for centuries, up to 1843, the common law relating to the concept of mental disorders as negativing responsibility for crimes was in the course of evolution, but I do not think it necessary for your Lordships to embark on an examination of the pre-1843 position. In that year, following the acquittal of one Daniel M'Naghten for shooting Sir Robert Peel's secretary, in what today would probably be termed a state of paranoia, the question of insanity and criminal responsibility was the subject of debate in the legislative chamber of the House of Lords, the relevant statute then in force being the Criminal Lunatics Act 1800, an Act 'for the safe custody of Insane Persons charged with Offences', which referred to persons who were 'insane' at the time of the commission of the offence, but contained no definition of insanity. The House invited the judges of the courts of common law to answer five abstract questions on the subject of insanity as a defence to criminal charges. The answer to the second and third of these questions combined was given by Tindal CJ on behalf of all the judges, except Maule J, and constituted what became known as the *M'Naghten* Rules. The judge's answer is in the following well-known terms (see *M'Naghten's Case* [1843–60] All ER Rep 229 at 233):

> '. . . the jurors ought to be told in all cases that every man is to be presumed to be sane, and to possess a sufficient degree of reason to be responsible for his crimes, until the contrary be proved to their satisfaction and that to establish a defence on the ground of insanity, it must be clearly proved that, at the time of the committing of the act, the party accused was labouring under a defect of reason, from disease of the mind, as not to know the nature and quality of the act he was doing or, if he did know it, that he did not know what he was doing was wrong.'

. . .

The *M'Naghten* Rules have been used as a comprehensive definition for this purpose by the courts for the last 140 years. . . .

The question before this House was whether, the jury having rejected the plea of insanity, there was any evidence of non-insane automatism fit to be left to the jury. The *ratio decidendi* of its dismissal of the appeal was that the jury having negatived the explanation that Bratty might have been acting unconsciously in the course of an attack of psychomotor epilepsy, there was no evidential foundation for the suggestion that he was acting unconsciously from any other cause.

. . .

My Lords, I can deal briefly with the various grounds on which it has been submitted that the instant case can be distinguished from what constituted the *ratio decidendi* in *Bratty's case*, and that it falls outside the ambit of the *M'Naghten* Rules.

First, it is submitted the medical evidence in the instant case shows that psychomotor epilepsy is not a disease of the mind, whereas in *Bratty's case* it was accepted by all the doctors that it was. The only evidential basis for this submission is that Dr Fenwick said that in medical terms to constitute a 'disease of the mind' or 'mental illness', which he appeared to regard as interchangeable descriptions, a disorder of brain functions (which undoubtedly occurs during a seizure in psychomotor epilepsy) must be prolonged for a period of time usually more than a day, while Dr Taylor would have it that the disorder must continue for a minimum of a month to qualify for the description 'a disease of the mind'.

The nomenclature adopted by the medical profession may change from time to time. Bratty was tried in 1961. But the meaning of the expression 'disease of the mind' as the cause of 'a defect of reason' remains unchanged for the purposes of the application of the *M'Naghten* Rules. I agree with what was said by Devlin J in *R v Kemp* [1957] 1 QB 399 at 407 that 'mind' in the *M'Naghten* Rules is used in the ordinary sense of the mental faculties of reason, memory and understanding. If the effect of a disease is to impair these faculties so severely as to have either of the consequences referred to in the latter part of the rules, it matters not whether the aetiology of the impairment is organic, as in epilepsy, or functional, or whether the impairment itself is permanent or is transient and intermittent, provided that it subsisted at the time of commission of the act. The purpose of the legislation relating to the defence of insanity, ever since its origin in 1880, has been to protect society against recurrence of the dangerous conduct. The duration of a temporary suspension of the mental faculties of reason, memory and understanding, particularly if, as in the appellant's case, it is recurrent, cannot on any rational ground be relevant to the application by the courts of the *M'Naghten* Rules, though it may be relevant to the course adopted by the Secretary of State, to whom the responsibility for how the defendant is to be dealt with passes after the return of the special verdict of not guilty by reason of insanity.

. . .

The only other submission in support of the appellant's appeal which I think it necessary to mention is that, because the expert evidence was to the effect that the appellant's acts in kicking Mr Payne were unconscious and thus 'involuntary' in the legal sense of that term, his state of mind was not one dealt with by the *M'Naghten* Rules at all, since it was not covered by the phrase 'as not to know the nature and quality of the act he was doing'. Quite apart from being contrary to all three speeches in this House in *Bratty's case*, the submission appears to me, with all respect to counsel, to be quite unarguable. Dr Fenwick himself accepted it as an accurate description of the appellant's mental state in the post-ictal stage of a seizure. The audience to whom the phrase in the *M'Naghten* Rules was addressed consisted of peers of the realm in the 1840s when a certain orotundity of diction had not yet fallen out of fashion. Addressed to an audience of jurors in the 1980s it might more aptly be expressed as: he did not know what he was doing.

My Lords, it is natural to feel reluctant to attach the label of insanity to a sufferer from psychomotor epilepsy of the kind to which the appellant was subject, even though the expression in the context of a special verdict of not guilty by reason of insanity is a technical one which includes a purely temporary and intermittent suspension of the mental faculties of reason, memory and understanding resulting from the occurrence of an epileptic fit. But the label is contained in the current statute, it has appeared in this statute's predecessors ever since 1800. It does not lie within the power of the courts to alter it. Only Parliament can do that. It has done so twice, it could do so once again.

Sympathise though I do with the appellant, I see no other course open to your Lordships than to dismiss this appeal.

Appeal dismissed.

So here the House of Lords confirmed that a defendant is presumed to be sane and approved the definition of insanity found in the *M'Naghten*[160] rules, first set out in 1843. This definition can be broken down into three requirements:

Disease of the mind

The phrase 'disease of the mind' is to be given its normal meaning:[161] it is not a medical term. What must be shown is that the defendant was suffering from a disease which affected the functioning of the mind. There is no need, therefore, to show that it was a disease of the brain as such.[162] This means that diabetes, for example, can amount to a disease of the mind if it produces a malfunctioning of the brain. Lord Denning in *Bratty*[163] suggested that a disease of the mind was a mental disorder which manifested itself in violence and was prone to reoccur. However, these *dicta* have since been rejected[164] and it is clear that a 'disease of the mind' need not be prone to recur nor manifest itself in violence.

It should also be stressed that just because there was a malfunctioning of the mind it does not follow that this was a disease. If the defendant was hit on the head by a brick and suffers concussion there might be no disease and so the concussion could not amount to a disease of the mind. Similarly, simply being intoxicated cannot form the basis of an insanity defence, even if the intoxication causes a psychotic episode:[165]

R v Coley
[2013] EWCA Crim 223

Sean Coley was convicted of attempted murder. At the time of the offence he was 17, described as 'quiet and pleasant', but a regular user of strong cannabis. He also enjoyed violent video games. One evening just before midnight he went into his neighbour's house and stabbed her partner causing serious injuries. He gave evidence that he had consumed a good deal of cannabis that day, and had no recollection of the events. There was evidence from psychologists that he might have suffered a 'brief psychotic episode' caused by the cannabis. The question on appeal was whether, if that evidence was accepted, the defendant could rely on the defence of automatism or insanity.

Lord Justice Hughes

16. We do not doubt that the possible state of mind in which this defendant stabbed the man next door can properly be called a mental abnormality (or, in the nineteenth century language of *M'Naghten*, a defect of reason) which is recognised medically by psychiatrists. As a matter of fact, some care may need to be exercised in discovering exactly how the expressions "psychosis" or "psychotic" are used, which was not much explored in the evidence in this case, save to explain that the doctors were speaking of a state in which the mind becomes detached, to a greater or lesser extent, from reality. Generally, as we understand it, these expressions are more often encountered as descriptions of symptoms than as constituting a mental illness in their own right. The underlying cause of such symptoms

---

[160] (1843) 10 Cl & F 200.   [161] *Kemp* [1957] 1 QB 399, 406.   [162] *Ibid*.
[163] [1963] AC 386.   [164] *Sullivan* [1984] AC 156.   [165] *Coley* [2013] EWCA Crim 223.

may vary. Well understood ones certainly include schizophrenia and bi-polar disorder, which are no doubt mental disorders or illnesses. Another well known possible cause of psychotic symptoms is drug abuse, which is not a mental disorder. But with that caveat, we agree that to speak of a psychotic episode is no doubt to speak of a temporary abnormality of the brain or mind and thus of a defect of reason for the purposes of the *M'Naghten* rules.

17. However, the key thing to understand is that whether there is or is not a "disease of the mind" for the purpose of the *M'Naghten* rules is, and has to be, a question of law and not of medical usage. It makes excellent sense for medical people to classify a great variety of conditions as recognised medically. It enables statistics to be gathered, resources allocated, diagnoses understood with reasonable consistency and treatment to be advised: see the discussion in the slightly different context of diminished responsibility in *R v Dowds* [2012] EWCA Crim 281. But the law has to cope with the synthesising of the law of insanity with the law of voluntary intoxication. The first calls for a special verdict of acquittal and very particular means of disposal. The latter is generally no defence at all, but may be relevant to whether the defendant formed a specific intention, if the offence in question is one which requires such: *DPP v Majewski* [1977] AC 443. In most, but not all, intoxication cases, the intoxication will be possibly relevant to a serious offence allegedly committed but will afford no defence to a lesser offence constituted by the same facts: for example causing grievous bodily harm with intent (s 18) and causing grievous bodily harm without such intent (s 20), or of course murder and manslaughter. In the development of the common law, intoxication was historically regarded chiefly as an aggravation of offending, rather than as an excuse for it. For all the reasons explained in *Majewski*, the law refuses as a matter of policy to afford a general defence to an offender on the basis of his own voluntary intoxication. The pressing social reasons for maintaining this general policy of the law are certainly no less present in modern conditions of substance abuse than they were in the past.

18. The precise line between the law of voluntary intoxication and the law of insanity may, we do not doubt, be difficult to identify in some borderline cases. But the present case falls comfortably on the side of the line covered by voluntary intoxication. It matters not that the condition of the defendant as observed in the aftermath of his attack on the neighbour was not that of conventional intoxication, in the sense that he was not, for example, staggering or unable to speak clearly. If the doctors were right about his state of mind, his mind was to an extent detached from reality by the direct and acute effects on it of the ingestion of cannabis. Every intoxicated person has his mind affected, and to an extent disordered, by the direct and acute effects of the ingestion of intoxicants; all intoxication operates through the brain. Not infrequently it would be perfectly legitimate to say of a very drunken man that his mind had become detached from reality by the intoxication; that is obviously true, for example, of the drunken man who suffers delusions as a result of the drink, but the proposition is not limited to that case. In order to engage the law of insanity, it is not enough that there is an effect on the mind, or, in the language of the *M'Naghten* rules, a 'defect of reason'. There must also be what the law classifies as a disease of the mind. Direct acute effects on the mind of intoxicants, voluntarily taken, are not so classified. That is the distinction drawn by Stephen J in *Davis* and maintained ever since.

Defect of reason

It must be shown that the disease of the mind gave rise to a defect of reason: the defendant's power of reasoning must be impaired. It is not enough to show that the power of reasoning was available but not used. Someone who absent-mindedly was unaware what he or she was doing cannot rely on insanity.[166]

---

[166] In any event absent-mindedness is not a disease of the mind (*Clarke* [1972] 1 All ER 219). Of course, absent-minded people may well be able to plead that they have no *mens rea*.

The defendant did not know the nature and quality of his or her act or that it was wrong

It must be shown that as a result of the defect of reason caused by the disease of the mind either (a) the defendant did not know the nature or quality of his or her act or (b) he or she did not know it was wrong:

Not knowing the nature and quality of the act

This requires proof that the defendant did not know what he or she was doing. This would be so in the following situations:

(1) The defendant had no awareness of what was happening.[167] For example, the defendant was suffering from a seizure of some kind.

(2) The defendant was aware what he or she was doing, but was deluded as to the material circumstances of his or her actions, rendering the act fundamentally different. For example, a defendant who thought he or she was killing a monstrous creature when in fact he or she was killing a person.

(3) A person who was unaware of the consequences of his or her act, for example he or she was unaware that his or her act would kill the victim. Stephen gave the example of a person who cut off the head of someone who was asleep because 'it would be great fun to see him looking for it when he woke up'.[168]

Not knowing that the act is wrong

'Wrong' here means that the act was illegal. This was held to be the law in *Windle*.[169] Although that view has been criticized,[170] it was followed in *Johnson*,[171] which preferred illegality as the test because what was or was not immoral was too uncertain.

The Human Rights Act 1998 and the definition of insanity

Article 5 of the ECHR states:

> Everyone has the right to liberty and security of person. No one shall be deprived of his liberty save in the following cases and in accordance with the procedures prescribed by law: . . .
>
> (e) the lawful detention . . . of persons of unsound mind.

The European Court of Human Rights in *Winterwerp v Netherlands*[172] explained that:

> In the Court's opinion, except in emergency cases, the individual concerned should not be deprived of his liberty unless he has been reliably shown to be of 'unsound mind'. The very nature of what has to be established before the competent national authority—that is, a true

---

[167] *Sullivan* [1983] 2 All ER 673.   [168] Stephen (1887: 166).   [169] [1952] 2 QB 826.
[170] Notably the High Court of Australia in *Stapleton* (1952) 86 CLR 358 refused to follow *Windle*.
[171] [2007] EWCA Crim 1978. The issue is discussed in Mackay (2009). Notably the Court of Appeal saw the case for considering reform of the law. Mackay, Mitchell, and Howe (2006) suggest that in practice defendants whose mental illness means (only) that they do not realize that what they are doing is morally wrong are often permitted to use the defence of insanity.
[172] (1979) 2 EHRR 387.

> mental disorder—calls for objective medical expertise. Further, the mental disorder must be of a kind or degree warranting compulsory confinement. What is more, the validity of the continued confinement depends upon the persistence of such a disorder.[173]

In the light of this decision on Article 5 the present law on the detention of those found not guilty by reason of insanity could be challenged under the Human Rights Act. The following arguments could be made:

(1) As already noted, the legal definition of insanity is far wider than the medical concept of mental disorder. It is certainly arguable that the detention of an epileptic who has been found not guilty by reason of insanity infringes Article 5 because such a person is not 'of unsound mind'.

(2) The *Winterwerp* requirement that there be 'objective medical expertise' could be used to challenge the English law on the basis that the doctors under English law have to use the legal, not medical, understanding of mental disorder.[174]

(3) A defendant is presumed sane unless the contrary is proved. The burden of proving the defence falls on the defendant on the balance of probabilities.[175] This is a departure from the normal rules governing defences, where the prosecution must disprove any defence raised by the defendant. The placing of the burden of proof on the defendant may be challengeable as contrary to the presumption of innocence that is protected under Article 6(2) of the ECHR.[176]

Insanity and offences of strict liability

In *DPP v Harper*[177] it was held that insanity was not a defence to a strict liability offence.[178] However, most commentators take the view that the decision is wrong. First, it made no reference to an earlier decision, *Hennessy*,[179] which had stated that insanity was a defence to a strict liability offence. Second, the reasoning used in *DPP v Harper* is suspect. It was claimed that insanity is a denial of *mens rea*.[180] However, if that was all insanity was there would be no need to have a special defence of insanity because any defendant who was legally insane would simply be able to claim he or she lacked the *mens rea* of the offence.

Insanity and intoxication

The leading case on insanity and intoxication is *Lipman*.[181] There the defendant took LSD and (he claimed) as a result had an hallucination in which he was attacked by a many-headed

---

[173] (1979) 2 EHRR 387, para. 39.

[174] It has only been since s. 1 of the Criminal Procedure (Insanity and Unfitness to Plead) Act 1991 that the jury, before finding insanity, must hear evidence from at least two registered medical practitioners (*R v Lederman* [2015] EWCA Crim 1308 confirms both must agree that the individual is unfit to plead). At least one of the doctors must be approved as having 'special experience in the diagnosis or treatment of mental disorder'. In part the statute was passed in order to comply with Art. 5 of the ECHR.

[175] *Bratty v Attorney-General for Northern Ireland* [1963] AC 386 (HL).

[176] *Kebelene* [1999] 3 WLR 972 makes it clear that reversals of the burden of proof are challengeable under the 1998 Act.

[177] [1998] RTR 200, discussed in Ward (1997).

[178] Driving with excess alcohol in his blood (Road Traffic Act 1988, s. 5(1)(a)).

[179] (1989) 89 Cr App R 10.

[180] The reasoning was that, as insanity was simply a denial of *mens rea*, that was no defence to an offence of strict liability, which requires no *mens rea*.

[181] [1970] 1 QB 152.

monster. He killed the monster. On recovering, he discovered that in fact he had killed his girlfriend. He was not permitted to plead insanity because it was his voluntary intoxication, rather than any disease of the mind, which had caused him to be unaware of the nature of his acts. If, however, a defendant can show that although intoxicated it was his or her disease of the mind that caused his or her lack of awareness then insanity may be available (*Burns*).[182]

9.2 A CLAIM THAT THE DEFENDANT WAS INSANE AT THE TIME OF THE TRIAL

When the accused is brought up for trial he or she may be found unfit to plead under sections 4 and 4A of the Criminal Procedure (Insanity) Act 1964.[183] The key issue is whether the accused is able to understand the charge and the difference between a plea of guilty and of not guilty. The accused must also be able to challenge jurors, to instruct counsel, and understand the evidence.[184] In summary the defendant's mental capabilities must be sufficient for him or her to be able to conduct his or her defence adequately.[185] Once it has been determined that the defendant is unfit to stand trial the judge has a wide discretion as to the appropriate course of action (except in the case of murder).[186] The 1991 Act includes disposals ranging from an absolute discharge to admission to hospital with a restraining order.

FURTHER READING

Baker, E. (1994) 'Human Rights, M'Naghten and the 1991 Act' *Criminal Law Review* 84.

Child, J. and Sullivan, G.R. (2014) 'When Does the Insanity Defence Apply? Some Recent Cases' *Criminal Law Review* 788.

Duff, R.A. (1994) 'Fitness to Plead and Fair Trials' *Criminal Law Review* 419.

Horder, J. (1993b) 'Pleading Involuntary Lack of Capacity' *Cambridge Law Journal* 52: 298.

Mackay, R. (1995) *Mental Condition Defences in the Criminal Law* (Oxford: OUP) is the leading work on English law on this topic.

Mackay, R. (2009) 'Righting the Wrong?—Some Observations on the Second Limb of the M'Naghten Rules' *Criminal Law Review* 80.

Mackay, R. and Kearns, G. (1999) 'More Fact(s) about the Insanity Defence' *Criminal Law Review* 714.

Mackay, R. and Kearns, G. (2000) 'An Upturn in Unfitness to Plead? Disability in Relation to the Trial under the 1991 Act' *Criminal Law Review* 532.

Mackay, R., Mitchell, B., and Howe, L. (2006) 'Yet More Facts about the Insanity Defence' *Criminal Law Review* 399.

Mackay, R., Mitchell, B., and Howe, L. (2007) 'A Continued Upturn in Unfitness to Plead—More Disability in Relation to the Trial under the 1991 Act' *Criminal Law Review* 530.

---

[182] (1984) 79 Cr App R 173 (CA).

[183] As amended by the Criminal Procedure (Insanity and Unfitness to Plead) Act 1991. See Howard (2011) for a discussion of the law and its possible reform.

[184] *Robertson* [1968] 1 WLR 1767.   [185] Grubin (1993); Duff (1994).

[186] When the court must order detention in hospital (Criminal Procedure (Insanity) Act 1964, s. 5(3)).

10 DIMINISHED RESPONSIBILITY

This is a defence only to a charge of murder. It is discussed in Chapter 5.

11 LOSS OF CONTROL

This is a defence only to a charge of murder. It is discussed in Chapter 5.

12 CHILDREN

Some children are exempt from criminal liability. It is necessary to distinguish between two age groups:

12.1 CHILDREN BELOW THE AGE OF 10

A child below the age of 10 cannot be convicted of a criminal offence.[187] This is an absolute rule. However deliberate or unpleasant the act committed by a child if he or she has not yet reached his or her tenth birthday he or she cannot be guilty. A child who commits a serious offence may be taken into care by the local authority, but this is a civil, not criminal, matter. One way of understanding the law's approach is to say that a child who commits a crime under the age of 10 needs the protection and support of social workers, rather than deserving the punishment and stigma of a criminal conviction.

12.2 A CHILD AGED 10 TO 14

A child aged between 10 and 14 can be convicted of a crime.[188] Section 34 of the Crime and Disorder Act 1998 abolished the common law presumption that a child between 10 and 14 was *doli incapax*, meaning that a child was not capable of committing a crime because he or she did not know the difference between right and wrong.[189] Section 34 states:

> **Abolition of rebuttable presumption that a child is doli incapax**
>
> The rebuttable presumption of criminal law that a child aged 10 or over is incapable of committing an offence is hereby abolished.

The House of Lords in *R v JTB*[190] has made it clear that the defence of *doli incapax* has now been abolished. So, once a child is over the age of 10 they can be convicted of an offence, as long as they have the necessary *mens rea*. The age of criminal responsibility is much

---

[187] Children and Young Persons Act 1933, s. 50.

[188] In *T v UK* [2000] Crim LR 187 the European Court of Human Rights rejected an argument that punishing children aged 10 was contrary to Art. 3 of the ECHR.

[189] For a detailed discussion of the criminal liability of young people, see Ashworth (2010); Crofts (2003); Keating (2007); Elliott (2011).

[190] [2009] UKHL 20.

lower than many other countries and the law has been criticized by numerous international bodies, including the UN Committee for the Rights of the Child.[191]

13 INTOXICATION

Technically intoxication is a not a defence, although it is often spoken of as such.[192] We have discussed in Chapter 3 the effect of intoxication on the law's understanding of *mens rea*. Here we shall consider whether there should be a special defence for those who commit crimes with the necessary *mens rea* after being involuntarily intoxicated. The leading case is *Kingston*:

R v Kingston
[1995] 2 AC 355 (HL)

Barry Kingston was in dispute with two former business associates. They hired Kevin Penn to photograph Kingston in compromising situations with a boy so that they could blackmail him. Penn lured a 15-year-old boy to his flat, gave him a drink which allegedly contained sedative drugs and some cannabis. The boy fell asleep on a bed and remembered nothing until he woke the next morning. Penn then invited Kingston to his flat and gave him some coffee. Kingston claimed that unknown to him Penn had drugged the coffee. Penn then showed Kingston the naked boy on the bed and Kingston and Penn assaulted him. Penn photographed and taped the indecent assault. Kingston's defence was based on the fact that he had been involuntarily intoxicated. Although he admitted he had paedophilic tendencies, he claimed to have always been able to keep these under control. Kingston explained that the drugs Penn had put in his coffee had caused him to lose his inhibitions and commit the offence. The trial judge directed the jury that if they found the defendant had intentionally assaulted the boy he was guilty, even if that intent had been induced by the drugs administered by Penn. On appeal to the Court of Appeal his conviction was quashed on the basis that if drugs were surreptitiously administered to a person who was thereby caused to lose his inhibitions and form an intent which he would not otherwise have formed this was not a criminal intent. The issue was referred to the House of Lords.

Lord Mustill

The starting point is the verdict of guilty coupled with the judge's direction on the necessity for intent. This implies that the majority either (a) were sure that the respondent had not involuntarily taken a drug or drugs at all or (b) were sure that whatever drug he may have taken had not had such an effect on his mind that he did not intend to do what he did. We are therefore not concerned with what is picturesquely called automatism; nor was it suggested that the effect of the drug was to produce a condition of temporary insanity. What then was said to have been the induced mental condition on which the respondent relies? Inevitably, since the judge's ruling meant that whatever medical evidence there may have been was not developed we cannot be sure. Still, the general nature of the case is clear

---

[191] Keating (2007).   [192] Simester (2009).

enough. In ordinary circumstances the respondent's paedophilic tendencies would have been kept under control, even in the presence of the sleeping or unconscious boy on the bed. The ingestion of the drug (whatever it was) brought about a temporary change in the mentality or personality of the respondent which lowered his ability to resist temptation so far that his desires overrode his ability to control them. Thus we are concerned here with a case of disinhibition. The drug is not alleged to have created the desire to which the respondent gave way, but rather to have enabled it to be released. The situation is therefore different from that which led to the acquittal of the accused in the first of the Scottish cases to which I shall refer, where the drug directly brought about the violent conduct with which he was charged.

On these facts there are three grounds on which the respondent might be held free from criminal responsibility. First, that his immunity flows from general principles of the criminal law. Secondly, that this immunity is already established by a solid line of authority. Finally, that the court should, when faced with a new problem acknowledge the justice of the case and boldly create a new common law defence.

It is clear from the passage already quoted that the Court of Appeal adopted the first approach. The decision was explicitly founded on general principle. There can be no doubt what principle the court relied upon, for at the outset the court recorded the submission of counsel for the respondent that 'the law recognises that, exceptionally, an accused person may be entitled to be acquitted if there is a possibility that, although his act was intentional, the intent itself arose out of circumstances for which he bears no blame' (see [1994] QB 81 at 87). The same proposition is implicit in the assumption by the court that if blame is absent the necessary *mens rea* must also be absent.

My Lords, with every respect I must suggest that no such principle exists or, until the present case, had ever in modern times been thought to exist. Each offence consists of a prohibited act or omission coupled with whatever state of mind is called for by the statute or rule of the common law which creates the offence. In those offences which are not absolute the state of mind which the prosecution must prove to have underlain the act or omission— the 'mental element'—will in the majority of cases be such as to attract disapproval. The mental element will then be the mark of what may properly be called a 'guilty mind'. The professional burglar is guilty in a moral as well as a legal sense; he intends to break into the house to steal, and most would confidently assert that this is wrong. But this will not always be so. In respect of some offences the mind of the defendant, and still less his moral judgment, may not be engaged at all. In others, although a mental activity must be the motive power for the prohibited act or omission the activity may be of such a kind or degree that society at large would not criticise the defendant's conduct severely or even criticise it at all. Such cases are not uncommon. Yet to assume that contemporary moral judgments affect the criminality of the act, as distinct from the punishment appropriate to the crime once proved, is to be misled by the expression '*mens rea*', the ambiguity of which has been the subject of complaint for more than a century. Certainly, the 'mens' of the defendant must usually be involved in the offence; but the epithet 'rea' refers to the criminality of the act in which the mind is engaged, not to its moral character. If support from the commentators for this proposition is necessary it may be found in Smith and Hogan *Criminal Law* (7th edn, 1992), pp 79–80, *Glanville Williams Textbook of Criminal Law* (2nd edn, 1983), p 221 and also p 75 and *Russell on Crime* (12th edn, 1964), vol 1, pp 80, 86.

. . . I would therefore reject that part of the respondent's argument which treats the absence of moral fault on the part of the appellant as sufficient in itself to negative the necessary mental element of the offence.

. . .

His second ground is more narrow, namely that involuntary intoxication is already recognised as a defence by authority which the House ought to follow.

[**Lord Mustill** referred to a variety of English and Commonwealth authorities, none of which he found persuasive support for the Court of Appeal's view.]

. . .

To recognise a new defence of this type would be a bold step. The common law defences of duress and necessity (if it exists) and the limited common law defence of provocation are all very old. Since counsel for the appellant was not disposed to emphasise this aspect of the appeal the subject was not explored in argument, but I suspect that the recognition of a new general defence at common law has not happened in modern times. Nevertheless, the criminal law must not stand still, and if it is both practical and just to take this step, and if judicial decision rather than legislation is the proper medium, then the courts should not be deterred simply by the novelty of it. So one must turn to consider just what defence is now to be created.

. . .

My Lords, since the existence or otherwise of the defence has been treated in argument at all stages as a matter of existing law the Court of Appeal had no occasion to consider the practical and theoretical implications of recognising this new defence at common law, and we do not have the benefit of its views. In their absence, I can only say that the defence appears to run into difficulties at every turn. In point of theory, it would be necessary to reconcile a defence of irresistible impulse derived from a combination of innate drives and external disinhibition with the rule that irresistible impulse of a solely internal origin (not necessarily any more the fault of the offender) does not in itself excuse although it may be a symptom of a disease of the mind: see *A-G for the State of South Australia v Brown* [1960] AC 432. Equally, the state of mind which founds the defence superficially resembles a state of diminished responsibility, whereas the effect in law is quite different. It may well be that the resemblance is misleading, but these and similar problems must be solved before the bounds of a new defence can be set.

On the practical side there are serious problems. Before the jury could form an opinion on whether the drug might have turned the scale witnesses would have to give a picture of the defendant's personality and susceptibilities, for without it the crucial effect of the drug could not be assessed; pharmacologists would be required to describe the potentially disinhibiting effect of a range of drugs whose identity would, if the present case is anything to go by, be unknown; psychologists and psychiatrists would express opinions, not on the matters of psychopathology familiar to those working within the framework of the Mental Health Acts but on altogether more elusive concepts. No doubt as time passed those concerned could work out techniques to deal with these questions. Much more significant would be the opportunities for a spurious defence. Even in the field of road traffic the 'spiked' drink as a special reason for not disqualifying from driving is a regular feature. Transferring this to the entire range of criminal offences is a disturbing prospect. The defendant would only have to assert, and support by the evidence of well-wishers, that he was not the sort of person to have done this kind of thing, and to suggest an occasion when by some means a drug might have been administered to him for the jury be sent straight to the question of a possible disinhibition. The judge would direct the jurors that if they felt any legitimate doubt on the matter—and by its nature the defence would be one which the prosecution would often have no means to rebut—they must acquit outright, all questions of intent, mental capacity and the like being at this stage irrelevant.

My Lords, the fact that a new doctrine may require adjustment of existing principles to accommodate it, and may require those involved in criminal trials to learn new techniques, is not of course a ground for refusing to adopt it, if that is what the interests of justice require. Here, however, justice makes no such demands, for the interplay between the wrong done to the victim, the individual characteristics and frailties of the defendant, and the pharmacological effects of whatever drug may be potentially involved can be far better recognised by a tailored choice from the continuum of sentences available to the judge than by the application of a single yea-or-nay jury decision. To this, there is one exception. The mandatory life sentence for murder, at least as present administered, leaves no room for the trial judge to put into practice an informed and sympathetic assessment of the kind just described. It is for this reason alone that I have felt any hesitation about rejecting the argument for the respondent. In the end however I have concluded that this is not a sufficient reason to force on the theory and practice of the criminal law an exception which would otherwise be unjustified. For many years mandatory sentences have impelled juries to return merciful but false verdicts, and have stimulated the creation of partial defences such as provocation and diminished responsibility whose lack of a proper foundation has made them hard to apply in practice. I do not think it right that the law should be further distorted simply because of this anomalous relic of the history of the criminal law.

All this being said, I suggest to your Lordships that the existing work of the Law Commission in the field of intoxication could usefully be enlarged to comprise questions of the type raised by this appeal, and to see whether by statute a merciful, realistic and intellectually sustainable statutory solution could be newly created. For the present, however, I consider that no such regime now exists, and that the common law is not a suitable vehicle for creating one.

Appeal allowed.

This decision makes it clear that if a defendant has the necessary *mens rea* for an offence the fact that he or she only committed it because he or she was involuntarily intoxicated provides no defence. It is, however, not clear what would happen in a case where the defendant was involuntarily intoxicated and committed a strict liability or negligence-based offence. Lord Mustill's reasoning appears to indicate that the defendant would still be guilty, but this is by no means beyond doubt. →7 (p.736)

14 MISTAKE

It is in fact technically incorrect to see mistake as a special category of defence.[193] Rather, a mistake can be a particular way of denying that the defendant has *mens rea* or asserting that the defendant has a defence, such as self-defence. Consider these four examples:

(1) **The mistake negates *mens rea*** Anna was out shooting rabbits and she saw something she thought was a rabbit and shot at it. In fact it was Tom who was hiding in some bushes, who died from the shot. Anna would have a defence of no *mens rea* to a charge of murder. Her mistake meant that she did not have an intention to kill or cause grievous bodily harm to a person.

---

[193] A point stressed by Lord Hailsham in *Morgan* [1976] AC 182, 214 (HL).

(2) **The mistake does not negate *mens rea*** Eva is a terrorist. She shoots Damien dead. Eva believes that Damien is a government minister, but she is mistaken and Damien is in fact a member of the public. Here Eva is guilty of murder, but her mistake did not negate her *mens rea* (she did intend to kill a person), nor did her mistake give rise to a defence.[194]

(3) **The mistaken belief forms the basis of a defence** Elizabeth mistakenly believes that Richard is about to attack her and so she stabs him dead. Elizabeth will be able to rely on the defence of self-defence.[195]

(4) **A mistake of law provides no defence** Grace buys some cannabis. She misunderstands an inaccurate report in a tabloid newspaper and believes that it is no longer an offence to possess cannabis. She is charged with possession of cannabis. It is no defence for her to claim that she thought what she was doing was legal.

We will now consider these examples in further detail:

14.1 A MISTAKE WHICH MAY NEGATE *MENS REA*

The simple question to ask in these cases is whether in the light of the mistake the defendant had the required *mens rea* or recklessness. The leading case on this area of the law is now *B v DPP*,[196] which was discussed in Chapter 4. There their Lordships confirmed that, unless a statutory offence states otherwise, if the defendant can demonstrate that he or she honestly (even if unreasonably) believed that an element of the *actus reus* did not exist then he or she can have a defence.

What if the reason for the defendant's mistake which led to his or her lack of *mens rea* is intoxication? The correct view, it is submitted, is to follow the general approach for intoxication. For example, in cases of voluntarily intoxication the mistaken belief can be introduced as evidence of no *mens rea* in cases of specific intent, but otherwise will not provide a defence. So in a murder case if the defendant was so drunk he thought the victim was a deer and shot him this could provide a defence: there was no intent to kill or seriously injure a person. This defendant would still be convicted of manslaughter. In cases of involuntary intoxication the drunken mistake can provide a defence if that mistake negates *mens rea*.[197]

14.2 MISTAKES AND DEFENCES

The law is not straightforward in cases where a defendant wishes to rely on a defence, such as self-defence or consent, but is mistaken as to one of the elements of the defence. An example is a defendant who uses force against a person he or she believes is attacking him or her, but who is not. The easiest way to deal with cases is to consider each defence separately and to consider three kinds of mistake:

(1) **A reasonable mistake**: a mistake that a reasonable person in the defendant's shoes might have made.

(2) **An unreasonable mistake**: a mistake that a reasonable person would not have made.

(3) **A drunken mistake**: a mistaken belief reached by someone who is drunk.

---

[194] See *R v Ellis, Street and Smith* (1987) 84 Cr App R 235 (CA) for a less straightforward case.
[195] *Beckford* [1998] AC 130.   [196] [2000] 2 WLR 452 (HL).
[197] *Kingston* [1995] 2 AC 355 (HL).

Now we shall consider each defence separately and how they deal with these three different kinds of mistake:

Lawful defence

(1) **Reasonable mistakes**: the defendant is to be judged on the facts as he or she believed them to be.[198] So if the defendant believes he or she is being attacked when he or she is not then the jury must ask themselves whether the amount of force used was reasonable assuming the facts to be as the defendant believed them to be. If it was the defendant can use lawful defence.

(2) **Unreasonable mistakes**: the defendant's belief that he or she is being attacked does not have to be reasonable.

(3) **Drunken mistakes**: a defendant cannot rely on a drunken belief that he or she is being attacked.[199] The question the jury must ask themselves is whether the drunkenness caused the mistake. This will be done by considering whether the defendant would have made the same mistake had he or she been sober. If he or she would have done then he or she can rely on lawful defence, but if he or she would not then he or she may not.

Duress

(1) **Reasonable mistakes**: the defendant can rely on duress (by threats or circumstances) if he or she has reasonable grounds for believing that the threats have been made or the threatening circumstances exist, even if in fact there is no such threat.[200]

(2) **Unreasonable mistakes**: the defendant probably[201] must have reasonable grounds for believing that the threat of death or serious injury has been made and that it will be carried out. If he or she does not have reasonable grounds he or she cannot rely on the defence.

(3) **Drunken mistakes**: an unreasonable drunken belief that the defendant is being threatened will not provide a defence.

Consent

(1) **Reasonable mistakes**: if the defendant mistakenly believes that the victim was consenting to the use of force, in circumstances in which consent would have provided a defence, then the defendant has a defence.

(2) **Unreasonable mistakes**: there is no need for the defendant to show that the belief in consent was reasonably held.[202]

(3) **Drunken mistakes**: general principles suggest that a drunken belief that the victim was consenting will not provide a defence.[203] There are, however, two cases which suggest that a drunken belief that the victim was consenting could provide a defence:

---

[198] *Williams* (1984) 78 Cr App R 276 (CA); *Beckford* [1988] AC 130 (PC).
[199] *Hatton* [2005] EWCA Crim 2951; *O'Grady* [1987] 3 WLR 321 (CA); *O'Connor* [1991] Crim LR 135 (CA).
[200] *Martin* [1989] 1 All ER 652 (CA); *Howe* [1987] 1 All ER 771 (HL); *Graham* [1982] 1 WLR 294 (CA).
[201] See the discussion at p.657.   [202] *Morgan* [1976] AC 182 (HL).
[203] *Fotheringham* (1989) 88 Cr App R 206 (CA).

(a) In *Richardson and Irvin*[204] the Court of Appeal suggested that a drunken mistaken belief that the victim was consenting to rough horseplay could provide a defence to a charge of assault occasioning actual bodily harm.

(b) In *Jaggard v Dickinson*[205] a drunken woman believed she was breaking the window of her friend's house so she could get in. In fact the house belonged to a stranger. It was held that her drunken mistaken belief that the owner would have consented provided a defence to criminal damage under section 5(2) and (3) of the Criminal Damage Act 1971.[206]

It is arguable that these two cases, neither of which was argued in depth, should not be regarded as conclusive. Indeed in *Magee v CPS*[207] Elias LJ held there was 'considerable doubt' whether *Jaggard v Dickinson* was good law.

The conflict between the case law requires a decision from the Court of Appeal to clarify the present state of the law.

Loss of control

(1) **Reasonable mistakes**: if a defendant mishears or misinterprets what is said or done and as a result loses his or her self-control he or she can rely on loss of control.

(2) **Unreasonable mistakes**: if the mistake is an unreasonable one the position is unclear. Section 55 of the Coroners and Justice Act 2009 refers to a 'fear of serious violence' being a qualifying trigger. The statute does not say it must be a reasonable fear. By contrast, in relation to the 'things done or said' trigger, the statute says they must constitute circumstances of an 'extremely grave character'. That suggests an unreasonable belief as to those circumstances will be insufficient.

(3) **Drunken mistakes**: it is unlikely that a drunken belief that there is a qualifying trigger will be sufficient to allow a defendant to use the defence.

14.3 MISTAKES OF LAW

In considering mistakes of law it is necessary to distinguish between mistakes of law that negate *mens rea* and those which do not:

(1) **Mistakes of law which do not negate *mens rea*** There is a well-known legal maxim: ignorance of the law is no excuse (*ignorantia juris neminem excusat*).[208] So it is no defence to a charge of rape that the defendant did not know that it was a criminal offence to have sexual intercourse with someone without her consent.[209] There are two exceptions to the principle:

(a) A person has a defence if he or she is charged with an offence created by a statutory instrument which has not been publicized[210] or a government Order if the person affected is unaware of the Order.[211]

---

[204] [1999] 1 Cr App R 392 (CA).   [205] [1981] QB 527 (QBD).

[206] Section 5(2) of the Criminal Damage Act 1971 provides a defence to a person who causes criminal damage, believing that the owner would have consented to the damage if he had known of the circumstances of the damage. Section 5(3) of the Act states: 'For the purposes of this section it is immaterial whether a belief is justified or not if it is honestly held.'

[207] [2014] EWHC 4089 (Admin).

[208] See the discussion in Ashworth (2011a); Power (2007); Segev (2006).

[209] This rule can produce great unfairness (see *Bailey* (1800) Russ & Ry 1).

[210] Statutory Instruments Act 1946, s. 3(2).   [211] *Lim Chin Aik v R* [1963] AC 160 (PC).

(b) If a person intends to do an act and seeks advice from a state agency as to whether the action is lawful and is told (wrongly) that it is lawful, then a subsequent prosecution may be halted by a judge as an abuse of process.[212]

(2) **Mistakes of law which do negate *mens rea*** A mistake of law can provide a defence if it means that the defendant lacks the *mens rea* of the offence. This is most relevant in property offences. Section 2(1)(a) of the Theft Act 1968, for example, specifically states that a person will not be dishonest if he or she believes he or she has, in law, the right to take the property. For example, if Jonathan is charged with the theft of David's car he has a defence if he can persuade the jury that he believed that because David owed him money he was legally entitled to seize his property. The mistake of law will establish that the defendant was not dishonest.

FURTHER READING

Fletcher, G. (1978) *Rethinking Criminal Law* (Boston, MA: Little, Brown), ch. 9.

Husak, D. and von Hirsch, A. (1993) 'Culpability and Mistake of Law' in S. Shute, J. Gardner, and J. Horder (eds) *Action and Value in Criminal Law* (Oxford: OUP).

Tur, R. (1993) 'Subjectivism and Objectivism: Towards Synthesis' in S. Shute, J. Gardner, and J. Horder (eds) *Action and Value in Criminal Law* (Oxford: OUP).

PART II: THE THEORY OF DEFENCES

15 DEFINING DEFENCES

15.1 THE TRADITIONAL APPROACH

There is much dispute over the correct way to classify defences.[213] Perhaps the most popular way is to draw a distinction between:

(1) the *actus reus* of the crime;

(2) the *mens rea* of the crime;

(3) a defence;

(4) mitigation.

---

[212] *Postermobile plc v Brent LBC* [1997] EWHC Admin 1002. Technically the offence is committed, but it is not possible to prosecute it.

[213] P. Robinson (1997: 11) suggests that defences are 'anything that prevents conviction of a defendant'. This is too wide because it would include the death of the defendant before the trial is completed (Husak 1999a).

The prosecution must prove the *actus reus* and *mens rea* of the offence, and once these have been proved the defendant will be guilty unless he or she is able to establish a defence. It should be noted that some defences are partial defences, meaning that they do not lead to a complete acquittal, but reduce the charge for which the defendant is convicted. A good example is loss of control which, if successful, reduces the charge from murder to manslaughter. Matters of mitigation will not affect whether or not the defendant is guilty of the offence charged but will affect the sentence imposed. For example, if the defendant was racially insulted and therefore hit the victim, the provocation will not amount to a defence (remember loss of control is a defence only to murder) but it may well mean that the defendant will receive a lower sentence than he or she would have received had it been an unprovoked assault.[214]

This apparently straightforward classification is beset with difficulties. Glanville Williams has written:

> what we think of as the definition of an offence and what we call a defence can only be regarded as depending largely upon the accidents of language, the convenience of legal drafting, or the unreasoning force of tradition.[215]

Indeed whether a matter raised by the defence is regarded as a denial of *actus reus*, a denial of *mens rea*, or a defence can be hard to tell.[216] Certainly the classification the courts have adopted is not that which you might at first expect: self-defence is regarded by the courts as a denial of *actus reus*, automatism is seen likewise as a denial of *actus reus*. This is not an argument that the classification cannot be supported but it demonstrates that some careful argumentation is needed to define these classifications.[217] ←1 (p.626)

15.2 ALTERNATIVES TO THE TRADITIONAL CLASSIFICATION

In the light of such difficulties some commentators have suggested alternatives or amendments to the traditional classification:

(1) **To add an additional category of exemption**: those to whom the criminal law is not addressed or who are outside the purview of the criminal law;[218] the argument being that some people lack the moral capacity necessary to be people to whom the law is appropriately addressed.[219] Children and the insane[220] would be two categories of defendant who clearly fall into this classification. Such people cannot be required or expected to comply with the standards expected of the criminal law because they lack the capacity to appreciate those standards or be responsible for their behaviour.[221] Supporters of the traditional classification claim that these 'exemptions' can be brought within the definition of excuses.[222]

---

[214] J. Gardner (1995a). If the defendant is morally blameless such factors may also influence the prosecution in its decision whether or not to prosecute.

[215] G. Williams (1982a: 256).   [216] Husak (1998).

[217] Of course, the fact that 'bright lines' cannot be drawn does not mean that generally the classification is not useful.

[218] Lacey (2000a).   [219] J. Gardner (2008a).

[220] Loughnan (2012). P. Robinson (1982) is sceptical about exemptions. He argues that although someone may be insane at the time of the offence, he may not generally be insane. To describe such a person as exempt from the criminal law sometimes and sometimes not creates unnecessary confusion in his view.

[221] See e.g. Horder (1997b) for further discussion.

[222] For arguments against the existence of exemptions, see W. Wilson (2002: 288–9).

(2) **To argue that all defences are in essence about redefining the offence definition:**[223] all offences would be made up of just two elements: the *actus reus* and *mens rea*, and all defences would be denials of the *actus reus* or *mens rea*. So the *actus reus* of the offence would be to do X (except in self-defence or acting under duress).

15.3 DOES ANY OF THIS MATTER?

You may by now be beginning to wonder whether any of this matters very much. Why should it matter whether we regard self-defence as a denial of the *actus reus*, the *mens rea*, or a defence? Is that not a matter which is only of interest to those academics who wish to describe criminal law in terms of nicely-defined boxes? Well, there is much to be said for such a point of view, and certainly there are grave dangers in expecting criminal law to fit into neat packages. However, there are cases where the distinctions have practical significance. For example, the prosecution has the burden of proving the *actus reus* and *mens rea* elements of the offence. The defence carries the burden of raising the defence. So whether self-defence (say) is an element of the *actus reus* or a defence matters here. If self-defence is a denial of the *actus reus* then it is for the prosecution to prove that the defendant was not acting in self-defence, whereas if it is a defence, if the defendant wishes to raise the matter he or she must introduce evidence of self-defence before the court.[224]

We will now turn to the wealth of material that has been produced examining the philosophical foundations for the defences recognized in the law. As you will see there are many theories that have been put forward as *the* theory of criminal defences. Perhaps before starting it is worth noting that many commentators[225] warn against adopting a single theory of criminal culpability. Rather, each defence and each crime needs careful consideration on its own. Certainly no one theory of culpability can explain the criminal law as it stands at present.

FURTHER READING

Alldridge, P. (1983) 'The Coherence of Defences' *Criminal Law Review* 665.

Campbell, K. (1987) 'Offence and Defence' in I. Dennis (ed.) *Criminal Law and Criminal Justice* (London: Sweet & Maxwell).

Duff, R.A. (2007) *Answering for Crime* (Oxford: Hart), ch. 11.

Fletcher, G. (1978) *Rethinking Criminal Law* (Boston, MA: Little, Brown), ch. 10.

Smith, A. (1978) 'On *Actus Reus* and *Mens Rea*' in P.R. Glazebrook (ed.) *Reshaping the Criminal Law* (London: Stevens).

Tadros, V. (2005a) *Criminal Responsibility* (Oxford: OUP).

Williams, G. (1982b) 'The Theory of Excuses' *Criminal Law Review* 732.

Wilson, W. (2005) 'The Structure of Criminal Defences' *Criminal Law Review* 371.

---

223 P. Robinson (1982).
224 Also, in offences of strict liability, where there is no need for the prosecution to prove any *mens rea*, whether an element is regarded as of *actus reus* or *mens rea* is important.
225 e.g. Horder (1993b).

16 JUSTIFICATIONS AND EXCUSES

One popular way of analysing defences is to distinguish between justifications and excuses.[226]

> **DEFINITION**
>
> A justification focuses on what the defendant did and claims that what he or she did was what the law permitted him or her to do. Normally that is because society has approved of what the defendant has done.
>
> With an excuse the defendant admits that what he or she did was not permissible, but that he or she does not deserve to be blamed. This may be because of his or her mental state, for example.[227]

As Paul Robinson has stated: 'An actor's conduct is justified; an actor is excused' (1999: 69).

Nicola Lacey describes the difference between an excuse and a justification, but then explains some of the difficulties in drawing the distinction:

N. Lacey, 'Community, Culture and Criminalization' in W. Kymlicka, C. Lernestedt, and M. Matravers (eds), *Criminal Law and Cultural Diversity* (Oxford: OUP, 2014), 58–9

Criminal law theorists have often distinguished between defenses which are primarily excusatory and those which are justificatory. While excuses bear primarily on the conditions or circumstances under which the defendant has acted, and hence on responsibility, justifications bear on the nature of the defendant's conduct. Justifications justify actions; excuses excuse actors. A justification's normative defense of conduct is precisely what has often made courts so wary of such defenses, which at root pitch the defendant's view of the proper standard of conduct against that of the law. Hence most advocates of cultural defenses are careful to pose them at the level of excuse or mitigation rather than justification: to defendants' levels of responsibility in acting rather than in terms of the normative quality of their conduct.

But the excuse/justification, actor/action distinction turns out, once again, to be a difficult line to hold. First, justificatory and excusatory elements are often blended in actual defense arguments. For example, though the provocation defense has gradually acquired a more excusatory character—a claim of psychological loss of self-control—as the codes of honor in which it originated as a partial justification have been dismantled, elements of justification continue to mark the reasonableness standard which the provocation must also meet (Horder 1992). Thus, second, even where a defense is placed on a firmly excusatory footing, evaluations of reasonableness come into play. A provoked reaction must be that of "a reasonable person"; the duress defense is available only where a person of "reasonable firmness" would have succumbed to the threat, and so on. Even in the case of strongly subjective defenses and principles of responsibility, the aims of the criminal process come

---

[226] Fletcher (1978: ch. 10); J.C. Smith (1989); P. Robinson (1982); G. Williams (1982b); Greenawalt (1984).

[227] W. Wilson (2004) emphasizes the role played by the fact the defendant was facing a crisis in determining whether there is an excuse.

into play. For example, though defendants in English law are generally entitled to be judged on the basis of the facts as they believed them to be, a mistake induced by voluntary intoxication will be ignored. There is no such thing as purely factual criminal responsibility or excuse: a normative case for the relevant cultural or other argument will always have to be provided. What we regard as an excuse is itself a function of our evaluation of the conduct in question.

16.1 JUSTIFICATIONS

A justification focuses on the act of the defendant and claims that the defendant performed a permissible act.[228] It is sometimes suggested that a justification is a claim that the defendant did the 'right' thing. This would be misleading. Consider this example: Nick is approached by two 7-year-old children who are playing with guns. They point the guns at Nick and place their fingers on the triggers. The only way Nick can save himself is to shoot the children dead, which he does. Now, whether what the defendant did is 'right' is a matter of great debate among ethicists. Some people would take the view that he ought to lay down his own life rather than kill 'the innocent children'. However, what is clear is that he is legally permitted to use force in these circumstances. So it is preferable to say that a justification involves actions that are permissible, rather than actions that are right.[229]

But how does the law decide what a defendant is permitted to do which would otherwise be a criminal offence? A number of different theories have been produced to explain justifications:[230]

(1) **Lesser of two evils** A justification applies when the defendant has performed the lesser of two evils.[231] In other words an act is justified if it causes more good than harm: there is no 'net societal harm'.[232] There are difficulties with such an explanation. It appears to provide a defence to a doctor who killed a nurse to use her organs to save two of his patients. It also does not explain why it is permissible to use slightly more force than is threatened to repel an attack.[233]

(2) **Moral forfeiture** This is the idea that the victim has forfeited his or her right not to be injured as a result of his or her morally wrong conduct, thereby authorizing the defendant's use of force against him or her.[234] This theory is (as we shall see) a popular way of justifying self-defence. By attacking the defendant the victim has forfeited his or her right not to be injured and therefore the defendant is entitled to use force to repel the victim's attack. The theory works less well in circumstances in which the victim is not morally to blame, but the

---

[228] One issue of some debate concerning justification is whether, if there is a justification, there is still a wrong committed against a victim. One view is that in the case of a justified act the defendant has still wronged the 'victim', but that this wrong has been outweighed by the good consequences flowing from the act. The opposite view is that if the act is justified then it is 'all right' and no legal wrong has been done. See the discussion in Fletcher (1998: ch. 1).

[229] See the discussion in Uniacke (1994) and Schopp (1998). Uniacke suggests a distinction between a strong justification (the act was morally right) and a weak justification (the act was permissible, although morally wrong). Both are justifications for the purpose of the law she argues.

[230] Dressler (1987). See also for further discussion Bergelson (2007a).

[231] Teichman (1986) suggests that a justification only arises if the defendant has done the greater of two goods.

[232] P. Robinson (1996b). For a detailed discussion, see Alexander (2005) and Simons (2005).

[233] Alexander (1999).   [234] See further Leverick (2006: ch. 2).

defendant is still justified in acting (e.g. where the defendant injures a child who is attacking him or her or a case of necessity). There are also some commentators who argue that fundamental rights should not be forfeited. We would not be happy with the idea that someone could forfeit his or her right not to be tortured; should we be any happier with someone losing the right to life?

(3) **Securing legal and moral rights** Here justifications are seen as upholding the defendant's legal (and moral) rights. Justifications, the argument goes, arise where the defendant is acting in order to protect or promote his or her rights. For example, in self-defence the defendant is acting in order to promote his or her right to personal autonomy. There are difficulties with this theory where there is a clash of rights. If after a shipwreck five people are in a life raft suitable for only four people, does each person have a right of autonomy which permits them to force off one of the others? If one is justified in pushing off the other, is the other justified in resisting the force?

(4) **Public authority justification** Under this theory public officers (e.g. police officers) are given authority on behalf of the state to use force in certain circumstances.
Which view is adopted on the nature of justification can affect your response to two scenarios which have been hotly debated by those interested in this subject:

The case of the unknown justification

This scenario under discussion[235] is best explained by way of an example. Bill sees in the distance his enemy, George. He pulls out his gun and shoots George dead. Unknown to Bill, George was in fact about to blow up a bomb which would have killed many people. So in fact Bill's actions produced a net social good, but he was unaware that he was doing so. Was Bill justified in acting the way he did? Commentators are deeply divided on the issue:

(1) **Bill is justified (the Robinson view)** Those who take this view argue that Bill did exactly what we would have wanted him to do. Because of his actions many lives were saved. We should therefore not criminalize him for what he did. The leading exponent of this view is Paul Robinson. His view has the benefit of simplicity: justifications are about what the defendant does, not what he or she thinks. He argues that it better reflects the common understanding of justification and enables the law to send a clear message about what conduct is permissible.[236] Robinson has been willing to accept that in our scenario Bill might be appropriately convicted of attempted murder: he tried to commit murder, but in fact carried out a lawful killing,[237] although other commentators have replied that to say an act both is justified and also constitutes a criminal offence of attempt is contradictory.[238]

(2) **Bill is not justified (the *Dadson* view)** This is the view taken in English law, following the *Dadson*[239] case. Only if one acts in a permissible way and for justifying reasons can one claim to be justified.[240] Some commentators have argued that the law does not want to encourage people to break the law if they are not aware of any justifying circumstances.

---

[235] Discussed in Christopher (1995); P. Robinson (1996b); J. Gardner (1996).
[236] P. Robinson (1996b).   [237] *Ibid*. He is supported on this by Gross (1979: 199).
[238] W. Wilson (2002: 273).   [239] (1850) 4 Cox CC 358.
[240] Hitchler (1931). Some commentators would add that the justifying circumstances must be one of the reasons for which the defendant acted.

The case of the mistaken justification

Again this is best explained by an example. Margaret is out for a late night walk. She hears running behind her, turns and see Ronald running towards her. Convinced that Ronald is about to rape her, she shoots him. In fact it turns out that Ronald was out for a jog and intended Margaret no harm. On the facts as Margaret believed them to be she was justi-fied in acting as she did, but on the facts as they actually were she was not justified. Paul Robinson argues that such an actor is not justified.[241] What Margaret did not produce was a net social good. He points out that if a passer-by (Neil) sees what is happening and tries to stop Margaret because he appreciates that she has made a mistake, then if we hold Margaret justified in her attack Neil will be committing an offence, whereas if we say she is only excused (as Robinson would have it) then Neil is justified.[242] Simester and Sullivan think it is arguable that Margaret in a case like this acts justifiably.[243] She did what was permitted, how society would have wanted her to act, *given her state of mind*. Kimberly Kessler Ferzan[244] suggests that if the victim was in some way acting culpably the defendant is justified even if the defendant mistakenly thought the threat was far greater than it was or failed to see an escape route.

Deeds v reasons

These two problems indicate a fundamental dispute over the nature of justification. In essence there are three views. A person is justified because:

(1) his or her deeds are justified (the 'deeds' view);[245]

(2) he or she acts for justifiable reasons (the 'reasons' view); or

(3) both his or her deeds and reasons are justified (the 'deeds and reasons' view).[246]

The practical differences between these views are demonstrated by the following points:

(1) A person who takes the 'deeds' view would find the unknown justified actor justified, but not the mistaken justified actor.

(2) The 'reasons' view would not find the unknown justified actor justified, but would find the mistaken justified actor justified.

(3) The 'deeds and reasons' view would find neither the unknown justified nor the mis-taken justified actor justified.

16.2 EXCUSES

Excuses are often said to be all about removing blame.[247] An excuse accepts that the defend-ant behaved in an unjustified way, but argues that he or she is not to blame for his or her action. Although, as was explained in Chapter 3, the *mens rea* requirements ensure that the defendant was to blame for bringing about the harm to the victim, *mens rea* can do only part of that job. For example, a defendant may intentionally injure a victim, but only do so

---

241 See also Horder (2004: ch. 5) and Ripstein (1996).

242 Remember that private defence is available only against an unjust threat (see Section 1.1, p.627).

243 Simester, Spencer, Sullivan, and Virgo (2013: 668).   244 Kessler Ferzan (2005).

245 P. Robinson (1996).   246 Fletcher (1998: 88–9) and J. Gardner (1996).

247 Kadish (1987a).

because he or she has been threatened with death. Marcia Baron[248] suggests that excuses can be divided into two categories: those that relate to the defendant and claim that there was something about the defendant which made it harder for him or her than most people to comply with the law (e.g. because he or she suffered a mental abnormality) and those that relate to the circumstances the defendant found him or herself in (e.g. he or she was facing a threat of death if he or she did not commit the crime). Excuses therefore complete the picture of the assessment of the defendant's blameworthiness.

So which defences are justifications and which are excuses?

Unfortunately it is not possible to produce a definitive list of which defences are justifications and which are excuses. The courts rarely talk about the distinction between a justification and an excuse, and there is no consensus over the proper classification of some defences. There is a general agreement that automatism and insanity are excuses.[249] Private defence and chastisement are usually seen as justifications.[250] Much more debate surrounds loss of control,[251] duress,[252] and mistaken private defence.

In the following passage, Jeremy Horder sets out what he sees as the essential elements of an excuse:

J. Horder, *Excusing Crime* (Oxford: OUP, 2004), 8–12

To be recognizable as such, it is a necessary condition of any claim to excuse that it is an explanation for engagement in wrongdoing (an explanation not best understood as a justification, as a simple claim of involuntariness, or as an out-and-out denial of responsibility) that sheds such a favourable moral light on D's conduct that it seems entirely wrong to convict, at least for the full offence. So defined, claims that are candidates for excuse overlap to some extent with claims treated as claims for mitigation of sentence; but claims that meet the necessary conditions for excuse are by no means just the most pressing of the claims for mitigation of sentence that D might plausibly make. Excuses are morally as well as legally distinctive in character. Excuses excuse the act or omission amounting to wrongdoing, by shedding favourable moral light on what D did through a focus on the reasons that D committed that wrongdoing, where those reasons played a morally 'active' role in D's conduct (meaning that what D did or what happened to D can be subject to critical moral evaluation). So long as those reasons did play a morally active role in D's conduct, it can still be appropriate to speak of the case for 'excusing' D, even when D combines a factor (duress, say, or provocation) with respect to which he or she was morally active, with a factor (mental disorder, say, or involuntariness), with respect to which he or she was morally 'passive'. The existence of a morally active dimension to what happened to D or to what D did, means that the event stands to be evaluated in the light of underlying 'guiding' reasons, reasons that dictate how D *ought* (not) to have behaved, in failing to control his or her nerves, or in losing his or her temper, as well as in striking someone, and so forth. The applicability of guiding reasons gives rise to the critical, judgmental or evaluative element in a claim, making it to

---

248 Baron (2006). See Horder (2007a), who is less convinced by this distinction.
249 Although many commentators would prefer to refer to insanity as an exemption.
250 There is of course much debate whether chastisement *should* be a defence at all.
251 See Chapter 5.   252 Huigens (2004).

at least some extent excusatory, even if its potential for success must sometimes turn in part on the influence of some morally passive physical or mental weakness or deficiency, on which guiding reasons can have no bearing. I will say more about the excusatory character and potential of reasons with respect to which D is morally active in a moment. It follows, though, that excuses ought to be distinguished from out-and-out denials of responsibility, of the kind constituted by a claim to acquittal focused solely on the effects of a severe mental disorder or deficiency (such as insanity). For, in such cases, guiding reasons—reasons concerned with how D ought to have behaved—have no moral significance, and we cannot judge D's conduct objectively in the light of an applicable moral standard.

Excusatory reasons, with respect to which one is morally active, can be divided into two general kinds, 'explanatory' reasons and 'adopted' reasons. Adopted reasons are reasons that (even in the blink of an eye) one positively chooses to or makes one's mind up to act on, whereas explanatory reasons are not. An explanatory reason is a reason why something happened to one or why one acted in a certain way, whether accidentally (as in the case of clumsiness) *or* intentionally, without choice or decision, but where there was still a morally active dimension to what happened or to what was done. If a dancer accidentally trips, and in so doing, treads on his or her partner's toes, the accident may be treated as a straightforward denial of voluntariness, on the basis that what happened was a freak accident that could have happened to anyone. There is, though, the potential for an excusatory issue to emerge from behind this categorization of what happens to the dancer. Guiding reasons—in the form of reasons not to tread on someone's toes—clearly have a particular moral salience when one is dancing with a partner; and one can seek to guard against accidents. So there will always potentially be an issue about whether the dancer could reasonably and should have done more to avoid tripping, bearing in mind the need, in context, to keep his or her dance movements fluid, spontaneous and well timed, etc. This is a classic capacity-focused, excusatory issue, where the dancer's plea, 'I could not, in the circumstances, reasonably have been expected to do more to avoid tripping and hence treading on my partner's toes', is an explanatory (excusatory) reason. We should note, further, that the dancer's claim remains in some sense excusatory in character, even if he or she puts the whole episode down to his or her clumsiness. In such a case, the dancer gives a reason why the accident occurred that relates to an individual condition or disposition (the clumsiness), with respect to which he or she should be regarded as to a degree morally active, and hence for the manifestation of which he or she must thus accept some moral responsibility. Even though the clumsy dancer's claim resembles a claim of simple involuntariness, clumsy people can usually try with some prospect of success to be less clumsy, if they absolutely have to (this is the morally active dimension to what the dancer did). So, the issue is whether the dancer could and should have done more to keep his or her tendencies to clumsiness under control, given the need also to keep his or her dance movements fluid, well timed, and so on. As in the initial example where the dancer simply trips, this issue involves a capacity-focused question of excuse, even though there is now a more 'individualized' character to that question than there is to the question how much, in general, competent dancers should do to avoid treading on their partner's toes. In that regard, the question how much care we can reasonably expect D him- or herself to take is an excusatory question, albeit not the same excusatory question as the question how much care we can expect of competent dancers in general. . . .

In the case of intentional conduct, when one seeks excuse by putting a killing down to an instantaneous loss of self-control (provocation), or ascribing to the impact of sheer terror an 'instinctive' defensive response that is too heavy-handed (excessive defence), one may also be giving an explanatory reason for the action. In such cases, the phenomenological strength of the desire at the heart of the emotion (the urge to kill; the desire to ensure the attack is thwarted) spontaneously eclipses or bypasses the restraining or moderating power of reason. So the actions taken, albeit intentional, are not chosen: they are not based on 'adopted' reasons. Indeed, in the kind of cases I have in mind, the actions bear some family resemblances to conduct that is involuntary, as in the case, say, of clumsy actions. Nonetheless, there is clearly still an evaluative dimension to what D does. . . . [W]e can still ask whether D should have let his or her temper, or terror, get the better of him or her to the extent that it did. As Derek Parfit puts it, conduct that is, 'not deserving the extreme charge "irrational" [may, nonetheless, be] open to rational criticism'. One must, however, take care with examples of this kind, in general (angry or fearful actions). People who are provoked to anger, or fearful of threats, can sometimes still remain in evaluative control of their consequent conduct throughout, and can hence make genuine reasoned choices, even if they are not the choices they would have made in a calm frame of mind. How do all such actions, actions based on an *adopted* reason (a reason D chose to act on) come to be excused, whether or not they are grounded in an emotional reaction?

There are different routes to excuse for such actions, actions based on adopted reasons, which is why it is important to have a broad understanding of the necessary conditions of excuse. Finding an understandable 'rational defect' in a morally salient motivating force or factor behind an action is perhaps the most commonly encountered route to excuse, particularly but not solely where the action is grounded in a strong emotional reaction. In a case of angry or fearful action, D might claim that the phenomenological strength of an understandable emotion (D's 'operating' reason) so diminished in significance any countervailing evaluative considerations that the wrongful course seemed overwhelmingly attractive or proper, in a way it could and should never rationally have done. By way of contrast with the examples discussed in the preceding paragraph, however, in such cases it is still correct to say that D chooses his or her action from the balance of applicable reasons. D's choice hence has some of the hallmarks of a rational choice, but is a defective example of such a choice, for the reasons just given. So, for example, in an excessive defence case, the fulfilment of the necessary conditions for excuse could hinge on a finding that the sheer strength of D's fear made the choice of a heavy-handed course of action as a means of thwarting an attack *seem* entirely rational and proper, but only because of the mental domination achieved by the desire to ensure that the attack is thwarted. To give a different kind of example, a morally salient rational defect in a motivating factor behind the action also underpins the excusatory element in many factual mistake cases where, as things turn out, the mistake leads D into wrong-doing. In such cases, D commonly acts for an adopted reason, deciding on or choosing a course of action in a normal way. So, D's choice appears to have some of the hallmarks of a rational choice. D chooses that course of action, though, in the more-or-less understandably mistaken belief that a state of affairs exists (D's 'auxiliary' reason) that makes a crucial—morally salient— difference to the rational justification for that course of action, when no such state of affairs really exists. So, there is a rational defect lying behind D's choice. These different kinds of rational defects in morally salient motivating forces or factors behind actions can, of course, combine. So, one might be mistaken about the existence or nature of provocation (one kind of rational defect) that then led one into precipitate action following a loss of self-control (another sort of rational defect).

These kinds of mistake cases, in which the existence of a rational defect in a morally salient motivating force or factor behind D's choice does important excusatory work, are very different from cases where the adopted reason for which D commits the wrongdoing reflects a salient *moral* mistake. This happens where, for example, D decides (adopted reason) to abide by the demands of his or her religion as a matter of conscience, even though to do so means D will perform acts regarded as wrong in law. . . . The defect in the motivation for D's choice here is not rational, but moral: he or she simply gets the balance of reasons wrong by sticking to what conscience demands. D (*ex hypothesi*) understands the demands of his or her religion well enough to know how believers mean them to influence the balance of reasons. So, the excusatory work is now being done by a sense that it is understandable, albeit morally mistaken, to get the balance of reasons wrong by putting conscience-based compliance with religious demands ahead of avoiding legal wrongdoing. Even so, as in all the examples discussed to date, what matters in this category of cases is a capacity-focused question . . .: could and should more have been expected of D, rationally or morally (as the case may be)? This category of case shares something else with those discussed earlier. It is as true of this category of cases as of all the 'adopted reason' cases briefly discussed so far, that the importance to the excuse of the rational or moral defect in a motivating force or factor behind the choice is that the adopted reason is given for doing the very thing that is, in fact, prohibited by law. In other cases . . . the excusatory focus is on reasons for action D adopted to *avoid* committing wrongdoing, in spite of which the wrongdoing occurred. This is so, for example, when D says he or she should be excused on a 'due diligence' basis (normally, in regulatory cases), because no more could reasonably have been expected than that he or she put in the effort he or she did put in, taking the steps he or she chose to take, to try to ensure that wrongdoing would be avoided. Given that the adopted reasons—the compliance strategy, in effect—bear on steps taken to avoid wrongdoing, rather than being reasons to commit the act involving wrongdoing itself, there is no need for them to manifest some rational or moral defect. Indeed, as we will see in chapter 6 below, it may be that we would not excuse, on a 'due diligence' basis, unless we could find no rational (and still less, moral) fault whatsoever with the compliance strategy D adopted.

Whilst mitigating circumstances can clearly bear on the explanatory or adopted reasons for the act or omission amounting to criminal wrongdoing, there is no necessary conceptual connection between them. It could be right to mitigate a sentence in response to developments after the commission of the act, such as V's forgiveness, or D's co-operation with the authorities. It could also be right to mitigate the sentence in response to, morally, purely passive factors underlying the crime's commission not amounting, as such, to a denial of responsibility, like D's deprived upbringing. Some factors can be mitigating in a non-excusatory way, or can be dealt with as excusatory claims, depending on what it is that 'counts' about them in context. For example, following the definition of the necessary conditions of excuse just given, youth can only be pleaded in an excusatory way if it is tendered as an argument (say) about the understandable nature of the impulsiveness or lack of adequate foresight (i.e. the rational defect in a morally salient motivating force or factor) that lay behind the act itself. Youth can also, though, be relevant to mitigation in a non-excusatory way, i.e. even if it did nothing to shed light on the reasons why D did as he or she did. This would be the case if the court believes that it would be wrong to sentence D for as long a period in prison as someone older, for the same offence, because the impact of the same period of experiencing imprisonment would be disproportionately harsh on a younger person. The example of youth shows, though, that even if a factor can be pleaded in a genuinely excusatory way (in that it meets the necessary conditions for excuse), this obviously does not mean that it ought to gain recognition as a formal excusing condition, rather than being left as a matter for mitigation of sentence. Whether a plea ought to gain recognition as a formal excuse must turn on *how* significant the sufficiency conditions for an excuse are, in a given kind of case.

16.3 DOES THE DISTINCTION BETWEEN JUSTIFICATIONS AND EXCUSES REALLY MATTER?

You may by now be thinking, does it really matter whether a defence is a justification or an excuse? Well, some commentators certainly think it does. Here are some of the possible points of significance:

(1) Paul Robinson[253] suggests that if the law provides a justification this in effect changes the law. He therefore argues that if a case came before a court in which a man shot his neighbour's dog which was attacking his baby and the court held he was justified in doing this, then the law would be changed to the extent that it would now be lawful for a person to shoot a dog which was attacking a baby.[254] By contrast, if a defendant is granted an excuse this is of no wider significance. No two people are identical, so the fact that one person was excused does not mean another will be.[255] A similar point is made by Jeremy Horder,[256] who argues that justification seeks to offer guidance to defendants before they act, while excuses assess the culpability of offenders once they have acted.[257]

(2) If a defendant is attacked by a person who is excused (e.g. the defendant is attacked by a person who is sleepwalking) the defendant can lawfully resist the attack.[258] However, if the person using force against the defendant is justified (e.g. the defendant is attacked by a police officer who is making a lawful arrest) then the defendant cannot lawfully resist the attack.[259]

(3) You can lawfully assist a person who is justified in using force, but not someone who is only excused.[260] If you assist a police officer to arrest a villain, you will be justified because the police officer is justified. If you assist an insane person to attack an innocent person, the insane person can rely on the excuse of insanity, but you will not therefore have an excuse.[261]

(4) Justificatory defences are applicable to offences of strict liability, but excuses are not. Some commentators would wish to modify this statement by stressing that exemption defences (e.g. infancy, insanity) would apply to strict liability offences, even though they are classified as excuses.

(5) Some commentators argue that if the defence is a justification defendants can still rely on a defence if they honestly believe the circumstances were justificatory, even if in fact they were not.[262] However, if defendants are relying on an excuse they must *reasonably* believe the circumstances to be those that provide them with an excuse.

(6) Some commentators suggest that a defendant who, through his or her own fault put him or herself in a position where he or she must choose between the lesser of two evils, can rely on a justification (we would still want him or her to do the lesser of the two evils even

---

[253] P. Robinson (1982).

[254] It is interesting to note that one of the reasons in *Dudley and Stephens* (1884) 14 QBD 273 the court was unwilling to accept that the defendants had a defence of necessity was that such a verdict might encourage others placed in a similar position to do as the defendants did.

[255] Although an argument could be made that once a particular medical condition gives rise to a defence then all sufferers can be entitled to an excuse.

[256] Horder (2002a).   [257] P. Robinson (1990).

[258] Gur-Arye (1986) suggests that a person's right to self-defence should not be lost even if the attack he or she is facing is justified or excused.

[259] Unless he is unaware that the other person is a police officer and believes he is a villain who is trying to kill him.

[260] Gur-Arye (1986) also rejects this on the basis that a person intervening to protect someone's life should have a legal defence whether the person whose life he is saving is facing a justified or an excused attack.

[261] *Quick and Paddison* [1973] QB 910 (CA).   [262] Although this is rejected by some.

though he or she is responsible for getting him or herself into that position), but an excuse is not available for a person who has brought about his or her own excusing state of mind.[263]

(7) Paul Robinson[264] recommends that when the jury acquits a defendant they should be required to make it clear whether they are acquitting the defendant because they thought he or she was excused or because he or she was justified or because the prosecution had failed to established the *mens rea* or *actus reus*. This would clarify the basis of the defendant's acquittal and enable the law to send a clear message about the requirements of the criminal law.[265]

(8) You might think that the legal test for a justification would be objective (was the defendant's *act* permissible?), while the legal test for an excuse subjective (was the defendant responsible?), but this is, in fact, rarely so. As this issue raises some interesting points about the nature of a justification and an excuse we will consider this in detail now under a separate heading.

16.4 SHOULD JUSTIFICATIONS BE OBJECTIVE AND EXCUSES SUBJECTIVE?

As just indicated it seems at first sight obvious that a justification would be objective (is what the defendant did permissible (or reasonable)?) and an excuse subjective (was the defendant's state of mind such that he or she was responsible for his or her actions?). However, if you look back at Part I you will find that most of the defences involve a mixture of objective and subjective elements. Why is this?

On the Robinson view all justifications would be purely objective because we would be simply concerned with the defendant's actions. However, on the *Dadson* view the state of mind of the defendant is relevant too. Remember that according to *Dadson* only if the defendant is aware of the justifying circumstances can the defendant plead a justification. So on the *Dadson* understanding of justifications we would expect to see some subjective elements (requiring that the defendant was aware of and acted because of the justificatory reasons).

Some excuses will in their nature be subjective (e.g. insanity), although much controversy surrounds whether all excuses should be purely subjective. Take duress: should the question be whether the defendant felt compelled to give in to the threat or whether it was reasonable for the defendant to give in to the threat? Of course those who regard duress as a justification have no difficulty with having the standard of the reasonable person here, but it is also supported by some of those who regard duress as an excuse. How can they support the use of a reasonable person test? Here are two possible explanations:

(1) To claim that one is blameless it is not enough to show that one was not responsible for one's actions, but also that one *ought* not to have been responsible for one's actions.[266] If Alan (a lover of rose bushes) is kidnapped by Charlie and told that she will destroy his rose bush unless he kills Dermot, Alan may feel himself in an awful dilemma and may feel compelled to kill Dermot, but this should not provide him with an excuse. He may feel greatly

---

[263] This proposition is contested by some who argue that a justification should not be available where the defendant has acted for the purpose of putting himself in the position where he has to choose between the two evils. e.g. the defendant who deliberately starts a fire so that he can 'justifiably' destroy his neighbour's house in order to avoid the fire spreading.

[264] P. Robinson (1982).

[265] Robinson suggested that this would open the way for potential detention or other coercive measures under the civil law where the defendant was merely excused.

[266] Horder (1992: ch. 8) argues that there is a justificatory element in excuses. See further Horder (2004).

pressurized, but he should not be. The law values people higher than rose bushes: this should have been an easy choice for Alan. So, the argument goes, in a duress case it must be shown that the defendant acted when faced with what he or she regarded as an appalling dilemma and that he or she ought to have found it an appalling dilemma.

(2) A different argument would be based on the character theory. If we are to decide that the defendant's actions did not reveal bad character then the objective test is an aspect of this. A person who injures an innocent third party after he or she has been threatened that he or she will be killed does not reveal bad character; a person who injures because his rose bush is threatened does.[267]

The following passage looks at several of the issues relating to justifications and excuses which we have been examining. John Gardner argues that there is a closer relationship between justifications and reasons than is often supposed. To claim you have a justification for doing or believing something is to claim you have good reasons for doing or so believing. He suggests reasons must be guiding or explanatory. Guiding reasons are reasons which dictate what you *ought* to do or believe. Explanatory reasons, by contrast, explain *why* you act in a particular way. A person may think their explanatory reasons are guiding reasons but they need not be. In simple terms a person may think he or she has a good reason for acting, but in fact that reason is not a good one. Gardner argues that to amount to a justification a person must have both guiding and explanatory reasons for being justified, and the guiding reason must correspond with the explanatory reasons. In simple terms you must have a justifiable reason for acting as you did and you must act *because of* that justifying reason. An excuse, he argues, is analogous to a justification in that an excused person must act for good explanatory reasons (e.g. believing that he or she is justified in acting the way he or she does) and then justify why he or she (wrongly) thought he or she was justified:

J. Gardner, 'Justifications and Reasons' in A. Simester and A. Smith (eds) *Harm and Culpability* (Oxford: OUP, 1996), 118–22

It is widely thought that excuses are more 'subjective' than justifications. In one sense of 'subjective', as we will see, this is perfectly true. But it is not true if we are using the labels 'subjective' and 'objective' to mark the contrast between explanatory and guiding reasons. Over a wide range of cases, excuses, just like justifications, depend on the union of explanatory and guiding reasons. Whenever excuses depend on the union of explanatory and guiding reasons, moreover, they do so precisely because justifications depend on the union of explanatory and guiding reasons. The structure of excuse derives, in other words, from the structure of justification, and thus shares in its combination of subjective (explanatory) and objective (guiding) rationality.

Some theorists have associated excuses with character traits. They are mistaken if they think that every excuse is concerned with character. Many excuses are of a technical nature. They relate to levels of skill rather than degrees of virtue. Their gist is that the person claiming them does not possess the skills needed to do better, and should not be expected to possess those skills. Whether one should be expected to possess certain skills, or skills to a certain degree, depends, to some extent, on one's form of life. A doctor who tries to excuse her blundering treatment by claiming lack of diagnostic skill should not get far, whereas an amateur first-aider may

---

[267] Ashworth (1973: 161). In Westen (2008) it is argued that the key question is whether the defendant's actions showed proper respect for the values upheld by the law.

be able to extinguish her blame, under similar conditions, by making exactly the same argument. But such excuses, even though they are of great legal importance, will not concern us here. Our concern will be with that major group of excuses which do indeed relate to character evaluation. These include excuses very familiar to criminal lawyers, such as excuses based on provocation and duress. Their gist is similar to that of technical excuses. It is that the person claiming them does not possess the virtues needed to do better, and should not be expected to possess those virtues. Again, which virtues one should be expected to possess, and to what extent, depends largely on one's form of life. A police officer is expected to exhibit more fortitude and courage than an ordinary member of the public, a friend is expected to be more considerate and atten-tive than a stranger, etc. What exactly does this mean? Essentially, it means that where there is a conflict of reasons, some people are expected to act for some reasons, whereas others are expected to act for other, often incompatible and incomparable, reasons. But obviously the need to claim an excuse from one's action arises only if one fails to establish a full justification. A fully justified action needs no excuse. So the point cannot be that those who act with excuse act for undefeated reasons, i.e., that it is alright for them to act for those reasons. That would yield a full justification for their actions. The point must be that there is something suspect about the reasons for which they act. And indeed there is. They are not valid reasons. They are what the person acting upon them takes to be valid reasons, *and justifiably so*. Thus the structure of excuse derives from the structure of justification. To excuse an action is not, of course, to justify that action. Rather, one justifies one's belief that the action is justified.

This explanation of non-technical excuses has to be modified and extended somewhat to accommodate unjustified actions upon justified emotions, attitudes, passions, desires, deci-sions, etc., as well as unjustified actions upon justified beliefs. Provocation, as Jeremy Horder has explained involves unjustified action out of justified anger. Duress, or a certain central kind of duress, can be similarly analysed as involving unjustified action out of justified fear. But these are, in a sense, derivative cases. Emotions like anger and fear are mediating forces between beliefs and actions. They enhance or constrain the motivating force of certain motiv-ating beliefs. Their justification therefore turns in part on the justification of the beliefs which partly constitute them. Of course, there is still a justificatory gap: an emotion is not fully justified merely by the justification of its cognitive component. But justified emotion (and in similar vein justified attitude or desire or decision) nevertheless entails justified belief. Thus the most basic or rudimentary case of non-technical excuse remains that of unjustified action upon justified belief. One must therefore consider what is needed to make a belief justified. It is of course one of the great problems of epistemology, and we cannot do justice to it here. Suffice it to say that the general account of justification applicable to action is also broadly applicable to belief. One must have an undefeated reason for one's belief, and that must moreover be the reason why one holds the belief. This explains the nature of epistemic faults, such as prejudice, gullibility, and superstition. One cannot understand these faults unless one appreciates that a belief is justified, not only by the reasons there are for holding it, but also by the process of reasoning by which it came to be held, i.e., not only by guiding reasons but also by explanatory reasons. The same facts also explain why a requirement of *reasonableness* has traditionally been imposed upon excuses in the criminal law. It is not enough that one made a mistake as to justification, if it was not a reasonable mistake, it is not enough that one was angry to the point of losing self-control, if one's anger was not reasonable, etc. By 'reasonable' here is meant, in my view, much the same as 'justified'. There must have been an undefeated reason for one's belief, emotion, etc., which also explains why one held the belief or experienced the emotion, etc. The fact that sometimes this element of reasonableness is dispensed with in the law does not show a drift towards a more purely 'subjective' account of excuses, i.e., one depending on explanatory reasons without regard for guiding reasons. It shows, rather, that some excuse-like arguments, in common with some justification-like arguments, may actually serve to negate an element of the offence rather than to excuse or justify its commission. Some mistakes, as the courts put it, may simply serve to negate the mens rea for the particular crime; and if, as may be, the mens rea required is, e.g., knowledge, then of course the reasonableness of one's mistake is neither here nor there. The extent to which legal systems will tolerate such arguments depends on many contingencies about them, including the extent to which and way in which they implement the demand for mens rea. But this has nothing to do with excuses, in which an element of reasonableness, at some level, is conceptually necessitated whether the crime is one of full subjective mens rea or one of no mens rea at all.

Requirements of 'reasonableness' in criminal excuses also sometimes go beyond what the logic of excuses requires, and in that case they normally serve another role. They serve to orientate the law towards general application to people living many different forms of life, rather than tailoring it to suit the expected virtues of a certain kind of person leading a certain kind of life. The debate about the extent to which the reasonable person should be 'individualized' to the characteristics of the defendant in the definition of criminal excuses is partly a debate about the extent to which the criminal law should aspire to this kind of generality. Should the 'reasonable person' in provocation become the 'reasonable police officer' when the defendant is a police officer? Should the 'reasonable person' in cases of drunken mistake become the 'reasonable drunkard'? Once again there is no universal theoretical solution to this problem. Within broad limits, legal systems may quite properly vary in their willingness to individualize excuses and the general principles, if any, upon which they do so. But legal systems cannot, consistent with the logic of (non-technical) excuses, vary in the importance they attach to the combination of guiding and explanatory reasons in the excusatory scheme of things. Thus they cannot altogether eliminate the essential 'objective' dimension of excusatory claims. They cannot ignore the important point that excuses rely on reason, not on the absence of it. That is, they rely on the ability of the person who claims to be excused to believe and feel as reason demands, and because reason demands it. Those people who cannot meet this condition do not need to bother making excuses. Such people are not responsible for their actions, and are free from blame as well as being improper targets for criminal liability, irrespective of both justification and excuse. Justification and excuse both belong to the realm of responsible agency, and that is precisely because both depend, to put it crudely, on the ability to live within reason.

The logical relationship between justification and (non-technical) excuse helps to explain the so-called 'quasi-justificatory drift' of many familiar excuses. In English law this is compounded by the law's cautious insistence on having a belt as well as braces: in general no excuse is accepted into the criminal law which is not also a partial justification, and no justification is accepted which is not also a partial excuse. The drift of the excuse is not so much quasi-justificatory as truly justificatory. But neither of these facts should obscure the crucial conceptual distinction between justification and excuse. Nor should one be distracted by the paradoxical sound of the claim that an action which is justifiably believed to be justified is excused rather than justified. It only goes to show that, as between the concepts of justification and excuse, justification is the more fundamental. The same proposition also brings out the true sense in which excuses may be regarded as more 'subjective' than justifications. For by their nature excuses take the world as the defendant justifiably sees it rather than as it is. They look to what the defendant believes to be applicable reasons for action, so long as she does so on the basis of genuinely applicable reasons for belief. Justifications, meanwhile, look directly to the genuinely applicable reasons for action, without stopping to look for applicable reasons for belief. But in this whole contrast the talk of 'reasons' is talk of guiding reasons. It leaves on one side the fact that, in both justification and excuse, explanatory reasons also play a key role, and that, in this sense and to this extent, each is just as subjective as the other.

16.5 PROBLEMS WITH JUSTIFICATIONS AND EXCUSES

As we have already noted, there are some commentators who deny the usefulness of the distinction between justifications and excuses. Their reasons include the following:

(1) The English and Welsh courts have not placed great weight on the distinction. The general refusal of the courts to engage in an analysis of the defences in terms of justifications and excuses may indicate the distinction lacks practical benefit.

(2) The fact that there is so much debate over whether duress or mistaken self-defence is a justification or excuse indicates that the distinction is too vague to be useful. As Kent Greenawalt stresses, there is not even agreement over whether justification should be judged on the basis of the facts that occurred or on the facts as they were believed to be.[268]

(3) Some commentators argue that our society lacks agreed moral standards which can be used to assess the justifiability or not of particular actions. The chastisement of children and the hunting of foxes with dogs, at present, are controversial issues over which there is no consensus. For the law to declare these actions justifiable or not is to impose a moral judgment when society lacks a sufficient consensus on the issue.

The passage by Nicola Lacey to be excerpted shortly considers some of the criticisms of the justification/excuse distinction.

FURTHER READING

Baron, M. (2012) 'The Standard of the Reasonable Person in the Criminal Law' in R.A. Duff, L. Farmer, S. Marshall, M. Renzo, and V. Tadros (eds) *The Structures of the Criminal Law* (Oxford: OUP).

Berman, M. (2003) 'Justification and Excuse, Law and Morality' *Duke Law Journal* 53: 1.

Gardner, J. (1996) 'Justifications and Reasons' in A. Simester and A. Smith (eds) *Harm and Culpability* (Oxford: OUP).

Gardner, J. (1998b) 'The Gist of Excuses' *Buffalo Criminal Law Review* 1: 575.

Greenawalt, K. (1984) 'The Perplexing Borders of Justification and Excuse' *Colorado Law Review* 84: 1897.

Horder, J. (2004) *Excusing Crime* (Oxford: OUP).

Nourse, V. (2008) 'After the Reasonable Man: Getting over the Subjectivity/Objectivity Question' *New Criminal Law Review* 11: 34.

Robinson, P. (1996b) 'Competing Theories of Justification: Deeds v Reasons' in A. Simester and A. Smith (eds) *Harm and Culpability* (Oxford: OUP).

Simester, A. (2012) 'On Justifications and Excuses' in L. Zedner and J. Roberts (eds) *Principles and Values in Criminal Law and Criminal Justice: Essays in Honour of Andrew Ashworth* (Oxford: OUP).

Simons, K. (2005) 'Exploring the Intricacies of the Lesser Evils Defense' *Law and Philosophy* 24: 645.

Westen, P. (2006) 'An Attitudinal Theory of Excuse' *Law and Philosophy* 25: 289.

---

[268] Greenawalt (1984). See also Norrie (2010b).

Westen, P. (2008) 'Individualizing the Reasonable Person in Criminal Law' *Criminal Law and Philosophy* 2: 137.

Westen, P. and Mangiafico, J. (2003) 'The Criminal Defense of Duress: A Justification, Not an Excuse—and Why It Matters' *Buffalo Criminal Law Review* 8: 833.

Wilson, W. (2004) 'The Filtering Role of Crisis in the Constitution of Criminal Excuses' *Canadian Journal of Law and Jurisprudence* 17: 387.

17 CHARACTER, CHOICE, AND CAPACITY

An alternative way of analysing defences is to examine their theoretical foundations.[269] There are three main schools of thought on the theoretical underpinning on defences, which will be outlined next. However, before that it should be stressed that within each school of thought there is a diversity of opinion as to the correct interpretation of the theory, and that there are of course many other theories that have been adopted. Also there are many commentators who decry any attempt to develop one overarching theory of culpability, arguing that there are different forms of culpability that may be appropriate in different kinds of offences. It is preferable, therefore, to consider offences and defences one by one and decide why we have them, rather than seek to force them all to abide by one guiding principle.[270]

First, we briefly summarize the main theories,[271] then we look at one academic's summary of the competing views, and then look in more detail at the strengths and weaknesses of the different theories:

(1) **The choice theory**[272] At the heart of this theory is the view that a defendant should be punished only for what he or she chose to do. We have seen in Chapter 3 that supporters of this theory tend to prefer subjective forms of *mens rea*, for example intention, *Cunningham* recklessness. Under this theory the law should provide a defence to a defendant who did not choose to act in the way he or she did, for example where the defendant is an automaton.

(2) **The capacity theory** A popular variant of the choice theory is to justify punishment not only for those who chose to commit the harm, but those who could have avoided causing the harm but did not. Applying this theory to defences then, they apply when the defendant did not and could not have chosen to obey the law. Hence, in the case of insanity the defendant, because of his or her mental illness, was not capable of acting otherwise. In the case of duress the defendant either did not choose or could not realistically have chosen to have acted otherwise.

(3) **The character theory** This theory focuses on an argument that the defendant's criminal act reflects the bad character of the defendant. Here a defence exists when the act does not reveal bad character. So, in a case of duress, the fact that the defendant acted in the way he or she did in response to the threats does not reveal bad character on his or her part if he or she responded reasonably.

---

[269] Considering the theoretical basis for defences in these ways can be complementary to or independent from analysing them in terms of justifications or excuses.

[270] e.g. Horder (1993b).   [271] See for a detailed discussion Horder (2004: ch. 3).

[272] The choice theory has also been called the responsibility principle and the voluntarism principle.

In this next passage, Nicola Lacey distinguishes between the capacity view and the reasons view of defences:

N. Lacey, 'Space, Time and Function: Intersecting Principles of Responsibility across the Terrain of Criminal Justice' (2007) 1 *Criminal Law and Philosophy* 233 at 236–40

'Capacity' principles: choice and opportunity

The dominant way of thinking about responsibility in contemporary British and American criminal law doctrine turns on the notion of human (or more rarely, corporate) capacity. On this view, the foundation of not only a person's status as a responsible agent answerable to the normative demands of the criminal law but also of an attribution of responsibility for specific actions lies in human capacities of cognition—knowledge of circumstances, assessment of consequences—and volition powers of self-control. The crucial factor is the way in which these human capacities—human agency—are engaged in advertent conduct: to put it crudely, responsible conduct is conduct which the agent chooses. This notion of capacity-based responsibility naturally issues in a focus on so-called subjective principles of mens rea: intention, recklessness or foresight of relevant consequences, knowledge and so on. These forms of mens rea essentially consist in subjective mental states on the part of the defendant. Prime examples in English case-law would include *R v Morgan* (now reversed by the Sexual Offences Act 2003) and *B v DPP*.

Many commentators have noted the increasing emphasis on this form of subjectivism, though there is considerable disagreement about the degree of its realisation and the timing of and reasons for its ascendancy . . . [B]oth Alan Norrie and I have argued that its progress may be explained partly in terms of its ability to provide a legitimating principle which is relatively independent of any evaluation of the relevant conduct. The proof of intention or subjective recklessness being a question of fact, the emphasis is simply on proof of the requisite mental state; a feature which may be useful in a system which criminalizes a huge range of conduct, much of it beyond the terrain of 'real' or 'quasi-moral' crime, and in which moral pluralism or value conflict risks tensions which a factual view of mens rea may help to keep out of the courtroom (Lacey, 2001; Norrie, 2001).

Whatever the merits of these competing or complementary accounts of the rise of choice-based principles of responsibility, it is clear that, both conceptually and practically, they are not the only way of looking at capacity principles of attribution. For the basic moral intuition underlying the capacity view can be interpreted in another way, with decisive implications for the shape of criminal law. If the basic moral intuition is that it is only legitimate to hold people criminally responsible for things which they had the capacity to avoid doing, we can realise this intuition in one of two ways. We can do so through proof of subjective choice in the sense of intention, awareness, knowledge (Williams, 1983) or we can ask—as Hart did (Hart, 1968)—whether the defendant had a fair opportunity to conform his or her behaviour to the criminal law standard. This second approach has the implication that not only subjective mental states but also 'objective' standards like negligence or the imposition of reasonableness constraints in the specification of defences may be accommodated. It also, therefore, offers an account more likely to be able to rationalise the actual shape of systems of criminal law. From the point of view of the argument which Norrie and I have advanced, this is however at the cost of revealing that a criminal trial is, inevitably, in the business of making a potentially controversial normative evaluation of the defendant's conduct. The question to be proven is no longer the relatively neutral, factual and dualistic: 'Did D cause P's death? If so, did s/he do so with intent to cause death or grievous bodily harm?'; 'Did D have sexual intercourse with P? If so, did s/he do so intentionally and aware that P was not consenting?' It is, rather, 'Did D do these things in circumstances in which we would say that they had had a fair opportunity to avoid them?' The answer to this question may, of course, be provided by proof of intent or subjective recklessness. But it might also be answered in terms of D's indifference or omission to advert to a risk which would have been obvious to a reasonable person, or to which it would be reasonable for us to expect D to advert, such that we would be inclined to say that D had a fair opportunity to avoid homicide or rape. So long as we are confident that D has the capacities of a reasonable person, this fair opportunity view is perfectly consistent with the moral intuition underlying the capacity principle of criminal responsibility. A further perceived advantage of the opportunity version of capacity responsibility is that it is less obviously susceptible than the choice version to the truth of determinism, in that the evaluation can be relative to socially pervasive reactive attitudes . . . The issue, in other words, is not what we 'could' have helped, whether we 'could' have chosen otherwise, but what prevailing social norms judge us to have had a fair opportunity to help or choose. Notice how this version of the opportunity theory implicitly maps responsibility doctrines onto a particular view of the aims and functions of the criminal law.

'Character' principles: overall character; expressed disposition towards the relevant criminal law norms

The idea that an attribution of criminal responsibility is in some sense an evaluation of character has been advanced in radically different guises by Michael Bayles (in Humean form and in relation to criminal responsibility in general) (Bayles, 1982), by John Gardner (in Aristotelian form and in relation to defences, conceptualised as mechanisms ensuring that we are not held responsible for things which are 'out of character'), in my own early work (Lacey, 1988) and most recently by Tadros (2005). In its most radical form, it is thought by capacity theorists to be morally unacceptable to the extent that, unless we are held to have capacity for our characters, character responsibility implies holding us accountable for things which we could not, or had no fair opportunity to, avoid; it has also been argued that it is premised on an inappropriately ambitious vision of the moral role of criminal law. Since my purpose in this paper is interpretive rather than normative, I shall set these objections aside for the moment. It is worth noting, however, that it is also possible for character and capacity notions to be combined, as Martin Wiener has persuasively argued they were in the early Victorian criminal justice project, which aspired not merely to hold people responsible for conduct disclosing bad character, but also to use the penal process to reshape character, in part precisely by engaging the capacity-based agency of subjects.

The more radical of the two character principles which I want to distinguish may be labelled the 'overall-character principle': it holds that the attribution of criminal responsibility is founded in a judgment that the defendant's conduct is evidence of a wrongful, bad, disapproved character trait: disregard of human life, indifference to sexual integrity, lack of respect for property rights and so on. The criminal law, on this view, seeks to convict, label and stigmatise those of bad character or disposition: the principle of responsibility-attribution is merely a function of the overall meaning and purpose of criminal law in its quasi-moral mode, and the criminal conduct is at root a symptom of the underlying rationale for conviction and punishment, namely bad or anti-social character. A crucial question therefore arises as to the scope of the conduct which is regarded as evidence relevant to this judgment of criminal character. Systems adhering to an overall-character principle would be those in which broad character evidence is admissible: not merely previous convictions of offences with similar facts, but criminal record in general and perhaps even general evidence about lifestyle, employment history and so on. (In case this sounds far fetched, it is perhaps worth remembering that systems of this kind are not unknown in the contemporary world; and, as I have argued elsewhere, broad character-based assessments of responsibility were standard in early modern English criminal trials (Lacey, 2001).)

In its more cautious form, however, character-responsibility restricts itself to an evaluation of the specific conduct which forms the basis for the present allegation. The relevant question becomes not 'Is D's conduct evidence of criminal character?' but rather 'Does D's conduct in causing P's death or having sexual intercourse with P express a settled disposition of hostility or indifference to the relevant norm of criminal law, or at least acceptance of such a disposition?' As Tadros puts it, 'does D's conduct qua moral agent display the sort of vice which calls for criminal law's communicative role of expressing moral indignation to be invoked?' This formulation opens up an obvious path to the elaboration of defences such as duress, provocation, self-defence or—possibly—mental incapacity. It also preserves the specific allegation of criminal conduct as central to the rationale for conviction and punishment, and is founded on a particular understanding of D's status as a moral agent: a reasoning being responsible for their beliefs, desires, emotions and values. While taking a more cautious view of relevant evidence, it would also naturally locate an attribution of responsibility within a broader time frame than that implied by the capacity principles. For the context within which an agent has acted—a history of domestic abuse, for example—will be relevant to an evaluation of the disposition which that action expresses.

We will now consider the capacity and character theories in greater detail.

17.1 THE CAPACITY THEORY

What is it?

The starting point for the capacity theory is that 'a person is not to be blamed for what he has done if he could not help doing it'.[273] In other words it is appropriate to punish only a person who is responsible for his or her actions.[274] Defences, then, should be available where the defendant lacked a fair opportunity to choose to act otherwise.[275] Michael Moore[276] has argued that the emphasis within the capacity theory on choice and the ability to choose reflects wider attitudes within our society. People regard the ability to choose as an important freedom. We would resent any attempt by the state to restrict our choice on how to live our lives. We want to have our choices respected. Moore argues that it flows from this that we should respect people's bad choices, and that involves making people responsible for them.

Problems with the capacity theory

The following are some of the problems that have been identified with the capacity theory:[277]

(1) A common complaint about the capacity theory is that the consideration of whether the defendant freely chose to commit the crime is too narrow. For example, arguments that the defendant committed the crime as a result of socio-economic pressures will not be countenanced by the court. There is evidence that people in certain socio-economic groups or from particular backgrounds are more likely to commit offences than others. Of course, this does not prove that, for example, being poor causes someone to commit crime. But it does indicate that, at least in statistical terms, people do not start on a level playing field as regards the likelihood that they will commit crime.

---

[273] Hart (1968: 174). For a discussion of the implications of such an approach, see Smith and Wilson (1993).
[274] Dressler (1988a: 701).   [275] Uniacke (2007).   [276] M. Moore (1999).
[277] Some of the problems with the capacity theory in relation to *mens rea* were discussed in Chapter 3.

(2) Another complaint made about the capacity theory is that in focusing on choice it does not take into account a wide enough range of factors in assessing the defendant's blameworthiness. Other relevant factors, for example, the emotion which led to the defendant acting in the way he or she did, are irrelevant for the capacity theory.[278] From the point of view of the capacity theory, the person who freely chooses to kill his or her relative in order to end the pain the relative is suffering from a terminal illness is treated in the same way as a person who kills the relative in order to gain an inheritance. The 'choice' element is the same in both. Yet, it is claimed, a proper assessment of the defendant's blameworthiness would regard the two cases as quite different.[279]

(3) John Gardner[280] suggests that the capacity theory is misleading. By asking, for example, in a duress case where the defendant unreasonably gave in to the threat, whether the defendant had the capacity to act more bravely is misconceived. If it is concluded that the defendant was as brave as he or she could be, then that is a reason for blame—not excuse. He or she should not be such a cowardly person.

17.2 THE CHARACTER THEORY

What is it?

The character theory assesses criminal liability on the basis of the extent to which the defendant's actions have displayed good or bad character.[281] As Glover has put it: '[T]o blame a person for an action is more than merely to say that he has brought about something we object to. We disapprove, not merely of the action or its consequences, but of him.'[282] Applying the theory to defences, a defence arises to rebut an inference from the causing of harm to a bad character trait.

The benefits of the character theory are said to be that it enables the law to undertake a sensitive assessment of the defendant's culpability.[283] Its supporters argue that it enables the law to take a wider range of factors than simply the element of choice, which is the focus of the capacity theory.

Problems with the character theory

The following are some of the problems that have been identified with the character theory:

(1) The character theory assumes that people are responsible for their characters. If you disagree with that controversial assumption[284] then the character theory loses its attraction.[285] There may be a temptation for the character theorist to reply that we are responsible for our character because we choose to be the kind of people we are.[286] However, such an argument is in danger of reducing the character theory to a version of the choice theory.

(2) One problem which critics are keen to point to is the difficulty for the character theory of actions which are 'out of character'. Imagine Gwen has worked as a cashier for a company

---

[278] Bennett (2012); Reilly (1998).   [279] W. Wilson (2004).   [280] J. Gardner (1998b).

[281] See especially Fletcher (1978: ch. 10); Nozick (1981); Bayles (1982); Lacey (1988); Arenella (1990); Mousourakis (1998a).

[282] Glover (1970: 64).

[283] See Mousourakis (1998a) for an argument that the character theory can explain some, but not all, defences.

[284] See Lelling (1998) for one psychological perspective.   [285] Vuoso (1987).

[286] M. Moore (1998: ch. 6).

for 20 years. She daily handles large sums of money and has always done so honestly, except on a single occasion when she took a small sum. Do we conclude that Gwen has a dishonest character and should be guilty of theft? Or rather that the fact she has worked for so long without taking money demonstrates her honesty, and the one lapse is 'out of character' and she should therefore have a defence?[287] Duff argues that such a person has shown a character flaw.[288] An honest person would *always* resist the temptation to be dishonest.[289]

(3) Why do we look only to criminal actions to decide whether or not the defendant has exhibited a criminal trait?[290] If everyone who knew a man was willing to state he was a dishonest person, even though he had never actually committed an offence, why, under the character theory, can you not convict such a person? Character theorists could rely on two possible responses:

(1) Antony Duff[291] argues that you cannot claim to have a certain characteristic unless you act in a way that reveals that characteristic.[292] You cannot claim to be a brave person unless you have acted at least once in a brave way. In the same way you cannot exhibit a criminal character trait unless you have acted at least once in that criminal way. So although in your private life you may have shown yourself to be a dishonest person, unless you act in a criminally dishonest way you have not shown yourself to be dishonest *in a criminal way.*[293]

(2) George Fletcher,[294] defending the character theory, replies that an important principle of privacy comes into play to prevent the conviction of a person with a criminally inclined character who has yet to act in a criminal way.

Differences between the character and capacity theories

In many situations the character and capacity theories would provide a defence in similar situations. A defendant who lacks the opportunity to comply with the law is not exhibiting bad character. However, there are two categories of cases where the theories may disagree:

(1) Imagine a person who commits a crime while overcome with anger or hatred so that he or she loses control of him or herself. It might be thought that the two theories would deal with these in different ways. A character theorist would have little problem in stating there is no defence because killing when overcome with hatred exhibits bad character. The case is perhaps harder for the capacity theorist. Can such a person claim he or she did not freely choose to act as he or she did and given his or her personality (e.g. being particularly short-tempered) he or she did not have a fair opportunity to act otherwise?

(2) Imagine a person who has had an exemplary life and is widely recognized by his community to be a considerate and kind person. One day his wife is killed in a tragic accident, he drinks

---

[287] e.g. a person who has been kidnapped and 'brainwashed' by his kidnappers into joining their criminal gang.

[288] Duff (1993).

[289] Even dishonest people regularly resist the temptation to be dishonest. This leads to a further difficulty for character theorists. How can one act reveal a character through a single action? Some character theorists suggest that a person is responsible only for stable character traits (Bayles 1982), but others reject such a requirement (Horder 1993a).

[290] Brudner (1987).   [291] Duff (1993).   [292] See also J. Gardner (1998b).

[293] Even this may not be a complete answer: a defendant could be examined by psychiatrists and found to be predisposed to commit criminal acts, even though he is yet to commit any. Should not the character theory be willing to convict such a person because 'we know' he has a criminal character?

[294] Fletcher (1976: 799–802).

too much and hits a barman. He has never in the past behaved in this way. The choice theorist would have little difficulty in convicting him of an assault. The character theorist has more problems here. In the light of his exemplary behaviour and the unusual circumstances of the assault can we say that his action reflects a character trait? Is not this kind of conduct simply out of character? The temptation is to say that any chosen behaviour is 'in character' (even if an aspect of the person's character we are yet to see), but this becomes very close to the choice theory.

Some commentators have argued that there is no effective difference between the choice and character theories.[295] Take duress. When successful the choice theorists say that there was no meaningful choice made to commit the crime. But how do they decide that a person has not exercised a meaningful choice? Inevitably an important issue is the gravity of the threat. A person facing a dire threat has less freedom of choice than a person facing a minor threat. However, the argument goes, then the questions whether the choice was genuine and whether the choice was one which reflects badly on the defendant's character merge together.

FURTHER READING

Bayles, M. (1982) 'Character, Purpose and Criminal Responsibility' *Law and Philosophy* 1: 5.

Duff, R.A. (1993) 'Choice, Character and Criminal Liability' *Law and Philosophy* 12: 345.

Duff, R.A. (2003) 'Virtue, Vice, and Criminal Liability: Do We Want an Aristotelian Criminal Law?' *Buffalo Criminal Law Review* 6: 147.

Horder, J. (1993a) 'Criminal Culpability: The Possibility of General Theory' *Law and Philosophy* 12: 193.

Lacey, N. (1988) *State Punishment* (London: Routledge).

Lacey, N. (2007b) 'Space, Time and Function: Intersecting Principles of Responsibility across the Terrain of Criminal Justice' *Criminal Law and Philosophy* 1: 233.

Lacey, N. (2011) 'The Resurgence of Character' in S. Green and R.A. Duff (eds) *Philosophical Foundations of Criminal Law* (Oxford: OUP).

Moore, M. (1997) *Placing Blame* (Oxford: OUP).

Spain, E. (2013) *The Role of Emotions in Criminal Law Defences* (Cambridge: Cambridge University Press).

Tadros, V. (2005a) *Criminal Responsibility* (Oxford: OUP).

---

18 DETERMINISM

Determinism is the theory that all our actions are determined by factors outside our control. There are many different forms of determinism, ranging from the view that all our actions are predetermined by God, to a view that we are genetically predetermined to do all we do.[296] If determinism is correct, it produces real problems for both the capacity and character theories, and indeed the blaming function of the criminal law.[297] If our actions are predetermined how can we blame people for the 'choices' they make? If our characters are a result of our genes to what extent can we hold people responsible for their characters?

---

[295] Duff (1993).   [296] Wells (1998).   [297] Kelman (1981); Norrie (2000); Kenny (1978).

The truth or otherwise of determinism is not known.[298] Perhaps the predominant view is that even if our actions are to a large extent affected by genetic, social, environmental,[299] and other factors outside our control, we still have an element of control over our actions.[300] Indeed our society is based on the assumption that we have free will. If we were all predetermined to do what we do our society would be a very different one. Many organizations and people, not least government, spend much time and effort in trying to persuade people to change (or not to change) their behaviour (e.g. advertising). All such activities would be pointless if our actions were predetermined.

A key question, then, is, accepting that to some extent our actions are affected by genetic, social, and economic factors, is the impact of those factors sufficient to justify providing a defence? After all there is evidence that those from deprived social backgrounds are more likely to commit offences than those who are better off.[301] This has led some commentators to argue for a defence of 'rotten social background'.[302]

QUESTIONS

1. If we are all predetermined is there any point discussing whether determinism is correct or not because you are predetermined to accept or reject the theory of determinism? You are also predetermined to get whatever mark you will get in your criminal law examination, so why revise?

2. If we accept Norrie's argument with what do we replace the current criminal law?

FURTHER READING

Dershowitz, A. (1994) *The Abuse Excuse and Other Cop-Outs, Sob Stories, and Evasions of Responsibility* (Boston, MA: Little, Brown).

Horder, J. (1996b) 'Criminal Law: Between Determinism, Liberalism and Criminal Justice' *Current Legal Problems* 96.

Westen, P. (2005) 'Getting the Fly Out of the Bottle: The False Problem of Free Will and Determinism' *Buffalo Criminal Law Review* 8: 599.

Williams, B. (1997) 'Moral Responsibility and Political Freedom' *Cambridge Law Journal* 56: 96.

---

19 INSANITY

19.1 PROBLEMS WITH THE PRESENT LAW

The position and treatment of mentally disordered people are problematic for society in many areas, not just the criminal law.[303] There are delicate balances to be made between protecting the interests of the mentally disordered person, his or her carers, and the interests of

---

[298] Ainsworth (2000).   [299] Bazelon (1976).
[300] Aristotle, *Nicomachean Ethics,* book iii, ch. 5; Wolf (1991); Dennett (1984).
[301] See Duff (2006) who argues that we are criminally responsible as citizens, but that if a group were systematically treated in an unjust way the state might lose the warrant to punish them.
[302] Delgado (1985); Bazelon (1976).   [303] Mason and Mercer (1999).

the wider community.[304] The popular media in particular have portrayed mentally ill people as dangerous. But consider these two findings:

(1) Gunn and Taylor point out that the risk of being killed by a serious mentally ill patient is 'small'. The risk that a mentally ill person will commit suicide is about 100 times greater.[305]

(2) In a 1982 study by Norval Morris[306] a cohort of mentally disordered people with a range of mental illnesses had no greater incidence of criminal offending than a same sized cohort of people randomly selected from the community. In fact he found that males aged between 14 and 22 from deprived inner-city areas had a far higher incidence of offending behaviour than the mentally disordered group.[307]

Such statements inevitably raise the question whether our society is more concerned with protecting the lives of the sane than the insane. The question is especially pertinent, given the distressingly high number of prisoners in normal prisons who suffer mental illness and are not getting the medical treatment they need.[308] ←6 (p.675)

The difficulties in finding the appropriate response of the criminal law to mental abnormalities include the following:

(1) One issue which may be thought significant is: did the defendant commit the crime because of his or her mental illness or would he or she have committed the offence even if he or she had not suffered from his or her illness?[309] Unfortunately this kind of question is extremely difficult to answer.[310] As Daniel Robinson puts it, neither neurology nor psychiatry has any 'magic lantern to light up the concealed corners of a defendant's mind'.[311]

(2) It is all too easy to merge the questions: should the defendant be convicted of a criminal offence and should the defendant be detained in order to receive compulsory treatment?[312] There the argument that 'the public need to be protected from dangerous people' pressures the law to ensure the detention of mentally ill people even if 'technically' they have not committed an offence. Also there are those who say 'we need to offer treatment to those who are mentally ill', again pressurizing the system to facilitate the detention of the mentally ill, even if no offence has been committed.[313]

(3) There has been much debate over which definition of insanity the courts should use. The starting point of the dispute is the source of the definition. Is it a question of medical expertise? A legal issue? Or should insanity be given its 'ordinary meaning', as understood by members of the public?[314] At present the legal definition of insanity is different from the medical one. This means that doctors giving evidence have the difficulty of matching the medical diagnoses with the legal terminology used. There is always the fear (or hope?) that doctors will manipulate the legal terminology to reach what in medical terms would be the 'right' result.

(4) Why should someone who is insane receive any special treatment under the law? An immediate answer may be that an insane person will lack the *mens rea* required for an offence,

---

[304] Home Office (1999) discusses the government's proposals regarding 'dangerous' people.
[305] Gunn and Taylor (1993: 335).   [306] N. Morris (1982).   [307] Bowden (1996).
[308] Home Office (1987); Simpson (1976); Gray, Laing, and Noaks (2002).   [309] Gross (1979).
[310] D. Robinson (1996).   [311] *Ibid*, 237. See also Morse (1996).
[312] Gostin (1986); Gray, Laing, and Noaks (2002).   [313] See Home Office (1999).
[314] D. Robinson (1996). e.g. Morse (1985) suggests directing the jury to consider whether the defendant was 'crazy'.

but if this is so he or she can rely on the defence of 'no *mens rea*' and will not require a special defence of insanity. Michael Moore justified the defence of insanity by arguing that the criminal law is addressed to those who are rational and have the capacity to comply with its rules.[315] A mentally ill person, lacking the capacity to comply with the rules of the law, is exempt from its requirements. However, as mentioned previously, deciding whether a mentally ill person could have avoided breaking the law is extremely difficult.[316]

In the following passage, Victor Tadros summarizes his objections to the *M'Naghten* test for insanity:

V. Tadros, *Criminal Responsibility* (Oxford: OUP, 2005), 347

I have shown that the M'Naghten Rules are both too broad and too narrow.

The rules are too broad because they suggest that *any* failure to appreciate the nature and quality of the act or that it was wrong will be sufficient to undermine responsibility. This fails to recognise the possibility that the defendant is fully responsible for his cognitive or evaluative failure. If the defendant has made a cognitive or evaluative error, it is only where the defendant's cognition or evaluation is radically detached from his background beliefs and values that he ought to be entitled to an excuse.

They are too narrow for three reasons. Firstly, they do not provide a defence for those who lack the autonomy to develop coherent and independent lives in general. They fail to appreciate that there may be defendants who understand the nature and quality of the act that they perform, but whose general capacities are sufficiently lacking that they do not have status-responsibility at all. Such defendants ought to be provided with an exemption. . . .

Secondly, the Rules fail to understand the significance of time for responsibility. They fail to appreciate that there may be defendants who have undergone personality change such that the beliefs and desires that they have are not reflective of their settled character. Such defendants may have all of the capacities of a healthy defendant at the time at which the action is performed, but they lack responsibility for their actions on the grounds that when the action was performed *they were not really themselves*.

Thirdly, the Rules do not include a volitional limb. They fail to appreciate that there may be defendants whose desires are radically detached from their system of beliefs and values in such a way that does not reflect on them *qua* agent. If those desires are sufficiently strong that an agent of good character would not be capable of resisting the desire, the defendant ought to be provided with a defence. In short, the argument that I am pressing is that the M'Naghten Rules have two overly broad limbs where there ought to be five narrower limbs to mental disorder defences.

19.2 REFORM OF THE PRESENT LAW

It is unacceptable that epileptics,[317] diabetics,[318] or sleepwalkers[319] are labelled insane when no one with medical expertise would accept that description.[320] In fact the term

---

[315] M. Moore (1997: ch. 2). See also Bonnie (1983).   [316] Slobogin (2000).

[317] *Sullivan* [1984] 1 AC 156. For a detailed examination of the way people suffering from epilepsy have been treated under the law, see Mackay and Reuber (2007).

[318] *Hennessy* [1989] 1 WLR 287.   [319] *Burgess* [1991] 2 QB 92.

[320] See also Loughnan (2007), who emphasizes the importance of the understanding of 'madness' that the general public have.

'insanity' is not used in this area by medical professionals, who prefer to use terms such as mental illness or mental disorder. Further, the distinction between external and internal factors, upon which the law's approach places a great deal of weight, can produce arbitrary distinctions. It is not surprising therefore that there have been many calls for reform of the law on insanity.[321] Although interestingly in the Law Commission's study it was found that despite the theoretical problems in practice the definition of insanity could be 'worked around' and caused few practical problems.[322] Three contrasting approaches will be examined here:

Abolishing the insanity defence

There are some who have argued that the insanity defence should be abolished.[323] Although this might sound like a surprising suggestion, several American writers have made this argument. Two arguments have been relied upon and will now be mentioned:

(1) The insane defendant should be able to rely on exactly the same defences as a sane defendant.[324] For example, if an insane person lacks *mens rea* he or she should be not guilty for that reason. If he or she believes God is telling him or her to commit a crime or else he or she will be struck by a thunderbolt he or she can plead duress. In other words there should be no special defence for insanity. The argument here is that if an insane person lacks the *mens rea* for a crime or has a defence, then like any other citizen he or she deserves to be acquitted.[325] His or her sanity becomes simply irrelevant. It should be added that this argument is not seeking to deal with the question of civil detention of those suffering mental illness. So an insane person who commits a crime unaware of what he or she is doing should be acquitted of a criminal offence but could be required to undergo compulsory treatment under civil law.[326] Those who reject this argument may point to strict liability offences or negligence-based offences where the insane person would (under this proposal) have no defence.

(2) An extreme view, most notably promoted by Thomas Szasz, is that mental illness is a fiction, a convenient myth created by the mentally ill and those who care for them.[327] Szasz argues that 'mental illness' is a form of survival mechanism which people use to cope with life. Few accept his thesis nowadays, especially now that mental illnesses are far more clearly defined than they were when he was writing. However, it is hard to deny his claim that the line between mental illness, eccentricity, and 'normality' is hard to draw. Maybe his thesis would have found greater support if he had claimed that everyone was insane, rather than claiming that everyone was sane! Certainly it is not difficult to find evidence of people classified as 'insane' who in fact should not have been.[328] Further, there is concerning evidence that the rate of mental illness correlates strongly with social and economic circumstances.[329]

---

[321] It is notable that very few defendants seek to rely on the defence of insanity. One study found that from 1975 to 1988 there were only 49 verdicts of 'not guilty by reason of insanity'. In the five years after the Criminal Procedure (Insanity and Unfitness to Plead) Act 1991 there were 44 findings of 'not guilty by reason of insanity' (Mackay (1990) and Mackay and Kearns (1999)).

[322] Law Commission (2013).   [323] Hogg (2015).   [324] N. Morris (1982); Slobogin (2000).
[325] Szasz (1970).   [326] Goldstein (1967).   [327] Szasz (1970).   [328] Rosenhan (1973).
[329] Hill (1983).

These arguments are explored further in this passage:

W. Sinnott-Armstrong and K. Levy, 'Insanity Defenses' in J. Deigh and
D. Dolinko (eds) *The Oxford Handbook of Philosophy of Criminal Law*
(Oxford: OUP, 2011), 318–21

Arguments for an Insanity Defense

. . .

The main argument for an insanity defense is simple:

If the insanity defense were abolished, the law would not take adequate account of the in-capacitating effects of severe mental illness. Some mentally ill defendants who were psychotic and grossly out of touch with reality may be said to have "intended" to do what they did but nonetheless may have been so severely disturbed that they were unable to understand or appreciate the significance of their actions. These cases do not arise frequently, but when they do a criminal conviction, which signifies the societal judgment that the defendant deserves to be punished, would offend the basic moral intuitions of the community. Judges and juries would be forced either to return a verdict of conviction, which they would regard as morally obtuse, or to acquit the defendant in defiance of the law. They should be spared that moral embarrassment.

Insanity removes moral responsibility, and criminal punishment without moral responsibil-ity is both morally and practically problematic. If the (main) purpose of punishment is either to repay moral wrongs or to express moral condemnation, then punishment seems inappropri-ate when the punished person was not morally responsible. Still, this conclusion is controver-sial because it is not clear that the (main) purpose of punishment is retribution or expression of moral condemnation rather than more consequentialist goals like rehabilitation, incapaci-tation, specific deterrence, general deterrence, victim healing, or protection of society.

. . .

Of course, abilities come in degrees. It is harder for some people than others to obey the law. Circumstances also matter. Some insane people can avoid breaking the law by seek-ing treatment during their lucid periods or by avoiding situations in which they will end up doing harm. Still, if insane people lack the degree of ability or control that is needed in order for them to be morally responsible on some occasions, then they should be excused from criminal punishment for acts that they perform on these occasions (assuming that these conditions can be proved by the applicable standards of evidence).

A separate set of arguments for the insanity defense comes from consequentialists. If someone really is insane in a way that removes the ability to avoid doing illegal acts, then threats of punishment will not deter this person from breaking the law. He will continue to commit the illegal acts regardless, in which case punishment would be pointless. Similarly, if the purpose of punishment is moral education of criminals or rehabilitation more generally, then these purposes cannot be served by punishing insane people who simply cannot learn or come to know right from wrong. Indeed, punishment and confinement might even ex-acerbate some mental illnesses, perhaps by removing support networks.

Arguments against an Insanity Defense

Other consequentialists argue on the opposite side of the issue that even if punishment cannot specifically deter, morally educate, or rehabilitate certain insane people, punishing the insane can still promote other benefits. These other benefits are sometimes claimed to justify abolishing or severely restricting the insanity defense.

One benefit is supposed to be general deterrence—that is, deterring people in society other than the specific individual who is punished. Punishing the insane can promote general deterrence in at least two ways. First, threats of punishment can deter *some* insane criminals. Even if fully insane people cannot be deterred or taught moral lessons, those who are only partially incapacitated can be affected by threats of punishment. Such threats can provide incentives that are strong enough to counteract their insane inclinations. . . .

The second way in which punishing the insane might promote general deterrence is by preventing sane criminals from hoping (usually mistakenly) that they might be able to avoid punishment by faking insanity. . . .

A second consequentialist argument against the insanity defense is that a verdict of not guilty by reason of insanity arguably creates the impression that the criminal "got away with it." After millions of television viewers watched Hinckley shoot President Reagan in 1981 and then be found not guilty by reason of insanity, many people thought that he got off at least partly because he was rich and had tricky lawyers and psychiatrists on his side. Whether or not this widespread belief was true, the impression that rich, devious people get away with crimes can decrease people's respect for the law and thereby their motivation to obey the law.

Third, many critics of the insanity defense fear that dangerous people are incapacitated for less time in mental institutions than in jails and, therefore, that the insanity defense might end up putting dangerous people back out on the street. . . .

Fourth, there is the fundamental problem of determining whether or not a particular defendant really is insane. In many cases, psychiatrists testify on both sides, and juries don't know which experts to believe. In addition, psychiatrists themselves often admit that even if they can determine what a person actually believed and intended to do, they cannot determine whether or not a particular defendant had the ability to do what she did not actually do or to believe what she did not actually believe. It is not even clear what kind of evidence could support claims about such abilities and counterfactuals. These evidentiary difficulties and difficult judgment calls make some results seem arbitrary. Indeed, some convicted criminals in prisons have more serious psychiatric problems than others who were found not guilty by reason of insanity.

Updating the definition of insanity

The Law Commission are considering reform of the law on insanity. The following is an extract of the summary of the core principle at the heart of their approach and then some of their key proposals for reform.

**Law Commission, *Criminal Liability: Insanity and Automatism—
A Discussion Paper* (London: TSO, 2013)**

A.117 In order to be criminally responsible, a person must be, at the time of the act, accountable. That means that he or she must be an agent, and have some basic concept of him or herself as an agent. It also means he or she must have had the capacity to conform to the law. A person might lack that capacity by being incapable of practical reasoning, and/or by being incapable of controlling his or her actions. Where there is such a complete breakdown of the normal human capacities of rationality and self-control, for reasons which are not the accused's fault, then the accused should not be held criminally responsible for what he or she is alleged to have done.

Proposal 2

10.7 We provisionally propose the creation of a new statutory defence of not criminally responsible by reason of recognised medical condition.

Proposal 3

10.8 The party seeking to raise the new defence must adduce expert evidence that at the time of the alleged offence the defendant wholly lacked the capacity:

(i) rationally to form a judgment about the relevant conduct or circumstances;

(ii) to understand the wrongfulness of what he or she is charged with having done; or

(iii) to control his or her physical acts in relation to the relevant conduct or circumstances as a result of a qualifying recognised medical condition.

Proposal 4

10.9 We provisionally propose that certain conditions would not qualify. These include acute intoxication or any condition which is manifested solely or principally by abnormally aggressive or seriously irresponsible behaviour.

FURTHER READING

Bonnie, R. (1993) 'The Moral Basis of the Insanity Defence' *American Bar Association Journal* 69: 194.

Duff, R.A. (1986) *Trials and Punishments* (Oxford: OUP).

Hogg, C. (2015) 'The Insanity Defence: An Argument for Abolition' *Journal of Criminal Law* 79: 250.

Howard, H. (2003) 'Reform of the Insanity Defence: Theoretical Issues' *Journal of Criminal Law* 67: 51.

Howard, H. (2011) 'Unfitness to Plead and the Vulnerable Defendant: An Examination of the Law Commission's Proposals for a New Capacity Test' *Journal of Criminal Law* 75: 194.

Law Commission (2010b) Consultation Paper 197, Unfitness to Plead (London: TSO).

Law Commission (2013) Criminal Liability: Insanity and Automatism—A Discussion Paper (London: TSO).

Loughnan, A. (2007) ' "Manifest Madness": Towards a New Understanding of the Insanity Defence' *Modern Law Review* 70: 379.

Loughnan, A. (2012a) 'Mental Incapacity Doctrines in Criminal Law' *New Criminal Law Review* 1.

Loughnan, A. (2012c) *Manifest Madness* (Oxford: OUP).

Mackay, R. (2011) 'Unfitness to Plead—Some Observations of the Law Commission's Consultation Paper' *Criminal Law Review* 433.

Moore, M. (1997) *Placing Blame* (Oxford: OUP), ch. 12.

Morse, S. (1994) 'Culpability and Control' *University of Pennsylvania Law Review* 142: 1587.

Scottish Law Commission (2003) *Discussion Paper on Insanity and Diminished Responsibility* (Edinburgh: TSO).

Tadros, V. (2001b) 'Insanity and the Capacity for Criminal Responsibility' *Edinburgh Law Review* 5: 325.

20 PRIVATE DEFENCE

20.1 THE MORAL BASIS OF PRIVATE DEFENCE

Why should the criminal law provide a defence to those who use force in order to protect themselves or others from an attack? This is a question which has troubled many lawyers and ethicists. Here are some of the most popular answers: ←2 (p. 627)

Consequentialist theory

This theory argues simply that where force is used in self-defence this produces better consequences than where it is not.[330] Simply, when faced with the alternatives of either the innocent person being attacked or the aggressor being repelled with force, the latter is the option which produces the greater good and so should be preferred. Sangero argues that it is better that the aggressor is harmed than the person being attacked because the aggressor devalues his interests by the attack. This explains why, when faced with either, the death of the aggressor is not as bad as the death of the person being attacked. The difficulty with this approach is that it contravenes the normal principle that all lives are equally valuable. It could also cause problems where the person being attacked has behaved badly too.[331] Sangero also argues the maintenance of 'the rule of law and order'[332] justifies giving greater weight to the person being attacked, although whether the existence of the defence discourages attacks and helps maintain order may be open to question.[333] Notably this argument would not support the existence of self-defence in a case where a person thinks they are being attacked, but they are not.

The forfeiture theory

The forfeiture theory states that by posing a threat to someone the victim (V) has forfeited his or her right not to have violence used against him or her. As Hugo Bedau put it: '[The wrong-doer] no longer merits our consideration, any more than an insect or a stone does'.[334] Suzanne Uniacke has developed perhaps the most sophisticated defence of this approach. She explains that a person's right to life or freedom from violence is conditional upon that person not posing a threat to other people. When posing a threat the person does not have those rights.[335] Although very popular, this theory is not without its critics whose arguments include:

(1) How does the theory explain that once the threat ceases V cannot be killed? So if V has hit D and then runs off, the law is clear that D cannot then shoot V. But why not if V has forfeited his or her right to be killed? Uniacke sees no difficulty with this. She claims that once the threat is no longer posed the victim reacquires the right to life. There will, though,

---

[330] Sangero (2006) is the leading work promoting this way of understanding the defence.

[331] Leverick (2007).   [332] Sangero (2006: 567).   [333] Leverick (2007).

[334] Bedau (1968: 570).   [335] Uniacke (1994: ch. 1). See also J. Thomson (1991).

be an ambiguous point in time (when the threat is diminishing, but still present) where there may be a legitimate argument about whether or not the right exists.

(2) How can you say a child or insane person forfeits his or her right by posing a threat? Although the forfeiture theory may have some appeal in saying that a person who chooses to try and kill another chooses to forfeit his or her right to life, can we say the same if they are children or insane and do not know what they are doing? Supporters of the forfeiture theory divide when faced with this question. Some reply that a right can be forfeited by your actions (in posing the threat) even if you are not morally responsible for your actions. This argument, that a blameless person can forfeit his rights, is controversial. Other supporters of the forfeiture theory accept that the theory has no application where the attackers are innocent. Instead they rely on an alternative theory to deal with such cases. For example, in the innocent attacker case we are faced with two innocent parties, one of whom is going to suffer pain. The recipient of the attack may legitimately prefer his or her own welfare over that of his or her equally innocent attacker. But if D is approached by five children all carrying machine guns, unaware of their dangerous nature, can D kill all five children?[336] It is difficult to justify such killing apart from referring to a right to defend yourself or a theory of forfeiture.

(3) How does the forfeiture requirement explain the proportionality requirement?[337] If I am attacked does my attacker lose all his or her rights and therefore I have the right to kill him or her? Supporters of the forfeiture theory reply that on posing a threat to another the attacker loses the right not to have force proportionate to the threatened force used against him or her. So if I make as if to slap you I do not lose my right to life, but do lose my right not to have moderate force used against me.

(4) Harder for supporters of the forfeiture theory is this: if V tries to kill D and thereby forfeits V's right to life, can D kill V in a particularly brutal way? For example, if V pulls out a gun and points it at D, if proportionate and necessary D could shoot V to save his or her life. But if D has two alternative means of stopping the attack by either shooting V or throwing into V's face acid which will slowly and painfully kill V, most commentators take the view that D must kill in the least painful way. But under the forfeiture theory V has lost his right to life and so D can choose.

Autonomy arguments for self-defence

An alternative theory in support of self-defence focuses not on V and his or her loss of rights (as the forfeiture theory does) but on D and his or her right to defend him or herself.[338] Supporters of such a view argue that it is part of your rights of autonomy that you can defend yourself from an unjust attack.[339] The difficulty with this argument is that it does not make it clear why self-defence is available only in the face of an unjust threat.[340]

---

[336] Alexander (1999) discusses this scenario further.

[337] For further discussion, see Uniacke (2010).

[338] One way of explaining the defence is that it is the responsibility of the state to protect its citizens from violence. If the state is unable to protect the citizen (because there is an imminent attack) then the citizen is able to intervene and use force. See e.g. Dressler (2002a).

[339] Nourse (2014) has distinguished between what she calls the pacifist position, with its focus on the right to life of the victim and stressing requirements of proportionality and necessity, with the libertarian view, which focuses on the defendant's right of autonomy.

[340] See Wallerstein (2005) for an excellent discussion.

In the following passage Victor Tadros explores the borderlines of self-defence by reference to the well-known Trolley Problem:

V. Tadros, *The Ends of Harm* (Oxford: OUP, 2013), 115

Trolley Driver. The driver of a trolley is hurtling down a track and he realizes that the brakes have failed. Five people are on the track in front of him, and if he does nothing the trolley will run into them and kill them. However, he can turn the trolley onto another track. If he does so, the trolley will run into one person, killing them.

Bridge. The driver of a trolley is hurtling down a track and the brakes have failed. Five people are on the track in front of the trolley. However, there are two people on the bridge between the trolley and the five. One of those is a large person, large enough to stop the trolley if he falls in front of it. The other is a very strong small person. The only way for the strong small person to prevent the trolley hitting the five is by knocking the large person off the bridge so that he will fall in front of it, killing him.

The problem is that it seems permissible for the driver to turn the trolley in *Trolley Driver* but wrong for the strong small person to push the large person off the bridge in *Bridge*. In both cases, there would be a net saving of four lives. So what's the difference between the cases?

One answer to this problem, the answer that I favour, is grounded in the means principle [which he has earlier explained in these terms: 'while it may be permissible to pursue the good where this will have, as one of its side effects, some lesser harm to others, it is not permissible to pursue the good where others will be used as a means to achieve that good'.] It is permissible to kill the one person in *Trolley Driver* because doing so produces a significantly greater good (a net saving of four lives). That is also true in *Bridge*. But in *Bridge* only using one person as a means can save the five. It is wrong to kill one person to save five if the one person is used as a means, but not if the death of the one is a side effect of the good-producing action.

20.2 MISTAKEN PRIVATE DEFENCE

It will be recalled from Part I that under English and Welsh law a defendant who mistakenly believes that he or she is being attacked can rely on private defence. But why is this?[341] The leading case on the topic was *Beckford*, which focused on the decision of the House of Lords in *Morgan* that unlawfulness is an element of all crimes of violence. As the *mens rea* of a crime must relate to all aspects of the *actus reus* the defendant must intend or be reckless as to the unlawfulness. Therefore, if the person believes the state of affairs to be such that he or she would have a defence to any criminal charge he or she lacks the intent or recklessness as to the unlawfulness part of the *actus reus*. Therefore, if a person believed he or she was acting in self-defence, even if that was based on an unreasonable mistake, he or she must be acquitted. Requiring people to know that they were being attacked would not be practical.[342]

---

[341] See the excellent discussion in Leverick (2006: ch. 9) and Norrie (2010b).   [342] Frowe (2010).

20.3 THE 'HOUSEHOLDER' PROVISIONS

As noted earlier the Crime and Courts Act 2013 (section 43) has introduced special provisions to deal with householders pleading self-defence after using violence against intruders.[343] In the following passage Nicola Wake criticizes these reforms:

N. Wake, 'Battered Women, Startled Householders and Psychological Self-defence: Anglo-Australian Perspectives' (2013) 77 *Journal of Criminal Law* 433

A significant number of commentators have suggested that s. 43 will not significantly alter the current law on self-defence since householders who react with fatal consequences are rarely prosecuted, suggesting that the change in the law may have more to do with political rhetoric than principled reform. Nevertheless, the revised test has the potential to raise the bar dangerously in terms of the amount of force which can legitimately be used in 'startled householder' cases: 'Do we really want to create a legal justice system where people are allowed to shoot dead someone who is only trying to steal their TV?'. Paul Mendelle QC has vehemently argued that:

> The law should encourage people to be reasonable, not unreasonable; to be proportionate, not disproportionate . . . [the legislation has] in effect, sanctioned extrajudicial execution or capital punishment for an offence, burglary, that carries a maximum of 14 years, which is the sentence that Parliament decided was appropriate.

The use of grossly disproportionate force may result in a murder conviction where the prosecution successfully prove the requisite *mens rea*. Determining the point at which force is to be regarded as grossly disproportionate is as decipherable as assessment of how many angels can dance on the head of a pin:

> If I manage to tackle a criminal and get him to the ground, I kick him once, and that's reasonable, I kick him twice and that's understandable, three times forgivable, four times, debatable, five times, disproportionate, six times it's very disproportionate, seven times extremely disproportionate—eight times, and it's grossly disproportionate. It is a horrible test. It sounds like state-sponsored revenge. [M. Wolkind QC]

It is disturbing that the government asserts that the line is crossed when it is abundantly clear that no further force is required, for example stabbing a burglar or stamping on his head while he is unconscious. Perplexed jurors will be required to engage in mental gymnastics in order to determine whether the defendant's conduct is to be regarded as reasonable, disproportionate or grossly disproportionate. There is also the question of how the changes will impact on the current law of mistaken belief. As noted, in cases involving mistaken belief, jurors are required to answer the hypothetical question of whether the force used by D was reasonable in the circumstances as he mistakenly perceived them to be. . . .

Arguments that the 'startled householder' defence can be justified on the basis that the general public support the provision are fundamentally flawed. The new provision is dangerous in terms of the level of violence that it permits and Parliament has failed to address the potential problems that the new legislation creates. It is now the judiciary and fact-finders who are charged with interpreting and applying this enigmatic piece of legislation and it may well be the general public who are put at risk. The government's decision to amend the law arbitrarily in favour of one discrete category of defendant is also odd. . . . New s. 76(5A) of the Criminal Justice and

---

[343] Dsouza (2015) justifies the provision on the basis that the defendant has a special entitlement to remain in their home.

Immigration Act 2008 effectively legitimises the use of disproportionate force in self-defence with a successful plea resulting in an outright acquittal in 'startled householder' cases, but not in cases like that of *Clegg*—this places the 'startled householder' in a better position than every other case of self defence, where the defence will fail if the use of force was disproportionate. Defending the contentious proposition, Grayling [a government minister], asserts:

> Being confronted by an intruder in your own home is terrifying, and the public should be in no doubt that the law is on their side. That is why I am strengthening the current law. Householders who act instinctively and honestly in self-defence are victims of crime and should be treated that way.

This rationale distinguishes *Clegg* from home invasion cases, but it cannot be convincingly reconciled with cases involving prolonged and systematic violent domestic abuse suffered in the familial home. The 'abused woman' who kills using disproportionate force in the home does not benefit from this change in the law because the person who attacks her is not a stranger, but the person she lives with. As previously noted, it will be more difficult for the 'abused woman', rather than the 'startled householder' to claim the partial defence as a result of the 'loss of control' conceptualisation.

FURTHER READING

Ashworth, A. (1975) 'Self-Defence and the Right to Life' *Cambridge Law Journal* 36: 272.

Christopher, R. (1998) 'Self-Defense and Objectivity' *Buffalo Criminal Law Review* 1: 537.

Frowe, H. (2010) 'A Practical Account of Self-Defence' *Law and Philosophy* 29: 245.

Horder, J. (1995b) 'Redrawing the Boundaries of Self-Defence' *Modern Law Review* 58: 431.

Kessler Ferzan, K. (2005) 'Justifying Self-Defense' *Law and Philosophy* 24: 711.

Lee, C. (1998) 'The Act–Belief Distinction in Self-Defense Doctrine: A New Dual Requirement Theory of Justification' *Buffalo Criminal Law Review* 2: 191.

Leverick, F. (2006) *Killing in Self-Defence* (Oxford: OUP).

Montague, P. (2010) 'Self-Defense, Culpability, and Distributive Justice' *Law and Philosophy* 29: 75.

Norrie, A. (2010b) 'The Problem of Mistaken Self-Defense: Citizenship, Chiasmus, and Legal Form' *New Criminal Law Review* 13: 357.

Schopp, R. (1998) *Justification Defences and Just Convictions* (Cambridge: Cambridge University Press).

Segev, R. (2005) 'Fairness, Responsibility and Self-Defense' *Santa Clara Law Review* 45: 383.

Simons, K. (2008) 'Self-Defense: Reasonable Beliefs or Reasonable Self-Control?' *New Criminal Law Review* 11: 51.

Uniacke, S. (1994) *Permissible Killing* (Cambridge: Cambridge University Press).

Uniacke, S. (2011) 'Proportionality and Self-Defense' *Law and Philosophy* 30: 253.

Wallerstein, S. (2005) 'Justifying the Right to Self-Defense: A Theory of Forced Consequences' *Virginia Law Review* 91: 999.

21 DURESS

There is much debate over the proper basis of the defence of duress. We will look at five possibilities: ←5 (p.653)

(1) **The 'no choice' model** This model argues that a defendant in the face of a threat of death or serious injury suffers such panic that he or she is incapable of rational thought. Duress in this model appears to be almost a form of temporary insanity.[344] Opponents of this approach argue that the law must consider whether the defendant ought to have found this such a difficult choice. If David is told that unless he injures his sister his collection of pornography will be burnt and David is so terrified that his beloved pornography collection will be destroyed that he is not able to think clearly and so injures his sister, should he have a defence? Surely not. Accepting that people can act impulsively in a panic, David should not have got into such a panic. This dilemma should not have been a difficult one for him.[345]

(2) **The 'lack of choice' model** Here it is said that even though the defendant may have been able carefully to consider the options before choosing to commit a crime, he or she should not be responsible for his or her choice.[346] As the capacity theory would have it he or she did not have a fair opportunity to choose to do otherwise.[347]

(3) **The 'character' model** The character model suggests that when acting under duress the defendant's behaviour does not reveal a bad character.[348] The model focuses on the appropriateness of the choice the defendant made: was it one which a morally good agent could make? It might be that the defendant made the morally correct choice (e.g. he or she committed a minor parking offence to escape from a threat of death) or it was the wrong choice, but bearing in mind that even morally well-disposed agents are affected by panic and fear, it is one such an agent might have made and so it does not reflect bad character on his or her part.[349]

(4) **Justification** Here the claim is that duress is a defence where the defendant made a morally permissible choice.[350] As the choice need be only permissible this means that the defendant will be justified if the harm he or she is required to commit is the same as[351] or less than the harm threatened.[352]

(5) **The 'no *mens rea*' model**[353] This view is that the defendant did not intend to harm the victim, but rather his or her purpose was to avoid the threat being carried out.[354] The defendant in a duress case therefore can claim not to have the *mens rea* necessary for an intent-based offence.

Although much has been written in support of these different theories it should be remembered that it is quite possible that more than one of these theories is correct. For example, it

---

[344] e.g. Widgery LJ in *Hudson and Taylor* [1971] 2 QB 202 (CA). The use of such terminology was rejected in *DPP for Northern Ireland v Lynch* [1975] AC 653, 679 (HL), per Lord Wilberforce.

[345] For an argument along these lines, see Morse (1994).   [346] M. Moore (1987: 1148).

[347] M. Moore (1999).   [348] Richards (1987).

[349] See the discussion in Horder (1994a); Alexander (1999).

[350] Wertheimer (1987), discussed by Honoré (1990). J. Gardner (2007b) suggests that a person should (not only may) kill if a terrorist says 'Unless you kill X I will kill five people'.

[351] Wertheimer (1987: 204).

[352] See Kessler Ferzan (2011) for a discussion of whether justification requires the act to be permissible or to be morally right.

[353] *Paquette* (1997) 70 DLR (3d) 129 (Sup. Ct of Canada).

[354] See Chapter 3, Part II, for a discussion of the different forms of *mens rea*.

could be argued that some defendants who successfully plead duress have a defence on the basis that their choice was justified, and others on the basis that their state of mind was such they were not responsible for that choice.[355]

The view one takes on the correct basis for the defence affects many of the controversial aspects of the definition of the offence.[356] For example, in relation to the debate over which characteristics of the accused should be attributable to the reasonable person test, if you take the justification view then you would not want any characteristics of the accused to affect the degree of bravery expected. However, Duff, supporting the character theory, suggests[357] 'we should ascribe to the reasonable person any of the defendant's actual characteristics that affected her response to the threat, *other than* characteristics which involve either some lack of reasonable regard for the law and its values, or a lack of reasonable courage.'

In the following passage, Kimberly Kessler Ferzan considers in more detail some of these explanations:

K. Kessler Ferzan, 'Justification and Excuse' in J. Deigh and D. Dolinko (eds)
The Oxford Handbook of Philosophy of Criminal Law (Oxford: OUP, 2011)

1 Choice, Reasoning, and Attitude

The choice theory flows from the law's concept of a person as practical reasoner. Just as the law presupposes that individuals act for reasons and thus can be guided by criminal-law rules, excuses set forth those conditions under which the defendant cannot be so guided. Choice theorists argue that the grounds for excusing an actor are that she lacked the rationality to appreciate the criminality of her conduct or the volitional ability to conform her conduct to the requirements of law. Notably, to the choice theorist, the fact that an action is *caused* is not sufficient to excuse it.

. . .

One critique of at least some forms of choice theory is that it is overinclusive, as it would arguably excuse the negligent who do not make choices. There are two general responses to this objection. First, Michael Moore has argued that there is a different culpability at work for negligence—the culpability of unexercised capacity. A prerequisite to negligence liability would then be having the rational capacity to understand that one's conduct could cause harm. Second, one might embrace this implication, and then argue that negligence should not be a basis for criminal liability. Of course, the latter path is the more radical, and requires the theorist to depart significantly from the extant criminal law.

2 Character Theories

Character theorists argue that an individual cannot be punished for a crime if it does not reflect the defendant's underlying character, motivation, or agency. In other words, people should not be punished for those actions that are "out of character." Underlying this theory is the view that one is ultimately responsible for one's character, and actions are just proxies for character.

---

[355] e.g. Herring (2013g: 297).   [356] K. Smith (1989).   [357] Duff (1996).

As summarized by Peter Westen, the character theories would excuse a defendant if:

(1) he made a reasonable and good-faith mistake that is consistent with his being of good character, (2) he was compelled by pressures over which he had no control (other that [*sic*] the pressures of settled character), (3) he was too young to have developed a settled character, (4) he acted from insanity rather than any settled character on his part, or (5) his conduct was out of character for him.

Hence, like choice theorists, character theorists seek to theorize a broad range of reasons why a defendant is not criminally blameworthy.

There are significant problems with character theories. First, it seems that even if an action is "out of character," that should not be sufficient to exculpate the defendant. Second, character theorists make the commission of a criminal act merely evidentiary, as opposed to providing the primary basis for responsibility. Not only does this shift radically refocus the criminal law but also this view of the relationship of character and action is utterly at odds with evidence law, which prohibits the use of character evidence to show that an action was or was not in conformity with the actor's character. Third, character theorists seem to get the relationship between character and action exactly backward—action is prior to, and constitutive of, character. To put the matter bluntly, one act of theft *makes* you a thief.

...

Still, there seems to be some grain of truth to character theories. An agent is not simply a choosing machine. As Antony Duff says, "[a] 'character' conception expresses a significant truth about *who* can be held criminally liable: that only moral agents, whose actions exhibit the structures of thought, attitude, and motivation that constitute 'character,' should be held liable." This sort of argument aligns itself with a theory of exemptions. That is, moral agency is a prerequisite to moral responsibility.

...

3 Reasons and Excuses

Just as one theory of justification analyzes the reasons for which the actor violates the prohibitory norm, so do some theories of excuse. These theorists essentially view the act of offering an excuse as one of *accepting responsibility* for the act but *denying liability* for it. Excuses look to the actor's reasons that thereby reveal him not to be blameworthy for the act. Notably, various theorists offer quite disparate views of how these reasons are said undermine blameworthiness. Three leading views are set forth below.

John Gardner's view is that the gist of excuses is *living up to societal expectations*. This view departs from other character theories by claiming that a defendant is not excused for acting out of character but precisely because she meets our normative expectations of her. For example, one is not entitled to an excuse for duress if one does not act with the proper reasonable firmness. Gardner also claims that this normative expectation may vary for differing roles.

Jeremy Horder also seeks to analyze excuses in terms of reasons. Like Gardner, Horder distinguishes excuses in terms of reasons from denials of responsibility, which fall within the category of exemptions, although Horder does make room for a partial excuse of diminished capacity. Although Horder's rather complicated views cannot be easily summarized here, Horder's general view is that excuses place the defendant's act in a more favorable light, when the "morally active" reasons for his conduct are scrutinized. Notably, unlike most excuse theories, Horder claims that the actor's reasons reflect on the *act*, not simply the *actor*.

QUESTIONS

1. Lacey and Wells have argued 'the duress defence is designed to excuse people invested with characteristics which are strongly marked as masculine in our society.' Do you agree?

2. The defendant suffers a medical condition which means that he will die unless he takes certain tablets every two hours. He runs out of medicine and asks his doctor for some more. The doctor says he will give the medicine only if the defendant injures his wife, which he does. Can the defendant plead duress? (NB: Is there a threat here or an offer?)

For guidance on answering this question, please visit the Online Resource Centre that accompanies this book: www.oxfordtextbooks.co.uk/orc/herringcriminal7e/.

FURTHER READING

Arenson, K. (2014) 'The Paradox of Disallowing Duress as a Defence to Murder' *Journal of Criminal Law* 78: 65.

Dressler, J. (1989) 'Exegesis of the Law of Duress: Justifying the Excuse and Searching for Its Proper Limits' *Southern California Law Review* 62: 1331.

Duff, R.A. (2002) 'Rule-Violations and Wrongdoings' in S. Shute and A. Simester (eds) *Criminal Law Theory* (Oxford: OUP).

Finkelstein, C. (2002b) 'Excuses and Dispositions in Criminal Law' *Buffalo Criminal Law Review* 6: 317.

Horder, J. (1994a) 'Occupying the Moral High Ground: The Law Commission on Duress' *Criminal Law Review* 334.

Huigens, K. (2004) 'Duress is Not a Justification' *Ohio Journal of Criminal Law* 2: 303.

Norrie, A. (2001) *Crime, Reason and History* (2nd edn, London: Butterworths).

Westen, P. and Mangiafico, J. (2003) 'The Criminal Defense of Duress: A Justification, Not an Excuse—and Why It Matters' *Buffalo Criminal Law Review* 8: 833.

22 NECESSITY

As mentioned in Part I, by 'necessity' in this book we mean a claim that the defendant did the lesser of two evils, although, as such, the defence is recognized by English and Welsh law only to a limited extent. The present law recognizes that necessity is available where the offence is committed which promotes the well-being of a 'victim' who is unable to consent. Such cases are based on the principle that if a person is unable to give consent, then others should treat him or her in a way which promotes his or her best interests. Such cases tend to be uncontroversial: few would deny that a doctor can operate on a person brought into a hospital unconscious after a car accident.[358] ←4 (p.643)

The reluctance to accept a general 'lesser of two evils' necessity defence at first sight seems hard to justify: how can it be proper to punish someone whose act has caused more

---

[358] Ashworth (1996: 190).

good than harm? The answer can be seen by considering an example: a doctor who kills one healthy patient and uses his organs to save three patients. The doctor could argue that killing one person to save three lives was the lesser of two evils, but very few people would regard his conduct as justified.

As the following extract by Simon Gardner demonstrates, there are not just practical difficulties with such a defence, but also political and theoretical ones:

S. Gardner, 'Direct Action and the Defence of Necessity' [2005] *Criminal Law Review* 371 at 379–82

The status of justificatory necessity as a matter of principle

. . .

The standard account of justificatory necessity depicts it as depending on a utilitarian assessment of the competing goods and harms. But making such an assessment is often, perhaps always, an ethically impossible exercise. Consider again *Re A (Children) (Conjoined Twins: Surgical Separation)*. In utilitarian terms, the question has to be: which involved the greater harm, killing Mary in order to save Josie, or allowing both to die? If one has to choose one, it may be hard not to choose the latter. But many, rejecting the medico-economic arguments adduced by Ward L.J., would regard the question as simply unanswerable, and not the less so for being addressed by judges. Or take *Jones*. A utilitarian assessment would require a decision not merely whether the coalition attack on Iraq was legal, but whether on balance it did good or harm; and, if harm, whether more or less harm than that involved in the acts allegedly done and planned by the accused at the airbase. We cannot expect judges to answer a question like that, and it would do no more than brush the difficulty under the carpet to leave it to be decided by the jury. As noted above, a utilitarian assessment does look more possible where human life and limb, or the interests of the state, are not at stake: say in the example given, where I break your £100 window to save my £200 chair from a fire. But to take a utilitarian approach even here is to disregard the value which I, and especially you, may subjectively attach to our property.

It is much more comfortable to think of necessity in terms of the vindication of rights. That is, I should have the defence if, committing what would otherwise be an offence, I act to vindicate a right that is recognised by the law but not otherwise reflected in the offence's definition, and that is superior to any right or interest that the offence exists to protect and that I injure by my action; and no less aggressive course of action (i.e. no course of action likewise calculated to vindicate the right, but less injurious of the rights and interests protected by the offence) was open to me.

Acceptance of this analysis does not destroy all space for an analysis in terms of 'best interests' or of utility. The 'best interests' doctrine will continue to operate in its own special niche. In the general run of necessity cases, an analysis focused on utility will remain viable where the two goods in question are sufficiently comparable. Perhaps the case of breaking a £100 window to save a £200 chair can be handled in this way after all, by suppressing the issue of the parties' subjective valuations as a luxury which cannot be allowed to obstruct the defence's availability. But where the two goods are not properly comparable and so a utilitarian approach cannot work (as at any rate in cases involving human life and limb), an approach focused on rights will provide a more robust analytical tool.

For in principle, the attraction of the rights analysis is that rights are (one of their raisons d'etre is to be) justiciable, in a way that the all-things-considered balance of advantage is commonly not. It is true that in England, until recently, this attraction existed more in theory than in practice, as it was hard to say whether a right had the necessary quality of recognition by the law. But, without necessarily saying that the Human Rights Act 1998 is the sole means by which rights can be recognised by English law, the coming into force of that Act has certainly meant that this analysis of necessity in terms of rights should be much more capable of ready practical operation.

Say I ruin your coat when, there being no less aggressive alternative, I use it to save a child from drowning. My act should be seen as justified because it is necessary in order to vindicate the child's right to life under Art 2 of the European Convention on Human Rights (ECHR). Or say I 'spring' those terrorism suspects whose detention without trial in Belmarsh Prison was declared unlawful in *A (FC) v Secretary of State for the Home Department*, as infringing Arts 5 and 14 of the ECHR. If there was no less aggressive alternative way to vindicate the detainees' rights, my act should be seen as justified on that ground. On the other hand, if I liberate some laboratory animals so as to save them from vivisection, I have no justification of this kind, as the interest I am promoting is not one recognised as a right by the law: either under the ECHR or, it is suggested, otherwise.

Care will however be needed over the question whether no less aggressive course of action was open to the accused. There is unlikely to be difficulty on this ground with my using your coat to rescue the drowning child, but it may well upset my defence when I 'spring' the Belmarsh detainees. In circumstances not involving an emergency, it should commonly be right to say that quite considerable time should be given for less drastic approaches to be tried, before a self-help approach would be justified.

Necessity and direct action

This last point surely means that the rights analysis of necessity is unlikely often to justify offences committed by way of political direct action. Such offences would be held justified only once democratic approaches had been exhaustively tried and had failed. It is tempting to say that, in the nature of democratic politics, this time might be something approaching never. But recall that the analysis under discussion is about vindicating the rights of particular individuals. The effluxion of the individuals' lives may create a more pressing timetable.

Peter Glazebrook[359] has argued that it is unjustifiable to support the 'lesser of two evils' in the circumstances of duress or self-defence, but not in other circumstances. Alan Norrie[360] picks up on this argument and points out that the existing defences are provided for the kinds of cases in which the more powerful people may find themselves (e.g. protecting themselves from mugging) but not in circumstances in which marginalized members of society are likely to find themselves (e.g. needing to steal food to escape hunger). Indeed an argument can be made that the 'rights' theory of necessity (referred to in Simon Gardner's passage in the previous excerpt) lets society off too much. It means that money cannot be stolen from a very rich person in order to pay for a life-saving operation. It upholds and helps maintain a society in which some people do not have enough money for the essentials of life and others have more than enough money. Jeremy Horder replies to such arguments by saying that even if this inequality is accepted as unjust the solution lies, not in allowing poor people to steal from rich people, but rather through reforming the taxation and social security systems. Indeed inequalities within society would be more fairly resolved

[359] Glazebrook (1972).   [360] Norrie (2001).

through taxation and social security systems than through permitting the poor to steal (which would be likely to favour the strong or the devious). Horder,[361] however, recognizes that there are some emergencies where such political alternatives are not available. He gives the example of a person trapped in a freezing storm on a mountainside who comes across a log cabin. Horder suggests he should be permitted to break in. This kind of emergency is not one to which Parliament could be expected to provide a political solution. Nor is this cabin scenario a case with wider ramifications. The starving thief scenario gives rise to a number of complex questions: how starving do you have to be to be able to steal and how rich does a person have to be for it to be permissible to steal from him? A further issue is a principle of constitutional law. In recognizing necessity are the courts, essentially, making law by in effect creating a new exception to a crime?[362] In the following passage, considering the *Nicklinson*[363] litigation, I make the case in favour of allowing necessity in exceptional cases involving terminally ill people who wish to be killed:[364]

J. Herring, 'Escaping the Shackles of Law at the End of Life' (2013) 21 *Medical Law Review* 487 at 493

This case is a further addition to the furious debate on how the law should respond to those who wish to die. That debate is skewed by the understandable temptation for lawyers to focus on the kind of cases which come to court. But, we should never forget that they are exceptional, when compared with the general case of a person who wishes to die. In 2010, there were 5,608 suicides in people aged fifteen years and over in the UK. In 2010, the Samaritans received over 500,000 contacts from people expressing a wish to commit suicide. They suggest around 5% of the population will attempt suicide at some point in their life. When considering how the law should respond to people who wish to die, we should remember that few suicides or attempted suicides are motivated by the kind of careful, calm, rational thinking expressed by, for example, Tony Nicklinson. Most are largely tragic cases involving individuals plagued by mental health problems, drug and alcohol misuse, and relationship difficulties. The central legal message we should be sending out to people wishing to commit suicide is 'please don't'. The official response must be one offering care, comfort, and support. If the primary message from the law to those seeking death and those dealing with them is 'you have a right to kill yourself if you want' something has gone badly wrong. Quite rightly, suicide prevention is at the heart of the public health response to this issue. It should be at the heart of the legal response too.

. . .

There are, of course, severe difficulties with using the law to send a message and it is inevitably crude. Given that, 'do not kill' and 'do not assist suicide' are not bad messages to send to those wishing to commit suicide and those dealing with them.

The difficulty is that we have our general principles but hard cases come along. The criminal law is familiar with this. We set out the definitions of offences, but a case arises which technically falls within the definition but deserves no conviction. The criminal law has a range of ways of dealing with these cases. We create 'wriggle room' through prosecutorial

---

361 Horder (2000).

362 See Thorburn (2008), who argues that in recognizing necessity the courts are reviewing the validity of the decision not to comply with the law, rather than changing the law itself.

363 *Nicklinson v Ministry of Justice* [2013] EWCA Civ 961.

364 See Stark (2013b and 2013c) for an alternative analysis.

discretion; the common sense of juries; providing minimal sentences; and the defence of necessity. This is because human life is complex. It does not fit into clear boxes. A few statutory lines cannot in their nature produce the full assessment of blame or capture all the nuances of morally complex scenarios. This is true for all crimes from battery through to murder. There is no breach of constitutional principle if the courts and prosecuting authorities use these devices to ensure there is no conviction in the rare case where the official response is inappropriate. Indeed, Parliament relies on these to make the criminal law workable. These devices are essential in an effective criminal law system. They are an acknowledgement of the limitations of language and an inability to deal in rules with all the minutiae of an individual case that are needed for an effective moral assessment. Without such devices, the individual defendant can bear the burden of the inevitably blunt nature of law.

. . .

I believe utilising the defence of necessity would have provided the ideal response of the law to the issues raised. The current law says to doctors and carers: You can let die, but do not kill. I think that is a pretty good standard message for the law to convey. That, however, needs to be tempered in the rare cases where upholding those principles works harshly for those seeking death or assisting them. We can acknowledge that in rare cases, compassion is met by not prosecuting or by using a defence of necessity.

FURTHER READING

Alexander, L. (2005) 'Lesser Evils: A Closer Look at the Paradigmatic Justification' *Law and Philosophy* 24: 611.

Brudner, A. (1987) 'A Theory of Necessity' *Oxford Journal of Legal Studies* 7: 338.

Freeman, M. (2001) 'Whose Life is It Anyway?' *Medical Law Review* 9: 259.

Harris, J. (2001) 'Human Being, Persons and Conjoined Twins' *Medical Law Review* 9: 221.

McEwan, J. (2001) 'Murder by Design: The "Feel-Good Factor" and the Criminal Law' *Medical Law Review* 9: 246.

Michalowski, S. (2002) 'Sanctity of Life—Are Some Lives More Sacred than Others?' *Legal Studies* 22: 377.

Norrie, A. (2001) *Crime, Reason and History* (London: Butterworths), ch. 8.

Parry, J. (1999) 'The Virtue of Necessity: Reshaping Culpability and the Rule of Law' *Houston Law Review* 36: 397.

Rogers, J. (2001) 'Necessity, Private Defence and the Killing of Mary' *Criminal Law Review* 515.

Schopp, R. (1998) *Justification Defences and Just Convictions* (Cambridge: Cambridge University Press).

Sheldon, S. and Wilkinson, S. (2001) ' "On the Sharpest Horns of a Dilemma": *Re A (Conjoined Twins)*' *Medical Law Review* 9: 201.

Stark, F. (2013c) ' "Necessity and *Nicklinson*" *Criminal Law Review* 947.

Uniacke, S. (2001) 'Was Mary's Death Murder?' *Medical Law Review* 9: 208.

Wilson, W. (2002) *Central Issues in Criminal Law Theory* (Oxford: Hart), ch. 10.

23 ISSUES WHICH FALL BETWEEN THE GAPS OF THE DEFENCES

We will now look at three controversial scenarios that do not fall neatly into any of the established defences:

23.1 *KINGSTON*

The case of *Kingston*[365] has been controversial. It will be recalled that the House of Lords held that the defendant, who was involuntarily intoxicated, could still be convicted of an offence providing he has the necessary *mens rea*. The approach of the Court of Appeal, that a defendant who suffered a disinhibition caused by a stratagem of a third party could have a defence, was rejected. Perhaps the most sophisticated support for providing *Kingston* with a defence comes from G.R. Sullivan:[366] ←7 (p.688)

G.R. Sullivan, 'Making Excuses' in A. Smith and G.R. Sullivan (eds) *Harm and Culpability* (Oxford: OUP, 1996), 131–4

The Possibility of Excuse

How can it be said that a state of involuntary intoxication may give rise to a finding of blame-lessness if it does not negate the mental element for the offence nor cause conduct to be compelled? If we take Hart's classic epitome of excusing conditions and ask whether Kingston lacked fair opportunity and capacity to conform his conduct to law, we arguably affirm, not refute, the decision of the House of Lords. The fact that his intoxication was involuntary pre-sumptively engages the issue of fair opportunity. Yet a claim of lack of fair opportunity may be said to founder on the fact that D's conduct was at most merely disinhibited and in no sense compelled. Although self-restraint was made more difficult for D, he seemingly remained in pos-session of sufficient volitional and cognitive resources with which to conform his conduct to law.

The Court of Appeal's decision to excuse D in such circumstances has been plausibly castigated as unprincipled indulgence. Under that court's reasoning, D merely has to adduce evidence that his state of intoxication was involuntary. Unless that evidence is refuted, the prosecution is faced with the onerous task of proving the hypothesis that D, had he been sober, would have committed the offence with which he is charged. A claim that one would not have indulged in some reprehensible conduct but for a state of disinhibition induced by drink or drugs is inherently plausible. Moreover, Lord Taylor, in giving judgment for the Court of Appeal, remarked that involuntary intoxication should be a defence for all crimes of specific or basic intent. In coming to this conclusion, he invoked an analogy with the defence of duress. There is, however, little point of contact between the respective defences apart from the fact that the involuntary intoxication in *Kingston* arose from the machinations of a third party. Duress, of course, arises only for cases of awful dilemma—offend or be killed or seriously hurt—states of psychic compulsion. By contrast, a condition of intoxication falling short of automatism does not make for involuntary conduct, however loosely the term 'invol-untary' is employed. Furthermore, duress is not available if the charge be murder. Although that limitation can be cogently criticized for confusing excuse with justification, granted its

---

[365] [1994] 3 All ER 353.   [366] See also Crosby (2010).

existence, to allow non-automatous involuntary intoxication as an excuse for all crimes would further undermine what coherence there is in the current provision of defences.

Lord Mustill was, with respect, correct in ruling that, taken by itself, a state of involuntary intoxication cannot excuse. In *Kingston*, *mens rea* was present and the conduct uncompelled. There was a powerful case to answer and, *pace* Lord Taylor, it was an insufficient response for D to maintain that he would not have so acted had he not been surreptitiously drugged. Many states of being—anger, apprehension, fatigue, etc.—may arise quite involuntarily and provide a necessary condition for conduct that otherwise would not have occurred. Ordinarily, such destabilization affords no more than mitigation.

Under the Model Penal Code, involuntary intoxication will found a defence to any crime if it deprived the defendant of 'substantial capacity to conform his conduct to law'. Arguably, a significant diminution in the capacity for self-control should excuse completely if the defendant's condition had more affinity with automatism than with a state of mere disinhibition. Absent a clear-cut state of automatism, however, the line is difficult to draw. Many jurisdictions in the United States which formerly used 'substantial capacity to conform conduct to law' as a limb of a Model Penal Code-inspired insanity test have abandoned it because of the impalpable questions to which it gave rise. The House of Lords was well advised to reject this test as a standard for an involuntary intoxication defence.

Nonetheless, there may have been principled reasons sufficient for the House of Lords to have upheld, rather than reversed, the Court of Appeal. An opportunity may have been missed for creative yet appropriate judicial law-making. Whether a defence should have been provided in *Kingston* depends, it will be argued, on conditions which may, or may not, have been present on the facts of that case. As stated already, disinhibition falling short of automatism cannot *of itself* excuse. But if such a condition arose blamelessly and induced conduct which would not otherwise have occurred, this will attenuate to some extent the culpability of the agent. That culpability would be further attenuated, it will be claimed, if, until the incident in question, the defendant had abstained from practising his paedophilia.

All we know of the defendant in *Kingston* is that he was a homosexual with paedophiliac predilections. The formative influences of sexual preference are obscure. In terms of orientation, our sexuality is something that we have rather than something we have made. If we are dealt a card marked for paedophilia, the most that can be asked of us is that we do not put it into play. The card cannot be surrendered and it would be a barbarity to punish for mere possession. Requiring forbearance in a matter so pervasive and unpredictable as sexual expression is to require a great deal, notwithstanding that the protection of a vulnerable class must always be the overriding concern. If a person of paedophiliac inclinations does not practise his paedophilia, he is entitled to that full dignity and respect which is due to all law-abiding citizens. Indeed, he may claim particular credit for sustaining a non-criminal status. If on a particular occasion he becomes blamelessly disinhibited by drugs and loses self-control when confronted with that temptation he otherwise avoids and resists, it is not obvious that the public interest requires him to suffer the total forfeit of credit which a conviction for a stigmatic offence entails.

The particularity of facts such as those related above renders the consequentialist claims of individual and general deterrence uncompelling. Retributivist claims are less clearly settled. It has already been suggested that his blameless state of disequilibrium must count in his favour, even if only as mitigation. It will be argued more fully below that mitigation may be upgraded to excuse if, until this particular occasion, the defendant had refrained from paedophiliac practices. However, were he a practising paedophile his conduct would not constitute an arguably condonable lapse from a standard he was able otherwise to sustain. Then, at most, he would be a candidate for mitigation. If he is, on the basis outlined above, a candidate for an acquittal, he may yet deservedly be convicted if the conduct for which he claims excuse was very grave, for example a killing. We are dealing with uncompelled conduct perpetrated with *mens rea*. In such cases previous good conduct and a blameless state of disequilibrium may be insufficient to outweigh the culpability evinced by a heinous wrong. We are not dealing with excusatory claims which, if made out, invariably sustain a plea for acquittal. It may depend on what it is the defendant has done.

In essence, this paper attempts to found the claim, adumbrated above, that involuntarily intoxicated persons of previous good character and others in similar cases can, if particular conditions be met, be excused for certain crimes. First, however, we should note the view taken by the House of Lords in *Kingston* that such cases are adequately treated by way of mitigation. This standpoint coheres with the unequivocal opinion of Lord Mustill that a conviction for a serious offence need not entail descriptively or prescriptively that the defendant was in any sense at fault. He endorsed a decision of the Privy Council to the effect that an undercover policeman acting with the knowledge and consent of his superiors and without recourse to entrapment or conduct to the prejudice of third parties would be guilty of trafficking in drugs notwithstanding that the 'trafficking' (carrying drugs out of the jurisdiction) was done solely in the interests of law enforcement. It follows that an involuntarily intoxicated person could at most hope for some degree of mitigation—the policeman's conduct seemed justified whereas the cases we are concerned with fall, at most, to be excused.

By contrast with the House of Lords, the view taken here is that a conviction for a stigmatic offence is a sanction in its own right and that sanctions should be confined to the blameworthy. The non-conviction of the blameless should be a pervasive principle of substantive criminal law limited only by the need to theorize and practise criminal law as a system of rules and by the exigencies of forensic practicability. Those limitations entail that many 'normal' life narratives cannot afford grounds of excuse, however exculpatory the force of the narrative may be. But other accounts, not currently represented in standard defences, can be brought within the framework of substantive criminal law. If it can be done it should be done in order to diminish the incidence of unnecessary criminal convictions.

FURTHER READING

Arenella, P. (1992) 'Convicting the Morally Blameless' *University of California Los Angeles Law Review* 39: 1511.

Brooks, T. (2015) 'Involuntary Intoxication: A New Six-Step Procedure' *Journal of Criminal Law* 79: 81.

Herring, J., Regan, C., Weinberg, D., and Withington, P. (eds) (2012) *Intoxication and Society* (Basingstoke: Palgrave Macmillan).

Horder, J. (1993b) 'Pleading Involuntary Lack of Capacity' *Cambridge Law Journal* 52: 298.

23.2 BATTERED WOMEN

What defence, if any, should be available to a woman who kills her sleeping partner following months of violence from him?[367] We shall briefly outline the options that may be available:

(1) **Loss of control** She may seek to argue that she lost her self-control and killed her husband. As we saw in Chapter 5, there can be great difficulties in proving such a

---

[367] Although this is the hypothetical scenario which most commentators discuss, Maguigan's (1991) American research suggests that in fact most battered women kill in the face of an attack.

defence in cases of this kind: most notably proving there was a loss of self-control, that the loss of self-control was 'sudden and temporary', and that the defendant's response was reasonable.[368]

(2) **Diminished responsibility** As discussed in Chapter 5, if the defendant can demonstrate that at the time of the offence she was suffering from an abnormality of mind (e.g. battered women's syndrome (BWS)[369]) she may be able to plead the partial defence of diminished responsibility. Some commentators oppose reliance on this defence, arguing that far from suffering from an abnormal mind the defendant was in fact acting in an entirely reasonable way, given the abuse she had been through.[370] Further, the defence is available only to a charge of murder.

(3) **Duress** It could be argued that she was responding reasonably to a threat of death or serious violence.[371] Dressler,[372] the leading proponent of this view, suggests that the question the law should ask is whether in the face of the threats of violence to come the defendant acted in a reasonable way. Horder[373] argues that duress is inappropriate because there is no threat which the defendant is giving in to and in cases of duress the person who is killed is innocent, which is not so here.

(4) **Self-defence** The woman may seek to claim that she was acting in self-defence to prevent future attacks. Due to his great physical strength she could only realistically prevent herself being attacked when he was asleep. The difficulty in English law in using self-defence is twofold. First, she has difficulty in satisfying the 'requirement' that she was defending herself from an imminent attack.[374] Second, it could be argued that she had the opportunity to escape from any prospective attack (by leaving the home) and therefore the use of violence was not necessary.[375]

In the following extract, Aileen McColgan considers the difficulties battered women face when seeking to use self-defence or other defences:[376]

A. McColgan, 'General Defences' in D. Nicolson and L. Bibbings (eds) *Feminist Perspectives on Criminal Law* (London: Cavendish, 1999), 221–4

I have argued elsewhere that, at least in those cases in which women kill when in fear for their lives, self-defence/justifiable force is more appropriate than either provocation or diminished responsibility.[377] This is partly because it fits the facts of cases when women kill abusive partners out of fear for their lives better than defences premised upon the defendant's rage or mental abnormality. In addition, and by contrast with the partial defences of

---

[368] See further Herring (2011b).

[369] Some commentators are sceptical about whether BWS exists as a syndrome (Loveless 2014).

[370] Coughlin (1998: 70); Shaffer (1997); Allen (1987). Others argue that BWS too easily provides women with a defence (Derschowitz 2000).

[371] Loveless (2014).   [372] Dressler (2002a). For a response to Dressler, see Krause (2007).

[373] Horder (2002a).

[374] Horder (2002a) believes there is no requirement of imminence as such, simply a question whether the defendant was acting reasonably.

[375] Dressler (2010).

[376] See also Herring (2009b: ch. 10); Stubbs and Tolmie (2005); Nourse (2001); McColgan (1993); Zipursky (1996); Fletcher (1996); Ayyildiz (1995).

[377] McColgan (1993).

provocation and diminished responsibility, its successful employment results in an acquittal. Satisfaction of the 'imminence requirement' does not demand immediate threat of attack, but extends to cases in which the threat is not of physical violence itself, but of being placed in a position where escape from such future threatened violence is impossible.

There is every argument that, as a matter of law, many women who kill abusive partners fulfil the 'necessity' requirement of self-defence (of which imminence is a factor). Some would do so on a purely objective test. Others kill in less apparently clear cut circumstances in which, particularly where the woman is not actually being assaulted at the time, some explanation might be required of why she needed to use force. In such cases, evidence of the perceived or actual difficulties of escape from abusive partners would be of benefit to the defence. Women are most likely to suffer fatal attack when they try to escape their abusers and it is almost impossible entirely to disappear from the sight of an abusive partner, not least because the courts generally grant batterers access to their children. Even if a woman's perception of the impossibility or futility of escape was adjudged inaccurate, the proper question is *what* she perceived, rather than whether that perception was reasonable. Where there was any significant doubt about the accuracy of such perception, evidence of BWS could be employed if relevant, as it was in Margaret Howell's case, to support the woman's claim that she regarded escape as impossible. But, in many cases, the danger or futility of attempted escape can be made apparent without resort to expert psychological evidence.

The next question concerns the proportionality of, rather than the necessity for, the force used in self-defence. Margaret Howell may have been convicted of manslaughter because her use of a shotgun was regarded as disproportionate to the threat faced by her. However, any assumption that an armed defence is disproportionate to an unarmed attack overlooks the fact that men are typically much stronger than the women they abuse and that the dozens of women who are killed by their partners every year are most likely to die at their hands, rather than at the receiving end of any other weapon. The irony is that men's ability to kill with their bare hands appears frequently to result in their conviction for manslaughter, rather than murder; prosecutors and juries being more likely to accept that such killings are unintentional or, in any event, less likely to have been premeditated than where weapons are used.

The question of proportionality, like that of necessity, is an objective one. The defendant must, however, be judged on the facts *as she believed them to be*. Evidence that the defendant 'honestly and instinctively' considered her use of force necessary and proportional is to be regarded as 'the most potent evidence' that it actually was.

Domestic violence typically follows a pattern of escalation, with the effect that a woman who has withstood previous assaults may well get to the point where she suspects, on good grounds, that an impending attack may be fatal. Even if (as in some US jurisdictions) a purely objective approach were to be taken, consideration of the typically escalating pattern of domestic violence suggests the accuracy or, at any rate, the reasonableness, of many defendants' perceptions that they had to act in order to avoid an assault of unprecedented severity. Unless we are to condemn many severely abused women to futile (and possibly fatal) attempts to escape their abusers or to passive acceptance of violence which may itself be life-threatening, we must recognize the necessity, on occasion, of using force in self-defence.

The question which arises is why, given the relatively generous contours of the English law of self-defence, so few women who kill their abusive partners manage, apparently regardless of the circumstances of their actions, to secure acquittals. It seems that the difficulty rests not with the formal legal rules, but with informal, almost extra-legal, models of self-defence. These models are constructed in the imagination, owe their contours to 'common sense' or traditional paradigms of human behaviour and operate to block real consideration of situations which, although arguably within the legal defences' contours, do not fit the model. The relative scarcity of female killers has resulted in a paradigmatically male 'ideal model', which requires a spontaneous reaction against an unknown assailant, the defender using only comparable methods of defence (weapon matched to weapon, bare hand to bare hand). Further, aggressive force is incompatible with stereotypical femininity.

The ideal model of self-defence, thus constructed, operates against women, because of their unequal physical size and strength and, in cases of domestic violence, their possible quasi-hostage status. Successful utilisation of the defence will require reconstruction of the ideal model to include women's experience of life and limb-threatening violence.

In the US, where the rules governing self-defence are generally more restrictive than those which prevail in England, substantial numbers of women argue self-defence in relation to the killings of abusive partners. A proportion of those women succeed with the defence. There, lawyers have used evidence that women were suffering from BWS to assist self-defence pleas *by* showing 'the battered woman's perception that danger or great bodily harm [wa]s imminent', sometimes 'in spite of the fact that her battering partner was passive at the time of the offence'. Evidence of BWS has also been used 'to rebut the prosecution's inference that the defendant could have left, rather than kill the spouse' to draw an analogy between the battered woman and a hostage or a prisoner of war and in order to refute prosecution claims that the 'defendant masochistically enjoyed the beatings her ex-husband had given her'.

The increasing use of BWS in the US has proven problematic. Not only have the courts, in general, been prepared to accept BWS evidence only in those cases in which, *independent of it*, the defendant satisfies the (generally very rigorous) requirements for self-defence, but such evidence sometimes serves only to provide another hurdle between the battered woman and acquittal: not only does she have to establish the elements of self-defence in the ordinary way, but she then has also to show that she is properly regarded as suffering from BWS. Where women fail to conform to the stereotypical pattern of the 'battered woman' (where, for example, a woman has defended herself before or was the main breadwinner), this itself appears sufficient to thwart any chance of an acquittal, even where the elements of self-defence appear to be made out.

FURTHER READING

Dressler, J. (2002a) 'Battered Women Who Kill Their Sleeping Tormentors' in S. Shute and A. Simester (eds) *Criminal Law Theory* (Oxford: OUP).

Dressler, J. (2006) 'Descent into Murder: Provocation's Stricture—The Prognosis for Women Who Kill Men Who Abuse Them' *Journal of Criminal Law* 29: 342.

Dressler, J. (2010) 'Feminist (or "Feminist") Reform of Self-defense Law: Some Critical Reflections' *Marquette Law Review* 93: 1475.

Herring, J. (2011b) 'The Serious Wrong of Domestic Abuse and the Loss of Control Defence' in A. Reed and M. Bohlander (eds) *Loss of Control and Diminished Responsibility: Domestic, Comparative and International Perspectives* (London: Ashgate).

Horder, J. (1992) *Provocation and Responsibility* (Oxford: OUP), ch. 9.

Horder, J. (2002a) 'Killing the Passive Abuser: A Theoretical Defence' in S. Shute and A. Simester (eds) *Criminal Law Theory* (Oxford: OUP).

Loveless, J. (2014) 'R. v GAC: Battered Woman "Syndromization"' *Criminal Law Review* 655.

McColgan, A. (1993) 'In Defence of Battered Women Who Kill' *Oxford Journal of Legal Studies* 13: 508.

Maguigan, H. (1991) 'Battered Women and Self-Defense' *University of Pennsylvania Law Review* 140: 379.

Nourse, V. (2014) 'Self-Defense' in M. Dubber and T. Hörnle (eds) *The Oxford Handbook of Criminal Law* (Oxford: OUP).

Rosen, C. (1993) 'On Self-Defense, Imminence, and Women Who Kill Their Batterers' *North Carolina Law Review* 71: 371.

Wake, N. (2013) 'Battered Women, Startled Householders and Psychological Self-Defence: Anglo-Australian Perspectives' *Journal of Criminal Law* 77: 433.

Zipursky, B. (1996) 'Self-Defense, Domination and the Social Contract' *University of Pennsylvania Law Review* 145: 579.

23.3 THE ZEEBRUGGE DISASTER

Is it easy to distinguish between a case of duress and a case of self-defence? At first sight it might be thought that the difference is obvious. Contrast these two cases:

(1) Martin kills Olive who is attacking him.

(2) Penelope kills Quinten after she has been told by Robin that unless she does so she will be killed.

In both cases Martin and Penelope are acting in order to protect their lives. But there is a crucial difference: Olive was not blameless; Quinten was. Hence in English and Welsh law duress is not a defence to murder; self-defence is. The law is said by some to be based on the principle that it cannot be justifiable to take an innocent person's life. But a moment's thought should show that it is not as straightforward as this. Is not a child or an insane person who is attacking not 'innocent'? Even leaving aside these problems, can a clear line be drawn between cases where the victim is or is not posing an unjust threat to the defendant?[378] In the following passage, Fiona Leverick considers a cases which demonstrates that the distinction between self-defence, duress, and necessity is far from straightforward, including an incident that occurred during the Zeebrugge ferry disaster:[379] ←3 (p.633)

F. Leverick, *Killing in Self-Defence* (Oxford: OUP, 2006), 6–11

1.4.1 Distinguishing self-defence and necessity

Self-defence can be distinguished from necessity (or indeed the English defence of duress of circumstances) on the basis that in the case of self-defence the act of the accused is directed towards someone who poses a direct threat to her life or physical integrity, whether

---

[378] Uniacke (1994: 39). For a discussion of whether it would be permissible to shoot down a plane which was full of passengers but being flown into a crowded place, see Bohlander (2006).

[379] See also Horder (1999b) and Alexander (1999).

as an aggressor or passive threat. Thus the defining feature of a claim of self-defence is that it involves defensive force being directed towards the *source* of the threat posed. As Kasachkoff states, '[t]he crucial point here is that for a killing to qualify as a killing in self-defence, it not only must have self-protection as its aim but be directed at the person but for whom we would stand in need of no protection'.

The defence of necessity is a plea by the accused that she broke the law because it was the least harmful of two (or more) alternative courses of action. Like self-defence, the defence of necessity can involve the infliction of harm on a person. Unlike self-defence, this would involve harming a *bystander* who was not posing a direct threat. An example might be the person who kills and eats one of her companions on a shipwreck in order to avoid starving to death. If this were to be recognised as a defence at all, then it would be properly classified as an act of necessity and not one of self-defence, on the basis that the victim posed no direct threat to the life of the accused.

That is not to say that the distinction between self-defence and necessity is always a clear one. There lie difficult cases at the borderline between the two defences, especially where passive threats are concerned. One example is the roped mountaineer, A, who falls off a cliff edge and is left dangling on a rope tied to her companion, B. If B can no longer hold A's weight without falling, and cuts the rope, causing A to fall to her death, opinion has differed on the appropriate defence for B to claim. It is suggested here that this is properly a case of self-defence. In terms of the distinctions above, A is a passive threat and, as such, poses a direct threat to the life of B. She is not culpable for doing so, but the culpability of the threat is not a necessary condition for an act to be classified as one of self-defence.

Other cases are more difficult to classify. For example, evidence was given in the inquest relating to the *Herald of Free Enterprise* disaster that a man, C, stood on a ladder blocking the path to safety of a number of other individuals, who were in freezing water and in danger of drowning. One of those in the water shouted at C, for ten minutes, asking him to move, but, when C did not, he instructed one of the other passengers to push C into the water where, it was presumed, C drowned.

The coroner described this as 'a reasonable act of self-preservation' but did not comment on whether the appropriate defence in these circumstances would be self-defence or necessity. The categorization was of considerable importance, given that while self-defence was accepted in English law as a complete defence to murder, necessity was not. The most appropriate classification is probably one of necessity, as the man might properly be regarded not as a direct threat, but as a bystander (the direct threat being the rising water), but this is by no means an obvious conclusion.

Another difficult case is that of the conjoined twins in *Re: A (Children)*. Here, two babies, named Mary and Jodie for the purposes of reporting the case, were born with a shared heart. In any operation to separate them, only Jodie, the stronger of the two, could survive. If separation did not take place, both twins would eventually die. The Court of Appeal was asked to rule on whether the separation of the twins would be lawful. The relevant issue is the nature of any defence the doctors undertaking the separation would have to a charge of Mary's murder, given that at least two members of the court accepted that performing the operation would involve the intentional killing of Mary.

One member of the court, Ward LJ, identified the appropriate defence as self-defence, whereas another, Brooke LJ, analysed the case in terms of necessity. Uniacke has doubted that the case is one of self-defence, on the basis that for Mary to be a direct threat to Jodie, there needs to be some prior position of Jodie's that Mary directly threatened. As the twins were born conjoined, Uniacke argues, it is difficult to think of what this prior position might be. This is not regarded here as a meaningful basis upon which to rule out the defence of self-defence. The threat that Mary posed to Jodie seems little different in nature to the passive but direct threat posed to the mountaineer by her roped companion and I would suggest that both *are* best classified as cases of self-defence. Regardless of the conclusion reached, what *Re: A (Children)* and the other cases discussed above demonstrate is the difficulty of distinguishing clearly between self-defence and necessity in cases that lie close to the borderline.

1.4.2 Distinguishing self-defence from duress

Distinguishing self-defence from duress is comparatively straightforward. Here, the distinction lies in the nature of the act undertaken by the accused. In a case of self-defence, the accused avoids harm by *warding off* or *blocking* a threat. In a case of duress, the accused avoids harm by *complying with the demands* of the threatener. For example, the accused, A, is threatened with death, by B, unless she commits theft. If A complies with the threat (and commits the theft), her act is one committed under duress. If A wards off the threat of death (for example by disabling or killing B), her act is one of self-defence.

This relatively clear-cut distinction has not stopped some from confusing acts of self-defence with acts committed under duress. Dressler, for example, has suggested that a battered woman acts under duress when she kills her violent partner while he is sleeping, in order to avoid future violence. This is on the basis that she chose to engage in conduct (killing her abusive partner) because she was coerced to do so by another person's (the abuser's) threat of future force. As Horder points out, this simply does not have the gist of a claim of duress. The battered woman is not complying with a demand issued by her partner, or indeed any other person. Her claim is closer to one of self-defence, although it is unlikely that she will be able to satisfy the conditions of the defence.

It is sometimes suggested that a further distinction can be made between self-defence and duress, based on the status of the victim. That is, in cases of self-defence, the accused harms someone who was a direct threat to her life or bodily integrity, whereas in cases of duress, the accused harms an innocent victim who was *not* the source of the threat. While this is undoubtedly true in the vast majority of claims of duress involving harm to a victim, it is not a necessary feature of the defence. It is possible to envisage a scenario where the person issuing the threats demands that the accused harms not an innocent victim, but the threatener herself. The threat from A that, unless B cuts off A's leg, A will kill B is an example of this nature.

1.4.3 A unified defence of 'necessary action'?

These conceptual distinctions have not prevented Clarkson from arguing that the defences of self-defence, necessity and duress should be brought together under a unified defence (termed 'necessary action') governed by the same rules. For Clarkson:

> . . . what unites these actions is more important than what separates them. In all of them a defendant is committing a prima facie wrong in order to avoid some sort of crisis. To protect herself and/or other persons the defendant is committing what would otherwise be a crime and the true issue is how the law should respond to these actions and in what circumstances it should afford a defence.

While it is true that the defences have much in common, there is nonetheless something to be said for treating necessity, duress, and self-defence as distinct defences.

Self-defence differs from necessity and duress in that it always involves action against one or more persons who pose a *direct threat* to life or bodily integrity. This fact alone is sufficient reason for having a set of distinct rules; distinct, that is, from those governing necessity and duress, where the victim, if indeed there was one, would not generally have posed such a threat. The most obvious example relates to whether or not the defence can be pled to a charge of murder. This is generally accepted in relation to self-defence *because* the murder victim was herself a direct threat to the life of the accused, but it is extremely controversial in relation to necessity and duress, where any victim was likely to have been an innocent bystander. Likewise, the public policy issues relating to each of the defences are not identical. For example, there is an argument for placing more stringent restrictions on duress than on the other two defences because of the risk that the defence is abused by terrorist groups or other criminal organizations. Indeed, this was precisely the reason given by the House of Lords in *R v Hasan* for imposing stricter conditions on the defence of duress (where the defendant is judged according to an objective test) than on the defence of self-defence (where a subjective test is applied).

Aside from anything else, there is an argument to be made for conceptual separation of the three defences on the grounds of fair labelling. The accused is surely entitled to the nature of her defensive act being labelled as accurately as possible by the courts, rather than subsumed under a general heading of 'necessary defence', because she may be morally judged by society on the basis of this label. 'I did this in self-defence' (a justification defence and thus a claim that her behaviour was acceptable) reflects more favourably on the accused than 'I did this under duress' (most commonly an excuse defence and thus a claim that her behaviour was unacceptable but not blameworthy).

FURTHER READING

Chan, W. and Simester, A. (2005) 'Duress, Necessity: How Many Defences?' *King's College Law Journal* 16: 121.

Horder, J. (1998b) 'Self-Defence, Necessity and Duress: Understanding the Relationship' *Canadian Journal of Law and Jurisprudence* 11: 143.

Leverick, F. (2006) *Killing in Self-Defence* (Oxford: OUP).

QUESTIONS

1. Is it possible to distinguish justifications and excuses? Is it useful to do so?

2. Does the choice or character theory better explain the defence of duress?

3. Are there any good reasons for not permitting duress as a defence to murder? For a discussion of this, see Arenson (2014).

4. Should any defence be available to a woman who kills a partner who has been persistently abusive to her? Which defence should it be?

5. If the Zeebrugge disaster case had come before the courts would any defence be available to the person who pushed the deceased off the ladder?

6. Quick and Wells (2006: 524) write: 'Domestic violence is about power and control. Male killing is about power and control. Women killing abusers is about avoiding

power and control.' Should greater account of the gender of the defendant be taken when considering the availability of defences?

7. If A, a racist, believes that B is about to attack him simply because of B's race, and A uses force in self-defence against B, should A have a defence? Some commentators argue not, because the law should demonstrate its opposition to racism. Others (e.g. Gravey (2008)) argue that to do so would be to punish A for his beliefs, rather than the wrongfulness of his conduct. What do you think?

24 CONCLUDING THOUGHTS

The fact that criminal law needs to have defences demonstrates that it is not possible to rely on *mens rea* and *actus reus* alone to obtain a complete assessment of the defendant's blameworthiness. The defences ensure that those who do not deserve the full censure of a criminal conviction escape it. However, the questions raised by the defences are complex and raise difficult political and moral questions. Some raise the issue of the extent to which the defendant is to be blamed for what has happened. Other defences raise the question of whether there may be occasions on which the defendant acted in an appropriate way in committing what would otherwise be a crime. The courts have strived to keep these defences within clear boundaries, for fear that otherwise they will provide too ready a way to escape from a criminal charge.

THE CRIMINAL LIABILITY OF CORPORATIONS

CENTRAL ISSUES

1. The Corporate Manslaughter and Corporate Homicide Act 2007 created a new offence of corporate manslaughter. This can be committed where the way in which a company's activities are managed or organized amounts to a gross negligence and causes someone's death.

2. In a limited number of crimes, a company can be guilty in respect of the acts of one of its employees under the doctrine of vicarious liability.

PART I: THE LAW ON CORPORATE CRIMINALITY

1 THE DIFFICULTY IN CONVICTING COMPANIES OF CRIMES

In recent years there has been increasing interest in convicting companies of crimes following tragedies including the Ladbroke Grove railway crash, the Zeebrugge ferry disaster, and the King's Cross fire. In particular, it has been felt that some of these awful events have been caused by the actions not just of an individual but of a whole company. It is felt that awarding damages in a civil case fails to recognize the severity of wrong that the company as a whole did towards the victims.

Imagine that a train passes through a red light, and as a result there is a crash. It might be easy simply to see the case as one where the train driver should be held responsible and that is the end of the story. However, such an approach may not pay attention to the fault of the train company in ensuring that signals were placed where they were clearly visible to drivers, or in having safety mechanisms on trains that inhibited drivers from passing through red lights.[1] To dismiss the crash as 'just the train driver's fault' would be to take a very narrow view of who is responsible for the accident. It is not difficult to imagine a case where the employee who directly caused the harm was less responsible than the managers who failed to install appropriate safety mechanisms.[2] →1 (p.752)

Despite the demands for criminal liability there are difficulties in explaining how a company can be guilty of a criminal offence. The company is a legal person,[3] separate from its directors and its shareholders, but there is a real problem in explaining how a company can be said to act or have *mens rea*. For some offences there is no difficulty in convicting a company because Parliament expressly provides for this.[4]

However, where there is no such provision, the courts have attempted to manipulate the concepts of *mens rea* and *actus reus*, as traditionally understood, so that it is possible to say that a company caused a result or intended or foresaw a consequence.

2   CORPORATE KILLING

The Corporate Manslaughter and Corporate Homicide Act 2007 created a new offence of corporate manslaughter.[5] The offence is defined in section 1(1):

> An organisation to which this section applies is guilty of an offence if the way in which its activities are managed or organised—
>
> (a) causes a person's death, and
>
> (b) amounts to a gross breach of a relevant duty of care owed by the organisation to the deceased.

The offence can be committed not only by companies but other bodies, including the police force and trade unions. The penalty is a fine.[6] The offence requires proof of a number of elements. →2 (p.752)

There must be a duty of care owed by the organization to the deceased. In section 2 this phrase is defined as referring to the duty of care in the law of tort.[7] However, sections 3 to 7 exclude certain activities from falling within the offence; these include decisions concerning military operations, policing, and child protection.

There must be a breach of the duty of care which is gross. Section 1(4)(b) explains that the breach will be gross 'if the conduct alleged to amount to a breach of that duty falls far below what can reasonably be expected of the organisation in the circumstances.' Further

---

[1] Reason (1997: 9). See Harding (2007) for a broader discussion of how individual and corporate responsibilities relate.

[2] Wells (2001: 161–3).

[3] The Interpretation Act 1978, s. 5 and Sch. 1 state that unless a contrary intention appears in every Act of Parliament 'person' includes (inter alia) a corporation.

[4] e.g. Theft Act 1968, s. 18.

[5] The offence of corporate homicide in the title applies only to Scotland. See Gobert (2008) and Ormerod and Taylor (2008) for useful discussions of the Act.

[6] The court can also order the company to take remedial steps in an attempt to ensure the breach does not reoccur (s. 9). See Davies (2010) for a discussion of sentencing under the Act.

[7] The duty of care can arise from the general principles of negligence or from the fact the organization is an employer or occupier of premises. Section 2(6) makes it clear that some of the special tort rules (e.g. *ex turpi causa* and *volenti non fit injuria*) will not apply.

guidance is provided by section 8 which sets out factors a jury should consider when looking at the 'gross' issue:

> (2) The jury must consider whether the evidence shows that the organisation failed to comply with any health and safety legislation that relates to the alleged breach, and if so—
>
> (a) how serious that failure was;
>
> (b) how much of a risk of death it posed.
>
> (3) The jury may also—
>
> (a) consider the extent to which the evidence shows that there were attitudes, policies, systems or accepted practices within the organisation that were likely to have encouraged any such failure as is mentioned in subsection (2), or to have produced tolerance of it;
>
> (b) have regard to any health and safety guidance that relates to the alleged breach.

It must be shown that the gross breach of the duty caused the death. Section 1(3) makes clear that an organization will only be guilty if 'the way in which its activities are managed or organised by its senior management is a substantial element in the breach.' This is an extremely important limitation on the scope of the offence. Often in corporate accidents although a junior employee may be found to have been clearly at fault it is harder to show that the management is responsible.

The phrase 'senior management' is defined in section 1(4)(c) as

> the persons who play significant roles in—
>
> (i) the making of decisions about how the whole or a substantial part of its activities are to be managed or organised, or
>
> (ii) the actual managing or organising of the whole or a substantial part of those activities.

A person may be regarded as the 'mind' of the company but still not responsible for making decisions about or actually organizing how the activities of the company are to be carried out. But clearly the acts of a low ranking employee with no decision-making authority cannot form the basis of a corporate manslaughter conviction.[8] Note also that it is not necessary under the Act to point to a particular individual who has been negligent. The prosecution can claim that the management as a group made decisions which were far below the standard that could be expected of the organization. Celia Wells,[9] however, complains that 'By requiring the "substantial" involvement of "senior management" and then defining this body as "those persons who play significant roles" the Act gives the lie to the Government's claimed commitment to an organisational version of fault that is not dependent on the actions of specified individuals.'

Since its enactment in 2007 there had been only three prosecutions by the end of 2012.[10] The three cases resulted in fines of £385,000, £187,500, and £480,000. This has led some commentators to question the extent to which the law is being properly enforced.[11]

---

[8] Note that an individual employee cannot be charged as an accessory to corporate manslaughter. See Gobert (2008) for a concern that the responsibility of individual managers is watered down by the Act.

[9] Wells (2014).

[10] *R v Cotswold Geotechnical Holdings Ltd* [2011] EWCA Crim 1337 is the only one reported fully.

[11] Slapper (2013).

FURTHER READING

Dobson, A. (2012) 'Shifting Sands: Multiple Counts in Prosecutions for Corporate Manslaughter' *Criminal Law Review* 200.

Glazebrook, P. (2002) 'A Better Way of Convicting Businesses of Avoiding Deaths and Injuries?' *Cambridge Law Journal* 61: 405.

Gobert, J. (2008) 'The Corporate Manslaughter and Corporate Homicide Act 2007—Thirteen Years in the Making but was It Worth the Wait?' *Modern Law Review* 71: 413.

Ormerod, D. and Taylor, R. (2008) 'The Corporate Manslaughter and Corporate Homicide Act 2007' *Criminal Law Review* 589.

Price, L. (2015) 'Finding Fault in Organisations—Reconceptualising the Role of Senior Managers in Corporate Manslaughter' *Legal Studies* 38: 385.

Wells, C. (2014) 'Corporate Criminal Liability: A Ten Year Review' *Criminal Law Review* 849.

3 VICARIOUS LIABILITY

3.1 WHAT IS VICARIOUS LIABILITY?

Normally a person is not liable in criminal law for the acts of another. One important exception to this rule is vicarious liability where the act, and in some cases even the *mens rea*, of another person is imputed to the defendant.[12] The defendant's conviction does not rest on anything said or done by the defendant, but on the acts and mental state of another. Vicarious liability is therefore different from accessorial liability (see Chapter 15), where a defendant's guilt flows from his or her acts of assistance to someone who goes on to commit the offence.

3.2 WHICH CRIMES CAN BE COMMITTED VICARIOUSLY?

Most vicarious liability operates where the offence is one of strict liability, but it is not limited to such crimes.[13] Whether an offence can be committed vicariously is a matter of statutory interpretation for each particular offence.[14] Sometimes the statute explicitly makes the offence one of vicarious liability (e.g. where the statute states that the defendant is guilty if he 'or by his servant or agent sell . . .'[15]). However, the court may decide by implication that the offence is one of vicarious liability.[16] The court is likely to do this if it thinks that the imposition of vicarious liability is necessary to give effect to legislation. Commonly in offences which involve the selling of goods the courts have interpreted the word 'sell' to include an employee selling, this being seen as giving the word 'sell' its normal meaning.[17] So in *Tesco Stores Ltd v Brent LBC*[18] it was held that Tesco Ltd had 'supplied'

---

[12] See also Gelsthorpe and Morris (1999) and the discussion of the circumstances in which a parent can be liable for the crimes of his or her children.

[13] *Tesco v Nattrass* [1972] AC 153 (HL).

[14] *Seaboard Offshore v Secretary of State for Transport* [1994] 1 WLR 541 (HL).

[15] Licensing Act 1964, s. 59(1).

[16] *Mousell Bros v London and North Western Rwy* [1917] 2 KB 836.

[17] *Coppen v Moore (No. 2)* [1898] 2 QB 306.   [18] [1993] 2 All ER 718.

an 18-rated video to a child, although, of course, the video was actually supplied by the check-out assistant. Similarly, it has been held that an employer is in possession of goods which his employee possesses in the course of his or her employment[19] and uses a car that his employee uses at work.[20] However, it has been held that driving cannot be committed vicariously: only the person in the driving seat can drive the car.[21] It appears that a defendant cannot be guilty for an attempt[22] or, as an accessory, vicariously.[23]

3.3 FOR WHOSE ACT CAN THE DEFENDANT BE VICARIOUSLY LIABLE?

If the offence is one that can be committed vicariously then the accused is responsible for the acts of anyone employed by him or authorized to act as his agent.[24] The accused will be vicariously liable only for an employee or agent who is acting within the scope of his or her employment. For example, in *Adams v Camfoni*[25] it was held that a licensee was not guilty of selling alcohol outside the permitted hours when his messenger boy (who had no authority to sell alcohol) had done so.

3.4 WHAT *MENS REA* MUST BE PROVED?

Normally, where an offence which requires *mens rea* is committed vicariously then the defendant himself must be proved to have that *mens rea*. So if the offence requires knowledge and the act is performed by an agent or employee it must be shown that the accused knew his employee or agent was doing that act. There appears to be one exception to this and that is where the defendant has delegated responsibility to an agent. In that case the *mens rea* of the agent can be transferred to the defendant. The House of Lords in *Vane v Yiannopoullos*[26] doubted the acceptability of transferring the *mens rea* from the employee and agent. In that case a waitress sold wine contrary to the conditions of a restaurant licence, while the accused, the licence holder, was on the premises. It was suggested that the *mens rea* of an employee could only be ascribed to the accused in a case of complete delegation: where the accused employs a person to stand fully in his shoes.[27] This has become known as the 'delegation principle'. However, in *Allen v Whitehead*[28] the owner of a café was convicted of knowingly 'permitting or suffering' prostitutes to meet at his premises. The owner in fact visited the café only once or twice a week, but he had installed a manager to look after the premises. The manager was aware the prostitutes were gathering at the café. The owner was held to have appointed the manager, not just as a person to serve drinks, but as his representative as the person in charge of the café. The owner had therefore delegated responsibility to the manager and so the manager's knowledge could be imputed to the owner. This case was distinguished from *Vane v Yiannopoullos* where the waitress could not be said to be representing the defendant, who indeed was present on the premises.

[19] *Melias Ltd v Preston* [1957] 2 QB 380 (CA).   [20] *Green v Burnett* [1955] 1 QB 78.
[21] *Thornton v Mitchell* [1940] 1 All ER 339.   [22] *Gardner v Akeroyd* [1952] 2 QB 743.
[23] *Ferguson v Weaving* [1951] 1 KB 814.
[24] *Quality Dairies (York) Ltd v Pedley* [1952] 1 KB 275.   [25] [1929] 1 KB 95.
[26] [1965] AC 486.   [27] Followed in *Winson* [1969] 1 QB 371.   [28] [1930] 1 KB 211.

PART II: THE THEORY OF CORPORATE LIABILITY

4 THEORETICAL ISSUES IN CORPORATE LIABILITY

4.1 THE REALITY OF CORPORATE CRIME

The Health and Safety Executive reports that for the year 2014/15 there were 142 fatal injuries to employees in the workplace and there were 77,593,000 injuries in the workplace.[29]

The Health and Safety Executive prosecuted 582 cases and were successful in 547 cases. That is a very high success rate.[30] The normal punishment was a fine with the average being a penalty of £18,944 per offence. Following the Southall rail disaster, which led to seven deaths, a £1.5 million fine was imposed.[31]

It is, perhaps, not surprising that the courts have been reluctant to impose huge fines. In the case of companies running public services there is a concern that such a fine in reality simply means that less is spent on improving those services.[32] If it is a public company it may be that those who really suffer are junior employees and shareholders, and not the senior management, who may be truly to blame.[33] ←1 (p.748)

The Law Commission[34] has produced a report on the use of the criminal law in areas of regulatory enforcement and corporate criminal liability. It encourages regulators to only use criminal law as a last resort. The criminal law should be used to deal with wrong-doers who deserve the stigma of punishment and criminal conviction, rather than using it whenever it is effective as a way of enforcing regulatory offences. Indeed they suggest many regulatory offences could be replaced with civil penalties.

4.2 THE CLAMOUR FOR CORPORATE LIABILITY

It is only in recent years that concerns about corporate killing have led to calls for companies to be criminally liable. In the following excerpt, Nicola Lacey considers why it is that interest in corporate crime has grown: ←2 (p.748)

N. Lacey, ' "Philosophical Foundations of the Common Law": Social Not Metaphysical' in J. Horder (ed.) *Oxford Essays in Jurisprudence* (Oxford: OUP, 2000), 33–5

Four main cultural arguments have been advanced to explain the recent steps towards recognition of corporate manslaughter. The first argument has to do with technological

---

[29] Health and Safety Executive (2015).　　[30] *Ibid.*

[31] See Baldwin (2004) and Almond (2014) for an argument that the government enforcement of regulations is becoming stricter.

[32] It should not be forgotten that companies are often the victims of crime (Gobert and Punch 2003: ch. 1).

[33] Norrie (1991: 101). Gobert (1998) and Fisse (1990) look at the options for punishing companies.

[34] Law Commission (2010a).

change: the growth of technology is argued to have increased the scope for huge disasters which cause so much harm that there is bound to be a strong social reaction. This change is reinforced, secondly, by developments in mass communications: where such disasters occur, everyone knows about them. Perhaps partly as a result of these two factors, sociologists have also noted a change, thirdly, in attitudes to both risk and responsibility. In the modern world, we are unwilling to ascribe tragedies to fate, chance, the gods; our scientific world view makes us look for causes, and in particular for causal agencies to which we can attribute responsibility—notably human beings. We assume that where such causes can be found, this implies that disasters were avoidable; and this makes us willing to attribute blame. This has led some sociologists to argue that in the late modern world, we become increasingly aware of failings which are proximate to the event but also systemic failings in the corporation's rules and procedures developed over a period of time.

In cases such as the *Herald* sinking, it is then argued that the relative importance of these systemic failings as compared with reckless or negligent individual acts or omissions proximate to the event renders the exclusive prosecution of junior employees who are often most directly involved unfair. Significantly, the Crown Prosecution Service recently proceeded against not only the train driver but also Great Western Trains in pursuing a manslaughter prosecution following the 1997 Southall rail disaster in which seven people were killed. Notwithstanding the fact that the corporate manslaughter charge was dismissed by the trial judge, the Crown Prosecution Service decision, as well as public reaction to the charge's dismissal, appear to signify the emergence of a social sense of corporate responsibility which is not a derivative of individually blameworthy acts. This development does not, of course, determine the normative question whether corporations *should* be held liable in criminal law. But it directly raises the question whether law *could* develop a conceptual framework for corporate liability presupposing a model of the firm which, though avoiding the metaphysical and anthropomorphic mystifications of the 'real entity' theory, goes beyond the 'aggregate/contractual' model to recognize both firms' distinctive capacity for collective action and citizens' interpretation of firms as autonomous and distinctive collectivities operating in the social world and oriented to risk, yet also increasingly intolerant of it. Finally, both the growing social significance of corporations and increasing public knowledge of their operations, as reflected by, for example, levels of media reporting, have engendered a willingness to blame collectivities as well as individuals. Hence we seem to be witnessing the emergence of (or perhaps a return to) a social construction of corporations as bodies who can be genuinely blameworthy, and whom it is both fair and appropriate to hold directly responsible for crime. The close analysis of how disasters such as the *Herald* sinking occur tend to illuminate the diffusion of responsibility and—as in the case of Sheen J's inquiry—single out not only individuals.

4.3 SHOULD A COMPANY BE GUILTY OF A CRIME?

A company is regarded as a person in the eyes of the law.[35] It is able therefore to enter contracts and commit torts. But should it be liable for committing a criminal offence? The arguments over this issue can be divided into those that focus on the practical benefits or disadvantages of corporate liability and those that consider the issue from a more theoretical perspective.

---

[35] Wells (2001: ch. 5) provides a useful history of corporate liability within the UK.

Practical issues

On the one side of the argument there are those who argue that if companies are made criminally liable for deaths or serious harms this will create a strong incentive on corporate managers to ensure that adequate safety systems are properly in place and adhered to.[36] However, to others regulation and non-criminal sanctions will be a more effective means of improving safety standards in corporate enterprise than the criminal law.[37] In particular it is claimed that companies will be more willing to own up to mistakes that have been made and open to discussion about safety problems if the stick of a criminal penalty is not held over them.[38]

Can companies be morally responsible?

Much of the debate over whether companies should be found guilty of serious criminal offences has centred on the question: Are companies morally responsible for their actions?[39] Bob Sullivan has challenged the theoretical basis for imposing corporate liability, arguing that companies are not 'moral agents' who can be held morally responsible for their actions.[40] However, he argues this does not mean that companies cannot be held criminally responsible. Those who reject arguments of the kind Sullivan makes suggest that companies do have an existence that is distinct from any identifiable employee.[41] It is possible, they argue, for companies to develop a 'corporate ethos'[42] (e.g. that safety issues are (or are not) important) which cannot be traced to a single person or group of people. It is therefore fair to hold a company morally responsible for its acts.[43] It is also possible to argue that even if not morally responsible a company can be held liable if to do so promotes another important aim of the criminal law: the avoidance of harm.[44]

4.4 IF THERE IS TO BE CORPORATE CRIME, WHAT FORM SHOULD IT TAKE?

If the law is to make companies liable for their crimes then the next question is what form should that take.[45] One option would be to use the present offences, but develop ways of finding that the company has a *mens rea* or can commit an *actus reus*. Theories such as the aggregation theory attempt to do this. Another would be to reject the idea that a company can be made to be like a person[46] and to pass legislation which creates specific corporate crimes, of the kind the government has enacted.

In the following extract, Celia Wells considers some of the alternative forms that corporate criminal liability could take:

---

[36] Lacey (2000b).   [37] Simpson (2002). See Almond (2014) for a detailed discussion.
[38] Khanna (1996).   [39] Stewart (2012).   [40] Sullivan (1996b). See also Wolf (1985).
[41] Certainly the notion of corporate crime appears to be gaining in acceptability among the general public. See generally the discussion in White and Haines (2000: 7) on the role of the media in defining crime.
[42] Bucy (1991).
[43] Wells (2001: 65); Gobert and Punch (2003: 46–9); French (1984). For a discussion of how a company can be seen as an actor, see Coleman (1974).
[44] Gobert and Punch (2003: 47).   [45] Lacey (2000b).   [46] Wells (2001: 71).

C. Wells, *Corporations and Criminal Responsibility* (2nd edn, Oxford: OUP, 2001), 154–60

3. People, Systems, and Culture

In the arguments about the appropriate basis for corporate criminal liability two distinct strands emerge. One line seeks to equate the corporate entity with the individual, to tease out those characteristics of corporations which can be correlated with the essence of individual responsibility. The other exploits the dissimilarities between individuals and the group entity. Corporations are different from human beings, their activities are not merely on a grander scale, their whole existence, function, and formation marks them apart. The contours of their culpability should reflect those differences. Although either route can lead to corporate liability, the second has more potential. Any argument which seeks to equiparate corporate with individual liability has to confront the group difference at some point; efforts to bring out corporate intentionality from corporate policy need to face the complexities of group structures with their lines of authority and internal power distributions. At the same time, the idea that humans are atomistic individuals acting without reference to the groups of which they are a part is unhelpful.

With the concentration on the group/individual comparison, it is easy to lose sight of the culpability criterion itself. Much of the corporate crime literature makes false assumptions about the nature of criminal fault requirements; commentators use 'intention' without acknowledging the alternative of recklessness. Debate about how best to capture corporate responsibility is often hampered by a failure to distinguish between culpability criteria such as intention and recklessness. This applies as much to discussions of aggregation as to other proposals introduced below. Aggregation is often conceived as a collective 'knowledge'. An attitudinal rather than a cognitive version of recklessness facilitates the attribution of blame to the corporate entity. Recklessness can be found in the practical indifference, the attitude, which an action manifests. A corporate action can be said to display such an indifference when it results from the decisions of its responsible officers. It is necessary then to adjust perceptions not only of groups and of individuals but also of culpability criteria; by so doing it is possible to emerge with a strengthened theory of corporate 'intentionality'. A theory which makes the corporation responsible for itself is also required. The two organizational models of organizational process and bureaucratic process lead to the recognition that responsibility can be found either in the individual corporate worker *or* in the corporate structure itself. The latter can have a number of forms, ranging from aggregate knowledge to full-blown corporate culture liability. It can also embrace compliance.

i. Extending Identification

Since it is proposed that this second holistic type of liability should be additional and not a substitute for derivative forms, it is necessary first to consider whether the current form of identification liability for *mens rea* offences is broad enough in scope. Many commentators regard the *respondeat superior* doctrine which has developed in the US federal courts as too wide for *mens rea* offences; conversely, the UK direct liability scheme is seen as too narrow. There are strong arguments in favour of extending identification so that the corporation is liable for the crimes of those with responsibility for particular spheres. Under the 'responsible officer' theory regional managers, for example, would be included. This is already reflected in Canadian law; as Schroeder J. put it in one case: 'He may have been but a satellite to a major planet, but his position in the galaxy was not an inferior one.' French proposes a test that at least includes anyone with a 'significant degree of autonomy with regard to making corporate decisions and instigating corporate actions'. The identification rule should reflect actual responsibility rather than formal duty.

ii. Aggregation

The aggregation of employees' knowledge means that corporate culpability does not have to be contingent on one individual employee's satisfying the relevant culpability criterion. Aggregation straddles agency and holistic forms of liability. It is used in the United States but has been rejected in English corporate manslaughter cases. Conceptually or epistemologically the notion of aggregation is problematic if it is taken to mean that the fragmented knowledge of a number of individuals is fitted together to make one culpable whole. This is less of a problem in offences based on recklessness where recklessness is conceived in terms of practical indifference. But even if the knowledge-of-risk model of recklessness were adopted, the difficulties could be overcome. Aggregation needs to be seen as a recognition that individuals within a company contribute to the whole machine; it is the whole which is judged, not the parts. So the question would not be whether employee X's knowledge plus employee Y's knowledge *added up* to recklessness or whatever, but whether, given the information held amongst a number of 'responsible officers', it can be said that the corporation itself was reckless. This is no more demanding a feat of the imagination than that required by so-called subjective mental states when the court determines by what can only be a matter of guesswork whether a defendant actually foresaw a risk or actually intended a result.

iii. Going Holistic

The images of the organization emerging from the discussion in section 1 suggest that a pure form of holistic liability is appropriate. Corporations can be seen as diverse and heterogeneous both within and amongst themselves, but with a core structure through which management exerts or attempts to exert control both over objectives and over attainment. The anthropomorphic image infusing much legal discourse is unhelpful if it is taken to imply that the mind cannot be responsible for the body. But in other ways the physiological metaphor could be used as the basis for a form of liability which better reflects the reality of the corporate organization. Corporate liability in the United Kingdom assumes that only a select few officers exert control or have any managerial autonomy over aspects of the enterprise for which they work. This does not seem borne out by theories of organizations. Thus a widening of primary liability would be indicated. We do not imagine that we are transacting with the managing director of Marks and Spencer when we shop there, nor that when a plane takes off the airline's board of directors has specific knowledge of its activities, route, or condition that day. We do, however, expect that large companies operate according to a set of rules and procedures and that these, particularly in relation to public transport systems, have addressed the potential risks and developed safety procedures to ensure that those risks are minimized.

The two organizational models referred to earlier, those of organizational process and bureaucratic process, suggest that a scheme of corporate liability should recognize that responsibility can both flow from the individual to the corporation and be found in the corporation's structures themselves. Current liability reflects the first: the corporation can be vicariously or directly liable for the wrongdoing of individuals within it. The second goes further and demands that liability be placed on the corporation in some instances even though no identifiable individual has committed an offence. This rejects the conventional analysis of identification liability as the only way in which a corporation can be said to act directly and knowingly, supplementing it with the notion that *the corporation* can be responsible for *the corporation's activities*.

Tigar advances the following arguments for a broader starting point. The first is the familiar one that identification is based on unwarranted assumptions about corporate managerial behaviour. Rules of liability should encourage management to have a preventive system: 'Broad rules of corporate criminal liability shape [the corporation's internal culture] towards law-abiding behaviour at all levels of the structure.' Secondly, a point which was mentioned in Chapter 2, the operation of collateral estoppel: corporate liability is a means of promoting, encouraging, and facilitating civil recovery which would otherwise be inaccessible. And lastly, if the only route to criminal liability is through the complicity or acquiescence of top management, then every corporate guilty plea puts management at serious risk of suit by shareholders. Another point can be added, which is that the narrower the system of liability, the more it favours larger enterprises: smaller companies have fewer bureaucratic layers and differentiate less between managerial and operational roles. Reliance on an identification model, even with a lower threshold of 'responsible officer', is insufficient. Concentration on the misdeeds of managerial officers ignores the reality of corporate decision-making. It is clear from what we know of the way large corporations organize themselves that power is both dispersed (within a clear structure) and that this is mediated by informal rules and rivalries. The identification doctrine applied to diffuse corporate structures can result in no one being liable, or improperly reflect the limits of moral responsibility. Management priorities set from above 'determine the social context within which a corporation's shop-floor workers make decisions about working practices'.

French has provided a philosophical model through which to justify the imposition of liability on a company for the actions of its subordinate members. A corporation's internal decision structures, its CIDs, are seen as incorporating recognition rules. A CID structure has three elements: an organizational flow-chart, procedural rules, and policies. The first provides the 'grammar' of the corporation, while the last two are 'corporate decision recognition rules'. Corporations then are mini-jurisdictions and their operating policies are broad, general principles. Where the corporate CID structure has contributed to the realization of a risk, an appropriate legal mechanism should be found in response. Again, organization theories reinforce the argument by showing that corporations usually have detailed configurations which place responsibility for specific aspects on different departments. Internal structure and culture affect a company's actions. While some corporate harms are caused by senior management (individually or collectively) engaging knowingly in fraudulent activity or acting recklessly in the sense described above, many occur through a system failure. The relevant question would then be whether the corporation can be blamed because its system, its operating policies, displayed a reckless attitude to safety. P&O's culpability in relation to the Zeebrugge tragedy provides an instructive example. In that case, the relevant issue was the company's failure to develop a safety policy, which was both a cause of the capsize and a large contributory factor in the failure of the prosecution. The very failures which caused the accident allowed the company to slip through the net of responsibility.

Once the idea that a corporation's fault can be approached through its policies is established, refinements such as compliance or reactive fault can be introduced. CIDs can be used both to lead a corporation towards liability but also to give it the opportunity to escape. The corporation should be able to rebut the attribution of corporate responsibility to any act of its high managerial staff on the grounds that it is against established internal policy. Such a defence will not be easy to mount because it will need evidence of the policy plus a lack of any previous examples whereby it has condoned similar failures: in other words, evidence that the illegal conduct was clearly and convincingly forbidden and of the development and implementation of reasonable safeguards designed to prevent corporate crime. Providing the equivalent of a due diligence defence may also counter those who oppose an extension of identification liability beyond the higher directorial echelons. Liability based either, as just discussed, on the company's structures, or on the wrongdoings of any of its employees, could be rebutted by proving that, as an organization, it exercised due diligence to prevent the crime. If the acts of top officials represent the practices and procedures of the corporation, their involvement in corporate criminal activity should almost always defeat a due diligence defence. This could amount to an effective deterrent, since the affirmative defence of due diligence would have to be preceded by the adoption of stringent procedures to combat illegal activity.

This would be a clear recognition that an act is corporate not only because of its form, but because of the policy it instantiates, displays, or manifests. A variation on this is Fisse's concept of reactive fault, that is: 'unreasonable corporate failure to devise and undertake satisfactory preventive or corrective measures in response to the commission of the *actus reus* of the offence.' Focusing on the corporation's reactions would mean unlocking the time-frame of *actus reus/mens rea*; it would also counter the argument that broadening the liability base could have an undesirable effect on the range of penalties by 'undercutting' the justification for imposing sanctions more severe than a fine or other monetary penalty. The concept of reactive fault approaches corporate blameworthiness through its CIDs, but extends the enquiry to allow for the situation, one which is probably common, where a corporation fails to adapt its policies in the light of past errors. This could be particularly useful in the areas of health and safety of workers, product safety, and pollution regulation, where it is easy to refute an allegation of recklessness if each 'offence' is considered in isolation.

As I suggested earlier, an advantage claimed for starting with a broad notion of liability based effectively on the actions of any corporate employee, which is then limited by proof of reasonable preventive strategies, is that it avoids the extremely difficult line-drawing exercise of deciding where in the corporation the threshold for liability should begin. Some clear models have now emerged. There is agency in one form or another—the strict *respondeat superior* version or the responsible officer version—or there is organizational liability which does not depend on the misdeeds of a specified individual. Each of these can be qualified by a compliance or due diligence component in the form of a positive liability requirement, an affirmative defence, or a sentencing discount. Lastly, liability can in some circumstances be imposed on the individual employee or manager as well. A combination of these models is probably optimal, none is sufficient in all conditions and circumstances. The Australian Criminal Code Act discussed in Chapter 7 remains the main example of legislation aiming to achieve such a combination. John Coffee's somewhat tighter version emphasises the relevance of preventive compliance programmes:

'A legal entity, including a corporation, partnership, union, or other form of business association, may be convicted of an offence if:

a. the offence is an offence (i) for which a legislative purpose to impose liability on such entity is plainly evident or (ii) in absence of such liability, there is significant risk that the legislature's purpose would be frustrated;

b. the commission of the offence was performed, authorised, requested, commanded, or recklessly tolerated by a senior managerial agent of the entity acting on behalf of the entity within the normal or foreseeable scope of such agent's authority and with an intent to benefit the entity; or;

c. the offence was a proximate and foreseeable consequence of the entity's failure to devise and implement reasonable preventive, monitoring, or safety controls or precautions, or to adopt and maintain a reasonable compliance programme, which

> failure under the circumstances constituted a serious departure from the standards and procedures then observed by similarly situated entities or that should have been observed by any such entity.'

Provision should be made to counter the ability of organizations to disappear or to be absorbed into a different enterprise. An important contributory factor cited by relatives of those killed in the *Piper Alpha* oil rig explosion when they eventually abandoned their efforts to mount a private prosecution was the sale of the rig company by its parent company, Occidental. This distinctive capacity of the company to disaggregate, dissolve, or reconstitute itself presents a challenge which is not peculiar to the enforcement of criminal law; plaintiffs in civil actions have this problem too. The range of possible devices which might be used to stay any such corporate escape moves have not been elaborated here. Where such devices fail, then of course the individual directors might be the only appropriate target. An additional, although related, problem is that identified by Collins as 'complex patterns of economic integration'. A construction site, for example, will often be worked by a number of separate capital units, different contractors working together but legally distinct. This creates problems, particularly with regard to recovery for economic loss in tort, but it has wider implications. 'Firms enjoy considerable freedom both in law and in practice to determine the limits of their boundaries.' Any adjustment of legal principles to reflect vertical integration will have clear implications for criminal liability, but it is not a matter to which I have devoted detailed attention here.

The Law Commission has recently considered the law on criminal liability in regulatory contexts. In the following section they set out the problems with an approach based on the identification doctrine.

Law Commission Consultation Paper 195, *Criminal Liability in Regulatory Contexts* (London: TSO, 2010)

The Weaknesses of the Identification Doctrine

Interpreting directing mind and will

5.81 First, it is important to note that directing mind and will is a phrase that has been interpreted in various ways. As Pinto and Evans have suggested, it, "appears to be less a term of art than a matter of construction depending on the context and the meaning of the section under consideration".

5.82 Further recognition of this uncertainty can be seen in the current editions of practitioner texts. For example, Blackstone's Criminal Practice states that:

> Precisely which employees or officers are identified with the company for these purposes is a matter of some debate . . . it seems that it will normally only be senior persons at or close to board level who will normally be identified with the company.

5.83 From an examination of the case law on the issue, it seems that the uncertainty over directing mind and will extends beyond merely differences of approach depending on context. *Nattrass* is often seen as the case which unequivocally applied the directing mind and will theory; yet even in that case three of their Lordships described the test in significantly different terms, capable of leading to different results if applied to a different set of facts than the one they faced.

Inappropriate method

5.84 Perhaps of greater concern regarding the identification doctrine is that, quite apart from the difficulties apparent in its application, it may simply be an inappropriate and ineffective method of establishing criminal liability of corporations. This wider concern may be particularly evident when the identification doctrine is applied in its strictest sense, in which case Smith & Hogan note that:

> Only the very senior managers will be likely to fit the description as the directing mind and will of the company. This illustrates one of the major shortcomings of the identification doctrine—that it fails to reflect the reality of the modern day large multinational corporation . . . it produces what many regard as an unsatisfactorily narrow scope for criminal liability.

5.85 This concern that the doctrine is inappropriate for modern corporations has been widely expressed, Professor Gobert has stated that the doctrine, "fails to capture the complexity of the modern company". By focusing on attributing the acts and state of minds of a limited range of senior people to the corporation, the identification doctrine fails to reflect the fact that, in modern corporations, a good deal of important policy or strategic decision-making may be de-centralised, or regional rather than national.

5.86 Further, Professor Clarkson notes that, "the doctrine ignores the reality of modern corporate decision-making which is often the product of corporate policies and procedures rather than individual decisions". This may be one of the reasons that the courts have in recent cases sought to avoid an application of the identification doctrine, undermining any status it might have had as a general principle. In that regard, one commentator, drawing on an analysis of recent cases, reaches the conclusion that "courts are beginning to recognise the 'corporateness' of corporate conduct, thus acknowledging the limitations inherent in the controlling officer, directing mind, conception of liability". Similarly, another commentator sees the confusion apparent in the latest authorities as indicating that, "a fundamental shift of direction has occurred".

5.87 A related difficulty with the identification doctrine, as a method of establishing corporate liability, is that it necessarily involves applying the same test to corporations of very different sizes, from one-man-bands to multinational corporations. This may create unfairness, as between the two groups. It is more likely that in small companies Directors (or equivalent persons) will have a direct hand in the running of the business at the front line, and hence will have the knowledge required to impute their individual fault to the company itself because they embody the directing mind and will of the company. In a large or multinational corporation, Directors are much less likely to take such an active front line role, and the policies that they set for those at the front line to follow may intentionally give considerable decision-making latitude to employees further down the line.

5.88 Accordingly, large or multinational corporations with complex multi-level organisational structures will find it easier to deny that individuals who took decisions that led to the commission of fault-based offences had a truly directing mind and will. The result is the company itself avoids liability for what was, in fact, the devolved decision of an employee, even though that employee might have been quite a senior employee. Professor Gobert recognised this weakness when he noted that:

> The identification doctrine propounds a test of corporate liability that works best in cases where it is needed least [small businesses] and works worst in cases where it is needed most [big business].

5.89 This situation can be contrasted with that generated in law by the extended vicarious liability approach adopted by the court in *Pioneer*, where Lord Nolan noted that:

Liability can only be escaped by completely effective preventative measures. How great a burden the devising of such measures will cast upon individual employers will depend upon the size and nature of a particular organisation.

Conclusion

5.90 It is clear from the examination of the main authorities dealing with the application of the identification doctrine that the law in this area suffers from considerable uncertainty. Professor Cartwright notes that "it is troubling that we are left with a series of cases which do not provide a definite answer to important issues of corporate and vicarious liability". Certainly, it would have been a considerable improvement if Parliament had stepped in long ago to define the nature and scope of the identification doctrine.

5.91 However, it is unlikely that having only one basis on which companies can be found criminally liable, however broadly stated, will prove to be workable or desirable across the board. Recent legislation in fact points in the opposite direction, namely in the direction of specially tailored solutions to fit different contexts in which crimes may come to be committed by, or on behalf of, companies.

In the following extract James Gobert considers the success of the 2007 Act:

J. Gobert, 'The Corporate Manslaughter and Corporate Homicide Act 2007—Thirteen Years in the Making but was It Worth the Wait?' (2008) 71 *Modern Law Review* 413 at 426–8

Prior to passage of the 2007 Act (and still with respect to other common law and statutory offences) the prevailing test of corporate criminal liability was to be found in the 'identification doctrine'. To convict a company of a crime, the prosecution had to show that a person who represented the 'directing mind and will of the company' had committed the offence with which the company was charged. If this could be proved, the offence could then be imputed to the company. The deficiencies of the identification doctrine have been well documented elsewhere, and it was to overcome these shortcomings that the Law Commission recommended a test of corporate liability that was not linked to personal fault. Under the Law Commission's proposals, systemic fault, embodied in the concept of 'management failure', was to be the basis of corporate liability. This methodological approach constituted a recognition that often deaths in a corporate context are due to the combined effect of flawed policies and the actions and inactions of more than one individual. Although a theory of aggregated fault intended to capture the latter dimension of corporate fault was advanced by the prosecution in the Herald case, it was rejected by the trial court. The 2007 Act appears to accept the concept of aggregation in limited form by its reference to 'senior management' in s. 1(3) and the linkage in s. 1(4) of senior management to persons (note the use of the plural) who play significant roles in the making or carrying out of corporate decisions. While the acts of the persons referred to in s. 1(4) only would need to be shown to be a substantial element in the breach, and not its sole cause, it nonetheless remains unclear whether wrongful acts of employees can be added to the wrongful acts of these individuals in determining whether a 'management failure' has occurred.

In dispensing with the need to identify a specific individual within the organization who has committed manslaughter, the 2007 Act represents a major improvement over the identification doctrine. Also, the category of senior management is doubtless more encompassing and realistic than the identification doctrine's restriction to persons who comprise the 'directing mind and will' of a company. Nevertheless, the 2007 Act's linkage of senior management to persons who play a significant role in the formulation and/or implementation of organisation policy appears, at least indirectly, to continue the identification doctrine's preoccupation with individual rather than systemic fault. In so doing, it may perpetuate many of the evidentiary problems associated with the identification doctrine, while adding new problems of its own. Under the identification doctrine, arguments over whether an individual was part of a company's 'directing mind and will' were commonplace. Under the Act, similar arguments can be anticipated in respect of which individuals play a 'significant' role in the making or carrying out of organisational policy. Added to this sticking point can be expected new disputes raised by the wording of the Act: how much of a role must an individual play in decision-making or managing before the role can be deemed to be 'significant'?; with how large a part of an organisation's activities must an individual be involved to satisfy the Act's requirement that the individual be involved in a 'substantial part' of the activities in question? In respect of the requirement that the way that 'senior management' managed or organised the relevant activities be shown to have constituted a 'substantial element' in the breach, it would seem inevitable that whether senior management's contributions to a breach were substantial or something less weighty will prove a point of contention. The wrangling can be expected to be particularly acute where there are failings at multiple levels, some managerial and some not, of a large company. In such a case the question that will arise is whether the contributions of senior management need to be viewed in isolation to see whether, standing on their own, they played a 'substantial' role in the death or whether the failings of other employees can be factored into the assessment of whether the senior management failure was a substantial element in the breach. It is submitted that in answering this question courts should be able to take into account oversight responsibilities.

QUESTIONS

1. Nowadays many of the large-scale corporate projects involve a number of companies working together (H. Collins 1990). Have the proposals concerning corporate liability paid sufficient attention to such cases?

2. If you are convinced by the argument that companies should be responsible for crimes why not schools being responsible for crimes of their pupils, universities of their students, families of their children? Cannot schools, universities, and families also have an 'ethos'?

For guidance on answering this question, please visit the Online Resource Centre that accompanies this book: www.oxfordtextbooks.co.uk/orc/herringcriminal7e/.

3. Is there a danger that focusing on corporate liability will lead to negligent managers not being prosecuted?

FURTHER READING

Almond, P. (2014) *Corporate Manslaughter and Regulatory Reform* (Basingstoke: Palgrave).

Beck, S. (2014) 'Corporate Criminal Liability' in M. Dubber and T. Hörnle (eds) *The Oxford Handbook of Criminal Law* (Oxford: OUP).

Bovens, M. (1998) *The Quest for Responsibility: Accountability and Citizenship in Complex Organisations* (Cambridge: Cambridge University Press).

Braithwaite, J. and Fisse, B. (1988) 'The Allocation of Responsibility for Corporate Crime' *Sydney Law Review* 11: 468.

Braithwaite, J. and Fisse, B. (1993) *Corporations, Crime and Accountability* (Cambridge: Cambridge University Press).

Clarkson, C. (2008) 'Corporate Manslaughter: Need for a Special Offence?' in C. Clarkson and S. Cunningham (eds) *Criminal Liability for Non-Aggressive Death* (Aldershot: Ashgate).

Clough, J. and Mulhern, C. (2002) *The Prosecution of Corporations* (Oxford: OUP).

Glazebrook, P. (2002) 'A Better Way of Convicting Businesses of Avoidable Deaths and Injuries?' *Cambridge Law Journal* 61: 405.

Gobert, J. (2008) 'The Corporate Manslaughter and Corporate Homicide Act 2007—Thirteen Years in the Making but was It Worth the Wait?' *Modern Law Review* 71: 413.

Gobert, J. and Punch, M. (2003) *Rethinking Corporate Crime* (London: Butterworths).

Gómez-Jara Díez, C. (2011) 'Corporate Culpability as a Limit to the Overcriminalization of Corporate Criminal Liability: The Interplay between Self-Regulation, Corporate Compliance, and Corporate Citizenship' *New Criminal Law Review* 14: 78.

Griffin, S. (2007) 'Corporate Manslaughter: A Radical Reform' *Journal of Criminal Law* 70: 151.

Horder, J. (2012a) *Homicide and the Politics of Law Reform* (Oxford: OUP), ch. 4.

Isaacs, T. (2011) 'Corporate Agency and Corporate Wrongdoing' *New Criminal Law Review* 16: 241.

Law Commission (2010a) Consultation Paper 195, *Criminal Liability in Regulatory Contexts* (London: TSO).

Lederman, L. (2000) 'Models for Imposing Corporate Criminal Liability: From Adaptation and Imitation toward Aggregation and the Search for Self-Identity' *Buffalo Criminal Law Review* 4: 642.

Lee, I. (2011) 'Corporate Criminal Responsibility as Team Member Responsibility' *Oxford Journal of Legal Studies* 31: 755.

Ntsanyu Nana, C. (2010) *Revisiting the Question of Imputation in Corporate Criminal Law* (Cambridge: Cambridge Scholars Publishing).

Slapper, G. and Tombs, S. (1999) *Corporate Crime* (Harlow: Longman).

Stewart, J. (2013) 'A Pragmatic Critique of Corporate Criminal Theory: Lessons from the Extremity' *New Criminal Law Review* 16: 261.

Sullivan, G.R. (1996b) 'The Attribution of Culpability to Limited Companies' *Cambridge Law Journal* 55: 515.

Tombs, S. (2007) '"Violence", Safety Crimes and Criminology' *British Journal of Criminology* 47: 531.

Wells, C. (2001) *Corporations and Criminal Responsibility* (2nd edn, Oxford: OUP).

Wells, C. (2011) 'Corporate Crime: Opening the Eyes of the Sentry' *Legal Studies* 30: 370.

5 CONCLUDING THOUGHTS

The criminal law has struggled to find ways of convicting companies. In part this is because the traditional notions of individual responsibility and blame do not transfer well to a consideration of corporate responsibility. Indeed it is noticeable that especially drafted legislation has proved necessary in order to enable the conviction of companies for manslaughter. The enthusiasm for corporate crime reflects the importance of the role that companies play in modern society. It also reflects a culture that strives to find ways of rendering companies accountable for what they do, and also a culture that seeks to find someone to blame when a person is killed.

INCHOATE OFFENCES

CENTRAL ISSUES

1. A defendant is guilty of attempting to commit a crime if he or she carries out an act which is more than merely preparatory to the commission of the offence, while intending to commit it.

2. The Serious Crime Act 2007 has created offences of encouraging or assisting another to commit an offence. These are committed whether or not the person encouraged or assisted goes on to commit a crime.

3. A criminal conspiracy arises where two or more people agree to pursue a course of conduct which involves committing an offence. To be guilty, the members of the conspiracy must intend the agreed actions to be done, but do not have to intend to play an active role themselves.

PART I: THE LAW ON INCHOATE OFFENCES

1 INCHOATE OFFENCES

DEFINITION

Inchoate offences are ones that seek to deal with defendants who have taken steps towards the commission of an offence but who have not (yet) committed it. The two best known examples are attempts and conspiracies.

The word inchoate means 'just begun' or 'undeveloped'. It is used to indicate that a substantive crime has not been committed, but the defendant has taken steps towards committing one or encouraging others to commit one. This chapter will discuss three inchoate offences of general application:

(1) attempts;

(2) offences under the Serious Crime Act 2007;

(3) conspiracies.

The offence of incitement, which used to be an important inchoate offence, was abolished by the Serious Crime Act 2007. In attempts cases the defendant has gone beyond mere preparation and taken steps towards carrying out a complete crime. Conspiracy involves agreeing with others to commit an offence. The Serious Crime Act 2007 offences involve encouraging or assisting a person to commit an offence. With all of these inchoate offences the defendant has not him or herself performed the *actus reus* but is sufficiently close to doing so, or persuading others to do so, for the law to find it appropriate to punish him or her. As we shall see in Part II of this chapter there is much debate about the justification for inchoate offences. There are some who emphasize the practical benefit of such offences: they permit the lawful arrest and punishment of those who plan to harm someone else, without having to wait until a victim is actually harmed. There are others who emphasize the moral blameworthiness of such conduct. It can be a matter of luck that, for example, an attempter failed to harm the victim. On the other hand there are those who are concerned that inchoate offences may infringe an important principle of criminal law: wicked thoughts alone do not deserve punishment.[1] It is for this reason that it is not enough that a defendant plans to harm another; he or she must put these plans into practice by taking steps to do so or by encouraging or agreeing with others to do so.[2]

2 ATTEMPT

> **DEFINITION**
>
> The *actus reus*: the defendant has done an act which is more than merely preparatory to the commission of the offence.
>
> The *mens rea*: normally an intention to commit the full offence. It is more difficult if the *actus reus* of the full offence requires proof that the defendant did an act in certain circumstances. Then the defendant must intend to do his or her act but need only be reckless as to the circumstances (if the *mens rea* for the full offence requires only recklessness as to the circumstances).

The criminal law on attempts is now governed by section 1(1) of the Criminal Attempts Act 1981. If, with intent to commit an offence to which this section applies, a person does an act which is more than merely preparatory to the commission of the offence, he or she is guilty of attempting to commit the offence.

---

[1] *Higgins* (1801) 2 East 5.
[2] For a discussion of 'double inchoate' offences, see Zimmerman (2000).

2.1 *MENS REA*

The *mens rea* is a crucial aspect of a criminal attempt. It can be what makes the difference between a harmless act and a criminal offence: Andrew meets William and raises his hand. This may or may not be an attempted assault: it all depends on whether Andrew is intending to punch William or give him a friendly pat on the back. The key *mens rea* requirement for an attempt as stated in section 1(1) is an intent to produce the *actus reus*. So, for example, attempted murder requires an intention to kill.[3] An intention to cause grievous bodily harm is not enough, even though such an intention is sufficient for the full offence of murder. Similarly for attempted criminal damage it must be shown there was an intention to cause criminal damage,[4] even though recklessness is enough for the full offence. However, unfortunately for students, as is so often the case, the law is not quite as straightforward as it may at first appear. There are the following difficulties: →1 (p.818)

What does 'intent' mean?

This is governed by *Pearman*.[5] This case confirms that the word 'intent' in the Criminal Attempts Act carries the same meaning as in the common law. In other words it includes direct intent and sometimes indirect intent. The meaning of intent is therefore the same as that set out in Chapter 3.

What about the circumstances or consequences of the act?

The law here is governed by two leading cases which need careful reading. The first (*Khan*) appears to suggest that recklessness as to circumstantial aspects of the *actus reus* of the full offence can sometimes be sufficient for an attempt; but this has been thrown into doubt by the second more recent case (*Pace and Rogers*):

R v Khan (Mohammed Iqbal); R v Dhokia; R v Banga; R v Faiz
[1990] 2 All ER 783 (CA)

Mohammed Iqbal Khan, Mahesh Dhokia, Jaswinder Singh Banga, and Navaid Faiz were charged with the attempted rape of a 16-year-old girl. The appellants and the victim met at a disco and then went to a house. Inside the house some young men had sexual intercourse with the victim and the appellants attempted unsuccessfully to have sexual intercourse with her. The trial judge directed the jury that if the defendants were reckless as to whether or not the victim would have consented to sexual intercourse they could be convicted of attempted rape. Recklessness here included a 'could not care less' attitude. They appealed on the basis that the jury should have been directed that they could be convicted of attempted rape only if they knew or intended that the victim was not consenting.

---

[3] *Whybrow* (1951) 35 Cr App R 141.   [4] *Millard and Vernon* [1987] Crim LR 393.
[5] (1984) 80 Cr App R 259.

Lord Justice Russell

In our judgment an acceptable analysis of the offence of rape is as follows: (1) the intention of the offender is to have sexual intercourse with a woman; (2) the offence is committed if, but only if, the circumstances are that: (a) the woman does not consent; AND (b) the defendant knows that she is not consenting or is reckless as to whether she consents.

Precisely the same analysis can be made of the offence of attempted rape: (1) the intention of the offender is to have sexual intercourse with a woman; (2) the offence is committed if, but only if, the circumstances are that: (a) the woman does not consent; AND (b) the defendant knows that she is not consenting or is reckless as to whether she consents.

The only difference between the two offences is that in rape sexual intercourse takes place whereas in attempted rape it does not, although there has to be some act which is more than preparatory to sexual intercourse. Considered in that way, the intent of the defendant is precisely the same in rape and in attempted rape and the mens rea is identical, namely, an intention to have intercourse plus a knowledge of or recklessness as to the woman's absence of consent. No question of attempting to achieve a reckless state of mind arises; the attempt relates to the physical activity; the mental state of the defendant is the same. A man does not recklessly have sexual intercourse, nor does he recklessly attempt it. Recklessness in rape and attempted rape arises not in relation to the physical act of the accused but only in his state of mind when engaged in the activity of having or attempting to have sexual intercourse.

If this is the true analysis, as we believe it is, the attempt does not require any different intention on the part of the accused from that for the full offence of rape. We believe this to be a desirable result which in the instant case did not require the jury to be burdened with different directions as to the accused's state of mind, dependent upon whether the individual achieved or failed to achieve sexual intercourse.

We recognise, of course, that our reasoning cannot apply to all offences and all attempts. Where, for example, as in causing death by reckless driving or reckless arson, no state of mind other than recklessness is involved in the offence, there can be no attempt to commit it.

In our judgment, however, the words 'with intent to commit an offence' to be found in section 1 of the Act of 1981 mean, when applied to rape, 'with intent to have sexual intercourse with a woman in circumstances where she does not consent and the defendant knows or could not care less about her absence of consent.' The only 'intent,' giving that word its natural and ordinary meaning, of the rapist is to have sexual intercourse. He commits the offence because of the circumstances in which he manifests that intent—i.e. when the woman is not consenting and he either knows it or could not care less about the absence of consent.

Accordingly we take the view that in relation to the four appellants the judge was right to give the directions that he did when inviting the jury to consider the charges of attempted rape.

Appeals dismissed.

R v Pace and Rogers
[2014] EWCA Crim 186

Pace and Rogers were scrap metal dealers. They were charged with the offence of attempting to convert criminal property contrary to section 327(1) of the Proceeds of Crime Act 2002. In fact, the property had not been stolen, and the property was part of a sting operation organized by the police. The full offence required proof that the offender suspected the property was stolen. The question for the Court of Appeal was what *mens rea* was required for the attempted offence. Was it the same as the full offence (suspicion), as the Crown argued, or was intent required, as the appellants claimed?

Lord Justice Davis

52. ... [T]he authority of *Khan* is not decisive for present purposes: and indeed, in fairness to Mr Farrell [counsel for the Crown], he did not suggest that it was. In *Khan*, the substantive offence admitted of recklessness as the mens rea: which is not the case here. In *Khan*, moreover, the appellants were charged with attempted rape solely because they had not succeeded in penetrating the victim, which is what they had intended to do. Had they succeeded in that act, as they had intended, the full offence of rape would have been made out. But that is not so in the present case. The two appellants here could never have been guilty of the substantive offence of converting criminal property: just because the property in question did not constitute or represent benefit from criminal conduct. Furthermore, the court in *Khan* had been careful to say (at p.35):

> "We recognise, of course, that our reasoning cannot apply to all offences and all attempts. Where, for example, as in causing death by reckless driving or reckless arson, no state of mind other than recklessness is involved in the offence, there can be no attempt to commit it."

53. We were also referred to . . . *AG's Reference (No 3 of 1992)* (1994) 98 CAR 383, which adopted broadly the same approach as in *Khan*. That too was a decision in a context different from the present case. It related to attempted arson being reckless whether life be endangered, contrary to s.1(2) of the Criminal Damage Act 1971. We have to say that we found, with respect, some of the passages in the judgment somewhat elliptical, if not self-contradictory: and the judgment is in fact subject to some adverse comment in Smith & Hogan's Criminal Law. We do not, at all events, think that it materially advances the Crown's argument. . . .

62. Turning, then, to s.1(1) we consider that, as a matter of ordinary language and in accordance with principle, an "intent to commit an offence" connotes an intent to commit all the elements of the offence. We can see no sufficient basis, whether linguistic or purposive, for construing it otherwise.

63. Once that is appreciated, the fault line in the Crown's argument is revealed. A constituent element of the offence of converting criminal property is, as we have said, that the property in question *is* criminal property. That is an essential part of the offence. Accordingly, an intent to commit the offence involves, in the present case, an intent to convert criminal property: and that connotes an intent that the property should *be* criminal property. But the Crown's argument glosses over that. Its argument connotes that the property in question which it is intended to be converted is *property* known or suspected to constitute or represent benefit from criminal conduct. It ignores the requirement for the substantive offence that the property concerned must be *criminal property* (as defined). The Crown, in effect, thus seeks to make it a criminal offence to intend to convert property suspecting, if not knowing, that it is stolen. But that is not what s.327, read with s.340(3), provides.

Appeal allowed.

It is fair to say that the law following *Pace and Rogers* is in disarray. Commentators have struggled to explain how *Pace and Rogers* and *Khan* can be reconciled. Here are some possible views:

(1) *Pace and Rogers* now represents the law and *Khan* must be treated as overruled.[6] For an attempted offence it must be shown that the defendant intended all the elements of the *actus reus* to be present. That is so even in cases where recklessness or suspicion are required for the full offence.

This view would emphasize the clear view of the Court of Appeal in *Pace and Rogers* that 'to s.1(1) we consider that, as a matter of ordinary language and in accordance with principle, an "intent to commit an offence" connotes an intent to commit all the elements of the offence', which appears to clearly contradict *Khan*. The problem with this view is that the Court of Appeal in *Pace and Rogers* discussed *Khan* and did not expressly overrule it. In any event, rules of precedent would prevent them doing that.

(2) *Khan* represents the law and *Pace and Rogers* should be dismissed as an error. For an attempted offence it must be shown the defendant intended all the elements of the *actus reus* save elements of the circumstances in cases where recklessness or suspicion are sufficient for the full offence.

This view would emphasize that as a matter of precedent *Pace and Rogers* should have followed *Khan*. *Khan* has represented the law for many years and *Pace and Rogers* does not clearly overrule it. It might also refer to the academic criticism that has been levelled at *Pace and Rogers*. Andrew Dyson[7] suggests that Pace and Rogers will in time be seen as a 'flash in the pan'. The difficulty with this view is that the Court of Appeal were clear that suspicion was not enough in *Pace and Rogers* and one cannot simply dismiss a case on the basis you do not agree with it.

(3) Both *Pace and Rogers* and *Khan* are correct. They are dealing with different situations. In a case of an 'impossible attempt' (e.g. where the facts were such that the defendant could never have committed the offence) it must be shown that the defendant intended the crime to take place, as *Pace and Rogers* states. However, in a 'possible attempt' case (where the defendant could have completed the crime, but failed to do so) the *mens rea* for an attempt can include recklessness as to circumstances.

The benefit of this view is that it provides a way of saying both cases are correct. The distinction between impossible and possible attempts could be said to be important because section 1(3) of the Criminal Attempts Act states that, if the defendant's intent would amount to an intent to commit an offence if the facts of the case had been as the defendant believed them to be, he should be regarded as having the intent to commit the offence. That would explain the conclusion in *Pace and Rogers* that suspicion was not enough for that impossible attempt.[8] The difficulty with this view is that the court did not explain the decision in this way. The statement quoted in view (1) seems to refer to a rule about attempts generally and not just impossible attempts.

(4) Both *Pace and Rogers* and *Khan* are correct. There are different rules for different crimes. *Khan* tells us about the *mens rea* for attempted rape and *Pace and Rogers* about the conversion of property offence. We will need to wait for future cases to tell us the *mens rea* for other attempted offences and to develop a more general rule.

Maybe that will be that in cases where recklessness is enough for the full offence *Khan* is to be followed and where suspicion is required *Pace and Rogers* will be followed.[9]

---

[6] Child and Hunt (2014) support this view. See also Child (2014).

[7] Dyson (2014).   [8] Virgo (2014).

[9] The court also suggested that *Khan* and *Pace and Rogers* could be distinguished on the basis that there could not be an impossible attempt in *Khan* but there could be in *Pace and Rogers*. That distinction has been widely rejected by commentators including Simester (2015) and Stark (2014) and is hard to justify.

The disadvantage of this approach is that it seems odd that the phrase 'intent to commit the offence' will have a different meaning depending on which crime is being charged.

None of these views is entirely satisfactory.

There is a dispute between commentators not only as to the law, but as to what it should be. Andrew Simester[10] supports the decision in *Pace and Rogers* because it fits in with the standard meaning of the word 'attempt':

> To "attempt" to do something is to *try* to do it. If only for the sake of speaking clearly to the citizens it is meant to guide, a law criminalising the "attempt" to do something should mean what it says, i.e. that trying to do the thing is a crime.

Opponents of the argument that *Pace and Rogers* should apply to all offences often rely on the offence of attempted rape. It seems that if *Pace and Rogers* has overruled *Khan* the law is that to be guilty of attempted rape the defendant must intend the victim not to consent. That will be very hard to prove because it means the defendant would regard his plan as having failed if it turned out the victim did consent. Only the most sadistic rapist would have that state of mind. Simester suggests that knowledge or settled belief that the victim was not consenting should be required. However, that too will be hard to prove—the defendant can easily claim they thought the victim might not be consenting but did not know for sure that she was not consenting and that would be hard to disprove. The *Khan* test, where it would be sufficient if the defendant realized the victim might not be consenting, seems the most workable test, but perhaps the test that is hardest to fit into the wording of the legislation. Simester argues it is contrary to the wording of the statute:

> A person who advertently runs the risk of harm is not thereby *trying* to cause that harm. Choosing to risk wrongdoing may be morally problematic, but it is not problematic in the same way: it is not a direct attack on the rights and interests of others but, rather, a form of endangerment.

Even if *Khan* does apply to the offence of attempted rape, there is still a question mark over how it applies to attempted rape. *Khan* made it clear that the *mens rea* for attempted rape is that the defendant intends to have sexual intercourse with the victim, being reckless as to whether the victim consents. However, that was based on the fact that at the time recklessness was the required *mens rea* for the offence of rape. Since the 2003 Sexual Offences Act the *mens rea*, is more complex, but involves proof that the defendant did not reasonably believe that the victim consented.[11] It remains to be seen whether following the 2003 Act the *mens rea* for an attempted rape will be an intention to have sexual intercourse, with a lack of reasonable belief in consent. Findlay Stark[12] believes the 2003 Act has altered the *mens rea* for rape so that:

> It can be assumed that the *mens rea* of attempted rape is, in a case involving non-consent, that the defendant has (i) an intention to penetrate the complainant's vagina, anus or mouth with his penis, and (ii) no reasonable belief in consent. In a case where there is consent, the defendant must have (i) an intention to penetrate the consenting person's vagina, anus or mouth with his penis, and (ii) the *belief* that this is not consented to.

---

[10] Simester (2015).   [11] See Chapter 7 for a discussion.   [12] Stark (2015).

Simester would claim such a reading would depart too much from the wording of the Act and the natural meaning of attempt. However, if the wrong of rape is penetration without a reasonable belief in consent then that is exactly what the person described by Stark is trying to do.[13]

Whichever test is used, as often in criminal law, much depends on the jury determining what was in the mind of the defendant. In *Ferriter*[14] the defendant went behind the bar of a pub, wrestled a barmaid to the floor 'got on top of her' and tried to pull her trousers down. She managed to escape before he was able to do anything more. His conviction for attempted rape was overturned by the Court of Appeal, although they substituted a conviction for attempted sexual assault. He denied any sexual motive and the Court of Appeal determined the jury could not be satisfied on the basis of what had happened there was an intent to rape, although they could be sure there was an intent to commit a sexual assault.

QUESTION

The Court of Appeal in *Attorney-General's Reference (No. 3 of 1992)*[15] proposed the 'missing element' test. This requires the court to decide what is the missing element in the attempt; that is, what is missing from the case which, if present, would mean that the full offence had been committed. The defendant will be guilty of an attempt if he or she intended to supply that missing element. The Court suggested this was not intended to be different from the *Khan* test. But consider the following scenario: Tim damages a watch, which he thinks belongs to Judith, but in fact belongs to him. The 'missing element' test would be applied thus: all that is preventing this being criminal damage is that the watch does not belong to another. Tim is therefore guilty of attempted criminal damage if he intends the watch to belong to another.

The 'circumstance' test would be applied in this way: the ownership of the watch is a circumstance, and because recklessness is sufficient as to that in the full offence of criminal damage, it is enough for an attempt. Tim is therefore guilty of attempted criminal damage if he is *reckless* as to whether the watch belongs to another.

Which test should the court use, assuming *Pace and Rogers* is not followed?

For guidance on answering this question, please visit the Online Resource Centre that accompanies this book: www.oxfordtextbooks.co.uk/orc/herringcriminal7e/.

Conditional intent

What of a case where the defendant has an intent to commit a crime only in certain circumstances? For example, Dave rushes into a bedroom with a gun raised, intending to kill his wife if he finds her in bed with another man or Sue rummages through someone's handbag intending to steal anything that she finds of value.

In *Husseyn*[16] the defendant was charged with attempting to steal sub-aqua equipment from a van. He had opened a bag and started to look in it to see if there was anything worth taking. The Court of Appeal held that because it could not be said that he had intended to take the sub-aqua equipment he could not be found guilty of attempting to steal it. Subsequently in *Attorney-General's Reference (Nos 1 and 2 of 1979)*[17] the Court

---

[13] Stark (2015).   [14] [2012] EWCA Crim 2211.   [15] (1994) 98 Cr App R 383.
[16] (1978) 67 Cr App R 131 (CA).   [17] [1979] 3 All ER 143.

of Appeal explained that a conditional intent (to steal anything that was worth stealing) could form the basis of an attempt charge if the indictment[18] was drafted carefully. In *Husseyn* the correct charge would be attempting to steal 'some or all of the contents of the holdall'. Smith and Hogan have suggested 'attempting to steal from a holdall' would be even better.[19]

2.2 ACTUS REUS

The *actus reus* of an attempt is defined in section 1(1) of the Criminal Attempts Act 1981 as doing an act which is more than merely preparatory to the commission of these offences. These words are to be given their normal meaning.[20] The word 'merely' is key here. It is clear that not every preparatory act constitutes an attack. If Neil buys a knife, planning to use it in a robbery weeks later, he may have begun to prepare for the robbery, but this is mere preparation and he is well short of an attempted robbery. In reality there is no hard and fast rule about when an act may be more than merely preparatory, but the following cases give some indication of the courts' attitudes: →2 (p.815)

R v Geddes
[1996] Crim LR 894 (CA)

Gary Geddes entered a boys' lavatory block in a school in Brighton. He had no right to be there. He was found in a cubicle with a cider can, a large knife, some rope, some orange toilet paper, and a roll of masking tape. The prosecution alleged that he was planning to kidnap a boy. At his trial it was argued, inter alia, that his actions could not constitute an attempt because he had done nothing that was more than merely preparatory. He was convicted and appealed.

Lord Bingham of Cornhill CJ [reading the judgment of the court]

In considering the question whether there was evidence before the jury which entitled them to hold that the appellant had done an act which was more than merely preparatory, it is helpful to begin with the judgment given by the Lord Chief Justice in *R v Rowley* (1992) 94 Cr App R 95. In that case the appellant had left notes in public places inviting boys to respond to him. The purpose of the notes was to initiate relationships for the appellant's sexual gratification, although the notes did not in terms say so. One of the charges against the appellant was of attempting to incite a child under 14 to commit acts of gross indecency with him. With reference to that part of the appeal, the Lord Chief Justice said at page 100:

> '. . . The effect of that latter subsection [Criminal Attempts Act 1981, section 4(3)] is that it is for the jury to determine whether the act is more than merely preparatory or not, but only in circumstances upon which the judge has to rule, where there is some evidence fit for their consideration on that issue.'

The Lord Chief Justice then went on to deal with the facts of that case.

---

[18] The indictment sets out the charge the defendant must face. [19] Ormerod (2007: 386).
[20] *Jones* [1990] 3 All ER 886 (CA).

In so stating the law, Lord Taylor CJ was echoing observations made by Lord Lane CJ in *R v Gullefer (Note)* [1990] 3 All ER 882, [1990] 1 WLR 1063. At page 1065B of the latter report Lord Lane, giving the judgment of this court, said:

'Thus the judge's task is to decide whether there is evidence upon which a jury could reasonably come to the conclusion that the appellant had gone beyond the realm of mere preparation and had embarked upon the actual commission of the offence. If not, he must withdraw the case from the jury. If there is such evidence, it is then for the jury to decide whether the defendant did in fact go beyond mere preparation. That is the way in which the judge approached this case. He ruled that there was sufficient evidence.'

At page 1066C Lord Lane added:

'It seems to us that the words of the Act of 1981 seek to steer a midway course. They do not provide, as they might have done, that the *Reg v Eagleton* test is to be followed, or that, as Lord Diplock suggested, the defendant must have reached a point from which it was impossible for him to retreat before the actus reus of an attempt is proved. On the other hand the words give perhaps as clear a guidance as is possible in the circumstances on the point of time at which Stephen's "series of acts" begin. It begins when the merely preparatory acts come to an end and the defendant embarks upon the crime proper. When that is will depend of course upon the facts in any particular case.'

The judge also considered *R v Campbell* 93 Cr App R 350. That was a case in which the appellant had been convicted of attempted robbery. The evidence showed that he had been loitering outside a sub-post office, equipped in a manner clearly indicating an intention to rob it. But he had been arrested before he had entered the sub-post office and when he was still outside. It was held, allowing the appeal:

'(1) In directing a jury as to an attempt to commit a crime the judge should restrict himself to the definition of an attempt in the Criminal Attempts Act 1981. In the present case the judge had also directed the jury with references to the law obtaining before that Act; that was wholly unnecessary. It is sufficient to direct the jury that before they could convict they must be satisfied so as to feel sure that the defendant intended to commit the offence and that, with that intent, he did an act which was more than an act of preparation to commit the offence. It was for the jury to decide whether the act relied upon by the prosecution was more than merely preparatory.

(2) In considering a submission that the case should be withdrawn from the jury at the close of the prosecution case the judge must form a judgment upon the Crown's evidence and determine whether or not that evidence is safe to be left to the jury. If he considers that the relevant circumstances could not amount to an attempt he should withdraw the matter from the jury. If he concludes that, although the matter is not as conclusive as that, it nevertheless would be unsafe to leave the evidence to the jury, he should direct a verdict of not guilty. It is only if he is satisfied that there is evidence upon which a jury can properly and safely consider whether or not there has been an attempt that he should allow the case to continue.

(3) In the present case a number of acts remained undone and the appellant's acts were indicative of mere preparation, even if he was still of a mind to rob the post office. If a person in such circumstances has not even gained the place where he

could be in a position to carry out the offence, it is extremely unlikely that it could ever be said that he had performed an act which could properly be said to be an attempt. It would be unwise to try to lay down hard and fast rules as to when, in varying circumstances, an attempt has begun. The matter has to be decided on a case by case basis.'

If one were to ask the simple question: did Campbell attempt to rob the post office, the answer would, in our judgment, be no. The evidence was strong that he had an intention of robbing the post office; he was very close in time and space to doing so; but he did not embark on the actual commission of the robbery.

This appeal is concerned not with the correctness of the jury's decision of fact, but the correctness of the judge's ruling of law. Was the evidence summarised in the admissions sufficient in law to support a finding that the appellant did an act which was more than merely preparatory to the commission of the offence charged? The cases show that the line of demarcation between acts which are merely preparatory and acts which may amount to an attempt is not always clear or easy to recognise. There is no rule of thumb test. There must always be an exercise of judgment based on the particular facts of the case. It is, we think, an accurate paraphrase of the statutory test and not an illegitimate gloss upon it to ask whether the available evidence, if accepted, could show that a defendant has done an act which shows that he has actually tried to commit the offence in question, or whether he has only got ready or put himself in a position or equipped himself to do so.

In the present case, as already indicated, there is not much room for doubt about the appellant's intention. Furthermore, the evidence is clearly capable of showing that he made preparations, that he equipped himself, that he got ready, that he put himself in a position to commit the offence charged. We question whether the cider can in the cubicle is of central importance, but would accept that in the absence of any explanation it could lead to the inference that the appellant had been in the cubicle. But was the evidence sufficient in law to support a finding that the appellant had actually tried or attempted to commit the offence of imprisoning someone? Had he moved from the realm of intention, preparation and planning into the area of execution or implementation? In *Campbell*, which was of course decided on its own facts, it was held that the appellant had not. Here it is true that the appellant had entered the school; but he had never had any contact or communication with any pupil; he had never confronted any pupil at the school in any way. That may well be no credit to him, and may indeed reflect great credit on the vigilance of the school staff. The whole story is one which fills the court with the gravest unease. Nonetheless, we cannot escape giving an answer to the fundamental legal question . . . So, for this purpose, must the contents of the rucksack, which give a clear indication as to what the appellant may have had in mind, but do not throw light on whether he had begun to carry out the commission of the offence. On the facts of this case we feel bound to conclude that the evidence was not sufficient in law to support a finding that the appellant did an act which was more than merely preparatory to wrongfully imprisoning a person unknown. In those circumstances we conclude that the appeal must be allowed and the conviction quashed.

Appeal allowed.

The Court of Appeal has avoided setting down any definite rule for the jury to apply, other than to say that the words 'more than merely preparatory' should be given their 'plain meaning'. Useful phrases that have been used by the judiciary to describe the *actus reus* of an attempt are 'on the job'[21] or 'embarks on the crime proper'.[22] In *Moore v DPP*[23] Toulson LJ found the following quote from a Law Commission Report helpful:

> To elaborate further, preparatory conduct by D which is sufficiently close to the final act to be properly regarded as part of the execution of D's plan can be an attempt . . . In other words, it covers the steps immediately preceding the final act necessary to effect D's plan and bring about the commission of the intended offence.

Here are some indications which may however be gleaned from the facts of some of the cases, although they do not represent hard and fast rules:

(1) If the defendant has done the last act before completing his offence the *actus reus* of an attempt will be made out.[24] So if A shoots at B, but B ducks and so avoids the bullet, clearly A will have committed the *actus reus* of an attempt.

(2) It is not necessary to show that the defendant has done the 'last act'[25] before committing the actual offence.[26] In other words even though the defendant may still have several actions to complete he or she may still be guilty of an attempt.

(3) Simply because an act is one of a series of acts which will lead to the commission of the crime does not mean that the act is necessarily sufficient to amount to attempt. Such acts will amount to preparation, but not necessarily more than mere preparation.[27]

(4) In a crime of violence unless the defendant is face to face with the victim it is unlikely that the act will be described as more than mere preparation.[28] Unlikely, but not impossible. No doubt a terrorist who plants a bomb under a victim's car will be held to have committed an attempt to kill, even though he or she has not met the victim.

When considering the *actus reus* of an attempt it is necessary to consider carefully the *actus reus* of the full offence. In *Toothill*[29] the defendant was charged with attempted burglary (with intent to rape). He had knocked on the door of the potential victim's house and was arrested in the victim's garden. He was guilty of an attempted burglary. This is because he was more than merely preparatory to entering the property as a trespasser (the *actus reus* of burglary).[30] →3 (p.811)

Attempt by omission

The 1981 Act requires there to be 'an *act* which is more than merely preparatory'. This seems to imply that an omission cannot constitute an attempt. This may seem obvious, but if a parent sees her child drowning and stands by doing nothing, but at the very last minute

---

[21] *Osborn* (1919) 84 JP 63.   [22] *Gullefer* [1990] 3 All ER 882.

[23] [2010] EWHC 1822 (Admin), para. 27.

[24] *Jones* [1990] 1 WLR 1057.   [25] A test proposed in *Eagleton* (1855) 6 Cox CC 559.

[26] *Gullefer* [1990] 3 All ER 882.   [27] *Gullefer* [1991] Crim LR 576.

[28] Compare *Kelly* [1992] Crim LR 181 and *Campbell* (1990) 93 Cr App R 350.

[29] [1998] Crim LR 876.

[30] There are quite a number of cases in which the Court of Appeal has considered the *actus reus* of an attempt. To get a wider flavour of how they approach such cases read: *Jones* (1990) 91 Cr App R 351; *Gullefer* [1990] 3 All ER 882; *Campbell* [1991] Crim LR 268; *Kelly* [1992] Crim LR 181; *Griffin* [1993] Crim LR 514; *Attorney-General's Reference (No. 1 of 1992)* [1993] Crim LR 274; *Tosti* [1997] Crim LR 746; *Nash* [1999] Crim LR 308.

someone intervenes and rescues the child, can the parent be successfully prosecuted for attempting to murder the child? After all, but for the fortunate intervention of the third party, the parent would be guilty of murder. We await definitive guidance from the courts on this question.

Is it possible to convict of an attempt if the attempt was successful?

Is it a defence to a charge of attempt if the defendant in fact succeeded? The answer (not surprisingly) is that the defendant can still be convicted of an attempted offence. Section 6(4) of the Criminal Law Act 1967 resolves the issue:

> where a person is charged on an indictment with attempting to commit an offence or with any assault or other act preliminary to an offence, but not with the completed offence, then (subject to the discretion of the court to discharge the jury with a view to the preferment of an indictment for the completed offence) he may be convicted of the offence charged notwithstanding that he is shown to be guilty of the completed offence.[31]

What can be attempted?

It is possible to convict a defendant of attempting to commit any offence except for the following:

(1) Conspiracy (either common law or statutory conspiracy).[32]

(2) Offences of assisting an arrestable offender or compounding an arrestable offence.[33]

(3) Offences of aiding, abetting, counselling, or procuring the commission of an offence.[34]

(4) Summary only offences. The explanation is that attempting to commit summary only offences (which are in their nature minor crimes) is not sufficiently serious to justify a criminal conviction. However, there are a few summary only offences in respect of which the statute has explicitly[35] stated that it is an offence to attempt to commit them.[36]

(5) Some commentators suggest that offences where there is a more serious offence with the same *actus reus* cannot be attempted: for example, manslaughter. To intend to commit manslaughter one must intend to kill, which is attempted murder.

(6) There are complex provisions dealing with attempting to commit offences abroad which are not covered here.

---

[31] *Webley v Buxton* [1977] QB 481 indicates that although s. 6(4) does not apply to summary offences, the common law rule is the same and a defendant can be convicted of an attempt to carry out a summary offence, even if in fact they have committed the full offence.

[32] Criminal Attempts Act 1981, s. 1(4).   [33] Criminal Law Act 1967, ss 4(1) and 5(1).

[34] *R v Kenning* [2008] EWCA Crim 1534. Although it should be noted that the Suicide Act 1961, s. 2(1), creates the offence of aiding the commission of suicide, and it is therefore possible to attempt to aid the commission of suicide. See Bohlander (2010a and 2010b) and Child (2010) for a debate on whether this provision is inconsistent with the offences in the Serious Crime Act 2007, Part 2; see Chapter 15.

[35] *Bristol Magistrates' Court, ex p E* [1998] 3 All ER 798 confirmed that either way offences can be attempted.

[36] e.g. the Road Traffic Act 1988, s. 5 (driving with alcohol concentration above the prescribed limit).

2.3 IMPOSSIBLE ATTEMPTS

The cases under consideration here are where a defendant is trying to commit an offence which he or she cannot complete. →4 (p.822) The following situations need to be distinguished:

'Legal impossibility'

The defendant is trying to perform an action which he or she believes to be illegal, but which is not. This is simply not an offence. In *Taaffe*[37] the defendant imported into the country packages which he believed contained foreign currency. He believed that it was illegal to import foreign currency, which it was not. He could not be convicted of attempting to import foreign currency. Similarly, if the defendant believed that taking topless photographs of his wife was an offence he would not be convicted of attempting to commit the imaginary crime. Less straightforward is a case where the mistake is of civil law. For example, the defendant is attempting to damage property which he or she believes under civil law is someone else's but which in fact is his or hers.[38] There are no cases directly on this situation.

'Impossibility through ineptitude'

This is where the defendant is trying to commit a crime but the means he or she is using are inadequate to commit the offence. The defendant is clearly guilty. For example, Ray tries to poison Lucy's tea, but puts in so little poison that it has no effect on her well-being. Clearly Ray is guilty of an attempt if he intended to kill Lucy.

More controversial is a much-debated hypothetical case where D sticks pins into a wax model of V genuinely believing that doing so will release evil powers which will kill V. If D is a devout believer he or she may think that sticking the pins into the model of V is as effective as stabbing V. Although there is a widespread view that the use of such 'radically deficient means' to attempt should not amount to an attempted murder, it is in fact hard to explain how it is different from the case where D shoots at V who is such a long way away that there is no way that a bullet could reach him or her. The best explanation is that offered by Duff who argues that such conduct 'failed to engage with the world as an attempt to commit [the] offence'.[39]

'Physical impossibility'

Here the reason for the failure is not the ineffective means used, but is that the crime simply cannot be committed. For example, D tries to kill V who he or she thinks is asleep, but is in fact dead. Or D plants seeds believing they will grow into a cannabis plant, but in fact he or she grows chives. In these cases the defendant can still be guilty. The law is governed by section 1(2) and (3) of the Criminal Attempts Act 1981:

> (2) A person may be guilty of attempting to commit an offence to which this section applies even though the facts are such that the commission of the offence is impossible.

---

[37] [1983] 2 All ER 625.

[38] A slightly different example is *Haughton v Smith* [1975] AC 476, where the defendant was charged with attempting to handle stolen goods. He handled the goods, but unknown to him they were not stolen.

[39] Duff (1996: 398). Probably the term 'facts' in s. 1(3) could not be said to include beliefs as to what the law is.

(3) In any case where—

    (a) apart from this subsection a person's intention would not be regarded as having amounted to an intent to commit an offence; but

    (b) if the facts of the case had been as he believed them to be, his intention would be so regarded, then, for the purposes of subsection (1) above, he shall be regarded as having had an intent to commit that offence.

The effect of these provisions is that what is key for the law on attempts in this area is the accused's intention. For the purposes of impossible attempts the facts are taken to be the facts as the defendant believed them. So if the defendant believes he or she is dealing in illegal drugs he or she can be convicted of an attempted drug-dealing offence, even if in fact what he or she is selling is chalk. He or she will be guilty of an attempt to deal in drugs.

DEFINITION

The jury must ask whether on the facts as the defendant believed them to be he or she was doing an act which was more than merely preparatory to the commission of an offence.

So if Max is dead, but Bob believes he is alive and approaches Max, intending to kill him, then the question is whether, if Max had been alive (that being what Bob believed), what Bob did was more than merely preparatory to killing him.

The leading case on impossible attempts is the following:

R v Shivpuri
[1987] AC 1 (HL)

Pyare Shivpuri was arrested by customs officers. He confessed that he was dealing in illegal drugs. However, on further analysis, it was found that the suitcase did not contain illegal drugs but snuff and harmless vegetable matter. He was charged with an attempt to commit the offence of being knowingly concerned in dealing with and harbouring prohibited drugs contrary to section 170(1)(b) of the Customs and Excise Management Act 1979. He appealed against his conviction on the basis that, as he did not have in his possession an illegal drug, he could not be charged in connection with an attempt to deal in such drugs. The Court of Appeal dismissed his appeal and he then appealed to the House of Lords.

Lord Bridge of Harwich

The certified question granted . . . reads:

'Does a person commit an offence under Section 1, Criminal Attempts Act, 1981, where, if the facts were as that person believed them to be, the full offence would have been committed by him, but where on the true facts the offence which that person set out to commit was in law impossible, e.g., because the substance imported and believed to be heroin was not heroin but a harmless substance?'

[**Lord Bridge** quoted section 1 of the Criminal Attempts Act 1981 and continued:]

Applying this language to the facts of the case, the first question to be asked is whether the appellant intended to commit the offences of being knowingly concerned in dealing with and harbouring drugs of class A or class B with intent to evade the prohibition on their importation. Translated into more homely language the question may be rephrased, without in any way altering its legal significance, in the following terms: did the appellant intend to receive and store (harbour) and in due course pass on to third parties (deal with) packages of heroin or cannabis which he knew had been smuggled into England from India? The answer is plainly Yes, he did. Next, did he, in relation to each offence, do an act which was more than merely preparatory to the commission of the offence? The act relied on in relation to harbouring was the receipt and retention of the packages found in the lining of the suitcase. The act relied on in relation to dealing was the meeting at Southall station with the intended recipient of one of the packages. In each case the act was clearly more than preparatory to the commission of the intended offence; it was not and could not be more than merely preparatory to the commission of the actual offence, because the facts were such that the commission of the actual offence was impossible. Here then is the nub of the matter. Does the 'act which is more than merely preparatory to the commission of the offence' in s. 1(1) of the 1981 Act (the *actus reus* of the statutory offence of attempt) require any more than an act which is more than merely preparatory to the commission of the offence which the defendant intended to commit? Section 1(2) must surely indicate a negative answer if it were otherwise, whenever the facts were such that the commission of the actual offence was impossible, it would be impossible to prove an act more than merely preparatory to the commission of that offence and sub-ss (1) and (2) would contradict each other.

This very simple, perhaps over-simple, analysis leads me to the provisional conclusion that the appellant was rightly convicted of the two offences of attempt with which he was charged. But can this conclusion stand with *Anderton v Ryan*? The appellant in that case was charged with an attempt to handle stolen goods. She bought a video recorder believing it to be stolen. On the facts as they were to be assumed it was not stolen. By a majority the House decided that she was entitled to be acquitted. I have re-examined the case with care. If I could extract from the speech of Lord Roskill or from my own speech a clear and coherent principle distinguishing those cases of attempting the impossible which amount to offences under the statute from those which do not, I should have to consider carefully on which side of the line the instant case fell. But I have to confess that I can find no such principle.

Running through Lord Roskill's speech and my own in *Anderton v Ryan* is the concept of 'objectively innocent' acts which, in my speech certainly, are contrasted with 'guilty acts' . . .

If we fell into error, it is clear that our concern was to avoid convictions in situations which most people, as a matter of common sense, would not regard as involving criminality. In this connection it is to be regretted that we did not take due note of para 2.97 of the Law Commission Report, Criminal Law: Attempt and Impossibility in Relation to Attempt, Conspiracy and Incitement (1980) (Law Com no 102) which preceded the enactment of the 1981 Act, which reads:

> 'If it is right in principle that an attempt should be chargeable even though the crime which it is sought to commit could not possibly be committed, we do not think that we should be deterred by the consideration that such a change in our law would also cover some extreme and exceptional cases in which a prosecution would be theoretically possible. An example would be where a person is offered goods at such a low price that he believes that they are stolen, when in fact they are not. If he actually purchases them, upon the principles which we have discussed he would be liable for an attempt to handle stolen goods. Another case which has been much debated is

> that raised in argument by Bramwell B. in *Reg. v. Collins*. If A takes his own umbrella, mistaking it for one belonging to B and intending to steal B's umbrella, is he guilty of attempted theft? Again, on the principles which we have discussed he would in theory be guilty, but in neither case would it be realistic to suppose that a complaint would be made or that a prosecution would ensue.'

The prosecution in *Anderton v Ryan* itself falsified the Commission's prognosis in one of the 'extreme and exceptional cases'. It nevertheless probably holds good for other such cases, particularly that of the young man having sexual intercourse with a girl over 16, mistakenly believing her to be under that age, by which both Lord Roskill and I were much troubled.

However that may be, the distinction between acts which are 'objectively innocent' and those which are not is an essential element in the reasoning in *Anderton v Ryan* and the decision, unless it can be supported on some other ground, must stand or fall by the validity of this distinction. I am satisfied on further consideration that the concept of 'objective innocence' is incapable of sensible application in relation to the law of criminal attempts. The reason for this is that any attempt to commit an offence which involves 'an act which is more than merely preparatory to the commission of the offence' but which for any reason fails, so that in the event no offence is committed, must ex hypothesi, from the point view of the criminal law, be 'objectively innocent'. What turns what would otherwise, from the point of view of the criminal law, be an innocent act into a crime is the intent of the actor to commit an offence. I say 'from the point of view of the criminal law' because the law of tort must surely here be quite irrelevant. A puts his hand into B's pocket. Whether or not there is anything in the pocket capable of being stolen, if A intends to steal his act is a criminal attempt, if he does not so intend his act is innocent. A plunges a knife into a bolster in a bed. To avoid the complication of an offence of criminal damage, assume it to be A's bolster. If A believes the bolster to be his enemy B and intends to kill him, his act is an attempt to murder B, if he knows the bolster is only a bolster, his act is innocent. These considerations lead me to the conclusion that the distinction sought to be drawn in *Anderton v Ryan* between innocent and guilty acts considered 'objectively' and independently of the state of mind of the actor cannot be sensibly maintained.

. . .

I am thus led to the conclusion that there is no valid ground on which *Anderton v Ryan* can be distinguished. I have made clear my own conviction, which as a party to the decision (and craving the indulgence of my noble and learned friends who agreed in it) I am the readier to express, that the decision was wrong. What then is to be done? If the case is indistinguishable, the application of the strict doctrine of precedent would require that the present appeal be allowed. Is it permissible to depart from precedent under the 1966 Practice Statement Note ([1966] 3 All ER 77, [1966] 1 WLR 1234) notwithstanding the especial need for certainty in the criminal law? The following considerations lead me to answer that question affirmatively. Firstly, I am undeterred by the consideration that the decision in *Anderton v Ryan* was so recent. The 1966 Practice Statement is an effective abandonment of our pretention to infallibility. If a serious error embodied in a decision of this House has distorted the law, the sooner it is corrected the better. Secondly, I cannot see how, in the very nature of the case, anyone could have acted in reliance on the law as propounded in *Anderton v Ryan* in the belief that he was acting innocently and now find that, after all, he is to be held to have committed a criminal offence. Thirdly, to hold the House bound to follow *Anderton v Ryan* because it cannot be distinguished and to allow the appeal in this case would, it seems to me, be tantamount to a declaration that the 1981 Act left the law of criminal attempts unchanged following the decision in *Haughton v Smith* [1975] AC 476. Finally, if, contrary to my present view, there is a valid ground on which it would be proper to distinguish cases similar to that considered in *Anderton v Ryan*, my present opinion on that point would not foreclose the option of making such a distinction in some future case.

I cannot conclude this opinion without disclosing that I have had the advantage, since the conclusion of the argument in this appeal, of reading an article by Professor Glanville Williams entitled 'The Lords and Impossible Attempts, or Quis Custodiet Ipsos Custodies?' [1986] CLJ 33. The language in which he criticises the decision in *Anderton v Ryan* is not conspicuous for its moderation, but it would be foolish, on that account, not to recognise the force of the criticism and churlish not to acknowledge the assistance I have derived from it.

I would answer the certified question in the affirmative and dismiss the appeal.

Appeal dismissed.

So in this decision their Lordships overruled their own decision in *Anderton v Ryan*[40] and held that if, on the facts as the defendant believed them to be, the defendant was doing something that was more than merely preparatory to the commission of the offence, he or she can be convicted of an attempt. *Shivpuri* does much to clarify the law, and it is simple to understand (although it is, of course, always difficult for the jury to work out what was in fact going on inside the defendant's mind). *Shivpuri* was applied in the case of *R v S*[41] where it was held that a defendant could be convicted of attempting to aid and abet a suicide even though the victim had no intention of committing suicide, if the defendant believed they did.

There is, however, one significant area of doubt, and that is what 'believe' means here. What if D has sexual intercourse with V who consents to the sexual intercourse, but D is not sure whether V consents. Is this doubt enough for 'believes' in section 1(2) of the Criminal Attempts Act 1981? In other words for the purposes of section 1(2), in deciding whether the defendant had performed an act which was more than merely preparatory on the facts as the defendant believed them to be, are suspected beliefs sufficient?

2.4 ATTEMPTS AND ABANDONMENT

There is no case which yet accepts a defence of abandonment in English criminal law on attempts.[42] So if the defendant has done an act which is more than merely preparatory, with intent to commit the full offence, but changes his or her mind and runs off at the very last minute, he or she could still be guilty of an attempt.[43]

QUESTION

Pete plans to have sexual intercourse with Emily. She has told him that she fancies him and Pete believes that this means she would like to have sexual intercourse with him. Pete kisses Emily, which she does not like, but she keeps quiet. When Pete starts to undress her, Emily pushes him away and says 'Please stop'. Pete continues to try to undress her and Emily's opposition becomes more vocal. Pete then is aware that Emily does not want sex and leaves. Has Pete committed any offences?

For guidance on answering this question, please visit the Online Resource Centre that accompanies this book: www.oxfordtextbooks.co.uk/orc/herringcriminal7e/.

---

[40] [1985] AC 560.　　[41] [2005] EWCA Crim 819.　　[42] See further Wasik (1980).
[43] Although the Crown Prosecution Service may decide not to prosecute him or her.

FURTHER READING

Buxton, R. (1984) 'Circumstances, Consequences and Attempted Rape' *Criminal Law Review* 365.

Christie, S. (2009) 'The Relevance of Harm as the Criterion for the Punishment of Impossible Attempts' *Journal of Criminal Law* 73: 153.

Duff, R.A. (1996) *Criminal Attempts* (Oxford: OUP).

Horder, J. (1994c) 'Varieties of Intention, Criminal Attempts and Endangerment' *Legal Studies* 14: 335.

Smith, K. (1991) 'Proximity at Attempt: Lord Lane's Midway Course' *Criminal Law Review* 576.

Temkin, J. (1976) 'Impossible Attempts: Another View' *Modern Law Review* 39: 55.

Williams, G. (1991b) 'Intents in the Alternative' *Cambridge Law Journal* 50: 120.

3 SERIOUS CRIME ACT 2007

Part 2 of the Serious Crime Act 2007 creates the following offences:[44]

44 Intentionally encouraging or assisting an offence

(1) A person commits an offence if—

   (a) he does an act capable of encouraging or assisting the commission of an offence; and

   (b) he intends to encourage or assist its commission.

(2) But he is not to be taken to have intended to encourage or assist the commission of an offence merely because such encouragement or assistance was a foreseeable consequence of his act.

45 Encouraging or assisting an offence believing it will be committed

A person commits an offence if—

   (a) he does an act capable of encouraging or assisting the commission of an offence; and

   (b) he believes—

      (i) that the offence will be committed; and

      (ii) that his act will encourage or assist its commission.

46 Encouraging or assisting offences believing one or more will be committed

(1) A person commits an offence if—

   (a) he does an act capable of encouraging or assisting the commission of one or more of a number of offences; and

   (b) he believes—

      (i) that one or more of those offences will be committed (but has no belief as to which); and

      (ii) that his act will encourage or assist the commission of one or more of them.

(2) It is immaterial for the purposes of subsection (1)(b)(ii) whether the person has any belief as to which offence will be encouraged or assisted.

---

[44] See Fortson (2008) for a helpful analysis of the Act.

(3) If a person is charged with an offence under subsection (1)—

    (a) the indictment must specify the offences alleged to be the 'number of offences' mentioned in paragraph (a) of that subsection; but

    (b) nothing in paragraph (a) requires all the offences potentially comprised in that number to be specified.

(4) In relation to an offence under this section, reference in this Part to the offences specified in the indictment is to the offences specified by virtue of subsection (3)(a).

. . .

50 Defence of acting reasonably

(1) A person is not guilty of an offence under this Part if he proves—

    (a) that he knew certain circumstances existed; and

    (b) that it was reasonable for him to act as he did in those circumstances.

(2) A person is not guilty of an offence under this Part if he proves—

    (a) that he believed certain circumstances to exist;

    (b) that his belief was reasonable; and

    (c) that it was reasonable for him to act as he did in the circumstances as he believed them to be.

(3) Factors to be considered in determining whether it was reasonable for a person to act as he did include—

    (a) the seriousness of the anticipated offence (or, in the case of an offence under section 44, the offences specified in the indictment);

    (b) any purpose for which he claims to have been acting;

    (c) any authority by which he claims to have been acting.

These provisions create three offences which render a defendant liable for offering encouragement or assistance, even where the offence is not committed. They provide, in effect, inchoate liability for accomplices. They should therefore be read alongside Chapter 15, which deals with the law on accomplices. The key difference between these offences and the law on accomplices is that for the latter the person encouraged or assisted must go on to commit an offence. However, for these Serious Crime Act offences there is no need to show that an offence resulted. So if Ashleigh gives Bobby a gun and asks him to kill Stephanie, Ashleigh should be charged as an accomplice if Bobby does indeed go on to kill; but under the Serious Crime Act if Bobby refuses to do what Ashleigh asks. That said, if Bobby does go on to commit murder there is no reason why Ashleigh would not be guilty of the Serious Crime Act offence: it is simply not the most serious charge the prosecution could bring. →5 (p.809)

The three offences are found in sections 44, 45, and 46 of the Act, quoted in the previous extract. They all involve doing 'an act capable of encouraging or assisting the commission of an offence'. They differ in the *mens rea* requirements. So first we will discuss the *actus reus* requirements which are the same for all three offences.

Doing an act which is capable of encouraging or assisting an offence

Although the offences do not require an actual crime to result, for all three of them the defendant must be shown to have done an act or omission[45] which is 'capable of encouraging

---

[45] Section 47(8) makes it clear that omissions are included.

or assisting an offence'. So, if the defendant wants to encourage or help another commit a crime, but his or her act is so inept that it could not help anyone commit a crime, no offence will be committed. However, this needs to be distinguished from a case where the defendant gives an act of encouragement or assistance which is in fact not helpful or encouraging, but if it was capable of being so could be an offence.[46] So, if Monica knows that Olive is planning to commit a murder, and posts her what she thinks is a bag of poison, but is in fact sugar, Monica could not be guilty of the offence, because the sugar was not capable of assisting the murder. However, if she sent poison, but Olive decided not to use it, Monica could be guilty, because her act was capable of being of assistance. This seems to set the hurdle for these offences very low: only on rare occasion will an act not be capable of assisting an offence at all. The statute does not say that the assistance has to be a substantial assistance and so, presumably, an act which is capable of assisting the commission of an offence to a small extent could be sufficient for the offence. Ormerod and Fortson suggest that 'the most marginal of acts might suffice'.[47] Indeed it also seems from the wording of the act that there is no need for the other party to know that the defendant had done the act capable of assisting or encouraging the offence. So in the example just discussed it would be irrelevant that Olive never received the package of poison. Monica's act of sending the poison was capable of assisting the offence and that is all that is required.

The court will consider whether there is encouragement looking at the broad context of the conversation. In *R v James Jones*[48] a shopkeeper whose shop stocked smoking equipment gave considerable advice to a client on how to grow 'tomatoes'. The prosecution argued that in reality the advice was about growing cannabis. The jury accepted this argument and convicted the defendant, a decision upheld on appeal.

Acts which help a person evade detection of an offence they have committed might be thought not to amount to assistance of an offence, but section 65(2) states that reducing the possibility of a criminal conviction can constitute assistance. This would suggest that helping someone escape from the scene of a crime, or to destroy evidence could amount to one of the Part 2 offences.[49]

The reference to 'encouragement' is ambiguous. If Mary tells Charles that she plans to kill Tom, and Charles says 'Well done'; would that be sufficient? Or will the courts require something more than an expression of support to amount to encouragement? Section 65(1) states that threats or pressurizing someone can amount to encouragement.

Mens rea requirements: section 44

The offences in sections 44, 45, and 46 all involve encouraging or assisting another to commit an offence, but there is a crucial difference in the *mens rea* required. For section 44 it must be shown that the defendant intended to encourage or assist in the commission of the offence,[50] while for section 45 or 46 the defendant needs simply to believe that the offence will be encouraged.[51] This makes section 44 a more serious offence than the other two.

---

[46] Section 47(9).   [47] Ormerod and Fortson (2009: 391).

[48] *R v James Jones* [2010] EWCA Crim 925.

[49] However, s. 65(3) makes it clear that failure to respond to a police officer's request for assistance is not included.

[50] Section 44(2) makes it clear that foreseeing that the act will be of assistance or encouragement is not enough for s. 44: there must be an intention.

[51] Section 47(2) makes it clear it is enough that the defendant wanted the other person to do the acts which would amount to an offence; the defendant does not have to know the conduct is a particular crime.

Section 45 or 46 would be appropriate where a person knows that what he or she is doing will assist or encourage, but does not particularly want to do so. Stark[52] argues that intention for the purposes of section 44 must be limited to direct intent and cannot cover indirect intent (see Chapter 3 for a discussion of the difference). He argues that this is because if the defendant simply foresees the results as virtually certain that will amount to a belief and so fall within section 45. This, however, might not follow. A defendant who foresees the result as virtually certain and is found to have intention under the *Woollin* direction might be guilty under both sections 44 and 45. It is not unusual for a defendant to be guilty of two crimes at the same time.[53]

There are a very complex set of provisions dealing with the question of whether the defendant (D) has to foresee that P (the person encouraged or assisted) will have the *mens rea* for the offence. Section 44 requires proof that D intended to encourage or assist the commission of an offence by P. This suggests that D must intend that P will have the necessary *mens rea* of the offence. Section 47(5), however, states that D will be guilty if he or she intends or foresees that P will have the necessary *mens rea*.[54] If the offence requires particular circumstances to be present then D must foresee or intend that that circumstances be present. So, to be guilty of the section 44 offence in relation to a charge of rape it must be shown that D intended P to sexually penetrate V; intending or foreseeing that P had the *mens rea* for rape and intending or foreseeing that V would not consent. To summarize, the *mens rea* for section 44 is that D:

- Intended to assist or encourage the commission of the offence.
- Foresaw or intended that P would have the *mens rea* for the offence.
- Foresaw or intended that any circumstances which are elements of the *actus reus* of the offence that is assisted or encouraged will be present.

There is some ambiguity over a case where the offence the defendant intends to encourage or assist is impossible. For example, what would the position be if Tracy encouraged Simon to kill Valerie, but Valerie was already dead. One reading of the statute is that as Tracy intended to encourage a murder and the acts were capable of encouraging a murder the offence is made out. Although it might be argued that the acts were not capable of encouraging 'the murder of Valerie' as that was an impossible offence. It is submitted that in such a case the correct charge would be an attempt to do an act capable of assistance or encouragement.[55]

Mens rea requirements: section 45

As already mentioned section 45 is to be used where the defendant (D) believes that the act will be of assistance or encouragement and that the offence will be committed. There is no need to show that D wants the offence to be committed. It is not made clear what degree of foresight would be sufficient. If a shopkeeper sells a kitchen knife to a dodgy looking customer, aware there is a risk that the knife will be used for the crime, would that be sufficient? As the statute refers to a belief that the offence will be committed, this indicates that

---

[52] Stark (2013a).

[53] e.g. a defendant may have committed both actual bodily harm and grievous bodily harm with a vicious wound.

[54] Section 47(5) also provides that D will be guilty if P lacks *mens rea*, but D would have the required fault if D had done the act. This provision is designed to deal with a case of innocent agency (see Chapter 15, Section 1.2, p.833).

[55] Section 47(8)(c) indicates that an attempt is included within the definition of the substantive offence.

a suspicion or fear will not be enough. Andrew Ashworth suggests that 'a belief is to act without any significant doubt on the matter.'[56] If the court follows that approach, which is the most natural reading of the section, the offence will not be as broad as might first be thought.

Schedule 3 to the Serious Crime Act lists a series of offences to which section 45 cannot apply. This includes conspiracies, attempts, and some statutory incitement offences.

Mens rea requirements: section 46

This offence is designed to deal with a situation where D encourages or assists P in committing a crime, but is unaware which crime P might commit. The section 46 offences involve D doing an act which is capable of encouraging or assisting one of a range of offences, believing that one of those offences will be committed. The *mens rea* is that D must believe his or her act will encourage or assist the commission of one of the offences. He or she must also believe that one of the offences will be committed. As discussed in relation to section 45, the reference to a belief that the offence 'will be committed' indicates there is a very strong belief that the offence will occur. A belief that an offence might occur will be insufficient. Also the section 46 offence will be made out if D believes one of a range of offences will be committed, but he is unsure which one it will be.[57] The Court of Appeal seeks to set out the *mens rea* for section 46 in this judgment:

R v Sadique
[2013] EWCA Crim 1150

Omar Sadique was convicted of assisting in the supply of controlled drugs of class A and class B contrary to section 46 of the Serious Crime Act 2007. The basis of the allegation was that he had supplied cutting agents like benzocaine and lignocaine. The appellant's defence was that he ran a legitimate business dealing in chemicals which he was perfectly entitled to supply, and he had no idea that they were being sold or supplied for misuse as cutting agents in the drugs trade. The problem at the heart of the case was that it was not known by Sadique if the agents were to be used for class A or class B drugs.

Lord Judge CJ

34. In our judgment the ingredients of the s.46 offence, and the ancillary provisions, and s.58(4)–(7) in particular, underline that an indictment charging a s.46 offence by reference to one or more offences is permissible, and covers the precise situation for which the legislation provides. Before the appellant in the present case could be convicted, the jury had to be satisfied that (a) he was involved in the supply of the relevant chemicals and (b) that, if misused criminally, the chemicals were capable of misuse by others to commit offences of supplying or being concerned in the supply of, or being in possession with intent to supply class A and/or class B drugs. None of this would be criminal unless it was also proved (c) that at the time when the relevant chemicals were being supplied, the appellant believed that what he was doing would encourage or assist the commission of one or more of these drug related offences and (d) that he also believed that this was the purpose, or one of the purposes, for which the chemicals would be used by those to whom he supplied them. If

---

[56] Ashworth (2009: 460).   [57] Section 47(4).

those ingredients were established, as the chemicals could be used for cutting agents for class A drugs or class B drugs, or both, it was not necessary for the Crown to prove that he had a specific belief about the particular drug related offence which those he was encouraging or assisting would or did commit.

In the following passage David Ormerod and Rudi Fortson seek to explain the *mens rea* required for the three offences:

D. Ormerod and R. Fortson, 'Serious Crime Act 2007: The Part 2 Offences' [2009] *Criminal Law Review* 389 at 404–8

(v) *Mens rea* elements

The principal differences between the new offences lie in the respective requirements. Each offence comprises a number of distinct mens rea elements:

- D's mens rea as to his own conduct;
- D's mens rea as to the assistance or encouragement that his conduct will provide;
- D's mens rea as to whether the anticipated offence will be committed by P;
- D's mens rea about P's likely mens rea if P were to commit the offence that D anticipates P will; and
- D's awareness of the existence of the proscribed circumstances and/or consequences of the offence that D anticipates that P will commit.

In order to identify the precise mens rea for each offence it is necessary to consider the language of ss.44–46 and, equally importantly, the extremely convoluted provisions of s.47. As noted, in interpreting the relevant mens rea it is useful to construe the actus reus of the anticipated offence as comprising external elements of (i) conduct, (ii) circumstances and (iii) consequences. This excessively technical approach to mens rea is drawn largely from the Law Commission's proposals in LC 300.

(a) D's mens rea as to his conduct. For each of the offences, D must intend to perform the conduct capable of encouraging P (for example, supplying a gun to P). This limb of the mens rea for the offences is not satisfied on proof of mere recklessness or negligence as to whether D's act might assist P, for example, where D leaves his gun in an unlocked cupboard and P helps himself to it.

(b) Mens rea as to the encouragement or assistance his conduct will provide. Under s.44 D must intend his acts to assist or encourage the commission of an offence. Under ss.45 and 46 it is sufficient that he believes they will (not might) assist or encourage. Each term deserves elaboration.

Intention

In relation to the s.44 offence, s.44(2) makes clear that "intention" is not satisfied by proof that the encouragement was a foreseeable consequence of the act. The provision is designed to make clear that the defendant's "intention" refers to his purpose and that the concept of "virtually certain consequences" has no part to play here. Thus, D might lend a gun to P and yet it might not have been D's purpose (intention) that, by giving the gun to P, the latter would use it to rob a bank, notwithstanding that it was "virtually certain" that P would do so. The section fails to make that as clear as it might. There is a further problem with the specific definition in relation to s.44. Because purposive intent is required here, but not commonly elsewhere in the criminal law (where oblique intent will usually suffice), jurors will be faced with two definitions of the same word in many cases to which s.44 applies, for example at the joint trial of D and P where D assisted by supplying the gun for P to murder V.

Belief

In s.45 D must believe that his act that is capable of assisting or encouraging will assist or encourage the anticipated offence and in s.46 that it will assist or encourage *one* of the possible anticipated offences. Belief is a mens rea concept which has given rise to difficulty in interpretation throughout the criminal law and its boundaries remain ambiguous, lying as it does between the equally vague concepts of suspicion and knowledge. No definition of "belief is attempted in the Act. It seems safe to assume that "belief" constitutes a state of subjective awareness short of knowledge, but greater than mere suspicion. Thus, in *Hall*, the Court of Appeal spoke of "belief" in the following terms:

> "Belief, of course, is something short of knowledge. It may be said to be the state of mind of a person who says to himself: 'I cannot say I know for certain that [the circumstance exists] but there can be no other reasonable conclusion in the light of all the circumstances, in the light of all that I have heard and seen.' "[58]

In *Moys* the court suggested that the question whether D knew or believed that the proscribed circumstance existed, is a subjective one, and that suspicion, even coupled with the fact that D shut his eyes to the circumstances, is not enough. By way of contrast, although in secondary liability the courts purport to apply a test of "knowledge" of what P might do, in practice they apply a much lower mens rea requirement satisfied by contemplation of the risk of a real possibility that P will commit it.

Whether the courts will be as prepared to dilute the meaning of belief in the context of the present offences is unclear. It is submitted that the offences are already broad enough, and that the principle of construing criminal statutes narrowly ought to apply.

(c) D's mens rea as to whether the anticipated offence will be committed by P. Again this mens rea element differs slightly for each offence. Under s.44 it is clear that D must intend the offence to be committed whilst under s.45 it is sufficient if he believes it will (not might) be committed and under s.46 that D believes that one or more of those offences will be committed (but has no belief as to which). Intention and belief share the meanings discussed in the previous paragraph.

(d) D's mens rea as to P's mens rea with regard to the conduct element of the offence. There is a further, crucial limb of the mens rea of each of the three offences under Pt 2 and this, in ordinary language, concerns D's state of mind in relation to what he *anticipates* P will do (i.e. with regard to the conduct element of the anticipated offence) *and with what state of mind*. In relation to all three offences, the mens rea is satisfied by D's belief that P will act with the requisite mens rea for the commission of the anticipated offence (s.47(5) (a)(i)) or, that D is reckless whether P will so act (s.47(5)(a)(ii)). Two criticisms can be made of this element of the mens rea. First, discovering that this is the mens rea is no easy task. For example, s.44 requires that D *intended* to encourage or assist the commission of an "offence". That must be construed in accordance with s.47(2), "it is sufficient to prove that

---

[58] *Hall* (1985) 81 Cr App R 260 at 264, [1985] Crim LR 377.

[D] intended to encourage or assist the *doing of an act* which would *amount to the commission of an offence*". Thus, D's intention must relate to "an act" that would be done by P which constitutes the *conduct element* only of the actus reus of the anticipated offence. Thereafter, D's liability turns on his state of mind—not P's—in relation to the anticipated offence elements of *conduct* (e.g. appropriating property), *circumstances* (e.g. belonging to another) and *consequences*. Section 47(5) and (8) provides [emphasis added]:

"(5) (a) if the offence is one requiring proof of *fault*, it must be proved that—

    (i) D *believed* that, were the act to be done, it would be done with that fault;

    (ii) D was *reckless* as to whether or not it would be done with that fault; or

    (iii) D's state of mind was such that, were he to do it, it would be done with that fault; and

(8) Reference in this section to the doing of an act includes reference to—

    (a) a failure to act;

    (b) the continuation of an act that has already begun;

    (c) an attempt to do an act (except an act amounting to the commission of the offence of attempting to commit another offence)."

It is important to recall that the expression "doing of an act" in s.47(8) refers to the act of the perpetrator (P)—not the actions of D.

The second criticism of the element of mens rea is that "recklessness" suffices for such broad-reaching inchoate offences. This might strike some readers as surprising, particularly as the concept of recklessness is not expressly mentioned in the Law Commission's draft Bill. However, it is arguable that the Law Commission did not need to make explicit reference to "recklessness" given that it had recommended that defendants ought to be liable if they are "prepared for a criminal act to be done not caring whether or not the circumstances element of the offence is present". The Law Commission did not think it necessary to make specific provision in its draft Bill to embrace "indifference", believing that the wording of cl.1(2)(a) and cl.2(3)(a)—on which s.47(5)(a)(i) and s.47(5)(a)(iii) are modelled—was adequate to capture such cases.

By s.47(5)(a)(iii) it is also sufficient if D would have mens rea were he to commit the anticipated crime even though he does not believe and is not reckless as to whether P would have it. For example, D encourages P to rape V. P has sex with V but lacks mens rea for rape. D is guilty of encouraging rape if D had the mens rea for rape (as for example in *Cogan and Leak*). Where this sub-paragraph is relied on, D is to be assumed to be able to do the act in question, so there is no defence of impossibility for him (s.47(6)). In this example, D can therefore be guilty for assisting or encouraging rape even if D is a woman. This goes further than the common law.

(e) D's mens rea as to circumstances and consequences of the anticipated crime. The final element of mens rea relates to D's state of mind as to the proscribed circumstances and consequences of the offence he anticipates. Once again we must return to the tortuous s.47. By s.47(5)(b) if the offence is one requiring proof of particular *circumstances or consequences* (or both), it must be proved that:

"(i) D *believed* [*intended or believed: s.44*] [*believed: ss.45 and 46*] that, were the act to be done, it would be done in those circumstances or with those consequences; or

    (ii) D was *reckless* as to whether or not it would be done in those circumstances or with those consequences." (Emphasis added.)

The effect of this is best explained by a series of examples. If D encourages P to have sex with V (aged 12), for s.44 D must intend, or believe, or be reckless as to whether the child whom he has encouraged P to touch sexually would be under 13 if the act (by P) was done (circumstances). As a second example, in a case where D2 encourages or assists P to use violence on V, D2 would only be liable for assisting or encouraging murder under s.44 if he intended, believed or was reckless as to the consequence (V's death) arising. As a further example, if D3 writes a letter to P, encouraging P to break V's window, to be liable D3 must believe, (or intend under s.44) or be reckless as to the consequence (V's property being damaged) arising. Explaining these elements and rules to a jury will be no mean achievement.

Defences

The Act provides a defence for a person acting reasonably. This is explained in section 50:

(1) A person is not guilty of an offence under this Part if he proves—
  (a) that he knew certain circumstances existed; and
  (b) that it was reasonable for him to act as he did in those circumstances.
(2) A person is not guilty of an offence under this Part if he proves—
  (a) that he believed certain circumstances to exist;
  (b) that his belief was reasonable; and
  (c) that it was reasonable for him to act as he did in the circumstances as he believed them to be.
(3) Factors to be considered in determining whether it was reasonable for a person to act as he did include—
  (a) the seriousness of the anticipated offence (or, in the case of an offence under section 46, the offences specified in the indictment);
  (b) any purpose for which he claims to have been acting;
  (c) any authority by which he claims to have been acting.

This section is particularly relevant for shopkeepers and others supplying items to the public, aware that it is possible the items they supply could assist an offence. If a shopkeeper sells a knife to a threatening individual, realizing that it could be used in a crime, the shopkeeper will have to rely on the jury finding his or her conduct reasonable.

Section 51 provides that if an offence is designed to protect a particular category of persons then they cannot be charged under the Serious Crime Act, Part 2 offences. This is most relevant in the case of sexual offences against children because it means that a child cannot be charged with encouraging a sexual offence against him or herself.

Assessment of the Act

David Ormerod and Rudi Fortson suggest that Part 2 of the Serious Crime Act 2007 'creates some of the most convoluted offences in decades' and refer to their 'excessive complexity' and 'unwarranted incoherence'.[59] These comments must be read in the light of the fact that they replaced the common law offence of incitement, which itself was notoriously complex. That said, it is hard not to agree with Ashworth's observation that 'simplicity and clarity were not high on the draftsman's agenda'.[60] While complexity might be a price one

[59] Ormerod and Fortson (2009: 389).   [60] Ashworth (2009: 462).

is willing to pay for clarity in the law, here there is the double whammy of both complexity and ambiguity.

These concerns have been acknowledged by the Justice Committee of the House of Commons:

House of Commons, Justice Committee, *Post-Legislative Scrutiny of Part 2 (Encouraging or Assisting Crime) of the Serious Crime Act 2007* (London: TSO, 2013)

The criticisms of Part 2 of the Act made by Professors Spencer and Virgo and Dr Child break down into the following topics:

a) **Unintelligible**—academics, practitioners and judges reported that the sections are very difficult to interpret. In the 2011 *Sadique* appeal Hooper LJ commented that "the provisions creating and defining section 46 are very complex." He added that the Court had needed extra time and further written submissions in order to try to understand how section 46 operated. Professor Graham Virgo said that he lectured on this topic to law undergraduates, and that:

> in my opinion, this is the worst piece of legislation to be enacted for a significant time. The unnecessary complexity and prolixity of Part 2 makes it very difficult to explain and to understand. A number of the students subsequently informed me that, if they, as bright students, find it very difficult to understand the law, what hope is there for jurors untrained in the law?

b) **Interrelation of sections**—the Law Commission's original proposal was adapted by the then Government and turned from two into three statutory sections. However, the individual sections cannot be interpreted on their own. In order to understand section 46, for example, the Court of Appeal in *Sadique* in 2011 and 2013 had to interpret sections 47–58 and 64–67. The three main sections do not contain all the basic information to interpret the *actus reus* or *mens rea* elements.

c) **The mental element—*mens rea***—Dr Child pointed out that inchoate offences are necessarily more complex in terms of the *mens rea* element of the offence, than normal offences:

> This is because D must perform the *actus reus* (assist or encourage) with certain *mens rea* both as to his own acts as well as certain *mens rea* as to the future acts of another (P). Indeed, in the context of two party offences (such as assisting and encouraging) D must also have a certain *mens rea* in relation to the *mens rea* of P. Such complexity is unavoidable if we wish to have a statute capable of setting out the full requirements of the offence, an approach that I firmly support.

However, as Dr Child and the other academics point out, the SCA drafting has actually increased the inherent complexity of inchoate offences. Under the SCA, D must intend (s.44) or believe (s.45–46) the act element of the future offence, but this is merely the use/ hitting of the hammer. In contrast, D need only be reckless as to whether P will damage property (result/consequences element) and whether that property will belong to another (circumstance element). Professor Ormerod and Rudi Fortson QC discuss this in their 2009 Criminal Law Review article. They suggest that:

> Crucial to understanding the operation of the offences is a recognition that the traditional interpretative tools of *actus reus* and *mens rea* will prove inadequate. Each offence must be analysed having regard to one or more of three external elements of the *actus reus* of the offence D anticipates P will commit, namely, (i) conduct, (ii)

circumstances, and (iii) consequences. (. . .) D's liability will turn on whether he has the distinct specified *mens rea* for each of these three separate elements of P's anticipated crime (s.47(5)(b)). (. . .) D must be proved to have *mens rea* (but not necessarily of the same type) in respect of each of those elements. But, not all offences subdivide so easily and, of course, not all offences have all three elements.

Applying this to a section 46 "one or more offence" case leads to the following analysis, which shows both the variety and difficulty of understanding and applying the different types of mental element; we bear in mind that often it will be a jury who must understand and apply these sections. D will be liable if:

i. D supplies a hammer which is capable of encouraging or assisting the commission by P of one or more of a number of offences (for example, criminal damage, assault, burglary); and

ii. D *believes* that his act of supplying the weapon to P *will* (not might) encourage or assist the commission of at least one of those offences; and

iii. Although it cannot be proved that D had a belief or intent as to which *one* will be committed, it can be proved that D *believes* that one or more such offences *will* (not might) be committed; and

iv. D *believes* or is *reckless* as to whether when P is to perform the *conduct* element of the offence (hitting the window with the hammer) P will do so with the *mens rea* required for that offence (or D's state of mind is sufficient itself if it is such that were he (D) to do it, it would be done with the fault required); and

v. D *believes* or is *reckless* as to whether, were P to perform the *conduct* element of the offence, P would do so in those *circumstances* (window belonged to another) or with those *consequences* (window is damaged) if any of which the anticipated offence requires proof.

. . .[61]

e) **Plugging the gap in the law**—Professor Spencer suggested that the *Sadique* judgment showed that the gap in the law he identified had been filled, but he did not think that this could be considered a success:

the complexity and obscurity of the provisions make it impossible to say that they have plugged the gap "successfully". [. . .] they are the legislative equivalent of the nursery rhyme about the Old Lady Who Swallowed a Fly—and then swallowed a spider to catch the fly, then swallowed a bird to catch the spider, and so on.

4 CONSPIRACY

DEFINITION

A conspiracy is an agreement by two or more people to engage in a course of conduct which amounts to a criminal offence (or corrupt public morals or fraud).

---

61 I have omitted criticism of case law which has since been overruled.

4.1 THE NATURE OF CONSPIRACY

It is an offence to conspire to commit:

(1) any criminal offence,[62] including aiding, abetting, counselling, procuring, or inciting an offence.[63] These are known as statutory conspiracies;

(2) a small number of activities which are not in and of themselves illegal, but which common law has decreed it is an offence to conspire to commit. They are:

   (a) to defraud; and

   (b) (maybe) to do an act which corrupts public morals.

These are known as common law conspiracies.

The vast majority of conspiracies are, therefore, statutory conspiracies, although a few are common law conspiracies. There is no rational reason why there should be these two categories of conspiracies, except to annoy law students. The distinction is particularly unfortunate because the law governing statutory conspiracies and common law conspiracies differs. The basis for the distinction between these two kinds of conspiracy is found in the wording of the Criminal Law Act 1977. Under section 1(1) it is an offence to agree to commit any offence. Section 5(1) and (2) reads as follows:

> (1) Subject to the following provisions of the section, the offence of conspiracy at common law is hereby abolished.
>
> (2) Subsection (1) above shall not affect the offence of conspiracy at common law so far as relates to conspiracy to defraud.

This was interpreted by the House of Lords in *Ayres*[64] to mean that all conspiracies which involve an agreement to commit a criminal offence are statutory conspiracies and cannot be common law conspiracies. →6 (p.823)

4.2 STATUTORY CONSPIRACIES

> **DEFINITION**
>
> To constitute a conspiracy there must be:
>
> (1) an agreement;
>
> (2) the agreement must be to pursue a course of conduct that will involve the commission of a crime;
>
> (3) the parties must intend to do the act which is required for the offence and must intend or know that the circumstances within the *actus reus* exist.

---

[62] The consent of the DPP is required before a charge of conspiracy to commit a summary offence can be brought (Criminal Law Act 1977, s. 4(1)).

[63] See e.g. *Booth* [1999] Crim LR 144.   [64] [1984] AC 447 (HL).

Section 1(1) of the Criminal Law Act 1977 (as amended by section 5 of the Criminal Attempts Act 1981) provides:

> Subject to the following provisions of this part of this Act, if a person agrees with any other person or persons that a course of conduct shall be pursued which, if the agreement is carried out in accordance with their intentions, either—
>
> (a) will necessarily amount to or involve the commission of any offence or offences by one or more parties to the agreement, or
>
> (b) would do so but for the existence of facts which render the commission of the offence or any offences impossible,
>
> he is guilty of conspiracy to commit the offence or offences in question.

This statutory definition indicates that a conspiracy is made up of the following elements:

An agreement

The need for an agreement

The key element of the *actus reus* of the offence of conspiracy is an agreement. The parties must have reached a decision to carry out the unlawful plan as a joint project. They must have gone beyond the stage of negotiation and reached the stage where there is an agreement.[65] It is not necessary to show that every member of the conspiracy has communicated with every other. What needs to be shown is that the common purpose has been communicated by the defendant to at least one other party to the conspiracy.[66] If Steve is aware that Jonathan and Bryony are conspiring to commit a crime and he does things to help them, this does not make him a conspirator: he must enter some kind of agreement with Jonathan and Bryony.[67] In some cases it can be difficult to decide whether many people happen to be pursuing the same crime independently (e.g. several members of the public carrying out the same kind of fraud on a company) or whether they are acting in concert.[68]

Once the parties have reached an agreement the *actus reus* of a conspiracy has occurred.[69] Therefore, if the parties agree to commit a crime, but then later decide not to go ahead with the plan, they may be convicted of a conspiracy.[70] Indeed the parties can be guilty of a conspiracy even though they have not taken any steps to implement the agreement.[71] Lord Nicholls in *Saik*[72] was very clear about this: 'The offence therefore lies in making an agreement. Implicitly, the subsection requires also that the parties intend to carry out their agreement. The offence is complete at that stage. The offence is complete even if the parties do not carry out their agreement.'

As long as the parties have reached a clear agreement to commit an offence it is not necessary to show that they have agreed all of the details of the plan. Two people may be guilty of

---

[65] *Walker* [1962] Crim LR 458; *Mills* (1963) 47 Cr App R 49.   [66] *Ardalan* [1972] 2 All ER 257.

[67] *Griffiths* (1965) 49 Cr App R 94 (CA); *contra Meyrick* (1929) 21 Cr App R 523 (CA).

[68] A person can be guilty of conspiracy by joining together with others who have already agreed to commit a crime (*Zezev* [2002] Crim LR 648).

[69] *Hussain, Bhatti and Bhatti* [2002] Crim LR 407.   [70] *Thomson* (1965) 50 Cr App R 1.

[71] *DPP v Nock* [1978] AC 979.   [72] [2006] UKHL 18, para. 3.

conspiring to burgle, even though they are yet to agree where and when they will commit that crime. It is also a conspiracy to reach a conditional agreement. It would, therefore, be a conspiracy to burgle if the agreement were that 'if the house is unoccupied we will burgle it'.[73]

Who can be the parties to a conspiracy?

To amount to a conspiracy there must be at least two parties to the agreement. However, agreements between certain people cannot be a conspiracy:

(1) An agreement between a husband and wife[74] or civil partners is not a conspiracy (Criminal Law Act 1977, section 2(2)(a)).[75] However, an agreement between a wife, a husband, and a third party can be.[76] The explanation for this rule is that the criminal law seeks to protect marital privacy.

(2) An agreement between one person and a person under the age of criminal responsibility cannot amount to a criminal conspiracy.[77]

(3) An agreement between the defendant and the intended victim[78] of the crime is not a criminal conspiracy.[79] So if D agrees with V illegally to cut off V's leg this does not amount to a conspiracy. However, it appears that if D conspires with others that drugs will be supplied to him or her, he or she can be guilty of a conspiracy.[80]

(4) There can be no conspiracy if the only two parties to the agreement are a company and the director of that company who is solely responsible for the conduct of the company's business.[81]

There must be at least two parties to the agreement who have the necessary *mens rea* for a conspiracy. If only one party has the *mens rea* then there cannot be a conspiracy. For example, if one party but not the other is aware of a fact that makes the proposed course of conduct illegal then there will be no conspiracy. If all parties to the alleged conspiracy are charged together it is not open to the jury to convict only one of them, unless the evidence against that one conspirator is markedly stronger than the evidence against the others, and the jury is convinced the person convicted conspired with someone, even if they are not sure who that was.[82]

An agreement to commit a crime

The conspirators must agree on a course of conduct which constitutes the *actus reus* of a crime. It is possible to conspire to attempt or to conspire to conspire. However, a conspiracy to aid, abet, counsel, or procure an offence is not itself a crime according to *Kenning*.[83]

But what exactly must the conspirators know if they are to be said to have agreed to commit a crime?

---

[73] *O'Hadhmaill* [1996] Crim LR 509.
[74] This rule does not apply to an unmarried cohabiting couple.
[75] Of course, if a husband and wife go on to commit a crime they will be guilty of the substantive offence.
[76] *Chrastny* [1991] 1 WLR 1381.   [77] Criminal Law Act 1977, s. 2(2)(b).
[78] The word 'victim' is not defined in the Criminal Law Act 1977.
[79] Criminal Law Act 1977, s. 2(2)(c).   [80] *Drew* [2000] 1 Cr App R 91.
[81] *McDonnell* [1966] 1 QB 233.
[82] Section 5(8) and (9) of the Criminal Law Act 1977; *Roberts* (1983) 78 Cr App R 41.
[83] [2008] EWCA Crim 1534. It is, however, possible to convict someone of conspiring to commit a statutory offence whose *actus reus* involves aiding or abetting something (e.g. aiding and abetting another's suicide (*Reed* [1982] Crim LR 819)).

(1) There is no need to show that the conspirators knew that their proposed course of conduct amounted to a crime.[84]

(2) The parties must intend the consequences of their actions which are parts of the *actus reus*. For example, it is not enough for a charge of a conspiracy to kill to show that the parties agreed to put poison in the victim's cup of tea; they must also intend the victim to die as a result.[85] If the agreement is to put poison in the victim's cup of tea with the intention of causing discomfort to the victim, but the victim dies, there is no conspiracy to kill[86] simply because the parties did not agree to kill. Even if the conspirators foresaw the risk that their conduct might kill a victim, there is no conspiracy to murder unless they intended the death.[87] Some doubt over the law as stated in this paragraph now exists as a result of the decision in *R v Saskavickas*,[88] where it was suggested that recklessness would be sufficient. However, subsequently, in *R v Harmer*[89] and *Ali*[90] the Court of Appeal confirmed the standard approach that the defendants must know or intend the facts to exist.

(3) Knowledge of essential facts. The conspirators must be aware of any circumstances which form part of the *actus reus* and therefore render their proposed conduct illegal or intend those facts to exist.[91] If two people reach an agreement to grow some plants unaware that the plants are cannabis or agree to have intercourse with a woman, being unsure whether or not she will consent, they will not be guilty of a conspiracy because they do not know[92] the circumstantial facts which are essential to the conspiracy. The Court of Appeal applied this reasoning in finding that an agreement to import Class B drugs is not sufficient to justify a conviction for an agreement to import Class A drugs.[93]

(4) Mistaken beliefs of the conspirators. The conspirators will be judged on their planned actions, not what actually happened. For example, if the parties agreed to plant seeds, believing that they would produce cannabis plants, but in fact the seeds were parsnip seeds, they would be guilty of a conspiracy to produce cannabis.

(5) Intention to commit a more serious crime. If D agrees with A to commit crime X, but secretly intends to commit a more serious crime, then D will be guilty of conspiring to commit crime X. However, if D agrees with A to commit crime X, but in fact intends to commit a lesser crime (e.g. D agrees with A to kill V, but intends just to beat V up) he or she will not be guilty of a conspiracy to commit crime X.[94] If they have both agreed to commit an offence, but differ over some details, this will not affect their criminal liability. So if one conspirator thought that the agreement was to produce one kind of Class A drug and the other conspirator thought the agreement was to produce a different kind of Class A drug, they could be said to be both guilty of conspiring to produce a Class A drug.[95]

---

[84] *Churchill v Walton* [1967] 2 AC 224.

[85] An intention to cause grievous bodily harm is therefore insufficient for a conspiracy to murder (*Siracusa* (1990) 90 Cr App R 340, 350).

[86] Although they may be guilty of murder.

[87] Although there might be a conspiracy to poison (Offences Against the Person Act 1861, ss 23 and 24).

[88] [2004] EWCA Crim 2686.   [89] [2005] EWCA Crim 1.   [90] [2005] Crim LR 864.

[91] *Saik* [2006] UKHL 18. For a discussion of the problems in correctly charging conspiracies, see Jarvis and Bisgrove (2014).

[92] In the rape example they suspect, but do not know, that the victim will not consent.

[93] *Taylor* [2002] Crim LR 205 (CA), although the Court of Appeal added that if one person thought that the agreement was to produce Class A drugs and the other thought it was to produce Class B drugs there could be no conspiracy.

[94] *Barnard* (1980) 70 Cr App R 28.   [95] *Broad* [1997] Crim LR 666 (CA).

The plan must necessarily involve the commission of a crime by one or more of the parties

Section 1(1) of the Criminal Law Act 1977 makes it clear that the plan must necessarily involve the commission of a crime. There are two points to consider further:

(1) The agreement must be that at least one of the parties to the conspiracy will commit the crime. So if a gang reaches an agreement that its leader will commit a crime, but the leader is not present at the meeting and so is not a party to the agreement, there is no conspiracy.

(2) The proposed course of conduct must necessarily involve the commission of a crime. The word 'necessarily' is problematic.[96] Very few agreements will inevitably involve the commission of the crime, not least because the conspirators are likely explicitly or implicitly to agree that the plan will not go ahead if there is a police officer at the scene of the crime. Fortunately the courts have refused to treat the word 'necessarily' in a strict way. Lord Nicholls in *Saik*[97] explained: 'A conspiracy to rob a bank tomorrow if the coast is clear when the conspirators reach the bank is not, by reason of this qualification, any less a conspiracy to rob. In the nature of things, every agreement to do something in the future is hedged about with conditions, implicit if not explicit.' In *Jackson*[98] four members of a gang arranged to shoot one of their members (W) in the leg. W was on trial for burglary and the hope was that the judge would be sympathetic to W because of his leg injury and pass a lower sentence than he would otherwise. They were charged with a conspiracy to pervert the course of justice. The conspirators argued that their plan did not necessarily involve the perversion of justice because W might have been acquitted of the offence. The Court of Appeal focused on the words 'if the agreement is carried out in accordance with their intentions' and held that the question to ask was if the 'plan worked' would an offence be committed? Here, if the plan worked, W would receive a lesser sentence. The Court of Appeal in *Jackson* expressly rejected an argument that 'necessarily' meant inevitably. Indeed the point was made that the conspirators might think that it was extremely unlikely that their plan would work but could still be held to have conspired to commit an offence.

The Court of Appeal in *Jackson* gave as an example of a plan which would not necessarily involve the commission of an offence an agreement by two people to drive to Edinburgh within a certain time which could be achieved if the traffic was especially light, but if the traffic congestion was at normal levels would require the parties to break the speed limits. In *O'Hadhmaill*[99] a man was charged with conspiring to cause an IRA explosion if the peace talks failed. He argued that he had not agreed on a course of conduct which necessarily amounted to an offence. He was convicted, which the Court of Appeal subsequently upheld.

QUESTION

Tom and Una agree to rob a bank. Tom suggests that if a police officer tries to arrest them they will kill him. Is this a conspiracy to kill? (Consider whether this is closer to *O'Hadhmaill* or closer to the drivers to Edinburgh discussed in *Jackson*.)

---

[96] Notably it is omitted from the Draft Criminal Code.   [97] [2006] UKHL 18, para. 5.
[98] [1985] Crim LR 444 (CA).   [99] [1996] Crim LR 509 (CA).

Intention that the plan be carried out

We have already seen that the parties' plan must involve the commission of an offence and that this requires them to know of any facts or circumstances which are aspects of the *actus reus*. Suspicion that the facts or circumstances might exist is insufficient.[100] However, the *mens rea* for a conspiracy goes further than this and requires each defendant to intend the conspiracy to be carried out. This is so even if the crime is one of strict liability.[101] It appears that foresight of a result as virtually certain can amount to intention, along the lines of the *Woollin* decision.[102]

This intent requirement appears to be straightforward. But this element of the offence was thrown into doubt by the following decision of the House of Lords in *Anderson*:[103]

R v Anderson
[1986] AC 27 (HL)

William Anderson was convicted of conspiring with others to effect the escape of Ahmed Andaloussi, a prisoner at Lewes Prison. The prosecution alleged that Anderson had been paid £20,000 for his part in the escape plan. He was to purchase and supply diamond wire of a kind capable of cutting through metal bars. This was to be smuggled into the prison by other conspirators. In fact, shortly after receiving the £20,000 Anderson was injured in a car accident and unable to supply the wire in pursuance of the plan. He claimed that he was going to supply the wire and then escape to Spain, playing no further role in the escape. He argued before the House of Lords that he lacked the *mens rea* for a conspiracy because he did not intend the escape plan to come into effect.

Lord Bridge of Harwich

The Court of Appeal, having dismissed his appeal, certified that its decision involved a point of law of general public importance in terms which can conveniently be divided into two parts, since, in truth, there are two separate questions involved:

> '[1] Is a person who "agrees" with two or more others, who themselves intend to pursue a course of conduct which will necessarily involve the commission of an offence, and who has a secret intention himself to participate in part only of that course of conduct, guilty himself of conspiracy to commit that offence under Section 1(1) of the Criminal Law Act 1977 [2] if not is he liable to be indicted as a principal offender under Section 8 of the Accessories and Abettors Act 1861?'

The present appeal is brought by leave of your Lordships' House.

Section 1(1) of the Criminal Law Act 1977 has been amended by the Criminal Attempts Act 1981, but the point of construction arising in this appeal is in no way affected by the

---

[100] *Saik* [2006] UKHL 18; *Suchedina* [2007] Crim LR 301 (CA).

[101] Criminal Law Act 1977, s. 1(2).

[102] *Cooke* [1986] AC 909 (HL), where British Rail employees were convicted of a conspiracy to defraud British Rail. The purpose of their plan was to make money for themselves, but they were aware that in doing so they were virtually certain to cause British Rail losses and so could be said to have intended to cause those losses.

[103] [1986] AC 27 (HL).

amendment. It is sufficient, therefore, for the present purposes, to set out the language of the subsection as originally enacted. It provides as follows:

'Subject to the following provisions of this Part of this Act, if a person agrees with any other person or persons that a course of conduct shall be pursued which will necessarily amount to or involve the commission of any offence or offences by one or more of the parties to the agreement if the agreement is carried out in accordance with their intentions, he is guilty of conspiracy to commit the offence or offences in question.'

The 1977 Act, subject to exceptions not presently material, abolished the offence of conspiracy at common law. It follows that the elements of the new statutory offence of conspiracy must be ascertained purely by interpretation of the language of s 1(1) of the 1977 Act. For purposes of analysis it is perhaps convenient to isolate the three clauses each of which must be taken as indicating an essential ingredient of the offence as follows: (1) 'if a person agrees with any other person or persons that a course of conduct shall be pursued' (2) 'which will necessarily amount to or involve the commission of any offence or offences by one or more of the parties to the agreement' (3) 'if the agreement is carried out in accordance with their intentions'.

Clause (1) presents, as it seems to me, no difficulty. It means exactly what it says and what it says is crystal clear. To be convicted, the party charged must have agreed with one or more others that 'a course of conduct shall be pursued'. What is important is to resist the temptation to introduce into this simple concept ideas derived from the civil law of contract. Any number of persons may agree that a course of conduct shall be pursued without undertaking any contractual liability. The agreed course of conduct may be a simple or an elaborate one and may involve the participation of two or any larger number of persons who may have agreed to play a variety of roles in the course of conduct agreed.

Again, clause (2) could hardly use simpler language. Here what is important to note is that it is not necessary that more than one of the participants in the agreed course of conduct shall commit a substantive offence. It is, of course, necessary that any party to the agreement shall have assented to play his part in the agreed course of conduct, however innocent in itself, knowing that the part to be played by one or more of the others will amount to or involve the commission of an offence.

It is only clause (3) which presents any possible ambiguity. The heart of the submission for the appellant is that in order to be convicted of conspiracy to commit a given offence the language of clause (3) requires that the party charged should not only have agreed that a course of conduct shall be pursued which will necessarily amount to or involve the commission of that offence by himself or one or more other parties to the agreement, but must also be proved himself to have intended that that offence should be committed. Thus, it is submitted here that the appellant's case that he never intended that Andaloussi should be enabled to escape from prison raised an issue to be left to the jury, who should have been directed to convict him only if satisfied that he did so intend. I do not find it altogether easy to understand why the draftsman of this provision chose to use the phrase 'in accordance with their intentions'. But I suspect the answer may be that this seemed a desirable alternative to the phrase 'in accordance with its terms' or any similar expression, because it is a matter of common experience in the criminal courts that the 'terms' of a criminal conspiracy are hardly ever susceptible of proof. The evidence from which a jury may infer a criminal conspiracy is almost invariably to be found in the conduct of the parties. This was so at common law and remains so under the statute. If the evidence in a given case justifies the inference of an agreement that a course of conduct should be pursued, it is a not inappropriate formulation of the test of the criminality of the inferred agreement to ask whether the further inference can be drawn that a crime would necessarily have been committed if the agreed course of conduct had been pursued in accordance with the several intentions of the parties. Whether that is an accurate analysis or not, I am clearly driven by consideration of the diversity of roles which parties may agree to play in criminal conspiracies to reject any construction of the statutory language which would require the prosecution to prove an intention on the part of each conspirator that the criminal offence or offences which will necessarily be committed by one or more of the conspirators if the agreed course of conduct is fully carried out should in fact be committed. A simple example will illustrate the absurdity to which this construction would lead. The proprietor of a car hire firm agrees for a substantial payment to make available a hire car to a gang for use in a robbery and to make false entries in his books relating to the hiring to which he can point if the number of the car is traced back to him in connection with the robbery. Being fully aware of the circumstances of the robbery in which the car is proposed to be used he is plainly a party to the conspiracy to rob. Making his car available for use in the robbery is as much a part of the relevant agreed course of conduct as the robbery itself. Yet, once he has been paid, it will be a matter of complete indifference to him whether the robbery is in fact committed or not. In these days of highly organised crime the most serious statutory conspiracies will frequently involve an elaborate and complex agreed course of conduct in which many will consent to play necessary but subordinate roles, not involving them in any direct participation in the commission of the offence or offences at the centre of the conspiracy. Parliament cannot have intended that such parties should escape conviction of conspiracy on the basis that it cannot be proved against them that they intended that the relevant offence or offences should be committed.

There remains the important question whether a person who has agreed that a course of conduct will be pursued which, if pursued as agreed, will necessarily amount to or involve the commission of an offence is guilty of statutory conspiracy irrespective of his intention, and, if not, what is the *mens rea* of the offence. I have no hesitation in answering the first part of the question in the negative. There may be many situations in which perfectly respectable citizens, more particularly those concerned with law enforcement, may enter into agreements that a course of conduct shall be pursued which will involve commission of a crime without the least intention of playing any part in furtherance of the ostensibly agreed criminal objective, but rather with the purpose of exposing and frustrating the criminal purpose of the other parties to the agreement. To say this is in no way to encourage schemes by which police act, directly or through the agency of informers, as agents provocateurs for the purpose of entrapment. That is conduct of which the courts have always strongly disapproved. But it may sometimes happen, as most of us with experience in criminal trials well know, that a criminal enterprise is well advanced in the course of preparation when it comes to the notice either of the police or of some honest citizen in such circumstances that the only prospect of exposing and frustrating the criminals is that some innocent person should play the part of an intending collaborator in the course of criminal conduct proposed to be pursued. The *mens rea* implicit in the offence of statutory conspiracy must clearly be such as to recognise the innocence of such a person, notwithstanding that he will, in literal terms, be obliged to agree that a course of conduct be pursued involving the commission of an offence.

I have said already, but I repeat to emphasise its importance, that an essential ingredient in the crime of conspiring to commit a specific offence or offences under s 1(1) of the 1977 Act is that the accused should agree that a course of conduct be pursued which he knows must involve the commission by one or more of the parties to the agreement of that offence or those offences. But, beyond the mere fact of agreement, the necessary *mens rea* of the crime is, in my opinion, established if, and only if, it is shown that the accused, when he entered into the agreement, intended to play some part in the agreed course of conduct in furtherance of the criminal purpose which the agreed course of conduct was intended to achieve. Nothing less will suffice nothing more is required.

Applying this test to the facts which, for the purposes of the appeal, we must assume, the appellant, in agreeing that a course of conduct be pursued that would, if successful, necessarily involve the offence of effecting Andaloussi's escape from lawful custody, clearly intended, by providing diamond wire to be smuggled into the prison, to play a part in the agreed course of conduct in furtherance of that criminal objective. Neither the fact that he intended to play no further part in attempting to effect the escape, nor that he believed the escape to be impossible, would, if the jury had supposed they might be true, have afforded him any defence.

Appeal dismissed.

Two particularly controversial points have been made by Lord Bridge in *Anderson*:

(1) The suggestion that a defendant could be convicted of conspiracy, even without intending the agreement to be carried out. There is wide acceptance of the view that this suggestion should not be regarded as an accurate statement of the law. There are three reasons why not:

  (a) On the facts of the case it was true that Anderson did not think that the plot had much chance of success and that he was just in the plan for the money, but neither of these points meant he did not intend the plan to be carried out. From the discussion in Chapter 3 it will be recalled that it is possible to intend a result without thinking one is likely to achieve it, and also that motive is not the same as intent. Here he assisted the project of his conspirators knowing that they were going to implement the plan and this was sufficient to constitute intent.

  (b) Applying Lord Bridge's logic it could be said that the parties conspired to commit a crime, even though none of them intended to carry out the plan! That would be bizarre.

  (c) The Court of Appeal has consistently failed to follow the House of Lords on this point.[104] Further the Privy Council in *Yip Chiu-Cheung* held that it did have to be shown that every alleged conspirator intended the agreement to be carried out.[105]

  In *R v G; R v F*[106] two men exchanged text messages about raping a boy. The Court of Appeal emphasized that the jury had to be convinced that the men intended to rape the boy if they were to be convicted of a conspiracy to rape. On the facts it was possible the exchanges were fantasy and so a conviction for conspiracy would not be appropriate.

(2) That a person is guilty of conspiracy if, and only if, it is established that he or she intended to play some part[107] in the agreed course of conduct. This was a novel suggestion. As mentioned previously, the key element of a conspiracy is an agreement, not the carrying out of the plan. The decision would lead to all kinds of difficulty in defining exactly what could be said to constitute carrying out an element of the

---

104 *Edwards* [1991] Crim LR 45; *Ashton* [1992] Crim LR 667; *Harvey* [1999] Crim LR 70.
105 *Yip Chiu-Cheung* [1995] 1 AC 111, although their Lordships did not refer to *Anderson* [1986] AC 27. See also *Edwards* [1991] Crim LR 45, which requires each conspirator to intend the plan to be carried out.
106 [2012] EWCA Crim 1756.   107 It is far from clear what 'play some part' means.

plan. In *Siracusa* (in the following extract) the Court of Appeal doubted whether it was an essential requirement of a conspiracy that each conspirator plays some active role:

R v Siracusa
(1989) 90 Cr App R 340 (CA)

Four men were charged with conspiracy to contravene section 170(2)(b) of the Customs and Excise Management Act 1979. The case concerned smugglers who were bringing heroin and cannabis into the UK by secreting it inside pieces of Thai and Kashmiri furniture. The appellants appealed against their conviction on the basis that the judge had wrongly directed the jury that the appellants would be guilty of conspiracy if they had agreed on a course of conduct which necessarily amounted to either the importation of cannabis or the importation of heroin.

Lord Justice O'Connor [reading the judgment of the court]

[Having considered passages from Lord Bridge's judgment in *Anderson* O'Connor LJ continued:]

We think it obvious that Lord Bridge cannot have been intending that the organiser of a crime who recruited others to carry it out would not himself be guilty of conspiracy unless it could be proved that he intended to play some active part himself thereafter. Lord Bridge had pointed out at p 259 that:

'in these days of highly organised crime the most serious statutory conspiracies will frequently involve an elaborate and complex agreed course of conduct in which many will consent to play necessary but subordinate roles, not involving them in any direct participation in the commission of the offence or offences at the centre of the conspiracy.'

The present case is a classic example of such a conspiracy. It is the hallmark of such crimes that the organisers try to remain in the background and more often than not are not apprehended. Secondly, the origins of all conspiracies are concealed and it is usually quite impossible to establish when or where the initial agreement was made, or when or where other conspirators were recruited. The very existence of the agreement can only be inferred from overt acts. Participation in a conspiracy is infinitely variable: it can be active or passive. If the majority shareholder and director of a company consents to the company being used for drug smuggling carried out in the company's name by a fellow director and minority shareholder, he is guilty of conspiracy. Consent, that is the agreement or adherence to the agreement, can be inferred if it is proved that he knew what was going on and the intention to participate in the furtherance of the criminal purpose is also established by his failure to stop the unlawful activity. Lord Bridge's dictum does not require anything more.

We return to the first sentence of this paragraph in Lord Bridge's speech. He starts by saying: 'I have said already, but I repeat to emphasise its importance. . . . ' We have cited what he had already said when dealing with his clause 2. It is clear that he was not intending to say anything different. So when he goes on to say:

'an essential ingredient in the crime of conspiring to commit a specific offence or offences under section 1(1) of the Act of 1977 is that the accused should agree that a

> course of conduct be pursued which he knows must involve the commission by one
> or more of the parties to the agreement of that offence or those offences,'
>
> he plainly does not mean that the prosecution have to prove that persons who agree to
> import prohibited drugs into this country know that the offence which will be committed will
> be a contravention of section 170(2) of the Customs and Excise Act. He is not to be taken as
> saying that the prosecution must prove that the accused knew the name of the crime. We
> are satisfied that Lord Bridge was doing no more than applying the words of section 1 of the
> Criminal Law Act 1977, namely, that when the accused agreed to the course of conduct, he
> knew that it involved the commission of an offence.
>
> The *mens rea* sufficient to support the commission of a substantive offence will not nec-
> essarily be sufficient to support a charge of conspiracy to commit that offence. An intent to
> cause grievous bodily harm is sufficient to support the charge of murder, but is not sufficient
> to support a charge of conspiracy to murder or of attempt to murder.
>
> We have come to the conclusion that if the prosecution charge a conspiracy to contravene
> section 170(2) of the Customs and Excise Management Act by the importation of heroin, then
> the prosecution must prove that the agreed course of conduct was the importation of heroin.
> This is because the essence of the crime of conspiracy is the agreement and in simple terms,
> you do not prove an agreement to import heroin by proving an agreement to import cannabis.
>
> *Appeals against convictions dismissed. Appeals against sentence by Siracusa, Monteleone,
> and Luciani allowed. Sentences varied. Appeal against sentence by Di Carlo dismissed.*

4.3   IMPOSSIBILITY AND STATUTORY CONSPIRACIES

Section 1(1)(b), quoted in the previous section, deals with the problem of impossibility where facts exist which render the commission of the agreed offence impossible: the defendants are judged on the facts as they believe them to be. So the defendants are guilty even if what they plan to do is in fact impossible, if they believe their plan to be feasible. So if Janet and James conspire to kill Michael they are guilty of conspiracy to kill even if Michael is already dead and so their plan is impossible.

4.4   COMMON LAW CONSPIRACIES

The present position is that the only common law conspiracies that exist are conspiracies to defraud and conspiracies to corrupt public morals. Section 12 of the Criminal Justice Act 1987 states:

> If—
>
> (a) a person agrees with any other person or persons that a course of conduct shall be
>   pursued; and
>
> (b) that course of conduct will necessarily amount to or involve the commission of any
>   offence or offences by one or more of the parties to the agreement if the agreement is
>   carried out in accordance with their intentions,
>
> the fact that it will do so shall not preclude a charge of conspiracy to defraud being brought
> against any of them in respect of the agreement.

This indicates that a conspiracy to defraud which also involves a criminal offence can be charged as either a statutory conspiracy or a common law conspiracy. Of course, a conspiracy to defraud which does not involve a criminal act can be charged only as a common law conspiracy.

It used to be thought there was also a common law conspiracy to outrage public decency, but in *Gibson*[108] it was confirmed that there was a substantive offence of outraging public decency, and so conspiring to outrage public decency should now be seen as a statutory conspiracy.[109]

Conspiracy to defraud

Actus reus

The most widely accepted definition of a conspiracy to defraud is found in Lord Dilhorne's *dicta* in *Scott v Metropolitan Police Commissioner*:[110]

> it is clearly the law that an agreement by two or more by dishonesty to deprive a person of something which is his or to which he is or would be entitled and an agreement by two or more by dishonesty to injure some proprietary right of his, suffices to constitute the offence of conspiracy to defraud.

As this quotation indicates, there are two key elements of a conspiracy to defraud:

(1) The conspiracy must involve dishonesty.

(2) If the agreement were carried out there would be some prejudice to the victim's property rights.[111]

The key notion of a conspiracy to defraud is, then, dishonest deprivation of the victim's proprietary rights. There is no need to show that if the plan were implemented anyone would be deceived, but there must be some property rights of the victims which are threatened.[112] Nor is it necessary to show that the ultimate fraud will be perpetrated by a party to the agreement. In *Hollinshead*[113] the House of Lords held that it was a conspiracy to defraud to produce devices designed to alter readings on electricity meters. The intention was that members of the public (rather than the conspirators) would use the devices to defraud the electricity companies. Price fixing cannot on its own amount to a conspiracy to defraud.[114] That is because it is unclear what kinds of price fixing arrangements would be regarded as criminal. It would be unfair, therefore, to include price fixing within the definition of the offence. However, if a price-fixing arrangement was combined with other features such as fraud, misrepresentation, violence, intimidation, or inducement of a breach of contract then that could amount to a conspiracy to defraud.[115]

---

[108] [1990] 2 QB 619 (CA). See also *Rowley* [1991] 4 All ER 649 (CA); *Rose v DPP* [2006] EWHC 852 (Admin); and *Hamilton* [2007] EWCA Crim 2062.

[109] See also *Lunderbech* [1991] Crim LR 784.   [110] [1975] AC 919 (HL).

[111] *Moses and Ansbro* [1991] Crim LR 617.

[112] *Adams* [1995] 1 WLR 52 (PC), where the property was information to which a company was entitled.

[113] [1985] AC 975 (HL).

[114] *Norris v Government of the United States of America* [2008] UKHL 16.

[115] *Goldshield Group plc* [2008] UKHL 17.

The leading case is *Scott*, but that is now interpreted by the Privy Council in the following case:

Wai Yu-tsang v R
[1992] 1 AC 269 (PC)

Wai Yu-tsang was the chief accountant of a Hong Kong bank. He did not report to the relevant authorities the fact that the bank had not honoured some cheques and he failed to register the dishonouring in the company's accounts. This created a false impression of the bank's financial position. He was charged with conspiring to defraud the bank, its existing and potential shareholders, creditors, and depositors. He claimed to be acting under the instructions of the managing director and acting in order to prevent a run on the bank, and therefore in the best interests of the bank. He appealed to the Privy Council on the basis that the judge's direction on the mental element of a conspiracy to defraud was erroneous. The judge had stated that it was sufficient if the defendant had intentionally imperilled economic interests or threatened financial prejudice of the company, whatever his motive.

Lord Goff of Chieveley [reading the judgment of the court]

This authority [*Welham v DPP* [1960] 1 All ER 805] establishes that the expression 'intent to defraud' is not to be given a narrow meaning, involving an intention to cause economic loss to another. In broad terms, it means simply an intention to practise a fraud on another, or an intention to act to the prejudice of another man's right.

. . .

In the context of conspiracy to defraud, it is necessary to bear in mind that such a conspiracy is an agreement to practise a fraud on somebody (cf *Welham v DPP* [1960] 1 All ER 805 at 815, [1961] AC 103 at 133 per Lord Denning). In *Allsop*'s case (1977) 64 Cr App R 29 what the defendant agreed to do was to present the company with false particulars, in reliance upon which, as he knew, the company would decide whether to enter into hire-purchase transactions. It is then necessary to consider whether that could constitute a conspiracy to defraud, notwithstanding that the defendant's underlying purpose or motive was not to damage any economic interest of the company but to ensure that the transaction went through so that he would earn his commission. Their Lordships can see no reason why such an agreement should not be a conspiracy to defraud the company, substantially for the reasons given by the Court of Appeal. The defendant was, for his own purposes, dishonestly supplying the company with false information which persuaded it to accept risks which it would or might not have accepted if it had known the true facts. Their Lordships cannot see why this was not an agreement to practise a fraud on the company, because, as Shaw LJ said, it was a dishonest agreement to employ a deceit which imperilled the economic interests of the company.

The attention of their Lordships was drawn to a critique of *Allsop*'s case in Smith and Hogan *Criminal Law* (6th edn, 1988) p 273, to which they have given careful consideration. The learned authors first criticise the reference by the Court of Appeal to *Hyam v DPP*. With this criticism, their Lordships are inclined to agree, doubting whether an authority on the mental element in the crime of murder throws much light on the nature of a conspiracy to defraud. However, the Court of Appeal only felt it necessary to pray in aid Lord Diplock's speech in *Hyam v DPP* in order to circumnavigate the dictum of Lord Diplock in *Scott*'s case, an exercise which their Lordships do not need to embark upon since they consider that dictum to be, for the reasons they have explained, too narrowly expressed. Next, the authors suggest that *Allsop*'s case can be explained on the basis that there was an intention on the part of the defendant to defraud the company, since he intended the company to pay, as indeed it did pay, money for cars which it would not have paid, even though in the outcome if suffered no loss. There is force in this suggestion, as was recognised by the Court of Appeal itself (see 64 Cr App R 29 at 32). But the Court of Appeal was concerned with the question whether the conviction could stand on the basis of the summing up of the trial judge; and their Lordships are now concerned with the correctness of the reasoning of the Court of Appeal on that question (at 31).

Lastly, it is suggested that, on the rationalisation which the authors prefer, the case was not about recklessness, and did not decide that anything less than intention in the strict sense would suffice for conspiracy to defraud. Their Lordships are however reluctant to allow this part of the law to become enmeshed in a distinction, sometimes artificially drawn, between intention and recklessness. The question whether particular facts reveal a conspiracy to defraud depends upon what the conspirators have dishonestly agreed to do, and in particular whether they have agreed to practise a fraud on somebody. For this purpose it is enough for example that, as in *R v Allsop* and in the present case, the conspirators have dishonestly agreed to bring about a state of affairs which they realise will or may deceive the victim into so acting, or failing to act, that he will suffer economic loss or his economic interests will be put at risk. It is however important in such a case, as the Court of Appeal stressed in *Allsop*'s case, to distinguish a conspirator's intention (or immediate purpose) dishonestly to bring about such a state of affairs from his motive (or underlying purpose). The latter may be benign to the extent that he does not wish the victim or potential victim to suffer harm; but the mere fact that it is benign will not of itself prevent the agreement from constituting a conspiracy to defraud. Of course, if the conspirators were not acting dishonestly, there will have been no conspiracy to defraud; and in any event their benign purpose (if it be such) is a matter which, if they prove to be guilty, can be taken into account at the stage of sentence.

In forming this view of the matter, their Lordships draw comfort from the fact that *R v Allsop* has been accepted as good authority by the Supreme Court of Canada in *R v Olan* [1978] 2 SCR 1175 at 1182 per Dickson J delivering the judgment of the court, in a passage subsequently followed by the Supreme Court of Canada in *Vezina v R, Cote v R* [1986] 1 SCR 2 at 22–23 per Lamer J likewise delivering the judgment of the court.

Appeal dismissed.

As this case indicates, although normally a conspiracy to defraud will, if implemented, lead to a financial loss to the victim there are two circumstances in which this need not be shown:

(1) Deceiving a person holding a public office into acting contrary to his public duty would be a conspiracy to defraud.[116]

(2) If the conspirators know that their actions will put at risk the victim's property then they are guilty of a conspiracy to defraud. This is so even where in fact the risk does not materialize and the victim does not suffer a loss.[117] For example, if the conspirators agree to use the victim's money to gamble this could be a conspiracy to defraud, even if in fact they win the gamble and the victim profits.

---

[116] e.g. *Welham v DPP* [1961] AC 103 (HL); *Terry* [1984] AC 374 (HL).
[117] *Wai Yu-tsang* [1991] 4 All ER 664 (PC); *Allsop* (1977) 64 Cr App R 29 (CA).

Mens rea

The *mens rea* for conspiracy to defraud is:

(1) an intention to defraud; and

(2) dishonesty.

At one time it was thought that what needs to be shown is the conspirators' purpose to cause prejudice to the victim.[118] In *Wai Yu-tsang* it was pointed out that often the conspirators' purpose is to make a profit and they may prefer the victims not to lose out if that is possible. The Privy Council suggested that the defendant's knowledge that his or her conduct might cause loss to the victim was sufficient for the *mens rea*, even if such loss was not their purpose as such.[119] The conspirators must be dishonest. The *Ghosh*[120] definition of dishonesty is used.

Conspiracy to corrupt public morals

There is yet to be an authoritative decision on whether there is a substantive offence of corrupting public morals. If there is such a substantive offence then a conspiracy to corrupt public morals should be charged as a statutory conspiracy, not a common law one. Whether or not there is such a substantive offence was left open in *Shaw v DPP*[121] and has not yet been resolved.[122]

The House of Lords in *Shaw v DPP*[123] held by a majority that it was an offence to conspire to corrupt public morals. The House of Lords upheld the conviction for conspiracy to corrupt public morals of a man who produced a 'Ladies Directory' giving the names, addresses, and talents of prostitutes. In *Knuller v DPP*[124] the House of Lords upheld the conviction of conspiracy to corrupt public morals of the accused who had published a magazine which included advertisements soliciting homosexual acts. In language which would seem surprising if used by their Lordships today they held that such advertisements could corrupt public morals as they could lead to conduct which is 'destructive to the very fabric of society'. However, in deciding whether the offence was committed, their Lordships added that 'the jury should be invited, where appropriate, to remember that they live in a plural society with a tradition of toleration towards minorities, and that this atmosphere of toleration is itself part of public decency.'[125]

As this implies it will be very rare that an agreement will amount to a conspiracy to corrupt public morals, and the offence is rarely prosecuted.[126] Perhaps an agreement to promote paedophilia or bestiality would be regarded by the jury as sufficient to involve a conspiracy to corrupt public morals.

4.5 IMPOSSIBILITY AND COMMON LAW OFFENCES

According to the House of Lords in *DPP v Nock*[127] impossibility is a defence to a charge of common law conspiracy. However, this is only where the conspiracy could never be achieved:

---

[118] *Scott v MPC* [1975] AC 819 (PC).   [119] *Cooke* [1986] AC 909 (HL).

[120] *Ghosh* [1982] QB 1053 (CA).   [121] [1962] AC 220 (HL).

[122] This was assumed to be a common law offence in *Armhouse Lee Ltd v Chappell* The Independent, 26 July 1996 (CA).

[123] [1962] AC 220 (HL).   [124] [1973] AC 435 (HL).   [125] *Knuller* [1973] AC 435, 439.

[126] In *Armhouse Lee Ltd v Chappell* The Independent, 26 July 1996 (CA) the Court of Appeal held that advertising phone numbers by which sexually explicit words and descriptions could be heard could not be regarded as corrupting public morals.

[127] [1978] AC 979 (HL).

impossibility is not a defence if the means used to achieve the purpose are impossible. So if A and B conspire to project indecent images into the night-time sky, the fact that such a display was not scientifically possible would not prevent the possibility of a conviction for conspiracy to corrupt public morals. An example of where impossibility would be a defence to a common law conspiracy is where A and B intend to defraud V, while V had already died. It should be stressed that impossibility is assessed at the time of the agreement. The fact that the plan subsequently becomes impossible (e.g. the company it was planned to defraud has ceased to exist) does not prevent the original conspiracy being committed.

FURTHER READING

Ashworth, A. (1987) 'Defining Criminal Offences without Harm' in P. Smith (ed.) *Criminal Law: Essays in Honour of J.C. Smith* (London: Butterworths).

Horder, J. (1996a) 'Crimes of Ulterior Intent' in A. Simester and G.R. Sullivan (eds) *Harm and Culpability* (Oxford: OUP).

Husak, D.N. (1995b) 'The Nature and Justifiability of Nonconsummate Offenses' *Arizona Law Review* 37: 151.

Ormerod, D. (2006) 'Making Sense of Mens Rea in Statutory Conspiracies' *Current Legal Problems* 185.

PART II: THEORY

5 INCHOATE OFFENCES

At first sight inconsummate offences do not fit naturally into the structure of criminal law. After all where is the harm to a victim where there is an attempt or conspiracy for example? Are not the offences discussed in Part I in essence punishing people for bad thoughts? In the following passage Michael Cahill sets out the reasons why you might think inchoate crimes should be punished: ←5 (p.784)

M. Cahill, 'Inchoate Crimes' in M. Dubber and T. Hörnle (eds) *The Oxford Handbook of Criminal Law* (Oxford: OUP, 2014), 516–18

---

1. The culpability-based view

One understanding of inchoate liability is that inchoate crimes are characterized by the offender's *intent* to engage in harmful or wrongful conduct. Under this view, a person's affirmative desire or purpose to bring about some criminal harm or wrong defines and justifies inchoate liability. Yet understanding inchoate crimes in terms of an offender's motivations or culpability poorly suits the task of specifying the nature and limits of that category or of the state's criminalization authority. Subjective intent is both over-inclusive and under-inclusive as a criterion for criminalization or for distinguishing inchoate crimes from consummate ones.

Basing criminalization on intent is over-inclusive in that it allows liability grounded solely on the offender's culpability, without requiring any showing of objective harm or wrong (or even risk of a harm or wrong). Such a focus is not without its adherents, but it would entail outcomes that strike many as troubling, as it either holds that culpability can make otherwise innocuous conduct wrongful without explaining when and why that is so, or else allows liability in the absence of wrongdoing without explaining when or why such liability is acceptable and proper. A culpability-based view cannot specify with any precision (descriptively or normatively) the point at which acceptable conduct, coupled with culpability as to future conduct, becomes criminal. If one's resolve to do things in the future is the ground for considering one a wrongdoer, then that ground arises as soon as the resolution forms; whether one is apprehended and punished at an early or late moment in the course of enacting that resolution seems more a matter of timing and happenstance than anything else. In any case, it is hard to quantify the point at which the enactment of one's resolve becomes wrongful. Yet it would be troubling to allow the resolution itself, standing alone, to support criminal punishment, in part because such a position denies the prospect of renunciation prior to completion of the contemplated conduct. In short, incomplete conduct, even if combined with a plan to engage in further conduct, does not itself constitute wrongdoing, and if only wrongdoing could properly be criminalized, it would be correct to conclude, with Alexander and Ferzan, that inchoate (in the sense of incomplete) conduct is not suitable for criminalization.

Basing criminalization on intent is also under-inclusive because criminal liability can and should attach to non-intentional, though culpable, actions in the direction of a criminal offense. For example, conduct that recklessly creates a substantial risk of harm is a common, and proper, object of criminal sanction, and preliminary conduct that is likely to culminate in such a risk may merit intervention on the same basis as intentional but preliminary conduct tending toward a criminalized harm or risk. The intent-based approach to inchoate liability draws an arbitrary line between intent and other forms of culpability.

2. The risk-based view

A different account of the nature and proper limits of inchoate liability, suggested by Douglas Husak, characterizes inchoate offenses as demanding the creation of a sufficient *risk* of harm, though harm itself need not occur. While it is certainly plausible to distinguish harm-based from risk-based offenses, that distinction might ultimately be less sturdy or useful than it first appears. As a matter of positive law, many crimes that intuitively seem like consummate offenses (particularly in that it seems uncontroversial to punish an inchoate attempt to commit them) might as easily be considered risk-based as harm-based: for example, theft violates property interests but, depending on how narrowly one frames the offense temporally, might not lead to harm insofar as the stolen property might ultimately be recovered or returned; fraud offenses involve deception but may not harm the person deceived; bribery risks, but need not entail, corruption in that a bribe might not actually affect the recipient's official conduct; even arson is often defined in a way that requires conduct (starting a fire) but does not demand any resulting property damage. Hence, aside from a handful of offenses against the person that clearly require harm, such as homicide and battery, there may be many offenses for which categorization as harm-based versus risk-based, and thus (on this view) consummate versus inchoate, will be slippery and unclear.

Moreover, such a distinction may not be especially helpful, as it does not change the underlying normative inquiry that would apply to assess the merits of recognizing a given crime. Even if not harmful, conduct that creates a significant risk of harm is wrongful, and the same general inquiry would apply for decisions to criminalize either harmful or risky conduct: does this conduct merit criminalization across the board, that is, does every provable case of a person engaging in this conduct provide a basis, without more, for punishment?

That question can be answered in the affirmative even for clearly risk-based crimes, such as reckless endangerment, that nonetheless address conduct that is wrongful per se.

. . .

3. The intervention-based view

I have elsewhere tentatively defended the proposition that "inchoate crimes" are properly defined as those involving as yet incomplete conduct:

> On this account, the category of inchoate crimes is defined by two features: (1) incomplete conduct toward some ultimate offense (this is what makes the crime inchoate, rather than consummate); and (2) the actor's firm commitment to the performance of the as-yet-unperformed conduct that would complete that offense (this is what makes the conduct worthy of punishment at all, rather than "mere thoughts" or "mere preparation").

The prior articulation of this position suggested that an actor's culpability as to future conduct might provide a basis for considering otherwise neutral preliminary conduct to be wrongful. As noted previously, that culpability-based view no longer strikes me as correct; rather, the better view is that preventive goals may support criminalization even though the actor's preliminary conduct is *not* (yet) wrongful.

. . .

This conceptualization of inchoate crime also partially explains, while offering some reason to critique aspects of, the doctrinal distinctions that exist between inchoate and consummate offenses under existing law. For example, many modern criminal codes recognize a *renunciation* defense that may apply for, but only for, inchoate offenses. The defense applies where one engages in preliminary conduct sufficient to constitute an inchoate crime (e.g. attempt), but then abandons one's efforts rather than pursuing the crime to completion. Yet no renunciation defense exists for consummate offenses such as, say, theft: one cannot undo one's liability for a pre-occurring act of larceny by returning the stolen item, even if one does so before anyone realizes it has gone missing.

6 THE THEORY OF CRIMINAL ATTEMPTS

6.1 WHY DO WE PUNISH ATTEMPTS?

Although you might at first think it is obvious that the law should punish attempts, further thought reveals that it is not a straightforward issue. After all, normally in an attempt no one has actually been harmed, and yet harm is normally seen as an essential element of an offence. In the following extract, George Fletcher sets out some of the difficulties in approaching this issue: ←3 (p.776)

G. Fletcher, *Basic Concepts of Criminal Law* (New York: OUP, 1998), 172–4

Historically, the attempt derives from the completed offense. But once attempts came to be recognized as a staple of nineteenth-century criminal prosecutions, theorists began to wonder whether with regard to at least some crimes, the attempt might indeed be the more basic offense. In cases of bringing about harmful consequences—homicide, arson, destruction of property—the actor might do everything in his power to [bring about the] result without succeeding. He might shoot to kill and hit the wall. She might throw a fire bomb with the intent of burning down a house and the bomb turns out to be a dud. He might swing an axe at his enemy and miss. This element of accident in cases of harmful consequences makes one wonder whether the attempt should be regarded as the basic offense and the completed homicide, arson, or battery merely an adventitious after effect of attempting with intent.

Our ordinary sensibilities tell us that, of course, it is worse to kill than to shoot and miss. The successful killer deserves a greater penalty than the unsuccessful attempter. At least that is what the woman on the street—or the man in the Clapham bus, as the English say, thinks. In law as in basketball, the rule usually is: No harm, no foul. No one with ordinary sensibilities would advocate the death penalty for someone who merely tried to kill. And yet many of the leading theorists of criminal law, at least in the English-speaking world, hold the view that the consummation of an intended offense is merely a matter of chance and therefore not a proper basis for aggravating the penalty designated for the attempt.

The basic argument for this position begins with the sensible premise that punishment should be imposed on the basis of blameworthiness or culpability. There follows a more controversial point: The only fair basis for culpability is the actions under one's control—that is, what can one be sure of bringing about with the extensions of one's body. This includes basic actions such as speaking, pulling the trigger of a gun, putting poison in coffee, planting a bomb. It does not include the consequences of these actions that depend on intervening forces of nature. It follows, according to the logic of this argument, that these consequences should not be charged to the account of the culpable actor. This is the reasoning that leads so many thoughtful writers to support the view that the attempt—which is supposedly within the control of the actor—should be the primary offense. The basis for punishment should, therefore, be the attempt and not its fortuitous after effects.

The more traditional way of thinking about crime and responsibility starts with the bringing about of harm and inquires: Who is responsible for this wrong and to what extent? The attempter merely approaches the harm, merely creates a risk of the harm, and therefore should be held liable for a lesser degree of wrongdoing. A lesser degree of wrongdoing implies mitigated punishment.

The search for the primary or basic offense implies, then, two different concepts of crime. The culpability-centered theory focuses exclusively on the actor who has formulated a criminal intent and has started to act upon it. Whether there is an actual victim, whether the action disturbs the peace, is irrelevant. What counts is the potential of the attempt to bring about harm, if it is not halted in its progression toward execution. The evil of the attempt lies primarily in its defiance of the legal norms designed to protect the interests of others.

The harm-centered conception of crime focuses on the victim. The evil of the offense lies in killing, raping, burning, destroying, maiming, threatening—in general in bringing about harm to a concrete individual. When there is no actual but only a potential victim, there is by definition a lesser wrong.

It is true that those who merely attempt but do not cause harm have lesser grounds for remorse and guilt. In *Crime and Punishment* Raskolnikov is properly haunted by the thought of having killed an old lady to take her money. If he tried to kill her and failed, it would be curiously neurotic for him to suffer the same pangs of guilt. Recognizing the role of remorse testifies to the close connection between wrong-doing and victimhood. That there is an actual victim—an irreversible harm to another human being—produces a human response that differs radically from the sense of impropriety that comes simply from violating a norm of the legal system.

We will now pick up some of the points that Fletcher makes in his extract. The first is the 'problem of moral luck'.

6.2 'THE PROBLEM OF MORAL LUCK'

Should the fact that the victim was wise enough not to take a larger sip or that the poison was not stronger be a reason for rendering her any less guilty than if she had succeeded? Such questions are addressed in the following passage:

A. Ashworth, 'Belief, Intent and Criminal Liability' in J. Eekelaar and J. Bell (eds) *Oxford Essays in Jurisprudence* (Oxford: OUP, 1987), 16–17

Is A, who shoots at X intending to kill him but misses because X unexpectedly moves, any less culpable than B, who shoots at Y intending to kill him and does so? An external description of both sets of events would probably not suggest that they have 'done' the same thing, whereas an account which paid more attention to the actor's point of view and to matters which lay within the actor's control would suggest that they both intended and tried, to the same extent, to do the same thing. The argument is that, because of the element of uncertainty in the outcome of things which we try to do, it would be wrong for assessments of culpability to depend on the occurrence or non-occurrence of the intended consequences. 'Success or failure . . . makes no difference at all to [an agent's] moral status in relation to his original act. His original act, strictly considered, was simply his trying and *that* is what moral assessment must concern itself with' (Winch, *Ethics and Action*, 1972, p. 139) . . . Moral blame and criminal liability should be based so far as possible on choice and control, on the trying and not on what actually happened thereafter.

What are the reasons for wishing to reduce the influence of chance upon criminal liability? It cannot be doubted that luck plays a considerable part. Actual results also play a considerable part in judgments of others, and tend to dominate assessments in such fields as business, sport, and education. Those who try hard but are unsuccessful often receive less recognition than those who achieve goals (no matter how little effort they put into it). But these are not moral assessments of the individuals or their characters. If one turns to moral and social judgments, it is doubtful whether outcomes should be proper criteria. It may be desirable overall to have fewer bad outcomes and more good outcomes in society, but that does not lead to the conclusion that moral praise and blame should be allocated solely according to result. Indeed, a bad outcome stemming from a good intent may be a better predictor of good outcomes than a good outcome born of a bad intent. From time to time we may praise someone for producing a good result, even though it was not what he was trying to do, but this is more a reflection of our pleasure at the outcome than an assessment of his conduct and character. If we turn to blaming, is it not unacceptable to blame people for causing results irrespective of whether they were caused intentionally, negligently, or purely accidentally? Blaming is a moral activity which is surely only appropriate where the individual had some choice or control over the matter. For this reason the criminal law should seek to minimize the effect of luck upon the incidence and scale of criminal liability.

To Andrew Ashworth, then, the law should not attach significance to matters which are a matter of luck. As the difference between an attempt and a successful crime can be regarded as a matter of luck, an argument can be made that all attempts should be treated in the same way as the complete crime.

But not everyone agrees with him. Read again the discussions on moral luck that we had in Chapter 2, Section 7.

FURTHER READING

Ashworth, A. (1988) 'Criminal Attempts and the Role of Resulting Harm under the Code in the Common Law' *Rutgers Law Journal* 19: 725.

Ben-Shahar, O. and Harel, A. (1996) 'The Economics of the Law of Criminal Attempts: A Victim-Centered Perspective' *University of Pennsylvania Law Review* 145: 299.

Blumoff, T. (2003) 'A Jurisprudence for Punishing Attempts Asymmetrically' *Buffalo Criminal Law Review* 6: 951.

Christopher, R. (2004) 'Does Attempted Murder Deserve Greater Punishment than Murder? Moral Luck and the Duty to Prevent Harm' *Notre Dame Journal of Law, Ethics and Public Policy* 18: 419.

Duff, R.A. (1996) *Criminal Attempts* (Oxford: OUP).

Duff, R.A. (2005b) 'Criminalizing Endangerment' in R.A. Duff and S. Green (eds) *Defining Crimes* (Oxford: OUP).

Enoch, D. and Marmor, A. (2007) 'The Case against Moral Luck' *Law and Philosophy* 26: 405.

Jareborg, N. (1993) 'Criminal Attempts and Moral Luck' *Israel Law Review* 27: 213.

Kadish, S. (1994) 'The Criminal Law and the Luck of the Draw' *Journal of Criminal Law and Criminology* 84: 1501.

Perlman, M. (1995) 'Punishing Acts and Counting Consequences' *Arizona Law Review* 37: 227.

Shachar, Y. (1987) 'The Fortuitous Gap in Law and Morality' *Criminal Justice Ethics* 6: 12.

Yaffe, G. (2009) 'Trying, Acting and Attempted Crimes' *Law and Philosophy* 28: 109.

6.3 *ACTUS REUS* OF ATTEMPT

When considering the law on attempts it is useful to contrast three different kinds of attempts.

Imagine Michael decides to kill Jane. He finds her and pulls out a gun. Contrast these three alternatives:

(1) Just before Michael is able to shoot a police officer grabs him and prevents him firing the gun.

(2) Michael fires the gun but Jane ducks at the last moment and the bullet misses.

(3) Michael fires the gun but, unknown to Michael, Jane is already dead.

All of these three cases are linked by the fact that in none of them is Jane actually harmed by Michael. But they can be distinguished. Ashworth argues that there is an important difference between complete and incomplete attempts.[128] A complete attempt is where the defendant has done everything that he or she intended to do, but the attempt nevertheless failed. In an incomplete case the defendant has been prevented from completing his or her course of actions. So case (1) is an example of an incomplete attempt, but cases (2) and (3) are complete attempts. ←2 (p.773)

There is little doubt that a complete attempt would constitute the *actus reus* of an attempt, but in the case of an incomplete attempt where should the line be drawn? Here are some possible approaches the law could take:

(1) **Last act**[129] It could be argued that the defendant should not be liable until he has committed the very last act before the offence is committed. This approach leaves the imposition of criminal liability until the very last moment. It would be supported by those who are wary of punishing attempts for fear of depriving the defendant of an opportunity to 'repent' and turn back from the offence. It would also appeal to those who are concerned about convicting people of simply having an 'evil mind'.

(2) **'Unequivocable act'**[130] It can be argued that what needs to be shown is an act which unequivocally demonstrates that the defendant intends to complete the crime.[131] In other words, that the defendant is close enough to committing the crime that there is no realistic chance of the defendant changing his or her mind.

(3) **The 'substantial step' test**[132] This test requires proof that the defendant has not simply started on his or her plan but has gone a significant way down the path. Opponents of this test claim that it will create too much uncertainty.

(4) **Dangerous proximity** This test requires proof that the defendant came 'proximately close' to committing the offence. To some commentators it is too vague to give practical guidance to the jury.

(5) **'More than merely preparatory'** This is the test which is adopted by English and Welsh law. It seeks to draw a line between those acts which are mere preparation and those which are embarking on the offence proper. Its difficulty is that in some cases the distinction can be hard to draw.

(6) **The 'first act' test**[133] This test requires proof that the defendant has simply done the first of a series of acts that the defendant intends will result in the offence being completed. It would appeal to those who see the *mens rea* as the key element of the offence and seek only an external act revealing that mental state. It also has the benefit of being an easy test to use. The difficulty with it is that different crimes require different levels of planning. Sometimes there will be a single act of preparation (e.g. raising a fist in order to assault); in others a larger number of actions may be required (e.g. before committing an armed robbery). Therefore, the first act may not be a ready indicator of the blameworthiness of the defendant.[134]

Antony Duff has proposed that the defendant should have committed the *actus reus* of an attempt if his or her conduct amounts to embarking on the commission of the offence he or she intends to commit.[135]

---

[128] Jareborg (1993) is not convinced by the placing of any weight on the distinction.
[129] *Eagleton* (1855) 6 Cox CC 559, although see the interpretation of this case in *Roberts* (1855) 169 ER 836.
[130] *Davey v Lee* [1968] 1 QB 366.   [131] Schulhofer (1974).
[132] Considered and rejected in *Roberts* (1855) 169 ER 836.   [133] *Scofield* [1784] Cald 397.
[134] Stewart (2001: 403).   [135] Duff (1996). See also Stewart (2001).

Duff admits that his proposed test, which is very similar, if not identical, to the one presently used by the courts, is open to a challenge of being indeterminate. To overcome this he suggests Parliament could list some examples of conduct which would constitute an attempt.[136] Duff claims that his test reflects the 'normal' meaning of an attempt, and to some extent this is supported by interviews among members of the public who appear to support the idea that an attempt should be committed shortly before the commission of the offence.[137] Other commentators, including Glanville Williams, are more sceptical about trying to discover the 'normal' meaning of the word 'attempt'.[138] He points out that throughout the criminal law there are divergences between the normal and legal meaning of words.[139]

C. Clarkson, 'Attempt: The Conduct Requirement' (2009) 29 *Oxford Journal of Legal Studies* 25 at 36–41

In order to determine the parameters of the new test, two related questions need to be addressed. First, what is the law of attempt for? What is its underlying rationale? Second, how serious an offence should it be? Should it be regarded as being as serious (or nearly as serious) as the completed crime or should it be a lesser offence?

There are several commonly stated rationales of the law of attempt. These are sometimes categorized as being either objectivist or subjectivist theories. Under an objectivist perspective, the defendant by intending to commit the crime and by committing acts closely connected with the crime has crossed a moral threshold ('crossed the Rubicon') and is displaying a degree of moral culpability similar to that involved in the commission of the full offence. Further, the actions involved in an attempt display 'vivid danger' and a 'clear threat of harm'. There is a manifest threat to the security interests of others. The victim in Jones was threatened or unnerved by the defendant's actions. This infringement of his security rights is a 'second-order harm'. These rationales suggest the defendant must come close to committing the crime. It was not until the defendant in Jones entered the car brandishing a loaded gun that his actions constituted this 'vivid danger' and that he had crossed a threshold making him sufficiently morally culpable for such a serious offence. On the other hand, under a 'subjectivist' rationale the main emphasis is on the mental element of the defendant. If someone intends to commit a crime, they are dangerous and need restraining; they also need rehabilitation and punishment is necessary to deter them and others from embarking on criminal plans. Under this approach, all that is required is some conduct corroborative of this intention. Accordingly, liability can be imposed at a much earlier stage. Even before entering the car, the defendant in Jones had, by shortening the gun and setting off in disguise to kill his victim, indicated his dangerousness. At this stage punishment is also appropriate to deter others from such actions. And, of course, the law should be structured so as to facilitate police intervention to prevent crimes. When a person planning robbery and armed with a gun or an imitation firearm, as was the defendant in Campbell, is only one yard from the door of the building wherein the robbery is planned, the police should not be forced to wait until he has entered the building and produced his gun to the victim.

In striking the balance between these rationales the competing interests of individual freedom and the countervailing interests of society have to be placed in the scales. As the Law

---

[136] Duff (1996: 394). For further discussion, see Culver (1998).
[137] Robinson and Darley (1995: 20–8).   [138] Williams (1991).
[139] See Horder (2012b) on the extent to which certainty is important.

Commission state: 'In a free and democratic society where the right to privacy, freedom of conduct and civil liberties generally are respected, the balance may come down firmly against imposing criminal liability.'

The weight to be given to these competing interests depends on the seriousness of the offence of attempt. If attempts are to continue to be treated as being as serious (in terms of potential punishment) as the complete offence, the balance should only be struck at a point when the defendant's moral culpability can be regarded as broadly equal to that of the person who commits the full crime. On the other hand, if the offence were to be regarded as less serious, liability could be imposed for conduct at an earlier stage. The emphasis would then be not so much on the broadly comparable culpability of the attempter but rather on the dangerousness of such an actor and the need to facilitate police intervention. In short, the less serious the offence of attempt, the earlier could the line be drawn.

There are strong reasons why the crime of attempt should continue to be regarded as being of (almost) comparable gravity to the complete offence. The labels attempted murder and attempted rape have a strong resonance with the public as being very serious offences. In many cases it could be sheer luck that the crime was not completed. The defendant has broadly the same mens rea (or greater) than that required for the full offence. There is, of course, an argument that attempts should generally be punished less severely than completed offences, as is done in many other jurisdictions. Put simply, it is worse to kill someone than try to kill someone and worse to rape someone than try to rape someone. However, most of those supporting this view still recognize the seriousness of the crime of attempt and that in some cases the penalty imposed should be the same as for the complete offence. For example, Duff has proposed that while the penalty imposed for an attempt should generally be lighter than that which would have been imposed had the offence been completed, nevertheless a person convicted of an attempt should potentially be liable to the same penalty as for the completed offence and 'in exceptional cases' should be punished at that level.

A further argument for insisting that conduct comes close to the actual commission of the crime is that it affords intending criminals an opportunity to abandon the criminal enterprise. In doing this, we are according the person respect as a responsible agent 'who is in principle susceptible to rational persuasion'.

Finally, drawing the line at an earlier point would result in an unwarranted extension of the criminal law. Any 'respectable theory of criminalisation' needs to accept the 'last resort principle'. This principle applies not only to the creation of new offences but to the expansion of existing offences. In order to respect freedom, civil liberties and privacy, any expansion of the criminal law should involve a thorough investigation into whether it is necessary. Such an investigation is easier when criminalizing specific acts of preparation, in that one is operating within a specific context with a clearly defined harm being targeted. Simply to allow the line at which conduct should be criminalized to drift backwards risks infringing this basic principle.

Accordingly, it is suggested that the primary rationale of a reformulated offence of attempt should be, as at present, that of punishing a person whose moral culpability can be regarded as broadly comparable to that of the completer. This is similar to Duff's proposal that the conduct required for an attempt should be 'constitutive of the agent's criminality'. Culpability being broadly comparable or constitutive of criminality is not the same as requiring it to be equal to that of the completer. Such equality would only exist when the defendant has done all she needs to do to commit the crime. To be broadly comparable or constitutive of criminality, the defendant must have crossed a (relevant) threshold and have commenced, or be about to commence, on the execution of the crime. What is needed is a test that captures this crossing of a threshold and conduct displaying a 'vivid danger' that the full offence will be committed. . . .

Of course, a major problem will be how to capture this new degree of proximity. Legislation cannot be framed in terms of vague concepts, such as crossing thresholds or displaying a vivid danger. This is where the use of examples becomes important. What is needed is a general reformulation of the actus reus of attempt backed up by a series of examples. . . .

A possible reformulation could run along the lines of imposing liability for attempt when a person: 'does an act which is more than merely preparatory to, and is closely connected to, the commission of the offence in terms of time, location and acts under the control of the accused remaining to be accomplished'. Such a test is necessarily broad and open to the accusation of vagueness and being capable of generating uncertainty. However, this test has the advantage of stressing that mere preparatory acts will not suffice. The actions of the defendant in Jones in buying and shortening his gun and in setting forth armed with his gun are all merely preparatory acts. Further, unlike the present law, it emphasizes that the defendant must have come close to committing the offence but not so close as to have embarked on the crime.

QUESTIONS

1. Are you convinced by any of the arguments for why the law should punish attempts? Given that the prisons are so overcrowded should not the law focus on offences where victims are directly harmed?

2. Glazebrook (1969) suggests that there is no need to have a special law of attempts if the law defines each substantive crime to include attempt. However, this would be to treat attempts under the same label as the completed offence. To some, this would not recognize the important moral difference between an attempted offence and a completed offence. What do you think?

3. Would the law on attempts be clearer if greater attention were paid to the difference between acts which generally endanger people (e.g. drink driving) and acts which are designed to harm a specific victim (e.g. where D shoots at V and misses)? (See Duff (2005b) and Chiao (2010).)

6.4 *MENS REA* FOR ATTEMPT

What is the appropriate *mens rea* for an attempt?[140] Again the issue depends in part on whether one takes a subjectivist or an objectivist approach to attempts. To subjectivists, because it is essentially a matter of chance whether or not the attempt succeeds, the *mens rea* for the attempt should be the same as that required for a completed offence.[141] For many objectivists an attempt requires an intention to 'make up' for the lower level of harm in an attempt. Other commentators have made reference to the 'normal meaning' of an attempt, which they suggest means intending to produce a certain result.[142] ←1 (p.767)

---

[140] White (1991: 15ff); Kugler (2002: 202–12).   [141] Robinson (1994: 890–6).

[142] Horder (1994c). For criticism of appeals to the normal meaning of attempt, see Kugler (2002: 202–12).

In the following passage, Antony Duff sets out his view on what the *mens rea* for an attempt should be:

R.A. Duff, *Criminal Attempts* (Oxford: OUP, 1996), 362–6

13.3 The Fault Element in Attempts: Why a Law of Attempts?

. . .

We have seen that strict subjectivists (if they can justify distinguishing inchoate and substantive offences at all) should require exactly the same fault element for the inchoate offence as for the relevant substantive offence: if recklessness as to the relevant result (as to death, injury, or damage, for example) suffices for a substantive offence, it should also suffice for the inchoate version of that offence. Can (or should) objectivists resist this conclusion? Can they argue that the non-occurrence of the result required for the substantive offence should make a difference, not just to the seriousness of the offence for which the defendant is convicted, or to the severity of the sentence she receives, but to the fault element required for conviction of the inchoate offence? That is, can they justify a general law of *attempts*, rather than a broader law of inchoate crimes?

I have argued that we should interpret the 'intent to commit an offence', which attempts are often said to require, as an intention such that the agent would necessarily commit an offence in carrying it out. To justify the claim that this should be the fault element of the general inchoate offence, I must show two things: first, why that inchoate offence should require intention even when the relevant substantive offence does not; and secondly, why it should not then require intention as to *all* aspects of the substantive offence. This will involve discussing the difference between *attempts* (or attacks) and actions of *endangerment*, and explaining why we should have a general law of attempts (rather than a broader law of endangerment) by showing how the non-occurrence of the prospective harmful result makes a greater difference to the culpable character of actions of endangerment than it does to that of attempts.

Attacks and Endangerments

I suggested earlier that intended action is the paradigm of action and of responsible agency: in so far as we are responsible agents, we are paradigmatically responsible for our intended actions. This suggests that intended criminal action, the intended doing of criminal harm, is the paradigm of criminality. The paradigm of murder, or wounding, is an intended killing or wounding, done without justification or excuse: that must count as murder, or wounding, if anything does; a responsible agent cannot deny responsibility for a death, or wound, which he causes with intent (whereas he might be able to deny culpable responsibility for deaths or wounds which he foresees even as certain side-effects of his action); and we count some actions, which are not intended to kill or wound, as murders, or woundings, in virtue of their closeness or resemblance to this paradigm.

We are of course also culpably responsible and may be criminally liable for harms which we cause recklessly, rather than with intent. Sometimes, indeed, we may see little moral difference between intention and an especially heinous recklessness . . . More often, however, we will see an agent's culpable responsibility for a harm which she causes as being qualified by the fact that she caused it recklessly rather than with intent. For she did not direct her action towards that harm; and she could consistently have hoped (as one who intends harm could not) not to cause it: her action (and she as its agent) is therefore less intimately related to that harm. We might then (particularly when the harm is very serious) mark this difference between the intending and the reckless agent by convicting the reckless agent of a lesser offence—of manslaughter rather than murder, for instance; or by convicting the reckless agent of the same offence, but mitigating her sentence.

In such cases there is a completed harm, which we ascribe to the agent: what gives her action its normative character, as a culpable killing or wounding for instance, is the fact that it did cause death or injury, as well as her culpable relationship to that death or injury. The same is true, of course, of actions that are intended to, and do, cause harm: they take their character as wrongfully harmful actions partly from the very fact of their success. What, though, if an action does not cause the harm which it was intended to cause, or risked causing? The distinction between intention and recklessness now becomes more significant, as the distinction between *attack* and *endangerment*—which is also the distinction between *essentially* and only *potentially* harmful action.

An action constitutes endangerment when it in fact threatens to cause harm; it endangers that which it threatens to harm. The threat may be unintentional and non-culpable (as when a driver whose brakes unexpectedly fail endangers others); endangerment is culpable when it is negligent (the driver failed to check her brakes), or reckless (she knew that her brakes might fail), or intentional (she drives at a pedestrian deliberately, intending to frighten him).

By contrast, intention is central to the notion of attack (as it is to that of attempt). The paradigm or standard case of attack is an action that is intended to cause harm, and that in fact causes or threatens to cause that intended harm: I attack another's life by acting with the intention of killing her, in a way that in fact directly threatens her life; or I attack another's property by acting with the intention of damaging what I know is her property, in a way that in fact threatens her property.

Attacks are essentially, not merely potentially, harmful. Consider actions intended to kill. An action is essentially murderous if murder is part of its intrinsic character, as the agent intends and engages in it: if it would be murder were it completed as the agent intends. That is, the action is essentially murderous if the agent intends [to kill] and the context is such that the killing would be murder. Likewise, an action is essentially homicidal if the agent intends [to kill], in a context such that the killing would be manslaughter rather than murder. To count an action as essentially murderous or homicidal is to say that the actual occurrence of death simply completes what was already its intrinsic character. It was already structured by the prospect of, and already directed towards, causing death: the occurrence of death objectively actualizes or completes that intrinsic character, rather than giving the action a homicidal character which previously it did not have.

By contrast, actions which constitute endangerment are only potentially harmful. An action is potentially murderous or homicidal if it would constitute murder, or manslaughter, were it to cause death, but the actual causation of death is no part of its intrinsic character as the agent conceives and engages in it.

. . .

To ask whether we should have a general law of attempts, defined in terms of an 'intent to commit an offence', is thus to ask whether we should have a general law of attacks rather than of endangerment: should we criminalize essentially harmful actions which in fact cause no harm more readily than those which are only potentially harmful?

Part of the answer to this question lies in the very difference between essentially and potentially harmful action. One who intends to do harm, whose action is essentially harmful, relates himself as an agent as closely as he can to that harm; his action falls short of the paradigm of wrongfully harmful action only in that its harmful character is not completely actualized; and that non-completion of its harmful character is the non-completion of the action itself, as he intends it. By contrast, one whose action is only potentially harmful relates himself less closely, as an agent, to the harm which he risks causing: if the harm does not ensue, his action is complete without causing harm; it is connected to the paradigm of wrongfully harmful action neither by the fact of causing harm nor by its intentional structure. Relatedly, one who intends to do harm cannot hope that that harm will not ensue, nor (without repenting his action) be relieved if it does not; while one who is only reckless as to a risk of harm can (it is consistent with the intentional structure of his action that he will) have such a hope and feel such relief.

It follows that if we should be criminally liable for our actions, in so far as they are culpably related to some criminal harm, we have stronger reason to criminalize actions which are essentially harmful than to criminalize those which are only potentially harmful: to criminalize failed attacks than to criminalize endangerments which cause no actual harm. For the former are more closely related to the harm which they are intended but fail to cause, than are the latter to the harm which they threaten to but do not actually cause.

FURTHER READING

Alexander, L. and Kessler, K. (1997) '*Mens Rea* and Inchoate Crimes' *Journal of Criminal Law and Criminology* 87: 1138.

Ashworth, A. (2011) 'Attempts' in J. Deigh and D. Dolinko (eds) *The Oxford Handbook of Philosophy of Criminal Law* (Oxford: OUP).

Chiao, V. (2010) 'Intention and Attempt' *Criminal Law and Philosophy* 4: 37.

Clarkson, C. (2009) 'Attempt: The Conduct Requirement' *Oxford Journal of Legal Studies* 29: 25.

Duff, R.A. (1991) 'The Circumstances of an Attempt' *Cambridge Law Journal* 50: 100.

Duff, R.A. (2007) *Answering for Crime* (Oxford: Hart), ch. 7.

Duff, R.A. (2008) 'Whose Luck is It Anyway' in C. Clarkson and S. Cunningham (eds) *Criminal Liability for Non-Aggressive Death* (Aldershot: Ashgate).

Rogers, J. (2008) 'The Codification of Attempts and the Case for "Preparation" ' *Criminal Law Review* 937.

Stannard, J. (1987) 'Making Up for the Missing Element: A Sideways Look at Attempts' *Legal Studies* 7: 194.

Sullivan, G.R. (1992) 'Intent, Subjective Recklessness and Culpability' *Oxford Journal of Legal Studies* 12: 380.

Williams, G. (1991b) 'Intents in the Alternative' *Cambridge Law Journal* 50: 120.

Wilson, W. (2013) 'Participating in Crime: Some Thoughts on the Retribution/Prevention Dichotomy in Preparation for Crime and How to Deal with It' in A. Reed and M. Bohlander (eds) *Participation in Crime* (Aldershot: Ashgate).

Wishart, J. (2013) 'Criminal Culpability, Criminal Attempts and the Erosion of Choice Theory' *Journal of Criminal Law* 77: 78.

Yaffe, G. (2010) *Attempts* (Oxford: OUP).

6.5 IMPOSSIBLE ATTEMPTS

In many cases of impossible attempts it is unlikely that the defendant will be charged because his or her conduct will be objectively innocent. If a man has sexual intercourse with a woman with her consent, believing her to be over 13, whereas in fact she is under 13, technically he is guilty of an attempt to have sexual intercourse with a girl under 13. In fact because what he has done is 'objectively innocent' it is unlikely the police will ever find out about this unless the man makes a confession. However, where there is evidence that the defendant believes he or she is committing an offence, even though in fact he or she is not (e.g. he or she is found with a bag of white powder and a drug-taking kit, but the white powder is found to be chalk) should there be an offence? ←4 (p.778)

Subjectivists are likely to take the view that the defendant was as blameworthy as if the facts had been true. He or she has shown a similar contempt for the values the law upholds and seeks to protect what a person who actually commits the offence has done. It could be claimed it is purely 'luck' that the facts were not as the defendant believed them to be. For objectivists the complete lack of harm means that it is illegitimate to punish an impossible attempt. There is no objective or manifest criminality. The House of Lords in *Shivpuri* adopted the subjective view.

QUESTIONS

1. Michael, of deep religious faith, prays that God will strike down his enemy, Brian, with a thunderbolt. He believes God will answer his prayer, but Brian is still alive. Cynthia invites her friend, Sophie, around for a cup of tea. She has prepared poison in the shape of a sugar cube. She intends to put it in Sophie's tea, but by mistake puts a normal sugar cube in Sophie's tea. Are these 'failed attacks'? Can they be distinguished?

2. George Fletcher (1978: 137ff) expressed the concern that for many cases of impossible attempts the only way the prosecution could get a conviction was if the defendant was foolish or vulnerable enough to confess. Is that a reason against punishing impossible attempts?

3. Duff (1996: 384) discusses the hypothetical example of a person putting pins into a model of the victim, believing that thereby he or she will release evil powers which will kill the victim. He argues such behaviour cannot amount to an attempt because 'it fails so radically to engage with the world that it does not even amount to a failed attack'. Is that a convincing argument?

FURTHER READING

Fletcher, G. (1978), *Rethinking Criminal Law* (Boston, MA: Little, Brown), 137ff.

Temkin, J. (1976) 'Impossible Attempts: Another View' *Modern Law Review* 39: 55.

Williams, G. (1991a) 'Criminal Omissions—The Conventional View' *Law Quarterly Review* 107: 87.

Yaffe, G. (2010) *Attempts* (Oxford: OUP).

6.6 REFORM OF THE LAW ON ATTEMPTS

The Law Commission have proposed reform of the law on attempts. They summarized their proposed reforms as follows:

Law Commission Report No. 318, *Conspiracy and Attempts* (London: TSO, 2009)

9.17 We recommend that the Criminal Attempts Act 1981 be amended to provide that, for the purposes of section 1(1), an intent to commit an offence includes a conditional intent to commit it.

9.18 We recommend that for substantive offences which have a circumstance requirement but no corresponding fault requirement, or which have a corresponding fault requirement which is objective (such as negligence), it should be possible to convict D of attempting to commit the substantive offence only if D was subjectively reckless as to the circumstance at the relevant time.

9.19 We recommend that where a substantive offence has fault requirements not involving mere negligence (or its equivalent) in relation to a fact or circumstance, it should be possible to convict D of attempting to commit the substantive offence if D possessed those fault requirements at the relevant time.

9.20 We recommend that the Criminal Attempts Act 1981 be amended so that D may be convicted of attempted *murder* if (with the intent to kill V) D failed to discharge his or her legal duty to V (where that omission, unchecked, could have resulted in V's death).

---

7 CONSPIRACY THEORY

Conspiracy is a controversial offence. In particular, the fact that the offence can be committed simply by a verbal agreement by two or more people to commit the crime, before any steps are taken to implement the plan.[143] In the following extract, Fred Abbate sets out some of the principal concerns with the offence and some of its possible justifications: ←6 (p.794)

F.J. Abbate, 'The Conspiracy Doctrine: A Critique' in M. Gorr and S. Harwood (eds) *Controversies in Criminal Law* (Boulder, CO: Westview, 1992), 56–9

Unlike other inchoate crimes, conspiracy has drawn criticism because of what are thought to be its peculiar features:

(1) The conspirational group may be punished for contemplating an objective for which as individuals they could not be punished. A lone person with felonious designs—even known felonious designs—cannot ordinarily be brought to trial. But if he plots with others, he has committed a crime.

(2) In order for a conspiracy to obtain, no formal agreement need be shown to have occurred. A 'tacit understanding' is enough, a 'unity of design and purpose.' Each conspirator need not even know the identity of all the others.

---

143 Law Commission Report No. 76 (1976: para. 1.5); Dennis (1977).

(3) Where the conspiracy is for an unlawful purpose, even if the conspirators have not yet decided on the means to accomplish it, they may still be prosecuted.

(4) Although most conspiracies are secret, openness does not immunize an agreement from prosecution for conspiracy.

(5) 'Each conspirator is liable for all consequences that naturally flow from the conspiracy and for the acts of all who participate with him in executing the unlawful purpose.' The 'acts' at issue need not be the agreed-upon methods, so long as they are in furtherance of the plan.

(6) Although one may join a conspiracy at a date later than that of the original agreement, he is not only liable for all acts done thereafter, but for the original agreement itself.

(7) Under many statutes no 'overt act' in furtherance of the agreement need be shown in order for the charge of conspiracy to be proven.

(8) Certain of the rules of evidence are relaxed in conspiracy trials, and there is often a higher penalty attached to the conspiracy crime than to the completed offense.

. . .

The classical general defense of the conspiracy doctrine is the 'group-danger' rationale. On the assumption that the criminal law has as one of its objectives the prevention of harm to the community, the claim is that, since combinations of persons with harmful intentions are more dangerous than lone persons with those same intentions, conspiracies themselves must be made a crime. The increased danger, the argument continues, is the result of several factors:

(a) An individual is more likely to carry out his group commitments than his purely private decisions.

(b) Having committed himself to others, it is now much more difficult for a person to reverse the original decision, since such a reversal would require the cooperation of others.

(c) There is now increased probability that the harm intended will be produced.

(d) There is now the prospect of a greater amount of harm than that intended by lone individuals.

These factors have been used to justify the state's stepping in at a stage even earlier than it does in the case of attempt. (The 'overt act' required in conspiracy need not be an attempt to carry out the plan.) This point has been expressed by an often quoted study of conspiracy by the *Harvard Law Review*:

'Since one who has decided to commit a crime does not confront the further choice whether to attempt that crime, the deterrent function of the proscription against attempt is not additional to that of the proscription against the completed offense. By contrast, conspiracy is simply a route by which a given criminal object can be approached. Because the antisocial potentialities of this route are peculiarly great, it is arguable that even those who have not been deterred by the penalty for the completed offense should nevertheless be discouraged from embarking upon their criminal venture in concert with others.'

Further,

'. . . the uneasiness produced by the consciousness that such groupings exist is in itself an important antisocial effect. Consequently, the State has an interest in stamping out conspiracy above and beyond its interest in preventing the commission of any specific substantive offense. This additional interest may explain, for example, why some courts have imposed cumulative sentences for a conspiracy and for the crime which was its object.'

By calling the group-danger rationale a 'general defense,' I mean to indicate that it seeks to justify conspiracy as a category of crime while still being neutral about the wisdom of the particular features of the doctrine. Indeed, critics of the procedural and other details of the doctrine often wish to retain the category purged of what they consider its objectionable features. Thus, the group-danger justification will not, without further argument, account for, say, the vicarious responsibility aspect of conspiracy law or the relaxation of the rules of evidence.

But does the group-danger rationale even do its general justifying task without problems? Consider (a) and (b) above, which assert that commitments to groups are less likely to be revised or left unaccomplished than individual decisions. Even if true, the argument would justify stepping in and prosecuting only those conspiracies that are based upon certain sorts of commitments of individuals to groups, not all those (as the category is framed at law) that are 'combinations' or 'agreements.' It has been noted that a 'tacit understanding' or 'unity of design and purpose' is all that is required for conspiracy, and although showing these might sometimes provide evidential support for the existence of 'commitment,' quite clearly it need not. From the fact that M and N have agreed to do or have an understanding that they will do A, it surely does not follow that M is in any clear sense 'committed' to N to do A. He may merely, for example, view his consorting with N as a means to carry out his own particular designs.

But even if M is committed to N, it does not follow that he is therefore more committed to the doing of A than he would be as a lone individual. A person who is morally committed to a course of action does not become more committed to it for having joined with others. Nor does his joining involve the clearer likelihood that now he will carry out his intentions. And stressing point (b) will not help much, since M's change of mind does not require the cooperation of others if his original intention to do A was not itself a result of his joining with others.

If we turn to (c) and (d) of the group-danger rationale, there are more questions. The mere addition of heads and hands does not of itself increase the potential for danger, even in cases where 'commitment' is an appropriate description. As a matter of empirical fact, a single (and single-minded) person might be much more dangerous to the public safety than a group. As Goldstein put it:

> 'More likely, empirical investigation would disclose that there is as much reason to believe that a large number of participants will increase the prospect that the plan will be leaked as that it will be kept secret; or that the persons involved will share their uncertainties and dissuade each other as that each will stiffen the others determination.'

The remark about secrecy (no longer essential to a conspiracy according to the Spock case) suggests another point. The claim, noted above, that is the 'uneasiness' aroused by knowing there are conspiracies afoot which helps justify the state's interference even before attempt, would work just as well as an argument for punishing lone individuals with harmful intentions. If 'uneasiness' is an important antisocial effect, then presumably any uneasiness will do. In addition, a group which has decided to do some harmful act, but has not yet decided upon the means, should cause less uneasiness than one person who has decided upon both, yet the former is as full-blown a conspiracy as is any other. We will take up the question of punishment for intentions in a moment, but the point to be made now is that the 'uneasiness' argument flatly justifies too much.

Nor will the distinction between attempt and conspiracy, as drawn above, hold much promise after closer scrutiny. It is true, of course, that one who has decided to commit a crime does not face the further choice of whether or not to attempt it, so that the proscription against attempts is, so to speak, 'built in' to the proscription against the accomplished objective. But this is also true with regard to certain kinds of conspiracies, namely, those in which the objective by its very nature requires a group effort. Consider a plot to seize and shut down a complicated waterworks. Given the nature of the crime, one does not (if one is rational) intend to do it unless one intends to do it with others. There are not two choices here—the decision to take over the waterworks *and* the decision to do it in concert with others. The conspiracy cannot be labeled a mere 'route by which a given criminal object can be approached,' and the parallel with attempts is obvious.

These objections to the group-danger rationale do not, of course, show that the invoking of it is always out of place. They do, however, show it to be a much weaker general defense than most who employ it seem to think. For the common-law conception of conspiracy is not what is being justified by the rationale, but rather a special sub-class of the category, viz., one where members are strongly committed to the group's cause and to each other, where the members are in actual fact more dangerous in combination than as individuals, where more than mere social uneasiness is the effect of the venture, and where the objective is such that it does not require a group effort by definition.

Clearly the purpose of the offence of conspiracy is to enable the police and prosecution authorities to intervene early and convict a group of criminals before having to wait until they actually commit the offence. However, there is, as Abbate points out, a remarkable contrast with attempts. In attempts law great care is taken not to put the *actus reus* of an attempt too early. Otherwise defendants could be punished for their evil thoughts, rather than what they have done. Hence the English law insists that the defendant has done an act which is more than merely preparatory. By contrast, in conspiracy there is only a need to demonstrate an agreement to commit the offence.[144] The key difference between a conspiracy and an attempt is the number of people involved.[145]

The argument that is most commonly put forward to justify conspiracy is, to use the words of Andrew Ashworth, 'In many cases group behaviour may acquire a momentum of its own, with individuals being afraid to withdraw and participants spurring each other on.'[146] But is there much dispute over whether there is evidence to support such a claim.[147]

The offence of conspiracy is also justifiable on the basis that an offence committed by a group dedicated to the same purpose involves doing the victim a different kind of wrong from that where there is only one offender. However, such an argument, although it may be convincing where a group has actually committed the offence, is hard to justify where there is no offence.

QUESTION

In 2009 (BBC News Online 2009b) two schoolboys were acquitted of conspiracy to murder and cause explosions after it was found they had discussed blowing up their school and wrote in journals about their plans. The defence claimed that the boys simply had overactive imaginations and that the prosecution had over-reacted to what was typical schoolboy imagination. Does this show the dangers of the use of conspiracy?

---

[144] Dressler (1987: 382).

[145] Bowne (1993: 224) has concerns for the disproportionate use of conspiracy offences on minority groups.

[146] Ashworth (1999: 475).   [147] Katyal (2003); Barloon (1996).

FURTHER READING

Alexander, L. and Kessler, K. (1997) '*Mens Rea* and Inchoate Crimes' *Journal of Law and Criminology* 87: 1138.

Dennis, I. (1977) 'The Rationale of Criminal Conspiracy' *Law Quarterly Review* 93: 39.

Law Commission (2002) Report No. 276, *Fraud* (London: TSO).

Law Commission (2009b) Report No. 318, *Conspiracy and Attempts* (London: TSO).

Levi, M. and Smith, A. (2002) *Organised Crime and Conspiracy Legislation* (London: Home Office).

Robbins, I. (1989) 'Double Inchoate Crimes' *Harvard Journal of Legislation* 26: 1.

8 THE RATIONALE FOR THE NEW SERIOUS CRIME ACT OFFENCES

In the following passage David Ormerod and Rudi Fortson challenge the need for the new offences:[148]

D. Ormerod and R. Fortson, 'Serious Crime Act 2007: The Part 2 Offences' [2009] *Criminal Law Review* 389 at 395–7

It is questionable whether all of these tortuously difficult offences in ss.44–46 are even necessary. The ease with which the offence of incitement was prosecuted is difficult to evaluate but, in practice, its apparent clarity was evidenced by the paucity of appellate decisions (compared, for example, to conspiracy). The Law Commission described it as "rarely troubling the courts". The Court of Appeal had settled on a definition of the offence from the draft Code which was repeatedly endorsed. Nevertheless, in LC 300 the Commission concluded that incitement displayed six "unsatisfactory features":

"(1) there is uncertainty as to whether it must be D's purpose that P should commit the offence that D is inciting;

(2) the fault element of the offence has been distorted by decisions of the Court of Appeal. These decisions have focused, wrongly, on the state of mind of P rather than on D's state of mind;

(3) there is uncertainty as to whether and, if so, to what extent it is a defence to act in order to prevent the commission of an offence or to prevent or limit the occurrence of harm;

(4) there is uncertainty as to the circumstances in which D is liable for inciting P to do an act which, if done by P, would not involve P committing an offence, for example because P is under the age of criminal responsibility or lacks a guilty mind;

(5) the rules governing D's liability in cases where D incites P to commit an inchoate offence have resulted in absurd distinctions;

---

148 See also Baker (2011c).

(6)   D may have a defence if the offence that he or she incites is impossible to commit whereas impossibility is not a defence to other inchoate offences, apart from common law conspiracies. The offence of incitement is therefore in need of clarification."

Arguably, none of these features provides a compelling case for reform. Admittedly, the courts had fallen into error on the mens rea of incitement in *Curr*, but had belatedly rectified that in *Claydon*. We accept that there may have been a case for putting on a statutory footing the definition of incitement and for clarifying a number of issues, such as liability for impossibility, to ensure coherence with other inchoate offences. That falls a long way short of accepting a compelling case for outright abolition of incitement and its replacement with a range of disturbingly wide offences. We acknowledge that this is not a universally held view. In reviewing what were then legislative proposals, Sullivan argued that the broad scheme is understandable given the need to challenge career criminals and terrorist support networks. We would counter that by suggesting that the activities of these categories of criminal are adequately met by the extremely wide offences enacted under, for example, the Terrorism Acts, and the Proceeds of Crime Act 2002. Some support for that is borne out by the willingness of agencies to prosecute for those offences, particularly under the Proceeds of Crime Act. More generally, we would suggest that legislation has, in recent years, been willing to extend the net of criminal liability to ensnare assisters and encouragers by its creation of offences such as those of "being knowingly concerned in" the principal wrongdoing. The argument for a range of broad general inchoate offences was far from clear.

Perhaps the longest standing and most persuasive argument for reform of incitement lay in the need for an offence of "facilitation". This deals with D who assisted P without also encouraging him to commit the anticipated offence in circumstances where P did *not* then go on to commit the anticipated crime, perhaps because P changed his mind, or because he was arrested before he could commit the offence. For example, if D sold a ladder to P, intending that P would use it to commit burglary, and P was arrested long before he could use the ladder for that purpose, then D might well have escaped liability because, (a) it does not necessarily constitute incitement since D did not "encourage" P to commit burglary, (although the likelihood of the courts adopting such a narrow view of incitement, unless constrained to do so, seems relatively remote); (b) D and P had not conspired to burgle, (c) no question of liability arises under the Criminal Attempts Act 1981, and (d) there could be no secondary liability (Accessories and Abettors Act 1861 s.8) because the substantive offence was not committed: D's intention in providing the ladder to P was to profit from its sale, not to burgle.

This argument for the creation of a facilitation offence was supported by the claim that absence of such an offence led to an extended definition of incitement and overuse of conspiracy. Examples cited by the Law Commission include the cases of *Anderson* and *Hollinshead*. The House of Lords extended the scope of conspiracy in *Anderson* to include cases in which none of the conspirators intend to carry out the agreement. However, that decision was gratefully distinguished by subsequent decisions and did not seem to have distorted the law as much as was feared. In the House of Lords' most recent pronouncement, Lord Nicholls expressly stated that the "conspirators must intend to do the act prohibited by the substantive offence". In *Hollinshead*, the House had held that D1 and D2 were guilty of conspiracy where they foresaw that X, who was not a conspirator, would be able to commit a fraud. An objection to the decision in *Hollinshead* is that the *purpose* of the accused was not to perpetrate a fraud by, for example, causing loss to an electricity board, but to make a profit (i.e. by manufacturing and selling devices that were intended to under-record the amounts of electricity used). However controversial, *Hollinshead* has not been overruled, and even without Pt 2 of the SCA [Serious Crime Act] 2007, the particular conduct involved gives rise to liability under s.7 of the Fraud Act 2006.

Whether these were powerful bases even for a new offence of facilitation is therefore highly debatable. Even if it were to be accepted that a new facilitation offence was desirable, if not necessary, we suggest that this might have been achieved with a simple provision comprising no more than a few lines of statute. Even that limited amendment would have begged many other questions including whether it ought to have rendered obsolete the range of existing facilitation offences in English criminal law.

9 CONCLUDING THOUGHTS

It can seem rather odd that criminal law should punish defendants in cases where the defendant has not actually caused a harm to the victim. Yet that is precisely the role performed by inchoate offences. Their existence shows that the concern of the law is not just with punishing those who cause harm, but with preventing the endangerment of others, and with the holding to account those who have behaved wrongfully. The extension of inchoate offences with the Serious Crime Act 2007 demonstrates the great concern that the public have about those who plan to commit major offences.

15

COMPLICITY

> **CENTRAL ISSUES**
>
> 1. The principal is the person who actually causes the harm to the victim, whilst the accomplice is the person who assists the principal in the commission of an offence.
>
> 2. A person can be an accomplice by aiding, abetting, counselling, or procuring another to commit an offence. Another way is by being a party to a joint enterprise during which the principal commits the offence.
>
> 3. To be an accomplice the defendant must intend to aid, abet, counsel, or procure the commission of the offence, and foresee that the principal might commit the offence.
>
> 4. The Law Commission has recommended radical reform of the law on accomplice liability.

PART I: THE LAW OF COMPLICITY

1 PRINCIPALS AND ACCOMPLICES

> **DEFINITION**
>
> The principal is the person whose acts or omission amount to the *actus reus* of the offence.
>
> The accomplice is a person who aids, abets, counsels, or procures the principal in the commission of the offence.[1]

This chapter deals with the legal position of those who help or encourage others who go on to commit crimes. The criminal law punishes not only those who directly harm a victim

---

[1] This distinction seems straightforward but see *DPP v Nedrick-Smith* [2006] EWHC 3015 (Admin), where (especially at para. 14) the court appears to become rather confused as to the difference between joint principals, joint enterprise, and accessories.

but also those who assist them. So if Bob stabs Steven to death, Bob is clearly guilty of murder. But if Charles has given Bob the knife, Diana has told Bob where Steven can be found and Edwina has encouraged Bob to kill Steven, then Charles, Diana, and Edwina can all also be guilty in connection with Steven's death. Those who help others commit crimes have been known by a number of different legal terms: accessories, secondary parties, or accomplices.[2]

It must be said at the outset that the law in this area is unclear in places. Professors Ashworth and Horder have stated:

> the English law of complicity is replete with uncertainties and conflicts. It betrays the worst features of the common law: what some would regard as flexibility appears here as a succession of opportunistic decisions by the courts, often extending the law, and resulting in a body of jurisprudence that has little coherence.[3]

As this quotation indicates, the subject of this chapter is not an easy one and commentators have struggled to present a clear guide to the present law. Not surprisingly, therefore, students find it difficult too. When reading this chapter always keep in mind the offences under Part 2 of the Serious Crime Act 2007, involving the encouragement and assistance of crime, and which are discussed in Chapter 14.

In order to understand the position of accomplices first it is necessary to distinguish them from principals. Generally in this chapter when discussing scenarios, where the letter P is used it represents the alleged principal and where the letter A is used it represents the alleged accomplice.

1.1 WHO IS THE PRINCIPAL?

The principal is the perpetrator of the crime. That is the person (or people) whose actions constitute the *actus reus* of the offence. For example, in a murder case it is the person whose act caused the death of the victim. By contrast, the accomplice will be the person who assisted or encouraged the principal to commit the crime. This appears a straightforward distinction, but it is important to contrast five different cases:[4]

(1) Val and Ian both stab Sara. The combined effect of the two wounds is that Sara dies. In such a case Val and Ian are guilty as joint principals.[5] It may be that they have different *mens rea* in which case they will be convicted of different offences (e.g. one of murder and one of manslaughter). Alternatively, they may have the same *mens rea* in which case they are guilty of the same crime.

(2) Laurie gives Stephen a knife, telling him to stab Agatha to death, which Stephen does. Stephen is clearly the principal and Laurie the accomplice.[6]

---

[2] At one point the common law distinguished between principals in the second degree (those who were assisting the principal and were present when the offence was committed) and accessories before the fact (those whose participation was limited to activities before the crime was committed). The law no longer draws this distinction.

[3] Ashworth and Horder (2013: 443).   [4] *Macklin and Murphy's Case* (1838) 2 Lew CC 225.

[5] See *Montague* [2013] EWCA Crim 1781, where the judgments display considerable confusion by calling a case of joint principals one of joint enterprise.

[6] *Kennedy* [2007] UKHL 38.

(3) Minnette and Dorothy, acting together, attack Peter. Evidence is unable to establish whether the fatal wound was inflicted by Minnette or Dorothy. They are both liable for murder. This is because it can be said of both Minnette and Dorothy: 'Either your stab wound caused Peter's death or you assisted the person whose stab wound caused Peter's death. Therefore, you are guilty of murder, either as the principal or the accomplice.'[7] This law is demonstrated in the rather unusual facts of *Giannetto*[8] (in the following extract).[9]

(4) Dick and Phyllis attack Tom at the same time, but without intending to assist each other or cooperate together. In such a case Dick and Phyllis are each individually responsible for their own actions, but not for each other's.[10] So if it was established that the cause of death was only the wound inflicted by Dick, Phyllis could not be convicted of murder or manslaughter (but could be guilty of the wounds she inflicted).

(5) Arthur gives Conan some poison, telling Conan it is medicine for Conan's child. Conan, believing Arthur, gives the poison to the child who dies. In such a case Arthur is guilty of murder as the principal and Conan is not guilty of any offence.

This last example is one of the 'doctrine of innocent agency', which needs to be considered in further detail. But first an extract from *Giannetto* which explains what the prosecution needs to show in order to establish that a defendant is a principal:

R v Giannetto
[1997] 1 Cr App R 1 (CA)

Robert Giannetto made threats to his wife Julia Giannetto and paid Welch to kill her. Giannetto was arrested after his wife's death. The prosecution was unable to establish who had killed her. He was convicted of murder on the basis that either he or someone acting on his behalf (maybe Welch) killed her. He appealed on the basis that the judge had failed to indicate to the jury that they had to be unanimous in deciding whether he was the principal or accessory.

Lord Justice Kennedy

Having considered the authorities with some care we are satisfied that in the circumstances of this case the trial judge was right not to direct the jury that before they could convict they must all be satisfied either that the appellant killed his wife or that he got someone else to do so. They were entitled to convict if they were all satisfied that if he was not the killer he at least encouraged the killing, and accordingly this ground of appeal fails.

There are two cardinal principles. The first is that the jury must be agreed upon the basis on which they find a defendant guilty. The second is that a defendant must know what case he has to meet. Where the Crown allege, fair and square, that on the evidence the defendant must have committed the offence either as principal or as secondary offender, and make it equally clear that they cannot say which, the basis on which the jury must be unanimous is that the defendant, having the necessary *mens rea*, by whatever means caused the result which is criminalised by the law. The Crown is not required to specify the means, because the legal definition of the crime does not require it; and the defendant knows perfectly well

---

[7] *Giannetto* [1997] 1 Cr App R 1; *Jogee* [2016] UKSC 8, para. 1. [8] [1997] 1 Cr App R 1.
[9] See also *Banfield* [2013] EWCA Crim 1394. [10] *Peters and Parfitt* [1995] Crim LR 501.

what case he has to meet. Of course, if (as will very often be so) the Crown nail their colours to a particular mast, their case will, generally, have to be established in the terms in which it is put. Our judgment should give no encouragement to prosecutors casting around for alternative possibilities where the essential evidence does not show a clear case against the defendant. But the facts of the present appeal are by no means an instance of that.

Appeal dismissed.

1.2 'INNOCENT AGENCY'

An innocent agent is a person whose act causes the harm to the victim, but who is 'innocent': either because he or she lacks criminal capacity (e.g. he or she is insane or under the age of criminal responsibility) or he or she is unaware of the criminal nature of the act he or she is doing (e.g. a passer-by who touches a booby trap bomb, setting it off).[11] Where an innocent agent is involved the principal is the person who 'causes' the innocent agent to perform the *actus reus* and the innocent agent is not guilty of any crime.

In the case law the best example of innocent agency is *Michael*,[12] where the defendant wished to kill her baby. She delivered poison to her nurse, telling her it was medicine and to administer it to the baby. The nurse decided not to administer the poison and left it on the shelf. A child then took the poison and administered it to the baby and killed him. The child and nurse in this case could be described as 'innocent agents'. Similarly, in *Stringer and Banks*[13] an employer told his employees to type letters and engage in accounting transactions which (unknown to the employees) resulted in fraudulent transfers. The employees were innocent agents and the principal was the employer.

Professor David Ormerod[14] has suggested that there are some crimes which cannot be committed through an innocent agent because 'it is impossible to say that D has personally committed the *actus reus*'. He suggests bigamy and rape as examples.[15] The argument in favour of this view is that to say a principal has committed rape when he or she used an innocent agent is an artificial description of what he or she has done. By contrast, in a case where the defendant has used an innocent agent to administer poison there is no artificiality in saying that the defendant has poisoned the victim.

FURTHER READING

Alldridge, P. (1990) 'The Doctrine of Innocent Agency' *Criminal Law Forum* 1: 45.

Alldridge, P. (1992) 'Common Sense, Innocent Agency, and Causation' *Criminal Law Forum* 3: 299.

Taylor, R. (2008) 'Procuring, Causation, Innocent Agency and the Law Commission' *Criminal Law Review* 32.

Williams, G. (1992) 'Innocent Agency and Causation' *Criminal Law Forum* 3: 289.

---

[11] See Taylor (2008) for a discussion of this doctrine.   [12] (1840) 9 C & P 356.
[13] [1991] Crim LR 639 (CA).   [14] Ormerod (2008: 181).
[15] However, in *Cogan and Leak* [1976] QB 217 (CA) a husband was convicted of raping his wife through the innocent agency of his friend. The Court of Appeal did suggest that an alternative way of examining the case was to see it as one of procuring rape, and this analysis was also preferred by the Divisional Court in *DPP v K and B* [1997] 1 Cr App R 36 (DC). For further discussion, see Yaffe (2012).

2 COMPLICITY: THE *ACTUS REUS*

DEFINITION

There are five ways that one can be an accomplice:[16]

(1) aiding;

(2) abetting;

(3) counselling;

(4) procuring;

(5) party to a joint enterprise.

It used to be thought that the law on joint enterprise was different from aiding, abetting, counselling, and procuring. However, the Supreme Court in the decision of *Jogee*[17] has made it clear that the principles underpinning joint enterprise are the same as those underpinning the other forms of being an accomplice.

Section 8 of the Accessories and Abettors Act 1861 states:[18]

> Whosoever shall aid, abet, counsel, or procure the commission of any indictable offence, whether the same be an offence at common law or by virtue of any act passed or to be passed, shall be liable to be tried, indicted, and punished as a principal offender.

This section makes three points of crucial importance to the law of accomplices:

(1) There must be an offence committed by the principal.[19] The significance of this is that if the accused offers aiding, abetting, counselling, or procuring to the principal, but the principal does not go on to commit an offence then the accused is not guilty as an accessory. Imagine this: Jeeves, a butler to Bertie, knowing that Gussie, a burglar, is intending to burgle Bertie's house, leaves his safe wide open. Jeeves commits no offence if Gussie does not burgle that night because he has a headache.[20] There is no such offence as an attempt to aid, abet, counsel, or procure. However, the new offences in sections 44 to 46 of the Serious Crime Act 2007 (see Chapter 14, Section 3) mean a person can be guilty of an offence for doing an act which was capable of giving assistance or encouragement to a crime, even if the principal does not go on to commit it. →1 (p.870)

(2) The accomplice is charged with the basic offence. For example, an accused will be charged with murder, even though the allegation is that he or she has been an accomplice to the murder.[21] This is particularly significant in the context of murder because a mandatory life sentence automatically follows a conviction of murder. The Supreme Court in *Jogee* explained that this was because the accomplice shared in the crime committed by the

---

[16] There are a few offences for which the *actus reus* involves assisting and encouraging, e.g. the Suicide Act 1961, s. 2 (assisting and encouraging suicide).

[17] [2016] UKSC 8.

[18] As amended by the Criminal Law Act 1977. The Magistrates' Courts Act 1980, s. 44, contains a similar provision for summary offences.

[19] *R v Kenning* [2008] EWCA Crim 1534.   [20] He may be guilty of a firearms offence.

[21] *Jogee* [2016] UKSC 8, para. 1.

principal 'even if it was not his hand which struck the blow, ransacked the house, smuggled the drugs or forged the cheque, he has encouraged or assisted those physical acts'.[22]

(3) The prosecution only need to prove that the defendant was an accomplice in one of the four ways listed in section 8 or is liable under the doctrine of joint enterprise. They do not need to specify in what way the defendant was an accomplice. In *Jogee*[23] it was suggested that the ways of being an accomplice could be reduced to two: that the accessory encouraged or assisted the principal in the commission of the offence.

Let us now consider the meaning of 'aiding', 'abetting', 'counselling', 'procuring', and 'joint enterprise'. The starting point is the following statement of Lord Widgery CJ in *Attorney-General's Reference (No. 1 of 1975)*:[24]

> We approach s. 8 of the 1861 Act on the basis that the words should be given their ordinary meaning, if possible. We approach the section on the basis also that if four words are employed here 'aid, abet, counsel or procure', the probability is that there is a difference between each of those four words and the other three, because, if there were no such difference, then Parliament would be wasting time in using four words where two or three would do.

The significance of this quotation is that it indicates that the words should be given their normal meaning. This is all well and good, but 'abetting', 'procuring', and 'counselling'[25] are not words in common usage and to give them a 'normal' meaning is therefore not straightforward. The second point that Lord Widgery has made is that the four words are to have distinct meanings.[26] Again this is a little problematic; in particular, commentators have struggled to find an independent meaning of the phrase 'to abet' that is not covered by aiding or counselling. Notably other cases (e.g. *Attorney-General v Able*[27]) have suggested that the four words are just synonyms of helping. →2 (p.885) Indeed in *Jogee*[28] the Supreme Court suggested that the forms of being an accomplice could be reduced to assisting and encouraging. Although the blurriness of the lines between the different forms of being an accomplice worries law students, the approach taken by the courts is that an accomplice can be convicted, even if it is a bit unclear exactly what kind of accomplice he or she was.

2.1 AIDING

Aiding covers offering help or assistance to someone. This includes giving someone a piece of equipment[29] or some information which helps them commit a crime.[30] It is not necessary to show that the assistance was essential to the commission of the crime, nor that without it the crime could not have taken place. Indeed, all that is required is that the assistance was of some help to the principal in committing the crime.[31] However, to constitute aiding an act must actually be of assistance in commission of the crime.[32] So if Harold tells Peter that

---

[22] *Ibid*, para. 1.   [23] *Ibid*, para. 8.   [24] [1975] 2 All ER 684, 686.

[25] The word 'counselling' is, of course, normally used in the context of giving someone advice or support on emotional issues, but that is not what is meant here.

[26] See Smith (1978) for an argument that the words should not be seen as four separate terms but as capturing the single common law concept of being an accomplice.

[27] [1984] QB 795.   [28] [2016] UKSC 8.   [29] e.g. *Bainbridge* [1960] 1 QB 129.

[30] e.g. *Attorney-General v Able* [1984] QB 795.   [31] *Bryce* [2004] 2 Cr App R 35.

[32] *Attorney-General v Able* [1984] QB 795.

he is going to kill Tim, and Peter (who hates Tim) gives Harold a knife, but Harold does not use the knife but instead shoots Tim, then Peter will not have aided the murder because his knife in no way assisted it. Two points, however, should be made about this example. The first is that the provision of the knife may amount to counselling (discussed in Section 2.3). The second is that if the knife gave Harold confidence to commit the crime, even though he did not use it, Peter might still be held to have aided Harold.

Many cases of aiding will involve the parties meeting so the assistance can be provided,[33] but there need be no meeting. Indeed the principal may not even be aware that he or she has been assisted. If a security guard, disgruntled with his employer, left a property unlocked, hoping that a passing burglar would take advantage of this, which he did, the security guard could be guilty of aiding a burglary. In *Stringer (Ian)*[34] the Court of Appeal firmly rejected an argument that an act of assistance had to occur at the time of the crime. As they pointed out, a defendant who gives the principal a gun, which he uses to murder, is undoubtedly an accomplice, even if the giving of the gun occurred some time before the murder.

2.2 ABETTING

To be honest, no one knows what abetting means. Abetting is defined in the *Oxford English Dictionary* as including 'to incite, instigate or encourage'.[35] As will be seen, these terms are those often used to define counselling.[36] If abetting is to be given a special meaning of its own the best suggestion is that of Devlin J in *NCB v Gamble*,[37] who proposed that abetting was encouragement at the time of the offence, while counselling was encouragement before the crime took place.

2.3 COUNSELLING

Counselling involves encouraging, inciting, or instigating the offence. This may involve urging someone to commit an offence or simply indicating that the commission of the offence would be desirable. There is no need to show that the counselling caused the offence. In *Giannetto*[38] the trial judge suggested that if a man said to a husband that he was about to kill his wife and the husband did 'as little as patting him on the back, nodding, saying "Oh goody"' this would be sufficient to amount to counselling. In *Calhaem*[39] the defendant hired a hit man to kill a woman. The hit man did kill her but in a panic when she started screaming. The defendant's conviction as a counsellor of the killing could be upheld even though at the time of the killing the principal did not kill because of the instructions, but because of his panic. The Court explained that the hit man had committed the crime requested and there was some causal link between the counselling and the offence.

The most authoritative on the current position is found in their Lordships' judgment in *Jogee*:[40]

---

[33] *Attorney-General's Reference (No. 1 of 1975)* [1975] QB 773.   [34] [2011] EWCA Crim 1396.
[35] Macdonald (2015: 497) uses this as the meaning of abet in the criminal law.
[36] J.C. Smith (1978).   [37] [1959] 1 QB 11.   [38] [1997] 1 Cr App R 1, 13.
[39] [1985] QB 808.   [40] [2016] UKSC 8, para. 12.

Once encouragement or assistance is proved to have been given, the prosecution does not have to go so far as to prove that it had a positive effect on [P]'s conduct or on the outcome: *R v Calhaem* [1985] QB 808. In many cases that would be impossible to prove. There might, for example, have been many supporters encouraging [P] so that the encouragement of a single one of them could not be shown to have made a difference. The encouragement might have been given but ignored, yet the counselled offence committed. Conversely, there may be cases where anything said or done by [A] has faded to the point of mere background, or has been spent of all possible force by some overwhelming intervening occurrence by the time the offence was committed. Ultimately it is a question of fact and degree whether [A]'s conduct was so distanced in time, place or circumstances from the conduct of [P] that it would not be realistic to regard [P]'s offence as encouraged or assisted by it.

2.4 PROCURING

To procure has been defined as 'to produce by endeavour'.[41] In other words, the accomplice has in a sense caused the principal to commit the offence.[42] At least, the principal acted as a consequence of the accomplice's acts. A good example of this is *Attorney-General's Reference (No. 1 of 1975)*,[43] where A added alcohol to P's drink. When P later drove he was driving with a blood-alcohol concentration higher than the prescribed limit.[44] A's act had procured P to commit a drink-driving offence. Another example of procuring is *Millward*,[45] where the defendant was convicted of procuring the causing of death by dangerous driving by instructing his employee to drive a tractor and trailer, aware that the hitch mechanism between the two was defective. Subsequently the employee drove the tractor and trailer, which became unhitched, causing the death of a passing motorist. These cases should be contrasted with *Beatty v Gillbanks*,[46] where the officers of the Salvation Army knew that a meeting in Weston-super-Mare was likely to produce a violent reaction from a group known as the Skeleton Army. Nevertheless, they decided that the meeting should go ahead, and indeed there was a violent reaction from the Skeleton Army, which included the breaking of shop windows. The Salvation Army officers could not be said to have procured the violence. The case may be explained on the basis that the officers were not *endeavouring* to cause the violence of the Skeleton Army, or on the basis that, unlike *Attorney-General's Reference (No. 1 of 1975)*[47] and *Millward*,[48] the principals (the Skeleton Army) knew exactly what they were doing and could be said to have made an independent decision to carry out the violence.

Procuring is closely linked with the doctrine of innocent agency discussed at Section 1.2; the crucial difference being that in procuring the principal is not entirely innocent (e.g. he or she does have the capacity to commit the crime and has the relevant *mens rea*).

---

[41] *Attorney-General's Reference (No. 1 of 1975)* [1975] 2 All ER 684, 686.   [42] *Ibid*, 687.
[43] [1975] 2 All ER 684.
[44] Road Traffic Act 1972, s. 6(1). The offence is now found in the Road Traffic Act 1988, s. 5.
[45] [1994] Crim LR 527.   [46] (1882) 9 QBD 308.   [47] [1975] 2 All ER 684.
[48] [1994] Crim LR 527.

2.5 JOINT ENTERPRISE

A joint enterprise involving accessory liability arises where two or more people together embark on the commission of a criminal offence (Crime A), during which one of them goes on to commit a further offence (Crime B).[49] The others will then be an accomplice under joint enterprise to the commission of Crime B. The two parties may expressly agree to commit Crime A or this may be an unspoken understanding.[50] A common example is where two people decide to commit a burglary together, during which one of them kills a security guard who interrupts them. In such a case clearly the killer is the principal, but the other burglar can be convicted as an accomplice to the murder.

Lords Phillips, Judge, and Wilson in *Gnango*[51] explained the doctrine in these terms:

> (i) D1 and D2 have a common intention to commit crime A (ii) D1, as an incident of committing crime A, commits crime B, and (iii) D2 had foreseen the possibility that he might do so.

In such a case D1 will be the principal to crime B and D2 the accomplice.

In a case of joint enterprise there is no need to show that the accomplice aided or encouraged the offence. It is enough that they were a party to the joint enterprise and had the *mens rea*.

It is important to keep separate the idea of joint principals (see Section 1.1) and joint enterprise. Chav and Sheila together burgle a house. They are both engaging in the *actus reus* of burglary and so are joint principals. However, if Chav kills a security guard who interrupts them then Chav will be the principal to murder and Sheila the accomplice to the murder under the principle of joint enterprise (because the killing took place during the commission of the burglary together).

An important limitation on the notion of joint enterprise is that the crime must be committed in the course of or incidental to Crime A.[52] So if David and Nick commit a burglary and on the way home Nick scratches his enemy's car for his own reasons, David would not be liable under the doctrine of joint enterprise. The scratching was not part of, nor incidental to, their common purpose. Similarly an accomplice cannot be party to a joint enterprise if they join in after the principal has committed the crime.

2.6 THE PROBLEM OF *GNANGO*

In 2011 the Supreme Court heard an appeal in the case of *Gnango*. The case has proved controversial and difficult. Its significance is unclear. It is interesting to note that while one leading textbook[53] devotes many pages to a discussion of it, another contains only a passing reference in a footnote.[54] Not only can commentators not agree on what the case says, they cannot even agree on whether it is important![55] The fact that in *Jogee*,[56] now the leading case

---

[49] See Buxton (2009) for a detailed discussion.

[50] *DPP v Nedrick-Smith* [2006] EWHC 3015 (Admin) suggests that it is possible to be part of a joint enterprise even if the person is not taking part in the attack, nor, at the time of the offence, encouraging it.

[51] [2011] UKSC 59, at para. 42.

[52] *Gnango* [2010] EWCA Crim 1691.   [53] Simester, Spencer, Sullivan, and Virgo (2013).

[54] Ashworth and Horder (2013).   [55] Sullivan (2013).   [56] [2016] UKSC 8.

on accomplices, does not refer to *Gnango* is perhaps indicative of the fact it raised complex issues which arose from the particular facts of the case.

R v Gnango
[2012] 1 AC 827

Armel Gnango and a man who was never identified (but was called Bandana Man at the trial) got into a gun fight with each other on a London street. They fired shots at each other. Magda Pniewska, a care worker, was passing by and was shot dead by a bullet from Bandana Man's gun. Gnango was convicted as an accomplice at his trial, but that was overturned by the Court of Appeal. The question, in brief, for the Supreme Court was:

> If (1) D1 and D2 voluntarily engage in fighting each other, each intending to kill or cause grievous bodily harm to the other and each foreseeing that the other has the reciprocal intention, and if (2) D1 mistakenly kills V in the course of the fight, in what circumstances, if any, is D2 guilty of the offence of murdering V?

There were seven judges sitting in the Supreme Court in this case. A majority upheld the conviction of Gnango for murder, as an accomplice, but disagreed on the basis:

Lord Phillips and Lord Judge (with whom Lord Wilson agrees)

No issue of parasitic accessory liability arises in this case

42. Parasitic accessory liability arises where (i) D1 and D2 have a common intention to commit crime A (ii) D1, as an incident of committing crime A, commits crime B, and (iii) D2 had foreseen the possibility that he might do so. Here there was no crime A and crime B. It cannot be said that the two protagonists had a joint intention to commit violence of a type that fell short of the violence committed. Either Bandana Man and the respondent had no common intention, or there was a common intention to have a shoot out. If they intended to have a shoot out, then each necessarily accepted that the other would shoot at him with the intention to kill or cause serious injury. Neither intended that the other should kill him but each accepted the risk that he might do so.

43. The Crown sought to suggest that there was a joint intention to have an affray, which was crime A, and that the killing by Bandana Man was crime B, for which the respondent was liable as an accessory because it was within his contemplation as a possible, albeit unintended, incident of crime A. The fallacy of this argument is that, if there was a joint intention to have an affray, that intention was to have an affray by shooting at each other with homicidal intent. It is artificial to treat the intention to have an affray as a separate intention from the intention to have a potentially homicidal shooting match.

The victim rule

44. Why was the Crown so keen to establish liability under the doctrine of parasitic accessory liability? The answer is, we believe, that the Crown believed that this route would enable it to by-pass what was perceived to be a barrier to the direct route to the respondent's liability for murder. The direct route was as follows:

   i)   Bandana Man attempted to kill the respondent;

ii) By agreeing to the shoot out, the respondent aided and abetted Bandana Man in this attempted murder;

iii) Bandana Man accidentally killed Miss Pniewska instead of the respondent. Under the doctrine of transferred malice he was guilty of her murder.

iv) The doctrine of transferred malice applied equally to the respondent as aider and abetter of Bandana Man's attempted murder. He also was guilty of Miss Pniewska's murder.

45. The Crown believed that there was a barrier to this direct route to the respondent's liability for murder. This was the application of the victim rule. Mr Altman, when discussing the law with the judge, stated that the respondent could not aid and abet his own attempted murder. If this proposition correctly represents the law, we do not see how the Crown can avoid its effect by invoking the doctrine of parasitic accessory liability. . . .

. . .

[After a careful consideration of the victim rule their lordships concluded it had no application in this case, stating:]

54. In the light of the conclusion that we have just reached, no question arises as to the application of the victim rule where, although the intended victim of the crime to which the defendant is party is the defendant himself, the actual victim proves to be a third party.

. . .

60. A guilty verdict in this case involves a combination of common law principles in relation to aiding and abetting and the common law doctrine of transferred malice, . . . We have considered whether to hold the respondent guilty of murder would be so far at odds with what the public would be likely to consider the requirements of justice as to call for a reappraisal of the application of the doctrine in this case. We have concluded to the contrary. On the jury's verdict the respondent and Bandana Man had chosen to indulge in a gunfight in a public place, each intending to kill or cause serious injury to the other, in circumstances where there was a foreseeable risk that this result would be suffered by an innocent bystander. It was a matter of fortuity which of the two fired what proved to be the fatal shot. In other circumstances it might have been impossible to deduce which of the two had done so. In these circumstances it seems to us to accord with the demands of justice rather than to conflict with them that the two gunmen should each be liable for Miss Pniewska's murder.

62. We have considered the judgments of Lord Brown and Lord Clarke. They essentially agree with our conclusions. Each, however, considers that the defendant was liable as a principal to the agreed joint activity of shooting with intent to kill or cause serious injury, rather than as an accessory to the act of firing the shot. This is not a difference of substance. It may well be that, in terms of the common law, Bandana Man was a principal in the first degree and the respondent was a principal in the second degree—see *Archbold*, 2011 edition, para 18-1. But as *Archbold* remarks at para 18.6:

"the distinction between a joint principal and an abettor is sometimes difficult, and unnecessary, to draw."

Whether the respondent is correctly described as a principal or an accessory is irrelevant to his guilt. . . .

64. On the jury's verdict, both men agreed to the joint enterprise of having a shoot-out. Whether, on strict analysis, that made the respondent guilty as a principal to Bandana Man's actus reus of firing the fatal shot, or guilty as one who had "aided, abetted[,] counselled or procured" his firing of that shot creates no practical difficulty on the facts of this case and does not affect the result.

65. For these reasons we would answer the certified question in the affirmative, allow this appeal and restore the respondent's conviction for murder.

Lord Brown

68.... [T]o my mind the all-important consideration here is that both A and B were intentionally engaged in a potentially lethal unlawful gunfight (a "shoot-out" as it has also been described) in the course of which an innocent passerby was killed. The general public would in my opinion be astonished and appalled if in those circumstances the law attached liability for the death only to the gunman who actually fired the fatal shot (which, indeed, it would not always be possible to determine). Is he alone to be regarded as guilty of the victim's murder? Is the other gunman really to be regarded as blameless and exonerated from all criminal liability for that killing? Does the decision of the Court of Appeal here, allowing A's appeal against his conviction for murder, really represent the law of the land?

69. To my mind the answer to these questions is a plain "no". Realistically this case is indistinguishable from the succession of authorities establishing criminal liability on the part of anyone who willingly involves himself in the use of unlawful violence between protagonists intent on killing or seriously injuring each other, be they duellers, prize-fighters or sado-masochists—see respectively *R v Young & Webber* (1838) 8 C & P 644, *R v Coney* (1882) 8 QBD 534 and *R v Brown* (*Anthony*) [1994] 1 AC 212. It is the very purpose of those engaging in these various activities that injuries will occur. The suggestion that certain of the perpetrators of such consensual violence, merely because they are also its prospective victims, cannot be liable for it, whether as principals or accessories by virtue of the decision in *R v Tyrrell* [1894] 1 QB 710 (discussed by Lord Phillips and Lord Judge at para 18 of their judgment), cannot be right. The principle underlying criminal liability for duelling, prize-fighting and so forth is not to be understood simply as the protection of those most directly at risk of the injuries intended. Rather it is the protection of society generally from the damaging consequences of such injuries and the discouragement of violent conduct as a whole. . . .

71. For my part I am not disposed to analyse A's liability for C's murder here in accessory terms—as the aider or abetter, counsellor or procurer of B's attempt to kill him (A himself) whose liability for C's death thus arises, *Tyrrell* constituting no obstacle, under the doctrine of transferred malice. Rather it seems to me that A is liable for C's murder as a principal—a direct participant engaged by agreement in unlawful violence (like a duel, a prize-fight or sado-masochism) specifically designed to cause and in fact causing death or serious injury. But whichever analysis is adopted, A's liability for C's murder seems to me clear and I would regard our criminal law as seriously defective were it otherwise.

Lord Clark

78. As Lord Phillips and Lord Judge have explained, the judge had ruled that it was open to the jury to find that the respondent and Bandana Man were engaged on a joint enterprise to commit an affray and that, if the jury found that the respondent foresaw that Bandana Man might shoot and kill an innocent passer-by this would found a verdict of murder on the part of the respondent. I agree with Lord Phillips and Lord Judge (at para 42) that no issue of what they call parasitic accessory liability could arise here because it cannot be said that the two protagonists had a joint intention to commit violence of a type that fell short of the violence committed. Either they had no common intention, or the common intention was to have a shoot-out, which involved each necessarily accepting that the other would shoot at him with the intention to kill or cause serious injury. It was thus open to the jury to find that there was

an agreement to that effect which may have been made on the spur of the moment but was in any event made before Bandana Man shot and killed the victim, Miss Pniewska.

79. My only concern has been whether, in the light of the judge's ruling, he intended to direct the jury that they could convict if the common intention fell short of an intention to shoot and be shot at. However, I agree with the conclusion of Lord Phillips and Lord Judge at para 57 that it is not realistic to think that the jury could have found such a common intention and with their conclusion at para 58 that the direction the judge in fact gave was an unequivocal direction that the jury could only convict if they were sure that the protagonists had formed a mutual plan or agreement to have a gun fight in which each would attempt to kill or seriously injure the other. It follows that I would not accept the conclusions of the Court of Appeal to the contrary. . . .

81. In reaching these conclusions, I entirely agree with Lord Brown's conclusions at paras 69 to 71. Like him, I am not disposed to analyse the respondent's liability for murder in accessory terms but as a principal to a joint enterprise (that is an agreement) to engage in unlawful violence specifically designed to cause death or serious injury, where death occurs as a result. I would be inclined to describe this as a form of principal and not secondary liability, but if it is a form of secondary liability, so be it. I also agree with Lord Brown that such a conclusion is consistent with public policy and, for the reasons he gives at para 72, does not extend criminal responsibility for death as widely as the Court of Appeal envisaged at paras 74 and 75 of their judgment.

82. For these reasons, I too would allow the appeal and restore the respondent's conviction for murder.

83. By way of postscript I would like to mention another possible basis of liability for murder which was touched upon in argument. It arises out of a consideration of the decision of the Court of Appeal in *R v Pagett* (1983) 76 Cr App Rep 279 to which Lord Judge drew attention in the course of the argument. It appears to me to be at least arguable that it was or would have been open to the jury to conclude that one of the effective causes of the death of the victim was the respondent shooting at Bandana Man. This is on the basis that it provoked (or caused) Bandana Man to shoot back with intent to kill or cause serious harm to the respondent as a result of which the victim was shot and killed. This analysis does not depend upon the respondent and Bandana Man being parties to a joint enterprise.

. . .

89. This case is not on all fours with *Pagett* because Bandana Man was not acting in reasonable self-defence. However, once the respondent became aware that Bandana Man had a gun and was willing to use it, even assuming that there was no joint enterprise, it was undoubtedly foreseeable that, if the respondent continued shooting at Bandana Man, he would shoot back with intent to kill him or cause serious harm. Indeed, the jury's verdict shows that the respondent foresaw precisely that. In these circumstances, it was open to the jury to conclude that the respondent's firing at Bandana Man was a cause of the latter shooting back. It was the very thing that might have been expected.

Lord Dyson

102. In his summing up, the judge did not direct the jury on aiding and abetting. He did not ask them in terms to consider whether, by shooting back, the respondent encouraged Bandana Man in turn to shoot back at him with intent to do so. In view of his ruling, these omissions on the part of the judge were not by an oversight: they were quite deliberate. But the question is whether, although the issue of aiding and abetting by encouragement was not before the jury in terms, they showed by their verdict on the issue that was before them

(parasitic accessory liability) that they were sure that the respondent and Bandana Man had a common purpose to shoot and be shot at and encouraged each other to give effect to that purpose.

103. This question has caused me considerable anxiety, not least because (i) this was a murder charge, (ii) a finding of aiding and abetting by encouragement did not accord with this careful judge's assessment of the facts and (iii) he did not direct the jury explicitly on the aiding and abetting issue. But I have been persuaded by the reasoning of Lord Phillips and Lord Judge that the jury must nevertheless have been satisfied that there was an agreement between the respondent and Bandana Man to shoot and be shot at and that they encouraged each other to carry that agreement into effect. The jury were directed that they had to be sure that the respondent and Bandana Man planned to use unlawful violence towards each other "by having a shootout whether that plan was made beforehand and the meeting was pre-arranged or was made on the spur of the moment when they saw each other and fired at each other from the steps and the car respectively". The judge gave the standard direction for joint enterprise (in the context of parasitic accessory liability) that the offence (in this case affray by gunfight) had to be the joint commission of an offence by two or more people who are "in it together as part of a joint plan". In my view, a shootout *pursuant to a plan* must mean an exchange of fire pursuant to an agreement to shoot and be shot at; and persons who *agree* to shoot at each other must by virtue of their agreement intend to encourage each other to do so. It differs from a simple exchange of fire. Nor is it relevant that each of the participants hopes that his shot will prove fatal and that there will be no return of fire. The fact that the jury convicted the respondent of the murder of Ms Pniewska following the judge's directions must mean that, if they had been asked in terms whether the respondent and Bandana Man (i) agreed to shoot and be shot at and (ii) thereby encouraged each other to that end (intending to do so), they would have answered both questions in the affirmative. In other words, the jury showed by their verdict that they considered that this was analogous to a duel.

104. I would, therefore, uphold the conviction on the basis that the jury must have been satisfied that the respondent aided and abetted the murder of Ms Pniewska by encouraging Bandana Man to shoot at him in the course of the planned shootout.

. . .

Causation

106. Lord Clarke has suggested, as an alternative, that the respondent caused Bandana Man to shoot back at him and thereby contributed to the death. This way of putting the case was not left to the jury and causation was a matter for the jury to determine. Furthermore, we heard very little argument on this point. It seems to me that, if Bandana Man's act of shooting at the respondent was a free, deliberate and informed act, it broke the chain of causation between the respondent's shooting at him and his shooting and killing Ms Pniewska: see *R v Kennedy (No 2)* [2007] UKHL 38; [2008] AC 269. As Professor Ormerod points out in his article (loc cit), it might be argued that Bandana Man's act of shooting was not a free, deliberate and informed act because he was acting in self-defence. But that seems very difficult on the facts of this case. It might also be argued that, even if Bandana Man was acting in a free, deliberate and informed manner, that is irrelevant if he and the respondent were acting in concert: see *R v Latif* [1996] 1 WLR 104, 115. None of these issues was explored by the jury. I agree with Lord Clarke that we cannot uphold the conviction on the basis that the respondent caused Bandana Man to fire the fatal shot.

Lord Kerr [dissenting]

115. Lord Phillips, Lord Judge and Lord Dyson have concluded that, although it was not left to the jury by the trial judge, the effect of their verdict is that Gnango was guilty because he aided and abetted B to fire at him. This was on the basis that both shared a common intention to shoot at one another. In particular, each intended to shoot at the other and to be shot at by him. The Court of Appeal concluded that the jury was "never asked to confront the question whether the shared common purpose was not only to shoot, but to be shot at" (para 59 of the Court of Appeal's judgment). This is unquestionably correct. The jury was not invited at any time during the judge's carefully composed charge to address the question whether the shared intention included what seems to be the supremely important element of the avowed aiding and abetting of this offence—the agreement to be shot at. . . .

. . .

121. The terms of any "plan" are critical to any conclusion that the parties to it must be taken to have encouraged each other to shoot. But an anterior question must be addressed. Can it be said that solely because there was an exchange of fire, this must be on foot of a plan? Agreement to shoot it out with an opponent, if reached in advance, would be such a plan although there is no evidence that this is what happened here. But where there has been what has been described as a "spontaneous agreement" to engage in a shoot-out, the question arises whether this can truly be said to be the product of an agreement in any real sense. Is it not at least as likely to be the result of a sudden, simultaneously reached, coincident intention by the two protagonists to fire at each other? I do not consider that because there was a shoot-out (whatever that term may mean) and because the jury were asked to consider that Gnango and B "joined together . . . to commit . . . unlawful violence", by returning a verdict of guilty, the jury must be taken to have concluded that there was a plan in the sense of an agreement between them.

122. But even if the jury's verdict can be taken as evidence of their conclusion that there had been a plan or agreement between Gnango and B, does it follow that an element of that plan *must* be that they agreed to be shot at, as well as to shoot? Agreeing to a shoot-out does not necessarily mean agreeing to be shot at. This is particularly so where the plan takes the form of (and here it could only take the form of) an instantaneous meeting of minds between Gnango and B on their first catching sight of each other on the occasion of the gunfight. That type of situation is quite different from a duel where participants meet at a pre-arranged place and an appointed time. The essence of a duel conducted with firearms is that there should be an exchange of fire. The parties to the duel anticipate—and may be said to impliedly consent to—being fired on as well as firing. But there is no basis on which to infer that such was the intention of the two protagonists here, much less to conclude that the jury's verdict can only be consistent with such implicit intention on the part of Gnango and B. It is at least just as likely that neither agreed to be fired on and that both hoped that they would avoid that unpleasant eventuality by hitting the target with their own shot. Put shortly, when the only material that the jury had to go on was that there was a shoot-out, it is, in my view, impossible to conclude that the finding of guilt can only be explained on the basis that it had been proved that there was a plan between Gnango and B to shoot and be shot at.

123. Even if it were possible so to conclude, however, it does not follow that this amounted to an intention on the part of Gnango or B to assist or encourage each other to shoot. One might be alive to the very real risk that firing, if the target was not hit, would prompt return fire, but that is a significantly different thing from saying that this was encouragement to fire back. Being prepared to run the risk does not equate with encouraging an opponent to fire at you. Before, therefore, one could be confident that the jury's verdict meant that they had found it established that Gnango had intended to encourage B to fire, it would have been

necessary for them to receive directions about that vital component of aiding and abetting. As the judge said, when ruling that he would not allow this to go to the jury as a possible basis of liability, "on the evidence, the defendant fired at Bandana Man in the hope of killing him or causing him grievous bodily harm, frightening him, or arguably, in self-defence". Being shot at was hardly likely to have been a desired outcome on the part of Gnango. Intending to encourage B to fire at him was even less likely.

. . .

125. It is, of course, true that, in considering whether there was an intention to encourage, intent must be clearly distinguished from desire or motive. In a trilogy of cases, *R v Moloney* [1985] AC 905; *R v Hancock* [1986] AC 455; and *R v Woollin* [1999] 1 AC 82 the House of Lords held that intention is not restricted to consequences that are wanted or desired, but includes consequences which a defendant might not want to ensue, but which the jury find (a) are the virtually certain result of the defendant's actions (barring some unforeseen intervention); and (b) are consequences which the defendant appreciated were virtually certain to occur. Before such an oblique intention could form the basis of a jury's verdict, of course, precise directions to this effect would have to be given. In the absence of a specific direction on Gnango's intention to encourage B to shoot at him, I do not consider that the verdict of the jury can be upheld on the basis that it was founded on their conclusion that he either had the requisite intention or that the virtually certain result of his firing at B was that he would return fire and that Gnango knew that this was virtually certain to occur.

126. This is particularly so because there is an obvious explanation for the jury's verdict other than that they concluded that there had been a plan which included an intention on the part of Gnango and B to encourage the other to shoot at him. The judge had put to the jury that if they were satisfied that Gnango and B had participated by agreement in an affray, in the course of which Gnango foresaw that B might commit intentional grievous bodily harm or kill, he could be found guilty on that account. For the reasons given by Lord Phillips, Lord Judge and Lord Dyson, with which I agree, this form of parasitic accessory liability was not a basis on which the jury could convict. But it seems to be likely in the extreme that this is the basis on which they did convict. That being so, there was no occasion for them to consider whether the requisite intention on the part of Gnango to found a verdict of guilty on the basis of aiding and abetting was present. Nor can their verdict be considered to supply the necessary ingredients of liability on that basis.

Liability as a joint principal

127. It is important at the start of this discussion to recognise the clear distinction that must be drawn between the concepts of joint principal liability and joint enterprise. Joint principal offending is a species of primary liability. In *Smith & Hogan's Criminal Law* (2011) 13th ed the following definition of joint principals is given: "D1 and D2 are joint principal offenders where each does an act which is a cause of the actus reus". Unlike the position in a joint enterprise, no common purpose is required in order to render those who cause or contribute to a cause of the actus reus guilty as joint principals. What is required is that each must contribute by his own act to the commission of the offence with the necessary mens rea.

128. By contrast, the doctrine of joint enterprise arises in situations where there are two offences, the first being that which has been jointly embarked on and the second the unplanned but foreseen offence committed by one of the participants alone. . . .

132. If B fired at Gnango first, it seems to me highly questionable (at least) that Gnango's returning fire *caused* B to fire again. The first shot surely betokened an intention on the part of B to fire at and to hit Gnango, irrespective of whether Gnango fired back. It might be said, to borrow the words of Professor Glanville Williams, that Gnango's firing on B made it much

more likely that B would fire again, but that is not enough to show that B was caused to fire because of Gnango's shot. I do not consider, therefore, that Gnango can be guilty of the murder of Ms Pniewska as a joint principal.

Conclusion

133. I would dismiss the appeal.

The facts of *Gnango* were relatively straightforward and yet it has proved an extraordinarily complex decision to analyse. This is revealed by the fact that the case generated such a diversity of views among the judiciary. It was clear that the majority (6 to 1) agree that Gnango should hold some criminal liability for the killing. But why? It may assist to look at some of the ways the legal analysis could work.[57] I will summarize the possible approach, explain which judges seem to support it, but then point out the problems.

(1) **Joint enterprise**

    (a) *Summary of the argument* Gnango (G) and Bandana Man (BM) were jointly engaging in a crime of affray. Under the principle of joint enterprise G was liable for the murder by BM because while committing the offence of affray with BM, BM murdered V and G foresaw that BM might commit murder.[58]

    (b) *Treatment in the case* This approach was rejected by the Court of Appeal and the Supreme Court.

    (c) *Problems with the approach* The weakness in the approach is that BM and G were not acting jointly in the affray. They were fighting each other, not embarking on an enterprise together. They were not acting in concert, but against each other.

(2) **Accessory**

    (a) *Summary of the argument* By engaging in a gun fight with BM, G had encouraged BM to fire at him. BM shot at G but missed and killed V. BM was guilty of murder under the doctrine of transferred malice. G was liable as an accomplice to that murder in that he had encouraged BM to act in that way.

    (b) *Treatment in the case* This argument was rejected by the Court of Appeal but accepted in the Supreme Court by Lords Phillips, Judge, Wilson, and Dyson. The Phillips/Judge judgment[59] stated that Lords Brown and Clarke agreed with them.[60] It can therefore be taken to represent the view of at least four and possibly six of the majority of the Supreme Court.

    (c) *Problems with the approach* One problem with this analysis is that G had not encouraged BM to shoot at him. G was trying to stop BM shooting at him, hardly encouraging him. True, by shooting at BM he had foreseen that BM would shoot back but there is a difference between encouragement and provocation. Critics of the accessory argument can note that if BM had shot G we would surely not have said that G encouraged his own murder. It should make no difference if the act of shooting at G had an unexpected result of killing V. Perhaps the best way of putting the encouragement argument is that by participating in the shoot-out G was 'egging BM to respond' as Richard Buxton has put it.[61]

---

[57] Buxton (2012).
[58] Note after *Jogee* [2016] UKSC 8 it would be necessary to show that G intended to assist BM's murder.
[59] Technically it was the judgment of Lords Phillips and Judge, with which Lord Wilson agreed.
[60] Something not explicitly stated by Lords Brown and Clarke.   [61] Buxton (2012: 276).

(3) **G as a principal**

(a) *Summary of the argument* G caused BM to fire back at him and thereby cause the death of V. G was therefore liable as a principal or joint principal.

(b) *Treatment in the case* This was the argument put forward by Lords Brown and Clarke in the Supreme Court as an alternative justification for the conviction.[62] Lord Dyson seemed to support it too. Oddly Lords Phillips and Judge (supported by Lord Wilson) did not explicitly reject the view of Lords Brown and Clarke because they thought it 'immaterial' in this case whether G was liable as an accomplice or principal. Buxton[63] takes these remarks to indicate support for the Brown/Clarke view, but it is suggested that had they wished to explicitly support the Brown/Clarke reasoning they would have made that clear. So this approach may have the agreement of three, or possibly five, members of the Supreme Court.

(c) *Problems with the approach* Lord Dyson and Lord Kerr made a powerful argument that the doctrine of *novus actus interveniens*,[64] meant that the free voluntary informed act of BM broke the chain of causation. Oddly Lord Dyson felt that despite this analysis it was still possible to find G liable as a principal. He did not explain how he overcame the very problem with the analysis he identified! It seems a fatal response to the argument.

(4) **G is not guilty in relation to the murder**

(a) *Summary of the argument* Although G may be guilty of affray and attempted murder of BM he was not responsible for BM's murder of V. It was not an act he encouraged or caused.

(b) *Treatment by the court* This was the argument that persuaded Lord Kerr in his dissenting judgment in the Supreme Court.[65]

(c) *Problems with the approach* As the majority indicated the conclusion that Gnango was not guilty in relation to the killing seems contrary to a common sense of justice.

So what is the reasoning which received the support of the court? This is disputed. Findlay Stark in his analysis concludes that:

> There is not one approach, then, in *Gnango* which received universal acclaim by the majority judges. At best, the primary liability analysis received the express assent of three judges, and the possible support of the other three, but the causal difficulties mentioned above make this approach seem unsustainable. The secondary liability analysis, which is at least theoretically viable, was adopted expressly by four judges, reservedly by one judge, and almost rejected by another. So the secondary liability basis for upholding Gnango's murder conviction presumably 'wins', but only by the slimmest of margins (on one view, 4:3).[66]

This seems correct and it is the view that Gnango was guilty of murder as an accomplice which has most support. It may be that one reason the Supreme Court struggled with this case was that they were too compartmentalized. It is true the case did not quite fit into

---

[62] As Buxton (2012) points out, this argument was not put to the jury and so could not be used to uphold the conviction.

[63] Buxton (2012).   [64] See Chapter 2.

[65] It has received some academic support too: see Stark (2013d).

[66] Stark (2013d); Virgo (2013).

aiding, abetting, counselling, procuring, or joint enterprise, but it had elements of all of those. In a general sense Gnango was clearly associated with and connected with Bandana Man's crime. It was not necessary to precisely identify the nature of the accompliceship here given the close connection he had to the killing.[67] →3 (p.882)

QUESTIONS

1. Professor David Ormerod has summarized the law: '(i) "Procuring" implies causation but not consensus; (ii) "abetting" and "counselling" imply consensus but not causation; (iii) "aiding" requires actual assistance but neither consensus nor causation' (2008: 189). Does it make sense to have these differences in the ways of being an accomplice?

2. The cases seem to suggest that acts that are of only minimal significance to the commission of the crime can be the *actus reus* of being an accomplice saying: 'Oh goody' or applauding an illegal performance. Is this too little to justify criminalization? (See Part II of this chapter for further discussion on this.)

3. Martin gives Clement seven good reasons why Clement should kill Edith. Clement rejects the suggestions. Dick overhears what Martin has said, is persuaded by his arguments, and kills Edith. What crimes, if any, has Martin committed?

For guidance on answering this question, please visit the Online Resource Centre that accompanies this book: www.oxfordtextbooks.co.uk/orc/herringcriminal7e/.

FURTHER READING

Sullivan, G.R. (2013) 'Accessories and Principals after *Gnango*' in A. Reed and M. Bohlander (eds), *Participation in Crime* (Aldershot: Ashgate).

2.7 OMISSIONS AND ACCOMPLICE LIABILITY

Simply being present at the scene of a crime does not of itself render you guilty as an accomplice.[68] This is because there is no duty to intervene and stop a crime taking place. So in *Clarkson*,[69] where the defendant came across a man committing a rape and simply watched, he was found not to be an accomplice to the rape. Similarly in *Willett*[70] simply being present in a car when the driver drives over the victim is insufficient to make you an accomplice. It would have to be shown that you encouraged the driver to act in that way. This is part of the general rule that omissions do not form the basis of criminal liability.[71] There are, however, some circumstances in which mere presence can render a person an accomplice:

(1) If a police constable requests that citizens assist in the suppression of a breach of the peace and they refuse to do so this can constitute an offence.[72]

(2) If under the normal law on omissions you are under a duty to protect a person in peril and you fail to do so you can be guilty of an offence. For example, a father who stands by

---

[67] See Virgo (2013), who uses this kind of approach. See Mirfield (2013) for objections to it.
[68] *Jogee* [2016] UKSC 8, para. 11; *L v CPS* [2013] EWHC 4127 (Admin).
[69] [1971] 3 All ER 344 (CMAC).   [70] [2010] EWCA Crim 1620.
[71] See the discussion on omissions in Chapter 2.   [72] *Brown* (1841) Car & M 314.

while someone injures his child or a security guard simply watches while people burgle the premises which he is meant to be guarding, then they may be guilty as accessories to the crimes.[73] Arguably, in such cases, the defendants could also be regarded as principals if their failure to perform their legal duty caused harm to the victims.

(3) Where a person has a legal power to intervene to prevent a crime and fails to do so then he or she may be responsible as an accessory. In *Rubie v Faulkner*[74] a driving instructor was convicted as an accessory to a dangerous driving offence after failing to intervene to prevent his pupil driving dangerously.[75] Examples of when people have a right to control the behaviour of the principal are where they have ownership or control of the property or premises used by the principal or where the principal is an employee of the accessory.[76]

(4) If the person's presence effectively encourages the principal then this may amount to being an accessory, but only if the accomplice is aware that the principal is encouraged by his or her presence.[77] Standing by, ready to help the principal if necessary, could certainly amount to encouragement.[78] As their Lordships noted in *Jogee:*[79] 'Most people are bolder when supported or fortified by others than they are when alone. And something done by a group is often a good deal more effective than the same thing done by an individual alone.' In *Francom*[80] the victim was subjected to appalling torture in a flat in which the defendant was present. It was held that, given the length of time for which he was present, the jury was entitled to infer that the defendant's presence must have encouraged the principals. Harder are cases where a group of people watch an illegal fight or musical performance.[81] Merely being present does not normally suffice as encouragement in such offences, but applauding or helping arrange the event would constitute counselling.[82] In 2008 a girl was convicted of aiding and abetting manslaughter when filming her friends attack the victim, who later died, in a so-called 'happy slapping' incident.[83] In these cases the courts will now have to bear in mind the right to freedom of assembly and association protected under the European Convention on Human Rights. This may, in the light of the Human Rights Act 1998, mean that mere presence at an illegal activity without more should not be regarded as sufficient for criminal liability.

The following case seems to be at the limits of when presence can create liability:

R v Daley
[2015] EWCA Crim 1515

Kyrone Daley had travelled with his friend Thomas by car to where the victim was. Daley knew Thomas had a loaded gun with him. Thomas shot the victim dead. The appeal turned on whether Daley's presence with Thomas was sufficient to amount to liability.

---

[73] See also *Forman and Ford* [1988] Crim LR 677 (Crown Ct).   [74] [1940] 1 KB 571.

[75] [1907] 1 KB 40. See also *Tuck v Robson* [1970] 1 All ER 1171 (DC), where the landlord of a pub was convicted of aiding and abetting his customers drinking after hours when standing by and watching them do so. Similarly in *Webster* [2006] EWCA Crim 415 the defendant let his drunken friend drive a car and was convicted as an accomplice to dangerous driving.

[76] *JF Alford Transport Ltd* [1997] 2 Cr App R 326 (CA).   [77] *Tait* [1993] Crim LR 538 (CA).

[78] *R v Robinson (Denis)* [2011] UKPC 3.   [79] [2016] UKSC 8, para. 11.

[80] [2001] 1 Cr App R 237.   [81] See *Coney* (1882) 8 QBD 534; *Wilcox v Jeffery* [1951] 1 All ER 464.

[82] *Wilcox v Jeffery* [1951] 1 All ER 464; *Allan* [1965] 1 QB 130 (CA).

[83] BBC News Online (2008a). 'Happy slapping' refers to an incident where the victim is attacked, on film. The purpose of the attack being to distribute the film for entertainment.

Lord Justice Hallett

44. . . . [T]here was ample evidence that the appellant had embarked upon a joint venture of possession of the loaded firearm and knowingly and voluntarily aligned himself with the gunman. He had a close and long-standing friendship with Thomas, he got into the car at the same time as Thomas placed the firearm and the ammunition into it, he knew there was a feud with Amir and that Thomas desired revenge, he and Thomas tracked the route taken by the victim for several miles, going out of their way to do so, they arrived on the same street within a matter of seconds or minutes of the victim and they ensured that the murder scene was free from potential witnesses. The appellant continued to associate with Thomas after he had witnessed, at close quarters, a cold blooded execution and they both then went to some lengths to cover their tracks. Finally, he told a large number of significant lies, including lies in relation to a memory card associated with his telephone, upon which there were images of a hand pointing a gun at someone's head.

45. In truth Mr Moloney [counsel for the appellant]'s complaint is not so much about the judge's directions but about the very existence of parasitic accessory liability and its extension to cases involving possession of weapons. We reject the argument that 'possession' is a unique offence so that to found parasitic accessory liability the prosecution must go further and establish that both the gunman and the companion are joint principals in a criminal enterprise and or involved in a criminal enterprise above and beyond that of possession of the gun. There is no support for this novel proposition, either in the authorities or in logic. . . .

46. Further we reject the assertion that the principle of parasitic accessory liability should not be applied to cases involving possession of deadly weapons. Far from extending the principle too far, as it seems to us, this is exactly the kind of offence to which the principle (as long as it exists) should be applied. On the jury's verdict the appellant lent himself to a criminal enterprise knowing a lethal weapon was to be carried and foreseeing it might be used to murder, as it was, and in his presence.

The argument seems to be that this was a case of joint enterprise. Thomas and Daley were committing the offence of possession together, during which the principal (Thomas) committed murder. As Daley had foreseen that Thomas might kill, he had the *mens rea* of murder.[84] The reasoning could be used in many cases where a person is present at the scene of the murder, which they had foreseen might take place. The use of the possession offence seems to place much weight on the fact they were travelling by car. Had they travelled by foot and Daley had carried the gun it would be harder to say they were engaging in joint possession. Interestingly, what seems to have particularly caught the attention of the court was that Daley had associated himself with Thomas. Perhaps it was that which was the key point behind the conviction.

3 MENS REA

DEFINITION

The *mens rea* requirement for an accomplice is that he or she does his or her acts of assistance intending to assist the principal in the commission of the offence.

---

[84] Following *Jogee* [2016] UKSC 8, it would now need to be shown that Daley had intended to assist Thomas in the killing.

Of course, to convict an accomplice it must be shown that at the time of the *actus reus*, he or she had the *mens rea*. →4 (p.874)

3.1 *MENS REA* FOR ACCOMPLICES: GENERAL PRINCIPLES

For a long time the law on the *mens rea* for accomplices was unclear. Fortunately, the Supreme Court in *Jogee*[85] has now provided authoritative guidance. It rejects the complex and sometimes contradictory approaches taken in previous cases. This book will not seek to make sense of the old law, but will focus on the current law.

R v Jogee
[2016] UKSC 8

Ameen Jogee was convicted of the murder of Paul Fyfe. Mr Fyfe was stabbed to death by Mohammed Hirsi, who pleaded guilty to murder. Mr Jogee had been with Hirsi during the evening of the killing. Jogee was outside Fyfe's flat when Hirsi was inside. Jogee was carrying a bottle and told Hirsi to 'do something' to Fyfe. He came to the door of the flat and threatened to hit Fyfe with the bottle. Hirsi stabbed Fyfe with a knife he found in the kitchen. The judge directed the jury that they could convict Jogee of murder if they concluded that he had taken part in the attack and realized it was possible Hirsi might use the knife with intent to cause serious harm.

[In their judgments their Lordships use D1 to refer to the principal and D2 to refer to the accomplice.]

Lord Hughes and Lord Toulson (with whom Lord Neuberger, Lady Hale and Lord Thomas agreed):

8. The requisite conduct element is that D2 has encouraged or assisted the commission of the offence by D1.

9. Subject to the question whether a different rule applies to cases of parasitic accessory liability, the mental element in assisting or encouraging is an intention to assist or encourage the commission of the crime and this requires knowledge of any existing facts necessary for it to be criminal . . .

10. If the crime requires a particular intent, D2 must intend to assist or encourage D1 to act with such intent. D2's intention to assist D1 to commit the offence, and to act with whatever mental element is required of D1, will often be co-extensive on the facts with an intention by D2 that that offence be committed. Where that is so, it will be seen that many of the cases discuss D2's mental element simply in terms of intention to commit the offence. But there can be cases where D2 gives intentional assistance or encouragement to D1 to commit an offence and to act with the mental element required of him, but without D2 having a positive intent that the particular offence will be committed. That may be so, for example, where at the time that encouragement is given it remains uncertain what D1 might do; an arms supplier might be such a case.

. . .

---

85 [2016] UKSC 8.

14. With regard to the mental element, the intention to assist or encourage will often be specific to a particular offence. But in other cases it may not be. D2 may intentionally assist or encourage D1 to commit one of a range of offences, such as an act of terrorism which might take various forms. If so, D2 does not have to 'know' (or intend) in advance the specific form which the crime will take. It is enough that the offence committed by D1 is within the range of possible offences which D2 intentionally assisted or encouraged him to commit (*Maxwell*).

. . .

17. Secondary liability does not require the existence of an agreement between the principal and the secondary party to commit the offence. If a person sees an offence being committed, or is aware that it is going to be committed, and deliberately assists its commission, he will be guilty as an accessory. But where two or more parties agree on an illegal course of conduct (or where one party encourages another to do something illegal), the question has often arisen as to the secondary party's liability where the principal has allegedly gone beyond the scope of what was agreed or encouraged.

. . .

Restatement of the principles

. . .

89. In cases of alleged secondary participation there are likely to be two issues. The first is whether the defendant was in fact a participant, that is, whether he assisted or encouraged the commission of the crime. Such participation may take many forms. It may include providing support by contributing to the force of numbers in a hostile confrontation.

90. The second issue is likely to be whether the accessory intended to encourage or assist D1 to commit the crime, acting with whatever mental element the offence requires of D1 (as stated in para 10 above). If the crime requires a particular intent, D2 must intend (it may be conditionally) to assist D1 to act with such intent. To take a homely example, if D2 encourages D1 to take another's bicycle without permission of the owner and return it after use, but D1 takes it and keeps it, D1 will be guilty of theft but D2 of the lesser offence of unauthorised taking, since he will not have encouraged D1 to act with intent permanently to deprive. In cases of concerted physical attack there may often be no practical distinction to draw between an intention by D2 to assist D1 to act with the intention of causing grievous bodily harm at least and D2 having the intention himself that such harm be caused. In such cases it may be simpler, and will generally be perfectly safe, to direct the jury (as suggested in *Wesley Smith* and *Reid*) that the Crown must prove that D2 intended that the victim should suffer grievous bodily harm at least. However, as a matter of law, it is enough that D2 intended to assist D1 to act with the requisite intent. That may well be the situation if the assistance or encouragement is rendered some time before the crime is committed and at a time when it is not clear what D1 may or may not decide to do. Another example might be where D2 supplies a weapon to D1, who has no lawful purpose in having it, intending to help D1 by giving him the means to commit a crime (or one of a range of crimes), but having no further interest in what he does, or indeed whether he uses it at all.

91. It will therefore in some cases be important when directing juries to remind them of the difference between intention and desire.

92. In cases of secondary liability arising out of a prior joint criminal venture, it will also often be necessary to draw the jury's attention to the fact that the intention to assist, and indeed the intention that the crime should be committed, may be conditional. The bank robbers who attack the bank when one or more of them is armed no doubt hope that it will not be necessary to use the guns, but it may be a perfectly proper inference that all were intending that if they met resistance the weapons should be used with the intent to do grievous bodily harm

at least. The group of young men which faces down a rival group may hope that the rivals will slink quietly away, but it may well be a perfectly proper inference that all were intending that if resistance were to be met, grievous bodily harm at least should be done.

93. Juries frequently have to decide questions of intent (including conditional intent) by a process of inference from the facts and circumstances proved. The same applies when the question is whether D2, who joined with others in a venture to commit crime A, shared a common purpose or common intent (the two are the same) which included, if things came to it, the commission of crime B, the offence or type of offence with which he is charged, and which was physically committed by D1. A time honoured way of inviting a jury to consider such a question is to ask the jury whether they are sure that D1's act was within the scope of the joint venture, that is, whether D2 expressly or tacitly agreed to a plan which included D1 going as far as he did, and committing crime B, if the occasion arose.

94. If the jury is satisfied that there was an agreed common purpose to commit crime A, and if it is satisfied also that D2 must have foreseen that, in the course of committing crime A, D1 might well commit crime B, it may in appropriate cases be justified in drawing the conclusion that D2 had the necessary conditional intent that crime B should be committed, if the occasion arose; or in other words that it was within the scope of the plan to which D2 gave his assent and intentional support. But that will be a question of fact for the jury in all the circumstances.

95. In cases where there is a more or less spontaneous outbreak of multi-handed violence, the evidence may be too nebulous for the jury to find that there was some form of agreement, express or tacit. But, as we have said, liability as an aider or abettor does not necessarily depend on there being some form of agreement between the defendants; it depends on proof of intentional assistance or encouragement, conditional or otherwise. If D2 joins with a group which he realises is out to cause serious injury, the jury may well infer that he intended to encourage or assist the deliberate infliction of serious bodily injury and/ or intended that that should happen if necessary. In that case, if D1 acts with intent to cause serious bodily injury and death results, D1 and D2 will each be guilty of murder.

96. If a person is a party to a violent attack on another, without an intent to assist in the causing of death or really serious harm, but the violence escalates and results in death, he will be not guilty of murder but guilty of manslaughter. So also if he participates by encouragement or assistance in any other unlawful act which all sober and reasonable people would realise carried the risk of some harm (not necessarily serious) to another, and death in fact results: *R v Church* [196[6]] 1 QB 59, approved in *Director of Public Prosecutions v Newbury* [1977] AC 500 and very recently re-affirmed in *R v F (J) & E (N)* [2015] EWCA Crim 351; [2015] 2 Cr App R 5. The test is objective. As the Court of Appeal held in *Reid*, if a person goes out with armed companions to cause harm to another, any reasonable person would recognise that there is not only a risk of harm, but a risk of the violence escalating to the point at which serious harm or death may result. Cases in which D2 intends some harm falling short of grievous bodily harm are a fortiori, but manslaughter is not limited to these.

97. The qualification to this (recognised in *Wesley Smith, Anderson and Morris* and *Reid*) is that it is possible for death to be caused by some overwhelming supervening act by the perpetrator which nobody in the defendant's shoes could have contemplated might happen and is of such a character as to relegate his acts to history; in that case the defendant will bear no criminal responsibility for the death.

98. This type of case apart, there will normally be no occasion to consider the concept of 'fundamental departure' as derived from *English*. What matters is whether D2 encouraged or assisted the crime, whether it be murder or some other offence. He need not encourage or assist a particular way of committing it, although he may sometimes do so. In particular, his intention to assist in a crime of violence is not determined only by whether he knows

what kind of weapon D1 has in his possession. The tendency which has developed in the application of the rule in *Chan Wing-Siu* to focus on what D2 knew of what weapon D1 was carrying can and should give way to an examination of whether D2 intended to assist in the crime charged. If that crime is murder, then the question is whether he intended to assist the intentional infliction of grievous bodily harm at least, which question will often, as set out above, be answered by asking simply whether he himself intended grievous bodily harm at least. Very often he may intend to assist in violence using whatever weapon may come to hand. In other cases he may think that D1 has an iron bar whereas he turns out to have a knife, but the difference may not at all affect his intention to assist, if necessary, in the causing of grievous bodily harm at least. Knowledge or ignorance that weapons generally, or a particular weapon, is carried by D1 will be evidence going to what the intention of D2 was, and may be irresistible evidence one way or the other, but it is evidence and no more.

99. Where the offence charged does not require mens rea, the only mens rea required of the secondary party is that he intended to encourage or assist the perpetrator to do the prohibited act, with knowledge of any facts and circumstances necessary for it to be a prohibited act: *National Coal Board v Gamble*.

As a result of the *Jogee* decision the *mens rea* of an accomplice is easy to state: the accomplice must intend to assist or encourage the principal to commit the crime (including that the principal has the necessary *mens rea*). An easy case would be where A gives P a gun hoping that P will murder A's wife. Quite obviously A will have assisted P to commit murder and A will have intended P to commit murder (both the *actus reus* and *mens rea* of murder).

It must be shown that A intended to assist P. So, if a security guard decides to go home early and not bother locking up an office and later that night there is a burglary, the security guard will not be an accomplice. They may even have foreseen that there would be a burglary as a result of them not doing their job properly, but they were not intending to assist a burglary.

Where the offence involves doing an act in particular circumstances the jury should ask whether the defendant 'knew the essential matters of the offence'.[86] So if, for example, it was a case of assisting the handling of stolen goods, it would need to be shown that the defendant knew the goods were stolen. Knowledge here includes a defendant who deliberately shuts his or her eyes to the circumstances.[87] It does not need to be shown that A knew the details of the crime that P was to commit. So if A gives P a crowbar to help P commit a burglary, A can be liable as an accomplice to burglary even if A does not know when or where the burglary is to take place. It is enough that A intended to assist P to commit a burglary; A does not need to know when or where.[88]

It must be shown that A intended to help P commit the offence, with P having the *mens rea* required. In *Jogee* the following 'homely example' was used:

[I]f [A] encourages [P] to take another's bicycle without permission of the owner and return it after use, but [P] takes it and keeps it, [P] will be guilty of theft but [A] of the lesser offence of unauthorised taking, since he will not have encouraged [P] to act with intent permanently to deprive.[89]

---

[86] *O'Neil v Gale* [2013] EWCA Civ 1554.   [87] *JF Alford Transport Ltd* [1997] 2 Cr App R 326.
[88] *Bainbridge* [1960] 1 QB 129.   [89] *Jogee* [2016] UKSC 8, para. 90.

Notice in this scenario that it is not that A is entirely innocent. A can be convicted of the offence with the *actus reus* that occurred (the taking of the bike) with the *mens rea* A had (taking without permission) which creates the offence of unauthorized taking of a conveyance without permission.[90] Similarly, their Lordships explained: 'If a person is a party to a violent attack on another, without an intent to assist in the causing of death or really serious harm, but the violence escalates and results in death, he will be not guilty of murder but guilty of manslaughter.'[91] In many cases of violence, however, asking whether A intended to assist P in the assault may be unnecessarily complex. In *Jogee* their Lordships said that in cases of a physical attack it might be simpler for the jury to ask whether A intended the victim to suffer the injury.[92]

We will discuss some of the more complex scenarios in the following sections.

3.2 *MENS REA* FOR ACCOMPLICES: CONDITIONAL INTENT

The Supreme Court in *Jogee* confirmed that an accomplice could be found to have the necessary intent to assist or encourage the principal to commit the offence relying on the notion of 'conditional intent'. This is best explained by an example. Imagine A knows P is off to rob a bank, and gives P a gun in case he is disturbed by a security guard. P is indeed disturbed by a security guard and shoots him with the gun. A can be held to be liable as an accomplice. Although A might say 'I did not intend P to kill the security guard because I hoped P would not be disturbed', the law would reply, 'you did intend to assist P whether P shot someone or not. In other words, you intended to assist P to kill, if that was necessary.' That is the concept of conditional intent: A intends to assist P in killing if the conditions require it.

This use of conditional intent is especially helpful in a case involving gangs. In *Jogee* this point was made:

> If the jury is satisfied that there was an agreed common purpose to commit crime [X], and if it is satisfied also that [A] must have foreseen that, in the course of committing crime [X], [P] might well commit crime [Y], it may in appropriate cases be justified in drawing the conclusion that A had the necessary conditional intent that crime [Y] should be committed, if the occasion arose.[93]

This scenario might be quite common. If a gang goes out to beat up members of a rival gang or destroy someone's property, the members may foresee that they might meet resistance from a rival gang and, if so, violence will be used. In that case the conditional intent argument could be used to say to a member that they did intend to assist the gang in their enterprise, even if violence was necessary.

Having explained the idea of conditional intent relied upon in *Jogee*, it must be admitted that it is a problematic idea. As the example with the gang used in the previous paragraph demonstrates, there is a fine line between saying 'you foresaw that other gang members would use violence' and saying 'you intended to help the gang if violence was necessary'. However, their Lordships in *Jogee* were quite clear that they were requiring more than simply that A assisted P, foreseeing that P might commit an offence. That was the old law which they were seeking to depart from. The difference is that if A has intentionally assisted

---

[90] Theft Act 1968, s. 12.   [91] *Jogee* [2016] UKSC 8, para. 96.   [92] *Ibid*, para. 90.   [93] *Ibid*, para. 94.

P to commit crime X, foreseeing that P might commit crime Y, that is evidence that A conditionally assisted crime Y. However, the jury are entitled to conclude that A did not have that intent. Unfortunately the Supreme Court gives little guidance on when it would or would not be appropriate to find conditional intent based simply on foresight. Perhaps the best guidance is that the jury should consider what A's attitude would be if P does indeed commit crime Y. If A is pleased, or at least accepts that P had to act that way, then the jury will find A to have conditional intent. However, if A is dismayed that P committed crime Y then they should not be found to have conditional intent, unless the notion of oblique intent can be used. We will discuss that next.

3.3 *MENS REA* FOR ACCOMPLICES: OBLIQUE INTENT

In *Jogee* it is clear that A must intend to assist or encourage P in committing the offence. This does not require proof that A wants P to commit the crime. So if A sells P a gun, knowing that P will use it to commit a crime of violence, A will be liable as an accomplice, even if he does not care whether P commits a crime. That is because his knowledge that P will commit the crime can constitute oblique intent (see Chapter 3). However, that will apply only where A knows for certain that P is going to commit a crime. So if P asks A for a steak knife and A gives it to him, hoping that it is for use on tough meat, but aware that it might be used to harm someone, A will not be liable. A does not want to assist P to commit a crime and so there is no direct intent. Although he foresees that P might commit a crime with the knife, that cannot amount to oblique intent because he is not sure if P will commit a crime.

3.4 *MENS REA* FOR ACCOMPLICES: WEAPONS

Under the old law there was a particular set of rules that dealt with cases where A assisted P, knowing that P had a weapon. The law after *Jogee* is that there is no particular rule about weapons, but if A knows that P has a weapon, that will be good evidence that A intended to assist P in an offence using the weapon. Their Lordships explained:

> Knowledge or ignorance that weapons generally, or a particular weapon, is carried by [P] will be evidence going to what the intention of [A] was, and may be irresistible evidence one way or the other, but it is evidence and no more.[94]

So imagine A and P are going on a burglary and during the burglary P shoots a security guard dead with a gun P had been carrying. If A knew P had the gun, it may well be that the jury will conclude from that knowledge that A intended to assist P to murder, if necessary (i.e. conditional intent). However, if A did not know P had the gun, it will be much harder to conclude that A intended to assist P to murder.

3.5 *MENS REA* FOR ACCOMPLICES: RANGE OF OFFENCES

In some cases A may intend to assist P in committing a crime, but be unsure precisely what offence P is going to commit. For example, A may agree to drive P, a known criminal, to a

---

[94] *Jogee* [2016] UKSC 8, para. 98.

particular place, knowing P intends to commit a crime there, but not being sure what that crime is. This issue too was addressed in *Jogee*:

> With regard to the mental element, the intention to assist or encourage will often be specific to a particular offence. But in other cases it may not be. D2 may intentionally assist or encourage D1 to commit one of a range of offences, such as an act of terrorism which might take various forms. If so, D2 does not have to 'know' (or intend) in advance the specific form which the crime will take. It is enough that the offence committed by D1 is within the range of possible offences which D2 intentionally assisted or encouraged him to commit.[95]

So, in the example given in the previous paragraph, if A was not sure when he drove P to an address whether P was going to commit murder, grievous bodily harm, or actual bodily harm then A could be guilty as an accomplice if, indeed, P committed one of those offences. If, however, P committed a crime which A had not considered (e.g. rape) then A can say 'I did not intend to assist P in committing a rape' and if the jury accepts that then A would need to be found not guilty of being an accomplice to rape.

3.6 SUMMARIZING THE CURRENT LAW ON ACCESSORIES

An attempt will now be made to summarize the law on accessories:

(1) The *actus reus* of being an accessory is aiding, abetting, counselling, or procuring the principal's offence. Alternatively, it is being a party to a joint enterprise at the time the principal commits the offence. This can be summarized as assisting or encouraging the commission of the principal's offence.

(2) The *mens rea* is that the defendant intended to assist or encourage the commission of the offence by the principal, including that the principal has the necessary *mens rea*.

QUESTIONS

1. Alfred and Mary decide to commit a burglary. Alfred knows that Mary has a gun, but she promises she will use it only if they are disturbed by the homeowner. They are disturbed by a passing police officer, whom Mary shoots. Consider Alfred's criminal liability.

2. Elizabeth knows that Henry would like to kill Anne. She tells him where Anne can be found. In fact when Henry finds Anne he only hits her on the nose. Discuss Elizabeth's criminal liability.

3. James and John decide to shoplift. James knows that John has a flick knife in his pocket. When they are stopped by a store detective, John produces a gun (which James did not know he had) and shoots the detective dead. What crimes have been committed?

For guidance on answering this question, please visit the Online Resource Centre that accompanies this book: www.oxfordtextbooks.co.uk/orc/herringcriminal7e/.

---

[95] *Ibid*, para. 14.

4 SECONDARY PARTICIPATION AND INCHOATE OFFENCES

The following statements summarize the interrelation of accomplice and inchoate offences:

(1) It is an offence to conspire or attempt to commit an offence.

(2) It is not an offence to attempt to aid, abet, counsel, or procure.[96]

(3) It is not an offence to conspire to aid, abet, counsel, or procure.[97]

(4) It is an offence to aid, abet, counsel, or procure an attempt to commit an offence.[98]

5 CONVICTION OF SECONDARY PARTY AND ACQUITTAL OF PRINCIPAL

Even if the principal has been acquitted it may still be appropriate to convict the accomplice. It is necessary to distinguish between the following scenarios:

(1) The principal has been acquitted because there is insufficient evidence that he or she committed the offence. In such a case as long as it is clear that *someone* committed the offence and that the accomplice aided, abetted, counselled, or procured him or her, the accomplice can be convicted.[99]

(2) The principal has been acquitted because he or she has no *mens rea*. In *Cogan and Leak*[100] Mr Leak terrorized his wife into submitting to sexual intercourse with Mr Cogan. He had told Mr Cogan that Mrs Leak wanted to have sexual intercourse with him. Here, although the principal (Mr Cogan) was acquitted because he lacked *mens rea*, Mr Leak could be convicted of procuring rape. So even though the principal is acquitted because he lacked *mens rea* the accomplice can still be convicted. The same principle was applied in *Millward*,[101] where the defendant instructed his employee to drive a vehicle on a road. The defendant knew that the vehicle was in a dangerous condition, but the employee did not. The employee was charged with causing death by reckless driving and the defendant of abetting the causing death by reckless driving. The employee was not found to be reckless and so was acquitted. The defendant could still be convicted of procuring the *actus reus* (the defendant had the *mens rea* necessary to be an accomplice).[102]

(3) The principal has been acquitted because there is no evidence that the *actus reus* was performed. In such a case no one can be convicted as an accomplice. In *Thornton v Mitchell*[103] a bus conductor negligently signalled to the driver of the bus that he should reverse the bus. The bus killed a pedestrian. The driver was acquitted of careless driving: quite simply his driving was not careless. It therefore followed that the conductor could not be convicted of procuring careless driving. It should be stressed this was not a case where the

---

96 Criminal Attempts Act 1981, s. 1(4)(b).

97 *Hollinshead* [1985] 1 All ER 850, 857–8 (CA). The case was considered by the House of Lords ([1985] AC 975), which did not express a view on *Hapgood and Wyatt* (1870) LR 1 CCR 221 (CCR) and whether such an offence existed.

98 *Hapgood and Wyatt* (1870) LR 1 CCR 221 (CCR).   99 *Hui Chi-Ming* [1991] 3 All ER 897.

100 [1976] QB 217 (CA).   101 [1994] Crim LR 527 (CA).

102 *DPP v K and B* [1997] 1 Cr App R 36.   103 [1940] 1 All ER 339 .

bus driver simply lacked the *mens rea*; he did not commit the *actus reus*: there was no careless driving.[104]

(4) The principal has been acquitted because he or she has a special defence. An example of such a situation may be *Bourne*.[105] The defendant compelled his wife to have sexual relations with their dog. The defendant was convicted of abetting the wife to commit buggery. This was even though the wife was never charged with buggery and had she been charged with that offence she was likely to be acquitted on the basis of the defence of coercion.[106]

(5) The principal has been convicted of an offence which the accessory could not have committed. For example, a woman has assisted a man in a rape. In such a case the accessory can be convicted.[107] The fact she could not have committed the offence herself is irrelevant.

6 CAN A SECONDARY PARTY EVER BE GUILTY OF A GREATER OFFENCE THAN THE PRINCIPAL?

What is the position if the accomplice has a more serious *mens rea* than the principal? Lord Mackay in *Howe* gave the following example:

> A hands a gun to B informing him that it is loaded with blank ammunition only and telling him to go and scare V by discharging it. The ammunition is in fact live (as A knows) and V is killed. B is convicted only of manslaughter . . . It would seem absurd that A should thereby escape conviction for murder.[108]

Lord Mackay added:

> I would affirm [the] view that where a person has been killed and that result is the result intended by another participant, the mere fact that the actual killer may be convicted only of the reduced charge of manslaughter for some reason special to himself does not, in my opinion in any way, result in a compulsory reduction for the other participant.[109]

So in such a case the accomplice would be convicted of a more serious offence than the principal. Glanville Williams has suggested that such cases should be regarded as examples of a 'semi-innocent agent' (although this expression has been disapproved of by others).[110] In *Richards*[111] a woman hired E and F to beat up her husband 'bad enough to put him in hospital for a month'.[112] E and F did beat up the husband but were acquitted of wounding with intent to cause grievous bodily harm[113] and convicted of unlawful wounding.[114] It was held that the woman could not be guilty of counselling wounding with intent to cause grievous bodily harm because she could not be convicted as an accomplice for a more serious offence

---

[104] See also *Loukes* [1996] Crim LR 341.

[105] (1952) 36 Cr App R 125 (CA).   [106] See Chapter 12; the defence has recently been abolished.

[107] *Ram and Ram* (1893) 17 Cox CC 609.

[108] *Burke* [1986] QB 626, 641–2, approved by Lord Mackay in the House of Lords ([1987] AC 417 (HL)).

[109] [1987] 1 All ER 771, 799.

[110] Kadish (1987b: 183) argues that this terminology only adds to the mystery.

[111] [1974] QB 776 (CA).

[112] She hoped by regularly visiting him in hospital she might win back his affections!

[113] Offences Against the Person Act 1861, s. 18.   [114] *Ibid*, s. 20.

than that committed by the principal. This reasoning was rejected in *Howe*. If *Richards* were heard today the defendant could be guilty of counselling wounding with intent to cause grievous bodily harm.

7 WITHDRAWAL BY A SECONDARY PARTY

What is the position where the accomplice is aiding, abetting, counselling, or procuring the principal, but then changes his mind and seeks to cease to be part of the criminal enterprise?[115] To escape such liability it is necessary to show that the withdrawal has taken place before the principal has committed the offence. To withdraw from an enterprise it is not enough just to have a change of heart; something must be done. It should be recalled that the *mens rea* for an accessory must be established at the time of the act of assistance, not at the time when the principal commits the offence. So any withdrawal must take place before the act of assistance is effective.

Exactly what amounts to a withdrawal differs from case to case. There are no hard and fast rules governing this area. The overarching test is that the communication of withdrawal must 'serve unequivocal notice upon the other party to the common unlawful cause that if he proceeds upon it he does so without the further aid and assistance of those who withdraw'.[116] If the defendant was the instigator of a gang's attack he may have to do more to demonstrate withdrawal than a more peripheral member of the gang.[117] In order to withdraw a defendant does not actually have to try and prevent the crime occurring.[118] The following case examines in further detail the circumstances in which the defence of withdrawal may be available:

R v Rook
[1993] 2 All ER 955 (CA)

Adrian Rook and Andrew Armstrong were recruited by a husband to kill his wife. They were to be paid £15,000 and given some jewellery. Rook recruited Mark Leivers to assist. The four met over a two- or three-day period to plan the killing. On the appointed day for the killing Rook could not be found. The husband nevertheless drove his wife to the agreed site and Leivers killed her. Rook gave evidence that he never intended to kill the wife, that his plan was to take the money and disappear. He appealed against his conviction for murder.

Lord Justice Lloyd

[I]f a person gives assistance and encouragement, such as would make him liable as a secondary party, and he then changes his mind, what must he do to make his withdrawal effective? Must he neutralise the assistance he has already given (to use the term adopted by Smith & Hogan, in *Criminal Law* (7th ed. 1992) at p. 154 and by Glanville Williams in *Criminal Law, The General Part* (2nd ed. 1961), para. 127)? Must he at least have done his best to

---

[115] Reed (2013).

[116] *Becerra* (1975) 62 Cr App R 212 (CA). In *Baker* [1994] Crim LR 444 (CA) saying 'I'm not doing it', turning around and moving a few feet away were far from unequivocal.

[117] *R v Gallant* [2008] EWCA Crim 1111.   [118] *Otway* [2011] EWCA Crim 3.

prevent the commission of the crime, by communicating his withdrawal to the other parties, or in some other way? Or is it enough that he should have absented himself on the day?

. . .

Mr. Maxwell [counsel for the Crown] submits that where a person has given assistance, for example by providing a gun, in circumstances which would render him liable as a secondary party if he does not withdraw, then in order to escape liability he must 'neutralise' his assistance. He must, so it was said, break the chain of causation between his act of assistance, and the subsequent crime, by recovering the gun, or by warning the victim to stay away, or by going to the police. Mr. Hockman [counsel for the appellant] submits, on the other hand, that the Crown must prove that the defendant continued ready to help until the moment the crime is committed; and if there is doubt as to the defendant's state of mind on the day in question, or his willingness to provide further help if required, then the jury must acquit.

As between these two extreme views, we have no hesitation in rejecting the latter. In *Croft* (1944) 29 Cr. App. R. 169, [1944] KB 295, the surviving party of a suicide pact was held to be guilty of murder. Lawrence J. giving the judgment of the Court said ([1944] K.B. 295 at 298):

'The authorities, however, such as they are, show, in our opinion, that the appellant, to escape being held guilty as an accessory before the fact, must establish that he expressly countermanded or revoked the advising, counselling, procuring or abetting which he had previously given.'

In *Whitehouse* [1941] 1 W.L.R. 112, 115, Sloan J.A. said:

'Can it be said on the facts of this case that a mere change of mental intention and a quitting of the scene of the crime just immediately prior to the striking of the fatal blow will absolve those who participate in the commission of the crime by overt acts up to that moment from all the consequences of its accomplishment by the one who strikes in ignorance of his companions' change of heart? I think not. After a crime has been committed and before a prior abandonment of the common enterprise may be found by a jury there must be, in my view, in the absence of exceptional circumstances, something more than a mere mental change of intention and physical change of place by those associates who wish to dissociate themselves from the consequences attendant upon their willing assistance up to the moment of the actual commission of that crime. I would not attempt to define too closely what must be done in criminal matters involving participation in a common unlawful purpose to break the chain of causation and responsibility. That must depend upon the circumstances of each case but it seems to me that one essential element ought to be established in a case of this kind: Where practicable and reasonable there must be timely communication of the intention to abandon the common purpose from those who wish to dissociate themselves from the contemplated crime to those who desire to continue in it. What is "timely communication" must be determined by the facts of each case, but where practicable and reasonable it ought to be such communication, verbal or otherwise, that will serve unequivocal notice upon the other party to the common unlawful cause that if he proceeds upon it he does so without the further aid and assistance of those who withdraw. The unlawful purpose of him who continues alone is then his own and not one in common with those who are no longer parties to it nor liable to its full and final consequences.'

In *Becerra* (1975) 62 Cr. App. R. 212 this Court approved that passage as a correct statement of the law. The facts of *Becerra* were that the victim was killed in the course of a burglary. The appellant had provided the knife shortly before the murder. The court held that the appellant's sudden departure from the scene of the crime with the words 'Come on let's go' was an insufficient communication of withdrawal. So the appellant's conviction as a secondary party to the murder was upheld. In *Whitefield* (1984) 79 Cr. App. R 36, 39, 40, Dunn L.J. stated the law as follows:

> 'If a person has counselled another to commit a crime, he may escape liability by withdrawal before the crime is committed, but it is not sufficient that he should merely repent or change his mind. If his participation is confined to advice or encouragement, he must at least communicate his change of mind to the other, and the communication must be such as will serve unequivocal notice upon the other party to the common unlawful cause that if he proceeds upon it he does so without the aid and assistance of those who withdraw.'

In the present case the appellant never told the others that he was not going ahead with the crime. His absence on the day could not possibly amount to 'unequivocal communication' of his withdrawal. In his evidence in chief, in a passage already quoted, he made it quite clear to himself that he did not want to be there on the day. But he did not make it clear to the others. So the minimum necessary for withdrawal from the crime was not established on the facts. In these circumstances, as in *Becerra*, it is unnecessary for us to consider whether communication of his withdrawal would have been enough, or whether he would have had to take steps to 'neutralise' the assistance he had already given.

Mr. Maxwell rightly drew our attention to a sentence in the judgment of Sloan J.A., already quoted, where he refers to the service of notice on the other party that if he proceeds he does so without further aid from those who withdraw. This may suggest that aid already afforded need not be neutralised. We agree with Mr. Maxwell that this attaches too much importance to a single word. But that is as far as we are prepared to go in this case. We are not prepared, as at present advised, to give our approval to his proposition in its extreme form. In his *Criminal Law, The General Part* (2nd ed., 1961), Glanville Williams quotes at paragraph 127 a graphic phrase from an American authority. (*Eldredge v. U.S.* 62 F 2d 449 (1932) per McDermott J.) 'A declared intent to withdraw from a conspiracy to dynamite a building is not enough. If the fuse has been set he must step on the fuse.' It may be that this goes too far. It may be that it is enough that he should have done his best to step on the fuse. Since this is as much a question of policy as a question of law, and since it does not arise on the facts of the present case, we say no more about it.

Appeal dismissed.

Do not forget that even where the defence of withdrawal succeeds the accused may still be guilty of an offence under the Serious Crimes Act 2007 or conspiracy.

The rules appear to be slightly different where the accessory and principal have joined together spontaneously to commit a crime, rather than formally planned it. In *Mitchell*[119] a fight involving six people broke out in a restaurant. A, B, and D were on one side and U, V, and W on the other. During the fight V was left prostrate. A, B, and D left, but D then returned to beat V further. The Court of Appeal held that where a group simply spontaneously attacks someone it is sufficient to withdraw, simply to walk away; there is no need to communicate a withdrawal. However, *Robinson*[120] restricted *Mitchell*[121] to the facts of its case, and in particular the fact that in *Mitchell* A, B, and D had walked away, ending their attack, and D's return was, in effect, starting a new attack. Where, as in *Robinson*, the parties join together for a spontaneous attack, then there must be a communicated withdrawal if someone wishes to disassociate herself from the attack.

---

[119] [1999] Crim LR 496 (CA).   [120] CA, 3 February 2000.   [121] [1999] Crim LR 496 (CA).

In *O'Flaherty*,[122] however, a gang (including the appellants) attacked a young man. He managed to escape, but some of the gang pursued him and found him. They attacked him again, this time killing him. One appellant claimed that although he was responsible for the injuries suffered during the first attack he was not responsible for the killing as he was not a party to that attack. The Court of Appeal suggested that it was for the jury to consider whether the second attack was in reality a continuation of the first, or a separate incident. However, they suggested the jury's main focus should be on whether the defendant had disengaged himself from the gang by the time the second attack took place by making an effective withdrawal.[123]

8 ACCESSORIES AND VICTIMS

Where a provision in a statute is designed to protect a class of persons it may be construed as impliedly excluding their liability as an accessory.[124] For example, in *Tyrell*[125] a girl under 16 abetted a man to have sexual intercourse with her. It was held that the girl could not be convicted of aiding and abetting the offence against her. The offence was designed to protect under-16-year-olds, not to criminalize them.[126]

9 ASSISTANCE AFTER THE OFFENCE

There are a number of offences which are committed by those who assist a person after he or she has committed an offence. It is, for example, an offence to impede the apprehension or prosecution of an arrestable offender[127] or to accept money (or other benefits) for not passing on information which would secure the prosecution or conviction of an offender.[128]

> **QUESTIONS**
>
> 1. In a South African case, *S v Robinson*,[129] P and two others agreed with V that V should be killed by P so that V could escape prosecution for fraud and others could obtain insurance monies. V withdrew his consent to the arrangement, not surprisingly, but P killed him nevertheless. The offence committed was the one planned. However, key to the plan was that the victim consented and this element of consent was missing. Did its absence mean that the two others should be convicted? (The South African court held them liable as accomplices to attempted murder only, because their complicity in murder was dependent on consent.)
>
> 2. Susan lends Paul a gun. Susan asks for it back. She looks very angry and Paul fears she may use it to shoot someone, but he still gives it to her. Susan uses the gun to commit a robbery. Is Paul an accessory to the robbery?

---

[122] [2004] EWCA Crim 526.

[123] See also *Mitchell* [2008] EWCA Crim 2552.

[124] For further discussion, see Herring (2013c).   [125] [1894] 1 QB 710 (CCR).

[126] More controversial is where one adult encourages another adult to cause him actual bodily harm (e.g. as part of a sadomasochistic activity). Can the 'victim' here be convicted of aiding and abetting the offence against himself?

[127] Criminal Law Act 1967, s. 4.   [128] *Ibid*, s. 5.   [129] (1968) (1) SA 666.

FURTHER READING

Buxton, R. (2009) 'Joint Enterprise' *Criminal Law Review* 233.

Dennis, I. (1988) 'Intention and Complicity: A Reply' *Criminal Law Review* 649.

Duff, R.A. (1990) ' "Can I Help You?" Accessorial Liability and the Intention to Assist' *Legal Studies* 10: 165.

Horder, J. (2012a) *Homicide and the Politics of Law Reform* (Oxford: OUP), ch. 7.

Krebs, B. (2010) 'Joint Criminal Enterprise' *Modern Law Review* 73: 578.

Law Commission (2007) Report No. 305, *Participation in Crime* (London: TSO).

Ormerod, D. and Fortson, R. (2009) 'Serious Crime Act 2007: The Part 2 Offences' *Criminal Law Review* 389.

Reed, A. (2013) 'Repentance and Forgiveness: Withdrawal from Participation Liability and the Proportionality Test' in A. Reed and M. Bohlander (eds) *Participation in Crime* (Aldershot: Ashgate).

Smith, K. (1991) *A Modern Treatise on the Law of Criminal Complicity* (Oxford: OUP).

Smith, K. (2001) 'Withdrawal in Complicity: A Restatement of Principles' *Criminal Law Review* 769.

Sullivan, G.R. (1988) 'Intent, Purpose and Complicity' *Criminal Law Review* 641.

Taylor, R. (1983) 'Complicity and Excuses' *Criminal Law Review* 656.

Wilson, W. (2008a) 'A Rational Scheme of Liability for Participating in Crime' *Criminal Law Review* 3.

Wilson, W. and Ormerod, D. (2015) 'Simply Harsh to Fairly Simple: Joint Enterprise Reform' *Criminal Law Review* 3.

PART II: ACCESSORIES AND THEORY

10   GENERAL THEORIES OF ACCESSORIAL LIABILITY

The person in the street, when asked to imagine a typical crime, is likely to think of an individual acting alone attacking a victim.[130] In fact, many crimes are committed by people not acting alone but alongside or with the support of others.[131] The involvement and encouragement of others in committing crimes can affect the nature of the crime in a number of ways:

(1) The victim may regard being the victim of an incident involving a number of offenders as more terrifying and therefore more serious.[132]

(2) The offenders may feel that it is harder to withdraw from the criminal enterprise and keep going with it when, acting alone, they would have desisted.[133]

---

[130] Wells (1999) argues that the criminal law is often based on an individualist model, which makes it difficult to criminalize group criminal behaviour.

[131] Some offences can be committed only by two or more people, such as the offence of riot (Public Order Act 1986, s. 1).

[132] Ashworth and Horder (2013: 404).

[133] Dressler (1985: 113) argues that there is no statistical support for the view that offenders in groups commit more serious offences than individuals acting alone.

(3) Where a group of offenders commits crimes together there is a greater likelihood of bystanders or anyone seeking to prevent the crime being harmed.[134]

(4) The offenders might be encouraged by others to commit an offence which they would otherwise shun. Indeed one criminologist has suggested that 'peer influence is the principal proximate cause of most criminal conduct, the last link in what is undoubtedly a longer causal chain.'[135]

As can be seen from the discussion in Part I of this chapter the law on accessories is in an uncertain state. This is partly because the law has failed to articulate clearly a single theory of accessorial liability. Indeed, arguably, we now have two parallel theories on accessory liability: an inchoate model based on Part 2 of the Serious Crime Act 2007; and the derivative theory, based on the general law on accessories. This part will outline three theoretical models which may explain why one person should be criminally responsible for helping or encouraging another to commit a criminal offence. We will then go on to consider how these theoretical models may assist in some of the questions of the *actus reus* and *mens rea* of accessories that have so troubled the courts. It should not, however, be thought that if the law adopted one theoretical model the law would be crystal clear because practical and policy issues may make the application of the principle undesirable.

10.1 DERIVATIVE THEORY OF ACCESSORIAL LIABILITY

Explanations of the theory

Under the derivative theory of liability the accomplice's liability derives from the offence committed by the principal. Supporters of the derivative theory have struggled to explain precisely what is meant by this, and various ways of explaining the theory have been used. It is said that accomplices are liable because they have associated themselves with the offence which the principal committed.[136] This is not an argument that accomplices cause principals to commit offences, but rather that in moral terms accomplices have placed themselves alongside the principals and identified themselves with the principals' offences.[137] Some commentators have put it in terms of the doctrine of agency: accomplices authorize the principal to commit the offence on behalf of both of them.[138] Joshua Dressler suggests that accomplices forfeit their right to be regarded as responsible only for their own actions by choosing to assist another in committing a criminal offence.[139] William Wilson puts it in this way:

> If liability here is derivative it derives not so much from any community of purpose between P and A as from the fact that A, being in a position to thwart P's criminal endeavour, failed culpably to do so.[140]

This rather controversial version of the derivative theory attaches liability to the failure of the accomplice to prevent the principal acting. In other words it is a form of liability for omissions.

---

[134] Ohana (2000).
[135] Warr (2002: 136).
[136] American law treats a conspirator as a perpetrator (*Pinkerton v US* 328 US 640 (1946)).
[137] Robinson (1997).   [138] W. Wilson (2002: 198).   [139] Dressler (1985).
[140] W. Wilson (2002: 203).

Criticisms of the theory

Critics of the derivative theory complain that this is all rather vague. It is normally regarded as a fundamental principle of the criminal law that individuals are autonomous agents who are responsible for their own actions but not the actions of others.[141] Only the most powerful of explanations should justify the infringement of such a central principle. It might be suggested that in cases where there is a very strong link between the accomplice's and the principal's acts some of the arguments used have force, but how can a person who offers a small amount of aid (e.g. babysitting for a person who is out burgling) be said to have fully associated herself with the principal's offence?

10.2 DOES THE THEORY EXPLAIN THE CURRENT LAW?

The following aspects of the current law appear to be in line with the derivative theory:

(1) The accessory is convicted of the same offence as the principal. So a person who assists in a murder is guilty of the offence of murder, and is liable to the mandatory sentence that follows.[142]

(2) If the principal does not commit the *actus reus* of an offence the accomplice is not liable for a complicity offence. If a husband hires a 'hit man' to kill his wife, he is not liable as an accomplice to murder if the 'hit man' does not commit the offence. There is no offence from which the husband's liability can derive.

(3) The *mens rea* for an accessory requires the accomplice (at least) to intend to assist the principal in their offence. Such an accomplice can be said to have adopted the principal's act as his or her own.

However, there are other aspects of the law which fit in less well with the theory. For example:

(1) The House of Lords in *Jogee*[143] explicitly rejected the notion that the acts of the principal must be desired by the accomplice, as is envisaged in some ways of explaining the derivative theory of liability.[144]

(2) The fact that even though the principal is acquitted it is possible still to convict an accomplice (e.g. if the principal has been able to rely on an excuse or lacks *mens rea*). This, it might be said, has weakened the claim that the accomplice's liability is flowing from the principal's guilt.[145] For example, it might be said that there has been no legal wrong if the principal has sexual intercourse with the victim, honestly believing that the victim consented.

(3) The *dicta* in *Howe*[146] that it is possible for an accomplice to be convicted of a more serious offence than that committed by the principal appear to be a departure from the derivative theory. However, it could be argued that in such cases the liability derives from the act performed by the principal.

---

[141] Kadish (1987).

[142] Under the German system the accomplice gets a maximum sentence of three-quarters of what the principal gets (Ashworth 1999: 415). Ashworth objects to this system because he suggests that sometimes the accomplice is more blameworthy than the principal.

[143] [2016] UKSC 8.   [144] Especially those who draw an analogy with agency.

[145] Kadish (1985).

[146] *Burke* [1986] QB 626, 641–2, approved by Lord Mackay in the House of Lords ([1987] AC 417 (HL)). Kadish (1985: 405) explains such cases on the basis that the principal is a 'semi-innocent agent'.

(4) The fact that the accomplice does not have to foresee the exact act of the principal may be said to undermine the derivative theory. Can a defendant be said to have authorized or associated him or herself with an attack which used a weapon the existence of which he or she was unaware?

In the following extract, William Wilson explains some of his concerns about the derivative theory:

W. Wilson, *Central Issues in Criminal Theory* (Oxford: Hart, 2002), 220–4

The criminal law treats the accessory as if he had committed the wrong himself because whether or not he can be deemed causally responsible it is not unfair to hold him accountable. It is for this reason that the accessory is usually punishable within the full range of punishments available for that offence. This is not necessarily so. Under the German system, for example, punishment for secondary parties is formally discounted to reflect their participatory rather than executory status. There is no such formal discounting in common law systems. This reflects the common law's more pragmatic approach which permits much theoretical rubbish to be swept under the carpet. It allows punishment and condemnation of all those who are associated with the offence, which is a good thing. It does not necessitate rules capable of distinguishing fairly and consistently between different levels and forms of participation, which is a bad thing, on the presumed ground that the creation of such rules would pose a serious legislative headache. The absence of such rules, however, means that differentiating degrees and forms of involvement still goes on but becomes a matter of prosecutorial and judicial discretion tailored to questions of individual fault and participatory role. So it allows for the kind of sentencing flexibility which can punish the (non-perpetrating) instigators of crime as severely, or more severely, than their hired-hands, while also allowing the more typical accessory to be punished less severely than the perpetrator. The theoretical problem thus posed is that this undermines the notion that the accessory's liability derives from what the perpetrator, rather than what he himself has done.

The range of problems left uncatered for by this fudging of the theoretical basis to accessorial liability spreads across the whole field of doctrine. Given that some cases of participation are equivalent under one analysis or another to perpetration while others are not, how can this best be instantiated in consistent doctrine? If liability is derivative, how do we deal with those cases where a co-adventurer goes beyond the common purpose if not what was contemplated? How do we deal with those cases where the principal commits a lesser/greater offence than that to which encouragement and assistance are offered? On what basis is it proper to deem a non-perpetrator to be guilty of the primary offence if for one reason or another it is not possible to convict the perpetrator, and so on?

A number of possible solutions may be mooted. An obvious solution is to abandon altogether the derivative basis to accessorial liability, already much disregarded, and render participation in crime an inchoate offence. This is the position adopted by the Law Commission which recommends replacing accessorial liability with two separate inchoate offences, namely assisting and encouraging crime. The advantage is that an inchoate basis to liability attacks the fiction that there is a necessary moral congruence between those who perpetrate crime and those who help or encourage its commission or that the principal was somehow acting as the secondary party's executive agent. It would, however, require complementary provisions for dealing with cases where, as in *Cogan and Leak* or *Bourne*, the secondary party procures the commission of the *actus reus* of the offence by an otherwise innocent or semi-innocent principal. The strong disadvantage of this proposal is that it ignores the intuition that it is often appropriate to ascribe authorship of a crime to someone other than the perpetrator. Such people should not be labelled, along with mere mechanical assisters and encouragers, as mere facilitators, but as principals. As Sir John Smith has argued in the context of murder,

> 'those who are instrumental in bringing about a killing should not have their responsibility set apart from those who directly perpetrate it because . . . (we) feel strongly that D is responsible for those deaths. If we are going to punish him because he bears that responsibility, we are going to punish him for the homicide; and if we are going to punish him for the homicide, then he ought to be charged with, and convicted of, homicide.'

Another possible solution is to retain a form of derivative liability but to tie liability as an accessory not to the principal's mental attitude but to that of the secondary party. Somebody who acts for the purpose of effecting a criminal wrong arguably commits a different wrong from someone who acts for the purpose only of assisting or encouraging another to commit such wrong. This is so although in given instances culpability may be comparable. The wrong most obviously attributable to the uncaring supplier of a murder weapon, whether a private individual or a state licensed corporate arms dealer, is that of being a killer's 'armourer' rather than a party to a killing/murder. So those who help or encourage because they want the substantive offence to take place could be treated as principal offenders. Those who help or encourage because they merely wish to be helpful or encourage the principal offender in the commission of the offence could be treated as facilitators. The problem with this latter approach is that the distinction between these two states of mind will often be paper-thin and certainly sufficiently insubstantial to make for easy prosecutions. Another response would be to hang accessorial liability upon the notion of control. Both instigator and 'principal in the second degree' are prime movers and so easy to associate with the principal's deed. So where A procures P to kill T, A is the prime mover since, although C pulled the trigger on the gun, it was W who pulled the trigger on H's life. Such an analysis is consistent with the rationale for the doctrine of innocent agency. In the former case we have a conscious, purposive agent. In the latter we have an innocent pawn. But both involve, as executor, an agent who does his principal's bidding which should be enough to warrant equal treatment and punishment. The objection to both *mens rea* and control tests is that they do not cover the case of those who, without being in a position to influence the commission of an offence, nevertheless provide crucial assistance so as to put them on an equivalent causal footing with the perpetrator. If a secondary party, say by providing crucial information or supplying an otherwise unobtainable tool necessary for the commission of the crime, is a *sine qua non* of the crime's successful commission should he not, along with the perpetrator be held accountable for the commission of that offence?

An altogether more satisfactory way of dealing with the problem of different degrees of causal influence might be to create a structure of offences reflecting such difference. It seems extraordinary that the common law, unlike say the German system, makes no formal distinction between a person who successfully incites another person to kill her husband and an ordinary retailer who knowingly supplies the murder weapon. This can be done by drawing a distinction between causal and non-causal participation in crime with the former punishable upon an accessorial basis and the latter, involving lesser acts of assistance and encouragement, upon an inchoate basis. It makes obvious sense to require a causal connection in the case of inciting someone to commit a crime, given that the inchoate offence is still available for (non-causal) encouragement. Cases of assistance might though be treated differently since charging an inchoate offence is not an option for (non-causal) acts of assistance and, as explained above, proving even a minimal but for causal connection would be next to impossible in most cases.

10.3 CAUSATION AND ACCOMPLICE LIABILITY

The theory

A second theory is based on the argument that liability for accomplices should be based on a finding that the accomplice partly caused the harm to the victim.[147] This theory argues that an accomplice is, in effect, a joint principal. Accomplices are not, therefore, being punished for the acts of the principal (as the derivative theory suggests), but rather are being punished for their own acts and their contribution towards the harm done to the victim.[148]

John Gardner has written supporting the causal theory. He sees it based on the fundamental principle that you are responsible for your own acts and their consequences, but not the acts of other people. So if the accomplice's act does not contribute to the eventual crime there should be no liability.

J. Gardner, 'Complicity and Causality' (2007) 1 *Criminal Law and Philosophy* 127 at 136

The distinction between principals and accomplices, as we discovered, is embedded in the structure of rational agency. As rational beings we cannot live without it. It enters our thought as soon as we begin to think about responsibility. I am responsible for my actions, and you are responsible for yours. My actions are mine to justify or excuse, and your actions are yours to justify or excuse. And yet my actions include my actions of contributing to your actions. So there is a sense in which my responsibility for my actions can extend out to your actions. I can be accused of failing to attend to reasons that are yours to conform to even though I cannot be accused of failing to conform to them myself. I fail to attend to them, in the relevant sense, by contributing to your non-conformity with them. The question which divides agent-relativists and agent-neutralists is merely how much of this kind of rational attention I should be giving to your reasons. Which contributions to your non-conformity make me complicit in it? The two sides differ in their response. But they can do so without disagreeing about what counts as principalship.

. . . [T]he contrast between principals and accomplices is embedded in the structure of rational agency. The pay-off that we have just discovered is that the distinction between principals and accomplices is therefore often marked in morality. Many moral wrongs, such as torture and rape and betrayal and deceit, are committed only by performing nonproxyable actions, such that anyone who contributes to their commission through another person's commission of them is an accomplice, not a principal, in their commission. If moral theory has lost sight of this distinction in recent times, we have the consequentialist revolutionaries to thank. Strict consequentialists insist that it matters only what consequences my action has, not how those consequences come about (where this has no further consequences). We have just found one reason why they cannot be right about this. They cannot be right because if they were right, an elementary truth about responsibility would be falsified. The elementary truth is that I am responsible for my actions, while you are responsible for yours. Each of us has a different relationship to our own actions from the relationship that we have to the actions of others. The relationship we have to our own actions is direct: we answer for them as such. The relationship we have to the actions of others is indirect: we answer for

---

[147] For support for the theory, see J. Gardner (2007b); Dressler (1985); and K. Smith (1991).
[148] Dressler (2007) suggests a substantial contribution should be required.

them only inasmuch as, by our own actions, we contribute to them. If strict consequentialists want to abandon the distinction between these two modes of responsibility for actions they need to abandon, not merely agent-relativism, but also the idea that we each have a special relationship to our own actions.

Criticism of the causation theory

Critics of the causation theory would say that there are important moral differences between the person who stabbed the victim and the person who supplied the knife.[149] To say they both caused the victim's death is quite simply wrong. Although it may be possible to imagine a case where, morally speaking, both the principal and accessory were equally causally effective in bringing about the death, in many cases there are important moral differences between the two.[150] John Gardner suggests that although an accomplice and a principal may in some cases by their actions produce the same result this does not mean they are morally equivalent:

The principal in murder acted against one action-reason (the reason not to kill) while the accomplice acted against a different action-reason (the reason not to procure a killing). But both acted against one and the same outcome-reason (the reason not to do anything in consequence of which someone will die).[151]

It is worth noting that even if one is not fully convinced by the causation theory one may want to distinguish accessories whose assistance or encouragement played a tangible role in the harm suffered by the victim and those whose acts had a minimal causal relevance to the offence committed.[152]

Does the current English and Welsh law reflect the theory?

As already indicated, one difficulty with the causation theory of accomplice liability is that under the normal rules of causation an accomplice cannot be said to have caused the principal to commit the crime.[153] If Fred tells Penelope that she should kill Pip and Penelope does so, Fred cannot in English law be said to have caused Pip's death unless Penelope can be regarded as an innocent agent (e.g. because she is insane or under the age of criminal responsibility). This is because of the doctrine of *novus actus interveniens*: a free, voluntary act of a third party breaks the chain of causation.[154] Supporters of the causation theory of accessorial liability could respond in two ways: ←1 (p.834)

(1) It might be said that the causation theory of complicity is not using causation in the sense of legal causation, but rather factual causation. In other words all that needs to be shown is that without the accomplice's act the offence would not have been committed at the time and in the place that it was committed.[155] Although the doctrine of *novus actus interveniens* explains why the accomplice is not a legal cause, the fact that he or she is a factual cause generates a good reason for holding him or her liable.[156] What is required is a moral causal responsibility, not strict legal causal responsibility.[157] Even with that caveat it

---

[149] For a powerful criticism of the causation theory, see Kadish (1985).
[150] J. Gardner (1998: 212).   [151] *Ibid.*   [152] Kreutzner (2008).   [153] Kadish (1985).
[154] See Chapter 2 for a full discussion of this doctrine.   [155] K. Smith (1991).
[156] Kadish (1987: 162).   [157] W. Wilson (2002: 202); J.C. Smith (2002: 132).

might be replied that the courts do not even appear to require that the accomplice's actions are even a factual cause.[158] Supporters of the causation approach might reply that such cases are simply wrong.

(2) It might be said that the doctrine of *novus actus interveniens* is honoured as much in the breach as in the observance and need not be regarded as a part of the law on causation. Indeed in the case of an innocent agent we accept that a defendant can be said to have caused a third party to act in a certain way. Chapter 2 considers some of the cases and arguments over the status of the *novus actus interveniens* doctrine.

10.4 INCHOATE MODEL

The inchoate model proposes that accomplice liability should be seen as an inchoate offence.[159] In other words, the accomplice's liability does not turn on the guilt of the principal, but rather on the act of the defendant in offering assistance to the principal, believing that the act will be one of assistance or encouragement. The inchoate model is reflected in the offences in Part 2 of the Serious Crime Act, in that they do not require proof that the principal went on to commit any kind of act. Crucially the inchoate model does not require that there is a principal who goes on to commit the crime or that the accomplice's acts were actually assisting or encouraging the principal. So if Alan asks Brian to kill Alan's wife he can be liable as an accomplice whether Brian says 'Certainly not' and reports Alan to the police, whether Brian goes ahead and kills as requested, or whether the evidence establishes that Brian killed Alan's wife but would have done so even if Alan had not asked him to. In other words, being an accessory involves offering what the defendant believes will be assistance or encouragement to commit a crime; what the principal subsequently did would be irrelevant.[160] Under the inchoate model it is enough if the acts of the accomplice could have assisted or encouraged the principal.[161]

In the following passage, the Law Commission sets out some of the arguments for and against an inchoate model of liability:[162]

Law Commission Report No. 300, *Inchoate Liability for Assisting and Encouraging Crime* (London: TSO, 2006), paras 4.4–4.15

The arguments in favour of inchoate liability for assisting

Combating serious crime

4.4 The police would be able to work more effectively, particularly in the context of serious organised crime. Under the common law, the police cannot proceed against D until another person has committed or attempted to commit the principal offence. The lack of a general inchoate liability for assisting crime sits uneasily with the developments in intelligence-led policing which is now an important weapon in the state's response to serious organised crime. A general inchoate offence that capturing all preliminary acts of assistance

[158] e.g. *Wilcox v Jeffery* [1951] 1 All ER 464 (DC).
[159] Kutz (2011).   [160] Law Commission Consultation Paper No. 131 (1993b).
[161] Kutz (2011).
[162] See also Spencer (1987) and Clarkson (1998). For further discussion of their proposals, see Buxton (2009) and W. Wilson (2008a).

regardless of whether the principal offence was subsequently committed or attempted would be a valuable addition to the state's resources in tackling serious organised crime.

The rationale underlying inchoate liability

4.5 Incitement, conspiracy and attempt, although distinct offences, share a common rationale. Each offence, by proscribing conduct that manifests an intention to bring about harm and enhances the prospect of harm occurring, enables the criminal law to intervene at a stage before the harm materialises. The utilitarian rationale underlying these offences is that the benefits of avoiding harm outweigh any disadvantages arising from what some might perceive as the criminal law's premature intervention. We believe that the utilitarian rationale is as strong when D's conduct consists of assisting as it is when D is encouraging or conspiring with P to bring about harm.

Eliminating the element of chance

4.6 In the CP [Consultation Paper], the Commission stated:

Under the present law it is a matter of chance, so far as D is concerned, whether he becomes guilty, that chance depending on whether P commits the principal crime.

It might be thought that criminal liability for culpable conduct that assists others to commit offences should not be a matter of chance or luck.

Sufficiently culpable conduct

4.7 Assisting another person to commit an offence is sufficiently culpable conduct to warrant the imposition of criminal liability even if that person does not commit or attempt to commit the offence. If D lends a gun to P so that P can and does murder V, we do not hesitate to label D's conduct as culpable. It is no less culpable merely because P for whatever reason does not commit the murder. As Professor Spencer [(1987: 148)] has observed:

'It is no fault of mine—or to be more accurate, it is not due to any lack of fault on my part—that the crime was never committed. If my behaviour was bad enough to punish where you actually made use of the help I gave you, it was surely bad enough to punish where I fully expected you to use it but you got caught before you had the chance.'

Deterrence

4.8 An inchoate offence of facilitation may have some deterrent effect. It would deter some individuals from assisting prospective perpetrators of offences if they were aware that there was an immediate risk of liability regardless of whether the offence they were assisting was committed or attempted.

A more coherent approach

4.9 The lack of a general inchoate offence of assisting crime has resulted in a piecemeal and haphazard approach. Having noted that there are numerous statutory offences that criminalise particular acts of assisting, Professor Spencer [(1987: 158)] stated:

'The present range of offences is quite inadequate to cover all the cases which ought to be covered, and the gaps between them produce some anomalies which suggest the criminal law has a very odd set of values. It is an offence under s 59 of the

Offences Against the Person Act 1861 to lend a knitting needle for an abortion, for example, but no offence at all to lend a knife to commit murder—unless of course the murder is attempted or committed.'

Labelling and punishment

4.10 In addition, the current piecemeal approach, besides being neither comprehensive nor rational, may inadequately label or punish D for his or her conduct. Thus, even where a statutory provision does criminalise a preliminary act of assistance, it may fail to adequately label and punish D for what he or she has sought to encourage or assist:

Example 4A

D goes to P's home and sells P a swordstick believing that P intends to use it to murder P's wife. Before P can attempt to kill his wife, he is arrested.

D is guilty only of the statutory offence of selling an offensive weapon. It is a summary offence, punishable with a maximum term of six months' imprisonment.

Restoring the proper boundaries of offences

4.11 The introduction of general inchoate liability for assisting crime would facilitate the process of restoring the proper boundaries of other inchoate offences, for example statutory conspiracy.

The arguments against inchoate liability for assisting

Liability for otherwise lawful conduct

4.12 Marginal activities, that would otherwise constitute lawful conduct, would qualify as criminal assistance. Professor K J M Smith [(1994: 239)] posits this example:

'D, a publican, or a generous host, believes that P is going to leave the premises in his car, but continues to ply him with drink to an extent that puts him well over the statutory limit. P does not in the event drive home.'

Premature intervention

4.13 It would result in premature intervention and might result in D being liable for assisting P who had no intention of committing an offence. In his response to the CP, Professor Sir John Smith provided an example of D supplying a weapon to P in the belief that P will use it to murder V whereas P merely intends to shoot rabbits. In the CP, the Commission cited the example of D agreeing to pay P, a builder doing repairs to his house, in cash knowing or believing that P wants payment in this form to assist him in defrauding the Inland Revenue. P subsequently makes a proper return to the revenue as he had always intended to.

Disparity between the liability of P and D

4.14 D will incur immediate liability for assisting P even though P, who may have requested the assistance, incurs no liability until he or she makes an attempt to commit the principal offence . . .

Vagueness and uncertainty

4.15 On one view, an inchoate offence of assisting with no requirement of knowledge or belief as to the future commission of any specific offence, but related to crime in general, would make the requirements for liability unduly vague and uncertain. On the other hand, a test of knowledge or belief in respect of a particular offence would give rise to problems in cases where assistance is provided and no principal offence is subsequently committed. It might be very difficult to prove that P had a particular offence in mind. The Crown Prosecution Service ('the CPS'), in its response to the CP, provided an example. D supplies P with a baseball bat in the belief that P will use it commit an offence. The CPS pointed out that P could use the bat to commit one or more of eleven potential offences and that those offences do not proscribe the same conduct or result and do not have an identical fault element.

Does the inchoate theory explain the law on accomplices in England and Wales?

It does not. The law is clear that if a principal does not commit the *actus reus* of an offence then an accomplice cannot be held liable, however much assistance or encouragement may have been offered. Of course, the law already recognizes incitement as an inchoate offence of encouraging another to commit an offence, and that crime is committed whether or not the incitee actually goes ahead and commits the offence. There is at present no comparative offence in relation to assistance.

11 THEORIES OF ACCESSORIAL *MENS REA*

What should the *mens rea* for an accessory be? As will be recalled from Part I of this chapter the law is far from clear.[163] The law is in part inevitably complex because of the number of different matters to which the *mens rea* must relate.[164] It must be decided what state of mind an accomplice must have in relation to the following:

(1) The accomplice's act.

(2) The act of the principal.

(3) The state of mind of the principal.

(4) The circumstances in which the principal acts.

Further, it must be decided whether in respect of these it is necessary to prove intention, recklessness, or negligence. Three approaches will be outlined here: ←4 (p.851)

11.1 PURPOSE

It could be argued that the prosecution should be required to show that it was the accomplice's intention that the principal commits the crime with the accomplice's assistance or encouragement. Supporters of such an approach may justify it on the basis that in the case of accomplice liability it is difficult to locate a harm to a victim directly caused by the

---

[163] Weiss (2002) provides a summary of the present American law.   [164] Weisberg (2000).

accomplice and therefore it is appropriate to have a higher standard for the *mens rea*. Such an argument is particularly likely to appeal to those who support the inchoate model of liability. Such an approach may also find support from those who are concerned with excessive criminalization.

11.2 RECKLESSNESS

It could be argued that it must be shown that the accomplice foresaw that the principal would go on to commit the crime with the accomplice's acts of assistance or encouragement. Those who adopt this view will accept that this may mean that the accomplice needs to have a lower *mens rea* than that required for the principal. The argument in favour of recklessness is based on some of the ideas behind derivative liability. In particular, the argument that by joining together with the principal, foreseeing that he or she will commit a crime, the accomplice adopts that offence as his or her own.

Those who take the recklessness view divide on the detail of what the defendant needs to foresee. Easy cases are those where the action was agreed in advance (e.g. 'we will burgle the house, but if the owner appears we will kill him') or where the agreed action was known to be dangerous (e.g. 'we will steal the car and drive it up the motorway as fast as possible'). Harder are cases where what was foreseen and what occurs slightly differ. If the defendant assists the principal foreseeing that the principal will stab the victim to death, should it matter whether the principal in fact shoots the victim?[165]

11.3 THE ACCOMPLICE'S *MENS REA* SHOULD BE THE SAME AS THAT REQUIRED FOR THE PRINCIPAL

This approach is in favour of requiring that the accomplice have the same *mens rea* as that required for a principal. So in a murder case it would be necessary to show that the accomplice intended the victim to suffer death or grievous bodily harm, while in a negligence-based offence, negligence would suffice.

In the following passage, Grace Mueller sets out some of the arguments in favour of this view:

G.E. Mueller, 'The *Mens Rea* of Accomplice Liability' (1988) 61 *Southern California Law Review* 2169 at 2173

A. Justifications for the Full *Mens Rea* Approach

There are several reasons for requiring that an accomplice possess the *mens rea* of the offense before finding him or her guilty. First, as a matter of social policy, people should not have to constantly look over their shoulders to make sure that they have done nothing which might later subject them to criminal liability. 'A pall would be cast on ordinary activity if we had to fear criminal liability for what others might do simply because our actions made their acts more probable.'[166]

---

[165] Clarkson (1998).   [166] Kadish (1985: 353).

Second, since the concept of culpability provides the basis for our criminal justice system, the act requirement is secondary to the mental element. An accomplice's mental state is one of the reasons we punish a non-perpetrator in the first place. In many cases, an act is required primarily as proof that mental culpability exists. Thus, since the notion of culpability is central to our views of just punishment, it seems absurd to punish an accomplice who did not possess the requisite *mens rea*.

The societal goals of deterrence and retribution do not undermine the argument for a full *mens rea* approach. An accomplice who possesses the *mens rea* of the substantive offense will be deterred as much as the perpetrator, since punishment upon conviction is the same. But it is difficult to deter if one cannot anticipate being connected to the crime. Therefore, only the smallest incremental increase in the deterrence may be anticipated if the accomplice is held liable on some lesser *mens rea*. Further, retribution is founded, in part, on culpability. Generally, society wishes to see criminals punished only to the extent that punishment is deserved. Desert is calculated by the level of culpability involved in the crime, and culpability is tied to the criminal's mental state. 'Deeply ingrained in our legal tradition is the idea that the more purposeful is the criminal conduct, the more serious is the offense, and, therefore, the more severely it ought to be punished.'[167]

A final argument for requiring proof of the *mens rea* of the substantive crime is inversely related to the culpability rationale discussed above. Since, by definition, an accomplice does not carry out the action which constitutes the act requirement for the offense, the requisite culpability can be demonstrated only by proving that the accomplice had the *mens rea* of the substantive offense. In order to demonstrate that the accomplice should be punished, solid proof of culpability is necessary. Those who accept the idea that knowing facilitation or foreseeability is sufficient for liability might argue that more objective criteria are needed, because actually proving subjective *mens rea* is too difficult. This criticism, however, is easily answered. When a perpetrator is charged with a crime that requires a certain mental state, the state looks to proof that this was indeed the accused's state of mind. It then allows the fact finder to decide whether the prosecution has met its burden of persuasion. The same types of evidence should prove as persuasive in the case of an accomplice, even though no equally clear act may be shown from which judges and juries may infer the mental state. These arguments suggest that the law should require proof that an accused accomplice possesses the *mens rea* of the substantive offense in order to punish the 'correct' people.

In the following extract, Andrew Simester explains why he does not accept that the accessory and principal need to have the same *mens rea*. In his view an accessory should only be liable if they have knowledge that the offence will be committed:

A. Simester, 'The Mental Element in Complicity' (2006) 123 *Law Quarterly Review* 578 at 589–92

At least where recklessness is sufficient to convict the principal of the relevant substantive offence, why *should* full knowledge be necessary on the part of the accomplice? If knowledge is required, S will escape liability in many cases where she willingly assists P to commit a crime, and has the same *mens rea* (i.e. recklessness) toward that crime as P. One might think that S has crossed the threshold justifying conviction, in terms of exhibiting culpable conduct: S has in fact assisted or encouraged P, and she has done so being aware of the potential to facilitate crime.

[167] *Tison v Arizona* 107 S Ct 1676 (1987).

The first step in answering this objection is to see that doctrines of complicity are quite separate from those concerning the perpetration of crime. The very basis of secondary liability is different from that of a principal. Although S is held responsible for P's crime, there is no suggestion that she actually commits it. The *actus reus* requirement is independent of the substantive offence: S must aid or abet P, and need not herself satisfy any of the *actus reus* of the substantive crime. This being so, there seems no reason why the *mens rea* requirement for participation should be determined by the principal offence.

Indeed, we can put this rather more strongly. The proper question to ask is not whether S is *culpable* in respect of the occurrence of P's crime, but whether the occurrence of that crime *can legitimately be attributed* to S (as well as to P). At issue is not culpability but *responsibility*—in particular, the principle of wrong responsibility identified above. Paradigmatically, both within and outwith the law, people are distinctively responsible for, and only for, the consequences of their own actions. Suppose, for example, that some teenager commits a murder. Depending on the circumstances, we may think that his parents have done a bad job of bringing him up, without adequately instilling the values that should have restrained him from killing V. But we are not inclined to treat the parents as murderers. This point rests upon the idea that individuals are separate, autonomous moral agents. In a liberal society, the right to be treated as separate individuals is fundamental. If the law is to acknowledge this, it must judge its citizens according to their own actions and not according to what others do. Sometimes, we do judge it apt to attribute responsibility for an event that D does not herself bring about, and criminal liability for omissions and complicity does just this. But such occasions are exceptional, and they need careful constraint. By contrast with, say, tort law, which is primarily concerned with reallocating losses, criminal liability is personal. As such, the citizen has a right not to be convicted and labelled as a criminal unless she is personally responsible, and blameworthy, *in respect of the crime of which she is convicted*.

This means that the mere occurrence of a prohibited harm, together with moral culpability on the part of S, is insufficient to convict S of the corresponding crime. She must be involved in that crime by virtue of some wrong that she herself commits. And here we come to the crux of the matter. The most a secondary party does is assist or encourage a crime, not perpetrate it. Since this is a far less stringent contribution than is required of the perpetrator, it is insufficient by itself to involve S in P's crime. S's conduct is, by itself, innocent and not a wrong at all—she does something that is permitted, e.g. lend or sell P a knife, say, or a jemmy—something that we may do innocently in ordinary life. Conduct of this sort has no inherent or necessary connection to crime.

When computer manufacturers make and sell computers, there is a recognised chance that their customers will use the machines to download and copy music illegally. Yet no one would say that those manufacturers are responsible for the illegal copying. Simply put: if my action is lawful and not wrong, someone else's crime does not become my lookout— and should not be my moral or legal responsibility—simply because I foresee its possibility. Something more is required. That 'something more' is supplied by my *mens rea*: by a requirement that I either intend, or at least know, that P means to commit a crime. It is only then that my helpful, but otherwise lawful, conduct becomes a wrong. Notice that *mens rea* quite often plays this role. Picking up someone else's property is not the stuff of crime unless it is done with intent to deprive. In the law of theft, *mens rea* does not operate simply to establish fault, because, in itself, the *actus reus* does not specify a wrong.

It is only when accompanied by *mens rea* that there is an action meriting the attention of the criminal law. So it is with complicity. In aiding and abetting, it is not her conduct *simpliciter* to which we object. There is nothing wrong with selling jemmies, for example, or computers. If that is so, it follows that the *mens rea* requirement does more than simply establish a connection between the eventual harm and S's culpability. It is also part of what makes S's conduct a wrong.

A person who sells a jemmy suspecting, but not knowing, of its intended criminal use, and without that being her purpose, does not identify or ally herself with the crime P then commits. The moral character of her action is innocent: she simply sells a jemmy. Just as many of our projects can miscarry, the jemmy may or may not be put to nefarious use by someone else. But if it is her *purpose* that the jemmy should be so used, then she involves herself in P's crime directly. Similarly, if she *knows* that it will be so used, then her conduct is no longer objectively innocent or ambiguous; its moral character of aiding or abetting crime is now unequivocal. She cannot evade the truth that, by her conduct, she is intentionally assisting P's crime. Thus her mental state is integral to the moral character of her action. Without it, there is no reason to think of her conduct as wrong. And it goes too far, and curtails S's freedom of action too greatly, that she should be prohibited from doing anything that *might* lead to crime by another.

A different view is proposed by Graham Virgo in this passage:

G. Virgo, 'Joint Enterprise Liability is Dead: Long Live Accessorial Liability' [2012] *Criminal Law Review* 850

Whether there is a valid distinction between joint enterprise and general accessorial liability has been a matter of some controversy. Some commentators consider that the two forms of liability remain distinct. This is also the view of the Law Commission and has sometimes been recognised by the courts. The distinction appears to turn on the significance of the common purpose to commit crime A, which is considered by some to affect the *mens rea* which needs to be established. For, where there is such a purpose, D2's intention that crime A be committed means that it is sufficient that he foresees that D1 might commit offence B. Where, however, there is no such common purpose, the liability of D2 as an accessory depends on proof of a more culpable fault element, either that D2 knew or believed that D1 would commit the substantive offence.

Other commentators disagree. Further, recent cases do not support such a distinction. Most significantly, in *Stringer* the Court of Appeal recognised that joint enterprise is not a legal term of art or an independent source of liability, but is simply secondary liability which involves the application of ordinary principles. This is surely correct. There are certain features of so-called "joint enterprise liability" which make it indistinguishable from general accessorial liability. First, D2 is usually convicted of the same offence as D1, so that D2's liability derives from that of D1; as is the case with general accessorial liability. Even if D2 is convicted of a different offence, for example manslaughter rather than murder, the liability is parasitic in that it depends on the commission of a crime by D1, again as is the case with general accessorial liability. Secondly, the *mens rea* is the same regardless of whether the liability is general accessorial liability or founded on a common purpose to commit crime A, namely that D2 must foresee the commission of the relevant offence by D1 as a possibility.

The only apparent differences between joint enterprise and accessorial liability relate to the identification of the *actus reus* component relating to D2's liability and the application of the rule that D2 will not be liable for crime B where it was a "fundamental departure" from the common purpose to commit crime A. But careful analysis of these differences suggests that either they do not exist or, if they do, they cannot be defended.

Actus reus

Today the *actus reus* of accessorial liability is usually described as assisting, encouraging or procuring the commission of the crime by D1. Where D2 had a common purpose with D1 to commit crime A and D1 committed crime B, whether D2's liability for crime B can be regarded as truly accessorial will turn on whether the common purpose to commit crime A can be regarded as assisting, encouraging or procuring crime B to be committed. In *Stringer* the Court of Appeal considered that participation in a joint criminal adventure did involve the provision of mutual encouragement and assistance so that D2 could be considered to be an accessory to crime B. But since the commission of crime B is by definition a departure from the common purpose to commit crime A, can D2 really be considered to have assisted or encouraged D1 to commit crime B? Whether this joint enterprise scenario can be considered to fall within the *actus reus* of accessorial liability requires careful analysis of the rationale behind accessorial liability generally. Why is D2 convicted of the same offence as that committed by D1? Three different explanations for this can be identified.

Causation

If D2 can be considered to have caused D1 to have committed the principal offence, then it is appropriate to consider D2 to be responsible in some way for the commission of that crime. This is encompassed by the use of the word "procuring" the commission of the substantive offence. But where D1 has freely acted in committing the crime then D2 cannot be considered to have caused that crime, because of the fundamental principle that the voluntary acts of D1 will break the chain of causation. The chain of causation will not, however, be broken where D1's commission of the crime cannot be considered to be truly voluntary, such as where D1 was mistaken or ignorant of all the facts relating to the commission of the crime. So, for example, where D2 laces D1's drink without D1's knowledge so that, when D1 drives his car he is over the limit, D1 will be guilty of the strict liability offence of drink driving, but his ignorance that his drinks were laced will mean that D2 can still be considered to be a contributory cause of the offence being committed.

But in most cases D1 will have acted wholly voluntarily and so D2 cannot be considered to have caused the substantive offence. Consequently, where D2 has simply assisted D1 to commit the crime or encouraged D1 to commit the crime, D2's liability cannot be founded on causation of that offence. Nevertheless, sometimes liability for assisting or encouraging a crime has been justified on the ground that D2 caused D1 to commit the crime. So for example in *Mendez* it was held that secondary liability was founded on causation, even where the assistance or encouragement related to the commission of crime A and D1 committed crime B. This is not, however, a test of "but for" causation, but simply whether D2 can be considered to have materially contributed to the commission of the offence by D1. It was even acknowledged that the assessment of such contribution may have a "moral component" as to whether it is just to hold D2 liable for the offence committed. In fact, this case recognised an attenuated form of causation, whereby it was sufficient that the act of assistance or encouragement objectively caused D1 to commit the substantive offence, even if D1 did not subjectively need such assistance or encouragement in order to commit the crime. But this distinction is meaningless; if the assistance or encouragement did not influence D1 then D2 cannot be considered to have caused the commission of the offence in any way. This has now been recognised in *Stringer* where two defendants chased the victim who was then killed by D1. It was held that the liability of the defendants did not depend on whether they were a cause of the killing. This is surely right. Outside of the limited doctrine of procuring, causation cannot explain how liability for assisting or encouraging a crime can be established. Some other explanation needs to be identified.

Connection

Instead of relying on causation as a justification for the imposition of liability for assisting or encouraging a crime, the Court of Appeal in *Stringer* recognised that such liability can be imposed where there is some connecting link so that D2's conduct can be considered to have made a contribution to the commission of the offence. The imposition of such liability is morally justified because D2 has involved himself in the commission of the crime by the act of assistance or encouragement.

This connection can be established as regards assistance by showing that the act of assistance had contributed to the commission of the offence simply by D2 having helped D1 to commit the crime in some way, and, as regards encouragement, by showing that the words or conduct of D2 had acted on the mind of D1 either directly or indirectly in his decision to commit the crime. A point will, however, be reached where the acts of assistance or encouragement are so remote, either in time or place, that it would not be appropriate to consider D1's conduct to have been influenced by the act of assistance or encouragement. In *Stringer* itself, where the defendants chased the victim who was then stabbed by D1, it was held that the act of chasing the victim was sufficiently connected to the stabbing because the gap in time between the chasing and the stabbing was so small that there was ample evidence that D1 had been encouraged or assisted in the attack by the victim being chased by the defendants, so that D1 had the comfort of knowing that he was not on his own but had the support of the defendants and a reasonable expectation that they would come to his assistance if needed.

This "connection" justification for accessorial liability is not subject to the limitation of causation, namely that the voluntary acts of D1 will break the chain of causation, but it does involve some form of link between D2 and D1 in that D1 must have been influenced by D2's contribution in some way. This is clear as regards assistance, since it will need to be shown that D2's act did help D1 to commit the crime, albeit that this help may have been limited and certainly it need not be necessary for D1 to commit the crime. Where D2 has encouraged D1 to commit a crime, the relevant connection will be established if it can be shown that D1 was influenced to commit the crime by the act of encouragement, even if D1 would still have committed the crime had there not been any encouragement. Where D2 has provided assistance to D1 which is not relied on by D1, such as where D2 provides a weapon which is not used, this might still be regarded as encouraging D1 to commit the crime, because D1 might take comfort from the support of D2.

In fact this notion of connection between D2 and D1's commission of the crime was expanded even further in *Stringer*, since Toulson L.J. recognised:

> "If D provides assistance or encouragement to P, and P does that which he has been encouraged or assisted to do, there is good policy reason for treating D's conduct as materially contributing to the commission of the offence, and therefore justifying D's punishment as a person responsible for the commission of the offence, whether or not P would have acted in the same way without such encouragement or assistance."

It follows that, as regards encouragement, for example, as long as it can be shown that D1 (P in the above dictum) was aware of the communication, it can be presumed that this influenced the crime committed by D1 as long as D1 happened to do that which he was encouraged to do. It follows that if D2 encouraged D1 to commit murder in a letter which was not received or by words which D1 did not hear, connection cannot be presumed. But if D1 reads the letter or hears the words and commits murder then the relevant connection can be presumed. This might be considered to be consistent with the approach adopted in *Calhaem*, where it was recognised that, as regards counselling, there is no need to establish any causal connection between the encouragement and the commission of the substantive offence, it being sufficient that the crime was committed within the scope of authority contemplated by D2. This notion of presumed connection might even be deployed to explain how D2 might be liable for the commission of crime B in departure from a common purpose to commit crime A. But where D1 has intentionally departed from the common purpose it is surely stretching the notion of even a presumed connection too far to say that D1 was influenced by D2 to commit crime B. So some other explanation needs to be identified for the imposition of such liability.

Association

If the imposition of accessorial liability cannot be justified on the facts by establishing causation or an actual or presumed connection with the crime committed by D1, there is a third way of justifying the imposition of such liability. This is that D2 should be liable for the commission of the substantive offence by D1 where D2 can be considered to be associated with the commission of that offence in some way. This principle of association was explicitly recognised in *A* to explain the imposition of joint enterprise liability. Hughes L.J. held that the liability of D2 in such circumstances rests on him having continued with the common venture to commit crime A, even though he realised, but may not have desired, that crime B might be committed by D1. In such circumstances D2 could be considered to have associated himself with crime B. This analysis was specifically approved by Lords Phillips, Judge and Wilson in *Gnango*.

Whereas the other explanations of accessorial liability, causation and connection, depend on establishing some effect on or link to the commission of the crime committed by D1, albeit that this may be a presumed connection, this need not be proved where the justification for the imposition of liability is association. The focus is instead on the conduct of D2 in its own right and whether this can be considered to establish that D2 is associated with the crime committed by D1, without resorting to any artificial presumption of effect on D1. Although Lords Phillips, Judge and Wilson in *Gnango* justified the imposition of "parasitical accessorial liability" on the basis that it is the joining in the common enterprise which renders the conduct of D2 an encouragement to D1 to commit crime B, this is a somewhat artificial notion of encouragement, both because it is not necessary to show that D1 was encouraged to commit crime B by virtue of the joint venture to commit crime A, and because D2 might not desire crime B to be committed, so cannot be considered to have intended to encourage it. But that should be irrelevant. By continuing with the joint venture, being aware that crime B might be committed, D2 is sufficiently associated with that crime to be regarded as responsible for its commission.

Whilst the principle of association might be a perfectly adequate explanation of joint enterprise liability, it is still necessary to consider whether this form of liability can be considered distinct from general accessorial liability. It need not be if the principle of association might operate within general accessorial liability as well. There are, in fact, a number of examples of this being the case, where D2 is liable for the crime committed by D1 by association with it, even though there is no joint venture to commit a different crime. So, for example, spectators at a prize fight can be considered to be accessories to the fight, not simply because of their voluntary presence, but, where their presence was not accidental, because they could be considered to have acted in concert with those who were fighting, so that they are associated with it, even though it cannot be proved that the fighters were actually encouraged by their presence and the fight would have occurred without their presence. Similarly, in *Wilcox v Jeffery*, where the defendant journalist had attended a concert given by a jazz musician knowing that a condition of his entry to the country was that he was not to perform, it was held that the defendant had encouraged the crime by his presence, even though the crime would still have been committed had he not been present. But, rather than identifying liability by reference to assumed encouragement, he could be considered to be associated with the commission of the offence by his knowing presence. Indeed, Lord Goddard C.J. said he was "present, taking part, concurring or encouraging, whichever word you like to use for expressing this conception", and it would have been different if he had gone there to protest rather than to "approve or encourage" the principal's performance. By approving of the concert, knowing of the conditions of entry to the country, he could simply be considered to be associated with the crime.

. . .

This principle of association provides the link to enable so-called "joint enterprise liability" to be treated as falling within general accessorial liability. If D2 can be considered to be associated with the crime committed by D1, then he will be liable for its commission as an accessory, as long, of course, as D2 foresaw the commission of that offence as a possibility. The principle of association can also be logically extended to impose accessorial liability where D2 assists or encourages D1 to commit crime A, foreseeing that crime B might be committed. Although there is not necessarily an agreed common purpose between D1 and D2 that crime A be committed, the fact that D2 has assisted or encouraged that crime, foreseeing the possibility of crime B being committed, should be regarded as sufficient evidence of D2's association with crime B to justify conviction of that offence.

12 THE THEORY OF JOINT ENTERPRISE

Is joint enterprise simply one way of being an accessory or should cases of joint enterprise be regarded as sufficiently different to justify different legal treatment?[168] The recent cases appear to suggest it is. In the following passage, the authors argue against that view: ←3 (p.848)

A.P. Simester, J. Spencer, G.R. Sullivan, and G. Virgo, *Criminal Law Theory and Doctrine* (Oxford: Hart, 2013), 228–30

'Intellectually', said Lord Mustill, 'there are problems with the concept of a joint venture, but they do not detract from its general practical worth . . .'[169] One may hesitate to distinguish so readily between matters of intellectual coherence and those of practicality, but it is true that the rationale for joint enterprise liability is somewhat unclear. *Smith and Hogan* claims that joint enterprise is simply an aspect of aiding, abetting, counselling, or procuring, which therefore falls to be 'governed by the ordinary principles of secondary participation.'[170] At

---

[168] See Krebs (2010). [169] *Powell; English* [1997] 4 All ER 545, 548 (HL).
[170] J.C. Smith (2002: 147).

least one judge in the Court of Appeal agrees, but the Law Commission does not. The Supreme Court appeared to treat 'parasitic accessorial liability' as a separate ground in *Gnango*. In our view joint enterprise should be treated as a special case of secondary participation and not merely a sub-species of assistance and encouragement. The core of a joint enterprise is its common unlawful purpose. It is this element of shared commitment to commit crime A that triggers the doctrines of joint enterprise liability.

Aiding/abetting and joint enterprise are structurally unalike. In cases of aiding and abetting S's liability for any crime by P is considered individually. S directly participates in each crime by her intended act of aiding or abetting that very crime. The wrong which makes S responsible for each crime is that deliberate assistance or encouragement: it is her act of directly associating herself with P's crime. In joint enterprise cases, the wrong is the agreement or confederacy. That agreement (to commit crime A) opens a wider door to liability; it exposes S to conviction for any foreseen crimes B, C, and D, committed by P in the course of executing the agreement. As such, S's connection to crime B is *indirect*. It operates only through the agreement.

It is important to recognise that aiding, abetting, counselling, and procuring are not doctrines that operate as ends in themselves. They exist as formally-recognised channels via which the law transcends the normal limitations of autonomy, individual responsibility, and causation doctrines in order to associate one person with responsibility for a crime committed by another. There is no reason, therefore, why the law should not recognise complementary doctrines where a similar rationale for extending responsibility applies. Joint enterprise presents just that situation.

Even so, we should ask, why should the agreement or confederacy make such a difference? Clearly, the law regards the joint unlawful enterprise as upping the ante, such that S becomes liable to be convicted of crimes to which she has in no way contributed.

The answer depends on the fact that S's common purpose is unlawful. This is quite different from aiding and abetting, where S's actions need not be in themselves wrongful. Lending someone a knife is unproblematic until we know what P's plans are. What makes S's actions the stuff of criminal law, in other words, is her mens rea with respect to P's conduct. . . .

This does not apply to joint enterprise. By entering into an agreement or joint enterprise, S becomes, through her own deliberate choice, a participant in a group action to commit a crime. Moreover, her new status has moral significance: she associates herself with the conduct of the other members of the group in a way that the mere aider or abettor, who remains an independent character throughout the episode, does not. The law has a particular hostility to criminal groups: conspiracy to defraud, for example, is an offence even where individual fraud is not. As with the inchoate crime of conspiracy, the rationale is partly one of dangerousness: 'experience has shown that joint criminal enterprises only too readily escalate into the commission of greater offences'. Criminal associations are dangerous. They present a threat to public safety that ordinary criminal prohibitions, addressed to individual actors, do not entirely address. Moreover, the danger is not just of an immediately physical nature. A group is a form of society, and a group constituted by a joint unlawful enterprise is a form of society that has set itself against the law and order of society at large. Individuals offending alone do not do this. Thus concerted wrongdoing imports additional and special reasons why the law must intervene.

In the following passage a powerful case is made against the operation of the current law on joint enterprise. Note that this was written before the decision of the Supreme Court in the *Jogee* case. You may want to consider whether that decision has dealt with the concerns raised, or exacerbated them:

W. Wilson and D. Ormerod, 'Simply Harsh to Fairly Simple: Joint Enterprise Reform' [2015] *Criminal Law Review* 3 at 12–13

Particularly in the case of murder, there is a significant injustice arising from the present state of the law founded on the joint enterprise approach. A conviction for being party to a joint enterprise may mean that D suffers all the consequences of a murder conviction, including the offence label and the mandatory sentence (ratcheted up in real terms by the Sch.21 tariffs to the Criminal Justice Act 2003), without necessarily having demonstrated any of the culpability or wrongdoing of the principal offender. Given that the wrong in murder is to kill with malice aforethought, to convict a secondary party of that crime simply upon proof of his contemplation or foresight that this may be what his principal has in mind takes considerable justification.

Simester offers one justification: it is not, in principle, wrong to punish D for the actions of P. By joining with P in a common criminal enterprise which has death as a foreseen outcome D changes his normative position in relation to that outcome. Rough justice it may be, he implies, but justice nevertheless, no less than GBH murder is. We cannot absolve ourselves from responsibility for the consequences of our actions by blaming an unruly fate. That is not how our moral universe is organised. The problem with this argument in the context of PAL ['parasitic accessory liability'], however, is, as has been explained, that it fails to pay full regard to a central and defining feature underpinning criminal doctrine: that we must take responsibility for our own choices and their outcomes, not the choices of others and their outcomes. Standard accessorial liability accommodates this problem to a degree by basing the liability of secondary parties on their lending (unconditional) support to the criminal projects of the principal. This is why contemplation alone sufficed in *DPP of Northern Ireland v Maxwell*. In *Maxwell* D did not know precisely the crime to be committed, but by assisting P in the knowledge that P might intentionally commit one of a number of crimes, D was deemed, quite fairly, to have lent his support to any of those crimes, if committed. The unknown crime constitutes their common purpose. But in PAL, having lent support to one *crime*, D is also deemed to lend support to another merely because, although it forms no part of their common purpose, he has foreseen, out of the corner of his eye, the possibility that P might commit this further crime. Unconditional support is lent only to crime A and only constructive support, in effect, to crime B, a crime indeed which D may even have counselled his principal *not* to commit or which was at the periphery of his thinking when lending his support to crime A. What moral principle demands that I take responsibility not simply for the consequences of my own choices and those choices of my co-adventurer which I happen to share but also those which I do not share but happen to contemplate that he may, with a following wind, make at some stage in the future? In the specific context of murder, of course, the problem is exacerbated. D is liable despite not having chosen to kill; and not even having chosen to cause serious injury. D's choice, and *pace* Simester admittedly he makes one, is simply not to back out of a criminal enterprise when he realises that P may have more on his mind than what has been agreed. A conviction for murder, rather than manslaughter, is, given the power of the label and the mandatory sentence, not rough justice. It is injustice.

FURTHER READING

Green, A. and McGourlay, C. (2015) 'The Wolf Packs in Our Midst and Other Products of Criminal Joint Enterprise Prosecutions' *Journal of Criminal Law* 79: 234.

13   *ACTUS REUS* ISSUES

It is striking what a wide range of behaviour is covered by the *actus reus* of being an accessory:[171] from on the one hand a bully who compels a weak-minded person into committing a crime on his or her behalf, to on the other the wife of a burglar who gives him a cup of tea to send him on his way on his nocturnal activities.[172] Indeed the range of activities involved has led several commentators to suggest that it is not possible to provide one set of legal regulations and approaches to deal with the whole range of forms of accessoryship. ←2 (p.835)

In fact, under English and Welsh law, actions which have only the most limited connection to the ultimate offence can generate accomplice liability. No doubt often those who could be prosecuted as accessories are not. As Sullivan[173] puts it: 'At present, we are governed by a very broad conception of complicity, considerably tempered by a lack of full enforcement.'

The following scenarios give a flavour of the kinds of cases which may be said to be problematic:

(1) Michael Allen[174] asks: 'A sees D, a motorist, standing beside a vehicle which has a punctured tyre. He offers to change the tyre. When performing this act of charity he notices that one of the other tyres is partially bald, and therefore illegal. If A completes the task, will he be liable for aiding and abetting D's offence of driving a vehicle on the road with a defective tyre?'

(2) Jerry, a generous host, provides copious amounts of alcohol at his parties. He does so even though he knows that several guests have driven to the party and will drive home with a blood-alcohol level above that permitted. Lord Widgery CJ in *Attorney-General's Reference (No. 1 of 1975)*[175] suggested he did not think such a host would be liable, but it is hard to see why not. Is it any different from a person who tells a group of friends about a house that is easy to burgle knowing that amongst the group there are likely to be some who will go on to burgle the property?

(3) If a shopkeeper sells something to someone (e.g. a hammer) aware that the person is likely to use that equipment to carry out a crime (e.g. an assault) is the shopkeeper liable as an accomplice if the assault subsequently takes place?[176] Several commentators have expressed concern that if shopkeepers were not permitted to sell anything to someone they thought might possibly use it illegally then this would place a great burden on shopkeepers. Such concerns could be met in two ways: it might be suggested that a distinction could be drawn between ordinary goods, where there would be no liability for shopkeepers, and items which are particularly dangerous (e.g. guns or explosives), where shopkeepers could be expected not to sell the items to those they feared would use them illegally.[177] Others have suggested that the solution is that shopkeepers should be liable only if they sell items with the purpose of assisting in the commission of a crime.[178] That, of course, would be rare.

---

[171] Glazebrook (1996) argues that the *actus reus* of an offence should be defined in such a way as to include what are presently defined as principals and accessories.

[172] G. Williams (1990) supports the idea of reducing accessoryship to influencing and helping. Help is much easier to understand than aid.

[173] Sullivan (1994: 254).

[174] Allen (2007: 217).   [175] [1975] QB 773 (CA).

[176] For a detailed discussion of the American law on this, see Rogers (1998).

[177] G. Williams (1990).   [178] Ashworth and Horder (2013: 412).

Other commentators are less concerned with the potential infringement of the rights of shopkeepers.[179] If someone thinks there is a real possibility that the item being sold will be used illegally the shopkeeper should not go ahead with the sale. The rights of the potential victims who may be injured in the possible offence outweigh concerns over interrupting the business activities of shopkeepers.

These examples demonstrate two concerns in particular: first, everyday common conduct which we would not expect to be an offence (offering a friend a drink) could constitute an offence.[180] Second, throwing the net of accomplice liability too wide could effectively constitute liability of omissions and possibly interfere with basic human rights.

14 REFORM OF THE LAW

There is considerable dissatisfaction with the current law. The complaints with the current law are summarized in this excerpt. Note again that this was written before the decision in *Jogee*:

B. Crewe, A. Liebling, N. Padfield, and G. Virgo, 'Joint Enterprise: The Implications of an Unfair and Unclear Law' [2015] *Criminal Law Review* 252 at 255–6

It is possible to identify four significant difficulties with the "law of joint enterprise":

(a) The language of "joint enterprise" is ambiguous, as is the apparent assumption that all participants in a joint enterprise are all in it together. Focusing on the language of being an accessory, and needing to be associated with the commission of the substantive offence, would focus attention on significant issues of responsibility for the commission of the substantive offence.

(b) Prosecution policy is unclear. Although, following a report of the House of Commons Justice Committee, the DPP published guidelines as to when accessories will be prosecuted, including in the joint enterprise context, it is unclear whether this has had much if any impact. Indeed, the Justice Committee correctly commented in its follow-up report that, whilst this guidance "contains a comprehensive and detailed account of the law", it is not possible to say whether the principal aim of the guidance, namely to reduce the risk of overcharging by prosecutors, has been fulfilled. The Justice Committee has recommended that the CPS commissions research into the use of the guidance by prosecutors in making charging decisions involving joint enterprise. This is to be welcomed.

(c) The state of the law is unnecessarily confused. The authorities are confused as to what it is the D2 must foresee where D1 departs from the common purpose and commits crime B. Further, careful consideration needs to be given to whether this is sufficient culpability to convict D2 of crime B. This is most marked where crime B is murder. To convict D1 of murder it must be shown that he or she caused death with the intention to kill or to cause serious injury. To convict D2 of murder as an accessory where murder is a departure from the common purpose, it is sufficient to show that D2 foresaw the commission of murder as a possibility.

---

[179] Schroth (2000) discusses the relevance of free speech to complicity.
[180] Kadish (1997). For a dramatic example, see Glazebrook (2001).

There is no need to establish any causative effect of D2 on D1, this being presumed by virtue of the common purpose to commit crime A. Both D1 and D2 will receive the mandatory life sentence, typically where the minimum tariff is high. So, for example, if a gang member goes along with other members of the gang and suspects that one of them might have a knife and might use that knife intentionally to kill, he or she will be guilty of murder if the knife is used to kill. The concern here is not that D2 is convicted of a crime in such circumstances, since there may well be sufficient culpability and responsibility in associating with a gang when there is awareness of the possession and previous use of knives. The concern arises from the injustice in using the blunderbuss of joint enterprise liability for murder where it is not possible to discriminate appropriately between the different culpabilities and responsibilities of D1 and D2.

(d) Joint enterprise cases are particularly complex for judge and jury. This is in part because of the complexity and uncertainty of the law, making judicial directions to the jury especially difficult. Further, many joint enterprise cases, especially those relating to murder, involve a significant number of defendants, making the forensic task of the jury even more difficult in determining who is responsible and their degree of association with the crime. It is inevitable in complex trials that jurors will infer from membership of a gang, where there is a culture of possession of knives, that all members of the gang must have foreseen the use of a knife with relevant intent. There is legitimate concern that prosecution policy is casting the net too wide to catch as many gang members as possible, making the task of the judge and the jury even more difficult.

The House of Commons Justice Committee[181] raises another concern. It refers to research indicating that 'in cases where there were four or more defendants in the period between 2005 and 2013 . . . [i]t is clear that a large proportion of those convicted of joint enterprise offences are young Black and mixed race men.' They quote evidence from Dr Ben Crewe as to why this might be so: 'BME [black and minority ethnic] men may be over-represented in the kinds of communities where young men typically hang around in groups that are labelled by outsiders as gangs' and 'an association may exist unconsciously in the minds of the police, prosecutors and juries between being a young ethnic minority male and being in a gang, and therefore being involved in forms of urban violence'.[182]

The Law Commission has produced two reports on reform of the law of accessories.[183] The first[184] makes the radical suggestion that there will be inchoate offences of assisting and encouraging crimes. These will be committed whether or not the principal commits the crime. So, to be clear, the proposal is that if A said to B 'I think you should go and burgle that house' and B said 'Certainly not', it would be open for A to be prosecuted under the proposed law. Of course, under the current law B could not be liable as an accomplice. One benefit of the proposal is that it would enable early intervention in a case where, for example, it was clear a gang of people were helping a terrorist prepare to commit an outrage, but it had not yet taken place.[185] A version of their model made its way into the offences in Part 2 of the Serious Crime Act 2007.

[181] House of Commons Justice Committee (2015).
[182] The Serious Crime Act 2015, s. 45 creates an offence of participating in activities of an organized crime group.
[183] Sullivan (2006a: 1050).
[184] Law Commission Report No. 300 (2006). For further discussion of their proposals, see Buxton (2009); Taylor (2008); W. Wilson (2008a); and Sullivan (2008).
[185] Sullivan (2006a: 1048).

The second report advocates retention, with slight modification, of the current law on accessories.[186] So, in effect, the Law Commission is advocating a use of both the derivative and inchoate models of liability.

FURTHER READING

Crewe, B., Liebling, A., Padfield, N., and Virgo, G. (2015) 'Joint Enterprise: The Implications of an Unfair and Unclear Law' *Criminal Law Review* 252.

Dressler, J. (1985) 'Reassessing the Theoretical Underpinnings of Accomplice Liability' *Hastings Law Journal* 37: 111.

Dyson, M. (2015) 'The Future of Joint-up Thinking: Living in a Post-Accessory Liability World' *Journal of Criminal Law* 79: 181.

Edwards, S. (2013) '"The Straw Woman" at Law's Precipice: An Unwilling Party' in A. Reed and M. Bohlander (eds) *Participation in Crime* (Aldershot: Ashgate).

Farmer, L. (2007) 'Complicity beyond Causality' *Criminal Law and Philosophy* 1: 151.

Gardner, J. (2007b) 'Complicity and Causality' *Criminal Law and Philosophy* 1: 127.

Glazebrook, P. (1996) 'Structuring the Criminal Code: Functional Approaches to Complicity, Incomplete Offences and General Defences' in A.P. Simester and G.R. Sullivan (eds) *Harm and Culpability* (Oxford: OUP).

Green, A. and McGourlay, C. (2015) 'The Wolf Packs in Our Midst and Other Products of Criminal Joint Enterprise Prosecutions' *Journal of Criminal Law* 79: 234.

House of Commons Justice Committee (2015) *Joint Enterprise: Follow-Up* (London: TSO).

Kadish, S. (1985) 'Complicity, Blame and Cause' *California Law Review* 73: 323.

Kadish, S. (1997) 'Reckless Complicity' *Journal of Criminal Law and Criminology* 87: 369.

Krebs, B. (2010) 'Joint Criminal Enterprise' *Modern Law Review* 73: 578.

Kutz, C. (2007) 'Causeless Complicity' *Criminal Law and Philosophy* 1: 289.

Kutz, C. (2011) 'The Philosophical Foundations of Complicity Law' in J. Deigh and D. Dolinko (eds) *The Oxford Handbook of Philosophy of Criminal Law* (Oxford: OUP).

Lanham, D. (2000) 'Primary and Derivative Criminal Liability: An Australian Perspective' *Criminal Law Review* 707.

Law Commission (2006a) Report No. 300, *Inchoate Liability for Assisting and Encouraging Crime* (London: TSO).

Law Commission (2007) Report No. 305, *Participating in Crime* (London: TSO).

Simester, A. (2006) 'The Mental Element in Complicity' *Law Quarterly Review* 123: 578.

Smith, K. (1991) *A Modern Treatise on the Law of Criminal Complicity* (Oxford: OUP).

Stewart, J. (2014) 'Complicity' in M. Dubber and T. Hörnle (eds) *The Oxford Handbook of Criminal Law* (Oxford: OUP).

Sullivan, G.R. (2008) ' "Participating in Crime": Law Com No. 305—Joint Criminal Ventures' *Criminal Law Review* 19.

---

[186] For criticism of this, see Sullivan (2006b).

Taylor, R. (2008) 'Procuring, Causation, Innocent Agency and the Law Commission' *Criminal Law Review* 32.

Wilson, W. (2002) *Central Issues in Criminal Theory* (Oxford: Hart), ch. 7.

Wilson, W. (2008a) 'A Rational Scheme of Liability for Participating in Crime' *Criminal Law Review* 3.

Wilson, W. (2013) 'Participating in Crime: Some Thoughts on the Retribution/Prevention Dichotomy in Preparation for Crime and How to Deal with It' in A. Reed and M. Bohlander (eds) *Participation in Crime* (Aldershot: Ashgate).

Yaffe, G. (2012) 'Moore on Causing, Acting and Complicity' *Legal Theory* 18: 437.

15 CONCLUDING THOUGHTS

The law on accomplices enables the punishment of not only those who actually harm the victim, but also those who help or encourage others to do such harm. This means that the law can deal with some of the worse criminals, who avoid doing any 'dirty work' themselves but arrange for others to do it. While the basic notion of accessorial liability is straightforward the law has developed in a surprisingly complex way. One can only feel sympathy for juries who seek to determine what *mens rea* A intended P would have. It is not only questions of proof that create difficulties: there is the more profound question of the extent to which one person should be responsible for the actions of another. Like so many questions in the criminal law that is a question with no easy answer, and leaving plenty of room for fierce debate.

NOTE ON BIBLIOGRAPHY

A comprehensive bibliography, including the references in this book, can be found on the accompanying Online Resource Centre. The bibliography is available alphabetically by author name, allowing you to quickly locate specific references.

In addition to this you can find all references within the Further Reading and footnotes throughout the text.

To access this bibliography and the other online resources (including useful weblinks, and guidance to answering the questions) go to:

www.oxfordtextbooks.co.uk/orc/herringcriminal7e/

BIBLIOGRAPHY AND FURTHER READING

ABBATE, F. (1992) 'The Conspiracy Doctrine: A Critique' in M. Gore and S. Harwood (eds) *Controversies in Criminal Law* (Boulder, CO: Westview).

AINSWORTH, P. (2000) *Psychology and Crime* (Harlow: Longman).

AKDENIZ, Y. (1996) 'Section 3 of the Computer Misuse Act 1990—An Antidote for Computer Viruses' *Web Journal of Current Legal Issues.*

ALCOHOL CONCERN (2005) www.alcoholconcern.org.uk/.

ALCOHOL CONCERN (2013) *Statistics on alcohol* (London: Alcohol Concern).

ALEXANDER, L. (1996) 'The Moral Magic of Consent (II)' *Legal Theory* 2: 165.

ALEXANDER, L. (1999) '*Propter Honoris Respectum*: A Unified Excuse of Pre-emptive Self-protection' *Notre Dame Law Review* 74: 1475.

ALEXANDER, L. (2000) 'Insufficient Concern: A Unified Conception of Criminal Culpability' *California Law Review* 88: 955.

ALEXANDER, L. (2002) 'Criminal Liability for Omissions' in S. Shute and A. Simester (eds) *Criminal Law Theory* (Oxford: Oxford University Press).

ALEXANDER, L. (2005) 'Lesser Evils: A Closer Look at the Paradigmatic Justification' *Law and Philosophy* 24: 611.

ALEXANDER, L. (2013) 'Causing the Conditions of One's Defense: A Theoretical Non-problem' *Criminal Law and Philosophy* 7: 623.

ALEXANDER, L. AND KESSLER, K. (1997) 'Mens Rea and Inchoate Crimes' *Journal of Law and Criminology* 87: 1138.

ALEXANDER, L. AND KESSLER FERZAN, K. (2009) *Crime and Culpability: A Theory of Criminal Law* (Oxford: Oxford University Press).

INDEX